ORACLE® *Oracle Press*™

Oracle9*i*: The Complete Reference

Oracle9*i*: The Complete Reference

Kevin Loney
George Koch
And the Experts at TUSC

McGraw-Hill/Osborne

New York Chicago San Francisco
Lisbon London Madrid Mexico City Milan
New Delhi San Juan Seoul Singapore Sydney Toronto

McGraw-Hill/Osborne
2600 Tenth Street
Berkeley, California 94710
U.S.A.

To arrange bulk purchase discounts for sales promotions, premiums, or fund-raisers, please contact **McGraw-Hill/Osborne** at the above address. For information on translations or book distributors outside the U.S.A., please see the International Contact Information page immediately following the index of this book.

Oracle 9*i*: The Complete Reference

1234567890 DOC DOC 0198765432
Book p/n 0-07-222707-9 and CD p/n 0-07-222708-7
parts of
ISBN 0-07-222521-1

Publisher	**Copy Editor**
Brandon A. Nordin	Margaret Berson
Vice President & Associate Publisher	**Proofreader**
Scott Rogers	Cheryl Abel
Acquisitions Editor	**Indexer**
Lisa McClain	James Minkin
Project Editor	**Computer Designers**
LeeAnn Pickrell	Tabitha M. Cagan, Lucie Ericksen
Acquisitions Coordinator	**Illustrators**
Athena Honore	Michael Mueller, Lyssa Wald
Technical Editor	**Cover Series Design**
Bob Bryla	Damore Johann Design, Inc.

This book was composed with Corel VENTURA™ Publisher.

To my parents, and to Sue, Emily, Rachel, and Jane
—K.L.

To Elwood Brant, Jr. (Woody), 1949–1990
—G.K.

About the Authors

Kevin Loney is a senior management technical consultant with TUSC (http://www.tusc.com), an Oracle-focused consultancy headquartered in Chicago. He is an expert in the administration, tuning, security, recovery, design, and development of Oracle databases and applications. An Oracle DBA and developer since 1987, he is the primary author of numerous books, including *Oracle9i DBA Handbook*, *Oracle9i Instant Scripts*, and *Oracle8 Advanced Tuning and Administration*, all published by Oracle Press. He is a frequent presenter at local and international Oracle user groups.

George Koch is a leading authority on relational database applications. A popular speaker and widely published author, he is also the creator of THESIS, the securities trading, accounting, and portfolio management system that was the first major commercial applications product in the world to employ a relational database (Oracle) and provide English language querying to its users. He is a former senior vice president of Oracle Corporation.

Contents at a Glance

PART III

PL/SQL

PART IV

Object-Relational Databases

PART V

Java in Oracle

PART VI

Hitchhiker's Guides

PART VII

Alphabetical Reference

Contents

PART I
Critical Database Concepts

PART II
SQL and SQL*PLUS

PART III
PL/SQL

PART IV
Object-Relational Databases

PART V

Java in Oracle

PART VI

Hitchhiker's Guides

PART VII

Alphabetical Reference

Acknowledgments

his book is dedicated to my family, who have allowed me the time to write it. Thank you for your patience and support and love.

Beyond that, this book is dedicated to the memory of two people: Stephen Jay Gould and Matthew Horning. Stephen Jay Gould inspired me to be a technical writer—his steady growth as a writer and his clarity of thought and expression made me believe this kind of writing was a possibility. He passed away as this book was being finished, and the world is poorer for his passing.

Matthew Horning was an Oracle DBA I worked with for several weeks during the summer of 2001 on the upper floors of #1 World Trade Center in New York City. He had the misfortune of being in the office early on 9/11. His coworkers were inspiring to work with during the recovery efforts that followed. In his obituary, Matt's family asked that donations in his memory be given to Heifer International (http://www.heifer.org). If an act of compassion can come out of such destruction, then there may always be hope. As Gould noted, "Ordinary kindness trumps paroxysmal evil by at least a million events to one."

This book is the product of many hands, and countless hours from many people. My thanks go out to all those who helped, whether through their comments, feedback, edits, or suggestions. For additional information about the book, see the publisher's site (http://www.osborne.com) and my site (http://www.kevinloney.com). Additional articles and presentations can be found on the company site at http://www.tusc.com.

Thanks to all of my colleagues at TUSC:

- To the contributors and reviewers there, including Brad Brown, Jay Urban, and Mike Holder.

- To the exemplary management, including Jake Van der Vort, Rich Niemiec, Joe Trezzo, Brad Brown, and others. It's a delight to work with an executive team who understands the requirements of this kind of undertaking and who shares a commitment to professional altruism. Thanks to the rest of the management team there who actively pursue the professional traits TUSC values.

- To my peers at TUSC, including Mike Ault, Bill Callahan, Patrick Callahan, Holly Clawson, Judy Corley, Mark Greenhalgh, Andy Hamilton, Mike Killough, Allen Peterson, Randy Swanson, Bob Taylor, Bob Yingst, and many others for their insights and contributions.

Special thanks to Bob Bryla, who served as technical editor for this edition. His thoroughness, corrections, and suggestions were greatly appreciated. Imagine being a technical editor on a 1400 page book covering such a range of content and you can begin to appreciate Bob's task—then do it while working on my schedule!

Thanks to my colleagues and friends, including Eyal Aronoff, John Beresniewicz, Steve Bobrowski, Rachel Carmichael, Steven Feuerstein, Mike McDonnell, Marlene Theriault, Mike Janesch, Craig Warman, and Vinny Smith. This book has benefited from the knowledge they have shared, and I have benefited from their friendship and guidance.

Thanks to the folks at McGraw-Hill/Osborne who guided this product through its stages: Scott Rogers, LeeAnn Pickrell, Athena Honore, Lisa McClain, and Jeremy Judson, and the others at Osborne with whom I never directly worked. Thanks also to the Oracle component of Oracle Press. This book would not have been possible without the earlier excellent work of George Koch and Robert Muller.

Thanks to the writers and friends along the way: Jerry Gross; Jan Riess; Robert Meissner; Marie Paretti; Br. Declan Kane, CFX; Br. William Griffin, CFX; Chris O'Neill; Cheryl Bittner; Bill Fleming; and Mike Restuccia.

Thanks to the First State Oracle User Group board (Pete Silva, Phil Stewart, Earl Shaffer, and Lori Kaupas) for its support (http://www.fsoug.org).

Special thanks to Sue, Emily, Rachel, Jane, and the rest of the home team. As always, this has been a joint effort.

—Kevin Loney

Preface

The Intriguing History of This Book

I first encountered Oracle in 1982, in the process of evaluating database management systems for a major commercial application that my company was preparing to design and build. At its conclusion, our evaluation was characterized by *ComputerWorld* as the single-most "grueling" study of DBMSs that had ever been conducted. The study was so tough on the vendors whose products we examined that word of it made the press as far away as New Zealand and publications as far afield as the *Christian Science Monitor*.

We began the study with 108 candidate companies, then narrowed the field to sixteen finalists, including most of the major database vendors of the time, and all types of databases: network, hierarchical, relational, and others. After the rigorous final round of questions, two of the major vendors participating asked that the results of the study of their products never be published. A salesman from a third vendor quit his job at the end of one of the sessions. We knew how to ask tough questions.

Oracle, known then as Relational Software, Inc., had fewer than 25 employees at the time, and only a few major accounts. Nevertheless, when the study was completed, we announced Oracle as the winner. We declared that Oracle was technically the best product on the market, and that the management team at RSI looked capable enough to carry the company forward successfully. Our radical proclamation was made at a time when few people even knew what the term relational meant, and those who did had very few positive things to say about it. Many IS executives loudly criticized our conclusions and predicted that Oracle and the relational database would go nowhere.

Oracle today is the largest database company, and the second largest software company in the world. The relational database is now the world standard.

Koch Systems Corporation, the company I owned and ran at the time, became Oracle's first Valued Added Reseller. We developed the world's first major commercial relational application, a securities trading and accounting system called THESIS. This product was used by major banks and corporations to manage their investment portfolios. Even IBM bought THESIS, and it allowed Oracle to be installed at IBM headquarters in spite of vigorous internal opposition. After all, IBM was the leading database company at the time, with IMS and DB2 as their flagship products.

Oracle was continuing to refine its young product, to understand the kinds of features and functionality that would make it productive and useful in the business world, and our development efforts at Koch Systems contributed to that refinement. Some of Oracle's features were the direct

results of requests that we made of Oracle's developers, and our outspoken advocacy of an end-user bias in application design and naming conventions has influenced a generation of programmers who learned Oracle in our shop or read articles which we published.

All of this intimate involvement with the development and use of Oracle led us to an early and unmatched expertise with the product and its capabilities. Since I have always loved sharing discoveries and knowledge—to help shorten the learning time necessary with new technologies and ideas, and save others the cost of making the same mistakes I did—I decided to turn what we'd learned into a book.

Oracle: The Complete Reference was conceived in 1988 to pull together all of the fundamental commands and techniques used across the Oracle product line, as well as give solid guidance in how to develop applications using Oracle and SQL. Part I of the book was aimed both at developers and end-users, so that they could share a common language and understanding during the application development process: developers and end users working side by side—a wild concept when the book was first conceived.

Linda Allen, a respected literary agent in San Francisco, introduced me to Liz Fisher, then the editor at McGraw-Hill/Osborne. Liz liked the idea very much. Contracts were drawn, and the first edition was scheduled to be released in 1989. But a now-departed senior executive at McGraw-Hill heard of the project and instantly canceled its development, pronouncing that Oracle is a flash in the pan. It is going nowhere. A year later, when Oracle Corporation had again doubled in size and the senior executive was gone, the effort was restarted, and the first edition finally arrived in 1990.

Almost immediately, it became the No. 1 book in its category, a position it has maintained for over a decade.

In July of 1990, I was hired by Oracle to run its Applications Division. I became senior vice president of the company and guided the division (with a lot of talented help) to worldwide success. While at Oracle, I also introduced McGraw-Hill/Osborne to Oracle senior management, and after opposition from an Oracle vice president who didn't see any value in the idea (he's no longer with Oracle), Oracle Press was born.

Oracle Press is now the leading publisher of Oracle-based reference manuals in the world.

In 1992, Bob Muller, a former developer at both Koch Systems and Oracle, took over responsibilities for technical updates to the book, as my duties at Oracle precluded any more than editorial review of changes. This produced *Oracle7: The Complete Reference*. This was Bob's first published book, and he has since gone on to write several other popular books on development and database design.

In 1994, I left Oracle to fulfill a long-held desire—full time ministry—and today I'm the pastor of Church of the Resurrection (http://www.resurrection.org) in West Chicago, Illinois. I continue to write in publications as diverse as the *Wall Street Journal* and *Christianity Today*, and I've recently published a book in England, *The Country Parson's Advice to His Parishioner*, from Monarch Books. I also sit on the board of directors of Apropos, a leading call center applications company, but I no longer work in Oracle application development.

Also in 1994, Kevin Loney, a highly respected independent Oracle consultant and author (http://www.kevinloney.com), took over the updating and rewriting responsibilities for the third edition of the book, and has continued ever since. He has contributed major new sections (such as the Hitchhiker's Guides, the PL/SQL, Java, and ORDBMS sections, among others), and fully integrated new Oracle product features into all sections of the book. He has also integrated many readers' comments into the structure and content of the book, making its current form the product of both its readers and its authors. Those efforts have allowed *Oracle: The Complete Reference* to

stay at the top of its field and continue to be the single-most comprehensive guide to Oracle, still unmatched in range, content, and authority. I am a real fan of Kevin's and am most impressed by his knowledge and thoroughness.

Oracle: The Complete Reference is now available in eight languages, and is found on the desks of developers and Oracle product users all over the world. Not only has it been No. 1 in its category (with two editions out, it was once both No. 1 and No. 4), it has also been regularly in the top 100 of *all* books sold through Amazon.com. At one point it was the No. 7 best-selling book of all books sold in Brazil! Its reputation and enduring success are unparalleled in its marketplace.

Like Oracle itself, the book has survived and prospered in spite of the recurring predictions of failure from many quarters. Perhaps this brief history can be an encouragement to others who face opposition but have a clear vision of what is needed in the years ahead.

As Winston Churchill said, "Never give in, never give in, never give in—in nothing great or small, large or petty—never give in except to convictions of honor and good sense."

George Byron Koch
GeorgeKoch@GeorgeKoch.com
Wheaton, Illinois

Introduction

racle is the most widely used database in the world. It runs on virtually every kind of computer. It functions virtually identically on all these machines, so when you learn it on one, you can use it on any other. This fact makes knowledgeable Oracle users and developers very much in demand, and makes your Oracle knowledge and skills very portable.

Oracle documentation is thoroughgoing and voluminous, currently spanning multiple CDs. *Oracle9i: The Complete Reference* is the first entity that has gathered all of the major Oracle definitions, commands, functions, features, and products together in a single, massive core reference—one volume that every Oracle user and developer can keep handy on his or her desk.

The audience for this book will usually fall into one of three categories:

- *An Oracle end user* Oracle can easily be used for simple operations such as entering data and running standard reports. But such an approach would ignore its great power; it would be like buying a high-performance racing car, and then pulling it around with a horse. With the introduction provided in the first two sections of this book, even an end user with little or no data processing background can become a proficient Oracle user—generating ad hoc, English-language reports; guiding developers in the creation of new features and functions; and improving the speed and accuracy of the real work done in a business. The language of the book is simple, clear English without data processing jargon, and with few assumptions about previous knowledge of computers or databases. It will help beginners to become experts with an easy-to-follow format and numerous real examples.

- *A developer who is new to Oracle* With as many volumes of documentation as Oracle provides, finding a key command or concept can be a time-consuming effort. This book attempts to provide a more organized and efficient manner of learning the essentials of the product. The format coaches a developer new to Oracle quickly through the basic concepts, covers areas of common difficulty, examines misunderstanding of the product and relational development, and sets clear guidelines for effective application building.

■ *An experienced Oracle developer* As with any product of great breadth and sophistication, there are important issues about which little, if anything, has been published. Knowledge comes through long experience, but is often not transferred to others. This book delves deeply into many such subject areas (such as precedence in UNION, INTERSECTION, and MINUS operators; inheritance and CONNECT BY; eliminating NOT IN with an outer join; using external tables; implementing the object-relational and Java options; and many others). The text also reveals many common misconceptions and suggests rigorous guidelines for naming conventions, application development techniques, and design and performance issues.

How This Book Is Organized

There are seven major parts to this book and a CD-ROM.

Part I is an introduction to "Critical Database Concepts." These chapters are essential reading for any Oracle user, new or veteran, from key-entry clerk to database administrator. They establish the common vocabulary that both end users and developers can use to coherently and intelligently share concepts and assure the success of any development effort. This introductory section is intended for both developers and end users of Oracle. It explores the basic ideas and vocabulary of relational databases and points out the dangers, classical errors, and profound opportunities in relational database applications.

Part II, "SQL and SQL*Plus," teaches the theory and techniques of relational database systems and applications, including SQL (Structured Query Language) and SQLPLUS. The section begins with relatively few assumptions about data processing knowledge on the part of the reader, and then advances step by step, through some very deep issues and complex techniques. The method very consciously uses clear, conversational English, with unique and interesting examples, and strictly avoids the use of undefined terms or jargon. This section is aimed primarily at developers and end users who are new to Oracle, or need a quick review of certain Oracle features. It moves step by step through the basic capabilities of SQL and Oracle's interactive query facility, SQLPLUS. When you've completed this section you should have a thorough understanding of all SQL key words, functions, and operators. You should be able to produce complex reports, create tables, and insert, update, and delete data from an Oracle database.

The later chapters of Part II provide some very advanced methods in SQLPLUS, Oracle's simple, command-line interface, and in-depth descriptions of the new and very powerful features of Oracle. This is intended for developers who are already familiar with Oracle, and especially those familiar with previous versions of Oracle, but who have discovered needs they couldn't readily fill. Some of these techniques are previously unpublished and, in some cases, have been thought impossible. The tips and advanced techniques covered here demonstrate how to use Oracle in powerful and creative ways. These include taking advantage of distributed database capabilities, loading data files, and performing advanced text-based searches. They also include the latest features, such as external tables, flashback queries, and new datatypes and functions.

Part III, "PL/SQL," provides coverage of PL/SQL. The topics include a review of PL/SQL structures, plus triggers, stored procedures, and packages.

Part IV, "Object-Relational Databases," provides extensive coverage of object-oriented features such as abstract datatypes, methods, object views, object tables, nested tables, varying arrays, and large objects.

Part V, "Java in Oracle," provides coverage of the Java features in the Oracle database. This section includes an overview of Java syntax as well as chapters on JDBC and SQLJ and Java stored procedures.

Part VI contains several "hitchhiker" guides: to the data dictionary, database optimizer, Oracle9i Application Server, database administration, and Oracle's XML implementation. These guides provide an overview of areas that developers may need to use in their application development and administration.

Part VII, the "Alphabetical Reference," is the complete reference for the Oracle server—a book unto itself. Reading the introductory pages to this reference will make its use much more effective and understandable. This section contains references for most major Oracle commands, keywords, products, features and functions, with extensive cross-referencing of topics. The reference is intended for use by both developers and users of Oracle but assumes some familiarity with the products. To make the most productive use of any of the entries, it would be worthwhile to read the first four pages of the reference. These explain in greater detail what is and is not included and how to read the entries.

The CD that accompanies this book contains a special electronic edition of *Oracle9i: The Complete Reference*. Now, with this electronic version, you can easily store all of the valuable information contained in the book on your PC while the print version of the book remains in your office or home. The CD also contains the table creation statements and row insertions for all of the tables used in this book. For anyone learning Oracle, having these tables available on your own Oracle ID, or on a practice ID, will make trying or expanding on the examples very easy.

Style Conventions Used in This Book

Except when testing for an equality (such as, City = 'CHICAGO'), Oracle ignores upper- and lowercase. In the formal listing of commands, functions, and their format (syntax) in the Alphabetical Reference, this book will follow Oracle's documentation style of putting all SQL in UPPERCASE, and all variables in lowercase italic.

Most users and developers of Oracle, however, never key all their SQL in uppercase. It's too much trouble, and Oracle doesn't care anyway. This book, therefore, will follow somewhat different style conventions in its examples (as opposed to its formal command and function formats, mentioned earlier), primarily for readability. They are as follows:

- Italic and boldface will not be used in example listings.

- **select**, **from**, **where**, **order by**, **having**, and **group by** will be in lowercase.

- SQLPLUS commands will be in lowercase: **column**, **set**, **save**, **ttitle**, and so on.

- SQL operators and functions will be in uppercase, such as **IN**, **BETWEEN**, **UPPER**, **SOUNDEX**, and so on.

- Columns will use upper- and lowercase, as in Feature, EastWest, Longitude, and so on.

- Tables will be in uppercase, such as in NEWSPAPER, WEATHER, LOCATION, and so on.

PART
I

Critical Database Concepts

CHAPTER
1

Sharing Knowledge
and Success

F or an Oracle9i application to be built and used rapidly and effectively, users and developers must share a common language and a deep and common understanding of both the business application and the Oracle tools.

This is a new approach to development. Historically, the systems analyst studied the business requirements and built an application to meet those needs. The user was involved only in describing the business and, perhaps, in reviewing the functionality of the application after it was completed.

With the new tools and approaches available, and especially with Oracle, applications can be built that more closely match the needs and work habits of the business—but only if a common understanding exists.

This book is aimed specifically at fostering this understanding, and at providing the means for both user and developer to exploit Oracle's full potential. The end user will know details about the business that the developer will not comprehend. The developer will understand internal functions and features of Oracle and the computer environment that will be too technically complex for the end user. But these areas of exclusive expertise will be minor compared with what both end users and developers can share in using Oracle. There is a remarkable opportunity here.

It is no secret that "business" people and "systems" people have been in conflict for decades. Reasons for this include differences in knowledge, culture, professional interests and goals, and the alienation that simple physical separation between groups can often produce. To be fair, this syndrome is not peculiar to data processing. The same thing occurs between people in accounting, personnel, or senior management, as members of each group gather apart from other groups on a separate floor or in a separate building or city. Relations between the individuals from one group and another become formalized, strained, and abnormal. Artificial barriers and procedures that stem from this isolationism become established, and these also contribute to the syndrome.

This is all very well, you say, and may be interesting to sociologists, but what does it have to do with Oracle?

Because Oracle isn't cloaked in arcane language that only systems professionals can comprehend, it fundamentally changes the nature of the relationship between business and systems people. Anybody can understand it. Anybody can use it. Information that previously was trapped in computer systems until someone in systems created a new report and released it now is accessible, instantly, to a business person, simply by typing an English query. This changes the rules of the game.

Where Oracle is used, it has radically improved the understanding between the two camps, has increased their knowledge of one another, and has even begun to normalize relations between them. This has also produced superior applications and end results.

Since its first release, Oracle has been based on the easily understood relational model (explained shortly), so nonprogrammers can readily understand what Oracle does and how it does it. This makes it approachable and unimposing.

Furthermore, Oracle was created to run identically on virtually any kind of computer. Thus, it doesn't matter which manufacturer sold you your equipment; Oracle works on it. These features all contributed directly to the profound success of the product and the company.

In a marketplace populated by computer companies with "proprietary" hardware, "proprietary" operating systems, "proprietary" databases, and "proprietary" applications, Oracle gives business users and systems departments new control over their lives and futures. They are no longer bound to the database product of a single hardware vendor. Oracle runs on nearly every kind of computer. This is a basic revolution in the workplace and in application development, with consequences that will extend far into the future.

Some individuals neither accept nor understand this yet, nor do they realize just how vital it is that the dated and artificial barriers between "users" and "systems" continue to fall. But the advent of cooperative development will profoundly affect applications and their usefulness.

However, many application developers have fallen into an easy trap with Oracle: carrying forward unhelpful methods from previous-generation system designs. There is a lot to unlearn. Many of the techniques (and limitations) that were indispensable to a previous generation of systems are not only unnecessary in designing with Oracle; they are positively counterproductive. In the process of explaining Oracle, the burden of these old habits and approaches must be lifted. Refreshing new possibilities are available.

Throughout this book, the intent will be to explain Oracle in a way that is clear and simple, in terms that both users and developers can understand and share. Outdated or inappropriate design and management techniques will be exposed and replaced.

The Cooperative Approach

Oracle is an *object-relational database.* A relational database is an extremely simple way of thinking about and managing the data used in a business. It is nothing more than a collection of tables of data. We all encounter tables every day: weather reports, stock charts, sports scores. These are all tables, with column headings and rows of information simply presented. Even so, the relational approach can be sophisticated and powerful enough for even the most complex of businesses. An object-relational database supports all of the features of a relational database while also supporting object-oriented concepts and features.

Unfortunately, the very people who can benefit most from a relational database—the business users—usually understand it the least. Application developers, who must build systems that these users need to do their jobs, often find relational concepts difficult to explain in simple terms. A common language is needed to make this cooperative approach work.

The first two parts of this book explain, in readily understandable terms, just what a relational database is and how to use it effectively in business. It may seem that this discussion is for the benefit of "users" only. An experienced relational application designer may be inclined to skip these early chapters and simply use the book as a primary source Oracle reference. Resist that temptation! Although much of this material may seem like elementary review, it is an opportunity for an application designer to acquire a clear, consistent, and workable terminology with which to talk to users about their needs and how these needs might be quickly met. If you are an application designer, this discussion may also help you unlearn some unnecessary and probably unconscious design habits. Many of these habits will be uncovered in the course of introducing the relational approach. It is important to realize that even Oracle's power can be diminished considerably by design methods appropriate only to nonrelational development.

If you are an end user, understanding the basic ideas behind object-relational databases will help you express your needs cogently to application developers and comprehend how those needs can be met. An average person working in a business role can go from beginner to expert in short order. With Oracle, you'll have the power to get and use information, have hands-on control over reports and data, and possess a clear-eyed understanding of what the application does and how it does it. Oracle gives you, the user, the ability to control an application or query facility expertly and *know* whether you are getting all the available flexibility and power.

You also will be able to unburden programmers of their least favorite task: writing new reports. In large organizations, as much as 95 percent of all programming backlog is composed

of new report requests. Because you can write your own reports, in minutes instead of months, you will be delighted to have the responsibility.

Everyone Has "Data"

A library keeps lists of members, books, and fines. The owner of a baseball card collection keeps track of players' names, dates, averages, and card values. In any business, certain pieces of information about customers, products, prices, financial status, and so on must be saved. These pieces of information are called *data*.

Information philosophers like to say that data is just data until it is organized in a meaningful way, at which point it becomes "information." If this is true, then Oracle is also a means of easily turning data into information. Oracle will sort through and manipulate data to reveal pieces of knowledge hidden there—such as totals, buying trends, or other relationships—which are as yet undiscovered. You will learn how to make these discoveries. The main point here is that you have data, and you do three basic things with it: acquire it, store it, and retrieve it.

Once you've achieved the basics, you can make computations with data, move it from one place to another, or modify it. This is called *processing*, and, fundamentally, it involves the same three steps that affect how information is organized.

You could do all of this with a cigar box, pencil, and paper, but as the volume of data increases, your tools tend to change. You may use a file cabinet, calculators, pencils, and paper. While at some point it makes sense to make the leap to computers, your tasks remain the same.

A *relational database management system* (often called an RDBMS for short) such as Oracle gives you a way of doing these tasks in an understandable and reasonably uncomplicated way. Oracle basically does three things:

■ Lets you put data into it

■ Keeps the data

■ Lets you get the data out and work with it

Figure 1-1 shows how simple this process is.

Oracle supports this in-keep-out approach and provides clever tools that allow you considerable sophistication in how the data is captured, edited, modified, and put in; how you keep it securely; and how you get it out to manipulate and report on it.

An *object-relational database management system (ORDBMS)* extends the capabilities of the RDBMS to support object-oriented concepts. You can use Oracle as an RDBMS or take advantage of its object-oriented features.

The Familiar Language of Oracle

The information stored in Oracle is kept in tables—much like the weather table from a daily newspaper shown in Figure 1-2.

This table has four columns: City, Temperature, Humidity, and Condition. It also has a row for each city from Athens to Sydney. Last, it has a table name: WEATHER.

FIGURE 1-1. *What Oracle does with data*

These are the three major characteristics of most tables you'll see in print: *columns, rows, and a name.* The same is true in a relational database. Anyone can understand the words and the ideas they represent, because the words used to describe the parts of a table in an Oracle database are the same words used in everyday conversation. The words have no special, unusual, or esoteric meanings. What you see is what you get.

Tables of Information

Oracle stores information in tables, an example of which is shown in Figure 1-3. Each of these tables has one or more columns. The column headings, such as City, Temperature, Humidity, and Condition shown in Figure 1-3, describe the kind of information kept in the column. The

WEATHER

City	Temperature	Humidity	Condition
Athens.......	97	89	Sunny
Chicago......	66	88	Rain
Lima.........	45	79	Rain
Manchester...	66	98	Fog
Paris........	81	62	Cloudy
Sparta.......	74	63	Cloudy
Sydney.......	29	12	Snow

FIGURE 1-2. *A weather table from a newspaper*

```
                                   Table name
                    A column          │
                        │             │
                        │          WEATHER
                        ▼             ▼
        City            Temperature     Humidity    Condition
        ----------      -----------     --------    ---------
        ATHENS                   97           89     SUNNY
        CHICAGO                  66           88     RAIN
        LIMA                     45           79     RAIN  ◄──────A row
        MANCHESTER               66           98     FOG
        PARIS                    81           62     CLOUDY
        SPARTA                   74           63     CLOUDY
        SYDNEY                   29           12     SNOW
```

FIGURE 1-3. *A WEATHER table from Oracle*

information is stored row after row (city after city). Each unique set of data, such as the temperature, humidity, and condition for the city of Manchester, gets its own row.

Oracle avoids specialized, academic terminology in order to make the product more approachable. In research papers on relational theory, a column may be called an "attribute," a row may be called a "tuple" (rhymes with "couple"), and a table may be called an "entity." For an end user, however, these terms are confusing. More than anything, they are an unnecessary renaming of things for which there are already commonly understood names in our shared everyday language. Oracle takes advantage of this shared language, and developers can too. It is imperative to recognize the wall of mistrust and misunderstanding that the use of unnecessary technical jargon produces. Like Oracle, this book will stick with "tables," "columns," and "rows."

Structured Query Language

Oracle was the first company to release a product that used the English-based *Structured Query Language,* or *SQL.* This language allows end users to extract information themselves, without using a systems group for every little report.

Oracle's query language has structure, just as English or any other language has structure. It has rules of grammar and syntax, but they are basically the normal rules of careful English speech and can be readily understood.

SQL, pronounced either "sequel" or "S.Q.L.," is an astonishingly capable tool, as you will see. Using it does not require any programming experience.

Here's an example of how you might use SQL. If someone asked you to select from the preceding WEATHER table the city where the humidity is 89, you would quickly respond "Athens." If you were asked to select cities where the temperature is 66, you would respond "Chicago and Manchester."

Oracle is able to answer these same questions, nearly as easily as you are, and in response to simple queries very much like the ones you were just asked. The keywords used in a query to Oracle are **select**, **from**, **where**, and **order by**. They are clues to Oracle to help it understand your request and respond with the correct answer.

A Simple Oracle Query

If Oracle had the example WEATHER table in its database, your first query (with a semicolon to tell Oracle to execute the command) would be simply this:

```
select City from WEATHER where Humidity = 89 ;
```

Oracle would respond:

```
City
----------
ATHENS
```

Your second query would be this:

```
select City from WEATHER where Temperature = 66 ;
```

For this query, Oracle would respond:

```
City
----------
MANCHESTER
CHICAGO
```

As you can see, each of these queries uses the keywords **select**, **from**, and **where**. What about **order by**? Suppose you wanted to see all the cities listed in order by temperature. You'd simply type this:

```
select City, Temperature from WEATHER
  order by Temperature ;
```

and Oracle would instantly respond with this:

```
City          Temperature
----------    -----------
SYDNEY             29
LIMA               45
MANCHESTER         66
CHICAGO            66
SPARTA             74
PARIS              81
ATHENS             97
```

Oracle has quickly reordered your table by temperature. (This table lists lowest temperatures first; in a later chapter, you'll learn how to specify whether you want low numbers or high numbers first.)

There are many other questions you can ask with Oracle's query facility, but these examples show how easy it is to obtain the information you need from an Oracle database in the form that will be most useful to you. You can build complicated requests from simple pieces of information,

but the method used to do this will always be understandable. For instance, you can combine the **where** and **order by** keywords, both simple by themselves, to tell Oracle to select those cities where the temperature is greater than 80, and show them in order by increasing temperature. You would type this:

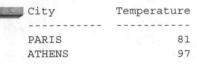

```
select City, Temperature from WEATHER
  where Temperature > 80
  order by Temperature ;
```

and Oracle would instantly respond with this:

```
City        Temperature
----------- -----------
PARIS               81
ATHENS              97
```

Or, to be even more specific, request cities where the temperature is greater than 80 and the humidity is less than 70:

```
select City, Temperature, Humidity from WEATHER
  where Temperature > 80
    and Humidity < 70
  order by Temperature ;
```

and Oracle would respond with this:

```
City        Temperature Humidity
----------- ----------- --------
PARIS               81       62
```

Why It Is Called "Relational"

Notice that the WEATHER table lists cities from several countries, and some countries have more than one city listed. Suppose you need to know in which country a particular city is located. You could create a separate LOCATION table of cities and their countries, as shown in Figure 1-4.

For any city in the WEATHER table, you can simply look at the LOCATION table, find the name in the City column, look over to the Country column in the same row, and see the country's name.

These are two completely separate and independent tables. Each contains its own information in columns and rows. They have one significant thing in common: the City column. For each city name in the WEATHER table, there is an identical city name in the LOCATION table.

For instance, what is the current temperature, humidity, and condition in an Australian city? Look at the two tables, figure it out, and then resume reading this.

How did you solve it? You found just one AUSTRALIA entry, under the Country column, in the LOCATION table. Next to it, in the City column of the same row, was the name of the city, SYDNEY. You took this name, SYDNEY, and then looked for it in the City column of the WEATHER table. When you found it, you moved across the row and found the Temperature, Humidity, and Condition: 29, 12, and SNOW.

WEATHER

City	Temperature	Humidity	Condition
ATHENS	97	89	SUNNY
CHICAGO	66	88	RAIN
LIMA	45	79	RAIN
MANCHESTER	66	98	FOG
PARIS	81	62	CLOUDY
SPARTA	74	63	CLOUDY
SYDNEY	29	12	SNOW

LOCATION

City	Country
ATHENS	GREECE
CHICAGO	UNITED STATES
CONAKRY	GUINEA
LIMA	PERU
MADRAS	INDIA
MADRID	SPAIN
MANCHESTER	ENGLAND
MOSCOW	RUSSIA
PARIS	FRANCE
ROME	ITALY
SHENYANG	CHINA
SPARTA	GREECE
SYDNEY	AUSTRALIA
TOKYO	JAPAN

FIGURE 1-4. *WEATHER and LOCATION tables*

Even though the tables are independent, you can easily see that they are related. The city name in one table is *related* to the city name in the other (see Figure 1-5). This relationship is the basis for the name *relational* database.

This is the basic idea of a relational database (sometimes called a *relational model*). Data is stored in tables. Tables have columns, rows, and names. Tables can be related to each other if each has a column with a common type of information.

That's it. It's as simple as it seems.

WEATHER

City	Temperature	Humidity	Condition
ATHENS	97	89	SUNNY
CHICAGO	66	88	RAIN
LIMA	45	79	RAIN
MANCHESTER	66	98	FOG
PARIS	81	62	CLOUDY
SPARTA	74	63	CLOUDY
SYDNEY	29	12	SNOW

LOCATION

City	Country
ATHENS	GREECE
CHICAGO	UNITED STATES
CONAKRY	GUINEA
LIMA	PERU
MADRAS	INDIA
MADRID	SPAIN
MANCHESTER	ENGLAND
MOSCOW	RUSSIA
PARIS	FRANCE
ROME	ITALY
SHENYANG	CHINA
SPARTA	GREECE
SYDNEY	AUSTRALIA
TOKYO	JAPAN

Relationship

FIGURE 1-5. *The relationship between the WEATHER and LOCATION tables*

Some Common, Everyday Examples

Once you understand the basic idea of relational databases, you'll begin to see tables, rows, and columns everywhere. Not that you didn't see them before, but you probably didn't think about them in quite the same way. Many of the tables that you are accustomed to seeing could be stored in Oracle. They could be used to quickly answer questions that would take you quite some time to answer using nearly any other method.

A typical stock market report in the paper might look like the one in Figure 1-6. This is a small portion of a dense, alphabetical listing that fills several narrow columns on several pages in a newspaper. Which stock traded the most shares? Which had the biggest percentage change in its price, either positively or negatively? The answers to these questions can be obtained through simple English queries in Oracle, which can find the answers much faster than you could by searching the columns on the newspaper page.

Figure 1-7 is an index to a newspaper. What's in section F? If you read the paper from front to back, in what order would you read the articles? The answers to these questions are obtainable via simple English queries in Oracle. You will learn how to do all of these queries, and even build the tables to store the information, in the course of using this reference.

Company	Close Yesterday	Close Today	Shares Traded
Ad Specialty	31.75	31.75	18,333,876
Apple Cannery	33.75	36.50	25,787,229
AT Space	46.75	48.00	11,398,323
August Enterprises	15.00	15.00	12,221,711
Brandon Ellipsis	32.75	33.50	25,789,769
General Entropy	64.25	66.00	7,598,562
Geneva Rocketry	22.75	27.25	22,533,944
Hayward Antiseptic	104.25	106.00	3,358,561
IDK	95.00	95.25	9,443,523
India Cosmetics	30.75	30.75	8,134,878
Isaiah James Storage	13.25	13.75	22,112,171
KDK Airlines	80.00	85.25	7,481,566
Kentgen Biophysics	18.25	19.50	6,636,863
LaVay Cosmetics	21.50	22.00	3,341,542
Local Development	26.75	27.25	2,596,934
Maxtide	8.25	8.00	2,836,893
MBK Communications	43.25	41.00	10,022,980
Memory Graphics	15.50	14.25	4,557,992
Micro Token	77.00	76.50	25,205,667
Nancy Lee Features	13.50	14.25	14,222,692
Northern Boreal	26.75	28.00	1,348,323
Ockham Systems	21.50	22.00	7,052,990
Oscar Coal Drayage	87.00	88.50	25,798,992
Robert James Apparel	23.25	24.00	19,032,481
Soup Sensations	16.25	16.75	22,574,879
Wonder Labs	5.00	5.00	2,553,712

FIGURE 1-6. *A stock market table*

Feature	Section	Page
Births	F	7
Bridge	B	2
Business	E	1
Classified	F	8
Comics	C	4
Doctor's In	F	6
Editorials	A	12
Modern Life	B	1
Movies	B	4
National News	A	1
Obituaries	F	6
Sports	D	1
Television	B	7
Weather	C	2

FIGURE 1-7. *A table based on sections of a newspaper*

Throughout this book, the examples use data and objects encountered frequently in business and everyday life. Similar data to use for your exercises should be as easy to find as your nearest bookshelf. You will learn how to enter and retrieve data in the pages ahead, using examples based on these everyday data sources.

CHAPTER
2

The Dangers in a
Relational Database

 s with any new technology or new venture, it's sensible to think through not only the benefits and opportunities that are presented, but also the costs and risks. Combine a relational database with a series of powerful and easy-to-use tools, as Oracle does, and the possibility of being seduced into disaster by its simplicity becomes real. Add in object-oriented and web capabilities, and the dangers increase. This chapter discusses some of the dangers that both developers and users need to consider.

Is It Really as Easy as They Say?

According to the database vendors—the industry evangelists—developing an application using a relational database and the associated "fourth-generation" tools will be as much as 20 times faster than traditional system development. And it will be very easy: ultimately, programmers and systems analysts will be used less, and end users will control their own destinies.

Critics of the relational approach warn that relational systems are inherently slower than others, that users who are given control of query and report writing will overwhelm computers, and that a company will lose face and fortune if a more traditional approach is not taken. The press cites stories of huge applications that simply failed to run when they were put into production.

So, what's the truth? The truth is that the rules of the game have changed. Fourth-generation development efforts make very different demands upon companies and management than do more traditional methods. There are issues and risks that are brand new and not obvious. Once these are identified and understood, the risk is no greater, and probably much smaller, than in traditional development.

What Are the Risks?

The primary risk is that developing relational database applications *is* as easy as they say. Understanding tables, columns, and rows isn't difficult. The relationship between two tables is conceptually simple. Even *normalization,* the process of analyzing the inherent or "normal" relationships between the various elements of a company's data, is fairly easy to learn.

Unfortunately, this often produces instant "experts," full of confidence but with little experience in building real, production-quality applications. For a tiny marketing database, or a home inventory application, this doesn't matter very much. The mistakes made will reveal themselves in time, the lessons will be learned, and the errors will be avoided the next time around. In an important application, however, this is a sure formula for disaster. This lack of experience is usually behind the press's stories of major project failures.

Older development methods are generally slower, primarily because the tasks of the older methods—coding, submitting a job for compilation, linking, and testing—result in a slower pace. The cycle, particularly on a mainframe, is often so tedious that programmers spend a good deal of time "desk-checking" in order to avoid going through the delay of another full cycle because of an error in the code.

Fourth-generation tools seduce developers into rushing into production. Changes can be made and implemented so quickly that testing is given short shrift. The elimination of virtually all desk-checking compounds the problem. When the negative incentive (the long cycle) that encouraged desk-checking disappeared, desk-checking went with it. The attitude of many seems to be, "If the application isn't quite right, we can fix it quickly. If the data gets corrupted, we can

patch it with a quick update. If it's not fast enough, we can tune it on the fly. Let's get it in ahead of schedule and show the stuff we're made of."

This problem is made worse by an interesting sociological phenomenon: Many of the developers of relational applications are recent college graduates. They've learned relational or object-oriented theory and design in school and are ready to make their mark. More seasoned developers, as a class, haven't learned the new technology. They're busy supporting and enhancing the technologies they know, which support their companies' current information systems. The result is that inexperienced developers tend to end up on the relational projects, are sometimes less inclined to test, and are less sensitive to the consequences of failure than those who have already lived through several complete application development cycles.

The testing cycle in an important Oracle project should be longer and more thorough than in a traditional project. This is true even if proper project controls are in place, and even if seasoned project managers are guiding the project, because there will be less desk-checking and an inherent overconfidence. This testing must check the correctness of data entry screens and reports, of data loads and updates, of data integrity and concurrence, and particularly of transaction and storage volumes during peak loads.

Because it really is as easy as they say, application development with Oracle's tools can be breathtakingly rapid. But this automatically reduces the amount of testing done as a normal part of development, and the planned testing and quality assurance must be consciously lengthened to compensate. This is not usually foreseen by those new to either Oracle or fourth-generation tools, but you must budget for it in your project plan.

The Importance of the New Vision

Many of us look forward to the day when we can simply type a "natural" language query in English, and have the answer back, on our screen, in seconds.

We are closer to this goal than most of us realize. The limiting factor is no longer technology, but rather the rigor of thought in our application designs. Oracle can straightforwardly build English-based systems that are easily understood and exploited by unsophisticated users. The potential is there, already available in Oracle's database and tools, but only a few have understood and used it.

Clarity and understandability should be the hallmarks of any Oracle application. Applications can operate in English, be understood readily by end users who have no programming background, and provide information based on a simple English query.

How? First of all, a major goal of the design effort must be to make the application easy to understand and simple to use. If you err, it must always be in this direction, even if it means consuming more CPU or disk space. The limitation of this approach is that you could make an application exceptionally easy to use by creating overly complex programs that are nearly impossible to maintain or enhance. This would be an equally bad mistake. However, all things being equal, an end-user orientation should never be sacrificed for clever coding.

Changing Environments

Consider that the cost to run a computer, expressed as the cost per million instructions per second (MIPS), has historically declined at the rate of 20 percent per year. Labor costs, on the other hand, have risen steadily, not just because of the general trend, but also because salaries of individual employees increase the longer they stay with a company and the better they become

at their jobs. This means that any work that can be shifted from human laborers to machines is a good investment.

Have we factored this incredible shift into our application designs? The answer is "somewhat," but terribly unevenly. The real progress has been in *environments,* such as the visionary work first done at Xerox Palo Alto Research Center (PARC), and then on the Macintosh, and now in MS-Windows, web-based browsers, and other graphical, icon-based systems. These environments are much easier to learn and understand than the older, character-based environments, and people who use them can produce in minutes what previously took days. The improvement in some cases has been so huge that we've entirely lost sight of how hard some tasks used to be.

Unfortunately, this concept of an accommodating and friendly environment hasn't been grasped by many application developers. Even when they work in these environments, they continue old habits that are just no longer appropriate.

Codes, Abbreviations, and Naming Standards

The problem of old programming habits is most pronounced in codes, abbreviations, and naming standards, which are almost completely ignored when the needs of end users are considered. When these three issues are thought about at all, usually only the needs and conventions of the systems groups are considered. This may seem like a dry and uninteresting problem to be forced to think through, but it can make the difference between great success and grudging acceptance, between an order-of-magnitude leap in productivity and a marginal gain, between interested, effective users and bored, harried users who make continual demands on the developers.

Here's what happened. Business records used to be kept in ledgers and journals. Each event or transaction was written down, line by line, in English. As we developed applications, codes were added to replace data values (such as "01" for "Accounts Receivable," "02" for "Accounts Payable," and so on). Key-entry clerks would actually have to know or look up most of these codes and type them in at the appropriately labeled fields on their screens. This is an extreme example, but literally thousands of applications take exactly this approach and are every bit as difficult to learn or understand.

This problem has been most pronounced in large, conventional mainframe systems development. As relational databases are introduced into these groups, they are used simply as replacements for older input/output methods such as Virtual Storage Access Method (VSAM) and Information Management System (IMS). The power and features of the relational database are virtually wasted when used in such a fashion.

Why Are Codes Used Instead of English?

Why use codes at all? Two primary justifications are usually offered:

■ A category has so many items in it that all of them can't reasonably be represented or remembered in English.

■ To save space in the computer.

The second point is an anachronism. Memory and permanent storage were once so expensive and CPUs so slow (with less power than a modern hand-held calculator) that

programmers had to cram every piece of information into the smallest possible space. Numbers, character for character, take half of the computer storage space of letters, and codes reduce the demands on the machine even more.

Because machines were expensive, developers had to use codes for *everything* to make *anything* work at all. It was a technical solution to an economic problem. For users, who had to learn all sorts of meaningless codes, the demands were terrible. Machines were too slow and too expensive to accommodate the humans, so the humans were trained to accommodate the machines. It was a necessary evil.

This economic justification for codes vanished years ago. Computers are now fast enough and cheap enough to accommodate the way people work, and use words that people understand. It's high time that they did so. Yet, without really thinking through the justifications, developers and designers continue to use codes.

The first point—that of too many items per category—is more substantive, but much less so than it first appears. One idea is that it takes less effort (and is therefore less expensive) for someone to key in the numeric codes than actual text string values like book titles. This justification is untrue in Oracle. Not only is it more costly to train people to know the correct customer, product, transaction, and other codes, and more expensive because of the cost of mistakes (which are high with code-based systems), but using codes also means not using Oracle fully; Oracle is able to take the first few characters of a title and fill in the rest of the name itself. It can do the same thing with product names, transactions (a "b" will automatically fill in with "buy," an "s" with "sell"), and so on, throughout an application. It does this with very robust pattern-matching abilities.

The Benefit of User Feedback

There is an immediate additional benefit: Key-entry errors drop almost to zero because the users get immediate feedback, in English, of the business information they're entering. Digits don't get transposed; codes don't get remembered incorrectly; and, in financial applications, money rarely is lost in accounts due to entry errors, with significant savings.

Applications also become much more comprehensible. Screens and reports are transformed from arcane arrays of numbers and codes into a readable and understandable format. The change of application design from code-oriented to English-oriented has a profound and invigorating effect on a company and its employees. For users who have been burdened by code manuals, an English-based application produces a tremendous psychological release.

How to Reduce the Confusion

Another version of the "too many items per category" justification is that the number of products, customers, or transaction types is just too great to differentiate each by name, or there are too many items in a category that are identical or very similar (customers named "John Smith," for instance). A category can contain too many entries to make the options easy to remember or differentiate, but more often this is evidence of an incomplete job of categorizing information: Too many dissimilar things are crammed into too broad a category. Developing an application with a strong English-based (or French, German, Spanish, and so on) orientation, as opposed to code-based, requires time spent with users and developers—taking apart the information about the business, understanding its natural relationships and categories, and then carefully constructing a database and naming scheme that simply and accurately reflects these discoveries.

There are three basic steps to doing this:

1. Normalize the data.

2. Choose English names for the tables and columns.

3. Choose English words for the data.

Each of these steps will be explained in order. The goal is to design an application in which the data is sensibly organized, is stored in tables and columns whose names are familiar to the user, and is described in familiar terms, not codes.

Normalization

Relations between countries, or between departments in a company, or between users and developers, are usually the product of particular historical circumstances, which may define current relations even though the circumstances have long since passed. The result of this can be abnormal relations, or, in current parlance, dysfunctional relations. History and circumstance often have the same effect on data—on how it is collected, organized, and reported. And data, too, can become abnormal and dysfunctional.

Normalization is the process of putting things right, making them normal. The origin of the term is the Latin word *norma,* which was a carpenter's square that was used for ensuring a right angle. In geometry, when a line is at a right angle to another line, it is said to be "normal" to it. In a relational database, the term also has a specific mathematical meaning having to do with separating elements of data (such as names, addresses, or skills) into *affinity groups,* and defining the normal, or "right," relationships between them.

The basic concepts of normalization are being introduced here so that users can contribute to the design of an application they will be using, or better understand one that's already been built. It would be a mistake, however, to think that this process is really only applicable to designing a database or a computer application. Normalization results in deep insights into the information used in a business and how the various elements of that information are related to each other. This will prove educational in areas apart from databases and computers.

The Logical Model

An early step in the analysis process is the building of a *logical model,* which is simply a normalized diagram of the data used by the business. Knowing why and how the data gets broken apart and segregated is essential to understanding the model, and the model is essential to building an application that will support the business for a long time, without requiring extraordinary support.

Normalization is usually discussed in terms of *form*: First, Second, and Third Normal Form are the most common, with Third representing the most highly normalized state. There are Fourth and Fifth normalization levels defined as well, but they are beyond the scope of this discussion.

Consider a bookshelf; for each book, you can store information about it—the title, publisher, authors, and multiple categories or descriptive terms for the book. Assume that this book-level data became the table design in Oracle. The table might be called BOOKSHELF, and the columns might be Title, Publisher, Author1, Author2, Author3, and Category1, Category2, and Category3.

The users of this table already have a problem: in the BOOKSHELF table, users are limited to listing just three authors or categories for a single book.

What happens when the list of acceptable categories changes? Someone has to go through every row in the BOOKSHELF table and correct all the old values. And what if one of the authors changes his or her name? Again, all of the related records must be changed. What will you do when a fourth author contributes to a book?

These are not really computer or technical issues, even though they became apparent because you were designing a database. They are much more basic issues of how to sensibly and logically organize the information of a business. They are the issues that normalization addresses. This is done with a step-by-step reorganization of the elements of the data into affinity groups, by eliminating dysfunctional relationships, and by ensuring normal relationships.

Normalizing the Data Step one of the reorganization is to put the data into First Normal Form. This is done by moving data into separate tables, where the data in each table is of a similar type, and giving each table a *primary key*—a unique label or identifier. This eliminates repeating groups of data, such as the authors on the bookshelf.

Instead of having only three authors allowed per book, each author's data is placed in a separate table, with a row per name and description. This eliminates the need for a variable number of authors in the BOOKSHELF table and is a better design than limiting the BOOKSHELF table to just three authors.

Next, you define the primary key to each table: What will uniquely identify and allow you to extract one row of information? For simplicity's sake, assume the titles and authors' names are unique, so AuthorName is the primary key to the AUTHOR table.

You now have split BOOKSHELF into two tables: AUTHOR, with columns AuthorName (the primary key) and Comments, and BOOKSHELF, with a primary key of Title, and with columns Publisher, and Category1, Category2, and Category3, Rating, and RatingDescription. A third table, BOOKSHELF_AUTHOR, provides the associations: Multiple authors can be listed for a single book and an author can write multiple books—known as a many-to-many relationship. Figure 2-1 shows these relationships and primary keys.

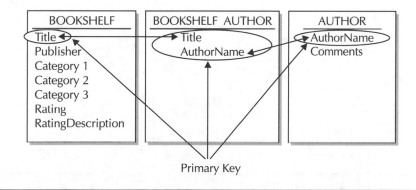

FIGURE 2-1. *The BOOKSHELF, AUTHOR, and BOOKSHELF_AUTHOR tables*

The next step in the normalization process, Second Normal Form, entails taking out data that's only dependent on a part of the key. If there are attributes that do not depend on the entire key, then those attributes should be moved to a new table. In this case, RatingDescription is not really dependent on Title—it's based on the Rating column value, so it should be moved to a separate table.

The final step, Third Normal Form, means getting rid of anything in the tables that doesn't depend solely on the primary key. In this example, the categories are interrelated; you would not list a title as both "Fiction" and "Nonfiction," and you would have different subcategories under the "Adult" category than you would have under the "Children" category. Category information is therefore moved to a separate table. Figure 2-2 shows the tables in Third Normal Form.

Any time the data is in Third Normal Form, it is already automatically in Second and First Normal Form. The whole process can therefore actually be accomplished less tediously than by going from form to form. Simply arrange the data so that the columns in each table, other than the primary key, are dependent only on the *whole primary key*. Third Normal Form is sometimes described as "the key, the whole key, and nothing but the key."

Navigating Through the Data

The bookshelf database is now in Third Normal Form. Figure 2-3 shows a sample of what these tables might contain. It's easy to see how these tables are related. You navigate from one to the other to pull out information on a particular author, based on the keys to each table. The primary key in each table is able to uniquely identify a single row. Choose Stephen Jay Gould, for instance, and you can readily discover his record in the AUTHOR table, because AuthorName is the primary key.

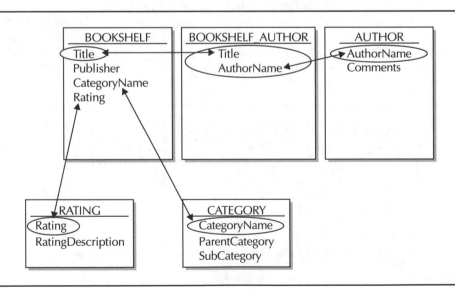

FIGURE 2-2. *BOOKSHELF and related tables*

```
AUTHOR
AuthorName                 Comments
--------------------       --------------------------------------------
DIETRICH BONHOEFFER        GERMAN THEOLOGIAN, KILLED IN A WAR CAMP
ROBERT BRETALL             KIERKEGAARD ANTHOLOGIST
ALEXANDRA DAY              AUTHOR OF PICTURE BOOKS FOR CHILDREN
STEPHEN JAY GOULD          SCIENCE COLUMNIST, HARVARD PROFESSOR
SOREN KIERKEGAARD          DANISH PHILOSOPHER AND THEOLOGIAN
HARPER LEE                 AMERICAN NOVELIST, PUBLISHED ONLY ONE NOVEL
LUCY MAUD MONTGOMERY       CANADIAN NOVELIST
JOHN ALLEN PAULOS          MATHEMATICS PROFESSOR
J. RODALE                  ORGANIC GARDENING EXPERT

RATING
Rating      RatingDescription
----------  -----------------
1           ENTERTAINMENT
2           BACKGROUND INFORMATION
3           RECOMMENDED
4           STRONGLY RECOMMENDED
5           REQUIRED READING

CATEGORY
CategoryName     ParentCategory   SubCategory
--------------   --------------   -----------
ADULTREF         ADULT            REFERENCE
ADULTFIC         ADULT            FICTION
ADULTNF          ADULT            NONFICTION
CHILDRENPIC      CHILDREN         PICTURE BOOK
CHILDRENFIC      CHILDREN         FICTION
CHILDRENNF       CHILDREN         NONFICTION

BOOKSHELF_AUTHOR
Title                                AuthorName
---------------------------------    ----------------------
TO KILL A MOCKINGBIRD                HARPER LEE
WONDERFUL LIFE                       STEPHEN JAY GOULD
INNUMERACY                           JOHN ALLEN PAULOS
KIERKEGAARD ANTHOLOGY                ROBERT BRETALL
KIERKEGAARD ANTHOLOGY                SOREN KIERKEGAARD
ANNE OF GREEN GABLES                 LUCY MAUD MONTGOMERY
GOOD DOG, CARL                       ALEXANDRA DAY
LETTERS AND PAPERS FROM PRISON DIETRICH BONHOEFFER
```

FIGURE 2-3. *Sample data from the BOOKSHELF tables*

```
BOOKSHELF
Title                           Publisher               CategoryName Rating
------------------------------- ----------------------- ------------ ------
TO KILL A MOCKINGBIRD           HARPERCOLLINS           ADULTFIC     5
WONDERFUL LIFE                  W.W.NORTON & CO.        ADULTNF      5
INNUMERACY                      VINTAGE BOOKS           ADULTNF      4
KIERKEGAARD ANTHOLOGY           PRINCETON UNIV PR       ADULTREF     3
ANNE OF GREEN GABLES            GRAMMERCY               CHILDRENFIC  3
GOOD DOG, CARL                  LITTLE SIMON            CHILDRENPIC  1
LETTERS AND PAPERS FROM PRISON  SCRIBNER                ADULTNF      4
```

FIGURE 2-3. *Sample data from the BOOKSHELF tables* (continued)

Look up Harper Lee in the AuthorName column of the BOOKSHELF_AUTHOR table and you'll see that she has published one novel, whose title is "To Kill A Mockingbird." You can then check the publisher, category, and rating for that book in the BOOKSHELF table. You can check the RATING table for a description of the rating.

When you looked up "To Kill A Mockingbird" in the BOOKSHELF table, you were searching by the primary key for the table. To find the author of that book, you could reverse your earlier search path, looking through BOOKSHELF_AUTHOR for the records that have that value in the Title column—the column 'Title' is a foreign key in the BOOKSHELF_AUTHOR table. When the primary key for BOOKSHELF appears in another table, as it does in the BOOKSHELF_AUTHOR table, it is called a *foreign key* to that table.

These tables also show real-world characteristics: There are ratings and categories that are not yet used by books on the bookshelf. Because the data is organized logically, you can keep a record of potential categories, ratings, and authors even if none of the current books use those values.

This is a sensible and logical way to organize information, even if the "tables" are written in a ledger book or on scraps of paper in cigar boxes. Of course, there is still some work to do to turn this into a real database. For instance, AuthorName probably ought to be broken into FirstName and LastName, and you might want to find a way to show which author is the primary author, or if one is an editor rather than an author.

This whole process is called normalization. It really isn't any trickier than this. There are some other issues involved in a good design, but the basics of analyzing the "normal" relationships among the various elements of data are just as simple and straightforward as they've just been explained. It makes sense regardless of whether or not a relational database or a computer is involved at all.

One caution needs to be raised, however. Normalization is a part of the process of analysis. It is not design. Design of a database application includes many other considerations, and it is a fundamental mistake to believe that the normalized tables of the logical model are the "design" for the actual database. This fundamental confusion of analysis and design contributes to the stories in the press about the failure of major relational applications. These issues are addressed for developers more fully later in this chapter.

English Names for Tables and Columns

Once the relationships between the various elements of the data in an application are understood and the data elements are segregated appropriately, considerable thought must be devoted to choosing names for the tables and columns into which the data will be placed. This is an area given too little attention, even by those who should know better. Table and column names are often developed without consulting end users and without rigorous review. Both of these failings have serious consequences when it comes to actually using an application.

For example, consider the tables shown in Figure 2-3. The table and column names are virtually all self-evident. An end user, even one new to relational ideas and SQL, would have little difficulty understanding or even replicating a query such as this:

```
select Title, Publisher
   from BOOKSHELF
 order by Publisher;
```

Users understand this because the words are all familiar. There are no obscure or ill-defined terms. When tables with many more columns in them must be defined, naming the columns can be more difficult, but a few consistently enforced rules will help immensely. Consider some of the difficulties commonly caused by lack of naming conventions. What if you had chosen these names instead?

```
BOOKSHELF        B_A         AUTHS          CATEGORIES
------------     --------    ------------   --------------
title            title       anam           cat
pub              anam        comms          p_cat
cat                                         s_cat
rat
```

The naming techniques in this table, as bizarre as they look, are unfortunately very common. They represent tables and columns named by following the conventions (and lack of conventions) used by several well-known vendors and developers.

Here are a few of the more obvious difficulties in the list of names:

- *Abbreviations are used without good reason.* This makes remembering the "spelling" of a table or column name virtually impossible. The names may as well be codes, because the users will have to look them up.

- *Abbreviations are inconsistent.*

- *The purpose or meaning of a column or table is not apparent from the name.* In addition to abbreviations making the spelling of names difficult to remember, they obscure the nature of the data the column or table contains. What is P_cat? Comms?

- *Underlines are used inconsistently.* Sometimes they are used to separate words in a name, but other times they are not. How will anyone remember which name does or doesn't have an underline?

- *Use of plurals is inconsistent.* Is it CATEGORY or CATEGORIES? Comm or Comms?

■ *Rules apparently used have immediate limitations.* If the first letter of the table name is to be used for a name column, as in Anam for a table whose table name starts with 'A', what happens when a second table beginning with the letter 'A' becomes necessary? Does the name column in that table also get called ANam? If so, why isn't the column in both simply called Name?

These are only a few of the most obvious difficulties. Users subjected to poor naming of tables and columns will not be able to simply type English queries. The queries won't have the intuitive and familiar "feel" that the BOOKSHELF table query has, and this will harm the acceptance and usefulness of the application significantly.

Programmers used to be required to create names that were a maximum of six to eight characters in length. As a result, names unavoidably were confused mixes of letters, numbers, and cryptic abbreviations. Like so many other restrictions forced on users by older technology, this one is just no longer applicable. Oracle allows table and column names up to 30 characters long. This gives designers plenty of room to create full, unambiguous, and descriptive names.

The difficulties outlined here imply solutions, such as avoiding abbreviations and plurals, and either eliminating underlines or using them consistently. These quick rules of thumb will go a long way in solving the naming confusion so prevalent today. At the same time, naming conventions need to be simple, easily understood, and easily remembered. In a sense, what is called for is a normalization of names. In much the same way that data is analyzed logically, segregated by purpose, and thereby normalized, the same sort of logical attention needs to be given to naming standards. The job of building an application is improperly done without it.

English Words for the Data

Having raised the important issue of naming conventions for tables and columns, the next step is to look at the data itself. After all, when the data from the tables is printed on a report, how self-evident the data is will determine how understandable the report is. In the BOOKSHELF example, Rating is a code value, and Category is a concatenation of multiple values. Is this an improvement? If you asked another person about a book, would you want to hear that it was a rated a 4 in AdultNF? Why should a machine be permitted to be less clear?

Additionally, keeping the information in English makes writing and understanding queries much simpler. The query should be as English-like as possible:

```
select Title, AuthorName
   from BOOKSHELF_AUTHOR;

Title                            AuthorName
-------------------------------  --------------------
TO KILL A MOCKINGBIRD            HARPER LEE
WONDERFUL LIFE                   STEPHEN JAY GOULD
INNUMERACY                       JOHN ALLEN PAULOS
KIERKEGAARD ANTHOLOGY            ROBERT BRETALL
KIERKEGAARD ANTHOLOGY            SOREN KIERKEGAARD
ANNE OF GREEN GABLES             LUCY MAUD MONTGOMERY
GOOD DOG, CARL                   ALEXANDRA DAY
LETTERS AND PAPERS FROM PRISON   DIETRICH BONHOEFFER
```

Capitalization in Names and Data

Oracle makes it slightly easier to remember table and column names by ignoring whether you type in capital letters, small letters, or a mixture of the two. It stores table and column names in its internal data dictionary in uppercase. When you type a query, it instantly converts the table and column names to uppercase, and then checks for them in the dictionary. Some other relational systems are case-sensitive. If users type a column name as "Ability," but the database thinks it is "ability" or "ABILITY" (depending on what it was told when the table was created), it will not understand the query.

NOTE
You can force Oracle to create tables and columns with mixed-case names, but doing so will make querying and working with the data difficult. Use the default uppercase behavior.

The ability to create case-sensitive table names is promoted as a benefit because it allows programmers to create many tables with, for instance, similar names. They can make a worker table, a Worker table, a wORker table, and so on. These will all be separate tables. How is anyone, including the programmer, supposed to remember the differences? This is a drawback, not a benefit, and Oracle was wise not to fall into this trap.

A similar case can be made for data stored in a database. There are ways to find information from the database regardless of whether the data is in uppercase or lowercase, but these methods impose an unnecessary burden. With few exceptions, such as legal text or form-letter paragraphs, it is much easier to store data in the database in uppercase. It makes queries easier and provides a more consistent appearance on reports. When and if some of this data needs to be put into lowercase, or mixed uppercase and lowercase (such as the name and address on a letter), then the Oracle functions that perform the conversion can be invoked. It will be less trouble overall, and less confusing, to store and report data in uppercase.

Looking back over this chapter, you'll see that this practice was not followed. Rather, it was delayed until the subject could be introduced and put in its proper context. From here on, with the exception of one or two tables and a few isolated instances, data in the database will be in uppercase.

Normalizing Names

Several query tools have come on the market whose purpose is to let you make queries using common English words instead of odd conglomerations. These products work by building a logical map between the common English words and the hard-to-remember, non-English column names, table names, and codes. The mapping takes careful thought, but once completed, it makes the user's interaction with the application easy. Why not put the care in at the beginning? Why create a need for yet another layer, another product, and more work, when much of the confusion can be avoided simply by naming things better the first time around?

For performance reasons, it may be that some of an application's data must still be stored in a coded fashion within the computer's database. These codes should *not* be exposed to users, either during data entry or retrieval, and Oracle allows them to be easily hidden.

The instant that data entry requires codes, key-entry errors increase. When reports contain codes instead of English, errors of interpretation begin. And when users need to create new or ad hoc reports, their ability to do so quickly and accurately is severely impaired both by codes and by not being able to remember strange column and table names.

Oracle gives users the power to see and work with English throughout the entire application. It is a waste of Oracle's power to ignore this opportunity, and it will without question produce a less understandable and less productive application. Developers should seize the opportunity. Users should demand it. Both will benefit immeasurably.

Good Design Has a Human Touch

At this point, if you are new to Oracle you may want to go right into working with Oracle and the SQL language. That is covered in the next chapter; the remainder of this chapter focuses on performance, naming, and design considerations. You can refer back to this section later when you are ready to design and implement an application.

This section of this chapter looks at a method of approaching a development project that takes into account the real business tasks your end users have to accomplish. This distinguishes it from the more common data orientation of many developers and development methodologies. Data normalization and CASE (Computer Aided Software Engineering) technologies have become so much the center of attention with relational application development that a focus on the data and the issues of referential integrity, keys, normalization, and table diagrams has become almost an obsession. They are so often confused with design—and even believed to *be* design—that the reminder that they are analysis is often met with surprise.

Normalization is analysis, not design. And it is only a part of the analysis necessary to understand a business and build a useful application. The goal of application development, after all, is to help the business run more successfully by improving the speed and efficiency with which business tasks are done and by making the environment in which people work as meaningful and supportive as possible. Give people control over their information, and intuitive, straightforward access to it, and they will respond gratefully and productively. Assign the control to a remote group, cloud the information in codes and user-hostile interfaces, and they will be unhappy and unproductive.

The methods outlined in this section are not intended to be a rigorous elucidation of the process, and the tools you use and are familiar with for data structures or flows are probably sufficient for the task. The purpose here is to disclose an approach that is effective in creating responsive, appropriate, and accommodating applications.

Understanding the Application Tasks

One of the often-neglected steps in building software is understanding the end user's job—the tasks that computer automation is intended to support. Occasionally, this is because the application itself is quite specialized; more often, it is because the approach to design tends to be data-oriented. Frequently, these are the major questions asked in the analysis:

- What data should be captured?
- How should the data be processed?
- How should the data be reported?

These questions expand into a series of subquestions, and include issues such as input forms, codes, screen layouts, computations, postings, corrections, audit trails, retention, storage volumes, processing cycles, report formatting, distribution, and maintenance. These are all vitally important areas. One difficulty, however, is that they all focus solely on data.

People *use* data, but they *do* tasks. One might argue that while this may be true of professional workers, key-entry clerks really only transfer data from an input form to a keyboard; their tasks are very data-oriented. This is a fair portrayal of these jobs today. But is this a consequence of the real job that needs to get done, or is it a symptom of the design of the computer application? Using humans as input devices, particularly for data that is voluminous, consistent in format (as on forms), and in a limited range of variability, is an expensive and antiquated, not to mention dehumanizing, method of capturing data. Like the use of codes to accommodate machine limitations, it's an idea whose time has passed.

This may sound like so much philosophy, but it has practical import in the way application design is done. People use data, but they do tasks. And they don't do tasks through to completion one at a time. They do several tasks that are subsets of or in intersection with each other, and they do them all at once, in parallel.

When designers allow this idea to direct the analysis and creation of an application, rather than focusing on the data orientation that has been historically dominant, the very nature of the effort changes significantly. Why have windowing environments been so successful? Because they allow a user to jump quickly between small tasks, keeping them all active without having to shut down and exit one in order to begin another. The windowing environment comes closer to mapping the way people really think and work than the old "one thing at a time" approach ever did. This lesson should not be lost. It should be built upon.

Understanding the application tasks means going far beyond identifying the data elements, normalizing them, and creating screens, processing programs, and reports. It means really understanding what the users do and what their tasks are, and designing the application to be responsive to those tasks, not just to capture the data associated with them. In fact, when the orientation is toward the data, the resulting design will inevitably *distort* the users' tasks rather than support them.

How do you design an application that is responsive to tasks rather than data? The biggest hurdle is simply understanding that focusing on tasks is necessary. This allows you to approach the analysis of the business from a fresh perspective.

The first step in the analysis process is to understand the tasks. For which tasks do the members of this group really need to use computers? What is the real service or product produced? This seems like a fundamental and even simplistic first question, but you'll find that a surprising number of businesspeople are quite unclear about the answer. An amazing number of businesses, from healthcare to banking, from shipping to manufacturing, used to think they were in the data processing business. After all, they input data, process it, and report it, don't they? This delusion is yet another symptom of the data orientation our systems designs have had that has led dozens of companies to attempt to market their imagined "real" product, data processing, with disastrous consequences for most of them.

Hence the importance of learning about a business application: You have to keep an open mind, and may often have to challenge pet notions about what the business is in order to learn what it really is. This is a healthy, if sometimes difficult, process.

And, just as it is essential that businesspeople become literate users of SQL and understand the basics of the relational model, so it is important that application designers really understand the service or product being delivered, and the tasks *necessary* to make that happen. A project

team that includes end users who have been introduced to the essentials of SQL and the relational approach, such as by reading this book, and designers who are sensitive to end users' needs and understand the value of a task-oriented, readable application environment, will turn out extraordinarily good systems. The members of such a project team check, support, and enhance each other's efforts.

One approach to this process is to develop two converging documents: a task document and a data document. It is in the process of preparing the task document that the deep understanding of the application comes about. The data document will help implement the vision and ensure that the details and rules are all accounted for, but the task document defines the vision of what the business is.

Outline of Tasks

The task document is a joint effort of the business users and the application designers. It lists the tasks associated with the business from the top down. It begins with a basic description of the business. This should be a simple declarative sentence of three to ten words, in the active voice, without commas and with a minimum of adjectives:

We sell insurance.

It should not be:

Amalgamated Diversified is a leading international supplier of financial resources, training, information processing, transaction capture and distribution, communications, customer support, and industry direction in the field of shared risk funding for health care maintenance, property preservation, and automobile liability.

There is a tremendous temptation to cram every little detail about a business and its dreams about itself into this first sentence. Don't do it. The effort of trimming the descriptive excesses down to a simple sentence focuses the mind wonderfully. If you can't get the business down to ten words, you haven't understood it yet.

But, as an application designer, creating this sentence isn't your task alone; it is a joint effort with the business user, and it initiates the task documentation process. It provides you with the opportunity to begin serious questioning about what the business does and how it does it. This is a valuable process for the business itself, quite independent of the fact that an application is being built. You will encounter numerous tasks and subtasks, procedures, and rules that will prove to be meaningless or of marginal use. Typically, these are artifacts of either a previous problem, long since solved, or of information or reporting requests from managers long since departed.

Some wags have suggested that the way to deal with too many reports being created, whether manually or by computer, is to simply stop producing them and see if anyone notices. This is a humorous notion, but the seed of truth it contains needs to be a part of the task documentation process. In fact, it proved quite useful in Y2K remediation efforts—many programs and reports didn't have to be fixed, simply because they were no longer used!

Your approach to the joint effort of documenting tasks allows you to ask skeptical questions and look at (and reevaluate the usefulness of) what may be mere artifacts. Be aware, however, that you need to proceed with the frank acknowledgment that you, as a designer, cannot

understand the business as thoroughly as the user does. There is an important line between seizing the opportunity of an application development to rationalize what tasks are done and why, and possibly offending the users by presuming to understand the "real" business better than they do.

Ask the user to describe a task in detail and explain to you the reason for each step. If the reason is a weak one, such as "We've always done it this way," or "I think they use this upstairs for something," red flags should go up. Say that you don't understand, and ask again for an explanation. If the response is still unsatisfactory, put the task and your question on a separate list for resolution. Some of these will be answered simply by someone who knows the subject better, others will require talking to senior management, and many tasks will end up eliminated because they are no longer needed. One of the evidences of a good analysis process is the improvement of existing procedures, independent of, and generally long before, the implementation of a new computer application.

General Format of the Task Document

This is the general format for the task document:

- Summary sentence describing the business (three to ten words)

- Summary sentences describing and numbering the major tasks of the business (short sentences, short words)

- Additional levels of task detail, as needed, within each of the major tasks

By all means, follow the summary sentence for every level with a short, descriptive paragraph, if you want, but don't use this as an excuse to avoid the effort of making the summary sentence clear and crisp. Major tasks are typically numbered 1.0, 2.0, 3.0, and so on, and are sometimes referred to as zero-level tasks. The levels below each of these are numbered using additional dots, as in 3.1 and 3.1.14. Each major task is taken down to the level where it is a collection of *atomic tasks*—tasks for which no subtask is meaningful in itself and that, once started, is either taken to completion or dropped entirely. Atomic tasks are never left half-finished.

Writing a check is an atomic task; filling in the dollar amount is not. Answering the telephone as a customer service representative is not an atomic task; answering the phone and fulfilling the customer's request is atomic. Atomic tasks must be meaningful and must complete an action.

The level at which a task is atomic will vary by task. The task represented by 3.1.14 may be atomic yet still have several additional sublevels. The task 3.2 may be atomic, or 3.1.16.4 may be. What is important is not the numbering scheme (which is nothing more than a method for outlining a hierarchy of tasks) but the decomposition to the atomic level. The atomic tasks are the fundamental building blocks of the business. Two tasks can still be atomic if one occasionally depends upon the other, but only if each can and does get completed independently. If two tasks always depend upon each other, they are not atomic. The real atomic task includes them both.

In most businesses, you will quickly discover that many tasks do not fit neatly into just one of the major (zero-level) tasks, but seem to span two or more, and work in a network or "dotted line" fashion. This is nearly always evidence of improper definition of the major tasks or incomplete atomization of the lower tasks. The goal is to turn each task into a conceptual "object," with a well-defined idea of what it does (its goal in life) and what resources (data, computation, thinking, paper, pencil, and so on) it uses to accomplish its goal.

Insights Resulting from the Task Document

Several insights come out of the task document. First, because the task document is task-oriented rather than data-oriented, it is likely to substantially change the way user screens are designed. It will affect what data is captured, how it is presented, how help is implemented, and how users switch from one task to another. The task orientation will help ensure that the most common kinds of jumping between tasks will not require inordinate effort from the user.

Second, the categorization of major tasks will change as conflicts are discovered; this will affect how both the designers and the business users understand the business.

Third, even the summary sentence itself will probably change. Rationalizing a business into atomic task "objects" forces a clearing out of artifacts, misconceptions, and unneeded dependencies that have long weighed down the business unnecessarily.

This is not a painless process, but the benefits in terms of the business's self-understanding, the cleanup of procedures, and the automation of the tasks will usually far exceed the emotional costs and time spent. It helps immensely if there is general understanding going into the project that uncomfortable questions will be asked, incorrect assumptions corrected, and step-by-step adjustments made to the task document until it is completed.

Understanding the Data

In conjunction with the decomposition and description of the tasks, the resources required at each step are described in the task document, especially in terms of the data required. This is done on a task-by-task basis, and the data requirements are then included in the data document. This is a conceptually different approach from the classical view of the data. You will not simply take the forms and screens currently used by each task and record the elements they contain. The flaw in this "piece of paper in a cigar box" approach lies in our tendency (even though we don't like to admit it) to accept anything printed on paper as necessary or true.

In looking at each task, you should determine what data is necessary to do the task, rather than what data elements are on the form you use to do the task. By requiring that the definition of the data needed come from the task rather than from any existing forms or screens, you force an examination of the true purpose of the task and the real data requirements. If the person doing the task doesn't know the use to which data is put, the element goes on the list for resolution. An amazing amount of garbage is eliminated by this process.

Once the current data elements have been identified, they must be carefully scrutinized. Numeric and letter codes are always suspect. They disguise real information behind counterintuitive, meaningless symbols. There are times and tasks for which codes are handy, easily remembered, or made necessary by sheer volume. But, in your final design, these cases should be rare and obvious. If they are not, you've lost your way.

In the scrutiny of existing data elements, codes should be set aside for special attention. In each case, ask yourself whether the element should be a code. Its continued use as a code should be viewed suspiciously. There must be good arguments and compelling reasons for perpetuating the disguise. The process for converting codes back into English is fairly simple, but is a joint effort. The codes are first listed, by data element, along with their meanings. These are then examined by users and designers, and short English versions of the meanings are proposed, discussed, and tentatively approved.

In this same discussion, designers and end users should decide on names for the data elements. These will become column names in the database, and will be regularly used in English queries, so the names should be descriptive (avoiding abbreviations, other than those

common to the business) and singular. Because of the intimate relationship between the column name and the data it contains, the two should be specified simultaneously. A thoughtful choice of a column name will vastly simplify determining its new English contents.

Data elements that are not codes also must be rigorously examined. By this point, you have good reason to believe that all of the data elements you've identified are necessary to the business tasks, but they are not necessarily well-organized. What appears to be one data element in the existing task may in fact be several elements mixed together that require separation. Names, addresses, and phone numbers are very common examples of this, but every application has a wealth of others.

First and last names were mixed together, for example, in the AUTHOR table. The AuthorName column held both first and last names, even though the tables were in Third Normal Form. This would be an extremely burdensome way to actually implement an application, in spite of the fact that the normalization rules were technically met. To make the application practical and prepare it for English queries, the AuthorName column needs to be decomposed into at least two new columns, LastName and FirstName. This same categorization process is regularly needed in rationalizing other data elements, and is often quite independent of normalization.

The degree of decomposition depends on how the particular data elements are likely to be used. It is possible to go much too far and decompose categories that, though made up of separable pieces, provide no additional value in their new state. Decomposition is application-dependent on an element-by-element basis. Once decomposition has been done, these new elements, which will become columns, need to be thoughtfully named, and the data they will contain needs to be scrutinized. Text data that will fall into a definable number of values should be reviewed for naming. These column names and values, like those of the codes, are tentative.

The Atomic Data Models

Now the process of normalization begins, and with it the drawing of the atomic data models. There are many good texts on the subject and a wide variety of analysis and design tools that can speed the process, so this book doesn't suggest any particular method, since recommending one method may hinder rather than help.

Each atomic transaction should be modeled, and should be labeled with the task number to which it applies. Included in the model are table names, primary and foreign keys, and major columns. Each normalized relationship should have a descriptive name, and estimated row counts and transaction rates should appear with each table. Accompanying each model is an additional sheet with all of the columns and datatypes, their ranges of value, and the tentative names for the tables, columns, and named values in the columns.

The Atomic Business Model

This data document is now combined with the task document. The combined document is a · business model. It's reviewed jointly by the application designers and end users for accuracy and completeness.

The Business Model

At this point, both the application designers and the end users should possess a clear vision of the business, its tasks, and its data. Once the business model is corrected and approved, the process of synthesizing the tasks and data models into an overall business model begins. This part of the

process sorts common data elements between tasks, completes final, large-scale normalization, and resolves consistent, definitive names for all of the parts.

This can be quite a large drawing for major applications, with supporting documentation that includes the tasks, the data models (with corrected element names, based on the full model), and a list of each of the full-scale tables and their column names, datatypes, and contents. A final check of the effort is made by tracing the data access paths of each transaction in the full business model to determine that all the data the transaction requires is available for selection or insertion, and that no tasks insert data with elements missing that are essential to the model's referential integrity.

With the exception of the effort spent to properly name the various tables, columns, and common values, virtually everything to this point has been analysis, not design. The aim has been to promote understanding of the business and its components.

Data Entry

Screen design does not proceed from the business model. It is not focused on tables, but rather on tasks, so screens are created that support the task orientation and the need to jump between subtasks when necessary. In practical terms, this will often map readily to a primary table used by the task, and to other tables that can be queried for values or updated as the primary table is accessed.

But there will also be occasions where there simply is no main table, but instead a variety of related tables, all of which will supply or receive data to support the task. These screens will look and act quite differently from the typical table-oriented screens developed in many applications, but they will significantly amplify the effectiveness of their users and their contribution to the business. And that's the whole purpose of this approach.

The interaction between the user and the machine is critical; the input and query screens should consistently be task-oriented and descriptive, in English. The use of icons and graphical interfaces plays an important role as well. Screens must reflect the way work is actually done, and be built to respond in the language in which business is conducted.

Query and Reporting

If anything sets apart the relational approach, and SQL, from more traditional application environments, it is the ability for end users to easily learn and execute ad hoc queries. These are those reports and one-time queries that are outside of the basic set usually developed and delivered along with the application code.

With SQLPLUS (and other reporting tools), end users are given unprecedented control over their own data. Both the users and developers benefit from this ability: the users, because they can build reports, analyze information, modify their queries, and reexecute them all in a matter of minutes, and the developers, because they are relieved of the undesirable requirement of creating new reports.

Users are granted the power to look into their data, analyze it, and respond with a speed and thoroughness unimaginable just a few years ago. This leap in productivity is greatly extended if the tables, columns, and data values are carefully crafted in English; it is greatly foreshortened if bad naming conventions and meaningless codes and abbreviations are permitted to infect the design. The time spent in the design process to name the objects consistently and descriptively will pay off quickly for the users, and therefore for the business.

Some people, typically those who have not built major relational applications, fear that turning query facilities over to end users will cripple the machine on which the facilities are used. The fear

is that users will write inefficient queries that will consume overwhelming numbers of CPU cycles, slowing the machine and every other user. Experience shows that this generally is not true. Users quickly learn which kinds of queries run fast, and which do not. Further, most business intelligence and reporting tools available today can estimate the amount of time a query will take, and restrict access—by user, time of day, or both—to queries that would consume a disproportionate amount of resources. In practice, the demands users make on a machine only occasionally get out of hand, but the benefits they derive far exceed the cost of the processing. Virtually any time you can move effort from a person to a machine, you save money.

The real goal of design is to clarify and satisfy the needs of the business and business users. If there is a bias, it must always be toward making the application easier to understand and use, particularly at the expense of CPU or disk, but less so if the cost is an internal complexity so great that maintenance and change become difficult and slow.

Toward Object Name Normalization

The basic approach to naming is to choose meaningful, memorable, and descriptive readable names, avoiding abbreviations and codes, and using underlines either consistently or not at all. In a large application, table, column, and data names will often be multiword, as in the case of ReversedSuspenseAccount or Last_GL_Close_Date. The goal of thoughtful naming methods is ease of use: The names must be easily remembered and must follow rules that are easily explained and applied. In the pages ahead, a somewhat more rigorous approach to naming is presented, with the ultimate goal of developing a formal process of object name normalization.

Level-Name Integrity

In a relational database system, the hierarchy of objects ranges from the database, to the table owners, to the tables, to the columns, to the data values. In very large systems, there may even be multiple databases, and these may be distributed within locations. For the sake of brevity, the higher levels will be ignored for now, but what is said will apply to them as well.

Each level in this hierarchy is defined within the level above it, and each level should be given names appropriate to its own level and should not incorporate names from outside its own level. For example, a table cannot have two columns called Name, and the account named George cannot own two tables named AUTHOR.

There is no requirement that each of George's tables have a name that is unique throughout the entire database. Other owners may have AUTHOR tables as well. Even if George is granted access to them, there is no confusion, because he can identify each table uniquely by prefixing its owner's name to the table name, as in Dietrich.AUTHOR. It would not be logically consistent to incorporate George's owner name into the name of each of his tables, as in GEOAUTHOR, GEOBOOKSHELF, and so on. This confuses and complicates the table name by placing part of its parent's name in its own, in effect a violation of *level-name integrity*.

Brevity should never be favored over clarity. Including pieces of table names in column names is a bad technique, because it violates the logical idea of levels, and the level-name integrity that this requires. It is also confusing, requiring users to look up column names virtually every time they want to write a query. Object names must be unique within their parent, but no incorporation of names from outside an object's own level should be permitted.

The support for abstract datatypes in Oracle strengthens your ability to create consistent names for attributes. If you create a datatype called ADDRESS_TY, it will have the same attributes

each time it is used. Each of the attributes will have a consistent name, datatype, and length, making their implementation more consistent across the enterprise. However, using abstract datatypes in this manner requires that you do both of the following:

- Properly define the datatypes at the start so that you can avoid the need to modify the datatype later

- Support the syntax requirements of abstract datatypes (see Chapter 4 for details)

Foreign Keys

The one area of difficulty with using brief column names is the occasional appearance of a foreign key in a table in which another column has the same name that the foreign key column has in its home table. One possible long-term solution is to allow the use of the full foreign key name, including the table name of its home table, as a column name in the local table (such as BOOKSHELF.Title as a column name).

The practical need to solve the same-name column problem requires one of the following actions:

- Invent a name that incorporates the source table of the foreign key in its name without using the dot (using an underline, for instance).

- Invent a name that incorporates an abbreviation of the source table of the foreign key in its name.

- Invent a name different from its name in its source table.

- Change the name of the conflicting column.

None of these is particularly attractive, but if you come across the same-name dilemma, you'll need to take one of these actions.

Singular Names

One area of great inconsistency and confusion is the question of whether objects should have singular or plural names. Should it be the AUTHOR table or the AUTHORS table? Should it be the Name column or the Names column?

There are two helpful ways to think about this issue. First, consider some columns common to nearly every database: Name, Address, City, State, and Zip. Other than the first column, does it ever occur to anyone to make these names plural? It is nearly self-evident when considering these names that they describe the contents of a single row, a record. Even though relational databases are "set-oriented," clearly the fundamental unit of a set is a row, and it is the content of that row that is well-described by singular column names. When designing a data entry screen to capture a person's name and address, should it look like this?

```
Names: _____

Addresses: _____

Cities: _____  States __  Zips _____-____
```

Or will you make these column names singular on the screen, since you're capturing *one* name and address at a time, but tell the users that when they write queries they must all be converted to plural? It is simply more intuitive and straightforward to restrict column names to singular.

If all objects are named consistently, neither you nor a user has to try to remember the rules for what is plural and what isn't. The benefit of this should be obvious. Suppose we decide that all objects will henceforth be plural. We now have an "s" or an "es" on the end of virtually every object, perhaps even on the end of each word in a long multiword object name. Of what possible benefit is it to key all of these extra letters all the time? Is it easier to use? Is it easier to understand? Is it easier to remember? Obviously, it is none of these.

Therefore, the best solution is this: All object names are always singular. The sole exception to this rule is any widely accepted term already commonly used in the business, such as "sales."

Brevity

As mentioned earlier, clarity should never be sacrificed for brevity, but given two equally meaningful, memorable, and descriptive names, always choose the shorter. During application development, propose alternative column and table names such as these to a group of users and developers and get their input on choosing the clearest name. How do you build lists of alternatives? Use a thesaurus and a dictionary. On a project team dedicated to developing superior, productive applications, every team member should be given a thesaurus and a dictionary as basic equipment, and then should be reminded over and over again of the importance of careful object naming.

Object Name Thesaurus

Ultimately, relational databases should include an object name thesaurus, just as they include a data dictionary. This thesaurus should enforce the company's naming standards and ensure consistency of name choice and abbreviation (where used).

Such standards may require the use of underlines in object naming to make the parsing of the name into component parts a straightforward task. This also helps enforce the consistent use of underlines, rather than the scattered, inconsistent usage within an application that underlines frequently receive now.

If you work directly with a government agency or large firm, that organization may already have object-naming standards. The object-naming standards of large organizations have over the years radiated into the rest of the commercial marketplace, and may form the basis for the naming standards used at your company. For example, those standards may provide the direction to choose between "Corporation" and "Firm." If they do not, you should develop your naming standards to be consistent both with those base standards and with the guidelines put forth in this chapter.

Intelligent Keys and Column Values

Intelligent keys are so named because they contain nontrivial combinations of information. The term is misleading in the extreme because it implies something positive or worthwhile. A more meaningful term might be "overloaded" keys. General ledger and product codes often fall into this category and contain all the difficulties associated with other codes, and more. Further, the difficulties found in overloaded keys also apply to non-key columns that are packed with more than one piece of meaningful data.

Typical of an overloaded key or column value is this description: "The first character is the region code. The next four characters are the catalog number. The final digit is the cost center code, unless this is an imported part, in which case an *I* is tagged onto the end of the number, or unless it is a high-volume item, such as screws, in which case only three digits are used for catalog number, and the region code is HD."

Eliminating overloaded key and column values is essential in good relational design. The dependencies built on pieces of these keys (usually foreign keys into other tables) are all at risk if the structure is maintained. Unfortunately, many application areas have overloaded keys that have been used for years and are deeply embedded in the company's tasks. Some of them were created during earlier efforts at automation, using databases that could not support multiple key columns for composite keys. Others came about through historical accretion, by forcing a short code, usually numeric, to mean more and to cover more cases than it was ever intended to at the beginning. Eliminating the existing overloaded keys may have practical ramifications that make it impossible to do immediately. This makes building a new, relational application more difficult.

The solution to this problem is to create a new set of keys, both primary and foreign, that properly normalizes the data; then, make sure that people can access tables only through these new keys. The overloaded key is then kept as an additional, and unique, table column. Access to it is still possible using historical methods (matching the overloaded key in a query, for instance), but the newly structured keys are promoted as the preferred method of access. Over time, with proper training, users will gravitate to the new keys. Eventually, the overloaded keys (and other overloaded column values) can simply be **NULL**ed out or dropped from the table.

Failing to eliminate overloaded keys and values makes extracting information from the database, validating the values, assuring data integrity, and modifying the structure all extremely difficult and costly.

The Commandments

All of the major issues in designing for productivity have now been discussed. It probably is worthwhile to sum these up in a single place—thus "The Commandments" (or perhaps "The Suggestions"). Their presentation does not assume that you need to be told what to do, but rather that you are capable of making rational judgments and can benefit from the experience of others facing the same challenges. The purpose here is not to describe the development cycle, which you probably understand better than you want to, but rather to bias that development with an orientation that will radically change how the application will look, feel, and be used. Careful attention to these ideas can dramatically improve the productivity and happiness of an application's users.

The Ten Commandments of Humane Design

1. Include users. Put them on the project team and teach them the relational model and SQL.

2. Name tables, columns, keys, and data jointly with the users. Develop an application thesaurus to ensure name consistency.

3. Use English words that are meaningful, memorable, descriptive, short, and singular. Use underlines consistently or not at all.

4. Don't mix levels in naming.

5. Avoid codes and abbreviations.

6. Use meaningful keys where possible.

7. Decompose overloaded keys.

8. Analyze and design from the tasks, not just the data. Remember that normalization is not design.

9. Move tasks from users to the machine. It is profitable to spend cycles and storage to gain ease of use.

10. Don't be seduced by development speed. Take time and care in analyses, design, testing, and tuning.

CHAPTER
3

The Basic Parts of
Speech in SQL

ith the Structured Query Language, or SQL, you tell Oracle which information you want it to **select**, **insert**, **update**, or **delete**. In fact, these four verbs are the primary words you will use to give Oracle instructions. As of Oracle9i, you can use an additional command, **merge**, to perform **insert**s and **update**s with a single command.

In Chapter 1, you saw what is meant by "relational," how tables are organized into columns and rows, and how to instruct Oracle to select certain columns from a table and show you the information in them row by row. In this and the following chapters, you will learn how to do this more completely for the different datatypes supported by Oracle. In this section, you will learn how to interact with SQL*PLUS, a powerful Oracle product that can take your instructions for Oracle, check them for correctness, submit them to Oracle, and then modify or reformat the response Oracle gives, based on orders or directions that you've set in place. It *interacts* with you, which means you can "talk" to it, and it will "talk" back. You can give it directions, and it will follow them precisely. It will tell you if it doesn't understand something you've told it to do.

It may be a little confusing at first to understand the difference between what SQL*PLUS is doing and what Oracle is doing, especially since the error messages that Oracle produces are simply passed on to you by SQL*PLUS, but you will see as you work through this book where the differences lie. As you get started, just think of SQL*PLUS as a coworker—an assistant who follows your instructions and helps you do your work more quickly. You interact with this coworker by typing on your keyboard.

You may follow the examples in this and subsequent chapters by typing the commands shown. Your Oracle and SQL*PLUS programs should respond just as they do in these examples. You do need to make certain that the tables used in this book have been loaded into your copy of Oracle.

You can understand what is described in this book without actually typing it in yourself; for example, you can use the commands shown with your own tables. It will probably be clearer and easier, though, if you have the same tables loaded into Oracle that are used here, and practice using the same queries.

The CD contains instructions on loading the tables. Assuming that you have done this, connect to SQL*PLUS and begin working by typing this:

```
sqlplus
```

(If you want to run SQL*PLUS from your desktop client machine, select the SQL Plus program option from the Application Development menu option under the Oracle software menu option.) This starts SQL*PLUS. (Note that you don't type the * that is in the middle of the official product name, and the asterisk doesn't appear in the program name, either. From here on, SQLPLUS will be referred to without the asterisk.) Since Oracle is careful to guard who can access the data it stores, it always requires that you enter an ID and password to connect to it. Oracle will display a copyright message, and then ask for your username and password. Log into your database using the account and password you created to hold the example tables (such as practice/practice). If you provide a valid username and password, SQLPLUS will announce that you're connected to Oracle, and then will display this prompt:

```
SQL>
```

You are now in SQLPLUS, and it awaits your instructions. If the command fails, there are several potential reasons: Oracle is not in your path, you are not authorized to use SQLPLUS, or Oracle hasn't been installed properly on your computer. If you get this message:

```
ERROR: ORA-1017: invalid username/password; logon denied
```

it means either that you've entered the username or password incorrectly, or that your username has not yet been set up properly on your copy of Oracle. After three unsuccessful attempts to enter a username and password that Oracle recognizes, SQLPLUS will terminate the attempt to log on, with this message:

```
unable to CONNECT to ORACLE after 3 attempts, exiting SQL*Plus
```

If you get this message, contact your company's database administrator. Assuming everything is in order, and the SQL> prompt has appeared, you may now begin working with SQLPLUS.

When you want to quit working and leave SQLPLUS, type this:

```
quit
```

Style

First, some comments on style. SQLPLUS doesn't care whether the SQL commands you type are in uppercase or lowercase. This command:

```
SeLeCt feaTURE, section, PAGE FROM newsPaPeR;
```

will produce exactly the same result as this one:

```
select Feature, Section, Page from NEWSPAPER;
```

Case matters only when SQLPLUS or Oracle is checking an alphanumeric value for equality. If you tell Oracle to find a row where Section = 'f' and Section is really equal to 'F', Oracle won't find it (since f and F are not identical). Aside from this use, case is completely irrelevant. (Incidentally, the letter 'F', as used here, is called a *literal,* meaning that you want Section to be tested literally against the letter 'F', not a column *named* F. The single quote marks enclosing the letter tell Oracle that this is a literal, and not a column name.)

As a matter of style, this book follows certain conventions about case to make the text easier to read:

- **select**, **from**, **where**, **order by**, **having**, and **group by** will always be lowercase and boldface.

- SQLPLUS commands also will be lowercase and boldface: **column**, **set**, **save**, **ttitle**, and so on.

- **IN**, **BETWEEN**, **UPPER**, and other SQL operators and functions will be uppercase and boldface.

44 Part I: Critical Database Concepts

- Column names will be mixed uppercase and lowercase without boldface: Feature, EastWest, Longitude, and so on.

- Table names will be uppercase without boldface: NEWSPAPER, WEATHER, LOCATION, and so on.

You may want to follow similar conventions in creating your own queries, or your company already may have standards it would like you to use, or you may choose to invent your own. The goal of any such standards should always be to make your work simple to read and understand.

Creating the NEWSPAPER Table

The examples in this book are based on the tables created by the scripts that are located on the CD. Each table is created via the **create table** command, which specifies the names of the columns in the table, as well as the characteristics of those columns. Here is the **create table** command for the NEWSPAPER table, which is used in many of the examples in this chapter:

```
create table NEWSPAPER (
Feature      VARCHAR2(15) not null,
Section      CHAR(1),
Page         NUMBER
);
```

In later chapters in this book, you'll see how to interpret all the clauses of this command. For now, you can read it as: "Create a table called NEWSPAPER. It will have three columns, named Feature (a variable-length character column), Section (a fixed-length character column), and Page (a numeric column). The values in the Feature column can be up to 15 characters long, and every row must have a value for Feature. Section values will all be 1 character long."

In later chapters, you'll see how to extend this simple command to add constraints, indexes, and storage clauses. For now, the NEWSPAPER table will be kept simple so that the examples can focus on SQL.

Using SQL to select Data from Tables

Figure 3-1 shows a table of features from a local newspaper. If this were an Oracle table, rather than just paper and ink on the front of the local paper, SQLPLUS would display it for you if you typed this:

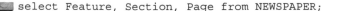

```
select Feature, Section, Page from NEWSPAPER;

FEATURE           S        PAGE
---------------   -   ----------
National News     A           1
Sports            D           1
Editorials        A          12
Business          E           1
Weather           C           2
Television        B           7
```

```
Births          F       7
Classified      F       8
Doctor Is In    F       6
Modern Life     B       1
Comics          C       4
Movies          B       4
Bridge          B       2
Obituaries      F       6

14 rows selected.
```

What's different between the table you created and the one shown in the output in Figure 3-1? Both tables have the same information, but the format differs. For example, the column headings differ slightly. In fact, they even differ slightly from the columns you just asked for in the **select** statement.

The column named Section shows up as just the letter 'S', and although you used uppercase and lowercase letters to type this:

```
select Feature, Section, Page from NEWSPAPER;
```

the column headings came back with all of the letters in uppercase.

Feature	Section	Page
Births	F	7
Bridge	B	2
Business	E	1
Classified	F	8
Comics	C	4
Doctor Is In	F	6
Editorials	A	12
Modern Life	B	1
Movies	B	4
National News	A	1
Obituaries	F	6
Sports	D	1
Television	B	7
Weather	C	2

FIGURE 3-1. *A NEWSPAPER table*

These changes are the result of the assumptions SQLPLUS makes about how information should be presented. You can change these assumptions, and you probably will, but until you give it different orders, this is how SQLPLUS changes what you input:

- It changes all the column headings to uppercase.

- It allows columns to be only as wide as the column is defined to be in Oracle.

- It squeezes out any spaces if the column heading is a function. (This will be demonstrated in Chapter 7.)

The first point is obvious. The column names you used were shifted to uppercase. The second point is not obvious. How *are* the columns defined? To find out, ask Oracle. Simply tell SQLPLUS to **describe** the table, as shown here:

```
describe NEWSPAPER

Name                                 Null?     Type
----------------------------------- --------- -------
FEATURE                             NOT NULL  VARCHAR2(15)
SECTION                                       CHAR(1)
PAGE                                          NUMBER
```

This display is a descriptive table that lists the columns and their definitions for the NEWSPAPER table; the **describe** command works for any table. Note that the details in this description match the **create table** command given earlier in this chapter.

The first column tells the names of the columns in the table being described.

The second column, Null?, is really a rule about the column named to its left. When the NEWSPAPER table was created, the **NOT NULL** rule instructed Oracle not to allow any user to add a new row to the table if he or she left the Feature column empty (**NULL** means empty). Of course, in a table such as NEWSPAPER, it probably would have been worthwhile to use the same rule for all three columns. What good is it to know the title of a Feature without also knowing what Section it's in and what Page it's on? But, for the sake of this example, only Feature was created with the rule that it could not be **NULL**.

Because Section and Page have nothing in the Null? column, they are allowed to be empty in any row of the NEWSPAPER table.

The third column, Type, tells the basic nature of the individual columns. Feature is a VARCHAR2 (variable-length character) column that can be up to 15 characters (letters, numbers, symbols, or spaces) long.

Section is a character column as well, but it is only one character long! The creator of the table knew that newspaper sections in the local paper are only a single letter, so the column was defined to be only as wide as it needed to be. It was defined using the CHAR datatype, which is used for fixed-length character strings. When SQLPLUS went to display the results of your query:

```
select Feature, Section, Page from NEWSPAPER;
```

it knew from Oracle that Section was a maximum of only one character. It assumed that you did not want to use up more space than this, so it displayed a column just one character wide, and used as much of the column name as it could: 'S'.

The third column in the NEWSPAPER table is Page, which is simply a number. Notice that the Page column shows up as ten spaces wide, even though no pages use more than two digits—numbers usually are not defined as having a maximum width, so SQLPLUS assumes a maximum just to get started.

You also may have noticed that the heading for the only column composed solely of numbers, Page, was *right-justified*—that is, it sits over on the right side of the column, whereas the headings for columns that contain characters sit over on the left. This is standard alignment for column headings in SQLPLUS. As with other column features, you'll see in Chapter 6 how to change alignment as needed.

Finally, SQLPLUS tells you how many rows it found in Oracle's NEWSPAPER table. (Notice the "14 rows selected" notation at the bottom of the display.) This is called *feedback*. You can make SQLPLUS stop giving feedback by setting the **feedback** option, as shown here:

```
set feedback off
```

or you can set a minimum number of rows for **feedback** to work:

```
set feedback 25
```

This last example tells Oracle that you don't want to know how many rows have been displayed until there have been at least 25. Unless you tell SQLPLUS differently, **feedback** is set to 6.

The **set** command is a SQLPLUS command, which means that it is an instruction telling SQLPLUS how to act. There are many SQLPLUS options, such as **feedback**, that you can set. Several of these will be shown and used in this chapter and in the chapters to follow. For a complete list, look up **set** in the Alphabetical Reference section of this book.

The **set** command has a counterpart named **show** that allows you to see what instructions you've given to SQLPLUS. For instance, you can check the setting of **feedback** by typing

```
show feedback
```

SQLPLUS will respond with

```
FEEDBACK ON for 25 or more rows
```

The width used to display numbers also is changed by the **set** command. You check it by typing

```
show numwidth
```

SQLPLUS will reply as shown here:

```
numwidth 9
```

Since 9 is a wide width for displaying page numbers that never contain more than two digits, shrink the display by typing

```
set numwidth 5
```

However, this means that all number columns will be five digits wide. If you anticipate having numbers with more than five digits, you must use a number higher than 5. Individual columns in the display also can be set independently. This will be covered in Chapter 6.

select, from, where, and order by

You will use four primary keywords in SQL when selecting information from an Oracle table: **select**, **from**, **where**, and **order by**. You will use **select** and **from** in every Oracle query you do.

The **select** keyword tells Oracle which columns you want, and **from** tells Oracle the name(s) of the table or tables those columns are in. The NEWSPAPER table example showed how these are used. In the first line that you entered, a comma follows each column name except the last. You'll notice that a correctly typed SQL query reads pretty much like an English sentence. A query in SQLPLUS usually ends with a semicolon (sometimes called the *SQL terminator*). The **where** keyword tells Oracle what qualifiers you'd like to put on the information it is selecting. For example, if you input this:

```
select Feature, Section, Page from NEWSPAPER
 where Section = 'F';

FEATURE          S  PAGE
--------------- - -----
Births           F     7
Classified       F     8
Obituaries       F     6
Doctor Is In     F     6
```

Oracle checks each row in the NEWSPAPER table before sending the row back to you. It skips over those without the single letter 'F' in their Section column. It returns those where the Section entry is 'F', and SQLPLUS displays them to you.

To tell Oracle that you want the information it returns sorted in the order you specify, use **order by**. You can be as elaborate as you like about the order you request. Consider these examples:

```
select Feature, Section, Page from NEWSPAPER
 where Section = 'F'
 order by Feature;

FEATURE          S  PAGE
--------------- - -----
Births           F     7
Classified       F     8
Doctor Is In     F     6
Obituaries       F     6
```

They are nearly reversed when ordered by page, as shown here:

```
select Feature, Section, Page from NEWSPAPER
  where Section = 'F'
  order by Page;

FEATURE          S  PAGE
---------------  -  -----
Obituaries       F     6
Doctor Is In     F     6
Births           F     7
Classified       F     8
```

In the next example, Oracle first puts the Features in order by Page (see the previous listing to observe the order they are in when they are ordered only by Page). It then puts them in further order by Feature, listing Doctor Is In ahead of Obituaries.

```
select Feature, Section, Page from NEWSPAPER
  where Section = 'F'
  order by Page, Feature;

FEATURE          S  PAGE
---------------  -  -----
Doctor Is In     F     6
Obituaries       F     6
Births           F     7
Classified       F     8
```

Using **order by** also can reverse the normal order, like this:

```
select Feature, Section, Page from NEWSPAPER
  where Section = 'F'
  order by Page desc, Feature;

FEATURE          S  PAGE
---------------  -  -----
Classified       F     8
Births           F     7
Doctor Is In     F     6
Obituaries       F     6
```

The **desc** keyword stands for *descending*. Because it followed the word "Page" in the **order by** line, it put the page numbers in descending order. It would have the same effect on the Feature column if it followed the word "Feature" in the **order by** line.

Notice that each of these keywords—**select**, **from**, **where**, and **order by**—has its own way of structuring the words that follow it. The groups of words including these keywords are often called *clauses*, as shown in Figure 3-2.

Select Feature, Section, Page	<--**select clause**
from NEWSPAPER	<--**from clause**
where Section = 'F'	<--**where clause**

FIGURE 3-2. *Clauses*

Logic and Value

Just as the **order by** clause can have several parts, so can the **where** clause, but with a significantly greater degree of sophistication. You control the extent to which you use **where** through the careful use of logical instructions to Oracle on what you expect it to return to you. These instructions are expressed using mathematical symbols called *logical operators.* These are explained shortly, and also are listed in the Alphabetical Reference section of this book.

The following is a simple example in which the values in the Page column are tested to see if any equals 6. Every row where this is true is returned to you. Any row in which Page is not equal to 6 is skipped (in other words, those rows for which Page = 6 is false).

```
select Feature, Section, Page
   from NEWSPAPER
 where Page = 6;

FEATURE         S  PAGE
--------------- - -----
Obituaries      F     6
Doctor Is In    F     6
```

The equal sign is called a *logical operator,* because it operates by making a logical test that compares the values on either side of it—in this case, the value of Page and the value 6—to see if they are equal.

In this example, no quotes are placed around the value being checked, because the column the value is compared to (the Page column) is defined as a NUMBER datatype. Number values do not require quotes around them during comparisons.

Single-Value Tests

You can use one of several logical operators to test against a single value, as shown in the upcoming sidebar "Logical Tests Against a Single Value." Take a few examples from any of the expressions listed in this sidebar. They all work similarly and can be combined at will, although they must follow certain rules about how they'll act together.

Logical Tests Against a Single Value

All of these operators work with letters or numbers, and with columns or literals.

EQUAL, GREATER THAN, LESS THAN, NOT EQUAL

Page=	6	Page is equal to 6
Page>	6	Page is greater than 6
Page>=	6	Page is greater than or equal to 6
Page<	6	Page is less than 6
Page<=	6	Page is less than or equal to 6
Page!=	6	Page is not equal to 6
Page^=	6	Page is not equal to 6
Page<>	6	Page is not equal to 6

Because some keyboards lack an exclamation mark (!) or a caret (^), Oracle allows three ways of typing the *not equal* operator. The final alternative, <>, qualifies as a *not equal* operator because it permits only numbers less than 6 (in this example) or greater than 6, but not 6 itself.

LIKE

Feature LIKE 'Mo%'	Feature begins with the letters Mo
Feature LIKE '_ _ l%'	Feature has an l in the third position
Feature LIKE '%o%o%'	Feature has two o's in it

LIKE performs pattern matching. An underline character (_) represents exactly one character. A percent sign (%) represents any number of characters, including zero characters.

IS NULL, IS NOT NULL

Precipitation IS NULL	Precipitation is unknown
Precipitation IS NOT NULL	Precipitation is known

NULL tests to see if data exists in a column for a row. If the column is completely empty, it is said to be **NULL**. The word **IS** must be used with **NULL** and **NOT NULL**; equal, greater than, or less than signs do not work with **NULL** and **NOT NULL**.

Equal, Greater Than, Less Than, Not Equal

Logical tests can compare values, both for equality and for relative value. Here, a simple test is made for all sections equal to B:

```
select Feature, Section, Page
   from NEWSPAPER
 where Section = 'B';

FEATURE          S  PAGE
--------------   -  -----
Television       B    7
Modern Life      B    1
Movies           B    4
Bridge           B    2
```

The following is the test for all pages greater than 4:

```
select Feature, Section, Page
   from NEWSPAPER
 where Page > 4;

FEATURE          S  PAGE
--------------   -  -----
Editorials       A   12
Television       B    7
Births           F    7
Classified       F    8
Obituaries       F    6
Doctor Is In     F    6
```

The following is the test for sections greater than B (this means later in the alphabet than B):

```
select Feature, Section, Page
   from NEWSPAPER
 where Section > 'B';

FEATURE          S  PAGE
--------------   -  -----
Sports           D    1
Business         E    1
Weather          C    2
Births           F    7
Classified       F    8
Comics           C    4
Obituaries       F    6
Doctor Is In     F    6
```

Just as a test can be made for greater than, so can a test be made for less than, as shown here (all page numbers less than 8):

```
select Feature, Section, Page
  from NEWSPAPER
 where Page < 8;
```

```
FEATURE           S      PAGE
--------------    -   ----------
National News     A         1
Sports            D         1
Business          E         1
Weather           C         2
Television        B         7
Births            F         7
Modern Life       B         1
Comics            C         4
Movies            B         4
Bridge            B         2
Obituaries        F         6
Doctor Is In      F         6
```

The opposite of the test for equality is the *not equal* test, as given here:

```
select Feature, Section, Page
  from NEWSPAPER
 where Page <> 1;
```

```
FEATURE           S      PAGE
--------------    -   ----------
Editorials        A        12
Weather           C         2
Television        B         7
Births            F         7
Classified        F         8
Comics            C         4
Movies            B         4
Bridge            B         2
Obituaries        F         6
Doctor Is In      F         6
```

NOTE
Be careful when using the greater than and less than operators against numbers that are stored in character datatype columns. All values in VARCHAR2 and CHAR columns will be treated as characters during comparisons. Therefore, numbers that are stored in those types of columns will be compared as if they were character strings, not numbers. If the column's datatype is NUMBER, then 12 is greater than 9. If it is a character column, then 9 is greater than 12, because the character '9' is greater than the character '1'.

LIKE

One of the most powerful features of SQL is a marvelous pattern-matching operator called **LIKE**, which is able to search through the rows of a database column for values that look like a pattern you describe. It uses two special characters to denote which kind of matching to do: a percent sign, called a *wildcard,* and an underline, called a *position marker.* To look for all of the Features that begin with the letters 'Mo', use the following:

```
select Feature, Section, Page from NEWSPAPER
  where Feature LIKE 'Mo%';

FEATURE          S    PAGE
--------------- - ----------
Modern Life      B        1
Movies           B        4
```

The percent sign (%) means anything is acceptable here: one character, a hundred characters, or no characters. If the first letters are 'Mo', **LIKE** will find the Feature. If the query had used 'MO%' as its search condition instead, then no rows would have been returned, due to Oracle's case-sensitivity in data values. If you want to find those Features that have the letter 'i' in the third position of their titles, and you don't care which two characters precede the 'i' or what set of characters follows, using two underlines (_ _) specifies that any character in those two positions is acceptable. Position three must have a lowercase 'i'; the percent sign after that says anything is okay.

```
select Feature, Section, Page from NEWSPAPER
  where Feature LIKE '__i%';

FEATURE          S    PAGE
--------------- - ----------
Editorials       A       12
Bridge           B        2
Obituaries       F        6
```

Multiple percent signs also can be used. To find those words with two lowercase 'o's anywhere in the Feature title, three percent signs are used, as shown here:

```
select Feature, Section, Page from NEWSPAPER
  where Feature LIKE '%o%o%';

FEATURE          S    PAGE
--------------- - ----------
Doctor Is In     F        6
```

For the sake of comparison, the following is the same query, but it is looking for two 'i's:

```
select Feature, Section, Page from NEWSPAPER
  where Feature LIKE '%i%i%';

FEATURE          S      PAGE
--------------- - ----------
Editorials       A        12
Television       B         7
Classified       F         8
Obituaries       F         6
```

This pattern-matching feature can play an important role in making an application friendlier by simplifying searches for names, products, addresses, and other partially remembered items.

NULL and NOT NULL

The NEWSPAPER table has no columns in it that are **NULL**, even though the **describe** you did on it showed that they were allowed. The following query on the COMFORT table contains, among other data, the precipitation for San Francisco, California and Keene, New Hampshire, for four sample dates during 2001:

```
select City, SampleDate, Precipitation
  from COMFORT;

CITY           SAMPLEDAT PRECIPITATION
-------------- --------- -------------
SAN FRANCISCO 21-MAR-01           .5
SAN FRANCISCO 22-JUN-01           .1
SAN FRANCISCO 23-SEP-01           .1
SAN FRANCISCO 22-DEC-01          2.3
KEENE          21-MAR-01          4.4
KEENE          22-JUN-01          1.3
KEENE          23-SEP-01
KEENE          22-DEC-01          3.9
```

You can find out the city and dates on which precipitation was not measured with this query:

```
select City, SampleDate, Precipitation
  from COMFORT
 where Precipitation IS NULL;

CITY           SAMPLEDAT PRECIPITATION
-------------- --------- -------------
KEENE          23-SEP-01
```

IS NULL essentially instructs Oracle to identify columns in which the data is missing. You don't know for that day whether the value should be 0, 1, or 5 inches. Because it is unknown, the

value in the column is not set to 0; it stays empty. By using **NOT**, you also can find those cities and dates for which data exists, with this query:

```
select City, SampleDate, Precipitation
  from COMFORT
 where Precipitation IS NOT NULL;

CITY          SAMPLEDAT PRECIPITATION
------------- --------- -------------
SAN FRANCISCO 21-MAR-01           .5
SAN FRANCISCO 22-JUN-01           .1
SAN FRANCISCO 23-SEP-01           .1
SAN FRANCISCO 22-DEC-01          2.3
KEENE         21-MAR-01          4.4
KEENE         22-JUN-01          1.3
KEENE         22-DEC-01          3.9
```

Oracle lets you use the relational operators (=, !=, and so on) with **NULL**, but this kind of comparison will not return meaningful results. Use **IS** or **IS NOT** for comparing values to **NULL**.

Simple Tests Against a List of Values

If there are logical operators that test against a single value, are there others that will test against many values, such as a list? The sidebar "Logical Tests Against a List of Values" shows just such a group of operators.

Logical Tests Against a List of Values

Logical tests with numbers:

Page IN (1,2,3)	Page is in the list (1,2,3)
Page NOT IN (1,2,3)	Page is not in the list (1,2,3)
Page BETWEEN 6 AND 10	Page is equal to 6, 10, or anything in between
Page NOT BETWEEN 6 AND 10	Page is below 6 or above 10

With letters (or characters):

Section IN ('A', 'C', 'F')	Section is in the list ('A', 'C', 'F')
Section NOT IN ('A', 'C', 'F')	Section is not in the list ('A', 'C', 'F')
Section BETWEEN 'B' AND 'D'	Section is equal to 'B', 'D', or anything in between (alphabetically)
Section NOT BETWEEN 'B' AND 'D'	Section is below 'B' or above 'D' (alphabetically)

Here are a few examples of how these logical operators are used:

```
select Feature, Section, Page
  from NEWSPAPER
 where Section IN ('A','B','F');
```

```
FEATURE           S      PAGE
--------------- - ----------
National News     A         1
Editorials        A        12
Television        B         7
Births            F         7
Classified        F         8
Modern Life       B         1
Movies            B         4
Bridge            B         2
Obituaries        F         6
Doctor Is In      F         6
```

```
select Feature, Section, Page
  from NEWSPAPER
 where Section NOT IN ('A','B','F');
```

```
FEATURE           S      PAGE
--------------- - ----------
Sports            D         1
Business          E         1
Weather           C         2
Comics            C         4
```

```
select Feature, Section, Page
  from NEWSPAPER
 where Page BETWEEN 7 and 10;
```

```
FEATURE           S      PAGE
--------------- - ----------
Television        B         7
Births            F         7
Classified        F         8
```

These logical tests also can be combined, as in this case:

```
select Feature, Section, Page
  from NEWSPAPER
 where Section = 'F'
   AND Page > 7;
```

```
FEATURE           S      PAGE
--------------- - ----------
Classified        F         8
```

The **AND** command has been used to combine two logical expressions and requires any row Oracle examines to pass *both* tests; both Section = 'F' and Page > 7 must be true for a row to be returned to you. Alternatively, **OR** can be used, and will return rows to you if *either* logical expression turns out to be true:

```
select Feature, Section, Page
   from NEWSPAPER
 where Section = 'F'
    OR Page > 7;

FEATURE          S  PAGE
--------------   -  -----
Editorials       A    12
Births           F     7
Classified       F     8
Obituaries       F     6
Doctor Is In     F     6
```

There are some Sections here that qualify even though they are not equal to 'F', because their Page is greater than 7, and there are other Sections whose Page is less than or equal to 7, but whose Section is equal to 'F'.

Finally, choose those features in Section F between pages 7 and 10 with this query:

```
select Feature, Section, Page
   from NEWSPAPER
 where Section = 'F'
   and Page BETWEEN 7 AND 10;

FEATURE          S  PAGE
--------------   -  -----
Births           F     7
Classified       F     8
```

There are a few additional *many-value operators* whose use is more complex; they will be covered in Chapter 8. They also can be found, along with those just discussed, in the Alphabetical Reference section of this book.

Combining Logic

Both **AND** and **OR** follow the commonsense meaning of the words. They can be combined in a virtually unlimited number of ways, but you must use care, because **AND**s and **OR**s get convoluted very easily.

Suppose you want to find the Features in the paper that the editors tend to bury, those that are placed somewhere past page 2 of section A or B. You might try this:

```
select Feature, Section, Page
   from NEWSPAPER
 where Section = 'A'
    or Section = 'B'
   and Page > 2;
```

```
FEATURE          S   PAGE
--------------   -   -----
National News    A     1
Editorials       A    12
Television       B     7
Movies           B     4
```

Note that the result you got back from Oracle is not what you wanted. Somehow, page 1 of section A was included. Why is this happening? Is there a way to get Oracle to answer the question correctly? Although both **AND** and **OR** are logical connectors, **AND** is stronger. It binds the logical expressions on either side of it more strongly than **OR** does (technically, **AND** is said to have *higher precedence*), which means this **where** clause:

```
where Section = 'A'
   or Section = 'B'
  and Page > 2;
```

is interpreted to read, "where Section = 'A', or where Section = 'B' *and* Page > 2." If you look at each of the failed examples just given, you'll see how this interpretation affected the result. The **AND** is always acted on first.

You can break this bonding by using parentheses that enclose those expressions you want to be interpreted together. Parentheses override the normal precedence:

```
select Feature, Section, Page
   from NEWSPAPER
 where Page > 2
   and ( Section = 'A' or Section = 'B' );
```

```
FEATURE           S PAGE
----------------- - ----
Editorials        A   12
Television        B    7
Movies            B    4
```

The result is exactly what you wanted in the first place. Note that while you can type this with the sections listed first, the result is identical because the parentheses tell Oracle what to interpret together. Compare this to the different results caused by changing the order in the first three examples, where parentheses were not used.

Another Use for where: Subqueries

What if the logical operators in the previous sidebars, "Logical Tests Against a Single Value" and "Logical Tests Against a List of Values," could be used not just with a single literal value (such as 'F') or a typed list of values (such as 4,2,7 or 'A','C','F'), but with values brought back by an Oracle query? In fact, this is a powerful feature of SQL.

Imagine that you are the author of the "Doctor Is In" feature, and each newspaper that publishes your column sends along a copy of the table of contents that includes your piece. Of course, each editor rates your importance a little differently, and places you in a section he or she deems suited to your feature. Without knowing ahead of time where your feature is, or with

what other features you are placed, how could you write a query to find out where a particular local paper places you? You might do this:

```
select Section from NEWSPAPER
 where Feature = 'Doctor Is In';
```

```
S
-
F
```

The result is 'F'. Knowing this, you could do this query:

```
select FEATURE from NEWSPAPER
 where Section = 'F';
```

```
FEATURE
---------------
Births
Classified
Obituaries
Doctor Is In
```

You're in there with births, deaths, and classified ads. Could the two separate queries have been combined into one? Yes, as shown here:

```
select FEATURE from NEWSPAPER
  where Section = (select Section from NEWSPAPER
                     where Feature = 'Doctor Is In');
```

```
FEATURE
---------------
Births
Classified
Obituaries
Doctor Is In
```

Single Values from a Subquery

In effect, the **select** in parentheses (called a *subquery*) brought back a single value, F. The main query then treated this F as if it were a literal 'F', as was used in the previous query. Remember that the equal sign is a single-value test. It can't work with lists, so if your subquery returned more than one row, you'd get an error message like this:

```
select * from NEWSPAPER
  where Section = (select Section from NEWSPAPER
                     where Page = 1);
```

```
ERROR: ORA-1427:  single-row subquery returns more than one row
```

All of the logical operators that test single values can work with subqueries, as long as the subquery returns a single row. For instance, you can ask for all of the features in the paper where

the section is *less than* (earlier in the alphabet) the section that carries your column. The asterisk in this **select** shows a shorthand way to request all the columns in a table without listing them individually. They will be displayed in the order in which they were created in the table.

```
select * from NEWSPAPER
  where Section < (select Section from NEWSPAPER
                   where Feature = 'Doctor Is In');
```

```
FEATURE         S   PAGE
--------------- -   -----
National News   A    1
Sports          D    1
Editorials      A    12
Business        E    1
Weather         C    2
Television      B    7
Modern Life     B    1
Comics          C    4
Movies          B    4
Bridge          B    2

10 rows selected.
```

Ten other features rank ahead of your medical advice in this local paper.

Lists of Values from a Subquery

Just as the single-value logical operators can be used on a subquery, so can the many-value operators. If a subquery returns one or more rows, the value in the column for each row will be stacked up in a list. For example, suppose you want to know the cities and countries where it is cloudy. You could have a table of complete weather information for all cities, and a LOCATION table for all cities and their countries, as shown here:

```
select City, Country from LOCATION;
```

```
CITY                          COUNTRY
----------------------------- ---------------------------
ATHENS                        GREECE
CHICAGO                       UNITED STATES
CONAKRY                       GUINEA
LIMA                          PERU
MADRAS                        INDIA
MANCHESTER                    ENGLAND
MOSCOW                        RUSSIA
PARIS                         FRANCE
SHENYANG                      CHINA
ROME                          ITALY
TOKYO                         JAPAN
SYDNEY                        AUSTRALIA
SPARTA                        GREECE
MADRID                        SPAIN
```

```
select City, Condition from WEATHER;

CITY          CONDITION
-----------   -----------
LIMA          RAIN
PARIS         CLOUDY
MANCHESTER    FOG
ATHENS        SUNNY
CHICAGO       RAIN
SYDNEY        SNOW
SPARTA        CLOUDY
```

First, you'd discover which cities were cloudy:

```
select City from WEATHER
 where Condition = 'CLOUDY';

CITY
-----------
PARIS
SPARTA
```

Then, you would build a list including those cities and use it to query the LOCATION table:

```
select City, Country from LOCATION
 where City IN ('PARIS', 'SPARTA');

CITY                        COUNTRY
-------------------------   -------------------------
PARIS                       FRANCE
SPARTA                      GREECE
```

The same task can be accomplished by a subquery, where the **select** in parentheses builds a list of cities that are tested by the **IN** operator, as shown here:

```
select City, Country from LOCATION
 where City IN (select City from WEATHER
                where Condition = 'CLOUDY');

CITY                        COUNTRY
-------------------------   -------------------------
PARIS                       FRANCE
SPARTA                      GREECE
```

The other many-value operators work similarly. The fundamental task is to build a subquery that produces a list that can be logically tested. The following are some relevant points:

- The subquery must either have only one column, or compare its selected columns to multiple columns in parentheses in the main query (covered in Chapter 12).

- The subquery must be enclosed in parentheses.

- Subqueries that produce only one row can be used with *either* single- or many-value operators.

- Subqueries that produce more than one row can be used *only* with many-value operators.

Combining Tables

If you've normalized your data, you'll probably need to combine two or more tables to get all the information you want.

Suppose you are the Oracle at Delphi. The Athenians come to ask about the forces of nature that might affect the expected attack by the Spartans, as well as the direction from which they are likely to appear:

```
select City, Condition, Temperature from WEATHER;

CITY         CONDITION    TEMPERATURE
-----------  -----------  -----------
LIMA         RAIN                  45
PARIS        CLOUDY                81
MANCHESTER   FOG                   66
ATHENS       SUNNY                 97
CHICAGO      RAIN                  66
SYDNEY       SNOW                  29
SPARTA       CLOUDY                74
```

You realize your geography is rusty, so you query the LOCATION table:

```
select City, Longitude, EastWest, Latitude, NorthSouth
   from LOCATION;

CITY                     LONGITUDE E LATITUDE N
-----------------------  --------- - -------- -
ATHENS                       23.43 E    37.58 N
CHICAGO                      87.38 W    41.53 N
CONAKRY                      13.43 W     9.31 N
LIMA                         77.03 W    12.03 S
MADRAS                       80.17 E    13.05 N
MANCHESTER                    2.15 W     53.3 N
MOSCOW                       37.35 E    55.45 N
PARIS                          2.2 E    48.52 N
SHENYANG                     123.3 E    41.48 N
ROME                         12.29 E    41.54 N
TOKYO                        139.5 E    35.42 N
SYDNEY                       151.1 E    33.52 S
SPARTA                       22.27 E    37.05 N
MADRID                        3.14 W    40.24 N
```

This is much more than you need, and it doesn't have any weather information. Yet these two tables, WEATHER and LOCATION, have a column in common: City. You can therefore put the information from the two tables together by joining them. You merely use the **where** clause to tell Oracle what the two tables have in common (this is similar to the example given in Chapter 1):

```
select WEATHER.City, Condition, Temperature, Latitude,
       NorthSouth, Longitude, EastWest
  from WEATHER, LOCATION
 where WEATHER.City = LOCATION.City;
```

CITY	CONDITION	TEMPERATURE	LATITUDE	N	LONGITUDE	E
ATHENS	SUNNY	97	37.58	N	23.43	E
CHICAGO	RAIN	66	41.53	N	87.38	W
LIMA	RAIN	45	12.03	S	77.03	W
MANCHESTER	FOG	66	53.3	N	2.15	W
PARIS	CLOUDY	81	48.52	N	2.2	E
SPARTA	CLOUDY	74	37.05	N	22.27	E
SYDNEY	SNOW	29	33.52	S	151.1	E

Notice that the only rows in this combined table are those where the same city is in *both* tables. The **where** clause is still executing your logic, as it did earlier in the case of the NEWSPAPER table. The logic you gave described the relationship between the two tables. It says, "select those rows in the WEATHER table and the LOCATION table where the cities are equal." If a city was only in one table, it would have nothing to be equal to in the other table. The notation used in the **select** statement is TABLE.ColumnName—in this case, WEATHER.City.

The **select** clause has chosen those columns from the two tables that you'd like to see displayed; any columns in either table that you did not ask for are simply ignored. If the first line had simply said this:

```
select City, Condition, Temperature, Latitude
```

then Oracle would not have known to which City you were referring. Oracle would tell you that the column name City was ambiguous. The correct wording in the **select** clause is WEATHER.City or LOCATION.City. In this example, it won't make a bit of difference which of these alternatives is used, but you will encounter cases where the choice of identically named columns from two or more tables will contain very different data.

The **where** clause also requires the names of the tables to accompany the identical column name by which the tables are combined: "where weather dot city equals location dot city"—that is, where the City column in the WEATHER table equals the City column in the LOCATION table.

Consider that the combination of the two tables looks like a single table with seven columns and seven rows. Everything that you excluded is gone. There is no Humidity column here, even though it is a part of the WEATHER table. There is no Country column here, even though it is a part of the LOCATION table. And of the 14 cities in the LOCATION table, only those that are in the WEATHER table are here in this table. Your **where** clause didn't allow the others to be selected.

A table that is built from columns in one or more tables is sometimes called a *projection,* or a *result table.*

Creating a View

There is even more here than meets the eye. Not only does this look like a new table, but you can give it a name and treat it like one. This is called *creating a view*. A *view* is a way of hiding the logic that created the joined table just displayed. It works this way:

```
create view INVASION AS
select WEATHER.City, Condition, Temperature, Latitude,
       NorthSouth, Longitude, EastWest
  from WEATHER, LOCATION
 where WEATHER.City = LOCATION.City;

View created.
```

Now you can act as if INVASION were a real table with its own rows and columns. You can even ask Oracle to describe it to you:

```
describe INVASION
```

Name	Null?	Type
CITY		VARCHAR2(11)
CONDITION		VARCHAR2(9)
TEMPERATURE		NUMBER
LATITUDE		NUMBER
NORTHSOUTH		CHAR(1)
LONGITUDE		NUMBER
EASTWEST		CHAR(1)

You can query it, too (note that you will not have to specify which table the City columns were from, because that logic is hidden inside the view):

```
select City, Condition, Temperature, Latitude, NorthSouth,
       Longitude, EastWest
  from INVASION;
```

CITY	CONDITION	TEMPERATURE	LATITUDE	N	LONGITUDE	E
ATHENS	SUNNY	97	37.58	N	23.43	E
CHICAGO	RAIN	66	41.53	N	87.38	W
LIMA	RAIN	45	12.03	S	77.03	W
MANCHESTER	FOG	66	53.3	N	2.15	W
PARIS	CLOUDY	81	48.52	N	2.2	E
SPARTA	CLOUDY	74	37.05	N	22.27	E
SYDNEY	SNOW	29	33.52	S	151.1	E

There will be some Oracle functions you won't be able to use on a view that you can use on a plain table, but they are few, and mostly involve modifying rows and indexing tables, which will be discussed in later chapters. For the most part, a view behaves and can be manipulated just like any other table.

NOTE
Views do not contain any data. Tables contain data. As of Oracle8i, you can create "materialized views" that contain data, but they are truly tables, not views.

Suppose now you realize that you don't really need information about Chicago or other cities outside of Greece, so you change the query. Will the following work?

```
select City, Condition, Temperature, Latitude, NorthSouth,
       Longitude, EastWest
  from INVASION
 where Country = 'GREECE';
```

SQLPLUS passes back this message from Oracle:

```
where Country = 'GREECE'
          *
ERROR at line 4: ORA-00904:  invalid column name
```

Why? Because even though Country is a real column in one of the tables behind the view called INVASION, it was not in the **select** clause when the view was created. It is as if it does not exist. So, you must go back to the **create view** statement and include only the country of Greece there:

```
create or replace view INVASION as
select WEATHER.City, Condition, Temperature, Latitude,
       NorthSouth, Longitude, EastWest
  from WEATHER, LOCATION
 where WEATHER.City = LOCATION.City
   and Country = 'GREECE';

View created.
```

Using the **create or replace view** command allows you to create a new version of a view without first dropping the old one. This command will make it easier to administer users' privileges to access the view, as will be described in Chapter 19.

The logic of the **where** clause has now been expanded to include both joining two tables and a single-value test on a column in one of those tables. Now, query Oracle. You'll get this response:

```
select City, Condition, Temperature, Latitude, NorthSouth,
       Longitude, EastWest
  from INVASION;
```

CITY	CONDITION	TEMPERATURE	LATITUDE	N	LONGITUDE	E
ATHENS	SUNNY	97	37.58	N	23.43	E
SPARTA	CLOUDY	74	37.05	N	22.27	E

This allows you to warn the Athenians that the Spartans are likely to appear from the southwest but will be overheated and tired from their march. With a little trigonometry, you could even make Oracle calculate how far they will have marched. The old Oracle at Delphi was always ambiguous in her predictions. She would have said, "The Spartans the Athenians will conquer." You can at least offer some facts.

Expanding the View

This power of views to hide or even modify data can be used for a variety of useful purposes. Very complex reports can be built up by the creation of a series of simple views, and specific individuals or groups can be restricted to seeing only certain pieces of the whole table.

In fact, any qualifications you can put into a query can become part of a view. You could, for instance, let supervisors looking at a payroll table see only their own salaries and those of the people working for them, or restrict operating divisions in a company to seeing only their own financial results, even though the table actually contains results for all divisions. Most importantly, views are *not* snapshots of the data at a certain point in the past. They are dynamic, and always reflect the data in the underlying tables. The instant data in a table is changed, any views created with that table change as well.

For example, you may create a view that restricts values based on column values. As shown here, a query that restricts the LOCATION table on the Country column could be used to limit the rows that are visible via the view:

```
create or replace view PERU_LOCATIONS as
select * from LOCATION
 where Country = 'PERU';
```

A user querying PERU_LOCATIONS would not be able to see any rows from any country other than Peru.

The queries used to define views may also reference *pseudo-columns*. A pseudo-column is a "column" that returns a value when it is selected, but is not an actual column in a table. The User pseudo-column, when selected, will always return the Oracle username that executed the query. So, if a column in the table contains usernames, those values can be compared against the User pseudo-column to restrict its rows, as shown in the following listing. In this example, the NAME table is queried. If the value of its Name column is the same as the name of the user entering the query, then rows will be returned.

```
create or replace view RESTRICTED_NAMES
select * from NAME
 where Name = User;
```

This type of view is very useful when users require access to selected rows in a table. It prevents them from seeing any rows that do not match their Oracle username.

Views are powerful tools. There will be more to come on the subject of views in Chapter 18.

The **where** clause can be used to join two tables based on a common column. The resulting set of data can be turned into a view (with its own name), which can be treated as if it were a regular table itself. The power of a view is in its ability to limit or change the way data is seen by a user, even though the underlying tables themselves are not affected.

CHAPTER
4

The Basics of
Object-Relational
Databases

 ou can extend your relational database to include object-oriented concepts and structures. In this chapter, you will see an overview of the major object-oriented features (first introduced in Oracle8) and the impact they have on SQL. You will see detailed descriptions of more advanced object-oriented features in later chapters; this chapter introduces the concepts and provides a general overview.

Do I Have to Use Objects?

Just because you use Oracle does not mean you have to use object-oriented programming (OOP) concepts when implementing your database. In fact, the database is referred to as an object-relational database management system (ORDBMS). The implication for developers is that three different "flavors" of Oracle are available:

Relational | The traditional Oracle relational database management system (RDBMS), as described in the preceding chapters

Object-relational | The traditional Oracle relational database, extended to include object-oriented concepts and structures such as abstract datatypes, nested tables, and varying arrays

Object-oriented | An object-oriented database whose design is based solely on object-oriented analysis and design

Oracle provides full support for all three implementations. If you have previously used Oracle as a relational database, you can continue to use it in the same manner. Since the OOP capabilities are extensions to the relational database, you can select which OOP features you want to use when enhancing existing relational applications. If you want to redesign and implement your application using only OOP features, you can also do that. Regardless of the method you choose, you should first be familiar with the functions and features of the core Oracle relational database. Even if you plan to use only OOP capabilities, you still need to know the functions and datatypes available in Oracle, as well as its programming languages (SQL and PL/SQL).

In this chapter, you will see the basic parts of speech for SQL extended to include object-relational structures. In the following chapters, you will find detailed descriptions of Oracle's functions, followed by sections on PL/SQL (Oracle's procedural programming language), triggers, and procedures. Following the chapters on PL/SQL and procedures, you will find several chapters on the implementation of OOP features. You should understand Oracle's functions, structures, and programming languages before implementing the more advanced OOP and object-relational structures.

Why Should I Use Objects?

Since you don't *have* to use objects, should you use them at all? At first, using OOP features may seem to complicate the design and implementation of your database systems—just as adding new features to any system may automatically increase its complexity. OOP adherents claim that objects reduce complexity by giving you an intuitive way of representing complex data and its relations. For example, if you want to move a car, you can either move the car (an object),

or you can break it into its components (tires, steering column, and so on), move the components individually, and then perform a join in the new location. Treating the car as an object is a more natural way of relating to it and simplifies your interaction with it.

Besides simplifying your interactions with data, objects may help you in other ways. In this chapter, you will see examples of three benefits that come from using OOP features:

- **Object reuse** If you write OOP code, you increase the chances of reusing previously written code modules. Similarly, if you create OOP database objects, you increase the chances that the database objects can be reused.

- **Standards adherence** If you create standard objects, you increase the chance that they will be reused. If multiple applications or tables use the same set of database objects, you have created a de facto standard for the database objects. For example, if you create standard datatypes to use for all addresses, then all the addresses in your database will use the same internal format.

- **Defined access paths** For each object, you can define the procedures and functions that act upon it—you can unite the data and the methods that access it. Having the access paths defined in this manner allows you to standardize the data access methods and enhance the reusability of the objects.

The costs of using objects are chiefly the added complexity of the system and the time it takes to learn how to implement the features. But, as you'll see in this chapter, the basics of extending the Oracle RDBMS to include OOP capabilities build easily upon the relational model presented in the earlier chapters. The short time required to develop and use abstract datatypes, as shown later in this chapter, should help you gauge the time required for learning OOP features.

Everybody Has Objects

Everybody has data, and everybody has methods of interacting with data. Since the combination of data and methods makes up an object, everybody has objects. Consider the bookshelf example from the preceding chapters. If you track book borrowers, each entry will hold basic contact information—name, address, and perhaps favorite type of book. You will usually have a standard for the structure of an address—it starts with a person's name, followed by street name, city name, and state or region. When you add a new person to your list of borrowers, you'll follow the same process each time. Methods for adding new borrower records could include the following:

Add_Borrower	For adding a person to the list
Update_Borrower	For updating a person's entry
Remove_Borrower	For deleting a person from the list
Count_Borrower	For counting the number of borrowers per favorite type of book

As shown by the Count_Borrower method, methods do not have to manipulate the data; they can report on the data. They can perform functions on the data and return the result of the function to the user. For example, if you stored borrowers' birth dates, an Age method could be used to calculate and report their ages.

Oracle supports many different types of objects. In the following sections, you will see descriptions of the major object types available.

Abstract Datatypes

Abstract datatypes are datatypes that consist of one or more subtypes. Rather than being constrained to the standard Oracle datatypes of NUMBER, DATE, and VARCHAR2, abstract datatypes can more accurately describe your data. For example, an abstract datatype for addresses may consist of the following columns:

```
Street   VARCHAR2(50)
City     VARCHAR2(25)
State    CHAR(2)
Zip      NUMBER
```

When you create a table that uses address information, you can create a column that uses the abstract datatype for addresses—and thus contains the Street, City, State, and Zip columns that are part of that datatype. Abstract datatypes can be nested; they can contain references to other abstract datatypes. You will see a detailed example of nested abstract datatypes in the next section of this chapter.

Two of the benefits listed earlier for objects—reuse and standards adherence— are realized from using abstract datatypes. When you create an abstract datatype, you create a standard for the representation of abstract data elements (such as addresses, people, or companies). If you use the same abstract datatype in multiple places, you can be sure that the same logical data is represented in the same manner in those places.

You can use abstract datatypes to create *object tables*. In an object table, the columns of the table map to the columns of the abstract datatype.

Nested Tables

A *nested table* is a collection of rows, represented as a column within the main table. For each record within the main table, the nested table may contain multiple rows. In one sense, it's a way of storing a one-to-many relationship within one table. Consider a table that contains information about departments, each of which may have many projects in progress at any one time. In a strictly relational model, you would create two separate tables—DEPARTMENT and PROJECT.

Nested tables allow you to store the information about projects within the DEPARTMENT table. The PROJECT table records can be accessed directly via the DEPARTMENT table, without the need to perform a join. The ability to select the data without traversing joins may make the data easier to access for users. Even if you do not define methods for accessing the nested data, you have clearly associated the department and project data. In a strictly relational model, the association between the DEPARTMENT and PROJECT tables would be accomplished via foreign key relationships. For examples of nested tables and other collection types, see Part IV.

Varying Arrays

A *varying array* is, like a nested table, a collection. A varying array is a set of objects, each with the same datatype, seen as a column within a table. The size of the array is limited when it is created. When you create a varying array in a table, the array is treated as a column in the main table. Conceptually, a varying array is a nested table with a limited number of rows.

Varying arrays, also known as VARRAYS, allow you to store repeating values in tables. For example, suppose you have a PROJECT table, and projects have workers assigned to them. In the example system, a project can have many workers, and a worker can work on multiple projects. In a strictly relational implementation, you can create a PROJECT table, a WORKER table, and an intersection table PROJECT_WORKER that stores the relationships between them.

You can use varying arrays to store the worker names in the PROJECT table. If projects are limited to ten workers or fewer, you can create a varying array with a limit of ten entries. The datatype for the varying arrays will be whatever datatype is appropriate for the worker name values. The varying array can then be populated, so that for each project, you can select the names of all of the project's workers—without querying the WORKER table. For each project record in the PROJECT table, there would be multiple entries in the varying array holding the worker names. For examples of varying arrays and other collection types, see Part IV.

Large Objects

A *large object,* or *LOB,* is capable of storing large volumes of data. The LOB datatypes available are BLOB, CLOB, NCLOB, and BFILE. The BLOB datatype is used for binary data, and can extend to 4GB in length. The CLOB datatype stores character data and can also store up to 4GB. The NCLOB datatype is used to store CLOB data for multibyte character sets. The data for BLOB, CLOB, and NCLOB datatypes is stored inside the database. Thus, you could have a single row in the database that is over 4GB in length.

The fourth LOB datatype, BFILE, is a pointer to an external file. The files referenced by BFILEs exist on the operating system; the database only maintains a pointer to the file. The size of the external file is limited only by the operating system. Since the data is stored outside the database, Oracle does not maintain the concurrency or integrity of the data.

You can use multiple LOBs per table. For example, you could have a table with a CLOB column and two BLOB columns. This is an improvement over the LONG datatype, since you can only have one LONG per table. Oracle provides a number of functions and procedures to manipulate and select LOB data. Part IV contains implementation details for LOBs.

References

Nested tables and varying arrays are *embedded objects*—they are physically embedded within another object. Another type of object, called a *referenced object,* is physically separate from the objects that refer to it. *References,* also known as REFs, are essentially pointers to row objects. A "row object" is different from a "column object." An example of a "column object" is a varying array—it is an object that is treated as a column in a table. A "row object," on the other hand, always represents a row.

The implementation of references is described in Part IV. As noted earlier in this chapter, you do not have to use all the available OOP capabilities within Oracle. References are typically among the last OOP features implemented when migrating a relational application to an object-relational or OOP approach.

Object Views

Object views allow you to add OOP structures on top of your existing relational tables. For example, you can create an abstract datatype based on an existing table's definition. Object views give you the benefits of relational table storage and OOP structures. Object views allow

you to begin to develop OOP features within your relational database—a bridge between the relational and OOP worlds.

Before using object views, you should be familiar with abstract datatypes and triggers. See Part IV for a full description of object views.

Naming Conventions for Objects

Chapter 2 included a discussion of the naming standards for tables and columns. In general, you should use common, descriptive words for table and column names. For the OOP examples in this book, the following rules will be enforced:

- Table and column names are singular (such as EMPLOYEE, Name, and State)

- Abstract datatype names are singular nouns with an _TY suffix (such as PERSON_TY or ADDRESS_TY)

- Table and datatype names are always uppercase (such as EMPLOYEE or PERSON_TY)

- Column names are always capitalized (such as State and Start_Date)

- Object view names are singular nouns with an _OV suffix (such as PERSON_OV or ADDRESS_OV)

- Nested table names are plural nouns with an _NT suffix (such as WORKERS_NT)

- Varying array names are plural nouns with an _VA suffix (such as WORKERS_VA)

The name of an object should consist of two parts: the core object name and the suffix. The core object name should follow your naming standards; the suffixes help to identify special types of objects.

A Common Object Example

Let's consider an object found in most systems: addresses. Even in a system as simple as the bookshelf system, addresses are maintained and selected. These addresses follow a standard format—the street address, city, and state or region. You can use this standard format as the basis for an abstract datatype for addresses. First, expand it to include additional address information, such as the Zip code. Next, use the **create type** command to create an abstract datatype:

```
create type ADDRESS_TY as object
(Street   VARCHAR2(50),
 City     VARCHAR2(25),
 State    CHAR(2),
 Zip      NUMBER);
/
```

The **create type** command is the most important command in object-relational databases. What the command in this example says is "create an abstract datatype named ADDRESS_TY. It will be represented as having four attributes, named Street, City, State, and Zip, using the defined datatypes and lengths for each column." So far, no methods have been created by the user—but the database has internally created methods that will be used whenever the ADDRESS_TY object

is accessed. For information on creating your own methods, see Part IV and the **create type body** command entry in the Alphabetical Reference.

Within the **create type** command, the **as object** clause explicitly identifies ADDRESS_TY as an OOP implementation.

Now that the ADDRESS_TY datatype exists, you can use it within other datatypes. For example, you may decide to create a standard datatype for people. People have names and addresses. Therefore, you can create the following type:

```
create type PERSON_TY as object
(Name      VARCHAR2(25),
 Address   ADDRESS_TY);
/
```

What did this command do? First, the datatype was given a name—PERSON_TY— and identified as an object via the **as object** clause. Then, two columns were defined. This line,

```
(Name      VARCHAR2(25),
```

defines the first column of PERSON_TY's representation. The second line,

```
Address   ADDRESS_TY);
```

defines the second column of PERSON_TY's representation. The second column, Address, uses the ADDRESS_TY abstract datatype previously created. What are the columns within ADDRESS_TY? According to the ADDRESS_TY definition, they are

```
create type ADDRESS_TY as object
(Street   VARCHAR2(50),
 City     VARCHAR2(25),
 State    CHAR(2),
 Zip      NUMBER);
/
```

Based on these definitions, a PERSON_TY entry will have Name, Street, City, State, and Zip columns—even though only one of those columns is explicitly defined within the PERSON_TY type definition.

You can imagine how this capability to define and reuse abstract datatypes can simplify data representation within your database. For example, a Street column is seldom used by itself; it is almost always used as part of an address. Abstract datatypes allow you to join elements together and deal with the whole—the address—instead of the parts—the Street and other columns that constitute the address.

You can now use the PERSON_TY datatype in the process of table creation.

The Structure of a Simple Object

Try as you might, you can't insert data into PERSON_TY. The reason is straightforward: A datatype describes data, it does not store data. You cannot store data in a NUMBER datatype, and you cannot store data in a datatype that you define, either. To store data, you have to create a table that uses your datatype.

The following command creates a table named CUSTOMER. A customer has a Customer_ID and all the attributes of a person (via the PERSON_TY datatype).

```
create table CUSTOMER
(Customer_ID    NUMBER,
 Person         PERSON_TY);
```

What happens if you **describe** the CUSTOMER table? The output will show the following column definitions:

```
describe CUSTOMER
```

```
Name                                 Null?     Type
--------------------------------- -------- ----
CUSTOMER_ID                                    NUMBER
PERSON                                         PERSON_TY
```

The **describe** command shows that the Person column of the CUSTOMER table has been defined using the PERSON_TY datatype. You can further explore the data dictionary to see the construction of the PERSON_TY datatype. The columns of an abstract datatype are referred to as its *attributes*. Within the data dictionary, the USER_TYPE_ATTRS view displays information about the attributes of a user's abstract datatypes.

NOTE
The data dictionary is a series of tables and views that contains information about the structures and users in the database. You can query the data dictionary for useful information about the database objects that you own or have been granted access to. See Part VI for a user-oriented guide to the data dictionary views available to you.

In the following query, the name, length, and datatype are selected for each of the attributes within the PERSON_TY datatype:

```
select Attr_Name,
       Length,
       Attr_Type_Name
  from USER_TYPE_ATTRS
 where Type_Name = 'PERSON_TY';
```

```
ATTR_NAME                          LENGTH ATTR_TYPE_NAME
--------------------------------- ---------- ------------------
NAME                                   25 VARCHAR2
ADDRESS                                   ADDRESS_TY
```

The query output shows that the PERSON_TY type consists of a Name column (defined as a VARCHAR2 column with a length of 25) and an Address column (defined using the ADDRESS_TY type). You can query USER_TYPE_ATTRS again to see the attributes of the ADDRESS_TY datatype:

```
select Attr_Name,
       Length,
       Attr_Type_Name
  from USER_TYPE_ATTRS
 where Type_Name = 'ADDRESS_TY';

ATTR_NAME                                LENGTH ATTR_TYPE_NAME
------------------------------------- ---------- ------------------

STREET                                       50 VARCHAR2
CITY                                         25 VARCHAR2
STATE                                         2 CHAR
ZIP                                             NUMBER
```

You can **describe** the abstract datatypes as well:

```
desc PERSON_TY

Name                          Null?       Type
-------------------------- --------  ----------------------------

NAME                                      VARCHAR2(25)
ADDRESS                                   ADDRESS_TY

desc ADDRESS_TY

Name                          Null?       Type
-------------------------- --------  ----------------------------

STREET                                    VARCHAR2(50)
CITY                                      VARCHAR2(25)
STATE                                     CHAR(2)
ZIP                                       NUMBER
```

You will not often be called upon to completely decompose the types that constitute a table; but if you need to, you can use the **describe** command or the queries shown in this section to "drill down" through the layers of abstraction. Once you know the structures of each of the abstract datatypes used by the table, you can **insert** records into it.

NOTE
If you do not own the tables and types you are trying to find information about, you can query ALL_TAB_COLUMNS and ALL_TYPE_ATTRS in place of USER_TAB_COLUMNS and USER_TYPE_ATTRS. The ALL_TAB_COLUMNS and ALL_TYPE_ATTRS views show all the columns and attributes for the tables and types that you either own or have been granted access to. Both ALL_TAB_COLUMNS and ALL_TYPE_ATTRS contain an Owner column that identifies the table's or type's owner. See Part VI for a description of the data dictionary views.

NOTE
*You can use the **set describe depth** command to see dependent types and attributes when you describe a table. See Chapter 30.*

Inserting Records into CUSTOMER

Oracle creates methods, called *constructor methods,* for data management when you create an abstract datatype. A constructor method is a program that is named after the datatype; its parameters are the names of the attributes defined for the datatype. When you need to insert records into a table based on abstract datatypes, you use the constructor methods. For example, the CUSTOMER table uses the PERSON_TY datatype, and the PERSON_TY datatype uses the ADDRESS_TY datatype. To insert a record into the CUSTOMER table, you need to insert a record using the PERSON_TY and ADDRESS_TY datatypes' constructor methods.

In the following example, a record is inserted into CUSTOMER using the constructor methods for the PERSON_TY and ADDRESS_TY datatypes. The constructor methods for these datatypes are shown in bold in the example; they have the same names as the datatypes:

```
insert into CUSTOMER values
(1,
 PERSON_TY('NEIL MULLANE',
         ADDRESS_TY('57 MT PLEASANT ST',
                 'FINN', 'NH', 11111)));

1 row created.
```

The **insert** command provides the values to be inserted as a row in the CUSTOMER table. The values provided must match the datatypes of the columns in the table.

In this example, a Customer_ID value of 1 is specified. Next, the values for the Person column are inserted, using the PERSON_TY constructor method (shown in bold). Within the PERSON_TY datatype, a Name is specified, and then the ADDRESS_TY constructor method is used to insert the Address values. So, for the record inserted in the example, the Name value is 'NEIL MULLANE', and the Street value is '57 MT PLEASANT ST'. Note that the parameters for the constructor method are in the same order as the attributes of the datatype.

A second record can be inserted into CUSTOMER, using the exact same format for the calls to the constructor methods (again shown in bold):

```
insert into CUSTOMER values
(2,
 PERSON_TY('SEYMOUR HESTER',
         ADDRESS_TY('1 STEPAHEAD RD',
                 'BRIANT', 'NH', 11111)));
```

The second record has now been inserted into the CUSTOMER table. You only need to use constructor methods when you are manipulating records in tables that use abstract datatypes.

Selecting from Abstract Datatypes

If you want to select the Customer_ID values from CUSTOMER, you simply query that column's values from the table:

```
select Customer_ID
   from CUSTOMER;

CUSTOMER_ID
-----------
          1
          2
```

Querying the Customer_ID values is straightforward, since that column is a standard datatype within the CUSTOMER table.

What if you want to select the person's name from CUSTOMER? You couldn't query it as shown here:

```
select Name       /* this will not work */
   from CUSTOMER;
```

because Name is not a column in CUSTOMER. You'll get the following error:

```
select Name
       *
ERROR at line 1:
ORA-00904: invalid column name
```

Oracle reports this error because Name is not a column within the CUSTOMER table. Name is an attribute within the PERSON_TY abstract datatype. To see the Name values, you need to query the Name attribute within the Person column. You can't query PERSON_TY directly; it's just a datatype, not a table. The query structure is shown in the following example:

```
select Customer_ID, C.Person.Name
   from CUSTOMER C;
```

Notice the syntax for the Name column:

```
           C.Person.Name
```

First, note that the access of the datatype's attribute requires the use of a table alias. A *table alias,* also known as a *correlation variable,* allows Oracle to resolve any ambiguity regarding the name of the object being selected.

As a column name, Person.Name points to the Name attribute within the PERSON_TY datatype. The format for the column name is

```
           Correlation.Column.Attribute
```

This may be a little confusing. During **insert**s, you use the name of the *datatype* (actually, you use the name of the constructor method, which is the same as the name of the datatype). During **select**s, you use the name of the *column.* You use the name of the *column* for **select**s because there may well be multiple columns using the same datatype in the table.

What if you want to **select** the Street values from the CUSTOMER table? The Street column is part of the ADDRESS_TY datatype, which in turn is part of the PERSON_TY datatype. To select this data, extend the Column.Attribute format to include the nested type. The format will be as follows:

```
Correlation.Column.Column.Attribute
```

Thus, to select the Street attribute of the Address attribute within the Person column, your query will be

```
select C.Person.Address.Street
   from CUSTOMER C;

PERSON.ADDRESS.STREET
-----------------------------------------------------
57 MT PLEASANT ST
1 STEPAHEAD RD
```

The syntax

```
select C.Person.Address.Street
```

tells Oracle exactly how to find the Street attribute. The correlation variable can be any name you choose (following Oracle's naming standards for tables) as long as it does not conflict with the name of any other table in the query.

If you use abstract datatypes, you can neither **insert** nor **select** values for the abstract datatypes' attributes without knowing the exact structure of the attributes. For example, you cannot **select** the CUSTOMER table's City values unless you know that City is part of the Address attribute, and that Address is part of the Person column. You cannot **insert** or **update** a column's values unless you know the datatype that it is a part of and the nesting of datatypes needed to reach it.

What if you need to reference the City column as part of a **where** clause? As in the prior examples, you can refer to City as part of the Address attribute, nested within the Person column, as shown next.

```
select C.Person.Name,
       C.Person.Address.City
  from CUSTOMER C
 where C.Person.Address.City like 'F%';

PERSON.NAME                  PERSON.ADDRESS.CITY
------------------------     ------------------------
NEIL MULLANE                 FINN
```

When updating data within abstract datatypes, refer to its attributes via the Column.Attribute syntax shown in the preceding examples. For example, to change the City value for the customers who live in Briant, NH, execute the following **update**:

```
update CUSTOMER C
   set C.Person.Address.City = 'HART'
 where C.Person.Address.City = 'BRIANT';
```

Oracle will use the **where** clause to find the right records to update, and the **set** clause to set the new values for the rows' City columns.

As shown in these examples, using abstract datatypes simplifies the representation of the data but may complicate the way in which you query and work with the data. You need to weigh the benefits of abstract datatypes—more intuitive representation of the data—against the potential increase in complexity of data access.

In later chapters, you will see descriptions of the use and implementation of additional OOP features, such as nested tables and varying arrays. Abstract datatypes provide a common starting point for implementing OOP features within an Oracle database. In Part IV, you will see further uses of abstract datatypes, nested tables, and varying arrays.

Object-Oriented Analysis and Design

In Chapter 2, you saw the basics of normalization—designing a relational database application. When you consider adding in OOP features, such as abstract datatypes, you need to approach database design from a slightly different perspective. For example, in traditional normalization, you try to relate each attribute to its primary key. In OOP design, you go beyond normalization and seek groups of columns that define a common object representation.

For example, in relational design, a CUSTOMER table may be created as follows:

```
create table CUSTOMER
(Customer_ID  NUMBER primary key,
 Name         VARCHAR2(25),
 Street       VARCHAR2(50),
 City         VARCHAR2(25),
 State        CHAR(2),
 Zip          NUMBER);
```

From a Third Normal Form perspective, this is a proper representation of the CUSTOMER table. Each of the attributes is related solely to the Customer_ID (the primary key of the table). But looking at the table, you can see that there are columns that, when grouped together, represent an object. The examples earlier in this chapter grouped the Street, City, State, and Zip columns into a single datatype called ADDRESS_TY. Creating the ADDRESS_TY abstract datatype allows you to use that datatype in multiple tables. If the abstract datatype is used in multiple relational tables, then you benefit from object reuse and from adherence to the standard definition of attribute structures.

Once you define abstract datatypes, you should look for relationships between them to see if they should be nested (as PERSON_TY and ADDRESS_TY are). When analyzing your database design for types, you should focus on those types that most likely will be reused or that will always behave in the same manner. Once you have defined the types, you can apply them in the creation of new database objects. If your tables already exist, you can use object views to overlay OOP designs on relational tables. See Part IV for information on object views.

Once your types are defined, you can create methods for each type. The methods define the behavior of data access involving the types. Usually, methods are created based on "use cases"—how is the data used? There should be methods to account for each manner in which the data is used. You will see examples of user-defined methods in Part IV.

Going Forward

Oracle enables you to use the database as a strictly relational database, as an object-relational database, or as an OOP database. At its core, Oracle is a relational database; the OOP features are implemented as extensions on the relational engine. Therefore, you should be very familiar with Oracle's relational features before starting to use its OOP features. This part of this book mirrors that approach. In Part II, you will see detailed descriptions of Oracle's implementation of the SQL language. That part of the book focuses on the implementation of SQL for relational tables; with some limitations, the same functions will work against tables that use OOP features such as abstract datatypes. Following the chapters on SQL usage, you will see sections on PL/SQL (Oracle's procedural extension to SQL) and Java. Once you know PL/SQL, you will be able to create your own methods for your datatypes, as explained in the OOP-related chapters. When planning to use the advanced features, remember that they are extensions to SQL; a firm grounding in SQL is essential to their effective use.

CHAPTER
5

Introduction to
Web-Enabled
Databases

any of the examples in this book focus on the use of SQL within the database. The examples assume that you can log in directly to an Oracle database, or that you are using a client-based tool that allows you to enter commands into a database. With the introduction of web-based technologies, your ability to interact with the database has been augmented by new options. You still need to know SQL, but to take advantage of these options, you may need to understand web listeners, new toolsets, languages such as Java, and application programming interfaces (APIs) such as JDBC and SQLJ.

The complexity of the environment may be daunting at first. Consider a simple architecture, shown in Figure 5-1, in which two computers are involved in the application—a client and a server. The database resides on the server, and the user interacts with the server via the client. The client and the server rely on the underlying network for their communications, and each runs a version of Oracle Net (known as Net8 in earlier versions). The server listens for Oracle Net requests issued by the client.

Now consider a three-tier architecture, shown in Figure 5-2. A three-tier architecture has three separate components: a client, an application server, and a database server. In implementing a three-tier architecture, you have many more choices available than you have in the traditional client-server architecture. The communications protocol used to communicate between the client and the application server can be different from that used to communicate between the application server and the database server. The workload distribution among the three components can vary widely across applications. The performance and reliability of the components in both stand-alone and networked mode can influence the success or failure of the application.

NOTE
In some three-tier implementations, the application server and the database server reside on the same physical server.

The three-tier architecture significantly increases your opportunities for distributing an application's workload over multiple servers. However, it also increases the number of points of failure in the architecture, and complicates the configuration of a preproduction test environment. Oracle supports many different ways of implementing a three-tier architecture, and you will need to select the architecture that best suits the needs of your application. You should reevaluate your environment needs for each new application rather than assume that a single architecture will seamlessly support every desired outcome.

FIGURE 5-1. *Client-server architecture*

FIGURE 5-2. *Three-tier architecture*

Most web-enabled databases rely on a three-tier model. Typically, an existing database server is made available for web-based access. To make the database available, the server must be accessible via an external network. To provide this network access, a second server is commonly used as a firewall, restricting the kinds of commands that can be passed to the database server. The application server can act as a firewall.

Consider the architecture shown in Figure 5-3. Based on Figure 5-2, it shows one possible configuration for a web-enabled database. In Figure 5-3, the client is a computer with access to the Internet, running a browser. That client communicates with the application server via the Hypertext Transfer Protocol (HTTP). The application server, in turn, executes commands against the database, formats the results in Hypertext Markup Language (HTML), and returns the results to the client.

In this configuration, the application server provides authentication services (to make sure the client is allowed to initiate the request), database connection services, and application processing services. The client's role is to initiate the request and display the results returned, while the database serves as the repository for the data. Clearly, you should restrict the privileges available to the application server to make sure only authorized commands can be performed on behalf of clients.

FIGURE 5-3. *Common web-based implementation*

Where Does SQL Fit In?

SQL is the standard language for accessing Oracle data, so where in a web-based architecture does it fit? SQL and Oracle's procedural language, PL/SQL, are commonly used in the following places:

- Within the database server, in the form of stored procedures and packages (see Part III)

- In commands executed to create and maintain the database structures

- In direct queries of the database

- In scripts and batch processes executed on the database server

- In commands issued by the application server

You may have additional places within your architecture where SQL is used, but the preceding are the most common. Since the client and the application server may not be communicating via SQL, you need to have a web listener running on the application server in order to receive HTTP requests. The application server will then be able to receive requests from clients (via HTTP) and begin to act on them. If the application server communicates with the database server via SQL, then the application server will require Oracle Net as well.

Instead of using standard SQL to communicate with the database server, the application server can use Java Database Connectivity (JDBC) and SQLJ (a precompiler that generates JDBC code). See Part V for details on the creation and use of JDBC and SQLJ programs. If you use JDBC or SQLJ, you still need to provide Oracle Net on the application server to support database connectivity. You also need to know SQL and the ways in which JDBC and SQLJ provide support for different result sets.

Where Does Java Fit In?

With the ubiquity of Java on the web, you may be tempted to create a fully Java-based database application. In that architecture, the client communicates with the application server via either HTTP or the Internet Inter-ORB Protocol (IIOP). Within the database, you can create Java classes, and the application server would interact with those Java classes via IIOP. Thus, you can create a web-enabled database that does not rely on Oracle Net for any of its connectivity.

Within the database, you can write your stored procedures in either PL/SQL (see Part III) or Java (see Part V). In general, you should use these languages for the functions they perform best: PL/SQL for database interaction and Java for non-database-related functions. If you use Java exclusively throughout your application, you should expect to encounter performance or functionality limitations during its production usage.

Java is well suited for use on the client and application server. In your application development process, you should test the implications of using Java in place of PL/SQL or SQL for your database access. PL/SQL has been part of the Oracle kernel for over a decade and is well suited for quick data retrieval and manipulation. Although Java technically fits into all the servers shown in Figure 5-3, you need to evaluate how well it performs for your purposes.

Where Does Oracle Portal Fit In?

Oracle Portal is an Oracle product that is used to create web sites and applications (known as WebDB in prior releases). The core data for the sites and applications is stored in Oracle tables. When a client accesses the site, the client's request is handled by a web listener, such as Oracle's 9i Application Server (9iAS). The web listener executes PL/SQL functions stored within the database. Those functions return the requested data embedded within HTML tags. The listener then returns that data to the client, and the site is displayed within the client's browser.

The table concept introduced in Chapter 1 may help to illustrate this process. To display the WEATHER table in a client browser, you could create an Oracle Portal application. The WEATHER table will reside within the database on the database server. To display the data in tabular format, the query by the application server will embed HTML table-formatting tags in the output. The result is an HTML file that contains the embedded HTML table-formatting tags along with the data from the WEATHER table's rows.

You can use Oracle Portal for many purposes, but you should consider your desired outcomes before implementing it. As Oracle Portal requires a three-tier architecture, you need to make sure this architecture fits your environment and your processing capabilities.

Within a web-enabled database, there is room for all technologies—PL/SQL in packages, SQL in scripts, Java in classes, Oracle Portal as a user interface, and other Oracle products as integrating technologies. As new development tools and integration components become available, look to complement your current architecture. Integrating your data access methods and data presentation technologies should simplify your application maintenance and design, giving you an extendable platform for your future application requirements.

PART
II

SQL and SQL*PLUS

CHAPTER
6

Basic SQL*PLUS
Reports and
Commands

QLPLUS is usually thought of as a kind of interactive report writer. It uses SQL to get information from the Oracle database, and lets you create reports by giving you easy control over titles, column headings, subtotals and totals, reformatting of numbers and text, and much more. It also can be used to change the database by using **insert**, **update**, and **delete** commands in SQL. SQLPLUS can even be used as a code generator, where a series of commands in SQLPLUS can dynamically build a program and then execute it.

In most production applications, more advanced report writers are used—such as Web-based parameter-driven reports. SQLPLUS is most commonly used for simple queries and printed reports. Getting SQLPLUS to format information in reports according to your taste and needs requires only a handful of *commands,* or keywords that instruct SQLPLUS how to behave. They are listed in Table 6-1. Detailed explanations, examples, and additional features of each of these commands are given in the Alphabetical Reference section of this book.

In this chapter, you will see a basic report that was written using SQLPLUS, along with an explanation of the features used to create it. If building a report seems a bit daunting at first, don't worry. Once you try the steps, you'll find them simple to understand, and they will soon become familiar.

You can write SQLPLUS reports while working interactively with SQLPLUS—that is, you can type commands about page headings, column titles, formatting, breaks, totals, and so on, and then execute a SQL query, and SQLPLUS will immediately produce the report formatted to your specifications. For quick answers to simple questions that aren't likely to recur, this is a fine approach. More common, however, are complex reports that need to be produced periodically, and that you'll want to print rather than just view on the screen. Unfortunately, when you quit SQLPLUS, it promptly forgets every instruction you've given it. If you were restricted to using SQLPLUS only in this interactive way, then running the same report at a later time would require typing everything all over again.

The alternative is very straightforward. You simply type the commands, line by line, into a file. SQLPLUS can then read this file as if it were a script, and execute your commands just as if you were typing them. In effect, you create a report program, but you do it without a programmer or a compiler. You create this file using any of the popular editor programs available or even (given certain restrictions) a word processor.

The editor is not a part of Oracle. Editors come in hundreds of varieties, and every company or person seems to have a favorite. Oracle realized this, and decided to let you choose which editor program to use, rather than packaging a program with Oracle and forcing you to use it. When you're ready to use your editor program, you suspend SQLPLUS, jump over to the editor program, create or change your SQLPLUS report program (also called a *start file*), and then jump back to SQLPLUS right at the spot you left and run that report (see Figure 6-1).

SQLPLUS also has a built-in editor of its own, sometimes called the *command line editor,* which allows you to quickly modify a SQL query without leaving SQLPLUS. Its use will be covered later in this chapter.

Command	Definition
remark	Tells SQLPLUS that the words to follow are to be treated as comments, not instructions.
set headsep	The heading separator identifies the single character that tells SQLPLUS to split a title into two or more lines.
ttitle	Sets the top title for each page of a report.
btitle	Sets the bottom title for each page of a report.
column	Gives SQLPLUS a variety of instructions on the heading, format, and treatment of a column.
break on	Tells SQLPLUS where to put spaces between sections of a report, or where to break for subtotals and totals.
compute sum	Makes SQLPLUS calculate subtotals.
set linesize	Sets the maximum number of characters allowed on any line of the report.
set pagesize	Sets the maximum number of lines per page.
set newpage	Sets the number of blank lines between pages.
spool	Moves a report you would normally see displayed on the screen into a file, so you can print it.
//**	Marks the beginning and ending of a comment within a SQL entry. Similar to **remark**.
--	Marks the beginning of an inline comment within a SQL entry. Treats everything from the mark to the end of the line as a comment. Similar to **remark**.
set pause	Makes the screen display stop between pages of display.
save	Saves the SQL query you're creating into the file of your choice.
host	Sends any command to the host operating system.
start or @	Tells SQLPLUS to follow (execute) the instructions you've saved in a file.
edit	Pops you out of SQLPLUS and into an editor of your choice.
define _editor	Tells SQLPLUS the name of the editor of your choice.
exit or quit	Terminates SQLPLUS.

TABLE 6-1. *Basic SQLPLUS Commands*

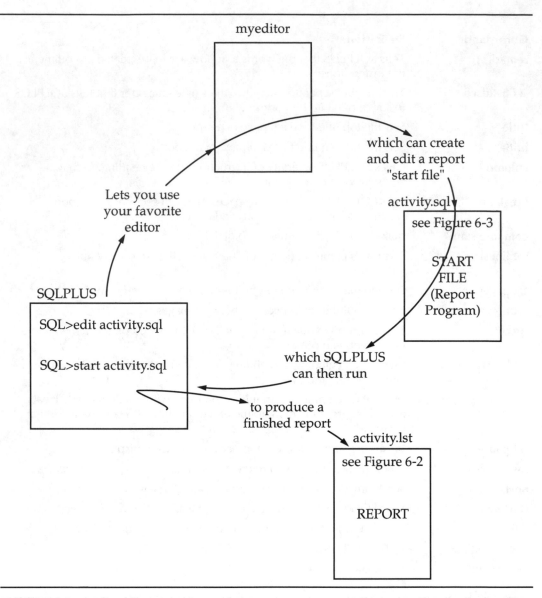

FIGURE 6-1. *Report creation process*

Building a Simple Report

Figure 6-2 shows a quick and easy report showing the dates books were checked out and returned.

Figure 6-3 shows the SQLPLUS start file that produced this report, in this case named activity.sql. To run this report program in SQLPLUS, type this:

```
start activity.sql
```

```
Thu Apr 04                                                     page 1
                     Checkout Log for 1/1/02-3/31/02

                                                             Days
NAME                  TITLE            CHECKOUTD RETURNEDD    Out
------------------    -----------      --------- ---------   -------
DORAH TALBOT          EITHER/OR        02-JAN-02 10-JAN-02    8.00
                      POLAR EXPRESS    01-FEB-02 15-FEB-02   14.00
                      GOOD DOG, CARL   01-FEB-02 15-FEB-02   14.00
                      MY LEDGER        15-FEB-02 03-MAR-02   16.00
*******************                                          -------
avg                                                          13.00

EMILY TALBOT          ANNE OF GREEN GABLES 02-JAN-02 20-JAN-02  18.00
                      MIDNIGHT MAGIC       20-JAN-02 03-FEB-02  14.00
                      HARRY POTTER AND THE 03-FEB-02 14-FEB-02  11.00
                      GOBLET OF FIRE
*******************                                          -------
avg                                                          14.33

FRED FULLER           JOHN ADAMS       01-FEB-02 01-MAR-02   28.00
                      TRUMAN           01-MAR-02 20-MAR-02   19.00
*******************                                          -------
avg                                                          23.50

GERHARDT KENTGEN      WONDERFUL LIFE   02-JAN-02 02-FEB-02   31.00
                      MIDNIGHT MAGIC   05-FEB-02 10-FEB-02    5.00
                      THE MISMEASURE OF 13-FEB-02 05-MAR-02   20.00
                      MAN
*******************                                          -------
avg                                                          18.67

JED HOPKINS           INNUMERACY       01-JAN-02 22-JAN-02   21.00
                      TO KILL A        15-FEB-02 01-MAR-02   14.00
                      MOCKINGBIRD
*******************                                          -------
avg                                                          17.50

PAT LAVAY             THE SHIPPING NEWS 02-JAN-02 12-JAN-02   10.00
                      THE MISMEASURE OF 12-JAN-02 12-FEB-02   31.00
                      MAN
*******************                                          -------
avg                                                          20.50

ROLAND BRANDT         THE SHIPPING NEWS 12-JAN-02 12-MAR-02   59.00
                      THE DISCOVERERS   12-JAN-02 01-MAR-02   48.00
                      WEST WITH THE NIGHT 12-JAN-02 01-MAR-02  48.00
*******************                                          -------
avg                                                          51.67

                                                            -------
avg                                                          22.58

                         from the Bookshelf
```

FIGURE 6-2. *Bookshelf checkout report output*

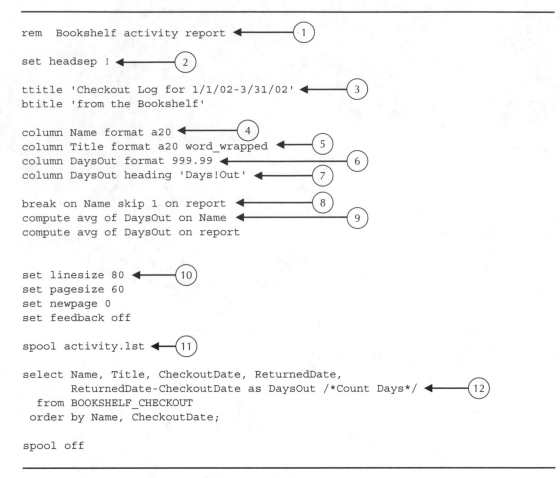

```
rem  Bookshelf activity report                              (1)

set headsep !                          (2)

ttitle 'Checkout Log for 1/1/02-3/31/02'                    (3)
btitle 'from the Bookshelf'

column Name format a20                          (4)
column Title format a20 word_wrapped            (5)
column DaysOut format 999.99                    (6)
column DaysOut heading 'Days!Out'               (7)

break on Name skip 1 on report                  (8)
compute avg of DaysOut on Name                  (9)
compute avg of DaysOut on report

set linesize 80                       (10)
set pagesize 60
set newpage 0
set feedback off

spool activity.lst          (11)

select Name, Title, CheckoutDate, ReturnedDate,
       ReturnedDate-CheckoutDate as DaysOut /*Count Days*/   (12)
  from BOOKSHELF_CHECKOUT
 order by Name, CheckoutDate;

spool off
```

FIGURE 6-3. *The activity.sql file*

How to Distinguish Between SQLPLUS and SQL

The **select** statement toward the bottom of Figure 6-3, beginning with the word "select" and ending with the semicolon (;), is Structured Query Language—the language you use to talk to the Oracle database. Every other command on the page is a SQLPLUS command, used to format the results of a SQL query into a report.

The SQLPLUS **start** command causes SQLPLUS to read the file activity.sql and execute the instructions you've placed in it. Reviewing this start file will show you the basic SQLPLUS instructions you can use to produce reports or change the way SQLPLUS interacts with you. Depending on your experience, this may seem formidable or elementary. It is made up of a series of simple instructions to SQLPLUS.

① remark

The first line of Figure 6-3, at Circle 1, is documentation about the start file itself. Documentation lines begin with

```
rem
```

which stands for **remark**. SQLPLUS ignores anything on a line that begins with **rem**, thus allowing you to add comments, documentation, and explanations to any start file you create. It is always a good idea to place remarks at the top of a start file, giving the filename, its creator and date of creation, the name of anyone who has modified it, the date of modification, what was modified, and an explanation of the purpose of the file. This will prove invaluable later on, as dozens of reports begin to accumulate.

② set headsep

The punctuation that follows **set headsep** (for **head**ing **sep**arator) at Circle 2 in Figure 6-3 tells SQLPLUS how you will indicate where you want to break a page title or a column heading that runs longer than one line. When you first activate SQLPLUS, the default **headsep** character is the vertical bar (|), but if you want to use vertical bars in your titles, you may find it simpler to use a different **headsep** character.

```
set headsep !
```

CAUTION

Choosing a character that may otherwise appear in a title or column heading will cause unexpected splitting.

③ ttitle and btitle

The line at Circle 3 in Figure 6-3:

```
ttitle 'Checkout Log for 1/1/02-3/31/02'
```

instructs SQLPLUS to put this **top title** at the top of each page of the report. The title you choose must be enclosed in single quotation marks. This line:

```
btitle 'from the Bookshelf'
```

works similarly to **ttitle**, except that it goes on the **b**ottom of each page (as the **b** indicates), and also must be in single quotation marks. Because single quotes are used to enclose the entire title, an apostrophe (the same character on your keyboard) would trick SQLPLUS into believing the title had ended.

NOTE

To use apostrophes in titles, put two single quotation marks right next to each other when you want to print a single quotation mark. Because both SQL and SQLPLUS rely on single quotation marks to enclose strings of characters, this technique is used throughout SQL and SQLPLUS whenever an apostrophe needs to be printed or displayed.

When using **ttitle** this way, SQLPLUS will always center the title you choose based on the **linesize** you set (**linesize** will be discussed later in the chapter), and will always place the weekday, month, and the day of the month the report was run in the upper-left corner, and the page number in the upper-right corner.

You can use the **repheader** and **repfooter** commands to create headers and footers for reports. See the Alphabetical Reference section of this book for descriptions of **repheader** and **repfooter**.

column

column allows you to change the heading and format of any column in a **select** statement. Look at the report in Figure 6-2. The fifth column, "Days Out", is not a column in the database, and is called DaysOut in the query shown in Figure 6-3. The line:

```
column DaysOut heading 'Days!Out'
```

(4) relabels the column and gives it a new heading. This heading breaks into two lines because it has the **headsep** character (**!**) embedded in it. The line at Circle 4

```
column Name format a20
```

sets the width for the Name column's display at 20. The *a* in a18 tells SQLPLUS that this is an alphabetic column, as opposed to a numeric column. The width can be set to virtually any value, irrespective of how the column is defined in the database.

(5) The Name column is defined as 25 characters wide, so it's possible that some names will have more than 20 characters. If you did nothing else in defining this column on the report, any Name more than 20 characters long would wrap onto the next line. Looking at Figure 6-2 again, you can see that four of the titles have wrapped; the Title column is defined as VARCHAR2(100) but is formatted as a20 (see Circle 5).

Instead of using the **word_wrapped** format, you could choose **truncated**, eliminating the display of any characters that exceed the specified format length for the column.

(6) Circle 6 in Figure 6-3 shows an example of formatting a number:

```
column DaysOut format 999.99
```

This defines a column with room for five digits and a decimal point. If you count the spaces in the report for the DaysOut column, you'll see seven spaces. Just looking at the **column** command might lead you to believe the column would be six spaces wide, but this would leave no room for a minus sign if the number were negative, so an extra space on the left is always provided for numbers.

(7) Circle 7 in Figure 6-3 refers to a column that didn't appear in the table when we had SQLPLUS describe it:

```
column DaysOut heading 'Days!Out'
```

What is DaysOut? Look at the **select** statement at the bottom of Figure 6-3. DaysOut appears in the line:

```
ReturnedDate-CheckoutDate as DaysOut /*Count Days*/
```

which tells SQL to perform date arithmetic—count the number of days between two dates—and give the computation a simpler column name. As a consequence, SQLPLUS sees a column named DaysOut, and all of its formatting and other commands will act as if it were a real column in the table. The **column** command for DaysOut is an example. "DaysOut" is referred to as a *column alias*—another name to use when referring to a column.

⑧ **break on**

Look at Circle 8 in Figure 6-3. Note on the report in Figure 6-2 how the checkout records for each Name are grouped together. This effect was produced by the line:

```
break on Name skip 1 on report
```

as well as by the line:

```
order by Name, CheckoutDate;
```

in the **select** statement near the end of the start file.

SQLPLUS looks at each row as it is brought back from Oracle, and keeps track of the value in Name. For the first four rows, this value is DORAH TALBOT, so SQLPLUS displays the rows it has gotten. On the fifth row, Name changes to EMILY TALBOT. SQLPLUS remembers your break instructions, which tell it that when Name changes, it should break away from the normal display of row after row, and skip one line. You'll notice one line between the Name sections on the report. Unless the names were collected together because of the **order by** clause, it wouldn't make sense for **break on** to skip one line every time the Name changed. This is why the **break on** command and the **order by** clause must be coordinated.

You also may notice that DORAH TALBOT is only printed on the first line of its section, as are the rest of the names. This is done to eliminate the duplicate printing of each of these names for every row in each section, which is visually unattractive. If you want, you can force it to duplicate the name on each row of its section, by altering the **break on** command to read

```
break on Name duplicate skip 1
```

The report output in Figure 6-2 shows an average for DaysOut for the entire report. To be able to get a grand total for a report, add an additional break using the **break on report** command. Be careful when adding breaks, since they all need to be created by a single command; entering two consecutive **break on** commands will cause the first command's instructions to be replaced by the second command. See Circle 8 for the **break on** command used for the report:

```
break on Name skip 1 on report
```

⑨ **compute avg**

The averages calculated for each section on the report were produced by the **compute avg** command at Circle 9. This command always works in conjunction with the **break on** command,

and the totals it computes will always be for the section specified by the **break on**. It is probably wise to consider these two related commands as a single unit:

```
break on Name skip 1 on report
compute avg of DaysOut on Name
compute avg of DaysOut on report
```

In other words, this tells SQLPLUS to compute the average of the DaysOut for each Name. SQLPLUS will do this first for DORAH TALBOT, then for each successive name. Every time SQLPLUS sees a new Name, it calculates and prints an average for the previous DaysOut values. **compute avg** also puts a row of asterisks below the column that **break on** is using, and prints the word "avg" underneath. For reports with many columns that need to be added, a separate **compute avg** (or **compute sum** if you're calculating sums) statement is used for each calculation. It also is possible to have several different kinds of breaks on a large report (for Name, Title, and dates, for example) along with coordinated **compute avg** commands.

You can use a **break on** command without a **compute sum** command, such as for organizing your report into sections where no totals are needed (addresses with a **break on** City would be an example), but the reverse is not true.

NOTE
*Every **compute avg** command must have a **break on** command to guide it, and the **on** portion of both commands must match (such as on Name in the preceding example, **break on Name skip 1 on report** and **compute avg of DaysOut on Name**).*

The following are the basic rules:

■ Every **break on** must have a related **order by**.

■ Every **compute avg** must have a related **break on**.

This makes sense, of course, but it's easy to forget one of the pieces. In addition to **compute avg**, you can also **compute sum**, **compute count**, **compute max**, or compute any other of Oracle's grouping functions on the set of records.

⑩ set linesize

The four commands at Circle 10 in Figure 6-3 control the gross dimensions of your report. The command **set linesize** governs the maximum number of characters that will appear on a single line. For letter-size paper, this number is usually around 70 or 80, unless your printer uses a very compressed (narrow) character font.

If you put more columns of information in your SQL query than will fit into the **linesize** you've allotted, SQLPLUS will wrap the additional columns down onto the next line and stack columns under each other. You actually can use this to very good effect when a lot of data needs to be presented.

SQLPLUS also uses **linesize** to determine where to center the **ttitle**, and where to place the date and page number. Both date and page number appear on the top line, and the distance

between the first letter of the date and the last digit of the page number will always equal the **linesize** you set.

set pagesize

The **set pagesize** command sets the total number of lines SQLPLUS will place on each page, including the **ttitle**, **btitle**, **column** headings, and any blank lines it prints. On letter- and computer-size paper, this is usually 66 [6 lines per inch times 11 inches (U.S.)]. **set pagesize** is coordinated with **set newpage**.

set newpage

A better name for **set newpage** might have been "set blank lines" because what it really does is print blank lines before the top line (date, page number) of each page in your report. This is useful both for adjusting the position of reports coming out on single pages on a laser printer, and for skipping over the perforations between the pages of continuous form computer paper.

NOTE
*set pagesize does not set the size of the body of the report (the number of printed lines from the date down to the **btitle**); it sets the total length of the page, measured in lines.*

Thus, if you type this:

```
set pagesize 66
set newpage 9
```

SQLPLUS produces a report starting with 9 blank lines, followed by 57 lines of information (counting from the date down to the **btitle**). If you increase the size of **newpage**, SQLPLUS puts fewer rows of information on each page, but produces more pages altogether.

That's understandable, you say, but what's been done at Circle 10 on Figure 6-3? It says

```
set pagesize 60
set newpage 0
```

This is a strange size for a report page—is SQLPLUS to put zero blank lines between pages? No. Instead, the 0 after **newpage** switches on a special property it has: **set newpage 0** produces a *top-of-form character* (usually a hex 13) just before the date on each page. Most modern printers respond to this by moving immediately to the top of the next page, where the printing of the report will begin. The combination of **set pagesize 60** and **set newpage 0** produces a report whose body of information is exactly 60 lines long, and which has a top-of-form character at the beginning of each page. This is a cleaner and simpler way to control page printing than jockeying around with blank lines and lines per page. You can also use the **set newpage none** command, which will result in no blank lines and no form feeds between report pages.

(11) spool

In the early days of computers, most file storage was done on spools of either magnetic wire or tape. Writing information into a file and spooling a file were virtually synonymous. The term has

survived, and *spooling* now generally refers to any process of moving information from one place to another. In SQLPLUS,

```
spool activity.lst
```

tells SQL to take all of the output from SQLPLUS and write it to the file named activity.lst. Once you've told SQLPLUS to spool, it continues to do so until you tell it to stop, which you do by inputting

```
spool off
```

This means, for instance, that you could type

```
spool work.fil
```

and then type a SQL query, such as

```
select Feature, Section, Page from NEWSPAPER
 where Section = 'F';

FEATURE          S  PAGE
--------------   -  ----
Births           F     7
Classified       F     8
Obituaries       F     6
Doctor Is In     F     6
```

or a series of SQLPLUS commands, such as:

```
set pagesize 60
column Section heading 'My Favorites'
```

or anything else. Whatever prompts SQLPLUS produces, whatever error messages you get, whatever appears on the computer screen while spooling—it all ends up in the file work.fil. Spooling doesn't discriminate. It records everything that happens from the instant you use the **spool** command until you use **spool off**, which brings us back to the report at Circle 11 of Figure 6-3:

```
spool activity.lst
```

This phrase is carefully placed as the command just before the **select** statement, and **spool off** immediately follows. Had **spool activity.lst** appeared any earlier, the SQLPLUS commands you were issuing would have ended up on the first page of your report file. Instead, they go into the file activity.lst, which is what you see in Figure 6-2: the results of the SQL query, formatted according to your instructions, and nothing more. You are now free to print the file, confident that a clean report will show up on your printer.

This set of commands will print the SQL query on the first page of the output, followed by the data starting on the second page. To not show the SQL query with the output, you can also change the order of commands: Type in the SQL query but without the concluding semicolon.

Press ENTER twice and the command will still be in SQLPLUS's buffer, unexecuted. You can then start spooling and execute the command:

```
(SQL command typed here)

spool activity.lst
/
spool off
```

(12) **/* */**

Circle 12 of Figure 6-3 shows how a comment can be embedded in a SQL statement. This is different in method and use from the **remark** statement discussed earlier. **remark** (or **rem**) must appear at the beginning of a line, and works only for the single line on which it appears. Furthermore, a multiple-line SQL statement is not permitted to have a **remark** within it. That is,

```
select Feature, Section, Page
rem this is just a comment
   from NEWSPAPER
 where Section = 'F';
```

is wrong. It will not work, and you'll get an error message. However, you can embed remarks in SQL following the method shown at Circle 12, or like this:

```
select Feature, Section, Page
  /* this is just a comment */
   from NEWSPAPER
 where Section = 'F';
```

The secret lies in knowing that **/*** tells SQLPLUS a comment has begun. Everything it sees from that point forward, even if it continues for many words and lines, is regarded as a comment until SQLPLUS sees ***/**, which tells it that the comment has ended. You can also use the characters "– –" to begin a comment. The end of the line ends the comment. This kind of comment works just like a single-line version of **/* */** except that you use – – (two dashes) instead.

Some Clarification on Column Headings

It's possible that the difference between the renaming that occurs in this:

```
        ReturnedDate-CheckoutDate as DaysOut
```

and the new heading given the column Item in this:

```
column DaysOut heading 'Days!Out'
```

is not quite clear, particularly if you look at this command:

```
compute avg of DaysOut on Name
```

SQLPLUS commands are aware only of columns that actually appear in the **select** statement. Every **column** command refers to a column in the **select** statement. Both **break on** and **compute** refer only to columns in the **select** statement. The only reason a **column** command or a **compute** command is aware of the column DaysOut is that it got its name in the **select** statement itself. The renaming of "ReturnedDate-CheckoutDate" to "DaysOut" is something done by SQL, *not* by SQLPLUS.

Other Features

It's not terribly difficult to look at a start file and the report it produces and see how all of the formatting and computation was accomplished. It's possible to begin by creating the start file, typing into it each of the commands you expect to need, and then running it in SQLPLUS to see if it was correct. But when creating reports for the first time, it is often much simpler to experiment interactively with SQLPLUS, adjusting column formats, the SQL query, the titles, and the totals, until what you really want begins to take shape.

Command Line Editor

When you type a SQL statement, SQLPLUS remembers each line as you enter it, storing it in what is called the *SQL buffer* (a fancy name for a computer scratchpad where your SQL statements are kept). Suppose you'd entered this query:

```
select Featuer, Section, Page
  from NEWSPAPER
 where Section = 'F';
```

SQLPLUS responds with the following:

```
select Featuer, Section, Page
       *
ERROR at line 1: ORA-0704:  invalid column name
```

You realize you've misspelled "Feature." You do not have to retype the entire query. The command line editor is already present and waiting for instructions. First, ask it to list your query:

```
list
```

SQLPLUS immediately responds with this:

```
  1    select Featuer, Section, Page
  2    from NEWSPAPER
  3*   where Section = 'F'
```

Notice that SQLPLUS shows all three lines and numbers them. It also places an asterisk next to line 3, which means it is the line your editing commands are able to affect. But you want to change line 1, so you type, and SQLPLUS lists, this:

```
list 1
```

```
  1* select Featuer, Section, Page
```

Line 1 is displayed and is now the current line. You can change it by typing this:

```
change /Featuer/Feature

   1* select Feature, Section, Page
```

You can check the whole query again with this:

```
list

   1  select Feature, Section, Page
   2     from NEWSPAPER
   3* where Section = 'F'
```

If you believe this is correct, enter a single slash after the prompt. This slash has nothing to do with the **change** command or the editor. Instead, it tells SQLPLUS to execute the SQL in the buffer.

```
/

FEATURE          S   PAGE
---------------  -   ----
Births           F    7
Classified       F    8
Obituaries       F    6
Doctor Is In     F    6
```

The **change** command requires that you mark the start and end of the text to be changed with a slash (/) or some other character. The line:

```
change $Featuer$Feature
```

would have worked just as well. SQLPLUS looks at the first character after the word "change" and assumes that is the character you've chosen to use to mark the start and end of the incorrect text (these markers are usually called *delimiters*). You can also delete the current line, as shown here:

```
list

   1  select Feature, Section, Page
   2     from NEWSPAPER
   3* where Section = 'F'

del

list

   1  select Feature, Section, Page
   2     from NEWSPAPER
```

del will delete just what is on the current line. You can pass the **del** command a range of line numbers, to delete multiple lines at once, by specifying the first and last line numbers for the

range of lines to delete. To delete lines 3 through 7, use **del 3 7**. Note this has a space before the number of the first line to delete (3) and another space before the number of the last line to delete (7). If you leave out the space between the 3 and the 7, SQLPLUS will try to delete line 37. To delete from line 2 to the end of the buffer, use **del 2 LAST**.

The word "delete" (spelled out) will erase all of the lines and put the word "delete" as line 1. This will only cause problems, so avoid typing the whole word "delete." If your goal is to clear out the **select** statement completely, type this:

```
clear buffer
```

If you'd like to append something to the current line, you can use the **append** command:

```
list 1

  1* select Feature, Section, Page

append  "WhereItIs"

  1* select Feature, Section, Page "WhereItIs"
```

append places its text right up against the end of the current line, with no spaces in between. To put a space in, as was done here, type *two* spaces between the word **append** and the text.

You may also **input** a whole new line after the current line, as shown here:

```
list

  1  select Feature, Section, Page "WhereItIs"
  2*    from NEWSPAPER

input where Section = 'A'

list

  1  select Feature, Section, Page "WhereItIs"
  2     from NEWSPAPER
  3* where Section = 'A'
```

and then set the column heading for the WhereItIs column:

```
column WhereItIs heading "Where It Is"
```

and then run the query:

```
/

FEATURE          S Where It Is
---------------  - -----------
National News    A           1
Editorials       A          12
```

To review, the command line editor can **list** the SQL statement you've typed, **change** or **del**ete the current line (marked by the asterisk), **append** something onto the end of the current line, or **input** an entire line after the current line. Once your corrections are made, the SQL statement will execute if you type a slash at the SQL> prompt. Each of these commands can be abbreviated to its own first letter, except **del**, which must be exactly the three letters **del**.

The command line editor can edit only your SQL statement. It cannot edit SQLPLUS commands. If you've typed **column Name format a18**, for instance, and want to change it to **column Name format a20**, you must retype the whole thing (this is in the SQLPLUS interactive mode—if you've got the commands in a file, you obviously can change them with your own editor). Also note that in interactive mode, once you've started to type a SQL statement, you must complete it before you can enter any additional SQLPLUS commands, such as **column** formats or **ttitle**. As soon as SQLPLUS sees the word **select**, it assumes everything to follow is part of the **select** statement until it sees *either* a semicolon (;) at the end of the last SQL statement line *or* a slash (/) at the beginning of the line after the last SQL statement line.

Either of these is correct:

```
select * from LEDGER;

select * from LEDGER
/
```

This is not:

```
select * from LEDGER/
```

set pause

During the development of a new report or when using SQLPLUS for quick queries of the database, it's usually helpful to set the **linesize** at 79 or 80, the **pagesize** at 24, and **newpage** at 1. You accompany this with two related commands, as shown here:

```
set pause 'More. . .'
set pause on
```

The effect of this combination is to produce exactly one full screen of information for each page of the report that is produced, and to pause at each page for viewing ("More. . ." will appear in the lower-left corner) until you press ENTER. After the various column headings and titles are worked out, the **pagesize** can be readjusted for a page of paper, and the pause eliminated with this:

```
set pause off
```

save

If the changes you want to make to your SQL statement are extensive, or you simply want to work in your own editor, save the SQL you've created so far, in interactive mode, by writing the SQL to a file, like this:

```
save fred.sql
```

SQLPLUS responds with

```
Created file fred.sql
```

Your SQL (but not any **column**, **ttitle**, or other SQLPLUS commands) is now in a file named fred.sql (or a name of your choice), which you can edit using your own editor.

If the file already exists, then you must use the **replace** option (abbreviated **rep**) of the **save** command to save the new query in a file with that name. For this example, the syntax would be

```
save fred.sql rep
```

store

You can use the **store** command to save your current SQLPLUS environment settings to a file. The following will create a file called my_settings.sql and will store the settings in that file:

```
store set my_settings.sql create
```

If the my_settings.sql file already existed, you could use the **replace** option instead of **create**, and replace the old file with the new settings. You could also use the **append** option to append the new settings to an existing file.

Editing

Everyone has a favorite editor. Word processing programs can be used with SQLPLUS, but only if you save the files created in them in ASCII format (see your word processor manual for details on how to do this). Editors are just programs themselves. They are normally invoked simply by typing their name at the operating system prompt. On UNIX, it usually looks something like this:

```
> vi fred.sql
```

In this example, vi is your editor's name, and fred.sql represents the file you want to edit (the start file described previously was used here only as an example—you would enter the real name of whatever file you want to edit). Other kinds of computers won't necessarily have the > prompt, but they will have something equivalent. If you can invoke an editor this way on your computer, it is nearly certain you can do it from within SQLPLUS, *except* that you don't type the name of your editor, but rather the word **edit**:

```
SQL> edit fred.sql
```

You should first tell SQLPLUS your editor's name. You do this while in SQLPLUS by *defining* the editor, like this:

```
define _editor = "vi"
```

(That's an underline before the *e* in editor.) SQLPLUS will then remember the name of your editor (until you **quit** SQLPLUS) and allow you to use it any time you want. See the sidebar "Using login.sql to Define the Editor" later in this chapter for directions on making this happen automatically.

Using login.sql to Define the Editor

If you'd like SQLPLUS to define your editor automatically, put the **define _editor** command in a file named login.sql. This is a special filename that SQLPLUS always looks for whenever it starts up. If it finds login.sql, it executes any commands in it as if you had entered them by hand. It looks first at the directory you are in when you type **SQLPLUS**. If it doesn't find login.sql there, it then looks in the home directory for Oracle. If it doesn't find login.sql there, it stops looking.

You can put virtually any command in login.sql that you can use in SQLPLUS, including both SQLPLUS commands and SQL statements; all of them will be executed before SQLPLUS gives you the SQL> prompt. This can be a convenient way to set up your own individual SQLPLUS environment, with all the basic layouts the way you prefer them. Here's an example of a typical login.sql file:

```
prompt Login.sql loaded.
set feedback off
set sqlprompt 'What now, boss? '
set sqlnumber off
set numwidth 5
set pagesize 24
set linesize 79
define _editor="vi"
```

Another file, named glogin.sql, is used to establish default SQLPLUS settings for all users of a database. This file, usually stored in the administrative directory for SQLPLUS, is useful in enforcing column and environment settings for multiple users.

The meaning of each of these commands can be found in the Alphabetical Reference section of this book.

host

In the unlikely event that none of the editing commands described in the previous section work, but you do have an editor you'd like to use, you can invoke it by typing this:

```
host vi fred.sql
```

host tells SQLPLUS that this is a command to simply hand back to the operating system for execution and is the equivalent of typing **vi fred.sql** at the > prompt. Incidentally, this same **host** command can be used to execute almost any operating system command from within SQLPLUS, including **dir**, **copy**, **move**, **erase**, **cls**, and others.

Adding SQLPLUS Commands

Once you've saved a SQL statement into a file, such as fred.sql, you can add to the file any SQLPLUS commands you want. Essentially, you can build it in a similar fashion to activity.sql

in Figure 6-3. When you've finished working on it, you can exit your editor and be returned to SQLPLUS.

start

Once you are back in SQLPLUS, test your editing work by executing the file you've just edited:

```
start fred.sql
```

All of the SQLPLUS and SQL commands in that file will execute, line by line, just as if you'd entered each one of them by hand. If you've included a **spool** and a **spool off** command in the file, you can use your editor to view the results of your work. This is just what was shown in Figure 6-2—the product of starting activity.sql and spooling its results into activity.lst.

To develop a report, use steps like these, in cycles:

1. Use SQLPLUS to build a SQL query interactively. When it appears close to being satisfactory, save it under a name such as **test.sql**. (The extension .sql is usually reserved for start files, scripts that will execute to produce a report.)

2. Edit the file test.sql using a favorite editor. Add **column**, **break**, **compute**, **set**, and **spool** commands to the file. You usually spool to a file with the extension .lst, such as test.lst. Exit the editor.

3. Back in SQLPLUS, the file test.sql is **start**ed. Its results fly past on the screen, but also go into the file test.lst. The editor examines this file.

4. Incorporate any necessary changes into test.sql and run it again.

5. Continue this process until the report is correct and polished.

Checking the SQLPLUS Environment

You saw earlier that the command line editor couldn't change SQLPLUS commands, because it could affect only SQL statements—those lines stored in the SQL buffer. You also saw that you could **save** SQL statements and **store** environment settings into files, where they could be modified using your own editor.

If you'd like to check how a particular column was defined, type

```
column DaysOut
```

without anything following the column name. SQLPLUS will then list all of the instructions you've given about that column, as shown here:

```
COLUMN   DaysOut ON
HEADING  'Days!Out' headsep '!'
FORMAT   999.99
```

If you type just the word **column**, without any column name following it, then *all* of the columns will be listed:

```
COLUMN    Title ON
FORMAT    a20
word_wrap

COLUMN    DaysOut ON
HEADING   'Days!Out' headsep '!'
FORMAT    999.99

COLUMN    Name ON
FORMAT    a20
```

ttitle, **btitle**, **break**, and **compute** are displayed simply by typing their names, with nothing following. SQLPLUS answers back immediately with the current definitions. The first line in each of the next examples is what you type; the following lines show SQLPLUS's replies:

```
Ttitle
ttitle ON and is the following 31 characters:
Checkout Log for 1/1/02-3/31/02

btitle
btitle ON and is the following 18 characters:
from the Bookshelf

break
break on report nodup
         on Name skip 1 nodup

compute
COMPUTE avg LABEL 'avg' OF DaysOut ON Name
COMPUTE avg LABEL 'avg' OF DaysOut ON report
```

Looking at those settings (also called *parameters*) that follow the **set** command requires using the word **show**:

```
show headsep
headsep "!" (hex 21)

show linesize
linesize 80

show pagesize
pagesize 60

show newpage
newpage 0
```

See the Alphabetical Reference section of this book under **set** and **show** for a complete list of parameters.

The **ttitle** and **btitle** settings can be disabled by using the **btitle off** and **ttitle off** commands. The following listing shows these commands. SQLPLUS does not reply to the commands.

```
ttitle off

btitle off
```

The settings for columns, breaks, and computes can be disabled via the **clear columns**, **clear breaks**, and **clear computes** commands. The first line in each example in the following listings is what you type; the following lines show what SQLPLUS replies:

```
clear columns
columns cleared

clear breaks
breaks cleared

clear computes
computes cleared
```

Building Blocks

This has been a fairly dense chapter, particularly if SQLPLUS is new to you, yet on reflection, you'll probably agree that what was introduced here is not really difficult. If Figure 6-3 looked daunting when you began the chapter, look at it again now. Is there any line on it that you don't understand, or don't have a sense of what is being done and why? You could, if you wanted, simply copy this file (activity.sql) into another file with a different name, and begin to modify it to suit your own tastes, and to query against your own tables. The structure of any reports you produce will, after all, be very similar.

There is a lot going on in activity.sql, but it is made up of simple building blocks. This will be the approach used throughout the book. Oracle provides building blocks, and lots of them, but each separate block is understandable and useful.

In the previous chapters, you learned how to select data out of the database, choosing certain columns and ignoring others, choosing certain rows based on logical restrictions you set up, and combining two tables to give you information not available from either one on its own.

In this chapter, you learned how to give orders that SQLPLUS can follow in formatting and producing the pages and headings of polished reports.

In the next several chapters, you'll change and format your data row by row. Your expertise and confidence should grow chapter by chapter; by the end of Part II of this book, you should be able to produce very sophisticated reports in short order, to the considerable benefit of your company and yourself.

CHAPTER
7

Getting Text Information
and Changing It

his chapter introduces *string functions,* which are software tools that allow you to manipulate a string of letters or other characters. To quickly reference individual functions, look them up by name in the Alphabetical Reference section of this book. This chapter focuses on the manipulation of text strings; to perform word searches (including word stem expansions and fuzzy matches), you should use Oracle Text, as described in Chapter 24.

Functions in Oracle work in one of two ways. Some functions create new objects from old ones; they produce a result that is a modification of the original information, such as turning lowercase characters into uppercase. Other functions produce a result that tells you something about the information, such as how many characters are in a word or sentence.

NOTE
If you are using PL/SQL, you can create your own functions with the **create function** *statement. See Part III for details.*

Datatypes

Just as people can be classified into different types based on certain characteristics (shy, outgoing, smart, silly, and so forth), different kinds of data can be classified into *datatypes* based on certain characteristics.

Datatypes in Oracle include NUMBER, CHAR (short for CHARACTER), DATE, VARCHAR2, LONG, RAW, LONG RAW, BLOB, CLOB, and BFILE. The first several are probably obvious. The rest are special datatypes that you'll encounter later. A full explanation of each of these can be found by name or under "Datatypes" in the Alphabetical Reference section of this book. Each datatype is covered in detail in the chapters ahead, as well as in Chapter 4. As with people, some of the "types" overlap and some are fairly rare.

If the information is the character (VARCHAR2 or CHAR) type of information—a mixture of letters, punctuation marks, numbers, and spaces (also called *alphanumeric*)—you'll need string functions to modify or inform you about it. Oracle's SQL provides quite a few such tools.

What Is a String?

A *string* is a simple concept: a bunch of things in a line, like houses, popcorn or pearls, numbers, or characters in a sentence.

Strings are frequently encountered in managing information. Names are strings of characters, as in Juan L'Heureaux. Phone numbers are strings of numbers, dashes, and sometimes parentheses, as in (415) 555-2676. Even a pure number, such as 5443702, can be considered as either a number or a string of characters.

NOTE
Datatypes that are restricted to pure numbers (plus a decimal point and minus sign, if needed) are called NUMBER, and are not usually referred to as strings. A number can be used in certain ways that a string cannot, and vice versa.

Strings that can include any mixture of letters, numbers, spaces, and other symbols (such as punctuation marks and special characters) are called *character strings,* or just *character* for short.

There are two string datatypes in Oracle. CHAR strings are always a fixed length. If you set a value to a string with a length less than that of a CHAR column, Oracle automatically pads the string with blanks. When you compare CHAR strings, Oracle compares the strings by padding them out to equal lengths with blanks. This means that if you compare "character " with "character" in CHAR columns, Oracle considers the strings to be the same. The VARCHAR2 datatype is a variable-length string. The VARCHAR datatype is synonymous with VARCHAR2, but this may change in future versions of Oracle, so you should avoid using VARCHAR. Use CHAR for fixed-length character string fields and VARCHAR2 for all other character string fields.

The simple Oracle string functions, explained in this chapter, are shown in Table 7-1.

Notation

Functions are shown with this kind of notation:

```
FUNCTION(string [,option])
```

The function itself will be in uppercase. The thing it affects (usually a string) will be shown in lowercase italics. Any time the word *string* appears, it represents either a literal string of characters or the name of a character column in a table. When you actually use a string function, any literal must be in single quotes; any column name must appear without single quotes.

Every function has only one pair of parentheses. The value that function works on, as well as additional information you can pass to the function, goes between the parentheses.

Some functions have *options,* parts that are not always required to make the function work as you want. Options are always shown in square brackets: []. See the discussion on **LPAD** and **RPAD** in the following section for an example of how options are used.

A simple example of how the **LOWER** function is printed follows:

```
LOWER(string)
```

The word "LOWER" with the two parentheses is the function itself, so it is shown here in uppercase. *string* stands for the actual string of characters to be converted to lowercase, and is shown in lowercase italics. Therefore,

```
LOWER('CAMP DOUGLAS')
```

would produce

```
camp douglas
```

The string 'CAMP DOUGLAS' is a literal (which you learned about in Chapter 3), meaning that it is literally the string of characters that the function **LOWER** is to work on. Oracle uses single quotation marks to denote the beginning and end of any literal string. The string in **LOWER**

Function Name	Use
\| \|	Glues or concatenates two strings together. The \| symbol is called a *vertical bar* or *pipe*.
ASCII	Returns the decimal representation in the database character set of the first character of the string.
CHR	Returns the character having the binary equivalent to the string in either the database character set or the national character set.
CONCAT	CONCATenates two strings together (same as \| \|).
INITCAP	INITial CAPital. Capitalizes the first letter of a word or series of words.
INSTR	Finds the location of a character IN a STRing.
LENGTH	Tells the LENGTH of a string.
LOWER	Converts every letter in a string to LOWERcase.
LPAD	Left PAD. Makes a string a certain length by adding a certain set of characters to the left.
LTRIM	Left TRIM. Trims all the occurrences of any one of a set of characters off the left side of a string.
RPAD	Right PAD. Makes a string a certain length by adding a certain set of characters to the right.
RTRIM	Right TRIM. Trims all the occurrences of any one of a set of characters off the right side of a string.
SOUNDEX	Finds words that SOUND like the EXample specified.
SUBSTR	SUBSTRing. Clips out a piece of a string.
TRIM	TRIMs all occurrences of any one of a set of characters off either or both sides of a string.
UPPER	Converts every letter in a string into UPPERcase.

TABLE 7-1. *Oracle String Functions*

also could have been the name of a column from a table, in which case the function would have operated on the contents of the column for every row brought back by a **select** statement. For example,

```
select City, LOWER(City), LOWER('City') from WEATHER;
```

would produce this result:

```
CITY          LOWER(CITY)  LOWER('CITY')
-----------   -----------  -------------
LIMA          lima         city
PARIS         paris        city
MANCHESTER    manchester   city
ATHENS        athens       city
CHICAGO       chicago      city
SYDNEY        sydney       city
SPARTA        sparta       city
```

At the top of the second column, in the **LOWER** function, CITY is not inside single quotation marks. This tells Oracle that it is a column name, not a literal.

In the third column's **LOWER** function, 'CITY' is inside single quotation marks. This means you literally want the function **LOWER** to work on the word "CITY" (that is, the string of letters C-I-T-Y), not the column by the same name.

Concatenation (||)

This notation:

```
string || string
```

tells Oracle to concatenate, or stick together, two strings. The strings, of course, can be either column names or literals. For example,

```
select City||Country from LOCATION;
```

```
CITY || COUNTRY
--------------------------------------------------
ATHENSGREECE
CHICAGOUNITED STATES
CONAKRYGUINEA
LIMAPERU
MADRASINDIA
MANCHESTERENGLAND
MOSCOWRUSSIA
PARISFRANCE
SHENYANGCHINA
ROMEITALY
TOKYOJAPAN
SYDNEYAUSTRALIA
SPARTAGREECE
MADRIDSPAIN
```

Here, the cities vary in width from 4 to 12 characters. The countries push right up against them. This is just how the concatenate function is supposed to work: it glues columns or strings together with no spaces in between.

This isn't very easy to read, of course. To make this a little more readable, you could list cities and countries with a comma and a space between them. You'd simply concatenate the City and Country columns with a literal string of a comma and a space, like this:

```
select City ||', '||Country from LOCATION;

CITY ||','||COUNTRY
------------------------------------------------------
ATHENS, GREECE
CHICAGO, UNITED STATES
CONAKRY, GUINEA
LIMA, PERU
MADRAS, INDIA
MANCHESTER, ENGLAND
MOSCOW, RUSSIA
PARIS, FRANCE
SHENYANG, CHINA
ROME, ITALY
TOKYO, JAPAN
SYDNEY, AUSTRALIA
SPARTA, GREECE
MADRID, SPAIN
```

Notice the column title. See Chapter 6 for a review of column titles.

You could also use the **CONCAT** function to concatenate strings. The query

```
select CONCAT(City, Country) from LOCATION;
```

is equivalent to

```
select City||Country from LOCATION;
```

How to Cut and Paste Strings

In this section, you learn about a series of functions that often confuse users: **LPAD**, **RPAD**, **LTRIM**, **RTRIM**, **TRIM**, **LENGTH**, **SUBSTR**, and **INSTR**. These all serve a common purpose: they allow you to *cut* and *paste*.

Each of these functions does some part of cutting and pasting. For example, **LENGTH** tells you how many characters are in a string. **SUBSTR** lets you clip out and use a *substring*—a portion of a string—starting at one position in the string and continuing for a given length. **INSTR** lets you find the location of a group of characters within another string. **LPAD** and **RPAD** allow you to easily concatenate spaces or other characters on the left or right side of a string. **LTRIM** and **RTRIM** clip characters off the ends of strings, and **TRIM** can clip characters from both ends at once. Most interesting is that all of these functions can be used in combination with each other, as you'll soon see.

RPAD and LPAD

RPAD and **LPAD** are very similar functions. **RPAD** allows you to "pad" the right side of a column with any set of characters. The character set can be almost anything: spaces, periods, commas, letters or numbers, pound signs (#), or even exclamation marks (!). **LPAD** does the same thing as **RPAD**, but to the left side.

Here are the formats for **RPAD** and **LPAD**:

```
RPAD(string,length [,'set'])

LPAD(string,length [,'set'])
```

string is the name of a CHAR or VARCHAR2 column from the database (or a literal string), *length* is the total number of characters long that the result should be (in other words, its width), and *set* is the set of characters that do the padding. The set must be enclosed in single quotation marks. The square brackets mean that the set (and the comma that precedes it) are optional. If you leave this off, the function will automatically pad with spaces. This is sometimes called the *default*; that is, if you don't tell the function which set of characters to use, it will use spaces by default.

Many users produce tables with dots to help guide the eye from one side of the page to the other. Here's how **RPAD** does this:

```
select RPAD(City,35,'.'), Temperature from WEATHER;

RPAD(CITY,35,'.')                     TEMPERATURE
----------------------------------- -----------
LIMA...............................          45
PARIS..............................          81
MANCHESTER.........................          66
ATHENS.............................          97
CHICAGO............................          66
SYDNEY.............................          29
SPARTA.............................          74
```

Notice what happened here. **RPAD** took each city, from Lima through Sparta, and concatenated dots on the right of it, adding just enough for each city so that the result (City plus dots) is exactly 35 characters long. The concatenate function (||) could not have done this. It would have added the same number of dots to every city, leaving a ragged edge on the right.

LPAD does the same sort of thing, but on the left. Suppose you want to reformat cities and temperatures so that the cities are right-justified (that is, they all align at the right):

```
select LPAD(City,11), Temperature from WEATHER;

LPAD(CITY,1 TEMPERATURE
----------- -----------
       LIMA          45
      PARIS          81
 MANCHESTER          66
     ATHENS          97
    CHICAGO          66
     SYDNEY          29
     SPARTA          74
```

LTRIM, RTRIM, and TRIM

LTRIM and **RTRIM** are like hedge trimmers. They trim off unwanted characters from the left and right ends of strings. For example, suppose you have a MAGAZINE table with a column in it that contains the titles of magazine articles, but the titles were entered by different people. Some people always put the titles in quotes, while others simply entered the words; some used periods, others didn't; some started titles with "The," while others did not. How do you trim these?

```
select Title from MAGAZINE;

TITLE
------------------------------------
THE BARBERS WHO SHAVE THEMSELVES.
"HUNTING THOREAU IN NEW HAMPSHIRE"
THE ETHNIC NEIGHBORHOOD
RELATIONAL DESIGN AND ENTHALPY
"INTERCONTINENTAL RELATIONS."
```

Here are the formats for **RTRIM** and **LTRIM**:

```
RTRIM(string [,'set'])

LTRIM(string [,'set'])
```

string is the name of the column from the database (or a literal string), and *set* is the collection of characters you want to trim off. If no set of characters is specified, the functions trim off spaces.

You can trim off more than one character at a time; to do so, simply make a list (a string) of the characters you want removed. First, let's get rid of the quotes and periods on the right, as shown here:

```
select RTRIM(Title,'."') from MAGAZINE
```

Set of characters being trimmed

The preceding produces this:

```
RTRIM(TITLE,'."')
------------------------------------
THE BARBERS WHO SHAVE THEMSELVES
"HUNTING THOREAU IN NEW HAMPSHIRE
THE ETHNIC NEIGHBORHOOD
RELATIONAL DESIGN AND ENTHALPY
"INTERCONTINENTAL RELATIONS
```

RTRIM removed both the double quotation marks and the periods from the right side of each of these titles. The *set* of characters you want to remove can be as long as you want. Oracle will check and recheck the right side of each title until every character in your string has been removed—that is, until it runs into the first character in the string that is *not* in your *set*.

Combining Two Functions

Now what? How do you get rid of the quotes on the left? There are two options, the first of which uses the **LTRIM** function. Title is buried in the middle of the **RTRIM** function. In this section, you learn how to combine functions.

You know that when you ran the **select** statement:

```
select Title from MAGAZINE;
```

the result you got back was the content of the Title column, as shown next.

```
THE BARBERS WHO SHAVE THEMSELVES.
"HUNTING THOREAU IN NEW HAMPSHIRE"
THE ETHNIC NEIGHBORHOOD
RELATIONAL DESIGN AND ENTHALPY
"INTERCONTINENTAL RELATIONS."
```

Remember that the purpose of this:

```
RTRIM(Title,'."')
```

is to take each of these strings and remove the quotes on the right side, effectively producing a result that is a *new* column whose contents are shown here:

```
THE BARBERS WHO SHAVE THEMSELVES
"HUNTING THOREAU IN NEW HAMPSHIRE
THE ETHNIC NEIGHBORHOOD
RELATIONAL DESIGN AND ENTHALPY
"INTERCONTINENTAL RELATIONS
```

Therefore, if you pretend that **RTRIM(Title,'."')** is simply a column name itself, you can substitute it for the *string* in this:

```
LTRIM(string,'set')
```

So you simply type your **select** statement to look like this:

```
select LTRIM(RTRIM(Title,'."'),'"') from MAGAZINE;
```

Taking this apart for clarity, you see

Is this how you want it? And what is the result of this combined function?

```
LTRIM(RTRIM(TITLE,'."'),'"')
-----------------------------------
THE BARBERS WHO SHAVE THEMSELVES
HUNTING THOREAU IN NEW HAMPSHIRE
THE ETHNIC NEIGHBORHOOD
RELATIONAL DESIGN AND ENTHALPY
INTERCONTINENTAL RELATIONS
```

Your titles are cleaned up.

Looking at a combination of functions the first (or the thousandth) time can be confusing, even for an experienced query user. It's difficult to assess which commas and parentheses go with which functions, particularly when a query you've written isn't working correctly; discovering where a comma is missing, or which parenthesis isn't properly matched with another, can be a real adventure.

One simple solution to this is to break functions onto separate lines, at least until they're all working the way you want. SQLPLUS doesn't care at all where you break a SQL statement, as long as it's not in the middle of a word or a literal string. To better visualize how this **RTRIM** and **LTRIM** combination works, you could type it like this:

```
select LTRIM(
            RTRIM(Title,'."')
                          ,'"')
   from MAGAZINE;
```

This makes what you are trying to do obvious, and it will work even if it is typed on four separate lines with lots of spaces. SQLPLUS simply ignores extra spaces.

Suppose now you decide to trim off THE from the front of two of the titles, as well as the space that follows it (and, of course, the double quote you removed before). You might do this:

```
select LTRIM(RTRIM(Title,'."'),'"THE ')
   from MAGAZINE;
```

which produces the following:

```
LTRIM(RTRIM(TITLE,'."'),'"THE')
-----------------------------------
BARBERS WHO SHAVE THEMSELVES
UNTING THOREAU IN NEW HAMPSHIRE
NIC NEIGHBORHOOD
RELATIONAL DESIGN AND ENTHALPY
INTERCONTINENTAL RELATIONS
```

What happened? The second and third row got trimmed more than expected. Why? Because **LTRIM** was busy looking for and trimming off anything that was a double quote, a *T*, an *H*, an *E*, or a space. It was not looking for the word THE. It was looking for the letters in it, and it didn't quit the first time it saw any of the letters it was looking for. It quit when it saw a character that wasn't in its *set*.

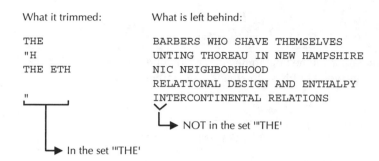

What it trimmed: What is left behind:

```
THE                       BARBERS WHO SHAVE THEMSELVES
"H                        UNTING THOREAU IN NEW HAMPSHIRE
THE ETH                   NIC NEIGHBORHHOOD
                          RELATIONAL DESIGN AND ENTHALPY
"                         INTERCONTINENTAL RELATIONS
```

NOT in the set '"THE'

In the set '"THE'

In other words, all of these:

```
'"THE'
'HET"'
'E"TH'
'H"TE'
'ET"H'
```

and many other combinations of the letters will have the same effect when used as the *set* of an **LTRIM** or **RTRIM**. The order of the letters of the *set* has no effect on how the function works. Note, however, that the *case* of the letters is important. Oracle will check the case of both the letters in the *set* and in the *string*. It will remove only those with an exact match.

 LTRIM and **RTRIM** are designed to remove any characters in a *set* from the left or right of a string. They're not intended to remove words. To do that requires clever use of **INSTR**, **SUBSTR**, and even **DECODE**, which you will learn about in Chapter 16.

 The previous example makes one point clear: It's better to make certain that data gets cleaned up or edited before it is stored in the database. It would have been a lot less trouble if the individuals typing these magazine article titles had simply avoided the use of quotes, periods, and the word THE.

Using the TRIM Function

The preceding example showed how to combine two functions—a useful skill when dealing with string manipulation. If you are trimming the exact same data from both the beginning and the end of the string, then you can use the **TRIM** function in place of an **LTRIM/RTRIM** combination.

 TRIM uses a unique syntax. The following example shows the use of the **TRIM** function with its associated **from** clause within the function. In this example, the double quotes are removed from the beginning and the end of the magazine article titles. Since the double quote is a character string, it is placed inside two single quotes:

```
select TRIM('"' from Title) from MAGAZINE;

TRIM('"'FROMTITLE)
-----------------------------------
THE BARBERS WHO SHAVE THEMSELVES.
HUNTING THOREAU IN NEW HAMPSHIRE
```

```
THE ETHNIC NEIGHBORHOOD
RELATIONAL DESIGN AND ENTHALPY
INTERCONTINENTAL RELATIONS.
```

The quotes have been removed from the beginning and ending of the strings. If you just want to trim one end of the strings, you could use the **leading** or **trailing** clauses, as shown in the following listing.

```
select TRIM(leading '"' from Title) from MAGAZINE;
select TRIM(trailing '"' from Title) from MAGAZINE;
```

Using **leading** makes **TRIM** act like **LTRIM**; **trailing** makes it act like **RTRIM**. The most powerful use of **TRIM** is its ability to act on both ends of the string at once, simplifying the code you have to write—provided the same characters are being removed from both ends of the string.

Adding One More Function

Suppose that you decide to **RPAD** your trimmed-up Title with dashes and carets, perhaps also asking for a magazine Name and Page number. Your query would look like this:

```
select Name, RPAD(RTRIM(LTRIM(Title,'"'),'."'),47,'-^'), Page
    from MAGAZINE;
```

```
NAME              RPAD(RTRIM(LTRIM(TITLE,'"'),'."'),47,'-^')   PAGE
----------------  ------------------------------------------  -----
BERTRAND MONTHLY  THE BARBERS WHO SHAVE THEMSELVES-^-^-^-^-^     70
LIVE FREE OR DIE  HUNTING THOREAU IN NEW HAMPSHIRE-^-^-^-^-^    320
PSYCHOLOGICA      THE ETHNIC NEIGHBORHOOD-^-^-^-^-^-^-^-^-^-    246
FADED ISSUES      RELATIONAL DESIGN AND ENTHALPY-^-^-^-^-^-^    279
ENTROPY WIT       INTERCONTINENTAL RELATIONS-^-^-^-^-^-^-^-^     20
```

Each function has parentheses that enclose the column it is going to affect, so the real trick in understanding combined functions in **select** statements is to read from the outside to the inside on both left and right, watching (and even counting) the pairs of parentheses.

LOWER, UPPER, and INITCAP

These three related and very simple functions often are used together. **LOWER** takes any string or column and converts any letters in it to lowercase. **UPPER** does the opposite, converting any letters to uppercase. **INITCAP** takes the initial letter of every word in a string or column and converts just those letters to uppercase.

Here are the formats for these functions:

```
LOWER(string)
UPPER(string)
INITCAP(string)
```

Returning to the WEATHER table, recall that each city is stored in uppercase letters, like this:

```
LIMA
PARIS
ATHENS
CHICAGO
MANCHESTER
SYDNEY
SPARTA
```

Therefore,

```
select City, UPPER(City), LOWER(City), INITCAP(LOWER(City))
   from WEATHER;
```

produces this:

```
City          UPPER(CITY)  LOWER(CITY)  INITCAP(LOW
-----------   -----------  -----------  -----------
LIMA          LIMA         lima         Lima
PARIS         PARIS        paris        Paris
MANCHESTER    MANCHESTER   manchester   Manchester
ATHENS        ATHENS       athens       Athens
CHICAGO       CHICAGO      chicago      Chicago
SYDNEY        SYDNEY       sydney       Sydney
SPARTA        SPARTA       sparta       Sparta
```

Look carefully at what is produced in each column, and at the functions that produced it in the SQL statement. The fourth column shows how you can apply **INITCAP** to **LOWER(City)** and have it appear with normal capitalization, even though it is stored as uppercase.

Another example is the Name column as stored in a MAGAZINE table:

```
NAME
----------------
BERTRAND MONTHLY
LIVE FREE OR DIE
PSYCHOLOGICA
FADED ISSUES
ENTROPY WIT
```

and then retrieved with the combined **INITCAP** and **LOWER** functions, as shown here:

```
select INITCAP(LOWER(Name)) from MAGAZINE;

INITCAP(LOWER(NA
----------------
Bertrand Monthly
```

```
Live Free Or Die
Psychologica
Faded Issues
Entropy Wit
```

and as applied to the Name, cleaned-up Title, and Page (note that you'll also rename the columns):

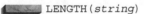

```
select INITCAP(LOWER(Name)) AS Name,
       INITCAP(LOWER(RTRIM(LTRIM(Title,'"'),'."'))) AS Title,
       Page
  from Magazine;
```

```
NAME            TITLE                                  PAGE
--------------- ------------------------------------- -----
Bertrand Monthly The Barbers Who Shave Themselves       70
Live Free Or Die Hunting Thoreau In New Hampshire      320
Psychologica     The Ethnic Neighborhood               246
Faded Issues     Relational Design And Enthalpy        279
Entropy Wit      Intercontinental Relations             20
```

LENGTH

This one is easy. **LENGTH** tells you how long a string is—how many characters it has in it, including letters, spaces, and anything else.

This is the format for **LENGTH**:

LENGTH(*string*)

For example,

```
select Name, LENGTH(Name) from MAGAZINE;
```

```
NAME            LENGTH(NAME)
--------------- ------------
BERTRAND MONTHLY         16
LIVE FREE OR DIE         16
PSYCHOLOGICA            12
FADED ISSUES            12
ENTROPY WIT             11
```

This isn't normally useful by itself, but it can be used as part of another function, for calculating how much space you'll need on a report, or as part of a **where** or an **order by** clause.

NOTE
*You cannot perform functions such as **LENGTH** on a column that uses a LONG datatype.*

SUBSTR

You can use the **SUBSTR** function to clip out a piece of a string.

This is the format for **SUBSTR**:

```
SUBSTR(string,start [,count])
```

This tells SQL to clip out a subsection of the *string*, beginning at position *start* and continuing for *count* characters. If you don't specify the *count*, **SUBSTR** will clip beginning at *start* and continuing to the end of the string. For example,

```
select SUBSTR(Name,6,4) from MAGAZINE;
```

gives you this:

```
SUBS
----
AND
FREE
OLOG
 ISS
PY W
```

You can see how the function works. It clipped out the piece of the magazine name starting in position 6 (counting from the left) and including a total of four characters.

A more practical use might be in separating out phone numbers from a personal address book. For example, assume that you have an ADDRESS table that contains, among other things, last names, first names, and phone numbers, as shown here:

```
select LastName, FirstName, Phone from ADDRESS;
```

LASTNAME	FIRSTNAME	PHONE
BAILEY	WILLIAM	213-293-0223
ADAMS	JACK	415-453-7530
SEP	FELICIA	214-522-8383
DE MEDICI	LEFTY	312-736-1166
DEMIURGE	FRANK	707-767-8900
CASEY	WILLIS	312-684-1414
ZACK	JACK	415-620-6842
YARROW	MARY	415-787-2178
WERSCHKY	ARNY	415-235-7387
BRANT	GLEN	415-526-7512
EDGAR	THEODORE	415-525-6252
HARDIN	HUGGY	617-566-0125
HILD	PHIL	603-934-2242
LOEBEL	FRANK	202-456-1414
MOORE	MARY	718-857-1638
SZEP	FELICIA	214-522-8383
ZIMMERMAN	FRED	503-234-7491

Suppose you want just those phone numbers in the 415 area code. One solution would be to have a separate column called AreaCode. Thoughtful planning about tables and columns will

eliminate a good deal of fooling around later with reformatting. However, in this instance, area codes and phone numbers are combined in a single column, so a way must be found to separate out the numbers in the 415 area code.

```
select LastName, FirstName, Phone from ADDRESS
  where Phone like '415-%';
```

```
LASTNAME                        FIRSTNAME                     PHONE
------------------------        ------------------------      ------------
ADAMS                           JACK                          415-453-7530
ZACK                            JACK                          415-620-6842
YARROW                          MARY                          415-787-2178
WERSCHKY                        ARNY                          415-235-7387
BRANT                           GLEN                          415-526-7512
EDGAR                           THEODORE                      415-525-6252
```

Next, since you do not want to dial your own area code when calling friends, you can eliminate this from the result by using another **SUBSTR**:

```
select LastName, FirstName, SUBSTR(Phone,5) from ADDRESS
  where Phone like '415-%';
```

```
LASTNAME                        FIRSTNAME                     SUBSTR(P
------------------------        ------------------------      --------
ADAMS                           JACK                          453-7530
ZACK                            JACK                          620-6842
YARROW                          MARY                          787-2178
WERSCHKY                        ARNY                          235-7387
BRANT                           GLEN                          526-7512
EDGAR                           THEODORE                      525-6252
```

Notice that the default version of **SUBSTR** was used here. **SUBSTR(Phone,5)** tells SQL to clip out the substring of the phone number, starting at position 5 and going to the end of the string. Doing this eliminates the area code.

Of course, this:

```
SUBSTR(Phone,5)
```

has exactly the same effect as the following:

```
SUBSTR(Phone,5,8)
```

You can combine this with the concatenation and column renaming techniques discussed in Chapter 6 to produce a quick listing of local friends' phone numbers, as shown here:

```
select LastName ||', '||FirstName AS Name,
       SUBSTR(Phone,5) AS Phone
```

```
      from ADDRESS
      where Phone like '415-%';
```

```
NAME                                                        PHONE
------------------------------------------------------     --------
ADAMS, JACK                                                 453-7530
ZACK, JACK                                                  620-6842
YARROW, MARY                                                787-2178
WERSCHKY, ARNY                                              235-7387
BRANT, GLEN                                                 526-7512
EDGAR, THEODORE                                             525-6252
```

To produce a dotted line following the name, add the **RPAD** function:

```
select RPAD(LastName ||', '||FirstName,25,'.') AS Name,
       SUBSTR(Phone,5) AS Phone
  from ADDRESS
 where Phone like '415-%';
```

```
NAME                        PHONE
-----------------------     --------
ADAMS, JACK..............   453-7530
ZACK, JACK...............   620-6842
YARROW, MARY.............   787-2178
WERSCHKY, ARNY...........   235-7387
BRANT, GLEN..............   526-7512
EDGAR, THEODORE..........   525-6252
```

The use of negative numbers in the **SUBSTR** function also works. Normally, the position value you specify for the starting position is relative to the start of the string. When using a negative number for the position value, it is relative to the *end* of the string. For example,

```
SUBSTR(Phone,-4)
```

would use the fourth position from the end of the Phone column's value as its starting point. Since no length parameter is specified in this example, the remainder of the string will be returned.

NOTE
*Use this feature only for VARCHAR2 datatype columns. Do not use this feature with columns that use the CHAR datatype. CHAR columns are fixed-length columns, so their values are padded with spaces to extend them to the full length of the column. Using a negative number for the **SUBSTR** position value in a CHAR column will determine the starting position relative to the end of the column, not the end of the string.*

The following example shows the result of this feature when it is used on a VARCHAR2 column:

```
select SUBSTR(Phone,-4)
  from ADDRESS
 where Phone like '415-5%';

SUBS
----
7512
6252
```

The *count* value of the **SUBSTR** function must always be positive or unspecified. Using a negative *count* will return a **NULL** result.

INSTR

The **INSTR** function allows for simple or sophisticated searching through a string for a set of characters, not unlike **LTRIM** and **RTRIM**, except that **INSTR** doesn't clip anything off. It simply tells you where in the string it found what you were searching for. This is similar to the **LIKE** logical operator described in Chapter 3, except that **LIKE** can only be used in a **where** or **having** clause, and **INSTR** can be used anywhere except in the **from** clause. Of course, **LIKE** can be used for complex pattern searches that would be quite difficult, if even possible, using **INSTR**.

This is the format for **INSTR**:

```
INSTR(string,set [,start [,occurrence ] ])
```

INSTR searches in the *string* for a certain *set* of characters. It has two options, one within the other. The first option is the default; it will look for the set starting at position 1. If you specify the location to *start*, it will skip over all the characters up to that point and begin its search there.

The second option is *occurrence*. A *set* of characters may occur more than once in a string, and you may really be interested only in whether something occurs more than once. By default, **INSTR** will look for the first occurrence of the set. By adding the option *occurrence* and making it equal to 3, for example, you can force **INSTR** to skip over the first two occurrences of the set and give the location of the third.

Some examples will make all of this simpler to grasp. Recall the table of magazine articles. Here is a list of their authors:

```
select Author from MAGAZINE;

AUTHOR
------------------------
BONHOEFFER, DIETRICH
CHESTERTON, G. K.
RUTH, GEORGE HERMAN
WHITEHEAD, ALFRED
CROOKES, WILLIAM
```

To find the location of the first occurrence of the letter *O*, **INSTR** is used without its options, and with *set* as 'O' (note the single quotation marks, since this is a literal), as shown in the following listing:

```
select Author, INSTR(Author,'O') from MAGAZINE;
```

```
AUTHOR                    INSTR(AUTHOR,'O')
------------------------  -----------------
BONHOEFFER, DIETRICH                      2
CHESTERTON, G. K.                         9
RUTH, GEORGE HERMAN                       9
WHITEHEAD, ALFRED                         0
CROOKES, WILLIAM                          3
```

This is, of course, the same as this:

```
select Author, INSTR(Author,'O',1,1) from MAGAZINE;
```

If it had looked for the second occurrence of the letter *O*, it would have found

```
select Author, INSTR(Author,'O',1,2) from MAGAZINE;
```

```
AUTHOR                    INSTR(AUTHOR,'O',1,2)
------------------------  ---------------------
BONHOEFFER, DIETRICH                          5
CHESTERTON, G. K.                             0
RUTH, GEORGE HERMAN                           0
WHITEHEAD, ALFRED                             0
CROOKES, WILLIAM                              4
```

INSTR found the second *O* in Bonhoeffer's name, at position 5, and in Crookes' name, at position 4. Chesterton has only one *O*, so for him, Ruth, and Whitehead, the result is zero, meaning no success—no second *O* was found.

To tell **INSTR** to look for the second occurrence, you also must tell it where to start looking (in this case, position 1). The default value of *start* is 1, which means that's what it uses if you don't specify anything, but the *occurrence* option requires a *start*, so you have to specify both.

If *set* is not just one character but several, **INSTR** gives the location of the first letter of the set, as shown here:

```
select Author, INSTR(Author,'WILLIAM') from MAGAZINE;
```

```
AUTHOR                    INSTR(AUTHOR,'WILLIAM')
------------------------  -----------------------
BONHOEFFER, DIETRICH                            0
CHESTERTON, G. K.                               0
RUTH, GEORGE HERMAN                             0
WHITEHEAD, ALFRED                               0
CROOKES, WILLIAM                               10
```

This has many useful applications. In the MAGAZINE table, for instance:

```
select Author, INSTR(Author,',') from MAGAZINE;
```

```
AUTHOR                       INSTR(AUTHOR,',')
------------------------     -----------------
BONHOEFFER, DIETRICH                        11
CHESTERTON, G. K.                           11
RUTH, GEORGE HERMAN                          5
WHITEHEAD, ALFRED                           10
CROOKES, WILLIAM                             8
```

Here, **INSTR** searched the strings of author names for a comma, and then reported back the position in the string where it found it.

Suppose you want to reformat the names of the authors from the formal "last name/comma/ first name" approach, and present them as they are normally spoken, as shown here:

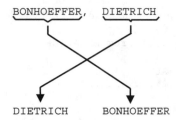

To do this using **INSTR** and **SUBSTR**, find the location of the comma, and use this location to tell **SUBSTR** where to clip. Taking this step by step, first find the comma:

```
select Author, INSTR(Author,',') from MAGAZINE;
```

```
AUTHOR                       INSTR(AUTHOR,',')
------------------------     -----------------
BONHOEFFER, DIETRICH                        11
CHESTERTON, G. K.                           11
RUTH, GEORGE HERMAN                          5
WHITEHEAD, ALFRED                           10
CROOKES, WILLIAM                             8
```

Two **SUBSTR**s will be needed, one that clips out the author's last name up to the position before the comma, and one that clips out the author's first name from two positions after the comma through to the end.

First, look at the one that clips from position 1 to just before the comma:

```
select Author, SUBSTR(Author,1,INSTR(Author,',')-1)
    from MAGAZINE;
```

```
AUTHOR                    SUBSTR(AUTHOR,1,INSTR(AUT
------------------------  ------------------------
BONHOEFFER, DIETRICH      BONHOEFFER
CHESTERTON, G. K.         CHESTERTON
RUTH, GEORGE HERMAN       RUTH
WHITEHEAD, ALFRED         WHITEHEAD
CROOKES, WILLIAM          CROOKES
```

Next, look at the one that clips from two positions past the comma to the end of the string:

```
select Author, SUBSTR(Author,INSTR(Author,',')+2) from MAGAZINE;
```

```
AUTHOR                    SUBSTR(AUTHOR,INSTR(AUTHO
------------------------  ------------------------
BONHOEFFER, DIETRICH      DIETRICH
CHESTERTON, G. K.         G. K.
RUTH, GEORGE HERMAN       GEORGE HERMAN
WHITEHEAD, ALFRED         ALFRED
CROOKES, WILLIAM          WILLIAM
```

Look at the combination of these two with the concatenate function putting a space between them, and a quick renaming of the column to ByFirstName:

```
column ByFirstName heading "By First Name"

select Author, SUBSTR(Author,INSTR(Author,',')+2)
               ||' ' ||
               SUBSTR(Author,1,INSTR(Author,',')-1)
               AS ByFirstName
  from MAGAZINE;
```

```
AUTHOR                    By First Name
------------------------  ------------------------
BONHOEFFER, DIETRICH      DIETRICH BONHOEFFER
CHESTERTON, G.K.          G.K. CHESTERTON
RUTH, GEORGE HERMAN       GEORGE HERMAN RUTH
WHITEHEAD, ALFRED         ALFRED WHITEHEAD
CROOKES, WILLIAM          WILLIAM CROOKES
```

It is daunting to look at a SQL statement like this one, but it was built using simple logic, and it can be broken down the same way. Bonhoeffer can provide the example.

The first part looks like this:

```
SUBSTR(Author,INSTR(Author,',')+2)
```

This tells SQL to get the **SUBSTR** of Author starting two positions to the right of the comma and going to the end. This will clip out DIETRICH—the author's first name.

The beginning of the author's first name is found by locating the comma at the end of his last name (**INSTR** does this), and then sliding over two steps to the right (where his first name begins).

The following illustration shows how the **INSTR** function (plus 2) serves as the *start* for the **SUBSTR** function:

This is the second part of the combined statement:

```
||' '||
```

which, of course, simply tells SQL to concatenate a space in the middle.

This is the third part of the combined statement:

```
SUBSTR(Author,1,INSTR(Author,',')-1)
```

This tells SQL to clip out the portion of the author's name starting at position 1 and ending one position before the comma, which results in the author's last name:

The fourth part simply assigns a column alias:

```
AS ByFirstName
```

It was only possible to accomplish this transposition because each Author record in the MAGAZINE table followed the same formatting conventions. In each record, the last name was always the first word in the string and was immediately followed by a comma. This allowed you to use the **INSTR** function to search for the comma. Once the comma's position was known, you could determine which part of the string was the last name, and the rest of the string was treated as the first name.

This is not often the case. Names are difficult to force into standard formats. Last names may include prefixes (such as von in von Hagel) or suffixes (such as Jr., Sr., and III). Using the previous example's SQL, the name Richards, Jr., Bob would have been transformed into Jr., Bob Richards.

Because of the lack of a standard formatting for names, many applications store the first and last names separately. Titles (such as MD) are usually stored in yet another column. A second option when storing such data is to force it into a single format and use **SUBSTR** and **INSTR** to manipulate that data when needed.

ASCII and CHR

The **ASCII** and **CHR** functions are seldom used during ad hoc queries. **CHR** converts numeric values to their ASCII character string equivalents:

```
select CHR(70)||CHR(83)||CHR(79)||CHR(85)||CHR(71)
    as ChrValues
  from DUAL;

CHRVA
-----
FSOUG
```

Oracle translated the **CHR(70)** to an 'F', **CHR(83)** to an 'S', and so on, based on the database's character set.

The **ASCII** function performs the reverse operation—but if you pass it a string, only the first character of the string will be acted upon:

```
select ASCII('FSOUG') from DUAL;

ASCII('FSOUG')
--------------
            70
```

To see each ASCII value, you will need to evaluate each of the letters via separate executions of the **ASCII** function.

order by and where with String Functions

String functions can be used in a **where** clause, as shown here:

```
select City
  from WEATHER
 where LENGTH(City) < 7;

CITY
-----------
LIMA
PARIS
ATHENS
SPARTA
SYDNEY
```

They can also be used in an **order by** clause, as shown here:

```
select City
   from WEATHER
 order by LENGTH(City);

CITY
-----------
LIMA
PARIS
ATHENS
SPARTA
SYDNEY
CHICAGO
MANCHESTER
```

These are simple examples; much more complex clauses could be used. For example, you could find all the authors with more than one *O* in their names by using **INSTR** in the **where** clause:

```
select Author from MAGAZINE
   where INSTR(Author,'O',1,2) > 0;

AUTHOR
------------------------
BONHOEFFER, DIETRICH
CROOKES, WILLIAM
```

This works by finding a second occurrence of the letter *O* in the author names. The **> 0** is a logical technique: recall that functions generally produce two different kinds of results, one that creates new objects, and the other that tells you something about existing objects.

The **INSTR** function tells something about a string, specifically the position of the set it has been asked to find. Here, it is asked to locate the second *O* in the Author string. Its result will be a number that will be greater than zero for those names with at least two *O*'s, and zero for those with one or less (when **INSTR** doesn't find something, its result is a zero). So, a simple test for a result greater than zero checks for the success of the **INSTR** search for a second *O*.

The **where** clause using **INSTR** produces the same result as this:

```
where Author LIKE '%O%O%'
```

Remember that the percent sign (**%**) is a wildcard, meaning it takes the place of anything, so the **like** clause here tells SQL to look for two *O*'s with anything before, between, or after them. This is probably easier to understand than the previous example of **INSTR**.

There are often several ways to produce the same result in Oracle. Some will be easier to understand, some will work more quickly, some will be more appropriate in certain situations, and some simply will be a matter of personal style.

SOUNDEX

There is one string function that is used almost exclusively in a **where** clause: **SOUNDEX**. It has the unusual ability to find words that sound like other words, virtually regardless of how either is spelled. This is especially useful when you're not certain how a word or name is really spelled.

This is the format for **SOUNDEX**:

```
SOUNDEX(string)
```

Here are a few of examples of its use:

```
select City, Temperature, Condition
  from WEATHER
 where SOUNDEX(City) = SOUNDEX('Sidney');

CITY          TEMPERATURE CONDITION
-----------   ----------- ---------
SYDNEY                 29 SNOW

select City, Temperature, Condition from WEATHER
 where SOUNDEX(City) = SOUNDEX('menncestr');

CITY          TEMPERATURE CONDITION
-----------   ----------- ---------
MANCHESTER             66 FOG

select Author from MAGAZINE
 where SOUNDEX(Author) = SOUNDEX('Banheffer');

AUTHOR
------------------------
BONHOEFFER, DIETRICH
```

SOUNDEX compares the sound of the entry in the selected column with the sound of the word in single quotation marks, and looks for a close match. **SOUNDEX** makes certain assumptions about how letters and combinations of letters are usually pronounced in English, and the two words being compared must begin with the same letter. It will not always find the word you're searching for or have misspelled, but it can help.

It is not necessary that one of the two **SOUNDEX**s in the **where** clause have a literal in it. **SOUNDEX** could be used to compare two columns to find those that sound alike.

One useful purpose for this function is cleaning up mailing lists. Many lists have duplicate entries with slight differences in spelling or format of the customers' names. By using **SOUNDEX** to list all the names that sound alike, many of these duplicates can be discovered and eliminated.

Let's apply this to the ADDRESS table:

```
select LastName, FirstName, Phone
  from ADDRESS;
```

LASTNAME	FIRSTNAME	PHONE
BAILEY	WILLIAM	213-293-0223
ADAMS	JACK	415-453-7530
SEP	FELICIA	214-522-8383
DE MEDICI	LEFTY	312-736-1166
DEMIURGE	FRANK	707-767-8900
CASEY	WILLIS	312-684-1414
ZACK	JACK	415-620-6842
YARROW	MARY	415-787-2178
WERSCHKY	ARNY	415-235-7387
BRANT	GLEN	415-526-7512
EDGAR	THEODORE	415-525-6252
HARDIN	HUGGY	617-566-0125
HILD	PHIL	603-934-2242
LOEBEL	FRANK	202-456-1414
MOORE	MARY	718-857-1638
SZEP	FELICIA	214-522-8383
ZIMMERMAN	FRED	503-234-7491

To find duplicates, you must force Oracle to compare each LastName in the table to all the others in the same table.

Join the ADDRESS table to itself by creating an alias for the table, calling it first **a** and then **b**. Now it is as if there are two tables, a and b, with the common column LastName.

In the **where** clause, any column where the LastName in one table is identical to the LastName in the other table is eliminated. This prevents a LastName from matching to itself.

Those that sound alike are then selected:

```
select a.LastName, a.FirstName, a.Phone
  from ADDRESS a, ADDRESS b
 where a.LastName != b.LastName
   and SOUNDEX(a.LastName) = SOUNDEX(b.LastName);
```

LASTNAME	FIRSTNAME	PHONE
SZEP	FELICIA	214-522-8383
SEP	FELICIA	214-522-8383

You can also perform SOUNDEX searches on individual words within a text entry. For examples of this and other complex text searches, see Chapter 24.

National Language Support

Oracle doesn't have to use English characters; it can represent data in any language through its implementation of *National Language Support.* By using characters made up of longer pieces of information than ordinary characters, Oracle can represent Japanese and other such strings. See **NLSSORT**, **NLS_INITCAP**, **NLS_LOWER**, and **NLS_UPPER** in the Alphabetical Reference section of this book. In addition to the **SUBSTR** function, Oracle supports **SUBSTRB** (using bytes instead of characters), **SUBSTRC** (using Unicode complete characters), **SUBSTR2** (using UCS2 codepoints), and **SUBSTR4** (using UCS4 codepoints).

Review

Data comes in several types, primarily DATE, NUMBER, and CHARACTER. Character data is basically a string of letters, numbers, or other symbols, and is often called a *character string*, or just a *string*. These strings can be changed or described by string functions. Oracle features two types of character datatypes: variable-length strings (the VARCHAR2 datatype) and fixed-length strings (the CHAR datatype). Values in CHAR columns are padded with spaces to the full column length if they are shorter than the defined length of the column.

Functions such as **RPAD**, **LPAD**, **LTRIM**, **RTRIM**, **TRIM**, **LOWER**, **UPPER**, **INITCAP**, and **SUBSTR** actually change the contents of a string or column before displaying them to you.

Functions such as **LENGTH**, **INSTR**, and **SOUNDEX** describe the characteristics of a string, such as how long it is, where in it a certain character is located, or what it sounds like.

All of these functions can be used alone or in combination to select and present information from an Oracle database. This is a straightforward process, built up from simple logical steps that can be combined to accomplish very sophisticated tasks.

CHAPTER
8

Playing the Numbers

 irtually everything we do, particularly in business, is measured, explained, and often guided by numbers. While Oracle cannot correct our obsession with numbers and the illusion of control they often give us, it will facilitate capable and thorough analysis of the information in a database. Good mathematical analysis of familiar numbers will often show trends and facts that were initially not apparent.

The Three Classes of Number Functions

Oracle functions deal with three classes of numbers: single values, groups of values, and lists of values. As with string functions (discussed in Chapter 7), some of these functions change the values they are applied to, while others merely report information about the values. The classes are distinguished in this way:

A *single value* is one number, such as these:

- A literal number, such as 544.3702

- A variable in SQLPLUS or PL/SQL

- One number from one column and one row of the database

Oracle single-value functions usually change these values through a calculation.

A *group of values* is all the numbers in one column from a series of rows, such as the closing stock price for all the rows of stocks in the STOCK table from Chapter 1. Oracle group-value functions tell you something about the whole group, such as average stock price, but not about the individual members of the group.

A *list of values* is a series of numbers that can include:

- Literal numbers, such as 1, 7.3, 22, 86

- Variables in SQLPLUS or PL/SQL

- Columns, such as OpeningPrice, ClosingPrice, Bid, Ask

Oracle list functions choose one member of a list of values.

Table 8-1 shows these functions by class. Some functions fit into more than one class. Other functions fall somewhere between string and number functions, or are used to convert data from one to the other. These are covered in Chapter 10.

Notation

Functions will be shown with this kind of notation:

```
FUNCTION(value [,option])
```

The function itself will be uppercase. Values and options will be shown in lowercase italics. Whenever the word *value* appears this way, it represents one of the following: a literal number, the name of a number column in a table, the result of a calculation, or a variable. Because Oracle does not allow numbers to be used as column names, a literal number should not be in single quotation marks (as a literal string would be in a string function). Column names also must not have single quotation marks.

Function	Definition
Single-Value Functions	
value1 + *value2*	Addition
value1 - *value2*	Subtraction
value1 * *value2*	Multiplication
value1 / *value2*	Division
ABS(*value*)	ABSolute *value*
ACOS(*value*)	Arc COSine of *value*, in radians
ASIN(*value*)	Arc SINe of *value*, in radians
ATAN(*value*)	Arc TANgent of *value*, in radians
ATAN2 (*value1, value2*)	ATAN2 returns the arc tangent of two values. Input vaules are unbounded, outputs are expressed in radians
BITAND (*value1, value2*)	BITwise AND of *value1* and *value2*, both of which must resolve to nonnegative integers, and returns an integer
CEIL(*value*)	Numeric CEILing: the smallest integer larger than or equal to *value*
COS(*value*)	COSine of *value*
COSH(*value*)	Hyperbolic COSine of *value*
EXP(*value*)	*e* raised to *value* EXPonent
FLOOR(*value*)	Largest integer smaller than or equal to *value*
LN(*value*)	Natural Logarithm of *value*
LOG(*value*)	Base 10 LOGarithm of *value*
MOD(*value, divisor*)	MODulus
NVL(*value, substitute*)	*substitute* for *value* if *value* is NULL
POWER(*value, exponent*)	*value* raised to an *exponent* POWER
ROUND(*value, precision*)	ROUNDing of *value* to *precision*
SIGN(*value*)	1 if *value* is positive, –1 if negative, 0 if zero
SIN(*value*)	SINe of *value*
SINH(*value*)	Hyperbolic SINe of *value*
SQRT(*value*)	SQuare RooT of *value*
TAN(*value*)	TANgent of *value*
TANH(*value*)	Hyperbolic TANgent of *value*

TABLE 8-1. *Numeric Functions*

Function	Definition
TRUNC(*value, precision*)	*value* TRUNCated to *precision*
VSIZE(*value*)	Storage SIZE of *value* in Oracle
Group-Value Functions	
AVG(*value*)	AVeraGe of *value* for group of rows
CORR(*value1, value2*)	Coefficient of CORRelation of a set of number pairs
COUNT(*value*)	COUNT of rows for column
COVAR_POP(*value1, value2*)	POPulation COVARiance of a set of number pairs
COVAR_SAMP(*value1, value2*)	SAMPle COVARiance of a set of number pairs
CUME_DIST(*value*)	CUMulative DISTribution of a value in a group of values
DENSE_RANK(*value*)	Rank of a row in an ordered group of rows
FIRST(*value*)	Analytic function performed on the row ranking FIRST in a set
GROUP_ID(*value*)	Distinguishes duplicate groups resulting from a GROUP BY specification
GROUPING(*expression*)	Used in conjunction with ROLLUP and CUBE functions to detect NULLs
GROUPING_ID	Returns a number corresponding to the GROUPING bit vector associated with a row
LAST(*value*)	Analytic function performed on the row ranking LAST in a set
MAX(*value*)	MAXimum of all *values* for group of rows
MIN(*value*)	MINimum of all *values* for group of rows
PERCENTILE_CONT(*value*)	Calculates the PERCENTILE ranking of a *value* in a set assuming a CONTinuous linear model
PERCENTILE_DISC(*value*)	Calculates the PERCENTILE ranking of a *value* in a set assuming a DISCrete distribution model
PERCENT_RANK(*value*)	Calculates the PERCENTILE ranking of a *value* in a set
RANK(*value*)	Calculates the RANK of a value in a group of values
STDDEV(*value*)	STanDard DEViation of all *values* for group of rows
STDDEV_POP(*value*)	POPulation STanDard DEViation
STDDEV_SAMP(*value*)	SAMPle STanDard DEViation
SUM(*value*)	SUM of all *values* for group of rows
VAR_POP(*value*)	POPulation VARiance

TABLE 8-1. *Numeric Functions* (continued)

Function	Definition
VAR_SAMP(*value*)	SAMPle VARiance
VARIANCE(*value*)	VARIANCE of all *values* for group of rows
List Functions	
COALESCE(*value1, value2, ...*)	Returns the first non-NULL *value* in the expression list
GREATEST*(value1, value2, ...)*	GREATEST *value* of a list
LEAST(*value1, value2, ...*)	LEAST *value* of a list

TABLE 8-1. *Numeric Functions* (continued)

Every function has only one pair of parentheses. The value that function works on, as well as additional information you can pass to the function, goes between the parentheses.

Some functions have *options,* or parts that are not required to make the function work but that can give you more control if you choose to use them. Options are always shown in square brackets: []. The necessary parts of a function always come before the optional parts.

Single-Value Functions

Most single-value functions are pretty straightforward. This section gives short examples of the major functions, and shows both the results of the functions and how they correspond to columns, rows, and lists. After the examples, you'll see how to combine these functions. The syntax for all of the functions is found in the Alphabetical Reference of this book.

A table named MATH was created to show the calculation effects of the many math functions. It has only four rows and four columns, as shown here:

```
select Name, Above, Below, Empty from MATH;

NAME          ABOVE    BELOW EMPTY
------------ ------- ------- -----
WHOLE NUMBER      11     -22
LOW DECIMAL    33.33  -44.44
MID DECIMAL     55.5   -55.5
HIGH DECIMAL  66.666 -77.777
```

This table is useful because it has values with a variety of characteristics, which are spelled out by the names of the rows. WHOLE NUMBER contains no decimal parts. LOW DECIMAL has decimals that are less than .5, MID DECIMAL has decimals equal to .5, and HIGH DECIMAL has decimals greater than .5. This range is particularly important when using **ROUND** and **TRUNC**ate functions, and in understanding how they affect the value of a number.

To the right of the Name column are three other columns: Above, which contains only numbers above zero (positive numbers); Below, which contains only numbers below zero; and Empty, which is **NULL**.

NOTE
*In Oracle, a number column may have no value in it at all: When
it is **NULL**, it is not zero; it is simply empty. This has important
implications in making computations, as you will see.*

Not all of the rows in this MATH table are needed to demonstrate how most math functions
work, so the examples primarily use the last row, HIGH DECIMAL. In addition, the SQLPLUS
column command has been used to explicitly show the precision of the calculation, so that the
results of functions that affect a number's precision can be clearly seen. To review the SQL and
SQLPLUS commands that produced the results that follow, look at the file math.sql (on the
accompanying CD-ROM). Chapter 14 discusses numeric formatting issues.

Addition, Subtraction, Multiplication, and Division (+, -, *, and /)

This query shows each of the four basic arithmetic functions, using Above and Below:

```
select Name, Above, Below, Empty,
       Above + Below  AS Plus,
       Above - Below  AS Subtr,
       Above * Below  AS Times,
       Above / Below  AS Divided
  from MATH
 where Name = 'HIGH DECIMAL';
```

NAME	ABOVE	BELOW	EMPTY	PLUS	SUBTR	TIMES	DIVIDED
HIGH DECIMAL	66.666	-77.777		-11.111	144.443	-5185.081482	-.857143

NULL

In the following example, the same four arithmetic operations are now done again, except instead
of using Above and Below, Above and Empty are used. Note that any arithmetic operation that
includes a **NULL** value has **NULL** as a result. The calculated columns (columns whose values are
the result of a calculation) Plus, Subtr, Times, and Divided are all empty.

```
select Name, Above, Below, Empty,
       Above + Empty  AS Plus,
       Above - Empty  AS Subtr,
       Above * Empty  AS Times,
       Above / Empty  AS Divided
  from MATH
 where Name = 'HIGH DECIMAL';
```

NAME	ABOVE	BELOW	EMPTY	PLUS	SUBTR	TIMES	DIVIDED
HIGH DECIMAL	66.666	-77.777					

What you see here is evidence that a **NULL** value cannot be used in a calculation. **NULL** isn't the same as zero; think of **NULL** as a value that is unknown. For example, suppose you have a table with the names of your friends and their ages, but the Age column for PAT SMITH is empty, because you don't know it. What's the difference in your ages? It's clearly not your age minus zero. Your age minus an unknown age is also unknown, or **NULL**. You can't fill in an answer because you don't have an answer. Because you can't make the computation, the answer is **NULL**.

This is also the reason you cannot use **NULL** with an equal sign in a **where** clause (see Chapter 3). It makes no sense to say x is unknown and y is unknown, therefore x and y are equal. If Mrs. Wilkins's and Mr. Adams's ages are unknown, it doesn't mean they're the same age.

There also will be instances where **NULL** means a value is irrelevant, such as an apartment number for a house. In some cases, the apartment number might be **NULL** because it is unknown (even though it really exists), while in other cases it is **NULL** because there simply isn't one. **NULL**s will be explored in more detail later in this chapter, under "NULLs in Group-Value Functions."

NVL: NULL-Value Substitution

The previous section states the general case about **NULL**s—that **NULL** represents an unknown or irrelevant value. In particular cases, however, although a value is unknown, you may be able to make a reasonable guess. If you're a package carrier, for instance, and 30 percent of the shippers that call you for pickups can't tell you the weight or volume of their packages, will you declare it completely impossible to estimate how many cargo planes you'll need tonight? Of course not. You know from experience the average weight and volume of your packages, so you'd plug in these numbers for those customers who didn't supply you with the information. Here's the information as supplied by your clients:

```
select Client, Weight from SHIPPING;

CLIENT          WEIGHT
------------- ------
JOHNSON TOOL      59
DAGG SOFTWARE     27
TULLY ANDOVER
```

This is what the **NULL**-value substitution (**NVL**) function does:

```
select Client, NVL(Weight,43) from SHIPPING;

CLIENT          NVL(WEIGHT,43)
------------- --------------
JOHNSON TOOL              59
DAGG SOFTWARE            27
TULLY ANDOVER            43
```

Here you know that the average package weight is 43 pounds, so you use the **NVL** function to plug in 43 any time a client's package has an unknown weight—that is, where the value in the column is **NULL**. In this case, TULLY ANDOVER didn't know the weight of their package when they called it in, but you can still total these and have a fair estimate.

This is the format for **NVL**:

```
NVL(value, substitute)
```

If *value* is **NULL**, this function is equal to *substitute*. If *value* is not **NULL**, this function is equal to *value*. *substitute* can be a literal number, another column, or a computation. If you really were a package carrier with this problem, you could even have a table join in your **select** statement where *substitute* was from a view that actually averaged the weight of all non-**NULL** packages.

NVL is not restricted to numbers. It can be used with CHAR, VARCHAR2, DATE, and other datatypes as well, but the *value* and *substitute* must be the same datatype, and it is really useful only in cases where the data is unknown, not where it's irrelevant.

ABS: Absolute Value

Absolute value is the measure of the magnitude of something. For instance, in a temperature change or a stock index change, the magnitude of the change has meaning in itself, regardless of the direction of the change (which is important in its own right). Absolute value is always a positive number.

This is the format for **ABS**:

```
ABS(value)
```

Note these examples:

```
ABS(146) = 146
ABS(-30) =  30
```

CEIL

CEIL (for ceiling) simply produces the smallest *integer* (or whole number) that is greater than or equal to a specific value. Pay special attention to its effect on negative numbers.

The following is the format for **CEIL** and some examples:

```
CEIL(value)
```

```
CEIL(2)    =  2
CEIL(1.3)  =  2
CEIL(-2)   = -2
CEIL(-2.3) = -2
```

FLOOR

FLOOR is the intuitive opposite of **CEIL**. This is the format for **FLOOR**, and some examples:

```
FLOOR(value)
```

```
FLOOR(2)    =  2
FLOOR(1.3)  =  1
FLOOR(-2)   = -2
FLOOR(-2.3) = -3
```

MOD

MODulus is an odd little function primarily used in data processing for esoteric tasks, such as "check digits," which helps assure the accurate transmission of a string of numbers. **MOD** divides a value by a divisor and tells you the remainder. For example, **MOD**(23,6) = 5 means divide 23 by 6. The answer is 3 with 5 left over, so 5 is the result of the modulus.

This is the format for **MOD**:

```
MOD(value,divisor)
```

Both *value* and *divisor* can be any real number. The value of **MOD** is zero if *divisor* is zero or negative. Note the following examples:

```
MOD(100,10)     =   0
MOD(22,23)      =  22
MOD(10,3)       =   1
MOD(-30.23,7)   =  -2.23
MOD(4.1,.3)     =    .2
```

The second example shows what **MOD** does whenever the divisor is larger than the dividend (the number being divided). It produces the dividend as a result. Also note this important case where *value* is an integer:

```
MOD(value,1)    = 0
```

The preceding is a good test to see if a number is an integer.

POWER

POWER is simply the ability to raise a value to a given positive exponent, as shown here:

```
POWER(value,exponent)
```

```
POWER(3,2)         =      9
POWER(3,3)         =     27
POWER(-77.777,2)   = 6049.261729
POWER(3,1.086)     =      3.297264
POWER(64,.5)       =      8
```

The exponent can be any real number.

SQRT: Square Root

Oracle has a separate square root function that gives results equivalent to **POWER**(*value*,.5):

```
SQRT(value)
```

```
SQRT(64)      = 8
SQRT(66.666)  = 8.16492
SQRT(4)       = 2
```

The square root of a negative number is an imaginary number. Oracle doesn't support imaginary numbers, so it returns an error if you attempt to find the square root of a negative number.

EXP, LN, and LOG

The **EXP, LN**, and **LOG** functions are rarely used in business calculations but are quite common in scientific and technical work. **EXP** is *e* (2.71828183...) raised to the specified power; **LN** is the "natural," or base *e*, logarithm of a value. The first two functions are reciprocals of one another; **LN(EXP(**i**))** = *value*. The **LOG** function takes a base and a positive value. **LN(***value***)** is the same as **LOG**(2.71828183,*value*).

```
EXP(value)

EXP(3)        =   20.085537
EXP(5)        = 148.413159

LN(value)

LN(3)         = 1.098612
LN(20.085536) = 3

LOG(value)

LOG(EXP(1),3) = 1.098612
LOG(10,100)   = 2
```

ROUND and TRUNC

ROUND and **TRUNC** are two related single-value functions. **TRUNC** truncates, or chops off, digits of precision from a number; **ROUND** rounds numbers to a given number of digits of precision.

Here are the formats for **ROUND** and **TRUNC**:

```
ROUND(value,precision)
TRUNC(value,precision)
```

There are some properties worth paying close attention to here. First, look at this simple example of a **select** from the MATH table. Two digits of precision are called for (counting toward the right from the decimal point).

```
select Name, Above, Below,
       ROUND(Above,2),
       ROUND(Below,2),
       TRUNC(Above,2),
       TRUNC(Below,2)
  from MATH;
```

NAME	ABOVE	BELOW	ROUND (ABOVE,2)	ROUND (BELOW,2)	TRUNC (ABOVE,2)	TRUNC (BELOW,2)
WHOLE NUMBER	11	-22	11	-22	11	-22

```
LOW DECIMAL      33.33  -44.44    33.33   -44.44    33.33   -44.44
MID DECIMAL      55.5   -55.5     55.5    -55.5     55.5    -55.5
HIGH DECIMAL     66.666 -77.777   66.67   -77.78    66.66   -77.77
```

Only the bottom row is affected, because only it has three digits beyond the decimal point. Both the positive and negative numbers in the bottom row were rounded or truncated: The 66.666 was rounded to a higher number, 66.67, but the -77.777 was rounded to a lower (more negative) number, -77.78. When rounding is done to zero digits, this is the result:

```
select Name, Above, Below,
       ROUND(Above,0),
       ROUND(Below,0),
       TRUNC(Above,0),
       TRUNC(Below,0)
   from MATH;
```

NAME	ABOVE	BELOW	ROUND (ABOVE,0)	ROUND (BELOW,0)	TRUNC (ABOVE,0)	TRUNC (BELOW,0)
WHOLE NUMBER	11	-22	11	-22	11	-22
LOW DECIMAL	33.33	-44.44	33	-44	33	-44
MID DECIMAL	55.5	-55.5	56	-56	55	-55
HIGH DECIMAL	66.666	-77.777	67	-78	66	-77

Note that the decimal value of .5 was rounded up when 55.5 went to 56. This follows the most common American rounding convention (some rounding conventions round up only if a number is larger than .5). Compare these results with **CEIL** and **FLOOR**. They have significant differences:

```
ROUND(55.5)  = 56     ROUND(-55.5)  = -56
TRUNC(55.5)  = 55     TRUNC(-55.5)  = -55
CEIL(55.5)   = 56     CEIL(-55.5)   = -55
FLOOR(55.5)  = 55     FLOOR(-55.5)  = -56
```

Finally, note that both **ROUND** and **TRUNC** can work with negative precision, moving to the left of the decimal point:

```
select Name, Above, Below,
       ROUND(Above,-1),
       ROUND(Below,-1),
       TRUNC(Above,-1),
       TRUNC(Below,-1)
   from MATH;
```

NAME	ABOVE	BELOW	ROUND (ABOVE,-1)	ROUND (BELOW,-1)	TRUNC (ABOVE,-1)	TRUNC (BELOW,-1)
WHOLE NUMBER	11	-22	10	-20	10	-20
LOW DECIMAL	33.33	-44.44	30	-40	30	-40

```
MID DECIMAL    55.5   -55.5        60       -60        50       -50
HIGH DECIMAL 66.666 -77.777        70       -80        60       -70
```

Rounding with a negative number can be useful when producing such things as economic reports, where populations or dollar sums need to be rounded up to the millions, billions, or trillions.

SIGN

SIGN is the flip side of absolute value. Whereas **ABS** tells you the magnitude of a value but not its sign, **SIGN** tells you the sign of a value but not its magnitude.

This is the format for **SIGN**:

```
SIGN(value)
```

```
Examples: SIGN(146) =  1  Compare to: ABS(146) = 146
          SIGN(-30) = -1              ABS(-30) =  30
```

The **SIGN** of 0 is 0:

```
SIGN(0)=0
```

The **SIGN** function is often used in conjunction with the **DECODE** function. **DECODE** will be described in Chapter 17.

SIN, SINH, COS, COSH, TAN, TANH, ACOS, ATAN, ATAN2, and ASIN

The trigonometric functions sine, cosine, and tangent are scientific and technical functions not used much in business. **SIN**, **COS**, and **TAN** give you the standard trigonometric function values for an angle expressed in radians (degrees multiplied by *pi* divided by 180). **SINH**, **COSH**, and **TANH** give you the hyperbolic functions for an angle.

```
SIN(value)
```

```
SIN(30*3.141593/180) = .5
```

```
COSH(value)
```

```
COSH(0)              = 1
```

The **ASIN**, **ACOS**, and **ATAN** functions return the arc sine, arc cosine, and arc tangent values (in radians) of the values provided. **ATAN2** returns the arc tangent of two values. Input values are unbounded; outputs are expressed in radians.

Group-Value Functions

Group-value functions are those statistical functions such as **SUM**, **AVG**, **COUNT**, and the like that tell you something about a group of values taken as a whole: the average age of all of the friends in the table mentioned earlier, for instance, or the oldest member of the group, or the youngest,

or the number of members in the group, and more. Even when one of these functions is supplying information about a single row—such as the oldest person—it is still information that is defined by the row's relation to the group.

As of Oracle9i, you can use a wide array of advanced statistical functions against your data—including regression testing and sampling. In the following discussions, you will see descriptions of the most commonly used group-value functions; for the others (all are listed in Table 8-1), see the Alphabetical Reference.

NULLs in Group-Value Functions

Group-value functions treat **NULL** values differently than single-value functions do. Group functions ignore **NULL** values and calculate a result in spite of them.

Take **AVG** as an example. Suppose you have a list of 100 friends and their ages. If you picked 20 of them at random, and averaged their ages, how different would the result be than if you picked a different list of 20, also at random, and averaged it, or if you averaged all 100? In fact, the averages of these three groups would be very close. What this means is that **AVG** is somewhat insensitive to missing records, even when the missing data represents a high percentage of the total number of records available.

> **NOTE**
> *AVG is not immune to missing data, and there can be cases where it will be significantly off (such as when missing data is not randomly distributed), but these cases will be less common.*

The relative insensitivity to missing data of **AVG** needs to be contrasted with, for instance, **SUM**. How close to correct is the **SUM** of the ages of only 20 friends to the **SUM** of all 100 friends? Not close at all. So if you had a table of friends, but only 20 out of 100 supplied their ages, and 80 out of 100 had **NULL** for their age, which would be a more reliable statistic about the whole group and less sensitive to the absence of data—the **AVG** age of those 20 names, or the **SUM** of them? Note that this is an entirely different issue than whether it is possible to estimate the sum of all 100 based on only 20 (in fact, it is precisely the **AVG** of the 20, times 100). The point is, if you don't know how many rows are **NULL**, you can use the following to provide a fairly reasonable result:

```
select AVG(Age) from LIST;
```

You cannot get a reasonable result from this, however:

```
select SUM(Age) from LIST;
```

This same test of whether or not results are reasonable defines how the other group functions respond to **NULLs**. **STDDEV** and **VARIANCE** are measures of central tendency; they, too, are relatively insensitive to missing data. (These will be covered in "STDDEV and VARIANCE," later in this chapter.)

MAX and **MIN** measure the extremes of your data. They can fluctuate wildly while **AVG** stays relatively constant: If you add a 100-year-old man to a group of 99 people who are 50 years old, the average age only goes up to 50.5—but the maximum age has doubled. Add a newborn baby, and the average goes back to 50, but the minimum age is now 0. It's clear that missing or unknown

NULL values can profoundly affect **MAX**, **MIN**, and **SUM**, so be cautious when using them, particularly if a significant percentage of the data is **NULL**.

Is it possible to create functions that also take into account how sparse the data is and how many values are **NULL** compared to how many have real values, and make good guesses about **MAX**, **MIN**, and **SUM**? Yes, but such functions would be statistical projections, which must make explicit their assumptions about a particular set of data. It is not an appropriate task for a general-purpose group function. Some statisticians would argue that these functions should return **NULL** if they encounter any **NULL**s, since returning any value can be misleading. Oracle returns something rather than nothing, but leaves it up to you to decide whether the result is reasonable.

COUNT is a special case. It can go either way with **NULL** values, but it always returns a number; it will never evaluate to **NULL**. Format and usage for **COUNT** will be shown shortly, but to simply contrast it with the other group functions, it will count all of the non-**NULL** rows of a column, or it will count all of the rows. In other words, if asked to count the ages of 100 friends, **COUNT** will return a value of 20 (since only 20 of the 100 gave their age). If asked to count the rows in the table of friends without specifying a column, it will return 100. An example of these differences is given in "DISTINCT in Group Functions," later in this chapter.

Examples of Single- and Group-Value Functions

Neither the group-value functions nor the single-value functions are particularly difficult to understand, but a practical overview of how each function works is helpful in fleshing out some of the options and consequences of their use.

The COMFORT table in these examples contains basic temperature data by city at noon and midnight on each of four sample days each year: the equinoxes (about March 21 and September 23) and the solstices (about June 22 and December 22). You ought to be able to characterize cities based on their temperatures on these days each year.

For the sake of these examples, this table has only eight rows: the data from the four dates in 2001 for San Francisco, California and Keene, New Hampshire. You can use Oracle's number functions to analyze these cities, their average temperature, the volatility of the temperature, and so on, for 2001. With more years and data on more cities, an analysis of temperature patterns and variability throughout the century could be made.

The table looks like this:

```
describe COMFORT

Name                                Null?     Type
----------------------------------- --------  ----
CITY                                NOT NULL  VARCHAR2(13)
SAMPLEDATE                          NOT NULL  DATE
NOON                                          NUMBER(3,1)
MIDNIGHT                                      NUMBER(3,1)
PRECIPITATION                                 NUMBER
```

It contains this temperature data:

```
select City, SampleDate, Noon, Midnight from COMFORT;
```

```
CITY            SAMPLEDAT NOON MIDNIGHT
------------    --------- ---- --------
SAN FRANCISCO   21-MAR-01 62.5     42.3
SAN FRANCISCO   22-JUN-01 51.1     71.9
SAN FRANCISCO   23-SEP-01          61.5
SAN FRANCISCO   22-DEC-01 52.6     39.8
KEENE           21-MAR-01 39.9     -1.2
KEENE           22-JUN-01 85.1     66.7
KEENE           23-SEP-01 99.8     82.6
KEENE           22-DEC-01 -7.2     -1.2
```

AVG, COUNT, MAX, MIN, and SUM

Due to a power failure, the noon temperature in San Francisco on September 23 did not get recorded. The consequences of this can be seen in the following query:

```
select AVG(Noon), COUNT(Noon), MAX(Noon), MIN(Noon), SUM(Noon)
  from COMFORT
 where City = 'SAN FRANCISCO';

AVG(NOON) COUNT(NOON) MAX(NOON) MIN(NOON) SUM(NOON)
--------- ----------- --------- --------- ---------
     55.4           3      62.5      51.1     166.2
```

AVG(Noon) is the average of the three temperatures that are known. **COUNT**(Noon) is the count of how many rows there are in the Noon column that are not **NULL**. **MAX** and **MIN** are self-evident. **SUM**(Noon) is the sum of only three dates because of the **NULL** for September 23. Note that

```
SUM(NOON)
---------
    166.2
```

is by no coincidence exactly three times the **AVG**(Noon).

Combining Group-Value and Single-Value Functions

Suppose you would like to know how much the temperature changes in the course of a day. This is a measure of *volatility*. Your first attempt to answer the question might be to subtract the temperature at midnight from the temperature at noon:

```
select City, SampleDate, Noon-Midnight
  from COMFORT
 where City = 'KEENE';

CITY            SAMPLEDAT NOON-MIDNIGHT
------------    --------- -------------
KEENE           21-MAR-01          41.1
KEENE           22-JUN-01          18.4
KEENE           23-SEP-01          17.2
KEENE           22-DEC-01            -6
```

With only four rows to consider in this table, you can quickly convert (or ignore) the pesky minus sign. Volatility in temperature is really a magnitude—which means it asks by how much the temperature changed. It doesn't include a sign, so the -6 isn't really correct. If it goes uncorrected, and is included in a further calculation, such as the average change in a year, the answer you get will be absolutely wrong, as shown here:

```
select AVG(Noon-Midnight)
  from COMFORT
 where City = 'KEENE';

AVG(NOON-MIDNIGHT)
------------------
           17.675
```

The correct answer requires an absolute value, as shown next.

```
select AVG(ABS(Noon-Midnight))
  from COMFORT
 where City = 'KEENE';

AVG(ABS(NOON-MIDNIGHT))
-----------------------
                20.675
```

Combining functions this way follows the same technique given in Chapter 7 in the section on string functions. An entire function such as

```
ABS(Noon-Midnight)
```

is simply plugged into another function as its value, like this:

```
AVG(value)
```

which produces

```
AVG(ABS(Noon-Midnight))
```

This shows both single-value and group-value functions at work. You see that you can place single-value functions inside group-value functions. The single-value functions will calculate a result for every row, and the group-value functions will view that result as if it were the actual value for the row. Single-value functions can be combined (*nested* inside each other) almost without limit. Group-value functions can contain single-value functions in place of their value. They can, in fact, contain many single-value functions in place of their value.

What about combining group functions? First of all, it doesn't make any sense to nest them this way:

```
select SUM(AVG(Noon)) from COMFORT;
```

The preceding will produce this error:

```
ERROR at line 1:
ORA-00978: nested group function without GROUP BY
```

Besides, if it actually worked, it would produce exactly the same result as this:

```
AVG(Noon)
```

because the result of **AVG**(Noon) is just a single value. The **SUM** of a single value is just the single value, so it is not meaningful to nest group functions. The exception to this rule is in the use of **group by** in the **select** statement, the absence of which is why Oracle produced the error message here. This is covered in Chapter 11.

It *can* be meaningful to add, subtract, multiply, or divide the results of two or more group functions. For example,

```
select MAX(Noon) - MIN(Noon)
  from COMFORT
 where City = 'SAN FRANCISCO';

MAX(NOON)-MIN(NOON)
-------------------
               11.4
```

gives the range of the temperatures in a year. In fact, a quick comparison of San Francisco and Keene could be done with just a bit more effort:

```
select City, AVG(Noon), MAX(Noon), MIN(Noon),
       MAX(Noon) - MIN(Noon) AS Swing
  from COMFORT
 group by City;

CITY           AVG(NOON) MAX(NOON) MIN(NOON) SWING
------------- --------- --------- --------- -----
KEENE              54.4      99.8      -7.2   107
SAN FRANCISCO      55.4      62.5      51.1  11.4
```

This query is a good example of discovering information in your data: The average temperature in the two cities is nearly identical, but the huge temperature swing in Keene, compared to San Francisco, says a lot about the yearly temperature volatility of the two cities, and the relative effort required to dress (or heat and cool a home) in one city compared to the other. The **group by** clause will be explained in detail in Chapter 11. Briefly, in this example it forced the group functions to work not on the total table, but on the subgroups of temperatures by city.

STDDEV and VARIANCE

Standard deviation and variance have their common statistical meanings, and use the same format as all group functions:

```
select MAX(Noon), AVG(Noon), MIN(Noon), STDDEV(Noon),
       VARIANCE(Noon)
```

```
  from COMFORT
 where City = 'KEENE';
```

```
MAX(NOON)  AVG(NOON)  MIN(NOON)  STDDEV(NOON)  VARIANCE(NOON)
---------  ---------  ---------  ------------  --------------
     99.8       54.4       -7.2       48.3338         2336.15
```

DISTINCT in Group Functions

All group-value functions have a **DISTINCT** versus **ALL** option. **COUNT** provides a good example of how this works.

This is the format for **COUNT** (I means "or"):

```
COUNT([DISTINCT | ALL] value)
```

Here is an example:

```
select COUNT(DISTINCT City), COUNT(City), COUNT(*)
  from COMFORT;
```

```
COUNT(DISTINCTCITY)  COUNT(CITY)  COUNT(*)
-------------------  -----------  --------
                  2            8         8
```

This query shows a couple of interesting results. First, **DISTINCT** forces **COUNT** to count only the number of unique city names. If asked to count the **DISTINCT** midnight temperatures, it would return 7, because two of the eight temperatures were the same. When **COUNT** is used on City but not forced to look at **DISTINCT** cities, it finds 8.

This also shows that **COUNT** can work on a character column. It's not making a computation on the values in the column, as **SUM** or **AVG** must; it is merely counting how many rows have a value in the specified column.

COUNT has another unique property: *value* can be an asterisk, meaning that **COUNT** tells you how many rows are in the table, regardless of whether any specific columns are **NULL**. It will count a row even if all of its fields are **NULL**.

The other group functions do not share **COUNT**'s ability to use an asterisk, nor its ability to use a character column for *value* (although **MAX** and **MIN** can). They do all share its use of **DISTINCT**, which forces each of them to operate only on unique values. A table with values such as this:

```
select FirstName, Age from BIRTHDAY;
```

```
FIRSTNAME        AGE
---------------  ----
GEORGE            42
ROBERT            52
NANCY             42
VICTORIA          42
FRANK             42
```

would produce this result:

```
select AVG(DISTINCT Age) AS Average,
       SUM(DISTINCT Age) AS Total
  from BIRTHDAY;

AVERAGE  TOTAL
-------  ------
     47      94
```

which, if you wanted to know the average age of your friends, is not the right answer. The use of **DISTINCT** other than in **COUNT** is likely to be extremely rare, except perhaps in some statistical calculations. **MAX** and **MIN** produce the same result with or without **DISTINCT**.

The alternative option to **DISTINCT** is **ALL**, which is the default. **ALL** tells SQL to check every row, even if the value is a duplicate of the value in another row. You do not need to type **ALL**; if you don't type **DISTINCT**, **ALL** is used automatically.

List Functions

Unlike the group-value functions, which work on a group of rows, the list functions work on a group of columns, either actual or calculated values, within a single row. In other words, list functions compare the values of each of several columns and pick either the greatest or least of the list. Consider the COMFORT table, shown here:

```
select City, SampleDate, Noon, Midnight from COMFORT;

CITY          SAMPLEDAT NOON  MIDNIGHT
------------- --------- ----  --------
SAN FRANCISCO 21-MAR-01 62.5      42.3
SAN FRANCISCO 22-JUN-01 51.1      71.9
SAN FRANCISCO 23-SEP-01           61.5
SAN FRANCISCO 22-DEC-01 52.6      39.8
KEENE         21-MAR-01 39.9      -1.2
KEENE         22-JUN-01 85.1      66.7
KEENE         23-SEP-01 99.8      82.6
KEENE         22-DEC-01 -7.2      -1.2
```

Now compare this query result with the following one. Note especially June and September in San Francisco, and December in Keene:

```
select City, SampleDate, GREATEST(Midnight,Noon) AS High,
       LEAST(Midnight,Noon) AS Low
  from COMFORT;

CITY          SAMPLEDAT HIGH  LOW
------------- --------- ----  ----
SAN FRANCISCO 21-MAR-01 62.5  42.3
SAN FRANCISCO 22-JUN-01 71.9  51.1
SAN FRANCISCO 23-SEP-01
SAN FRANCISCO 22-DEC-01 52.6  39.8
KEENE         21-MAR-01 39.9  -1.2
```

```
KEENE            22-JUN-01  85.1   66.7
KEENE            23-SEP-01  99.8   82.6
KEENE            22-DEC-01  -1.2   -7.2
```

September in San Francisco has a **NULL** result because **GREATEST** and **LEAST** couldn't legitimately compare an actual midnight temperature with an unknown noon temperature. In the other two instances, the midnight temperature was actually higher than the noon temperature.

These are the formats for **GREATEST** and **LEAST**:

```
GREATEST(value1,value2,value3. . .)
LEAST(value1,value2,value3. . .)
```

Both **GREATEST** and **LEAST** can be used with many values, and the values can be columns, literal numbers, calculations, or combinations of other columns. **GREATEST** and **LEAST** can also be used with character columns. For example, they can choose the names that fall last (**GREATEST**) or first (**LEAST**) in alphabetical order:

```
GREATEST('Bob','George','Andrew','Isaiah') = Isaiah
    LEAST('Bob','George','Andrew','Isaiah') = Andrew
```

As of Oracle9i, you can use the **COALESCE** function to evaluate multiple values for non-**NULL** values. Given a string of values, **COALESCE** will return the first non-**NULL** value encountered; if all are **NULL**, then a **NULL** result will be returned.

In the COMFORT table, there is a **NULL** value for Noon for one of the San Francisco measurements. The following query returns

```
select COALESCE(Noon, Midnight) from COMFORT
  where City = 'SAN FRANCISCO';

COALESCE(NOON,MIDNIGHT)
-----------------------
                   62.5
                   51.1
                   61.5
                   52.6
```

In the first two records of the output, the value displayed is the Noon value. In the third record, Noon is **NULL** so Midnight is returned instead. Oracle's **DECODE** and **CASE** functions provide similar functionality, as described in Chapter 17.

Finding Rows with MAX or MIN

Which city had the highest temperature ever recorded, and on what date? The answer is easy with just eight rows to look at, but what if you have data from every city in the country and for every day of every year for the last 50 years? Assume for now that the highest temperature for the year occurred closer to noon than midnight. The following won't work:

```
select City, SampleDate, MAX(Noon)
   from COMFORT;
```

Oracle flags the City column and gives this error message:

```
select City, SampleDate, MAX(Noon)
       *
ERROR at line 1:
ORA-00937:  not a single-group group function
```

This error message is a bit opaque. It means that Oracle has detected a flaw in the logic of the question. Asking for columns means you want individual rows to appear; asking for **MAX**, a group function, means you want a group result for all rows. These are two different kinds of requests. The first asks for a set of rows, but the second requests just one computed row, so there is a conflict. Here is how to construct the query:

```
select City, SampleDate, Noon
   from COMFORT
 where Noon = (select MAX(Noon) from COMFORT);

CITY          SAMPLEDAT  NOON
------------  ---------- -----
KEENE         23-SEP-01  99.8
```

This only produces one row. You might think, therefore, that the combination of a request for the City and SampleDate columns along with the **MAX** of noon is not so contradictory as was just implied. But what if you'd asked for minimum temperature instead?

```
select City, SampleDate, Midnight
   from COMFORT
 where Midnight = (select MIN(Midnight) from COMFORT);

CITY          SAMPLEDAT MIDNIGHT
------------  --------- --------
KEENE         21-MAR-01     -1.2
KEENE         22-DEC-01     -1.2
```

Two rows! More than one satisfied the **MIN** request, so there is a conflict in trying to combine a regular column request with a group function.

It is also possible to use two subqueries, each with a group-value function in it (or two subqueries, where one does and the other doesn't have a group function). Suppose you want to know the highest and lowest noon temperatures for the year:

```
select City, SampleDate, Noon
   from COMFORT
 where Noon = (select MAX(Noon) from COMFORT)
    or Noon = (select MIN(Noon) from COMFORT);
```

```
CITY          SAMPLEDAT  NOON
------------- ---------- -----
KEENE         23-SEP-01  99.8
KEENE         22-DEC-01  -7.2
```

Precedence and Parentheses

When more than one arithmetic or logical operator is used in a single calculation, which one is executed first, and does it matter what order they are in? Consider the following query of the DUAL table (a one-column, one-row table provided by Oracle):

```
select 2/2/4 from DUAL;

2/2/4
-----
  .25
```

When parentheses are introduced, although the numbers and the operation (division) stay the same, the answer changes considerably:

```
select 2/(2/4) from DUAL;

2/(2/4)
-------
      4
```

The reason for this is *precedence*. Precedence defines the order in which mathematical computations are made, not just in Oracle but in mathematics in general. The rules are simple: Operations within parentheses have the highest precedence, then multiplication and division, then addition and subtraction. When an equation is computed, any calculations inside parentheses are made first. Multiplication and division are next. Finally, any addition and subtraction are completed. When operations of equal precedence are to be performed, they are executed from left to right. Here are a few examples:

```
2*4/2*3 = 12          (the same as ( (2*4)/2 )*3)
(2*4)/(2*3) = 1.333
4-2*5 = -6            (the same as 4 - (2*5))
(4-2)*5 = 10
```

AND and **OR** also obey precedence rules, with **AND** having the higher precedence. Observe the effect of the **AND**, and also the left-to-right order, in these two queries:

```
select * from NEWSPAPER
  where Section = 'B' AND Page = 1 OR Page = 2;

FEATURE         S  PAGE
--------------- -  -----
Weather         C    2
Modern Life     B    1
Bridge          B    2
```

```
3 rows selected.

select * from NEWSPAPER
 where Page = 1 OR Page = 2 AND Section = 'B';

FEATURE          S  PAGE
---------------  -  -----
National News    A     1
Sports           D     1
Business         E     1
Modern Life      B     1
Bridge           B     2

5 rows selected.
```

If what you really want is page 1 or 2 in Section B, then parentheses are needed to overcome the precedence of the **AND**. Parentheses override any other operations.

```
select * from NEWSPAPER
 where Section = 'B' AND (Page = 1 OR Page = 2);

FEATURE          S  PAGE
---------------  -  -----
Modern Life      B     1
Bridge           B     2

2 rows selected.
```

The truth is that even experienced programmers and mathematicians have trouble remembering what will execute first when they write a query or an equation. It is always wise to make explicit the order you want Oracle to follow. Use parentheses whenever there could be the slightest risk of confusion.

Review

Single-value functions work on values in a row-by-row fashion. List functions compare columns and choose just one, again in a row-by-row fashion. Single-value functions almost always change the value of the column they are applied to. This doesn't mean, of course, that they have modified the database from which the value was drawn, but they do make a calculation with that value, and the result is different than the original value.

List functions don't change values in this way, but rather they simply choose (or report) the **GREATEST** or **LEAST** of a series of values in a row. Both single-value and list functions will not produce a result if they encounter a value that is **NULL**.

Both single-value and list functions can be used anywhere an expression can be used, such as in the **select** and **where** clauses.

The group-value functions tell something about a whole group of numbers—all of the rows in a set. The group-value functions tell you the average of those numbers, or the largest of them, or how many there are, or the standard deviation of the values, and so on. Group functions ignore

NULL values, and this fact must be kept firmly in mind when reporting about groups of values; otherwise, there is considerable risk of misunderstanding the data.

Group-value functions also can report information on subgroups within a table, or be used to create a summary view of information from one or more tables. Chapter 11 gives details on these additional features.

Finally, mathematical and logical precedence affect the order in which queries are evaluated, and this can have a dramatic effect on query results. Get into the habit of using parentheses to make the order you want both explicit and easy to understand.

CHAPTER
9

Dates: Then, Now, and the Difference

ne of Oracle's strengths is its ability to store and calculate dates, and the number of seconds, minutes, hours, days, months, and years between dates. In addition to basic date functions, Oracle supports a wide array of time zone conversion functions. It also has the ability to format dates in virtually any manner you can conceive of, from a simple 01-MAY-02, to May 1st in the 776th Year of the Reign of Louis IX. You probably won't use many of these date-formatting and computing functions, but the most basic ones will prove to be very important.

Date Arithmetic

DATE is an Oracle datatype, just as VARCHAR2 and NUMBER are, and it has its own unique properties. The DATE datatype is stored in a special internal Oracle format that includes not just the month, day, and year, but also the hour, minute, and second. The benefit of all this detail should be obvious. If you have, for instance, a customer help desk, for each call that is logged in, Oracle can automatically store the date and time of the call in a single DATE column. You can format the DATE column on a report to show just the date, or the date and the hour, or the date, hour, and minute, or the date, hour, minute, and second. You can use the TIMESTAMP datatype to store fractional seconds. See the "Using the TIMESTAMP Datatypes" section later in this chapter for details.

SQLPLUS and SQL recognize columns that are of the DATE datatype, and understand that instructions to do arithmetic with them call for *date arithmetic,* not regular math. Adding one to a date, for instance, will give you another *date:* the next day. Subtracting one date from another will give you a *number:* the count of days between the two dates.

However, since Oracle dates can include hours, minutes, and seconds, doing date arithmetic can prove to be tricky, since Oracle could tell you the difference between today and tomorrow is .516 days! (This will be explained later in this chapter.)

SYSDATE, CURRENT_DATE, and SYSTIMESTAMP

Oracle taps into the computer's operating system for the current date and time. It makes these available to you through a special function called SYSDATE. Think of SYSDATE as a function whose result is always the current date and time, and that can be used anywhere any other Oracle function can be used. You also can regard it as a hidden column or pseudo-column that is in every table. Here, SYSDATE shows today's date:

```
select SysDate from DUAL;

SYSDATE
---------
15-MAR-02
```

NOTE
DUAL is a small but useful Oracle table created for testing functions or doing quick calculations. Later in this chapter, the sidebar "The DUAL Table for Quick Tests and Calculations" describes DUAL.

A second function, CURRENT_DATE, reports the system date in the session's time zone:

```
select Current_Date from DUAL;

CURRENT_D
---------
15-MAR-02
```

Another function, SYSTIMESTAMP, reports the system date in the TIMESTAMP datatype format:

```
select SysTimeStamp from DUAL;

SYSTIMESTAMP
---------------------------------------------
15-MAR-02 02.41.31.000000 PM -05:00
```

See the "Using the TIMESTAMP Datatypes" section later in this chapter for details on the TIMESTAMP datatype and time zone format and functions. The following sections focus on the use of the DATE datatype, since DATE will satisfy most date processing requirements.

The Difference Between Two Dates

HOLIDAY is a table of some secular holidays in the United States during 2002:

```
select Holiday, ActualDate, CelebratedDate from HOLIDAY;

HOLIDAY                    ACTUALDAT CELEBRATE
------------------------   --------- ---------
NEW YEAR DAY               01-JAN-02 01-JAN-02
MARTIN LUTHER KING, JR.    15-JAN-02 17-JAN-02
LINCOLNS BIRTHDAY          12-FEB-02 18-FEB-02
WASHINGTONS BIRTHDAY       22-FEB-02 18-FEB-02
FAST DAY, NEW HAMPSHIRE    22-FEB-02 22-FEB-02
MEMORIAL DAY               30-MAY-02 27-MAY-02
INDEPENDENCE DAY           04-JUL-02 04-JUL-02
LABOR DAY                  02-SEP-02 02-SEP-02
COLUMBUS DAY               12-OCT-02 14-OCT-02
THANKSGIVING               28-NOV-02 28-NOV-02
```

Which holidays are not celebrated on the actual date of their anniversary during 2002? This can be easily answered by subtracting the CelebratedDate from the ActualDate. If the answer is not zero, then there is a difference between the two dates:

```
select Holiday, ActualDate, CelebratedDate
   from Holiday
 where CelebratedDate - ActualDate != 0;

HOLIDAY                    ACTUALDAT CELEBRATE
------------------------   --------- ---------
MARTIN LUTHER KING, JR.    15-JAN-02 17-JAN-02
LINCOLNS BIRTHDAY          12-FEB-02 18-FEB-02
WASHINGTONS BIRTHDAY       22-FEB-02 18-FEB-02
MEMORIAL DAY               30-MAY-02 27-MAY-02
COLUMBUS DAY               12-OCT-02 14-OCT-02
```

The DUAL Table for Quick Tests and Calculations
DUAL is a tiny table Oracle provides with only one row and one column in it:

```
describe DUAL

Name                                    Null?         Type
-------------------------------------   -----------   -------------
DUMMY                                                 VARCHAR(1)
```

Since Oracle's many functions work on both columns and literals, using DUAL lets you see some functioning using just literals. In these examples, the **select** statement doesn't care which columns are in the table, and a single row is sufficient to demonstrate a point. For example, suppose you want to quickly calculate **POWER**(4,3)—four "cubed":

```
select POWER(4,3) from DUAL;

POWER(4,3)
----------
        64
```

The actual column in DUAL is irrelevant. This means that you can experiment with date formatting and arithmetic using the DUAL table and the date functions in order to understand how they work. Then, those functions can be applied to actual dates in real tables.

Date Functions
The major functions performed on DATE datatype columns are as follows:

- **ADD_MONTHS**(*date,count*) Adds *count* **months** to *date*.
- **CURRENT_DATE** Returns the **current date** in the session's time zone.
- **CURRENT_TIMESTAMP** Returns the **current timestamp** with the active time zone information.
- **DBTIMEZONE** Returns the current **database timezone**, in UTC format.
- **EXTRACT**(*timeunit FROM datetime*) **Extract**s a portion of a date from a date value—such as extracting the month value from a date column's values.
- **FROM_TZ**(*timestamp*) Converts a timestamp value to a timestamp with timezone value.

- **GREATEST**(*date1,date2,date3,...*) Picks latest date from list of dates.

- **LEAST**(*date1,date2,date3,...*) Picks earliest date from list of dates.

- **LAST_DAY**(*date*) Gives date of **last day** of month that *date* is in.

- **LOCALTIMESTAMP** Returns the **local timestamp** in the active time zone, with no time zone information shown.

- **MONTHS_BETWEEN**(*date2,date1*) Gives *date2–date1* in **months** (can be fractional months).

- **NEW_TIME**(*date,'this','other'*) Gives the *date* (and time) in *this* time zone. *this* will be replaced by a three-letter abbreviation for the current time zone. *other* will be replaced by a three-letter abbreviation for the other time zone for which you'd like to know the time and date.

Time zones are as follows:

AST/ADT	Atlantic standard/daylight time
BST/BDT	Bering standard/daylight time
CST/CDT	Central standard/daylight time
EST/EDT	Eastern standard/daylight time
GMT	Greenwich mean time
HST/HDT	Alaska-Hawaii standard/daylight time
MST/MDT	Mountain standard/daylight time
NST	Newfoundland standard time
PST/PDT	Pacific standard/daylight time
YST/YDT	Yukon standard/daylight time

- **NEXT_DAY**(*date,'day'*) Gives date of **next day** after *date*, where '*day*' is 'Monday', 'Tuesday', and so on.

- **NUMTODSINTERVAL**(*'value','dateunit'*) Converts *value* to an INTERVAL DAY TO SECOND literal, where '*dateunit*' is 'DAY', 'HOUR', 'MINUTE', or 'SECOND'.

- **NUMTOYMINTERVAL** (*'value','dateunit'*) Converts *value* to an INTERVAL YEAR TO MONTH literal, where '*dateunit*' is 'YEAR' or 'MONTH'.

- **ROUND**(*date,'format'*) Without *format* specified, **round**s a *date* to 12 A.M.

(midnight, the beginning of that day) if time of *date* is before noon; otherwise, **round**s up to next day. For use of *format* for rounding, see **ROUND** in the Alphabetical Reference.

- **SESSIONTIMEZONE** Returns the value of the current **session**'s **timezone**.

- **SYS_EXTRACT_UTC** Extracts the Coordinated Universal Time (UTC) from the current date.

- **SYSTIMESTAMP** Returns the system date, including fractional seconds and time zone of the database.

- **SYSDATE** Returns the current date and time.

- **TO_CHAR**(*date*,'*format*') Reformats *date* according to *format*.*

- **TO_DATE**(*string*,'*format*') Converts a *string* in a given *format* into an Oracle date. Will also accept a *number* instead of a *string*, with certain limits. *format* is restricted.

- **TO_DSINTERVAL**('*value*') Converts *value* of CHAR, VARCHAR2, NCHAR, or NVARCHAR2 datatype to an INTERVAL DAY TO SECOND type.

- **TO_TIMESTAMP**('*value*') Converts *value* of CHAR, VARCHAR2, NCHAR, or NVARCHAR2 datatype to a value of TIMESTAMP datatype.

- **TO_TIMESTAMP_TZ**('*value*') Converts *value* of CHAR, VARCHAR2, NCHAR, or NVARCHAR2 datatype to a value of TIMESTAMP WITH TIMEZONE datatype.

- **TO_YMINTERVAL**('*value*') Converts *value* of CHAR, VARCHAR2, NCHAR, or NVARCHAR2 datatype to a value of INTERVAL YEAR TO MONTH datatype.

- **TRUNC**(*date*,'*format*') Without *format* specified, sets a *date* to 12 A.M. (midnight, the beginning of that day). For use of *format* for truncating, see **TRUNC** in the Alphabetical Reference.

- **TZ_OFFSET**('*value*') Returns the time zone offset corresponding to the *value* entered based on the date the statement is executed.

*See the sidebar "Date Formats" later in this chapter.

Adding Months

If February 22 is "Fast Day" in New Hampshire, perhaps six months later could be celebrated as "Feast Day." If so, what would the date be? Simply use the **ADD_MONTHS** function, adding a *count* of six months, as shown here:

```
column FeastDay heading "Feast Day"

select ADD_MONTHS(CelebratedDate,6) AS FeastDay
  from HOLIDAY
 where Holiday like 'FAST%';

Feast Day
---------
22-AUG-02
```

Subtracting Months

If picnic area reservations have to be made at least six months before Columbus Day, what's the last day you can make them? Take the CelebratedDate for Columbus Day, and use **ADD_MONTHS**, adding a *negative count* of six months (this is the same as subtracting months). This will tell you the date six months before Columbus Day. Then subtract one day.

```
column LastDay heading "Last Day"

select ADD_MONTHS(CelebratedDate,-6) - 1 AS LastDay
  from HOLIDAY
 where Holiday = 'COLUMBUS DAY';

Last Day
---------
13-APR-02
```

GREATEST and LEAST

Which comes first for each of the holidays that were moved to fall on Mondays, the actual or the celebrated date? The **LEAST** function chooses the earliest date from a list of dates, whether columns or literals; **GREATEST** chooses the latest date. These **GREATEST** and **LEAST** functions are exactly the same ones that are used with numbers and character strings:

```
select Holiday, LEAST(ActualDate, CelebratedDate) AS First,
       ActualDate, CelebratedDate
  from HOLIDAY
 where ActualDate - CelebratedDate != 0;

HOLIDAY                    FIRST     ACTUALDAT CELEBRATE
-------------------------- --------- --------- ---------
MARTIN LUTHER KING, JR.    15-JAN-02 15-JAN-02 17-JAN-02
LINCOLNS BIRTHDAY          12-FEB-02 12-FEB-02 18-FEB-02
WASHINGTONS BIRTHDAY       18-FEB-02 22-FEB-02 18-FEB-02
MEMORIAL DAY               27-MAY-02 30-MAY-02 27-MAY-02
COLUMBUS DAY               12-OCT-02 12-OCT-02 14-OCT-02
```

Here, **LEAST** worked just fine, because it operated on DATE columns from a table. What about literals?

```
select LEAST('20-JAN-02','20-DEC-02') from DUAL;

LEAST('20
---------
20-DEC-02
```

This is quite wrong, almost as if you'd said **GREATEST** instead of **LEAST**. December 20, 2002, is not earlier than January 20, 2002. Why did this happen? Because **LEAST** treated these literals as *strings*.

It did not know to treat them as dates. The **TO_DATE** function converts these literals into an internal DATE format that Oracle can use for its date-oriented functions:

```
select LEAST( TO_DATE('20-JAN-02'), TO_DATE('20-DEC-02') )
   from DUAL;

LEAST(TO_
---------
20-JAN-02
```

NEXT_DAY

NEXT_DAY computes the date of the next named day of the week (that is, Sunday, Monday, Tuesday, Wednesday, Thursday, Friday, or Saturday) after the given date. For example, suppose payday is always the first Friday after the 15th of the month. The table PAYDAY contains only the pay cycle dates, each one being the 15th of the month, with one row for each month of the year:

```
select CycleDate from PAYDAY;

CYCLEDATE
---------
15-JAN-02
15-FEB-02
15-MAR-02
15-APR-02
15-MAY-02
15-JUN-02
15-JUL-02
15-AUG-02
15-SEP-02
15-OCT-02
15-NOV-02
15-DEC-02
```

A Warning About GREATEST and LEAST

Unlike many other Oracle functions and logical operators, the **GREATEST** and **LEAST** functions will not evaluate literal strings that are in date format as dates. The dates are treated as strings:

```
select Holiday, CelebratedDate
  from HOLIDAY
 where CelebratedDate =  LEAST('17-JAN-02', '02-SEP-02');

HOLIDAY                   CELEBRATE
----------------------    ---------
LABOR DAY                 02-SEP-02
```

In order for **LEAST** and **GREATEST** to work properly, the function **TO_DATE** must be applied to the literal strings:

```
select Holiday, CelebratedDate
  from HOLIDAY
 where CelebratedDate = LEAST( TO_DATE('17-JAN-02'),
                               TO_DATE('02-SEP-02') );

HOLIDAY                   CELEBRATE
-------------------------    ---------
MARTIN LUTHER KING, JR.   17-JAN-02
```

What will be the actual payment dates?

```
column Payday heading "Pay Day"

select NEXT_DAY(CycleDate,'FRIDAY') AS Payday
  from PAYDAY;

Pay Day
---------
18-JAN-02
22-FEB-02
22-MAR-02
19-APR-02
17-MAY-02
21-JUN-02
19-JUL-02
16-AUG-02
20-SEP-02
```

```
18-OCT-02
22-NOV-02
20-DEC-02
```

This is nearly correct, except for February, March, and November, because **NEXT_DAY** is the date of the *next* Friday after the cycle date. Since February 15, March 15, and November 15 are Fridays, this (wrongly) gives the following Friday instead. The correct version is as follows:

```
column Payday heading "Pay Day"

select NEXT_DAY(CycleDate-1,'FRIDAY') AS PayDay
  from PAYDAY;
```

NEXT_DAY is really a "greater than" kind of function. It asks for the next date *greater than* the given date that falls on a specific day of the week. To catch those cycle dates that are already on Friday, subtract one from the cycle date. This makes every cycle date appear one day earlier to **NEXT_DAY**. The paydays are then always the correct Friday.

LAST_DAY

LAST_DAY produces the date of the last day of the month. Suppose that commissions and bonuses are always paid on the last day of the month. What are those dates in 2002?

```
column EndMonth heading "End Month"

select LAST_DAY(CycleDate) AS EndMonth
  from PAYDAY;

End Month
---------
31-JAN-02
28-FEB-02
31-MAR-02
30-APR-02
31-MAY-02
30-JUN-02
31-JUL-02
31-AUG-02
30-SEP-02
31-OCT-02
30-NOV-02
31-DEC-02
```

MONTHS_BETWEEN Two Dates

You recently came across a file containing the birthdates of a group of friends. You load the information into a table called BIRTHDAY and display it:

```
select FirstName, LastName, BirthDate from BIRTHDAY;
```

```
FIRSTNAME          LASTNAME           BIRTHDATE
---------------    ---------------    ---------
GEORGE             SAND               12-MAY-46
ROBERT             JAMES              23-AUG-37
NANCY              LEE                02-FEB-47
VICTORIA           LYNN               20-MAY-49
FRANK              PILOT              11-NOV-42
```

To calculate each person's age, compute the months between today's date and their birthdates, and divide by 12 to get the years:

```
select FirstName, LastName, Birthdate,
       MONTHS_BETWEEN(SysDate,Birthdate)/12 AS Age
  from BIRTHDAY;
```

```
FIRSTNAME          LASTNAME           BIRTHDATE   AGE
---------------    ---------------    ---------   -------
GEORGE             SAND               12-MAY-46   55.8728
ROBERT             JAMES              23-AUG-37   64.5933
NANCY              LEE                02-FEB-47   55.1497
VICTORIA           LYNN               20-MAY-49   52.8509
FRANK              PILOT              11-NOV-42   59.3755
```

The division will print the Age with a decimal component. Since most people over the age of seven don't report their age using portions of years, you may want to apply a **FLOOR** function to the computation.

Combining Date Functions

You are hired on March 15, 2002 at a great new job, with a starting salary that is lower than you had hoped, but with a promise of a review the first of the month after six months have passed. If the current date is March 15, 2002, when is your review date?

```
select SysDate AS Today,
       LAST_DAY(ADD_MONTHS(SysDate,6)) + 1 Review
  from DUAL;
```

```
TODAY       REVIEW
---------   ---------
15-MAR-02   01-OCT-02
```

ADD_MONTHS takes the SysDate and adds six months to it. **LAST_DAY** takes this result and figures the last day of that month. You then add 1 to the date to get the first day of the next month. How many days until that review? You simply subtract today's date from it. Note the use of parentheses to ensure the proper order of the calculation:

```
select (LAST_DAY(ADD_MONTHS(SysDate,6))+ 1)-SysDate  Wait
  from DUAL;
```

```
WAIT
-----
 200
```

ROUND and TRUNC in Date Calculations

Assume that this is today's SysDate:

```
SYSDATE
---------
15-MAR-02
```

In the beginning of the chapter, it was noted that Oracle could subtract one date from another, such as tomorrow minus today, and come up with an answer other than a whole number. Let's look at it:

```
select TO_DATE('16-MAR-02') - SysDate from DUAL;

TO_DATE('16-MAR-02')-SYSDATE
----------------------------
                        .516
```

The reason for the fractional number of days between today and tomorrow is that Oracle keeps hours, minutes, and seconds with its dates, and SysDate is always current, up to the second. It is obviously less than a full day until tomorrow.

To simplify some of the difficulties you might encounter using fractions of days, Oracle makes a couple of assumptions about dates:

- A date entered as a literal, such as '16-MAR-02', is given a default time of 12 A.M. (midnight) at the beginning of that day.

- A date entered through SQLPLUS, unless a time is specifically assigned to it, is set to 12 A.M. (midnight) at the beginning of that day.

- SysDate always includes both the date and the time, unless you intentionally round it off. The **ROUND** function on any date sets it to 12 A.M. of that day if the time is before exactly noon, and to 12 A.M. the next day if it is after noon. The **TRUNC** function acts similarly, except that it sets the time to 12 A.M. for any time up to and including one second before midnight.

To get the rounded number of days between today and tomorrow, use this:

```
select TO_DATE('16-MAR-02') - ROUND(SysDate) from DUAL;

TO_DATE('16-MAR-02')-ROUND(SYSDATE)
-----------------------------------
                                  1
```

If the current time is after noon, the rounded difference will be 0 days.

ROUND, without a '*format*' (see the earlier sidebar, "Date Functions"), always rounds a date to 12 A.M. of the closest day. If dates that you will be working with contain times other than noon, either use ROUND or accept possible fractional results in your calculations. TRUNC works similarly, but sets the time to 12 A.M. of the current day.

TO_DATE and TO_CHAR Formatting

TO_DATE and TO_CHAR are alike insofar as they both have powerful formatting capabilities. They are opposite insofar as TO_DATE converts a character string or a number into

Date Formats

These date formats are used with both TO_CHAR and TO_DATE:

MM	Number of month: 12
RM	Roman numeral month: XII
MON	Three-letter abbreviation of month: AUG
MONTH	Month fully spelled out: AUGUST, padded with blanks to 9 characters
DDD	Number of days in year, since Jan 1: 354
DD	Number of days in month: 23
D	Number of days in week: 6
DY	Three-letter abbreviation of day: FRI
DAY	Day fully spelled out, padded to 9 characters
YYYY	Full four-digit year: 1946
Y,YYY	Year, with comma
SYYYY	Signed year: 1000 B.C. = -1000
YYY	Last three digits of year: 946
YY	Last two digits of year: 46
Y	Last one digit of year: 6
IYYY	Four-digit year from ISO standard*
IYY	Three-digit year from ISO standard
IY	Two-digit year from ISO standard
I	One-digit year from ISO standard
RR	Last two digits of year relative to current date
RRRR	Rounded year, accepting either two- or four-digit input

CC	Century (20 for 1999)
SCC	Century, with BC dates prefixed with -
YEAR	Year spelled out: NINETEEN-FORTY-SIX
SYEAR	Year, with - before BC dates
Q	Number of quarter: 3
WW	Number of weeks in year, where week 1 starts on the first day of the year
IW	Number of weeks in year from ISO standard
W	Number of weeks in month where week 1 starts on the first day of the month
J	"Julian"—days since December 31, 4712 B.C.: 2422220
HH	Hours of day, always 1-12: 11
HH12	Same as HH
HH24	Hours of day, 24-hour clock: 17
MI	Minutes of hour: 58
SS	Seconds of minute: 43
SSSSS	Seconds since midnight, always 0-86399: 43000
FF	Fractional seconds as in HH.MI.SS.FF
X	Local radix character
/,-:.;	Punctuation to be incorporated in display for **TO_CHAR** or ignored in format for **TO_DATE**
A.M.	Displays A.M. or P.M., depending upon time of day
P.M.	Same effect as A.M.
AM or PM	Same as A.M. but without periods
B.C.	Displays B.C. or A.D., depending upon date
A.D.	Same as B.C.
BC or AD	Same as B.C. but without periods
E	Abbreviated era name, for Asian calendars
EE	Full era name, for Asian calendars
TZD	Daylight savings time information
TZH	Time zone hour

TZM	Time zone minute
TZR	Time zone region

These date formats work only with **TO_CHAR**. They do not work with **TO_DATE**:

"string"	*string* is incorporated in display for **TO_CHAR**.
fm	Prefix to Month or Day: fmMONTH or fmday. Suppresses padding of Month or Day (defined earlier) in format. Without fm, all months are displayed at same width. Similarly true for days. With fm, padding is eliminated. Months and days are only as long as their count of characters.
Fx	Format Exact: specifies exact format matching for the character argument and the date format model.
TH	Suffix to a number: ddTH or DDTH produces 24th or 24TH. Capitalization comes from the case of the number—DD—not from the case of the TH. Works with any number in a date: YYYY, DD, MM, HH, MI, SS, and so on.
SP	Suffix to a number that forces number to be spelled out: DDSP, DdSP, or ddSP produces THREE, Three, or three. Capitalization comes from case of number—DD—not from the case of SP. Works with any number in a date: YYYY, DD, MM, HH, MI, SS, and so on.
SPTH	Suffix combination of TH and SP that forces number to be both spelled out and given an ordinal suffix: Ddspth produces Third. Capitalization comes from case of number—DD—not from the case of SP. Works with any number in a date: YYYY, DD, MM, HH, MI, SS, and so on.
THSP	Same as SPTH.

*ISO is the International Standards Organization, which has a different set of standards for dates than the U.S. formats.

an Oracle date, whereas **TO_CHAR** converts an Oracle date into a character string. The formats for these two functions are as follows:

```
TO_CHAR(date[,'format'[,'NLSparameters']])

TO_DATE(string[,'format'[,'NLSparameters']])
```

date must be a column defined as a DATE datatype in Oracle. It cannot be a string even if it is in the default date format of DD-MON-YY. The only way to use a string where *date* appears in the **TO_CHAR** function is to enclose it within a **TO_DATE** function.

string is a literal string, a literal number, or a database column containing a string or a number. In every case but one, the format of *string* must correspond to that described by the *format*. Only if a *string* is in the default format can the *format* be left out. The default starts out as 'DD-MON-YY', but you can change this with

```
alter session set NLS_DATE_FORMAT = "DD/MON/YYYY";
```

for a given SQL session or with the NLS_DATE_FORMAT init.ora parameter.

format is a collection of many options, which can be combined in virtually an infinite number of ways. The sidebar "Date Formats" lists these options with explanations. Once you understand the basic method of using the options, putting them into practice is simple.

NLSparameters is a string that sets the NLS_DATE_LANGUAGE option to a specific language, as opposed to using the language for the current SQL session. You shouldn't need to use this option often. Oracle will return day and month names in the language set for the session with **alter session**.

NOTE
*In many cases, you can use the **EXTRACT** function in place of **TO_CHAR**. See the "Using the **EXTRACT** Function" section later in this chapter for examples.*

TO_CHAR will be used as an example of how the options work. Defining a column format for the **TO_CHAR** function results is the first task, because without it, **TO_CHAR** will produce a column in SQLPLUS nearly 100 characters wide. By renaming the column (so its heading is intelligible) and setting its format to 30 characters, a practical display is produced:

```
column Formatted format a30 word_wrapped
select BirthDate,
       TO_CHAR(BirthDate,'MM/DD/YY') AS Formatted
  from BIRTHDAY
 where FirstName = 'VICTORIA';

BIRTHDATE FORMATTED
--------- ------------------------------
20-MAY-49 05/20/49
```

BirthDate shows the default Oracle date format: DD-MON-YY, or day of month, dash, three-letter abbreviation for month, dash, last two digits of year. The **TO_CHAR** function in the **select** statement is nearly self-evident. MM, DD, and YY in the **TO_CHAR** statement are key symbols to Oracle in formatting the date. The slashes (/) are just punctuation, and Oracle will accept a wide variety of punctuation. It doesn't even need to be sensible. For example, here you see > used as punctuation:

```
select BirthDate, TO_CHAR(BirthDate,'YYMM>DD') Formatted
    from BIRTHDAY
 where FirstName = 'VICTORIA';
```

```
BIRTHDATE FORMATTED
--------- -----------------------------
20-MAY-49 4905>20
```

In addition to standard punctuation, Oracle allows you to insert text into the *format*. This is done by enclosing the desired text in *double* quotation marks:

```
select BirthDate,
       TO_CHAR(BirthDate,'Month, DDth "in, um,"
                YyyY') AS Formatted
  from BIRTHDAY ;

BIRTHDATE FORMATTED
--------- -----------------------------
12-MAY-46 May       , 12TH   in, um,
           1946
23-AUG-37 August    , 23RD   in, um,
           1937
02-FEB-47 February  , 02ND   in, um,
           1947
20-MAY-49 May       , 20TH   in, um,
           1949
11-NOV-42 November  , 11TH   in, um,
           1942
```

Several consequences of the *format* are worth observing here. The full word Month told Oracle to use the full name of the month in the display. Because it was typed with the first letter in uppercase and the remainder in lowercase, each month in the result was formatted the same way. The options for month are as follows:

Format	Result
Month	August
month	august
Mon	Aug
mon	aug

The day of the month is produced by the DD in the *format*. A suffix of **th** on DD tells Oracle to use *ordinal* suffixes, such as "TH", "RD", and "ND" with the number. In this instance, the suffixes are also case-sensitive, but their case is set by the DD, not the **th**:

Format	Result
DDth or DDTH	11TH
Ddth or DdTH	11Th
ddth or ddTH	11th

This same approach holds true for all numbers in the *format*, including century, year, quarter, month, week, day of the month (DD), Julian day, hours, minutes, and seconds.

The words between double quotation marks are simply inserted where they are found. Spaces between any of these format requests are reproduced in the result (look at the three spaces before the word "in" in the preceding example). YyyY is included simply to show that case is irrelevant unless a suffix such as Th is being used. For simplicity's sake, consider this format request:

```
select BirthDate, TO_CHAR(BirthDate,'Month, ddth, YyyY')
       AS Formatted
  from BIRTHDAY;

BIRTHDATE FORMATTED
--------- ------------------------------
12-MAY-46 May       , 12th, 1946
23-AUG-37 August    , 23rd, 1937
02-FEB-47 February  , 02nd, 1947
20-MAY-49 May       , 20th, 1949
11-NOV-42 November  , 11th, 1942
```

This is a reasonably normal format. The days are all aligned, which makes comparing the rows easy. This is the default alignment, and Oracle accomplishes it by padding the month names on the right with spaces up to a width of nine spaces. There will be circumstances when it is more important for a date to be formatted normally, such as at the top of a letter. The spaces between the month and the comma would look odd. To eliminate the spaces, **fm** is used as a prefix for the words "month" or "day":

Format	Result
Month, ddth	August, 20th
fmMonth, ddth	August, 20th
Day, ddth	Monday, 20th
fmDay, ddth	Monday, 20th

This is illustrated in the following:

```
select BirthDate, TO_CHAR(BirthDate,'fmMonth, ddth, YyyY')
       AS Formatted
  from BIRTHDAY;

BIRTHDATE FORMATTED
--------- ------------------------------
12-MAY-46 May, 12th, 1946
23-AUG-37 August, 23rd, 1937
02-FEB-47 February, 2nd, 1947
20-MAY-49 May, 20th, 1949
11-NOV-42 November, 11th, 1942
```

By combining all of these format controls and adding hours and minutes, you can produce a birth announcement:

```
select FirstName, Birthdate, TO_CHAR(BirthDate,
'"Baby Girl on" fmMonth ddth, YYYY, "at" HH:MI "in the Morning"')
      AS Formatted
  from BIRTHDAY
 where FirstName = 'VICTORIA';

FIRSTNAME       BIRTHDATE FORMATTED
--------------- --------- ----------------------------
VICTORIA        20-MAY-49 Baby Girl on May 20th, 1949,
                          at 3:27 in the Morning
```

Suppose that after looking at this, you decide you'd rather spell out the date. Do this with the **sp** control:

```
select FirstName, Birthdate, TO_CHAR(BirthDate,
'"Baby Girl on the" Ddsp "of" fmMonth, YYYY, "at" HH:MI')
      AS Formatted
  from BIRTHDAY
 where FirstName = 'VICTORIA';

FIRSTNAME       BIRTHDATE FORMATTED
--------------- --------- ----------------------------
VICTORIA        20-MAY-49 Baby Girl on the Twenty of
                          May, 1949, at 3:27
```

Well, 20 was spelled out, but it still doesn't look right. Add the **th** suffix to the **sp**:

```
select FirstName, Birthdate, TO_CHAR(BirthDate,
'"Baby Girl on the" Ddspth "of" fmMonth, YYYY, "at" HH:MI')
      AS Formatted
  from BIRTHDAY
 where FirstName = 'VICTORIA';

FIRSTNAME       BIRTHDATE FORMATTED
--------------- --------- ----------------------------
VICTORIA        20-MAY-49 Baby Girl on the Twentieth of
                          May, 1949, at 3:27
```

But was it 3:27 A.M. or 3:27 P.M.? These could be added inside double quotation marks, but then the result would always say "A.M." or "P.M.", regardless of the actual time of the day (since double quotation marks enclose a literal). Instead, Oracle lets you add *either* "A.M." or "P.M." after the time, but not in double quotation marks. Oracle then interprets this as a request to display whether it is A.M. or P.M. Note how the **select** has this formatting control entered as P.M., but the result shows A.M., because the birth occurred in the morning:

```
select FirstName, Birthdate, TO_CHAR(BirthDate,
'"Baby Girl on the" Ddspth "of" fmMonth, YYYY, "at" HH:MI P.M.')
```

```
        AS Formatted
  from BIRTHDAY
 where FirstName = 'VICTORIA';

FIRSTNAME       BIRTHDATE FORMATTED
--------------- --------- --------------------------------------
VICTORIA        20-MAY-49 Baby Girl on the Twentieth of
                          May, 1949, at 3:27 A.M.
```

Consult the sidebar "Date Formats," earlier in the chapter, for a list of all the possible date options. How would you construct a date format for the 776th Year of the Reign of Louis IX? Use date arithmetic to alter the year from A.D. to A.L. (Louis's reign began in 1226, so subtract 1,226 years from the current year) and then simply format the result using **TO_CHAR**.

The Most Common TO_CHAR Error

Always check the date formats when using the **TO_CHAR** function. The most common error is to interchange the 'MM' (Month) format with the 'MI' (Minutes) format when formatting the time portion of a date.

For example, to view the current time, use the **TO_CHAR** function to query the time portion of SysDate:

```
select TO_CHAR(SysDate,'HH:MI:SS') Now
  from DUAL;

NOW
--------
10:01:30
```

This example is correct, since it uses 'MI' to show the minutes. However, users often select 'MM' instead—partly because they are also selecting two other pairs of double letters, 'HH' and 'SS'. Selecting 'MM' will return the month, not the minutes:

```
select TO_CHAR(SysDate,'HH:MM:SS') NowWrong
  from DUAL;

NOWWRONG
--------
10:03:30
```

This time is incorrect, because the month was selected in the minutes place. Since Oracle is so flexible and has so many different supported date formats, it does not prevent you from making this error.

NEW_TIME: Switching Time Zones

The **NEW_TIME** function tells you the time and date of a date column or literal date in other time zones. This is the format for **NEW_TIME**:

```
NEW_TIME(date,'this','other')
```

date is the date (and time) in *this* time zone. *this* will be replaced by a three-letter abbreviation for the current time zone. *other* will be replaced by a three-letter abbreviation of the other time zone for which you'd like to know the time and date. The time zone options are given in the sidebar "Date Functions," earlier in this chapter. To compare just the date, without showing the time, of Victoria's birth between Eastern standard time and Hawaiian standard time, use this:

```
select Birthdate, NEW_TIME(Birthdate,'EST','HST')
  from BIRTHDAY
 where FirstName = 'VICTORIA';

BIRTHDATE NEW_TIME(
--------- ---------
20-MAY-49 19-MAY-49
```

But how could Victoria have been born on two different days? Since every date stored in Oracle also contains a time, it is simple enough using **TO_CHAR** and **NEW_TIME** to discover both the date and the time differences between the two zones. This will answer the question:

```
select TO_CHAR(Birthdate,'fmMonth Ddth, YYYY "at" HH:MI AM') AS Birth,
       TO_CHAR(NEW_TIME(Birthdate,'EST','HST'),
       'fmMonth ddth, YYYY "at" HH:MI AM') AS Birth
  from BIRTHDAY
 where FirstName = 'VICTORIA';

BIRTH                          BIRTH
------------------------------ ------------------------------
May 20th, 1949 at 3:27 AM      May 19th, 1949 at 10:27 PM
```

TO_DATE Calculations

TO_DATE follows the same formatting conventions as **TO_CHAR**, with some restrictions. The purpose of **TO_DATE** is to turn a literal string, such as MAY 20, 1949, into an Oracle date format. This allows the date to be used in date calculations.

This is the format for **TO_DATE**:

```
TO_DATE(string[,'format'])
```

To put the string 22-FEB-02 into Oracle date format, use this:

```
select TO_DATE('22-FEB-02','DD-MON-YY') from DUAL;

TO_DATE('
---------
22-FEB-02
```

Note, however, that the 22-FEB-02 format is already in the default format in which Oracle displays and accepts dates. When a literal string has a date in this format, the *format* in the **TO_DATE** can be left out, with exactly the same result:

```
select TO_DATE('22-FEB-02') from DUAL;

TO_DATE('
---------
22-FEB-02
```

But what century is the date in? Is it 1902 or 2002? If you do not specify the full four-year value for the year, then you are relying on the database to default to the proper century value.

If the string is in a familiar format, but not the default Oracle format of DD-MON-YY, **TO_DATE** fails:

```
select TO_DATE('02/22/02') from DUAL;

ERROR: ORA-01843: not a valid month
```

When the format matches the literal string, the string is successfully converted to a date and is then displayed in default date format:

```
select TO_DATE('02/22/02','MM/DD/YY') from DUAL;

TO_DATE('
---------
22-FEB-02
```

Suppose you need to know the day of the week of February 22. The **TO_CHAR** function will not work, even with the literal string in the proper format, because **TO_CHAR** requires a date (see its format at the very beginning of the "TO_DATE and TO_CHAR Formatting" section):

```
select TO_CHAR('22-FEB-02','Day') from DUAL;
ORA-01722: invalid number
```

The message is somewhat misleading, but the point is that the query fails. You could use the EXTRACT function, but this query will also work if you first convert the string to a date. Do this by combining the two functions **TO_CHAR** and **TO_DATE**:

```
select TO_CHAR( TO_DATE('22-FEB-02'), 'Day') from DUAL;

TO_CHAR(TO_DATE('22-FEB-02'),'DAY')
-----------------------------------
Friday
```

TO_DATE can also accept numbers, without single quotation marks, instead of strings, as long as they are formatted consistently. Here is an example:

```
select TO_DATE(11051946,'MMDDYYYY') from DUAL;

TO_DATE(1
---------
05-NOV-46
```

The punctuation in the *format* is ignored, but the number must follow the order of the format controls. The number itself must not have punctuation.

How complex can the format control be in **TO_DATE**? Suppose you simply reversed the **TO_CHAR select** statement shown earlier, put its result into the **string** portion of **TO_DATE**, and kept its format the same as **TO_CHAR**:

```
select TO_DATE('Baby Girl on the Twentieth of May, 1949,
        at 3:27 A.M.',
        '"Baby Girl on the" Ddspth "of" fmMonth, YYYY,
        "at" HH:MI P.M.')
        AS Formatted
   from BIRTHDAY
  where FirstName = 'VICTORIA';

ERROR: ORA-01858: a non-numeric character was found
 where a numeric was expected
```

This clearly failed. As it turns out, only a limited number of the *format* controls can be used. These are the restrictions on *format* that govern **TO_DATE**:

- No literal strings are allowed, such as "Baby Girl on the".

- Days cannot be spelled out. They must be numbers.

- Punctuation is permitted.

- fm is not necessary. If used, it is ignored.

- If Month is used, the month in the string must be spelled out. If Mon is used, the month must be a three-letter abbreviation. Uppercase and lowercase are ignored.

This **select** does work:

```
select TO_DATE('May 20, 1949, 3:27 A.M. ', 'Month Dd,
        YYYY, HH:MI P.M.')
        AS Formatted
   from BIRTHDAY
 where FirstName = 'VICTORIA';

FORMATTED
---------
20-AUG-49
```

Dates in where Clauses

Early in this chapter, you saw an example of date arithmetic used in a **where** clause:

```
select Holiday, ActualDate, CelebratedDate
   from Holiday
 where CelebratedDate - ActualDate != 0;

HOLIDAY                   ACTUALDAT CELEBRATE
------------------------- --------- ---------
MARTIN LUTHER KING, JR.   15-JAN-02 17-JAN-02
LINCOLNS BIRTHDAY         12-FEB-02 18-FEB-02
WASHINGTONS BIRTHDAY      22-FEB-02 18-FEB-02
MEMORIAL DAY              30-MAY-02 27-MAY-02
COLUMBUS DAY              12-OCT-02 14-OCT-02
```

Dates can be used with other Oracle logical operators as well, with some warnings and restrictions. The **BETWEEN** operator will do date arithmetic if the column preceding it is a date, even if the test dates are literal strings:

```
select Holiday, CelebratedDate
   from HOLIDAY
 where CelebratedDate BETWEEN
       '01-JAN-02' and '22-FEB-02';

HOLIDAY                   CELEBRATE
------------------------- ---------
NEW YEAR DAY              01-JAN-02
MARTIN LUTHER KING, JR.   17-JAN-02
LINCOLNS BIRTHDAY         18-FEB-02
WASHINGTONS BIRTHDAY      18-FEB-02
FAST DAY, NEW HAMPSHIRE   22-FEB-02
```

The logical operator **IN** works as well with literal strings:

```
select Holiday, CelebratedDate
   from HOLIDAY
 where CelebratedDate IN ('01-JAN-02', '22-FEB-02');

HOLIDAY                   CELEBRATE
------------------------- ---------
NEW YEAR DAY              01-JAN-02
FAST DAY, NEW HAMPSHIRE   22-FEB-02
```

If you cannot rely on 2000 being the default century value, then you can use the **TO_DATE** function to specify the century values for the dates within the **IN** operator:

```
select Holiday, CelebratedDate
   from HOLIDAY
```

```
where CelebratedDate IN
      (TO_DATE('01-JAN-2002','DD-MON-YYYY'),
       TO_DATE('22-FEB-2002','DD-MON-YYYY'));
```

```
HOLIDAY                      CELEBRATE
------------------------     ---------
NEW YEAR DAY                 01-JAN-02
FAST DAY, NEW HAMPSHIRE      22-FEB-02
```

LEAST and **GREATEST** do not work, because they assume the literal strings are *strings,* not *dates.* Refer to the sidebar "A Warning About GREATEST and LEAST," earlier in this chapter, for an explanation of **LEAST** and **GREATEST**.

Dealing with Multiple Centuries

If your applications use only two-digit values for years, then you may encounter problems related to the year 2000. If you only specify two digits of a year (such as '98' for '1998'), then you are relying on the database to specify the century value (the '19') when the record is inserted. If you are putting in dates prior to the year 2000 (for example, birthdates), then you may encounter problems with the century values assigned to your data.

In Oracle, all date values have century values. If you only specify the last two digits of the year value, then Oracle will, by default, use the current century as the century value when it inserts a record. For example, the following listing shows an **insert** into the BIRTHDAY table.

```
insert into BIRTHDAY
(FirstName, LastName, BirthDate)
values
('ALICIA', 'ANN', '21-NOV-39');
```

In the preceding example, no century value is specified for the BirthDate column, and no age is specified. If you use the **TO_CHAR** function on the BirthDate column, you can see the full BirthDate that Oracle inserted—it defaulted to the current century:

```
select TO_CHAR(BirthDate,'DD-MON-YYYY') AS Bday
   from BIRTHDAY
 where FirstName = 'ALICIA'
   and LastName = 'ANN';
```

```
BDAY
-----------
21-NOV-2039
```

For dates that can properly default to the current century, using the default does not present a problem. Alicia's BirthDate value is 21-NOV-2039—wrong by 100 years! Wherever you insert date values, you should specify the full four-digit year value.

Using the **EXTRACT** Function

As of Oracle9i, you can use the **EXTRACT** function in place of the **TO_CHAR** function when you are selecting portions of date values—such as just the month or day from a date. The **EXTRACT** function's syntax is

```
EXTRACT
( { { YEAR
    | MONTH
    | DAY
    | HOUR
    | MINUTE
    | SECOND
    }
  | { TIMEZONE_HOUR
    | TIMEZONE_MINUTE
    }
  | { TIMEZONE_REGION
    | TIMEZONE_ABBR
    }
  }
  FROM { datetime_value_expression | interval_value_expression }
)
```

For instance, to extract the month in which Victoria was born, you could execute the following:

```
select BirthDate,
       EXTRACT(Month from BirthDate) AS Month
  from BIRTHDAY
 where FirstName = 'VICTORIA';

BIRTHDATE    MONTH
---------  ----------
20-MAY-49        5
```

For more complex extractions, you will need to use **TO_CHAR**, but **EXTRACT** can support many common date value queries.

Using the **TIMESTAMP** Datatypes

As of Oracle9i, you can take advantage of several new datatypes. The DATE datatype stores date and time to the second; the TIMESTAMP datatypes store date to the billionth of a second.

The base datatype for timestamp values is called TIMESTAMP. Like DATE, it stores the year, month, day, hour, minute, and second. It also includes a *fractional_seconds_precision* setting that determines the number of digits in the fractional part of the seconds field. By default, the precision is 6; valid values are 0 to 9.

In the following example, a table is created with the TIMESTAMP datatype, and is populated via the SYSTIMESTAMP function:

```
create table X1
(tscol  TIMESTAMP(5));

insert into X1 values (SYSTIMESTAMP);
```

Now select that value from the table:

```
select * from X1;

TSCOL
---------------------------------
15-MAR-02 04.58.06.00542 PM
```

The output shows the second the row was inserted, down to five places after the decimal.

The SYSTIMESTAMP function returns data in the form of the TIMESTAMP (*fractional seconds precision*) WITH TIME ZONE datatype. The exact same row, inserted into a column that is defined with the TIMESTAMP(5) WITH TIME ZONE datatype, returns the data in the following format:

```
create table X2
(tscol  TIMESTAMP(5) WITH TIME ZONE);

select * from X2;

TSCOL
---------------------------------
15-MAR-02 04.58.06.00542 PM -05:00
```

In this output, the time zone is displayed as an offset of Coordinated Universal Time (UTC). The database is presently set to a time zone that is five hours prior to UTC.

Oracle also supports a TIMESTAMP (*fractional seconds precision*) WITH LOCAL TIME ZONE datatype, which is similar to TIMESTAMP WITH TIME ZONE. It differs in that the data is normalized to the database time zone when it is stored in the database, and during retrievals the users see data in the session time zone.

In addition to the TIMESTAMP datatypes, Oracle also supports two interval datatypes: INTERVAL YEAR (*year_precision*) TO MONTH and INTERVAL DAY (*day_precision*) TO SECOND (*fractional_seconds_precision*). INTERVAL YEAR TO MONTH stores a period of time in years and months, where the precision is the number of digits in the YEAR field (ranging from 0 to 9; default is 2 digits). The INTERVAL DAY TO SECOND datatype stores a period of time in days, hours, minutes, and seconds; the precision for the day and seconds accepts values from 0 to 9. The INTERVAL datatypes are mostly used during statistical analysis and data mining.

CHAPTER
10

Conversion and
Transformation
Functions

his chapter looks at functions that convert, or transform, one datatype into another. Four major datatypes and their associated functions have been covered thus far:

- CHAR (fixed-length character strings) and VARCHAR2 (variable-length character strings) include any letter of the alphabet, any number, and any of the symbols on the keyboard. Character literals must be enclosed in single quotation marks: 'Sault Ste. Marie!'

- NUMBER includes just the digits 0 through 9, a decimal point, and a minus sign, if necessary. NUMBER literals are not enclosed in quotation marks: -246.320

- DATE is a special type that includes information about the date, time, and time zone. It has a default format of DD-MON-YY, but can be displayed in many ways using the **TO_CHAR** function, as you saw in Chapter 9. DATE literals must be enclosed in single quotation marks: '26-AUG-81'

Each of these datatypes has a group of functions designed especially to manipulate data of its own type, as shown in Chapters 7, 8, and 9. String functions are used with character columns or literals, arithmetic functions are used with NUMBER columns or literals, and date functions are used with DATE columns or literals. Most group and miscellaneous functions work with any of these types. Some of these functions change the object they affect (whether CHAR, VARCHAR2, NUMBER, or DATE), while others report information about the object.

In one sense, most of the functions studied so far have been *transformation functions,* meaning they changed their objects. However, the functions covered in this chapter change their objects in an unusual way: They transform them from one datatype into another, or they make a profound transformation of the data in them. Table 10-1 describes these functions.

Function Name	Definition
ASCIISTR	Translates a string in any character set and returns an ASCII STRing in the database character set.
BIN_TO_NUM	Converts a BINary value TO its NUMerical equivalent.
CAST	CASTs one built-in or collection type to another; commonly used with nested tables and varying arrays.
CHARTOROWID	CHARacter TO ROW IDentifier. Changes a character string to act like an internal Oracle row identifier, or RowID.
COMPOSE	Translates a string in any datatype to a Unicode string in its fully normalized form in the same character set as the input.
CONVERT	CONVERTs a character string from one national language character set to another.

TABLE 10-1. *Transformation Functions*

Function Name	Definition
DECODE	DECODEs a CHAR, VARCHAR2, or NUMBER into any of several different character strings or NUMBERs, based on value. This is a very powerful *if, then, else* function. Chapter 17 is devoted to DECODE.
DECOMPOSE	Translates a string in any datatype to a Unicode string after canonical decomposition in the same character set as the input.
HEXTORAW	HEXadecimal TO RAW. Changes a character string of hex numbers into binary.
NUMTODSINTERVAL	Converts a NUMber to an INTERVAL DAY TO SECOND literal.
NUMTOYMINTERVAL	Converts a NUMber to an INTERVAL YEAR TO MONTH literal.
RAWTOHEX	RAW TO HEXadecimal. Changes a string of binary numbers to a character string of hex numbers.
RAWTONHEX	RAW TO NHEX. Converts raw to an NVARCHAR2 character value containing its hexadecimal equivalent.
ROWIDTOCHAR	ROW Identifier TO CHARacter. Changes an internal Oracle row identifier, or RowID, to a character string.
ROWIDTONCHAR	RAW TO NCHAR. Converts a RowID value to an NVARCHAR2 datatype.
TO_CHAR	TO CHARacter. Converts a NUMBER or DATE to a character string.
TO_CLOB	TO CLOB. Converts NCLOB values in a LOB column or other character strings to CLOB values.
TO_DATE	TO DATE. Converts a NUMBER, CHAR, or VARCHAR2 to a DATE (an Oracle datatype).
TO_DSINTERVAL	Converts a character string of CHAR, VARCHAR2, NCHAR, or NVARCHAR2 datatype to an INTERVAL DAY TO SECOND type.
TO_LOB	TO LOB. Converts a LONG to a LOB as part of an **insert as select**.
TO_MULTI_BYTE	TO MULTI_BYTE. Converts the single-byte characters in a character string to multibyte characters.
TO_NCHAR	TO NCHAR. Converts a character string, NUMBER, or DATE from the database character set to the national character set.
TO_NCLOB	TO NCLOB. Converts CLOB values in a LOB column or other character strings to NCLOB values.
TO_NUMBER	TO NUMBER. Converts a CHAR or VARCHAR2 to a number.
TO_SINGLE_BYTE	TO SINGLE BYTE. Converts the multibyte characters in a CHAR or VARCHAR2 to single bytes.

TABLE 10-1. *Transformation Functions* (continued)

Function Name	Definition
TO_YMINTERVAL	Converts a character string of CHAR, VARCHAR2, NCHAR, or NVARCHAR2 datatype to an INTERVAL YEAR TO MONTH type.
TRANSLATE	TRANSLATEs characters in a string into different characters.
UNISTR	Converts a string into Unicode in the database Unicode character set.

TABLE 10-1. *Transformation Functions* (continued)

The use of two of these functions, **TO_CHAR** and **TO_DATE**, has already been demonstrated in Chapter 9. **TO_CHAR** transforms a date into a character string (in the format you request). **TO_CHAR** can convert not just DATEs but also NUMBERs into character strings. **TO_DATE** is also a transformation function. It takes either a character string or a number and converts it into the DATE datatype. It then can be used in date arithmetic to calculate **MONTHS_BETWEEN**, **NEXT_DAY**, and other date functions.

Elementary Conversion Functions

Although there are many conversion functions listed in Table 10-1, the most commonly used are three whose purpose is to convert one datatype into another:

- **TO_CHAR** transforms a DATE or NUMBER into a character string.
- **TO_DATE** transforms a NUMBER, CHAR, or VARCHAR2 into a DATE.
- **TO_NUMBER** transforms a CHAR or VARCHAR2 into a NUMBER.

Why are these transformations important? **TO_DATE** is obviously necessary to accomplish date arithmetic. **TO_CHAR** allows you to manipulate a number as if it were a string, using string functions. **TO_NUMBER** allows you to use a string that happens to contain only numbers as if it were a number; by using it, you can add, subtract, multiply, divide, and so on.

This means that if you stored a nine-digit ZIP code as a number, you could transform it into a string, and then use **SUBSTR** and concatenation to add a dash (such as when printing addresses on envelopes):

```
select SUBSTR(TO_CHAR(948033515),1,5)||'-'||
       SUBSTR(TO_CHAR(948033515),6)  AS Zip
  from DUAL;

ZIP
----------------------------------------
94803-3515
```

Here, the **TO_CHAR** function transforms the pure number 948033515 (notice that it has no single quotation marks around it, as a CHAR or VARCHAR2 string must) into a character string.

SUBSTR then clips out positions 1 to 5 of this "string," producing 94803. A dash is concatenated on the right end of this string, and then another **TO_CHAR** creates another "string," which another **SUBSTR** clips out from position 6 to the end. The second string, 3515, is concatenated after the dash. The whole rebuilt string is relabeled Zip, and Oracle displays it: 94803-3515. This **TO_CHAR** function lets you use string manipulation functions on numbers (and dates) as if they were actually strings. Handy? Yes. But watch this:

```
select SUBSTR(948033515,1,5)||'-'||
       SUBSTR(948033515,6) AS Zip
  from DUAL;

ZIP
-----------------------------------------
94803-3515
```

This shouldn't work, because 948033515 is a NUMBER, not a character string. Yet the string function **SUBSTR** clearly worked anyway. Would it work with an actual NUMBER database column? Here's a table with Zip as a NUMBER:

```
describe ADDRESS

Name                            Null?     Type
------------------------------- --------- ----
LASTNAME                                  VARCHAR2(25)
FIRSTNAME                                 VARCHAR2(25)
STREET                                    VARCHAR2(50)
CITY                                      VARCHAR2(25)
STATE                                     CHAR(2)
ZIP                                       NUMBER
PHONE                                     VARCHAR2(12)
EXT                                       VARCHAR2(5)
```

Select just the ZIP code for all the Marys in the table:

```
select SUBSTR(Zip,1,5)||'-'||
       SUBSTR(Zip,6)  AS Zip
  from ADDRESS
 where FirstName = 'MARY';

ZIP
-----------------------------------------
94941-4302
60126-2460
```

SUBSTR works here just as well as it does with strings, even though Zip is a NUMBER column from the ADDRESS table. Will other string functions also work?

```
select Zip, RTRIM(Zip,20)
  from ADDRESS
```

```
where FirstName = 'MARY';

      ZIP RTRIM(ZIP,20)
---------- ---------------------------------------
 949414302 9494143
 601262460 60126246
```

The column on the left demonstrates that Zip is a NUMBER; it is even right-justified, as numbers are by default. But the **RTRIM** column is left-justified, just as strings are, and it has removed zeros and twos from the right side of the ZIP codes. Something else is peculiar here. Recall from Chapter 7 the format for **RTRIM**, shown here:

RTRIM(*string* [,'*set*'])

The *set* to be removed from the string is enclosed within single quotation marks, yet in this example,

RTRIM(Zip,20)

there are no quotation marks. So what is going on?

Automatic Conversion of Datatypes

Oracle is automatically converting these numbers, both the Zip and the 20, into strings, almost as if they both had **TO_CHAR** functions in front of them. In fact, with a few clear exceptions, Oracle will automatically transform any datatype into any other datatype, based on the function that is going to affect it. If it's a string function, Oracle will convert a NUMBER or a DATE instantly into a string, and the string function will work. If it's a DATE function and the column or literal is a string in the format DD-MON-YY, Oracle will convert it into a DATE. If the function is arithmetic and the column or literal is a character string, Oracle will convert it into a NUMBER and do the calculation.

Will this always work? No. To have Oracle automatically convert one datatype into another, the first datatype must already "look" like the datatype it is being converted to. The basic guidelines are as follows:

- Any NUMBER or DATE can be converted to a character string. Any string function can be used on a NUMBER or DATE column. Literal NUMBERs do not have to be enclosed in single quotation marks when used in a string function; literal DATEs do.

- A CHAR or VARCHAR2 value will be converted to a NUMBER if it contains only NUMBERs, a decimal point, or a minus sign on the left.

- A CHAR or VARCHAR2 value will be converted to a DATE only if it is in the default date format (usually DD-MON-YY). This is true for all functions except **GREATEST** and **LEAST**, which will treat the value as a string, and is true for **BETWEEN** only if the column to the left after the word **BETWEEN** is a DATE. Otherwise, **TO_DATE** must be used, with proper format.

These guidelines may be confusing, so favor the use of **TO_DATE** and other conversion functions to make sure the values are treated properly. The following examples should help to clarify the guidelines. The following are the effects of several randomly chosen string functions on NUMBERs and DATEs:

```
select INITCAP(LOWER(SysDate)) from DUAL;

INITCAP(LOWER(SYSDATE))
-----------------------
26-Mar-02
```

Note that the **INITCAP** function put the first letter of "mar" into uppercase even though "mar" was buried in the middle of the string "26-mar-02." This is a feature of **INITCAP** that is not confined to dates, although it is illustrated here for the first time. It works because the following works:

```
select INITCAP('this-is_a.test,of:punctuation;for+initcap')
   from DUAL;

INITCAP('THIS-IS_A.TEST,OF:PUNCTUATION;FO
-----------------------------------------
This-Is_A.Test,Of:Punctuation;For+Initcap
```

INITCAP puts the first letter of every word into uppercase. It determines the beginning of a word based on its being preceded by any character other than a letter. You can also cut and paste dates using string functions, just as if they were strings:

```
select SUBSTR(SysDate,4,3) from DUAL;

SUB
---
MAR
```

Here, a DATE is left-padded with 9s for a total length of 20:

```
select LPAD(SysDate,20,'9') from DUAL;

LPAD(SYSDATE,20,'9')
--------------------
9999999999926-MAR-02
```

LPAD, or any other string function, also can be used on NUMBERs, whether literal (as shown here) or as a column:

```
select LPAD(9,20,0) from DUAL;

LPAD(9,20,0)
--------------------
00000000000000000009
```

These examples show how string functions treat both NUMBERs and DATEs as if they were character strings. The result of the function (what you see displayed) is itself a character string. In this next example, a string (note the single quotation marks) is treated as a NUMBER by the number function **FLOOR**:

```
select FLOOR('-323.78') from DUAL;

FLOOR('-323.78')
----------------
            -324
```

Here, two literal character strings are converted to DATEs for the DATE function **MONTHS_BETWEEN**. This works only because the literal strings are in the default date format DD-MON-YY:

```
select MONTHS_BETWEEN('16-MAY-02','01-NOV-02') from DUAL;

MONTHS_BETWEEN('16-MAY-02','01-NOV-02')
---------------------------------------
                              -5.516129
```

One of the guidelines says that a DATE will not be converted to a NUMBER. Yet, here is an example of addition and subtraction with a DATE. Does this violate the guideline?

```
select SysDate, SysDate + 1, SysDate - 1 from DUAL;

SYSDATE   SYSDATE+1 SYSDATE-1
--------- --------- ---------
26-MAR-02 27-MAR-02 25-MAR-02
```

It does not, because the addition and subtraction is date arithmetic, not regular arithmetic. Date arithmetic (covered in Chapter 9) works only with addition and subtraction, and only with DATEs. Most functions will automatically convert a character string in default date format into a DATE. An exception is this attempt at date addition with a literal:

```
select '26-MAR-02' + 1 from DUAL;

ERROR: ORA-01722: invalid number
```

Date arithmetic, even with actual DATE datatypes, works only with addition and subtraction. Any other arithmetic function attempted with a date will fail. Dates are not converted to numbers, as this attempt to divide a date by 2 illustrates:

```
select SysDate / 2 from DUAL;
       *
ERROR at line 1: ORA-00932: inconsistent data types
```

Finally, a NUMBER will never be automatically converted to a DATE, because a pure number cannot be in the default format for a DATE, which is DD-MON-YY:

```
select NEXT_DAY(032602,'FRIDAY') from DUAL;
                      *
ERROR at line 1: ORA-00932: inconsistent data types
```

To use a NUMBER in a date function, **TO_DATE** is required.

A Warning About Automatic Conversion

The issue of whether it is a good practice to allow SQL to do automatic conversion of datatypes has arguments on either side. On one hand, this practice considerably simplifies and reduces the functions necessary to make a **select** statement work. On the other hand, if your assumption about what will be in the column is wrong (for example, you assume a particular character column will always have a number in it, meaning you can use it in a calculation), then, at some point, a query will stop working, Oracle will produce an error, and time will have to be spent trying to find the problem. Further, another person reading your **select** statement may be confused by what appear to be inappropriate functions at work on characters or numbers. Using TO_NUMBER makes it clear that a numeric value is always expected even if the column uses the VARCHAR2 datatype.

A simple rule of thumb might be that it is best to use functions where the risk is low, such as string manipulation functions on numbers, rather than arithmetic functions on strings. For your benefit and that of others using your work, always put a note near the **select** statement signaling the use of automatic type conversion.

Specialized Conversion Functions

As shown in Table 10-1, Oracle includes several specialized conversion functions. If you expect to use SQLPLUS and Oracle simply to produce reports, you probably won't ever need any of these functions. On the other hand, if you plan to use SQLPLUS to **update** the database, expect to build Oracle applications; or if you are using National Language Support, this information will eventually prove valuable. The functions can be found, by name, in the Alphabetical Reference section of this book.

NOTE
*The **CAST** function is used with nested tables and varying arrays; see Chapter 31 for details. The **DECODE** function is covered in Chapter 17.*

The conversion functions generally take a single value as input and return a single converted value as output. For example, the BIN_TO_NUM function converts binary values to decimal numeric values. Its input value is a list of the digits of a binary value, separated by commas and treated as a single input string:

```
select BIN_TO_NUM(1,1,0,1) from DUAL;

BIN_TO_NUM(1,1,0,1)
-------------------
              13
```

```
select BIN_TO_NUM(1,1,1,0) from DUAL;

BIN_TO_NUM(1,1,1,0)
-------------------
                 14
```

Transformation Functions

Although in one sense any function that changes its object could be called a transformation function, there are two unusual functions that you can use in many interesting ways to control your output based on your input, instead of simply transforming it. These functions are **TRANSLATE** and **DECODE**.

TRANSLATE

TRANSLATE is a simple function that does an orderly character-by-character substitution in a string. This is the format for **TRANSLATE**:

```
TRANSLATE(string,if,then)
```

TRANSLATE looks at each character in *string*, and then checks *if* to see whether that character is there. If it is, it notes the position in *if* where it found the character, and then looks at the same position in *then*. **TRANSLATE** substitutes whichever character it finds there for the character in *string*. Normally, the function is written on a single line, like this:

```
select TRANSLATE(7671234,234567890,'BCDEFGHIJ')
   from DUAL;

TRANSLA
-------
GFG1BCD
```

But it might be easier to understand if simply broken onto two lines (SQLPLUS doesn't care, of course):

```
select TRANSLATE(7671234,234567890,
                          'BCDEFGHIJ')
   from DUAL;

TRANSLA
-------
GFG1BCD
```

When **TRANSLATE** sees a 7 in the *string*, it looks for a 7 in the *if*, and translates it to the character in the same position in the *then* (an uppercase *G*). If the character is not in the *if*, it is not translated (observe what **TRANSLATE** did with the 1).

TRANSLATE is technically a string function, but, as you can see, it will do automatic data conversion and work with a mix of strings and numbers. The following is an example of a very simple code cipher, where every letter in the alphabet is shifted one position. Many years ago, spies used such character-substitution methods to encode messages before sending them. The recipient simply reversed the process. Do you remember the smooth-talking computer, HAL, in

the movie *2001: A Space Odyssey*? If you **TRANSLATE** HAL's name with a one-character shift in the alphabet, you get this:

```
select TRANSLATE('HAL','ABCDEFGHIJKLMNOPQRSTUVWXYZ',
                       'BCDEFGHIJKLMNOPQRSTUVWXYZA') AS Who
   from DUAL;

WHO
---
IBM
```

DECODE

If **TRANSLATE** is a character-by-character substitution, **DECODE** can be considered a value-by-value substitution. For every value it sees in a field, **DECODE** checks for a match in a series of *if/then* tests. **DECODE** is an incredibly powerful function, with a broad range of areas where it can be useful. Chapter 17 is devoted entirely to advanced use of **DECODE**.

This is the format for **DECODE**:

```
DECODE(value,if1,then1,if2,then2,if3,then3,. . .,else)
```

Only three *if/then* combinations are illustrated here, but there is no practical limit. To see how this function works, recall the NEWSPAPER table you saw in earlier chapters:

```
select * from NEWSPAPER;

FEATURE          S  PAGE
--------------   -  -----
National News    A    1
Sports           D    1
Editorials       A   12
Business         E    1
Weather          C    2
Television       B    7
Births           F    7
Classified       F    8
Modern Life      B    1
Comics           C    4
Movies           B    4
Bridge           B    2
Obituaries       F    6
Doctor Is In     F    6
```

Suppose you want to change the name of a couple of the regular features. **DECODE** will check each Feature *value*, row by row. If the *value* it finds is 'Sports', then it will substitute 'Games People Play'; if it finds 'Movies', then it will substitute 'Entertainment'; if it finds anything else in the value, then it will use the value of Feature.

In the next example, the page number is decoded. If the page number is 1, then the words 'Front Page' are substituted. If the page number is anything else, the words 'Turn to' are

concatenated with the page number. This illustrates that *else* can be a function, a literal, or another column.

```
select Feature, Section,
       DECODE(Page,'1','Front Page','Turn to '||Page)
  from NEWSPAPER;

FEATURE          S DECODE(PAGE,'1','FRONTPAGE','TURNTO'||PAGE)
---------------  - -----------------------------------------------
National News    A Front Page
Sports           D Front Page
Editorials       A Turn to 12
Business         E Front Page
Weather          C Turn to 2
Television       B Turn to 7
Births           F Turn to 7
Classified       F Turn to 8
Modern Life      B Front Page
Comics           C Turn to 4
Movies           B Turn to 4
Bridge           B Turn to 2
Obituaries       F Turn to 6
Doctor Is In     F Turn to 6
```

There are some restrictions on datatypes in the list of *if*s and *then*s, which will be covered in Chapter 17.

Review

Most functions in Oracle, although they are intended for a specific datatype, such as CHAR, VARCHAR2, NUMBER, and DATE, will actually work with other datatypes as well. They do this by performing an automatic type conversion. With a few logical exceptions, and the hope of future compatibility, they will do this as long as the data to be converted "looks" like the datatype required by the function.

Character functions will convert any NUMBER or DATE. NUMBER functions will convert a CHAR or VARCHAR2 if it contains the digits 0 through 9, a decimal point, or a minus sign on the left. NUMBER functions will not convert DATEs. DATE functions will convert character strings if they are in the format DD-MON-YY. They will not convert NUMBERs.

Two functions, **TRANSLATE** and **DECODE**, will fundamentally change the data they act on. **TRANSLATE** will do a character substitution according to any pattern you specify, and **DECODE** will do a value substitution for any pattern you specify.

CHAPTER
11

Grouping Things Together

p to this point, you've seen how SQL can **select** rows of information from database tables, how the **where** clause can limit the number of rows being returned to only those that meet certain rules that you define, and how the rows returned can be sorted in ascending or descending sequence using **order by**. You've also seen how the values in columns can be modified by character, NUMBER, and DATE functions, and how group functions can tell you something about the whole set of rows.

Beyond the group functions you've seen, there are also two group clauses: **having** and **group by**. These are parallel to the **where** and **order by** clauses except that they act on groups, not on individual rows. These clauses can provide very powerful insights into your data.

The Use of group by and having

If you want to generate a count of titles on the bookshelf, categorized by the type of book, you would write a query like this:

```
select CategoryName, COUNT(*)
  from BOOKSHELF
 group by CategoryName;
```

and Oracle would respond with:

```
CATEGORYNAME              COUNT(*)
-------------------- ----------
ADULTFIC                      6
ADULTNF                      10
ADULTREF                      6
CHILDRENFIC                   5
CHILDRENNF                    1
CHILDRENPIC                   3
```

Notice the mix of a column name, CategoryName, and the group function **COUNT** in the **select** clause. This mix is possible only because CategoryName is referenced in the **group by** clause. If it were not there, the opaque message first encountered in Chapter 8 would have resulted in this:

```
SQL> select CategoryName, COUNT(*) from BOOKSHELF;
select CategoryName, COUNT(*) from BOOKSHELF
       *
ERROR at line 1:
ORA-00937: not a single-group group function
```

This result occurs because the group functions, such as **SUM** and **COUNT**, are designed to tell you something about a group of rows, not the individual rows of the table. The error is avoided by using CategoryName in the **group by** clause, which forces the **COUNT** to count all the rows grouped within each CategoryName.

The **having** clause works very much like a **where** clause except that its logic is only related to the results of group functions, as opposed to columns or expressions for individual rows, which can still be selected by a **where** clause. Here, the rows in the previous example are further restricted to just those where there are more than five books in a category:

```
select CategoryName, COUNT(*)
   from BOOKSHELF
  group by CategoryName
having COUNT(*) > 5;

CATEGORYNAME           COUNT(*)
-------------------- ----------
ADULTFIC                      6
ADULTNF                      10
ADULTREF                      6
```

To determine the average rating by category, you can use the **AVG** function, as shown in the following listing:

```
select CategoryName, COUNT(*), AVG(Rating)
   from BOOKSHELF
  group by CategoryName;

CATEGORYNAME           COUNT(*) AVG(RATING)
-------------------- ---------- -----------
ADULTFIC                      6  3.66666667
ADULTNF                      10         4.2
ADULTREF                      6  3.16666667
CHILDRENFIC                   5         2.8
CHILDRENNF                    1           3
CHILDRENPIC                   3           1
```

Rating is a character column, defined as a VARCHAR2, but it contains numeric values, so Oracle can perform numeric functions on it (see Chapter 10). What is the overall average rating?

```
select AVG(Rating) from BOOKSHELF;

AVG(RATING)
-----------
 3.32258065
```

In this case, there is no **group by** clause because the entire set of rows in the BOOKSHELF table is treated as the group. Now you can use this result as part of a larger query: what categories have average ratings that are greater than the average rating of all books?

```
select CategoryName, COUNT(*), AVG(Rating)
   from BOOKSHELF
  group by CategoryName
```

```
having AVG(Rating) >
     (select AVG(Rating) from BOOKSHELF);

CATEGORYNAME            COUNT(*) AVG(RATING)
-------------------- ---------- -----------
ADULTFIC                      6  3.66666667
ADULTNF                      10         4.2
```

Looking back at the earlier listings, this result is correct—only two of the groups have average Rating values greater than the overall average.

Although the results are sorted by the CategoryName column, the purpose of **group by** is not to produce a desired sequence but rather to collect "like" things together. The order they appear in is a by-product of how **group by** works; **group by** is not meant to be used to change the sorting order.

Adding an order by

The solution for creating an alternative order for display is the addition of an **order by** clause following the **having** clause. You could add this:

```
order by CategoryName desc
```

which would reverse the order of the list:

```
select CategoryName, COUNT(*)
  from BOOKSHELF
 group by CategoryName
 order by CategoryName desc;

CATEGORYNAME            COUNT(*)
-------------------- ----------
CHILDRENPIC                   3
CHILDRENNF                    1
CHILDRENFIC                   5
ADULTREF                      6
ADULTNF                      10
ADULTFIC                      6
```

or you could use this instead:

```
order by COUNT(*) desc
```

yielding

```
CATEGORYNAME            COUNT(*)
-------------------- ----------
ADULTNF                      10
ADULTFIC                      6
ADULTREF                      6
CHILDRENFIC                   5
```

```
CHILDRENPIC                    3
CHILDRENNF                     1
```

Although you can use the column alias as part of the **order by** clause, you can't use it as part of the **having** clause. Giving **COUNT**(*) an alias of "Counter" and attempting to use **having Counter > 1** as a clause in this query will result in an "invalid column name" error:

```
select CategoryName, COUNT(*) as Counter
   from BOOKSHELF
 group by CategoryName
having Counter > 1
 order by COUNT(*) desc;

having Counter > 1
        *
ERROR at line 4:
ORA-00904: invalid column name
```

Order of Execution

The previous query has quite a collection of competing clauses! Here are the rules Oracle uses to execute each of them, and the order in which execution takes place:

1. Choose rows based on the **where** clause.

2. Group those rows together based on the **group by** clause.

3. Calculate the results of the group functions for each group.

4. Choose and eliminate groups based on the **having** clause.

5. Order the groups based on the results of the group functions in the **order by** clause. The **order by** clause must use either a group function or a column specified in the **group by** clause.

The order of execution is important because it has a direct impact on the performance of your queries. In general, the more records that can be eliminated via **where** clauses, the faster the query will execute. This performance benefit is due to the reduction in the number of rows that must be processed during the **group by** operation.

If a query is written to use a **having** clause to eliminate groups, then you should check to see if the **having** condition can be rewritten as a **where** clause. In many cases, this rewrite won't be possible. It is usually only available when the **having** clause is used to eliminate groups based on the grouping columns.

For example, if you have this query:

```
select CategoryName, COUNT(*), AVG(Rating)
   from BOOKSHELF
 where Rating > 1
 group by CategoryName
```

```
having CategoryName like 'A%'
 order by COUNT(*) desc;

CATEGORYNAME           COUNT(*) AVG(RATING)
-------------------- ---------- -----------
ADULTNF                     10         4.2
ADULTFIC                     6  3.66666667
ADULTREF                     6  3.16666667
```

then the order of execution would be:

1. Eliminate rows based on

 where Rating > 1

2. Group the remaining rows based on

 group by CategoryName

3. For each CategoryName, calculate the

 COUNT(*)

4. Eliminate groups based on

 having CategoryName like 'A%'

5. Order the remaining groups.

This query will run faster if the *groups* eliminated in Step 4 can be eliminated as *rows* in Step 1. If they are eliminated at Step 1, fewer rows will be grouped (Step 2), fewer calculations will be performed (Step 3), and no groups will be eliminated (Step 4). Each of these steps in the execution will run faster.

Since the **having** condition in this example is not based on a calculated column, it is easily changed into a **where** condition:

```
select CategoryName, COUNT(*), AVG(Rating)
   from BOOKSHELF
 where Rating > 1
   and CategoryName like 'A%'
 group by CategoryName
 order by COUNT(*) desc;
```

In the modified version, fewer rows will be grouped, resulting in a performance savings. As the number of rows in your tables increases, the performance savings from early row elimination can grow dramatically.

Views of Groups

In Chapter 3, a view called INVASION was created for the Oracle at Delphi, which joined together the WEATHER and LOCATION tables. This view appeared to be a table in its own right, with columns and rows, but each of its rows contained columns that actually came from two separate tables.

The same process of creating a view can be used with groups. The difference is that each row will contain information about a group of rows—a kind of subtotal table. For example, consider this group query:

```
select CategoryName, COUNT(*)
   from BOOKSHELF
 group by CategoryName;
```

You can create a view based on this query, and you can then query the view:

```
create or replace view CATEGORY_COUNT as
select CategoryName, COUNT(*) AS Counter
   from BOOKSHELF
 group by CategoryName;

desc CATEGORY_COUNT
```

Name	Null?	Type
CATEGORYNAME		VARCHAR2(20)
COUNTER		NUMBER

```
select * from CATEGORY_COUNT;
```

CATEGORYNAME	COUNTER
ADULTFIC	6
ADULTNF	10
ADULTREF	6
CHILDRENFIC	5
CHILDRENNF	1
CHILDRENPIC	3

NOTE
*Since the **COUNT**(*) column is a function, you have to give it a column alias (in this case, Counter) when using the query as the basis for a view.*

Renaming Columns with Aliases

Notice the name Counter in the **select** clause. The **AS Counter** clause *renames* the column it follows. The new names are called *aliases,* because they are used to disguise the real names of the underlying columns (which are complicated because they have functions).

When you query the view, you can (and must) now use the new column names:

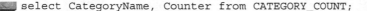
```
select CategoryName, Counter from CATEGORY_COUNT;
```

"Counter" is referred to as a *column alias*—another name to use when referring to a column. In the description of the view, and in the query, there is no evidence of the grouping function performed—just the Counter column name. It is as if the view CATEGORY_COUNT was a real table with rows of monthly sums. Why?

Oracle automatically takes a single word, without quotes, and uses it to rename the column it follows. When it does this, Oracle forces the word—the alias—into uppercase, regardless of how it was typed. You can see evidence of this by comparing the column names in the **create view** and the **describe** commands. When creating a view, *never put double quotes around your column aliases.* Always leave aliases in **create view** statements without quotes. This will cause them to be stored in uppercase, which is required for Oracle to find them. See the sidebar "Aliases in View Creation" for a warning on aliases.

You now have Category counts collected in a view. A total for the entire bookshelf could also be created, using BOOKCOUNT as both the view name and the column alias for **COUNT**(*):

```
create or replace view BOOKCOUNT as
select COUNT(*) BOOKCOUNT
   from BOOKSHELF;

View created.
```

If you query the view, you'll discover it has only one record:

```
select BOOKCOUNT
   from BOOKCOUNT;

BOOKCOUNT
---------
       31
```

As new rows are added and committed to the BOOKSHELF table, the BOOKCOUNT and CATEGORY_COUNT views will reflect the changes to the counts.

Aliases in View Creation

Internally, Oracle works with all column and table names in uppercase. This is how they are stored in its data dictionary, and this is how it always expects them to be. When aliases are typed to create a view, they should always be naked—without quotation marks around them. Putting double quotation marks around an alias can force the column name stored internally by Oracle to be in mixed case. If you do this, Oracle will not be able to find the column when you execute a **select** unless you enclose the column name within quotes during all of your queries.

Never use double quotation marks in creating aliases for a view.

The Power of Views of Groups

Now you'll see the real power of a relational database. You've created views containing totals by groups: Category and for the entire group. These views can now be *joined* together, just as the tables were in Chapter 3, to reveal information never before apparent. For instance, what percentage of the books are in each category?

```
select CategoryName, Counter, (Counter/BookCount)*100 as Percent
   from CATEGORY_COUNT, BOOKCOUNT
  order by CategoryName;

CATEGORYNAME             COUNTER    PERCENT
-------------------- ---------- ----------
ADULTFIC                      6 19.3548387
ADULTNF                      10 32.2580645
ADULTREF                      6 19.3548387
CHILDRENFIC                   5 16.1290323
CHILDRENNF                    1 3.22580645
CHILDRENPIC                   3 9.67741935
```

In this query, two views are listed in the **from** clause, but they are not joined in a **where** clause. Why not? In this particular case, no **where** clause is necessary, because one of the views, BOOKCOUNT, will only return one row (as shown in the previous listing). The one row in BOOKCOUNT is joined to each row in CATEGORY_COUNT, yielding one row of output for each row in CATEGORY_COUNT. The same results could have been obtained by directly joining the BOOKSHELF *table* with the BOOKCOUNT *view,* but as you can see, the query is more complicated and difficult to understand—and as the number of groups expands, the query will grow even more cumbersome:

```
select CategoryName, COUNT(*),
    (COUNT(*)/MAX(BookCount))*100 as Percent
  from BOOKSHELF, BOOKCOUNT
 group by CategoryName
 order by CategoryName;
```

Notice the percentage calculation:

```
    (COUNT(*)/MAX(BookCount))*100 as Percent
```

Since this result is part of a grouping function, each of the values must be grouped. Thus, an initial attempt such as this would fail:

```
    (COUNT(*)/BookCount)*100 as Percent
```

since BookCount is not grouped. As there is only one row in the BOOKCOUNT view, you can perform a **MAX** function on it to return that single row, grouped by itself.

To create queries that compare one grouping of rows with another grouping of rows, at least one of the groupings must be a view or an "inline view" created in the **from** clause of the query. Beyond this technical restriction, however, it is just simpler and easier to understand doing the

queries with views. Compare the last two examples, and the difference in clarity is apparent. Views hide complexity.

To use the inline view method, put the view's text within the **from** clause and give its columns aliases there:

```
select CategoryName, Counter, (Counter/BookCount)*100 as Percent
  from CATEGORY_COUNT,
       (select COUNT(*) as BookCount from BOOKSHELF)
 order by CategoryName;
```

In this example, the BOOKCOUNT view has been removed from the **from** clause, replaced by its base query. In that query, the BookCount alias is given to the result of a **COUNT**(*) performed against the BOOKSHELF table. In the main query, that BookCount alias is then used as part of a calculation. Using this coding method, there is no need to create the BOOKCOUNT view. Be careful when working with multiple grouping levels within the same query—creating views commonly helps to simplify the creation and maintenance of the code.

order by in views

From a strictly theoretical perspective, there is no reason to have an **order by** clause stored in a view—you can issue an **order by** clause when you query the view. As of Oracle8i, Oracle supports the **order by** clause within views, as shown here:

```
create view BOOKSHELF_SORTED
as select * from BOOKSHELF
order by Title;
```

Having the data sorted in the view may simplify your application development. For example, if your code steps through a set of records, having those records presorted may make your processing and error checking simpler. In your application development, you will know that the data will always be returned to you in an ordered fashion. The following query selects the Title values, using the RowNum pseudo-column to limit the output to nine records:

```
select Title from BOOKSHELF_SORTED
  where Rownum < 10;

TITLE
----------------------------------------
ANNE OF GREEN GABLES
BOX SOCIALS
CHARLOTTE'S WEB
COMPLETE POEMS OF JOHN KEATS
EITHER/OR
EMMA WHO SAVED MY LIFE
GOOD DOG, CARL
GOSPEL
HARRY POTTER AND THE GOBLET OF FIRE
```

The views also give you more power to use the many character, NUMBER, and DATE datatypes at will, without worrying about things like months appearing in alphabetical order.

Logic in the having Clause

In the **having** clause, the choice of the group function, and the column on which it operates, might bear no relation to the columns or group functions in the **select** clause:

```
select CategoryName, COUNT(*),
    (COUNT(*)/MAX(BookCount))*100 as Percent
  from BOOKSHELF, BOOKCOUNT
 group by CategoryName
having Avg(Rating) > 4
 order by CategoryName;

CATEGORYNAME               COUNT(*)    PERCENT
--------------------    ----------   ----------
ADULTNF                          10  32.2580645
```

Here, the **having** clause selected only those categories (the **group by** collected all the rows into groups by CategoryName) with an average rating greater than 4. All other groups are eliminated. For the group that met that criterion, the percentage of the total count was calculated.

The **having** clause is very effective for determining which rows in a table have duplicate values in specific columns. For example, if you are trying to establish a new unique index on a column (or set of columns) in a table, and the index creation fails due to uniqueness problems with the data, then you can easily determine which rows caused the problem.

First, select the columns that you want to be unique, followed by a **COUNT**(*) column. **Group by** the columns you want to be unique, and use the **having** clause to return only those groups having **COUNT**(*)>1. The only records returned will be duplicates. The following query shows this check being performed for the AuthorName column of the AUTHOR table:

```
select AuthorName, COUNT(*)
  from AUTHOR
 group by AuthorName
having COUNT(*)>1
 order by AuthorName;

no rows selected
```

Which books have more than one author? Select the titles from BOOKSHELF_AUTHOR for which the group (by Title) has more than one member:

```
column Title format a40

select Title, COUNT(*)
from BOOKSHELF_AUTHOR
group by Title
```

```
having COUNT(*)>1;

TITLE                                     COUNT(*)
---------------------------------------- ----------
COMPLETE POEMS OF JOHN KEATS                      2
JOURNALS OF LEWIS AND CLARK                       4
KIERKEGAARD ANTHOLOGY                             2
RUNAWAY BUNNY                                     2
```

Who are those ten authors? You could create a view based on this query, or try it as an inline view:

```
column Title format a40
column AuthorName format a30

select Title, AuthorName
from BOOKSHELF_AUTHOR,
   (select Title as GroupedTitle, COUNT(*) as TitleCounter
      from BOOKSHELF_AUTHOR
    group by Title
    having COUNT(*) > 1)
where Title = GroupedTitle
order by Title, AuthorName;

TITLE                                     AUTHORNAME
---------------------------------------- --------------------
COMPLETE POEMS OF JOHN KEATS             JOHN BARNARD
COMPLETE POEMS OF JOHN KEATS             JOHN KEATS
JOURNALS OF LEWIS AND CLARK             BERNARD DE VOTO
JOURNALS OF LEWIS AND CLARK             MERIWETHER LEWIS
JOURNALS OF LEWIS AND CLARK             STEPHEN AMBROSE
JOURNALS OF LEWIS AND CLARK             WILLIAM CLARK
KIERKEGAARD ANTHOLOGY                    ROBERT BRETALL
KIERKEGAARD ANTHOLOGY                    SOREN KIERKEGAARD
RUNAWAY BUNNY                            CLEMENT HURD
RUNAWAY BUNNY                            MARGARET WISE BROWN
```

This query may look complicated (and using a view would make it simpler to read), but it is based on the concepts covered in this chapter: An inline view performs a **group by** function and uses a **having** clause to return only those titles with multiple authors. Those titles are then used as the basis of a query against the BOOKSHELF_AUTHOR table. In a single query, the BOOKSHELF_AUTHOR table is queried for grouped data and individual row data.

order by with Columns and Group Functions

The **order by** clause is executed after the **where**, **group by**, and **having** clauses. It can employ group functions, or columns from the **group by**, or a combination. If it uses a group function, that function operates on the groups, and then the **order by** sorts the *results* of the function in order. If the **order by** uses a column from the **group by**, it sorts the rows that are returned based on that

column. Group functions and single columns (so long as the column is in the **group by**) can be combined in the **order by**.

In the **order by** clause, you can specify a group function and the column it affects even though they have nothing at all to do with the group functions or columns in the **select**, **group by**, or **having** clause. On the other hand, if you specify a column in the **order by** clause that is not part of a group function, it must be in the **group by** clause. Let's take the last example and modify the **order by** clause:

```
order by TitleCounter desc, Title, AuthorName
```

The titles and authors will now be ordered based on the number of authors (with the greatest number first), then by Title and AuthorName:

```
TITLE                                        AUTHORNAME
-------------------------------------------- -----------------------
JOURNALS OF LEWIS AND CLARK                  BERNARD DE VOTO
JOURNALS OF LEWIS AND CLARK                  MERIWETHER LEWIS
JOURNALS OF LEWIS AND CLARK                  STEPHEN AMBROSE
JOURNALS OF LEWIS AND CLARK                  WILLIAM CLARK
COMPLETE POEMS OF JOHN KEATS                 JOHN BARNARD
COMPLETE POEMS OF JOHN KEATS                 JOHN KEATS
KIERKEGAARD ANTHOLOGY                        ROBERT BRETALL
KIERKEGAARD ANTHOLOGY                        SOREN KIERKEGAARD
RUNAWAY BUNNY                                CLEMENT HURD
RUNAWAY BUNNY                                MARGARET WISE BROWN
```

Join Columns

As explained in Chapters 1 and 3, joining two tables together requires that they have a relationship defined by a common column. This is also true in joining views, or tables and views. The only exception is when one of the tables or views has just a single row, as the BOOKCOUNT table does. In this case, SQL joins the single row to every row in the other table or view, and no reference to the joining columns needs to be made in the **where** clause of the query.

Any attempt to join two tables that both have more than one row without specifying the joined columns in the **where** clause will produce what's known as a *Cartesian product,* usually a giant result where every row in one table is joined with every row in the other table. A small 80-row table joined to a small 100-row table in this way would produce 8,000 rows in your display, and few of them would be at all meaningful.

Review

Tables in Oracle can be grouped into collections of related rows, such as by Title, AuthorName, or CategoryName. This is done using the **group by** clause, which collects only those rows in the table that pass the logical test of the **where** clause:

```
where CategoryName like 'A%'
group by CategoryName
```

The **having** clause looks at these groups and eliminates any based on whether they pass the logical test of the group function used in the **having** clause, such as:

```
having COUNT(*) > 1
```

Those groups whose **COUNT**(*) is greater than one are returned to you. Each group has just one row in the resulting table that is displayed. The **having** clause need not (and often will not) correspond to the group functions in the **select** clause. After these rows have been chosen by the **having** clause, they can be placed in the desired sequence by an **order by**:

```
order by COUNT(*)
```

The **order by** must use either a column named in the **group by** or any appropriate group function that can reference any column without regard to the **select** or the **having** clause. Its group function will make its computation row by row for each group created by the **group by** clause.

All of these powerful grouping features can be combined to create complex summary views of the underlying table, which appear very simple. Once created, their columns can be manipulated, and their rows selected, just as with any other table. These views also can be joined to each other, and to tables, to produce deep insights into the data. You can use inline views to reduce the number of objects you maintain. You can use **order by** clauses within views. For commonly used groupings, consider the use of views to simplify your application development. In the following chapters, you will see additional functions and methods that allow you to perform even more complex data manipulation.

CHAPTER
12

When One Query
Depends upon Another

his chapter and Chapter 13 introduce more difficult concepts than we've previously seen. While many of these concepts are rarely used in the normal course of running queries or producing reports, there will be occasions that call for the techniques taught in these chapters. If they seem too challenging as you study them, read on anyway. The odds are good that by the time you need these methods, you'll be able to use them.

Advanced Subqueries

You've encountered *subqueries*—those **select** statements that are part of a **where** clause in a preceding **select** statement—in earlier chapters. Subqueries also can be used in **insert**, **update**, and **delete** statements. This use will be covered in Chapter 15.

Often, a subquery will provide an alternative approach to a query. For example, suppose you want to know what categories of books have been checked out. The following three-way join provides this information:

```
select distinct C.ParentCategory, C.SubCategory
   from CATEGORY C, BOOKSHELF B, BOOKSHELF_CHECKOUT BC
 where C.CategoryName = B.CategoryName
   and B.Title = BC.Title;

PARENTCA SUBCATEGORY
-------- --------------------
ADULT    FICTION
ADULT    NONFICTION
ADULT    REFERENCE
CHILDREN FICTION
CHILDREN PICTURE BOOK
```

Three tables are joined in the same way that two tables are. The common columns are set equal to each other in the **where** clause, as shown in the preceding listing. To join three tables together, two of them must each be joined to a third. In this example, the CATEGORY table is joined to the BOOKSHELF table, and the result of that join is joined to the BOOKSHELF_CHECKOUT table. The **distinct** clause tells Oracle to return only the distinct combinations of ParentCategory and SubCategory.

NOTE
Not every table is joined to every other table. In fact, the number of links between the tables is usually one less than the number of tables being joined.

Once the tables are joined, as shown in the first two lines of the **where** clause, then you can determine the count of checkouts by parent category and subcategory.

Correlated Subqueries

Is there another way to perform multitable joins? Recall that a **where** clause can contain a subquery **select**. Subquery **select**s can be nested—that is, a **where** clause in a subquery also can contain a **where** clause with a subquery, which can contain a **where** clause with a subquery—on down for more levels than you are ever likely to need. The following shows three **select**s, each connected to another through a **where** clause:

```
select distinct C.ParentCategory, C.SubCategory
   from CATEGORY C
 where CategoryName in
       (select CategoryName from BOOKSHELF
         where Title in
                 (select Title from BOOKSHELF_CHECKOUT)
       );

PARENTCA SUBCATEGORY
-------- --------------------
ADULT    FICTION
ADULT    NONFICTION
ADULT    REFERENCE
CHILDREN FICTION
CHILDREN PICTURE BOOK
```

This query selects any categories containing books that have been checked out. It does this simply by requesting a book whose Title is in the BOOKSHELF table and whose checkout record is in the BOOKSHELF_CHECKOUT table. In a subquery, Oracle assumes the columns to be from the first **select** statement, the one that contains the subquery in its **where** clause. This is called a *nested* subquery, because for every CategoryName in the main (outer) query, the CategoryName may be correlated in the second **where** clause.

Said differently, a subquery may refer to a column in a table used in its main query (the query that has the subquery in its **where** clause). Consider the following query:

```
select Title from BOOKSHELF_AUTHOR
 where Title in
       (select Title from BOOKSHELF
         where AuthorName = 'STEPHEN JAY GOULD');

TITLE
----------------------------------------------------
WONDERFUL LIFE
THE MISMEASURE OF MAN
```

Why does this query work? Taken on its own, the subquery would fail:

```
select Title from BOOKSHELF
  where AuthorName = 'STEPHEN JAY GOULD';
```

```
where AuthorName = 'STEPHEN JAY GOULD'
       *
ERROR at line 2:
ORA-00904: invalid column name
```

When executed as a subquery, it is correlated to the parent query—you can reference columns of the first **select** in the subquery. You'll see additional examples of correlated subqueries in this chapter and the chapters that follow.

Coordinating Logical Tests

If a reader is looking for more books in a particular category, what authors should he or she read? Suppose that Fred Fuller, who has checked out two biographies, asks for recommendations. Who else should you recommend?

```
select distinct AuthorName from BOOKSHELF_AUTHOR
  where Title in
    (select Title from BOOKSHELF
      where CategoryName in
        (select distinct CategoryName from BOOKSHELF
          where Title in
            (select Title
               from BOOKSHELF_CHECKOUT bc
              where BC.Name = 'FRED FULLER')));
```

That may look a daunting at first, but it's easy to follow if you talk through the code. Start at the innermost query: Get a list of the titles that Fred Fuller has checked out. For those titles, go to the BOOKSHELF table and get a list of the distinct CategoryName values those books are assigned to. Now go to BOOKSHELF a second time and get all the titles in those categories. For those titles, go to the BOOKSHELF_AUTHOR table and generate the list of authors. Here are the results:

```
AUTHORNAME
--------------------
BERNARD DE VOTO
BERYL MARKHAM
DANIEL BOORSTIN
DAVID MCCULLOUGH
DIETRICH BONHOEFFER
G. B. TALBOT
JOHN ALLEN PAULOS
MERIWETHER LEWIS
STEPHEN AMBROSE
STEPHEN JAY GOULD
WILLIAM CLARK
```

Fred is asking for recommendations for new authors, so let's exclude the ones he's already read. To see who Fred has read, simply query the BOOKSHELF_CHECKOUT and BOOKSHELF_AUTHOR tables:

```
select distinct AuthorName
   from BOOKSHELF_AUTHOR ba, BOOKSHELF_CHECKOUT bc
  where ba.Title = bc.Title
    and bc.Name = 'FRED FULLER';
```

```
AUTHORNAME
-----------------------
DAVID MCCULLOUGH
```

Now let's exclude that author from the list we're going to provide. We'll do that by adding an extra **and** clause to the query:

```
select distinct AuthorName from BOOKSHELF_AUTHOR
  where Title in
    (select Title from BOOKSHELF
      where CategoryName in
        (select distinct CategoryName from BOOKSHELF
          where Title in
            (select Title
              from BOOKSHELF_CHECKOUT bc
             where BC.Name = 'FRED FULLER')))
    and AuthorName not in
      (select AuthorName
        from BOOKSHELF_AUTHOR ba, BOOKSHELF_CHECKOUT bc
       where ba.Title = bc.Title
         and bc.Name = 'FRED FULLER');
```

```
AUTHORNAME
--------------------
BERNARD DE VOTO
BERYL MARKHAM
DANIEL BOORSTIN
DIETRICH BONHOEFFER
G. B. TALBOT
JOHN ALLEN PAULOS
MERIWETHER LEWIS
STEPHEN AMBROSE
STEPHEN JAY GOULD
WILLIAM CLARK
```

This **and** is a part of the main query, even though it follows the subquery. Also note that some of the tables are queried at multiple points within the script; each of those queries is treated as a separate access of the table.

Using EXISTS and Its Correlated Subquery

EXISTS is a test for existence. It is placed the way **IN** might be placed with a subquery, but differs in that it is a logical test for the return of rows from a query, not for the rows themselves.

How many authors have written more than one book on the bookshelf?

```
select AuthorName, COUNT(*)
  from BOOKSHELF_AUTHOR
 group by AuthorName
having COUNT(*) > 1;

AUTHORNAME                          COUNT(*)
------------------------------ ----------
DAVID MCCULLOUGH                      2
DIETRICH BONHOEFFER                   2
E. B. WHITE                           2
SOREN KIERKEGAARD                     2
STEPHEN JAY GOULD                     2
W. P. KINSELLA                        2
WILTON BARNHARDT                      2
```

Attempting to find both AuthorName and Title fails, however, because the **group by** made necessary by the **COUNT**(*) is on the primary key of the BOOKSHELF_AUTHOR table (AuthorName, Title). Since each primary key, by definition, uniquely identifies only one row, the count of titles for that one row can never be greater than one, so the **having** clause always tests false—it doesn't find any rows:

```
no rows selected.
```

EXISTS provides a solution. The following subquery asks, for each AuthorName selected in the outer query, whether an AuthorName exists in the BOOKSHELF_AUTHOR table with a count of Titles greater than one. If the answer for a given name is yes, the **EXISTS** test is true, and the outer query **select**s an AuthorName and Title. The author names are correlated by the "BA" alias given to the first BOOKSHELF_AUTHOR table.

```
select AuthorName, Title
  from BOOKSHELF_AUTHOR BA
 where EXISTS
       (select *
          from BOOKSHELF_AUTHOR  BA2
         where BA.AuthorName = BA2.AuthorName
         group by BA2.AuthorName
        having COUNT(BA2.Title) > 1)
order by AuthorName, Title;

AUTHORNAME               TITLE
------------------------ ------------------------------
DAVID MCCULLOUGH         JOHN ADAMS
DAVID MCCULLOUGH         TRUMAN
DIETRICH BONHOEFFER      LETTERS AND PAPERS FROM PRISON
DIETRICH BONHOEFFER      THE COST OF DISCIPLESHIP
E. B. WHITE              CHARLOTTE'S WEB
E. B. WHITE              TRUMPET OF THE SWAN
```

```
SOREN KIERKEGAARD          EITHER/OR
SOREN KIERKEGAARD          KIERKEGAARD ANTHOLOGY
STEPHEN JAY GOULD          THE MISMEASURE OF MAN
STEPHEN JAY GOULD          WONDERFUL LIFE
W. P. KINSELLA             BOX SOCIALS
W. P. KINSELLA             SHOELESS JOE
WILTON BARNHARDT           EMMA WHO SAVED MY LIFE
WILTON BARNHARDT           GOSPEL
```

The two queries are correlated—note that the subquery references the BA.AuthorName column even though that column is in the outer query, not the subquery. Within the subquery, the BA2 alias is not required but helps make the code easier to maintain.

This same query could have been built using **IN** and a test on the column Name. No correlated subquery is necessary here:

```
select AuthorName, Title
    from BOOKSHELF_AUTHOR BA
  where AuthorName in
        (select AuthorName
            from BOOKSHELF_AUTHOR
          group by AuthorName
          having COUNT(Title) > 1)
  order by AuthorName, Title;
```

Outer Joins

The syntax for outer joins has changed considerably in Oracle9i. In the following examples, you will see both the Oracle9i syntax and the pre-Oracle9i syntax. The pre-Oracle9i syntax is still supported in Oracle9i, but its use should be discontinued. New development should use the new syntax. The new syntax complies with ANSI SQL standards, while the old syntax does not.

Pre-Oracle9i Syntax for Outer Joins

What books were checked out during the time period tracked in the BOOKSHELF_CHECKOUT table?

```
select distinct Title
  from BOOKSHELF_CHECKOUT;
```

```
TITLE
----------------------------------------
ANNE OF GREEN GABLES
EITHER/OR
GOOD DOG, CARL
HARRY POTTER AND THE GOBLET OF FIRE
INNUMERACY
JOHN ADAMS
MIDNIGHT MAGIC
MY LEDGER
POLAR EXPRESS
```

```
THE DISCOVERERS
THE MISMEASURE OF MAN
THE SHIPPING NEWS
TO KILL A MOCKINGBIRD
TRUMAN
WEST WITH THE NIGHT
WONDERFUL LIFE
```

That's a correct report, but it doesn't show the 0 counts—the books that were not checked out. If you need to see the inventory of all books along with the checkout list, you'll need to join BOOKSHELF_CHECKOUT to BOOKSHELF:

```
select distinct B.Title
   from BOOKSHELF_CHECKOUT BC, BOOKSHELF B
where BC.Title = B.Title;
```

But that query will return the exact same records—the only rows in BOOKSHELF that can meet the join criteria are those that have been checked out. To list the rest of the books, you'll need to use an *outer join*—telling Oracle to return a row even if the join does not produce a match. Pre-Oracle9i, the syntax for an outer join uses a (+) on the side of the join that will be returning additional rows. In this case, that's BOOKSHELF_CHECKOUT. The following query shows the maximum number of days each book was checked out:

```
select B.Title, MAX(BC.ReturnedDate - BC.CheckoutDate)
        "Most Days Out"
  from BOOKSHELF_CHECKOUT BC, BOOKSHELF B
 where BC.Title (+) = B.Title
 group by B.Title;
```

TITLE	Most Days Out
ANNE OF GREEN GABLES	18
BOX SOCIALS	
CHARLOTTE'S WEB	
COMPLETE POEMS OF JOHN KEATS	
EITHER/OR	8
EMMA WHO SAVED MY LIFE	
GOOD DOG, CARL	14
GOSPEL	
HARRY POTTER AND THE GOBLET OF FIRE	11
INNUMERACY	21
JOHN ADAMS	28
JOURNALS OF LEWIS AND CLARK	
KIERKEGAARD ANTHOLOGY	
LETTERS AND PAPERS FROM PRISON	
MIDNIGHT MAGIC	14
MY LEDGER	16
POLAR EXPRESS	14
PREACHING TO HEAD AND HEART	
RUNAWAY BUNNY	

```
SHOELESS JOE
THE COST OF DISCIPLESHIP
THE DISCOVERERS                                   48
THE GOOD BOOK
THE MISMEASURE OF MAN                             31
THE SHIPPING NEWS                                 59
TO KILL A MOCKINGBIRD                             14
TRUMAN                                            19
TRUMPET OF THE SWAN
UNDER THE EYE OF THE CLOCK
WEST WITH THE NIGHT                               48
WONDERFUL LIFE                                    31
```

All of the Titles in BOOKSHELF are returned, even those that do not meet the join criteria. If you display the BOOKSHELF_CHECKOUT.Title values instead, you will see that those values are **NULL**. Think of the (+), which must immediately follow the join column of the shorter table, as saying "add an extra (**NULL**) row of BC.Title any time there's no match for B.Title."

Oracle9i Syntax for Outer Joins

As of Oracle9i, you can use the ANSI SQL standard syntax for outer joins. In the **from** clause, you can tell Oracle to perform a **left**, **right**, or **full outer** join. Let's start with the example from the last section:

```
select B.Title, MAX(BC.ReturnedDate - BC.CheckoutDate)
       "Most Days Out"
  from BOOKSHELF_CHECKOUT BC, BOOKSHELF B
 where BC.Title (+) = B.Title
 group by B.Title;
```

In this case, the BOOKSHELF_CHECKOUT table is having rows returned from it during the join even if no matches are found. This can be rewritten as:

```
select B.Title, MAX(BC.ReturnedDate - BC.CheckoutDate)
       "Most Days Out"
  from BOOKSHELF_CHECKOUT BC right outer join BOOKSHELF B
    on BC.Title = B.Title
 group by B.Title;
```

Note the use of the **on** clause as part of the outer join syntax. Note that

```
from BOOKSHELF_CHECKOUT BC right outer join BOOKSHELF B
```

is equivalent to

```
from BOOKSHELF B left outer join BOOKSHELF_CHECKOUT BC
```

You can replace the **on** clause with a **using** clause along with the name of the column the tables have in common—do not qualify the column name with a table name or table alias.

```
select Title, MAX(BC.ReturnedDate - BC.CheckoutDate)
       "Most Days Out"
  from BOOKSHELF_CHECKOUT BC right outer join BOOKSHELF B
 using (Title)
 group by Title;
```

Note that you cannot specify a table alias for the columns listed in the **using** clause—even in the **group by** and **select** clauses.

As with the old syntax, the side used as the driving table for the outer join makes a difference; doing a **left outer join** will not return all of the titles.

```
select B.Title, MAX(BC.ReturnedDate - BC.CheckoutDate)
       "Most Days Out"
  from BOOKSHELF_CHECKOUT BC left outer join BOOKSHELF B
    on BC.Title = B.Title
 group by B.Title;
```

```
TITLE                                     Most Days Out
----------------------------------------- -------------
ANNE OF GREEN GABLES                                 18
EITHER/OR                                             8
GOOD DOG, CARL                                       14
HARRY POTTER AND THE GOBLET OF FIRE                  11
INNUMERACY                                           21
JOHN ADAMS                                           28
MIDNIGHT MAGIC                                       14
MY LEDGER                                            16
POLAR EXPRESS                                        14
THE DISCOVERERS                                      48
THE MISMEASURE OF MAN                                31
THE SHIPPING NEWS                                    59
TO KILL A MOCKINGBIRD                                14
TRUMAN                                               19
WEST WITH THE NIGHT                                  48
WONDERFUL LIFE                                       31

16 rows selected.
```

The third option, **full outer join**, returns all rows from both tables. Rows that do not satisfy the **on** condition return **NULL** values.

```
select B.Title, MAX(BC.ReturnedDate - BC.CheckoutDate)
       "Most Days Out"
  from BOOKSHELF_CHECKOUT BC full outer join BOOKSHELF B
    on BC.Title = B.Title
 group by B.Title;
```

Prior to Oracle9i, you can generate the **full outer join** results by performing two separate outer joins—using each table as the outer table—and using a **union** operation to combine the results in a single query.

Replacing NOT IN with an Outer Join

The various logical tests that can be done in a **where** clause all have their separate performance measures. A **NOT IN** test may force a full read of the table in the subquery **select**. For example, what books were not checked out? You could write a query like this:

```
select Title
  from BOOKSHELF
 where Title not in
       (select Title from BOOKSHELF_CHECKOUT)
 order by Title;

TITLE
----------------------------------------
BOX SOCIALS
CHARLOTTE'S WEB
COMPLETE POEMS OF JOHN KEATS
EMMA WHO SAVED MY LIFE
GOSPEL
JOURNALS OF LEWIS AND CLARK
KIERKEGAARD ANTHOLOGY
LETTERS AND PAPERS FROM PRISON
PREACHING TO HEAD AND HEART
RUNAWAY BUNNY
SHOELESS JOE
THE COST OF DISCIPLESHIP
THE GOOD BOOK
TRUMPET OF THE SWAN
UNDER THE EYE OF THE CLOCK
```

This is typically the way such a query would be written, even though experienced Oracle users know it may be slow—you may be forcing Oracle to perform a time-intensive full table scan on the BOOKSHELF_CHECKOUT table. The following query uses an outer join and produces the same result. The difference is that this one will be efficient since the optimizer can take advantage of indexes on the join columns:

```
select distinct B.Title
  from BOOKSHELF_CHECKOUT BC right outer join BOOKSHELF B
    on BC.Title = B.Title
 where BC.Title is NULL
 order by B.Title;

TITLE
----------------------------------------
BOX SOCIALS
CHARLOTTE'S WEB
COMPLETE POEMS OF JOHN KEATS
EMMA WHO SAVED MY LIFE
GOSPEL
JOURNALS OF LEWIS AND CLARK
```

```
KIERKEGAARD ANTHOLOGY
LETTERS AND PAPERS FROM PRISON
PREACHING TO HEAD AND HEART
RUNAWAY BUNNY
SHOELESS JOE
THE COST OF DISCIPLESHIP
THE GOOD BOOK
TRUMPET OF THE SWAN
UNDER THE EYE OF THE CLOCK
```

Why does it work and give the same results as the **NOT IN**? The outer join between the two tables ensures that all rows are available for the test, including those Titles for whom no checkout records are listed in the BOOKSHELF_CHECKOUT table. The line

```
where BC.Title is NULL
```

produces only those Titles that don't appear in the BOOKSHELF_CHECKOUT table (and are therefore returned as NULL titles by Oracle). The logic here is obscure, but it works. The best way to use this technique is simply to follow the model. Save this method for use when a **NOT IN** will be searching a big table, and put plenty of explanatory comments nearby.

Replacing NOT IN with NOT EXISTS

A more common way of performing this type of query requires using the **NOT EXISTS** clause. **NOT EXISTS** is typically used to determine which values in one table do not have matching values in another table. In usage, it is identical to the **EXISTS** clause; in the following example, you'll see the difference in the query logic and the records returned.

NOT EXISTS allows you to use a correlated subquery to eliminate from a table all records that may successfully be joined to another table. For this example, that means you can eliminate from the BOOKSHELF table all Titles that are present in the Title column of the BOOKSHELF_CHECKOUT table. The following query shows how this is done:

```
select B.Title
  from BOOKSHELF B
 where not exists
       (select 'x' from BOOKSHELF_CHECKOUT BC
        where BC.Title = B.Title)
 order by B.Title;

TITLE
----------------------------------------
BOX SOCIALS
CHARLOTTE'S WEB
COMPLETE POEMS OF JOHN KEATS
EMMA WHO SAVED MY LIFE
GOSPEL
JOURNALS OF LEWIS AND CLARK
KIERKEGAARD ANTHOLOGY
```

```
LETTERS AND PAPERS FROM PRISON
PREACHING TO HEAD AND HEART
RUNAWAY BUNNY
SHOELESS JOE
THE COST OF DISCIPLESHIP
THE GOOD BOOK
TRUMPET OF THE SWAN
UNDER THE EYE OF THE CLOCK
```

This query shows the books that have not been checked out, as previously shown via the **not in** and outer join methods. How does this query work?

For each record in the BOOKSHELF table, the **NOT EXISTS** subquery is checked. If the join of that record to the BOOKSHELF_CHECKOUT table returns a row, then the results of the subquery **EXIST**. **NOT EXISTS** tells the query to reverse that return code; therefore, any row in BOOKSHELF that can be successfully joined to BOOKSHELF_CHECKOUT will not be returned by the outer query. The only rows left are the BOOKSHELF rows that do not have a matching row in BOOKSHELF_CHECKOUT.

NOT EXISTS is a very efficient way to perform this type of query, especially when multiple columns are used for the join. Because it uses a join, **NOT EXISTS** is frequently able to use available indexes, whereas **NOT IN** may not be able to use those indexes. The ability to use indexes for this type of query can have a dramatic impact on the query's performance.

NATURAL and INNER Joins

As of Oracle9i, you can use the **natural** keyword to indicate that a join should be performed based on all columns that have the same name in the two tables being joined. For example, what titles in BOOK_ORDER match those already in BOOKSHELF?

```
select Title
   from BOOK_ORDER natural join BOOKSHELF;

TITLE
----------------------------------------
GOSPEL
SHOELESS JOE
```

The natural join returned the results as if you had typed in:

```
select BO.Title
  from BOOK_ORDER BO, BOOKSHELF
 where BO.Title = BOOKSHELF.Title
   and BO.Publisher = BOOKSHELF.Publisher
   and BO.CategoryName = BOOKSHELF.CategoryName;
```

The join was performed based on the columns the two tables had in common.

Support for **inner** join syntax was introduced in Oracle9i. Inner joins are the default—they return the rows the two tables have in common, and are the alternative to outer joins. Note that

they support the **on** and **using** clauses, so you can specify your join criteria as shown in the following listing:

```
select BO.Title
  from BOOK_ORDER BO inner join BOOKSHELF B
    on BO.Title = B.Title;

TITLE
----------------------------------------
GOSPEL
SHOELESS JOE
```

UNION, INTERSECT, and MINUS

Sometimes you need to combine information of a similar type from more than one table. A classic example of this is merging two or more mailing lists prior to a mailing campaign. Depending upon the purpose of a particular mailing, you might want to send letters to any of these combinations of people:

- Everyone in both lists (while avoiding sending two letters to someone who happens to be in both lists)

- Only those people who are in both lists

- Those people in only one of the lists

These three combinations of lists are known in Oracle as **UNION**, **INTERSECT**, and **MINUS**. In the following examples you will see how to use these three clauses to manage the results of multiple queries. The examples will compare the books on hand (BOOKSHELF) with those on order (BOOK_ORDER).

To see all of the books, **UNION** the two tables. To reduce the size of the output, only the BOOKSHELF entries from the first half of the alphabet are selected:

```
select Title from BOOKSHELF
 where Title < 'M%';
```

returns 14 rows.

```
select Title from BOOK_ORDER;
```

returns 6 rows. If we **UNION** them together, how many rows are returned?

```
select Title from BOOKSHELF
 where Title < 'M%'
union
select Title from BOOK_ORDER;
```

```
TITLE
----------------------------------------
ANNE OF GREEN GABLES
BOX SOCIALS
CHARLOTTE'S WEB
COMPLETE POEMS OF JOHN KEATS
EITHER/OR
EMMA WHO SAVED MY LIFE
GALILEO'S DAUGHTER
GOOD DOG, CARL
GOSPEL
HARRY POTTER AND THE GOBLET OF FIRE
INNUMERACY
JOHN ADAMS
JOURNALS OF LEWIS AND CLARK
KIERKEGAARD ANTHOLOGY
LETTERS AND PAPERS FROM PRISON
LONGITUDE
ONCE REMOVED
SHOELESS JOE
SOMETHING SO STRONG

19 rows selected.
```

Where did the extra record go? The problem is that one of the Title values in BOOK_ORDER is already in the BOOKSHELF table. To show the duplicates, use **UNION ALL** instead of **UNION**:

```
select Title from BOOKSHELF
  where Title < 'M%'
union all
select Title from BOOK_ORDER
  order by Title;

TITLE
----------------------------------------
ANNE OF GREEN GABLES
BOX SOCIALS
CHARLOTTE'S WEB
COMPLETE POEMS OF JOHN KEATS
EITHER/OR
EMMA WHO SAVED MY LIFE
GALILEO'S DAUGHTER
GOOD DOG, CARL
GOSPEL
GOSPEL
HARRY POTTER AND THE GOBLET OF FIRE
INNUMERACY
JOHN ADAMS
JOURNALS OF LEWIS AND CLARK
KIERKEGAARD ANTHOLOGY
LETTERS AND PAPERS FROM PRISON
```

```
LONGITUDE
ONCE REMOVED
SHOELESS JOE
SOMETHING SO STRONG

20 rows selected.
```

The duplicate title is now listed twice.

In the following, the two lists of books are intersected. This list contains only those names that are in *both* underlying tables (note that the restriction on Title < 'M%' has been eliminated for this example):

```
select Title from BOOKSHELF
intersect
select Title from BOOK_ORDER
 order by Title;

TITLE
----------------------------------------
GOSPEL
SHOELESS JOE
```

Next, the list of new books (in BOOK_ORDER but not already in BOOKSHELF) is generated, via the **MINUS** operator:

```
select Title from BOOK_ORDER
minus
select Title from BOOKSHELF
 order by Title;

TITLE
----------------------------------------
GALILEO'S DAUGHTER
LONGITUDE
ONCE REMOVED
SOMETHING SO STRONG
```

You could have also used **MINUS** to show which books had not been checked out:

```
select Title from BOOKSHELF
 minus
select Title from BOOKSHELF_CHECKOUT;

TITLE
-------------------------------
BOX SOCIALS
CHARLOTTE'S WEB
COMPLETE POEMS OF JOHN KEATS
EMMA WHO SAVED MY LIFE
GOSPEL
```

```
JOURNALS OF LEWIS AND CLARK
KIERKEGAARD ANTHOLOGY
LETTERS AND PAPERS FROM PRISON
PREACHING TO HEAD AND HEART
RUNAWAY BUNNY
SHOELESS JOE
THE COST OF DISCIPLESHIP
THE GOOD BOOK
TRUMPET OF THE SWAN
UNDER THE EYE OF THE CLOCK

15 rows selected.
```

You've just learned the basics of **UNION**, **INTERSECT**, and **MINUS**. Now let's go into details. In combining two tables, Oracle does not concern itself with column names on either side of the combination operator—that is, Oracle will require that each **select** statement be valid and have valid columns for its own table(s), but the column names in the first **select** statement do not have to be the same as those in the second. Oracle does have these stipulations:

- The **select** statements must have the same number of columns. If the two tables being queried have differing numbers of columns selected, you can select strings in place of columns to make the two queries' column lists match.

- The corresponding columns in the **select** statements must be the same datatype (they needn't be the same length).

When ordering the output, Oracle uses the column names from the first **select** statement in giving the query results. Consequently, only column names from the first **select** statement can be used in the **order by**.

You can use combination operators with two or more tables, but when you do, precedence becomes an issue, especially if **INTERSECT** and **MINUS** appear. Use parentheses to force the order you want.

IN Subqueries

Combination operators can be used in subqueries, but you must be careful with precedence. A query of the form:

```
select ColA from TABLE_A
 where ColA in
(select Col1 from TABLE_1)
 union
(select Col2 from TABLE_2);
```

is poorly written and ambiguous. Which will be performed first, the **union** of the two queries as part of a single **where** clause, or the **in** clause based on the query of TABLE_1, followed by a **union** of that result with TABLE_2? Use parentheses to clarify your meaning and enforce the proper precedence of operations. The **in** clause is always given a higher precedence than **union**

unless you use parentheses to alter the way the query is executed. If you want the **union** to have higher precedence, use parentheses:

```
select ColA from TABLE_A
 where ColA in
(select Col1 from TABLE_1
 union
 select Col2 from TABLE_2);
```

Restrictions on UNION, INTERSECT, and MINUS

Queries that use a **UNION**, **INTERSECT**, or **MINUS** in their **where** clause must have the same number and type of columns in their **select** list. Note that the equivalent **IN** construction does not have that limitation.

The use of combination operators in place of **IN**, **AND**, and **OR** is a matter of personal style. Most SQL users regard **IN**, **AND**, and **OR** as being clearer and easier to understand than combination operators.

CHAPTER
13

Some Complex
Possibilities

his chapter continues the study of the more complex Oracle functions and features. Of particular interest here is the creation of simple and group queries that can be turned into views, the use of totals in calculations, and the creation of reports showing tree structure. Like the techniques covered in Chapter 12, these techniques are not essential for most reporting needs. If they look overly difficult, don't be frightened off. If you are new to Oracle and the use of its query facilities, it is enough to know that these capabilities exist and you can turn to them if needed.

Complex Groupings

Views can build upon each other. In Chapter 11, you saw the concept of creating a view of a grouping of rows from a table. As shown in Chapter 11, you can easily join views to other views and tables to produce additional views to simplify the task of querying and reporting.

As your groupings grow more complex, you will find that views are invaluable to your coding efforts; they simplify the representation of data at different grouping levels within your application. They also make it easier to use the more advanced statistical functions available in Oracle9i.

Consider the CATEGORY_COUNT view, first encountered in Chapter 11:

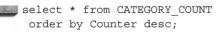

```
create or replace view CATEGORY_COUNT as
select CategoryName, COUNT(*) as Counter
  from BOOKSHELF
 group by CategoryName;

select * from CATEGORY_COUNT;

CATEGORYNAME             COUNTER
-------------------- ----------
ADULTFIC                      6
ADULTNF                      10
ADULTREF                      6
CHILDRENFIC                   5
CHILDRENNF                    1
CHILDRENPIC                   3
```

Order the results by their Counter column values, with the highest first:

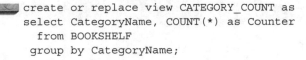

```
select * from CATEGORY_COUNT
  order by Counter desc;

CATEGORYNAME             COUNTER
-------------------- ----------
ADULTNF                      10
ADULTFIC                      6
ADULTREF                      6
CHILDRENFIC                   5
CHILDRENPIC                   3
CHILDRENNF                    1
```

The output shows the ranking of the categories; the ADULTNF category ranks first in terms of the number of books. Without displaying this list, you could determine where a different Counter value would be in the rankings. To do this, we'll use the **RANK** function. As shown in the following listing, the **RANK** function takes a value as its input, and has several additional clauses—**within group** and an **order by** clause that tells Oracle how to do the ranking. Where would a Counter value of 3 rank?

```
select RANK(3) within group
(order by Counter desc)
  from CATEGORY_COUNT;

RANK(3)WITHINGROUP(ORDERBYCOUNTERDESC)
--------------------------------------
                                     5
```

A Counter value of 3 would be the fifth-highest Counter value. How about a Counter value of 8?

```
select RANK(8) within group
(order by Counter desc)
  from CATEGORY_COUNT;

RANK(8)WITHINGROUP(ORDERBYCOUNTERDESC)
--------------------------------------
                                     2
```

Adding those five books to the category would move it up to second place. From a percentile basis, what would the percentile ranking for that category be?

```
select PERCENT_RANK(8) within group
(order by Counter desc)
  from CATEGORY_COUNT;

PERCENT_RANK(8)WITHINGROUP(ORDERBYCOUNTERDESC)
----------------------------------------------
                                    .166666667
```

As expected, it would be in the top one-sixth of the categories.

With this technique of using both summary views and analytic functions, you can create views and reports that include weighted averages, effective yield, percentage of total, percentage of subtotal, and many similar calculations. There is no effective limit to how many views can be built on top of each other, although even the most complex calculations seldom require more than three or four levels of views built upon views. Note that you can also create inline views in the **from** clause, as shown in Chapter 11.

Using Temporary Tables

You can create a table that exists solely for your session, or whose data persists for the duration of your transaction. You can use temporary tables to support specialized rollups or specific application processing requirements.

To create a temporary table, use the **create global temporary table** command. When you create a temporary table, you can specify whether it should last for the duration of your session (via the **on commit preserve rows** clause) or whether its rows should be deleted when the transaction completes (via the **on commit delete rows** clause).

Unlike a permanent table, a temporary table does not automatically allocate space when it is created. Space will be dynamically allocated for the table as rows are inserted:

```
create global temporary table YEAR_ROLLUP (
    Year    NUMBER(4),
    Month   VARCHAR2(9),
    Counter NUMBER)
on commit preserve rows;
```

You can see the duration of your data in YEAR_ROLLUP by querying the Duration column of USER_TABLES for this table. In this case the value of Duration is SYS$SESSION.

Now that the YEAR_ROLLUP table exists, you can populate it, such as via an **insert as select** command with a complex query. You can then query the YEAR_ROLLUP table as part of a join with other tables. You may find this method simpler to implement than the methods shown in the prior sections.

Using ROLLUP, GROUPING, and CUBE

How can you perform grouping operations, such as totals, within a single SQL statement rather than via SQL*Plus commands? As of Oracle8i, you can use the **ROLLUP** and **CUBE** functions to enhance the grouping actions performed within your queries. Let's see how this enables us to manage the data related to the book returns. The book loaner program has become more popular, so the loan time is now limited to 14 days, with a $0.20 fee per extra day. The following report shows the late charges by person:

```
set headsep !
column Name format a20
column Title format a20 word_wrapped
column DaysOut format 999.99 heading 'Days!Out'
column DaysLate format 999.99 heading 'Days!Late'

break on Name skip 1 on report
compute sum of LateFee on Name
set linesize 80
set pagesize 60
set newpage 0

select Name, Title, ReturnedDate,
       ReturnedDate-CheckoutDate as DaysOut /*Count days*/,
       ReturnedDate-CheckoutDate -14  DaysLate,
       (ReturnedDate-CheckoutDate -14)*0.20  LateFee
  from BOOKSHELF_CHECKOUT
 where ReturnedDate-CheckoutDate > 14
 order by Name, CheckoutDate;
```

NAME	TITLE	RETURNEDD	Days Out	Days Late	LATEFEE
DORAH TALBOT	MY LEDGER	03-MAR-02	16.00	2.00	.4
********************					----------
sum					.4
EMILY TALBOT	ANNE OF GREEN GABLES	20-JAN-02	18.00	4.00	.8
********************					----------
sum					.8
FRED FULLER	JOHN ADAMS	01-MAR-02	28.00	14.00	2.8
	TRUMAN	20-MAR-02	19.00	5.00	1
********************					----------
sum					3.8
GERHARDT KENTGEN	WONDERFUL LIFE	02-FEB-02	31.00	17.00	3.4
	THE MISMEASURE OF MAN	05-MAR-02	20.00	6.00	1.2
********************					----------
sum					4.6
JED HOPKINS	INNUMERACY	22-JAN-02	21.00	7.00	1.4
********************					----------
sum					1.4
PAT LAVAY	THE MISMEASURE OF MAN	12-FEB-02	31.00	17.00	3.4
********************					----------
sum					3.4
ROLAND BRANDT	THE SHIPPING NEWS	12-MAR-02	59.00	45.00	9
	THE DISCOVERERS	01-MAR-02	48.00	34.00	6.8
	WEST WITH THE NIGHT	01-MAR-02	48.00	34.00	6.8
********************					----------
sum					22.6

We can eliminate the DaysOut display and focus on the late fees, showing the fees due on each of the return dates:

```
clear compute
clear break
select ReturnedDate, Name,
       SUM((ReturnedDate-CheckoutDate -14)*0.20)  LateFee
  from BOOKSHELF_CHECKOUT
 where ReturnedDate-CheckoutDate > 14
 group by ReturnedDate, Name
 order by ReturnedDate, Name;
```

```
RETURNEDD NAME                    LATEFEE
--------- -------------------- ----------
20-JAN-02 EMILY TALBOT                 .8
22-JAN-02 JED HOPKINS                 1.4
02-FEB-02 GERHARDT KENTGEN            3.4
12-FEB-02 PAT LAVAY                   3.4
01-MAR-02 FRED FULLER                 2.8
01-MAR-02 ROLAND BRANDT              13.6
03-MAR-02 DORAH TALBOT                 .4
05-MAR-02 GERHARDT KENTGEN            1.2
12-MAR-02 ROLAND BRANDT                 9
20-MAR-02 FRED FULLER                   1
```

and then modify it further to group the late fees by month:

```
select TO_CHAR(ReturnedDate,'MONTH'), Name,
       SUM((ReturnedDate-CheckoutDate -14)*0.20)   LateFee
  from BOOKSHELF_CHECKOUT
 where ReturnedDate-CheckoutDate > 14
 group by TO_CHAR(ReturnedDate,'MONTH'), Name;

TO_CHAR(R NAME                    LATEFEE
--------- -------------------- ----------
FEBRUARY  GERHARDT KENTGEN            3.4
FEBRUARY  PAT LAVAY                   3.4
JANUARY   EMILY TALBOT                 .8
JANUARY   JED HOPKINS                 1.4
MARCH     DORAH TALBOT                 .4
MARCH     FRED FULLER                 3.8
MARCH     GERHARDT KENTGEN            1.2
MARCH     ROLAND BRANDT              22.6
```

Instead of simply grouping by Month and Name, you can use the **ROLLUP** function to generate subtotals and totals. In the following example, the **group by** clause is modified to include a **ROLLUP** function call. Notice the additional rows generated at the end of the result set and after each month.

```
select TO_CHAR(ReturnedDate,'MONTH'), Name,
       SUM((ReturnedDate-CheckoutDate -14)*0.20)   LateFee
  from BOOKSHELF_CHECKOUT
 where ReturnedDate-CheckoutDate > 14
 group by ROLLUP(TO_CHAR(ReturnedDate,'MONTH'), Name);

TO_CHAR(R NAME                    LATEFEE
--------- -------------------- ----------
FEBRUARY  GERHARDT KENTGEN            3.4
FEBRUARY  PAT LAVAY                   3.4
FEBRUARY                             6.8
JANUARY   EMILY TALBOT                 .8
JANUARY   JED HOPKINS                 1.4
JANUARY                              2.2
```

```
MARCH        DORAH TALBOT                 .4
MARCH        FRED FULLER                 3.8
MARCH        GERHARDT KENTGEN            1.2
MARCH        ROLAND BRANDT              22.6
MARCH                                     28
                                          37
```

For each month, Oracle has calculated the total LateFee, and shown it with a NULL name value. The output shows two separate charges of $3.40 in February, and a monthly total of $6.80. For the quarter, the total of the late charges is $37.00. You could have calculated these via SQLPLUS commands (see Chapter 6), but this method allows you to generate these sums via a single SQL command regardless of the tool used to query the database.

Let's refine the appearance of the report. You can use the **GROUPING** function to determine whether the row is a total or subtotal (generated by the **ROLLUP**) or corresponds to a **NULL** value in the database. In the **select** clause, the Name column will be selected as follows:

```
select DECODE(GROUPING(Name),1, 'All names',Name),
```

The **GROUPING** function will return a value of 1 if the column's value is generated by a **ROLLUP** action. This query uses **DECODE** (discussed at length in Chapter 17) to evaluate the result of the **GROUPING** function. If the **GROUPING** output is 1, the value was generated by the **ROLLUP** function, and Oracle will print the phrase 'All names'; otherwise, it will print the value of the Name column. We will apply similar logic to the Date column. The full query is shown in the following listing, along with its output:

```
select DECODE(GROUPING(TO_CHAR(ReturnedDate,'MONTH')),1,
         'All months',TO_CHAR(ReturnedDate,'MONTH')),
       DECODE(GROUPING(Name),1, 'All names',Name),
       SUM((ReturnedDate-CheckoutDate -14)*0.20)  LateFee
  from BOOKSHELF_CHECKOUT
 where ReturnedDate-CheckoutDate > 14
 group by ROLLUP(TO_CHAR(ReturnedDate, 'MONTH'), Name);

DECODE(GRO DECODE(GROUPING(NAME),1,'     LATEFEE
---------- ------------------------   ----------
FEBRUARY   GERHARDT KENTGEN              3.4
FEBRUARY   PAT LAVAY                     3.4
FEBRUARY   All names                     6.8
JANUARY    EMILY TALBOT                   .8
JANUARY    JED HOPKINS                   1.4
JANUARY    All names                     2.2
MARCH      DORAH TALBOT                   .4
MARCH      FRED FULLER                   3.8
MARCH      GERHARDT KENTGEN              1.2
MARCH      ROLAND BRANDT                22.6
MARCH      All names                      28
All months All names                      37
```

You can use the **CUBE** function to generate subtotals for all combinations of the values in the **group by** clause. The following query uses the **CUBE** function to generate this information:

```
select DECODE(GROUPING(TO_CHAR(ReturnedDate,'MONTH')),1,
        'All months',TO_CHAR(ReturnedDate,'MONTH')),
     DECODE(GROUPING(Name),1, 'All names',Name),
     SUM((ReturnedDate-CheckoutDate -14)*0.20)  LateFee
  from BOOKSHELF_CHECKOUT
 where ReturnedDate-CheckoutDate > 14
 group by CUBE(TO_CHAR(ReturnedDate, 'MONTH '), Name);
```

```
DECODE(GRO DECODE(GROUPING(NAME),1,'    LATEFEE
---------- ------------------------ ----------
FEBRUARY   GERHARDT KENTGEN               3.4
FEBRUARY   PAT LAVAY                      3.4
FEBRUARY   All names                      6.8
JANUARY    EMILY TALBOT                    .8
JANUARY    JED HOPKINS                    1.4
JANUARY    All names                      2.2
MARCH      DORAH TALBOT                    .4
MARCH      FRED FULLER                    3.8
MARCH      GERHARDT KENTGEN               1.2
MARCH      ROLAND BRANDT                 22.6
MARCH      All names                       28
All months DORAH TALBOT                    .4
All months EMILY TALBOT                    .8
All months FRED FULLER                    3.8
All months GERHARDT KENTGEN               4.6
All months JED HOPKINS                    1.4
All months PAT LAVAY                      3.4
All months ROLAND BRANDT                 22.6
All months All names                       37
```

The **CUBE** function provided the summaries generated by the **ROLLUP** option, plus it shows the sums by Name for the 'All months' category. Being able to perform these summaries in standard SQL greatly enhances your ability to pick the best reporting tool for your users.

Family Trees and connect by

One of Oracle's more interesting but little used or understood facilities is its **connect by** clause. Put simply, it is a method to report in order the branches of a *family tree*. Such trees are encountered often: the genealogy of human families, livestock, horses, corporate management, company divisions, manufacturing, literature, ideas, evolution, scientific research, and theory—even views built upon views.

The **connect by** clause provides a means to report on all of the family members in any of these many trees. It lets you exclude branches or individual members of a family tree, and allows

you to travel through the tree either up or down, reporting on the family members encountered during the trip.

The earliest ancestor in the tree is technically called the *root node.* In everyday English, this would be called the trunk. Extending from the trunk are branches, which have other branches, which have still other branches. The forks where one or more branches split away from a larger branch are called *nodes,* and the very end of a branch is called a *leaf,* or a *leaf node.* Figure 13-1 shows a picture of such a tree.

The following is a table of cows and bulls born between January 1900 and October 1908. As each offspring is born, it is entered as a row in the table, along with its sex, parents (the cow and bull), and birthdate. If you compare the Cows and Offspring in this table with Figure 13-1, you'll find they correspond. EVE has no recorded cow or bull parent, because she was born on a different farm, and ADAM and BANDIT are bulls brought in for breeding, again with no parents in the table.

```
column Cow format a6
column Bull format a6
column Offspring format a10
column Sex format a3

select * from BREEDING
 order by Birthdate;
```

OFFSPRING	SEX	COW	BULL	BIRTHDATE
BETSY	F	EVE	ADAM	02-JAN-00
POCO	M	EVE	ADAM	15-JUL-00
GRETA	F	EVE	BANDIT	12-MAR-01
MANDY	F	EVE	POCO	22-AUG-02
CINDY	F	EVE	POCO	09-FEB-03
NOVI	F	BETSY	ADAM	30-MAR-03
GINNY	F	BETSY	BANDIT	04-DEC-03
DUKE	M	MANDY	BANDIT	24-JUL-04
TEDDI	F	BETSY	BANDIT	12-AUG-05
SUZY	F	GINNY	DUKE	03-APR-06
PAULA	F	MANDY	POCO	21-DEC-06
RUTH	F	GINNY	DUKE	25-DEC-06
DELLA	F	SUZY	BANDIT	11-OCT-08
EVE	F			
ADAM	M			
BANDIT	M			

Next, a query is written to illustrate the family relationships visually. This is done using **LPAD** and a special column, Level, that comes along with **connect by**. Level is a number, from 1 for EVE to 5 for DELLA, that is really the *generation.* If EVE is the first generation of cattle, then DELLA is the fifth generation. Whenever the **connect by** clause is used, the Level column can be used in the **select** statement to discover the generation of each row. Level is a *pseudo-column,* like SysDate and User. It's not really a part of the table, but it is available under specific circumstances. The next listing shows an example of using Level.

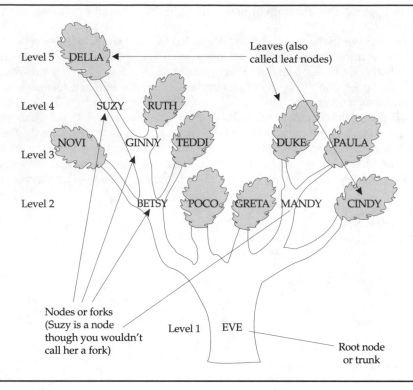

FIGURE 13-1. *Eve's descendants*

The results of this query are apparent in the following table, but why did the **select** statement produce this? How does it work?

```
column Offspring format a30
select Cow, Bull, LPAD(' ',6*(Level-1))||Offspring AS Offspring,
       Sex, Birthdate
  from BREEDING
 start with Offspring = 'EVE'
 connect by Cow = PRIOR Offspring;
```

```
COW    BULL   OFFSPRING                        SEX BIRTHDATE
------ ------ -------------------------------- --- ---------
              EVE                              F
EVE    ADAM         BETSY                      F   02-JAN-00
BETSY  ADAM               NOVI                 F   30-MAR-03
BETSY  BANDIT             GINNY                F   04-DEC-03
GINNY  DUKE                     SUZY           F   03-APR-06
SUZY   BANDIT                         DELLA    F   11-OCT-08
GINNY  DUKE                     RUTH           F   25-DEC-06
BETSY  BANDIT             TEDDI                F   12-AUG-05
```

```
EVE      ADAM          POCO                            M   15-JUL-00
EVE      BANDIT        GRETA                           F   12-MAR-01
EVE      POCO          MANDY                           F   22-AUG-02
MANDY    BANDIT              DUKE                      M   24-JUL-04
MANDY    POCO                PAULA                     F   21-DEC-06
EVE      POCO          CINDY                           F   09-FEB-03
```

Note that this is really Figure 13-1 turned clockwise onto its side. EVE isn't centered, but she is the root node (trunk) of this tree. Her children are BETSY, POCO, GRETA, MANDY, and CINDY. BETSY's children are NOVI, GINNY, and TEDDI. GINNY's children are SUZY and RUTH. And SUZY's child is DELLA. MANDY also has two children, DUKE and PAULA.

This tree started with EVE as the first "offspring." If the SQL statement had said **start with** MANDY, only MANDY, DUKE, and PAULA would have been selected. **start with** defines the beginning of that portion of the tree that will be displayed, and it includes only branches stretching out from the individual that **start with** specifies. **start with** acts just as its name implies.

The **LPAD** in the **select** statement is probably somewhat confusing. Recall from Chapter 7 the format for **LPAD**:

```
LPAD(string,length [,'set'])
```

That is, take the specified *string* and left-pad it for the specified *length* with the specified *set* of characters. If no set is specified, left-pad the string with blanks. Compare this syntax to the **LPAD** in the **select** statement shown earlier:

```
LPAD(' ',6*(Level-1))
```

In this case, the *string* is a single character, a space (indicated by the literal space enclosed in single quotation marks). The 6*(Level-1) is the *length*, and since the **set** is not specified, spaces will be used. In other words, this tells SQL to take this string of one space and left-pad it to the number of spaces determined by 6*(Level-1), a calculation made by first subtracting 1 from the Level and then multiplying this result by 6. For EVE the Level is 1, so 6*(1-1), or 0 spaces, is used. For BETSY, the Level (her generation) is 2, so an **LPAD** of 6 is used. Thus, for each generation after the first, six additional spaces will be concatenated to the left of the Offspring column. The effect is obvious in the result just shown. The name of each Offspring is indented by left-padding with the number of spaces corresponding to its Level or generation.

Why is this done, instead of simply applying the **LPAD** directly to Offspring? For two reasons. First, a direct **LPAD** on Offspring would cause the names of the Offspring to be right-justified. The names at each level would end up having their last letters lined up vertically. Second, if Level-1 is equal to 0, as it is for EVE, the resulting **LPAD** of EVE will be 0 characters wide. EVE will vanish:

```
select Cow, Bull, LPAD(Offspring,6*(Level-1),' ') AS Offspring,
       Sex, Birthdate   from BREEDING
 start with Offspring = 'EVE'
connect by Cow = PRIOR Offspring;

COW     BULL    OFFSPRING                             SEX BIRTHDATE
------  ------  ------------------------------------- --- ---------
                                                      F
EVE     ADAM    BETSY                                 F   02-JAN-00
```

```
BETSY    ADAM            NOVI                      F    30-MAR-03
BETSY    BANDIT          GINNY                     F    04-DEC-03
GINNY    DUKE                    SUZY              F    03-APR-06
SUZY     BANDIT                       DELLA        F    11-OCT-08
GINNY    DUKE                    RUTH              F    25-DEC-06
BETSY    BANDIT          TEDDI                     F    12-AUG-05
EVE      ADAM     POCO                             M    15-JUL-00
EVE      BANDIT   GRETA                            F    12-MAR-01
EVE      POCO     MANDY                            F    22-AUG-02
MANDY    BANDIT          DUKE                      M    24-JUL-04
MANDY    POCO            PAULA                     F    21-DEC-06
EVE      POCO     CINDY                            F    09-FEB-03
```

Thus, to get the proper spacing for each level, to ensure that EVE appears, and to make the names line up vertically on the left, the **LPAD** should be used with the concatenation function, and not directly on the Offspring column.

Now, how does **connect by** work? Look again at Figure 13-1. Starting with NOVI and traveling downward, which cows are the offspring prior to NOVI? The first is BETSY, and the offspring just prior to BETSY is EVE. Even though it is not instantly readable, this clause:

```
connect by Cow = PRIOR Offspring
```

tells SQL to find the next row in which the value in the Cow column is equal to the value in the Offspring column in the prior row. Look at the table and you'll see that this is true.

Excluding Individuals and Branches

There are two methods of excluding cows from a report. One uses the normal **where** clause technique, and the other uses the **connect by** clause itself. The difference is that the exclusion using the **connect by** clause will exclude not just the cow mentioned, but all of its children as well. If you use **connect by** to exclude BETSY, then NOVI, GINNY, TEDDI, SUZY, RUTH, and DELLA all vanish. The **connect by** really tracks the tree structure. If BETSY had never been born, none of her offspring would have been either. In this example, the **and** clause modifies the **connect by** clause:

```
select Cow, Bull, LPAD(' ',6*(Level-1))||Offspring AS Offspring,
       Sex, Birthdate
  from BREEDING
 start with Offspring = 'EVE'
connect by Cow = PRIOR Offspring
   and Offspring != 'BETSY';

COW     BULL    OFFSPRING                          SEX BIRTHDATE
------  ------  ---------------------------------- --- ---------
                EVE                                F
EVE     ADAM          POCO                         M   15-JUL-00
EVE     BANDIT        GRETA                        F   12-MAR-01
EVE     POCO          MANDY                        F   22-AUG-02
MANDY   BANDIT              DUKE                    M   24-JUL-04
```

```
MANDY   POCO                   PAULA                  F    21-DEC-06
EVE     POCO          CINDY                           F    09-FEB-03
```

The **where** clause removes only the cow or cows it mentions. If BETSY dies, she is removed from the chart, but her offspring are not. In fact, notice that BETSY is still there under the Cow column as mother of her children, NOVI, GINNY, and TEDDI:

```
select Cow, Bull, LPAD(' ',6*(Level-1))||Offspring AS Offspring,
       Sex, Birthdate
  from BREEDING
 where Offspring != 'BETSY'
 start with Offspring = 'EVE'
connect by Cow = PRIOR Offspring;
```

```
COW     BULL    OFFSPRING                             SEX BIRTHDATE
------  ------  ------------------------------        --- ---------
                EVE                                   F
BETSY   ADAM                    NOVI                  F    30-MAR-03
BETSY   BANDIT                  GINNY                 F    04-DEC-03
GINNY   DUKE                          SUZY            F    03-APR-06
SUZY    BANDIT                              DELLA     F    11-OCT-08
GINNY   DUKE                          RUTH            F    25-DEC-06
BETSY   BANDIT                  TEDDI                 F    12-AUG-05
EVE     ADAM          POCO                            M    15-JUL-00
EVE     BANDIT        GRETA                           F    12-MAR-01
EVE     POCO          MANDY                           F    22-AUG-02
MANDY   BANDIT                  DUKE                  M    24-JUL-04
MANDY   POCO                   PAULA                  F    21-DEC-06
EVE     POCO          CINDY                           F    09-FEB-03
```

The order in which the family tree is displayed when using **connect by** is basically level by level, left to right, as shown in Figure 13-1, starting with the lowest level, Level 1. For example, you may want to alter this order to collect the cows and their offspring by birthdate:

```
select Cow, Bull, LPAD(' ',6*(Level-1))||Offspring AS Offspring,
       Sex, Birthdate    from BREEDING
 start with Offspring = 'EVE'
connect by Cow = PRIOR Offspring
 order by Cow, Birthdate;
```

```
COW     BULL    OFFSPRING                             SEX BIRTHDATE
------  ------  ------------------------------        --- ---------
BETSY   ADAM                    NOVI                  F    30-MAR-03
BETSY   BANDIT                  GINNY                 F    04-DEC-03
BETSY   BANDIT                  TEDDI                 F    12-AUG-05
EVE     ADAM          BETSY                           F    02-JAN-00
EVE     ADAM          POCO                            M    15-JUL-00
EVE     BANDIT        GRETA                           F    12-MAR-01
EVE     POCO          MANDY                           F    22-AUG-02
EVE     POCO          CINDY                           F    09-FEB-03
```

```
GINNY   DUKE                    SUZY           F   03-APR-06
GINNY   DUKE                    RUTH           F   25-DEC-06
MANDY   BANDIT          DUKE                   M   24-JUL-04
MANDY   POCO            PAULA                  F   21-DEC-06
SUZY    BANDIT                        DELLA    F   11-OCT-08
                EVE                            F
```

The generations are still obvious in the display, but siblings are more closely grouped with each other. Another way to look at the same family tree is by Birthdate, as follows:

```
select Cow, Bull, LPAD(' ',6*(Level-1))||Offspring AS Offspring,
       Sex, Birthdate
  from BREEDING
 start with Offspring = 'EVE'
connect by Cow = PRIOR Offspring
 order by Birthdate;
```

```
COW     BULL    OFFSPRING                      SEX BIRTHDATE
------  ------  -----------------------------  --- ---------
EVE     ADAM        BETSY                      F   02-JAN-00
EVE     ADAM        POCO                       M   15-JUL-00
EVE     BANDIT      GRETA                      F   12-MAR-01
EVE     POCO        MANDY                      F   22-AUG-02
EVE     POCO        CINDY                      F   09-FEB-03
BETSY   ADAM            NOVI                   F   30-MAR-03
BETSY   BANDIT          GINNY                  F   04-DEC-03
MANDY   BANDIT          DUKE                   M   24-JUL-04
BETSY   BANDIT          TEDDI                  F   12-AUG-05
GINNY   DUKE                    SUZY           F   03-APR-06
MANDY   POCO            PAULA                  F   21-DEC-06
GINNY   DUKE                    RUTH           F   25-DEC-06
SUZY    BANDIT                        DELLA    F   11-OCT-08
                EVE                            F
```

Now, the order of the rows no longer shows generations, as in a tree, but the indenting still preserves this information. You can't tell what offspring belong to which parents without looking at the Cow and Bull columns, though. Not knowing Eve's BirthDate clearly disrupts the display of the family tree.

Traveling Toward the Roots

Thus far, the direction of travel in reporting on the family tree has been from parents toward children. Is it possible to start with a child, and move backward to parent, grandparent, great-grandparent, and so on? To do so, the word **prior** is simply moved to the other side of the equal sign. The following traces DELLA's ancestry:

```
select Cow, Bull, LPAD(' ',6*(Level-1))||Offspring AS Offspring,
       Sex, Birthdate
  from BREEDING
```

```
start with Offspring = 'DELLA'
connect by Offspring = PRIOR Cow;

COW     BULL    OFFSPRING                        SEX BIRTHDATE
------  ------  -------------------------------  --- ---------
SUZY    BANDIT  DELLA                             F   11-OCT-08
GINNY   DUKE            SUZY                       F   03-APR-06
BETSY   BANDIT                GINNY               F   04-DEC-03
EVE     ADAM                        BETSY         F   02-JAN-00
                                          EVE     F
```

This shows DELLA's own roots, but is a bit confusing if compared to the previous displays. It looks as if DELLA is the ancestor, and EVE the great-great-granddaughter. Adding an **order by** for Birthdate helps, but EVE is still further to the right:

```
select Cow, Bull, LPAD(' ',6*(Level-1))||Offspring AS Offspring,
       Sex, Birthdate
  from BREEDING
 start with Offspring = 'DELLA'
connect by Offspring = PRIOR Cow
 order by Birthdate;

COW     BULL    OFFSPRING                        SEX BIRTHDATE
------  ------  -------------------------------  --- ---------
EVE     ADAM                        BETSY         F   02-JAN-00
BETSY   BANDIT                GINNY               F   04-DEC-03
GINNY   DUKE            SUZY                       F   03-APR-06
SUZY    BANDIT  DELLA                             F   11-OCT-08
                                          EVE     F
```

The solution is simply to change the calculation in the **LPAD**:

```
select Cow, Bull, LPAD(' ',6*(5-Level))||Offspring Offspring,
       Sex, Birthdate
  from BREEDING
 start with Offspring = 'DELLA'
connect by Offspring = PRIOR Cow
 order by Birthdate;

COW     BULL    OFFSPRING                        SEX BIRTHDATE
------  ------  -------------------------------  --- ---------
EVE     ADAM            BETSY                     F   02-JAN 00
BETSY   BANDIT                GINNY               F   04-DEC-03
GINNY   DUKE                        SUZY          F   03-APR-06
SUZY    BANDIT                              DELLA  F   11-OCT-08
                EVE                               F
```

Finally, look how different this report is when the **connect by** tracks the parentage of the Bull. Here are Adam's offspring:

```
select Cow, Bull, LPAD(' ',6*(Level-1))||Offspring AS Offspring,
       Sex, Birthdate
  from BREEDING
 start with Offspring = 'ADAM'
connect by PRIOR Offspring = Bull;
```

COW	BULL	OFFSPRING		SEX	BIRTHDATE
		ADAM		M	
EVE	ADAM	BETSY		F	02-JAN-00
EVE	ADAM	POCO		M	15-JUL-00
EVE	POCO		MANDY	F	22-AUG-02
EVE	POCO		CINDY	F	09-FEB-03
MANDY	POCO		PAULA	F	21-DEC-06
BETSY	ADAM	NOVI		F	30-MAR-03

ADAM and BANDIT were the original bulls at the initiation of the herd. To create a single tree that reports both ADAM's and BANDIT's offspring, you would have to invent a "father" for the two of them, which would be the root of the tree. One of the advantages that these alternative trees have over the type of tree shown earlier is that many inheritance groups, from families to projects to divisions within companies, can be accurately portrayed in more than one way:

```
select Cow, Bull, LPAD(' ',6*(Level-1))||Offspring AS Offspring,
       Sex, Birthdate
  from BREEDING
 start with Offspring = 'BANDIT'
connect by PRIOR Offspring = Bull;
```

COW	BULL	OFFSPRING		SEX	BIRTHDATE
		BANDIT		M	
EVE	BANDIT	GRETA		F	12-MAR-01
BETSY	BANDIT	GINNY		F	04-DEC-03
MANDY	BANDIT	DUKE		M	24-JUL-04
GINNY	DUKE		SUZY	F	03-APR-06
GINNY	DUKE		RUTH	F	25-DEC-06
BETSY	BANDIT	TEDDI		F	12-AUG-05
SUZY	BANDIT	DELLA		F	11-OCT-08

The Basic Rules

Using **connect by** and **start with** to create tree-like reports is not difficult, but certain basic rules must be followed:

- The order of the clauses when using **connect by** is as follows:

 select
 from

where
start with
connect by
order by

- **prior** forces reporting to be from the root out toward the leaves (if the **prior** column is the parent) or from a leaf toward the root (if the **prior** column is the child).

- A **where** clause eliminates individuals from the tree, but not their descendants (or ancestors, if **prior** is on the right side of the equal sign).

- A qualification in the **connect by** (particularly a not equal) eliminates both an individual and all of its descendants (or ancestors, depending on how you trace the tree).

- **connect by** cannot be used with a table join in the **where** clause.

This particular set of commands is one that few people are likely to remember correctly. However, with a basic understanding of the tree and inheritance, constructing a proper **select** statement to report on a tree should just be a matter of referring to this chapter for correct syntax.

CHAPTER
14

Building a Report in SQL*PLUS

hapter 6 showed basic formatting of reports, and Chapters 3 and 11 gave methods for using groups and views. This chapter looks at more advanced formatting methods as well as more complex computations of weighted averages. This chapter will review the interrelationships among various SQLPLUS commands as well.

Advanced Formatting

Chapter 1 showed an example of a stock table from the newspaper. Here, you will actually manipulate that table to draw non-obvious information from it. For the sake of brevity, the stocks examined will be limited to a small number in three industries: electronics, space, and medical. These are the column commands in effect:

```
column Net format 99.90
column Industry format a11
column Company format a18
column CloseToday heading 'Close|Today' format 999.90
column CloseYesterday heading 'Close|Yest.' format 999.90
column Volume format 999,999,999
```

As shown in Figure 14-1, the first **select** simply retrieves the stocks in the three industries, calculates the difference in closing prices between today and yesterday, and sorts the stocks in order by Industry and Company.

This is a good beginning, but to make it more meaningful, some additional features must be added. A new column is calculated to show the percentage of change between one day's trading and the next day's trading:

```
(CloseToday/CloseYesterday)*100 - 100 AS Percent,
```

The calculation is given the alias Percent, and column formatting is put in place for it. Additionally, both Company and Industry columns are cut back considerably to make room for additional columns, which will be added shortly. Of course, on a wide report, such as one with 132 columns, this may not be necessary. It is done here for space considerations.

```
column Percent heading 'Percent|Change' format 9999.90
column Company format a8 trunc
column Industry heading 'Ind' format a5 trunc
```

See Figure 14-2 for the report including the Percent column and the modified formatting.

break on

Next, a **break on** command is set up to put a blank line between the end of an Industry group and the beginning of the next Industry; the sum of the daily Volume, by Industry, is then computed. Note the coordination between **break on** and **compute sum** in Figure 14-2.

```
select Industry, Company,
       CloseYesterday, CloseToday,
       (CloseToday - CloseYesterday) AS Net,
       Volume    from STOCK
 where Industry in ('ELECTRONICS', 'SPACE', 'MEDICAL')
 order by Industry, Company
/
```

```
                                   Close  Close
INDUSTRY     COMPANY               Yest.  Today   NET       VOLUME
----------   ------------------    ------ ------  ------  -----------
ELECTRONICS  IDK                    95.00  95.25    .25    9,443,523
ELECTRONICS  MEMORY GRAPHICS        15.50  14.25  -1.25    4,557,992
ELECTRONICS  MICRO TOKEN            77.00  76.50   -.50   25,205,667
MEDICAL      AT SPACE               46.75  48.00   1.25   11,398,323
MEDICAL      AUGUST ENTERPRISES     15.00  15.00    .00   12,221,711
MEDICAL      HAYWARD ANTISEPTIC    104.25 106.00   1.75    3,358,561
MEDICAL      KENTGEN BIOPHYSICS     18.25  19.50   1.25    6,636,863
SPACE        BRANDON ELLIPSIS       32.75  33.50    .75   25,789,769
SPACE        GENERAL ENTROPY        64.25  66.00   1.75    7,598,562
SPACE        GENEVA ROCKETRY        22.75  27.25   4.25   22,533,944
SPACE        NORTHERN BOREAL        26.75  28.00   1.25    1,348,323
SPACE        OCKHAM SYSTEMS         21.50  22.00    .50    7,052,990
SPACE        WONDER LABS             5.00   5.00    .00    2,553,712
```

FIGURE 14-1. *Closing stock prices and volumes*

The **break on** and **compute sum** are now expanded, as shown in Figure 14-3. The order of the columns in the **break on** is critical, as will be explained shortly. The **compute sum** has been instructed to calculate the Volume on breaks of both the Industry and Report columns. Volume is shown for each industry, as before, but now a total volume for all industries has been added. The **compute** command has been expanded to allow you to **compute** the sum on **Report**. This must be coordinated with the **break on**:

```
break on Report on Industry skip 1
compute sum of Volume on Industry Report
```

This will produce a sum of Volume for the entire report. This is the **break on** and **compute** that appear in Figure 14-3. The placement of **on Report** in the **break on** command is unimportant: **on Report** will always be the final break.

```
break on Industry skip 1

compute sum of Volume on Industry

select Industry,
       Company,
       CloseYesterday, CloseToday,
       (CloseToday - CloseYesterday) AS Net,
       (CloseToday/CloseYesterday)*100 - 100 AS Percent,
       Volume
  from STOCK
 where Industry in ('ELECTRONICS', 'SPACE', 'MEDICAL')
 order by Industry, Company
/
```

```
              Close   Close          Percent
Ind   COMPANY Yest.   Today   NET    Change        VOLUME
----- ------- ------- ------- ------ -------- ------------
ELECT IDK      95.00   95.25    .25      .26    9,443,523
      MEMORY G 15.50   14.25  -1.25    -8.06    4,557,992
      MICRO TO 77.00   76.50   -.50     -.65   25,205,667
*****                                         ------------
sum                                             39,207,182

MEDIC AT SPACE 46.75   48.00   1.25     2.67   11,398,323
      AUGUST E 15.00   15.00    .00      .00   12,221,711
      HAYWARD 104.25  106.00   1.75     1.68    3,358,561
      KENTGEN  18.25   19.50   1.25     6.85    6,636,863
*****                                         ------------
sum                                             33,615,458

SPACE BRANDON  32.75   33.50    .75     2.29   25,789,769
      GENERAL  64.25   66.00   1.75     2.72    7,598,562
      GENEVA R 22.75   27.25   4.50    19.78   22,533,944
      NORTHERN 26.75   28.00   1.25     4.67    1,348,323
      OCKHAM S 21.50   22.00    .50     2.33    7,052,990
      WONDER L  5.00    5.00    .00      .00    2,553,712
*****                                         ------------
sum                                             66,877,300
```

FIGURE 14-2. *Stock Report with a **break on** Industry and **compute sum** of Volume*

Next, the report is given a top title and a bottom title, using the extensive formatting capabilities of **ttitle** and **btitle**. See the sidebar "ttitle and btitle Formatting Commands" for an explanation of this.

```
ttitle left 'Current Portfolio' -
       right 'March 1st, 2002'      skip 1 -
       center 'Industry Listings  '  skip 2;

btitle left 'portfoli.sql';
```

```
break on Report on Industry skip 1
ttitle left 'Current Portfolio' -
       right 'March 1st, 2002'       skip 1 -
       center 'Industry Listings   '  skip 2;
btitle left 'portfoli.sql';

compute sum of Volume on Industry Report

select Industry,
       Company,
       CloseYesterday,
       CloseToday,
       (CloseToday - CloseYesterday) AS Net,
       (CloseToday/CloseYesterday)*100 - 100 AS Percent,
       Volume
  from STOCK
 where Industry in ('ELECTRONICS', 'SPACE', 'MEDICAL')
 order by Industry, Company
/
```

```
Current Portfolio                          March 1st, 2002
                      Industry Listings
              Close   Close         Percent
Ind  COMPANY  Yest.   Today   NET   Change       VOLUME
---- -------- ------- ------- ----- ------- -----------
ELECT IDK      95.00   95.25   .25    .26     9,443,523
      MEMORY G 15.50   14.25 -1.25  -8.06     4,557,992
      MICRO TO 77.00   76.50  -.50   -.65    25,205,667
*****                                      -----------
sum                                         39,207,182

MEDIC AT SPACE 46.75   48.00  1.25   2.67    11,398,323
      AUGUST E 15.00   15.00   .00    .00    12,221,711
      HAYWARD 104.25  106.00  1.75   1.68     3,358,561
      KENTGEN  18.25   19.50  1.25   6.85     6,636,863
*****                                      -----------
sum                                         33,615,458

SPACE BRANDON  32.75   33.50   .75   2.29    25,789,769
      GENERAL  64.25   66.00  1.75   2.72     7,598,562
      GENEVA R 22.75   27.25  4.50  19.78    22,533,944
      NORTHERN 26.75   28.00  1.25   4.67     1,348,323
      OCKHAM S 21.50   22.00   .50   2.33     7,052,990
      WONDER L  5.00    5.00   .00    .00     2,553,712
*****                                      -----------
sum                                         66,877,300

                                           -----------
                                           139,699,940
portfoli.sql
```

FIGURE 14-3. *Stock report with a **break on** Industry and Report and **compute sum** of Volume*

Order of Columns in break on

You can get into trouble if the order of the columns in **break on** is incorrect. Suppose that you want to report on revenues by company, division, department, and project (where a division has departments, and departments have projects). If you input this:

```
break on Project on Department on Division on Company
```

then the totals for each of these entities would be calculated every time the project changed, and they wouldn't be accumulated totals, only those for the project. This would be worthless. Instead, the **break on** must be in order from the largest grouping to the smallest, like this:

```
break on Company on Division on Department on Project
```

break on Row

SQLPLUS also allows **compute**s and **break**s to be made **on Row**. Like **on Report**, the **break on** and **compute** must be coordinated.

ttitle and btitle Formatting Commands

The results of these **ttitle** and **btitle** commands can be seen later in this chapter in Figure 14-5:

```
ttitle left 'Current Portfolio' -
       right xINDUSTRY                    skip 1 -
       center 'Industry Listings    '    skip 4;
```

left, **right**, and **center** define where the string that follows is to be placed on the page. A dash at the end of a line means another line of title commands follows. **skip** tells how many blank lines to print after printing this line. Text in single quotation marks is printed as is. Words not inside single quotation marks are usually variables. If they've been defined by **accept**, **NEW_VALUE**, or **define**, their values will print in the title. If they have not been defined, the name of the variable will print instead.

```
btitle left 'portfoli.sql on ' xTODAY -
       right 'Page ' format 999 sql.pno;
```

sql.pno is a variable that contains the current page number. Formatting commands can be placed anywhere in a title, and they will control formatting for any variables from there forward in the **ttitle** or **btitle** unless another formatting command is encountered.

For additional options for these commands, look in the Alphabetical Reference at the end of this book under **ttitle**.

Adding Views

In order for the report to be useful, computations of each stock in relation to its industry segment and to the whole are important. Two views are therefore created, shown next. The first summarizes stock Volume, grouped by Industry. The second summarizes total stock volume.

```
create or replace view INDUSTRY as
select Industry, SUM(Volume) AS Volume
  from STOCK
 where Industry in ('ELECTRONICS', 'SPACE', 'MEDICAL')
 group by Industry
/

create or replace view MARKET as
select SUM(Volume) AS Volume
  from STOCK
 where Industry in ('ELECTRONICS', 'SPACE', 'MEDICAL')
/
```

This practice of creating views in a SQLPLUS report is intended only for views that will be repeatedly used. For single-use views, you can create inline views in the **from** clause to achieve your goals (see Chapter 11).

Columns Used with ttitle and btitle

Some additional column definitions are now added, along with a new column, PartOfInd (explained later in the chapter). See Circle A in Figure 14-4.

Two columns that will appear in **ttitle** and **btitle** are put in with the **NEW_VALUE** command. Look at Circle B in Figure 14-4, and its effect in Circle 1 in Figure 14-5. The column Today was used to produce today's date in the **btitle**. How did this work? First of all, Today is an alias for a formatted SysDate in the **select** statement:

```
TO_CHAR(SysDate,'fmMonth ddth, yyyy') AS Today
```

NEW_VALUE placed the contents of the Today column (March 1st, 2002 in this example) into a variable named xToday, which is then used in **btitle**:

```
btitle left 'portfoli.sql on ' xToday -
       right 'Page ' format 999 sql.pno
```

The variable could have had any name. xToday was chosen to make it easy to spot in the listing, but it could even have the same name as the column Today, or something else, such as DateVar or XYZ. **portfoli.sql** is simply the name of the start file used to produce this report. It's a useful practice to print somewhere on the report the name of the start file used to create the report, so that if it needs to be rerun, it can be found quickly.

The last part of **format 999 sql.pno**, **sql.pno**, is a variable that always contains the current page number. You can use it anywhere in either **ttitle** or **btitle**. If you place it in the **btitle** after the word "right," it shows up on the bottom-right corner of each page.

```
column User noprint

column PartOfInd heading 'Part|of Ind' format 999.90  ◄────── Ⓐ

column Today    NEW_VALUE xTODAY noprint format a1 trunc
column Industry NEW_VALUE xINDUSTRY                     ◄────── Ⓑ

ttitle left 'Current Portfolio' -
       right xINDUSTRY              skip 1 -
       center 'Industry Listings  '  skip 4
btitle left 'portfoli.sql on ' xTODAY -
       right 'Page ' format 999 sql.pno

clear breaks  ◄──── Ⓒ
clear computes

break on Report page on Industry page  ◄────── Ⓓ

compute sum of Volume on Report Industry
compute sum of PartOfInd on Industry  ◄────── Ⓔ
compute avg of Net Percent on Industry
compute avg of Net Percent PartOfInd on Report

select S.Industry,
       Company,
       CloseYesterday, CloseToday,
       (CloseToday - CloseYesterday) AS Net,
       (CloseToday - CloseYesterday)*(S.Volume/I.Volume) AS PartOfInd,
       (CloseToday/CloseYesterday)*100 - 100 AS Percent,
       S.Volume,
       TO_CHAR(SysDate,'fmMonth ddth, yyyy') AS Today
  from STOCK S, INDUSTRY I
 where S.Industry = I.Industry
   AND I.Industry in ('ELECTRONICS', 'SPACE', 'MEDICAL')
 order by I.Industry, Company
/
```

FIGURE 14-4. *SQLPLUS commands for report by Industry*

The **format 999** that precedes it designates the format for the page number. Any time a formatting command like this appears in **ttitle** or **btitle**, it defines the format of any number or characters in the variables that follow it, all the way to the end of the **ttitle** or **btitle** command, unless another format command is encountered.

```
Current Portfolio                         2          ELECTRONICS
                        Industry Listings

               Close    Close           Part Percent
   Ind  COMPANY Yest.    Today    NET  of Ind  Change       VOLUME
   ----  ---------- ------- ------- ------ ------- ------- -----------
   ELECT IDK      95.00   95.25    .25     .06     .26    9,443,523
         MEMORY G 15.50   14.25  -1.25    -.15   -8.06    4,557,992
         MICRO TO 77.00   76.50   -.50    -.32    -.65   25,205,667
   *****                        ------ ------- ------- -----------
   avg                            -.50           -2.82
   sum                                    -.41          39,207,182

   portfoli.sql on March 1st, 2002        1              Page     1
```

```
Current Portfolio                         3          MEDICAL
                        Industry Listings

               Close    Close           Part Percent
   Ind  COMPANY Yest.    Today    NET  of Ind  Change       VOLUME
   -----  ---------- ------- ------- ------ ------- ------- -----------
   MEDIC AT SPACE  46.75   48.00   1.25    .42    2.67   11,398,323
         AUGUST E  15.00   15.00    .00    .00     .00   12,221,711
         HAYWARD  104.25  106.00   1.75    .17    1.68    3,358,561
         KENTGEN   18.25   19.50   1.25    .25    6.85    6,636,863
   *****                        ------ ------- ------- -----------
   avg                            1.06           2.80
   sum                                    .85          33,615,458
   portfoli.sql on March 1st, 2002                      Page     2
```

FIGURE 14-5. *Report by Industry, one industry per page*

A Warning About Variables

There are two other items of importance in the **column** command:

```
column Today NEW_VALUE xToday noprint format a1 trunc
```

noprint tells SQLPLUS not to display this column when it prints the results of the SQL statement. Without it, the date would appear on every row of the report. **format a1 trunc** is a bit more esoteric. Dates that have been reformatted by **TO_CHAR** get a default width of about 100 characters (this

FIGURE 14-5. *Report by Industry, one industry per page* (continued)

was discussed in Chapter 9). Even though the **noprint** option is in effect, SQLPLUS gets confused and counts the width of the Today column when deciding whether **linesize** has been exceeded. The effect is to completely foul up the formatting of the rows as they are displayed or printed. By changing the format to **a1 trunc**, you minimize this effect.

The other column with **NEW_VALUE** is Industry. This column already has some column definitions in effect:

```
column Industry heading 'Ind' format a5 trunc
```

And now a new one is added as shown in the following listing (remember that different instructions for a column may be given on several lines).

```
column Industry NEW_VALUE xIndustry
```

Like Today, this **column** command inserts the contents of the column from the **select** statement into a variable called xIndustry. The value in this variable is coordinated with the **break on**. It gets the value of Industry when the *first* row is read, and keeps it until a new value is encountered and the **break on** forces a new page, as shown at Circles 2, 3, and 4 in Figure 14-5.

Here's what SQLPLUS does:

1. Delays printing anything on a page until the **break on** detects a change in the value of Industry or enough rows are retrieved to fill the page.

2. Prints the **ttitle** with the value xIndustry had before the value changed (or the page got full).

3. Moves the value of xIndustry into an OLD_VALUE variable and saves it.

4. Prints the rows on the page.

5. Loads the new value into xIndustry.

6. Prints the **btitle**.

7. Begins collecting rows for the next page, and goes back to the first step.

What this means is that if xIndustry had been placed in the **btitle** instead of the **ttitle**, it would contain the Industry for the following page, instead of the one being printed. MEDICAL (Circle 3) would be at the bottom of page 1, SPACE (Circle 4) would be at the bottom of page 2, and so on. To use the **btitle** properly for column values retrieved in the query, you would use this:

```
column Industry OLD_VALUE xIndustry
```

More on break on and compute

Circle C in Figure 14-4 immediately precedes the **break on** and **compute** commands. Once a **compute** command is in place, it continues to be active until you either clear it or leave SQLPLUS. This means you can have **compute** commands from previous reports that will execute on a current report, producing all sorts of unwanted effects.

The **break on** command also persists, although any new **break on** command will completely replace it. It is good practice to **clear breaks** and **clear computes** just before setting up new ones.

Here are the options available for **break on**:

- **break on** *column*
- **break on row**
- **break on report**

column can be a column name, an alias, or an expression such as **SUBSTR**(Industry,1,4). Each of these options can be followed by one of these actions:

- **skip** *n*
- **skip page**

or by nothing. **break on** *column* produces the action any time the value in the selected column changes. **break on row** forces a break with every row. **break on report** takes the specified action every time a report ends.

The **skip** actions are to skip one or more lines (that is, print them blank) or to go to the top of a new page. Recall from Chapter 3 that **break on** is used only once, with all of the columns and actions you want. See Circle D in Figure 14-4.

The command **compute**, on the other hand, can be reused for each type of computation and for one or more columns at once. Circle E shows a variety of ways in which it can be used. Note how columns appear on either side of the **on** in the **compute** commands. No commas are used anywhere in either **break on** or **compute** commands.

Here are possible computations:

compute avg	compute num
compute count	compute sum
compute max	compute std
compute min	compute var

These have the same meanings for a column in a SQLPLUS report that **AVG()**, **COUNT()**, **MAX()**, **MIN()**, **STDDEV()**, **SUM()**, and **VARIANCE()** have in SQL. All of them except **num** ignore **NULL**s, and none of them is able to use the **DISTINCT** keyword. **compute num** is similar to **compute count**, except that **compute count** produces the count of non-**NULL** rows, and **compute num** produces the count of *all* rows.

Displaying Current breaks and computes

Entering just the word **break** or **compute** in SQLPLUS will cause it to display the **break**s and **compute**s it has in effect at the moment.

Running Several computes at Once

Figure 14-4 contains the following **compute** statements:

```
compute sum of Volume on Report Industry
compute sum of PartOfInd on Industry
compute avg of Net Percent on Industry
compute avg of Net Percent PartOfInd on Report
```

Look at Circles 5 and 6 in Figure 14-5 and you'll see the effects of all of these. Observe that the **avg** calculation for each column appears on one line, and the **sum** (where there is one) appears on the following line. Further, the words **sum** and **avg** appear *under the column* that follows the word **on** in the **compute** statement. They're missing at Circle 6 for the grand totals

because these are made on Report, and Report is not a column, so **sum** and **avg** can't appear under a column.

The Volume **sum** at Circle 5 is just for the Space industry stocks. The Volume **sum** at Circle 6 is for all industries (page 4 of this report contains only the grand totals and averages). Note that the first **compute** here is for the **sum** of one column, Volume, on both Report and Industry. (Incidentally, the order of the columns in a **compute** is irrelevant, unlike in a **break on**.)

The next **compute**, for PartOfInd on Industry, requires some explanation. (PartOfInd refers to its part of the industry point shift or a change in stock price over all the stocks in the industry.) PartOfInd comes from a portion of the **select** statement:

```
(CloseToday - CloseYesterday)*(S.Volume/I.Volume) AS PartOfInd,
```

This calculation weights the net change in a stock versus the other stocks in its Industry, based on the volume traded. Compare the actual Net change between BRANDON and NORTHERN in the SPACE industry. BRANDON changed only .75 but traded over 25 million shares. NORTHERN changed 1.25 but traded only about 1 million shares. The contribution of BRANDON to the upward shift in the SPACE industry is thus considerably greater than that of NORTHERN; this is reflected in the relative values for the two under the PartOfInd column.

Now compare the **sum** of the PartOfInd column, 2.08, with the **avg** of the Net column, 1.46 (from the very next **compute**). Which is more representative of the change in stock price in this industry? It is the **sum** of PartOfInd, because its values are weighted by stock volume. This example is given to show the difference between a simple average in a column and a weighted average, and to show how summary information is calculated. In one case, it is done by averaging; in another it's done by summing.

This is not the place to launch a detailed discussion of weighted averages, percentages, or statistical calculations, but it is appropriate to point out that significant differences will result from various methods of calculation. This will often affect decisions that are being made, so care and caution are in order.

The final **compute** calls for the average of Net, Percent, and PartOfInd on Report. These values are shown at Circle 6 as .88, .19, and 2.66, respectively. Look at the last line of Figure 14-6. This is the same report as that in Figure 14-5, with a few exceptions. It is on one page instead of four; its upper-right title is the date, not the industry segment; and its bottom line has an additional and different result for averages and totals:

```
Market Averages and Totals       1.09       2.66  139,699,940
```

These are the correct results, and they differ from those that are or can be calculated from the columns displayed using *any* **compute** statement, because the **compute** statements lack the weighting of the total industry volume. So, how was this result produced? The answer is in Figure 14-7. At Circle F, the **btitle** was turned off, and at Circle G (just following the **select** that produced the main body of the report) is an additional **select** that includes the label Market Averages and Totals, and a proper calculation of them.

This **select** statement is preceded by **set heading off** and **ttitle off**. These are necessary because a new **select** will normally force a new top title to print. The **set heading off** command is used to turn off the *column* titles that normally would appear above this line. The **btitle** at Circle F had to be turned off before the first **select** executed, because the completion of the first **select** would cause the **btitle** to print before the second **select** could even execute.

```
Current Portfolio                                March 1st, 2002
                       Industry Listings

         Close    Close            Part Percent
Ind COMPANY Yest.   Today   NET  of Ind Change        VOLUME
----- ------- ------- ------- ------ ------- ------- ------------
ELECT IDK      95.00   95.25    .25    .06     .26    9,443,523
      MEMORY G 15.50   14.25  -1.25   -.15   -8.06    4,557,992
      MICRO TO 77.00   76.50   -.50   -.32    -.65   25,205,667
*****                         ------ ------- ------- ------------
avg                            -.50          -2.82
sum                                   -.41           39,207,182

MEDIC AT SPACE 46.75   48.00   1.25    .42    2.67   11,398,323
      AUGUST E 15.00   15.00    .00    .00     .00   12,221,711
      HAYWARD 104.25  106.00   1.75    .17    1.68    3,358,561
      KENTGEN  18.25   19.50   1.25    .25    6.85    6,636,863
*****                         ------ ------- ------- ------------
avg                            1.06           2.80
sum                                    .85           33,615,458

SPACE BRANDON  32.75   33.50    .75    .29    2.29   25,789,769
      GENERAL  64.25   66.00   1.75    .20    2.72    7,598,562
      GENEVA R 22.75   27.25   4.50   1.52   19.78   22,533,944
      NORTHERN 26.75   28.00   1.25    .03    4.67    1,348,323
      OCKHAM S 21.50   22.00    .50    .05    2.33    7,052,990
      WONDER L  5.00    5.00    .00    .00     .00    2,553,712
*****                         ------ ------- ------- ------------
avg                            1.46           5.30
sum                                   2.08           66,877,300

                              ------ ------- ------- ------------
avg                             .88    .19    2.66
sum                                                 139,699,940

Market Averages and Totals     1.09          2.66  139,699,940
```

FIGURE 14-6. *Revised report with correct market averages and totals*

```
column User noprint
column Today    NEW_VALUE xTODAY noprint format a1 trunc
column Industry NEW_VALUE xINDUSTRY
column Net format 99.90
column Industry format a11
column Company format a18
column CloseToday heading 'Close|Today' format 999.90
column CloseYesterday heading 'Close|Yest.' format 999.90
column Volume format 999,999,999
column Percent heading 'Percent|Change' format 9999.90
```

FIGURE 14-7. *How the correct market averages and totals were produced*

```
column Company format a8 trunc
column Industry heading 'Ind' format a5 trunc

ttitle left 'Current Portfolio'    right xTODAY skip 1 -
       center 'Industry Listings'      skip 2;

btitle off  ◄──────── (F)

clear breaks
clear computes

break on Report on Industry skip 1

compute sum of Volume on Report Industry
compute sum of PartOfInd on Industry
compute avg of Net Percent on Industry
compute avg of Net Percent PartOfInd on Report

select S.Industry,
       Company,
       CloseYesterday, CloseToday,
       (CloseToday - CloseYesterday) AS Net,
       (CloseToday - CloseYesterday)*(S.Volume/I.Volume) AS PartOfInd,
       (CloseToday/CloseYesterday)*100 - 100 AS Percent,
       S.Volume, User,
       To_CHAR(SysDate,'fmMonth ddth, yyyy') AS Today
  from STOCK S, INDUSTRY I
 where S.Industry = I.Industry
   AND I.Industry in ('ELECTRONICS', 'SPACE', 'MEDICAL')
 order by I.Industry, Company
/
set heading off
ttitle off
clear computes
select 'Market Averages and Totals    ',          ◄──────── (G)
       SUM(((CloseToday-CloseYesterday)*S.Volume)/M.Volume) AS Net,
       '           ',
       AVG((CloseToday/CloseYesterday))*100 - 100 AS Percent,
       SUM(S.Volume) AS Volume
  from STOCK S, MARKET M
 where Industry in ('ELECTRONICS', 'SPACE', 'MEDICAL')
/
```

FIGURE 14-7. *How the correct market averages and totals were produced* (continued)

As shown in the sample report outputs in this chapter (Figures 14-2, 14-3, 14-5, and 14-6), when a **compute** command is used, the computed value is labeled with the function that was executed. For example, in Figure 14-6, both an **AVG** and a **SUM** function are computed; the output shows a label of "avg" for the **AVG** calculation, and "sum" for the **SUM** calculation. You can override the default labels and specify your own labels for computed functions in the **compute**

command. See the **label** clause of **compute** in the Alphabetical Reference for details. To avoid having the **compute** commands apply to the Volume column of the second query, the **clear computes** command is executed after the first query.

set termout off and set termout on

Another useful pair of commands is **set termout off** and **set termout on**. The former is often used in a start file just before the **spool** command, and the latter is often used just after it. The effect is to suppress the display of the report to the screen. For reports that are going to be printed, this saves time (they'll run faster) and avoids the annoying rolling of data across the screen. The spooling to a file continues to work properly.

Variables in SQLPLUS

If you're using SQLPLUS interactively, you can check on the current **ttitle** and **btitle** at any time by typing their names alone on a line. SQLPLUS immediately shows you their contents:

```
ttitle
ttitle OFF and is the following 92 characters:

left 'Current Portfolio'    right xTODAY
skip 1          center 'Industry Listings'      skip 2
```

Note the presence of xTODAY, which is a variable, rather than its current contents. SQLPLUS is capable of storing and using many variables—those used in **ttitle** and **btitle** are only some of them. The current variables and their values can be discovered by typing **define**:

```
define
DEFINE _SQLPLUS_RELEASE = "900010000" (CHAR)
DEFINE _EDITOR          = "Notepad" (CHAR)
DEFINE _O_VERSION       = "Oracle9i Enterprise Edition Release 9.0.1.0.0
With the Partitioning option
JServer Release 9.0.1.0.0 - Beta" (CHAR)
DEFINE _O_RELEASE       = "900010000" (CHAR)
DEFINE XINDUSTRY        = "SPACE" (CHAR)
DEFINE XTODAY           = "April 10th, 2002" (CHAR)
```

The _EDITOR variable is the editor you use when you type the word **edit**. You saw how to set this up in your login.sql file back in Chapter 6. The other variables identify which version and release of Oracle you are using.

The last variables are defined in the stock market queries, and their contents are just those displayed in the reports. SQLPLUS stores variables for **ttitle** and **btitle** by defining them as equal to some value, and then allows you to use them whenever a query is being executed. In fact, variables can be used many places in a report other than in titles.

Suppose your stock database were updated automatically by a pricing service, and you wanted to check regularly the closing prices and volumes on a stock-by-stock basis. This could be easily accomplished with variables in the **where** clause. Normally, you would type this query:

```
select Company, CloseYesterday, CloseToday, Volume
   from STOCK  where Company = 'IDK';
```

```
                        Close   Close
COMPANY                 Yest.   Today       VOLUME
------------------      -------  -------  ------------
IDK                     95.00   95.25    9,443,523
```

Alternatively, you could type this into a start file named, for example, closing.sql:

```
set heading on
column CloseToday heading 'Close|Today' format 999.90
column CloseYesterday heading 'Close|Yest.' format 999.90
column Volume format 999,999,999
column Company format a20

accept xCompany prompt 'Enter Company name: '

select Company, CloseYesterday, CloseToday, Volume
   from STOCK
 where Company = '&xCompany';
```

In this file, xCompany is a variable you have invented, such as xIndustry or xToday. **accept** tells SQLPLUS to accept input from the keyboard, and **prompt** tells it to display a message. Note that the variable name must be preceded by the ampersand (&) when it appears in the SQL **select** statement, but not when it appears in the **accept** or in a title. Then, when you type this:

```
start closing.sql
```

the screen displays this:

```
Enter Company name:
```

You then type **MEMORY GRAPHICS**. SQLPLUS will display the following:

```
select Company, CloseYesterday, CloseToday, Volume
   from STOCK
 where Company = '&xCompany';

old    3:   where Company = '&xCompany'
new    3:   where Company = 'MEMORY GRAPHICS'
```

```
                        Close   Close
COMPANY                 Yest.   Today       VOLUME
------------------      -------  -------  ------------
MEMORY GRAPHICS         15.50   14.25    4,557,992
```

First, it shows you the query you have set up. Next, it shows you the **where** clause—first with the variable in it, and then with the value you typed. Finally, it shows you the results of the query.

If you then typed **start closing.sql** again, but typed **IDK** for Company name, the **old** and **new** would show this:

```
old    3:   where Company = '&xCompany'
new    3:   where Company = 'IDK'
```

and the result would be for IDK. It is unnecessary for the **select** and the **old** and **new** to be displayed each time. Both of these can be controlled, the first by the **set echo** command and the second by **set verify**. To see what these are set at currently, type the **show** command followed by the keyword **verify** or **echo**:

```
show verify
verify ON

show echo
echo OFF
```

The revised version of the start file looks like this:

```
column CloseToday heading 'Close|Today' format 999.90
column CloseYesterday heading 'Close|Yest.' format 999.90
column Volume format 999,999,999
column Company format a20
set echo off
set verify off
set sqlcase upper
accept xCompany prompt 'Enter Company name: '

select Company, CloseYesterday, CloseToday, Volume
  from STOCK
 where Company = '&xCompany';
```

set sqlcase upper tells SQLPLUS to convert anything keyed into the variable (using the **accept**) to uppercase before executing the query. This can be helpful if you've stored your data in uppercase (which is a good practice) but don't want to force people to type in uppercase any time they run a query. Now when the start file is executed, this is what happens:

```
start closing.sql

Enter Company name: memory graphics

                          Close    Close
COMPANY                   Yest.    Today       VOLUME
------------------        -------  -------  ------------
MEMORY GRAPHICS           15.50    14.25    4,557,992
```

The use of variables in start files can be very helpful, particularly for reports in which the basic format of the report stays the same but certain parameters change, such as date, company division, stock name, project, client, and so on. When the report starts, it asks the person using it for these

details and then it runs. As just shown, typing only the word **define** will result in a list of all the variables currently defined. Typing **define** with just one name will show only that variable's contents:

```
define xCompany

DEFINE XCOMPANY        = "memory graphics" (CHAR)
```

After a start file has completed, any variables are held by SQLPLUS until you exit or intentionally **undefine** them:

```
undefine xCompany
```

An attempt now to see the variable's value produces the following:

```
define xCompany

SP2-0135: symbol xcompany is UNDEFINED
```

You also can define a variable within the start file without using the **accept** command. Simply assign a value directly, as shown here:

```
define xCompany = 'IDK'
```

Any place that &xCompany appears in the start file will have IDK substituted.

Other Places to Use Variables

Any variable that you define using either **accept** or **define** can be used directly in a **btitle** or **ttitle** command without using the **NEW_VALUE** column command. **NEW_VALUE** simply takes the contents of a column and issues its own **define** command for the variable name following **NEW_VALUE**. The single difference in using the variable in titles, as opposed to the SQL statement, is that in titles the variable is not preceded by an ampersand.

Variables also can be used in a setup start file, as explained later in this chapter in "Using mask.sql."

Numeric Formatting

The default method SQLPLUS uses for formatting numbers is to right-justify them in a column, without commas, using decimal points only if the number is not an integer. The table NUMBERTEST contains columns named Value1 and Value2, which have identical numbers in each column. These will be used to show how numeric formatting works. The first query shows the default formatting:

```
select Value1, Value2 from NUMBERTEST;

      VALUE1        VALUE2
------------  ------------
           0             0
       .0001         .0001
        1234          1234
```

```
       1234.5          1234.5

       1234.56         1234.56
       1234.567        1234.567
      98761234.6       98761234.6
```

Row five is **NULL**. Notice how the decimal point moves from row to row. Just as columns can be formatted individually in queries, the default format can be changed:

```
set numformat 9,999,999

select Value1, Value2 from NUMBERTEST;

     VALUE1       VALUE2
 ----------   ----------
          0            0
          0            0
      1,234        1,234
      1,235        1,235

      1,235        1,235
      1,235        1,235
 ##########   ##########
```

Now, row eight is filled with pound signs. The problem with row eight is that the format defined is too narrow. You can fix this by adding another digit on the left, as shown here:

```
set numformat 99,999,999

select Value1, Value2 from NUMBERTEST;

      VALUE1        VALUE2
 -----------   -----------
           0             0
           0             0
       1,234         1,234
       1,235         1,235

       1,235         1,235
       1,235         1,235
  98,761,235    98,761,235
```

Using mask.sql

Columns used in one report may also need to be used regularly in several reports. Instead of retyping the formatting commands for these columns in every start file, it can be useful to keep all the basic column commands in a single file. This file might be called mask.sql, because it contains formatting (also called *masking*) information for columns. For example, the file might look like the following:

```
REM      File mask.sql
set numwidth 12
set numformat 999,999,999.90

column Net format 99.90
column Industry format a11
column Company format a18
column CloseToday heading 'Close|Today' format 999.90
column CloseYesterday heading 'Close|Yest.' format 999.90
column Volume format 999,999,999

define xDepartment = 'Systems Planning Dept. 3404'
```

This is then effectively embedded in a start file (usually near the top) simply by including this line:

```
start mask.sql
```

show all and spooling

You've seen several commands that use the **set** command, and whose current status can be determined using the **show** command, such as **feedback**, **echo**, **verify**, **heading**, and so on. There are actually about 50 such commands that can be **set**. These can all be displayed at once using this:

```
show all
```

Unfortunately, these fly by so quickly on the screen that it's impossible to read most of them. You can solve this problem by spooling. Simply **spool** to a file, as in the previous example, execute **show all**, and then **spool off**. You can now look at the current status of all the **set** commands using your editor on the file. You can look up these commands in the Alphabetical Reference at the end of this book under **set**. The rows returned by the **show all** command will be ordered alphabetically.

As an alternative, you can use the **store** command described in Chapter 6 to save your current SQLPLUS environment settings to a file (like mask.sql). You can then execute this file at a later date to reset your environment settings.

Folding onto New Lines

Information retrieved from a database is often just fine with only one line of column titles, and columns of data stacked below them. Occasionally, however, a different kind of layout is preferable. Sometimes, this can be accomplished using literal columns of nothing but blank spaces, to properly position real data on more than one line and have it line up properly. These literal columns are given an alias in the SQL and then a blank heading in the **column** command. The technique parallels what was done for the total line in Figure 14-6. For example, look at this:

```
column Industry format a14 trunc
column B format a21 heading ' '
column Company format a20
column Volume format 999,999,999 justify left
set linesize 60
```

```
select Industry, ' ' AS B,
       Company,
       CloseYesterday, CloseToday,
       (CloseToday - CloseYesterday) AS Net,
       Volume
  from STOCK
 where Industry in ('ADVERTISING','GARMENT')
 order by Industry, Company;

INDUSTRY                                COMPANY
-------------- --------------------     --------------------
  CLOSEYESTERDAY      CLOSETODAY           NET VOLUME
-------------- --------------- --------------- -----------
ADVERTISING                             AD SPECIALTY
          31.75           31.75             .00  18,333,876

                                        MBK COMMUNICATIONS
          43.25           41.00           -2.25  10,022,980

                                        NANCY LEE FEATURES
          13.50           14.25             .75  14,222,692

GARMENT                                 ROBERT JAMES APPAREL
          23.25           24.0             .75  19,032,481
```

A literal column of one space, given an alias of *B*, is defined by the **column** command as 21 characters wide with a blank heading. This is used specifically to move the company names over so that the columns line up as desired, with stock Volume directly below the Company name, and column B for CloseToday and Net lining up with the blank.

fold_after and fold_before

Next, look at how the column command **fold_after** affects every column in the **select**. Notice how the **fold_after** essentially puts these columns on their own lines.

```
clear columns
column Net format 99.90
column A format a15 fold_after 1
column Company format a20 fold_after 1
column CloseToday heading 'Close|Today' format 999.90 -
   fold_after
column CloseYesterday heading 'Close|Yest.' format 999.90 -
   fold_after 1
column Net fold_after 1
column Volume format 999,999,999 fold_after 1
set heading off
```

```
select  Industry||',' AS A,
        Company,
        CloseYesterday,
        CloseToday, (CloseToday - CloseYesterday) AS Net,
        Volume
   from STOCK
  where Industry in ('ADVERTISING','GARMENT')
  order by Industry, Company;
```

The previous query produces the following output. Note that even though CloseToday had no number following its **fold_after** clause, SQLPLUS used a default of 1.

```
ADVERTISING,
AD SPECIALTY
   31.75
   31.75
    .00
   18,333,876

ADVERTISING,
MBK COMMUNICATIONS
   43.25
   41.00
  -2.25
   10,022,980

ADVERTISING,
NANCY LEE FEATURES
   13.50
   14.25
    .75
   14,222,692

GARMENT,
ROBERT JAMES APPAREL
   23.25
   24.00
    .75
   19,032,481
```

Additional Reporting Controls

Many of the commands illustrated here, as well as in other chapters, have options considerably beyond those used in these examples. All of the options for each of these commands can be found in the Alphabetical Reference, under the individual command names.

CHAPTER
15

Changing Data:
insert, update,
merge, and delete

ntil now, virtually everything you've learned about Oracle, SQL, and SQLPLUS has related to selecting data from tables in the database. This chapter shows how to *change* the data in a table: how to insert new rows, update the values of columns in rows, and delete rows entirely. Although these topics have not been covered explicitly, nearly everything you already know about SQL, including datatypes, calculations, string formatting, **where** clauses, and the like can be used here, so there really isn't much new to learn. Oracle gives you a transparent, distributed database capability that inserts, updates, and deletes data in remote databases as well (see Chapter 22). As you'll see in this chapter, Oracle9i introduces two new capabilities in this area: multitable inserts and the **merge** command to support inserts and updates in a single command.

insert

The SQL command **insert** lets you place a row of information directly into a table (or indirectly, through a view). The COMFORT table tracks temperatures at noon and midnight and daily precipitation, city by city, for four sample dates through the year:

```
describe COMFORT
```

Name	Null?	Type
CITY	NOT NULL	VARCHAR2(13)
SAMPLEDATE	NOT NULL	DATE
NOON		NUMBER(3,1)
MIDNIGHT		NUMBER(3,1)
PRECIPITATION		NUMBER

To add a new row to this table, use this:

```
insert into COMFORT
values ('WALPOLE', '21-MAR-01'),
       56.7, 43.8, 0);

1 row created.
```

The word **values** must precede the list of data to be inserted. A character string must be in single quotation marks. Numbers can stand by themselves. Each field is separated by commas, and the fields must be in the same order as the columns are when the table is described.

A date must be in single quotation marks and in the default Oracle date format. To insert a date not in the default format, use the **TO_DATE** function, with a formatting mask, as shown in the following:

```
insert into COMFORT
values ('WALPOLE', TO_DATE('06/22/2001','MM/DD/YYYY'),
       56.7, 43.8, 0);

1 row created.
```

Inserting a Time

Inserting dates without time values will produce a default time of midnight, the very beginning of the day. If you want to insert a date with a time other than midnight, simply use the **TO_DATE** function and include a time:

```
insert into COMFORT
values ('WALPOLE', TO_DATE('06/22/2001 1:35',
        'MM/DD/YYYY HH24:MI'), 56.7, 43.8, 0);

1 row created.
```

> **NOTE**
> *To store fractional seconds, you can use the TIMESTAMP and TIMESTAMP WITH TIME ZONE datatypes, as described in Chapter 9.*

Columns also can be inserted out of the order they appear when described, if you first (before the word **values**) list the order the data is in. This doesn't change the fundamental order of the columns in the table. It simply allows you to list the data fields in a different order. (See Part IV for information on inserting data into user-defined datatypes.)

You also can "insert" a **NULL**. This simply means the column will be left empty for this row, as shown in the following:

```
insert into COMFORT
        (SampleDate,  Precipitation, City, Noon, Midnight)
values ('23-SEP-01', NULL,
        'WALPOLE', 86.3, 72.1);

1 row created.
```

insert with select

You also can insert information that has been selected from a table. Here, a mix of columns selected from the COMFORT table, together with literal values for SampleDate (22-DEC-01) and City (WALPOLE), are inserted. Note the **where** clause in the **select** statement, which will retrieve only one row. Had the **select** retrieved five rows, five new ones would have been inserted; it ten rows had been retrieved, then ten new rows would have been inserted; and so on.

```
insert into COMFORT
        (SampleDate, Precipitation, City, Noon, Midnight)
select '22-DEC-01', Precipitation,
        'WALPOLE', Noon, Midnight
  from COMFORT
 where City = 'KEENE'
   and SampleDate = '22-DEC-01';

1 row created.
```

NOTE
*You cannot use the **insert into...select from** syntax with LONG datatypes unless you are using the **TO_LOB** function to insert the LONG data into a LOB column.*

Of course, you don't need to simply insert the value in a selected column. You can modify the column using any of the appropriate string, date, or number functions within the **select** statement. The results of those functions are what will be inserted. You can attempt to **insert** a value in a column that exceeds its width (for character datatypes) or its magnitude (for number datatypes). You have to fit within the constraints you defined on your columns. These attempts will produce a "value too large for column" or "mismatched datatype" error message. If you now query the COMFORT table for the city of Walpole, the results will be the records you inserted:

```
select * from COMFORT
 where City = 'WALPOLE';

CITY          SAMPLEDAT     NOON   MIDNIGHT PRECIPITATION
------------- --------- ---------- ---------- -------------
WALPOLE       21-MAR-01     56.7       43.8             0
WALPOLE       22-JUN-01     56.7       43.8             0
WALPOLE       22-JUN-01     56.7       43.8             0
WALPOLE       23-SEP-01     86.3       72.1
WALPOLE       22-DEC-01     -7.2       -1.2           3.9

5 rows selected.
```

There are two records shown for '22-JUN-01' because one of them has a time component. Use the TO_CHAR function to see the time:

```
select City, SampleDate,
       TO_CHAR(SampleDate,'HH24:MI:SS') AS TimeofDay, Noon
  from COMFORT
 where City = 'WALPOLE';

CITY          SAMPLEDAT TIMEOFDA       NOON
------------- --------- -------- ----------
WALPOLE       21-MAR-01 00:00:00       56.7
WALPOLE       22-JUN-01 00:00:00       56.7
WALPOLE       22-JUN-01 01:35:00       56.7
WALPOLE       23-SEP-01 00:00:00       86.3
WALPOLE       22-DEC-01 00:00:00       -7.2
```

Using the APPEND Hint to Improve insert Performance

As you will learn in Chapter 38, Oracle uses an optimizer to determine the most efficient way to perform each SQL command. For **insert** statements, Oracle tries to insert each new record into an existing block of data already allocated to the table. This execution plan optimizes the use of space required to store the data. However, it may not provide adequate performance for an **insert**

with a **select** command that inserts multiple rows. You can override the execution plan by using the APPEND hint to improve the performance of large inserts. The APPEND hint will tell the database to find the last block into which the table's data has ever been inserted. The new records will be inserted starting in the next block following the last previously used block. Since the data is being written into new blocks of the table, there is much less space management work for the database to do during the **insert**. Therefore, the **insert** may complete faster when the APPEND hint is used.

You specify the APPEND hint within the **insert** command. A hint looks like a comment—it starts with /* and ends with */. The only difference is that the starting set of characters includes a + before the name of the hint. The following example shows an **insert** command whose data is appended to the table:

```
insert /*+ APPEND */ into BOOKSHELF (Title)
select Title from BOOK_ORDER
 where Title not in (select Title from BOOKSHELF);
```

The records from the BOOK_ORDER table will be inserted into the BOOKSHELF table. Instead of attempting to reuse previously used space within the BOOKSHELF table, the new records will be placed at the end of the table's physical storage space.

Since the new records will not attempt to reuse available space that the table has already used, the space requirements for the BOOKSHELF table may increase. In general, you should use the APPEND hint only when inserting large volumes of data into tables with little reusable space. The point at which appended records will be inserted is called the table's *high-water mark*—and the only way to reset the high-water mark is to **truncate** the table. Since **truncate** will delete all records and cannot be rolled back, you should make sure you have a backup of the table's data prior to performing the **truncate**. See **truncate** in the Alphabetical Reference for further details.

rollback, commit, and autocommit

When you insert, update, or delete data from the database, you can reverse, or *roll back,* the work you've done. This can be very important when an error is discovered. The process of committing or rolling back work is controlled by two SQLPLUS commands, **commit** and **rollback**. Additionally, SQLPLUS has the facility to automatically commit your work without your explicitly telling it to do so. This is controlled by the **autocommit** feature of **set**. Like other **set** features, you can **show** it, like this:

```
show autocommit

autocommit OFF
```

OFF is the default. You can also specify a number for the **autocommit** value; this value will determine the number of commands after which Oracle will issue a **commit**. This means **insert**s, **update**s, and **delete**s are not made final until you **commit** them:

```
commit;

commit complete
```

Until you **commit**, only you can see how your work affects the tables. Anyone else with access to these tables will continue to get the old information. You will see *new* information whenever you **select** from the table. Your work is, in effect, in a "staging" area, which you interact with until you **commit**. You can do quite a large number of **insert**s, **update**s, and **delete**s, and still undo the work (return the tables to the way they used to be) by issuing this command:

```
rollback;

rollback complete
```

However, the message "rollback complete" can be misleading. It means only that Oracle has rolled back any work that hasn't been committed. If you **commit** a series of transactions, either explicitly with the word **commit** or implicitly by another action, the "rollback complete" message won't really mean anything.

Using savepoints

You can use *savepoints* to roll back portions of your current set of transactions. Consider the following commands:

```
insert into COMFORT
values ('WALPOLE', '22-APR-01',50.1, 24.8, 0);

savepoint A;

insert into COMFORT
values ('WALPOLE', '27-MAY-01',63.7, 33.8, 0);

savepoint B;

insert into COMFORT
values ('WALPOLE', '07-AUG-01',83.0, 43.8, 0);
```

Now, select the data from COMFORT for Walpole:

```
select * from COMFORT
  where City = 'WALPOLE';
```

CITY	SAMPLEDAT	NOON	MIDNIGHT	PRECIPITATION
WALPOLE	21-MAR-01	56.7	43.8	0
WALPOLE	22-JUN-01	56.7	43.8	0
WALPOLE	22-JUN-01	56.7	43.8	0
WALPOLE	23-SEP-01	86.3	72.1	
WALPOLE	22-DEC-01	-7.2	-1.2	3.9
WALPOLE	22-APR-01	50.1	24.8	0
WALPOLE	27-MAY-01	63.7	33.8	0
WALPOLE	07-AUG-01	83	43.8	0

The output shows the five former records plus the three new rows we've added. Now roll back just the last insert:

```
rollback to savepoint B;
```

If you now query COMFORT, you'll see that the last **insert** has been rolled back, but the others are still there:

```
select * from COMFORT
 where City = 'WALPOLE';
```

CITY	SAMPLEDAT	NOON	MIDNIGHT	PRECIPITATION
WALPOLE	21-MAR-01	56.7	43.8	0
WALPOLE	22-JUN-01	56.7	43.8	0
WALPOLE	22-JUN-01	56.7	43.8	0
WALPOLE	23-SEP-01	86.3	72.1	
WALPOLE	22-DEC-01	-7.2	-1.2	3.9
WALPOLE	22-APR-01	50.1	24.8	0
WALPOLE	27-MAY-01	63.7	33.8	0

The last two records are still not committed; you need to execute a **commit** command or another command to force a commit to occur. You can still roll back the second insert (to savepoint A) or roll back all of the inserts (via a **rollback** command).

Implicit commit

The actions that will force a **commit** to occur, even without your instructing it to, are **quit**, **exit** (the equivalent of **quit**), and any Data Definition Language (DDL) command. Using any of these commands forces a **commit**.

Auto rollback

If you've completed a series of **insert**s, **update**s, or **delete**s, but have not yet explicitly or implicitly committed them, and you experience serious difficulties, such as a computer failure, Oracle will automatically roll back any uncommitted work. If the machine or database goes down, it does this as cleanup work the next time the database is brought back up.

Multitable Inserts

As of Oracle9i, you can perform multiple inserts in a single command. You can perform all of the inserts unconditionally or you can specify conditions—using a **when** clause to tell Oracle how to manage the multiple inserts. If you specify **all**, then all of the **when** clauses will be evaluated; specifying **first** tells Oracle to skip subsequent **when** clauses after it finds one that is true for the row being evaluated. You can also use an **else** clause to tell Oracle what to do if none of the **when** clauses evaluates to true.

To illustrate this functionality, let's create a new table with a slightly different structure than COMFORT:

```
drop table COMFORT_TEST;
create table COMFORT_TEST (
City            VARCHAR2(13) NOT NULL,
SampleDate      DATE NOT NULL,
Measure         VARCHAR2(10),
Value           NUMBER(3,1)
);
```

COMFORT_TEST will have multiple records for each record in COMFORT—its Measure column will have values like 'Midnight', 'Noon', and 'Precip', allowing us to store a greater number of measures for each city on each sample date.

Now populate COMFORT_TEST with data from COMFORT, unconditionally:

```
insert ALL
        into COMFORT_TEST (City, SampleDate, Measure, Value)
      values (City, SampleDate, 'NOON', Noon)
        into COMFORT_TEST (City, SampleDate, Measure, Value)
      values (City, SampleDate, 'MIDNIGHT', Midnight)
        into COMFORT_TEST (City, SampleDate, Measure, Value)
      values (City, SampleDate, 'PRECIP', Precipitation)
select City, SampleDate, Noon, Midnight, Precipitation
  from COMFORT
 where City = 'KEENE';

12 rows created.
```

This query tells Oracle to insert multiple rows for each row returned from the COMFORT table. The query of COMFORT returns four rows. The first **into** clause inserts the Noon value, along with a text string of 'NOON' in the Measure column. The second **into** clause inserts the Midnight values, and the third inserts the Precipitation values, as shown in the query of COMFORT_TEST following the **insert**:

```
select * from COMFORT_TEST;

CITY          SAMPLEDAT MEASURE         VALUE
------------- --------- ---------- ----------
KEENE         21-MAR-01 NOON            39.9
KEENE         22-JUN-01 NOON            85.1
KEENE         23-SEP-01 NOON            99.8
KEENE         22-DEC-01 NOON            -7.2
KEENE         21-MAR-01 MIDNIGHT        -1.2
KEENE         22-JUN-01 MIDNIGHT        66.7
KEENE         23-SEP-01 MIDNIGHT        82.6
KEENE         22-DEC-01 MIDNIGHT        -1.2
KEENE         21-MAR-01 PRECIP           4.4
KEENE         22-JUN-01 PRECIP           1.3
```

```
KEENE          23-SEP-01 PRECIP
KEENE          22-DEC-01 PRECIP              3.9

12 rows selected.
```

What if you had used the **first** keyword instead of the **all** keyword? Unless you use **when** clauses, you can't use the **first** keyword. The following example shows the use of the **when** clause to restrict which **insert**s are performed within the multi-insert command. For this example, the **all** keyword is used:

```
delete from COMFORT_TEST;
commit;

insert ALL
        when Noon > 80 then
          into COMFORT_TEST (City, SampleDate, Measure, Value)
        values (City, SampleDate, 'NOON', Noon)
        when Midnight > 70 then
          into COMFORT_TEST (City, SampleDate, Measure, Value)
        values (City, SampleDate, 'MIDNIGHT', Midnight)
        when Precipitation is not null then
          into COMFORT_TEST (City, SampleDate, Measure, Value)
        values (City, SampleDate, 'PRECIP', Precipitation)
select City, SampleDate, Noon, Midnight, Precipitation
  from COMFORT
 where City = 'KEENE';

6 rows created.
```

What six rows were inserted? The two Noon values that met this condition:

```
        when Noon > 80 then
```

and the one Midnight value that met this condition:

```
        when Midnight > 70 then
```

and the three Precipitation values that met this condition:

```
        when Precipitation is not null then
```

You can see the results in COMFORT_TEST:

```
select * from COMFORT_TEST;

CITY            SAMPLEDAT MEASURE         VALUE
-------------   --------- ----------- ----------
KEENE           22-JUN-01 NOON              85.1
KEENE           23-SEP-01 NOON              99.8
```

```
KEENE          23-SEP-01 MIDNIGHT          82.6
KEENE          21-MAR-01 PRECIP             4.4
KEENE          22-JUN-01 PRECIP             1.3
KEENE          22-DEC-01 PRECIP             3.9
```

What if you had used **first** instead?

```
delete from COMFORT_TEST;
commit;

insert FIRST
        when Noon > 80 then
          into COMFORT_TEST (City, SampleDate, Measure, Value)
        values (City, SampleDate, 'NOON', Noon)
        when Midnight > 70 then
          into COMFORT_TEST (City, SampleDate, Measure, Value)
        values (City, SampleDate, 'MIDNIGHT', Midnight)
        when Precipitation is not null then
          into COMFORT_TEST (City, SampleDate, Measure, Value)
        values (City, SampleDate, 'PRECIP', Precipitation)
select City, SampleDate, Noon, Midnight, Precipitation
  from COMFORT
 where City = 'KEENE';

4 rows created.
```

Four rows are inserted:

```
select * from COMFORT_TEST;

CITY          SAMPLEDAT MEASURE         VALUE
------------- --------- ---------- ----------
KEENE         21-MAR-01 PRECIP           4.4
KEENE         22-DEC-01 PRECIP           3.9
KEENE         22-JUN-01 NOON            85.1
KEENE         23-SEP-01 NOON            99.8
```

What happened to the MIDNIGHT value? The only record that passed the MIDNIGHT **when** clause:

```
        when Midnight > 70 then
```

also passed the NOON **when** clause:

```
        when Noon > 80 then
```

so its Noon value (99.8) was inserted. Since the **first** keyword was used, and the condition that was evaluated first (Noon), was true, Oracle did not check the rest of the conditions for that row. The same process happened to the PRECIP measures—the other non-NULL Precipitation value was on the same record as the Noon reading of 85.1.

What if none of the conditions had been met? To show that option, let's create a third table, COMFORT2, with the same structure as COMFORT:

```
create table COMFORT2 (
City          VARCHAR2(13) NOT NULL,
SampleDate    DATE NOT NULL,
Noon          NUMBER(3,1),
Midnight      NUMBER(3,1),
Precipitation NUMBER
);
```

Now, we'll execute an **insert** for all cities (using the **first** clause) along with an **else** clause specifying that any rows that fail the conditions will be placed into the COMFORT2 table. For this example, the **when** conditions are changed to limit the number of rows that pass the conditions.

```
delete from COMFORT_TEST;
delete from COMFORT2;
commit;

insert FIRST
       when Noon > 80 then
          into COMFORT_TEST (City, SampleDate, Measure, Value)
       values (City, SampleDate, 'NOON', Noon)
       when Midnight > 100 then
          into COMFORT_TEST (City, SampleDate, Measure, Value)
       values (City, SampleDate, 'MIDNIGHT', Midnight)
       when Precipitation >100 then
          into COMFORT_TEST (City, SampleDate, Measure, Value)
       values (City, SampleDate, 'PRECIP', Precipitation)
    else
          into COMFORT2
select City, SampleDate, Noon, Midnight, Precipitation
  from COMFORT
where City = 'KEENE';

4 rows created.
```

The feedback tells you how many rows were created, but not which table they were created in. The total reported is for all inserts combined. In this case, two records were inserted into COMFORT_TEST and two were inserted into COMFORT2 because of the **else** condition:

```
select * from COMFORT_TEST;

CITY            SAMPLEDAT MEASURE        VALUE
-------------   --------- ----------  ----------
KEENE           22-JUN-01 NOON             85.1
KEENE           23-SEP-01 NOON             99.8
```

```
select * from COMFORT2;

CITY          SAMPLEDAT      NOON   MIDNIGHT PRECIPITATION
------------- ---------  ---------- ---------- -------------
KEENE         21-MAR-01      39.9       -1.2           4.4
KEENE         22-DEC-01      -7.2       -1.2           3.9
```

delete

Removing a row or rows from a table requires the **delete** command, as seen in the examples in the last section. The **where** clause is essential to removing only the rows you intend. **delete** without a **where** clause will empty the table completely. The following command deletes the Walpole entries from the COMFORT table.

```
delete from COMFORT where City = 'WALPOLE';
```

Of course, a **where** clause in a **delete**, just as in an **update** or a **select** that is part of an **insert**, can contain as much logic as any **select** statement, and may include subqueries, unions, intersects, and so on. You can always **rollback** a bad **insert**, **update**, or **delete**, but you really should experiment with the **select** before actually making the change to the database, to make sure you are doing the right thing.

Now that you've just deleted the rows where City = 'WALPOLE', you can test the effect of that **delete** with a simple query:

```
select * from COMFORT
 where City = 'WALPOLE';

no rows selected
```

Now **rollback** the **delete** and run the same query:

```
rollback;
rollback complete

select * from COMFORT
 where City = 'WALPOLE';

CITY          SAMPLEDAT      NOON   MIDNIGHT PRECIPITATION
------------- ---------  ---------- ---------- -------------
WALPOLE       21-MAR-01      56.7       43.8             0
WALPOLE       22-JUN-01      56.7       43.8             0
WALPOLE       22-JUN-01      56.7       43.8             0
WALPOLE       23-SEP-01      86.3       72.1
WALPOLE       22-DEC-01      -7.2       -1.2           3.9
```

```
WALPOLE        22-APR-01        50.1        24.8                0
WALPOLE        27-MAY-01        63.7        33.8                0
```

7 rows selected.

This illustrates that recovery is possible, so long as a **commit** hasn't occurred.

An additional command for deleting records, **truncate**, does not behave the same as **delete**. Whereas **delete** allows you to **commit** or **rollback** the deletion, **truncate** automatically deletes all records from the table. The action of the **truncate** command cannot be rolled back or committed; the truncated records are unrecoverable. See the **truncate** command in the Alphabetical Reference for further details.

update

update requires setting specific values for each column you want to change, and specifying which row or rows you want to affect by using a carefully constructed **where** clause:

```
update COMFORT set Precipitation = .5, Midnight = 73.1
  where City = 'KEENE'
    and SampleDate = '22-DEC-2001';
```

1 row updated.

Here is the effect, shown in the 22-DEC-01 record:

```
select * from COMFORT
  where City = 'KEENE';
```

CITY	SAMPLEDAT	NOON	MIDNIGHT	PRECIPITATION
KEENE	21-MAR-01	39.9	-1.2	4.4
KEENE	22-JUN-01	85.1	66.7	1.3
KEENE	23-SEP-01	99.8	82.6	
KEENE	22-DEC-01	-7.2	73.1	.5

4 rows selected.

What if you later discover that the thermometer used in Keene consistently reports its temperatures too high by one degree? You also can do calculations, string functions, and almost any other legitimate function in setting a value for the **update** (just as you can for an **insert**, or in the **where** clause of a **delete**). Here, each temperature in Keene is decreased by one degree:

```
update COMFORT set Midnight = Midnight - 1, Noon = Noon - 1
  where City = 'KEENE';
```

4 rows updated.

Here is the effect of the **update**:

```
select * from COMFORT
  where City = 'KEENE';

CITY           SAMPLEDAT       NOON   MIDNIGHT PRECIPITATION
-------------  ---------  ----------  ---------- -------------
KEENE          21-MAR-01       38.9       -2.2          4.4
KEENE          22-JUN-01       84.1       65.7          1.3
KEENE          23-SEP-01       98.8       81.6
KEENE          22-DEC-01       -8.2       72.1           .5
```

NOTE
*If your **update** violates the column definitions or constraints, it will fail. In this case, setting Noon or Midnight to values of 100 or greater will violate the numeric scale of the columns.*

As with **delete**, the **where** clause is critical. Without one, every row in the database will be updated. With an improperly constructed **where** clause, the wrong rows will be updated, often in ways that are hard to discover or fix, especially if your work has been committed. Always **set feedback on** when doing **update**s, and look at the feedback to be sure the number of rows updated is what you expected it to be. Query the rows after you **update** to see if the expected change took place.

update with Embedded select

It is possible to set values in an **update** by embedding a **select** statement right in the middle of it. Note that this **select** has its own **where** clause, picking out the temperature for the city of MANCHESTER from the WEATHER table, and the **update** has its own **where** clause to affect just the city of Keene on a certain day:

```
update COMFORT set Midnight =
        (select Temperature
           from WEATHER
          where City = 'MANCHESTER')
 where City = 'KEENE'
   and SampleDate = '22-DEC-01';

1 row updated.
```

Here is the effect of the **update**:

```
select * from COMFORT
  where City = 'KEENE';
```

CITY	SAMPLEDAT	NOON	MIDNIGHT	PRECIPITATION
KEENE	21-MAR-01	38.9	-2.2	4.4
KEENE	22-JUN-01	84.1	65.7	1.3
KEENE	23-SEP-01	98.8	81.6	
KEENE	22-DEC-01	-8.2	66	.5

```
4 rows selected.
```

When using subqueries with **update**s, you must be certain that the subquery will return no more than one record for each of the records to be updated; otherwise, the **update** will fail. See Chapter 12 for details on correlated queries.

You also can use an embedded **select** to **update** multiple columns at once. The columns must be in parentheses and separated by a comma, as shown here:

```
update COMFORT set (Noon, Midnight) =
        (select Humidity, Temperature
           from WEATHER
          where City = 'MANCHESTER')
 where City = 'KEENE'
   and SampleDate = '22-DEC-01';
```

```
1 row updated.
```

Here is the effect:

```
select * from COMFORT
 where City = 'KEENE';
```

CITY	SAMPLEDAT	NOON	MIDNIGHT	PRECIPITATION
KEENE	21-MAR-01	38.9	-2.2	4.4
KEENE	22-JUN-01	84.1	65.7	1.3
KEENE	23-SEP-01	98.8	81.6	
KEENE	22-DEC-01	98	66	.5

```
4 rows selected.
```

update with NULL

You also can update a table and set a column equal to **NULL**. This is the sole instance of using the equal sign with **NULL**, instead of the word "is." For example,

```
update COMFORT set Noon = NULL
  where City = 'KEENE'
```

```
      and SampleDate = '22-DEC-01';

1 row updated.
```

will set the noon temperature to **NULL** for Keene on December 22, 2001.

> **NOTE**
> *The primary issues with **insert**, **update**, and **delete** are careful
> construction of **where** clauses to affect (or **insert**) only the rows you
> really want, and the normal use of SQL functions within these **insert**s,
> **update**s, and **delete**s. It is extremely important that you exercise
> caution about committing work before you are certain it is correct.
> These commands extend the power of Oracle well beyond simple
> queries, and allow direct manipulation of data.*

Using the merge Command

As of Oracle9i, you can use the **merge** command to perform **insert**s and **update**s into a single
table in a single command. Based on the conditions you specify, Oracle will take the source
data—either a table, view, or a query—and update existing values if the conditions are met. If
the conditions are not met, the row will be inserted.

For the example, change the rows in the COMFORT2 table created earlier in this chapter:

```
update COMFORT2 set Noon = 55;
insert into COMFORT2 values ('KEENE', '16-MAY-01', 55, 55, 1);
commit;
```

The data in COMFORT2 should now look like this:

```
select * from COMFORT2;
```

CITY	SAMPLEDAT	NOON	MIDNIGHT	PRECIPITATION
KEENE	21-MAR-01	55	-2.2	4.4
KEENE	22-DEC-01	55	66	.5
KEENE	16-MAY-01	55	55	1

The Keene data in COMFORT is:

```
select * from COMFORT where City = 'KEENE';
```

CITY	SAMPLEDAT	NOON	MIDNIGHT	PRECIPITATION
KEENE	21-MAR-01	38.9	-2.2	4.4
KEENE	22-JUN-01	84.1	65.7	1.3

```
KEENE          23-SEP-01      98.8        81.6
KEENE          22-DEC-01                    66            .5
```

With COMFORT2 as the data source, we can now perform a **merge** on the COMFORT table. For the rows that match (the '21-MAR-01' and '22-DEC-01' entries, we'll update the Noon values in COMFORT. The rows that exist only in COMFORT2 (the '16-MAY-01' row) will be inserted into COMFORT. The following listing shows the command to use.

```
merge into COMFORT    C1
using (select City, SampleDate, Noon, Midnight,
              Precipitation from COMFORT2)    C2
   on (C1.City = C2.City and C1.SampleDate=C2.SampleDate)
 when matched then
      update set Noon = C2.Noon
 when not matched then
      insert (C1.City, C1.SampleDate, C1.Noon,
              C1.Midnight, C1.Precipitation)
      values (C2.City, C2.SampleDate, C2.Noon,
              C2.Midnight, C2.Precipitation);

3 rows merged.
```

The output tells you the number of rows processed from the source table, but does not tell you how many rows were inserted or updated. You can see the changes by querying COMFORT (note the Noon=55 records):

```
select * from COMFORT where City = 'KEENE';
```

CITY	SAMPLEDAT	NOON	MIDNIGHT	PRECIPITATION
KEENE	21-MAR-01	55	-2.2	4.4
KEENE	22-JUN-01	84.1	65.7	1.3
KEENE	23-SEP-01	98.8	81.6	
KEENE	22-DEC-01	55	66	.5
KEENE	16-MAY-01	55	55	1

Take a look at the command to see how this was accomplished. In the first line, the target table is named and given an alias of C1:

```
merge into COMFORT    C1
```

In the next two lines, the **using** clause provides the source data for the **merge**, and the source is given the alias C2:

```
using (select City, SampleDate, Noon, Midnight,
              Precipitation from COMFORT2)    C2
```

The condition for the merge is then specified in the **on** clause. If the source data's City and SampleDate values match those in the target table, then the data will be updated. The **when matched then** clause, followed by an **update** command, tells Oracle what columns to update in the source table:

```
   on (C1.City = C2.City and C1.SampleDate=C2.SampleDate)
when matched then
      update set Noon = C2.Noon
```

If there is no match, then the row should be inserted, as specified in the **when not matched** clause:

```
when not matched then
        insert (C1.City, C1.SampleDate, C1.Noon,
               C1.Midnight, C1.Precipitation)
        values (C2.City, C2.SampleDate, C2.Noon,
               C2.Midnight, C2.Precipitation);
```

You can use the **merge** command to simplify operations in which many rows are inserted and updated from a single source. As with all **update**s, you should be very careful to use the appropriate **where** clauses in the **using** clause of your **merge** commands.

CHAPTER
16

Advanced Use of
Functions and
Variables

n previous chapters, you've seen definitions and examples for character, number, and date functions, as well as for the use of variables. The examples ranged from simple to fairly complex, and enough explanation was provided so that you could construct rather sophisticated combined functions on your own.

This chapter expands on some of the earlier uses and shows examples of how functions can be combined to solve more difficult problems. Oracle has made solving some of these problems easier using SQL itself, but the examples in this chapter can expand your thinking about how to apply functions to solve real problems.

Functions in order by

Functions can be used in an **order by** to change the sorting sequence. Here, these **SUBSTR** functions cause the list of authors to be put in alphabetical order by first name:

```
select Author
  from MAGAZINE
 order by SUBSTR(Author,INSTR(Author,',')+2);

AUTHOR
------------------------
WHITEHEAD, ALFRED
BONHOEFFER, DIETRICH
CHESTERTON, G.K.
RUTH, GEORGE HERMAN
CROOKES, WILLIAM
```

Bar Charts and Graphs

You also can produce simple bar charts and graphs in SQLPLUS, using a mix of **LPAD** and a numeric calculation. The following bar chart shows the average number of days books have been checked out by each patron. First, look at the column formatting commands that will be used:

```
column Name format a16
column DaysOut Format 999
column Graph Heading 'Day|    1    2    3    4    5    6    7-
|....0....0....0....0....0....0....0' justify c
column Graph format a35
```

The first two of these commands (lines) are straightforward. The third requires some explanation. The dash at the end of the third line tells SQLPLUS the **column** command is wrapped onto the next line. If the dash appears at the end of a line, SQLPLUS assumes that it means another line of this command follows. Here is the SQL statement that produced the horizontal bar chart in the following listing.

```
select Name,
       AVG(ReturnedDate-CheckOutDate) DaysOut,
```

```
       LPAD('o',ROUND(AVG(ReturnedDate-CheckOutDate)/2,0),'o')
          AS Graph
  from BOOKSHELF_CHECKOUT
group by Name
order by AVG(ReturnedDate-CheckOutDate);
```

| | | Day | | | | | | |
| | | 1 | 2 | 3 | 4 | 5 | 6 | 7 |
NAME	DAYSOUT	o....o....o....o....o....o....o
DORAH TALBOT	13	ooooooo
EMILY TALBOT	14	ooooooo
JED HOPKINS	18	ooooooooo
GERHARDT KENTGEN	19	ooooooooo
PAT LAVAY	21	oooooooooo
FRED FULLER	24	oooooooooooo
ROLAND BRANDT	52	oooooooooooooooooooooooooo

```
7 rows selected.
```

This use of **LPAD** is similar to what was done in Chapter 13, where the cows and bulls were shown in their family tree. Basically, a lowercase *o* is the column here, and it is padded on the left with a number of additional lowercase *o*'s, to the maximum width determined by **ROUND**(AVG(ReturnedDate-CheckOutDate)/2,0).

Notice that the scale of the column heading is in increments of two. A simple change to the SQL will produce a classic graph rather than a bar chart. The literal column is changed from an *o* to a lowercase *x*, and the padding on the left is done by spaces.

```
select Name,
       AVG(ReturnedDate-CheckOutDate) DaysOut,
       LPAD('x',ROUND(AVG(ReturnedDate-CheckOutDate)/2,0),' ')
          AS Graph
  from BOOKSHELF_CHECKOUT
group by Name
order by AVG(ReturnedDate-CheckOutDate);
```

| | | Day | | | | | | |
| | | 1 | 2 | 3 | 4 | 5 | 6 | 7 |
NAME	DAYSOUT	o....o....o....o....o....o....o
DORAH TALBOT	13	x
EMILY TALBOT	14	x
JED HOPKINS	18	x
GERHARDT KENTGEN	19	x
PAT LAVAY	21	x
FRED FULLER	24	x
ROLAND BRANDT	52	x

```
7 rows selected.
```

Another way to graph the data is by its distribution rather than by person. First, a view is created that puts each number of days out into its decile. Thus 13, 14, 18, and 19 become 10; 20 through 29 become 20; 30 through 39 become 30; and so on:

```
create or replace view DaysOutRange as
select ROUND((ReturnedDate-CheckOutDate),-1) Decile,
       COUNT(*) Counter
  from BOOKSHELF_CHECKOUT
 group by ROUND((ReturnedDate-CheckOutDate),-1);
```

Next, a column heading is set up, similar to the previous heading although shorter and in increments of one:

```
column Graph Heading 'Count|         1     1|....5....0....5'-
justify c
column Graph format a15
```

The next SQL determines the count of values that are represented in each decile.

```
select Decile, Counter,
       LPAD('o',Counter,'o') AS Graph
  from DAYSOUTRANGE;

                         Count
                           1     1
    DECILE     COUNTER ....5....0....5
---------- ---------- ----------------
        10          8 oooooooo
        20          5 ooooo
        30          3 ooo
        50          2 oo
        60          1 o
```

If one of the dates were **NULL**, the **group by** output would include a **NULL** group, with a count and display similar to those shown in this listing. If you want to customize how Oracle handles books with **NULL** ReturnedDate values, you can use the **NVL** function to replace the **NULL** value with one of your choosing (such as SysDate). For more complex data replacement logic, you can use **DECODE** and **CASE**, as introduced later in this chapter and more fully described in Chapter 17.

Using TRANSLATE

TRANSLATE converts characters in a string into different characters, based on a substitution plan you give it, from *if* to *then*:

```
TRANSLATE(string,if,then)
```

In the following SQL, the letters in a sentence are replaced. Any time an uppercase *T* is detected, it is replaced by an uppercase *T*. In effect, nothing changes. Any time an uppercase vowel is detected, however, it is replaced by a lowercase version of the same vowel. Any letter not in the TAEIOU string is left alone. When a letter is found in TAEIOU, its position is checked in the TAEIOU string, and the letter there is substituted. Thus, the letter *E*, at position 3 in TAEIOU, is replaced by *e*, in position 3 of Taeiou:

```
select TRANSLATE('NOW VOWELS ARE UNDER ATTACK','TAEIOU','Taeiou')
   from DUAL;

TRANSLATE('NOWVOWELSAREUNDE
---------------------------
NoW VoWeLS aRe uNDeR aTTaCK
```

Eliminating Characters

Extending this logic, what happens if the *if* string is TAEIOU and the *then* string is only *T* ? Checking for the letter *E* (as in the word VOWELS) finds it in position 3 of TAEIOU. There is no position 3 in the *then* string (which is just the letter *T*), so the value in position 3 is nothing. So *E* is replaced by nothing. This same process is applied to all of the vowels. They appear in the *if* string, but not in the *then* string. As a result, they disappear, as shown here:

```
select TRANSLATE('NOW VOWELS ARE UNDER ATTACK','TAEIOU','T')
   from DUAL;

TRANSLATE('NOWVOWE
------------------
NW VWLS R NDR TTCK
```

This feature of **TRANSLATE**, the ability to eliminate characters from a string, can prove very useful in cleaning up data. Recall the magazine titles in Chapter 7:

```
select Title from MAGAZINE;

TITLE
-------------------------------------
THE BARBERS WHO SHAVE THEMSELVES.
"HUNTING THOREAU IN NEW HAMPSHIRE"
THE ETHNIC NEIGHBORHOOD
RELATIONAL DESIGN AND ENTHALPY
"INTERCONTINENTAL RELATIONS."
```

The method used in Chapter 7 to clean out the periods and double quotes was a nested combination of **LTRIM** and **RTRIM**:

```
select LTRIM( RTRIM(Title,'."') ,'"') from MAGAZINE;
```

The same goal can be accomplished with a single use of **TRANSLATE**:

```
select TRANSLATE(Title,'T".','T') AS TITLE
   from MAGAZINE;

TITLE
----------------------------------------
THE BARBERS WHO SHAVE THEMSELVES
HUNTING THOREAU IN NEW HAMPSHIRE
THE ETHNIC NEIGHBORHOOD
RELATIONAL DESIGN AND ENTHALPY
INTERCONTINENTAL RELATIONS
```

In the listing, you have to include one character in the *then* string—in this case, the letter *T* translates to the letter *T*. All other characters in the *if* set are eliminated.

Complex Cut and Paste

The NAME table contains a list of names as you might receive them from a mailing list company or another application. First name, last name, and initials are all in one column:

```
column Name format a25

select Name from NAME;

NAME
-------------------------
HORATIO NELSON
VALDO
MARIE DE MEDICIS
FLAVIUS JOSEPHUS
EDYTHE P. M. GAMMIERE
```

Suppose you want to cut and paste these names and put them into a table with FirstName and LastName columns. How would you go about it? The technique you learned in Chapter 7 involved using **INSTR** to locate a space, and using the number it returns in a **SUBSTR** to clip out the portion up to that space. Here's an attempt to do just that for the first name:

```
select SUBSTR(Name,1,INSTR(Name,' '))
   from NAME;

SUBSTR(NAME,1,INSTR(NAME,
-------------------------
HORATIO

MARIE
FLAVIUS
EDYTHE
```

VALDO has vanished! The problem is that these names are not as consistent as the authors' names were in Chapter 7. One of these names (probably a magician) is only one name long, so there is no space for the **INSTR** to find. When **INSTR** has an unsuccessful search, it returns a 0. The **SUBSTR** of the name VALDO, starting at position 1 and going for 0 positions, is nothing, so he disappears. This is solved with **DECODE**. In place of this:

```
INSTR(Name,' ')
```

you put the entire expression, like this:

```
DECODE(INSTR(Name,' '),0,99,INSTR(Name,' '))
```

DECODE's format is this:

```
DECODE(value,if1,then1[,if2,then2,if3,then3]...,else)
```

In the preceding example, **DECODE** tests the value of **INSTR**(Name, ' '). If it is equal to 0, **DECODE** substitutes 99; otherwise, it returns the default value, which is also **INSTR**(Name, ' '). The choice of 99 as a substitute is arbitrary. It will create an effective **SUBSTR** function for VALDO that looks like this:

```
SUBSTR('VALDO',1,99)
```

This works because **SUBSTR** will clip out text from the starting number, 1, to the ending number or the end of the string, whichever comes first. With the **DECODE** function in place, the first names are retrieved correctly:

```
select SUBSTR(Name,1,
       DECODE(INSTR(Name,' '),0,99,INSTR(Name,' ')))
  from NAME;

SUBSTR(NAME,1,DECODE(INST
-------------------------
HORATIO
VALDO
MARIE
FLAVIUS
EDYTHE
```

How about the last names? You could use **INSTR** again to search for a space, and use the location of the space in the string, plus one (+1), as the starting point for **SUBSTR**. No ending point is required for **SUBSTR**, because you want it to go to the end of the name. This is what happens:

```
select SUBSTR(Name,INSTR(Name,' ')+1)
  from NAME;
```

```
SUBSTR(NAME,INSTR(NAME,''
--------------------------
NELSON
VALDO
DE MEDICIS
JOSEPHUS
P. M. GAMMIERE
```

This didn't quite work. One solution is to use three **INSTR** functions, looking successively for the first, second, or third occurrence of a space in the name. Each of these **INSTR**s will return either the location where it found a space or a 0 if it didn't find any. In a name with only one space, the second and third **INSTR**s will both return 0. The **GREATEST** function, therefore, will pick the number returned by the **INSTR** that found the space furthest into the name:

```
select SUBSTR(Name,
GREATEST(INSTR(Name,' '),INSTR(Name,' ',1,2),
        INSTR(Name,' ',1,3)) +1)
  from NAME;

SUBSTR(NAME,GREATEST(INST
-------------------------
NELSON
VALDO
MEDICIS
JOSEPHUS
GAMMIERE
```

Except for the fact that you also got VALDO again, this worked. (**GREATEST** also could have been used similarly in place of **DECODE** in the previous example.) There is a second and simpler method:

```
select SUBSTR(Name,INSTR(Name,' ',-1)+1)
  from NAME;

SUBSTR(NAME,INSTR(NAME,''
-------------------------
NELSON
VALDO
MEDICIS
JOSEPHUS
GAMMIERE
```

The -1 in the **INSTR** tells it to start its search in the final position and go *backward*, or right to left, in the Name column. When it finds the space, **INSTR** returns its position, counting from the left as usual. The -1 simply makes **INSTR** start searching from the end rather than from the beginning. A -2 would make it start searching from the second position from the end, and so on.

The +1 in the **SUBSTR** command has the same purpose as in the previous example: Once the space is found, **SUBSTR** has to move one position to the right to begin clipping out the Name. If no space is found, the **INSTR** returns 0, and **SUBSTR** therefore starts with position 1. That's why VALDO made the list.

How do you get rid of VALDO? Add an ending position to the **SUBSTR** instead of its default (which goes automatically all the way to the end). The ending position is found by using this:

```
DECODE(INSTR(Name,' '),0,0,LENGTH(Name))
```

which says, "Find the position of a space in the Name. If the position is 0, return 0; otherwise, return the **LENGTH** of the Name." For VALDO, the **DECODE** produces 0 as the ending position for **SUBSTR**, so nothing is displayed. For any other name, because there is a space somewhere, the **LENGTH** of the Name becomes the ending position for the **SUBSTR**, so the whole last name is displayed.

This is similar to the **DECODE** used to extract the first name, except that the value 99 used there has been replaced by **LENGTH**(Name), which will always work, whereas 99 would fail for a name longer than 99 characters. This won't matter here, but in other uses of **DECODE** and **SUBSTR**, it could be important:

```
select SUBSTR(Name,
       INSTR(Name,' ',-1)+1,
       DECODE(INSTR(Name,' '), 0, 0, LENGTH(Name)))
  from NAME;

SUBSTR(NAME,INSTR(NAME,''
------------------------
NELSON

MEDICIS
JOSEPHUS
GAMMIERE
```

This **DECODE** also could have been replaced by a **GREATEST**:

```
select SUBSTR(Name,
       INSTR(Name,' ',-1)+1,
       GREATEST(INSTR(Name,' '),0))
  from NAME;
```

A third method to accomplish the same end uses **RTRIM**. Remember that **RTRIM** eliminates everything specified in its *set* from the right side of a string until it encounters any character not in its *set*. The **RTRIM** here effectively erases all the letters on the right until it hits the first space (just before the last name) or reaches the beginning of the string:

```
select
SUBSTR(Name,LENGTH(RTRIM(NAME,'ABCDEFGHIJKLMNOPQRSTUVWXYZ'))
    +1)
  from NAME;

SUBSTR(NAME,LENGTH(RTRIM(
------------------------
NELSON
```

```
MEDICIS
JOSEPHUS
GAMMIERE
```

LENGTH then measures the resulting string (with the last name erased). This tells you the position of the space before the last name. Add 1 to this number, do a **SUBSTR** starting there, and you'll get just the last name. Let's create a table with FirstName and LastName columns (you'll see complete details on creating tables in Chapter 18):

```
create table TWONAME(
FirstName    VARCHAR2(25),
LastName     VARCHAR2(25)
);
```

```
Table created.
```

Now, use an **insert** with a subquery to load the table data with the first and last names from the NAME table:

```
insert into TWONAME (FirstName, LastName)
select
    SUBSTR(Name,1,DECODE(INSTR(Name,' '),0,99,INSTR(Name,' '))),
    SUBSTR(Name,LENGTH(RTRIM(NAME,'ABCDEFGHIJKLMNOPQRSTUVWXYZ'))+1)
    from NAME;
```

Check the contents of the TWONAME table:

```
select * from TWONAME;

FIRSTNAME                 LASTNAME
------------------------- -------------------------
HORATIO                   NELSON
VALDO
MARIE                     MEDICIS
FLAVIUS                   JOSEPHUS
EDYTHE                    GAMMIERE
```

You can use similar techniques to extract the middle initial or initials, and apply these methods elsewhere as well, such as to addresses, product descriptions, company names, and so on.

When moving data from an old system to a new one, reformatting is frequently necessary and often difficult. The facilities exist in SQL, but they require some knowledge of how the functions work and some thoughtfulness to avoid the kinds of difficulties shown in the examples so far in this chapter.

Counting String Occurrences Within Larger Strings

You can use a combination of the **LENGTH** and **REPLACE** functions to determine how many times a string (such as ABC) occurs within a larger string (such as ABCDEFABC). The **REPLACE** function replaces a character or characters in a string with zero or more characters. Thus,

```
REPLACE('ADAH', 'A', 'BLAH')
```

will evaluate the string ADAH. Everywhere an *A* is found, it will be replaced with the string BLAH. Thus, the function shown in this example will return the string BLAHDBLAHH.

You can use the **REPLACE** function to eliminate characters from strings. For example, you can replace the character string you're searching for with **NULL** values. Thus,

```
REPLACE('GEORGE', 'GE', NULL)
```

returns a value of OR. The two separate occurrences of GE in GEORGE were each set to **NULL**.

You can use the **REPLACE** function to determine how many times a string (like GE) is found in a larger string (like GEORGE). First, replace the string with **NULL** values:

```
select REPLACE('GEORGE', 'GE', NULL)
   from DUAL;
```

The result of that query will be OR:

```
RE
--
OR
```

More importantly, the **LENGTH** of the result of that query will provide information about how many times the string was found. The following query will tell you how long the resulting string is:

```
select LENGTH(REPLACE('GEORGE', 'GE', NULL))
   from DUAL;

LENGTH(REPLACE('GEORGE','GE',NULL))
-----------------------------------
                 2
```

Now you can tell how many times the string was found. If you subtract the length of the shortened string from the original string and divide that difference by the length of the search string, the result will be the number of times the search string was found:

```
select (LENGTH('GEORGE')
       - LENGTH(REPLACE('GEORGE', 'GE', NULL)) )
       / LENGTH('GE')    AS Counter
  from DUAL;

  COUNTER
----------
        2
```

This example uses strings instead of character columns in order to be simpler to understand; in real applications, you would replace the original string (GEORGE) with your column name. The length of the string GEORGE is six characters. The length of GEORGE after GE is replaced with **NULL** is two characters. Therefore, the difference in the lengths of the original and shortened strings is four characters. Dividing four characters by the length of the search string (two characters) tells you that the string was found twice.

The only problem with this method occurs when the search string is zero characters in length (since you cannot divide by zero). Searching for a zero-length string may indicate a problem with the application logic that initiated the search.

Additional Facts About Variables

The command **accept** forces SQLPLUS to **define** the variable as equal to the entered value, and it can do this with a text message, with control over the datatype entered, and even with the response blanked out from viewing (such as for passwords; see the entry for **accept** in the Alphabetical Reference).

You can pass arguments to a start file when it is started by embedding numbered variables in the **select** statements (rather than variables with names).

To select all of the checkout records between one date and another, the **select** statement might look like this:

```
select * from BOOKSHELF_CHECKOUT
 where CheckOutDate BETWEEN '&1' AND '&2';
```

That query can be saved as a file (such as checkout.sql) and started from within SQLPLUS:

```
start checkout.sql 01-JAN-02 31-JAN-02
```

The start file checkout.sql would begin, with 01-JAN-02 substituted for &1, and 31-JAN-02 substituted for &2. As with other variables, character and DATE datatypes must be enclosed in single quotation marks in the SQL statement. One limitation of this is that each argument following the word **start** must be a single word without spaces.

Variable substitutions are not restricted to the SQL statement. The start file also may use variables for such things as SQLPLUS commands.

Variables can be concatenated simply by pushing them together. You can concatenate a variable with a constant by using a period:

```
select * from BOOKSHELF_CHECKOUT
 where CheckOutDate BETWEEN '01-&StartMonth.-02' AND '01-&EndMonth.-02';
```

This **select** statement will query for a starting month and an ending month, then build the two dates using a period as a concatenation operator.

> **NOTE**
> *No period is necessary before the variable—only after it. The ampersand (&) tells SQLPLUS that a variable is beginning.*

Related set Commands

Normally, the ampersand denotes a variable. This can be changed with **set define** followed by the single symbol that you'd prefer to use to denote a variable.

set escape defines a character you can place just in front of the ampersand (or other defined symbol) so that SQLPLUS will treat the symbol as a literal, not as denoting a variable.

set concat can change the default concatenation operator for variables, which is the period, to another single symbol. This variable concatenation is used in addition to, and separately from, the SQL concatenation operator, which is usually two vertical bars (II).

set scan turns variable substitution **off** or **on** for the SQL statement. If **scan** is **off**, any variable in a **select** statement is treated as a literal—for example, **&Test** is treated as the literal word **&Test**, not as the value it is defined as. Variables used in SQLPLUS commands, however, are still substituted as before.

As of Oracle9i, **set scan on/off** is deprecated—use **set define** in place of **set scan**.

See the **set** command in the Alphabetical Reference for additional environment configuration options.

CHAPTER
17

DECODE and CASE:
if, then, and else in SQL

he **DECODE** function is without doubt one of the most powerful in Oracle's SQL. It is one of several extensions Oracle added to the standard SQL language. This chapter will explore a number of ways that **DECODE** can be used, including the generation of "cross-tab" reports. As of Oracle9i, you can also use the **CASE** function and the **COALESCE** function to execute complex logical tests within your SQL statements.

This is an advanced and often difficult chapter. Most of what is illustrated here is unnecessary for the vast majority of reporting; don't be concerned if it seems beyond your needs. Its real value is more for sophisticated reporting and programming.

if, then, else

In programming and logic, a common construction of a problem is in the pattern *if, then, else*. For example, *if* this day is a Saturday, *then* Adah will play at home; *if* this day is a Sunday, *then* Adah will go to her grandparent's home; *if* this day is a holiday, *then* Adah will go over to Aunt Dora's; *else* Adah will go to school. In each case, "this day" was tested, and if it was one of a list of certain days, then a certain result followed, or else (if it was none of those days) another result followed. **DECODE** follows this kind of logic. Chapter 10 provided an introduction that demonstrated the basic structure and usage of **DECODE**.

This is **DECODE**'s format:

```
DECODE(value,if1,then1,if2,then2,if3,then3,. . . ,else)
```

value represents any column in a table (regardless of datatype) or any result of a computation, such as one date minus another, a **SUBSTR** of a character column, one number times another, and so on. *value* is tested for each row. If *value* equals *if1*, then the result of the **DECODE** is *then1*; if *value* equals *if2*, then the result of the **DECODE** is *then2*; and so on, for virtually as many *if/then* pairs as you can construct. If *value* equals none of the *if*s, then the result of the **DECODE** is *else*. Each of the *if*s, *then*s, and the *else* also can be a column or the result of a function or computation. You can have up to 255 elements within the parentheses.

Let's consider the checkout history for the bookshelf, as recorded in the BOOKSHELF_ CHECKOUT table:

```
column Name format a16
column Title format a24 word_wrapped
set pagesize 60

select * from BOOKSHELF_CHECKOUT;

NAME              TITLE                     CHECKOUTD RETURNEDD
----------------  ------------------------  --------- ---------
JED HOPKINS       INNUMERACY                01-JAN-02 22-JAN-02
GERHARDT KENTGEN  WONDERFUL LIFE            02-JAN-02 02-FEB-02
DORAH TALBOT      EITHER/OR                 02-JAN-02 10-JAN-02
EMILY TALBOT      ANNE OF GREEN GABLES      02-JAN-02 20-JAN-02
PAT LAVAY         THE SHIPPING NEWS         02-JAN-02 12-JAN-02
ROLAND BRANDT     THE SHIPPING NEWS         12-JAN-02 12-MAR-02
```

```
ROLAND BRANDT      THE DISCOVERERS        12-JAN-02 01-MAR-02
ROLAND BRANDT      WEST WITH THE NIGHT    12-JAN-02 01-MAR-02
EMILY TALBOT       MIDNIGHT MAGIC         20-JAN-02 03-FEB-02
EMILY TALBOT       HARRY POTTER AND THE   03-FEB-02 14-FEB-02
                   GOBLET OF FIRE
PAT LAVAY          THE MISMEASURE OF MAN  12-JAN-02 12-FEB-02
DORAH TALBOT       POLAR EXPRESS          01-FEB-02 15-FEB-02
DORAH TALBOT       GOOD DOG, CARL         01-FEB-02 15-FEB-02
GERHARDT KENTGEN   THE MISMEASURE OF MAN  13-FEB-02 05-MAR-02
FRED FULLER        JOHN ADAMS             01-FEB-02 01-MAR-02
FRED FULLER        TRUMAN                 01-MAR-02 20-MAR-02
JED HOPKINS        TO KILL A MOCKINGBIRD  15-FEB-02 01-MAR-02
DORAH TALBOT       MY LEDGER              15-FEB-02 03-MAR-02
GERHARDT KENTGEN   MIDNIGHT MAGIC         05-FEB-02 10-FEB-02
```

As you look through the checkout list, you realize that some of the books were checked out for a rather long time. You can order by the number of days checked out to highlight the readers who keep books for the longest time:

```
select Name, Title, ReturnedDate-CheckOutDate DaysOut
  from BOOKSHELF_CHECKOUT
 order by DaysOut desc;
```

```
NAME              TITLE                       DAYSOUT
---------------   ------------------------    ----------
ROLAND BRANDT     THE SHIPPING NEWS                59
ROLAND BRANDT     THE DISCOVERERS                  48
ROLAND BRANDT     WEST WITH THE NIGHT              48
GERHARDT KENTGEN  WONDERFUL LIFE                   31
PAT LAVAY         THE MISMEASURE OF MAN            31
FRED FULLER       JOHN ADAMS                       28
JED HOPKINS       INNUMERACY                       21
GERHARDT KENTGEN  THE MISMEASURE OF MAN            20
FRED FULLER       TRUMAN                           19
EMILY TALBOT      ANNE OF GREEN GABLES             18
DORAH TALBOT      MY LEDGER                        16
EMILY TALBOT      MIDNIGHT MAGIC                   14
DORAH TALBOT      POLAR EXPRESS                    14
DORAH TALBOT      GOOD DOG, CARL                   14
JED HOPKINS       TO KILL A MOCKINGBIRD            14
EMILY TALBOT      HARRY POTTER AND THE             11
                  GOBLET OF FIRE
PAT LAVAY         THE SHIPPING NEWS                10
DORAH TALBOT      EITHER/OR                         8
GERHARDT KENTGEN  MIDNIGHT MAGIC                    5
```

But is it specific readers who are the issue, or is it that there are certain categories of books that take longer to read? There are multiple variables involved, and looking at them in isolation

may lead to incorrect decisions. What is the average number of days out for the books in each category?

```
select B.CategoryName,
       MIN(BC.ReturnedDate-BC.CheckOutDate) MinOut,
       MAX(BC.ReturnedDate-BC.CheckOutDate) MaxOut,
       AVG(BC.ReturnedDate-BC.CheckOutDate) AvgOut
  from BOOKSHELF_CHECKOUT BC, BOOKSHELF B
 where BC.Title = B.Title
 group by B.CategoryName;
```

CATEGORYNAME	MINOUT	MAXOUT	AVGOUT
ADULTFIC	10	59	27.6666667
ADULTNF	16	48	29.1111111
ADULTREF	8	8	8
CHILDRENFIC	5	18	12
CHILDRENPIC	14	14	14

This is more useful, but it doesn't factor in the impact of the different people checking out books in the categories. To accomplish that, you could use an additional level of grouping, but it will be easier to use if you create a *cross-tab* report. The following listing generates a report that shows the minimum, maximum, and average days out by person by category. This query uses the **DECODE** function to perform the calculations.

```
column CategoryName format a11

select B.CategoryName,
       MAX(DECODE(BC.Name, 'FRED FULLER',
                  BC.ReturnedDate-BC.CheckOutDate,NULL)) MaxFF,
       AVG(DECODE(BC.Name, 'FRED FULLER',
                  BC.ReturnedDate-BC.CheckOutDate,NULL)) AvgFF,
       MAX(DECODE(BC.Name, 'DORAH TALBOT',
                  BC.ReturnedDate-BC.CheckOutDate,NULL)) MaxDT,
       AVG(DECODE(BC.Name, 'DORAH TALBOT',
                  BC.ReturnedDate-BC.CheckOutDate,NULL)) AvgDT,
       MAX(DECODE(BC.Name, 'GERHARDT KENTGEN',
                  BC.ReturnedDate-BC.CheckOutDate,NULL)) MaxGK,
       AVG(DECODE(BC.Name, 'GERHARDT KENTGEN',
                  BC.ReturnedDate-BC.CheckOutDate,NULL)) AvgGK
  from BOOKSHELF_CHECKOUT BC, BOOKSHELF B
 where BC.Title = B.Title
 group by B.CategoryName;
```

CATEGORYNAM	MAXFF	AVGFF	MAXDT	AVGDT	MAXGK	AVGGK
ADULTFIC						
ADULTNF	28	23.5	16	16	31	25.5
ADULTREF			8	8		
CHILDRENFIC					5	5
CHILDRENPIC			14	14		

The output now shows the borrowers across the top—Fred Fuller's maximum checkout time is the MaxFF column, Dorah Talbot's is the MaxDT column, and Gerhardt Kentgen's is the MaxGK column. The output shows that the AdultNF category has the longest average checkout time for each of the borrowers shown, and that in Gerhardt Kentgen's case it is significantly longer than the average checkout time in the other category he checked out.

How was this report generated? In the query, the grouping is by CategoryName. The MaxFF column query is shown here:

```
select B.CategoryName,
       MAX(DECODE(BC.Name, 'FRED FULLER',
                  BC.ReturnedDate-BC.CheckOutDate,NULL)) MaxFF,
```

DECODE is performing an if-then check on the data: If the BC.Name column value in a row is 'FRED FULLER', then calculate the difference between the ReturnedDate and CheckOutDate, else return a **NULL**. That list of values is then evaluated and the maximum value is returned. A similar set of operations returns the average checkout time for Fred Fuller:

```
       AVG(DECODE(BC.Name, 'FRED FULLER',
                  BC.ReturnedDate-BC.CheckOutDate,NULL)) AvgFF,
```

Replacing Values via DECODE

In the last example, **DECODE** was used to return values conditionally, depending on the Name of the person who checked out a book. You can also use **DECODE** to replace values in a list. For example, selecting the category names from BOOKSHELF yields:

```
select distinct CategoryName from BOOKSHELF;

CATEGORYNAM
-----------
ADULTFIC
ADULTNF
ADULTREF
CHILDRENFIC
CHILDRENNF
CHILDRENPIC
```

To replace these names, you could join BOOKSHELF to CATEGORY and select the ParentCategory and SubCategory from the CATEGORY table. If the list of categories is static, you could avoid the join to the CATEGORY table and perform the replacement via a **DECODE** function, as shown in the following listing. Note how **DECODE** supports multiple *if-then* combinations within a single call.

```
select distinct
       DECODE(CategoryName,'ADULTFIC','Adult Fiction',
                           'ADULTNF','Adult Nonfiction',
```

```
                                 'ADULTREF','Adult Reference',
                                 'CHILDRENFIC','Children Fiction',
                                 'CHILDRENNF','Children Nonfiction',
                                 'CHILDRENPIC','Children Picturebook',
                                 CategoryName)
       from BOOKSHELF;

DECODE(CATEGORYNAME,
--------------------
Adult Fiction
Adult Nonfiction
Adult Reference
Children Fiction
Children Nonfiction
Children Picturebook
```

In this case, the data is static; for volatile data, hard-coding the translations into the application code would not be an acceptable programming practice. The technique shown here is useful for transaction processing systems in which you are trying to minimize the number of database calls performed. In this example, there is no database access required to change 'ADULTNF' to 'Adult Nonfiction'; the change occurs within the **DECODE** function call. Note that if there are any other categories found, the *else* condition in the **DECODE** function returns the original CategoryName column value.

DECODE within DECODE

You can **DECODE** function calls within other **DECODE** function calls. Let's say you want to charge late fees, with different late fee rates for different categories of books. Adult category books may be kept later, but the penalty for late days will be higher.

Start with a basic flat rate charge of $0.20 per day for books checked out for more than 14 days:

```
column Name format a16
column Title format a20 word_wrapped
column DaysOut format 999.99 heading 'Days Out'
column DaysLate format 999.99 heading 'Days Late'
set pagesize 60
break on Name

select Name, Title, ReturnedDate,
       ReturnedDate-CheckoutDate as DaysOut /*Count days*/,
       ReturnedDate-CheckoutDate -14  DaysLate,
       (ReturnedDate-CheckoutDate -14)*0.20  LateFee
  from BOOKSHELF_CHECKOUT
where ReturnedDate-CheckoutDate > 14
 order by Name, CheckoutDate;
```

NAME	TITLE	RETURNEDD	Days Out	Days Late	LATEFEE
DORAH TALBOT	MY LEDGER	03-MAR-02	16.00	2.00	.4
EMILY TALBOT	ANNE OF GREEN GABLES	20-JAN-02	18.00	4.00	.8
FRED FULLER	JOHN ADAMS	01-MAR-02	28.00	14.00	2.8
	TRUMAN	20-MAR-02	19.00	5.00	1
GERHARDT KENTGEN	WONDERFUL LIFE	02-FEB-02	31.00	17.00	3.4
	THE MISMEASURE OF MAN	05-MAR-02	20.00	6.00	1.2
JED HOPKINS	INNUMERACY	22-JAN-02	21.00	7.00	1.4
PAT LAVAY	THE MISMEASURE OF MAN	12-FEB-02	31.00	17.00	3.4
ROLAND BRANDT	THE SHIPPING NEWS	12-MAR-02	59.00	45.00	9
	THE DISCOVERERS	01-MAR-02	48.00	34.00	6.8
	WEST WITH THE NIGHT	01-MAR-02	48.00	34.00	6.8

For books in the Adult categories, increase the allowed days late to 21 days. This won't change the number of days out, but will change the DaysLate column calculation. Since CategoryName is not a column in BOOKSHELF_CHECKOUT, this modification also requires the addition of the BOOKSHELF table to the **from** clause.

```
select BC.Name, BC.Title, BC.ReturnedDate,
       BC.ReturnedDate-BC.CheckoutDate as DaysOut /*Count days*/,
       DECODE(SUBSTR(CategoryName,1,5), 'ADULT',
          BC.ReturnedDate-BC.CheckoutDate -21,
          BC.ReturnedDate-BC.CheckoutDate -14 ) DaysLate,
       DECODE(SUBSTR(CategoryName,1,5), 'ADULT',
          (BC.ReturnedDate-BC.CheckoutDate -21)*0.30,
          (BC.ReturnedDate-BC.CheckoutDate -14)*0.20 ) LateFee
  from BOOKSHELF_CHECKOUT BC, BOOKSHELF B
 where BC.Title = B.Title
   and BC.ReturnedDate-BC.CheckoutDate >
       DECODE(SUBSTR(CategoryName,1,5), 'ADULT',21,14)
 order by BC.Name, BC.CheckoutDate;
```

NAME	TITLE	RETURNEDD	Days Out	Days Late	LATEFEE
EMILY TALBOT	ANNE OF GREEN GABLES	20-JAN-02	18.00	4.00	.8
FRED FULLER	JOHN ADAMS	01-MAR-02	28.00	7.00	2.1
GERHARDT KENTGEN	WONDERFUL LIFE	02-FEB-02	31.00	10.00	3
PAT LAVAY	THE MISMEASURE OF MAN	12-FEB-02	31.00	10.00	3
ROLAND BRANDT	THE SHIPPING NEWS	12-MAR-02	59.00	38.00	11.4
	THE DISCOVERERS	01-MAR-02	48.00	27.00	8.1
	WEST WITH THE NIGHT	01-MAR-02	48.00	27.00	8.1

In the **select** clause, the query logic for the DaysLate column is

```
DECODE(SUBSTR(CategoryName,1,5), 'ADULT',
    BC.ReturnedDate-BC.CheckoutDate -21,
    BC.ReturnedDate-BC.CheckoutDate -14 ) DaysLate
```

In **DECODE**'s if-then-else format, this says "If the first five characters of the CategoryName column match the string 'ADULT', then subtract 21 from the number of days late; otherwise, subtract 14 days." The LateFee calculation uses similar logic. The **where** clause uses a **DECODE** to determine the limiting value for the rows returned—for ADULT category books, allow 21 days; otherwise, allow 14:

```
and BC.ReturnedDate-BC.CheckoutDate >
    DECODE(SUBSTR(CategoryName,1,5), 'ADULT',21,14)
```

Now add an additional rule: For Adult fiction category books, the late fee will be double the late fee for other Adult books. From the last query, the calculation for LateFee is:

```
DECODE(SUBSTR(CategoryName,1,5), 'ADULT',
    (BC.ReturnedDate-BC.CheckoutDate -21)*0.30,
    (BC.ReturnedDate-BC.CheckoutDate -14)*0.20 ) LateFee
```

The new rule requires an additional category check within the **DECODE** already performed. The new LateFee calculation is shown here:

```
DECODE(SUBSTR(CategoryName,1,5), 'ADULT',
    DECODE(SUBSTR(CategoryName,6,3),'FIC',
    (BC.ReturnedDate-BC.CheckoutDate -21)*0.60,
    (BC.ReturnedDate-BC.CheckoutDate -21)*0.30),
    (BC.ReturnedDate-BC.CheckoutDate -14)*0.20 ) LateFee
```

Reading through the preceding listing, the first **DECODE** function tells Oracle that if the first five letters of the CategoryName are 'ADULT', then perform the second **DECODE** function. The second **DECODE** tells Oracle that if letters 6, 7, and 8 of the CategoryName are 'FIC', then the late fee is $0.60 per day after the twenty-first day; otherwise, it is $0.30 per day after the twenty-first day. At that point, the inner **DECODE** function completes. For the first **DECODE** function, the **else** clause (for non-ADULT category books) then specifies the late fee calculation. The query and result are shown in the following listing; you can see the impact by comparing the LateFee column for 'THE SHIPPING NEWS' in this report and the last report.

```
select BC.Name, BC.Title, BC.ReturnedDate,
    BC.ReturnedDate-BC.CheckoutDate as DaysOut /*Count days*/,
    DECODE(SUBSTR(CategoryName,1,5), 'ADULT',
        BC.ReturnedDate-BC.CheckoutDate -21,
        BC.ReturnedDate-BC.CheckoutDate -14 ) DaysLate,
    DECODE(SUBSTR(CategoryName,1,5), 'ADULT',
        DECODE(SUBSTR(CategoryName,6,3),'FIC',
        (BC.ReturnedDate-BC.CheckoutDate -21)*0.60,
        (BC.ReturnedDate-BC.CheckoutDate -21)*0.30),
        (BC.ReturnedDate-BC.CheckoutDate -14)*0.20 ) LateFee
  from BOOKSHELF_CHECKOUT BC, BOOKSHELF B
 where BC.Title = B.Title
   and BC.ReturnedDate-BC.CheckoutDate >
```

```
         DECODE(SUBSTR(CategoryName,1,5), 'ADULT',21,14)
order by BC.Name, BC.CheckoutDate;
```

NAME	TITLE	RETURNEDD	Days Out	Days Late	LATEFEE
EMILY TALBOT	ANNE OF GREEN GABLES	20-JAN-02	18.00	4.00	.8
FRED FULLER	JOHN ADAMS	01-MAR-02	28.00	7.00	2.1
GERHARDT KENTGEN	WONDERFUL LIFE	02-FEB-02	31.00	10.00	3
PAT LAVAY	THE MISMEASURE OF MAN	12-FEB-02	31.00	10.00	3
ROLAND BRANDT	THE SHIPPING NEWS	12-MAR-02	59.00	38.00	22.8
	THE DISCOVERERS	01-MAR-02	48.00	27.00	8.1
	WEST WITH THE NIGHT	01-MAR-02	48.00	27.00	8.1

You can nest **DECODE**s within other **DECODE**s to support complex logic within your data processing. For example, you may choose to print one column if it has a non-**NULL** value, and a second column if the first is **NULL**. With **DECODE**, that is a simple function call:

```
DECODE(Column1, NULL, Column2, Column1)
```

If Column1 is **NULL**, Column2 will be returned; otherwise, Column1's non-**NULL** value will be returned. You could also use **NVL** or the Oracle9i **COALESCE** and **NULLIF** functions to perform similar logic.

COALESCE will return the first non-NULL value encountered in a list of values. The last **DECODE** example could be rewritten as

```
COALESCE(Column1, Column2)
```

Since **COALESCE** is a new function and its name does not clearly convey its usage, be sure to provide comments within your code to explain the logical tests performed.

Greater Than and Less Than in DECODE

DECODE supports logic checks, but how do you do numeric comparisons in this format? The simplest solution is often to use the **SIGN** function. **SIGN** returns a 1 if the number is positive, 0 if it is 0, and –1 if the number is negative. Because **SIGN** operates on numbers, you can evaluate any function that returns a number, including date arithmetic.

Let's modify the LateFee business rule again. Using the same base calculation, we'll modify the outcome so that we will not collect late fees that are less than or equal to $4.00. Here is the original LateFee calculation:

```
DECODE(SUBSTR(CategoryName,1,5), 'ADULT',
     DECODE(SUBSTR(CategoryName,6,3),'FIC',
     (BC.ReturnedDate-BC.CheckoutDate -21)*0.60,
     (BC.ReturnedDate-BC.CheckoutDate -21)*0.30),
     (BC.ReturnedDate-BC.CheckoutDate -14)*0.20 ) LateFee
```

If that value is less than 4, we will return a 0; otherwise, we will return the calculated value. To implement this requirement, subtract 4 from the LateFee value; if the result is positive (its **SIGN** value is 1), return that result; otherwise, return a 0.

```
DECODE(SIGN(
        DECODE(SUBSTR(CategoryName,1,5),  'ADULT',
            DECODE(SUBSTR(CategoryName,6,3),'FIC',
            (BC.ReturnedDate-BC.CheckoutDate -21)*0.60,
            (BC.ReturnedDate-BC.CheckoutDate -21)*0.30),
            (BC.ReturnedDate-BC.CheckoutDate -14)*0.20 ) -4),
        1,
        DECODE(SUBSTR(CategoryName,1,5),  'ADULT',
            DECODE(SUBSTR(CategoryName,6,3),'FIC',
            (BC.ReturnedDate-BC.CheckoutDate -21)*0.60,
            (BC.ReturnedDate-BC.CheckoutDate -21)*0.30),
            (BC.ReturnedDate-BC.CheckoutDate -14)*0.20 ),
        0) LateFee
```

Building from a simple foundation, this series of **DECODE** function calls allows you to perform very complex logic on the LateFee calculations. The first **DECODE** evaluates the **SIGN** of the next **DECODE** function result when 4 is subtracted from it. If that number is positive, the calculated late fee is returned; otherwise, a 0 is returned. The following listing shows this calculation and the output that results.

```
select BC.Name, BC.Title, BC.ReturnedDate,
        BC.ReturnedDate-BC.CheckoutDate as DaysOut /*Count days*/,
        DECODE(SUBSTR(CategoryName,1,5),  'ADULT',
            BC.ReturnedDate-BC.CheckoutDate -21,
            BC.ReturnedDate-BC.CheckoutDate -14 ) DaysLate,
DECODE(SIGN(
        DECODE(SUBSTR(CategoryName,1,5),  'ADULT',
            DECODE(SUBSTR(CategoryName,6,3),'FIC',
            (BC.ReturnedDate-BC.CheckoutDate -21)*0.60,
            (BC.ReturnedDate-BC.CheckoutDate -21)*0.30),
            (BC.ReturnedDate-BC.CheckoutDate -14)*0.20 ) -4),
        1,
        DECODE(SUBSTR(CategoryName,1,5),  'ADULT',
            DECODE(SUBSTR(CategoryName,6,3),'FIC',
            (BC.ReturnedDate-BC.CheckoutDate -21)*0.60,
            (BC.ReturnedDate-BC.CheckoutDate -21)*0.30),
            (BC.ReturnedDate-BC.CheckoutDate -14)*0.20 ),
        0) LateFee
  from BOOKSHELF_CHECKOUT BC, BOOKSHELF B
 where BC.Title = B.Title
   and BC.ReturnedDate-BC.CheckoutDate >
        DECODE(SUBSTR(CategoryName,1,5),  'ADULT',21,14)
 order by BC.Name, BC.CheckoutDate;
```

```
NAME                 TITLE                 RETURNEDD Days Out Days Late   LATEFEE
----------------     ---------------       --------- -------- ---------   ----------
EMILY TALBOT         ANNE OF GREEN GABLES  20-JAN-02   18.00     4.00           0
FRED FULLER          JOHN ADAMS            01-MAR-02   28.00     7.00           0
GERHARDT KENTGEN     WONDERFUL LIFE        02-FEB-02   31.00    10.00           0
PAT LAVAY            THE MISMEASURE OF     12-FEB-02   31.00    10.00           0
                     MAN
ROLAND BRANDT        THE SHIPPING NEWS     12-MAR-02   59.00    38.00        22.8
                     THE DISCOVERERS       01-MAR-02   48.00    27.00         8.1
                     WEST WITH THE NIGHT   01-MAR-02   48.00    27.00         8.1
```

You can eliminate the display of the first four rows (with $0 late fees) by making a similar modification to the **where** clause.

Using CASE

As of Oracle9i, you can use the **CASE** function in place of **DECODE**. The **CASE** function uses the keywords **when**, **then**, **else**, and **end** to indicate the logic path followed, which may make the resulting code easier to follow than an equivalent **DECODE**.

Consider this simple **DECODE** example from earlier in this chapter:

```
select distinct
       DECODE(CategoryName,'ADULTFIC','Adult Fiction',
                           'ADULTNF','Adult Nonfiction',
                           'ADULTREF','Adult Reference',
                           'CHILDRENFIC','Children Fiction',
                           'CHILDRENNF','Children Nonfiction',
                           'CHILDRENPIC','Children Picturebook',
                           CategoryName)
    from BOOKSHELF;
```

The equivalent **CASE** function is

```
select distinct
       CASE CategoryName
          when  'ADULTFIC' then 'Adult Fiction'
          when  'ADULTNF' then 'Adult Nonfiction'
          when  'ADULTREF' then 'Adult Reference'
          when  'CHILDRENFIC' then 'Children Fiction'
          when  'CHILDRENNF' then 'Children Nonfiction'
          when  'CHILDRENPIC' then 'Children Picturebook'
          else CategoryName
       end
    from BOOKSHELF;

CASECATEGORYNAMEWHEN
--------------------
Adult Fiction
Adult Nonfiction
Adult Reference
```

```
Children Fiction
Children Nonfiction
Children Picturebook
```

CASE evaluates the first **when** clause and returns a match if the limiting condition is met. As with **DECODE**, you can nest **CASE** function calls. How would you perform the LateFee column calculations using **CASE**?

The **DECODE** function began by calculating a higher rate for ADULT category books:

```
DECODE(SUBSTR(CategoryName,1,5), 'ADULT',
    (BC.ReturnedDate-BC.CheckoutDate -21)*0.30,
    (BC.ReturnedDate-BC.CheckoutDate -14)*0.20 ) LateFee
```

The **CASE** equivalent is

```
CASE SUBSTR(CategoryName,1,5)
    when 'ADULT' then (BC.ReturnedDate-BC.CheckoutDate -21)*0.30
    else (BC.ReturnedDate-BC.CheckoutDate -14)*0.20
end
```

The second rule (ADULTFIC books have doubled late fees) requires a nested **CASE** command:

```
CASE SUBSTR(CategoryName,1,5)
    when 'ADULT' then
        CASE SUBSTR(CategoryName,6,3)
            when 'FIC' then (BC.ReturnedDate-BC.CheckoutDate -21)*0.60
            else (BC.ReturnedDate-BC.CheckoutDate -21)*0.30
            end
    else (BC.ReturnedDate-BC.CheckoutDate -14)*0.20
end
```

This is more complex, but the logic is very easy to follow, and will usually be simpler to maintain than the equivalent **DECODE** clause. Now consider the final condition: If the calculated late fee is less than or equal to $4, return a 0. Since we are using the **CASE** function, we do not need to use a **SIGN** function—we can just use a "<" comparison as part of the command processing. The following example shows how to add this check: An additional **CASE** function is added, and the inner **CASE** function call is enclosed in parentheses. The result is compared to $4:

```
CASE when
    (CASE SUBSTR(CategoryName,1,5)
      when 'ADULT' then
          CASE SUBSTR(CategoryName,6,3)
              when 'FIC' then (BC.ReturnedDate-BC.CheckoutDate -21)*0.60
              else (BC.ReturnedDate-BC.CheckoutDate -21)*0.30
              end
      else (BC.ReturnedDate-BC.CheckoutDate -14)*0.20
    end)
    < 4 then 0
```

The **else** clause for this **CASE** function call is the same as the inner **CASE** execution—it calculates the late fee.

```
else
    CASE SUBSTR(CategoryName,1,5)
      when 'ADULT' then
          CASE SUBSTR(CategoryName,6,3)
              when 'FIC' then (BC.ReturnedDate-BC.CheckoutDate -21)*0.60
              else (BC.ReturnedDate-BC.CheckoutDate -21)*0.30
              end
      else (BC.ReturnedDate-BC.CheckoutDate -14)*0.20
    end
end
```

The full query is shown in the following listing, along with its output.

```
column LateFee format 999.99

select BC.Name, BC.Title, BC.ReturnedDate,
       BC.ReturnedDate-BC.CheckoutDate as DaysOut /*Count days*/,
       DECODE(SUBSTR(CategoryName,1,5), 'ADULT',
            BC.ReturnedDate-BC.CheckoutDate -21,
            BC.ReturnedDate-BC.CheckoutDate -14 ) DaysLate,
CASE when
    (CASE SUBSTR(CategoryName,1,5)
      when 'ADULT' then
          CASE SUBSTR(CategoryName,6,3)
              when 'FIC' then (BC.ReturnedDate-BC.CheckoutDate -21)*0.60
              else (BC.ReturnedDate-BC.CheckoutDate -21)*0.30
              end
      else (BC.ReturnedDate-BC.CheckoutDate -14)*0.20
    end)
  < 4 then 0 else
  CASE SUBSTR(CategoryName,1,5)
    when 'ADULT' then
        CASE SUBSTR(CategoryName,6,3)
            when 'FIC' then (BC.ReturnedDate-BC.CheckoutDate -21)*0.60
            else (BC.ReturnedDate-BC.CheckoutDate -21)*0.30
            end
    else (BC.ReturnedDate-BC.CheckoutDate -14)*0.20
  end
end  AS LateFee
  from BOOKSHELF_CHECKOUT BC, BOOKSHELF B
 where BC.Title = B.Title
   and BC.ReturnedDate-BC.CheckoutDate >
        DECODE(SUBSTR(CategoryName,1,5), 'ADULT',21,14)
 order by BC.Name, BC.CheckoutDate;
```

NAME	TITLE	RETURNEDD	Days Out	Days Late	LATEFEE
EMILY TALBOT	ANNE OF GREEN GABLES	20-JAN-02	18.00	4.00	.00
FRED FULLER	JOHN ADAMS	01-MAR-02	28.00	7.00	.00
GERHARDT KENTGEN	WONDERFUL LIFE	02-FEB-02	31.00	10.00	.00
PAT LAVAY	THE MISMEASURE OF MAN	12-FEB-02	31.00	10.00	.00
ROLAND BRANDT	THE SHIPPING NEWS	12-MAR-02	59.00	38.00	22.80
	THE DISCOVERERS	01-MAR-02	48.00	27.00	8.10
	WEST WITH THE NIGHT	01-MAR-02	48.00	27.00	8.10

Comparing the **CASE** version to the **DECODE** version earlier in this chapter, you can see that the **CASE** command is six lines longer but is simpler to read and maintain. For Oracle9i databases, **CASE** offers a powerful alternative to **DECODE**—and both **CASE** and **DECODE** provide solid solutions when you need to perform logic within your queries.

CHAPTER
18

Creating, Dropping, and Altering Tables and Views

 ntil now, the emphasis of this book has been on using tables. This chapter looks at creating, dropping, and changing tables, creating views, and options such as index-organized or partitioned tables. You've seen numerous **create table** commands to this point; this chapter will reinforce those examples and show how to use the latest options.

Creating a Table

Consider the TROUBLE table. This is similar to the COMFORT table discussed earlier in the book, but is used to track cities with unusual weather patterns.

```
describe TROUBLE
```

```
Name                             Null?     Type
-------------------------------- --------  ----
CITY                             NOT NULL  VARCHAR2(13)
SAMPLEDATE                       NOT NULL  DATE
NOON                                       NUMBER(3,1)
MIDNIGHT                                   NUMBER(3,1)
PRECIPITATION                              NUMBER
```

The columns in the TROUBLE table represent the three major datatypes in Oracle—VARCHAR2, DATE, and NUMBER. Here is the SQL that created this Oracle table:

```
create table TROUBLE (
City          VARCHAR2(13) NOT NULL,
SampleDate    DATE NOT NULL,
Noon          NUMBER(3,1),
Midnight      NUMBER(3,1),
Precipitation NUMBER
);
```

These are the basic elements of this command:

- The words **create table**
- The name of the table
- An opening parenthesis
- Column definitions
- A closing parenthesis
- A SQL terminator

The individual column definitions are separated by commas. There is no comma after the last column definition. The table and column names must start with a letter of the alphabet, but may include letters, numbers, and underscores. Names may be 1 to 30 characters in length, must be

unique within the table, and cannot be an Oracle reserved word (see "Object Names" in the Alphabetical Reference of this book).

If the names are not within double quotes, case does not matter in creating a table. There are no options for DATE datatypes. Character datatypes must have their maximum length specified. NUMBERs may be either high-precision (up to 38 digits) or specified-precision, based on the maximum number of digits and the number of places allowed to the right of the decimal (an Amount field for U.S. currency, for instance, would have only two decimal places).

NOTE
Do not enclose table and column names within double quotes, or case will matter. This can be disastrous for your users or developers.

See Part IV of this book for additional **create table** options for object-relational features.

Character Width and NUMBER Precision

Specifying the maximum length for character (CHAR and VARCHAR2) columns and the precision for NUMBER columns has consequences that must be considered during the design of the table. Improper decisions can be corrected later, using the **alter table** command, but the process can be difficult.

Deciding on a Proper Width

A character column that is not wide enough for the data you want to put in it will cause an **insert** to fail and result in this error message:

```
ERROR at line 1: ORA-01401: inserted value too large for column
```

The maximum width for CHAR (fixed-length) columns is 2,000 characters. VARCHAR2 (varying-length character) columns can have up to 4,000 characters. In assigning width to a column, allot enough space to allow for all future possibilities. A CHAR(15) for a city name, for instance, is just going to get you in trouble later on. You'll have to either alter the table or truncate or distort the names of some cities.

NOTE
*There is no penalty in Oracle for defining a wide VARCHAR2 column. Oracle is clever enough not to store blank spaces at the end of VARCHAR2 columns. The city name SAN FRANCISCO, for example, will be stored in 13 spaces even if you've defined the column as VARCHAR2(50). And if a column has nothing in it (**NULL**), Oracle will store nothing in the column, not even a blank space (it does store a couple of bytes of internal database control information, but this is unaffected by the size you specify for the column). The only effect that choosing a higher number will have is in the default SQLPLUS column formatting. SQLPLUS will create a default heading the same width as the VARCHAR2 definition.*

Choosing NUMBER Precision

A NUMBER column with incorrect precision will have one of two consequences. Oracle will either reject the attempt to **insert** the row of data, or drop some of the data's precision. Here are four rows of data about to be entered into Oracle:

```
insert into TROUBLE values
     ('PLEASANT LAKE','21-MAR-01',
     39.99,  -1.31, 3.6);

insert into TROUBLE values
     ('PLEASANT LAKE','22-JUN-01',
     101.44,  86.2, 1.63);

insert into TROUBLE values
     ('PLEASANT LAKE','23-SEP-01',
     92.85,  79.6, 1.00003);

insert into TROUBLE values
     ('PLEASANT LAKE','22-DEC-01',
     -17.445, -10.4, 2.4);
```

These are the results of this attempt:

```
insert into TROUBLE values ('PLEASANT LAKE',
   '21-MAR-01', 39.99, -1.31, 3.6);

1 row created.

insert into TROUBLE values ('PLEASANT LAKE',
  '22-JUN-01', 101.44, 86.2, 1.63);
'22-JUN-01', 101.44, 86.2, 1.63)
              *
ERROR at line 2:
ORA-01438: value larger than specified precision allows for this column

insert into TROUBLE values ('PLEASANT LAKE',
  '23-SEP-01', 92.85, 79.6, 1.00003);

1 row created.

insert into TROUBLE values ('PLEASANT LAKE',
  '22-DEC-01', -17.445, -10.4, 2.4);

1 row created.
```

The first, third, and fourth rows were inserted, but the second **insert** failed because 101.44 exceeded the precision set in the **create table** statement, where Noon was defined as NUMBER(3,1). The 3 here indicates the maximum number of digits Oracle will store. The 1 means that one of those three digits is reserved for a position to the right of the decimal point. Thus, 12.3 would be a legitimate number, but 123.4 would not be.

Note that the error here is caused by the 101, not the .44, because NUMBER(3,1) leaves only two positions available to the left of the decimal point. The .44 will not cause the "value larger than specified precision" error. It would simply be rounded to one decimal place. This will be demonstrated shortly, but first, look at the results of a query of the four rows we've attempted to **insert**:

```
select * from TROUBLE;

CITY          SAMPLEDAT    NOON MIDNIGHT PRECIPITATION
------------- --------- -------- -------- -------------
PLEASANT LAKE 21-MAR-01       40     -1.3           3.6
PLEASANT LAKE 23-SEP-01     92.9     79.6       1.00003
PLEASANT LAKE 22-DEC-01    -17.4    -10.4           2.4
```

The three rows were successfully inserted; only the problematic row is missing. Oracle automatically backed out the single **insert** statement that failed.

Rounding During Insertion

If you correct the **create table** statement and increase the number of digits available for Noon and Midnight, as shown here:

```
drop table TROUBLE;
create table TROUBLE (
City          VARCHAR2(13) NOT NULL,
SampleDate    DATE NOT NULL,
Noon          NUMBER(4,1),
Midnight      NUMBER(4,1),
Precipitation NUMBER
);
```

then the four **insert** statements will all be successful. A query now will reveal this:

```
insert into TROUBLE values
    ('PLEASANT LAKE','21-MAR-01',
    39.99,  -1.31, 3.6);

insert into TROUBLE values
    ('PLEASANT LAKE','22-JUN-01',
    101.44,  86.2, 1.63);

insert into TROUBLE values
    ('PLEASANT LAKE','23-SEP-01',
    92.85,  79.6, 1.00003);

insert into TROUBLE values
    ('PLEASANT LAKE','22-DEC-01',
    -17.445, -10.4, 2.4);

select * from TROUBLE;
```

```
CITY          SAMPLEDAT   NOON MIDNIGHT PRECIPITATION
------------- --------- -------- -------- -------------
PLEASANT LAKE 21-MAR-01       40     -1.3           3.6
PLEASANT LAKE 22-JUN-01    101.4     86.2          1.63
PLEASANT LAKE 23-SEP-01     92.9     79.6       1.00003
PLEASANT LAKE 22-DEC-01    -17.4    -10.4           2.4
```

Look at the first **insert** statement. The value for Noon is 39.99. In the query, it is rounded to 40. Midnight in the **insert** is -1.31. In the query it is -1.3. Oracle rounds the number based on the digit just to the right of the allowed precision. Table 18-1 shows the effects of precision in several examples. See Chapter 8 for examples of the **ROUND** function.

Value in insert Statement	Actual Value in Table
For precision of NUMBER(4,1)	
123.4	123.4
123.44	123.4
123.45	123.5
123.445	123.4
1234.5	**insert** fails
For precision of NUMBER(4)	
123.4	123
123.44	123
123.45	123
123.445	123
1234.5	1235
12345	**insert** fails
For precision of NUMBER(4,-1)	
123.4	120
123.44	120
123.45	120
123.445	120
125	130
1234.5	1230

TABLE 18-1. *Results of inserts into NUMBER Datatype Columns*

Value in insert Statement	Actual Value in Table
12345	**insert** fails
For precision of NUMBER	
123.4	123.4
123.44	123.44
123.45	123.45
123.445	123.445
125	125
1234.5	1234.5
12345.6789012345678	12345.6789012345678

TABLE 18-1. *Results of inserts into NUMBER Datatype Columns* (continued)

Constraints in create table

The **create table** statement lets you enforce several different kinds of constraints on a table: candidate keys, primary keys, foreign keys, and check conditions. A **constraint** clause can constrain a single column or group of columns in a table. The point of these constraints is to get Oracle to do most of the work in maintaining the integrity of your database. The more constraints you add to a table definition, the less work you have to do in applications to maintain the data. On the other hand, the more constraints there are in a table, the longer it takes to update the data.

There are two ways to specify constraints: as part of the column definition (a *column* constraint) or at the end of the **create table** statement (a *table* constraint). Clauses that constrain several columns must be table constraints.

The Candidate Key

A *candidate key* is a combination of one or more columns, the values of which uniquely identify each row of a table. The following listing shows the creation of a UNIQUE constraint for the TROUBLE table:

```
drop table TROUBLE;

create table TROUBLE (
City          VARCHAR2(13) NOT NULL,
SampleDate    DATE NOT NULL,
Noon          NUMBER(4,1),
Midnight      NUMBER(4,1),
Precipitation NUMBER,
constraint TROUBLE_UQ UNIQUE (City, SampleDate)
);
```

The key of this table is the combination of City and SampleDate. Notice that both columns are also declared to be **NOT NULL**. This feature allows you to prevent data from being entered into the table without certain columns having data in them. Clearly, temperature and precipitation information is not useful without knowing where or when it was collected. This technique is common for columns that are the primary key of a table, but is also useful if certain columns are critical for the row of data to be meaningful. If **NOT NULL** isn't specified, the column can have **NULL** values.

The Primary Key

The *primary key* of a table is one of the candidate keys that you give some special characteristics. You can have only one primary key, and a primary key column cannot contain **NULL**s:

```
drop table TROUBLE;
create table TROUBLE (
City          VARCHAR2(13),
SampleDate    DATE,
Noon          NUMBER(4,1),
Midnight      NUMBER(4,1),
Precipitation NUMBER,
constraint TROUBLE_PK PRIMARY KEY (City, SampleDate)
);
```

This **create table** statement has the same effect as the previous one, except that you can have several UNIQUE constraints but only one PRIMARY KEY constraint.

For single-column primary or candidate keys, you can define the key on the column with a column constraint instead of a table constraint:

```
create table AUTHOR
(AuthorName  VARCHAR2(50) primary key,
Comments     VARCHAR2(100));
```

In this case, the AuthorName column is the primary key, and Oracle will generate a name for the PRIMARY KEY constraint. This is not recommended if you want to enforce a common naming standard for keys, as discussed later in "Naming Constraints."

Designating Index Tablespaces

UNIQUE and PRIMARY KEY constraints create indexes. Unless you tell Oracle differently, those indexes will be placed in your default tablespace (tablespaces are described fully in Chapter 20). To specify a different tablespace, use the **using index tablespace** clause of the **create table** command, as shown in the following listing:

```
create table AUTHOR2
(AuthorName  VARCHAR2(50),
Comments     VARCHAR2(100),
constraint AUTHOR_PK primary key (AuthorName)
         using index tablespace USERS);
```

The index associated with the AUTHOR_PK primary key constraint will be placed in the USERS tablespace. See Chapter 20 for details on the use of tablespaces.

> **NOTE**
> *In a default installation, the USERS tablespace is created and is the*
> *default tablespace.*

The Foreign Key

A *foreign key* is a combination of columns with values based on the primary key values from another table. A foreign key constraint, also known as a *referential integrity constraint,* specifies that the values of the foreign key correspond to actual values of the primary key in the other table. In the BOOKSHELF table, for example, the CategoryName column refers to values for the CategoryName column in the CATEGORY table:

```
create table BOOKSHELF
(Title        VARCHAR2(100) primary key,
Publisher     VARCHAR2(20),
CategoryName VARCHAR2(20),
Rating        VARCHAR2(2),
constraint CATFK foreign key (CategoryName)
references CATEGORY(CategoryName));
```

You can refer to a primary or unique key, even in the same table. However, you can't refer to a table in a remote database in the **references** clause. You can use the table form (which is used here to create a PRIMARY KEY on the TROUBLE table) instead of the column form to specify foreign keys with multiple columns.

Sometimes you may want to delete these dependent rows when you delete the row they depend on. In the case of BOOKSHELF and CATEGORY, if you delete a CategoryName from CATEGORY, you may want to make the matching BOOKSHELF CategoryName column values **NULL**. In another case, you might want to delete the whole row. The clause **on delete cascade** added to the **references** clause tells Oracle to delete the dependent row when you delete the corresponding row in the parent table. This action automatically maintains referential integrity. For more information on the clauses **on delete cascade** and **references**, consult "Integrity Constraint" in the Alphabetical Reference of this book.

The CHECK Constraint

Many columns must have values that are within a certain range or that satisfy certain conditions. With a *CHECK constraint,* you can specify an expression that must always be true for every row in the table. For example, the RATING table stores the valid ratings; to limit the available values beyond the limits enforced by the column definition, you can use a CHECK constraint, as shown in the following listing:

```
create table RATING_WITH_CHECK
(Rating  VARCHAR2(2) CHECK (Rating <= 9),
RatingDescription VARCHAR2(50));
```

A column-level CHECK constraint can't refer to values in other rows; it can't use the pseudo-columns SysDate, UID, User, UserEnv, CurrVal, NextVal, Level, or RowNum. You can use the table constraint form (as opposed to the column constraint form) to refer to multiple columns in a CHECK constraint.

Naming Constraints

You can name your constraints. If you use an effective naming scheme for your constraint names, you will be better able to identify and manage the constraints. The name of a constraint should identify the table it acts upon and the type of constraint it represents. For example, the primary key on the TROUBLE table could be named TROUBLE_PK.

You can specify a name for a constraint when you create the constraint. If you do not specify a name for the constraint, then Oracle will generate a name. Most of Oracle's generated constraint names are of the form SYS_C######; for example, SYS_C000145. Since the system-generated constraint name does not tell you anything about the table or the constraint, you should name your constraints.

In the following example, the PRIMARY KEY constraint is created, and named, as part of the **create table** command for the TROUBLE table. Notice the **constraint** clause:

```
create table TROUBLE (
City            VARCHAR2(13),
SampleDate      DATE,
Noon            NUMBER(4,1),
Midnight        NUMBER(4,1),
Precipitation NUMBER,
constraint TROUBLE_PK PRIMARY KEY (City, SampleDate)
);
```

The **constraint** clause of the **create table** command names the constraint (in this case, TROUBLE_PK). You may use this constraint name later when enabling or disabling constraints.

Dropping Tables

Dropping tables is very simple. You use the words **drop table** and the table name, as shown here:

```
drop table TROUBLE;

Table dropped.
```

You drop a table only when you no longer need it. In Oracle, the **truncate** command lets you remove all the rows in the table and reclaim the space for other uses without removing the table definition from the database.

Truncating is also very simple:

```
truncate table TROUBLE;

Table truncated.
```

Truncating can't be rolled back. If there are triggers that delete rows that depend on rows in the table, truncating does not execute those triggers. You should be *sure* you really want to **truncate** before doing it.

Altering Tables

Tables can be altered in one of three ways: by adding a column to an existing table; by changing a column's definition; or by dropping a column. Adding a column is straightforward, and similar to creating a table. Suppose you decide to add two new columns to the TROUBLE table: Condition, which you believe should be **NOT NULL**, and Wind, for the wind speed. The first attempt starts by creating the table and populating it with a few records:

```
create table TROUBLE (
City          VARCHAR2(13),
SampleDate    DATE,
Noon          NUMBER(4,1),
Midnight      NUMBER(4,1),
Precipitation NUMBER);

insert into TROUBLE values
    ('PLEASANT LAKE','21-MAR-01',
    39.99,  -1.31, 3.6);

insert into TROUBLE values
    ('PLEASANT LAKE','22-JUN-01',
    101.44,  86.2, 1.63);

insert into TROUBLE values
    ('PLEASANT LAKE','23-SEP-01',
    92.85,  79.6, 1.00003);

insert into TROUBLE values
    ('PLEASANT LAKE','22-DEC-01',
    -17.445, -10.4, 2.4);
```

The first attempt at adding the new columns looks like this:

```
alter table TROUBLE add (
Condition    VARCHAR2(9) NOT NULL,
Wind         NUMBER(3)
);

alter table TROUBLE add (
             *
ERROR at line 1: ORA-01758: table must be empty to add
mandatory (NOT NULL) column
```

You get an error message because you cannot add a column defined as **NOT NULL**—when you try to add it, the column won't have anything in it. Each row in the table would have a new empty column defined as **NOT NULL**.

The **alter table** command's **add** clause will work with a **NOT NULL** column if the table is empty, but usually, it is impractical to empty a table of all its rows just to add a **NOT NULL** column. And you can't use Export and Import if you add a column after Exporting but before Importing.

The alternative is to first alter the table by adding the column without the **NOT NULL** restriction:

```
alter table TROUBLE add (
Condition     VARCHAR2(9),
Wind          NUMBER(3)
);

Table altered.
```

Then, fill the column with data for every row (either with legitimate data or a placeholder until legitimate data can be obtained):

```
update TROUBLE set Condition = 'SUNNY';
```

Finally, alter the table again, and modify the column definition to **NOT NULL**:

```
alter table TROUBLE modify (
Condition     VARCHAR2(9) NOT NULL,
City          VARCHAR2(17)
);

Table altered.
```

Note that the City column was also modified to enlarge it to 17 characters (just to show how this is done). When the table is described, it shows this:

```
describe TROUBLE
```

Name	Null?	Type
CITY	NOT NULL	VARCHAR2(17)
SAMPLEDATE	NOT NULL	DATE
NOON		NUMBER(4,1)
MIDNIGHT		NUMBER(4,1)
PRECIPITATION		NUMBER
CONDITION	NOT NULL	VARCHAR2(9)
WIND		NUMBER(3)

The table contains the following:

```
select * from TROUBLE;
```

```
CITY             SAMPLEDAT   NOON MIDNIGHT PRECIPITATION CONDITION WIND
---------------  --------- ------ -------- ------------- --------- ----
PLEASANT LAKE    21-MAR-99     40     -1.3           3.6 SUNNY
PLEASANT LAKE    22-JUN-99  101.4     86.2          1.63 SUNNY
PLEASANT LAKE    23-SEP-99   92.9     79.6       1.00003 SUNNY
PLEASANT LAKE    22-DEC-99  -17.4    -10.4           2.4 SUNNY
```

Here you see the effect of the changes. City is now 17 characters wide instead of 13. Condition has been added to the table as **NOT NULL** and is SUNNY (temporarily). WIND has been added, and is **NULL**.

To make a **NOT NULL** column nullable, use the **alter table** command with the **NULL** clause, as follows:

```
alter table TROUBLE modify
(Condition NULL);
```

The Rules for Adding or Modifying a Column

These are the rules for adding a column to a table:

- You may add a column at any time if **NOT NULL** isn't specified.

- You may add a **NOT NULL** column in three steps:

 1. Add the column without **NOT NULL** specified.

 2. Fill every row in that column with data.

 3. Modify the column to be **NOT NULL**.

NOTE
*If you use the **default** clause when adding a column, Oracle will update each row with that default value when it adds the column; these updates fire any AFTER UPDATE triggers defined on the table (see Chapter 28).*

These are the rules for modifying a column:

- You can increase a character column's width at any time.

- You can increase the number of digits in a NUMBER column at any time.

- You can increase or decrease the number of decimal places in a NUMBER column at any time.

In addition, if a column is **NULL** for every row of the table, you can make any of these changes:

- You can change the column's datatype.

- You can decrease a character column's width.

- You can decrease the number of digits in a NUMBER column.

You can only change the datatype of a column if the column is empty (**NULL**) in all rows of the table.

Exceptions for LONG-LOB Column Changes

There is one notable exception to the restrictions on datatype changes. Oracle supports the changing of LONG datatype columns to LOB datatypes even if there is data already in the LONG column. The following listing illustrates this functionality:

```
create table LONGTEST
(Col1    NUMBER,
Longcol  LONG);

Table created.

insert into LONGTEST values (1,'This is a LONG value');

1 row created.

alter table LONGTEST modify (Longcol CLOB);

Table altered.

desc LONGTEST

 Name                                      Null?    Type
 ----------------------------------------- -------- ---------
 COL1                                               NUMBER
 LONGCOL                                            CLOB

select Longcol from LONGTEST;

LONGCOL
-----------------------------------
This is a LONG value
```

Dropping a Column

As of Oracle8i, you can drop a column from a table. Dropping a column is more complicated than adding or modifying a column, because of the additional work that Oracle has to do. Just removing the column from the list of columns in the table—so it doesn't show up when you **select** * from the table—is easy. It's recovering the space that was actually taken up by the column values that is more complex, and potentially very time-consuming for the database. For this reason, you can drop a column immediately or you can mark it as "unused," to be dropped at a later time. If the column is dropped immediately, the action may impact performance. If the column is marked as unused, there will be no impact on performance. The column can actually be dropped at a later time when the database is less heavily used.

To drop a column, use either the **set unused** clause or the **drop** clause of the **alter table** command. You cannot drop a pseudo-column, a column of a nested table, or a partition key column.

In the following example, column Wind is dropped from the TROUBLE table:

```
alter table TROUBLE drop column Wind;
```

Alternatively, you can mark the Wind column as unused:

```
alter table TROUBLE set unused column Wind;
```

Marking a column as "unused" does not release the space previously used by the column, until you drop the unused columns:

```
alter table TROUBLE drop unused columns;
```

You can query USER_UNUSED_COL_TABS, DBA_UNUSED_COL_TABS, and ALL_UNUSED_COL_TABS to see all tables with columns marked as unused.

NOTE
Once you have marked a column as "unused," you cannot access that column.

You can drop multiple columns in a single command, as shown in the following listing:

```
alter table TROUBLE drop (Condition, Wind);
```

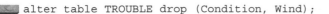

NOTE
*When dropping multiple columns, the **column** keyword of the **alter table** command should not be used; it causes a syntax error. The multiple column names must be enclosed in parentheses, as shown in the preceding listing.*

If the dropped columns are part of primary keys or unique constraints, then you will need to also use the **cascade constraints** clause as part of your **alter table** command. If you drop a column that belongs to a primary key, Oracle will drop both the column and the primary key index.

Creating a View

Since you've already seen the techniques for creating a view in prior chapters, they will not be reviewed here. However, this section gives several additional points about views that will prove useful.

If a view is based on a single underlying table, you can **insert**, **update**, or **delete** rows in the view. This will actually insert, update, or delete rows in the underlying table. There are restrictions on your ability to do this, although the restrictions are quite sensible:

■ You cannot **insert** if the underlying table has any **NOT NULL** columns that don't appear in the view.

■ You cannot **insert** or **update** if any one of the view's columns referenced in the **insert** or **update** contains functions or calculations.

■ You cannot **insert**, **update**, or **delete** if the view contains **group by**, **distinct**, or a reference to the pseudo-column RowNum.

You can **insert** into a view based on multiple tables if Oracle can determine the proper rows to insert. In a multitable view, Oracle determines which of the tables are *key-preserved*. If a view contains enough columns from a table to identify the primary key for that table, then the key is preserved and Oracle may be able to insert rows into the table via the view.

Stability of a View

Remember that the results of querying a view are built instantly from a table (or tables) when you execute the query. Until that moment, the view has no data of its own, as a table does. It is merely a description (a SQL statement) of what information to pull out of other tables and how to organize it. As a consequence, if a table is dropped, the validity of a view is destroyed. Attempting to query a view where the underlying table has been dropped will produce an error message about the view.

NOTE
The sole exception to this rule is the use of materialized views, introduced in Oracle8i. In fact, a materialized view is actually a table that stores data one would normally query via a view. Materialized views are described in detail in Chapter 23.

In the following sequence, a view is created on an existing table, the table is dropped, and the view then is queried.
First, the view is created:

```
create view RAIN as
select City, Precipitation
   from TROUBLE;

View created.
```

The underlying table is dropped:

```
drop table TROUBLE;

Table dropped.
```

The view is queried:

```
select * from RAIN;
               *
ERROR at line 1: ORA-04063: view "PRACTICE.RAIN" has errors
```

Similarly, a view is created using the asterisk in the view creation:

```
create view RAIN as
select * from TROUBLE;

View created.
```

But then the underlying table is altered:

```
alter table TROUBLE add (
Warning       VARCHAR2(20)
);

Table altered.
```

Despite the change to the view's base table, the view is still valid, although the columns in the view are only those that existed at the time of the CREATE VIEW.

After altering the table, replace the view. To re-create a view while keeping in place all the privileges that have been granted for it, use the **create or replace view** command, as shown in the following listing. This command will replace the view text of an existing view with the new view text, while the old grants on the view will not be affected.

```
create or replace view RAIN as
select * from TROUBLE;
```

order by in Views

As of Oracle8i, you can use an **order by** in a **create view** statement, as shown in the following listing based on the re-created TROUBLE table. Note that queries against this view will incur a performance penalty because of the additional sort activity they perform.

```
create view TROUBLE_SORTED
    as select * from TROUBLE
 order by City, SampleDate;

View created.

select * from TROUBLE_SORTED;

CITY          SAMPLEDAT    NOON    MIDNIGHT PRECIPITATION
------------- --------- ---------- ---------- -------------
PLEASANT LAKE 21-MAR-01         40       -1.3           3.6
PLEASANT LAKE 22-JUN-01      101.4       86.2          1.63
PLEASANT LAKE 23-SEP-01       92.9       79.6       1.00003
PLEASANT LAKE 22-DEC-01      -17.4      -10.4           2.4
```

Creating a Read-Only View

You can use the **with read only** clause of the **create view** command to prevent users from manipulating records via the view. Consider the RAIN view created in the previous section:

```
create or replace view RAIN as
select * from TROUBLE;
```

If a user has the ability to **delete** records from the TROUBLE table, then the user could **delete** the TROUBLE records via the RAIN view:

```
delete from RAIN;
```

The user could also **insert** or **update** the records in the TROUBLE table by performing those operations against the RAIN view. If the view is based on a join of multiple tables, then the user's ability to **update** the view's records is limited; a view's base tables cannot be updated unless only one table is involved in the **update** and the updated table's full primary key is included in the view's columns.

To prevent modifications to the base tables via a view, you can use the **with read only** clause of the **create view** command. If you use the **with read only** clause when creating a view, users will *only* be able to **select** records from the view. Users will be unable to manipulate the records obtained from the view even if the view is based on a single table:

```
create or replace view RAIN_READ_ONLY as
select * from TROUBLE
  with read only;
```

You can also use INSTEAD OF triggers to manage the data manipulation commands executed against views. See Chapter 30 for details on INSTEAD OF triggers.

Creating a Table from a Table

The RAIN view that was previously created from the TROUBLE table could alternatively have been a table. Oracle lets you create a new table on the fly, based on a **select** statement on an existing table:

```
create table RAIN_TABLE as
select City, Precipitation
  from TROUBLE;

Table created.
```

NOTE
*The **create table ... as select ...** command will not work if one of the selected columns uses the LONG datatype.*

When the new table is described, it reveals that it has "inherited" its column definitions from the TROUBLE table. A table created in this fashion can include all columns, using an asterisk if you like, or a subset of columns from another table. It also can include "invented" columns, which are the product of functions or the combination of other columns, just as in a view. The character column definitions will adjust to the size necessary to contain the data in the invented columns. NUMBER columns that had specified precision in the source table, but undergo computation in inventing a new column, will simply be NUMBER columns, with no specified precision, in the new table. When the table RAIN is described, it shows its column definitions:

```
describe RAIN_TABLE

Name                               Null?     Type
-------------------------------- -------- ------------
CITY                             NOT NULL VARCHAR2(13)
PRECIPITATION                             NUMBER
```

When RAIN_TABLE is queried, it contains just the columns and data selected from the TROUBLE table as it existed when RAIN_TABLE was created:

```
select * from RAIN_TABLE;

CITY            PRECIPITATION
-------------- --------------
PLEASANT LAKE            3.6
PLEASANT LAKE           1.63
PLEASANT LAKE        1.00003
PLEASANT LAKE            2.4
```

You also can use this technique to create a table with column definitions like that of the source table, but with no rows in it, by building a **where** clause that will select no rows from the old table:

```
create table RAIN_EMPTY as
select City, Precipitation
  from TROUBLE
 where 1=2;

Table created.
```

Querying this table will show there is nothing in it:

```
select * from RAIN_EMPTY;

no rows selected.
```

You can create a table based on a query without generating *redo log entries* (chronological records of database actions used during database recoveries). Avoiding the generation of these entries is accomplished by using the **nologging** keyword in the **create table** command. When the redo log entries are circumvented in this way, the performance of the **create table** command will improve, since less work is being done; the larger the table, the greater the impact. However, since the new table's creation is not being written to the *redo log files* (which record the redo log entries), the table will not be re-created if, following a database failure, those redo log files are used to recover the database. Therefore, you should consider performing a backup of the database soon after using the **nologging** option if you want to be able to recover the new table.

The following example shows how to use the **nologging** keyword during table creations based on queries. By default, table creations based on queries generate redo log entries.

```
create table RAIN_NOLOG
nologging
```

```
as
select * from TROUBLE;

Table created.
```

Note that you can specify **nologging** at the partition level and at the LOB level. The use of **nologging** will improve the performance of the operations that create the initial data in the table.

Creating an Index-Organized Table

An *index-organized table* keeps its data sorted according to the primary key column values for the table. Index-organized tables store their data as if the entire table was stored in an index. Indexes are described more fully in Chapter 20; in Oracle, they serve two main purposes:

- **To enforce uniqueness** When a PRIMARY KEY or UNIQUE constraint is created, Oracle creates an index to enforce the uniqueness of the indexed columns.

- **To improve performance** When a query can use an index, the performance of the query may dramatically improve. See Chapter 38 for details on the conditions under which a query may use an index.

An index-organized table allows you to store the entire table's data in an index. A normal index only stores the indexed columns in the index; an index-organized table stores all of the table's columns in the index.

To create an index-organized table, use the **organization index** clause of the **create table** command, as shown in the following example:

```
create table TROUBLE_IOT (
City            VARCHAR2(13),
SampleDate      DATE,
Noon            NUMBER(4,1),
Midnight        NUMBER(4,1),
Precipitation NUMBER,
constraint TROUBLE_IOT_PK PRIMARY KEY (City, SampleDate))
organization index;
```

To create TROUBLE as an index-organized table, you must create a PRIMARY KEY constraint on it.

An index-organized table is appropriate if you will always be accessing the TROUBLE data by the City and SampleDate columns (in the **where** clauses of your queries). To minimize the amount of active management of the index required, you should use index-organized tables only if the table's data is very static. If the table's data changes frequently, or if you need to index additional columns of the table, then you should use a regular table, with indexes as appropriate.

In general, index-organized tables are most effective when the primary key constitutes a large part of the table's columns. If the table contains many frequently accessed columns that are not part of the primary key, then the index-organized table will need to repeatedly access its overflow area. Despite this drawback, you may choose to use index-organized tables to take advantage of a key feature that is not available with standard tables: the ability to use the **move online** option

of the **alter table** command. You can use that option to move a table from one tablespace to another while it is being accessed by **insert**s, **update**s, and **delete**s. You cannot use the **move online** option for partitioned index-organized tables. Partitioning is described in the next section.

Using Partitioned Tables

As of Oracle8, you can divide the rows of a single table into multiple parts. Dividing a table's data in this manner is called *partitioning* the table; the table that is partitioned is called a *partitioned table,* and the parts are called *partitions*.

Partitioning is useful for very large tables. By splitting a large table's rows across multiple smaller partitions, you accomplish several important goals:

- The performance of queries against the tables may improve, since Oracle may have to only search one partition (one part of the table) instead of the entire table to resolve a query.

- The table may be easier to manage. Since the partitioned table's data is stored in multiple parts, it may be easier to load and delete data in the partitions than in the large table.

- Backup and recovery operations may perform better. Since the partitions are smaller than the partitioned table, you may have more options for backing up and recovering the partitions than you would have for a single large table.

The Oracle optimizer will know that the table has been partitioned; as shown later in this section, you can also specify the partition to use as part of the **from** clause of your queries.

Creating a Partitioned Table

To create a partitioned table, you specify how to set up the partitions of the table's data as part of the **create table** command. Typically, tables are partitioned by ranges of values.

Consider the BOOKSHELF table:

```
create table BOOKSHELF
(Title        VARCHAR2(100) primary key,
Publisher    VARCHAR2(20),
CategoryName VARCHAR2(20),
Rating       VARCHAR2(2),
Constraint CATFK foreign key (CategoryName)
references CATEGORY(CategoryName));
```

If you will be storing a large number of records in the BOOKSHELF table, you may want to separate the rows across multiple partitions. To partition the table's records, use the **partition by range** clause of the **create table** command, as shown next. The ranges will determine the values stored in each partition.

```
create table BOOKSHELF_RANGE_PART
(Title        VARCHAR2(100) primary key,
Publisher    VARCHAR2(20),
CategoryName VARCHAR2(20),
Rating       VARCHAR2(2),
```

```
constraint CATFK2 foreign key (CategoryName)
references CATEGORY(CategoryName)
)
partition by range (CategoryName)
 (partition PART1   values less than ('B')
     tablespace PART1_TS,
  partition PART2   values less than (MAXVALUE)
     tablespace PART2_TS);
/
```

The BOOKSHELF table will be partitioned based on the values in the CategoryName column:

```
partition by range (CategoryName)
```

For any Category values less than *B* (the ADULT categories), the record will be stored in the partition named PART1. The PART1 partition will be stored in the PART1_TS tablespace (see Chapter 20 for details on tablespaces). Any other category will be stored in the PART2 partition. Note that in the PART2 partition definition, the range clause is

```
partition PART2   values less than (MAXVALUE)
```

You do not need to specify a maximum value for the last partition; the **maxvalue** keyword tells Oracle to use the partition to store any data that could not be stored in the earlier partitions.

You can create multiple partitions, each with its own upper value defined. For each partition, you only specify the maximum value for the range. The minimum value for the range is implicitly determined by Oracle.

Range partitions were the only type of partition available in Oracle8. Oracle8i introduced *hash partitions.* A hash partition determines the physical placement of data by performing a hash function on the values of the partition key. In *range partitioning,* consecutive values of the partition key are usually stored in the same partition. In *hash partitioning,* consecutive values of the partition key are not necessarily stored in the same partition. Hash partitioning distributes a set of records over a greater set of partitions than range partitioning does, potentially decreasing the likelihood for I/O contention.

To create a hash partition, use the **partition by hash** clause in place of the **partition by range** clause, as shown in the following listing:

```
create table BOOKSHELF_HASH_PART
(Title        VARCHAR2(100) primary key,
Publisher     VARCHAR2(20),
CategoryName VARCHAR2(20),
Rating        VARCHAR2(2),
constraint CATFK_HASH foreign key (CategoryName)
references CATEGORY(CategoryName)
)
partition by hash (CategoryName)
partitions 10;
```

You can name each partition and specify its tablespace, just as you would for range partitioning, as shown here:

```
create table BOOKSHELF_HASH_PART
(Title        VARCHAR2(100) primary key,
Publisher     VARCHAR2(20),
CategoryName  VARCHAR2(20),
Rating        VARCHAR2(2),
constraint CATFK_HASH foreign key (CategoryName)
references CATEGORY(CategoryName)
)
partition by hash (CategoryName)
partitions 2
store in (PART1_TS, PART2_TS);
```

Following the **partition by hash (CategoryName)** line, you have two choices for format:

- As shown in the preceding listing, you can specify the number of partitions and the tablespaces to use:

```
partitions 2
store in (PART1_TS, PART2_TS);
```

This method will create partitions with system-generated names of the format SYS_P*nnn*. The number of tablespaces specified in the **store in** clause does not have to equal the number of partitions. If more partitions than tablespaces are specified, the partitions will be assigned to the tablespaces in a round-robin fashion.

- You can specify named partitions:

```
partition by hash (CategoryName)
(partition PART1 tablespace PART1_TS,
 partition PART2 tablespace PART2_TS);
```

In this method, each partition is given a name and a tablespace, with the option of using an additional **lob** or **varray** storage clause (see Chapters 31 and 32). This method gives you more control over the location of the partitions, with the added benefit of letting you specify meaningful names for the partitions.

Creating Subpartitions

As of Oracle8i, you can create *subpartitions*—partitions of partitions. You can use subpartitions to combine the two types of partitions: range partitions and hash partitions. You can use hash partitions in combination with range partitions, creating hash partitions of the range partitions. For very large tables, this composite partitioning may be an effective way of separating the data into manageable and tunable divisions.

The following example range-partitions the BOOKSHELF table by the Title column, and hash-partitions the Title partitions by CategoryName values:

```
create table BOOKSHELF_RANGE_HASH_PART
(Title        VARCHAR2(100) primary key,
Publisher     VARCHAR2(20),
CategoryName  VARCHAR2(20),
Rating        VARCHAR2(2),
constraint CATFK3 foreign key (CategoryName)
```

```
references CATEGORY(CategoryName)
)
partition by range (Title)
subpartition by hash (CategoryName)
subpartitions 6
 (partition PART1   values less than ('M')
     tablespace PART1_TS,
  partition PART2   values less than (MAXVALUE)
     tablespace PART2_TS);
```

The BOOKSHELF table will be range-partitioned into two partitions, using the Title value ranges specified for the named partitions. Each of those partitions will be hash-partitioned on the CategoryName column.

List Partitioning

As of Oracle9i, you can use list partitions in place of range and hash partitioning. In list partitioning, you tell Oracle all of the possible values, and designate the partitions into which the corresponding rows should be inserted. The following example shows the BOOKSHELF entries list partitioned by CategoryName:

```
create table BOOKSHELF_LIST_PART
(Title        VARCHAR2(100) primary key,
Publisher     VARCHAR2(20),
CategoryName VARCHAR2(20),
Rating        VARCHAR2(2),
constraint CATFK4 foreign key (CategoryName)
references CATEGORY(CategoryName)
)
partition by list (CategoryName)
 (partition PART1   values ('ADULTFIC', 'ADULTNF', 'ADULTREF')
     tablespace PART1_TS,
  partition PART2   values
       ('CHILDRENFIC', 'CHILDRENNF', 'CHILDRENPIC')
     tablespace PART1_TS);
```

> **NOTE**
> In Oracle9i Release 9.0.1, if you attempt to **insert** a row with a value
> that does not exist in the list partition definitions—in this case, a
> different category name—the **insert** attempt will result in an error.
> This restriction is to be eliminated in a later version of Oracle9i.

Indexing Partitions

When you create a partitioned table, you should create an index on the table. The index may be partitioned according to the same range values that were used to partition the table. In the following listing, the **create index** command for the BOOKSHELF_LIST_PART (list partitioned) table is shown. The index partitions are placed in the PART1_NDX_TS and PART2_NDX_TS tablespaces.

```
create index BOOKSHELF__LIST_CATEGORY
  on BOOKSHELF_LIST_PART(CategoryName)
   local
   (partition PART1
     tablespace PART1_NDX_TS,
    partition PART2
     tablespace PART2_NDX_TS);
```

Notice the **local** keyword. In this **create index** command, no ranges are specified. Instead, the **local** keyword tells Oracle to create a separate index for each partition of the BOOKSHELF_ LIST_PART table. There were two partitions created on BOOKSHELF_LIST_PART. This index will create two separate indexes—one for each partition. Since there is one index per partition, the indexes are "local" to the partitions.

You can also create "global" indexes. A global index may contain values from multiple partitions.

```
create index BOOKSHELF_LIST_CATEGORY_G
on BOOKSHELF_LIST_PART(Publisher)
 global;
)
```

The **global** clause in this **create index** command allows you to create a non-partitioned index (as shown here) or to specify ranges for the index values that are different from the ranges for the table partitions. Local indexes may be easier to manage than global indexes; however, global indexes may perform uniqueness checks faster than local (partitioned) indexes perform them.

NOTE
You cannot create global indexes for hash partitions or subpartitions.

Managing Partitioned Tables

You can use the **alter table** command to **add**, **drop**, **exchange**, **move**, **modify**, **rename**, **split**, and **truncate** partitions. These **alter table** command options allow you to alter the existing partition structure, as may be required after a partitioned table has been used heavily. For example, the distribution of the CategoryName values within the partitioned table may have changed, or the maximum value may have increased. See the "ALTER TABLE" entry in the Alphabetical Reference for information on these options.

Querying Directly from Partitions

If you know the partition from which you will be retrieving your data, you can specify the name of the partition as part of the **from** clause of your query. For example, suppose you want to query the records for the books in the ADULT categories. The optimizer should be able to use the partition definitions to determine that only the PART1 partition could contain data that can resolve this query; but if you want, you can explicitly tell Oracle to use PART1 as part of your query:

```
insert into BOOKSHELF_LIST_PART select * from BOOKSHELF;

select COUNT(*) from BOOKSHELF_LIST_PART partition (part1);
```

```
COUNT(*)
----------
        22
```

This example explicitly names the partition in which Oracle is to search for the ADULT category records. If the partition is modified (for example, if its range of values is altered), then PART1 may no longer be the partition that contains these records. Thus, you should use great care when using this syntax.

In general, this syntax is not necessary, because Oracle stores the range definitions for the partitions. When you query from the partitioned table, Oracle determines which partitions should be involved in resolving the query. This process may result in a small number of rows being searched for the query, thus improving query performance. Additionally, the partitions may be stored in different tablespaces (and thus on separate disk devices), helping to reduce the potential for disk I/O contention during the processing of the query.

During an **insert** into the partitioned table, Oracle uses the partitions' definitions to determine which partition the record should be inserted into. Thus, you can use a partitioned table as if it were a single table, and rely on Oracle to manage the internal separation of the data.

Online Redefinition of Tables

As described earlier in this chapter, you can perform many object redefinition commands online—including moving index-organized tables, replacing views, and dropping columns. As of Oracle9i, you can redefine tables online; you can even partition a non-partitioned table while it is accessible to users. You can use this feature to move tables among tablespaces in online transaction processing applications.

To accomplish this while the database is being accessed, use the DBMS_REDEFINITION package provided with Oracle9i. There are some significant restrictions on this process (from the *Oracle9i Administrator's Guide*), as shown here:

- Tables must have primary keys to be candidates for online redefinition.

- The table to be redefined and the final redefined table must have the same primary key column.

- Tables that have materialized views and materialized view logs defined on them cannot be redefined online.

- Tables that are materialized view container tables and Advanced Queuing tables cannot be redefined online.

- The overflow table of an index-organized table cannot be redefined online.

- Tables with user-defined types (objects, REFs, collections, typed tables) cannot be redefined online.

- Tables with FILE columns cannot be redefined online.

- Tables with LONG columns cannot be redefined online. Tables with LOB columns are acceptable.

- The table to be redefined cannot be part of a cluster.

- Tables in the SYS and SYSTEM schema cannot be redefined online.

- Temporary tables cannot be redefined.

- There is no horizontal subsetting support (in other words, no **where** clause can be specified on the source table).

- Only simple deterministic expressions can be used when mapping the columns in the interim table to those of the original table. For example, subqueries are not allowed.

- If new columns (which are not instantiated with existing data for the original table) are being added as part of the redefinition, then they must not be declared NOT NULL until the redefinition is complete.

- There cannot be any referential constraints between the table being redefined and the interim table.

If your tables meet those criteria, you can now start the redefinition process. The redefinition process has six steps:

1. Verify that the table can be rebuilt online.

2. Create the interim table and its indexes, grants, constraints, and triggers.

3. Start the redefinition.

4. Optionally, abort the process or sync the source/destination tables.

5. Finish the redefinition process.

6. Clean up the interim table.

The following steps show the redefinition of the AUTHOR table as it is partitioned while being accessible to users.

1. Verify That the Table Can Be Rebuilt Online
To verify that the table can be rebuilt online, execute the CAN_REDEF_TABLE procedure, providing the schema owner and table name as input:

```
execute DBMS_REDEFINITION.CAN_REDEF_TABLE('PRACTICE','AUTHOR');
```

If an error stack is reported, the first error listed will tell you what the problem is; later errors concerning the DBMS_REDEFINITION package can be ignored.

2. Create the Interim Table
What do you want AUTHOR to look like in the new tablespace? Create an interim table that will be used during the redefinition process. To simplify matters, keep the column names and order the same as the source AUTHOR table.

```
create table AUTHOR_INTERIM
(AuthorName    VARCHAR2(50) primary key,
 Comments      VARCHAR2(100)
```

```
)
partition by range (AuthorName)
(partition PART1 values less than ('M'),
partition PART2 values less than (MAXVALUE)
);
```

In this example, the AUTHOR_INTERIM table will serve as the interim table during the redefinition. Once the process is complete, AUTHOR_INTERIM will replace the old AUTHOR table—and the only indexes, constraints, triggers, and grants available for AUTHOR then will be those that you create on AUTHOR_INTERIM prior to the final step (Step 5 in this description). You can optionally create the indexes, triggers, grants, and constraints after the redefinition process completes, but creating them now avoids the need for locks on active tables later.

3. Start the Redefinition

The START_REDEF_TABLE procedure begins the redefinition. The AUTHOR_INTERIM table will now be populated with the committed data in the AUTHOR table, so the time and undo segment (transaction size) requirements for this step depend on the size of the AUTHOR table. As parameters, pass the schema owner, old table name, and the interim table name:

```
execute DBMS_REDEFINITION.START_REDEF_TABLE -
  ('PRACTICE','AUTHOR','AUTHOR_INTERIM');
```

If AUTHOR_INTERIM had a different column list than AUTHOR, that column list would be passed as the fourth parameter to the START_REDEF_TABLE procedure. Once this procedure has completed, you can query AUTHOR_INTERIM to verify its data contents—Oracle will have populated it with the data from AUTHOR.

4(a). OPTIONAL—Abort the Process

If you need to abort the redefinition process at this point, use the ABORT_REDEF_TABLE procedure, with the schema owner, source table, and interim table as input parameters.

```
execute DBMS_REDEFINITION.ABORT_REDEF_TABLE -
  ('PRACTICE','AUTHOR','AUTHOR_INTERIM');
```

After aborting the redefinition, you should consider truncating the interim (AUTHOR_INTERIM) table as well to reclaim its space allocation.

4(b). OPTIONAL—Sync the Tables

During the conclusion of the redefinition process, Oracle will sync the data between the source and interim tables. To shorten the time required by that part of the process, you can sync the tables prior to the final step. This optional step allows you to instantiate the latest production data in the interim table, minimizing later impact on your online users.

To sync the source and interim tables, use the SYNC_INTERIM_TABLE procedure, with the schema owner, source table, and interim table as input parameters.

```
execute DBMS_REDEFINITION.SYNC_INTERIM_TABLE -
  ('PRACTICE','AUTHOR','AUTHOR_INTERIM');
```

5. Finish the Redefinition Process

To complete the redefinition process, execute the FINISH_REDEF_TABLE procedure, as shown in the following examples. The input parameters are the owner, source table, and interim table names.

```
execute DBMS_REDEFINITION.FINISH_REDEF_TABLE -
  ('PRACTICE','AUTHOR','AUTHOR_INTERIM');
```

During this step, the AUTHOR table will take over the characteristics of the AUTHOR_INTERIM table—it will become a partitioned table, and will take over AUTHOR_INTERIM's internal object ID value.

Since the AUTHOR table should now be partitioned, you can verify its redefinition by querying USER_TAB_PARTITIONS:

```
select Table_Name, Tablespace_Name, High_Value
  from USER_TAB_PARTITIONS
 where Table_Name = 'AUTHOR';

TABLE_NAME     TABLESPACE_NAME HIGH_VALUE
------------   --------------- ----------
AUTHOR         USERS           MAXVALUE
AUTHOR         USERS           'M'
```

As shown in the preceding listing, the AUTHOR table partitions both reside in the USERS tablespace. At this point, you should verify that the foreign keys on AUTHOR are enabled; that all necessary grants are in place; that the indexes are all in place; and that all triggers are enabled.

6. Clean Up the Interim Table

Although AUTHOR has taken over the AUTHOR_INTERIM definitions, the AUTHOR_INTERIM table is still out there! AUTHOR and AUTHOR_INTERIM have switched places—AUTHOR_INTERIM is now a non-partitioned table. Once you have verified that the new AUTHOR table is correct, you should clean up the AUTHOR_INTERIM table—either by truncating it or dropping it to free the space it had allocated.

CHAPTER
19

By What Authority?

I nformation is vital to success, but when damaged or in the wrong hands, it can threaten success. Oracle provides extensive security features to safeguard your information from both unauthorized viewing and intentional or inadvertent damage. This security is provided by granting or revoking privileges on a person-by-person and privilege-by-privilege basis, and is in addition to (and independent of) any security your computer system already has. Oracle uses the **create user**, **create role**, and **grant** commands to control data access.

Users, Roles, and Privileges

Every Oracle user has a name and password, and owns any tables, views, and other resources that he or she creates. An Oracle *role* is a set of *privileges* (or the type of access that each user needs, depending on his or her status and responsibilities). You can grant or bestow specific privileges to roles and then assign roles to the appropriate users. A user can also grant privileges directly to other users.

Database system privileges let you execute specific sets of commands. The CREATE TABLE privilege, for example, lets you create tables. The GRANT ANY PRIVILEGE privilege allows you to grant any system privilege.

Database object privileges give you the ability to perform some operation on various objects. The DELETE privilege, for example, lets you delete rows from tables and views. The SELECT privilege allows you to query with a **select** from tables, views, sequences, and snapshots (materialized views).

See "Privilege" in the Alphabetical Reference at the end of this book for a complete list of system and object privileges.

Creating a User

The Oracle system comes with many users already created, including SYSTEM and SYS. The SYS user owns the core internal tables Oracle uses to manage the database; SYSTEM owns additional tables and views. You can log on to the SYSTEM user to create other users, since SYSTEM has that privilege.

When installing Oracle, you (or a system administrator) first create a user for yourself. This is the format for the **create user** command:

```
create user user identified {by password | externally};
```

Other privileges can be set via this command; see the **create user** command in the Alphabetical Reference for details.

To connect your computer system's userid and password into Oracle's security so that only one logon is required for host-based users, use **externally** instead of giving a password. A system administrator (who has a great many privileges) may want the extra security of having a separate password. Let's call the system administrator Dora in the following examples:

```
create user Dora identified by avocado;
```

Dora's account now exists and is secured by a password.

You also can set up the user with specific *tablespaces* (space on disk for the user's tables—discussed in the following chapter) and *quotas* (limits) for space and resource usage. See **create user** in the Alphabetical Reference and Chapter 20 for a discussion of tablespaces and resources.

To change a password, use the **alter user** command:

```
alter user Dora identified by psyche;
```

Now Dora has the password "psyche" instead of "avocado." However, Dora cannot log into her account until she first has the CREATE SESSION system privilege:

```
grant CREATE SESSION to Dora;
```

You'll see additional examples of system privilege grants later in this chapter.

Password Management

Passwords can expire, and accounts may be locked due to repeated failed attempts to connect. When you change your password, a password history may be maintained to prevent reuse of previous passwords.

The expiration characteristics of your account's password are determined by the profile assigned to your account. Profiles, which are created by the **create profile** command, are managed by the DBA (database administrator, discussed later in the chapter). See the "CREATE PROFILE" entry in the Alphabetical Reference for full details on the **create profile** command. Relative to passwords and account access, profiles can enforce the following:

- The "lifetime" of your password, which determines how frequently you must change it
- The grace period following your password's "expiration date" during which you can change the password
- The number of consecutive failed connect attempts allowed before the account is automatically "locked"
- The number of days the account will remain locked
- The number of days that must pass before you can reuse a password
- The number of password changes that must take place before you can reuse a password

Additional password management features allow the minimum length and complexity of passwords to be enforced.

In addition to the **alter user** command, you can use the **password** command in SQLPLUS to change your password. If you use the **password** command, your new password will not be displayed on the screen as you type. Database administrators can change any user's password via the **password** command; other users can change only their own password.

When you enter the **password** command, you will be prompted for the old and new passwords, as shown in the following listing:

```
connect dora/psyche
password
Changing password for dora
Old password:
New password:
Retype new password:
```

When the password has been successfully changed, you will receive the feedback:

```
Password changed
```

Enforcing Password Expiration

You can use profiles to manage the expiration, reuse, and complexity of passwords. You can limit the lifetime of a password, and lock an account whose password is too old. You can also force a password to be at least moderately complex, and lock any account that has repeated failed login attempts.

For example, if you set the FAILED_LOGIN_ATTEMPTS resource of the user's profile to 5, then four consecutive failed login attempts will be allowed for the account; the fifth will cause the account to be locked.

NOTE
If the correct password is supplied on the fifth attempt, then the 'failed login attempt count' is reset to 0, allowing for five more consecutive unsuccessful login attempts before the account is locked.

In the following listing, the LIMITED_PROFILE profile is created, for use by the user JANE:

```
create profile LIMITED_PROFILE limit
FAILED_LOGIN_ATTEMPTS 5;

create user JANE identified by EYRE
profile LIMITED_PROFILE;

grant CREATE SESSION to JANE;
```

If there are five consecutive failed connects to the JANE account, the account will be automatically locked by Oracle. When you then use the correct password for the JANE account, you will receive an error.

```
connect jane/eyre
ERROR: ORA-28000: the account is locked
```

To unlock the account, use the **account unlock** clause of the **alter user** command (from a DBA account), as shown in the following listing:

```
alter user JANE account unlock;
```

Following the unlocking of the account, connections to the JANE account will once again be allowed. You can manually lock an account via the **account lock** clause of the **alter user** command.

```
alter user JANE account lock;
```

If an account becomes locked due to repeated connection failures, it will automatically become unlocked when its profile's PASSWORD_LOCK_TIME value is exceeded. For example, if PASSWORD_LOCK_TIME is set to 1, then the JANE account in the previous example would be locked for one day, at which point the account would be unlocked.

You can establish a maximum lifetime for a password via the PASSWORD_LIFE_TIME resource within profiles. For example, you could force users of the LIMITED_PROFILE profile to change their passwords every 30 days.

```
alter profile LIMITED_PROFILE limit
PASSWORD_LIFE_TIME 30;
```

In this example, the **alter profile** command is used to modify the LIMITED_PROFILE profile. The PASSWORD_LIFE_TIME value is set to 30, so each account that uses that profile will have its password expire after 30 days. If your password has expired, you must change it the next time you log in unless the profile has a specified grace period for expired passwords. The grace period parameter is called PASSWORD_GRACE_TIME. If the password is not changed within the grace period, the account expires.

NOTE
If you are going to use the PASSWORD_LIFE_TIME parameter, then you need to give the users a way to change their passwords easily.

An "expired" account is different from a "locked" account. A locked account, as shown earlier in this section, may be automatically unlocked by the passage of time. An expired account, however, requires manual intervention by the DBA to be re-enabled.

NOTE
If you use the password expiration features, make sure the accounts that own your applications have different profile settings; otherwise, they may become locked and the application may become unusable.

To re-enable an expired account, you will need to execute the **alter user** command, as shown in the following example. In this example, the DBA manually expires JANE's password:

```
alter user jane password expire;

User altered.
```

Next, JANE attempts to connect to her account. When she provides her password, she is immediately prompted for a new password for the account.

```
connect jane/eyre
ERROR: ORA-28001: the account has expired

Changing password for jane
Old password:
New password:
Retype new password:
Password changed
Connected.
```

You can also force users to change their passwords when they first access their accounts, via the **password expire** clause of the **create user** command. The **create user** command does not, however, allow you to set an expiration date for the new password set by the user; to do that, you must use the PASSWORD_LIFE_TIME profile parameters shown in the previous examples.

To see the password expiration date of any account, query the Expiry_Date column of the DBA_USERS data dictionary view. Users who want to see the password expiration date for their accounts can query the Expiry_Date column of the USER_USERS data dictionary view (via either SQL*Plus or a client-based query tool).

Enforcing Password Reuse Limitations

To prevent a password from being reused, you can use one of two profile parameters: PASSWORD_REUSE_MAX or PASSWORD_REUSE_TIME. These two parameters are mutually exclusive; if you set a value for one of them, the other must be set to UNLIMITED.

The PASSWORD_REUSE_TIME parameter specifies the number of days that must pass before a password can be reused. For example, if you set PASSWORD_REUSE_TIME to 60, then you cannot reuse the same password within 60 days.

The PASSWORD_REUSE_MAX parameter specifies the number of password changes that must occur before a password can be reused. If you attempt to reuse the password before the limit is reached, Oracle will reject your password change.

For example, you can set PASSWORD_REUSE_MAX for the LIMITED_PROFILE profile created earlier in this chapter.

```
alter profile LIMITED_PROFILE limit
PASSWORD_REUSE_MAX 3
PASSWORD_REUSE_TIME UNLIMITED;
```

If the user JANE now attempts to reuse a recent password, the password change attempt will fail. For example, suppose she changes her password, as in the following line:

```
alter user JANE identified by austen;
```

and then changes it again:

```
alter user JANE identified by whitley;
```

During her next password change, she attempts to reuse a recent password, and the attempt fails.

```
alter user jane identified by austen;
alter user jane identified by austen
                                    *
ERROR at line 1:
ORA-28007: the password cannot be reused
```

She cannot reuse any of her recent passwords; she will need to come up with a new password.

Password histories are stored in the table named USER_HISTORY$ under the SYS schema. In this table, Oracle stores the userid, encrypted password value, and the date/timestamp for the creation of the password. When the PASSWORD_REUSE_TIME value is exceeded or the number of changes exceeds PASSWORD_REUSE_MAX, the old password records are deleted from the SYS.USER_HISTORY$ table. If a new encryption matches an existing encryption, the new password is rejected.

Because the old passwords are stored in a table owned by SYS, the data is stored in the SYSTEM tablespace. Therefore, if you plan to maintain a very large password history for a very large number of users who are forced to change passwords frequently, the space requirements of the password history table (SYS.USER_HISTORY$) may impact the space requirements of your SYSTEM tablespace.

Three Standard Roles

Now that Dora has an account, what can she do in Oracle? At this point, nothing—Dora has no system privileges.

Oracle provides three standard roles for compatibility with previous versions: CONNECT, RESOURCE, and DBA.

The CONNECT Role

Occasional users will usually be given only the CONNECT role or the CREATE SESSION privilege. CONNECT gives users the ability to log in and perform basic functions. This ability becomes meaningful with the addition of access to specific tables belonging to other users, and the privilege to **select**, **insert**, **update**, and **delete** rows in these tables, as each of these rights is granted. In addition to creating sessions, users who have the CONNECT role may also create tables, views, sequences, clusters, synonyms (discussed in this chapter), and links to other databases (see Chapter 22).

The RESOURCE Role

More sophisticated and regular users of the database may be granted the RESOURCE role. RESOURCE gives users the additional rights to create their own tables, sequences, procedures, triggers, datatypes (see Part IV of this book), operators, indextypes, indexes, and clusters. See Part III of this book for a discussion of stored procedures and triggers.

The DBA Role

The DBA (*database administrator*) role has all system privileges—including unlimited space quotas—and the ability to grant all privileges to other users. In this chapter, *dba* refers to the

person who is the database administrator and has the DBA role, while *DBA* refers just to those privileges encompassed by the DBA role. SYSTEM is for use by a DBA user. Some of the rights that are reserved for the dba are never given to, or needed by, normal users. Little time will be spent here on those rights. Other rights typically used by dbas are also regularly used by and important to users. This subset of DBA privileges will be explained shortly.

Format for the grant Command

Here is the format for the **grant** command for system privileges:

```
grant {system privilege | role | all [privileges] }
     [, {system privilege | role | all [privileges] }. . .]
     to {user | role} [, {user | role}]. . .
     [identified by password ]
     [with admin option]
```

By using the **grant** command, you can grant any system privilege or role to another user, to another role, or to **public**. The **with admin option** clause permits the grantee to bestow the privilege or role on other users or roles. The **all** clause grants the user or role all privileges except the SELECT ANY DICTIONARY system privilege.

The grantor can revoke a role from a user as well.

Revoking Privileges

Privileges granted can be taken away. The **revoke** command is similar to the **grant** command:

```
revoke {system privilege | role | all [privileges] }
      [, {system privilege | role | all [privileges] }. . .]
      from {user | role} [, {user | role}]. . .
```

An individual with the DBA role can revoke CONNECT, RESOURCE, DBA, or any other privilege or role from anyone, including another dba. This, of course, is dangerous, and is why DBA privileges should be given neither lightly nor to more than a tiny minority who really need them.

> **NOTE**
> *Revoking everything from a given user does not eliminate that user from Oracle, nor does it destroy any tables that user had created; it simply prohibits that user's access to them. Other users with access to the tables will still have exactly the same access they've always had.*

To remove a user and all the resources owned by that user, use the **drop user** command like this:

```
drop user username [cascade];
```

The **cascade** option drops the user along with all the objects owned by the user, including referential integrity constraints. The **cascade** option invalidates views, synonyms, stored

procedures, functions, or packages that refer to objects in the dropped user's schema. If you don't use the **cascade** option and there are still objects owned by the user, Oracle does not drop the user and instead returns an error message.

What Users Can Grant

A user can grant privileges on any object he or she owns. The dba can grant any system privilege (because the DBA role has the GRANT ANY and the GRANT ANY ROLE privileges).

Suppose that user Dora owns the COMFORT table and is a dba. She creates two new users, Bob and Judy, with these privileges:

```
create user Judy identified by sarah;

User created.

grant CONNECT to Judy;

Grant succeeded.

create user Bob identified by carolyn;

User created.

grant CONNECT, RESOURCE to bob;

Grant succeeded.
```

This sequence of commands gives both Judy and Bob the ability to connect to Oracle, and gives Bob some extra capabilities. But can either do anything with Dora's tables? Not without explicit access.

To give others access to your tables, use a second form of the **grant** command:

```
grant { object privilege | all [privileges] }
    [(column [, column] . . .)]
    [, { object privilege | all [privileges] }
    [(column [, column] . . .)] ] . . .
    on object to {user | role}
    [with grant option]
    [with hierarchy option];
```

The privileges a user can grant include these:

- On the user's tables, views, and materialized views:
 INSERT
 UPDATE (all or specific columns)
 DELETE
 SELECT

The INSERT, UPDATE, and DELETE privileges can only be granted on materialized views if they are updateable. See Chapter 23 for details on the creation of materialized views.

- On tables, you can also grant:
 ALTER (table—all or specific columns)
 REFERENCES
 INDEX (columns in a table)
 ON COMMIT REFRESH
 QUERY REWRITE
 ALL (of the items previously listed)

- On procedures, functions, packages, abstract datatypes, libraries, indextypes, and operators:
 EXECUTE

- On sequences:
 SELECT
 ALTER

- On directories (for BFILE LOB datatypes and external tables):
 READ
 WRITE

- On abstract datatypes and views:
 UNDER (for the ability to create subviews under a view, or subtype under a type)

The privilege granted must be one of the object privileges (ALL, ALTER, DELETE, EXECUTE, INDEX, INSERT, ON COMMIT REFRESH, QUERY REWRITE, READ, REFERENCES, SELECT, UNDER, UPDATE, or WRITE). These privileges give the grantee the ability to take some action on the object. The object can be one of the objects listed here or a synonym for any of these objects.

When you execute another user's procedure or function, it is typically executed using the privileges of its owner. This means that you don't need explicit access to the data the procedure or function uses; you see only the result of the execution, not the underlying data. You can also create stored procedures that execute under the privileges of the invoking user instead of the procedure owner; see Chapter 29 for details.

Dora gives Bob SELECT access to the COMFORT table:

```
grant select on COMFORT to Bob;

Grant succeeded.
```

The **with grant option** clause of the **grant** command allows the recipient of that grant to pass along the privileges he or she has received to other users. If the user Dora grants privileges on her tables to the user Bob **with grant option**, then Bob can make grants on Dora's tables to other users (Bob can only pass along those privileges—such as SELECT—that he has been granted). If

you intend to create views based on another user's tables and grant access to those views to other users, you first must be granted access **with grant option** to the base tables.

Moving to Another User with connect

To test the success of her grant, Dora connects to Bob's username with the **connect** command. This command may be used via one of the following methods:

- By entering both the username and password on the same line as the command
- By entering the command alone and then responding to prompts
- By entering the command and username and responding to the prompt for the password

The latter two methods suppress display of the password and are therefore inherently more secure. The following listing shows a sample connection to the database.

```
connect Bob/carolyn

Connected.
```

Once connected, Dora selects from the table to which Bob has been given SELECT access.

NOTE
Unless a synonym is used, the table name must be preceded by the username of the table's owner. Without this, Oracle will say the table does not exist.

```
select * from Dora.COMFORT;
```

CITY	SAMPLEDAT	NOON	MIDNIGHT	PRECIPITATION
SAN FRANCISCO	21-MAR-01	62.5	42.3	.5
SAN FRANCISCO	22-JUN-01	51.1	71.9	.1
SAN FRANCISCO	23-SEP-01		61.5	.1
SAN FRANCISCO	22-DEC-01	52.6	39.8	2.3
KEENE	21-MAR-01	39.9	-1.2	4.4
KEENE	22-JUN-01	85.1	66.7	1.3
KEENE	23-SEP-01	99.8	82.6	
KEENE	22-DEC-01	-7.2	-1.2	3.9

For convenience, a view named COMFORT is created, which is simply a straight **select** from the table Dora.COMFORT:

```
create view COMFORT as select * from Dora.COMFORT;

View created.
```

Selecting from this view will produce exactly the same results as selecting from Dora.COMFORT:

```
select * from COMFORT;

CITY          SAMPLEDAT  NOON MIDNIGHT PRECIPITATION
------------- --------- ----- -------- -------------
SAN FRANCISCO 21-MAR-01  62.5     42.3            .5
SAN FRANCISCO 22-JUN-01  51.1     71.9            .1
SAN FRANCISCO 23-SEP-01           61.5            .1
SAN FRANCISCO 22-DEC-01  52.6     39.8           2.3
KEENE         21-MAR-01  39.9     -1.2           4.4
KEENE         22-JUN-01  85.1     66.7           1.3
KEENE         23-SEP-01  99.8     82.6
KEENE         22-DEC-01  -7.2     -1.2           3.9
```

Now Dora returns to her own username and creates a view that selects only a part of the COMFORT table:

```
connect Dora/psyche
Connected.

create view SOMECOMFORT as
select * from COMFORT
 where City = 'KEENE';

View created.
```

She then grants both SELECT and UPDATE privileges to Bob *on this view,* and revokes all privileges from Bob (via the **revoke** command) for the whole COMFORT table:

```
grant select, update on SOMECOMFORT to Bob;

Grant succeeded.

revoke all on COMFORT from Bob;

Revoke succeeded.
```

Dora then reconnects to Bob's username to test the effects of this change:

```
connect Bob/carolyn
Connected.

select * from COMFORT;
              *
ERROR at line 1: ORA-04063: view "BOB.COMFORT" has errors
```

Attempting to select from his COMFORT view fails because the underlying table named in Bob's view was the Dora.COMFORT table. Not surprisingly, attempting to select from

Dora.COMFORT would produce exactly the same message. Next, an attempt to select from Dora.SOMECOMFORT is made:

```
select * from Dora.SOMECOMFORT;

CITY          SAMPLEDAT NOON MIDNIGHT PRECIPITATION
------------- --------- ----- -------- -------------
KEENE         21-MAR-01 39.9     -1.2           4.4
KEENE         22-JUN-01 85.1     66.7           1.3
KEENE         23-SEP-01 99.8     82.6
KEENE         22-DEC-01 -7.2     -1.2           3.9
```

This works perfectly well, even though direct access to the COMFORT table had been revoked, because Dora gave Bob access to a portion of COMFORT through the SOMECOMFORT view. It is just that portion of the table related to KEENE.

This shows a powerful security feature of Oracle: You can create a view using virtually any restrictions you like or any computations in the columns, and then give access to the view, rather than to the underlying tables, to other users. They will see only the information the view presents. This can even be extended to be user-specific. The "Security by User" section later in this chapter gives complete details on this feature.

Now, the view LITTLECOMFORT is created under Bob's username, on top of the view SOMECOMFORT:

```
create view LITTLECOMFORT as select * from Dora.SOMECOMFORT;

View created.
```

and the row for September 23, 2001, is updated:

```
update LITTLECOMFORT set Noon = 88
 where SampleDate = '23-SEP-01';

1 row updated.
```

When the view LITTLECOMFORT is queried, it shows the effect of the **update**:

```
select * from LITTLECOMFORT;

CITY          SAMPLEDAT NOON MIDNIGHT PRECIPITATION
------------- --------- ----- -------- -------------
KEENE         21-MAR-01 39.9     -1.2           4.4
KEENE         22-JUN-01 85.1     66.7           1.3
KEENE         23-SEP-01   88     82.6
KEENE         22-DEC-01 -7.2     -1.2           3.9
```

A query of Dora.SOMECOMFORT would show the same results, as would a query of COMFORT itself if Dora made it on her own username. The update was successful against the underlying table even though it went through two views (LITTLECOMFORT and SOMECOMFORT) to reach it.

NOTE
You need to grant users SELECT access to any table in which they can update or delete records. This is in keeping with the evolving ANSI standard and reflects the fact that a user who only had UPDATE or DELETE privilege on a table could use the database's feedback comments to discover information about the underlying data.

create synonym

An alternative method to creating a view that includes an entire table or view from another user is to create a synonym:

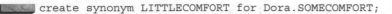

```
create synonym LITTLECOMFORT for Dora.SOMECOMFORT;
```

This synonym can be treated exactly like a view. See the **create synonym** command in the Alphabetical Reference.

Using Ungranted Privileges

Let's say an attempt is made to delete the row you just updated:

```
delete from LITTLECOMFORT where SampleDate = '23-SEP-01';
             *
ERROR at line 1: ORA-01031: insufficient privileges
```

Bob has not been given DELETE privileges by Dora, so the attempt fails.

Passing on Privileges

Bob can grant authority for other users to access his tables, but cannot bestow on other users access to tables that don't belong to him. Here, he attempts to give INSERT authority to Judy:

```
grant insert on Dora.SOMECOMFORT to Judy;
       *
ERROR at line 1: ORA-01031: insufficient privileges
```

Because Bob does not have this authority, he fails to give it to Judy. Next, Bob tries to pass on the privilege he does have, SELECT:

```
grant select on Dora.SOMECOMFORT to Judy;
       *
ERROR at line 1: ORA-01031: insufficient privileges
```

He cannot grant this privilege, either, because the view SOMECOMFORT does not belong to him. If he had been granted access to SOMECOMFORT **with grant option**, then the preceding

grant command would have succeeded. The view LITTLECOMFORT does belong to him, though, so he can try to pass authority to that on to Judy:

```
grant select on LITTLECOMFORT to Judy;

ERROR at line 1:
ORA-01720: grant option does not exist for 'DORA.SOMECOMFORT'
```

Since the LITTLECOMFORT view relies on one of Dora's views, and Bob was not granted SELECT **with grant option** on that view, Bob's grant fails.

In addition, a new table, owned by Bob, is created and loaded with the current information from his view LITTLECOMFORT:

```
create table NOCOMFORT as
select * from LITTLECOMFORT;

Table created.
```

SELECT privileges on it are granted to Judy as well:

```
grant select on NOCOMFORT to Judy;

Grant succeeded.
```

Queries are made from Judy's account against the table for which Bob granted the SELECT privilege to Judy:

```
connect Judy/sarah
select * from Bob.NOCOMFORT;

CITY          SAMPLEDAT NOON MIDNIGHT PRECIPITATION
------------- --------- ---- -------- -------------
KEENE         21-MAR-01 39.9     -1.2           4.4
KEENE         22-JUN-01 85.1     66.7           1.3
KEENE         23-SEP-01 88       82.6
KEENE         22-DEC-01 -7.2     -1.2           3.9
```

This grant was successful. A NOCOMFORT table was created, and owned, by Bob's username. He was able to successfully give access to this table.

If Dora wants Bob to be able to pass on his privileges to others, she can add another clause to the **grant** statement:

```
connect Dora/psyche
grant select, update on SOMECOMFORT to Bob with grant option;

Grant succeeded.
```

The **with grant option** clause enables Bob to pass on access to SOMECOMFORT to Judy through his LITTLECOMFORT view. Note that attempts to access a table to which a user does not have the SELECT privilege always result in this message:

```
ERROR at line 1: ORA-00942: table or view does not exist
```

This message appears rather than a message about not having access privilege so that a person without permission to query a table doesn't know that it even exists.

Creating a Role

In addition to the three system roles shown earlier in this chapter—CONNECT, RESOURCE, and DBA—you can create your own roles within Oracle. The roles you create can comprise table or system privileges or a combination of both. In the following sections, you will see how to create and administer roles.

To create a role, you need to have the CREATE ROLE system privilege. The syntax for role creation is shown in the following listing:

```
create role role_name
[not identified
|identified {by password | using [schema.]package
|externally | globally }];
```

When a role is first created, it has no privileges associated with it. Password options for roles are discussed in "Adding a Password to a Role," later in this chapter.

Two sample **create role** commands are shown in the following example:

```
create role CLERK;
create role MANAGER;
```

The first command creates a role called CLERK, which will be used in the examples in the following sections of this chapter. The second command creates a role called MANAGER, which will also be featured in those examples.

Granting Privileges to a Role

Once a role has been created, you may grant privileges to it. The syntax for the **grant** command is the same for roles as it was for users. When granting privileges to roles, you use the role name in the **to** clause of the **grant** command, as shown in the following listing:

```
grant select on COMFORT to CLERK;
```

As shown in this example, the role name takes the place of the username in the **grant** command. The privilege to select from the COMFORT table will now be available to any user of the CLERK role.

If you are a dba, or have been granted the GRANT ANY PRIVILEGE system role, then you may grant system privileges—such as CREATE SESSION, CREATE SYNONYM, and CREATE VIEW—to roles. These privileges will then be available to any user of your role.

The ability to log into the database is given via the CREATE SESSION system privilege. In the following example, this privilege is granted to the CLERK role. This privilege is also granted to the MANAGER role, along with the CREATE DATABASE LINK system privilege.

```
grant CREATE SESSION to CLERK;
grant CREATE SESSION, CREATE DATABASE LINK to MANAGER;
```

Granting a Role to Another Role

Roles can be granted to other roles. You can do this via the **grant** command, as shown in the following example:

```
grant CLERK to MANAGER;
```

In this example, the CLERK role is granted to the MANAGER role. Even though you have not directly granted any table privileges to the MANAGER role, it will now inherit any privileges that have been granted to the CLERK role. Organizing roles in this way is a common design for hierarchical organizations.

When granting a role to another role (or to a user, as in the following section), you may grant the role using the **with admin option** clause, as shown in the following listing:

```
grant CLERK to MANAGER with admin option;
```

If the **with admin option** clause is used, then the grantee has the authority to grant the role to other users or roles. The grantee can also alter or drop the role.

Granting a Role to Users

Roles can be granted to users. When granted to users, roles can be thought of as named sets of privileges. Instead of granting each privilege to each user, you grant the privileges to the role and then grant the role to each user. This greatly simplifies the administrative tasks involved in the management of privileges.

NOTE
Privileges that are granted to users via roles cannot be used as the basis for views, procedures, functions, packages, or foreign keys. When creating these types of database objects, you must rely on direct grants of the necessary privileges.

You can grant a role to a user via the **grant** command, as shown in the following example:

```
grant CLERK to Bob;
```

The user Bob in this example will have all of the privileges that were granted to the CLERK role (CREATE SESSION and SELECT privileges on COMFORT).

When granting a role to a user, you may grant the role using the **with admin option** clause, as shown in the following listing:

```
grant MANAGER to Dora with admin option;
```

Dora now has the authority to grant the MANAGER role to other users or roles, or to alter or drop the role.

Adding a Password to a Role

You can use the **alter role** command for only one purpose: to change the authority needed to enable it. By default, roles do not have passwords associated with them. To enable security for a role, use the **identified** keyword in the **alter role** command. There are two ways to implement this security.

First, you can use the **identified by** clause of the **alter role** command to specify a password, as shown in the following listing:

```
alter role MANAGER identified by cygnusxi;
```

Any time a user tries to activate that role, the password will be required. If, however, that role is set up as a default role for the user, then no password will be required for that role when the user logs in. See the upcoming "Enabling and Disabling Roles" section of this chapter for more details on these topics.

Roles can be tied to operating system privileges as well. If this capability is available on your operating system, then you use the **identified externally** clause of the **alter role** command. When the role is enabled, Oracle will check the operating system to verify your access. Altering a role to use this security feature is shown in the following example:

```
alter role MANAGER identified externally;
```

In most UNIX systems, the verification process uses the /etc/group file. To use this file for any operating system, the OS_ROLES database startup parameter in the init.ora file must be set to TRUE.

The following example of this verification process is for a database instance called "Local" on a UNIX system. The server's /etc/group file may contain the following entry:

```
ora_local_manager_d:NONE:1:dora
```

This entry grants the MANAGER role to the account named Dora. The **_d** suffix indicates that this role is to be granted by default when Dora logs in. An **_a** suffix would indicate that this role is to be enabled **with admin option**. If this role were also the user's default role, then the suffix would be **_ad**. If more than one user were granted this role, then the additional usernames would be appended to the /etc/group entry, as shown in the following listing:

```
ora_local_manager_d:NONE:1:dora,judy
```

If you use this option, all roles in the database will be enabled via the operating system.

Removing a Password from a Role

To remove a password from a role, use the **not identified** clause of the **alter role** command, as shown in the following listing. By default, roles do not have passwords.

```
alter role MANAGER not identified;
```

Enabling and Disabling Roles

When a user's account is altered, a list of default roles for that user can be created via the **default role** clause of the **alter user** command. The default action of this command sets all of a user's roles as default roles, enabling all of them every time the user logs in.

NOTE
The maximum number of roles a user can have enabled at any time is set via the MAX_ENABLED_ROLES database initialization parameter.

The syntax for this portion of the **alter user** command is as follows:

```
alter user username
default role {[role1, role2]
[all | all except role1, role2] [NONE]};
```

As shown by this syntax, a user can be altered to have, by default, specific roles enabled, all roles enabled, all except specific roles enabled, or no roles enabled. For example, the following **alter user** command will enable the CLERK role whenever Bob logs in:

```
alter user Bob
default role CLERK;
```

To enable a nondefault role, use the **set role** command, as shown in this example:

```
set role CLERK;
```

You may also use the **all** and **all except** clauses that were available in the **alter user** command:

```
set role all;
set role all except CLERK;
```

If a role has a password associated with it, that password must be specified via an **identified by** clause:

```
set role MANAGER identified by cygnusxi;
```

To disable a role in your session, use the **set role none** command, as shown in the following listing. This will disable all roles in your current session. Once all of the roles have been disabled, re-enable the ones you want.

```
set role none;
```

Since you may find it necessary to execute a **set role none** command from time to time, you may want to grant the CREATE SESSION privilege to users directly rather than via roles.

Revoking Privileges from a Role

To revoke a privilege from a role, use the **revoke** command, described earlier in this chapter. Specify the privilege, object name (if it is an object privilege), and role name, as shown in the following example:

```
revoke SELECT on COMFORT from CLERK;
```

Users of the CLERK role will then be unable to query the COMFORT table.

Dropping a Role

To drop a role, use the **drop role** command, as shown in the following example:

```
drop role MANAGER;
drop role CLERK;
```

The roles you specify, and their associated privileges, will be removed from the database entirely.

Granting UPDATE to Specific Columns

You may want to grant users the SELECT privilege to more columns than you want to grant them the UPDATE privilege. Since SELECT columns can be restricted through a view, to further restrict the columns that can be updated requires a special form of the user's **grant** command. Here is an example for two columns in the COMFORT table:

```
grant update (Noon, Midnight) on COMFORT to Judy;
```

Revoking Object Privileges

If object privileges can be granted, they can also be taken away. This is similar to the **grant** command:

```
revoke { object privilege | all [privileges] }
        [(column [, column]. . . )]
[, { object privilege | all [privileges] }
        [(column [, column]. . . )]]. . . .]
on object
from {user | role} [,{user | role}]
[cascade constraints] [force];
```

revoke all removes any of the privileges listed previously, from SELECT through INDEX; revoking individual privileges will leave intact others that had also been granted. The **with grant option** is revoked along with the privilege to which it was attached.

If a user defines referential integrity constraints on the object, Oracle drops these constraints if you revoke privileges on the object using the **cascade constraints** option. The **force** option applies to user-defined datatypes (see Chapter 31). The **force** option revokes the EXECUTE privilege on user-defined datatype objects with table or type dependencies; all dependent objects

will be marked as invalid and data in dependent tables will become inaccessible until the necessary privilege is re-granted.

Security by User

Access to tables can be granted specifically, table by table, and view by view, to each user. There is, however, an additional technique that will simplify this process in some cases. Recall the bookshelf checkout records:

```
select Name, SUBSTR(Title,1,30) from BOOKSHELF_CHECKOUT;

NAME                        SUBSTR(TITLE,1,30)
--------------------------  ---------------------------
JED HOPKINS                 INNUMERACY
GERHARDT KENTGEN            WONDERFUL LIFE
DORAH TALBOT                EITHER/OR
EMILY TALBOT                ANNE OF GREEN GABLES
PAT LAVAY                   THE SHIPPING NEWS
ROLAND BRANDT               THE SHIPPING NEWS
ROLAND BRANDT               THE DISCOVERERS
ROLAND BRANDT               WEST WITH THE NIGHT
EMILY TALBOT                MIDNIGHT MAGIC
EMILY TALBOT                HARRY POTTER AND THE GOBLET OF
PAT LAVAY                   THE MISMEASURE OF MAN
DORAH TALBOT                POLAR EXPRESS
DORAH TALBOT                GOOD DOG, CARL
GERHARDT KENTGEN            THE MISMEASURE OF MAN
FRED FULLER                 JOHN ADAMS
FRED FULLER                 TRUMAN
JED HOPKINS                 TO KILL A MOCKINGBIRD
DORAH TALBOT                MY LEDGER
GERHARDT KENTGEN            MIDNIGHT MAGIC
```

To enable each borrower to access this table, but restrict the access given to a view of only each borrower's own single row, you could create 19 separate views, each with a different name in the **where** clause, and you could make separate grants to each of these views for each borrower. Alternatively, you could create a view whose **where** clause contained User, the pseudo-column, like this:

```
create view MY_CHECKOUT as
select * from BOOKSHELF_CHECKOUT
 where SUBSTR(Name,1,INSTR(Name,' ')-1) = User;
```

The owner of the BOOKSHELF_CHECKOUT table can create this view and grant SELECT on it to users. A user can then query the BOOKSHELF_CHECKOUT table through the MY_CHECKOUT view. The **where** clause will find his or her username in the Name column (see the **where** clause), and return just that user's records.

In the following example, a user name Jed is created and granted access to the MY_CHECKOUT view. Selecting from that view yields just those books checked out by him.

```
create user jed identified by hop;

User created.

grant CREATE SESSION to jed;

Grant succeeded.

grant select on MY_CHECKOUT to jed;

Grant succeeded.

connect jed/hop

Connected.

select * from Practice.MY_CHECKOUT;

NAME
------------------------
TITLE
------------------------------------------------------------
CHECKOUTD RETURNEDD
--------- ---------
JED HOPKINS
INNUMERACY
01-JAN-02 22-JAN-02

JED HOPKINS
TO KILL A MOCKINGBIRD
15-FEB-02 01-MAR-02
```

Whenever MY_CHECKOUT is queried, it will return records depending on the pseudo-column User—the user of SQLPLUS at the moment the view is queried.

Granting Access to the Public

Rather than grant access to every worker, the **grant** command can be generalized to the public:

```
grant select on MY_CHECKOUT to public;
```

This gives everyone access, including users created after this grant was made. However, each user will still have to access the table using the owner's username as a prefix. To avoid this, a dba may create a *public synonym* (which creates a name accessible to all users that stands for Practice.MY_CHECKOUT):

```
create public synonym MY_CHECKOUT for Practice.MY_CHECKOUT;
```

From this point forward, anyone can access MY_CHECKOUT without prefixing it with the schema owner (Practice in this case). This approach gives tremendous flexibility for security.

Workers could see only their own salaries, for instance, in a table that contains salaries for everyone. If, however, a user creates a table or view with the same name as a public synonym, any future SQL statements by this user will act on this new table or view, and not on the one by the same name to which the public has access.

> **NOTE**
> *All of these accesses—and all attempts at system-level operations, such as logins—may be audited. See AUDIT in the Alphabetical Reference for an introduction to Oracle's security auditing capabilities.*

Granting Limited Resources

When granting resource quotas in an Oracle database, the **quota** parameter of the **create user** or **alter user** command is used, as shown in the following listing. In this example, Bob is granted a quota of 100MB in the USERS tablespace.

```
alter user Bob
quota 100M on USERS;
```

A user's space quota may be set when the user is created, via the **create user** command. If you want to remove limits on a user's space quota, you can grant that user the UNLIMITED TABLESPACE system privilege. See the **create user** and **alter user** commands in the Alphabetical Reference for further details on these commands.

Profiles can also be used to enforce other resource limits, such as the amount of CPU time or idle time a user's requests to Oracle can take. A profile detailing these resource limits is created and then assigned to one or more users. See the **create profile** and **alter user** command entries in the Alphabetical Reference for full details.

Advanced Options

In addition to the functions described in this chapter, Oracle supports advanced security features. Oracle's Virtual Private Database (VPD) feature offers a security model similar to that described in the "Security by User" section earlier in this chapter. VPD automatically adds **where** clauses to all of the commands issued by different users, allowing you to create complex security programs that are enforced within the database. With VPD, you can create policies that allow you to have data from multiple business areas in the same table while users querying the table only see their business area's data. Within VPD, you can use a procedure to validate a role instead of embedding a role in an application (**create role *rolename* identified using *procedurename***).

A second security option, Oracle Label Security, allows you to assign security labels to rows. You could, for example, create a system in which managers could see all rows while lower levels within an organization could only see a subset of the rows. Each row's security label is compared to the user's security privileges during data access. Oracle Label Security is an appropriate solution when your row-level security rules are best enforced via hierarchical groupings of rows by users.

For details on VPD and Oracle Label Security, see the Oracle9i Security Products and Features guide and the Oracle9i Security Overview documentation.

Database administrators can create functions to manage password complexity; for documentation and an example, see the utlpwdmg.sql file in the /rdbms/admin directory under the Oracle software home directory.

CHAPTER
20

Changing the
Oracle Surroundings

 ike Chapter 19, this chapter looks at that subset of database administrator (DBA) functions used by most Oracle users—functions not restricted to DBAs. These include indexes on tables, clusters, sequence generators, and allocations of space for tables and indexes. This chapter shows how Oracle's databases are structured internally, which helps in understanding how Oracle's many features actually work and how they interrelate. Only limited options of the **create index**, **create tablespace**, and **create cluster** commands will be shown in this chapter. Full options are described in Chapter 40 and are shown in the Alphabetical Reference later in this book.

Indexes

An *index* is a simple concept. It is typically a listing of *keywords* accompanied by the *location* of information on a subject. To find information on indexes, for instance, you look up the word "indexes" in the index at the back of this book. It will give the number of the page you are reading now. The word "indexes" is the key, and the page numbers given point you to the location of discussions about indexes in this book. This is related to the idea of primary keys in Oracle, which was described in Chapter 2.

While indexes are not strictly necessary to running Oracle, they do speed the process. For example, while you could find the information on indexes simply by reading through this book until you encountered the page with the information on it, this would be slow and time-consuming. Because the index at the back of the book is in alphabetical order, you can quickly go to the appropriate spot in the index (without reading every entry) where "index" is found. If the word is not common, this is quicker than reading through the book from front to back. These same principles apply to Oracle indexes. For example, if you are searching for a particular book, you can query with a limiting condition on the Title column:

```
select * from BOOKSHELF
  where Publisher = 'SCHOLASTIC';
```

If BOOKSHELF does not have an index on the Publisher column, Oracle has to read every row in the table until it finds all publishers that match the **where** clause of your query. If the table is small, that may not cause a performance problem. As the table grows in size, the time required to return all the matching rows to the user may impact the performance of the application and the business process it supports.

To speed the data retrieval, you can create an index on the Publisher column. Then, when you execute the same query, Oracle first looks in the index, which is sorted, thus finding the publisher named 'SCHOLASTIC' very quickly (Oracle doesn't read every entry, but jumps directly to the close vicinity of the name, much as you would in looking through the index of a book). The index entry then gives Oracle the exact location in the table (and on disk) of the row(s) for that publisher.

Knowing this, it is clear how indexing an important column (one that's likely to appear in a **where** clause) will speed up Oracle's response to a query. Indexing will likewise speed up queries where two tables are joined, if the columns that are related (by the **where** clause) are indexed. These are the basics of indexing; the rest of this chapter shows a number of additional features and issues related to indexing that will affect how quickly it works. For the impact of indexes on the optimization of your queries, see Chapter 38.

Creating an Index

You create an index via the **create index** command. When you designate a primary key or a unique column during table creation or maintenance, Oracle will automatically create a unique index to support that constraint. The full command syntax for **create index** is shown in the Alphabetical Reference. Its most commonly used format is as follows:

```
create [bitmap | unique] index index on table(column [,column]. . .)
[reverse];
```

index must be a unique name and follow the naming conventions of Oracle columns. *table* is simply the name of the table on which the index will be established, and *column* is the name of the column.

Bitmap indexes allow you to create useful indexes on columns with very few distinct values; see "Creating a Bitmap Index," later in this chapter. The **reverse** keyword tells Oracle to reverse the bytes of the indexed value, which may improve the data and processing distribution during the insert of many sequential data values.

You can establish a single index on multiple columns by listing the columns one after the other, separated by commas. For the following examples, the BOOKSHELF_AUTHOR table was created without a primary key:

```
create table BOOKSHELF_AUTHOR
(Title        VARCHAR2(100),
AuthorName  VARCHAR2(50),
constraint TitleFK Foreign key (Title) references BOOKSHELF(Title),
constraint AuthorNameFK Foreign key (AuthorName)
references AUTHOR(AuthorName));
```

Enforcing Uniqueness

Recall from Chapter 2 that a set of tables is said to be in Third Normal Form if all of the columns in each table's rows are dependent only on the primary key. In the BOOKSHELF_AUTHOR table, the primary key is the combination of the columns Title and AuthorName. In other tables, a primary key might be an employee ID, a client ID, an account number, or, in a bank, a combination of branch number and account number.

In each of these cases, the uniqueness of the primary key is critical. A bank with duplicate account numbers, or a billing system with duplicate client IDs, would wreak havoc as transactions were posted to accounts belonging to different people but having the same primary key (this is why names usually are not commonly used as primary keys—there are too many duplicates). To avoid this danger, have your database help prevent the creation of duplicate primary keys. Oracle offers two facilities that help:

- You can guarantee the uniqueness of a key through either indexing or constraints.

- You can use the sequence generators (discussed later in this chapter).

Creating a Unique Index

You can create a unique index on the combination of Title and AuthorName in the BOOKSHELF_ AUTHOR table in three ways: by creating a primary key constraint, by creating a unique constraint,

or by creating a unique index. If you create a constraint, you will be able to create foreign keys that refer to it. If you create the unique index first, you will still be able to create a primary key on the table—Oracle will use the existing index as the primary key index.

The following listing shows the **create index** command for this multicolumn index:

```
create unique index BA$TITLE_AUTHOR
    on BOOKSHELF_AUTHOR(Title, AuthorName);
```

The primary key method is shown here:

```
alter table BOOKSHELF_AUTHOR
  add constraint BA_PK primary key (Title, AuthorName);
```

To create a unique constraint, just replace the **primary key** clause with **unique**. When you attempt to create a unique index on a table that already has data in it, the command will fail if any duplicates exist. If the **create unique index** statement succeeds, then any future attempt to **insert** (or **update**) a row that would create a duplicate key will fail and result in this error message:

```
ERROR at line 1: ORA-00001: unique constraint (BOOKSHELF_AUTHOR.BA_PK) violated
```

When you create an index, it requires storage space. See "Placing an Index in the Database," later in this chapter, for details concerning the location of the created indexes.

Creating a Bitmap Index

To help tune queries that use nonselective columns in their limiting conditions, you can use bitmap indexes. Bitmap indexes should only be used if the data is infrequently updated, because they add to the cost of all data manipulation transactions against the tables they index.

Bitmap indexes are appropriate when nonselective columns are used as limiting conditions in a query. For example, if there are very few distinct Rating values in a very large BOOKSHELF table, then you would not usually create a traditional B-tree index on Rating, even if it is commonly used in **where** clauses. However, Rating may be able to take advantage of a bitmap index.

Internally, a bitmap index maps the distinct values for the columns to each record. For this example, assume there are five Rating values (1, 2, 3, 4, and 5) in a very large BOOKSHELF table. Since there are five Rating values, there are five separate bitmap entries for the Rating bitmap index. If the first five rows in the table have a Rating value of 1, and the next five have a Rating value of 2, then the Rating bitmap entries would resemble those shown in the following listing:

```
Rating bitmaps:
  1: < 1 1 1 1 1 0 0 0 0 0 >
  2: < 0 0 0 0 0 1 1 1 1 1 >
  3: < 0 0 0 0 0 0 0 0 0 0 >
  4: < 0 0 0 0 0 0 0 0 0 0 >
  5: < 0 0 0 0 0 0 0 0 0 0 >
```

In the preceding listing, each column of 0s and 1s represents a row in the BOOKSHELF table. Since ten rows are considered, ten bitmap values are shown. Reading the bitmap for Rating, the first five records have a Rating value of 1 (the '1' values), and the next five do not (the '0' values). There is a separate bitmap entry for each possible value.

The Oracle optimizer can dynamically convert bitmap index entries to RowIDs during query processing. This conversion capability allows the optimizer to use indexes on columns that have many distinct values (via B-tree indexes) and on those that have few distinct values (via bitmap indexes).

To create a bitmap index, use the **bitmap** clause of the **create index** command, as shown in the following listing. You should indicate its nature as a bitmap index within the index name so that it will be easy to detect during tuning operations.

```
create bitmap index BOOKSHELF$BITMAP_RATING
    on BOOKSHELF(Rating);
```

If you choose to use bitmap indexes, you will need to weigh the performance benefit during queries against the performance cost during data manipulation commands. The more bitmap indexes there are on a table, the greater the cost will be during each transaction. You should not use bitmap indexes on a column that frequently has new values added to it. Each addition of a new value to the Rating column will require that a corresponding new bitmap be created.

When to Create an Index

Indexes are most useful on larger tables, on columns that are likely to appear in **where** clauses either as a simple equality, such as this shown next:

```
where AuthorName = 'STEPHEN JAY GOULD'
   and Rating = '5'
```

or in joins, such as this:

```
where BOOKSHELF.Title = BOOKSHELF_AUTHOR.Title
```

See Chapter 38 for details on the usage of indexes by the optimizer. If there is no **where** clause, no index is used.

Variety in Indexed Columns

Traditional (B-tree) indexes are most useful on columns with a significant amount of variety in their data. For instance, a column that indicates whether a company is a current client with a *Y* or *N* would be a poor choice for a traditional index, and could actually slow down a query; a bitmap index would be a much better choice for that example. A telephone number column would be a good candidate for a B-tree index. An area code column would be marginal, depending on the distribution of unique area code values in the table.

In a multicolumn index, put the column likely to be accessed most often first. As of Oracle9i, you can use the optimizer's skip-scan feature to use multicolumn indexes even if the leading column is not mentioned in the query. See Chapter 38 for examples of index usage.

Small tables may be better left unindexed, except to enforce uniqueness in the primary key. A small table is one that takes fewer than five database blocks; beyond that, indexing will nearly always be productive.

Bitmap indexes present a viable indexing alternative for columns that have very few distinct values. Bitmap indexes are commonly used for "flag" columns that are restricted to values such as Y and N. Bitmap indexes are particularly effective when multiple bitmap indexes are used in a query; the optimizer can quickly evaluate the bitmaps and determine which rows meet all of the criteria for which bitmap indexes are available.

How Many Indexes to Use on a Table

You can create many indexes on a single table, with many columns in each index. The tradeoff for indexing too many columns is the speed of inserting new rows: Every index also must have a new entry made in it when an **insert** is done. If your table will be used primarily for queries, the only cost of indexing as many columns as you can (that have variety, and will be used in **where** clauses, of course) is using some extra disk space. Strictly from a data loading performance perspective, it is better to have a small number of indexes with many columns than to have many indexes with a small number of columns in each.

Except in cluster indexes (discussed later in this chapter), columns that are **NULL** will not appear in an index. Indexes based on more than one column will have an entry if any of the columns are not **NULL**. If all columns are **NULL** for a given row, no entry will appear for it in the index.

Placing an Index in the Database

You can specify where the index to a table is placed by assigning it to a specific tablespace. As was briefly mentioned in Chapter 19, a *tablespace* is a logical division of the database, corresponding to one or more datafiles. Datafiles provide the physical storage for the database— sections of disk where tables and indexes are stored. Databases have several tablespaces, each with its own name. To reduce the potential for disk contention, an index for a table should be placed in a tablespace that is on a physically separate disk drive than its corresponding table.

To specify the tablespace in which to locate an index, the normal **create index** statement is simply followed by the word **tablespace** and the tablespace name, as shown here:

```
create unique index BA$TITLE_AUTHOR
    on BOOKSHELF_AUTHOR(Title, AuthorName)
tablespace BA_INDEXES;
```

In this example, BA_INDEXES is the name given to a tablespace previously created by the database administrator. The use of the **tablespace** option in a **create index** statement lets you physically separate your tables from their associated indexes.

When you create a primary key or unique constraint, Oracle will automatically create an index to enforce uniqueness. Unless you specify otherwise, that index will be created in the same tablespace as the table that the constraint modifies, and will use the default storage parameters for that tablespace. Since that storage location is typically undesirable, you should take advantage of the **using index** clause when creating primary key and unique constraints.

The **using index** clause allows you to specify the storage parameters and tablespace location for an index created by a constraint. In the following example, a primary key is created on the

BOOKSHELF_AUTHOR table and is placed in the BA_INDEXES tablespace. This example assumes that there is not an existing index on the specified columns.

```
alter table BOOKSHELF_AUTHOR
   add constraint BA_PK primary key (Title, AuthorName)
using index tablespace BA_INDEXES;
```

See "Integrity Constraint" in the Alphabetical Reference for further options for the **using index** clause, and see **create index** in the Alphabetical Reference for performance-related index creation options.

Rebuilding an Index

Oracle provides a *fast index rebuild* capability that allows you to re-create an index without having to drop the existing index. The currently available index is used as the data source for the index, instead of using the table as the data source. During the index rebuild, you can change its **storage** parameters and **tablespace** assignment.

In the following example, the BA_PK index is rebuilt (via the **rebuild** clause). Its storage parameters are changed to use an initial extent size of 8MB and a next extent size of 4MB, in the BA_INDEXES tablespace.

```
alter index BA_PK rebuild
storage (initial 8M next 4M pctincrease 0)
tablespace BA_INDEXES;
```

NOTE
When the BA_PK index is rebuilt, there must be enough space for both the old index and the new index to exist simultaneously. After the new index has been created, the old index will be dropped and its space will be freed.

When you create an index that is based on previously indexed columns, Oracle may be able to use the existing indexes as data sources for the new index. For example, if you create a two-column index on the Title and AuthorName columns, and later decide to create an index on just the Title column, Oracle will use the existing index as the data source for the new index. As a result, the performance of your **create index** commands will improve—if you create the indexes in an order that can take advantage of this feature.

As of Oracle8i, you can rebuild indexes while they are being accessed via the **rebuild online** clause of the **alter index** command.

Function-based Indexes

As of Oracle8i, you can create *function-based indexes*. Prior to Oracle8i, any query that performed a function on a column could not use that column's index. Thus, this query could not use an index on the Title column:

```
select * from BOOKSHELF
  where UPPER(Title) = 'MY LEDGER';
```

but this query could:

```
select * from BOOKSHELF
  where Title = 'MY LEDGER';
```

since the second query does not perform the **UPPER** function on the Title column. As of Oracle8i, you can create indexes that allow function-based accesses to be supported by index accesses. Instead of creating an index on the column Title, you can create an index on the column expression UPPER(Title), as shown in the following listing:

```
create index BOOKSHELF$UPPER_TITLE on
BOOKSHELF(UPPER(Title));
```

Although function-based indexes can be useful, be sure to consider the following questions when creating them:

- Can you restrict the functions that will be used on the column? If so, can you restrict all functions from being performed on the column?

- Do you have adequate storage space for the additional indexes?

- When you drop the table, you will be dropping more indexes (and therefore more extents) than before; how will that impact the time required to drop the table?

Function-based indexes are useful, but you should implement them sparingly. The more indexes you create on a table, the longer all **insert**s, **update**s, and **delete**s will take.

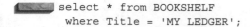

NOTE
Your DBA must enable the "query rewrite" capabilities in the database in order for you to use function-based indexes. The QUERY_REWRITE_ENABLED initialization parameter defaults to FALSE.

Tablespaces and the Structure of the Database

People who have worked with computers for any period of time are familiar with the concept of a file; it's a place on disk where information is stored, and it has a name. Its size is usually not fixed: if you add information to the file, it can grow larger and take up more disk space, up to the maximum available. This process is managed by the operating system, and often involves distributing the information in the file over several smaller sections of the disk that are not physically near each other. The operating system handles the logical connection of these smaller sections without your being aware of it at all. To you, the file looks like a single whole.

Oracle uses files as a part of its organizational scheme, but its logical structure goes beyond the concept of a file. A datafile is an operating system file used to store Oracle data. Each datafile is assigned to a tablespace—a logical division within the database. Tablespaces commonly include the SYSTEM tablespace (for Oracle's internal data dictionary), USERS (for user objects), and others for application tables, indexes, and additional database structures.

The datafiles can have a fixed size or can be allowed to extend themselves automatically when they fill, up to a defined limit. To add more space to a tablespace, you can manually extend your datafiles or add new datafiles. New rows can then be added to existing tables, and those tables may then have rows in multiple datafiles.

Each table has a single area of disk space, called a *segment,* set aside for it in the tablespace. Each segment, in turn, has an initial area of disk space, called the *initial extent,* set aside for it in the tablespace. Once the segment has used up this space, the *next extent,* another single area of disk space, is set aside for it. When it has used this up as well, yet another next extent is set aside. This process continues with every table until the whole tablespace is full. At that point, someone has to add a new file to the tablespace or extend the tablespace's files before any more growth in the tables can take place.

Every database also contains a SYSTEM tablespace. It contains the data dictionary, and the names and locations of all the tablespaces, tables, indexes, and clusters for this database. The objects within the SYSTEM tablespace are owned by the SYS and SYSTEM users; no other users should own objects in this tablespace, as they may impact the rest of the database.

create tablespace

The **create tablespace** command allows one or more files to be assigned immediately to the tablespace. It also specifies a default storage clause for any tables created without an explicit storage clause mentioned in the **create table** or **create index** statement. You must have DBA privileges to create tablespaces; see Chapter 40 for a discussion of the creation and management of tablespaces.

The default values for storage are operating-system-specific. The minimum and maximum values for each of these options are available in the Alphabetical Reference under **create table** and "Storage." These options may be changed with the **alter tablespace** command. The **create table** command for the BOOKSHELF table, placed in the PRACTICE tablespace, looks like this:

```
create table BOOKSHELF
(Title        VARCHAR2(100) primary key,
Publisher     VARCHAR2(20),
CategoryName VARCHAR2(20),
Rating        VARCHAR2(2),
constraint CATFK foreign key (CategoryName)
references CATEGORY(CategoryName)
)
tablespace PRACTICE
;
```

In this form, the BOOKSHELF table will inherit the default storage definitions of the PRACTICE tablespace. To override these defaults, the **storage** clause is used in the **create table** command:

```
create table BOOKSHELF
(Title        VARCHAR2(100) primary key,
Publisher     VARCHAR2(20),
CategoryName VARCHAR2(20),
Rating        VARCHAR2(2),
```

```
constraint CATFK foreign key (CategoryName)
references CATEGORY(CategoryName)
)
tablespace PRACTICE
storage (initial 4M next 4M minextents 2 pctincrease 0)
;
```

If you use temporary tables (see Chapter 13), you can create a tablespace dedicated to their storage needs. Use the **create temporary tablespace** command (fully described in the Alphabetical Reference) to support this special type of table.

As of Oracle8i, you can create locally managed tablespaces; as of Oracle9i, locally managed tablespaces are the default. In a locally managed tablespace, Oracle maintains a bitmap in the datafile headers to manage the location of data within the datafiles. If you are not using a locally managed tablespace, the extent management information is maintained by tables in the data dictionary (a dictionary-managed tablespace). In general, locally managed tablespaces provide a simpler and more consistent way to manage the space within your tablespaces. Space management is covered in greater detail in Chapter 40.

DBAs can alter a tablespace via the **alter tablespace** command. Tablespaces may be altered to be read-only:

```
alter tablespace PRACTICE read only;
```

or changed from read-only to writable:

```
alter tablespace PRACTICE read write;
```

The data in a read-only tablespace cannot be altered. As of Oracle8i, you can move tablespaces among databases; this concept, called a transportable tablespace, requires that the tablespaces to be moved first be placed in a read-only state. See the *Oracle9i DBA Handbook* for details on the management of datafiles and tablespaces.

Temporary Tablespaces

When you execute a command that performs a sorting or grouping operation, Oracle may create a temporary segment to manage the data. The temporary segment is created in a temporary tablespace, and the user executing the command does not have to manage that data. Oracle will dynamically create the temporary segment and will release its space once the operation has completed. If there is not enough temporary space available and the temporary tablespace datafiles cannot autoextend, the command will fail. Each user in the database has an associated temporary tablespace—there may be just one such tablespace for all users to share. As of Oracle9i, DBAs can define a default temporary tablespace for all users. See the *Oracle9i DBA Handbook* for further details.

Rollback Segments and System-Managed Undo

The SQL command **rollback** allows users to undo transactions that have been made against a database. The **rollback** command is available for any **update**, **insert**, or **delete** transaction; it is not available for changes to database objects (such as **alter table** commands). When you **select**

data that another user is changing, Oracle uses the rollback segments to show you the data as it existed before the changes began.

How the Database Uses Rollback Segments

Rollback segments are involved in every transaction that occurs within the database. The number and size of rollback segments available are specified by the DBA during database creation (see the **create rollback segment** entry in the Alphabetical Reference). Because rollback segments are created in tablespaces, their maximum size is limited to the amount of space in the tablespaces' datafiles.

The database assigns transactions to rollback segments in a least recently used/round-robin fashion, resulting in a fairly even distribution of the number of transactions across the pool of rollback segments. Although you can specify which rollback segment a transaction should use, most transactions use the default. Because of the round-robin assignment method used, it is usually not advantageous to have rollback segments of varied sizes.

If you use rollback segments, you should work with your DBA to understand any variations in size that exist among them. Some databases may have very large rollback segments available for large transactions; the same transactions would fail if executed while using smaller rollback segments.

If your transaction exceeds the amount of space available in its rollback segment, and the rollback segment cannot extend further, the transaction will fail. If you execute a long-running query, and the data it relies on has changed and the prior version of that data is no longer available in the rollback segments, your query will fail. It is critical for application developers to understand how the DBAs have configured the rollback segments and how their applications modify data.

Using Undo Tablespaces

As of Oracle9i, you can use automatic *undo management* to place all undo data in a single tablespace. When the DBA creates an undo tablespace, Oracle manages the storage, retention, and space utilization for your rollback data via system-managed undo (SMU). When a retention time is set (in the database's initialization parameter file), Oracle will make a best effort to retain all committed undo data in the database for the specified number of seconds. With that setting, any query taking less than the retention time should not result in an error as long as the undo tablespace has been sized properly. While the database is running, DBAs can change the UNDO_RETENTION parameter value via the **alter system** command.

Clusters

Clustering is a method of storing tables that are intimately related and often joined together into the same area on disk. For example, instead of the BOOKSHELF table being in one section of the disk and the BOOKSHELF_AUTHOR table being somewhere else, their rows could be interleaved together in a single area, called a *cluster*. The *cluster key* is the column or columns by which the tables are usually joined in a query (for example, Title for the BOOKSHELF and BOOKSHELF_AUTHOR tables). To cluster tables, you must own the tables you are going to cluster together.

The following is the basic format of the **create cluster** command:

```
create cluster cluster (column datatype [,column
    datatype]. . .) [other options];
```

The *cluster* name follows the table-naming conventions, and *column datatype* is the name and datatype you will use as the cluster key. The *column* name may be the same as one of the columns of a table you will put in this cluster, or it may be any other valid name. Here's an example:

```
create cluster BOOKandAUTHOR (Col1 VARCHAR2(100));
```

```
Cluster created.
```

This creates a cluster (a space is set aside, as it would be for a table) with nothing in it. The use of Col1 for the cluster key is irrelevant; you'll never use it again. However, its definition should match the primary key of the table to be added. Next, tables are created to be included in this cluster:

```
create table BOOKSHELF
(Title        VARCHAR2(100) primary key,
Publisher     VARCHAR2(20),
CategoryName VARCHAR2(20),
Rating        VARCHAR2(2),
constraint CATFK foreign key (CategoryName)
references CATEGORY(CategoryName)
)
cluster BOOKandAUTHOR (Title);
```

Prior to inserting rows into BOOKSHELF, you must create a cluster index:

```
create index BOOKandAUTHORndx
on cluster BOOKandAUTHOR;
```

Recall that the presence of a **cluster** clause here precludes the use of a **tablespace** or **storage** clause. Note how this structure differs from a standard **create table** statement:

```
create table BOOKSHELF
(Title        VARCHAR2(100) primary key,
Publisher     VARCHAR2(20),
CategoryName VARCHAR2(20),
Rating        VARCHAR2(2),
constraint CATFK foreign key (CategoryName)
references CATEGORY(CategoryName)
);
```

In the first **create table** statement, the cluster **BOOKandAUTHOR (Title)** clause *follows* the closing parenthesis of the list of columns being created in the table. **BOOKandAUTHOR** is the name of the cluster previously created. Title is the column in this table that will be stored in the

cluster key Col1. It is possible to have multiple cluster keys in the **create cluster** statement, and to have multiple columns stored in those keys in the **create table** statement. Notice that nowhere does either statement say explicitly that the Title column goes into the Col1 cluster key. The matchup is done by position only: Col1 and Title were both the first objects mentioned in their respective cluster statements. Multiple columns and cluster keys are matched first to first, second to second, third to third, and so on. Now a second table is added to the cluster:

```
create table BOOKSHELF_AUTHOR
(Title       VARCHAR2(100),
AuthorName  VARCHAR2(50),
constraint TitleFK Foreign key (Title) references BOOKSHELF(Title),
constraint AuthorNameFK Foreign key (AuthorName)
references AUTHOR(AuthorName)
)
cluster BOOKandAUTHOR (Title);
;
```

When these two tables are clustered, each unique Title is actually stored only once, in the cluster key. To each Title are attached the columns from both of these tables.

The data from both of these tables is actually stored in a single location, almost as if the cluster were a big table containing data drawn from both of the tables that make it up.

An additional cluster option, a *hash cluster,* uses the cluster column values to determine the physical location in which the row is stored. See the entry for the **create cluster** command in the Alphabetical Reference.

Sequences

You can assign unique numbers, such as customer IDs, to columns in your database by using a sequence; you don't need to create a special table and code to keep track of the unique numbers in use. This is done by using the **create sequence** command, as shown here:

```
create sequence CustomerID increment by 1 start with 1000;
```

This will create a sequence that can be accessed during **insert** and **update** commands (also **select**, although this is rare). Typically, the unique sequence value is created with a statement like the following:

```
insert into CUSTOMER
          (Name, Contact, ID)
values
          ('COLE CONSTRUCTION','VERONICA',CustomerID.NextVal);
```

The NextVal attached to CustomerID tells Oracle you want the next available sequence number from the CustomerID sequence. This is guaranteed to be unique; Oracle will not give it to anyone else. To use the same number more than once (such as in a series of **insert**s into related tables), CurrVal is used instead of NextVal, *after the first use.* That is, using NextVal ensures that the sequence table gets incremented and that you get a unique number, so you have to use NextVal first. Once you've used NextVal, that number is stored in CurrVal for your use

anywhere, until you use NextVal again, at which point both NextVal and CurrVal change to the new sequence number.

If you use both NextVal and CurrVal in a single SQL statement, both will contain the value retrieved by NextVal. Neither of these can be used in subqueries, as columns in the **select** clause of a view, with **DISTINCT**, **UNION**, **INTERSECT**, or **MINUS**, or in the **order by**, **group by**, or **having** clause of a **select** statement.

You can also cache sequence values in memory for faster access, and you can make the sequence cycle back to its starting value once a maximum value is reached. See **create sequence** in the Alphabetical Reference.

CHAPTER
21

Using SQL*Loader
to Load Data

n the scripts provided in Appendix A, a large number of **insert** commands are executed. In place of those **insert**s, you could create a file containing the data to be loaded and then use Oracle's SQL*Loader utility to load the data. This chapter provides you with an overview of the use of SQL*Loader and its major capabilities. Two additional data-movement utilities, Export and Import, are covered in Chapter 40. SQL*Loader, Export, and Import are described in great detail in the *Oracle9i Database Utilities* provided with the standard Oracle documentation set.

SQL*Loader loads data from external files into tables in the Oracle database. SQL*Loader requires two primary files: the datafile, which contains the information to be loaded, and the control file, which contains information on the format of the data, the records and fields within the file, the order in which they are to be loaded, and even, when needed, the names of the multiple files that will be used for data. You can also combine the control file information into the datafile itself, although the two are usually separated to make it easier to reuse the control file.

When executed, SQL*Loader will automatically create a log file and a "bad" file. The log file records the status of the load, such as the number of rows processed and the number of rows committed. The "bad" file will contain all the rows that were rejected during the load due to data errors, such as nonunique values in primary key columns.

Within the control file, you can specify additional commands to govern the load criteria. If these criteria are not met by a row, the row will be written to a "discard" file. The log, bad, and discard files will have the extensions .log, .bad, and .dsc, respectively. Control files are typically given the extension .ctl.

SQL*Loader is a powerful utility for loading data, for several reasons:

- It is highly flexible, allowing you to manipulate the data as it is being loaded.

- You can use SQL*Loader to break a single large data set into multiple sets of data during commit processing, significantly reducing the size of the transactions processed by the load.

- You can use its Direct Path loading option to perform loads very quickly.

To start using SQL*Loader, you should first become familiar with the control file, as described in the next section.

The Control File

The control file tells Oracle how to read and load the data. The control file tells SQL*Loader where to find the source data for the load and the tables into which to load the data, along with any other rules that must be applied during the load processing. These rules can include restrictions for discards (similar to **where** clauses for queries) and instructions for combining multiple physical rows in an input file into a single row during an **insert**. SQL*Loader will use the control file to create the **insert** commands executed for the data load.

The control file is created at the operating-system level, using any text editor that enables you to save plain text files. Within the control file, commands do not have to obey any rigid formatting requirements, but standardizing your command syntax will make later maintenance of the control file simpler.

The following listing shows a sample control file for loading data into the BOOKSHELF table:

```
LOAD DATA
INFILE 'bookshelf.dat'
INTO TABLE BOOKSHELF
(Title            POSITION(01:100)    CHAR,
 Publisher        POSITION(101:120)   CHAR,
 CategoryName     POSITION(121:140)   CHAR,
 Rating           POSITION(141:142)   CHAR)
```

In this example, data is loaded from the file bookshelf.dat into the BOOKSHELF table. The bookshelf.dat file contains the data for all four of the BOOKSHELF columns, with whitespace padding out the unused characters in those fields. Thus, the Publisher column value always begins at space 101 in the file, even if the Title value is less than 100 characters. Although this formatting makes the input file larger, it may simplify the loading process. No length needs to be given for the fields, since the starting and ending positions within the input data stream effectively give the field length.

The **infile** clause names the input file, and the **into table** clause specifies the table into which the data will be loaded. Each of the columns is listed, along with the position where its data resides in each physical record in the file. This format allows you to load data even if the source data's column order does not match the order of columns in your table.

To perform this load, the user executing the load must have INSERT privilege on the BOOKSHELF table.

Loading Variable-Length Data

If the columns in your input file have variable lengths, you can use SQL*Loader commands to tell Oracle how to determine when a value ends. In the following example, a comma separates the input values:

```
LOAD DATA
INFILE 'bookshelf.dat'
BADFILE '/user/load/bookshelf.bad'
TRUNCATE
INTO TABLE BOOKSHELF
FIELDS TERMINATED BY ","
(Title, Publisher, CategoryName, Rating)
```

The **fields terminated by ","** clause tells SQL*Loader that during the load, each column value will be terminated by a comma. Thus, the input file does not have to be 142 characters wide for each row, as was the case in the first load example. The lengths of the columns are not specified in the control file, since they will be determined during the load.

In this example, the name of the bad file is specified by the **badfile** clause. In general, the name of the bad file is only given when you want to redirect the file to a different directory.

This example also shows the use of the **truncate** clause within a control file. When this control file is executed by SQL*Loader, the BOOKSHELF table will be **truncate**d before the start

of the load. Since **truncate** commands cannot be rolled back, you should use care when using this option. In addition to **truncate**, you can use the following options:

- **append** Adds rows to the table.

- **insert** Adds rows to an empty table. If the table is not empty, the load will abort with an error.

- **replace** Empties the table and then adds the new rows. The user must have DELETE privilege on the table.

Starting the Load

To execute the commands in the control file, you need to run SQL*Loader with the appropriate parameters. SQL*Loader is started via the **SQLLDR** command at the operating system prompt.

NOTE
*The SQL*Loader executable may consist of the name SQLLDR followed by a version number. Consult your platform-specific Oracle documentation for the exact name. For Oracle9i, the executable file should be named SQLLDR.*

When you execute **SQLLDR**, you need to specify the control file, username/password, and other critical load information, as shown in Table 21-1.

SQLLDR Keyword	Description
Userid	Username and password for the load, separated by a slash.
Control	Name of the control file.
Log	Name of the log file.
Bad	Name of the bad file.
Discard	Name of the discard file.
Discardmax	Maximum number of rows to discard before stopping the load. The default is to allow all discards.
Skip	Number of logical rows in the input file to skip before starting to load data. Usually used during reloads from the same input file following a partial load. The default is 0.
Load	Number of logical rows to load. The default is all.
Errors	Number of errors to allow. The default is 50.

TABLE 21-1. *SQL*Loader Options*

SQLLDR Keyword	Description
Rows	Number of rows to commit at a time. Use this parameter to break up the transaction size during the load. The default for conventional path loads is 64; the default for Direct Path loads is all rows.
Bindsize	Size of conventional path bind array, in bytes. The default is operating-system-dependent.
Silent	Suppress messages during the load.
Direct	Use Direct Path loading. The default is FALSE.
Parfile	Name of the parameter file that contains additional load parameter specifications.
Parallel	Perform parallel loading. The default is FALSE.
File	File to allocate extents from (for parallel loading).
Skip_Unusable_Indexes	Allows loads into tables that have indexes in unusable states. The default is FALSE.
Skip_Index_Maintenance	Stops index maintenance for Direct Path loads, leaving them in unusable states. The default is FALSE.
Readsize	Size of the read buffer; default is 1MB.
External_table	Use external table for load; default is NOT_USED; other valid values are GENERATE_ONLY and EXECUTE.
Columnarrayrows	Number of rows for direct path column array; default is 5,000.
Streamsize	Size in bytes of the direct path stream buffer; default is 256,000.
Multithreading	A flag to indicate if multithreading should be used during a direct path load.
Resumable	A TRUE/FALSE flag to enable or disable resumable operations for the current session; default is FALSE.
Resumable_name	Text identifier for the resumable operation.
Resumable_timeout	Wait time for resumable operation; default is 7200 seconds.

TABLE 21-1. *SQL*Loader Options (continued)*

Each load must have a control file, since none of the input parameters specifies critical information for the load—the input file and the table being loaded.

If you want, you can separate the arguments to **SQLLDR** with commas. Enter them with the keywords (such as **userid** or **log**), followed by the parameter value. Keywords are always followed by an equal sign (=) and the appropriate argument.

If the **userid** keyword is omitted, you will be asked for it. If a slash is given after the equal sign, an externally identified account will be used. You also can use an Oracle Net database

specification string to log in to a remote database and load the data into it. For example, your command may start

```
sqlldr userid=usernm/mypass@dev
```

The **direct** keyword, which invokes the Direct Path load option, is described in "Direct Path Loading" later in this chapter.

The SILENT parameter tells **SQLLDR** to suppress certain informative data:

- HEADER suppresses the SQL*LOADER header.

- FEEDBACK suppresses the feedback at each commit point.

- ERRORS suppresses the logging (in the log file) of each record that caused an Oracle error, although the count is still logged.

- DISCARDS suppresses the logging (in the log file) of each record that was discarded, although the count is still logged.

- PARTITIONS disables the writing of the per-partition statistics to the log file.

- ALL suppresses all of the preceding.

If more than one of these is entered, separate each with a comma and enclose the list in parentheses. For example, you can suppress the **header** and **errors** information via the following keyword setting:

```
silent=(HEADER,ERRORS)
```

NOTE
Commands in the control file override any in the calling command line.

Let's load a sample set of data into the BOOKSHELF table, which has four columns (Title, Publisher, CategoryName, and Rating). The data to be loaded is in a file called bookshelf.txt, and consists of two records:

```
Good Record,Some Publisher, ADULTNF, 3
Another Title, Some Publisher, ADULTPIC, 4
```

NOTE
Each line is ended by a carriage return. Even though the first line's last value is not as long as the column it is being loaded into, the row will stop at the carriage return.

The data is separated by commas, and we don't want to delete the data previously loaded into BOOKSHELF, so the control file will look like this:

```
LOAD DATA
INFILE 'bookshelf.txt'
APPEND
INTO TABLE BOOKSHELF
FIELDS TERMINATED BY ","
(Title, Publisher, CategoryName, Rating)
```

Save that file as bookshelf.ctl, in the same directory as the input data file. Next, run **SQLLDR** and tell it to use the control file:

```
sqlldr practice/practice control=bookshelf.ctl log=bookshelf.log
```

When the load completes, you should have one successfully loaded record and one failure. The successfully loaded record will be in the BOOKSHELF table:

```
select Title
   from BOOKSHELF
 where Publisher like '%Publisher';

TITLE
-----------------------------------------
Good Record
```

A file named bookshelf.bad will be created, and will contain one record:

```
Another Title,Some Publisher,ADULTPIC,4
```

Why was that record rejected? Check the log file, bookshelf.log, which will say, in part:

```
Record 2: Rejected - Error on table BOOKSHELF.
ORA-02291: integrity constraint (PRACTICE.CATFK) violated -
parent key not found

Table BOOKSHELF:
  1 Row successfully loaded.
  1 Row not loaded due to data errors.
```

Row 2, the "Another Title" row, was rejected because the value for the CategoryName column violated the foreign key constraint—ADULTPIC is not listed as a category in the CATEGORY table.

Because the rows that failed are isolated into the bad file, you can use that file as the input for a later load once the data has been corrected.

Logical and Physical Records

In Table 21-1, several of the keywords refer to "logical" rows. A *logical* row is a row that is inserted into the database. Depending on the structure of the input file, multiple physical rows may be combined to make a single logical row.

For example, the input file may look like this:

```
Good Record,Some Publisher, ADULTNF, 3
```

in which case there would be a one-to-one relationship between that physical record and the logical record it creates. But the datafile may look like this instead:

```
Good Record,
Some Publisher,
ADULTNF,
3
```

To combine the data, you need to use continuation rules. In this case, the column values are split one to a line, so there is a set number of physical records for each logical record. To combine them, use the **concatenate** clause within the control file. In this case, you would specify **concatenate 4** to create a single logical row from the four physical rows.

The logic for creating a single logical record from multiple physical records can be much more complex than a simple concatenation. You can use the **continueif** clause to specify the conditions that cause logical records to be continued. You can further manipulate the input data to create multiple logical records from a single physical record (via the use of multiple **into table** clauses). See the control file syntax in the "SQLLDR" entry of the Alphabetical Reference in this book and the notes in the following section.

You can use SQL*Loader to generate multiple inserts from a single physical row (similar to the multitable insert capability described in Chapter 15). For example, suppose the input data is denormalized, with fields City and Rainfall, while the input data is in the format City, Rainfall1, Rainfall2, Rainfall3. The control file would resemble the following (depending on the actual physical stop and start positions of the data in the file):

```
into table RAINFALL
when City != '     '
(City        POSITION(1:5)      CHAR,
 Rainfall    POSITION(6:10)     INTEGER EXTERNAL)     -- 1st row
--
into table RAINFALL
when City != '     '
(City        POSITION(1:5)      CHAR,
 Rainfall    POSITION(11:16)    INTEGER EXTERNAL)     -- 2nd row
--
into table RAINFALL
when City != '     '
(City        POSITION(1:5)      CHAR,
 Rainfall    POSITION(16:21)    INTEGER EXTERNAL)     -- 3rd row
```

Note that separate **into table** clauses operate on each physical row. In this example, they generate separate rows in the RAINFALL table; they could also be used to insert rows into multiple tables.

Control File Syntax Notes

The full syntax for SQL*Loader control files is shown in the "SQLLDR" entry in the Alphabetical Reference, so it is not repeated here.

Within the **load** clause, you can specify that the load is **recoverable** or **unrecoverable**. The **unrecoverable** clause only applies to Direct Path loading, and is described in "Tuning Data Loads" later in this chapter.

In addition to using the **concatenate** clause, you can use the **continueif** clause to control the manner in which physical records are assembled into logical records. The **this** clause refers to the current physical record, while the **next** clause refers to the next physical record. For example, you could create a two-character continuation character at the start of each physical record. If that record should be concatenated to the preceding record, set that value equal to '******'. You could then use the **continueif next (1:2)='**'** clause to create a single logical record from the multiple physical records. The '******' continuation character will not be part of the merged record.

The syntax for the **into table** clause includes a **when** clause. The **when** clause, shown in the following listing, serves as a filter applied to rows prior to their insertion into the table. For example, you can specify

```
when Rating>'3'
```

to load only books with ratings greater than 3 into the table. Any row that does not pass the **when** condition will be written to the discard file. Thus, the discard file contains rows that can be used for later loads, but that did not pass the current set of **when** conditions. You can use multiple **when** conditions, connected with **and** clauses.

Use the **trailing nullcols** clause if you are loading variable-length records for which the last column does not always have a value. With this clause in effect, SQL*Loader will generate **NULL** values for those columns.

As shown in an example earlier in this chapter, you can use the **fields terminated by** clause to load variable-length data. Rather than being terminated by a character, the fields can be **terminated by whitespace** or **enclosed by** characters or **optionally enclosed by** other characters.

For example, the following entry loads AuthorName values and sets the values to uppercase during the insert. If the value is blank, a **NULL** is inserted:

```
AuthorName POSITION(10:34)  CHAR  TERMINATED BY WHITESPACE
     NULLIF AuthorName=BLANKS  "UPPER(:AuthorName)"
```

When you load DATE datatype values, you can specify a date mask. For example, if you had a column named ReturnDate and the incoming data is in the format Mon-DD-YYYY in the first 11 places of the record, you could specify the ReturnDate portion of the load as follows:

```
ReturnDate POSITION (1:11) DATE "Mon-DD-YYYY"
```

Within the **into table** clause, you can use the **recnum** keyword to assign a record number to each logical record as it is read from the datafile, and that value will be inserted into the assigned column of the table. The **constant** keyword allows you to assign a constant value to a column during the load. For character columns, enclose the constant value within single quotes. If you use the **sysdate** keyword, the selected column will be populated with the current system date and time.

```
CheckOutDate SYSDATE
```

If you use the **sequence** option, SQL*Loader will maintain a sequence of values during the load. As records are processed, the sequence value will be increased by the increment you specify. If the rows fail during **insert** (and are sent to the bad file), those sequence values will not be reused. If you use the **max** keyword within the sequence option, the sequence values will use the current maximum value of the column as the starting point for the sequence. The following listing shows the use of the **sequence** option:

```
Seqnum_col   SEQUENCE(MAX,1)
```

You can also specify the starting value and increment for a sequence to use when inserting. The following example inserts values starting with a value of 100, incrementing by 2. If a row is rejected during the **insert**, its sequence value is skipped.

```
Seqnum_col   SEQUENCE(100,2)
```

If you store numbers in VARCHAR2 columns, avoid using the **sequence** option for those columns. For example, if your table already contains the values 1 through 10 in a VARCHAR2 column, then the maximum value within that column is 9—the greatest character string. Using that as the basis for a **sequence** option will cause SQL*Loader to attempt to **insert** a record using 10 as the newly created value—and that may conflict with the existing record.

SQL*Loader control files can support complex logic and business rules. For example, your input data for a column holding monetary values may have an implied decimal; 9990 would be inserted as 99.90. In SQL*Loader, you could insert this by performing the calculation during the data load:

```
money_amount    position (20:28) external decimal(9) ":tax_amount/100"
```

See the "SQL*Loader Case Studies" of the *Oracle9i Utilities Guide* for additional SQL*Loader examples and sample control files.

Managing Data Loads

Loading large data volumes is a batch operation. Batch operations should not be performed concurrently with the small transactions prevalent in many database applications. If you have many concurrent users executing small transactions against a table, you should schedule your batch operations against that table to occur at a time when no users are accessing the table.

Oracle maintains *read consistency* for users' queries. If you execute the SQL*Loader job against the table at the same time that other users are querying the table, Oracle will internally

maintain undo entries to enable those users to see their data as it existed when they first queried the data. To minimize the amount of work Oracle must perform to maintain read consistency (and to minimize the associated performance degradation caused by this overhead), schedule your long-running data load jobs to be performed when few other actions are occurring in the database. In particular, avoid contention with other accesses of the same table.

Design your data load processing to be easy to maintain and reuse. Establish guidelines for the structure and format of the input datafiles. The more standardized the input data formats are, the simpler it will be to reuse old control files for the data loads. For repeated scheduled loads into the same table, your goal should be to reuse the same control file each time. Following each load, you will need to review and move the log, bad, data, and discard files so they do not accidentally get overwritten.

Within the control file, use comments to indicate any special processing functions being performed. To create a comment within the control file, begin the line with two dashes, as shown in the following example:

```
-- Limit the load to LA employees:
when Location='LA'
```

If you have properly commented your control file, you will increase the chance that it can be reused during future loads. You will also simplify the maintenance of the data load process itself, as described in the next section.

Repeating Data Loads

Data loads do not always work exactly as planned. Many variables are involved in a data load, and not all of them will always be under your control. For example, the owner of the source data may change its data formatting, invalidating part of your control file. Business rules may change, forcing additional changes. Database structures and space availability may change, further affecting your ability to load the data.

In an ideal case, a data load will either fully succeed or fully fail. However, in many cases, a data load will partially succeed, making the recovery process more difficult. If some of the records have been inserted into the table, then attempting to reinsert those records should result in a primary key violation. If you are generating the primary key value during the insert (via the **sequence** option), then those rows may not fail the second time—and will be inserted twice.

To determine where a load failed, use the log file. The log file will record the commit points as well as the errors encountered. All of the rejected records should be in either the bad file or the discard file. You can minimize the recovery effort by forcing the load to fail if many errors are encountered. To force the load to abort before a large number of errors is encountered, use the **errors** keyword of the **SQLLDR** command. You can also use the **discardmax** keyword to limit the number of discarded records permitted before the load aborts.

If you set **errors** to 0, the first error will cause the load to fail. What if that load fails after 100 records have been inserted? You will have two options: identify and delete the inserted records and reapply the whole load, or skip the successfully inserted records. You can use the **skip** keyword of **SQLLDR** to skip the first 100 records during its load processing. The load will then continue with record 101 (which, we hope, has been fixed prior to the reload attempt). If you cannot identify the rows that have just been loaded into the table, you will need to use the **skip** option during the restart process.

The proper settings for **errors** and **discardmax** depend on the load. If you have full control over the data load process, and the data is properly "cleaned" before being extracted to a load file, you may have very little tolerance for errors and discards. On the other hand, if you do not have control over the source for the input datafile, you need to set **errors** and **discardmax** high enough to allow the load to complete. After the load has completed, you need to review the log file, correct the data in the bad file, and reload the data using the original bad file as the new input file. If rows have been incorrectly discarded, you need to do an additional load using the original discard file as the new input file.

After modifying the errant CategoryName value, you can rerun the BOOKSHELF table load example using the original bookshelf.dat file. During the reload, you have two options when using the original input datafile:

- Skip the first row by specifying **skip=1** in the **SQLLDR** command line.

- Attempt to load both rows, whereby the first row fails because it has already been loaded (and thus causes a primary key violation).

Alternatively, you can use the bad file as the new input datafile and not worry about errors and skipped rows.

Tuning Data Loads

In addition to running the data load processes at off-peak hours, you can take other steps to improve the load performance. The following steps all impact your overall database environment, and must be coordinated with the database administrator. The tuning of a data load should not be allowed to have a negative impact on the database or on the business processes it supports.

First, batch data loads may be timed to occur while the database is in NOARCHIVELOG mode. While in NOARCHIVELOG mode, the database does not keep an archive of its online redo log files prior to overwriting them. Eliminating the archiving process improves the performance of transactions. Since the data is being loaded from a file, you can re-create the loaded data at a later time by reloading the datafile rather than recovering it from an archived redo log file.

However, there are significant potential issues with disabling NOARCHIVELOG mode. You will not be able to perform a point-in-time recovery of the database unless archiving is enabled. If there are non-batch transactions performed in the database, you will probably need to run the database in ARCHIVELOG mode all the time, including during your loads. Furthermore, switching between ARCHIVELOG and NOARCHIVELOG modes requires you to shut down the instance. If you switch the instance to NOARCHIVELOG mode, perform your data load, and then switch the instance back to ARCHIVELOG mode, you should perform a backup of the database (see Chapter 40) immediately following the restart.

Instead of running the entire database in NOARCHIVELOG mode, you can disable archiving for your data load process by using the **unrecoverable** keyword within SQL*Loader. The **unrecoverable** option disables the writing of redo log entries for the transactions within the data load. You should only use this option if you will be able to re-create the transactions from the input files during a recovery. If you follow this strategy, you must have adequate space to store old input files in case they are needed for future recoveries. The **unrecoverable** option is only available for Direct Path loads, as described in the next section.

Rather than control the redo log activity at the load process level, you can control it at the table or partition level. If you define an object as **nologging**, then block-level inserts performed by SQL*Loader Direct Path loading and the **insert /*+ APPEND */** command will not generate redo log entries.

If your operating environment has multiple processors, you can take advantage of the CPUs by parallelizing the data load. The **parallel** option of **SQLLDR**, as described in the next section, uses multiple concurrent data load processes to reduce the overall time required to load the data.

In addition to these approaches, you should work with your database administrator to make sure the database environment and structures are properly tuned for data loads. Tuning efforts should include the following:

- Preallocate space for the table, to minimize dynamic extensions during the loads.

- Allocate sufficient memory resources to the shared memory areas, including the log buffer area.

- Streamline the data writing process by creating multiple database writer (DBWR) processes for the database.

- Remove any unnecessary triggers during the data loads. If possible, disable or remove the triggers prior to the load, and perform the trigger operations on the loaded data manually after it has been loaded.

- Remove or disable any unnecessary constraints on the table. You can use SQL*Loader to dynamically disable and re-enable constraints.

- Remove any indexes on the tables. If the data has been properly cleaned prior to the data load, then uniqueness checks and foreign key validations will not be necessary during the loads. Dropping indexes prior to data loads significantly improves performance.

If you leave indexes on during a data load, Oracle must manage and rebalance the index with each inserted record. The larger your data load is, the more work Oracle will have to do to manage the associated indexes. If you can, you should consider dropping the indexes prior to the load and then re-creating them after the load completes. The only time indexes do not cause a penalty for data load performance is during a Direct Path load, as described in the next section.

Direct Path Loading

SQL*Loader, when inserting records, generates a large number of **insert** statements. To avoid the overhead associated with using a large number of **insert**s, you may use the Direct Path option in SQL*Loader. The Direct Path option creates preformatted data blocks and inserts those blocks into the table. As a result, the performance of your load can dramatically improve. To use the Direct Path option, you must not be performing any functions on the values being read from the input file.

Any indexes on the table being loaded will be placed into a temporary DIRECT LOAD state (you can query the index status from USER_INDEXES). Oracle will move the old index values to a temporary index it creates and manages. Once the load has completed, the old index values will be merged with the new values to create the new index, and Oracle will drop the temporary index it created. When the index is once again valid, its status will change to VALID. To minimize

the amount of space necessary for the temporary index, presort the data by the indexed columns. The name of the index for which the data is presorted should be specified via a **sorted indexes** clause in the control file.

To use the direct path option, specify

```
DIRECT=TRUE
```

as a keyword on the **SQLLDR** command line or include this option in the control file.

If you use the Direct Path option, you can use the **unrecoverable** keyword to improve your data load performance. This instructs Oracle not to generate redo log entries for the load. If you need to recover the database at a later point, you will need to re-execute the data load in order to recover the table's data. All conventional path loads are recoverable, and all Direct Path loads are recoverable by default.

Direct Path loads are faster than conventional loads, and **unrecoverable** Direct Path loads are faster still. Since performing **unrecoverable** loads impacts your recovery operations, you need to weigh the costs of that impact against the performance benefit you will realize. If your hardware environment has additional resources available during the load, you can use the **parallel** Direct Path load option to divide the data load work among multiple processes. The parallel Direct Path operations may complete the load job faster than a single Direct Path load.

Instead of using the **parallel** option, you could partition the table being loaded (see Chapter 18). Since SQL*Loader allows you to load a single partition, you could execute multiple concurrent SQL*Loader jobs to populate the separate partitions of a partitioned table. This method requires more database administration work (to configure and manage the partitions), but it gives you more flexibility in the parallelization and scheduling of the load jobs.

As of Oracle9i, you can take advantage of multithreaded loading functionality for Direct Path loads to convert column arrays to stream buffers and perform stream buffer loading in parallel. Use the **streamsize** parameter and **multithreading** flag to enable this feature.

Direct Path loading may impact the space required for the table's data. Since Direct Path loading inserts blocks of data, it does not follow the usual methods for allocating space within a table. The blocks are inserted at the end of the table, after its *high-water mark,* which is the highest block into which the table's data has ever been written. If you **insert** 100 blocks worth of data into a table and then **delete** all of the rows, the high-water mark for the table will still be set at 100. If you then perform a conventional SQL*Loader data load, the rows will be inserted into the already allocated blocks. If you instead perform a Direct Path load, Oracle will insert new blocks of data following block 100, potentially increasing the space allocation for the table. The only way to lower the high-water mark for a table is to **truncate** it (which deletes all rows and cannot be rolled back) or to drop and re-create it. You should work with your database administrator to identify space issues prior to starting your load.

Additional Oracle9i Enhancements

In addition to features noted earlier in this chapter, SQL*Loader features support for Unicode and expanded datatypes. As of Oracle9i, SQL*Loader can load integer and zoned/packed decimal datatypes across platforms with different byte ordering and accept EBCDIC-based zoned or packed decimal data encoded in IBM format. SQL*Loader also offers support for loading XML columns, loading object types with subtypes (see Chapter 30), and Unicode (UTF16 character set).

SQL*Loader also provides native support for the new Oracle9i date, time, and interval-related datatypes (see Chapter 9).

If a SQL*Loader job fails, you may be able to resume it where it failed using the **resumable**, **resumable_name**, and **resumable_timeout** options. For example, if the segment to which the loader job was writing could not extend, you can disable the load job, fix the space allocation problem, and resume the job. Your ability to perform these actions depends on the configuration of the database; work with your DBA to make sure the resumable features are enabled and adequate undo history is maintained for your purposes.

As of Oracle9i, you can access external files as if they are tables inside the database. This "external table" feature, described in Chapter 25, allows you to potentially avoid loading large volumes of data into the database. The syntax for external table definitions very closely resembles that of the SQL*Loader control file. Although they are limited in some significant ways (you cannot perform DML on external tables, for example), you should consider external tables as alternatives to data loads. See Chapter 25 for implementation details.

CHAPTER
22

Accessing
Remote Data

 s your databases grow in size and number, you will very likely need to share data among them. Sharing data requires a method of locating and accessing the data. In Oracle, remote data accesses such as queries and updates are enabled through the use of database links. As described in this chapter, database links allow users to treat a group of distributed databases as if they were a single, integrated database. In this chapter, you will also find information about direct connections to remote databases, such as those used in client-server applications.

Database Links

Database links tell Oracle how to get from one database to another. You may also specify the access path in an ad hoc fashion (see "Dynamic Links: Using the SQLPLUS copy Command," later in this chapter). If you will frequently use the same connection to a remote database, then a database link is appropriate.

How a Database Link Works

A database link requires that Oracle Net (previously known as SQL*Net and Net8) be running on each of the machines (*hosts*) involved in the remote database access. Oracle Net is usually started by the database administrator (DBA) or the system manager. A sample architecture for a remote access using a database link is shown in Figure 22-1. This figure shows two hosts, each running Oracle Net. There is a database on each of the hosts. A database link establishes a connection from the first database (named LOCAL, on the Branch host) to the second database (named REMOTE, on the Headquarters host). The database link shown in Figure 22-1 is located in the Local database.

Database links specify the following connection information:

- The communications protocol (such as TCP/IP) to use during the connection

- The host on which the remote database resides

- The name of the database on the remote host

- The name of a valid account in the remote database

- The password for that account

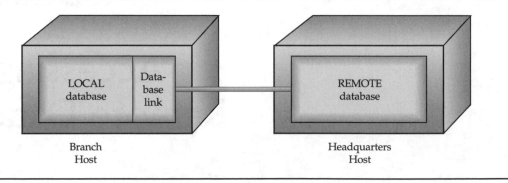

FIGURE 22-1. *Sample architecture for a database link*

When used, a database link actually logs in as a user in the remote database, and then logs out when the remote data access is complete. A database link can be *private,* owned by a single user, or *public,* in which case all users in the Local database can use the link.

The syntax for creating a database link is shown in "Syntax for Database Links," later in this chapter.

Using a Database Link for Remote Queries

If you are a user in the Local database shown in Figure 22-1, you can access objects in the Remote database via a database link. To do this, simply append the database link name to the name of any table or view that is accessible to the remote account. When appending the database link name to a table or view name, you must precede the database link name with an @ sign.

For local tables, you reference the table name in the **from** clause:

```
select *
  from BOOKSHELF;
```

For remote tables, use a database link named REMOTE_CONNECT. In the **from** clause, reference the table name followed by @REMOTE_CONNECT:

```
select *
  from BOOKSHELF@REMOTE_CONNECT;
```

When the database link in the preceding query is used, Oracle will log in to the database specified by the database link, using the username and password provided by the link. It will then query the BOOKSHELF table in that account and return the data to the user who initiated the query. This is shown graphically in Figure 22-2. The REMOTE_CONNECT database link shown in Figure 22-2 is located in the Local database.

As shown in Figure 22-2, logging in to the Local database and using the REMOTE_CONNECT database link in your **from** clause returns the same results as logging in directly to the remote database and executing the query without the database link. It makes the remote database seem local.

NOTE
The maximum number of database links that can be used in a single query is set via the OPEN_LINKS parameter in the database's initialization parameter file. This parameter defaults to four.

FIGURE 22-2. *Using a database link for a remote query*

There are restrictions to the queries that are executed using database links. You should avoid using database links in queries that use the **connect by**, **start with**, and **prior** keywords. Some queries using these keywords will work (for example, if **prior** is not used outside of the **connect by** clause, and **start with** does not use a subquery), but most uses of tree-structured queries will fail when using database links.

Using a Database Link for Synonyms and Views

You may create local synonyms and views that reference remote objects. To do this, reference the database link name, preceded by an @ sign, wherever you refer to a remote table. The following example shows how to do this for synonyms. The **create synonym** command in this example is executed from an account in the Local database.

```
create synonym BOOKSHELF_SYN
    for BOOKSHELF@REMOTE_CONNECT;
```

In this example, a synonym called BOOKSHELF_SYN is created for the BOOKSHELF table accessed via the REMOTE_CONNECT database link. Every time this synonym is used in a **from** clause of a query, the remote database will be queried. This is very similar to the remote queries shown earlier; the only real change is that the database link is now defined as part of a local object (in this case, a synonym).

What if the remote account that is accessed by the database link does not own the table being referenced? In that event, any synonyms that are available to the remote account (either private or public) can be used. If no such synonyms exist for a table that the remote account has been granted access to, then you must specify the table owner's name in the query, as shown in the following example:

```
create synonym BOOKSHELF_SYN
    for Practice.BOOKSHELF@REMOTE_CONNECT;
```

In this example, the remote account used by the database link does not own the BOOKSHELF table, nor does the remote account have a synonym called BOOKSHELF. It does, however, have privileges on the BOOKSHELF table owned by the remote user Practice in the Remote database. Therefore, the owner and table name are specified; both are interpreted in the Remote database. The syntax for these queries and synonyms is almost the same as if everything were in the local database; the only addition is the database link name.

To use a database link in a view, simply add it as a suffix to table names in the **create view** command. The following example creates a view in the local database of a remote table using the REMOTE_CONNECT database link:

```
create view LOCAL_BOOKSHELF_VIEW
as
select * from BOOKSHELF@REMOTE_CONNECT
 where Title >  'M';
```

The **from** clause in this example refers to BOOKSHELF@REMOTE_CONNECT. Therefore, the base table for this view is not in the same database as the view. Also note that a **where** clause is placed on the query, to limit the number of records returned by it for the view.

This view may now be treated the same as any other view in the local database. Access to this view can be granted to other users, provided those users also have access to the REMOTE_CONNECT database link.

Using a Database Link for Remote Updates

The database link syntax for remote **update**s is the same as that for remote queries. Append the name of the database link to the name of the table being updated. For example, to change the Rating values for books in a remote BOOKSHELF table, you would execute the **update** command shown in the following listing:

```
update BOOKSHELF@REMOTE_CONNECT
    set Rating = '5'
 where Title = 'INNUMERACY';
```

This **update** command will use the REMOTE_CONNECT database link to log in to the remote database. It will then **update** the BOOKSHELF table in that database, based on the **set** and **where** conditions specified.

You can use subqueries in the **set** portion of the **update** command (refer to Chapter 15). The **from** clause of such subqueries can reference either the local database or a remote database. To refer to the remote database in a subquery, append the database link name to the table names in the **from** clause of the subquery. An example of this is shown in the following listing:

```
update BOOKSHELF@REMOTE_CONNECT         /*in remote database*/
    set Rating =
        (select Rating
         from BOOKSHELF@REMOTE_CONNECT  /*in remote database*/
          where Title = 'WONDERFUL LIFE')
where Title = 'INNUMERACY';
```

NOTE
*If you do not append the database link name to the table names in the **from** clause of **update** subqueries, tables in the local database will be used. This is true even if the table being updated is in a remote database.*

In this example, the remote BOOKSHELF table is updated based on the Rating value on the remote BOOKSHELF table. If the database link is not used in the subquery, as in the following example, then the BOOKSHELF table in the local database will be used instead. If this is unintended, it will cause local data to be mixed into the remote database table. If you're doing it on purpose, be *very* careful.

```
update BOOKSHELF@REMOTE_CONNECT         /*in remote database*/
    set Rating =
        (select Rating
         from BOOKSHELF                 /*in local database*/
          where Title = 'WONDERFUL LIFE')
where Title = 'INNUMERACY';
```

Syntax for Database Links

You can create a database link with the following command:

```
create [shared] [public] database link REMOTE_CONNECT
connect to {current_user | username identified by password [authentication clause]}
using 'connect string';
```

The specific syntax to use when creating a database link depends upon two criteria:

- The "public" or "private" status of the database link
- The use of default or explicit logins for the remote database

These criteria and their associated syntax are described in turn in the following sections.

> **NOTE**
> *To create a database link, you must have CREATE DATABASE LINK system privilege. The account to which you will be connecting in the remote database must have CREATE SESSION system privilege. Both of these system privileges are included as part of the CONNECT role in Oracle.*

Public vs. Private Database Links

A *public* database link is available to all users in a database. By contrast, a *private* database link is only available to the user who created it. It is not possible for one user to grant access on a private database link to another user. The database link must either be public (available to all users) or private.

To specify a database link as public, use the **public** keyword in the **create database link** command, as shown in the following example.

```
create public database link REMOTE_CONNECT
connect to username identified by password
  using 'connect string';
```

> **NOTE**
> *To create a public database link, you must have CREATE PUBLIC DATABASE LINK system privilege. This privilege is included in the DBA role in Oracle.*

Default vs. Explicit Logins

In place of the **connect to ... identified by ...** clause, you can use **connect to current_user** when creating a database link. If you use the **current_user** option, then when that link is used, it will attempt to open a session in the remote database that has the same username and password as the local database account. This is called a *default login,* since the username/password combination will default to the combination in use in the local database.

The following listing shows an example of a public database link created with a default login (the use of default logins is described further in "Using the User Pseudo-column in Views," later in this chapter):

```
create public database link REMOTE_CONNECT
connect to current_user
 using 'connect string';
```

When this database link is used, it will attempt to log in to the remote database using the current user's username and password. If the current username is not valid in the remote database, or if the password is different, then the login attempt will fail. This failure will cause the SQL statement using the link to fail.

An *explicit* login specifies a username and password that the database link will use while connecting to the remote database. No matter which local account uses the link, the same remote account will be used. The following listing shows the creation of a database link with an explicit login:

```
create public database link REMOTE_CONNECT
connect to WAREHOUSE identified by ACCESS339
  using 'connect string';
```

This example shows a common usage of explicit logins in database links. In the remote database, a user named Warehouse was created, and was given the password ACCESS339. The Warehouse account can then be granted SELECT access to specific tables, solely for use by database links. The REMOTE_CONNECT database link then provides access to the remote Warehouse account for all local users.

Connect String Syntax

Oracle Net uses *service names* to identify remote connections. The connection details for these service names are contained in files that are distributed to each host in the network. When a service name is encountered, Oracle checks the local Oracle Net configuration file (called tnsnames.ora) to determine which protocol, host name, and database name to use during the connection. All of the connection information is found in external files.

When using Oracle Net, you must know the name of the service that points to the remote database. For example, if the service name HQ specifies the connection parameters for the database you need, then HQ should be used as the connect string in the **create database link** command. The following example shows a private database link, using a default login and an Oracle Net service name:

```
create database link REMOTE_CONNECT
connect to current_user
 using 'HQ';
```

When this link is used, Oracle checks the tnsnames.ora file on the local host to determine which database to connect to. When it attempts to log in to that database, it uses the current user's username and password.

The tnsnames.ora files for a network of databases should be coordinated by the DBAs for those databases. A typical entry in the tnsnames.ora file (for a network using the TCP/IP protocol) is shown in the following listing:

```
HQ =(DESCRIPTION=
       (ADDRESS_LIST =
              (ADDRESS = (PROTOCOL=TCP)
              (HOST=host1)
              (PORT=1521))
        )
       (CONNECT DATA=
              (SERVICE_NAME = HQ.host1)
        )
     )
```

In this listing, the HQ service name is mapped to a connect descriptor that tells the database which protocol to use (TCP/IP), and which host (host1) and database (HQ) to connect to. The "port" information refers to the port on the host that will be used for the connection; that data is environment-specific. Different protocols will have different keywords, but they all must convey the same content.

Using Shared Database Links

If you use the Shared Server option for your database connections and your application will employ many concurrent database link connections, you may benefit from using *shared database links*. A shared database link uses shared server connections to support the database link connections. If you have multiple concurrent database link accesses into a remote database, you can use shared database links to reduce the number of server connections required.

To create a shared database link, use the **shared** keyword of the **create database link** command. As shown in the following listing, you will also need to specify a schema and password for the remote database:

```
create shared database link HR_LINK_SHARED
connect to current_user
authenticated by HR identified by puffin55556d
using 'hq';
```

The HR_LINK_SHARED database link uses the connected user's username and password when accessing the 'hq' database, as specified via the **connect to current_user** clause. In order to prevent unauthorized attempts to use the shared link, shared links require the **authenticated by** clause. In this example, the account used for authentication is an application account, but you can also use an empty schema for authentication. The authentication account must have the CREATE SESSION system privilege. During usage of the HR_LINK_SHARED link, connection attempts will include authentication against the HR link account.

If you change the password on the authentication account, you will need to drop and re-create each database link that references it. To simplify maintenance, create an account that is only used for authentication of shared database link connections. The account should have only the CREATE SESSION system privilege, and should not have any privileges on any of the application tables.

If your application uses database links infrequently, you should use traditional database links without the **shared** clause. Without the **shared** clause, each database link connection requires a separate connection to the remote database.

Using Synonyms for Location Transparency

Over the lifespan of an application, its data very likely will move from one database to another, or from one host to another. Therefore, it will simplify application maintenance if the exact physical location of a database object is shielded from the user (and the application).

The best way to implement such location transparency is through the use of synonyms. Instead of writing applications (or SQLPLUS reports) that contain queries that specify a table's owner, such as

```
select *
   from Practice.BOOKSHELF;
```

you should create a synonym for that table, and then reference the synonym in the query:

```
create synonym BOOKSHELF
    for Practice.BOOKSHELF;

select *
   from BOOKSHELF;
```

The logic required to find the data has thus been moved out of your application and into the database. Moving the table location logic to the database will be a benefit any time you move the table (for example, when moving from a development database to a test database).

In addition to hiding the ownership of tables from an application, you can hide the data's physical location through the use of database links and synonyms. By using local synonyms for remote tables, you move another layer of logic out of the application and into the database. For example, the local synonym BOOKSHELF, as defined in the following listing, refers to a table that is located in a different database, on a different host. If that table ever moves, only the link has to be changed; the application code, which uses the synonym, will not change.

```
create synonym BOOKSHELF
    for BOOKSHELF@REMOTE_CONNECT;
```

If the remote account used by the database link is not the owner of the object being referenced, then you have two options. First, you can reference an available synonym in the remote database:

```
create synonym BOOKSHELF
    for BOOKSHELF@REMOTE_CONNECT;
```

where BOOKSHELF, in the remote account used by the database link, is a synonym for another user's BOOKSHELF table.

The second option is to include the remote owner's name when creating the local synonym, as shown in the following listing.

```
create synonym BOOKSHELF
    for Practice.BOOKSHELF@REMOTE_CONNECT;
```

These two examples will result in the same functionality for your queries, but there are differences between them. The second example, which includes the owner name, is potentially more difficult to maintain, because you are not using a synonym in the remote database. The two examples also have slightly different functionality when the **describe** command is used. If the remote account accesses a synonym (instead of a table), you will not be able to **describe** that table, even though you can **select** from it. For **describe** to work correctly, you need to use the format shown in the last example and specify the owner.

Using the User Pseudo-column in Views

The User pseudo-column is very useful when you are using remote data access methods. For example, you may not want all remote users to see all records in a table. To solve this problem, you must think of remote users as special users within your database. To enforce the data restriction, you need to create a view that the remote accounts will access. But what can you use in the **where** clause to properly restrict the records? The User pseudo-column, combined with properly selected usernames, allows you to enforce this restriction.

As you may recall from Chapter 19, queries used to define views may also reference *pseudo-columns.* A pseudo-column is a "column" that returns a value when it is selected, but it is not an actual column in a table. The User pseudo-column, when selected, always returns the Oracle username that executed the query. So, if a column in the table contains usernames, those values can be compared against the User pseudo-column to restrict its records, as shown in the following example. In this example, the NAME table is queried. If the value of the first part of the Name column is the same as the name of the user entering the query, then records will be returned.

```
create view MY_CHECKOUT as
select * from BOOKSHELF_CHECKOUT
  where SUBSTR(Name,1,INSTR(Name,' ')-1) = User;
```

> **NOTE**
> *We need to shift our point of view for this discussion. Since the discussion concerns operations on the database that owns the table being queried, that database will be referred to as the "local" database, and the users from other databases will be referred to as "remote" users.*

When restricting remote access to the rows of your table, you should first consider which columns would be the best to use for the restriction. There are usually logical divisions to the data within a table, such as Department or Region. For each distinct division, create a separate user account in your local database. For this example, let's add a Region column to the BOOKSHELF table. We will now be able to record the list of books from multiple distributed locations in a single table:

```
alter table BOOKSHELF
add
(Region VARCHAR2(10));
```

Suppose you have four major regions represented in your BOOKSHELF table, and you have created an Oracle account for each region. You could then set up each remote user's database link to use his or her specific user account in your local database. For this example, assume the regions are called NORTH, EAST, SOUTH, and WEST. For each of the regions, a specific database link would be created. For example, the members of the SOUTH department would use the database link shown in the following listing:

```
create database link SOUTH_LINK
connect to SOUTH identified by PAW
   using 'HQ';
```

The database link shown in this example is a private database link with an explicit login to the SOUTH account in the remote database.

When remote users query via their database links (such as SOUTH_LINK from the previous example), they will be logged in to the HQ database, with their Department name (such as SOUTH) as their username. Thus, the value of the User column for any table that the user queries will be SOUTH.

Now create a view of your base table, comparing the User pseudo-column to the value of the Department column in the view's **where** clause (this use of the User pseudo-column was first demonstrated in Chapter 19):

```
create or replace view RESTRICTED_BOOKSHELF
     as select *
  from BOOKSHELF
 where Region = User;
```

A user who connects via the SOUTH_LINK database link—and thus is logged in as the SOUTH user—would only be able to see the BOOKSHELF records that have a Region value equal to 'SOUTH'. If users are accessing your table from a remote database, then their logins are occurring via database links—and you know the local accounts they are using because you set them up.

This type of restriction can also be performed in the remote database rather than in the database where the table resides. Users in the remote database may create views within their databases of the following form:

```
create or replace view SOUTH_BOOKSHELF
     as select *
  from BOOKSHELF@REMOTE_CONNECT
 where Region = 'SOUTH';
```

In this case, the Region restriction is still in force, but it is administered locally, and the Region restriction is coded into the view's query. Choosing between the two restriction options (local or remote) is based on the number of accounts required for the desired restriction to be enforced.

To secure your production database, you should limit the privileges granted to the accounts used by database links. Grant those privileges via roles, and use views (with the **with read only** or **with check option** clause) to further limit the ability of those accounts to be used to make unauthorized changes to the data.

Dynamic Links: Using the SQLPLUS copy Command

The SQLPLUS **copy** command is an underutilized, underappreciated command. It allows data to be copied between databases (or within the same database) via SQLPLUS. Although it allows you to select which columns to copy, it works best when all the columns of a table are being chosen. The greatest benefit from using this command is its ability to **commit** after each array of data has been processed (explained shortly). This in turn generates transactions that are of a manageable size.

Consider the case of a large table, such as BOOKSHELF_CHECKOUT. What if the BOOKSHELF_CHECKOUT table has 100,000 rows that use a total of 100MB of space, and you need to make a copy of that table into a different database? The easiest option involves creating a database link and then using that link in a **create table … as select** command, as shown next.

```
create database link REMOTE_CONNECT
connect to PRACTICE identified by PRACTICE
  using 'HQ';

create table BOOKSHELF_CHECKOUT
as
select * from BOOKSHELF_CHECKOUT@REMOTE_CONNECT;
```

The first command creates the database link, and the second creates a new table based on all the data in the remote table.

Unfortunately, this option creates a very large transaction (all 100,000 rows would be **insert**ed into the new table as a single transaction) that places a large burden on internal Oracle structures called *rollback segments*. Rollback segments and system-managed undo (see Chapter 40) store the prior image of data until that data is committed to the database. Since this table is being populated by a single **insert**, a single, large transaction is generated, which may exceed the space in the currently available rollback segments. This failure will in turn cause the table creation to fail.

To break the transaction into smaller entries, use the SQLPLUS **copy** command, which has the following syntax:

```
copy from
[remote username/remote password@connect string]
[to username/password@connect string]
{append|create|insert|replace}
table name
using subquery;
```

If the current account is to be the destination of the copied data, then the word **to** and the local username, password, and connect string are not necessary. If the current account is to be the source of the copied data, then the remote connection information for the data source is not necessary.

To set the transaction entry size, use the SQLPLUS **set** command to set a value for the **arraysize** parameter. This determines the number of records that will be retrieved in each batch. The **copycommit** parameter tells SQLPLUS how many batches should be committed at one time.

Option	Description
APPEND	Inserts the rows into the destination table. Automatically creates the table if it does not exist.
CREATE	Creates the table and then inserts the rows.
INSERT	Inserts the rows into the destination table if it exists; otherwise, returns an error. When using INSERT, all columns must be specified in the **using** subquery.
REPLACE	Drops the existing destination table and replaces it with a new table containing the copied data.

TABLE 22-1. *COPY Command Options*

The following SQLPLUS script accomplishes the same data-copying goal that the **create table as** command met; however, it breaks up the single transaction into multiple transactions. In this example, the data is committed after every 1,000 records. This reduces the transaction's rollback segment entry size needed from 100MB to 1MB.

```
set copycommit 1
set arraysize 1000

copy from PRACTICE/PRACTICE@HQ -
create BOOKSHELF_CHECKOUT -
using -
select * from BOOKSHELF_CHECKOUT
```

NOTE
*Except for the last line, each line in the **copy** command must be terminated with a dash (-), since this is a SQLPLUS command.*

The different data options within the **copy** command are described in Table 22-1.

The feedback provided by the **copy** command may be confusing at first. After the final commit is complete, the database reports to the user the number of records that were committed in the *last* batch. It does not report the total number of records committed (unless they are all committed in a single batch).

Connecting to a Remote Database

In addition to the inter-database connections described earlier in this chapter, you may connect directly to a remote database via an Oracle tool. Thus, instead of typing

```
sqlplus username/password
```

and accessing your local database, you can go directly to a remote database. To do this, enter your username and password along with the Oracle Net connect string for the remote database:

```
sqlplus username/password@HQ
```

This command will log you in directly to the HQ database. The host configuration for this type of login is shown in Figure 22-3; the Branch host has the Oracle tools (such as SQLPLUS) on it and is running Oracle Net, and the Remote host is running Oracle Net and has an Oracle database. There may or may not be a database on the Branch host; specifying the Oracle Net connect string to the remote database forces Oracle to ignore any local databases.

As Figure 22-3 shows, there are very few hardware requirements for the Branch host. All it has to support is the front-end tool and Oracle Net—a typical configuration for client-server applications. A client machine, such as the Branch host, is used primarily for presentation of the data via the database access tools. The server side, such as the Headquarters host, is used to maintain the data and process the data access requests from users.

Regardless of the configuration you use and the configuration tools available, you need to tell Oracle Net how to find the remote database. Work with your DBA to make sure the remote server is properly configured to listen for new connection requests, and to make sure the client machines are properly configured to issue those requests.

FIGURE 22-3. *Sample architecture for a remote connection*

CHAPTER
23

Using Materialized Views

o improve the performance of an application, you can make local copies of remote tables that use distributed data, or create summary tables based on **group by** operations. Oracle provides *materialized views* to store copies of data or aggregations. In previous versions of Oracle, materialized views based on remote data were known as "snapshots." Materialized views can be used to replicate all or part of a single table, or to replicate the result of a query against multiple tables; refreshes of the replicated data can be done automatically by the database at time intervals that you specify. In this chapter, you will see the general usage of materialized views, including their refresh strategies, followed by a description of the optimization strategies available.

Functionality

Materialized views are copies (also known as *replicas*) of data, based upon queries. In its simplest form, a materialized view can be thought of as a table created by a command such as the following:

```
create table LOCAL_BOOKSHELF
as
select * from BOOKSHELF@REMOTE_CONNECT;
```

In this example, a table named LOCAL_BOOKSHELF is created in the local database and is populated with data from a remote database (defined by the database link named REMOTE_CONNECT). Once the LOCAL_BOOKSHELF table is created, though, its data may immediately become out of sync with the master table (BOOKSHELF@REMOTE_CONNECT). Also, LOCAL_BOOKSHELF may be updated by local users, further complicating its synchronization with the master table.

Despite these synchronization problems, there are benefits to replicating data in this way. Creating local copies of remote data may improve the performance of distributed queries, particularly if the tables' data does not change frequently. You may also use the local table creation process to restrict the rows returned, restrict the columns returned, or generate new columns (such as by applying functions to selected values). This is a common strategy for decision-support environments, in which complex queries are used to periodically "roll up" data into summary tables for use during analyses.

Materialized views automate the data replication and refresh processes. When materialized views are created, a *refresh interval* is established to schedule refreshes of replicated data. Local updates can be prevented, and transaction-based refreshes can be used. Transaction-based refreshes, available for some types of materialized views, send from the master database only those rows that have changed for the materialized view. This capability, described later in this chapter, may significantly improve the performance of your refreshes.

Required System Privileges

To create a materialized view, you must have the privileges needed to create the underlying objects it will use. You must have the CREATE MATERIALIZED VIEW or CREATE SNAPSHOT privilege, as well as the CREATE TABLE or CREATE ANY TABLE system privileges. In addition, you must have either the UNLIMITED TABLESPACE system privilege or a sufficient specified

space quota in a local tablespace. To create a refresh-on-commit materialized view, you must also have the ON COMMIT REFRESH system privilege on any tables you do not own, or the ON COMMIT REFRESH system privilege.

NOTE
Oracle9i supports the keyword **snapshot** *in place of* **materialized view** *for backward compatibility.*

Materialized views of remote tables require queries of remote tables; therefore, you must have privileges to use a database link that accesses the remote database. The link you use can be either public or private. If the database link is private, you need to have the CREATE DATABASE LINK system privilege. See Chapter 22 for further information on database links.

If you are creating materialized views to take advantage of the *query rewrite* feature (in which the optimizer dynamically chooses to select data from the materialized view instead of the underlying table), you must have the QUERY REWRITE privilege. If the tables are in another user's schema, you must have the GLOBAL QUERY REWRITE privilege.

Required Table Privileges

When creating a materialized view, you can reference tables in a remote database via a database link. The account that the database link uses in the remote database must have access to the tables and views used by the database link. You cannot create a materialized view based on objects owned by the user SYS.

Within the local database, you can grant SELECT privilege on a materialized view to other local users. Since most materialized views are read-only (although they can be updatable), no additional grants are necessary. If you create an updatable materialized view, you must grant users UPDATE privilege on both the materialized view and the underlying local table it accesses. For information on the local objects created by materialized views, see "Local and Remote Objects Created," later in this chapter.

Read-Only vs. Updatable

A read-only materialized view cannot pass data changes from itself back to its master table. An updatable materialized view can send changes to its master table.

Although that may seem to be a simple distinction, the underlying differences between these two types of materialized views are not simple. A read-only materialized view is implemented as a **create table as select** command. When transactions occur, they occur only within the master table; the transactions are sent to the read-only materialized view. Thus, the method by which the rows in the materialized view change is controlled—the materialized view's rows only change following a change to the materialized view's master table.

In an updatable materialized view, there is less control over the method by which rows in the materialized view are changed. Rows may be changed based on changes in the master table, or rows may be changed directly by users of the materialized view. As a result, you need to send records from the master table to the materialized view, *and* vice versa. Since multiple sources of changes exist, multiple masters exist (referred to as a *multimaster configuration*).

If you use updatable materialized views, you need to treat the materialized view as a master, complete with all of the underlying replication structures and facilities normally found at master sites. You also need to decide how the records will be propagated from the materialized view back to the master. During the transfer of records from the materialized view to master, you need to decide how you will reconcile conflicts. For example, what if the record with ID=1 is deleted at the materialized view site, while at the master site, a record is created in a separate table that references (via a foreign key) the ID=1 record? You cannot delete the ID=1 record from the master site, since that record has a "child" record that relates to it. You cannot insert the child record at the materialized view site, since the parent (ID=1) record has been deleted. How do you plan to resolve such conflicts?

Read-only materialized views let you avoid the need for conflict resolution by forcing all transactions to occur in the controlled master table. This may limit your functionality, but it is an appropriate solution for the vast majority of replication needs. If you need multimaster replication, see the *Oracle9i Replication* guide for guidelines and detailed implementation instructions.

create materialized view Syntax

The basic syntax for creating a materialized view is shown in the following listing. See the Alphabetical Reference for the full command syntax. Following the command description, examples are given that illustrate the creation of local replicas of remote data.

```
create materialized view [user.]name
[ organization index iot_clause]
[ { { segment attributes clauses }
  | cluster cluster (column [, column] ...) }
  [ {partitioning clause | parallel clause | build clause } ]
  | on prebuilt table [ {with | without} reduced precision ] ]
[ using index
 [ { physical attributes clauses| tablespace clause }
   [ physical attributes clauses| tablespace clause ]
   | using no index ]
[ refresh clause ]
[ for update ] [{disable | enable} query rewrite]
 as subquery;
```

The **create materialized view** command has four major sections. The first section is the header, in which the materialized view is named (the first line in the listing):

```
create materialized view [user.]name
```

The materialized view will be created in your user account (schema) unless a different username is specified in the header. In the second section, the storage parameters are set:

```
[ organization index iot_clause]
[ { { segment attributes clauses }
  | cluster cluster (column [, column] ...) }
  [ {partitioning clause | parallel clause | build clause } ]
```

```
 | on prebuilt table [ {with | without} reduced precision ] ]
[ using index
 [ { physical attributes clauses| tablespace clause }
   [ physical attributes clauses| tablespace clause ]
   | using no index ]
```

The storage parameters will be applied to a table that will be created in the local database. For information about the available storage parameters, see the "Storage" entry in the Alphabetical Reference. If the data has already been replicated to a local table, you can use the **on prebuilt table** clause to tell Oracle to use that table as a materialized view.

NOTE
You can specify the storage parameters to be used for the index that is automatically created on the materialized view.

In the third section, the refresh options are set:

```
[ refresh clause ]
```

The syntax for *refresh clause* is

```
{ refresh
    { { fast | complete | force }
    | on { demand | commit }
    | { start with | next } date
    | with { primary key | rowid }
    | using
      { default [ master | local ] rollback segment
      | [ master | local ] rollback segment rollback_segment
      }
      [ default [ master | local ] rollback segment
      | [ master | local ] rollback segment rollback_segment
      ]...
    }
    [ { fast | complete | force }
    | on { demand | commit }
    | { start with | next } date
    | with { primary key | rowid }
    | using
      { default [ master | local ] rollback segment
      | [ master | local ] rollback segment rollback_segment
      }
      [ default [ master | local ] rollback segment
      | [ master | local ] rollback segment rollback_segment
      ]...
    ]...
  }
| never refresh
}
```

The **refresh** option specifies the mechanism Oracle should use when refreshing the materialized view. The three options available are **fast**, **complete**, and **force**. Fast refreshes are only available if Oracle can match rows in the materialized view directly to rows in the base table(s); they use tables called *materialized view logs* to send specific rows from the master table to the materialized view. Complete refreshes completely re-create the materialized view. The **force** option for refreshes tells Oracle to use a fast refresh if it is available; otherwise, a complete refresh will be used. If you have created a simple materialized view but want to use complete refreshes, specify **refresh complete** in your **create materialized view** command. The refresh options are further described in "Refreshing Materialized Views," later in this chapter. Within this section of the **create materialized view** command, you also specify the mechanism used to relate values in the materialized view to the master table—whether RowIDs or primary key values should be used. By default, primary keys are used.

If the master query for the materialized view references a join or a single-table aggregate, you can use the **on commit** option to control the replication of changes. If you use **on commit**, changes will be sent from the master to the replica when the changes are committed on the master table. If you specify **on demand**, the refresh will occur when you manually execute a refresh command.

The fourth section of the **create materialized view** command is the query that the materialized view will use:

```
[ for update ] [{disable | enable} query rewrite]
 as subquery
```

If you specify **for update**, the materialized view will be updatable; otherwise, it will be read-only. Most materialized views are read-only replicas of the master data. If you use updatable materialized views, you need to be concerned with issues such as two-way replication of changes and the reconciliation of conflicting data changes. Updatable materialized views are an example of multimaster replication; for full details on implementing a multimaster replication environment, see the *Oracle9i Replication* guide.

NOTE
The query that forms the basis of the materialized view should not use the User or SysDate pseudo-columns.

The following example creates a read-only materialized view called LOCAL_BOOKSHELF in a local database, based on a remote table named BOOKSHELF that is accessible via the REMOTE_CONNECT database link. The materialized view is placed in the USERS tablespace.

```
create materialized view LOCAL_BOOKSHELF
storage (initial 100K next 100K pctincrease 0)
tablespace USERS
refresh force
start with SysDate next SysDate+7
with primary key
as
select * from BOOKSHELF@REMOTE_CONNECT;
```

Oracle responds with:

```
Materialized view created.
```

The command shown in the preceding example will create a read-only materialized view called LOCAL_BOOKSHELF. Its underlying table will be created with the specified storage parameters in a tablespace named USERS. Since the data in the materialized view's local base table will be changing over time, in production databases you should store materialized views in their own tablespace. The **force** refresh option is specified because no materialized view log exists on the base table for the materialized view; Oracle will try to use a fast refresh but will use a complete refresh until the materialized view log is created. The materialized view's query specifies that the entire BOOKSHELF table, with no modifications, is to be copied to the local database. As soon as the LOCAL_BOOKSHELF materialized view is created, its underlying table will be populated with the BOOKSHELF data. Thereafter, the materialized view will be refreshed every seven days. The storage parameters that are not specified will use the default values for those parameters for the USERS tablespace.

The following example creates a materialized view named LOCAL_CATEGORY_COUNT in a local database, based on a remote table named BOOKSHELF in a database accessed via the REMOTE_CONNECT database link.

```
create materialized view LOCAL_CATEGORY_COUNT
storage (initial 50K next 50K pctincrease 0)
tablespace USERS
refresh force
start with SysDate next SysDate+7
as
select CategoryName, COUNT(*) CountPerCat
  from BOOKSHELF@REMOTE_CONNECT
 group by CategoryName;
```

The query in the LOCAL_CATEGORY_COUNT materialized view counts the number of books in each category in the remote BOOKSHELF table.

There are a few important points to note about the two examples shown in this section:

- The **group by** query used in the LOCAL_CATEGORY_COUNT materialized view could be performed in SQLPLUS against the LOCAL_BOOKSHELF materialized view. That is, the **group by** operation can be performed outside of the materialized view.

- Since LOCAL_CATEGORY_COUNT uses a **group by** clause, it is a complex materialized view and may only be able to use complete refreshes. LOCAL_BOOKSHELF, as a simple materialized view, can use fast refreshes.

The two materialized views shown in the preceding examples reference the same table. Since one of the materialized views is a simple materialized view that replicates all columns and all rows of the master table, the second materialized view may at first appear to be redundant. However, sometimes the second, complex materialized view is the more useful of the two.

How can this be? First, remember that these materialized views are being used to service the query needs of *local* users. If those users always perform **group by** operations in their queries,

and their grouping columns are fixed, then LOCAL_CATEGORY_COUNT may be more useful to them. Second, if the transaction volume on the master BOOKSHELF table is very high, or the master BOOKSHELF table is very small, there may not be a significant difference in the refresh times of the fast and complete refreshes. The most appropriate materialized view is the one that is most productive for your users.

RowID vs. Primary Key–Based Materialized Views

You can base materialized views on primary key values of the master table instead of basing them on the master table's RowIDs. You should decide between these options based on several factors:

- **System stability** If the master site is not stable, then you may need to perform database recoveries involving the master table. When you use Oracle's Export and Import utilities to perform recoveries, the RowID values of rows are likely to change. If the system requires frequent Exports and Imports, you should use primary key–based materialized views.

- **Amount of data replicated** If you normally don't replicate the primary key columns, you can reduce the amount of data replicated by replicating the RowID values instead.

- **Amount of data sent during refreshes** During refreshes, RowID-based materialized views usually require less data to be sent to the materialized view than primary key–based materialized views require (unless the primary key is a very short column).

- **Size of materialized view log table** Oracle allows you to store the changes to master tables in separate tables called *materialized view logs* (described later in this chapter). If the primary key consists of many columns, the materialized view log table for a primary key–based materialized view may be considerably larger than the materialized view log for a comparable RowID-based materialized view.

- **Referential integrity** To use primary key–based materialized views, you must have defined a primary key on the master table. If you cannot define a primary key on the master table, then you must use RowID-based materialized views.

Underlying Objects Created

When you create a materialized view, a number of objects are created in the local and remote databases. The supporting objects created within a database are the same for both simple and complex materialized views. With simple materialized views, you have the ability to create additional objects called *materialized view logs,* which are discussed in "create materialized view log Syntax," later in this chapter.

Consider the simple materialized view shown in the last section:

```
create materialized view LOCAL_BOOKSHELF
storage (initial 100K next 100K pctincrease 0)
tablespace USERS
refresh force
start with SysDate next SysDate+7
with primary key
as
select * from BOOKSHELF@REMOTE_CONNECT;
```

Within the local database, this command will create the following objects in the materialized view owner's schema in addition to the materialized view object:

■ A table named LOCAL_BOOKSHELF that is the *local base table* for the materialized view of the remote table. This table contains the replicated data.

■ An index on the materialized view's local base table (LOCAL_BOOKSHELF). See the following section, "Indexing Materialized View Tables." The index in this example is created on the Title column, the primary key of the source table for the materialized view.

There is only one permissible change that should be made to these underlying objects: The LOCAL_BOOKSHELF table should be indexed to reflect the query paths that are normally used by local users. When you index the materialized view's local base table, you need to factor in your indexes' storage requirements when you estimate the materialized view's space needs. See the following section, "Indexing Materialized View Tables," for further details.

No supporting objects are created in the remote database unless you use materialized view logs to record changes to rows in the master table. Materialized view logs are described in "create materialized view log Syntax," later in this chapter.

Indexing Materialized View Tables

As noted in the preceding discussion, the local base table contains the data that has been replicated. Because that data has been replicated with a goal in mind (usually to improve performance in the database or the network), it is important to follow through to that goal after the materialized view has been created. Performance improvements for queries are usually gained through the use of indexes. Columns that are frequently used in the **where** clauses of queries should be indexed; if a set of columns is frequently accessed in queries, then a concatenated index on that set of columns can be created. (See Chapter 38 for more information on the Oracle optimizer.)

Oracle does not automatically create indexes for complex materialized views on columns other than the primary key. You need to create these indexes manually. To create indexes on your local base table, use the **create index** command (see the Alphabetical Reference). Do *not* create any constraints on the materialized view's local base table.

Since no indexes are created on the columns that users are likely to query from the materialized view, you should create indexes on the materialized view's local base table.

Using Materialized Views to Alter Query Execution Paths

For a large database, a materialized view may offer several performance benefits. You can use materialized views to influence the optimizer to change the execution paths for queries. This feature, called *query rewrite,* enables the optimizer to use a materialized view in place of the table queried by the materialized view, even if the materialized view is not named in the query. For example, if you have a large SALES table, you may create a materialized view that sums the SALES data by region. If a user queries the SALES table for the sum of the SALES data for a region, Oracle can redirect that query to use your materialized view in place of the SALES table. As a result, you can reduce the number of accesses against your largest tables, improving the system performance. Further, since the data in the materialized view is already grouped by region, summarization does not have to be performed at the time the query is issued.

NOTE
*You must specify **query rewrite** in the materialized view definition for the view to be used as part of a query rewrite operation.*

To use the query rewrite capability effectively, you should create a dimension that defines the hierarchies within the table's data. For example, countries are part of continents, and you can create tables to support this hierarchy:

```
create dimension GEOGRAPHY
    level COUNTRY_ID      is COUNTRY.Country
    level CONTINENT_id    is CONTINENT.Continent
    hierarchy COUNTRY_ROLLUP (
        COUNTRY_ID            child of
        CONTINENT_ID
    join key COUNTRY.Continent references CONTINENT_id);
```

If you summarize your SALES data in a materialized view at the country level, then the optimizer will be able to redirect queries for country-level SALES data to the materialized view. Since the materialized view should contain less data than the SALES table, the query of the materialized view should yield a performance improvement over a similar query of the SALES table.

To enable a materialized view for query rewrite, all of the master tables for the materialized view must be in the materialized view's schema, and you must have the QUERY REWRITE system privilege. If the view and the tables are in separate schemas, you must have the GLOBAL QUERY REWRITE system privilege. In general, you should create materialized views in the same schema as the tables on which they are based; otherwise, you will need to manage the permissions and grants required to create and maintain the materialized view.

Refreshing Materialized Views

The data in a materialized view may be replicated either once (when the view is created) or at intervals. The **create materialized view** command allows you to set the refresh interval, delegating the responsibility for scheduling and performing the refreshes to the database. In the following sections, you will see how to perform both manual and automatic refreshes.

What Kind of Refreshes Can Be Performed?

To see what kind of refresh and rewrite capabilities are possible for your materialized views, you can query the MV_CAPABILITIES_TABLE table. The capabilities may change between versions, so you should re-evaluate your refresh capabilities following Oracle software upgrades. To create this table, execute the utlxmv.sql script located in the /rdbms/admin directory under the Oracle software home directory.

The columns of MV_CAPABILITIES TABLE are

```
desc MV_CAPABILITIES_TABLE
```

Name	Null?	Type
STATEMENT_ID		VARCHAR2(30)

```
MVOWNER                                         VARCHAR2(30)
MVNAME                                          VARCHAR2(30)
CAPABILITY_NAME                                 VARCHAR2(30)
POSSIBLE                                        CHAR(1)
RELATED_TEXT                                    VARCHAR2(2000)
RELATED_NUM                                     NUMBER
MSGNO                                           NUMBER(38)
MSGTXT                                          VARCHAR2(2000)
SEQ                                             NUMBER
```

To populate the MV_CAPABILITIES_TABLE table, execute the DBMS_MVIEW.EXPLAIN_MVIEW procedure, using the name of the materialized view as the input value as shown in the following listing.

```
execute DBMS_MVIEW.EXPLAIN_MVIEW('local_bookshelf');
```

The utlxmv.sql script provides guidance on the interpretation of the column values, as shown in the following listing.

```
CREATE TABLE MV_CAPABILITIES_TABLE
(STATEMENT_ID      VARCHAR(30),   -- Client-supplied unique statement identifier
 MVOWNER           VARCHAR(30),   -- NULL for SELECT based EXPLAIN_MVIEW
 MVNAME            VARCHAR(30),   -- NULL for SELECT based EXPLAIN_MVIEW
 CAPABILITY_NAME   VARCHAR(30),   -- A descriptive name of the particular
                                  -- capability:
                                  -- REWRITE
                                  --    Can do at least full text match
                                  --    rewrite
                                  -- REWRITE_PARTIAL_TEXT_MATCH
                                  --    Can do at least full and partial
                                  --    text match rewrite
                                  -- REWRITE_GENERAL
                                  --    Can do all forms of rewrite
                                  -- REFRESH
                                  --    Can do at least complete refresh
                                  -- REFRESH_FROM_LOG_AFTER_INSERT
                                  --    Can do fast refresh from an mv log
                                  --    or change capture table at least
                                  --    when update operations are
                                  --    restricted to INSERT
                                  -- REFRESH_FROM_LOG_AFTER_ANY
                                  --    can do fast refresh from an mv log
                                  --    or change capture table after any
                                  --    combination of updates
                                  -- PCT
                                  --    Can do Enhanced Update Tracking on
                                  --    the table named in the RELATED_NAME
                                  --    column.  EUT is needed for fast
                                  --    refresh after partitioned
                                  --    maintenance operations on the table
```

```
                                    --    named in the RELATED_NAME column
                                    --    and to do non-stale tolerated
                                    --    rewrite when the mv is partially
                                    --    stale with respect to the table
                                    --    named in the RELATED_NAME column.
                                    --    EUT can also sometimes enable fast
                                    --    refresh of updates to the table
                                    --    named in the RELATED_NAME column
                                    --    when fast refresh from an mv log
                                    --    or change capture table is not
                                    --    possible.
     POSSIBLE          CHARACTER(1), -- T = capability is possible
                                    -- F = capability is not possible
     RELATED_TEXT      VARCHAR(2000),-- Owner.table.column, alias name, etc.
                                    -- related to this message.  The
                                    -- specific meaning of this column
                                    -- depends on the MSGNO column.  See
                                    -- the documentation for
                                    -- DBMS_MVIEW.EXPLAIN_MVIEW() for details
     RELATED_NUM       NUMBER,      -- When there is a numeric value
                                    -- associated with a row, it goes here.
                                    -- The specific meaning of this column
                                    -- depends on the MSGNO column.  See
                                    -- the documentation for
                                    -- DBMS_MVIEW.EXPLAIN_MVIEW() for details
     MSGNO             INTEGER,     -- When available, QSM message #
                                    -- explaining why not possible or more
                                    -- details when enabled.
     MSGTXT            VARCHAR(2000),-- Text associated with MSGNO.
     SEQ               NUMBER);     -- Useful in ORDER BY clause when
                                    -- selecting from this table.
```

Once the EXPLAIN_MVIEW procedure has been executed, you can query MV_CAPABILITIES_ TABLE to determine your options.

```
select Capability_Name, Msgtxt
  from MV_CAPABILITIES_TABLE
 where Msgtxt is not null;
```

For the LOCAL_BOOKSHELF materialized view, the query returns:

```
CAPABILITY_NAME
-------------------------------
MSGTXT
-----------------------------------------------------------------
PCT_TABLE
relation is not a partitioned table

REFRESH_FAST_AFTER_INSERT
the detail table does not have a materialized view log
```

```
REFRESH_FAST_AFTER_ONETAB_DML
see the reason why REFRESH_FAST_AFTER_INSERT is disabled

REFRESH_FAST_AFTER_ANY_DML
see the reason why REFRESH_FAST_AFTER_ONETAB_DML is disabled

REFRESH_FAST_PCT
PCT is not possible on any of the detail tables in the
materialized view

REWRITE_FULL_TEXT_MATCH
query rewrite is disabled on the materialized view

REWRITE_PARTIAL_TEXT_MATCH
query rewrite is disabled on the materialized view

REWRITE_GENERAL
query rewrite is disabled on the materialized view

REWRITE_PCT
general rewrite is not possible and PCT is not possible on
any of the detail tables
```

Since the **query rewrite** clause was not specified during the creation of the materialized view, the query rewrite capabilities are disabled for LOCAL_BOOKSHELF. Fast refresh capabilities are not supported because the base table does not have a materialized view log. If you change your materialized view or its base table, you should regenerate the data in MV_CAPABILITIES_TABLE to see the new capabilities.

Automatic Refreshes

Consider the LOCAL_BOOKSHELF materialized view described earlier. Its refresh schedule settings, defined by its **create materialized view** command, are shown in bold in the following listing:

```
create materialized view LOCAL_BOOKSHELF
storage (initial 100K next 100K pctincrease 0)
tablespace USERS
refresh force
start with SysDate next SysDate+7
with primary key
as
select * from BOOKSHELF@REMOTE_CONNECT;
```

The refresh schedule has three components. First, the type of refresh (**fast**, **complete**, or **force**) is specified. Fast refreshes use *materialized view logs* (described later in this chapter) to send changed rows from the master table to the materialized view. Complete refreshes completely re-create the materialized view. The **force** option for refreshes tells Oracle to use a fast refresh if it is available; otherwise, a complete refresh will be used.

The **start with** clause tells the database when to perform the first replication from the master table to the local base table. It must evaluate to a future point in time. If you do not specify a **start**

with time but specify a **next** value, Oracle will use the **next** clause to determine the start time. To maintain control over your replication schedule, you should specify a value for the **start with** clause.

The **next** clause tells Oracle how long to wait between refreshes. Since it will be applied to a different base time each time the materialized view is refreshed, the **next** clause specifies a date expression instead of a fixed date. In the previous example, the expression is

```
next SysDate+7
```

Every time the materialized view is refreshed, the next refresh will be scheduled for seven days later. Although the refresh schedule in this example is fairly simple, you can use many of Oracle's date functions to customize a refresh schedule. For example, if you want to refresh every Monday at noon, regardless of the current date, you can set the **next** clause to

```
NEXT_DAY(TRUNC(SysDate),'MONDAY')+12/24
```

This example will find the next Monday after the current system date; the time portion of that date will be truncated, and 12 hours will be added to the date. (For information on date functions in Oracle, see Chapter 9.)

For automatic materialized view refreshes to occur, you must have at least one background snapshot refresh process running in your database. The refresh process, called J*nnn* (where *nnn* is a number from 000 to 999), periodically "wakes up" and checks whether any materialized views in the database need to be refreshed. The number of J*nnn* processes running in your database is determined by an initialization parameter called JOB_QUEUE_PROCESSES. That parameter must be set (in your initialization parameter file) to a value greater than 0; for most cases, a value of 1 should be sufficient. A coordinator process starts job queue processes as needed.

If the database is not running the J*nnn* processes, you need to use manual refresh methods, described in the next section.

Manual Refreshes

In addition to the database's automatic refreshes, you can perform manual refreshes of materialized views. These override the normally scheduled refreshes; the new **start with** value will be based on the time of your manual refresh.

To refresh a single materialized view, use DBMS_MVIEW.REFRESH. Its two main parameters are the name of the materialized view to be refreshed and the method to use. For this method, you can specify 'c' for a complete refresh, 'f' for fast refresh, and '?' for force. For example:

```
execute DBMS_MVIEW.REFRESH('local_bookshelf','c');
```

If you are refreshing multiple materialized views via a single execution of DBMS_MVIEW.REFRESH, list the names of all of the materialized views in the first parameter, and their matching refresh methods in the second parameter, as shown here:

```
execute DBMS_MVIEW.REFRESH('local_bookshelf,local_category_count','?c');
```

In this example, the materialized view named LOCAL_BOOKSHELF will be refreshed via a fast refresh if possible (force), while the second materialized view will use a complete refresh.

You can use a separate procedure in the DBMS_MVIEW package to refresh all of the materialized views that are scheduled to be automatically refreshed. This procedure, named REFRESH_ALL, will refresh each materialized view separately. It does not accept any parameters. The following listing shows an example of its execution:

```
execute DBMS_MVIEW.REFRESH_ALL;
```

Since the materialized views will be refreshed via REFRESH_ALL consecutively, they are not all refreshed at the same time. Therefore, a database or server failure during the execution of this procedure may cause the local materialized views to be out of sync with each other. If that happens, simply rerun this procedure after the database has been recovered. As an alternative, you can create refresh groups, as described in the next section.

Another procedure within DBMS_MVIEWS, REFRESH_ALL_MVIEWS, refreshes all materialized views that have the following properties:

- The materialized view has not been refreshed since the most recent change to a master table or master materialized view on which it depends.

- The materialized view and all of the master tables or master materialized views on which it depends are local.

- The materialized view is in the view DBA_MVIEWS.

Enforcing Referential Integrity Among Materialized Views

The referential integrity between two related tables, both of which have simple materialized views based on them, may not be enforced in their materialized views. If the tables are refreshed at different times, or if transactions are occurring on the master tables during the refresh, it is possible for the materialized views of those tables to not reflect the referential integrity of the master tables.

For example, BOOKSHELF and BOOKSHELF_CHECKOUT are related to each other via a primary key/foreign key relationship, so simple materialized views of these tables may contain violations of this relationship, including foreign keys without matching primary keys. In this example, that could mean records in the BOOKSHELF_CHECKOUT materialized view with Title values that do not exist in the BOOKSHELF materialized view.

There are a number of potential solutions to this problem. First, time the refreshes to occur when the master tables are not in use. Second, perform the refreshes manually (see the following section for information on this) immediately after locking the master tables or quiescing the database. Third, you may join the tables in the materialized view, creating a complex materialized view that will be based on the master tables (which will be properly related to each other).

Using refresh groups is a fourth solution to the referential integrity problem. You can collect related materialized views into *refresh groups*. The purpose of a refresh group is to coordinate the refresh schedules of its members. Materialized views whose master tables have relationships with other master tables are good candidates for membership in refresh groups. Coordinating the refresh schedules of the materialized views will maintain the master tables' referential integrity in

the materialized views as well. If refresh groups are not used, the data in the materialized views may be inconsistent with regard to the master tables' referential integrity.

Manipulation of refresh groups is performed via the DBMS_REFRESH package. The procedures within that package are MAKE, ADD, SUBTRACT, CHANGE, DESTROY, and REFRESH, as shown in the following examples. Information about existing refresh groups can be queried from the USER_REFRESH and USER_REFRESH_CHILDREN data dictionary views.

NOTE
Materialized views that belong to a refresh group do not have to belong to the same schema, but they do have to be all stored within the same database.

Create a refresh group by executing the MAKE procedure in the DBMS_REFRESH package, whose structure is shown in the following listing:

```
DBMS_REFRESH.MAKE
(name IN VARCHAR2,
 list IN VARCHAR2, |
  tab IN DBMS_UTILITY.UNCL_ARRAY,
 next_date IN DATE,
 interval IN VARCHAR2,
 implicit_destroy IN BOOLEAN := FALSE,
 lax IN BOOLEAN := FALSE,
 job IN BINARY INTEGER := 0,
 rollback_seg IN VARCHAR2 := NULL,
 push_deferred_rpc IN BOOLEAN := TRUE,
 refresh_after_errors IN BOOLEAN := FALSE,
 purge_option IN BINARY_INTEGER := NULL,
 parallelism IN BINARY_INTEGER := NULL,
 heap_size IN BINARY_INTEGER := NULL);
```

All but the first four of the parameters for this procedure have default values that are usually acceptable. The *list* and *tab* parameters are mutually exclusive. You can use the following command to create a refresh group for materialized views named LOCAL_BOOKSHELF and LOCAL_CATEGORY_COUNT. The command is shown here separated across several lines, with continuation characters at the end of each line; you can also enter it on a single line.

```
execute DBMS_REFRESH.MAKE -
(name => 'book_group', -
 list => 'local_bookshelf, local_category_count', -
 next_date => SysDate, -
 interval => 'SysDate+7');
```

NOTE
The list *parameter, which is the second parameter in the listing, has
a single quote at its beginning and at its end, with none between.
In this example, two materialized views—LOCAL_BOOKSHELF and
LOCAL_CATEGORY_COUNT—are passed to the procedure via a
single parameter.*

The preceding command will create a refresh group named BOOK_GROUP, with two
materialized views as its members. The refresh group name is enclosed in single quotes, as is
the *list* of members—but not each member.

If the refresh group is going to contain a materialized view that is already a member of
another refresh group (for example, during a move of a materialized view from an old refresh
group to a newly created refresh group), then you must set the *lax* parameter to TRUE so that
Oracle will automatically remove the materialized view from the previous refresh group. A
materialized view can only belong to one refresh group at a time.

To add materialized views to an existing refresh group, use the ADD procedure of the
DBMS_REFRESH package, whose structure is

```
DBMS_REFRESH.ADD
(name IN VARCHAR2,
 list IN VARCHAR2, |
  tab IN DBMS_UTILITY.UNCL_ARRAY,
 lax IN BOOLEAN := FALSE);
```

As with the MAKE procedure, the ADD procedure's *lax* parameter does not have to be
specified unless a materialized view is being moved between two refresh groups. When this
procedure is executed with the *lax* parameter set to TRUE, the materialized view is moved to
the new refresh group and is automatically deleted from the old refresh group.

To remove materialized views from an existing refresh group, use the SUBTRACT procedure
of the DBMS_REFRESH package, as in the following:

```
DBMS_REFRESH.SUBTRACT
(name IN VARCHAR2,
 list IN VARCHAR2, |
  tab IN DBMS_UTILITY.UNCL_ARRAY,
 lax IN BOOLEAN := FALSE);
```

As with the MAKE and ADD procedures, a single materialized view or a list of materialized
views (separated by commas) may serve as input to the SUBTRACT procedure. You can alter the
refresh schedule for a refresh group via the CHANGE procedure of the DBMS_REFRESH package.

```
DBMS_REFRESH.CHANGE
(name IN VARCHAR2,
 next_date IN DATE := NULL,
 interval IN VARCHAR2 := NULL,
 implicit_destroy IN BOOLEAN := NULL,
```

```
rollback_seg IN VARCHAR2 := NULL,
push_deferred_rpc IN BOOLEAN := NULL,
refresh_after_errors IN BOOLEAN := NULL,
purge_option IN BINARY_INTEGER := NULL,
parallelism IN BINARY_INTEGER := NULL,
heap_size IN BINARY_INTEGER := NULL);
```

The *next_date* parameter is analogous to the **start with** clause in the **create materialized view** command. The *interval* parameter is analogous to the **next** clause in the **create materialized view** command. For example, to change the BOOK_GROUP's schedule so that it will be replicated every three days, you can execute the following command (which specifies a **NULL** value for the *next_date* parameter, leaving that value unchanged):

```
execute DBMS_REFRESH.CHANGE
(name => 'book_group',
 next_date => null,
 interval => 'SysDate+3');
```

After this command is executed, the refresh cycle for the BOOK_GROUP refresh group will be changed to every three days.

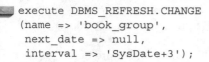

NOTE
Refresh operations on refresh groups may take longer than comparable materialized view refreshes. Group refreshes may also require significant undo segment space to maintain data consistency during the refresh.

You may manually refresh a refresh group via the REFRESH procedure of the DBMS_REFRESH package. The REFRESH procedure accepts the name of the refresh group as its only parameter. The command shown in the following listing will refresh the refresh group named BOOK_GROUP:

```
execute DBMS_REFRESH.REFRESH('book_group');
```

To delete a refresh group, use the DESTROY procedure of the DBMS_REFRESH package, as shown in the following example. Its only parameter is the name of the refresh group.

```
execute DBMS_REFRESH.DESTROY(name => 'book_group');
```

You may also implicitly destroy the refresh group. If you set the *implicit_destroy* parameter to TRUE when you create the group with the MAKE procedure, the refresh group will be deleted (destroyed) when its last member is removed from the group (usually via the SUBTRACT procedure).

Additional Materialized View Management Options
There are two additional packages that you can use to manage and evaluate your materialized views: DBMS_MVIEW and DBMS_OLAP. To create these packages for materialized views, you must run dbmssnap.sql and dbmssum.sql respectively.

The DBMS_MVIEW package options are shown in Table 23-1.

Subprogram	Description
BEGIN_TABLE_REORGANIZATION	A process to preserve the data needed for a materialized view refresh is performed, used prior to reorganizing the master table.
END_TABLE_REORGANIZATION	Ensures that the materialized view master table is in the proper state and that the master table is valid, at the end of a master table reorganization.
EXPLAIN_MVIEW	Explains what is possible with an existing or proposed materialized view (is it fast refreshable, is query rewrite available?).
EXPLAIN_REWRITE	Explains why a query failed to rewrite, or which materialized views will be used if it rewrites.
I_AM_A_REFRESH	The value of the I_AM_A_REFRESH package state is returned, called during replication.
PMARKER	Used for Partition Change Tracking, returns a partition marker from a RowID.
PURGE_DIRECT_LOAD_LOG	Used with data warehousing, this subprogram purges rows from the direct loader log after they are no longer needed by a materialized view.
PURGE_LOG	Purges rows from the materialized view log.
PURGE_MVIEW_FROM_LOG	Purges rows from the materialized view log.
REFRESH	Refreshes one or more materialized views that are not members of the same refresh group.
REFRESH_ALL_MVIEW	Refreshes all materialized views that do not reflect changes to their master table or master materialized view.
REFRESH_DEPENDENT	Refreshes all table-based materialized views that depend on either a specified master table or master materialized view. The list can contain one or more master tables or master materialized views.
REGISTER_MVIEW	Enables an individual materialized view's administration.
UNREGISTER_MVIEW	Used to unregister a materialized view at a master site or master materialized view site.

TABLE 23-1. *DBMS_MVIEW Subprograms*

The DBMS_MVIEW package is used to perform management actions such as evaluating, registering, or refreshing a materialized view.

The DBMS_OLAP package can be used to determine whether a materialized view would enhance your database query performance, generate materialized view creation scripts, estimate

the size the materialized view would be, and so on. The DMBS_OLAP package has the following options shown in Table 23-2.

See the *Oracle9i Supplied PL/SQL Packages and Types Reference* guide for details on this package.

Subprogram	Description
ADD_FILTER_ITEM	Filters the contents used during the recommendation process.
CREATE_ID	Creates an internal ID used by a new workload collection, a new filter, or a new advisor run.
ESTIMATE_MVIEW_SIZE	Estimates the size of a materialized view in bytes and rows that you could create.
EVALUATE_MVIEW_STRATEGY	Measures the utilization of each existing materialized view.
GENERATE_MVIEW_REPORT	Generates an HTML-based report on the given Advisor run.
GENERATE_MVIEW_SCRIPT	Generates a simple script containing the SQL commands to implement recommendations made in the Summary Advisor report.
LOAD_WORKLOAD_CACHE	Obtains a SQL cache workload.
LOAD_WORKLOAD_TRACE	Loads a workload collected by Oracle Trace.
LOAD_WORKLOAD_USER	Loads a user-defined workload.
PURGE_FILTER	Deletes a specific filter or all filters.
PURGE_RESULTS	Removes all results or those for a specific run.
PURGE_WORKLOAD	Deletes a specific collection or all workloads.
RECOMMEND_MVIEW_STRATEGY	Generates a set of recommendations about which materialized views should be created, retained, or dropped.
SET_CANCELLED	Stops the Advisor. If the Advisor is taking too long to report results, stops the Advisor.
VALIDATE_DIMENSION	Verifies that the relationships specified in a dimension are correct.
VALIDATE_WORKLOAD_CACHE	Validates the SQL Cache workload before performing load operations.
VALIDATE_WORKLOAD_TRACE	Validates the Oracle Trace workload before performing load operations.
VALIDATE_WORKLOAD_USER	Validates the user-supplied workload before performing load operations.

TABLE 23-2. *DBMS_OLAP Subprograms*

create materialized view log Syntax

In simple materialized views, each record in the materialized view is based on a single row in a single master table. When simple materialized views are used, a *materialized view log* can be created on the master table. The materialized view log is a table that records the date on which every changed row within the master table last replicated. The record of changed rows can then be used during refreshes to send out to the materialized views only those rows that have changed in the master table. Multiple simple materialized views based on the same table can use the same materialized view log.

The full syntax for the **create materialized view log** command is shown in the Alphabetical Reference. The following listing shows part of the syntax; as you may note from its syntax, it has all of the parameters normally associated with tables:

```
create materialized view log on [schema .] table
[{ physical_attributes_clause
 | tablespace tablespace
 | { logging | nologging }
 | { cache | nocache }
 }
 [ physical_attributes_clause
 | tablespace tablespace
 | { logging | nologging }
 | { cache | nocache }
 ]...
]
[parallel_clause] [partitioning_clauses]
[with
 { object id | primary key | rowid | sequence | ( column [, column]... ) }
 [, { object id | primary key | rowid | sequence | ( column [, column]... ) }]...
]
[{ including | excluding } new values];
```

The **create materialized view log** command is executed in the master table's database, usually by the owner of the master table. Materialized view logs should not be created for tables that are only involved in complex materialized views (since they wouldn't be used). No name is specified for the materialized view log.

A materialized view log for the BOOKSHELF table can be created via the following command, executed from within the account that owns the table:

```
create materialized view log on BOOKSHELF
 tablespace USERS
storage (initial 40K next 40K pctincrease 0)
with primary key;
```

The command shown in this example creates a materialized view log in a tablespace named USERS. Because materialized view logs may grow unpredictably over time, in production databases, you should store their associated objects in tablespaces that are dedicated to materialized view logs. The LOCAL_BOOKSHELF materialized view was created using the **with**

primary key clause, so the materialized view log for the BOOKSHELF table should also be created using the **with primary key** clause.

Required System Privileges

To create the materialized view log, you must have CREATE TABLE and CREATE TRIGGER system privileges. If you are creating the materialized view log from a user account that does not own the master table, you need to have CREATE ANY TABLE, COMMENT ANY TABLE, and CREATE ANY TRIGGER system privileges as well as SELECT privilege on the materialized view master table.

Local and Remote Objects Created

When a materialized view log is created, two objects are created in the master table's schema. From the perspective of the materialized view owner, the **create materialized view log** command occurs in the remote database, and the objects it creates are all in the remote database. The materialized view log creates a table and a trigger:

- A table is created to store the identifiers of the rows that change in the master table, along with a separate timestamp column to record the time the changed rows were last replicated.

- An internal trigger is created to insert the key values—either RowIDs or primary key values—and refresh timestamps of updated, inserted, or deleted rows into the materialized view log table.

The columns shown in the **create materialized view log** command are related to the use of subqueries within materialized view queries. You can use a subquery within a materialized view query only if the subquery completely preserves the key values of the replicated data. Subqueries can be used only with primary key–based materialized views.

Altering Materialized Views and Logs

You may alter the storage parameters, refresh option, and refresh schedule for existing materialized views. If you are unsure of the current settings for a snapshot, check the USER_MVIEWS data dictionary view.

The syntax for the **alter materialized view** command is shown in the Alphabetical Reference. The command in the following listing alters the refresh option used by the LOCAL_BOOKSHELF materialized view:

```
alter materialized view LOCAL_BOOKSHELF
refresh complete;
```

All future refreshes of LOCAL_BOOKSHELF will refresh the entire local base table.

To alter a materialized view, you must either own the materialized view or have the ALTER ANY MATERIALIZED VIEW system privilege.

The storage parameters for materialized view logs may be modified via the **alter materialized view log** command. The syntax for this command is shown in the Alphabetical Reference.

Changing the storage-related parameters for a materialized view log will change the storage parameters on the materialized view log's table. For example, the following command will change the **next** parameter within the **storage** clause for the materialized view log (assuming the tablespace is dictionary-managed):

```
alter materialized view log on BOOKSHELF
storage (next 100K);
```

To alter a materialized view log, you must own the table, have ALTER privilege for the table, or have ALTER ANY TABLE system privilege.

Dropping Materialized Views and Logs

To drop a materialized view, you must have the system privileges required to drop both the materialized view and all of its related objects. You need to have DROP MATERIALIZED VIEW if the object is in your schema, or DROP ANY MATERIALIZED VIEW system privilege if the materialized view is not in your schema.

The following command drops the LOCAL_CATEGORY_COUNT materialized view created earlier in this chapter:

```
drop materialized view LOCAL_CATEGORY_COUNT;
```

Materialized view logs can be dropped via the **drop materialized view log** command. Once the materialized view log is dropped from a master table, no fast refreshes can be performed for simple materialized views based on that table. A materialized view log should be dropped when no simple materialized views are based on the master table. The following command drops the materialized view log that was created on the BOOKSHELF table earlier in this chapter:

```
drop materialized view log on BOOKSHELF;
```

To drop a materialized view log, you must have the ability to drop both the materialized view log and its related objects. If you own the materialized view log, you must have the DROP TABLE and DROP TRIGGER system privileges. If you do not own the materialized view log, you need the DROP ANY TABLE and DROP ANY TRIGGER system privileges to execute this command.

CHAPTER
24

Using Oracle Text
for Text Searches

As the amount of text in your database increases, so does the complexity of the text queries performed against the database. Instead of just performing string matches, you will need new text-search features—such as weighting the terms in a search of multiple terms or ranking the results of a text search.

You can use Oracle Text to perform text-based searches. In prior versions, this feature was known as the ConText Cartridge and interMedia Text. If you have previously used ConText, you may find the configuration for Oracle Text to be simpler and better integrated with the Oracle kernel. As of Oracle9i, new features such as index sets have been added to further enhance text-searching capabilities.

You can use Oracle Text to perform wildcard searching, "fuzzy matches," relevance ranking, proximity searching, term weighting, and word expansions. In this chapter, you'll see how to configure and use Oracle Text.

Adding Text to the Database

Text can be added to the database either by physically storing the text in a table or by storing pointers to external files in the database. That is, for the books on the bookshelf, you can store reviews either in the database or in external files. If you store the reviews in external files, then you store the filenames in the database.

To store the reviews in the database, create the BOOK_REVIEW tables. In this chapter, you will see examples of two types of indexes: CONTEXT and CTXCAT. To support these examples, two separate tables will be created: BOOK_REVIEW_CONTEXT and BOOK_REVIEW_CTXCAT, both loaded with the same data.

```
create table BOOK_REVIEW_CONTEXT
(Title          VARCHAR2(100) primary key,
Reviewer       VARCHAR2(25),
Review_Date    DATE,
Review_Text    VARCHAR2(4000));

insert into BOOK_REVIEW_CONTEXT values
('MY LEDGER', 'EMILY TALBOT', '01-MAY-02',
'A fascinating look into the transactions and finances of G. B. Talbot
and Dora Talbot as they managed a property in New Hampshire around 1900.
The stories come through the purchases - for medicine, doctor visits and
gravesites - for workers during harvests - for gifts at the general store
at Christmas.  A great read. ');

create table BOOK_REVIEW_CTXCAT
(Title          VARCHAR2(100) primary key,
Reviewer       VARCHAR2(25),
Review_Date    DATE,
Review_Text    VARCHAR2(4000));

insert into BOOK_REVIEW_CTXCAT values
('MY LEDGER', 'EMILY TALBOT', '01-MAY-02',
'A fascinating look into the transactions and finances of G. B. Talbot
and Dora Talbot as they managed a property in New Hampshire around 1900.
```

The stories come through the purchases - for medicine, doctor visits and gravesites - for workers during harvests - for gifts at the general store at Christmas. A great read. ');

The Review_Text column of the BOOK_REVIEW tables is defined as having a VARCHAR2(4000) datatype. For longer values, consider the use of CLOB datatypes. See Chapter 32 for details on CLOB datatypes. You can select the review text from the database:

```
set linesize 70
select Review_Text
  from BOOK_REVIEW_CONTEXT
 where Title = 'MY LEDGER';
REVIEW_TEXT

--------------------------------------------------------------------
A fascinating look into the transactions and finances of G. B. Talbot
and Dora Talbot as they managed a property in New Hampshire around 190
0.  The stories come through the purchases - for medicine, doctor visi
its and gravesites - for workers during harvests - for gifts at the gen
earl store at Christmas.  A great read.
```

Text Queries and Text Indexes

Querying text is different from querying data because words have shades of meaning, relationships to other words, and opposites. You may want to search for words that are near each other, or words that are related to others. These queries would be extremely difficult if all you had available was the standard relational operators. By extending SQL to include text indexes, Oracle Text permits you to ask very complex questions about the text.

To use Oracle Text, you need to create a *text index* on the column in which the text is stored. "Text index" is a slightly confusing term—it is actually a collection of tables and indexes that store information about the text stored in the column.

There are several different types of text indexes available in Oracle9i. The first, CONTEXT, is supported in Oracle8i as well as Oracle9i. As of Oracle9i, you can use the CTXCAT text index to further enhance your text index management and query capabilities. In this chapter, you will see examples of both types of indexes. You can use a third type of index, CTXRULE, to build a content-based document classification application. See the *Oracle Text Application Developer's Guide* for details on the use of CTXRULE indexes.

NOTE
Before creating a text index on a table, you must create a primary key for the table (if one does not already exist).

You can create a text index via a special version of the **create index** command. For a CONTEXT index, specify the Ctxsys.Context index type, as shown in the following listing:

```
create index Review_Context_Index on BOOK_REVIEW_CONTEXT(Review_Text)
indextype is ctxsys.context;
```

When the text index is created, Oracle creates a number of indexes and tables in your schema to support your text queries. You can rebuild your text index via the **alter index** command, just as you would for any other index.

As of Oracle9i, you can use a CTXCAT index type in place of the CONTEXT index type:

```
create index Review_CtxCat_Index on BOOK_REVIEW_CTXCAT(Review_Text)
indextype is ctxsys.ctxcat;
```

The CTXCAT index type supports the transactional synchronization of data between the base table (BOOK_REVIEW_CTXCAT) and its text index. With CONTEXT indexes, you need to manually tell Oracle to update the values in the text index after data changes in the base table. CTXCAT index types do not generate "score" values during text queries (as CONTEXT indexes do), but the query syntax is largely the same for the two types. The following sections illustrate the types of text queries you can perform via Oracle Text.

Text Queries

Once a text index is created on the Review_Text column of the BOOK_REVIEW_CONTEXT table, text-searching capabilities increase dramatically. You can now look for any book review that contains the word 'property':

```
select Title
  from BOOK_REVIEW_CONTEXT
 where CONTAINS(Review_Text, 'property')>0;
```

The **CONTAINS** function takes two parameters—the column name and the search string—and checks the text index for the Review_Text column. If the word "property" is found in the Review_Text column's text index, then a *score* greater than 0 is returned by the database, and the matching Title value is returned. The score is an evaluation of how well the record being returned matches the criteria specified in the **CONTAINS** function.

If you create a CTXCAT index, use the **CATSEARCH** function in place of **CONTAINS**. **CATSEARCH** takes three parameters: the column name, the search string, and the name of the index set. Index sets are described in the "Index Sets" section later in this chapter. For this example, there is no index set, so that parameter is set to **NULL**:

```
select Title
  from BOOK_REVIEW_CTXCAT
 where CATSEARCH(Review_Text, 'property', NULL)>0;
```

CATSEARCH does not compute a score but uses the >0 syntax, simplifying your migration from CONTEXT indexes to CTXCAT indexes.

How a Text Query Works

When a function such as **CONTAINS** or **CATSEARCH** is used in a query, the text portion of the query is processed by Oracle Text. The remainder of the query is processed just like a regular query within the database. The results of the text query processing and the regular query processing are merged to return a single set of records to the user.

Available Text Query Expressions

Oracle Text would be rather limited if it allowed you to search only for exact matches of words. Oracle Text offers a broad array of text-searching capabilities you can use to customize your queries. Most of the text-searching capabilities are enabled via the **CONTAINS** and **CATSEARCH** functions, which can appear only in the **where** clause of a **select** statement; never in the **where** clauses of **insert**s, **update**s, or **delete**s.

The operators within **CONTAINS** allow you to perform the following text searches:

- Exact matches of a word or phrase
- Exact matches of multiple words, using Boolean logic to combine searches
- Searches based on how close words are to each other in the text
- Searches for words that share the same word "stem"
- "Fuzzy" matches of words
- Searches for words that sound like other words

CATSEARCH supports the exact match search functions as well as the creation of "index sets," described later in this chapter. In the following sections, you will see examples of these types of text searches, along with information about the operators you can use to customize text searches.

Searching for an Exact Match of a Word

The following query of the BOOK_REVIEW tables returns the title for all reviews including the word "property":

```
REM  CONTAINS method for CONTEXT indexes:
select Title
  from BOOK_REVIEW_CONTEXT
 where CONTAINS(Review_Text, 'property')>0;

REM  CATSEARCH method for CTXCAT indexes:
select Title
  from BOOK_REVIEW_CTXCAT
 where CATSEARCH(Review_Text, 'property', NULL)>0;
```

Within the function calls, the > sign is called a *threshold* operator. The preceding text search can be translated to the following:

```
select all the Title column values
from the BOOK_REVIEW_CONTEXT table
where the score for the text search of the Review_Text column
for an exact match of the word 'property'
exceeds a threshold value of 0.
```

The threshold analysis compares the score—the internal score Oracle calculated when the text search was performed—to the specified threshold value. Score values for individual searches range from 0 to 10 for each occurrence of the search string within the text. For CONTEXT indexes, you can display the score as part of your query.

To show the text-search score, use the **SCORE** function, which has a single parameter—a label you assign to the score within the text search:

```
column Title format a30

select Title, SCORE(10)
  from BOOK_REVIEW_CONTEXT
 where CONTAINS(Review_Text, 'property', 10)>0;

TITLE                            SCORE(10)
------------------------------   ----------
MY LEDGER                                 3
```

In this listing, the **CONTAINS** function's parameters are modified to include a label (10) for the text-search operation performed. The **SCORE** function will display the score of the text search associated with that label.

For CONTEXT indexes, you can use the **SCORE** function in the **select** list (as shown in the preceding query) or in a **group by** clause or an **order by** clause.

Searching for an Exact Match of Multiple Words

What if you want to search the text for multiple words? You can use Boolean logic (ANDs and ORs) to combine the results of multiple text searches in a single query. You can also search for multiple terms within the same function calls and let Oracle resolve the search results.

For example, if you wanted to search for reviews that had the words "property" and "harvests" in the review text, you could enter the following query:

```
REM   CONTAINS method for CONTEXT indexes:
select Title
  from BOOK_REVIEW_CONTEXT
 where CONTAINS(Review_Text, 'property AND harvests')>0;

REM   CATSEARCH method for CTXCAT indexes:
select Title
  from BOOK_REVIEW_CTXCAT
 where CATSEARCH(Review_Text, 'property AND harvests', NULL)>0;
```

> **NOTE**
> *This search does not look for the phrase "property and harvests" but rather for two individual words anywhere in the searched text. You will see the syntax for phrase searches in the next section.*

Instead of using AND in the CONTEXT index query, you could have used an ampersand (&). Before using this method in SQLPLUS, **set define off** so the & character will not be seen as part of a variable name:

```
set define off

REM  CONTAINS method for CONTEXT indexes:
select Title
  from BOOK_REVIEW_CONTEXT
 where CONTAINS(Review_Text, 'property & harvests')>0;
```

For the CTXCAT index, the word AND can be left out entirely:

```
REM  CATSEARCH method for CTXCAT indexes:
select Title
  from BOOK_REVIEW_CTXCAT
 where CATSEARCH(Review_Text, 'property harvests', NULL)>0;
```

Using either the & character or the word AND denotes an AND operation—so the **CONTAINS** function will return a row only if the review text includes *both* the words "property" and "harvests." Each search must pass the threshold criteria defined for the search scores. If you want to search for more than two terms, just add them to the **CONTAINS** or **CATSEARCH** clause, as shown in the following listing:

```
REM  CONTAINS method for CONTEXT indexes:
select Title
  from BOOK_REVIEW_CONTEXT
 where CONTAINS(Review_Text, 'property AND harvests AND workers')>0;

REM  CATSEARCH method for CTXCAT indexes:
select Title
  from BOOK_REVIEW_CTXCAT
 where CATSEARCH(Review_Text, 'property harvests workers', NULL)>0;
```

The query in this listing returns a row only if its search scores for "property," "harvests," and "workers" are each greater than 0.

In addition to AND, you can use the OR operator—in which case a record is returned if either of the search conditions meets the defined threshold. The symbol for OR in Oracle Text is a vertical line (|), so the following two queries are processed identically:

```
REM  CONTAINS method for CONTEXT indexes:
select Title
  from BOOK_REVIEW_CONTEXT
 where CONTAINS(Review_Text, 'property OR harvests')>0;

select Title
```

```
  from BOOK_REVIEW_CONTEXT
 where CONTAINS(Review_Text, 'property | harvests')>0;
```

When these queries are executed, a record is returned if either of the two separate searches (for "property" and "harvests") returns a score greater than 0. The **CATSEARCH** function does not support the use of the term **or**; only the | symbol is supported:

```
REM  CATSEARCH method for CTXCAT indexes:

select Title
  from BOOK_REVIEW_CTXCAT
 where CATSEARCH(Review_Text, 'property | harvests', NULL)>0;
```

The ACCUM (accumulate) operator provides another method for combining searches. ACCUM adds together the scores of the individual searches and compares the accumulated score to the threshold value. The symbol for ACCUM is a comma (,), so the two queries shown in the following listing are equivalent:

```
REM  CONTAINS method for CONTEXT indexes:
select Title
  from BOOK_REVIEW_CONTEXT
 where CONTAINS(Review_Text, 'property ACCUM harvests')>0;

select Title
  from BOOK_REVIEW_CONTEXT
 where CONTAINS(Review_Text, 'property , harvests')>0;
```

The ACCUM syntax is supported in **CATSEARCH** function calls but should not be used, since **CATSEARCH** does not calculate a score to compare to the threshold value.

You can also use Oracle Text to subtract the scores from multiple searches before comparing the result to the threshold score. The MINUS operator in **CONTAINS** subtracts the score of the second term's search from the score of the first term's search. The queries in the following listing will determine the search score for "property" and subtract from it the search score for "house" and compare the difference to the threshold score.

```
REM  CONTAINS method for CONTEXT indexes:
select Title
  from BOOK_REVIEW_CONTEXT
 where CONTAINS(Review_Text, 'property MINUS house')>0;

select Title
  from BOOK_REVIEW_CONTEXT
 where CONTAINS(Review_Text, 'property - house')>0;
```

You can use the symbol – in place of the MINUS operator, as shown in the preceding listing.

For CONTEXT indexes, the – operator reduces the score when comparing the overall search score to the threshold value, but does not eliminate the row from consideration. To eliminate rows based on search terms in CONTEXT indexes, use the "~" as the "not" operator.

For CTXCAT indexes, the symbol "–" has a different meaning than it does with CONTEXT indexes. For CTXCAT indexes, "–" tells Oracle Text not to return the row if the search term after the "–" is found (like "~" in CONTEXT indexes). If the second term is found, **CATSEARCH** will not return the row. For **CATSEARCH** queries, you can replace "–" with the word "not".

You can use parentheses to clarify the logic within your search criteria. If your search uses both ANDs and ORs, you should use parentheses to clarify the way in which the rows are processed. For example, the following query returns a row if the searched text contains either the word "house" or both the words "workers" and "harvests":

```
REM  CONTAINS method for CONTEXT indexes:
select Title
  from BOOK_REVIEW_CONTEXT
 where CONTAINS(Review_Text, 'house OR (workers AND harvests)')>0;
```

CATSEARCH does not require the word AND between "workers" and "harvests":

```
REM  CATSEARCH method for CTXCAT indexes:
select Title
  from BOOK_REVIEW_CTXCAT
 where CATSEARCH(Review_Text, 'house | (workers harvests)', NULL)>0;
```

If you change the location of the parentheses, you change the logic of the text search. The following query returns a row if the searched text contains either "house" or "workers" and also contains the word "harvests":

```
select Title
  from BOOK_REVIEW_CONTEXT
 where CONTAINS(Review_Text, '(house OR workers) AND harvests')>0;
```

When evaluating the scores of multiple searches against CONTEXT indexes, you can tell Oracle Text to weigh the scores of some searches more heavily than others. For example, if you want the search score for "harvests" to be doubled when compared to the threshold score, you can use the asterisk symbol (*) to indicate the factor by which the search score should be multiplied.

The following query will double the search score for "harvests" when it is evaluated in an OR condition:

```
select Title, SCORE(10)
  from BOOK_REVIEW_CONTEXT
 where CONTAINS(Review_Text, 'harvests*2 OR property*1',10)>5;
```

When using CONTEXT indexes, you can weight the search scores to indicate the relevance of the terms in the search. If one term is the most important term in the search, then give that term the highest weighting. Through the use of the AND, OR, ACCUM, and MINUS operators, you should be able to search for any combination of word matches. In the next section, you will see how to search for phrases.

Searching for an Exact Match of a Phrase

When searching for an exact match for a phrase, you specify the whole phrase as part of the search string. If your phrase includes reserved words (such as "and," "or," or "minus"), then you need to use the escape characters shown in this section so that the search is executed properly.

The following query searches for any title whose review entry includes the phrase "doctor visits."

```
REM  CONTAINS method for CONTEXT indexes:
select Title
  from BOOK_REVIEW_CONTEXT
 where CONTAINS(Review_Text, 'doctor visits')>0;

REM  CATSEARCH method for CTXCAT indexes:
select Title
  from BOOK_REVIEW_CTXCAT
 where CATSEARCH(Review_Text, 'doctor visits',NULL)>0;
```

If the search phrase includes a reserved word within Oracle Text, then you must use curly braces ({}) to enclose the text. The following query searches for the phrase "transactions and finances." The word "and" is enclosed in braces.

```
REM  CONTAINS method for CONTEXT indexes:
select Title
  from BOOK_REVIEW_CONTEXT
 where CONTAINS(Review_Text, 'transactions {and} finances')>0;

REM  CATSEARCH method for CTXCAT indexes:
select Title
  from BOOK_REVIEW_CTXCAT
 where CATSEARCH(Review_Text, 'transactions {and} finances',NULL)>0;
```

The query of 'transactions {and} finances' is different from a query of 'transactions and finances'. The query of 'transactions {and} finances' returns a record only if the *phrase* "transactions and finances" exists in the searched text. The query of 'transactions and finances' returns a record if the search score for the *word* "transactions" and the search score for the *word* "finances" are both above the threshold score (or in a CTXCAT index, if both are found).

You can enclose the entire phrase within curly braces, in which case any reserved words within the phrase will be treated as part of the search criteria, as shown in the following example:

```
REM  CONTAINS method for CONTEXT indexes:
select Title
  from BOOK_REVIEW_CONTEXT
 where CONTAINS(Review_Text, '{transactions and finances}')>0;
```

Searches for Words That Are Near Each Other

You can use the *proximity search* capability to perform a text search based on how close terms are to each other within the searched document. A proximity search returns a high score for words that are next to each other, and returns a low score for words that are far apart. If the words are next to each other, the proximity search returns a score of 100.

To use proximity searching against CONTEXT indexes, use the keyword NEAR, as shown in the following example:

```
REM   CONTAINS method for CONTEXT indexes:
select Title
  from BOOK_REVIEW_CONTEXT
 where CONTAINS(Review_Text, 'workers NEAR harvests')>0;
```

You can replace the NEAR operator with its equivalent symbol, the semicolon (;). The revised query is shown in the following listing:

```
REM   CONTAINS method for CONTEXT indexes:
select Title
  from BOOK_REVIEW_CONTEXT
 where CONTAINS(Review_Text, 'workers ; harvests')>0;
```

In CONTEXT index queries, you can specify the maximum number of words between the search terms. For example, for words within 10 words of each other, you may use a search string of 'NEAR((workers, harvests),10)'.

You can use the phrase- and word-searching methods shown in this chapter to search for exact matches of words and phrases, as well as to perform proximity searches of exact words and phrases. Thus far, all the searches have used exact matches of the search terms as the basis for the search. In the next four sections, you will see how to expand the search terms via four methods: wildcards, word stems, fuzzy matches, and SOUNDEX searches.

Using Wildcards During Searches

In the previous examples in this chapter, the queries selected text values that exactly match the criteria specified. For example, the search terms included "workers" but not "worker." You can use wildcards to expand the list of valid search terms used during your query.

Just as in regular text-string wildcard processing, two wildcards are available:

Character	Description
%	Percent sign; multiple-character wildcard
_	Underscore; single-character wildcard

The following query will search for all text matches for all words that start with the characters "worker":

```
REM   CONTAINS method for CONTEXT indexes:
select Title
  from BOOK_REVIEW_CONTEXT
 where CONTAINS(Review_Text, 'worker%')>0;
```

The following query limits the expansion of the text string to exactly three characters. In place of the % sign in the preceding query, three underscores (_ _ _) are used. Since the underscore is a single-character wildcard, the text string cannot expand beyond three characters during the

search. For example, the word "workers" could be returned by the text search, but the word "workplace" would be too long to be returned.

```
REM  CONTAINS method for CONTEXT indexes:
select Title
  from BOOK_REVIEW_CONTEXT
 where CONTAINS(Review_Text, 'work___')>0;
```

You should use wildcards when you are certain of some of the characters within the search string. If you are uncertain of the search string, you should use one of the methods described in the following sections—word stems, fuzzy matches, and SOUNDEX matches.

Searching for Words That Share the Same Stem

Rather than using wildcards, you can use *stem-expansion* capabilities to expand the list of text strings. Given the "stem" of a word, Oracle will expand the list of words to search for to include all words having the same stem. Sample expansions are shown here:

Stem	Sample Expansions
Play	plays played playing playful
Works	working work worked workman workplace
Have	had has haven't hasn't
Story	stories

Since "works" and "work" have the same stem, a stem-expansion search using the word "works" will return text containing the word "work."

To use stem expansion within a query, you need to use the dollar sign ($) symbol. Within the search string, the '$' should immediately precede the word to be expanded, with no space between the '$' and the word.

The following listing shows the result of a query against BOOK_REVIEW_CONTEXT for all reviews that contain a word sharing the stem of the word "manage":

```
REM  CONTAINS method for CONTEXT indexes:
select Title
  from BOOK_REVIEW_CONTEXT
 where CONTAINS(Review_Text, '$manage')>0;
```

When this query is executed, Oracle expands the word "$manage" to include all words with the same stem, and then performs the search. If a review contains one of the words with a stem of "manage", the record will be returned to the user.

The expansion of terms via word stems simplifies the querying process for the user. You no longer need to know what form of a verb or noun was used when the text was entered—all forms are used as the basis for the search. You do not need to specify specific text strings, as you do when querying for exact matches or using wildcards. Instead, you specify a word, and Oracle Text dynamically determines all the words that should be searched for, based on the word you specified.

Searching for Fuzzy Matches

A *fuzzy match* expands the specified search term to include words that are spelled similarly but that do not necessarily have the same word stem. Fuzzy matches are most helpful when the text contains misspellings. The misspellings can be either in the searched text or in the search string specified by the user during the query.

For example, 'MY LEDGER' will not be returned by this query because its review does not contain the word "hardest":

```
REM  CONTAINS method for CONTEXT indexes:
select Title
  from BOOK_REVIEW_CONTEXT
 where CONTAINS(Review_Text, 'hardest')>0;
```

It does, however, contain the word "harvest." A fuzzy match will return reviews containing the word "harvest," even though "harvest" has a different word stem than the word used as the search term.

To use a fuzzy match, precede the search term with a question mark, with no space between the question mark and the beginning of the search term. The following example illustrates the use of the fuzzy match capability.

```
REM  CONTAINS method for CONTEXT indexes:
select Title
  from BOOK_REVIEW_CONTEXT
 where CONTAINS(Review_Text, '?hardest')>0;
```

Searches for Words That Sound Like Other Words

Stem-expansion searches expand a search term to multiple terms based on the stem of the word. Fuzzy matches expand a search term based on similar words in the text index. A third kind of search-term expansion, SOUNDEX, expands search terms based on how the word sounds. The SOUNDEX expansion method uses the same text-matching logic available via the **SOUNDEX** function in SQL.

To use the SOUNDEX option, you must precede the search term with an exclamation mark (!), with no space between the exclamation mark and the search term. During the search, Oracle evaluates the SOUNDEX values of the terms in the text index and searches for all words that have the same SOUNDEX value.

As shown in the following query, you can search for all reviews that include the word "great," using a SOUNDEX match technique:

```
REM  CONTAINS method for CONTEXT indexes:
select Title
  from BOOK_REVIEW_CONTEXT
 where CONTAINS(Review_Text, '!grate')>0;
```

The 'MY LEDGER' review is returned because the words "grate" and "great" have the same SOUNDEX value.

You can also *nest* operators, allowing you to perform stem expansions on the terms returned by a fuzzy match. In the following example, a fuzzy match is performed on the word "stir," and the terms returned from the fuzzy match are expanded using stem expansion:

```
REM  CONTAINS method for CONTEXT indexes:
select Title
  from BOOK_REVIEW_CONTEXT
 where CONTAINS(Review_Text, '$?stir')>0;
```

The major search options for **CONTAINS** are summarized in Table 24-1. For a list of all supported syntax (including thesaurus use, synonym expansion, and XML support), see the *Oracle Text Reference* guide. The search options for **CATSEARCH** are summarized in Table 24-2. Table 24-2 does not list the deprecated **CONTAINS** features such as ACCUM that are not documented as supported features for **CATSEARCH**.

Operator	Description	
OR	Returns a record if either search term has a score that exceeds the threshold	
		Same as OR
AND	Returns a record if both search terms have a score that exceeds the threshold	
&	Same as AND	
ACCUM	Returns a record if the sum of the search terms' scores exceeds the threshold	
,	Same as ACCUM	
MINUS	Returns a record if the score of the first search minus the score of the second search exceeds the threshold	
–	Same as MINUS	
*	Assigns different weights to the score of the searches	
NEAR	The score will be based on how near the search terms are to each other in the searched text	
;	Same as NEAR	
NOT	Excludes the row if the term after the NOT is found	
~	Same as NOT	
EQUIV	Treats two terms (term1 equiv term2) as the same during search scoring	
=	Same as EQUIV	
{}	Encloses reserved words such as AND if they are part of the search term	
%	Multiple-character wildcard	

TABLE 24-1. *Major CONTAINS Options*

Operator	Description
_	Single-character wildcard
$	Performs stem expansion of the search term prior to performing the search
?	Performs a fuzzy match of the search term prior to performing the search
!	Performs a SOUNDEX search
()	Specifies the order in which search criteria are evaluated

TABLE 24-1. *Major CONTAINS Options* (continued)

Using the ABOUT Operator

In Oracle Text, you can search on themes of documents. Thematic searching is integrated with text-term searching. You can use the ABOUT operator to search for terms that have to do with the theme of the document rather than the specific terms within the document. For example:

```
REM   CONTAINS method for CONTEXT indexes:
select Review_Text
  from BOOK_REVIEW_CONTEXT
 where CONTAINS(Review_Text, 'ABOUT(medicine)')>0;

REM   CATSEARCH method for CTXCAT indexes:
select Title
  from BOOK_REVIEW_CTXCAT
 where CATSEARCH(Review_Text, 'ABOUT(medicine)', NULL)>0;
```

Operator	Description
\|	Returns a record if either search term is found
AND	Returns a record if both search terms are found. This is the default action, so (a b) is treated as (a AND b).
–	Returns rows that contain the term preceding the "–" and do not contain the term following it.
NOT	Same as –.
" "	Encloses phrases.
()	Specifies the order in which search criteria are evaluated.

TABLE 24-2. *CATSEARCH Options*

Index Synchronization

When using CONTEXT indexes, you need to manage the text index contents; the text indexes are not updated when the base table is updated. As soon as a Review_Text value is updated, its text index is out of sync with the base table. To sync the index, execute the SYNC_INDEX procedure of the CTX_DDL package, as shown in the following listing:

```
execute CTX_DDL.SYNC_INDEX('REVIEW_INDEX');
```

Index Sets

Historically, problems with queries of text indexes have occurred when other criteria are used alongside text searches as part of the **where** clause. For example, are **where** clauses on non-text columns applied before or after the text searches are completed, and how are the results properly ordered? To improve the "mixed" query capability, Oracle9i features index sets. The indexes within the index set may be on structured relational columns or on text columns.

To create an index set, use the CTX_DDL package to create the index set and add indexes to it. When you create a text index, you can then specify the index set it belongs to. To execute this example, you should first drop the REVIEW_CTXCAT_INDEX text index created earlier in this chapter on the BOOK_REVIEW_CTXCAT table:

```
drop index REVIEW_CTXCAT_INDEX;
```

To create an index set named Reviews, use the CREATE_INDEX_SET procedure:

```
execute CTX_DDL.CREATE_INDEX_SET('Reviews');
```

You can now add indexes to the index set via the ADD_INDEX procedure. First, add a standard, non-text index:

```
execute CTX_DDL.ADD_INDEX('Reviews', 'Reviewer');
execute CTX_DDL.ADD_INDEX('Reviews', 'Review_Date');
```

Now create a CTXCAT text index. Specify Ctxsys.Ctxcat as the index type, and list the index set in the **parameters** clause:

```
create index REVIEW_CTXCAT_INDEX
    on BOOK_REVIEW_CTXCAT(Review_Text)
 indextype is CTXSYS.CTXCAT
parameters ('index set Reviews');
```

You can now order your results by the result of the combined index set search.

```
select * from BOOK_REVIEW_CTXCAT
  where CATSEARCH(Review_Text, 'great',
               'Reviewer=''EMILY TALBOT''
                  order by Review_Date desc')>0;
```

To resolve this query, Oracle Text will use the index set, allowing you to order the results properly. Note that there are two quotes around the string 'EMILY TALBOT', since that is a text string search—it will be converted to a set of single quotes when the query is executed.

Index sets can contain up to 99 indexes on NUMBER, DATE, CHAR, and VARCHAR2 datatypes. No column in an index set index can exceed 30 bytes (so in this example, the Title column cannot be indexed as part of an index set). The indexed columns must not contain **NULL** values.

For more details on index sets, text index management, and text application development, see *Oracle Text Application Developer's Guide* and *Oracle Text Reference*, both provided as part of the standard Oracle documentation set.

CHAPTER
25

Using External Tables

s of Oracle9i, you can use the external table feature to access external files as if they are tables inside the database. When you create an external table, you define its structure and location within Oracle. When you query the table, Oracle reads the external table and returns the results just as if the data had been stored within the database. But since the data is outside the database, you do not have to be concerned about the process for loading it into the database—a potentially significant benefit for data warehouses and large databases.

External tables have limits—you cannot **insert**, **update**, or **delete** their rows from within Oracle, and you cannot index them. Since they are part of the database application, you will have to account for them as part of your backup and recovery processes. Despite these complications, external tables can be a powerful addition to your database architecture plans.

Accessing the External Data

To access external files from within Oracle, you must first use the **create directory** command to define a directory object pointing to the external file location. Users who will access the external files must have the READ privilege on the directory.

NOTE
*Before you start, verify that the external directory exists, and that the user who will be issuing the **create directory** command has the CREATE ANY DIRECTORY system privilege.*

The following example creates a directory named BOOK_DIR and grants READ and WRITE access to the Practice schema:

```
create directory BOOK_DIR as 'e:\oracle\external';
grant read on directory BOOK_DIR to practice;
grant write on directory BOOK_DIR to practice;
```

The Practice user can now read files in the e:\oracle\external directory as if they were inside the database. Because Practice has also been granted WRITE privilege on that directory, the Practice user can create log, discard, and bad files within the directory—just as if that user were executing the SQL*Loader utility (see Chapter 21).

The following listing generates two files for sample data, one from BOOKSHELF and one from BOOKSHELF_AUTHOR. Note that the **spool** command cannot use the directory name created via **create directory**; you need to specify the full operating system directory name.

```
connect practice/practice

set pagesize 0 newpage 0 feedback off
select Title||'~'||Publisher||'~'||CategoryName||'~'||Rating||'~'
  from BOOKSHELF
 order by Title

spool e:\oracle\external\bookshelf_dump.lst
```

```
/
spool off

select Title||'~'||AuthorName||'~'
  from BOOKSHELF_AUTHOR
 order by Title

spool e:\oracle\external\book_auth_dump.lst
/
spool off
```

In addition to the data, the output files will contain a single line at the top with a "/" and a final line that reads "SQL> spool off". To simplify data management, you should manually edit the file at the operating system level to delete these extra lines.

If another user is to access the data in the bookshelf_dump.lst and book_auth_dump.lst files, you must grant that user READ privilege on the BOOK_DIR directory:

```
grant read on directory BOOK_DIR to another_user;
```

and the files themselves must be readable by the Oracle user at the operating system level.

Creating an External Table

Now that the external data is available and accessible, you can create a table structure that accesses it. To do so, you need to use the **organization external** clause of the **create table** command. Within that clause, you can specify the data structure much as you would for a SQL*Loader control file. The following listing shows the creation of the BOOKSHELF_EXT table, based on the data in the bookshelf.lst spool file created in the prior section:

```
set feedback on heading on newpage 1 pagesize 60

create table BOOKSHELF_EXT
(Title        VARCHAR2(100),
Publisher     VARCHAR2(20),
CategoryName  VARCHAR2(20),
Rating        VARCHAR2(2)
)
organization external
(type ORACLE_LOADER
 default directory BOOK_DIR
 access parameters (records delimited by newline
 fields terminated by "~"
                  (Title        CHAR(100),
                   Publisher    CHAR(20),
                   CategoryName CHAR(20),
                   Rating       CHAR(2)
                  ))
 location ('bookshelf_dump.lst')
);
```

Oracle will respond with:

```
Table created.
```

although no data will have been created inside the Oracle database.

Similarly, you can create a table based on the book_auth_dump.lst spool file:

```
create table BOOKSHELF_AUTHOR_EXT
(Title          VARCHAR2(100),
AuthorName      VARCHAR2(50)
)
organization external
(type ORACLE_LOADER
 default directory BOOK_DIR
 access parameters (records delimited by newline
                    fields terminated by "~"
                   (Title        CHAR(100),
                    AuthorName    CHAR(50)
                   ))
 location ('book_auth_dump.lst')
);
```

NOTE
Oracle will perform only cursory validation when the external table is created. You will not see most errors until you attempt to query the table. The syntax for the access parameters is very specific, and minor errors in the access definition may prevent all of the rows from being accessed.

You can verify the contents of the external tables by querying from them and comparing them to the source tables, as shown in the following listing:

```
select Title from BOOKSHELF
 where CategoryName = 'CHILDRENPIC';

TITLE
-----------------------------------------
GOOD DOG, CARL
POLAR EXPRESS
RUNAWAY BUNNY

3 rows selected.

select Title from BOOKSHELF_EXT
 where CategoryName = 'CHILDRENPIC';

TITLE
-------------------------------------------
```

```
GOOD DOG, CARL
POLAR EXPRESS
RUNAWAY BUNNY

3 rows selected.

select COUNT(*) from BOOKSHELF_AUTHOR;

  COUNT(*)
----------
        37

select COUNT(*) from BOOKSHELF_AUTHOR_EXT;

  COUNT(*)
----------
        37
```

You can join the "internal" table BOOKSHELF_AUTHOR to its external counterpart, BOOKSHELF_AUTHOR_EXT, to verify there are no rows missing or added:

```
select * from BOOKSHELF_AUTHOR BA
where not exists
(select 'x' from BOOKSHELF_AUTHOR_EXT BAE
  where BA.Title = BAE.Title
    and BA.AuthorName = BAE.AuthorName);

no rows selected
```

The BOOKSHELF_AUTHOR_EXT table points to the book_auth_dump.lst file. If you alter the data in the file, the data in BOOKSHELF_AUTHOR_EXT will change. As illustrated here, you can query external tables the same way you query standard tables—in joins, as part of views, and so on. You can perform functions on the external table columns during queries just as you would for standard tables.

You can query the USER_EXTERNAL_TABLES data dictionary view for information about your external tables, including the default directory and access definitions:

```
desc USER_EXTERNAL_TABLES
```

Name	Null?	Type
TABLE_NAME	NOT NULL	VARCHAR2(30)
TYPE_OWNER		CHAR(3)
TYPE_NAME	NOT NULL	VARCHAR2(30)
DEFAULT_DIRECTORY_OWNER		CHAR(3)
DEFAULT_DIRECTORY_NAME	NOT NULL	VARCHAR2(30)
REJECT_LIMIT		VARCHAR2(40)
ACCESS_TYPE		VARCHAR2(7)
ACCESS_PARAMETERS		VARCHAR2(4000)

For example, the BOOKSHELF_AUTHOR_EXT table uses BOOK_DIR as its default directory, as shown in the following listing:

```
select * from USER_EXTERNAL_TABLES
 where Table_Name = 'BOOKSHELF_AUTHOR_EXT';

TABLE_NAME                              TYP TYPE_NAME                          DEF
--------------------------------        --- --------------------------------   ---
DEFAULT_DIRECTORY_NAME                  REJECT_LIMIT                           ACCESS_
--------------------------------        ---------------------------------------------- -------
ACCESS_PARAMETERS
--------------------------------------------------------------------------------
BOOKSHELF_AUTHOR_EXT                    SYS ORACLE_LOADER                      SYS
BOOK_DIR                                0                                      CLOB
records delimited by newline
                    fields terminated by "~"
                (Title          CHAR(100),
                 AuthorName     CHAR(50)
               )
```

USER_EXTERNAL_TABLES does not show the name of the external file (or files) the table references. To see that information, query USER_EXTERNAL_LOCATIONS:

```
select * from USER_EXTERNAL_LOCATIONS;

TABLE_NAME
------------------------------
LOCATION
------------------------------------------------
DIR DIRECTORY_NAME
--- ------------------------------
BOOKSHELF_AUTHOR_EXT
book_auth_dump.lst
SYS BOOK_DIR

BOOKSHELF_EXT
bookshelf_dump.lst
SYS BOOK_DIR
```

External Table Creation Options

Within the **organization external** clause, there are four main subclauses: **type**, **default directory**, **access parameters**, and **location**. When you create an external table, you can use these clauses to customize the way Oracle views the external data.

Type and Default Directory

The syntax for the **type** component is

```
( [type access_driver_type] external_data_properties )
[reject limit { integer | unlimited }]
```

For external tables, the access driver is the API used to transform the external data. Use **type ORACLE_LOADER** for your external tables—the only type available at this time—as shown in the examples earlier in this chapter.

NOTE
Because the access driver is part of the Oracle software, only files accessible by the database can be accessed as external tables. Files the Oracle user cannot access cannot be used as external tables.

Following the **type** declaration, you can set a "reject limit" value. By default, no rows can be rejected—any problem with any row will cause the **select** statement to return an error. Let's generate another copy of the BOOKSHELF data to a separate file, and this time leave in the extra lines SQL*Plus inserts during the **spool** operation:

```
set pagesize 0 newpage 0 feedback off
select Title||'~'||Publisher||'~'||CategoryName||'~'||Rating||'~'
  from BOOKSHELF
 order by Title

spool e:\oracle\external\bookshelf_dump_2.lst
/
spool off
```

Now create a new table that references this spool file, telling Oracle to skip the first record (**skip 1**) and to allow one other error (**reject limit 1**). That will account for the "/" in the first line and the "SQL> spool off" in the last line:

```
set feedback on heading on newpage 1 pagesize 60

create table BOOKSHELF_EXT_2
(Title         VARCHAR2(100),
Publisher      VARCHAR2(20),
CategoryName   VARCHAR2(20),
Rating         VARCHAR2(2)
)
organization external
(type ORACLE_LOADER
 default directory BOOK_DIR
 access parameters (records delimited by newline
skip 1
                fields terminated by
                "~"
                (Title        CHAR(100),
                 Publisher    CHAR(20),
                 CategoryName CHAR(20),
                 Rating       CHAR(2)
                ) )
 location ('bookshelf_dump_2.lst')
)
```

```
reject limit 1
;
```

You can now verify the number of rows in the table:

```
set feedback on heading on newpage 1 pagesize 60
select COUNT(*) from BOOKSHELF_EXT_2;

  COUNT(*)
----------
        31
```

The **default directory** clause specifies the directory object to be used for all datafiles that do not specify another directory. If you use multiple external files located in multiple directories, you can name one of them as the default directory and specify the others by directory name in the **location** clause. You must use directory object names (such as BOOK_DIR) in the **location** clause, not the full directory path name.

Access Parameters

The **access parameters** clause tells Oracle how to map the rows in the file to rows in the table. Its syntax is shown in the following illustration:

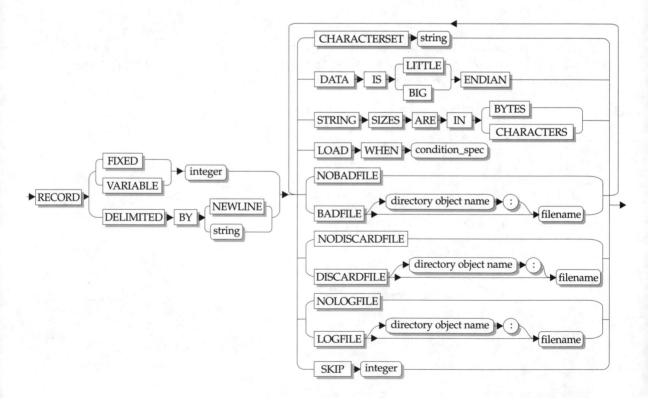

Within the **access parameters** clause, you first tell Oracle how to create a record—whether its length is fixed or variable, and how rows are delimited. In the case of the BOOKSHELF_EXT example, the records are delimited by newlines. If there were multiple rows on a single line, you could use a character string as a separator between rows. Since the external data may come from a non-Oracle database, Oracle supports multiple character sets and string sizes.

As with SQL*Loader, you can specify a **when** clause to limit which rows are selected. In the following listing, the BOOKSHELF_EXT_3 table is created, with a **when** clause (shown in bold) to limit it to only books in the CHILDRENPIC category.

```
create table BOOKSHELF_EXT_3
(Title        VARCHAR2(100),
Publisher     VARCHAR2(20),
CategoryName  VARCHAR2(20),
Rating        VARCHAR2(2)
)
organization external
(type ORACLE_LOADER
 default directory BOOK_DIR
 access parameters (records delimited by newline
                 load when CategoryName = 'CHILDRENPIC'
                                    skip 1
                 fields terminated by "~"
                 (Title          CHAR(100),
                  Publisher      CHAR(20),
                  CategoryName   CHAR(20),
                  Rating         CHAR(2)
                 ) )
 location ('bookshelf_dump_2.lst')
)
reject limit 1
;
```

You can see the result here:

```
select SUBSTR(Title, 1,30), CategoryName
  from BOOKSHELF_EXT_3;

SUBSTR(TITLE,1,30)                CATEGORYNAME
------------------------------    --------------------
GOOD DOG, CARL                    CHILDRENPIC
POLAR EXPRESS                     CHILDRENPIC
RUNAWAY BUNNY                     CHILDRENPIC

3 rows selected.
```

BOOKSHELF_EXT_3 accesses the same file as BOOKSHELF_EXT_2, but it only shows the records for the CHILDRENPIC category due to its **load when** clause.

As with SQL*Loader, you can create a log file, a bad file, and a discard file. Rows that fail the **load when** condition will be written to the discard file. Rows that fail the **access parameters**

conditions will be written to the bad file, and the load details will be written to the log file. For all three types of files, you can specify a directory object along with the filename so that you can write the output to a directory other than your input datafile directory. You can specify **nodiscardfile**, **nobadfile**, and **nologfile** to prevent these files from being created. Use directory object names (such as BOOK_DIR in this chapter's examples) when specifying locations for discard files, bad files, and log files. If you don't specify locations for log files, bad files, and discard files, Oracle creates them in the default directory with system-generated names.

Within the **access parameters** clause, you also specify the field definitions and delimiters, such as

```
fields terminated by "~"
(Title          CHAR(100),
 Publisher      CHAR(20),
 CategoryName   CHAR(20),
 Rating         CHAR(2))
```

You can use the **missing field values are null** clause to set values for **NULL** column values, but you must exercise caution when using this option. For example, the AUTHOR table has **NULL** values in its Comments column. The external table creation for AUTHOR_EXT is shown in the following listing:

```
set pagesize 0 newpage 0 feedback off
select AuthorName||'~'||Comments||'~'
  from AUTHOR
 order by AuthorName

spool e:\oracle\external\author_dump.lst
/
spool off

set feedback on heading on newpage 1 pagesize 60
create table AUTHOR_EXT
(AuthorName    VARCHAR2(50),
 Comments      VARCHAR2(100)
)
organization external
(type ORACLE_LOADER
 default directory BOOK_DIR
 access parameters (records delimited by newline
                    skip 1
                    fields terminated by "~"
                    missing field values are null
                    (AuthorName    CHAR(50),
                     Comments      CHAR(100)
                    ) )
 location ('author_dump.lst')
)
reject limit 1
;
```

But this is not correct—if you select the AuthorName values from AUTHOR_EXT, you will see that the values include:

```
select AuthorName from AUTHOR_EXT
  where AuthorName like 'S%';

AUTHORNAME
-------------------------------------------------
SOREN KIERKEGAARD
STEPHEN AMBROSE
STEPHEN JAY GOULD
SQL> spool off

4 rows selected.
```

Because of the **missing field values are null** clause, the "SQL> spool off" line at the end of the listing was read as an AuthorName value, with a **NULL** Comments value. This highlights the problem with coding exceptions into your loader definitions—you need to make sure you fully understand the source data and the way the loader will treat it. In most cases, your data integrity will be better served by forcing rows to fail (into bad files or discard files) and evaluating the failed rows apart from your general loads.

See the SQL*Loader entry in the Alphabetical Reference for the full syntax available for the **access parameters** clause.

Location

In the **location** clause, you specify the datafiles to use as the source data for the table. You can name multiple files in the **location** clause if they all exist in directory objects the user has READ privilege on. The following example combines two separate BOOKSHELF spool files to illustrate the ability to combine multiple files into a single external table.

```
create table BOOKSHELF_EXT_4
(Title        VARCHAR2(100),
Publisher     VARCHAR2(20),
CategoryName VARCHAR2(20),
Rating        VARCHAR2(2)
)
organization external
(type ORACLE_LOADER
 default directory BOOK_DIR
 access parameters (records delimited by newline
                    skip 1
                    fields terminated by "~"
                    (Title        CHAR(100),
                     Publisher     CHAR(20),
                     CategoryName CHAR(20),
                     Rating        CHAR(2)
                    ) )
location ('bookshelf_dump_2.lst', 'bookshelf_dump.lst')
)
```

```
reject limit 1
;
```

The order of the files is important—the skip 1 applies to the first file, not to the second file. The second file, bookshelf_dump.lst, is the file that was previously edited to eliminate the non-data rows in its first and last rows. The result, reflecting the rows in both, is shown in the following listing:

```
select COUNT(*) from BOOKSHELF_EXT_4;

  COUNT(*)
----------
        62
```

Limitations, Benefits, and Potential Uses of External Tables

External tables have limitations that may make them inappropriate for some online transaction procession applications. You cannot perform any **insert**, **update**, or **delete** operations on external tables. The more dynamic the table is, the less appropriate external files may be. As shown in the examples earlier in this chapter, you can change the file dynamically at the operating system level. If your application generates **insert**s only, you may be able to write those inserted records into an external file instead of a database table.

You cannot index external tables. The lack of indexes on external tables does not have to be a negative factor in application performance. Queries of external tables complete very quickly, even though a full table scan is required with each access. There is I/O involved, but modern I/O systems use caching and RAID techniques to significantly reduce the performance penalty associated with repeated full scans of the same file.

You cannot specify constraints on an external table. Even creating a NOT NULL or foreign key constraint fails:

```
alter table BOOKSHELF_EXT add constraint CATFK
foreign key (CategoryName) references CATEGORY(CategoryName);

foreign key (CategoryName) references CATEGORY(CategoryName)
*
ERROR at line 2:
ORA-30657: operation not supported on external organized table
```

Despite these limitations, external tables offer many useful features. You can join external tables (to each other, or to standard tables). You can use hints to force the optimizer to choose different join paths, and you can see the results in the query execution paths (see Chapter 38 for details on hints and the Oracle optimizer).

As an alternative to data loading, external tables offer DBAs and application developers the possibility of accessing data without supporting long-running load programs. Because the files can be edited at the operating system level, you can quickly replace a table's data without worrying about outstanding transactions modifying the table. For example, you could use this

capability to create multiple external tables and create a **union all** view across them, creating a partition view across multiple files. You can then manage each table's data separately at the file system level, replacing their contents as needed.

Because the external table can be queried, you can use the external table as the data source for an **insert as select** command. During that operation, Oracle will attempt to load the external files in parallel, potentially improving performance. To further improve performance of the **insert as select** operation, you should use the APPEND hint to force block-level inserts. When you specify the degree of parallelism for the **insert as select** operation, Oracle starts multiple ORACLE_LOADER access drivers to process the data in parallel. To further enhance load performance, avoid using variable-length fields, delimited fields, character set conversion, NULLIF, DEFAULTIF, and datatype conversion operations. Turning off **badfile** (with **nobadfile**) eliminates the costs associated with the file creation and the maintenance of the original row's context.

During the **insert as select**, you can perform functions on the data as it is processed. You can perform the functions either in the **insert as select** command syntax or in the external table definition. This capability highlights an important benefit of external tables—you can centralize the representation and processing requirements for your data, building translation routines into your table definitions. There is no processing data stored in SQL*Loader control files or PL/SQL routines; all of the logic is built into the table definition, accessible via USER_EXTERNAL_TABLES.

During queries, external tables allow you to select specific data sets (via the **load when** clause, as illustrated in this chapter). If you have multiple data sources for a data warehouse load, you can choose which data will be made available even while the data is outside the database. You can use this feature to maintain application availability during data loads. These loads can occur in parallel if the external file has a FIXED file format.

The limited access feature also allows you to enforce complex security rules concerning data access. For example, you may keep sensitive data outside the database, in a secure directory. Users with READ access to that directory would be able to use the external table and join it to other tables; users without that access would be limited to the data inserted into the publicly accessible tables. Highly secure data, or lightly accessed dynamic data, need not be inserted into the database until it is needed, if at all.

If you use external tables in your database architecture, you must make sure your backup and recovery plans account for those files as well as the rest of your database. If the external files change more rapidly than the database files, you may need to back them up more frequently in order to take advantage of Oracle's full recovery capabilities.

CHAPTER
26

Using Flashback
Queries

s part of its read consistency model, Oracle displays data that has been committed to the database. As of Oracle9i, you can query data as it existed prior to a transaction being committed. If you accidentally **commit** an errant **update** or **delete**, you can use this capability—called a flashback query—to see the data as it existed prior to the **commit**. You can use the results of the flashback query to restore the data. Flashback queries are limited. To use them, your database must be using system-managed undo, a feature introduced in Oracle9i to replace rollback segments; see your DBA to determine if this feature is enabled in your environment. The DBA must create an undo tablespace, enable automatic undo management, and establish an undo retention time window. Oracle will attempt to maintain enough undo information in the undo tablespace to support flashback queries during the retention time period. The retention time setting and the amount of space available in the undo tablespace can significantly impact your ability to successfully execute a flashback query.

NOTE
Oracle uses undo to roll back transactions and support flashback queries. Oracle uses redo (captured in the online redo log files) to apply transactions during database recoveries.

As you will see in the examples in this chapter, flashback queries are not simple. While syntax improvements have been documented as included in Oracle9i Release 2, flashback queries still require non-standard SQL commands. You should not rely on flashback queries as part of your application design because of their complexity, because you cannot predict their performance, and because of their dependence on system elements outside of the application developer's control (such as the number of transactions during a time period and the size of the undo tablespace). Rather, you should treat them as an option during critical periods of testing, support, and data recovery. For example, you could use them to create copies of tables at multiple past points in time for use when reconstructing changed data.

NOTE
To use flashback queries, you must have EXECUTE privilege on the DBMS_FLASHBACK package.

Time-based Flashback Example

The BOOK_ORDER table has six records, as shown in the following listing:

```
select * from BOOK_ORDER;

TITLE                          PUBLISHER                CATEGORYNAME
------------------------------ ------------------------ ------------
SHOELESS JOE                   MARINER                  ADULTFIC
GOSPEL                         PICADOR                  ADULTFIC
SOMETHING SO STRONG            PANDORAS                 ADULTNF
GALILEO'S DAUGHTER             PENGUIN                  ADULTNF
LONGITUDE                      PENGUIN                  ADULTNF
```

```
ONCE REMOVED                    SANCTUARY PUB         ADULTNF

6 rows selected.
```

A shipment has arrived, and the old BOOK_ORDERS records are deleted and the deletion is committed. Unfortunately, not all of the books were in the shipment, so the **delete** is inappropriate:

```
delete from BOOK_ORDER;
commit;
```

How can you reconstruct the unreceived records from the BOOK_ORDER table, since you only have the received books in hand? You could perform a database recovery by using **import** to restore the table, or performing a physical database recovery. With flashback queries, you can avoid the need to perform these recovery operations.

First, let's query the old data from the database. Since flashback mode only supports queries, doing more with the data (such as saving it to a separate table) will be addressed in a more complex example in the next section. To enter flashback mode, use the ENABLE_AT_TIME procedure of the DBMS_FLASHBACK package. In the following example, the flashback is enabled at a time five minutes in the past (SysDate-5/1440).

```
select COUNT(*) from BOOK_ORDER;

  COUNT(*)
----------
         0

execute DBMS_FLASHBACK.ENABLE_AT_TIME(SysDate-5/1440);

PL/SQL procedure successfully completed.

select COUNT(*) from BOOK_ORDER;

  COUNT(*)
----------
         6
```

Once the query is complete, disable flashback mode:

```
execute DBMS_FLASHBACK.DISABLE;

PL/SQL procedure successfully completed.
```

NOTE
You must disable flashback mode before enabling it again.

When you execute a flashback query, only the state of the data is changed. The current system time is used (as you can see by querying the SysDate value) and the current data dictionary is used.

NOTE
You cannot execute a flashback query against a remote table across a database link.

Saving the Data

As shown in the BOOK_ORDER example, flashback queries are simple to implement, provided the undo management of the database is properly configured and the undo information is available. But how can you work with the flashback data? While in flashback mode, you cannot perform DDL or DML operations, so you cannot execute a **create table as select** command to save old data to a temporary work table.

To perform DDL and DML operations against flashback data, you will need to use PL/SQL, Oracle's procedural language extension to the SQL programming language (see Chapter 27). The sequence of commands for the PL/SQL used to save flashback data is as follows:

1. Define the cursor that queries the data and a variable to hold the data.

2. Begin the PL/SQL block.

3. Enable flashback query mode.

4. Open the cursor.

5. Disable flashback query mode.

6. Loop through the selected records, exiting when there are no more records.

Let's save the old data. With flashback mode disabled, create a new table with the same structure as BOOK_ORDER but with no records in it:

```
drop table BOOK_ORDER_FLASH;
create table BOOK_ORDER_FLASH
(Title        VARCHAR2(100) primary key,
Publisher     VARCHAR2(20),
CategoryName VARCHAR2(20));

Table created.
```

Now, execute a PL/SQL block. In the cursor definition, you can specify the rows and columns you want returned. In this example, the entire table is selected.

```
declare cursor OLD_BOOK_ORDER is select * from BOOK_ORDER;
        OBO     BOOK_ORDER%ROWTYPE;
begin
  DBMS_FLASHBACK.ENABLE_AT_TIME(SysDate-30/1440);
  open OLD_BOOK_ORDER;
  DBMS_FLASHBACK.DISABLE;
  loop
```

```
    fetch OLD_BOOK_ORDER into OBO;
    exit when OLD_BOOK_ORDER%NOTFOUND;
    insert into BOOK_ORDER_FLASH
       values (OBO.Title, OBO.Publisher, OBO.CategoryName);
  end loop;
  close OLD_BOOK_ORDER;
  commit;
end;
/
```

Oracle responds with:

```
PL/SQL procedure successfully completed.
```

You can now verify that the flashback data has been saved:

```
column Title format a30

select * from BOOK_ORDER_FLASH;

TITLE                          PUBLISHER            CATEGORYNAME
------------------------------ -------------------- ------------
SHOELESS JOE                   MARINER              ADULTFIC
GOSPEL                         PICADOR              ADULTFIC
SOMETHING SO STRONG            PANDORAS             ADULTNF
GALILEO'S DAUGHTER             PENGUIN              ADULTNF
LONGITUDE                      PENGUIN              ADULTNF
ONCE REMOVED                   SANCTUARY PUB        ADULTNF

6 rows selected.
```

If the flashback query attempted to use an index created after the flashback point in time, the query would fail. In that event, you should use hints to tell the optimizer which data access method to use (a full table scan or a different index); see Chapter 38 for details on the use of hints.

Limitations of Time-Based Flashbacks

The preceding examples showed how to use the system timestamp during your flashback query. However, Oracle internally uses the System Change Number (SCN), not the system timestamp, to generate the flashback data. The system timestamp is matched to SCN values every five minutes; the table SYS.SMON_SCN_TIME shows at least the last five days worth of SCN/system timestamp matches. When you flashback to a point in time, Oracle uses the most recent five-minute timestamp preceding the requested time. If SMON_SCN_TIME has a record for 1:00 P.M. and 1:05 P.M., a request for a flashback to 1:04 P.M. will return the data from 1:00 P.M.

SMON_SCN_TIME only maintains the most recent 1,440 entries, so flashback queries that go beyond the most recent five days in an always-open database must use an SCN-based approach as described in the next section. If you shut down your database periodically (such as for offline backups), the 1,440 records in SMON_SCN_TIME will span more than five days.

SCN-based Flashback Example

When you perform time-based flashbacks, you are really doing SCN-based flashbacks; you're just relying on Oracle to find an SCN near the time you specified. If you know the exact SCN, you can perform a flashback with a great degree of precision. In place of the ENABLE_AT_TIME procedure, you will call the ENABLE_AT_SYSTEM_CHANGE_NUMBER procedure, as shown in the following example.

To begin an SCN-based flashback, you must first know the SCN of your transaction. To get the latest change number, issue a **commit** and then execute the GET_SYSTEM_CHANGE_NUMBER function of the DBMS_FLASHBACK package prior to executing your transaction. The following example shows this process as part of a transaction against the BOOK_ORDER_FLASH table created and populated in the first part in this chapter. First, the current SCN is assigned to a variable named SCN_FLASH and displayed via the SQL*Plus **print** command:

```
commit;

variable SCN_FLASH number;
execute :SCN_FLASH :=DBMS_FLASHBACK.GET_SYSTEM_CHANGE_NUMBER;

PL/SQL procedure successfully completed.

print SCN_FLASH

 SCN_FLASH
----------
   1589270
```

Next, the **delete** command is issued and the result is committed:

```
delete from BOOK_ORDER_FLASH;

6 rows deleted.

commit;
```

You can now query the flashback data. Although the SCN value is known, you can continue to use the SCN_FLASH variable value if you are within the same session:

```
execute DBMS_FLASHBACK.ENABLE_AT_SYSTEM_CHANGE_NUMBER(:SCN_FLASH);

PL/SQL procedure successfully completed.

select COUNT(*) from BOOK_ORDER_FLASH;
```

```
     fetch OLD_BOOK_ORDER into OBO;
     exit when OLD_BOOK_ORDER%NOTFOUND;
     insert into BOOK_ORDER_FLASH
        values (OBO.Title, OBO.Publisher, OBO.CategoryName);
  end loop;
  close OLD_BOOK_ORDER;
  commit;
end;
/
```

Oracle responds with:

```
PL/SQL procedure successfully completed.
```

You can now verify that the flashback data has been saved:

```
column Title format a30

select * from BOOK_ORDER_FLASH;

TITLE                           PUBLISHER            CATEGORYNAME
------------------------------  -------------------  ------------
SHOELESS JOE                    MARINER              ADULTFIC
GOSPEL                          PICADOR              ADULTFIC
SOMETHING SO STRONG             PANDORAS             ADULTNF
GALILEO'S DAUGHTER              PENGUIN              ADULTNF
LONGITUDE                       PENGUIN              ADULTNF
ONCE REMOVED                    SANCTUARY PUB        ADULTNF

6 rows selected.
```

If the flashback query attempted to use an index created after the flashback point in time, the query would fail. In that event, you should use hints to tell the optimizer which data access method to use (a full table scan or a different index); see Chapter 38 for details on the use of hints.

Limitations of Time-Based Flashbacks

The preceding examples showed how to use the system timestamp during your flashback query. However, Oracle internally uses the System Change Number (SCN), not the system timestamp, to generate the flashback data. The system timestamp is matched to SCN values every five minutes; the table SYS.SMON_SCN_TIME shows at least the last five days worth of SCN/system timestamp matches. When you flashback to a point in time, Oracle uses the most recent five-minute timestamp preceding the requested time. If SMON_SCN_TIME has a record for 1:00 P.M. and 1:05 P.M., a request for a flashback to 1:04 P.M. will return the data from 1:00 P.M.

SMON_SCN_TIME only maintains the most recent 1,440 entries, so flashback queries that go beyond the most recent five days in an always-open database must use an SCN-based approach as described in the next section. If you shut down your database periodically (such as for offline backups), the 1,440 records in SMON_SCN_TIME will span more than five days.

SCN-based Flashback Example

When you perform time-based flashbacks, you are really doing SCN-based flashbacks; you're just relying on Oracle to find an SCN near the time you specified. If you know the exact SCN, you can perform a flashback with a great degree of precision. In place of the ENABLE_AT_TIME procedure, you will call the ENABLE_AT_SYSTEM_CHANGE_NUMBER procedure, as shown in the following example.

To begin an SCN-based flashback, you must first know the SCN of your transaction. To get the latest change number, issue a **commit** and then execute the GET_SYSTEM_CHANGE_NUMBER function of the DBMS_FLASHBACK package prior to executing your transaction. The following example shows this process as part of a transaction against the BOOK_ORDER_FLASH table created and populated in the first part in this chapter. First, the current SCN is assigned to a variable named SCN_FLASH and displayed via the SQL*Plus **print** command:

```
commit;

variable SCN_FLASH number;
execute :SCN_FLASH :=DBMS_FLASHBACK.GET_SYSTEM_CHANGE_NUMBER;

PL/SQL procedure successfully completed.

print SCN_FLASH

 SCN_FLASH
----------
   1589270
```

Next, the **delete** command is issued and the result is committed:

```
delete from BOOK_ORDER_FLASH;

6 rows deleted.

commit;
```

You can now query the flashback data. Although the SCN value is known, you can continue to use the SCN_FLASH variable value if you are within the same session:

```
execute DBMS_FLASHBACK.ENABLE_AT_SYSTEM_CHANGE_NUMBER(:SCN_FLASH);

PL/SQL procedure successfully completed.

select COUNT(*) from BOOK_ORDER_FLASH;
```

```
COUNT(*)
----------
         6

execute DBMS_FLASHBACK.DISABLE;
```

You can now use the flashback data in BOOK_ORDER_FLASH, accessed by the ENABLE_AT_SYSTEM_CHANGE_NUMBER procedure, to populate BOOK_ORDER:

```
declare cursor OLD_BOOK_ORDER is select * from BOOK_ORDER_FLASH;
        OBO BOOK_ORDER_FLASH%ROWTYPE;
begin
  DBMS_FLASHBACK.ENABLE_AT_SYSTEM_CHANGE_NUMBER(:SCN_FLASH);
  open OLD_BOOK_ORDER;
  DBMS_FLASHBACK.DISABLE;
  loop
    fetch OLD_BOOK_ORDER into OBO;
    exit when OLD_BOOK_ORDER%NOTFOUND;
    insert into BOOK_ORDER
      values (OBO.Title, OBO.Publisher, OBO.CategoryName);
  end loop;
  close OLD_BOOK_ORDER;
  commit;
end;
/

PL/SQL procedure successfully completed.

select COUNT(*) from BOOK_ORDER;

COUNT(*)
----------
         6
```

> **NOTE**
> *DDL operations that alter the structure of a table invalidate the old undo data for the table, and flashback capabilities are limited to the time since the DDL was executed. Space-related changes (such as changing **pctfree**) do not invalidate the old undo data.*

For DBAs, flashback queries may offer a means of avoiding recovery operations. If the data can be reconstructed via flashback queries, and if the data volume is not overwhelming, you may be able to save the results of multiple flashback queries in separate tables. You could then compare the data in the tables via the SQL options shown in prior chapters—correlated subqueries, **exists**, **not exists**, **minus**, and so on. If you cannot avoid the need for a recovery operation, you should be able to pinpoint the time period to be used for a time-based recovery operation.

For application developers and application administrators, flashback queries provide an important tool for reconstructing data. Flashback queries may be particularly critical during testing and support operations. Rather than making flashback queries part of your production application design, you should use them as a fallback option for those support cases that cannot be resolved before data is affected.

PART

III

PL/SQL

CHAPTER
27

An Introduction to PL/SQL

L/SQL is Oracle's procedural language (PL) superset of the Structured Query Language (SQL). You can use PL/SQL to do such things as codify your business rules through the creation of stored procedures and packages, trigger database events to occur, or add programming logic to the execution of SQL commands.

The steps involved in the creation of triggers, stored procedures, and packages are described in the following chapters in this section of this book. In this chapter, you will see the basic structures and syntax used in PL/SQL.

PL/SQL Overview

PL/SQL code is grouped into structures called *blocks*. If you create a stored procedure or package, you give the block of PL/SQL code a name; if the block of PL/SQL code is not given a name, then it is called an *anonymous block*. The examples in this chapter will feature anonymous blocks of PL/SQL code; the following chapters in this section illustrate the creation of named blocks.

A block of PL/SQL code contains three sections:

Section	Description
Declarations	Defines and initializes the variables and cursors used in the block
Executable Commands	Uses flow-control commands (such as **if** commands and loops) to execute the commands and assign values to the declared variables
Exception Handling	Provides customized handling of error conditions

Within a PL/SQL block, the first section is the Declarations section. Within the Declarations section, you define the variables and cursors that the block will use. The Declarations section starts with the keyword **declare** and ends when the Executable Commands section starts (as indicated by the keyword **begin**). The Executable Commands section is followed by the Exception Handling section; the **exception** keyword signals the start of the Exception Handling section. The PL/SQL block is terminated by the **end** keyword.

The structure of a typical PL/SQL block is shown in the following listing:

```
declare
  <declarations section>
begin
  <executable commands>
 exception
  <exception handling>
end;
```

In the following sections of this chapter, you will see descriptions of each section of the PL/SQL block.

Declarations Section

The Declarations section begins a PL/SQL block. The Declarations section starts with the **declare** keyword, followed by a list of variable and cursor definitions. You can define variables to have constant values, and variables can inherit datatypes from existing columns and query results as shown in the following examples.

In the following listing, the area of a circle is calculated. The result is stored in a table named AREAS. The AREAS table has two columns, to store radius and area values. The area of the circle is calculated by squaring the value for the circle's radius and multiplying that value times the constant *pi*:

```
declare
  pi       constant NUMBER(9,7) := 3.1415927;
  radius INTEGER(5);
  area    NUMBER(14,2);
begin
  radius := 3;
  area := pi*power(radius,2);
  insert into AREAS values (radius, area);
end;
```

The **end;** signals the end of the PL/SQL block; depending on the tool you use, you may need to add a **/** to execute the PL/SQL block. When the PL/SQL block is executed, you will receive the following response from Oracle:

```
PL/SQL procedure successfully completed.
```

To verify that the PL/SQL block completed correctly, you can select from the database the rows that were inserted by the PL/SQL code. The query and results in the following listing show the row the PL/SQL block created in the AREAS table.

```
select *
  from AREAS;

    RADIUS       AREA
---------- ----------
         3     28.27
```

The output shows that a single row was inserted into the AREAS table by the PL/SQL block. Only one row was created because only one Radius value was specified.

In the first section of the PL/SQL block, shown in the following listing, three variables are declared. You must declare the variables that will be used in the Executable Commands section of the PL/SQL block.

```
declare
  pi       constant NUMBER(9,7) := 3.1415927;
  radius INTEGER(5);
  area    NUMBER(14,2);
```

The first variable declared is *pi,* which is set to a constant value via the **constant** keyword. Because it is declared as a **constant**, the value of the variable *pi* cannot be changed in the Executable Commands section. The value is assigned via the **:=** operator:

```
pi      constant NUMBER(9,7) := 3.1415927;
```

You can also assign constant values via the **default** keyword:

```
pi      NUMBER(9,7) DEFAULT 3.1415927;
```

The next two variables are defined but are not given default values:

```
radius INTEGER(5);
area    NUMBER(14,2);
```

You can assign an initial value to a variable in the Declarations section. To set an initial value for a variable, simply follow its datatype specification with the value assignment, as shown in the following listing:

```
radius INTEGER(5)   := 3;
```

In the example, the datatypes include NUMBER and INTEGER. PL/SQL datatypes include all of the valid SQL datatypes as well as complex datatypes based on query structures. Table 27-1 lists the supported PL/SQL datatypes.

In the following example, a cursor is declared to retrieve a record from the RADIUS_VALS table. RADIUS_VALS is a table with one column, named Radius, that holds radius values to be used in these examples. The cursor is declared in the Declarations section, and a variable named *rad_val* is declared with a datatype based on the cursor's results.

```
declare
  pi      constant NUMBER(9,7) := 3.1415927;
  area    NUMBER(14,2);
  cursor rad_cursor is
      select * from RADIUS_VALS;
  rad_val rad_cursor%ROWTYPE;
begin
  open rad_cursor;
  fetch rad_cursor into rad_val;
    area := pi*power(rad_val.radius,2);
    insert into AREAS values (rad_val.radius, area);
  close rad_cursor;
end;
```

For this example, the table RADIUS_VALS contains a single row with a Radius value of 3.

In the first part of the Declarations section, the *pi* and *area* variables are defined, as they were in the examples earlier in this chapter. The radius variable is not defined; instead, a cursor named *rad_cursor* is defined. The cursor definition consists of a cursor name (*rad_cursor*) and a query

Scalar Datatypes

BINARY_INTEGER	INT	NVARCHAR2	STRING
BOOLEAN	INTEGER	NUMBER	TIMESTAMP
CHAR	INTERVAL DAY TO SECOND	NUMERIC	TIMESTAMP WITH LOCAL TIME ZONE
CHARACTER	INTERVAL YEAR TO MONTH	PLS_INTEGER	TIMESTAMP WITH TIME ZONE
DATE	LONG	POSITIVE	UROWID
DEC	LONG RAW	POSITIVEN	VARCHAR
DECIMAL	NATURAL	REAL	VARCHAR2
DOUBLE PRECISION	NATURALN	SIGNTYPE	RAW
FLOAT	NCHAR	SMALLINT	ROWID

Composite Types

RECORD	TABLE	VARRAY

Reference Types

REF CURSOR	REF *object_type*

LOB Types

BFILE	BLOB	CLOB	NCLOB

TABLE 27-1. *PL/SQL Datatypes*

(**select * from RADIUS_VALS;**). A cursor holds the results of a query for processing by other commands within the PL/SQL block:

```
declare
   pi     constant NUMBER(9,7) := 3.1415927;
   area   NUMBER(14,2);
   cursor rad_cursor is
       select * from RADIUS_VALS;
```

A final declaration creates a variable whose structure is anchored by the cursor's result set:

```
   rad_val rad_cursor%ROWTYPE;
```

The *rad_val* variable will be able to reference each column of the query's result set. In this example, the query only returns a single column, but if the table contained multiple columns, you would be able to reference all of them via the *rad_val* variable.

In addition to the %ROWTYPE declaration, you can use the %TYPE declaration to inherit datatype information. If you use the %ROWTYPE declaration, the variable inherits the column and datatype information for all the columns in the cursor's result set. If you use the %TYPE declaration, then the variable only inherits the definition of the column used to define it. You can even base %TYPE definitions on cursors, as shown in the following example.

```
cursor rad_cursor is
    select * from RADIUS_VALS;
rad_val rad_cursor%ROWTYPE;
rad_val_radius  rad_val.Radius%TYPE;
```

In the preceding listing, the *rad_val* variable inherits the datatypes of the result set of the *rad_cursor* cursor. The *rad_val_radius* variable inherits the datatype of the Radius column within the *rad_val* variable.

The advantage of datatype anchoring using %ROWTYPE and %TYPE definitions is that it makes the datatype definitions in your PL/SQL code independent of the underlying data structures. If the RADIUS_VALS Radius column is changed from a NUMBER(5) datatype to a NUMBER(4,2) datatype, you do not need to modify your PL/SQL code; the datatype assigned to the associated variables will be determined dynamically at runtime.

Executable Commands Section

In the Executable Commands section, you manipulate the variables and cursors declared in the Declarations section of your PL/SQL block. The Executable Commands section always starts with the keyword **begin**. In the following listing, the first PL/SQL block example from the Declarations section is repeated: the area of a circle is calculated, and the results are inserted into the AREAS table:

```
declare
  pi      constant NUMBER(9,7) := 3.1415927;
  radius INTEGER(5);
  area    NUMBER(14,2);
begin
  radius := 3;
  area := pi*power(radius,2);
  insert into AREAS values (radius, area);
end;
```

In the preceding listing, the Executable Commands section is

```
begin
  radius := 3;
  area := pi*power(radius,2);
  insert into AREAS values (radius, area);
end;
```

Following the **begin** keyword, the PL/SQL block's work begins. First, a value is assigned to the radius variable, and the radius variable and the *pi* constant value are used to determine the value of the *area* variable. The Radius and Area values are then inserted into the AREAS table.

The Executable Commands section of the PL/SQL block may contain commands that execute the cursors declared in the Declarations section. In the following example (from the "Declarations Section" section of this chapter), the Executable Commands section features several commands that reference the *rad_cursor* cursor:

```
declare
  pi      constant NUMBER(9,7) := 3.1415927;
  area    NUMBER(14,2);
  cursor rad_cursor is
      select * from RADIUS_VALS;
  rad_val rad_cursor%ROWTYPE;
begin
  open rad_cursor;
  fetch rad_cursor into rad_val;
    area := pi*power(rad_val.radius,2);
    insert into AREAS values (rad_val.radius, area);
  close rad_cursor;
end;
```

In the first command involving the cursor, the **open** command is used:

```
  open rad_cursor;
```

When the *rad_cursor* cursor is **open**ed, the query declared for that cursor is executed and the records to be returned are identified. Next, records are **fetch**ed from the cursor:

```
  fetch rad_cursor into rad_val;
```

In the Declarations section, the *rad_val* variable was declared to anchor its datatypes to the *rad_cursor* cursor:

```
  cursor rad_cursor is
      select * from RADIUS_VALS;
  rad_val rad_cursor%ROWTYPE;
```

When you **fetch** a record from the cursor into the *rad_val* variable, you can still address each column value selected via the cursor's query. When the cursor's data is no longer needed, you can **close** the cursor, as shown in the following listing:

```
  close rad_cursor;
```

The Executable Commands section may contain conditional logic, such as **if** commands and loops. In the following sections, you will see examples of each of the major types of flow-control operations permitted in PL/SQL. You can use the flow-control operations to alter the manner in which the fetched records and executable commands are managed.

Conditional Logic

Within PL/SQL, you can use **if**, **else**, **elsif**, and **case** commands to control the flow of commands within the Executable Commands section. The formats of the **if** clauses are shown in the following listing:

```
if   <some condition>
  then  <some command>
elsif  <some condition>
  then  <some command>
else  <some command>
end if;
```

You can nest **if** conditions within each other, as shown in the following listing:

```
if   <some condition>
  then
    if  <some condition>
    then  <some command>
    end if;
else  <some command>
end if;
```

By nesting **if** conditions, you can quickly develop complex logic flows within your Executable Commands section. When nesting **if** conditions, make sure you are not making the flow control more complex than it needs to be; always check to see whether logical conditions can be combined into simpler orders.

The area of a circle example used in the previous section will now be modified to include conditional logic. In the following listing, the Executable Commands section of the PL/SQL block has been modified to include **if** and **then** commands:

```
declare
   pi      constant NUMBER(9,7) := 3.1415927;
   area    NUMBER(14,2);
   cursor rad_cursor is
       select * from RADIUS_VALS;
   rad_val rad_cursor%ROWTYPE;
begin
  open rad_cursor;
  fetch rad_cursor into rad_val;
    area := pi*power(rad_val.radius,2);
    if  area >30
    then
      insert into AREAS values (rad_val.radius, area);
    end if;
  close rad_cursor;
end;
```

In the preceding listing, an **if** condition is used to control the flow of commands within the Executable Commands section of the PL/SQL block. The flow-control commands are shown in the following listing:

```
if  area >30
  then
     insert into AREAS values (rad_val.radius, area);
  end if;
```

The flow-control commands in this example begin after the *area* variable's value has been determined. If the value is greater than 30, then a record will be inserted into the AREAS table; if the value is less than 30, then no record will be inserted into the table. You can use this sort of flow control to direct which of several SQL statements are to be executed, based on the conditions in your **if** conditions.

The following listing shows syntax for flow control involving SQL commands:

```
if  area>30
  then   <some command>
elsif  area<10
  then   <some command>
else   <some command>
end if;
```

Loops

You can use loops to process multiple records within a single PL/SQL block. PL/SQL supports three types of loops:

Simple loops	A loop that keeps repeating until an **exit** or **exit when** statement is reached within the loop
FOR loops	A loop that repeats a specified number of times
WHILE loops	A loop that repeats while a condition is met

In the following sections, you will see examples of each type of loop. The loop examples will use as their starting point the PL/SQL blocks used previously in this chapter. You can use loops to process multiple records from a cursor.

Simple Loops

In the following listing, a simple loop is used to generate multiple rows in the AREAS table. The loop is started by the **loop** keyword, and the **exit when** clause determines when the loop should be exited. An **end loop** clause identifies the end of the loop.

```
declare
  pi      constant NUMBER(9,7) := 3.1415927;
  radius INTEGER(5);
  area    NUMBER(14,2);
begin
  radius := 3;
```

```
loop
   area := pi*power(radius,2);
      insert into AREAS values (radius, area);
   radius := radius+1;
   exit when area >100;
end loop;
end;
```

The loop section of the example establishes the flow control for the commands in the Executable Commands section of the PL/SQL block. The steps within the loop are described in the following commented version of the **loop** commands:

```
loop
      /* Calculate the area, based on the radius value.   */
   area := pi*power(radius,2);
      /* Insert the current values into the AREAS table.  */
   insert into AREAS values (radius, area);
      /* Increment the radius value by 1.                 */
   radius := radius+1;
      /* Evaluate the last calculated area.  If the value */
      /* exceeds 100, then exit.  Otherwise, repeat the   */
      /* loop using the new radius value.                 */
   exit when area >100;
      /* Signal the end of the loop.                      */
end loop;
```

The loop should generate multiple entries in the AREAS table. The first record will be the record generated by a Radius value of 3. Once an *area* value exceeds 100, no more records will be inserted into the AREAS table.

Sample output following the execution of the PL/SQL block is shown in the following listing:

```
select *
  from AREAS
 order by Radius;
```

```
    RADIUS       AREA
---------- ----------
         3      28.27
         4      50.27
         5      78.54
         6      113.1
```

Since the *area* value for a Radius value of 6 exceeds 100, no further Radius values are processed and the PL/SQL block completes.

Simple Cursor Loops

You can use the attributes of a cursor—such as whether or not any rows are left to be fetched—as the exit criteria for a loop. In the following example, a cursor is executed until no more rows are

returned by the query. To determine the status of the cursor, the cursor's attributes are checked. Cursors have four attributes you can use in your program:

%FOUND	A record can be fetched from the cursor
%NOTFOUND	No more records can be fetched from the cursor
%ISOPEN	The cursor has been opened
%ROWCOUNT	The number of rows fetched from the cursor so far

The %FOUND, %NOTFOUND, and %ISOPEN cursor attributes are Booleans; they are set to either TRUE or FALSE. Because they are Boolean attributes, you can evaluate their settings without explicitly matching them to values of TRUE or FALSE. For example, the following command will cause an exit to occur when rad_cursor%NOTFOUND is TRUE:

```
exit when rad_cursor%NOTFOUND;
```

In the following listing, a simple loop is used to process multiple rows from a cursor:

```
declare
    pi      constant NUMBER(9,7) := 3.1415927;
    area    NUMBER(14,2);
    cursor rad_cursor is
        select * from RADIUS_VALS;
    rad_val rad_cursor%ROWTYPE;
begin
  open rad_cursor;
  loop
    fetch rad_cursor into rad_val;
    exit when rad_cursor%NOTFOUND;
      area := pi*power(rad_val.radius,2);
      insert into AREAS values (rad_val.radius, area);
  end loop;
  close rad_cursor;
end;
```

The loop section of the PL/SQL block uses values from the RADIUS_VALS table as its input. Instead of basing the exit criteria on the Area value, the cursor's %NOTFOUND attribute is checked. If no more rows are found in the cursor, then %NOTFOUND will be TRUE—and thus, the loop will be exited. The commented version of the loop is shown in the following listing:

```
loop
        /*  Within the loop, fetch a record.            */
      fetch rad_cursor into rad_val;
        /*  If the fetch attempt reveals no more        */
        /*  records in the cursor, then exit the loop.  */
      exit when rad_cursor%NOTFOUND;
        /*  If the fetch attempt returned a record,     */
        /*  then process the Radius value and insert    */
        /*  a record into the AREAS table.              */
```

```
      area := pi*power(rad_val.radius,2);
      insert into AREAS values (rad_val.radius, area);
      /*  Signal the end of the loop.                  */
   end loop;
```

When the preceding PL/SQL block is executed, every record in the RADIUS_VALS table will be processed by the loop. So far, the RADIUS_VALS table only contains one record—a Radius value of 3. Prior to executing the PL/SQL block for this section, add two new Radius values to the RADIUS_VALS table: 4 and 10.

The following listing shows the addition of the new records to the RADIUS_VALS table:

```
insert into RADIUS_VALS values (4);
insert into RADIUS_VALS values (10);
commit;

select *
  from RADIUS_VALS
 order by Radius;

    RADIUS
----------
         3
         4
        10
```

Once the new records have been added to the RADIUS_VALS table, execute the PL/SQL block shown earlier in this section. The output of the PL/SQL block is shown in the following listing:

```
select *
  from AREAS
 order by Radius;

    RADIUS        AREA
----------  ----------
         3       28.27
         4       50.27
        10      314.16
```

The query of the AREAS table shows that every record in the RADIUS_VALS table was fetched from the cursor and processed. Once there were no more records to process in the cursor, the loop was exited and the PL/SQL block completed.

FOR Loops

In simple loops, the loop executes until an **exit** condition is met. In a FOR loop, the loop executes a specified number of times. An example of a FOR loop is shown in the following listing. The FOR loop's start is indicated by the keyword **for**, followed by the criteria used to determine when the processing is complete and the loop can be exited. Since the number of times the loop is executed is set when the loop is begun, an **exit** command isn't needed within the loop.

In the following example, the areas of circles are calculated based on Radius values ranging from 1 through 7, inclusive.

```
declare
   pi      constant NUMBER(9,7) := 3.1415927;
   radius INTEGER(5);
   area    NUMBER(14,2);
begin
   for radius in 1..7 loop
     area := pi*power(radius,2);
     insert into AREAS values (radius, area);
   end loop;
end;
```

The steps involved in processing the loop are shown in the following commented listing:

```
   /*  Specify the criteria for the number of loop      */
   /*  executions.                                       */
   for radius in 1..7 loop
     /*  Calculate the area using the current Radius     */
     /*  value.                                          */
     area := pi*power(radius,2);
     /*  Insert the area and radius values into the AREAS */
     /*  table.                                          */
     insert into AREAS values (radius, area);
     /*  Signal the end of the loop.                     */
   end loop;
```

Note that there is no line that says

```
radius := radius+1;
```

in the FOR loop. Since the specification of the loop specifies

```
for radius in 1..7 loop
```

the Radius values are already specified. For each value, all of the commands within the loop are executed (these commands can include other conditional logic, such as **if** conditions). Once the loop has completed processing a Radius value, the limits on the **for** clause are checked, and either the next Radius value is used or the loop execution is complete.

Sample output from the FOR loop execution is shown in the following listing:

```
select *
  from AREAS
 order by Radius;

    RADIUS       AREA
---------- ----------
         1       3.14
```

```
2        12.57
3        28.27
4        50.27
5        78.54
6        113.1
7        153.94
```

7 rows selected.

Cursor FOR Loops

In FOR loops, the loop executes a specified number of times. In a Cursor FOR loop, the results of a query are used to dynamically determine the number of times the loop is executed. In a Cursor FOR loop, the opening, fetching, and closing of cursors is performed implicitly; you do not need to explicitly specify these actions.

The following listing shows a Cursor FOR loop that queries the RADIUS_VALS table and inserts records into the AREAS table:

```
declare
   pi      constant NUMBER(9,7) := 3.1415927;
   area    NUMBER(14,2);
   cursor rad_cursor is
       select * from RADIUS_VALS;
begin
   for rad_val in rad_cursor
     loop
       area := pi*power(rad_val.radius,2);
       insert into AREAS values (rad_val.radius, area);
     end loop;
end;
```

In a Cursor FOR loop, there is no **open** or **fetch** command. The command

```
   for rad_val in rad_cursor
```

implicitly opens the *rad_cursor* cursor and fetches a value into the *rad_val* variable. When no more records are in the cursor, the loop is exited and the cursor is closed. In a Cursor FOR loop, there is no need for a **close** command. Note that *rad_val* is not explicitly declared in the block.

The loop portion of the PL/SQL block is shown in the following listing, with comments to indicate the flow of control. The loop is controlled by the existence of a fetchable record in the *rad_cursor* cursor. There is no need to check the cursor's %NOTFOUND attribute—that is automated via the Cursor FOR loop.

```
    /*  If a record can be fetched from the cursor,      */
    /*  then fetch it into the rad_val variable.  If      */
    /*  no rows can be fetched, then skip the loop.       */
  for rad_val in rad_cursor
    /*  Begin the loop commands.                          */
    loop
       /*  Calculate the area based on the Radius value */
```

```
      /*  and insert a record into the AREAS table.    */
      area := pi*power(rad_val.radius,2);
      insert into AREAS values (rad_val.radius, area);
   /*  Signal the end of the loop commands.           */
   end loop;
```

Sample output is shown in the following listing; for this example, the RADIUS_VALS table has three records, with Radius values of 3, 4, and 10:

```
select *
  from RADIUS_VALS
 order by Radius;

    RADIUS
----------
         3
         4
        10
```

The execution of the PL/SQL block with the Cursor FOR loop will generate the following records in the AREAS table:

```
select *
  from AREAS
 order by Radius;

    RADIUS       AREA
---------- ----------
         3      28.27
         4      50.27
        10     314.16
```

WHILE Loops

In a WHILE loop, the loop is processed until an exit condition is met. Instead of specifying the exit condition via an **exit** command within the loop, the exit condition is specified in the **while** command that initiates the loop.

In the following listing, a WHILE loop is created so that multiple Radius values will be processed. If the current value of the Radius variable meets the **while** condition in the loop's specification, then the loop's commands are processed. Once a Radius value fails the **while** condition in the loop's specification, the loop's execution is terminated:

```
declare
   pi      constant NUMBER(9,7) := 3.1415927;
   radius INTEGER(5);
   area    NUMBER(14,2);
begin
   radius := 3;
   while radius<=7
     loop
```

```
      area := pi*power(radius,2);
      insert into AREAS values (radius, area);
   radius := radius+1;
 end loop;
end;
```

The WHILE loop is similar in structure to the simple loop, since it terminates the loop based on a variable's value. The following listing shows the steps involved in the loop, with embedded comments:

```
    /*  Set an initial value for the Radius variable.   */
radius := 3;
    /*  Establish the criteria for the termination of   */
    /*  the loop.  If the condition is met, execute the */
    /*  commands within the loop.  If the condition is  */
    /*  not met, then terminate the loop.               */
while radius<=7
    /*  Begin the commands to be executed.              */
   loop
     /*  Calculate the area based on the current        */
     /*  Radius value and insert a record in the        */
     /*  AREAS table.                                   */
    area := pi*power(radius,2);
    insert into AREAS values (radius, area);
    /*  Set a new value for the Radius variable.  The   */
    /*  new value of Radius will be evaluated against   */
    /*  the termination criteria and the loop commands  */
    /*  will be executed for the new Radius value or    */
    /*  the loop will terminate.                        */
   radius := radius+1;
    /*  Signal the end of the commands within the loop. */
 end loop;
```

When executed, the PL/SQL block in the previous listing will generate records in the AREAS table. The output of the PL/SQL block is shown in the following listing:

```
select *
  from AREAS
 order by Radius;

    RADIUS        AREA
---------- ----------
         3       28.27
         4       50.27
         5       78.54
         6       113.1
         7      153.94
```

Because of the value assigned to the Radius variable prior to the loop, the loop is forced to execute at least once. You should verify that your variable assignments meet the conditions used to limit the loop executions.

CASE Statements

As of Oracle9i, you can use **case** statements to control the branching logic within your PL/SQL blocks. For example, you can use them to assign values conditionally or to transform values prior to inserting them. In the following example, **case** expressions use the Radius values to determine which rows to insert into the AREAS table:

```
declare
   pi       constant NUMBER(9,7) := 3.1415927;
   area     NUMBER(14,2);
   cursor rad_cursor is
       select * from RADIUS_VALS;
   rad_val rad_cursor%ROWTYPE;
begin
  open rad_cursor;
  loop
    fetch rad_cursor into rad_val;
    exit when rad_cursor%NOTFOUND;
    area := pi*power(rad_val.radius,2);
    case
      when rad_val.Radius = 3
       then
          insert into AREAS values (rad_val.radius, area);
      when rad_val.Radius = 4
       then
          insert into AREAS values (rad_val.radius, area);
      when rad_val.Radius = 10
       then
          insert into AREAS values (0, 0);
      else raise CASE_NOT_FOUND;
    end case;
  end loop;
  close rad_cursor;
end;
```

This block generates the following output. The **case** clause forced the **insert** for the Radius value of 10 to user Radius and Area values of 0:

```
select * from AREAS;

    RADIUS        AREA
---------- ----------
         3       28.27
         4       50.27
         0           0
```

The keyword **case** begins the clause:

```
case
  when rad_val.Radius = 3
    then
      insert into AREAS values (rad_val.radius, area);
```

The **when** clauses are evaluated sequentially. The **else** keyword within the **case** clause works similarly to the **else** keyword within an **if-then** clause. If you omit the **else** keyword, PL/SQL adds the following implicit **else** clause:

```
else raise CASE_NOT_FOUND;
```

The **end case** clause ends the **case** clause. The **case** clause is commonly used to translate lists of values to their descriptions, as in the case of the bookshelf category names:

```
case CategoryName
   when  'ADULTFIC' then 'Adult Fiction'
   when  'ADULTNF' then 'Adult Nonfiction'
   when  'ADULTREF' then 'Adult Reference'
   when  'CHILDRENFIC' then 'Children Fiction'
   when  'CHILDRENNF' then 'Children Nonfiction'
   when  'CHILDRENPIC' then 'Children Picturebook'
   else CategoryName
end;
```

See Chapter 17 for examples of the complex uses of **case**.

Exception Handling Section

When user-defined or system-related exceptions (errors) are encountered, the control of the PL/SQL block shifts to the Exception Handling section. Within the Exception Handling section, the **when** clause is used to evaluate which exception is to be "raised"—that is, executed.

If an exception is raised within the Executable Commands section of your PL/SQL block, the flow of commands immediately leaves the Executable Commands section and searches the Exception Handling section for an exception matching the error encountered. PL/SQL provides a set of system-defined exceptions and allows you to add your own exceptions. Examples of user-defined exceptions are shown in Chapters 28 and 29.

The Exception Handling section always begins with the keyword **exception**, and it precedes the **end** command that terminates the Executable Commands section of the PL/SQL block. The placement of the Exception Handling section within the PL/SQL block is shown in the following listing:

```
declare
  <declarations section>
begin
  <executable commands>
 exception
  <exception handling>
end;
```

The Exception Handling section of a PL/SQL block is optional—none of the PL/SQL blocks shown previously in this chapter included an Exception Handling section. However, the examples shown in this chapter have been based on a very small set of known input values with very limited processing performed.

In the following listing, the simple loop for calculating the area of a circle is shown, with two modifications (shown in bold). A new variable named *some_variable* is declared in the Declarations section, and a calculation to determine the variable's value is created in the Executable Commands section.

```
declare
  pi      constant NUMBER(9,7) := 3.1415927;
  radius INTEGER(5);
  area    NUMBER(14,2);
  some_variable   NUMBER(14,2);
begin
  radius := 3;
  loop
    some_variable := 1/(radius-4);
    area := pi*power(radius,2);
      insert into AREAS values (radius, area);
    radius := radius+1;
    exit when area >100;
  end loop;
end;
```

Because the calculation for *some_variable* involves division, you may encounter a situation in which the calculation attempts to divide by zero—an error condition. The first time through the loop, the Radius variable (with an initial value of 3) is processed and a record is inserted into the AREAS table. The second time through the loop, the Radius variable has a value of 4—and the calculation for *some_variable* encounters an error:

```
declare
*
ERROR at line 1:
ORA-01476: divisor is equal to zero
ORA-06512: at line 9
```

Since an error was encountered, the first row inserted into AREAS is rolled back, and the PL/SQL block terminates.

You can modify the processing of the error condition by adding an Exception Handling section to the PL/SQL block, as shown in the following listing.

```
declare
  pi      constant NUMBER(9,7) := 3.1415927;
  radius INTEGER(5);
  area    NUMBER(14,2);
  some_variable   NUMBER(14,2);
begin
  radius := 3;
```

```
loop
  some_variable := 1/(radius-4);
  area := pi*power(radius,2);
    insert into AREAS values (radius, area);
  radius := radius+1;
  exit when area >100;
end loop;
exception
 when ZERO_DIVIDE
  then insert into AREAS values (0,0);
end;
```

The Exception Handling section of the PL/SQL block is repeated in the following listing:

```
exception
 when ZERO_DIVIDE
  then insert into AREAS values (0,0);
```

When the PL/SQL block encounters an error, it scans the Exception Handling section for the defined exceptions. In this case, it finds the ZERO_DIVIDE exception, which is one of the system-defined exceptions available in PL/SQL. In addition to the system-defined exceptions and user-defined exceptions, you can use the **when others** clause to address all exceptions not defined within your Exception Handling section. The command within the Exception Handling section for the matching exception is executed and a row is inserted into the AREAS table. The output of the PL/SQL block is shown in the following listing:

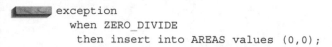

```
select *
  from AREAS;

    RADIUS       AREA
---------- ----------
         3      28.27
         0          0
```

The output shows that the first Radius value (3) was processed, and the exception was encountered on the second pass through the loop.

NOTE
*Once an exception is encountered, you cannot return to your normal flow of command processing within the Executable Commands section. If you need to maintain control within the Executable Commands section, you should use **if** conditions to test for possible exceptions before they are encountered by the program or create a nested block with its own local exception handling.*

The available system-defined exceptions are listed in the "Exceptions" entry in the Alphabetical Reference. Examples of user-defined exceptions are shown in Chapters 28 and 29.

CHAPTER
28

Triggers

trigger defines an action the database should take when some database-related event occurs. Triggers may be used to supplement declarative referential integrity, to enforce complex business rules, or to audit changes to data. The code within a trigger, called the *trigger body,* is made up of PL/SQL blocks (see Chapter 27).

The execution of triggers is transparent to the user. Triggers are executed by the database when specific types of data manipulation commands are performed on specific tables. Such commands may include **insert**s, **update**s, and **delete**s. Updates of specific columns may also be used as triggering events. As of Oracle8i, triggering events may also include DDL commands and database events (such as shutdowns and logins).

Because of their flexibility, triggers may supplement referential integrity; they should not be used to replace it. When enforcing the business rules in an application, you should first rely on the declarative referential integrity available with Oracle; use triggers to enforce rules that cannot be coded through referential integrity.

Required System Privileges

To create a trigger on a table, you must be able to alter that table. Therefore, you must either own the table, have the ALTER privilege for the table, or have the ALTER ANY TABLE system privilege. In addition, you must have the CREATE TRIGGER system privilege; to create triggers in another user's account (also called a *schema*), you must have the CREATE ANY TRIGGER system privilege. The CREATE TRIGGER system privilege is part of the RESOURCE role provided with Oracle.

To *alter* a trigger, you must either own the trigger or have the ALTER ANY TRIGGER system privilege. You may also alter triggers by altering the tables they are based on, which requires that you have either the ALTER privilege for that table or the ALTER ANY TABLE system privilege. For information on altering triggers, see "Enabling and Disabling Triggers," later in this chapter.

To create a trigger on a database-level event, you must have the ADMINISTER DATABASE TRIGGER system privilege.

Required Table Privileges

Triggers may reference tables other than the one that initiated the triggering event. For example, if you use triggers to audit changes to data in the BOOKSHELF table, then you may insert a record into a different table (say, BOOKSHELF_AUDIT) every time a record is changed in BOOKSHELF. To do this, you need to have privileges to insert into BOOKSHELF_AUDIT (to perform the triggered transaction).

NOTE
The privileges needed for triggered transactions cannot come from roles; they must be granted directly to the creator of the trigger.

Types of Triggers

A trigger's type is defined by the type of triggering transaction and by the level at which the trigger is executed. In the following sections, you will see descriptions of these classifications, along with relevant restrictions.

Row-Level Triggers

Row-level triggers execute once for each row affected by a DML statement. For the BOOKSHELF table auditing example described earlier, each row that is changed in the BOOKSHELF table may be processed by the trigger. Row-level triggers are the most common type of trigger; they are often used in data auditing applications. Row-level triggers are also useful for keeping distributed data in sync. Materialized views, which use internal row-level triggers for this purpose, are described in Chapter 23.

Row-level triggers are created using the **for each row** clause in the **create trigger** command. The syntax for triggers is shown in "Trigger Syntax," later in this chapter.

Statement-Level Triggers

Statement-level triggers execute once for each DML statement. For example, if a single INSERT statement inserted 500 rows into the BOOKSHELF table, a statement-level trigger on that table would only be executed once. Statement-level triggers therefore are not often used for data-related activities; they are normally used to enforce additional security measures on the types of actions that may be performed on a table.

Statement-level triggers are the default type of trigger created via the **create trigger** command. The syntax for triggers is shown in "Trigger Syntax," later in this chapter.

BEFORE and AFTER Triggers

Because triggers are executed by events, they may be set to occur immediately before or after those events. Since the events that execute triggers include database DML statements, triggers can be executed immediately before or after **insert**s, **update**s, and **delete**s. For database-level events, additional restrictions apply; you cannot trigger an event to occur before a login or startup takes place.

Within the trigger, you can reference the old and new values involved in the DML statement. The access required for the old and new data may determine which type of trigger you need. "Old" refers to the data as it existed prior to the DML statement; **update**s and **delete**s usually reference old values. "New" values are the data values that the DML statement creates (such as the columns in an inserted record).

If you need to set a column value in an inserted row via your trigger, then you need to use a BEFORE INSERT trigger to access the "new" values. Using an AFTER INSERT trigger would not allow you to set the inserted value, since the row will already have been inserted into the table.

AFTER row-level triggers are frequently used in auditing applications, since they do not fire until the row has been modified. The row's successful modification implies that it has passed the referential integrity constraints defined for that table.

INSTEAD OF Triggers

You can use INSTEAD OF triggers to tell Oracle what to do *instead of* performing the actions that invoked the trigger. For example, you could use an INSTEAD OF trigger on a view to redirect **insert**s into a table or to **update** multiple tables that are part of a view. You can use INSTEAD OF triggers on either object views (see Chapter 30) or relational views.

For example, if a view involves a join of two tables, your ability to use the **update** command on records in the view is limited. However, if you use an INSTEAD OF trigger, you can tell Oracle how to **update**, **delete**, or **insert** records in the view's underlying tables when a user attempts to

change values via the view. The code in the INSTEAD OF trigger is executed *in place of* the **insert**, **update**, or **delete** command you enter.

In this chapter, you will see how to implement basic triggers. INSTEAD OF triggers, which were initially introduced to support object views, are described in Chapter 30.

Schema Triggers

You can create triggers on schema-level operations such as **create table**, **alter table**, **drop table**, **audit**, **rename**, **truncate**, and **revoke**. You can even create triggers to prevent users from dropping their own tables! For the most part, schema-level triggers provide two capabilities: preventing DDL operations and providing additional security monitoring when DDL operations occur.

Database-Level Triggers

You can create triggers to be fired on database events, including errors, logins, logoffs, shutdowns, and startups. You can use this type of trigger to automate database maintenance or auditing actions.

Trigger Syntax

The full syntax for the **create trigger** command is shown in the Alphabetical Reference section of this book. The following listing contains an abbreviated version of the command syntax:

```
create [or replace] trigger [schema .] trigger
{ before | after | instead of }
{ dml_event_clause
| { ddl_event [or ddl_event]...
  | database_event [or database_event]...
  }
  on { [schema .] schema | database }
}
[when ( condition ) ]
{ pl/sql_block | call_procedure_statement }
```

The syntax options available depend on the type of trigger in use. For example, a trigger on a DML event will use the *dml_event_clause*, which follows this syntax:

```
{ delete | insert | update [of column [, column]...] }
[or { delete | insert | update [of column [, column]...] }]...
on { [schema .] table | [nested table nested_table_column of] [schema .] view }
[referencing_clause] [for each row]
```

Clearly, there is a great deal of flexibility in the design of a trigger. The **before** and **after** keywords indicate whether the trigger should be executed before or after the triggering event. If the **instead of** clause is used, the trigger's code will be executed instead of the event that caused the trigger to be invoked. The **delete**, **insert**, and **update** keywords (the last of which may include a column list) indicate the type of data manipulation that will constitute a triggering event. When referring to the old and new values of columns, you can use the defaults ("old" and "new") or you can use the **referencing** clause to specify other names.

When the **for each row** clause is used, the trigger will be a row-level trigger; otherwise, it will be a statement-level trigger. The **when** clause is used to further restrict when the trigger is executed. The restrictions enforced in the **when** clause may include checks of old and new data values.

For example, suppose we want to track any changes to the Rating value in the BOOKSHELF table whenever rating values are lowered. First, we'll create a table that will store the audit records:

```
drop table BOOKSHELF_AUDIT;
create table BOOKSHELF_AUDIT
(Title         VARCHAR2(100),
Publisher      VARCHAR2(20),
CategoryName   VARCHAR2(20),
Old_Rating     VARCHAR2(2),
New_Rating     VARCHAR2(2),
Audit_Date     DATE);
```

The following row-level BEFORE UPDATE trigger will be executed only if the Rating value is lowered. This example also illustrates the use of the **new** keyword, which refers to the new value of the column, and the **old** keyword, which refers to the old value of the column.

```
create or replace trigger BOOKSHELF_BEF_UPD_ROW
before update on BOOKSHELF
for each row
when (new.Rating < old.Rating)
begin
  insert into BOOKSHELF_AUDIT
    (Title, Publisher, CategoryName,
     Old_Rating, New_Rating, Audit_Date)
  values
    (:old.Title, :old.Publisher, :old.CategoryName,
     :old.Rating, :new.Rating, Sysdate);
end;
```

Breaking this **create trigger** command into its components makes it easier to understand. First, the trigger is named:

```
create or replace trigger BOOKSHELF_BEF_UPD_ROW
```

The name of the trigger contains the name of the table it acts upon and the type of trigger it is. (See "Naming Triggers," later in this chapter, for information on naming conventions.)

This trigger applies to the BOOKSHELF table; it will be executed **before update** transactions have been committed to the database:

```
before update on BOOKSHELF
```

Because the **for each row** clause is used, the trigger will apply to each row changed by the **update** statement. If this clause is not used, then the trigger will execute at the statement level.

```
for each row
```

The **when** clause adds further criteria to the triggering condition. The triggering event not only must be an **update** of the BOOKSHELF table, but also must reflect a lowering of the Rating value:

```
when (new.Rating < old.Rating)
```

The PL/SQL code shown in the following listing is the trigger body. The commands shown here are to be executed for every **update** of the BOOKSHELF table that passes the **when** condition. For this to succeed, the BOOKSHELF_AUDIT table must exist, and the owner of the trigger must have been granted privileges (directly, not via roles) on that table. This example **insert**s the old values from the BOOKSHELF record into the BOOKSHELF_AUDIT table before the BOOKSHELF record is updated.

```
begin
  insert into BOOKSHELF_AUDIT
    (Title, Publisher, CategoryName,
     Old_Rating, New_Rating, Audit_Date)
  values
    (:old.Title, :old.Publisher, :old.CategoryName,
     :old.Rating, :new.Rating, Sysdate);
end;
```

NOTE
*When the **new** and **old** keywords are referenced in the PL/SQL block, they are preceded by colons (:).*

This example is typical of auditing triggers. The auditing activity is completely transparent to the user who performs the **update** of the BOOKSHELF table. However, the transaction against the BOOKSHELF table is dependent on the successful execution of the trigger.

Combining DML Trigger Types

Triggers for multiple **insert**, **update**, and **delete** commands on a table can be combined into a single trigger, provided they are all at the same level (row level or statement level). The following example shows a trigger that is executed whenever an **insert** or an **update** occurs. Several points (shown in bold) should stand out in this example:

- The **update** portion of the trigger occurs only when the Rating column's value is updated.

- An **if** clause is used within the PL/SQL block to determine which of the two commands invoked the trigger.

- In this example the column to be changed is specified in the *dml_event_clause* instead of in the **when** clause as in prior examples.

```
drop trigger BOOKSHELF_BEF_UPD_ROW;

create or replace trigger BOOKSHELF_BEF_UPD_INS_ROW
```

```
before insert or update of Rating on BOOKSHELF
for each row
begin
 if INSERTING then
  insert into BOOKSHELF_AUDIT
   (Title, Publisher, CategoryName,
    New_Rating, Audit_Date)
  values
   (:new.Title, :new.Publisher, :new.CategoryName,
    :new.Rating, Sysdate);
 else -- if not inserting then we are updating the Rating
  insert into BOOKSHELF_AUDIT
   (Title, Publisher, CategoryName,
    Old_Rating, New_Rating, Audit_Date)
  values
   (:old.Title, :old.Publisher, :old.CategoryName,
    :old.Rating, :new.Rating, Sysdate);
 end if;
end;
```

Again, look at the trigger's component parts. First, it is named and identified as a **before insert** and **before update** (of Rating) trigger, executing **for each row**:

```
create or replace trigger BOOKSHELF_BEF_UPD_INS_ROW
before insert or update of Rating on BOOKSHELF
for each row
```

The trigger body then follows. In the first part of the trigger body, shown in the following listing, the type of transaction is checked via an **if** clause. Valid transaction types are INSERTING, DELETING, and UPDATING. In this case, the trigger checks to see if the record is being inserted into the BOOKSHELF table. If it is, then the first part of the trigger body is executed. The INSERTING portion of the trigger body inserts the new values of the record into the BOOKSHELF_AUDIT table.

```
begin
 if INSERTING then
  insert into BOOKSHELF_AUDIT
   (Title, Publisher, CategoryName,
    New_Rating, Audit_Date)
  values
   (:new.Title, :new.Publisher, :new.CategoryName,
    :new.Rating, Sysdate);
```

Other transaction types can then be checked. In this example, because the trigger executed, the transaction must be either an **insert** or an **update** of the Rating column. Since the **if** clause in the first half of the trigger body checks for **insert**s, and the trigger is only executed for **insert**s and **update**s, the only conditions that should execute the second half of the trigger body are **update**s of Rating. Therefore, no additional **if** clauses are necessary to determine the DML event type. This

portion of the trigger body is the same as in the previous example: prior to being updated, the old values in the row are written to the BOOKSHELF_AUDIT table.

```
else -- if not inserting then we are updating the Rating
  insert into BOOKSHELF_AUDIT
   (Title, Publisher, CategoryName,
    Old_Rating, New_Rating, Audit_Date)
  values
   (:old.Title, :old.Publisher, :old.CategoryName,
    :old.Rating, :new.Rating, Sysdate);
```

Combining trigger types in this manner may help you to coordinate trigger development among multiple developers, since it consolidates all the database events that depend on a single table.

Setting Inserted Values

You may use triggers to set column values during **insert**s and **update**s. The previous examples in this chapter set the BOOKSHELF_AUDIT.Audit_Date value to the result of the SYSDATE function. You may also use updates to support different application needs, such as storing an uppercase version of a value along with the mixed-case version entered by users. In that case, you may have partially denormalized your table to include a column for the derived data. Storing this data in an uppercase format (for this example, in the column UpperPerson) allows you to display data to the users in its natural format while using the uppercase column during queries.

Since the uppercase version of the value is derived data, it may become out of sync with the user-entered column. Unless your application supplies a value for the uppercase version during **insert**s, that column's value will be **NULL** when a new row is entered.

To avoid this synchronization problem, you can use a database trigger. Put a BEFORE INSERT and a BEFORE UPDATE trigger on the table; they will act at the row level. As shown in the following listing, this approach can set a new value for UpperName every time the Name column's value is changed in BOOKSHELF_CHECKOUT:

```
alter table BOOKSHELF_CHECKOUT add (UpperName VARCHAR2(25));

create or replace trigger BOOKSHELF_CHECKOUT_BUI_ROW
before insert or update of Name on BOOKSHELF_CHECKOUT
for each row
begin
  :new.UpperName := UPPER(:new.Name);
end;
```

In this example, the trigger body determines the value for UpperName by using the **UPPER** function on the Name column. This trigger will be executed every time a row is inserted into BOOKSHELF_CHECKOUT and every time the Name column is updated. The Name and UpperName columns will thus be kept in sync.

Maintaining Duplicated Data

The method of setting values via triggers, shown in the previous section, can be combined with the remote data access methods described in Chapter 22. As with materialized views, you may replicate all or some of the rows in a table.

For example, you may want to create and maintain a second copy of your application's audit log. By doing so, you safeguard against a single application erasing the audit log records created by multiple applications. Duplicate audit logs are frequently used in security monitoring.

Consider the BOOKSHELF_AUDIT table used in the examples in this chapter. A second table, BOOKSHELF_AUDIT_DUP, could be created, possibly in a remote database. For this example, assume that a database link called AUDIT_LINK can be used to connect the user to the database in which BOOKSHELF_AUDIT_DUP resides (refer to Chapter 22 for details on database links).

```
drop table BOOKSHELF_AUDIT_DUP;
create table BOOKSHELF_AUDIT_DUP
(Title        VARCHAR2(100),
Publisher     VARCHAR2(20),
CategoryName  VARCHAR2(20),
Old_Rating    VARCHAR2(2),
New_Rating    VARCHAR2(2),
Audit_Date    DATE);
```

To automate populating the BOOKSHELF_AUDIT_DUP table, the following trigger could be placed on the BOOKSHELF_AUDIT table:

```
create or replace trigger BOOKSHELF_AUDIT_AFT_INS_ROW
after insert on BOOKSHELF_AUDIT
for each row
begin
 insert into BOOKSHELF_AUDIT_DUP@AUDIT_LINK
   (Title, Publisher, CategoryName,
    New_Rating, Audit_Date)
   values (:new.Title, :new.Publisher, :new.CategoryName,
    :new.New_Rating, :new.Audit_Date);
end;
```

As the trigger header shows, this trigger executes for each row that is inserted into the BOOKSHELF_AUDIT table. It inserts a single record into the BOOKSHELF_AUDIT_DUP table in the database defined by the AUDIT_LINK database link. AUDIT_LINK may point to a database located on a remote server. For asynchronous replication requirements, consider using materialized views instead (see Chapter 23).

You can see the actions of these triggers by inserting a row into BOOKSHELF:

```
insert into BOOKSHELF
(Title, Publisher, CategoryName, Rating) values
('HARRY POTTER AND THE CHAMBER OF SECRETS',
'SCHOLASTIC','CHILDRENFIC','4');

1 row created.

select Title from BOOKSHELF_AUDIT;
```

```
TITLE
----------------------------------------------------
HARRY POTTER AND THE CHAMBER OF SECRETS

select Title from BOOKSHELF_AUDIT_DUP;

TITLE
----------------------------------------------------
HARRY POTTER AND THE CHAMBER OF SECRETS
```

Customizing Error Conditions

Within a single trigger, you may establish different error conditions. For each of the error conditions you define, you may select an error message that appears when the error occurs. The error numbers and messages that are displayed to the user are set via the RAISE_APPLICATION_ERROR procedure, which may be called from within any trigger.

The following example shows a statement-level BEFORE DELETE trigger on the BOOKSHELF table. When a user attempts to **delete** a record from the BOOKSHELF table, this trigger is executed and checks two system conditions: that the day of the week is neither Saturday nor Sunday, and that the Oracle username of the account performing the **delete** begins with the letters "LIB." The trigger's components will be described following the listing.

```
create or replace trigger BOOKSHELF_BEF_DEL
before delete on BOOKSHELF
declare
  weekend_error EXCEPTION;
  not_library_user EXCEPTION;
begin
if TO_CHAR(SysDate,'DY') = 'SAT' or
    TO_CHAR(SysDate,'DY') = 'SUN' THEN
   RAISE weekend_error;
end if;
if SUBSTR(User,1,3) <> 'LIB' THEN
   RAISE not_library_user;
end if;
EXCEPTION
  WHEN weekend_error THEN
    RAISE_APPLICATION_ERROR (-20001,
      'Deletions not allowed on weekends');
  WHEN not_library_user THEN
    RAISE_APPLICATION_ERROR (-20002,
      'Deletions only allowed by Library users');
end;
```

The header of the trigger defines it as a statement-level BEFORE DELETE trigger:

```
create or replace trigger BOOKSHELF_BEF_DEL
before delete on BOOKSHELF
```

There are no **when** clauses in this trigger, so the trigger body is executed for all **delete**s.

The next portion of the trigger declares the names of the two exceptions that are defined within this trigger:

```
declare
   weekend_error EXCEPTION;
   not_library_user EXCEPTION;
```

The first part of the trigger body contains an **if** clause that uses the **TO_CHAR** function on the SysDate function. If the current day is either Saturday or Sunday, then the WEEKEND_ERROR error condition is raised. This error condition, called an *exception*, must be defined within the trigger body.

```
if TO_CHAR(SysDate,'DY') = 'SAT' or
   TO_CHAR(SysDate,'DY') = 'SUN' THEN
   RAISE weekend_error;
end if;
```

A second **if** clause checks the User pseudo-column to see if its first three letters are "LIB." If the username does not begin with "LIB," then the NOT_LIBRARY_USER exception is raised. In this example, the operator <> is used; this is equivalent to != (meaning "not equals").

```
if SUBSTR(User,1,3) <> 'LIB' THEN
   RAISE not_library_user;
end if;
```

The final portion of the trigger body tells the trigger how to handle the exceptions. It begins with the keyword **exception**, followed by a **when** clause for each of the exceptions. Each of the exceptions in this trigger calls the RAISE_APPLICATION_ERROR procedure, which takes two input parameters: the error number (which must be between –20001 and –20999), and the error message to be displayed. In this example, two different error messages are defined, one for each of the defined exceptions:

```
EXCEPTION
   WHEN weekend_error THEN
     RAISE_APPLICATION_ERROR (-20001,
       'Deletions not allowed on weekends');
   WHEN not_library_user THEN
     RAISE_APPLICATION_ERROR (-20002,
       'Deletions only allowed by Library users');
```

The use of the RAISE_APPLICATION_ERROR procedure gives you great flexibility in managing the error conditions that may be encountered within your trigger. For a further description of procedures, see Chapter 29.

NOTE
*The exceptions will still be raised even if the **delete** operations find no rows to delete.*

When a non-"LIB" user attempts to delete a row from BOOKSHELF, this is the result:

```
delete from BOOKSHELF
where Title = 'MY LEDGER';
```

```
delete from BOOKSHELF
            *
ERROR at line 1:
ORA-20002: Deletions only allowed by Library users
ORA-06512: at "PRACTICE.BOOKSHELF_BEF_DEL", line 17
ORA-04088: error during execution of trigger 'PRACTICE.BOOKSHELF_BEF_DEL'
```

Calling Procedures Within Triggers

Rather than creating a large block of code within a trigger body, you can save the code as a stored procedure and call the procedure from within the trigger, by using the **call** command. For example, if you create an INSERT_BOOKSHELF_AUDIT_DUP procedure that inserts rows into BOOKSHELF_AUDIT_DUP, you can call it from a trigger on the BOOKSHELF_AUDIT table, as shown in the following listing:

```
create or replace trigger BOOKSHELF_AFT_INS_ROW
after insert on BOOKSHELF_AUDIT
for each row
begin
call INSERT_BOOKSHELF_AUDIT_DUP(:new.Title, :new.Publisher,
   :new.CategoryName, :new.Old_Rating, :new.New_Rating,
   :new.Audit_Date);
end;
```

Naming Triggers

The name of a trigger should clearly indicate the table it applies to, the DML commands that trigger it, its before/after status, and whether it is a row-level or statement-level trigger. Since a trigger name cannot exceed 30 characters in length, you need to use a standard set of abbreviations when naming. In general, the trigger name should include as much of the table name as possible. Thus, when creating a BEFORE UPDATE, row-level trigger on a table named BOOKSHELF_CHECKOUT, you should not name the trigger BEFORE_UPDATE_ROW_LEVEL_BC. A better name would be BOOKSHELF_CHECKOUT_BEF_UPD_ROW.

Creating DDL Event Triggers

You can create triggers that are executed when a DDL event occurs. If you are planning to use this feature solely for security purposes, you should investigate using the **audit** command instead. For example, you can use a DDL event trigger to execute the trigger code for **create**, **alter**, and **drop** commands performed on a cluster, function, index, package, procedure, role, sequence, synonym, table, tablespace, trigger, type, user, or view. If you use the **on schema** clause, the trigger will execute for any new data dictionary objects created in your schema. The following example will execute a procedure named INSERT_AUDIT_RECORD whenever objects are created within your schema:

```
create or replace trigger CREATE_DB_OBJECT_AUDIT
after create on schema
begin
  call INSERT_AUDIT_RECORD (ora_dict_obj_name);
end;
```

Chapter 28: Triggers **521**

As shown in this example, you can reference system attributes such as the object name. The available attributes are listed in Table 28-1.

To protect the objects within a schema, you may want to create a trigger that is executed for each attempted **drop table** command. That trigger will have to be a BEFORE DROP trigger:

```
create or replace trigger PREVENT_DROP
  before drop on Practice.schema
begin
  if ora_dict_obj_owner = 'PRACTICE'
    and ora_dict_obj_name like 'BOO%'
    and ora_dict_obj_type = 'TABLE'
  then
    RAISE_APPLICATION_ERROR (
      -20002, 'Operation not permitted.');
  end if;
end;
```

Attribute	Type	Description	Example		
ora_client_ip_ address	VARCHAR	Returns the IP address of the client in a LOGON event, when the underlying protocol is TCP/IP.	`if (ora_sysevent = 'LOGON')` `then addr :=` `ora_client_ip_address;` `end if;`		
ora_database_ name	VARCHAR2(50)	Database name.	`DECLARE` `  db_name VARCHAR2(50);` `BEGIN` `    db_name :=` `ora_database_name;` `END;`		
ora_des_ encrypted_ password	VARCHAR2	The DES encrypted password of the user being created or altered.	`IF (ora_dict_obj_type = 'USER')` `  THEN INSERT INTO` `event_table` `(ora_des_encrypted_` `password);` `END IF;`		
ora_dict_obj_ name	VARCHAR(30)	Name of the dictionary object on which the DDL operation occurred.	`INSERT INTO event_table` `('Changed object is '		` `ora_dict_obj_name');`

TABLE 28-1. *System Event Attributes*

Attribute	Type	Description	Example
ora_dict_obj_ name_list (name_list OUT ora_name_list_t)	BINARY_INTEGER	Returns the list of object names of objects being modified in the event.	if (ora_sysevent = 'ASSOCIATE STATISTICS') then number_modified := ora_dict_obj_name_list (name_list); end if;
ora_dict_obj_ owner	VARCHAR(30)	Owner of the dictionary object on which the DDL operation occurred.	INSERT INTO event_table ('object owner is' \|\| ora_dict_obj_owner');
ora_dict_obj_ owner_list(own er_list OUT ora_name_list_t)	BINARY_INTEGER	Returns the list of object owners of objects being modified in the event.	if (ora_sysevent = 'ASSOCIATE STATISTICS') then number_of_modified_ objects := ora_dict_obj_owner_list (owner_list); end if;
ora_dict_ obj_type	VARCHAR(20)	Type of the dictionary object on which the DDL operation occurred.	INSERT INTO event_table ('This object is a ' \|\| ora_dict_obj_type);
ora_grantee(user_list OUT ora_name_list_t)	BINARY_INTEGER	Returns the grantees of a grant event in the OUT parameter; returns the number of grantees in the return value.	if (ora_sysevent = 'GRANT') then number_of_users := ora_grantee(user_list); end if;
ora_instance_ num	NUMBER	Instance number.	IF (ora_instance_num = 1) THEN INSERT INTO event_table ('1'); END IF;

TABLE 28-1. *System Event Attributes* (continued)

Attribute	Type	Description	Example
ora_is_alter_ column(Column_name IN VARCHAR2)	BOOLEAN	Returns TRUE if the specified column is altered.	```
if (ora_sysevent =
'ALTER' and
ora_dict_obj_type =
'TABLE')
 then alter_column :=
ora_is_alter_column
('FOO');
end if;
``` |
| ora_is_creating_ nested_table | BOOLEAN | Returns TRUE if the current event is creating a nested table. | ```
if (ora_sysevent =
'CREATE' and
ora_dict_obj_type =
'TABLE' and
ora_is_creating_
nested_table)
  then insert into
event_tab
values ('A nested table is
created');
end if;
``` |
| ora_is_drop_ column(Column_name IN VARCHAR2) | BOOLEAN | Returns TRUE if the specified column is dropped. | ```
if (ora_sysevent =
'ALTER' and
ora_dict_obj_type =
'TABLE')
 then drop_column :=
ora_is_drop_column
('FOO');
end if;
``` |
| ora_is_ servererror | BOOLEAN | Returns TRUE if given error is on error stack, FALSE otherwise. | ```
IF
(ora_is_servererror
(error_number
))
  THEN INSERT INTO
event_table
('Server error!!');
END IF;
``` |
| ora_login_user | VARCHAR2(30) | Login user name. | ```
SELECT ora_login_user
FROM dual;
``` |

**TABLE 28-1.**   *System Event Attributes* (continued)

| Attribute | Type | Description | Example |
|---|---|---|---|
| ora_partition_pos | BINARY_INTEGER | In an INSTEAD OF trigger for CREATE TABLE, the position within the SQL text where you could insert a PARTITION clause. | `-- Retrieve ora_sql_txt into`<br>`-- sql_text variable first.`<br><br>`n := ora_partition_pos;`<br>`new_stmt :=`<br>`substr(sql_text, 1, n-1)`<br>`\|\|`<br>`` ` ` `` `\|\|`<br>`my_partition_clause \|\|`<br>`` ` ` `` `\|\| substr(sql_text,`<br>`n));` |
| ora_privileges( Privilege_list OUT ora_name_list_t) | BINARY_INTEGER | Returns the list of privileges being granted by the grantee or the list of privileges revoked from the revokee in the OUT parameter; returns the number of privileges in the return value. | `if (ora_sysevent = 'GRANT' or`<br>`ora_sysevent = 'REVOKE')`<br>`  then`<br>`number_of_privileges :=`<br>`ora_privileges(priv_list);`<br>`end if;` |
| ora_revokee ( User_list OUT ora_name_list_t) | BINARY_INTEGER | Returns the revokees of a revoke event in the OUT parameter; returns the number of revokees in the return value. | `if (ora_sysevent = 'REVOKE')`<br>`then`<br>`number_of_users :=`<br>`ora_revokee(user_list);` |
| ora_server_error | NUMBER | Given a position (1 for top of stack), it returns the error number at that position on error stack. | `INSERT INTO event_table`<br>`('top`<br>`stack error ' \|\|`<br>`ora_server_error(1));` |
| ora_server_error_depth | BINARY_INTEGER | Returns the total number of error messages on the error stack. | `n := ora_server_error_depth;`<br>`-- This value is used with`<br>`-- other functions such as`<br>`-- ora_server_error` |

**TABLE 28-1.** *System Event Attributes* (continued)

| Attribute | Type | Description | Example | | | | |
|---|---|---|---|---|---|---|---|
| ora_server_error_msg (position in BINARY_INTEGER) | VARCHAR2 | Given a position (1 for top of stack), it returns the error message at that position on error stack. | `INSERT INTO event_table ('top stack error message' || ora_server_error_msg(1));` |
| ora_server_error_num_params (position in binary_integer) | BINARY_INTEGER | Given a position (1 for top of stack), it returns the number of strings that have been substituted into the error message using a format like "%s". | `n := ora_server_error_num_params(1);` |
| ora_server_error_param (position in binary_integer, param in binary_integer) | VARCHAR2 | Given a position (1 for top of stack) and a parameter number, returns the matching "%s", "%d", and so on substitution value in the error message. | `-- E.g. the 2nd %s in a message` `-- like "Expected %s, found %s"` `param := ora_server_error_param(1,2);` |
| ora_sql_txt (sql_text out ora_name_list_t) | BINARY_INTEGER | Returns the SQL text of the triggering statement in the OUT parameter. If the statement is long, it is broken up into multiple PL/SQL table elements. The function return value specifies how many elements are in the PL/SQL table. | `sql_text ora_name_list_t;` `stmt VARCHAR2(2000);` `...` `n := ora_sql_txt(sql_text);` `FOR i IN 1..n LOOP` `stmt := stmt || sql_text(i);` `END LOOP;` `INSERT INTO event_table ('text of triggering statement: ' || stmt);` |
| ora_sysevent | VARCHAR2(20) | System event firing the trigger: Event name is same as that in the syntax. | `INSERT INTO event_table (ora_sysevent);` |

**TABLE 28-1.** *System Event Attributes* (continued)

| Attribute | Type | Description | Example | | | | | | | | |
|---|---|---|---|---|---|---|---|---|---|---|---|
| ora_with_grant_ option | BOOLEAN | Returns TRUE if the privileges are granted with grant option. | `if (ora_sysevent = 'GRANT' and ora_with_grant_option = TRUE)`<br>`  then insert into event_table ('with grant option');`<br>`end if;` |
| space_error_info( error_number OUT NUMBER, error_type OUT VARCHAR2, object_owner OUT VARCHAR2, table_space_ name OUT VARCHAR2, object_name OUT VARCHAR2, sub_object_ name OUT VARCHAR2) | BOOLEAN | Returns TRUE if the error is related to an out-of-space condition, and fills in the OUT parameters with information about the object that caused the error. | `if (space_error_ info(eno, typ, owner, ts, obj, subobj) = TRUE)`<br>`then`<br>`dbms_output.put_line('The object ' || obj || ' owned by '`<br>`|| owner || ' has run out of`<br>`space.');`<br>`end if;` |

**TABLE 28-1.** *System Event Attributes* (continued)

Note that the trigger references the event attributes within its **if** clauses. Attempting to drop a table in the Practice schema whose name starts with BOO results in the following:

```
drop table BOOKSHELF_AUDIT_DUP;

drop table BOOKSHELF_AUDIT_DUP
*
ERROR at line 1:
ORA-00604: error occurred at recursive SQL level 1
ORA-20002: Operation not permitted.
ORA-06512: at line 6
```

You can use the RAISE_APPLICATION_ERROR procedure to further customize the error message displayed to the user.

## Creating Database Event Triggers

Like DML events, database events can execute triggers. When a database event occurs (a shutdown, startup, or error), you can execute a trigger that references the attributes of the event (as with DDL events). You could use a database event trigger to perform system maintenance functions immediately after each database startup.

For example, the following trigger pins packages on each database startup. Pinning packages is an effective way of keeping large PL/SQL objects in the shared pool of memory, improving performance and enhancing database stability. This trigger, PIN_ON_STARTUP, will run each time the database is started.

```
create or replace trigger PIN_ON_STARTUP
after startup on database
begin
 DBMS_SHARED_POOL.KEEP (
 'SYS.STANDARD', 'P');
end;
```

This example shows a simple trigger that will be executed immediately after a database startup. You can modify the list of packages in the trigger body to include those most used by your applications.

Startup and shutdown triggers can access the ora_instance_num, ora_database_name, ora_login_user, and ora_sysevent attributes listed in Table 28-1. See the Alphabetical Reference for the full **create trigger** command syntax.

# Enabling and Disabling Triggers

Unlike declarative integrity constraints (such as NOT NULL and PRIMARY KEY), triggers do not necessarily affect all rows in a table. They only affect operations of the specified type, and then only while the trigger is enabled. Any data created prior to a trigger's creation will not be affected by the trigger.

By default, a trigger is enabled when it is created. However, there are situations in which you may want to disable a trigger. The two most common reasons involve data loads. During large data loads, you may want to disable triggers that would execute during the load. Disabling the triggers during data loads may dramatically improve the performance of the load. After the data has been loaded, you need to manually perform the data manipulation that the trigger would have performed had it been enabled during the data load.

The second data load–related reason for disabling a trigger occurs when a data load fails and has to be performed a second time. In such a case, it is likely that the data load partially succeeded—and thus the trigger was executed for a portion of the records loaded. During a subsequent load, the same records would be inserted. Thus, it is possible that the same trigger will be executed twice for the same insert operation (when that insert operation occurs during both loads). Depending on the nature of the operations and the triggers, this may not be desirable. If the trigger was enabled during the failed load, then it may need to be disabled prior to the start of a second data load process. After the data has been loaded, you need to manually perform the data manipulation that the trigger would have performed had it been enabled during the data load.

To enable a trigger, use the **alter trigger** command with the **enable** keyword. To use this command, you must either own the table or have the ALTER ANY TRIGGER system privilege. A sample **alter trigger** command is shown in the following listing:

```
alter trigger BOOKSHELF_BEF_UPD_INS_ROW enable;
```

A second method of enabling triggers uses the **alter table** command, with the **enable all triggers** clause. You may not enable specific triggers with this command; you must use the **alter trigger** command to do that. The following example shows the usage of the **alter table** command:

```
alter table BOOKSHELF enable all triggers;
```

To use the **alter table** command, you must either own the table or have the ALTER ANY TABLE system privilege.

You can disable triggers using the same basic commands (requiring the same privileges) with modifications to their clauses. For the **alter trigger** command, use the **disable** clause:

```
alter trigger BOOKSHELF_BEF_UPD_INS_ROW disable;
```

For the **alter table** command, use the **disable all triggers** clause:

```
alter table BOOKSHELF disable all triggers;
```

You can manually compile triggers. Use the **alter trigger compile** command to manually compile existing triggers that have become invalid. Since triggers have dependencies, they can become invalid if an object the trigger depends on changes. The **alter trigger debug** command allows PL/SQL information to be generated during trigger recompilation.

# Replacing Triggers

The status of a trigger is the only portion that can be altered. To alter a trigger's body, the trigger must be re-created or replaced. When replacing a trigger, use the **create or replace trigger** command (refer to "Trigger Syntax" and the examples earlier in the chapter).

# Dropping Triggers

Triggers may be dropped via the **drop trigger** command. To drop a trigger, you must either own the trigger or have the DROP ANY TRIGGER system privilege. An example of this command is shown in the following listing:

```
drop trigger BOOKSHELF_BEF_UPD_INS_ROW;
```

# CHAPTER
# 29

# Procedures, Functions, and Packages

ophisticated business rules and application logic can be stored as *procedures* within Oracle. Stored procedures—groups of SQL, PL/SQL, and Java statements—enable you to move code that enforces business rules from your application to the database. As a result, the code will be stored once for use by multiple applications. Because Oracle supports stored procedures, the code within your applications should become more consistent and easier to maintain.

**NOTE**
*For details on Java and its use in stored procedures, see Chapters 34, 35, and 36. This chapter will focus on PL/SQL procedures.*

You may group procedures and other PL/SQL commands into *packages*. In the following sections, you will see implementation details and recommendations for packages, procedures, and *functions* (procedures that can return values to the user).

You may experience performance gains when using procedures, for two reasons:

■   The processing of complex business rules may be performed within the database—and therefore by the server. In client-server or three-tier applications, shifting complex processing from the application (on the client) to the database (on the server) may dramatically improve performance.

■   Because the procedural code is stored within the database and is fairly static, you may also benefit from the reuse of the same queries within the database. The Shared SQL Area in the System Global Area (SGA) will store the parsed versions of the executed commands. Thus, the second time a procedure is executed, it may be able to take advantage of the parsing that was previously performed, improving the performance of the procedure's execution.

In addition to these advantages, your application development efforts may also benefit. Business rules that are consolidated within the database no longer need to be written into each application, thus saving you time during application creation and simplifying the maintenance process.

# Required System Privileges

To create a procedural object, you must have the CREATE PROCEDURE system privilege (which is part of the RESOURCE role). If the procedural object will be in another user's schema, then you must have the CREATE ANY PROCEDURE system privilege.

## Executing Procedures

Once a procedural object has been created, it may be executed. When a procedural object is executed, it may rely on the table privileges of its owner, or may rely on the privileges of the user who is executing it. When the procedure is created using the definer's rights, a user executing the procedure does not need to be granted access to the tables that the procedure accesses.

In prior versions of Oracle, the only option was for the procedural objects to be executed under the privileges of the procedure owner (called *definer rights*). As an alternative, you can use *invoker rights,* in which case the procedures execute under the privileges of the user executing the procedure. If a procedure uses invoker rights, the user must have access to all of the database objects accessed by the procedure. Unless stated otherwise, the examples in this chapter assume users are executing procedures under the owner's privileges.

To allow other users to execute your procedural object, **grant** them the EXECUTE privilege on that object, as shown in the following example:

```
grant execute on MY_PROCEDURE to Dora;
```

The user Dora will now be able to execute the procedure named MY_PROCEDURE. If you do not **grant** the EXECUTE privilege to users, they must have the EXECUTE ANY PROCEDURE system privilege in order to execute the procedure.

When executed, procedures usually have variables passed to them. For example, a procedure that interacts with the BOOKSHELF table may accept a value for the Title column as its input. In this example, we will assume that the procedure creates a new record in the BOOKSHELF table when a new book is received (from the list of books in the BOOK_ORDER table). This procedure can be called from any application within the database (provided the user calling the procedure has been granted the EXECUTE privilege for it).

The syntax used to execute a procedure depends on the environment from which the procedure is called. From within SQL*Plus, a procedure can be executed by using the **execute** command, followed by the procedure name. Any arguments to be passed to the procedure must be enclosed in parentheses following the procedure name, as shown in the following example (which uses a procedure called NEW_BOOK):

```
execute NEW_BOOK('ONCE REMOVED');
```

The command will execute the NEW_BOOK procedure, passing to it the value ONCE REMOVED.

From within another procedure, function, package, or trigger, the procedure can be called without the **execute** command. If the NEW_BOOK procedure was called from a trigger on the BOOK_ORDER table, the body of that trigger may include the following command:

```
NEW_BOOK(:new.Title);
```

The NEW_BOOK procedure will be executed using the new value of the Title column as its input. (See Chapter 28 for further information on the use of old and new values within triggers.)

To execute a procedure owned by another user, you must either create a synonym for that procedure or reference the owner's name during the execution, as shown in the following listing:

```
execute Practice.NEW_BOOK('ONCE REMOVED');
```

The command will execute the NEW_BOOK procedure in the Practice schema.

Alternatively, a synonym for the procedure could be created by using the following command:

```
create synonym NEW_BOOK for Practice.NEW_BOOK;
```

The owner of that synonym would then no longer need to refer to the procedure's owner to execute the procedure. You could simply enter the command:

```
execute NEW_BOOK('ONCE REMOVED');
```

and the synonym would point to the proper procedure.

When you execute remote procedures, the name of a database link must be specified (see Chapter 22 for information on database links). The name of the database link must immediately follow the procedure's name and precede the variables, as shown in the following example:

```
execute NEW_BOOK@REMOTE_CONNECT('ONCE REMOVED');
```

The command uses the REMOTE_CONNECT database link to access a procedure called NEW_BOOK in a remote database.

To make the location of the procedure transparent to the user, a synonym may be created for the remote procedure, as shown in the following example:

```
create synonym NEW_BOOK
 for NEW_BOOK@REMOTE_CONNECT;
```

Once this synonym has been created, the user may refer to the remote procedure by using the name of the synonym. Oracle assumes that all remote procedure calls involve updates in the remote database.

# Required Table Privileges

Procedural objects may reference tables. For the objects to execute properly, the owner of the procedure, package, or function being executed must have privileges on the tables it uses. Unless you are using invoker rights, the user who is executing the procedural object does not need privileges on its underlying tables.

**NOTE**
*The privileges needed for procedures, packages, and functions cannot come from roles; they must be granted directly to the owner of the procedure, package, or function.*

# Procedures vs. Functions

Functions can return a value to the caller, and functions can be directly referenced in queries. This value is returned through the use of the **return** keyword within the function. Examples of functions are shown in "create function Syntax," later in this chapter.

# Procedures vs. Packages

Packages are groups of procedures, functions, variables, and SQL statements grouped together into a single unit. To execute a procedure within a package, you must first list the package name, and then list the procedure name, as shown in the following example:

```
execute BOOK_INVENTORY.NEW_BOOK('ONCE REMOVED');
```

Here, the NEW_BOOK procedure within the BOOK_INVENTORY package was executed.

Packages allow multiple procedures to use the same variables and cursors. Procedures within packages may be either available to the public (as is the NEW_BOOK procedure in the prior example) or private, in which case they are only accessible via commands from within the package (such as calls from other procedures). Examples of packages are shown in "create package Syntax," later in this chapter.

Packages may also include commands that are to be executed each time the package is called, regardless of the procedure or function called within the package. Thus, packages not only group procedures but also give you the ability to execute commands that are not procedure-specific. See "Initializing Packages," later in this chapter, for an example of code that is executed each time a package is called.

## create procedure Syntax

The syntax for the **create procedure** command is shown in the Alphabetical Reference. The syntax is

```
create [or replace] procedure [schema .] procedure
[(argument [in | out | in out] [nocopy] datatype
 [, argument [in | out | in out] [nocopy] datatype]...
)]
[authid { current_user | definer }]
{ is | as } { pl/sql_subprogram_body |
 language { java name 'string'| c [name name] library lib_name
[agent in (argument)]
[with context] [parameters (parameters)]
}};
```

Both the header and the body of the procedure are created by this command.

The NEW_BOOK procedure is created by the command shown in the following listing:

```
create or replace procedure NEW_BOOK (aTitle IN VARCHAR2,
 aPublisher IN VARCHAR2, aCategoryName IN VARCHAR2)
as
begin
 insert into BOOKSHELF (Title, Publisher, CategoryName, Rating)
 values (aTitle, aPublisher, aCategoryName, NULL);
 delete from BOOK_ORDER
 where Title = aTitle;
end;
```

Here, the NEW_BOOK procedure will accept a book's title, publisher, and category as its input. It can be called from any application. It inserts a record into the BOOKSHELF table, with a **NULL** value for the Rating column, and deletes the matching Title from the BOOK_ORDER table.

If a procedure already exists, you may replace it via the **create or replace procedure** command. The benefit of using this command (instead of dropping and re-creating the old procedure) is that the EXECUTE privilege grants previously made on the procedure will remain in place.

The IN qualifier is used for arguments for which values must be specified when calling the procedure. In the NEW_BOOK example, the aTitle, aPublisher, and aCategoryName arguments are declared as IN. The OUT qualifier signifies that the procedure passes a value back to the caller through this argument. The IN OUT qualifier signifies that the argument is both an IN and an OUT: A value must be specified for this argument when the procedure is called, and the procedure will return a value to the caller via this argument. If no qualifier type is specified, then the default value is IN.

In the **create procedure** syntax, **authid** refers to the type of authentication: definer rights (the default) or invoker rights (the **current_user**). The **nocopy** keyword tells Oracle to pass the variable value back to the user as quickly as possible.

By default, a procedure consists of a block of code written in PL/SQL (*block* refers to the code that the procedure will execute when called). In the NEW_BOOK example, the block is as follows:

```
begin
 insert into BOOKSHELF (Title, Publisher, CategoryName, Rating)
 values (aTitle, aPublisher, aCategoryName, NULL);
 delete from BOOK_ORDER
 where Title = aTitle;
end;
```

The PL/SQL block shown is fairly simple, consisting of a single SQL statement. PL/SQL blocks within procedures can include any DML statement; they cannot be used for DDL statements (such as **create view**).

Alternatively, **language** refers to the language in which the code is written. For Java examples, see Chapter 36.

The following listing shows the execution of the NEW_BOOK procedure, and the resulting changes to the BOOK_ORDER and BOOKSHELF tables.

```
select Title from BOOK_ORDER;

TITLE

SHOELESS JOE
GOSPEL
SOMETHING SO STRONG
GALILEO'S DAUGHTER
LONGITUDE
ONCE REMOVED

execute NEW_BOOK('ONCE REMOVED','SANCTUARY PUB','ADULTNF');

PL/SQL procedure successfully completed.

select Title from BOOK_ORDER;

TITLE

SHOELESS JOE
```

```
GOSPEL
SOMETHING SO STRONG
GALILEO'S DAUGHTER
LONGITUDE

select * from BOOKSHELF
 where Title = 'ONCE REMOVED';

TITLE
--
PUBLISHER CATEGORYNAME RA
------------------- -------------------- --
ONCE REMOVED
SANCTUARY PUB ADULTNF
```

# create function Syntax

The syntax for the **create function** command is more complicated than the syntax for the **create procedure** command. At a high level, the syntax is

```
create [or replace] function [schema .] function
[(argument [in | out | in out] [nocopy] datatype
 [, argument [in | out | in out] [nocopy] datatype]...
)]
return datatype
[{ invoker_rights_clause | deterministic | parallel_enable_clause }
 [invoker_rights_clause | deterministic | parallel_enable_clause]...
]
{ { aggregate | pipelined } using [schema .] implementation_type
| [pipelined] { is | as } { pl/sql_function_body | call_spec }};
```

Both the header and the body of the function are created by this command.

The **return** keyword specifies the datatype of the function's return value. This can be any valid PL/SQL datatype (see Chapter 27). Every function must have a **return** clause, since the function must, by definition, return a value to the calling environment.

The following example shows a function named OVERDUE_CHARGES, which returns the overdue book charges by person, based on calculations against the BOOKSHELF_CHECKOUT table. The input is the person's name, while the output is the balance for that person.

```
create or replace function OVERDUE_CHARGES (aName IN VARCHAR2)
 return NUMBER
 is
 owed_amount NUMBER(10,2);
begin
 select SUM(((ReturnedDate-CheckoutDate) -14)*0.20)
 into owed_amount
 from BOOKSHELF_CHECKOUT
```

```
 where Name = aName;
 RETURN(owed_amount);
end;
```

To show the differences between procedures and functions, we'll look at this function piece by piece. First, the function is named and the input is specified:

```
create or replace function OVERDUE_CHARGES (aName IN VARCHAR2)
```

Next, we define the characteristics of the value to be returned. The definition of the variable whose value will be returned has three parts: its datatype, its name, and its length. The datatype in this example is set via the **return NUMBER** clause. The variable is then named *owed_amount*, and is defined as a NUMBER(10,2). Thus, all three parts of the variable—its datatype, its name, and its length—have been defined.

```
 return NUMBER
 is
 owed_amount NUMBER(10,2);
```

The PL/SQL block follows. In the SQL statement, the sum of all late charges ($0.20 per day over 14 days) is calculated. The sum is selected into a variable called *owed_amount* (which we previously defined). The **RETURN(owed_amount)** command line then returns the value in the *owed_amount* variable to the calling program.

```
begin
 select SUM(((ReturnedDate-CheckoutDate) -14)*0.20)
 into owed_amount
 from BOOKSHELF_CHECKOUT
 where Name = aName;
 RETURN(owed_amount);
end;
```

If a function already exists, you may replace it via the **create or replace function** command. If you use the **or replace** clause, any EXECUTE grants previously made on the function will remain in place.

If the function is to be created in a different account (also known as a *schema*), then you must have the CREATE ANY PROCEDURE system privilege. If no schema is specified, then the function will be created in your schema. To create a function in your schema, you must have been granted the CREATE PROCEDURE system privilege (which is part of the RESOURCE role). Having the privilege to create procedures gives you the privilege to create functions and packages as well.

You can check the function by creating a variable and setting its value equal to the function's returned value:

```
variable owed number;
execute :owed := OVERDUE_CHARGES('FRED FULLER');

PL/SQL procedure successfully completed.
```

You can verify the results by printing the variable's value:

```
print owed

 OWED

 3.8
```

## Referencing Remote Tables in Procedures

Remote tables can be accessed by the SQL statements in procedures. A remote table can be queried via a database link in the procedure, as shown in the following example. In this example, the NEW_BOOK procedure inserts a record into the BOOKSHELF table in the database defined by the REMOTE_CONNECT database link while deleting from a local copy of BOOK_ORDER.

```
create or replace procedure NEW_BOOK (aTitle IN VARCHAR2,
 aPublisher IN VARCHAR2, aCategoryName IN VARCHAR2)
as
begin
 insert into BOOKSHELF@REMOTE_CONNECT
 (Title, Publisher, CategoryName, Rating)
 values (aTitle, aPublisher, aCategoryName, NULL);
 delete from BOOK_ORDER
 where Title = aTitle;
end;
```

Procedures may also use local synonyms. For example, you may create a local synonym for a remote table, as follows:

```
create synonym BOOKSHELF for BOOKSHELF@REMOTE_CONNECT;
```

You can then rewrite your procedure to remove the database link specifications:

```
create or replace procedure NEW_BOOK (aTitle IN VARCHAR2,
 aPublisher IN VARCHAR2, aCategoryName IN VARCHAR2)
as
begin
 insert into BOOKSHELF
 (Title, Publisher, CategoryName, Rating)
 values (aTitle, aPublisher, aCategoryName, NULL);
 delete from BOOK_ORDER
 where Title = aTitle;
end;
```

Removing database link names from procedures allows you to remove the details of the table's physical location from the procedure. If the table changes location, only the synonym will change, while the procedure will still be valid.

# Debugging Procedures

The SQLPLUS **show errors** command displays all the errors associated with the most recently created procedural object. This command checks the USER_ERRORS data dictionary view for the errors associated with the most recent compilation attempt for that object. **show errors** displays the line and column number for each error, as well as the text of the error message.

To view errors associated with previously created procedural objects, you may query USER_ERRORS directly, as shown in the following listing. This example queries USER_ERRORS for error messages encountered during the creation of the OVERDUE_CHARGES function shown earlier in this chapter.

```
select Line, /*Line number of the error. */
 Position, /*Column number of the error.*/
 Text /*Text of the error message.*/
 from USER_ERRORS
 where Name = 'OVERDUE_CHARGES'
 and Type = 'FUNCTION'
 order by Sequence;
```

Valid values for the Type column are VIEW, PROCEDURE, PACKAGE, FUNCTION, and PACKAGE BODY.

Two other data dictionary view levels—ALL and DBA—may also be used to retrieve information about errors involving procedural objects. For information on these views, see Chapter 37.

## Using the DBMS_OUTPUT Package

In addition to the debugging information provided by the **show errors** command, you may use the DBMS_OUTPUT package, one of a set of packages that is automatically installed when you create an Oracle database.

To use DBMS_OUTPUT, you must issue the **set serveroutput on** command before executing the procedural object you will be debugging.

DBMS_OUTPUT allows you to use three debugging functions within your package:

| | |
|---|---|
| PUT | Puts multiple outputs on the same line |
| PUT_LINE | Puts each output on a separate line |
| NEW_LINE | Used with PUT; signals the end of the current output line |

PUT and PUT_LINE are used to generate the debugging information you want to display. For example, if you are debugging a procedure that includes a loop (refer to Chapter 27), you may want to track the changes in a variable with each pass through the loop. To track the variable's value, you may use a command similar to the one shown in the following listing. In this example, the value of the Owed_Amount column is printed, prefixed by the literal string 'Owed:'.

```
DBMS_OUTPUT.PUT_LINE('Owed:'||Owed_Amount);
```

You may also use PUT and PUT_LINE outside of loops, but such uses may be better accomplished via the use of the **RETURN** command in functions (refer to "create function Syntax," earlier in this chapter).

# Creating Your Own Functions

Rather than just calling custom functions via **execute** commands, you may use them within SQL expressions. This enables you to extend the functionality of SQL, customizing it to your needs. Such functions can be used in the same manner as Oracle-provided functions, such as **SUBSTR** and **TO_CHAR**. Custom functions cannot be used in CHECK or DEFAULT constraints and cannot manipulate any database values.

You can call either stand-alone functions (created via the **create function** command shown in the previous sections) or functions declared in package specifications (to be covered in "create package Syntax" later in this chapter). Procedures are not directly callable from SQL, but may be called by the functions you create.

For example, consider the OVERDUE_CHARGES function shown earlier in this chapter, which calculated the total owed for overdue books. It had a single input variable—the person's name. However, to see the OVERDUE_CHARGES results for all of the book borrowers, you would normally need to execute this procedure once for each record in the BOOKSHELF_ CHECKOUT table.

You can improve the overdue charges calculation process. Consider the following query:

```
create view BOOK_BORROWERS
 as select distinct Name from BOOKSHELF_CHECKOUT;

select Name,
 OVERDUE_CHARGES(Name)
 from BOOK_BORROWERS;
```

Oracle returns the following output:

```
NAME OVERDUE_CHARGES(NAME)
------------------------ ---------------------
DORAH TALBOT -.8
EMILY TALBOT .2
FRED FULLER 3.8
GERHARDT KENTGEN 2.8
JED HOPKINS 1.4
PAT LAVAY 2.6
ROLAND BRANDT 22.6

7 rows selected.
```

This single query uses the custom OVERDUE_CHARGES function to calculate the overdue charges for all book borrowers. It's not quite correct—people are getting credit for books they returned early. You can use the **create or replace function** command to add a **where** clause to the function's query:

```
create or replace function OVERDUE_CHARGES (aName IN VARCHAR2)
 return NUMBER
 is
 owed_amount NUMBER(10,2);
begin
```

```
 select SUM(((ReturnedDate-CheckoutDate) -14)*0.20)
 into owed_amount
 from BOOKSHELF_CHECKOUT
 where Name = aName
 and ReturnedDate-CheckoutDate > 14;
 RETURN(owed_amount);
end;
```

The corrected output is shown in the following listing:

```
select Name,
 OVERDUE_CHARGES(Name)
 from BOOK_BORROWERS;

NAME OVERDUE_CHARGES(NAME)
------------------------------ ---------------------
DORAH TALBOT .4
EMILY TALBOT .8
FRED FULLER 3.8
GERHARDT KENTGEN 4.6
JED HOPKINS 1.4
PAT LAVAY 3.4
ROLAND BRANDT 22.6
```

The query selected each name from BOOK_BORROWERS; for each name, it executed the OVERDUE_CHARGES function, which selected data from BOOKSHELF_CHECKOUT.

To take advantage of this feature, your functions must follow the same guidelines as Oracle's functions. Most notably, they must not update the database, and must contain only IN parameters.

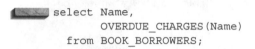

**NOTE**
*Although this technique works, it has performance costs. The more data there is in the table, the bigger the performance penalty will be when comparing this method to a traditional join.*

## Customizing Error Conditions

You may establish different error conditions within procedural objects (refer to Chapter 28 for examples of customized error conditions within triggers). For each of the error conditions you define, you may select an error message that will appear when the error occurs. The error numbers and messages that are displayed to the user are set by you via the RAISE_APPLICATION_ERROR procedure, which may be called from within any procedural object.

You can call RAISE_APPLICATION_ERROR from within procedures, packages, and functions. It requires two inputs: the message number and the message text. You get to assign both the message number and the text that will be displayed to the user. This is a very powerful addition to the standard exceptions that are available in PL/SQL (see "Exception" in the Alphabetical Reference).

The following example shows the OVERDUE_CHARGES function defined earlier in this chapter. Now, however, it has an additional section (shown in bold). Titled EXCEPTION, this section tells

Oracle how to handle nonstandard processing. In this example, the NO_DATA_FOUND exception's standard message is overridden via the RAISE_APPLICATION_ERROR procedure.

```
create or replace function OVERDUE_CHARGES (aName IN VARCHAR2)
 return NUMBER
 is
 owed_amount NUMBER(10,2);
begin
 select SUM(((ReturnedDate-CheckoutDate) -14)*0.20)
 into owed_amount
 from BOOKSHELF_CHECKOUT
 where Name = aName
 and (ReturnedDate-CheckoutDate) > 14;
 RETURN(owed_amount);
EXCEPTION
when NO_DATA_FOUND THEN
RAISE_APPLICATION_ERROR(-20100,
'No books borrowed.');
end;
```

In the preceding example, the NO_DATA_FOUND exception was used. If you want to define custom exceptions, you need to name the exception in a Declarations section of the procedure, which immediately precedes the **begin** command. As shown in the following listing, this section should include entries for each of the custom exceptions you have defined, listed as type EXCEPTION:

```
declare
some_custom_error EXCEPTION;
```

**NOTE**
*If you are using the exceptions already defined within PL/SQL, you do not need to list them in the Declarations section of the procedural object. See "Exception" in the Alphabetical Reference for a list of the predefined exceptions.*

In the **exception** portion of the procedural object's code, you tell the database how to handle the exceptions. It begins with the keyword **exception**, followed by a **WHEN** clause for each exception. Each exception may call the RAISE_ APPLICATION_ERROR procedure, which takes two input parameters: the error number (which must be between -20001 and -20999) and the error message to be displayed. In the preceding example, only one exception was defined. Multiple exceptions can be defined, as shown in the following listing; you may use the **when others** clause to handle all nonspecified exceptions:

```
EXCEPTION
 when NO_DATA_FOUND THEN
 RAISE_APPLICATION_ERROR(-20100,
 'No books borrowed.');
 when some_custom_error THEN
```

```
RAISE_APPLICATION_ERROR (-20101,
 'Some custom error message.');
```

The use of the RAISE_APPLICATION_ERROR procedure gives you great flexibility in managing the error conditions that may be encountered within procedural objects.

## Naming Procedures and Functions

Procedures and functions should be named according to the business function they perform or business rule they enforce. There should be no ambiguity about their purpose.

The NEW_BOOK procedure shown earlier should be renamed. NEW_BOOK performs a business function—inserting records into BOOKSHELF and deleting them from BOOK_ORDER—so its name should reflect that function. A better choice for the name would be RECEIVE_BOOK_ORDER. Since it performs a function, a verb (in this case, "receive") must describe what it does. The name of the procedure should also include the name of the major table(s) it impacts. If the tables are properly named, then the name of the table should be the direct object upon which the verb acts (in this case, BOOK_ORDER or BOOKSHELF). For the sake of consistency, we will continue to refer to the procedure as NEW_BOOK for the remainder of this chapter.

# create package Syntax

When creating packages, the package specification and the package body are created separately. Thus, there are two commands to use: **create package** for the package specification, and **create package body** for the package body. Both of these commands require that you have the CREATE PROCEDURE system privilege. If the package is to be created in a schema other than your own, then you must have the CREATE ANY PROCEDURE system privilege.

Here is the syntax for creating package specifications:

```
create [or replace] package [user.] package
[authid {definer | current_user}]
{is | as}
 package specification;
```

A *package specification* consists of the list of functions, procedures, variables, constants, cursors, and exceptions that will be available to users of the package.

A sample **create package** command is shown in the following listing. In this example, the BOOK_MANAGEMENT package is created. The OVERDUE_CHARGES function and NEW_BOOK procedure seen earlier in this chapter are included in the package.

```
create or replace package BOOK_MANAGEMENT
as
 function OVERDUE_CHARGES(aName IN VARCHAR2) return NUMBER;
 procedure NEW_BOOK (aTitle IN VARCHAR2,
 aPublisher IN VARCHAR2, aCategoryName IN VARCHAR2);
end BOOK_MANAGEMENT;
```

**NOTE**
*You may append the name of the procedural object to the **end** clause, as shown in the preceding example. This may make it easier to coordinate the logic within your code.*

A *package body* contains the blocks and specifications for all of the public objects listed in the package specification. The package body may include objects that are not listed in the package specification; such objects are said to be *private* and are not available to users of the package. Private objects may only be called by other objects within the same package body. A package body may also include code that is run every time the package is invoked, regardless of the part of the package that is executed—see "Initializing Packages," later in this chapter, for an example.

The syntax for creating package bodies is

```
create [or replace] package body [user.] package body
{is | as}
 package body;
```

The name of the package body should be the same as the name of the package specification.

Continuing the BOOK_MANAGEMENT example, its package body can be created via the **create package body** command shown in the following example:

```
create or replace package body BOOK_MANAGEMENT
as
function OVERDUE_CHARGES (aName IN VARCHAR2)
 return NUMBER
 is
 owed_amount NUMBER(10,2);
begin
 select SUM(((ReturnedDate-CheckoutDate) -14)*0.20)
 into owed_amount
 from BOOKSHELF_CHECKOUT
 where Name = aName
 and (ReturnedDate-CheckoutDate) > 14;
 RETURN(owed_amount);
 EXCEPTION
 when NO_DATA_FOUND THEN
 RAISE_APPLICATION_ERROR(-20100,
 'No books borrowed.');
end OVERDUE_CHARGES;
procedure NEW_BOOK (aTitle IN VARCHAR2,
 aPublisher IN VARCHAR2, aCategoryName IN VARCHAR2)
is
begin
 insert into BOOKSHELF
 (Title, Publisher, CategoryName, Rating)
 values (aTitle, aPublisher, aCategoryName, NULL);
 delete from BOOK_ORDER
 where Title = aTitle;
```

```
end NEW_BOOK;
end BOOK_MANAGEMENT;
```

The **create or replace package body** command shown in the preceding example combines the **create function** command for the OVERDUE_CHARGES function with the **create procedure** command for the NEW_BOOK procedure. The **end** clauses all have the names of their associated objects appended to them (shown in bold in the prior listing). Modifying the **end** clauses in this manner helps to clarify the ending points of the object's source code.

Additional functions, procedures, exceptions, variables, cursors, and constants may be defined within the package body, but they will not be available to the public unless they have been declared within the package specification (via the **create package** command). If a user has been granted the EXECUTE privilege on a package, then that user can access any of the public objects that are declared in the package specification.

## Initializing Packages

Packages may include code that is to be run the first time a user executes a function or procedure in the package within each session. In the following example, the BOOK_MANAGEMENT package body is modified to include a SQL statement that records the current user's username and the timestamp for the first time a package component is executed within the session. Two new variables must also be declared in the package body to record these values.

Since the two new variables are declared within the package body, they are not available to the public. Within the package body, they are separated from the procedures and functions. The package initialization code is shown in bold in the following listing:

```
create or replace package body BOOK_MANAGEMENT
as
User_Name VARCHAR2(30);
Entry_Date DATE;
function OVERDUE_CHARGES (aName IN VARCHAR2)
 return NUMBER
 is
 owed_amount NUMBER(10,2);
begin
 select SUM(((ReturnedDate-CheckoutDate) -14)*0.20)
 into owed_amount
 from BOOKSHELF_CHECKOUT
 where Name = aName
 and (ReturnedDate-CheckoutDate) > 14;
 RETURN(owed_amount);
 EXCEPTION
 when NO_DATA_FOUND THEN
 RAISE_APPLICATION_ERROR(-20100,
 'No books borrowed.');
end OVERDUE_CHARGES;
procedure NEW_BOOK (aTitle IN VARCHAR2,
 aPublisher IN VARCHAR2, aCategoryName IN VARCHAR2)
is
begin
```

```
 insert into BOOKSHELF
 (Title, Publisher, CategoryName, Rating)
 values (aTitle, aPublisher, aCategoryName, NULL);
 delete from BOOK_ORDER
 where Title = aTitle;
end NEW_BOOK;
begin
 select User, SysDate
 into User_Name, Entry_Date
 from DUAL;
end BOOK_MANAGEMENT;
```

**NOTE**
*The code that is to be run the first time that a component of the*
*package is executed is stored in its own PL/SQL block at the bottom*
*of the package body. It does not have its own **end** clause; it uses the*
*package body's **end** clause.*

The first time a BOOK_MANAGEMENT package component is executed in the user's session, the *User_Name* and *Entry_Date* variables will be populated by the query shown in the previous listing. These two variables can then be used by the functions and procedures within the package, although this example does not use them in the interest of brevity.

To **execute** a procedure or function that is within a package, specify both the package name and the name of the procedure or function in the **execute** command, as follows:

```
execute BOOK_MANAGEMENT.NEW_BOOK('SOMETHING SO STRONG','PANDORAS','ADULTNF');
```

# Viewing Source Code for Procedural Objects

The source code for existing procedures, functions, packages, and package bodies can be queried from the following data dictionary views:

| | |
|---|---|
| USER_SOURCE | For procedural objects owned by the user |
| ALL_SOURCE | For procedural objects owned by the user or to which the user has been granted access |
| DBA_SOURCE | For all procedural objects in the database |

Select information from the USER_SOURCE view via a query similar to the one shown in the following listing. In this example, the Text column is selected, ordered by the Line number. The Name of the object and the object Type are used to define which object's source code is to be displayed. The following example uses the NEW_BOOK procedure shown earlier in this chapter:

```
select Text
 from USER_SOURCE
 where Name = 'NEW_BOOK'
 and Type = 'PROCEDURE'
```

```
 order by Line;

TEXT

procedure NEW_BOOK (aTitle IN VARCHAR2,
 aPublisher IN VARCHAR2, aCategoryName IN VARCHAR2)
as
begin
 insert into BOOKSHELF (Title, Publisher, CategoryName, Rating)
 values (aTitle, aPublisher, aCategoryName, NULL);
 delete from BOOK_ORDER
 where Title = aTitle;
end;
```

As shown in this example, the USER_SOURCE view contains one record for each line of the NEW_BOOK procedure. The sequence of the lines is maintained by the Line column; therefore, the Line column should be used in the **order by** clause.

Valid values for the Type column are PROCEDURE, FUNCTION, PACKAGE, PACKAGE BODY, JAVA SOURCE, TYPE, and TYPE BODY.

# Compiling Procedures, Functions, and Packages

Oracle compiles procedural objects when they are created. However, procedural objects may become invalid if the database objects they reference change. The next time the procedural objects are executed, they will be recompiled by the database.

You can avoid this runtime compiling—and the performance degradation it may cause—by explicitly recompiling the procedures, functions, and packages. To recompile a procedure, use the **alter procedure** command, as shown in the following listing. The **compile** clause is the only valid option for this command.

```
alter procedure NEW_BOOK compile;
```

To recompile a procedure, you must either own the procedure or have the ALTER ANY PROCEDURE system privilege.

To recompile a function, use the **alter function** command, with the **compile** clause:

```
alter function OVERDUE_CHARGES compile;
```

To recompile a function, you must either own the function or have the ALTER ANY PROCEDURE system privilege.

When recompiling packages, you may either recompile both the package specification and the body or just recompile the package body. By default, both the package specification and the package body are recompiled. You cannot use the **alter function** or **alter procedure** command to recompile functions and procedures stored within a package.

If the source code for the procedures or functions within the package body has changed but the package specification has not, you may want to recompile only the package body. In most cases, it is appropriate to recompile both the specification and the package body.

The following is the syntax for the **alter package** command:

```
alter package [user.] package_name
compile [debug] [package | body | specification];
```

To recompile a package, use the preceding **alter package** command with the **compile** clause, as follows:

```
alter package BOOK_MANAGEMENT compile;
```

To recompile a package, you must either own the package or have the ALTER ANY PROCEDURE system privilege. Since neither PACKAGE nor BODY was specified in the preceding example, the default of PACKAGE was used, resulting in the recompilation of both the package specification and the package body.

# Replacing Procedures, Functions, and Packages

Procedures, functions, and packages may be replaced via their respective **create or replace** command. Using the **or replace** clause keeps in place any existing grants that have been made for those objects. If you choose to drop and re-create procedural objects, you have to regrant any EXECUTE privileges that had previously been granted.

# Dropping Procedures, Functions, and Packages

To drop a procedure, use the **drop procedure** command, as follows:

```
drop procedure NEW_BOOK;
```

To drop a procedure, you must either own the procedure or have the DROP ANY PROCEDURE system privilege.

To drop a function, use the **drop function** command, as follows:

```
drop function OVERDUE_CHARGES;
```

To drop a function, you must either own the function or have the DROP ANY PROCEDURE system privilege.

To drop a package (both the specification and the body), use the **drop package** command, as follows:

```
drop package BOOK_MANAGEMENT;
```

To drop a package, you must either own the package or have the DROP ANY PROCEDURE system privilege.

To drop a package body, use the **drop package** command with the **body** clause, as follows:

```
drop package body BOOK_MANAGEMENT;
```

To drop a package body, you must either own the package or have the DROP ANY PROCEDURE system privilege.

# PART
# IV

# Object-Relational
# Databases

# CHAPTER
# 30

# Implementing Types, Object Views, and Methods

n this chapter, you will see further details on the use of abstract datatypes, first introduced in Chapter 4. This chapter covers topics such as security administration for abstract datatypes and the indexing of abstract datatype attributes. The creation of methods for abstract datatypes is also shown, along with the use of object views and INSTEAD OF triggers.

To use the information provided in this chapter, you should be familiar with abstract datatypes (see Chapter 4), views (see Chapter 18), the **grant** command (see Chapter 19), indexes (see Chapter 20), and PL/SQL procedures and triggers (Chapters 27, 28, and 29). Elements of each of these topics play a part in the implementation of an object-relational database. The first section of this chapter provides a high-level review of the abstract datatypes shown in Chapter 4.

# Revisiting Abstract Datatypes

As described in Chapter 4, you can use abstract datatypes to group related columns into objects. For example, columns that are part of address information can be grouped into an ADDRESS_TY datatype via the **create type** command:

```
create type ADDRESS_TY as object
(Street VARCHAR2(50),
 City VARCHAR2(25),
 State CHAR(2),
 Zip NUMBER);
```

**NOTE**
*Depending on the tool you use, you may need to add a "/" to the end to execute this command.*

The **create type** command in the preceding listing creates an ADDRESS_TY abstract datatype. You can use ADDRESS_TY when creating additional database objects. For example, the following **create type** command creates the PERSON_TY datatype, using the ADDRESS_TY datatype as the datatype for its Address column:

```
create type PERSON_TY as object
(Name VARCHAR2(25),
 Address ADDRESS_TY);
```

Because the Address column of the PERSON_TY datatype uses the ADDRESS_TY datatype, it holds not one value but four—the four columns that constitute the ADDRESS_TY datatype.

## Security for Abstract Datatypes

The previous example assumed that the same user owned both the ADDRESS_TY datatype and the PERSON_TY datatype. What if the owner of the PERSON_TY datatype were different from the ADDRESS_TY datatype's owner?

For example, what if the account named Dora owns the ADDRESS_TY datatype, and the user of the account named George tries to create the PERSON_TY datatype? George executes the following command:

```
create type PERSON_TY as object
(Name VARCHAR2(25),
 Address ADDRESS_TY);
```

If George does not own the ADDRESS_TY abstract datatype, then Oracle will respond to this **create type** command with the following message:

```
Warning: Type created with compilation errors.
```

The compilation errors are caused by problems creating the *constructor method*—a special method created by Oracle when the datatype is created. Oracle cannot resolve the reference to the ADDRESS_TY datatype, since George does not own a datatype with that name. George could issue the **create type** command again (using the **or replace** clause) to specifically reference Dora's ADDRESS_TY datatype:

```
create or replace type PERSON_TY as object
(Name VARCHAR2(25),
 Address Dora.ADDRESS_TY);
```

```
Warning: Type created with compilation errors.
```

To see the errors associated with the datatype creation, use the **show errors** command:

```
show errors
Errors for TYPE PERSON_TY:

LINE/COL ERROR
-------- --
0/0 PL/SQL: Compilation unit analysis terminated
3/11 PLS-00201: identifier 'DORA.ADDRESS_TY' must be declared
```

George will not be able to create the PERSON_TY datatype (which includes the ADDRESS_TY datatype) unless Dora first **grant**s him EXECUTE privilege on her type. The following listing shows this grant:

```
grant EXECUTE on ADDRESS_TY to George;
```

Now that the proper grants are in place, George can create a datatype that is based on Dora's ADDRESS_TY datatype, as shown in the following listing.

```
create or replace type PERSON_TY as object
(Name VARCHAR2(25),
 Address Dora.ADDRESS_TY);
```

Using another user's datatypes is not trivial. For example, during **insert** operations, you must specify the owner of each type. George can create a table based on his PERSON_TY datatype (which includes Dora's ADDRESS_TY datatype), as shown in the following listing:

```
create table CUSTOMER
(Customer_ID NUMBER,
 Person PERSON_TY);
```

If George owned the PERSON_TY and ADDRESS_TY datatypes, an **insert** into CUSTOMER would use the format:

```
insert into CUSTOMER values
(1,PERSON_TY('SomeName',
 ADDRESS_TY('StreetValue','CityValue','ST',11111)));
```

Since George does not own the ADDRESS_TY datatype, this command will fail. During the **insert**, the ADDRESS_TY constructor method is used—and Dora owns it. Therefore, the **insert** command must be modified to specify Dora as the owner of ADDRESS_TY. The following example shows the corrected **insert** statement, with the reference to Dora shown in bold:

```
insert into CUSTOMER values
(1,PERSON_TY('SomeName',
 Dora.ADDRESS_TY('StreetValue','CityValue','ST',11111)));
```

Can George use a synonym for Dora's datatype? No. Although George *can* create a synonym named ADDRESS_TY:

```
create synonym ADDRESS_TY for Dora.ADDRESS_TY;
```

this synonym cannot be used:

```
create type PERSON2_TY
(Name VARCHAR2(25),
 Address ADDRESS_TY);
/
```

```
Warning: Type created with compilation errors.
```

You cannot use a synonym for another user's datatype. Therefore, you will need to refer to the datatype's owner during each **insert** command.

**NOTE**
*When you create a synonym, Oracle does not check the validity of the object for which you are creating a synonym. When you **create synonym x for y**, Oracle does not check to make sure that y is a valid object name or valid object type. The validity of that object is only checked when the object is accessed via the synonym.*

Be sure to drop the synonym before continuing with the examples:

```
drop synonym ADDRESS_TY;
```

In a relational-only implementation of Oracle, you grant the EXECUTE privilege on procedural objects, such as procedures and packages. Within the object-relational implementation of Oracle, the EXECUTE privilege is extended to cover abstract datatypes as well. The EXECUTE privilege is appropriate because abstract datatypes can include *methods*—PL/SQL functions and procedures that operate on the datatype. If you grant someone the privilege to use your datatype, you are granting the user the privilege to execute the methods you have defined on the datatype. Although Dora did not yet define any methods on the ADDRESS_TY datatype, Oracle automatically creates constructor methods to access the data. Any object (such as PERSON_TY) that uses the ADDRESS_TY datatype uses the constructor method associated with ADDRESS_TY. Even if you haven't created any methods for your abstract datatype, there are still procedures associated with it.

You can describe CUSTOMER:

```
describe CUSTOMER
```

```
Name Null? Type
-- -------- ---------
CUSTOMER_ID NUMBER
PERSON PERSON_TY
```

You can use the **set describe depth** command in SQL*Plus to show the datatype attributes for tables that use object-relational features. You can specify depth values from 1 to 50:

```
set describe depth 2
```

```
desc CUSTOMER
```

```
Name Null? Type
-- -------- ----------------
CUSTOMER_ID NUMBER
PERSON PERSON_TY
 NAME VARCHAR2(25)
 ADDRESS DORA.ADDRESS_TY
```

```
set describe depth 3
```

```
desc customer
```

```
Name Null? Type
-- -------- ----------------
CUSTOMER_ID NUMBER
PERSON PERSON_TY
 NAME VARCHAR2(25)
 ADDRESS DORA.ADDRESS_TY
 STREET VARCHAR2(50)
 CITY VARCHAR2(25)
 STATE CHAR(2)
 ZIP NUMBER
```

## Indexing Abstract Datatype Attributes

In the example from Chapter 4, the CUSTOMER table was created. As shown in the following listing, the CUSTOMER table contains a normal column (Customer_ID) and a Person column that is defined by the PERSON_TY abstract datatype:

```
create table CUSTOMER
(Customer_ID NUMBER,
 Person PERSON_TY);
```

From the datatype definitions shown in the previous section of this chapter, you can see that PERSON_TY has one column (Name) followed by an Address column defined by the ADDRESS_TY datatype.

As shown in Chapter 4, you fully qualify the datatype attributes when referencing columns within the abstract datatypes, by prefacing the attribute name with the column name, and by prefacing the column name with a correlation variable. For example, the following query returns the Customer_ID column along with the Name column. The Name column is an attribute of the datatype that defines the Person column, so you refer to the attribute as Person.Name:

```
select Customer_ID, C.Person.Name
 from CUSTOMER C;
```

**NOTE**
*When querying the attributes of an abstract datatype, you must use a correlation variable for the table, as shown in this example.*

To set the display attributes for an abstract datatype's attributes in SQL*Plus, use the **column** command, specifying the name of the datatype and the attribute:

```
column Customer_ID format 9999999
column Person.Name format A25
```

You can refer to attributes within the ADDRESS_TY datatype by specifying the full path through the related columns. For example, the Street column is referred to as Person.Address.Street, fully describing its location within the structure of the table. In the following example, the City column is referenced twice: once in the list of columns to select, and once within the **where** clause. In each reference, a correlation variable (in this example, *C*) is required.

```
select C.Person.Name,
 C.Person.Address.City
 from CUSTOMER C
 where C.Person.Address.City like 'F%';
```

Because the City column is used with a range search in the **where** clause, the Oracle optimizer may be able to use an index when resolving the query. If an index is available on the City column, then Oracle can quickly find all the rows that have City values starting with the letter *F*, as requested by the query.

**NOTE**
*The inner workings of the Oracle optimizer—and the conditions under which indexes are used—are described in Chapter 38. See that chapter for guidelines regarding the columns to index.*

To create an index on a column that is part of an abstract datatype, you need to specify the full path to the column as part of the **create index** command. To create an index on the City column (which is part of the Address column), you can execute the following command:

```
create index I_CUSTOMER$CITY
on CUSTOMER(Person.Address.City);
```

This command will create an index named I_CUSTOMER$CITY on the Person.Address.City column. Whenever the City column is accessed, the Oracle optimizer will evaluate the SQL used to access the data and determine if the new index can be useful to improve the performance of the query.

**NOTE**
*In the **create index** command, you do not use correlation variables when referencing the attributes of abstract datatypes.*

When creating tables based on abstract datatypes, you should consider how the columns within the abstract datatypes will be accessed. If, like the City column in the previous example, certain columns will commonly be used as part of limiting conditions in queries, then they should be indexed. In this regard, the representation of multiple columns in a single abstract datatype may hinder your application performance, since it may obscure the need to index specific columns within the datatype. When using abstract datatypes, you become accustomed to treating a group of columns as a single entity, such as the Address columns or the Person columns. It is important to remember that the optimizer, when evaluating query access paths, will consider the columns individually. In addition, remember that indexing the City column in one table that uses the ADDRESS_TY datatype does not affect the City column in a second table that uses the ADDRESS_TY datatype. For example, if there is a second table named BRANCH that uses the ADDRESS_TY datatype, then *its* City column will not be indexed unless you create an index for it. The fact that there is an index on the City column in the CUSTOMER table will have no impact on the City column in the BRANCH table.

Thus, one of the advantages of abstract datatypes—the ability to improve adherence to standards for logical data representation—does not extend to the physical data representation. You need to address each physical implementation separately.

# Implementing Object Views

The CUSTOMER table created in the previous section of this chapter assumed that a PERSON_TY datatype already existed. When implementing object-relational database applications, you should first use the relational database design methods described in the first part of this book. After the database design is properly normalized, you should look for groups of columns (or individual

columns) that constitute the representation of an abstract datatype. You can then create your tables based on the abstract datatypes, as shown earlier in this chapter.

But what if your tables already exist? What if you had previously created a relational database application and now want to implement object-relational concepts in your application without rebuilding and re-creating the entire application? To do this, you need the ability to overlay object-oriented (OO) structures, such as abstract datatypes, on existing relational tables. Oracle provides *object views* as a means for defining objects used by existing relational tables.

**NOTE**
*Throughout the examples in this book, the names of object views will always end with the suffix OV.*

In the examples earlier in this chapter, the order of operations was as follows:

1. Create the ADDRESS_TY datatype.

2. Create the PERSON_TY datatype, using the ADDRESS_TY datatype.

3. Create the CUSTOMER table, using the PERSON_TY datatype.

If the CUSTOMER table already existed, you could create the ADDRESS_TY and PERSON_TY datatypes, and use object views to relate them to the CUSTOMER table. In the following listing, the CUSTOMER table is created as a relational table, using only the built-in datatypes:

```
drop table CUSTOMER;

create table CUSTOMER
(Customer_ID NUMBER primary key,
 Name VARCHAR2(25),
 Street VARCHAR2(50),
 City VARCHAR2(25),
 State CHAR(2),
 Zip NUMBER);
```

If you want to create another table or application that stores information about people and addresses, you may choose to create the ADDRESS_TY and PERSON_TY datatypes. However, for consistency, they should be applied to the CUSTOMER table as well.

With the CUSTOMER table already created (and possibly containing data), you should create the abstract datatypes. First, create ADDRESS_TY:

```
drop type PERSON_TY;
drop type ADDRESS_TY;
create or replace type ADDRESS_TY as object
(Street VARCHAR2(50),
 City VARCHAR2(25),
 State CHAR(2),
 Zip NUMBER);
```

Next, create PERSON_TY, which uses ADDRESS_TY:

```
create or replace type PERSON_TY as object
(Name VARCHAR2(25),
 Address ADDRESS_TY);
```

Now, create an object view based on the CUSTOMER table using the datatypes you have defined. An object view starts with the **create view** command. Within the **create view** command, you specify the query that will form the basis of the view. You'll use the datatypes you just created. The code for creating the CUSTOMER_OV object view is shown in the following listing:

```
create view CUSTOMER_OV (Customer_ID, Person) as
select Customer_ID,
 PERSON_TY(Name,
 ADDRESS_TY(Street, City, State, Zip))
 from CUSTOMER;
```

Let's look at this command closely. In the first line, the object view is named:

```
create view CUSTOMER_OV (Customer_ID, Person) as
```

The CUSTOMER_OV view will have two columns: the Customer_ID column and the Person column (the latter is defined by the PERSON_TY datatype). Note that you cannot specify "object" as an option within the **create view** command.

In the next section of the **create view** command, you create the query that will form the basis for the view:

```
select Customer_ID,
 PERSON_TY(Name,
 ADDRESS_TY(Street, City, State, Zip))
 from CUSTOMER;
```

This example presents several important syntax issues. When a table is built on existing abstract datatypes, you select column values from the table by referring to the names of the columns (such as Person and Address in earlier examples) instead of their constructor methods. When creating the object view, however, you refer to the names of the constructor methods (PERSON_TY and ADDRESS_TY) instead.

**NOTE**
*See Chapter 4 for examples of queries that refer to columns defined by abstract datatypes.*

You can use a **where** clause in the query that forms the basis of the object view. In the following example, the CUSTOMER_OV is modified to include a **where** clause that limits it to showing the CUSTOMER values for which the State column has a value of 'DE':

```
create or replace view CUSTOMER_OV (Customer_ID, Person) as
select Customer_ID,
 PERSON_TY(Name,
 ADDRESS_TY(Street, City, State, Zip))
 from CUSTOMER
 where State = 'DE';
```

Note that when you create the object view CUSTOMER_OV, the **where** clause of the view's base query does not refer to the abstract datatype. Instead, it refers directly to the CUSTOMER table. The **where** clause refers directly to the State column because the query refers directly to the CUSTOMER table—a relational table that is not based on any abstract datatypes.

To create object views based on relational tables, the order of operations is as follows:

1. Create the CUSTOMER table if it does not already exist.

2. Create the ADDRESS_TY datatype.

3. Create the PERSON_TY datatype, using the ADDRESS_TY datatype.

4. Create the CUSTOMER_OV object view, using the defined datatypes.

There are two main benefits to using object views. First, they allow you to create abstract datatypes that operate against tables that already exist. Since you can use the same abstract data-types in multiple tables within your application, you can improve your application's adherence to standard representation of data and your ability to reuse existing objects. Since you can define methods for the abstract datatypes, the methods will apply to the data within any new tables you create as well as to your existing tables.

Second, object views provide two different ways to enter data into the base table. The flexibility of data manipulation for object views—being able to treat the base table as either a relational table or an object table—is a significant benefit for application developers. In the next section, you will see the data-manipulation options available for object views.

## Manipulating Data via Object Views

You can update the data in the CUSTOMER table via the CUSTOMER_OV object view, or you can update the CUSTOMER table directly. By treating CUSTOMER as just a table, you can insert data into it via a normal SQL **insert** command, as shown in the following example:

```
insert into CUSTOMER values
(123,'SIGMUND','47 HAFFNER RD','LEWISTON','NJ',22222);
```

This **insert** command inserts a single record into the CUSTOMER table. Even though you have created an object view on the table, you can still treat the CUSTOMER table as a regular relational table.

Since the object view has been created on the CUSTOMER table, you can **insert** into CUSTOMER via the constructor methods used by the view. As previously shown in this chapter, when you insert data into an object that uses abstract datatypes, you specify the names of the constructor methods within the **insert** command. The example shown in the following listing inserts a single record into the CUSTOMER_OV object view using the CUSTOMER_TY, PERSON_TY, and ADDRESS_TY constructor methods:

```
insert into CUSTOMER_OV values
 (234,
 PERSON_TY('EVELYN',
 ADDRESS_TY('555 HIGH ST','LOWLANDS PARK','NE',33333)));
```

Since you can use either method to insert values into the CUSTOMER_OV object view, you can standardize the manner in which your application performs data manipulation. If your **insert**s are all based on abstract datatypes, then you can use the same kind of code for **insert**s regardless of whether the abstract datatypes were created before or after the table.

You can query the rows just entered from either CUSTOMER or CUSTOMER_OV; but because the view has a **where** clause, CUSTOMER_OV will only show the rows that pass that limiting condition.

# Using INSTEAD OF Triggers

If you create an object view, you can use an INSTEAD OF trigger. Views cannot use the standard table-based triggers described in Chapter 28. You can use INSTEAD OF triggers to tell Oracle how to update the underlying tables that are part of the view. You can use INSTEAD OF triggers on either object views or standard relational views.

For example, if a view involves a join of two tables, your ability to **update** records in the view is limited. However, if you use an INSTEAD OF trigger, you can tell Oracle how to **update**, **delete**, or **insert** records in tables when a user attempts to change values via the view. The code in the INSTEAD OF trigger is executed *in place of* the **insert**, **update**, or **delete** command you enter.

For example, you may have a view that joins the BOOKSHELF table to BOOKSHELF_AUTHOR:

```
create or replace view AUTHOR_PUBLISHER as
select BA.AuthorName, Title, B.Publisher
 from BOOKSHELF_AUTHOR BA inner join BOOKSHELF B
 using (Title);
```

You can select values from this view—and if you use INSTEAD OF triggers, you can also perform data manipulation via this view. Consider these records:

```
select AuthorName, Publisher from AUTHOR_PUBLISHER
 where AuthorName = 'W. P. KINSELLA';

AUTHORNAME PUBLISHER
-- ----------
W. P. KINSELLA MARINER
W. P. KINSELLA BALLANTINE
```

If we attempt to update the Publisher value, the update fails:

```
update AUTHOR_PUBLISHER
 set Publisher = 'MARINER'
 where AuthorName = 'W. P. KINSELLA';

set Publisher = 'MARINER'
 *
ERROR at line 2:
ORA-01779: cannot modify a column which maps to a
 non key-preserved table
```

The problem is that Oracle cannot determine which publisher in which record to update in BOOKSHELF. To perform the update via the view, you will need to use an INSTEAD OF trigger. In the following listing, an INSTEAD OF trigger for the AUTHOR_PUBLISHER view is created:

```
create trigger AUTHOR_PUBLISHER_UPDATE
instead of UPDATE on AUTHOR_PUBLISHER
for each row
begin
 if :old.Publisher <> :new.Publisher
 then
 update BOOKSHELF
 set Publisher = :new.Publisher
 where Title = :old.Title;
 end if;
 if :old.AuthorName <> :new.AuthorName
 then
 update BOOKSHELF_AUTHOR
 set AuthorName = :new.AuthorName
 where Title = :old.Title;
 end if;
end;
```

In the first part of this trigger, the trigger is named and its purpose is described via the **instead of** clause. The trigger has been named to make its function clear: It is used to support **update** commands executed against the AUTHOR_PUBLISHER view. It is a row-level trigger; each changed row will be processed, as shown next.

```
create trigger AUTHOR_PUBLISHER_UPDATE
instead of UPDATE on AUTHOR_PUBLISHER
for each row
```

The next section of the trigger tells Oracle how to process the **update**. In the first check within the trigger body, the Publisher value is checked. If the old Publisher value is equal to the new Publisher value, then no changes are made. If the values are not the same, then the BOOKSHELF table is updated with the new Publisher value:

```
begin
 if :old.Publisher <> :new.Publisher
 then
 update BOOKSHELF
 set Publisher = :new.Publisher
 where Title = :old.Title;
 end if;
```

In the next section of the trigger, the AuthorName value is evaluated. If the AuthorName value has changed, then the BOOKSHELF table is updated to reflect the new AuthorName value:

```
if :old.AuthorName <> :new.AuthorName
then
 update BOOKSHELF_AUTHOR
 set AuthorName = :new.AuthorName
 where Title = :old.Title;
end if;
```

Thus, the view relies on two tables—BOOKSHELF and BOOKSHELF_AUTHOR—and an **update** of the view can update *either* or *both* of the tables. The INSTEAD OF trigger, introduced to support object views, is a powerful tool for application development.

You can now **update** the AUTHOR_PUBLISHER view directly and have the trigger **update** the proper underlying table. For example, the following command will update the BOOKSHELF table:

```
update AUTHOR_PUBLISHER
 set Publisher = 'MARINER'
 where AuthorName = 'W. P. KINSELLA';

2 rows updated.
```

Verify the **update** by querying the BOOKSHELF table:

```
select Publisher from BOOKSHELF
 where Title in
(select Title from BOOKSHELF_AUTHOR
 where AuthorName = 'W. P. KINSELLA');

PUBLISHER

MARINER
MARINER
```

INSTEAD OF triggers are very powerful. As shown in this example, you can use them to perform operations against different database tables, using the flow-control logic available within PL/SQL. In dealing with object views, you can use the INSTEAD OF triggers to redirect DML against the object views to the base tables for the views.

# Methods

When you created an object view on the CUSTOMER table, you defined abstract datatypes that the table used. Those datatypes help to standardize the representation of data, but they serve another purpose as well. You can define methods that apply to datatypes, and by applying those datatypes to existing tables, you can apply those methods to the data in those tables.

Consider the CUSTOMER_OV object view:

```
create or replace view CUSTOMER_OV (Customer_ID, Person) as
select Customer_ID,
 PERSON_TY(Name,
 ADDRESS_TY(Street, City, State, Zip))
 from CUSTOMER;
```

This view applies the PERSON_TY and ADDRESS_TY abstract datatypes to the data in the CUSTOMER table. If any methods are associated with those datatypes, they will apply to the data in the table. When you create an abstract datatype, you use the **create type** command. When you create a method, you use the **create type body** command.

# Syntax for Creating Methods

Before creating the body for a method, you must name the method within the datatype declaration. For example, let's create a new datatype, ANIMAL_TY. The datatype definition for ANIMAL_TY is shown in the following listing:

```
create or replace type ANIMAL_TY as object
(Breed VARCHAR2(25),
 Name VARCHAR2(25),
 BirthDate DATE,
member function AGE (BirthDate IN DATE) return NUMBER);
```

The ANIMAL_TY datatype could be used as part of an object view on the BREEDING table used in Chapter 13. In the BREEDING table, the name of an offspring, its sex, its parents, and its birthdate are recorded.

Within the **create type** command, this line:

```
member function AGE (BirthDate IN DATE) return NUMBER)
```

names the function that is a "member" of the ANIMAL_TY datatype. Since AGE will return a value, it is a function (see Chapter 29). To define the AGE function, use the **create type body** command, whose full syntax is shown in the Alphabetical Reference.

Let's create the AGE function as a member function within the ANIMAL_TY datatype. The AGE function will return the age, in days, of the animals:

```
create or replace type body ANIMAL_TY as
member function Age (BirthDate DATE) return NUMBER is
 begin
 RETURN ROUND(SysDate - BirthDate);
 end;
end;
```

If you had additional functions or procedures to code, you would specify them within the same **create type body** command, before the final **end** clause.

Now that the AGE function has been created, it is associated with the ANIMAL_TY datatype. If a table uses this datatype, then it can use the AGE function. However, there is a problem with the way in which the function is specified. The AGE function, as previously defined in the **create type body** command, does not explicitly restrict **update**s. The AGE function does not update any data, but there is no guarantee that the type body will not later be changed to cause AGE to update data. To call a member function within a SQL statement, you need to make sure that the function cannot update the database. Therefore, you need to modify the function specification in the **create type** command. The modification is shown in bold in the following listing:

```
create or replace type ANIMAL_TY as object
(Breed VARCHAR2(25),
 Name VARCHAR2(25),
 BirthDate DATE,
member function AGE (BirthDate IN DATE) return NUMBER,
PRAGMA RESTRICT_REFERENCES(AGE, WNDS));
```

**NOTE**
*You cannot drop or re-create a type that is in use by a table.*
*Therefore, it is critical that you make this modification before*
*creating a table that uses the ANIMAL_TY datatype.*

The following line

```
PRAGMA RESTRICT_REFERENCES(AGE, WNDS));
```

tells Oracle that the AGE function operates in the Write No Database State—it cannot modify the database. Other available restrictions are Read No Database State (RNDS—no queries performed), Write No Package State (WNPS—no values of packaged variables are changed), and Read No Package State (RNPS—no values of packaged variables are referenced).

You can now use the AGE function within a query. If ANIMAL_TY is used as the datatype for a column named Animal in the table named ANIMAL, then the table structure could be as follows:

```
create table ANIMAL
(ID NUMBER,
 Animal ANIMAL_TY);

insert into ANIMAL values
(11,ANIMAL_TY('COW','MIMI',TO_DATE('01-JAN-1997','DD-MON-YYYY')));
```

You can now invoke the AGE function, which is part of the ANIMAL_TY datatype. Like the attributes of an abstract datatype, the member methods are referenced using the column names that use the datatypes (in this case, Animal.AGE):

```
select A.Animal.AGE(A.Animal.BirthDate)
 from ANIMAL A;

A.ANIMAL.AGE(A.ANIMAL.BIRTHDATE)

 1987
```

The A.Animal.AGE(A.Animal.BirthDate) call executes the AGE method within the ANIMAL_TY datatype. Therefore, you do not have to store variable data such as age within your database. Instead, you can store static data—such as birthdate—in your database and use function and procedure calls to derive the variable data.

**NOTE**
*In this example, you need to use correlation variables in two places—when calling the AGE method and when passing the name of the Birthdate column to that method.*

## Managing Methods

You can add new methods to a datatype by altering the datatype (via the **alter type** command). When altering a datatype, list all of its methods, both the old and the new. After altering the datatype, alter the datatype's body, listing all of the datatype's methods in a single command.

You do not need to grant EXECUTE privilege on the member functions and procedures of abstract datatypes. If you grant another user EXECUTE privilege on the ANIMAL_TY datatype, that user automatically has EXECUTE privilege on the methods that are part of the datatype. Thus, the grant of access to the datatype includes both the data representation and its data access methods, in accordance with OO concepts.

When creating member functions, you can specify them as being map methods or order methods (or neither, as in the case of the ANIMAL_TY.Age member function). A *map method* returns the relative position of a given record in the ordering of all records within the object. A type body can contain only one map method, which must be a function.

An *order method* is a member function that takes a record in the object as an explicit argument and returns an integer value. If the returned value is negative, zero, or positive, the implicit "self" argument of the function is less than, equal to, or greater than, respectively, that of the explicitly specified record. When multiple rows within an object are compared in an **order by** clause, the order method is automatically executed to order the rows returned. A datatype specification can contain only one order method, which must be a function with the return type INTEGER.

The notion of ordering within the rows of an abstract datatype may have more relevance when you consider the implementation of *collectors*—datatypes that hold multiple values per row. Oracle offers two types of collectors, called *nested tables* and *varying arrays*. In the next chapter, you will see how to implement these collector types.

# CHAPTER
# 31

# Collectors
# (Nested Tables and
# Varying Arrays)

 ollectors make use of abstract datatypes. You should be familiar with the creation and implementation of abstract datatypes (see Chapters 4 and 30) before attempting to use varying arrays and nested tables.

# Varying Arrays

A varying array allows you to store repeating attributes of a record in a single row. For example, suppose you want to track which of your tools were borrowed by which of your neighbors. You could model this in a relational database by creating a BORROWER table:

```
create table BORROWER
(Name VARCHAR2(25),
 Tool VARCHAR2(25),
constraint BORROWER_PK primary key (Name, Tool));
```

Even though the worker's Name value does not change, it is repeated in each record because it is part of the primary key. Collectors such as varying arrays allow you to repeat *only* those column values that change, potentially saving storage space. You can use collectors to accurately represent relationships between datatypes in your database objects. In the following sections, you will see how to create and use collectors.

## Creating a Varying Array

You can create a varying array based on either an abstract datatype or one of Oracle's standard datatypes (such as NUMBER). For example, you could create a new datatype, TOOL_TY, as shown in the following listing, which has only one column; you should limit varying arrays to one column. If you need to use multiple columns in an array, consider using nested tables (described later in this chapter).

```
create type TOOL_TY as object
(ToolName VARCHAR2(25));
```

You do not have to create the base type—in this case, TOOL_TY—before you can create a varying array (to be named TOOLS_VA). Since the varying array is based on only one column, you can create the TOOLS_VA type in a single step. To create the varying array, use the **as varray()** clause of the **create type** command:

```
create or replace type TOOLS_VA as varray(5) of VARCHAR2(25);
```

When this **create type** command is executed, a type named TOOLS_VA is created. The **as varray(5)** clause tells Oracle that a varying array is being created, and it will hold a maximum of five entries per record. The name of the varying array is pluralized TOOLS instead of TOOL to show that this type will be used to hold multiple records. The suffix VA makes it clear that the type is a varying array. You can now use this type as the basis for a column definition, as shown in the following listing.

```
create table BORROWER
(Name VARCHAR2(25),
 Tools TOOLS_VA,
constraint BORROWER_PK primary key (Name));
```

## Describing the Varying Array

The BORROWER table will contain one record for each borrower, even if that borrower has multiple tools. The multiple tools will be stored in the Tools column, using the TOOLS_VA varying array. You can describe the BORROWER table as follows:

```
desc BORROWER

Name Null? Type
------------------------------ -------- ----
NAME NOT NULL VARCHAR2(25)
TOOLS TOOLS_VA
```

Note that the **set describe depth** command shown in Chapter 30 will not affect this output. You can query similar information from USER_TAB_COLUMNS:

```
select Column_Name,
 Data_Type
 from USER_TAB_COLUMNS
 where Table_Name = 'BORROWER';

COLUMN_NAME DATA_TYPE
------------------------------ ---------------------------
NAME VARCHAR2
TOOLS TOOLS_VA
```

USER_TYPES shows TOOLS_VA is a collection, with no attributes:

```
select TypeCode,
 Attributes
 from USER_TYPES
 where Type_Name = 'TOOLS_VA';

TYPECODE ATTRIBUTES
------------------------------ ----------
COLLECTION 0
```

For more details on TOOLS_VA, query the USER_COLL_TYPES data dictionary view, as shown in the following listing.

```
select Coll_Type,
 Elem_Type_Owner,
 Elem_Type_Name,
 Upper_Bound,
 Length
```

```
 from USER_COLL_TYPES
 where Type_Name = 'TOOLS_VA';

COLL_TYPE ELEM_TYPE_OWNER
------------------------------ ------------------------------
ELEM_TYPE_NAME UPPER_BOUND LENGTH
------------------------------ ----------- ----------
VARYING ARRAY
VARCHAR2 5 25
```

If you base a varying array on an existing abstract datatype, then the datatype's owner will be displayed in the Elem_Type_Owner column, and the datatype's name will be displayed in the Elem_Type_Name column. Since TOOLS_VA uses VARCHAR2 instead of an abstract datatype, the Elem_Type_Owner column's value is **NULL**.

## Inserting Records into the Varying Array

When a datatype is created, the database automatically creates a method called a *constructor method* for the datatype. As shown in Chapter 30, you need to use the constructor method when inserting records into columns that use an abstract datatype. Since a varying array is an abstract datatype, you need to use constructor methods to **insert** records into tables that use varying arrays. Furthermore, since the varying array is itself an abstract datatype, you may need to nest calls to multiple constructor methods to **insert** a record into a table that uses a varying array.

The columns of the BORROWER table are Name and Tools (a varying array using the TOOLS_VA datatype). The following command will **insert** a single record into the BORROWER table. In this example, the record will have a single Name column value and three Tools values.

```
insert into BORROWER values
('JED HOPKINS',
 TOOLS_VA('HAMMER','SLEDGE','AX'));
```

This **insert** command first specifies the value for the Name column. Because the Name column is not part of any abstract datatype, it is populated in the same way you would **insert** values into any relational column:

```
insert into BORROWER values
('JED HOPKINS',
```

The next part of the **insert** command inserts records into the Tools column. Because the Tools column uses the TOOLS_VA varying array, you need to use the TOOLS_VA constructor method:

```
TOOLS_VA('HAMMER','SLEDGE','AX'));
```

Since this is a varying array, you can pass multiple values to the TOOLS_VA constructor method. That is what is shown in the preceding listing; for the single neighbor name, three tools are listed in a single **insert**. If the varying array had been based on the TOOL_TY datatype, you would have instead nested calls to the TOOL_TY within the TOOLS_VA calls:

```
insert into BORROWER values
('JED HOPKINS',
 TOOLS_VA(
 TOOL_TY('HAMMER'),
 TOOL_TY('SLEDGE'),
 TOOL_TY('AX')));
```

Basing the varying array on an Oracle-supplied datatype (such as NUMBER) instead of an abstract or user-defined datatype simplifies the **insert** command by eliminating the nested calls to additional constructor methods.

The TOOLS_VA varying array was defined to have up to five values. In this **insert** command, only three values were entered for the row; the other two are uninitialized. If you want to set the uninitialized values to **NULL**, then you can specify that in the **insert** command:

```
insert into BORROWER values
('JED HOPKINS',
 TOOLS_VA('HAMMER','SLEDGE','AX',NULL,NULL));
```

If you specify too many values to insert into the varying array, Oracle responds with:

```
ORA-22909: exceeded maximum VARRAY limit
```

You cannot insert records into a table that contains a varying array unless you know the structure and datatypes within the array. This example assumed that all the datatypes used by the BORROWER table were within the schema used to create the BORROWER table. If the datatypes are owned by a separate schema, the creator of the BORROWER table will need EXECUTE privilege on those datatypes. During **insert**s, the creator of the BORROWER table needs to specify the owners of the datatypes. See Chapter 30 for examples of using datatypes created under other schemas.

## Selecting Data from Varying Arrays

When you insert records into a varying array, you need to make sure that the number of entries you insert does not exceed the varying array's maximum. The maximum number of entries is specified when the varying array is created, and can be queried from USER_COLL_TYPES, as shown in the previous section of this chapter.

You can query the varying array to determine its maximum number of entries per row, called its LIMIT, and the current number of entries per row, called its COUNT. However, this query cannot be performed directly, via a SQL **select** command. To retrieve the COUNT, LIMIT, and data from a varying array, you need to use PL/SQL. You can use a set of nested Cursor FOR loops, as shown in the next listing.

**NOTE**
*For an overview of PL/SQL and Cursor FOR loops, see Chapter 27.*

```
set serveroutput on
declare
 cursor borrower_cursor is
```

```
 select * from BORROWER;
begin
 for borrower_rec in borrower_cursor
 loop
 dbms_output.put_line('Contact Name: '||borrower_rec.Name);
 for i in 1..borrower_rec.Tools.Count
 loop
 dbms_output.put_line(borrower_rec.Tools(i));
 end loop;
 end loop;
end;
```

The following is the output of this PL/SQL script:

```
Contact Name: JED HOPKINS
HAMMER
SLEDGE
AX

PL/SQL procedure successfully completed.
```

The script uses several PL/SQL features to retrieve data from the varying array. The data will be displayed via the PUT_LINE procedure of the DBMS_OUTPUT package (see Chapter 29), so you must first enable PL/SQL output to be displayed:

```
set serveroutput on
```

In the Declarations section of the PL/SQL block, a cursor is declared; the cursor's query selects all the values from the BORROWER table:

```
declare
 cursor borrower_cursor is
 select * from BORROWER;
```

The Executable Commands section of the PL/SQL block contains two nested FOR loops. In the first loop, each record from the cursor is evaluated and the Name value is printed via PUT_LINE:

```
begin
 for borrower_rec in borrower_cursor
 loop
 dbms_output.put_line('Contact Name: '||borrower_rec.Name);
```

**NOTE**
*You should only print character data via PUT_LINE. PL/SQL will print numeric values via PUT_LINE, but you cannot concatenate them to expressions before printing. Therefore, you may need to use the **TO_CHAR** function on numeric data before printing it via PUT_LINE.*

In the next section of the PL/SQL block, the rows are evaluated further to retrieve the data stored in the varying array. A second FOR loop, nested within the first loop, is executed. The inner FOR loop is limited by the number of values in the array, as defined by the **COUNT** method (the maximum number of values in the array is available via the **LIMIT** method).

The values in the Tools array will be printed, one by one, by this loop:

```
for i in 1..borrower_rec.Tools.Count
 loop
 dbms_output.put_line(borrower_rec.Tools(i));
```

The notation

```
Tools(i)
```

tells Oracle to print the array value that corresponds to the value of *i*. Thus, the first time through the loop, the first value in the array is printed; then the value of *i* is incremented, and the second value in the array is printed.

The last part of the PL/SQL block closes the two nested loops and ends the block:

```
 end loop;
 end loop;
end;
```

Because this method involves nested loops within PL/SQL, selecting data from varying arrays is not trivial.

You can use the **TABLE** function in the **from** clause to simplify the process of selecting data from varying arrays. Consider the following query and its output:

```
select B.Name, N.*
 from BORROWER B, TABLE(B.Tools) N;
```

| NAME | COLUMN_VALUE |
| --- | --- |
| JED HOPKINS | HAMMER |
| JED HOPKINS | SLEDGE |
| JED HOPKINS | AX |

How did that work? The **TABLE** clause took as its input the name of the varying array, and its output is given the alias *N*. The values within *N* are selected, generating the second column of the output. This method is simpler than the PL/SQL method, but because of its unique syntax it may be more confusing for users.

Note that we may get a different number of tools for each borrower—anywhere from zero to five. For example, the following row would insert a row with just one entry in the varying array:

```
insert into BORROWER values
('FRED FULLER',
 TOOLS_VA('HAMMER'));
```

You can select that data via PL/SQL, via the **TABLE** function, or via SQL:

```
select * from BORROWER;

NAME

TOOLS

JED HOPKINS
TOOLS_VA('HAMMER', 'SLEDGE', 'AX')

FRED FULLER
TOOLS_VA('HAMMER')
```

For greater flexibility in selecting data from collectors, you should consider the use of nested tables, as described in the next section.

# Nested Tables

Whereas varying arrays have a limited number of entries, a second type of collector, a *nested table,* has no limit on the number of entries per row. A nested table is, as its name implies, a table within a table. In this case, it is a table that is represented as a column within another table. You can have multiple rows in the nested table for each row in the main table.

For example, if you have a table of animal breeders, you may also have data about their animals. Using a nested table, you could store the information about breeders and all of their animals within the same table. Consider the ANIMAL_TY datatype introduced in Chapter 30:

```
create or replace type ANIMAL_TY as object
(Breed VARCHAR2(25),
 Name VARCHAR2(25),
 BirthDate DATE);
```

**NOTE**
*To keep this example simple, this version of the ANIMAL_TY datatype does not include any methods.*

**NOTE**
*For this example, you should drop the ANIMAL table if it exists in your practice schema.*

The ANIMAL_TY datatype contains a record for each animal—its breed, name, and birthdate. To use this datatype as the basis for a nested table, you need to create a new datatype:

```
create type ANIMALS_NT as table of ANIMAL_TY;
```

The **as table of** clause of this **create type** command tells Oracle that you will be using this type as the basis for a nested table. The name of the type, ANIMALS_NT, has a pluralized root to indicate that it stores multiple rows, and has the suffix NT to indicate that it will be a nested table.

You can now create a table of breeders, using the ANIMALS_TY datatype:

```
create table BREEDER
(BreederName VARCHAR2(25),
 Animals ANIMALS_NT)
 nested table ANIMALS store as ANIMALS_NT_TAB;
```

In this **create table** command, the BREEDER table is created. The first column of the BREEDER table is a BreederName column. The second column is a column named Animals, whose definition is the nested table ANIMALS_NT:

```
create table BREEDER
(BreederName VARCHAR2(25),
 Animals ANIMALS_NT)
```

When creating a table that includes a nested table, you must specify the name of the table that will be used to store the nested table's data. That is, the data for the nested table is not stored "inline" with the rest of the table's data. Instead, it is stored apart from the main table. The data in the Animals column will be stored in one table, and the data in the BreederName column will be stored in a separate table. Oracle will maintain pointers between the tables. In this example, the "out-of-line" data for the nested table is stored in a table named ANIMALS_NT_TAB:

```
nested table ANIMALS store as ANIMALS_NT_TAB;
```

This example highlights the importance of naming standards for collectors. If you pluralize the column names ("Animals" instead of "Animal") and consistently use suffixes (TY, NT, and so forth), you can tell what an object is just by its name. Furthermore, since nested tables and varying arrays may be based directly on previously defined datatypes, their names may mirror the names of the datatypes on which they are based. Thus, a datatype named ANIMAL_TY could be used as the basis for a varying array named ANIMALS_VA or a nested table named ANIMALS_NT. The nested table would have an associated out-of-line table named ANIMALS_NT_TAB. If you know that a table named ANIMALS_NT_TAB exists and you are consistent in your object naming, you automatically know that it stores data based on a datatype named ANIMAL_TY.

## Inserting Records into a Nested Table

You can **insert** records into a nested table by using the constructor methods for its datatype. For the Animals column, the datatype is ANIMALS_NT; thus, you will use the ANIMALS_NT constructor method. The ANIMALS_NT type, in turn, uses the ANIMAL_TY datatype. As shown in the following example, inserting a record into the BREEDER table requires you to use both the ANIMALS_NT and ANIMAL_TY constructor methods. In the example, three animals are listed for the breeder named Jane James.

```
insert into BREEDER values
('JANE JAMES',
 ANIMALS_NT(
```

```
 ANIMAL_TY('DOG', 'BUTCH', '31-MAR-01'),
 ANIMAL_TY('DOG', 'ROVER', '05-JUN-01'),
 ANIMAL_TY('DOG', 'JULIO', '10-JUN-01')
));
```

This **insert** command first specifies the name of the breeder:

```
insert into BREEDER values
('JANE JAMES',
```

Next, the value for the Animals column is entered. Since the Animals column uses the ANIMALS_NT nested table, the ANIMALS_NT constructor method is called:

```
ANIMALS_NT(
```

The ANIMALS_NT nested table uses the ANIMAL_TY datatype, so the ANIMAL_TY constructor method is called for each value inserted:

```
 ANIMAL_TY('DOG', 'BUTCH', '31-MAR-01'),
 ANIMAL_TY('DOG', 'ROVER', '05-JUN-01'),
 ANIMAL_TY('DOG', 'JULIO', '10-JUN-01')
));
```

You can see the datatypes that constitute the table and its nested table via the **describe** command. Use the **set describe depth** SQL*Plus command to enable the display of the datatype attributes.

```
set describe depth 2

desc breeder
```

| Name | Null? | Type |
|------|-------|------|
| BREEDERNAME | | VARCHAR2(25) |
| ANIMALS | | ANIMALS_NT |
| BREED | | VARCHAR2(25) |
| NAME | | VARCHAR2(25) |
| BIRTHDATE | | DATE |

You can query this metadata from USER_TAB_COLUMNS, USER_TYPES, USER_COLL_TYPES, and USER_TYPE_ATTRS data dictionary views as in the examples earlier in this chapter.

# Querying Nested Tables

Nested tables support a great variety of queries. A nested table is a column within a table. To support queries of the columns and rows of a nested table, use the **TABLE** function introduced earlier in this chapter. The **THE** clause used in prior versions of Oracle is supported for backward compatibility, but is being deprecated.

To see how the **TABLE** function is used, first consider the nested table by itself. If it were a normal column of a relational table, you would be able to query it via a normal **select** command:

```
select BirthDate /* This won't work.*/
 from ANIMALS_NT
 where Name = 'JULIO';
```

ANIMALS_NT is not a normal table; it's a datatype. To select columns (such as BirthDate) from the nested table, you first need to "flatten" the table so it can be queried. First, apply the **TABLE** function to the nested table column (BREEDER.Animals), as shown in the following listing:

```
select BreederName, N.Name, N.BirthDate
 from BREEDER, TABLE(BREEDER.Animals) N;
```

```
BREEDERNAME NAME BIRTHDATE
------------------------ ---------------------- ---------
JANE JAMES BUTCH 31-MAR-01
JANE JAMES ROVER 05-JUN-01
JANE JAMES JULIO 10-JUN-01
```

With the data in this format, it is simple to retrieve the proper row:

```
select BreederName, N.Name, N.BirthDate
 from BREEDER, TABLE(BREEDER.Animals) N
 where N.Name = 'JULIO';
```

```
BREEDERNAME NAME BIRTHDATE
------------------------ ---------------------- ---------
JANE JAMES JULIO 10-JUN-01
```

### inserts, updates, and deletes with the TABLE function

You can use the **TABLE** function whenever you need to perform **insert**s or **update**s directly against the nested table. For example, a breeder probably will have more animals as time goes by, so you need the ability to add new records to the ANIMALS_NT nested table within the BREEDER table. You will have to **insert** records into the nested table without adding new records into the BREEDER table, and you will need to relate the new Animal records to breeders who are already in the BREEDER table.

The following **insert** statement adds a new record to the nested table in Jane James' BREEDER record:

```
insert into TABLE(select Animals
 from BREEDER
 where BreederName = 'JANE JAMES')
values
(ANIMAL_TY('DOG','MARCUS','01-AUG-01'));
```

The **insert** does not provide a value for the BreederName column; we are only inserting into the nested table of a breeder's row. The **TABLE** function is again used to "flatten" the nested table in the Animals column (for Jane's row) and the new values are inserted. Note the use of the **where** clause within the **TABLE** function call to specify the rows to be acted on.

You can also update the dog's birthdate. Julio's birthdate was originally entered as 10-JUN-01 but has since been discovered to be 01-SEP-01. The following **update** changes the nested table's

BirthDate value for Julio. Its syntax and structure are very close to the query examples shown earlier in this chapter.

```
update TABLE(select Animals
 from BREEDER
 where BreederName = 'JANE JAMES') N
 set N.BirthDate = '01-SEP-01'
 where N.Name = 'JULIO';
```

You can verify this change by querying the nested table data:

```
select BreederName, N.Name, N.BirthDate
 from BREEDER, TABLE(BREEDER.Animals) N;
```

| BREEDERNAME | NAME | BIRTHDATE |
|-------------|------|-----------|
| JANE JAMES  | BUTCH  | 31-MAR-01 |
| JANE JAMES  | ROVER  | 05-JUN-01 |
| JANE JAMES  | JULIO  | 01-SEP-01 |
| JANE JAMES  | MARCUS | 01-AUG-01 |

You can delete nested table entries as well:

```
delete TABLE(select Animals
 from BREEDER
 where BreederName = 'JANE JAMES') N
 where N.Name = 'JULIO';
```

```
1 row deleted.
```

```
select BreederName, N.Name, N.BirthDate
 from BREEDER, TABLE(BREEDER.Animals) N;
```

| BREEDERNAME | NAME | BIRTHDATE |
|-------------|------|-----------|
| JANE JAMES  | BUTCH  | 31-MAR-01 |
| JANE JAMES  | ROVER  | 05-JUN-01 |
| JANE JAMES  | MARCUS | 01-AUG-01 |

# Management Issues for Nested Tables and Varying Arrays

The administrative tasks required for nested tables and varying arrays have several differences, which are discussed in the following sections, along with advice on which collector type may best meet your criteria.

# Managing Large Collections

When storing data that is related to a table, you can choose one of three methods: a varying array, a nested table, or a separate table. If you have a limited number of rows, a varying array may be appropriate. As the number of rows increases, however, you may begin to encounter performance problems while accessing the varying array. These problems may be caused by a characteristic of varying arrays: They cannot be indexed. Nested tables and standard relational tables, however, can be indexed. As a result, the performance of a varray collector may worsen as it grows in size.

**NOTE**
*As of Oracle9i, transportable tablespaces can have varying arrays.*

Varying arrays are further burdened by the difficulty in querying data from them. If varying arrays are not a good solution for your application, which alternative should you use: a nested table or a separate relational table? It depends. Nested tables and relational tables serve different purposes, so your answer depends on what you are trying to do with the data. The key differences are as follows:

- Nested tables are abstract datatypes, created via the **create type** command. Therefore, they can have methods associated with them. If you plan to attach methods to the data, then you should use nested tables instead of relational tables. Alternatively, you could consider using object views with methods, as described in Chapter 30.

- Relational tables are easily related to other relational tables. If the data may be related to many other tables, then it may be best not to nest the data within one table. Storing it in its own table will give you the greatest flexibility in managing the data relationships.

# Variability in Collectors

As noted in Chapter 4, abstract datatypes can help you to enforce standards within your database. However, you may not be able to realize the same standardization benefits when you are using collectors. Consider the TOOLS_VA varying array shown earlier in this chapter. If another application or table wants to use a TOOLS_VA varying array, that application must use the same definition for the array, including the same maximum number of values. However, the new application may have a different value for the maximum number of tools. Thus, the array must be altered to support the greatest possible number of values it may contain in any of its implementations. As a result, the usefulness of the array's limiting powers may diminish. To support multiple array limits, you would need to create multiple arrays—eliminating any object reuse benefits you may have received from creating the varying arrays. You would then need to manage the different array limits and know what the limit is in each array.

You may also find that multiple nested tables are similar, with a difference in only one or two columns. You may be tempted to create a single, all-inclusive nested table type that is used in multiple tables, but that table would also encounter management problems. You would need to know which columns of the nested table were valid for which implementations. If you cannot use the same column structure, with the same meaning and relevance of the columns in each instance, then you should not use a shared nested table datatype. If you want to use nested tables

in that environment, you should create a separate nested table datatype for each instance in which you will use the nested table, and manage them all separately. Having multiple nested table datatypes will complicate the management of the database.

## Location of the Data

In a varying array, the data in the array is stored with the rest of the data in the table. In nested tables, however, the data may be stored out-of-line. As a result, the amount of data scanned during queries that do not involve the collector data may be less for a nested table than for a varying array. That is, during a query, the database will not need to read through the data in the nested table; if a varying array is used, then the database may need to read through the varying array's data to find the data it needs. Out-of-line data, as used by nested tables, can improve the performance of queries.

Out-of-line collector data mimics the way the data would be stored in a normal relational database application. For example, in a relational application, you would store related data (such as workers and skills) in separate tables, and the tables would be physically stored apart. Out-of-line nested tables store their data apart from the main table but maintain a relationship with the main table. Out-of-line data may improve the performance of queries by distributing across multiple tables the I/O performed against the table.

Out-of-line data is also used to store the large objects (LOBs) that are stored internally (as opposed to BFILEs, which are pointers to LOBs external to the database). In the next chapter, you will see how to create and manipulate LOB values up to 4GB in length. The combination of abstract datatypes, object views, collectors, and LOBs provides a strong foundation for the implementation of an object-relational database application. In Chapter 33, you will see how to extend these objects further toward the creation of an object-oriented database.

# CHAPTER
# 32

# Using Large Objects

ou can use a LONG datatype to store character data up to 2GB in length per row; the LONG RAW datatype provides storage for long binary data. In place of LONG and LONG RAW, you can use the LOB datatypes (BLOB, CLOB, NCLOB, and BFILE) for storage of long data up to 4GB in length. While Oracle still allows LONG and LONG RAW columns to be created, Oracle recommends that you create new columns using the LOB datatypes and that you convert existing LONG and LONG RAW columns to CLOB or BLOB columns, respectively. If you use one of these datatypes to store large objects (LOBs), you can take advantage of new capabilities for viewing and manipulating the data. You can also use Oracle Text (see Chapter 24) to perform text searches on CLOB data.

In this chapter, you will see how to use the LOB datatypes and how to manipulate the data—which does not even have to be stored within the database!

# Available Datatypes

Four types of LOBs are supported:

| LOB Datatype | Description |
| --- | --- |
| BLOB | Binary LOB; binary data, up to 4GB in length, stored in the database |
| CLOB | Character LOB; character data, up to 4GB in length, stored in the database |
| BFILE | Binary File; read-only binary data stored outside the database, the length of which is limited by the operating system |
| NCLOB | A CLOB column that supports a multibyte character set |

You can create multiple LOBs per table. For example, suppose you want to create a PROPOSAL table to track formal proposals you submit. Your proposal records may consist of a series of word processing files and spreadsheets used to document and price the proposed work. The PROPOSAL table will contain VARCHAR2 datatypes (for columns such as the name of the proposal recipient) plus LOB datatypes (containing the word processing and spreadsheet files). The **create table** command in the following listing creates the PROPOSAL table:

```
create table PROPOSAL
(Proposal_ID NUMBER(10),
 Recipient_Name VARCHAR2(25),
 Proposal_Name VARCHAR2(25),
 Short_Description VARCHAR2(1000),
 Proposal_Text CLOB,
 Budget BLOB,
 Cover_Letter BFILE,
constraint PROPOSAL_PK primary key (Proposal_ID));
```

Since you may submit multiple proposals to the same recipient, assign each proposal a Proposal_ID number. The PROPOSAL table stores the recipient of the proposal, the name of

the proposal, and a short description. Then, taking advantage of the LOB datatypes available in Oracle, add three columns:

| | |
|---|---|
| Proposal_Text | A CLOB containing the text of the proposal |
| Budget | A BLOB containing a spreadsheet showing calculations of the cost and profit for the proposed work |
| Cover_Letter | A binary file (BFILE) stored outside the database that contains your cover letter that accompanies the proposal |

Each row in the PROPOSAL table will have up to three LOB values stored. Oracle will use the normal database capabilities to support data integrity and concurrency for the Proposal and Budget entries, but not for the Cover_Letter values. Since the Cover_Letter column uses the BFILE datatype, its data is stored outside the database. Internally, the database stores only a locator value that allows it to find the external file. Oracle does not guarantee the data integrity of BFILE files stored outside the database. Also, Oracle does not validate that the file exists when you insert a record using a BFILE datatype. Data concurrency and integrity are maintained only for internally stored LOBs.

The data for the LOB columns, whether stored inside or outside the database, may not be physically stored within the PROPOSAL table. Within the PROPOSAL table, Oracle stores locator values that point to data locations. For BFILE datatypes, the locator points to an external file; for BLOB and CLOB datatypes, the locator points to a separate data location that the database creates to hold the LOB data. Thus, the LOB data is not necessarily stored directly with the rest of the data in the PROPOSAL table.

Storing the data *out-of-line* like this allows the database to avoid having to scan the LOB data each time it reads multiple rows from the database. The LOB data will only be read when it is required; otherwise, only its locator values will be read. You can specify the storage parameters (tablespace and sizing) for the area used to hold the LOB data, as described in the next section.

# Specifying Storage for LOB Data

When you create a table that includes a LOB column, you can specify the storage parameters for the area used for the LOB data. Thus, for a table that has no LOB columns, you would have a **storage** clause in the **create table** command (see Chapter 20). If the table has at least one LOB column, then you also need an additional **lob** clause within your **create table** command.

Consider the PROPOSAL table, this time with **storage** and **tablespace** clauses:

```
create table PROPOSAL
(Proposal_ID NUMBER(10),
 Recipient_Name VARCHAR2(25),
 Proposal_Name VARCHAR2(25),
 Short_Description VARCHAR2(1000),
 Proposal_Text CLOB,
 Budget BLOB,
 Cover_Letter BFILE,
constraint PROPOSAL_PK primary key (Proposal_ID))
```

```
storage (initial 50K next 50K pctincrease 0)
tablespace PROPOSALS;
```

Since there are three LOB columns, the **create table** command should be modified to include the storage specifications for the out-of-line LOB data. Two of the LOB columns—Proposal_Text and Budget—will store data within the database. The revised version of the **create table** command, with the LOB storage clause specified, is shown in the following listing.

```
create table PROPOSAL
(Proposal_ID NUMBER(10),
 Recipient_Name VARCHAR2(25),
 Proposal_Name VARCHAR2(25),
 Short_Description VARCHAR2(1000),
 Proposal_Text CLOB,
 Budget BLOB,
 Cover_Letter BFILE,
constraint PROPOSAL_PK primary key (Proposal_ID))
storage (initial 50K next 50K pctincrease 0)
tablespace PROPOSALS
lob (Proposal_Text, Budget) store as
(tablespace Proposal_Lobs
 storage (initial 100K next 100K pctincrease 0)
 chunk 16K pctversion 10 nocache logging);
```

The last four lines of the **create table** command tell Oracle how to store the out-of-line LOB data. The instructions are as follows:

```
lob (Proposal_Text, Budget) store as
(tablespace Proposal_Lobs
 storage (initial 100K next 100K pctincrease 0)
 chunk 16K pctversion 10 nocache logging);
```

The **lob** clause tells Oracle that the next set of commands deals with the out-of-line storage specifications for the table's LOB columns. The two LOB columns (Proposal_Text and Budget) are explicitly listed. When the two columns' values are stored out-of-line, they are stored in a segment as specified via the **lob** clause:

```
lob (Proposal_Text, Budget) store as
```

**NOTE**
*If there were only one LOB column, you could specify a name for the LOB segment. You would name the segment immediately after the **store as** clause in the preceding command.*

The next two lines specify the tablespace and storage parameters for the out-of-line LOB storage. The **tablespace** clause assigns the out-of-line data to the PROPOSAL_LOBS tablespace, and the **storage** clause is used to specify the **initial**, **next**, and **pctincrease** values the out-of-line

data storage will use. See the entry for the **storage** clause in the Alphabetical Reference for an explanation of the available storage parameters for segments.

```
(tablespace Proposal_Lobs
 storage (initial 100K next 100K pctincrease 0)
```

Since the segments are for storing LOB data, several additional parameters are available, and they are specified within the **lob** clause:

```
 chunk 16K pctversion 10
```

The **chunk** LOB storage parameter tells Oracle how much space to allocate during each LOB value manipulation. The default **chunk** size is 1K, going up to a maximum value of 32K.

The **pctversion** parameter is the maximum percentage of overall LOB storage space used for creating new versions of the LOB. By default, older versions of the LOB data will not be overwritten until 10 percent of the available LOB storage space is used.

The last two parameters of the LOB storage space tell Oracle how to handle the LOB data during reads and writes:

```
 nocache logging);
```

The **nocache** parameter in the **lob** storage clause specifies that the LOB values are not stored in memory for faster access during queries. The default **lob** storage setting is **nocache**; its opposite is **cache**.

The **logging** parameter specifies that all operations against the LOB data will be recorded in the database's redo log files. The opposite of **logging**, **nologging**, keeps operations from being recorded in the redo log files, thereby improving the performance of table-creation operations. You can also specify the **tablespace** and **storage** parameters for a LOB index. See the **create table** command entry in the Alphabetical Reference for the full syntax related to LOB indexes.

Now that the table has been created, you can begin to enter records into it. In the next section, you will see how to insert LOB values into the PROPOSAL table and how to use the DBMS_LOB package to manipulate the values.

# Manipulating and Selecting LOB Values

LOB data can be selected or manipulated in several ways. As of Oracle9i, you can use the character string functions you would use on VARCHAR2 columns against LOB datatypes. For large LOB values ( > 100KB in length), or for more complex operations against the data, you should manipulate LOB data via the DBMS_LOB package. Other methods for manipulating LOB data include using application programming interface (API) and Oracle Call Interface (OCI) programs. In this section, you will see the use of the string functions plus an overview of the DBMS_LOB package. As these examples demonstrate, LOBs are much more flexible than LONG datatypes in terms of data manipulation possibilities.

## Initializing Values

Consider the PROPOSAL table again. The Proposal_ID column is the primary key column for the PROPOSAL table. The PROPOSAL table contains three LOB columns—one BLOB column, one

CLOB, and one BFILE. For each of the LOB columns, Oracle will store a *locator value* that tells it where to find any out-of-line data stored for the record.

When you insert a record into a table that contains LOBs, you use functions to tell Oracle to create an empty locator value for the internally stored LOB columns. An empty locator value is different from a **NULL** value. If an internally stored LOB column's value is **NULL**, then you have to set it to an empty locator value before updating it to a non-**NULL** value.

Suppose you begin to work on a proposal and enter a record in the PROPOSAL table. At this point, you have neither a budget spreadsheet nor a cover letter. The **insert** command is shown in the following listing:

```
insert into PROPOSAL
(Proposal_ID, Recipient_Name, Proposal_Name, Short_Description,
 Proposal_Text,
 Budget, Cover_Letter)
values
(1, 'DOT RODALE', 'MAINTAIN ORGANIC GARDEN', NULL,
 'This is the text of a proposal to maintain an organic garden.',
 EMPTY_BLOB(),NULL);
```

The inserted record has a Proposal_ID of 1 and a Recipient_Name of DOT RODALE. The Proposal_Name value is MAINTAIN ORGANIC GARDEN and the Short_Description column is left **NULL** for now. The Proposal_Text column is set equal to a short character string for now. To set the Budget column to an empty locator value, the EMPTY_BLOB function is used. If you had wanted to set a CLOB datatype column equal to an empty locator value, then you would have used the EMPTY_CLOB function. The Cover_Letter column, since it is an externally stored BFILE value, is set to **NULL**.

To set a LOB column to an empty locator value, you have to know its datatype:

| | |
|---|---|
| BLOB | Use EMPTY_BLOB() |
| CLOB | Use EMPTY_CLOB() |
| NCLOB | Use EMPTY_CLOB() |
| BFILE | Use BFILENAME |

You use the BFILENAME procedure to point to a directory and filename combination. Before entering a value for the directory in the BFILENAME function, a user with the DBA role or CREATE ANY DIRECTORY system privilege must create the directory. To create a directory, use the **create directory** command, as shown in the following example:

```
create directory proposal_dir as '/u01/proposal/letters';
```

When inserting BFILE entries, you refer to the logical directory name—such as proposal_dir—instead of the physical directory name on the operating system. Users with DBA authority can grant READ access to the directory names to users. See the entry for the **create directory** command in the Alphabetical Reference for further details.

You can now enter a second PROPOSAL record; this record will have a Cover_Letter value:

```
insert into PROPOSAL
(Proposal_ID, Recipient_Name, Proposal_Name, Short_Description,
 Proposal_Text, Budget,
Cover_Letter)
values
(2, 'BRAD OHMONT', 'REBUILD FENCE', NULL,
 EMPTY_CLOB(), EMPTY_BLOB(),
 BFILENAME('proposal_dir','P2.DOC'));
```

In this listing, a second proposal—rebuilding a fence—is inserted into the PROPOSAL table. The EMPTY_CLOB() and EMPTY_BLOB() functions are used to insert empty locator values in the table. The BFILENAME function tells Oracle exactly where to find the cover letter—it's in the proposal_dir directory and its name is P2.DOC. Within the BFILENAME function, the first parameter is always the directory name, and the second parameter is the name of the file within that directory.

> **NOTE**
> *The P2.DOC file does not have to exist for this record to be inserted*
> *successfully.*

When you select the value from a LOB column, Oracle uses the locator value to find the data that is associated with the LOB data. You never need to know or specify the locator values. And, as you'll see in the following sections, you can do things with LOB values that are impossible to do with LONG datatypes.

## insert with Subqueries

What if you want to duplicate a proposal record? For example, suppose you begin to work on a third proposal, and it is very similar to the first proposal:

```
insert into PROPOSAL
(Proposal_ID, Recipient_Name, Proposal_Name, Short_Description,
 Proposal_Text, Budget, Cover_Letter)
select 3, 'SKIP GATES', 'CLEAR GATES FIELD', NULL,
 Proposal_Text, Budget, Cover_Letter
 from PROPOSAL
 where Proposal_ID = 1;
```

This **insert** command tells Oracle to find the PROPOSAL record with a Proposal_ID value of 1. Take the Proposal_Text, Budget, and Cover_Letter column values and the literal values specified (3, SKIP GATES, and so forth) and insert a new record into the PROPOSAL table. Note that the inserted columns will be set to empty locator values. The ability to perform **insert**s based on queries is a significant advantage of using LOB datatypes—you cannot perform this type of **insert** if a LONG column is part of the query.

**NOTE**
*If you use **insert as select** to populate LOB values, you may have multiple BFILE values pointing to the same external file. You may need to **update** the new values to point to the correct external files. Oracle does not maintain data integrity for the external files.*

## Updating LOB Values

In the third record that was created, the Proposal_Text value was copied from the first record. To update the Proposal_Text value of the record that has a Proposal_ID of 3, execute the following command:

```
update PROPOSAL
 set Proposal_Text = 'This is the new proposal text.'
 where Proposal_ID = 3;
```

You can also **update** the Cover_Letter column to point to the correct cover letter. Use the BFILENAME function to point to the correct file:

```
update PROPOSAL
 set Cover_Letter = BFILENAME('proposal_dir', 'P3.DOC')
 where Proposal_ID = 3;
```

You can update **NULL** values of BFILE columns without first setting them to empty locator values. If you had inserted a record with a **NULL** value for Budget (a BLOB column), you could not update the Budget column's value unless you first set its value to EMPTY_BLOB() via an **update** command. After setting the value to EMPTY_BLOB() and establishing an empty locator value, you could then **update** the Budget column value.

## Using String Functions to Manipulate LOB Values

As of Oracle9i, you can use the Oracle-provided string functions against CLOB values. For example, you can use **SUBSTR**, **INSTR**, **LTRIM**, and **INITCAP** to modify the strings. See Chapter 7 for descriptions of the built-in string functions.

In the PROPOSAL table, the Proposal_Text column is defined as a CLOB datatype. Here are the three Proposal_Text values (the second is **NULL**).

```
select Proposal_Text from PROPOSAL;

PROPOSAL_TEXT
--
This is the text of a proposal to maintain an organic garden.

This is the new proposal text.
```

Applying **INITCAP** to the third record yields this result:

```
select INITCAP(Proposal_Text) from PROPOSAL
 where Proposal_ID = 3;

INITCAP(PROPOSAL_TEXT)

This Is The New Proposal Text.
```

Applying **INSTR** to all three rows returns the expected result:

```
select INSTR(Proposal_Text,'new',1,1) from PROPOSAL;

INSTR(PROPOSAL_TEXT,'NEW',1,1)

 0
 0
 13
```

You can use **SUBSTR** to return the first ten characters of the text:

```
select SUBSTR(Proposal_Text,1,10) from PROPOSAL
 where Proposal_ID = 3;

SUBSTR(PROPOSAL_TEXT,1,10)

This is th
```

However, you cannot perform **NVL** and **DECODE** on the CLOB columns:

```
select NVL(Proposal_Text, 'Null') from PROPOSAL;
 *
ERROR at line 1:
ORA-00932: inconsistent datatypes
```

For complex manipulations, you should use the DBMS_LOB package, as described in the following sections.

# Using DBMS_LOB to Manipulate LOB Values

You can use the DBMS_LOB package to change or select LOB values. In the following sections, you will see how to perform SQL functions such as **SUBSTR** and **INSTR** on LOB values, as well as how to append to LOB values, compare LOB values, and read LOB values.

The string comparison and manipulation procedures and functions available within the DBMS_LOB package are listed in Table 32-1.

The major procedures and functions available within the DBMS_LOB package are described in the following sections. When using BFILEs, the maximum number of files you can concurrently have open is limited by the setting of the SESSION_MAX_OPEN_FILES parameter in the database's system parameter file. The default maximum number of concurrently open BFILE files is 10; the maximum is either 50 or the value of the MAX_OPEN_FILES parameter, whichever is lower.

In the following examples, the Proposal_Text CLOB column is used to show the impact of the major procedures and functions.

| Subprogram | Description |
| --- | --- |
| APPEND Procedure | Appends the contents of the source LOB to the destination LOB |
| CLOSE Procedure | Closes a previously opened internal or external LOB |
| COMPARE Function | Compares two entire LOBs or parts of two LOBs |
| COPY Procedure | Copies all, or part, of the source LOB to the destination LOB |
| CREATETEMPORARY Procedure | Creates a temporary BLOB or CLOB and its corresponding index in the user's default temporary tablespace |
| ERASE Procedure | Erases all or part of a LOB |
| FILECLOSE Procedure | Closes the file |
| FILECLOSEALL Procedure | Closes all previously opened files |
| FILEEXISTS Function | Checks if the file exists on the server |
| FILEGETNAME Procedure | Gets the directory alias and filename |
| FILEISOPEN Function | Checks if the file was opened using the input BFILE locators |
| FILEOPEN Procedure | Opens a file |
| FREETEMPORARY Procedure | Frees the temporary BLOB or CLOB in the user's default temporary tablespace |
| GETCHUNKSIZE Function | Returns the amount of space used in the LOB chunk to store the LOB value |
| GETLENGTH Function | Gets the length of the LOB value |
| INSTR Function | Returns the matching position of the *nth* occurrence of the pattern in the LOB |
| ISOPEN Function | Checks to see if the LOB was already opened using the input locator |
| ISTEMPORARY Function | Checks if the locator is pointing to a temporary LOB |
| LOADFROMFILE Procedure | Loads BFILE data into an internal LOB |
| OPEN Procedure | Opens a LOB (internal, external, or temporary) in the indicated mode |
| READ Procedure | Reads data from the LOB starting at the specified offset |
| SUBSTR Function | Returns part of the LOB value starting at the specified offset |
| TRIM Procedure | Trims the LOB value to the specified shorter length |
| WRITE Procedure | Writes data to the LOB from a specified offset |
| WRITEAPPEND Procedure | Writes a buffer to the end of a LOB |

**TABLE 32-1.** *DBMS_LOB Subprograms*

## READ

The READ procedure reads a piece of a LOB value. In the PROPOSAL table example, the Proposal_
Text for the first row is

```
select Proposal_Text
 from PROPOSAL
 where Proposal_ID = 1;

PROPOSAL_TEXT

This is the text of a proposal to maintain an organic garden.
```

This is a fairly short description, so it could have been stored in a VARCHAR2 datatype column.
Since it is stored in a CLOB column, though, its maximum length is much greater than it would
have been if it had been stored in a VARCHAR2 column—it can expand to 4GB in length. For
these examples, we'll use this short string for purposes of demonstration; you can use the same
functions and operations against longer CLOB strings, as well.

The READ procedure has four parameters, which must be specified in this order:

1. The LOB locator (for either a BLOB, CLOB, or BFILE)

2. The number of bytes or characters to be read

3. The offset (starting point of the read) from the beginning of the LOB value

4. The output data from the READ procedure

If the end of the LOB value is reached before the specified number of bytes is read, the READ
procedure will return an error.

Because the READ procedure requires the LOB locator as input, the READ procedure is executed
within PL/SQL blocks. You will need to select the LOB locator value, provide that as input to the
READ procedure, and then display the text read via the DBMS_OUTPUT package.

**A WORD ABOUT THE DBMS_OUTPUT PACKAGE**     As noted in Chapter 29, you can
use the DBMS_OUTPUT package to display the values of variables within a PL/SQL block. The
PUT_LINE procedure within DBMS_OUTPUT displays the specified output on a line. Before
using the DBMS_OUTPUT package, you should first execute the **set serveroutput on** command.
In the next section, you'll see how to create the PL/SQL block that will read the data from a LOB.

**A READ EXAMPLE**     To use the READ procedure, you need to know the locator value of the
LOB you want to read. The locator value must be selected from the table that contains the LOB.
Since the locator value must be supplied as input to the READ procedure, you should use PL/SQL
variables to hold the locator value. The READ procedure, in turn, will place its output in a
PL/SQL variable. You can use the DBMS_OUTPUT package to display the output value. The
structure of the PL/SQL block for this example is as follows:

```
declare
 variable to hold locator value
 variable to hold the amount (the number of characters/bytes to read)
```

```
 variable to hold the offset
 variable to hold the output
begin
 set value for amount_var;
 set value for offset_var;
 select locator value into locator var from table;
 DBMS_LOB.READ(locator var, amount var, offset var, output var);
 DBMS_OUTPUT.PUT_LINE('Output:' || output var);
end;
```

> **NOTE**
> *See Chapter 27 for an overview of PL/SQL blocks and their*
> *components.*

For the PROPOSAL table, selecting the first ten characters from the Proposal_Text column would look like this:

```
declare
 locator_var CLOB;
 amount_var INTEGER;
 offset_var INTEGER;
 output_var VARCHAR2(10);
begin
 amount_var := 10;
 offset_var := 1;
 select Proposal_Text into locator_var
 from PROPOSAL
 where Proposal_ID = 1;
 DBMS_LOB.READ(locator_var, amount_var, offset_var, output_var);
 DBMS_OUTPUT.PUT_LINE('Start of proposal text: ' || output_var);
end;
```

When the preceding PL/SQL block is executed, the output will match the SQL **SUBSTR** example shown earlier:

```
Start of proposal text: This is th

PL/SQL procedure successfully completed.
```

The output shows the first ten characters of the Proposal_Text value, starting at the first character of the LOB value.

The PL/SQL block in the preceding example first declared the variables to use:

```
declare
 locator_var CLOB;
 amount_var INTEGER;
 offset_var INTEGER;
 output_var VARCHAR2(10);
```

Next, values were assigned to the variables:

```
begin
 amount_var := 10;
 offset_var := 1;
```

The locator value was selected from the table and stored in a variable named *locator_var* :

```
select Proposal_Text into locator_var
 from PROPOSAL
 where Proposal_ID = 1;
```

Next, the READ procedure was called, using the values that had been assigned so far:

```
DBMS_LOB.READ(locator_var, amount_var, offset_var, output_var);
```

As a result of the execution of the READ procedure, the *output_var* variable will be populated with the data that was read. The PUT_LINE procedure displays that data:

```
DBMS_OUTPUT.PUT_LINE('Start of proposal text: ' || output_var);
```

This format for PL/SQL blocks will be used throughout the rest of this chapter. You can optionally set the variable values when they are declared.

If you want to select a different portion of the Proposal_Text CLOB, just change the amount and offset variables. If you change the number of characters read, you need to change the size of the output variable, too. In the following example, 12 characters are read from the Proposal_Text, starting from the tenth character:

```
declare
 locator_var CLOB;
 amount_var INTEGER;
 offset_var INTEGER;
 output_var VARCHAR2(12);
begin
 amount_var := 12;
 offset_var := 10;
 select Proposal_Text into locator_var
 from PROPOSAL
 where Proposal_ID = 1;
 DBMS_LOB.READ(locator_var, amount_var, offset_var, output_var);
 DBMS_OUTPUT.PUT_LINE('Part of proposal text: ' || output_var);
end;
```

Output from this PL/SQL block is shown in the following listing:

```
Part of proposal text: he text of a

PL/SQL procedure successfully completed.
```

If Proposal_Text had been created as a VARCHAR2 column, you could have selected this data using the **SUBSTR** function. However, you would have been limited to a maximum column length of 4,000 characters. Also, note that the LOB column can contain binary data (BLOB datatypes), and you can use the READ procedure to select data from BLOBs in the same way you select from CLOBs. For BLOBs, you should **declare** the output buffer to use the RAW datatype. In PL/SQL, RAW and VARCHAR2 datatypes (used for the output variables for CLOB and BLOB reads) have a maximum length of 32,767 characters.

## SUBSTR

The SUBSTR function within the DBMS_LOB package performs the SQL **SUBSTR** function on a LOB value. This function has three input parameters, which must be specified in this order:

1. The LOB locator

2. The number of bytes or characters to be read

3. The offset (starting point of the read) from the beginning of the LOB value

Because SUBSTR is a function, there is no output variable value returned directly from SUBSTR, as there was with READ. For the READ procedure, you declared an output variable and then populated it within the READ procedure call. The PL/SQL block used for the READ procedure is shown in the following listing, with the lines related to the output variable shown in bold:

```
declare
 locator_var CLOB;
 amount_var INTEGER;
 offset_var INTEGER;
 output_var VARCHAR2(12);
begin
 amount_var := 12;
 offset_var := 10;
 select Proposal_Text into locator_var
 from PROPOSAL
 where Proposal_ID = 1;
 DBMS_LOB.READ(locator_var, amount_var, offset_var, output_var);
 DBMS_OUTPUT.PUT_LINE('Section of proposal text: ' || output_var);
end;
```

Since SUBSTR is a function, you will populate the output variable differently. The format is

```
output_var := DBMS_LOB.SUBSTR(locator_var, amount_var, offset_var);
```

The preceding PL/SQL statement uses the SUBSTR function of the DBMS_LOB package to select 12 characters from the Proposal_Text LOB column, starting at the tenth character. The output is shown in the following listing.

```
Section of proposal text: he text of a
PL/SQL procedure successfully completed.
```

The equivalent SQL function call is

```
select SUBSTR(Proposal_Text,10,12)
 from PROPOSAL
 where Proposal_ID = 1;
```

The SUBSTR example differs from the READ example in only two ways: the name of the function call, and the manner of assigning a value to the output variable. As with the READ procedure example, the PUT_LINE procedure of the DBMS_OUTPUT package is used to display the results.

In general, you should use the SUBSTR function whenever you are interested in selecting only a specific section of the LOB value. The READ function can be used to select only a portion of a text string (as in the previous examples), but it is more often used within a loop. For example, suppose the LOB value is larger than the largest allowed RAW or VARCHAR2 variable in PL/SQL (32,767 characters). In that case, you can use the READ procedure within a loop to read all the data from the LOB value. Refer to Chapter 27 for details on the different loop options available in PL/SQL.

## INSTR

The INSTR function within the DBMS_LOB package performs the SQL **INSTR** function on a LOB value.

The INSTR function has four input parameters, which must be specified in this order:

1. The LOB locator

2. The pattern to be tested for (RAW bytes for BLOBs, character strings for CLOBs)

3. The offset (starting point of the read) from the beginning of the LOB value

4. The occurrence of the pattern within the LOB value

The INSTR function within DBMS_LOB searches the LOB for a specific pattern of bytes or characters. The occurrence variable allows you to specify which occurrence of the pattern within the searched value should be returned. The output of the INSTR function is the position of the start of the pattern within the searched string. For example, in SQL,

```
INSTR('ABCABC', 'A', 1, 1) = 1
```

means that within the string ABCABC, the pattern A is searched for, starting at the first position of the string, and looking for the first occurrence. The A is found in the first position of the searched string. If you start the search at the second position of the string, the answer will be different:

```
INSTR('ABCABC', 'A', 2, 1) = 4
```

Since this **INSTR** starts at the second position, the first A is not part of the value that is searched. Instead, the first A found is the one in the fourth position.

If you change the last parameter in the SQL **INSTR** to look for the second occurrence of the string A, starting at the second position, then the pattern is not found:

```
INSTR('ABCABC', 'A', 2, 2) = 0
```

If the SQL **INSTR** function cannot find the matching occurrence of the pattern, then a 0 is returned. The INSTR function of the DBMS_LOB package operates in the same manner.

Because INSTR is a function, you need to assign its output variable in the same manner as the SUBSTR function's output variable was assigned. In the following listing, the Proposal_Text CLOB value is searched for the string 'pr'. A *position_var* variable is declared to hold the output of the INSTR function.

```
declare
 locator_var CLOB;
 pattern_var VARCHAR2(2);
 offset_var INTEGER;
 occur_var INTEGER;
 position_var INTEGER;
begin
 pattern_var := 'pr';
 offset_var := 1;
 occur_var := 1;
 select Proposal_Text into locator_var
 from PROPOSAL
 where Proposal_ID = 1;
 position_var := DBMS_LOB.INSTR(locator_var, pattern_var,
offset_var, occur_var);
 DBMS_OUTPUT.PUT_LINE('Found string at position: ' || position_var);
end;
```

The output would be

```
Found string at position: 23

PL/SQL procedure successfully completed.
```

The output shows that the search string 'pr' is found within the Proposal_Text, starting at the twenty-third character of the LOB value. Since Oracle9i supports SQL string functions against CLOB columns, this function call is equivalent to the following query:

```
select INSTR(Proposal_Text ,'pr',1,1)
 from PROPOSAL
 where Proposal_ID = 1;
```

## GETLENGTH

The GETLENGTH function of the DBMS_LOB package returns the length of the LOB value. The DBMS_LOB.GETLENGTH function is similar in function to the SQL **LENGTH** function, but is used only for LOB values.

The GETLENGTH function of the DBMS_LOB package has only one input parameter: the locator value for the LOB. In the following listing, variables are declared to hold the locator value and the output value. The GETLENGTH function is then executed, and the result is reported via the PUT_LINE procedure:

```
declare
 locator_var CLOB;
 length_var INTEGER;
begin
 select Proposal_Text into locator_var
 from PROPOSAL
 where Proposal_ID = 1;
 length_var := DBMS_LOB.GETLENGTH(locator_var);
 DBMS_OUTPUT.PUT_LINE('Length of LOB: ' || length_var);
end;
```

The following is the GETLENGTH output:

```
Length of LOB: 61

PL/SQL procedure successfully completed.
```

If the LOB value is **NULL**, then the GETLENGTH function will return a value of **NULL**.
   The equivalent SQL function for CLOB values is

```
select LENGTH(Proposal_Text)
 from PROPOSAL
 where Proposal_ID = 1;
```

## COMPARE
The COMPARE function of the DBMS_LOB package compares two LOB values. If the two LOB
values are the same, then the COMPARE function returns a 0; otherwise, it returns a non-zero
integer value (usually 1 or -1). To execute the COMPARE function, the DBMS_LOB package
essentially performs two READ functions and compares the results. Thus, for each of the LOB
values to be compared, you need to supply a locator value and an offset value; the number of
characters or bytes to be compared will be the same for both LOB values. You can only compare
LOBs of the same datatype.
   The COMPARE function has five input parameters, which must be specified in this order:

1. The LOB locator for the first LOB

2. The LOB locator for the second LOB

3. The amount variable (the number of bytes or characters to compare)

4. The offset (starting point of the read) from the beginning of the first LOB value

5. The offset (starting point of the read) from the beginning of the second LOB value

Since the two LOBs being compared can have different offset values, you can compare the first
part of one LOB value with the second part of a different LOB value. The example in the following

listing compares the first 25 characters of the Proposal_Text values from two entries: the Proposal_ID 1 record, and the Proposal_ID 3 record:

```
declare
 first_locator_var CLOB;
 second_locator_var CLOB;
 amount_var INTEGER;
 first_offset_var INTEGER;
 second_offset_var INTEGER;
 output_var INTEGER;
begin
 amount_var := 25;
 first_offset_var := 1;
 second_offset_var := 1;
 select Proposal_Text into first_locator_var
 from PROPOSAL
 where Proposal_ID = 1;
 select Proposal_Text into second_locator_var
 from PROPOSAL
 where Proposal_ID = 3;
 output_var :=DBMS_LOB.COMPARE(first_locator_var, second_locator_var,
 amount_var, first_offset_var, second_offset_var);
 DBMS_OUTPUT.PUT_LINE('Comparison value (0 if the same): '||
 output_var);
end;
```

The following is the output:

```
Comparison value (0 if the same): 1

PL/SQL procedure successfully completed.
```

If the two strings are the same, then the COMPARE function will return a 0.

In the following listing, the same two LOBs are compared, but this time only their first five characters are used for the comparison. Since both start with the characters "This ", the COMPARE will return a 0.

```
declare
 first_locator_var CLOB;
 second_locator_var CLOB;
 amount_var INTEGER;
 first_offset_var INTEGER;
 second_offset_var INTEGER;
 output_var INTEGER;
begin
 amount_var := 5;
 first_offset_var := 1;
 second_offset_var := 1;
 select Proposal_Text into first_locator_var
 from PROPOSAL
```

```
 where Proposal_ID = 1;
 select Proposal_Text into second_locator_var
 from PROPOSAL
 where Proposal_ID = 3;
 output_var :=DBMS_LOB.COMPARE(first_locator_var, second_locator_var,
 amount_var, first_offset_var, second_offset_var);
 DBMS_OUTPUT.PUT_LINE('Comparison value (0 if the same): ' ||
 output_var);
end;

Comparison value (0 if the same): 0

PL/SQL procedure successfully completed.
```

The COMPARE function allows you to compare character strings to character strings and compare binary data to binary data. If you are using the COMPARE function on BLOB columns, you should define the locator variables as RAW datatypes.

## WRITE

The WRITE procedure of the DBMS_LOB package allows you to write data in specific locations of the LOB. For example, you can write binary data into a section of a BLOB, overwriting the existing data there. You can write character data into CLOB fields using the WRITE procedure. This procedure has four input parameters, which must be specified in this order:

1. The LOB locator for the LOB

2. The amount variable (the number of bytes or characters to write)

3. The offset (starting point of the write) from the beginning of the LOB value

4. The buffer variable assigned to the character string or binary data being added

Because the WRITE procedure updates the LOB value, you should first lock the row via a **select for update**, as shown in bold in the following listing. In this example, a record is selected and locked. The text ADD NEW TEXT is then written to the LOB value, overwriting the data starting in position 10 (as defined by the offset variable).

```
declare
 locator_var CLOB;
 amount_var INTEGER;
 offset_var INTEGER;
 buffer_var VARCHAR2(12);
begin
 amount_var := 12;
 offset_var := 10;
 buffer_var := 'ADD NEW TEXT';
 select Proposal_Text into locator_var
 from PROPOSAL
 where Proposal_ID = 3
```

```
 for update;
 DBMS_LOB.WRITE(locator_var, amount_var, offset_var, buffer_var);
commit;
end;
```

Since the WRITE procedure changes the data, a **commit** command is added before the **end** clause of the PL/SQL block.

For the WRITE procedure, no output is provided. To see the changed data, you need to either call the READ procedure (within the same PL/SQL block, if you want) or select the LOB value from the table again:

```
select Proposal_Text
 from PROPOSAL
 where Proposal_ID = 3;

PROPOSAL_TEXT
--
This is tADD NEW TEXTsal text.
```

The WRITE procedure overwrote 12 characters, starting at the tenth character of the Proposal_Text. You can use the WRITEAPPEND procedure to append new data to the end of an existing LOB value.

For CLOB data, you can rewrite this using an **update** statement combined with **SUBSTR** and concatenation functions.

## APPEND

The APPEND procedure of the DBMS_LOB package appends data from one LOB to a second LOB. Since this amounts to an update of a LOB value, the record being updated should be locked prior to executing the APPEND procedure.

The APPEND procedure takes only two parameters: the locator value for the destination LOB, and the locator value for the source LOB. If either parameter is **NULL**, the APPEND procedure will return an error.

In the following example, two locator variables are defined. The first locator variable is named *dest_locator_var*; this is the locator value for the LOB into which the data is to be appended. The second locator variable, *source_locator_var*, is the locator value for the source data that is to be appended to the destination LOB. The destination LOB, since it is being updated, is locked via a **select for update** command. In this example, the Proposal_Text value for the Proposal_ID 1 record is appended to the Proposal_Text value for the Proposal_ID 3 record:

```
declare
 dest_locator_var CLOB;
 source_locator_var CLOB;
begin
 select Proposal_Text into dest_locator_var
 from PROPOSAL
 where Proposal_ID = 3
 for update;
 select Proposal_Text into source_locator_var
 from PROPOSAL
```

```
 where Proposal_ID = 1;
 DBMS_LOB.APPEND(dest_locator_var, source_locator_var);
commit;
end;
```

To see the changed data, you can select the record from the PROPOSAL table:

```
select Proposal_Text
 from PROPOSAL
 where Proposal_ID = 3;

PROPOSAL_TEXT
--
This is tADD NEW TEXTsal text.This is the text of a proposal to
maintain an orga
```

What happened to the rest of the text? By default, only 80 characters of LONG and LOB values are displayed during queries. To see the rest of the text, use the **set long** command:

```
set long 1000

select Proposal_Text
 from PROPOSAL
 where Proposal_ID = 3;

PROPOSAL_TEXT
--
This is tADD NEW TEXTsal text.This is the text of a proposal to
maintain an organic garden.
```

In this example, the first 1,000 characters of the LOB value were displayed. If you need to know how long the LOB is, use the GETLENGTH function as described earlier in this chapter.

In addition to allowing you to append CLOB values, the APPEND procedure allows you to append BLOB values. When appending BLOB data, you need to be aware of the format of the BLOB data and the impact of appending new data on the end of the BLOB value. For BLOB values, the APPEND function may be most useful for applications in which the BLOB contains only raw data (such as digital data transmissions) rather than formatted binary data (such as spreadsheet files formatted by a program).

For CLOB data, you could rewrite this with an **update** statement, setting the Proposal_Text value equal to the concatenation of multiple values.

## ERASE

You can use the ERASE procedure of the DBMS_LOB package to erase the characters or bytes in any part of a LOB. You can use ERASE to erase the entire LOB value, or you can specify which section of the LOB to erase. ERASE is similar in function to WRITE. If you ERASE data in a BLOB value, the data is replaced with zero-byte filler. If you ERASE data in a CLOB value, spaces are inserted into the CLOB.

Since you are updating a LOB value, you should follow the standard procedures for LOB updates: lock the row and commit when the procedure has completed.

In the following PL/SQL block, a portion of the Proposal_Text for the record with Proposal_ID 3 is erased. The erased characters will start at an offset of 10 and continue for 17 characters. The parameters for the ERASE procedure, in order, are

**1.** The LOB locator for the LOB

**2.** The amount variable (the number of bytes or characters to erase)

**3.** The offset (starting point of the erasure) from the beginning of the LOB value

```
declare
 locator_var CLOB;
 amount_var INTEGER;
 offset_var INTEGER;
begin
 amount_var := 17;
 offset_var := 10;
 select Proposal_Text into locator_var
 from PROPOSAL
 where Proposal_ID = 3
 for update;
 DBMS_LOB.ERASE(locator_var, amount_var, offset_var);
commit;
end;
```

The change to the record can be seen by querying the Proposal_Text value:

```
select Proposal_Text
 from PROPOSAL
 where Proposal_ID = 3;

PROPOSAL_TEXT

This is t ext.This is the text of a proposal to
maintain an organic garden.
```

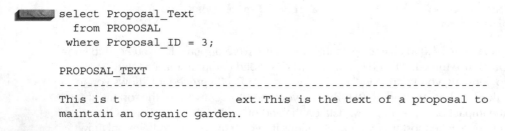

**NOTE**
*The space previously held by the erased data is replaced by blanks; the rest of the data in the LOB does not change its position.*

For CLOB data, you can rewrite this operation using an **update** statement, setting a new value for Proposal_Text by concatenating **SUBSTR** results and a blank string.

## TRIM
You can use the TRIM procedure of the DBMS_LOB package to reduce the size of a LOB value by trimming characters or bytes from the end of the value (such as the SQL **RTRIM** function). When the TRIM procedure is executed, you specify the locator value for the LOB and the LOB's new length.

In the following listing, the Proposal_Text for the Proposal_ID 3 record is trimmed to its first ten characters. Since the TRIM procedure changes the data, a **commit** command is added before the **end** clause of the PL/SQL block.

```
declare
 locator_var CLOB;
 new_length_var INTEGER;
begin
 new_length_var := 10;
 select Proposal_Text into locator_var
 from PROPOSAL
 where Proposal_ID = 3
 for update;
 DBMS_LOB.TRIM(locator_var, new_length_var);
commit;
end;
```

For the TRIM procedure, no output is provided. To see the changed data, you need to select the LOB value from the table again:

```
select Proposal_Text
 from PROPOSAL
 where Proposal_ID = 3;

PROPOSAL_TEXT
--
This is t
```

The sample output shows the results of the TRIM procedure following the ERASE procedure executed in the preceding section. For CLOB data, you could rewrite this as a simple **update**:

```
update PROPOSAL
 set Proposal_Text = SUBSTR(Proposal_Text,1,10)
 where Proposal_ID = 3;
```

## COPY

You can use the COPY procedure of the DBMS_LOB package to copy data from a part of one LOB into a second LOB. Unlike the APPEND procedure, you do not have to copy the full text of one LOB value into another. During the COPY procedure, you can specify the offset to read from and the offset to write to. The five parameters of the COPY procedure are, in order:

1. The destination LOB locator

2. The source LOB locator

3. The amount (the number of characters or bytes to copy)

4. The offset to start writing to within the destination LOB value

5. The offset to start reading from within the destination LOB value

COPY is a combination of the READ and WRITE capabilities. Like the WRITE operation, the COPY procedure modifies the LOB value. Therefore, the record should first be locked, and the PL/SQL block must contain a **commit** command. In the following example, the first 61 characters of the Proposal_ID 1 record are copied to the Proposal_ID 3 record. Since the destination LOB uses an offset of 1, the copied data will *overwrite* data within the destination LOB.

```
declare
 dest_locator_var CLOB;
 source_locator_var CLOB;
 amount_var INTEGER;
 dest_offset_var INTEGER;
 source_offset_var INTEGER;
begin
 amount_var := 61;
 dest_offset_var := 1;
 source_offset_var := 1;
 select Proposal_Text into dest_locator_var
 from PROPOSAL
 where Proposal_ID = 3
 for update;
 select Proposal_Text into source_locator_var
 from PROPOSAL
 where Proposal_ID = 1;
 DBMS_LOB.COPY(dest_locator_var, source_locator_var,
 amount_var, dest_offset_var, source_offset_var);
commit;
end;
```

The COPY procedure displays no output. To see the changed data, you need to select the LOB value from the table again:

```
select Proposal_Text
 from PROPOSAL
 where Proposal_ID = 3;

PROPOSAL_TEXT
--
This is the text of a proposal to maintain an organic garden.
```

## Using the BFILE Functions and Procedures

Since BFILE values are stored externally, several functions and procedures are used to manipulate the files prior to executing READ, SUBSTR, INSTR, GETLENGTH, or COMPARE operations on BFILE LOBs. The BFILE-related procedures and functions within DBMS_LOB, shown earlier in Table 32-1, allow you to open files, close files, get the filename, check whether a file exists, and check whether a file is open. The existence-check function is necessary because Oracle does not maintain the data stored in the external file; Oracle only maintains the pointer created via the BFILENAME procedure when the record is inserted or updated. You should use the procedures and functions in Table 32-1 to control the files used by your PL/SQL code. For example, to read the first ten bytes from the Cover_Letter BFILE for the Proposal_ID 2 record, you would OPEN the

In the following listing, the Proposal_Text for the Proposal_ID 3 record is trimmed to its first ten characters. Since the TRIM procedure changes the data, a **commit** command is added before the **end** clause of the PL/SQL block.

```
declare
 locator_var CLOB;
 new_length_var INTEGER;
begin
 new_length_var := 10;
 select Proposal_Text into locator_var
 from PROPOSAL
 where Proposal_ID = 3
 for update;
 DBMS_LOB.TRIM(locator_var, new_length_var);
commit;
end;
```

For the TRIM procedure, no output is provided. To see the changed data, you need to select the LOB value from the table again:

```
select Proposal_Text
 from PROPOSAL
 where Proposal_ID = 3;
```

```
PROPOSAL_TEXT
--
This is t
```

The sample output shows the results of the TRIM procedure following the ERASE procedure executed in the preceding section. For CLOB data, you could rewrite this as a simple **update**:

```
update PROPOSAL
 set Proposal_Text = SUBSTR(Proposal_Text,1,10)
 where Proposal_ID = 3;
```

## COPY

You can use the COPY procedure of the DBMS_LOB package to copy data from a part of one LOB into a second LOB. Unlike the APPEND procedure, you do not have to copy the full text of one LOB value into another. During the COPY procedure, you can specify the offset to read from and the offset to write to. The five parameters of the COPY procedure are, in order:

1. The destination LOB locator

2. The source LOB locator

3. The amount (the number of characters or bytes to copy)

4. The offset to start writing to within the destination LOB value

5. The offset to start reading from within the destination LOB value

COPY is a combination of the READ and WRITE capabilities. Like the WRITE operation, the COPY procedure modifies the LOB value. Therefore, the record should first be locked, and the PL/SQL block must contain a **commit** command. In the following example, the first 61 characters of the Proposal_ID 1 record are copied to the Proposal_ID 3 record. Since the destination LOB uses an offset of 1, the copied data will *overwrite* data within the destination LOB.

```
declare
 dest_locator_var CLOB;
 source_locator_var CLOB;
 amount_var INTEGER;
 dest_offset_var INTEGER;
 source_offset_var INTEGER;
begin
 amount_var := 61;
 dest_offset_var := 1;
 source_offset_var := 1;
 select Proposal_Text into dest_locator_var
 from PROPOSAL
 where Proposal_ID = 3
 for update;
 select Proposal_Text into source_locator_var
 from PROPOSAL
 where Proposal_ID = 1;
 DBMS_LOB.COPY(dest_locator_var, source_locator_var,
 amount_var, dest_offset_var, source_offset_var);
commit;
end;
```

The COPY procedure displays no output. To see the changed data, you need to select the LOB value from the table again:

```
select Proposal_Text
 from PROPOSAL
 where Proposal_ID = 3;

PROPOSAL_TEXT

This is the text of a proposal to maintain an organic garden.
```

## Using the BFILE Functions and Procedures

Since BFILE values are stored externally, several functions and procedures are used to manipulate the files prior to executing READ, SUBSTR, INSTR, GETLENGTH, or COMPARE operations on BFILE LOBs. The BFILE-related procedures and functions within DBMS_LOB, shown earlier in Table 32-1, allow you to open files, close files, get the filename, check whether a file exists, and check whether a file is open. The existence-check function is necessary because Oracle does not maintain the data stored in the external file; Oracle only maintains the pointer created via the BFILENAME procedure when the record is inserted or updated. You should use the procedures and functions in Table 32-1 to control the files used by your PL/SQL code. For example, to read the first ten bytes from the Cover_Letter BFILE for the Proposal_ID 2 record, you would OPEN the

file and then execute the READ procedure. The PUT_LINE procedure of the DBMS_OUTPUT package can then be called to show the data that was read.

If you use an Exception Handling section in your PL/SQL block, then you need to be sure to include FILECLOSE procedure calls within the declared exceptions. (Refer to Chapter 27 for further details on exception handling within PL/SQL blocks.)

To move data from an external file into a BLOB datatype, you can create a BFILE datatype in a table and use the **BFILENAME** function to create a LOB locator that points to the external file. The **BFILENAME** function takes two parameters: the directory name and the filename. For example:

```
insert into PROPOSAL (Proposal_ID, Cover_Letter)
values (4, BFILENAME ('proposal_dir','extfile.doc'));
```

You can then open the file and use the LOADFROMFILE procedure to load the BLOB datatype with the data from the external file.

If the data is presently in a LONG datatype, you can change it to a CLOB or NCLOB column via the **alter table** command. You can also use **alter table** to change a LONG RAW column to a BLOB datatype column. For **insert as select** operations, you can use the **TO_LOB** SQL function to move the data from the LONG column to a BLOB column.

# Deleting LOBS

When you delete LOB values, the locator value is deleted. If the deleted value is an internal LOB (BLOB, CLOB, or NCLOB), then both the locator and the LOB value are deleted. If the deleted value is an external LOB (BFILE), then only the locator value is deleted; you will need to manually delete the file to which the locator points.

# CHAPTER
## 33

# Advanced
# Object-Oriented
# Concepts

o far, all of the object-oriented programming (OOP) features of Oracle shown in this book have shared two characteristics: They are embedded objects, and they are column objects. An *embedded object* is one that is completely contained within another. For example, a nested table is contained within a table, so it is an embedded object. Although a nested table's data is stored apart from the main table, its data can only be accessed via the main table. A *column object* is one that is represented as a column in a table. For example, a varying array is represented as a column in a table, so it is a column object.

To take advantage of OOP capabilities, a database must also support *row objects*—objects that are represented as rows instead of columns. The row objects are not embedded objects; instead, they are *referenced objects,* accessible via references from other objects. In this chapter, you will see how row objects are created and referenced.

As you will see in this chapter, row objects can be extended for use within some of the objects discussed in prior chapters (such as object views). In addition to row objects, this chapter covers the application of objects to PL/SQL—creating *object PL/SQL.*

# Row Objects vs. Column Objects

The distinction between row objects and column objects is critical. First, consider column objects. Column objects are based on extensions of features already in the database. An abstract datatype or a varying array can be embedded as a column within a table. A nested table or a large object (LOB) can be stored in a single column of a table. In each case, the object is represented as a column within a table.

Nested tables and LOBs, however, involve data that is stored out-of-line from the main table. When you use a LOB (refer to Chapter 32), you specify the storage values for the table that will store the LOB data, and Oracle creates LOB locators that point from the main table to the rows in the LOB table. When you create a nested table, you specify the name of the table in which the nested table's records will be stored—and Oracle creates pointers from the main table to the records in the nested tables. Thus, the main table and its embedded nested table are related.

In row objects, the objects are represented as rows, not columns. The data is not embedded within the main table; instead, the main table contains a reference to another table. Nested tables, since they are stored apart from the main table, provide a useful tool for understanding row objects. What if the nested table's data is not embedded within the main table, and each of its rows is a row object? The main table will define references to the related data.

The object-relational features of Oracle described in earlier chapters relied on column objects. In this chapter, the focus is on the advanced OOP capabilities, which are based on row objects. You use row objects to create references between the rows of different tables.

# Object Tables and OIDs

In an *object table,* each row is a row object. An object table differs from a normal relational table in several ways. First, each row within the object table has an *OID*—an object identifier value—assigned by Oracle when the row is created. Second, the rows of an object table can be referenced by other objects within the database.

You can create an object table via the **create table** command. Consider the ANIMAL_TY datatype shown in previous chapters:

```
create or replace type ANIMAL_TY as object
(Breed VARCHAR2(25),
 Name VARCHAR2(25),
 BirthDate DATE);
```

> **NOTE**
> *To keep this example simple, the ANIMAL_TY datatype is created without any member functions.*

To create an object table of the ANIMAL_TY datatype, issue the following **create table** command:

```
create table ANIMAL of ANIMAL_TY;

Table created.
```

Note that the command has an unusual syntax—creating the table **of** an abstract datatype. The resulting table may first appear to be a normal relational table:

```
describe ANIMAL

Name Null? Type
------------------------------ ------- --------
BREED VARCHAR2(25)
NAME VARCHAR2(25)
BIRTHDATE DATE
```

The ANIMAL table's columns map to the attributes of the ANIMAL_TY datatype. However, there are significant differences in how you can use the table, since it is an object table. As noted earlier in this section, each row within the object table will have an OID value, and the rows can be referenced as objects.

## Inserting Rows into Object Tables

Because ANIMAL is an object table, you can use its datatype's constructor method when **insert**ing data into the table. Since the ANIMAL table is based on the ANIMAL_TY abstract datatype, the ANIMAL_TY constructor method can be used when **insert**ing values into ANIMAL.

> **NOTE**
> *Refer to Chapters 4 and 30 for detailed discussions of constructor methods.*

In the following listing, three rows are **insert**ed into the ANIMAL object table. In each command, the ANIMAL_TY constructor method is called.

```
insert into ANIMAL values
 (ANIMAL_TY('MULE','FRANCES', '01-APR-02'));
insert into ANIMAL values
```

```
 (ANIMAL_TY('DOG','BENJI', '03-SEP-01'));
insert into ANIMAL values
 (ANIMAL_TY('CROCODILE','LYLE', '14-MAY-00'));
```

If the abstract datatype on which the object table is based is itself based on a second abstract datatype, you may need to nest calls to multiple constructor methods within your **insert** command. (Refer to Chapter 4 for examples of nested abstract datatypes.)

**NOTE**
*If an object table is based on a datatype that does not contain any nested datatypes, you can also **insert** records into the object table using the normal **insert** command syntax for relational tables.*

When you **insert** a row into an object table, Oracle assigns an OID to the row. Having an OID allows you to use the row as a referenceable object. OID values are not reused.

## Selecting Values from Object Tables

When the ANIMAL table was created, it was based entirely on the ANIMAL_TY datatype:

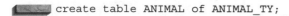
```
create table ANIMAL of ANIMAL_TY;
```

When you select from a table that contains an abstract datatype, you refer to the abstract datatype's columns as part of the table's columns. That is, if you used the ANIMAL_TY datatype as the basis for a *column* named Animal, then you would select the animal names by selecting Animal.Name from the table.

An object table, though, is based on a datatype—it has no other columns. Therefore, you do not need to reference the datatype when accessing the columns. To select the names from the ANIMAL table, just query the datatype's attributes directly:

```
select Name
 from ANIMAL;

NAME

FRANCES
BENJI
LYLE
```

You can refer to the columns within the **where** clause just as if ANIMAL were a relational table:

```
select Name
 from ANIMAL
 where Breed = 'CROCODILE';

NAME

LYLE
```

If the ANIMAL_TY datatype used another abstract datatype for one of its columns, that datatype's column would be referenced during all **select**s, **update**s, and **delete**s. (Refer to Chapter 4 for examples of queries from nested abstract datatypes.)

## Updates and Deletes from Object Tables

If the object table is based on an abstract datatype that uses no other abstract datatypes, then an **update** or **delete** of an object table uses the same format as you would use for relational tables. In this example, the ANIMAL_TY datatype does not use any other abstract datatype for one of its columns, so your **update**s and **delete**s from the ANIMAL object table behave the same as if ANIMAL were a relational table.

In the following command, one of the rows of ANIMAL is **update**d:

```
update ANIMAL
 set BirthDate = '01-MAY-00'
 where Name = 'LYLE';

1 row updated.
```

Note that during the **update**, the columns of the object table are referred to as if ANIMAL were a relational table. During a **delete**, you use the same means to reference the object table's columns in the **where** clause:

```
delete from ANIMAL
 where Name = 'LYLE';

1 row deleted.
```

Keeping a crocodile alongside mules and dogs probably wasn't such a good idea anyway.

## The REF Function

The **REF** function allows you to reference existing row objects. For example, the ANIMAL table has (after the deletion of one row, shown in the previous section) two row objects, each of which has an OID value assigned to it. You can see the OID assigned to each row by using the **REF** function, as shown here:

```
select REF(A)
 from ANIMAL A
 where Name = 'FRANCES';

REF(A)
--
0000280209FFD8EC317DA111D6B008444553544200FFD8EC307
DA111D6B0084445535442000041231600000
```

**NOTE**
*Your REF value should be different than the one shown here, but should have the same format.*

In this example, the ANIMAL table was given the alias *A*, and that alias was used as input to the **REF** function. The output shows the OID for the row object that met the limiting condition of the query.

**NOTE**
*The REF function takes as its input the alias given to the object table. The other functions shown later in this chapter also take aliases as inputs, so you should be familiar with this syntax.*

Since the **REF** function can only reference row objects, you cannot use it to reference column objects. Column objects include abstract datatypes, LOBs, and collectors.

As you can see, the **REF** function by itself does not give you any useful information. You need to use another function—**DEREF**—that translates the **REF** output into values. You can then use **REF** and **DEREF** to reference row object values, as described in the next section.

# Using the DEREF Function

The **REF** function takes a row object as its argument and returns a reference value. The **DEREF** function does the opposite—it takes a reference value (the OID generated for a reference) and returns the value of the row object.

Earlier in this chapter, the ANIMAL object table was created using the ANIMAL_TY abstract datatype:

```
create table ANIMAL of ANIMAL_TY;
```

To see how **DEREF** and **REF** work together, consider a table that is related to the ANIMAL table. The KEEPER table will track the people who take care of the animals. It will have a column for the name of the keeper (KeeperName) and a reference to the ANIMAL object table (AnimalKept), as shown in the following listing:

```
create table KEEPER
(KeeperName VARCHAR2(25),
 AnimalKept REF ANIMAL_TY);
```

The first part of the **create table** command looks normal:

```
create table KEEPER
(KeeperName VARCHAR2(25),
```

but the last line shows a new feature:

```
AnimalKept REF ANIMAL_TY);
```

The AnimalKept column references data that is stored elsewhere. The **REF** function points the AnimalKept column to a row object of the ANIMAL_TY datatype. Since ANIMAL is an object table of the ANIMAL_TY datatype, the AnimalKept column can point to the row objects within the ANIMAL object table. You can point the REF to any object table of that type.

When you **describe** the KEEPER table, you can see that its AnimalKept column relies on a **REF**:

```
describe KEEPER

Name Null? Type
----------------------------------- -------- ----
KEEPERNAME VARCHAR2(25)
ANIMALKEPT REF OF ANIMAL_TY
```

To see the full details, use a higher value for the describe depth:

```
set describe depth 2

desc KEEPER

Name Null? Type
--------------------------------------- -------- ----------------
KEEPERNAME VARCHAR2(25)
ANIMALKEPT REF OF ANIMAL_TY
 BREED VARCHAR2(25)
 NAME VARCHAR2(25)
 BIRTHDATE DATE
```

Now, **insert** a record into KEEPER. You need to use the **REF** function to store the ANIMAL references in the AnimalKept column.

```
insert into KEEPER
select 'CATHERINE WEILZ',
 REF(A)
 from ANIMAL A
 where Name = 'BENJI';
```

Let's look at this **insert** command closely. First, the KeeperName value is selected as a literal value:

```
insert into KEEPER
select 'CATHERINE WEILZ',
```

Next, the value for the AnimalKept column must be specified. But the datatype of AnimalKept is REF OF ANIMAL_TY, so you must select the reference from the ANIMAL object table to populate the AnimalKept column:

```
 REF(A)
 from ANIMAL A
 where Name = 'BENJI';
```

What's going on here? First, the ANIMAL object table is queried, and the **REF** function returns the OID for the row object selected. The OID is then stored in the KEEPER table as a pointer to that row object in the ANIMAL object table.

Does the KEEPER table contain the animal information? No. KEEPER contains the name of the keeper and a reference to a row object in the ANIMAL table. You can see the reference OID by querying KEEPER:

```
select * from KEEPER;

KEEPERNAME

ANIMALKEPT
--
CATHERINE WEILZ
0000220208FFD8EC327DA111D6B008444553544200FFD8EC307DA111D6B0084445
53544200
```

The AnimalKept column, as shown in this listing, contains the reference to the row object, not the value of the data stored in the row object.

You can't see the referenced value unless you use the **DEREF** function. When you select from KEEPER, Oracle will use the OID to evaluate the reference (**REF**). The **DEREF** function will take the reference and return a value.

In the following query, the value of the AnimalKept column in KEEPER is the parameter passed to the **DEREF** function. **DEREF** will take the OID from AnimalKept and find the referenced object; the function will evaluate the reference and return the values to the user.

```
select DEREF(K.AnimalKept)
 from KEEPER K
 where KeeperName = 'CATHERINE WEILZ';

DEREF(K.ANIMALKEPT)(BREED, NAME, BIRTHDATE)

ANIMAL_TY('DOG', 'BENJI', '03-SEP-01')
```

**NOTE**
*The parameter for the **DEREF** function is the column name of the REF column, not the table name.*

The result shows that the CATHERINE WEILZ record in KEEPER references an ANIMAL record for the animal named BENJI. A few aspects of this query are noteworthy:

- The query used a reference to a row object to travel from one table (KEEPER) to a second (the ANIMAL object table). Thus, a join is performed in the background, without you specifying the join criteria.

■ The object table itself is not mentioned in the query. The only table listed in the query is KEEPER. You do not need to know the name of the object table to **DEREF** its values.

■ The entire referenced row object was returned, not just part of the row.

These are significant differences that separate object queries from relational queries. Thus, when querying your tables, you need to know the way in which their relationships are established. Are the relationships based on foreign keys and primary keys, or on object tables and **REF** datatypes? To help smooth the transition between relational and object-oriented approaches, Oracle allows you to create object views that contain **REF**s superimposed on existing relational tables. See "Object Views with REFs," later in this chapter.

## The VALUE Function

The **DEREF** function was applied to the relational table—the KEEPER table, in this case. The **DEREF** function returns the value of the reference that goes from the relational table to the object table.

What about querying from the object table? Can you select from ANIMAL?

```
select * from ANIMAL;

BREED NAME BIRTHDATE
------------------------ ------------------------ ---------
MULE FRANCES 01-APR-02
DOG BENJI 03-SEP-01
```

Even though ANIMAL is an object table, you can select from it as if it were a relational table. This is consistent with the examples of **insert**s and **select**s shown earlier in this chapter. However, that is not what was shown via the **DEREF**. The **DEREF** showed the full structure of the abstract datatype used by the ANIMAL object table:

```
select DEREF(K.AnimalKept)
 from KEEPER K
 where KeeperName = 'CATHERINE WEILZ';

DEREF(K.ANIMALKEPT)(BREED, NAME, BIRTHDATE)

ANIMAL_TY('DOG', 'BENJI', '03-SEP-01')
```

To see the same structures from a query of the ANIMAL object table, use the **VALUE** function. As shown in the following listing, **VALUE** shows you the data in the same format that **DEREF** will use. The parameter for the **VALUE** function is the table alias.

```
select VALUE(A)
 from ANIMAL A
 where Name = 'BENJI';
```

```
VALUE(A)(BREED, NAME, BIRTHDATE)

ANIMAL_TY('DOG', 'BENJI', '03-SEP-01')
ANIMAL_TY('DOG', 'BENJI', '03-SEP-01')
```

The **VALUE** function is useful when debugging references and within PL/SQL, as shown in "Object PL/SQL," later in this chapter. Since it allows you to query the formatted values directly from the object table, you can select those values without using the **DEREF** query of KEEPER's AnimalKept column.

## Invalid References

You can **delete** the object to which a reference points. For example, you can **delete** a row from the ANIMAL object table to which a KEEPER record points:

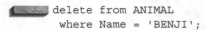
```
delete from ANIMAL
 where Name = 'BENJI';
```

The record in KEEPER that references this ANIMAL record will now have what is called a *dangling REF*. If you **insert** a new ANIMAL row for the animal named BENJI, it won't be recognized as being part of the same reference established earlier. The reason is that the first time you **insert**ed a BENJI row, Oracle generated an OID for the row object, and that is what the KEEPER column referenced. When you **delete**d the row object, the OID went away—and Oracle does not reuse OID numbers. Therefore, when the new BENJI record is entered, it is given a *new* OID value—and the KEEPER record still points to the old value.

This is a critical difference between relational and OOP systems. In a relational system, the join between two tables is dependent only on the current data. In an OOP system, the join is between objects—and just because two objects have the same data, that doesn't mean they are the same.

# Object Views with REFs

You can use object views to superimpose OOP structures on existing relational tables (refer to Chapter 30). For example, you can create abstract datatypes and use them within the object view of an existing table. Using object views allows you to access the table via either relational command syntax or abstract datatype syntax. As a result, object views provide an important technological bridge from existing relational applications to object-relational applications.

## A Quick Review of Object Views

This example from Chapter 30 will serve as part of the basis for the advanced object views in this chapter. First, a CUSTOMER table is created, with the Customer_ID column as its primary key:

```
create table CUSTOMER
(Customer_ID NUMBER constraint CUSTOMER_PK primary key,
 Name VARCHAR2(25),
 Street VARCHAR2(50),
```

```
City VARCHAR2(25),
State CHAR(2),
Zip NUMBER);
```

Next, two abstract datatypes are created. The first, ADDRESS_TY, contains attributes for addresses: Street, City, State, and Zip. The second, PERSON_TY, contains a Name attribute plus an Address attribute that uses the ADDRESS_TY datatype, as shown in the following listing:

```
create or replace type ADDRESS_TY as object
(Street VARCHAR2(50),
 City VARCHAR2(25),
 State CHAR(2),
 Zip NUMBER);

create or replace type PERSON_TY as object
(Name VARCHAR2(25),
 Address ADDRESS_TY);
```

Since the CUSTOMER table was created without using the ADDRESS_TY and PERSON_TY datatypes, you need to use object views in order to access CUSTOMER data via object-based accesses (such as methods). You can create an object view that specifies the abstract datatypes that apply to the CUSTOMER table. In the following listing, the CUSTOMER_OV object view is created:

```
create view CUSTOMER_OV (Customer_ID, Person) as
select Customer_ID,
 PERSON_TY(Name,
 ADDRESS_TY(Street, City, State, Zip))
 from CUSTOMER;
```

In the creation of the CUSTOMER_OV object view, the constructor methods for the two abstract datatypes (ADDRESS_TY and PERSON_TY) are specified. You can now access the CUSTOMER table directly (as a relational table) or via the constructor methods for the abstract datatypes.

The CUSTOMER table will be used in the next set of examples in this chapter.

## Object Views Involving References

If the CUSTOMER table shown in the previous section is related to another table, you can use object views to create a reference between the tables. That is, Oracle will use the existing primary key/foreign key relationships to simulate OIDs for use by **REF**s between the tables. You will thus be able to access the tables either as relational tables or as objects. When you treat the tables as objects, you will be able to use the **REF**s to automatically perform joins of the tables (refer to "Using the **DEREF** Function," earlier in this chapter, for examples).

The CUSTOMER table has a primary key of Customer_ID. Let's create a small table that will contain a foreign key reference to the Customer_ID column. In the following listing, the CUSTOMER_CALL table is created. The primary key of the CUSTOMER_CALL table is the combination of Customer_ID and Call_Number. The Customer_ID column of CUSTOMER_CALL is a foreign

key back to CUSTOMER—you cannot record a call for a customer who does not already have a record in CUSTOMER. A single nonkey attribute, Call_Date, is created within the CUSTOMER_CALL table.

```
create table CUSTOMER_CALL
(Customer_ID NUMBER,
 Call_Number NUMBER,
 Call_Date DATE,
 constraint CUSTOMER_CALL_PK
 primary key (Customer_ID, Call_Number),
 constraint CUSTOMER_CALL_FK foreign key (Customer_ID)
 references CUSTOMER(Customer_ID));
```

For example, you could have the following CUSTOMER and CUSTOMER_CALL entries:

```
insert into CUSTOMER values
(123,'SIGMUND','47 HAFFNER RD','LEWISTON','NJ',22222);
insert into CUSTOMER values
(234,'EVELYN','555 HIGH ST','LOWLANDS PARK','NE',33333);

insert into CUSTOMER_CALL values
(123,1,TRUNC(SysDate)-1);
insert into CUSTOMER_CALL values
(123,2,TRUNC(SysDate));
```

The foreign key from CUSTOMER_CALL to CUSTOMER defines the relationship between the tables. From an OOP point of view, the records in CUSTOMER_CALL reference the records in CUSTOMER. Therefore, we must find a way to assign OID values to the records in CUSTOMER and generate references in CUSTOMER_CALL.

## How to Generate OIDs

First, use an object view to assign OIDs to the records in CUSTOMER. Remember that OIDs are assigned to records in an object table—and an object table, in turn, is based on an abstract datatype. Therefore, we first need to create an abstract datatype that has the same structure as the CUSTOMER table:

```
create or replace type CUSTOMER_TY as object
(Customer_ID NUMBER,
 Name VARCHAR2(25),
 Street VARCHAR2(50),
 City VARCHAR2(25),
 State CHAR(2),
 Zip NUMBER);
```

Now, create an object view based on the CUSTOMER_TY type, while assigning OID values to the records in CUSTOMER:

```
create or replace view CUSTOMER_OV of CUSTOMER_TY
with object identifier (Customer_ID) as
```

```
select Customer_ID, Name, Street, City, State, Zip
 from CUSTOMER;
```

The first part of this **create view** command gives the view its name (CUSTOMER_OV) and tells Oracle that the view's structure is based on the CUSTOMER_TY datatype:

```
create or replace view CUSTOMER_OV of CUSTOMER_TY
```

The next part of the **create view** command tells the database how to construct OID values for the rows in CUSTOMER. The **with object identifier** clause is followed by the column to use for the OID—in this case, the Customer_ID value. This will allow you to address the rows within the CUSTOMER table as if they were referenceable row objects within an object table.

```
with object identifier (Customer_ID) as
```

> **NOTE**
> The **with object identifier** clause replaces the **with object OID** clause used in earlier versions of Oracle. The **with object OID** syntax is still supported for backward compatibility.

The final part of the **create view** command gives the query on which the view's data access will be based. The columns in the query must match the columns in the view's base datatype.

```
select Customer_ID, Name, Street, City, State, Zip
 from CUSTOMER;
```

The rows of CUSTOMER are now accessible as row objects via the CUSTOMER_OV view. The OID values generated for the CUSTOMER_OV rows are called *pkOIDs*, because they are based on CUSTOMER's primary key values. Relational tables can be accessed as row objects if you create object views for them.

### How to Generate References

The rows of CUSTOMER_CALL reference rows in CUSTOMER. From a relational perspective, the relationship is determined by the foreign key pointing from the CUSTOMER_CALL.Customer_ID column to the CUSTOMER.Customer_ID column. Now that the CUSTOMER_OV object view has been created, and the rows in CUSTOMER can be accessed via OIDs, you need to create reference values in CUSTOMER_CALL that reference CUSTOMER. Once the **REF**s are in place, you will be able to use the **DEREF** function (shown earlier in this chapter) to access the CUSTOMER data from within CUSTOMER_CALL.

The **create view** command for the object view of CUSTOMER_CALL is shown in the following listing. It uses a new function, **MAKE_REF**, which is described following the listing.

```
create view CUSTOMER_CALL_OV as
select MAKE_REF(CUSTOMER_OV, Customer_ID) Customer_ID,
 Call_Number,
 Call_Date
 from CUSTOMER_CALL;
```

With the exception of the **MAKE_REF** operation, this **create view** command looks like a normal **create view** command. The **MAKE_REF** operation is shown in this line:

```
select MAKE_REF(CUSTOMER_OV, Customer_ID) Customer_ID,
```

The **MAKE_REF** function takes as arguments the name of the object view being referenced and the name of the column (or columns) that form the foreign key in the local table. In this case, the Customer_ID column of the CUSTOMER_CALL table references the column that is used as the basis of OID generation in the CUSTOMER_OV object view. Therefore, two parameters are passed to **MAKE_REF**: CUSTOMER_OV and Customer_ID. The result of the **MAKE_REF** operation is given the column alias Customer_ID. Since this command creates a view, the result of an operation must be given a column alias.

What does **MAKE_REF** do? It creates references (called *pkREFs*, since they are based on primary keys) from the CUSTOMER_CALL_OV view to the CUSTOMER_OV view. You can now query the two views as if CUSTOMER_OV were an object table and CUSTOMER_CALL_OV were a table that contains a REF datatype that references CUSTOMER_OV.

### Querying the Object Views

The queries of the object views with REFs mirror the structure of the queries of table REFs. You use the **DEREF** function to select the value of the referenced data, as shown earlier in this chapter. Applied to the object views, the query will be

```
select DEREF(CCOV.Customer_ID)
 from CUSTOMER_CALL_OV CCOV
 where Call_Date = TRUNC(SysDate);

DEREF(CCOV.CUSTOMER_ID)(CUSTOMER_ID, NAME, STREET, CITY, STATE,ZIP)

CUSTOMER_TY(123, 'SIGMUND', '47 HAFFNER RD', 'LEWISTON','NJ',22222)
```

The query found the record in CUSTOMER_CALL for which the Call_Date value was the current system date. It then took the Customer_ID value from that record and evaluated its reference. That Customer_ID value, from the **MAKE_REF** function, pointed to a pkOID value in the CUSTOMER_OV object view. The CUSTOMER_OV object view returned the record whose pkOID matched the referenced value. The **DEREF** function then returned the value of the referenced row. The query thus returned rows from CUSTOMER even though the user only queried CUSTOMER_CALL.

Object views of column objects enable you to work with tables as if they were both relational tables and object-relational tables. When extended to row objects, object views enable you to generate OID values based on established foreign key/primary key relationships. Object views allow you to continue to use the existing constraints and standard **insert**, **update**, **delete**, and **select** commands. They also allow you to use OOP features such as references against the object tables. Object views thus provide an important technological bridge for migrating to an OOP database architecture.

As described earlier in this chapter, Oracle performs joins that resolve the references defined in the database. When the referenced data is retrieved, it brings back the entire row object that

was referenced. To reference the data, you need to establish pkOIDs in the table that is the "primary key" table in the relationship, and use **MAKE_REF** to generate references in the table that is the "foreign key" table in the relationship. You can then work with the data as if it were stored in object tables.

# Object PL/SQL

PL/SQL programs can use the abstract datatypes you have created. Whereas earlier versions of PL/SQL could only use the Oracle-provided datatypes (such as DATE, NUMBER, and VARCHAR2), you can now use your own user-defined datatypes as well. The result is the merging of SQL, procedural logic, and OOP extensions—a combination referred to as *object PL/SQL.*

The following anonymous PL/SQL block uses object PL/SQL concepts. The CUSTOMER_TY abstract datatype is used as the datatype for the *Cust1* variable, and its value is populated by a query of the CUSTOMER_OV object view.

```
set serveroutput on
declare
 Cust1 CUSTOMER_TY;
begin
 select VALUE(COV) into Cust1
 from CUSTOMER_OV COV
 where Customer_ID = 123;
 DBMS_OUTPUT.PUT_LINE(Cust1.Name);
 DBMS_OUTPUT.PUT_LINE(Cust1.Street);
end;
```

The output of this PL/SQL block is

```
SIGMUND
47 HAFFNER RD
```

In the first part of the PL/SQL block, a variable is declared using the CUSTOMER_TY datatype:

```
declare
 Cust1 CUSTOMER_TY;
```

The *Cust1* variable value is selected from the CUSTOMER_OV object view (created in the previous section of this chapter). The **VALUE** function is used to retrieve the data in the structure of the abstract datatype. Since the data will be selected in the format of the abstract datatype, you need to use the CUSTOMER_OV object view created on the CUSTOMER table.

```
begin
 select VALUE(COV) into Cust1
 from CUSTOMER_OV COV
 where Customer_ID = 123;
```

The Cust1.Name and Cust1.Street values are then retrieved from the attributes of the *Cust1* variable and displayed. You cannot pass the entire *Cust1* variable to the PUT_LINE procedure.

```
DBMS_OUTPUT.PUT_LINE(Cust1.Name);
DBMS_OUTPUT.PUT_LINE(Cust1.Street);
end;
```

This is a deliberately simple example, but it shows the power of object PL/SQL. You can use object PL/SQL anywhere you use abstract datatypes. Your PL/SQL is thus no longer bound to the Oracle-provided datatypes, and may more accurately reflect the objects in your database. In this example, an object view was queried to illustrate that the queries can access either column objects or row objects. You can then select the attributes of the abstract datatype and manipulate or display them. If you have defined methods for the abstract datatype, you can apply them as well.

For example, you can call the datatype's constructor methods within your PL/SQL blocks. In the following example, a variable named *NewCust* is defined using the CUSTOMER_TY datatype. The *NewCust* variable is then set equal to a set of values using the CUSTOMER_TY constructor method. The *NewCust* variable's set of values is then **insert**ed via the CUSTOMER_OV object view.

```
declare
 NewCust CUSTOMER_TY;
begin
 NewCust :=
 CUSTOMER_TY(345,'NewCust','StreetVal', 'City','ST',00000);
 insert into CUSTOMER_OV
 values (NewCust);
end;
```

You can see the result of the **insert** by querying CUSTOMER_OV:

```
select Customer_ID, Name from CUSTOMER_OV;

CUSTOMER_ID NAME
----------- ------------------------
 123 SIGMUND
 234 EVELYN
 345 NewCust
```

In addition to calling constructor methods, you can call the methods you have created on your abstract datatypes. If you will be comparing the values of variables that use the abstract datatypes, you will need to define map or order methods for the datatypes. This capability allows you to further extend object PL/SQL—you define the datatypes and the functions at the database level, and they are callable within any of your PL/SQL programs. Object PL/SQL represents a significant enhancement over traditional PL/SQL.

# Objects in the Database

The features available in Oracle—column objects, row objects, and object extensions to PL/SQL—enable you to implement objects in your database without sacrificing the investment you have already made in analysis and design. You can continue to create systems based on relational design techniques and tune them based on relational access methods. The tools that Oracle provides allow you to create an OOP layer above your relational tables. Once you have that layer in place, you can access the relational data as if it were stored in a fully OOP database.

Having an OOP layer allows you to realize some of the benefits of an OOP system, such as abstraction and encapsulation. You can apply the methods for each abstract datatype across a set of consistently implemented objects, and benefit from object reuse and standards enforcement. At the same time, you can benefit from Oracle's relational features. The ability to use both relational and object technology within an application lets you use the proper tool for the proper job within the database.

When implementing the object portion of an object-relational database, start by defining the abstract datatypes that are the core components of your business. Every object-relational feature, whether it relates to column objects or row objects, is based on an abstract datatype. The better you have defined your datatypes and their methods, the better you will be able to implement objects. If necessary, nest objects so that you can have multiple variations of the same core datatype. The result will be a database that is properly designed to take advantage of the relational and OOP features Oracle provides now, and will provide in versions to come.

# PART
# V

## Java in Oracle

# CHAPTER
# 34

## An Introduction to Java

n this chapter, you will see an overview of Java as it relates to Oracle database applications. There are numerous uses of Java beyond Oracle applications, and there are many features of the language that will not be used by most Oracle developers. The goal of this chapter is to provide developers who have a background in SQL and PL/SQL with an understanding of the Java language structures. This is not an exhaustive review of Java (there are numerous books that accomplish that goal) but rather a short overview of the Java language components most commonly used by Oracle developers.

Although there are many cases in which PL/SQL and Java correlate well to each other, there are significant differences in terminology and usage. That shouldn't be surprising, since the two programming languages were developed independently. Furthermore, PL/SQL's object-oriented capabilities were not part of its initial implementation, whereas Java has been object-oriented since its inception. To use Java effectively, you need to take a different approach than the one you may have taken in the past with PL/SQL.

Chapter 27 presented an introduction to the PL/SQL language structures and flow control. This chapter mirrors that approach: You will see the structures used by Java and the basic flow-control methods provided. Where applicable, you will also see the matching PL/SQL structures. You should be familiar with PL/SQL (Chapter 27); packages, functions, and procedures (Chapter 29); and abstract datatypes and methods (Chapter 30) before reading this chapter.

# Java vs. PL/SQL: An Overview

In comparing PL/SQL to Java, you get no further than the basic PL/SQL structure—a block—before you encounter a significant difference in terminology between the two languages. In PL/SQL, a *block* is a structured piece of code that has a Declarations section, an Executable Commands section, and an Exception Handling section. For a PL/SQL block, the structure may be represented as follows:

```
declare
 <declarations section>
begin
 <executable commands>
 exception
 <exception handling>
end;
```

In Java, the term *block* refers to a much smaller subset of code. In Java, a block is a collection of statements enclosed by curly braces, { and }. For example, the following pseudocode contains two Java blocks:

```
if (some condition) {
 block of code to process if condition is met
}
else {
 block of code to process if condition is not met
}
```

Within PL/SQL, that entire code section would be merely one part of a larger block; within Java, it contains two separate blocks. Throughout this chapter, all references to "blocks" refer to Java blocks unless otherwise specified.

A second major difference between PL/SQL and Java is in the declaration of variables. In a PL/SQL block, you define your variables before you begin the Executable Commands section. In a Java program, you can define variables where they are needed within the program. A Java program has no Declarations section comparable to the one used in PL/SQL blocks.

Throughout this chapter, you will see a number of other differences between PL/SQL and Java. It's important to remember that Java does not replace PL/SQL within your applications—you can continue to use PL/SQL for Oracle applications. For data-retrieval operations, you should test the performance of PL/SQL and Java before deciding on a technical direction to follow.

# Getting Started

To use the examples in this section, you need a copy of the Java Development Kit (JDK), which is available for free download from http://java.sun.com. You need to install the JDK on the server on which you will be running the Java programs. As of the time of this writing, JDK 1.4 is the most recent production release; most development efforts use JDK 1.3.1. At a minimum, you should use JDK 1.2.2.

# Declarations

Within Java, you can declare variables as needed. A variable has a name and a datatype, and is used to store a data value during the program's execution. A variable also has a scope, allowing it to be publicly accessible or private—similar to the manner in which procedures within packages can have private variables.

Examples of Java variable declarations include:

```
char aCharVariable = 'J';
boolean aBooleanVariable = false;
```

By convention, Java variables always start with a lowercase letter, as shown in this example. In the example, the datatypes are CHAR and BOOLEAN, and each variable is assigned an initial value. Note that the assignment character in Java is =, as opposed to := or => in PL/SQL. Each declaration is terminated with a semicolon.

The available primitive datatypes in Java are listed in Table 34-1.

| Datatype | Description |
|---|---|
| byte | Byte-length integer |
| short | Short integer |
| int | Integer |

**TABLE 34-1.** *Primitive Java Datatypes*

| Datatype | Description |
|----------|-------------|
| long | Long integer |
| float | Single-precision floating-point real number |
| double | Double-precision floating-point real number |
| char | A single Unicode character |
| boolean | A Boolean value, true or false |

**TABLE 34-1.** *Primitive Java Datatypes* (continued)

In addition to the primitive datatypes listed in Table 34-1, you can use reference datatypes, which are based on the contents of variables. You may note that there is no primitive datatype for variable-length character strings—Java provides a String class for that purpose. Classes are discussed later in this chapter.

## Executable Commands

You can assign values to variables via the use of expressions and statements. The arithmetic operators supported by Java include:

| Operator | Description |
|----------|-------------|
| * | Multiplication |
| / | Division |
| + | Addition |
| - | Subtraction |
| % | Modulus |

In addition to these operators, you can use Java's unary operators to simplify your coding. For example, you can increment variables via the ++ operator:

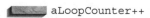

```
aLoopCounter = aLoopCounter++;
```

or you could simply write:

```
aLoopCounter++
```

**NOTE**
*The ++ operator is called a unary operator because it has only one operand. If an operator requires two operands (such as *), it is called a binary operator.*

In PL/SQL, that would have been written:

```
aLoopCounter := aLoopCounter +1;
```

If the **++** operator is placed in front of the variable name, then it is a *preincrement* operator rather than a *postincrement* operator:

```
int anotherCounter = ++aLoopCounter;
```

In this example, the variable *anotherCounter* is set to the incremented value of *aLoopCounter*. By contrast,

```
int anotherCounter = aLoopCounter++;
```

sets *anotherCounter* to the value of *aLoopCounter* before it is incremented. You can decrement a variable's value, via the **--** unary operator:

```
aLoopCounter = aLoopCounter--;
```

You can also combine the assignment of values with an operation. For example, instead of writing

```
aNumberVariable = aNumberVariable * 2;
```

you can write

```
aNumberVariable *= 2;
```

You can perform similar combinations using /=, %=, +=, and -=.

If you perform multiple arithmetic operations, you should use parentheses to clearly indicate the order in which the operations should be evaluated, as shown in the following example.

```
aNumberVariable = (aNumberVariable*2) +2;
```

Terminating these operations with semicolons makes them *statements*—complete units of execution.

## Conditional Logic

You can evaluate variables by using expressions and statements. To do so, you may use one or more of the fundamental classes provided as part of Java. A full listing of those methods is beyond the scope of this book; see Sun's Java documentation site or one of the many Java books available for the functionality currently provided.

**NOTE**
*The number of supplied classes changes dramatically with each release of Java.*

Part V: Java in Oracle

In the following listing, the Character.isUpperCase method is used to evaluate the *aCharVariable* declared earlier:

```
if (Character.isUpperCase(aCharVariable)) {
 some commands to execute
}
```

If the *aCharVariable* value is uppercase, the commands in the following block will be executed; otherwise, flow will continue to the next part of the program.

The following is the general syntax for **if** clauses:

```
if (expression) {
 statement
}
```

Notice the lack of a **then** clause. If the expression being evaluated is true, the following block is automatically executed.

You can also have **else** clauses to evaluate different conditions, as shown in the following listing:

```
if (expression) {
 statement
}
else {
 statement
}
```

If you have multiple conditions to check, you can use the **else if** clause to evaluate each in turn, ending with an **else** clause. The following listing illustrates the use of **else if** clauses.

```
if (aCharVariable == 'V') {
 statement
}
else if (aCharVariable == 'J') {
 statement
}
else {
 statement
}
```

In addition to supporting **if** clauses for conditional logic, Java features a **switch** clause. Used in conjunction with its **break** clause and statement labels, the **switch** clause can approximate the functionality of **goto** clauses (which Java does not support). First, let's look at a simple **switch** example. Using the **case** statement, multiple values of the *aMonth* variable are evaluated. Depending on the *aMonth* value, the text name for the month is displayed, and the processing leaves the **switch** block by means of a **break**.

```
int aMonth=2;
switch (aMonth) {
 case 1:
```

```
 System.out.println("January");
 break;
 case 2:
 System.out.println("February");
 break;
 case 3:
 System.out.println("March");
 break;
 default:
 System.out.println("Out of range");
 break;
}
```

This kind of code is much more complex to write than a simple **TO_CHAR**, but it illustrates the **switch** usage. The **switch** operator takes the *aMonth* variable as its input, and evaluates its value. If the value matches a **case** value, then the System.out.println method is called to print the month's name, and processing control leaves the **switch** block by means of a **break**. If the value does not match one of the **case** clauses, then the **default** option is executed.

Where does control go? By default, it goes to the next section of the program. However, you have the option of creating labels for sections of your code, and passing the name of those labels to the **break** clause. The following listing shows an example of a label and a **break** clause:

```
somelabel:
if (aCharVariable == 'V') {
 statement
}
else {
 statement
}
int aMonth=2;
switch (aMonth) {
 case 1:
 System.out.println("January");
 break somelabel;
 case 2:
 System.out.println("February");
 break someotherlabel;
 case 3:
 System.out.println("March");
 break somethirdlabel;
 default:
 System.out.println("Out of range");
 break;
}
```

In this example, the **if** clause is evaluated, followed by the **switch** clause. Note that the *aMonth* variable is not declared until just before it is needed. For this example, the *aMonth* variable is assigned a value of 2, so the program will display the word "February" and will then branch over to the section of code identified by the someotherlabel label. If the *aMonth* value had been 1, the **if** clause at the beginning of the code listing would have been reexecuted.

Java also supports a *ternary* operator—an operator that takes three operands and whose function is similar to that of **DECODE**. Acting as an inline if-else combination, the ternary operator evaluates an expression. If the expression evaluates to true, then the second operand is returned, else the third is returned. The syntax is as follows:

```
expression ? operand1 : operand2
```

The following listing shows a sample ternary operation:

```
aStatusVariable = (aCharVariable == 'V') ? "OK" : "Invalid";
```

In this example, the expression

```
(aCharVariable == 'V')
```

is evaluated. If it is true, "OK" is returned; otherwise, "Invalid" is returned.
You can use the ternary operator to simulate the use of a **GREATEST** function:

```
double greatest = (a > b) ? a : b;
```

In this example, the expression (a>b) is evaluated, where *a* and *b* are the names of variables. If that expression is true, *a*'s value is returned; otherwise, *b*'s value is returned.

**NOTE**
*Java has a "greatest" method for numeric values—the*
*Max method within the java.lang.Math class. The ternary*
*example in the preceding listing can be rewritten as*
***double greatest = Math.max(a, b);***

You can combine multiple logic checks via the use of AND and OR operations. In Java, an AND operation is represented by the **&&** operator:

```
if (aCharVariable == 'V' && aMonth == 3) {
 statement
}
```

The OR operation is represented by ||, as shown in the following listing:

```
if (aCharVariable == 'V' || aMonth == 3) {
 statement
}
```

For performance reasons, the && and || operations are carried out only if required; the second expression is not evaluated if the first expression determines the result. In the case of the **AND** operator, if the first value is false, then the evaluation ends at that point and the Boolean value false is returned. In the case of the **OR** operator, if the first expression is false, the second expression will still be evaluated because only one of the test conditions needs to be true for the

Boolean value true to be returned. If the first value of the **OR** operator were true, then subsequent expressions would not need to be evaluated and true would be returned.

The & and | operators are bitwise AND and OR; they are not short-circuited as && and | | are. All expressions will always be evaluated. This functionality can be important if you are testing the return values of method calls and you need to make sure the methods are executed.

# Loops

Java supports three main types of loops: WHILE loops, DO-WHILE loops, and FOR loops. In this section, you will see examples of each type of loop. Since Java is not written as an extension of SQL, it does not support cursor FOR loops as PL/SQL does.

## WHILE Loops and DO-WHILE Loops

A **while** clause evaluates a condition; if the condition is true, the associated block of statements is executed. The syntax for a WHILE loop is of the following form:

```
while (expression) {
 statement
 statement
}
```

The WHILE loop executes the block of statements (the section within the { and } braces) repeatedly until the *expression* is no longer true:

```
int aNumberVariable = 3;
while (aNumberVariable < 7) {
 some_processing_statement
 aNumberVariable++;
}
```

In this example, a counter variable (*aNumberVariable*) is created and initialized. The variable's value is then evaluated via the **while** clause. If the value is less than 7, the associated statement block is executed. As part of that block, the variable is incremented. When the block completes, the variable is again evaluated and the loop continues.

**NOTE**
*For examples of WHILE loop processing, see "Classes" later in this chapter.*

You could also write this as a DO-WHILE loop:

```
int aNumberVariable = 3;
do {
 some_processing_statement
 aNumberVariable++;
} while (aNumberVariable < 7);
```

In a DO-WHILE loop, the expression's value is not evaluated until the block has been processed at least one time.

## FOR Loops

You can use a FOR loop to repeatedly execute a block of code. In a FOR loop, you specify an initial value, a termination value, and an increment for the loop counter. The loop counter will be incremented each time through the loop by the increment you specify until the termination value is reached. The following is the syntax for a FOR loop:

```
for (initialization; termination; increment) {
 statement;
}
```

The prior section's WHILE example can be rewritten with a **for** clause, as shown in the following listing:

```
for (int aNumberVariable=3; aNumberVariable<7; aNumberVariable++) {
 some_processing_statement
}
```

The **for** clause version for this example is much shorter than the **while** version. In this example, the *aNumberVariable* variable is declared and initialized within the FOR loop. As long as the variable's value does not exceed 7, the block will be executed. For each pass through the loop, the variable's value is incremented by 1 via the **++** unary operator.

Within a loop, you can use the **continue** clause to jump to another statement within the loop. If you just use the **continue** clause by itself, the process flow will jump to the end of the loop body and evaluate the loop's termination test. If you use **continue** with a label (as shown previously in the section on the **switch** clause), processing will continue at the next iteration of the labeled loop.

## Cursors and Loops

Within PL/SQL, you can use cursor FOR loops to iterate through the results of a query. You can use Java's WHILE and FOR loops to simulate the functionality of a PL/SQL cursor FOR loop. The examples provided with Oracle9i show how this can be accomplished. Java examples are found in the /jdbc/demo directory under the Oracle software home directory. The Employee.java file found there creates the Employee class within Java. As part of that class, the example issues the following commands:

```
Statement stmt conn.createStatement();
ResultSet rset = stmt.executeQuery ("select ENAME from EMP");
//iterate through the result set and print the employee names
while (rset.next ())
 System.out.println (rset.getString (1));
```

This example assumes that a connection to the database has already been established. The first line of the example creates a variable called *stmt*, based on a connection variable called *conn* (not shown in this partial listing). The second line of the example creates a variable called *rset*, based on the result set that the query *stmt* will return. Following a comment (prefixed by //),

a **while** clause fetches each row in the result set. If the fetch retrieves a row from the result set, the ENAME from that EMP row is printed; otherwise, the loop will end.

From a programming perspective, you should be specific in the data returned. The example provided by Oracle can be modified to use the column name returned, instead of an absolute column number, as shown in the following listing:

```
Statement stmt conn.createStatement();
ResultSet rset = stmt.executeQuery ("select ENAME from EMP");
//iterate through the result set and print the employee names
while (rset.next()) {
System.out.println (rset.getString ("ENAME"));
}
```

The JDBC (Java Database Connectivity; see Chapter 35) demos provided by Oracle show samples of queries involving procedure calls, LOBs, and DML. In most cases, your Java code will be performing in a similar manner to the previous example: Write the process flow-control language in Java and pass it a statement to execute. Based on the outcome of that statement, you can direct different actions to occur via the use of **while**, **for**, **if**, **break**, **continue**, and **switch** clauses, as shown earlier in this chapter.

# Exception Handling

Java provides a robust set of error-handling routines and enables you to create complex error-handling procedures. In PL/SQL, you **raise** an exception; in Java, you **throw** exceptions. If an exception is thrown, you need to use the Java **catch** clause to capture and properly process the exception.

Java's exception-handling syntax is based on three blocks: **try**, **catch**, and **finally**. The **try** block includes the statements that might throw an exception. The **catch** block immediately following the **try** block associates exception handlers with the exceptions that may be thrown by the **try** block. The **finally** block cleans up any system resources not properly cleaned up during the **catch** block processing. The general structure is as follows:

```
try {
 statements
}
catch () {
 statements
}
catch () {
 statements
}
finally {
 statements
}
```

For example, the following code comes from the PLSQL.java example file provided as part of Oracle9i:

```
try {
 Statement stmt = conn.createStatement ();
```

```
 stmt.execute ("drop table plsqltest");
}
catch (SQLException e) {
}
```

In this example, a variable named *stmt* is created to execute a **drop table** command. If the execution fails—for example, if the table does not exist—how will that error be processed? The **catch** clause tells Java to handle it via an exception object called SQLException, a standard part of Java's SQL implementation. As shown in the example, the **catch** clause takes two parameters (an exception object and a variable name) and is optionally followed by a block of statements to execute.

The **try** block can contain multiple statements, or you can create separate **try** blocks for each statement. In general, it is easier to manage exception handling if you consolidate your **catch** blocks, so consolidating your **try** blocks will help you manage your code as it changes and grows.

The **finally** block cleans up the state of the current code section before passing control to any subsequent parts of the program. At runtime, the contents of the **finally** block are always executed, regardless of the outcome of the **try** block. For example, you could use the **finally** block to close a database connection.

## Reserved Words

The reserved words in Java are listed in Table 34-2. You cannot use these words as the names of classes, methods, or variables.

| | | | |
|---|---|---|---|
| abstract | else | interface | super |
| boolean | extends | long | switch |
| break | false | native | synchronized |
| byte | final | new | this |
| case | finally | null | throw |
| catch | float | package | throws |
| char | for | private | transient |
| class | goto | protected | true |
| const | if | public | try |
| continue | implements | return | void |
| default | import | short | volatile |
| do | instanceof | static | while |
| double | int | strictfp | |

**TABLE 34-2.** *Java Reserved Words*

# Classes

In the prior sections of this chapter, you saw the basic syntax structures for Java. In this section, you will see how to use that syntax to create and use objects. A simple program for printing the word "Oracle" is shown in the following listing:

```
public class HelloOracle {
 public static void main (String[] args) {
 System.out.println("Oracle");
 }
}
```

This example creates a *class* called HelloOracle. Within the HelloOracle class, a public method called *main* is created. The main method prints the word "Oracle." This is significantly more complex than

```
select 'Oracle' from dual;
```

but the Java version has features lacking in the SQL version. HelloOracle is a class, and as such its methods can be called from within other classes. HelloOracle could have multiple methods; in this example, it has only the main method.

The main method's declaration (**public static void main**) has a number of keywords that you should become familiar with:

| | |
|---|---|
| public | Defining the class as **public** allows all classes to call this method. |
| static | Declares that this is a class method; you use **static** to declare class methods. An additional option is the keyword **final** for methods and variables whose values cannot change (similar to PL/SQL's **constant** option). |
| void | Specifies the return value's data type from the procedure. Since this procedure does not return values, its type is **void**. |

In this example, the method is given the name main because that will simplify running the class's method. Now that the class has been created, you can compile and load it.

**NOTE**
*To compile and execute a Java class, you must have the JDK on your server. The following examples assume that the binaries that are part of that kit are located in a directory that is automatically searched via the PATH environment variable, and the directory containing your .class files is included in the CLASSPATH environment variable. The programs referenced here (javac and java) are located in the /bin subdirectory of the JDK software directory.*

First, save the program as a plain text file called HelloOracle.java. Next, compile it:

```
javac HelloOracle.java
```

A new file, called HelloOracle.class, will be created on your server. You can then run the class:

```
java HelloOracle
```

And the output will be displayed:

```
Oracle
```

As shown in the HelloOracle example, the class is first given a name, along with other optional attributes related to its inheritance of other classes' attributes. In the class body, all of the class variables and methods are defined. As with abstract datatypes in Oracle, Java classes have methods associated with them for the manipulation of their related data.

Let's consider a more complex example. The following listing is a Java program that computes the area of a circle, given a radius value as input (see Chapter 27 for the PL/SQL version):

```
// AreaOfCircle.java
//
public class AreaOfCircle {
 public static void main(String[] args) {
 try {
 int input = Integer.parseInt(args[0]);
 double result=area(input);
 System.out.println(result);
 }
 catch (ArrayIndexOutOfBoundsException oob) {
 System.out.println("You did not provide the radius of the circle.");
 System.out.println("Usage: java AreaOfCircle 10");
 }
 catch (NumberFormatException nfe) {
 System.out.println("Enter a valid number for the radius.");
 System.out.println("Usage: java AreaOfCircle 10");
 }
 } /// main

 public static double area (int rad) {
 double pi=3.1415927;
 double areacircle=pi*rad*rad;
 return areacircle;
 } /// area
} ///AreaOfCircle
```

**NOTE**
*Be sure to include a closing brace, }, for each block. In the examples shown in this chapter, the closing braces are always on a line by themselves to simplify debugging and processing flow-control errors that may arise.*

First, note that the class and the name of the file must be the same. In this case, the class is named AreaOfCircle, so this text is stored in a file called AreaOfCircle.java. The class has two methods, called main and area. When you execute the class, the main method is automatically executed. The main method takes the string provided as input and parses it as an integer into the *input* variable:

```
int input=Integer.parseInt(args[0]);
```

There are at least two possible exceptions that could be thrown when running this code. The first exception handled, ArrayIndexOutOfBoundsException, occurs when you try to reference a position in an array that doesn't exist. As the code explicitly references the first position of the array named args (args[0]), an exception will be thrown if no data was passed to the program. The other possible error, NumberFormatException, would occur if a non-numeric value was passed in. For example, if you ran the program by entering, "java AreaOfCircle XYZ" instead of "java AreaOfCircle 123", the NumberFormatException would be thrown because XYZ isn't a valid number. Both of these exceptions are handled by the two **catch** statements that provide the user with useful feedback regarding the cause of the error:

```
catch (ArrayIndexOutOfBoundsException oob) {
 System.out.println("You did not provide the radius of the circle.");
 System.out.println("Usage: java AreaOfCircle 10");
}
catch (NumberFormatException nfe) {
 System.out.println("You did not enter a valid number for the radius.");
 System.out.println("Usage: java AreaOfCircle 10");
}
```

Next, a variable named *result* is declared, and set equal to the value returned by the call to **area(input)**:

```
double result=area(input);
```

To process that directive, the area method is executed, using the *input* variable's value as its input. That method is as follows:

```
public static double area (int rad) {
 double pi=3.1415927;
 double areacircle=pi*rad*rad;
 return areacircle;
}
```

In its definition, the area method specifies that it will accept one variable, an integer type named *rad*. That variable's value (passed from the *input* variable in the main method) is then processed, and a variable named *areacircle* is calculated and returned to main. In main, that value is then printed:

```
 double result=area(input);
 System.out.println(result);
```

Testing the program is straightforward:

```
javac AreaOfCircle.java
java AreaOfCircle 10
```

The following is the output:

```
314.15927
```

Let's extend this example to include WHILE loop processing. In this example, the area method will be called repeatedly until the resulting input value exceeds a given value:

```
// AreaOfCircleWhile.java
//
public class AreaOfCircleWhile {
 public static void main(String[] args) {
 try {
 int input=Integer.parseInt(args[0]);
 while (input < 7) {
 double result=area(input);
 System.out.println(result);
 input++;
 }
 }
 catch (ArrayIndexOutOfBoundsException oob) {
 System.out.println("You did not provide the radius of the circle.");
 System.out.println("Usage: java AreaOfCircle 10");
 }
 catch (NumberFormatException nfe) {
 System.out.println("Enter a valid number for the radius.");
 System.out.println("Usage: java AreaOfCircle 10");
 }
 } /// main
 public static double area (int rad) {
 double pi=3.1415927;
 double areacircle=pi*rad*rad;
 return areacircle;
 } /// area
} /// AreaOfCircleWhile
```

In this listing, the area method and the exception handling blocks are unchanged from the prior example. The change is in the main method:

```
 int input=Integer.parseInt(args[0]);
 while (input < 7) {
 double result=area(input);
 System.out.println(result);
 input++;
 }
```

While the input value is less than 7, the input value will be processed. After the area for that radius value has been calculated and printed, the input value is incremented:

```
input++;
```

and the loop is evaluated again. Sample output is shown in the following listing.

```
javac AreaOfCircleWhile.java
java AreaOfCircleWhile 4

50.2654832
78.5398175
113.0973372
```

The output shows the area calculations for input radius values of 4, 5, and 6.

This example is not as complete as a finished program—you may need additional exception handling to handle non-integers, for example—but the structure is the important lesson to learn from this example. In addition to the methods shown in this example, you could create a constructor for the AreaOfCircleWhile class. All Java classes have constructors to initialize new objects based on the class. The constructor's name is the same as the name of the class. If you create a class with no constructor, then Java will create a default constructor at runtime. Like a method, the constructor body can contain local variable declarations, loops, and statement blocks. The constructor initializes these variables for the class.

In the following chapters, you will see how to implement Java within Oracle: within stored procedures and via SQLJ/JDBC. Those chapters assume that you have the basic knowledge of Java that is provided in this chapter. For additional information about the Java language, please see the Sun Microsystems web site and the variety of books devoted to Java.

# CHAPTER
## 35

# JDBC and SQLJ
# Programming

ava Database Connectivity (JDBC) and SQLJ build on the Java and programming basics described earlier in this book. The discussions and examples in this chapter assume you are familiar with the Java syntax and structures described in Chapter 34. This chapter does not cover every aspect of JDBC and SQLJ but focuses on the basic configuration and usage of these tools.

You can use JDBC to execute dynamic SQL statements in Java programs. Oracle provides sample files with its standard software installation. The following listing is from the Employee.java demo file, located with the file /jdbc/demo/demo.zip under the Oracle software home directory. The Employee.java demo issues the following commands after establishing a database connection:

```
Statement stmt conn.createStatement();
ResultSet rset = stmt.executeQuery ("select ENAME from EMP");
//iterate through the result set and print the employee names
while (rset.next ())
 System.out.println (rset.getString (1));
```

When you execute a SQL statement via JDBC—in this case, **select Ename from EMP**—the SQL statement is not checked for errors until it is run. The JDBC program that contains the SQL command will compile even if the SQL statement is invalid.

By contrast, SQLJ performs a precompilation step that includes syntax checks for the SQL embedded within the program. SQLJ also performs type checking and schema checking to make sure the data can be properly retrieved and processed. When the SQLJ precompilation is complete, the result is a Java program that runs via JDBC calls. SQLJ and JDBC, though distinct, are interrelated.

# Getting Started

To use the examples in this section, you need a copy of the Java Development Kit (JDK), which is available for free download from http://java.sun.com. You need to install the JDK on the server on which you will be developing and running the Java programs. As of the time of this writing, JDK 1.4 is the most recent production release; most development efforts use JDK 1.3.1. At a minimum, you should use JDK 1.2.2. The examples in this chapter assume JDK 1.3.1 is in use.

## Additional Steps for NT Users

If you will be accessing Oracle9i, you must set the CLASSPATH environment variable to find the classes12.zip file (for JDK 1.2.2 or 1.3.1) provided by Oracle. The file is located in the /jdbc/lib directory beneath your Oracle home directory or available for download from http://technet.oracle.com. For JDK 1.1.8, use the classes111.zip file found in the /jdbc/lib directory.

**NOTE**
*This step is not performed by the standard Oracle9i installation, so you need to do it manually. If the system variables are not properly set, you will not be able to compile Java classes that use Oracle's JDBC classes.*

To set your system variables, click the System icon in the Control Panel. Choose the Environment tab to list the environment variables and their definitions. The PATH variable should already be set, so select it and edit its value. Add the new entry to the end of the list, as shown in the following listing. This value should be separated from the other values in the list by a semicolon.

```
E:\Oracle\Ora91\jdbc\lib\classes12.zip
```

Replace "E:\Oracle\Ora91" with your Oracle software home directory. You should also add the JDK binaries directory to the PATH setting. The next listing shows the PATH setting expanded to include a JDK 1.3.1 binaries directory (replace "E:\jdk131" with the directory in which you installed the JDK):

```
E:\jdk131\bin
```

Next, create an environment variable named CLASSPATH if it doesn't already exist (it won't for an initial Java setup). This variable must have two entries, separated by a semicolon. The first entry must be a period, which denotes the current directory. The second entry must be the directory for the classes12.zip file, using the same form and value as you used for the PATH value:

```
.;E:\Oracle\Ora91\jdbc\lib\classes12.zip
```

If CLASSPATH is not set correctly, you will get a NoClassDefFoundError error when you run a compiled class.

**NOTE**
*Be sure to use a version of the JDK that is compatible with the Oracle release you are using. If you use a new release of the JDK with an older release of Oracle's drivers, you may encounter "access violation" errors when executing your programs.*

# Testing Your Connection

Oracle provides a sample program called JdbcCheckup.java that you can use to verify your JDBC configuration. This file may be in a Zip file (demo.zip on the /jdbc/demo directory), in which case you need to extract it before running the program. Compile and execute the JdbcCheckup.java class:

```
javac JdbcCheckup.java
java JdbcCheckup
```

When you execute JdbcCheckup, you are prompted for a username, password, and connect string for a database. That connection information will be used to attempt a connection; if successful, that attempt will return the following output:

```
Connecting to the database...Connecting...
connected.
Hello World.
Your JDBC installation is correct.
```

If you don't receive feedback telling you that your installation is correct, you need to check your configuration. Common problems include incorrectly set environment variables (PATH and CLASSPATH) and mismatched versions of database connection drivers. If you change the environment variable values, you need to shut down and restart the command windows for the changes to take effect.

# Using the JDBC Classes

JDBC is implemented in Oracle via a set of Oracle-provided classes whose names begin with oracle.sql, while the standard JDBC classes provided with the JDK begin with java.sql. The JdbcCheckup.java class, shown in the following listing, provides a good roadmap for beginning JDBC programmers. The JdbcCheckup.java class assumes you are using Oracle Net to connect to the database.

**NOTE**
*The following code is provided by Oracle. Your programming standards may implement these commands differently, such as by calling System.out.println in place of System.out.print, or by placing the brackets in different places.*

```
/*
 * This sample can be used to check the JDBC installation.
 * Just run it and provide the connect information. It will select
 * "Hello World" from the database.
 */

// You need to import the java.sql package to use JDBC
import java.sql.*;

// We import java.io to be able to read from the command line
import java.io.*;

class JdbcCheckup
{
 public static void main (String args [])
 throws SQLException, IOException
 {
 // Load the Oracle JDBC driver
 DriverManager.registerDriver(new oracle.jdbc.driver.OracleDriver());

 // Prompt the user for connect information
 System.out.println ("Please enter information to test connection
to the database");
 String user;
 String password;
 String database;

 user = readEntry ("user: ");
```

```
 int slash_index = user.indexOf ('/');
 if (slash_index != -1)
{
 password = user.substring (slash_index + 1);
 user = user.substring (0, slash_index);
 }
 else {
 password = readEntry ("password: ");
 }
 database = readEntry ("database (a TNSNAME entry): ");

 System.out.print ("Connecting to the database...");

 System.out.flush ();

 System.out.println ("Connecting...");
 Connection conn =
 DriverManager.getConnection ("jdbc:oracle:oci8:@" + database,
 user, password);

 System.out.println ("connected.");

 // Create a statement
 Statement stmt = conn.createStatement ();

 // Run a query
 ResultSet rset=stmt.executeQuery("select 'Hello World' from dual");
 // Loop through the query results
 while (rset.next ()) {
 System.out.println (rset.getString (1));
 }

 System.out.println ("Your JDBC installation is correct.");

 // close the resultSet
 rset.close();

 // Close the statement
 stmt.close();

 // Close the connection
 conn.close();
 }

 // Utility function to read a line from standard input
 static String readEntry (String prompt)
{
 try
{
 StringBuffer buffer = new StringBuffer ();
```

```
 System.out.print (prompt);
 System.out.flush ();
 int c = System.in.read ();
 while (c != '\n' && c != -1)
{
 buffer.append ((char)c);
 c = System.in.read ();
 }
 return buffer.toString ().trim ();
 }
 catch (IOException e)
{
 return "";
 }
 }
 }
}
```

**NOTE**
*Production applications would be expected to include many more
exception handling sections than shown in this brief example. See
Chapter 34 for an example of exception handling.*

Starting at the top, this script first imports the java.sql classes provided by Sun Microsystems:

```
import java.sql.*;
```

and the Oracle-provided JDBC driver is then registered:

```
DriverManager.registerDriver(new oracle.jdbc.driver.OracleDriver());
```

When you are prompted for information, the *user* variable is populated via a call to the readEntry function:

```
user = readEntry ("user: ");
```

The readEntry function is defined later in the class, in the section beginning

```
// Utility function to read a line from standard input
 static String readEntry (String prompt)
```

Once the connection data has been input, a *connection object* is created to maintain the state of the database session. The getConnection call in the following listing starts the connection:

```
Connection conn =
 DriverManager.getConnection ("jdbc:oracle:oci8:@" + database,
 user, password);
```

If you receive an error during the connection, this step is usually the cause. An incorrect username/password combination, a mismatched set of drivers, or failure to install and configure Oracle Net will cause this step to fail.

By default, a connection object is created with **autocommit** turned on—every transaction is automatically committed. To change that setting, you can use the following command (assuming you name the connection object conn, as shown in the example):

```
conn.setAutoCommit(false);
```

The class then creates a statement, executes a hard-coded query, and prints the output:

```
// Create a statement
 Statement stmt = conn.createStatement ();
// Run a query
 ResultSet rset =stmt.executeQuery("select 'Hello World' from dual");
 while (rset.next ()) {
 System.out.println (rset.getString (1));
 }
```

The resultset, statement, and connection are then closed and the program completes. Note that there are two steps in executing the statement: First, it's created via the call to the createStatement method, and then it's executed via the executeQuery method. In place of executeQuery, you can use execute or, if running an insert, update, or delete SQL statement, executeUpdate. If you select a column value (instead of just a text string), you should specify that column value in the print command, as shown in the following listing.

```
 ResultSet rset =stmt.executeQuery("select User from dual");
 while (rset.next ()) {
 System.out.println (rset.getString ("USER"));
```

## Using JDBC for Data Manipulation

Let's combine the pieces that have been described so far: the basic connection syntax from this chapter with the Java classes from Chapter 34. The example in this section will query the RADIUS_VALS table, calculate an area for each value, and insert those values into the AREAS table. Thus, it requires the use of the Java equivalent of a cursor FOR loop, along with support for executable commands and **insert**s.

For the example, put three records into the RADIUS_VALS table:

```
delete from RADIUS_VALS;
insert into RADIUS_VALS(Radius) values (3);
insert into RADIUS_VALS(Radius) values (4);
insert into RADIUS_VALS(Radius) values (10);
commit;
```

The following listing, JdbcCircle.java, contains the connection components from JdbcCheckup.java. The executable commands for the circle area start in the section called RetrieveRadius, shown in bold in the listing.

```java
// You need to import the java.sql package to use JDBC
import java.sql.*;
// We import java.io to be able to read from the command line
import java.io.*;

class JdbcCircle {

 public static void main (String args [])
 throws SQLException, IOException {

 // Load the Oracle JDBC driver
 DriverManager.registerDriver(new oracle.jdbc.driver.OracleDriver());
 // Prompt the user for connect information
 System.out.println ("Please enter information for connection");
 String user;
 String password;
 String database;

 user = readEntry ("user: ");
 int slash_index = user.indexOf ('/');
 if (slash_index != -1) {

 password = user.substring (slash_index + 1);
 user = user.substring (0, slash_index);
 }
 else {
 password = readEntry ("password: ");
 }
 database = readEntry ("database (a TNSNAME entry): ");
 System.out.println ("Connecting to the database...");

 Connection conn =
 DriverManager.getConnection ("jdbc:oracle:oci8:@" + database,
 user, password);
 System.out.println ("connected.");

 // Create a statement
 Statement stmt = conn.createStatement ();

 // RetrieveRadius
 ResultSet rset =stmt.executeQuery("select Radius from RADIUS_VALS");

 while (rset.next ()) {
 // if you wish to print the values:
 // System.out.println (rset.getInt ("RADIUS"));
```

```
 int radInput = rset.getInt ("RADIUS");

 // Retrieve Radius value, calculate area:
 double result = area(radInput);

 // insert the value into AREAS
 String sql = "insert into AREAS values ("+radInput+","+result+ ")";
 // If you want to print the SQL statement:
 // System.out.println(sql);

 // Create a statement for the insert:
 Statement insArea = conn.createStatement();
 // Execute the insert:
 boolean insertResult = insArea.execute(sql);
 }

 // close the resultSet
 rset.close();
 // Close the statement
 stmt.close();
 // Close the connection
 conn.close();
}

// Utility function to calculate the area
public static double area (int rad) {
 double pi=3.1415927;
 double areacircle=pi*rad*rad;
 return areacircle;
}

// Utility function to read a line from standard input
static String readEntry (String prompt) {

 try {

 StringBuffer buffer = new StringBuffer ();
 System.out.print (prompt);
 System.out.flush ();
 int c = System.in.read ();
 while (c != '\n' && c != -1) {

 buffer.append ((char)c);
 c = System.in.read ();
 }
 return buffer.toString ().trim ();
 }
 catch (IOException e) {

 return "";
```

```
 }
 }
 }
```

In the RetrieveRadius section, the query to be executed is passed to the executeQuery method. The result of the query is stored in a variable named *rset*.

```
// RetrieveRadius
 ResultSet rset =stmt.executeQuery("select Radius from RADIUS_VALS");
```

As noted in Chapter 34, you can use a WHILE loop in Java to approximate the functionality of a PL/SQL cursor FOR loop. The following section of the RetrieveRadius section uses the getInt method to retrieve the integer Radius value from the result set. If the value had been a string, then the getString method would have been used instead.

```
 while (rset.next ()) {
 // if you wish to print the values:
 // System.out.println (rset.getInt ("RADIUS"));
 int radInput = rset.getInt ("RADIUS");
```

The *radInput* variable, assigned in the preceding listing, can now be used as input to the area calculation. The area calculation is performed via a utility function (see the full JdbcCircle listing) based on the code examples presented in Chapter 34.

```
// Retrieve Radius value, calculate area:
 double result = area(radInput);
```

We now have the radius value (the *radInput* variable) and the area value (the *result* variable) to use when populating the AREAS table. Let's build the **insert** statement to perform the insert. First, use the string concatenation functions in Java to concatenate text with the variable values. Make sure not to include a semicolon at the end of the generated command string.

```
 // insert the value into AREAS
 String sql = "insert into AREAS values ("+radInput+","+result+ ")";
 // If you want to print the SQL statement:
 // System.out.println(sql);
```

Next, create a statement and execute the **insert** command (via a call to the *sql* variable that contains the command text):

```
 // Create a statement for the insert:
 Statement insArea = conn.createStatement();
 // Execute the insert:
 boolean insertResult = insArea.execute(sql);
```

Did it work? Compile and execute the JdbcCircle.java file, and then check the AREAS table:

```
select * from AREAS
 order by Radius;
```

```
 RADIUS AREA
 --------- ---------
 3 28.27
 4 50.27
 10 314.16
```

This example is based on a simple calculation—the area of a circle—but illustrates the key concepts in JDBC development: connecting to the database, retrieving data, implementing a cursor FOR loop, assigning variables, generating a dynamic SQL statement, and executing DML. In the next section, you will see this example written in SQLJ to illustrate the functionality and coding differences between the two languages.

# SQLJ

SQLJ is a preprocessor that embeds SQL commands as JDBC calls within a Java program. Unlike JDBC, SQLJ performs syntax checking on SQL statements during the compilation process. In the next section, you will see how to configure SQLJ. SQLJ requires the use of an additional set of classes, in the translator.zip file, to generate the Java classes.

## Additional Setup Steps for SQLJ

If you will be accessing Oracle9i using SQLJ, you must set the CLASSPATH system variable to include the translator.zip file (for all JDK versions) provided by Oracle. The file is located in the /sqlj/lib directory beneath the Oracle home directory.

**NOTE**
*This step is not performed by the standard Oracle9i installation, so you need to do it manually. If the system variables are not properly set, you will not be able to compile Java classes that use Oracle's SQLJ classes.*

To set your system variables, click the System icon in your Control Panel. Choose the Environment tab to list the environment variables and their definitions. If you did not add the JDK binaries to your PATH setting (as shown earlier in this chapter), then you must add them before using SQLJ.

**NOTE**
*The SQLJ program, sqlj.exe, must also be in your path. By default, Oracle will install this program to the /bin directory beneath the Oracle home directory.*

Replace "E:\Oracle\Ora91" with your Oracle software home directory, and replace "E:\jdk131" with the directory in which you downloaded the JDK. The CLASSPATH environment variable for SQLJ developers is different from that used by JDBC developers. For JDBC development, you only need the classes12.zip file to be in the classpath.

For SQLJ, you need to add the SQLJ translator.zip and runtime12.zip file directory, usually the /sqlj/lib directory under the Oracle software home directory. In the following listing, the one-line CLASSPATH setting is shown on multiple lines.

```
.;E:\Oracle\Ora91\jdbc\lib\classes12.zip;
E:\Oracle\Ora91\sqlj\lib\runtime12.zip;
E:\Oracle\Ora91\sqlj\lib\translator.zip
```

**NOTE**
*Replace "E:\Oracle\Ora91" with your Oracle software home directory.*

If you encounter errors when compiling the SQLJ examples in this chapter, check your CLASSPATH environment variable. You may need to shut down and restart your command window for changes to your CLASSPATH settings to take effect.

**NOTE**
*Be sure to use a version of the JDK that is compatible with the Oracle release you are using. If you use a new release of the JDK with an older release of Oracle's drivers, you may encounter "access violation" errors when executing your programs.*

## Testing Your SQLJ Configuration

Oracle provides a test script called TestInstallSQLJ.sqlj in the /sqlj/demo directory below the Oracle software home directory. TestInstallSQLJ.sqlj, in turn, reads a file named connect.properties in the same directory. The connect.properties file identifies the database, username, and password to be used for the demonstration connection. For example, the connect.properties file may contain the following entries:

```
sqlj.url=jdbc:oracle:oci8:@
sqlj.user=scott
sqlj.password=tiger
```

**NOTE**
*Add the name of your database directly after the @ in the sqlj.url entry, and use your test username and password in place of the preceding listing's example values.*

The TestInstallSQLJ.sqlj demo file inserts a row into a table named SALES, which has a column named Item_Name. For the purposes of this demo, you can create the SALES table with the following command:

```
create table SALES
 (Item_Number NUMBER,
```

```
Item_Name CHAR(30),
Sales_Date DATE,
Cost NUMBER,
Sales_Rep_Number NUMBER,
Sales_Rep_Name CHAR(20));
```

If you already have a SCOTT/TIGER account in your database, you can use that account and its SALES table for the connection test (although doing so will delete the rows presently in that table). If you prefer using JDBC for your table creation, you can run the TestInstallCreateTable.java class provided in the /sqlj/demo directory to create the SALES table. The TestInstallCreateTable.java file relies on the connection information specified in the connect.properties file.

With the SALES table in place and the connect.properties file properly configured, translate the TestInstallSQLJ.sqlj file:

```
sqlj TestInstallSQLJ.sqlj
```

This step should complete with no reported errors. As part of the SQLJ translation, the Java class will be compiled, so you can execute:

```
java TestInstallSQLJ
```

If your configuration is correct, you should see the following output:

```
Hello, SQLJ!
```

**NOTE**
*The longest part of the translation step is the Java compilation. If the translation process generates a JAVA file, you can manually compile that file (via* **javac**). *Depending on the errors encountered during compilation, manually compiling the file may provide you with more relevant debugging information than the translator provides.*

# Using the SQLJ Classes

When you translated the TestInstallSQLJ.sqlj file, several new files were created, including a TestInstallSQL.java file and a compiled TestInstallSQLJ.class file. Having seen a JDBC file earlier in this chapter, you should skim through the TestInstallSQLJ.java file to see what the translator did. You will see that it creates a class called MyIter:

```
class MyIter
extends sqlj.runtime.ref.ResultSetIterImpl
implements sqlj.runtime.NamedIterator
{
 public MyIter(sqlj.runtime.profile.RTResultSet resultSet)
 throws java.sql.SQLException
{
 super(resultSet);
 ITEM_NAMENdx = findColumn("ITEM_NAME");
```

```
 }
 public String ITEM_NAME()
 throws java.sql.SQLException
{
 return resultSet.getString(ITEM_NAMENdx);
 }
 private int ITEM_NAMENdx;
}
```

The MyIter class is a SQLJ iterator—a structure used to iterate through the results of queries returning multiple rows. Later in the file, the iterator is used as the basis for the query:

```
 MyIter iter;

// #sql iter = { SELECT ITEM_NAME FROM SALES };
```

And the query is executed:

```
 sqlj.runtime.profile.RTResultSet __sJT_result =
__sJT_execCtx.executeQuery();
 iter = new MyIter(__sJT_result);
```

SQLJ screens the JDBC details from you; you do not need to manually enter all the query-management code yourself. For each SQL statement, SQLJ creates the code needed to execute it via JDBC and Java. First, it creates a *connection context* object. The connection context maintains the JDBC connection. Each statement that is executed uses a different connection context object. For example, the TestInstallSQLJ.java file contains the following command to create a connection context:

```
 sqlj.runtime.ConnectionContext __sJT_connCtx =
sqlj.runtime.ref.DefaultContext.getDefaultContext();
```

In the preceding command, a connection context object is created based on the default context options. A default context supports a connection that your classes can use to access the database without having to specify a connection context object.

Within the connection context, all the commands are executed via *execution context* objects. Within TestInstallSQLJ.java, you should see commands similar to the following to create an execution context:

```
 sqlj.runtime.ExecutionContext __sJT_execCtx =
__sJT_connCtx.getExecutionContext();
 if (__sJT_execCtx == null)
 sqlj.runtime.error.RuntimeRefErrors.raise_NULL_EXEC_CTX();
 synchronized (__sJT_execCtx) {
 sqlj.runtime.profile.RTStatement __sJT_stmt =
__sJT_execCtx.registerStatement(__sJT_connCtx,
 TestInstallSQLJ_SJProfileKeys.getKey(0), 0);
```

The last line of the preceding listing refers to *profile keys*. When you translated
the TestInstallSQLJ.sqlj file, Oracle automatically created several files in addition to the
TestInstallSQLJ.java file. The translator retrieves the SQL statements from the SQLJ file you created
and creates two files: a file with a .ser extension that stores the statement profiles, and a file with
a .class extension that stores the profile keys. Thus, when you read the TestInstallSQLJ.java file,
you will see that the SQL commands are commented out, as shown in the following listing:

```
// #sql iter = { SELECT ITEM_NAME FROM SALES };
```

The actual SQL commands executed by the program are not visible unless you have the
source code (either the .sqlj file or the .java file created by the translator).

## Using SQLJ for Data Manipulation

Using TestInstallSQLJ.sqlj as a basis, you can develop a program that retrieves data from the
RADIUS_VALS table, performs the circle area calculation, and inserts the results into the AREAS
table. Because SQLJ handles the JDBC connection management, the logic flow of the SQLJ program
should be simpler to follow than the JDBC program, for people with a background in PL/SQL.

The following listing is the SqljCircle.sqlj file. As in the JdbcCircle.java example earlier in this
chapter, the area calculation is performed via a utility function. The most relevant part for this
example—the commands needed to extract and manipulate the data—is shown in bold.

```
/* Import SQLExceptions class. The SQLException comes from
 JDBC. Executable #sql clauses result in calls to JDBC, so methods
 containing executable #sql clauses must either catch or throw
 SQLException.
 */
import java.sql.SQLException ;
import oracle.sqlj.runtime.Oracle;

// iterator for the select
#sql iterator MyIter (int Radius);

class SqljCircle {

 //Main method
 public static void main (String args[]) {

 try {
 /* if you're using a non-Oracle JDBC Driver, add a call here to
 DriverManager.registerDriver() to register your Driver
 */
 // set the default connection to the URL, user, and password
 // specified in your connect.properties file
 Oracle.connect(SqljCircle.class, "connect.properties");
 SqljCircle ti = new SqljCircle();
 ti.runExample();
 } catch (SQLException e) {
 System.err.println("Error running the example: " + e);
 }
```

```
 } //End of method main

 //Method that runs the example
 void runExample() throws SQLException {

 MyIter iter;

 #sql iter = { select Radius from RADIUS_VALS};
 while (iter.next()) {
 // To see the radius values:
 //System.out.println(iter.Radius());

 int radInput = iter.Radius();
 double result=area(radInput);
 // To see the result values:
 //System.out.println(result);

 #sql { insert into AREAS values(:radInput,:result)};
 #sql {commit};
 }
 iter.close();
 }

 // Utility function to calculate the area
 public static double area (int rad) {
 double pi=3.1415927;
 double areacircle=pi*rad*rad;
 return areacircle;
 }
}
```

Since the query of RADIUS_VALS will return multiple rows, an iterator is specified within the SQLJ file. If you prefer, you can create and use JDBC result sets instead (see the JDBC examples earlier in this chapter). When you execute the query for the program, the result is passed as the value for the iterator:

```
#sql iter = { select Radius from RADIUS_VALS};
```

Next, use a WHILE loop to evaluate the rows:

```
 while (iter.next()) {
 // To see the radius values:
 //System.out.println(iter.Radius());
```

For each row passed to the iterator, capture the Radius value and use that as the *radInput* value. Then, create the *result* variable to hold the calculated area value based on the Radius value.

```
 int radInput = iter.Radius();
 double result=area(radInput);
```

```
// To see the result values:
//System.out.println(result);
```

Now that the values have been calculated, you can insert them into the AREAS table. This example assumes that the AREAS table is empty prior to executing the SqljCircle class. Within the **insert** command, the *radInput* and *result* variables are prefixed by a colon. Note that the entire command is enclosed within curly braces, {}, and that no semicolon appears within the braces. Each row is committed following each insert.

```
#sql { insert into AREAS values(:radInput,:result)};
#sql {commit};
```

This example contains an explicit **commit** command so that you can add additional criteria to control the commit frequency within the application.

Now, close the iterator:

```
iter.close();
```

and you're done. You can check the AREAS table for the result.

For the example, put three records into the RADIUS_VALS table:

```
delete from AREAS;
delete from RADIUS_VALS;
insert into RADIUS_VALS(Radius) values (3);
insert into RADIUS_VALS(Radius) values (4);
insert into RADIUS_VALS(Radius) values (10);
commit;
```

The connect.properties file should resemble the following, where "orcl" is the name of the instance to connect to:

```
sqlj.url=jdbc:oracle:oci8:@orcl
sqlj.user=practice
sqlj.password=practice
```

The following listing shows the compilation and execution of SqljCircle.sqlj:

```
sqlj SqljCircle.sqlj
java SqljCircle
```

You can verify the results from within SQL*Plus:

```
select * from AREAS
 order by Radius;

 RADIUS AREA
--------- ---------
 3 28.27
 4 50.27
 10 314.16
```

Because it supports SQL calls so easily, SQLJ is attractive to first-time JDBC programmers. By comparison, the SqljCircle.java file generated by the translator is three times longer than the SqljCircle.sqlj file. See the Oracle documentation for further information on the options available for implementing and managing iterators.

This chapter provides an overview of SQLJ's capabilities—queries, data manipulation, multirow result set management, variable assignments, and DML operations. For additional information regarding SQLJ's capabilities, please see Oracle's SQLJ documentation.

# CHAPTER
# 36

# Java Stored
# Procedures

ou can write stored procedures, triggers, object type methods, and functions that call Java classes. In this chapter, you will see a sample set of Java procedures, along with the commands required to execute a procedure. To get the most from this chapter, you should already be familiar with Java structures (refer to Chapter 34) and the uses of Java classes, JDBC, and SQLJ (refer to Chapter 35). You should also be familiar with the basic syntax and usage of stored procedures (refer to Chapter 29).

To focus on the database access operations of the Java classes, the example in this chapter is brief. The following class, called AreasDML, contains methods to insert and delete records from the AREAS table. In this example, the calculation of the area is not performed; rather, all required values are supplied during the **insert**. The following listing shows the AreasDML.sqlj file:

```
import sqlj.runtime.*;
import sqlj.runtime.ref.*;
import java.sql.SQLException ;
import oracle.sqlj.runtime.Oracle;
import java.sql.*;

class AreasDML {

 //Insert method
 public static void insert (
 oracle.sql.NUMBER radius,
 oracle.sql.NUMBER area) throws SQLException {
 try {
 #sql {insert into AREAS values
 (:radius, :area) };
 }
 catch (SQLException e) {
 System.err.println(e.getMessage());
 }
 }//End of method insert

 //Delete method
 public static void delete (
 oracle.sql.NUMBER radius,
 oracle.sql.NUMBER area) throws SQLException {
 try {
 #sql {delete from AREAS
 where Radius = :radius};
 }
 catch (SQLException e) {
 System.err.println(e.getMessage());
 }
 } //End of method delete
}
```

The AreasDML.sqlj file defines the AreasDML class. Within the AreasDML class, there are separate methods for processing **insert**s and **delete**s. In each of the method specifications, the datatypes for the AREAS table's columns are listed:

```
public static void insert (
 oracle.sql.NUMBER radius,
 oracle.sql.NUMBER area)
```

These parameters use the datatypes provided as part of Oracle's class libraries. If you use the standard Java datatypes, you may encounter datatype-related problems during the class execution.

**NOTE**
*If you import the oracle.sqlj.* libraries, you can use NUMBER in place of oracle.sql.NUMBER.*

The next part of the insert method inserts the values into the AREAS table:

```
#sql {insert into AREAS values
 (:radius, :area) };
```

Note that the variable names are case-sensitive—they must exactly match the names declared earlier.

The delete method is very similar in structure. Its SQL statement is

```
#sql {delete from AREAS
 where Radius = :radius};
```

Note that no part of the class creates a connection to the database, in contrast with the examples in Chapter 35. The connection used to invoke this class will provide the connection context for the class's methods.

Verify that the class compiles properly by processing it via the SQLJ preprocessor:

```
sqlj AreasDML.sqlj
```

This step should complete successfully. If you encounter errors during this compilation step, check your SQLJ environment configuration (see Chapter 35).

# Loading the Class into the Database

Before loading a class into the database, confirm that it compiles properly via SQLJ. You can then use the loadjava utility to load the class into the database. The syntax for the loadjava utility is as follows:

```
loadjava {-user | -u} username/password[@database]
 [-option_name -option_name ...] filename filename ...
```

The options available for the loadjava utility are shown in Table 36-1.

For example, to load the AreasDML.sqlj file into the Practice schema in an instance named "orcl", you can use the following command:

```
loadjava -u Practice/practice@orcl.world -verbose AreasDML.sqlj
```

Option	Description
<filenames>	Any number and combination of .java, .class, .sqlj, .ser, .jar, .zip, and resource filename arguments, in any order.
andresolve	Compiles source files and resolves each class file as it is loaded.
debug	Generates debugging information.
definer	Specifies that the methods of uploaded classes will execute with the privileges of their definer, not their invoker. By default, methods execute with the privileges of their invoker.
encoding	Sets (or resets) the option -*encoding* in the database table JAVA$OPTIONS to the specified value.
fileout	Prints messages to an output file.
force	Forces the loading of Java class files regardless of whether they have been loaded before. By default, previously loaded class files are rejected.
grant	Grants EXECUTE privilege on uploaded classes to the listed users and roles.
help	Prints loadjava help text.
javaresource	Directs loadjava to load a JAR file without unpacking it.
nousage	Suppresses the usage message given if either no option is specified or if the -*help* option is specified.
noserverside	Changes the behavior of the server-side loadjava tool to use a JDBC driver to access objects.
noverify	Causes the classes to be loaded without bytecode verification. You must be granted oracle.aurora.security.JServerPermission(Verifier) to execute this option. In addition, this option must be used in conjunction with -r.
oci8	Directs loadjava to communicate with the database using the OCI JDBC driver. This option (the default) and -*thin* are mutually exclusive.
resolve	Resolves all external references in the loaded and compiled classes. If this option is not specified, files are loaded but not compiled or resolved until runtime.
resolver	Binds newly created class schema objects to a user-defined resolver spec.
schema	Specifies the schema for newly created objects.
stdout	Causes the output to be directed to stdout, rather than to stderr.
synonym	Automatically creates a public synonym for the uploaded classes.

**TABLE 36-1.** *loadjava Options*

Option	Description
tableschema	Creates the loadjava internal tables within this specified schema, rather than in the Java file destination schema.
thin	Directs loadjava to communicate with the database using the thin JDBC driver. This option and *–oci8* are mutually exclusive.
time	Prints a timestamp on every message.
unresolvedok	When combined with *-resolve*, ignores unresolved errors.
user	Specifies a user, password, and database connect string for the load.
verbose	Enables the display of progress messages during loadjava execution.

**TABLE 36-1.**   *loadjava Options* (continued)

You should see the following output:

```
arguments: '-u' 'practice/practice@orcl.world' '-verbose' 'AreasDML.sql'
created :JAVA$CLASS$MD5$TABLE
creating : source AreasDML
created :CREATE$JAVA$LOB$TABLE
loading : source AreasDML
creating : AreasDML
```

**NOTE**
*The name of the class should not match the name of any of the existing objects in your schema.*

The AreasDML class is now loaded into the database. Here's what it created (you can query new objects from USER_OBJECTS based on their object creation timestamps):

```
OBJECT_NAME OBJECT_TYPE
-- ------------------
AreasDML JAVA CLASS
AreasDML JAVA SOURCE
AreasDML_SJProfileKeys JAVA CLASS
CREATE$JAVA$LOB$TABLE TABLE
JAVA$CLASS$MD5$TABLE TABLE
JAVA$OPTIONS TABLE
SYS_C002684 INDEX
SYS_C002685 INDEX
SYS_LOB0000032362C00002$$ LOB

9 rows selected.
```

(The names of the indexes and LOB, which start with SYS_ , will be different in your database, since each name includes a sequence number that is database-specific.) The AreasDML source, class, and profile keys should be familiar from the SQLJ examples in Chapter 35.

# How to Access the Class

Now that the AreasDML class has been loaded into the database, you must create a procedure to call each of the methods. The **create procedure** command in the following listing creates a procedure called InsertAreaViaJava:

```
create or replace procedure InsertAreaViaJava
(Radius NUMBER,
 Area NUMBER)
as
language java
name 'AreasDML.insert(oracle.sql.NUMBER, oracle.sql.NUMBER)';
/
```

This brief procedure has two parameters—Radius and Area. Its **language java** clause tells Oracle that the procedure is calling a Java method. The name of the method is specified in the **name** clause (be sure to be consistent with your use of capital letters). The formats for the Java method call are then specified.

A separate procedure will delete the AREA table's records via a method call:

```
create or replace procedure DeleteAreaViaJava
(Radius NUMBER,
 Area NUMBER)
as
language java
name 'AreasDML.delete(
 oracle.sql.NUMBER, oracle.sql.NUMBER)';
/
```

Now, go into SQL*Plus and use the **call** command to execute the Java classes. For this example, start with the AREAS table empty:

```
delete from AREAS;
commit;

call InsertAreaViaJava(10,314.15);
```

You will see this response:

```
Call completed.
```

The **call** command will pass the values 10 and 314.15 as parameters to the InsertAreaViaJava stored procedure. It will format them according to the specifications in the **name** clause and will pass them to the AreasDML.insert method. That method will use your current connection to

execute its SQLJ commands, and the row will be inserted. Most of these libraries and classes will not have been loaded yet within the database. That's a lot of steps to go through, so the performance will be affected the first time you run the Java stored procedure, but subsequent executions will be much faster. You can verify its success by querying the AREAS table:

```
select * from AREAS;

 RADIUS AREA
--------- ---------
 10 314.15
```

And you can delete that record via a call to DeleteAreaViaJava:

```
call DeleteAreaViaJava(10,314.15);
```

Oracle will reply

```
Call completed.
```

The call to DeleteAreaViaJava will complete much faster than the call to InsertAreaViaJava, because your Java libraries will have been loaded the first time you executed InsertAreaViaJava.

Check out the error handling by passing a character string to be inserted:

```
call InsertAreaViaJava('J',314.15);
 *
ERROR at line 1:
ORA-01722: invalid number
```

As expected, the datatype mismatch caused a problem—in this case, Oracle detects that the data being passed to the PL/SQL procedure does not match the datatype of the procedure's parameter.

When debugging Java stored procedures, you can call System.err.println from within your Java code, as shown in the AreasDML.sqlj listing earlier in this chapter. To display the output within your SQL*Plus session, you must first execute the following commands:

```
set serveroutput on
call DBMS_JAVA.SET_OUTPUT(10000);
```

Calling DBMS_JAVA.SET_OUTPUT will redirect the output of System.out.println to DBMS_OUTPUT.PUT_LINE. Otherwise, the System.out.println output will only go to the database's log file.

## Where to Perform Commands

The AreasDML example is intended to provide an overview of the implementation of Java stored procedures. Suppose you now want to make the procedures more complex. Since area and radius are directly related to each other, you only need to accept the radius value as input to the procedure. You could then calculate the area and insert the calculated value. As shown in Chapters 27, 34, and 35, you can perform those calculations either in Java or in PL/SQL.

Your choice of a platform and language for your data processing will impact your performance. In general, you will pay a performance penalty the first time you execute a Java stored procedure (as the classes are loaded), but subsequent executions will not pay the same penalty. If you repeatedly execute the same commands, the performance impact of the first execution will be minimal.

For example, multiple executions of the InsertAreaViaJava procedure completed in 0.5 seconds, 0.2 seconds, 0.2 seconds, and 0.2 seconds. A series of **insert**s into the AREAS table completed in an average of 0.18 seconds.

Logging out and logging back in impacts your performance, but not nearly as much as the first execution of the procedure. When you use Java stored procedures, you must therefore be aware of the way in which the application interacts with Oracle. If your users frequently log out and log back in, then they will pay a performance penalty the first time they execute the procedure following each login. Furthermore, the first execution of the procedure following a database startup will pay the most severe performance penalty. The performance impact of these actions must be taken into account during the design stage of your application development.

To reduce the performance penalties associated with the Java stored procedure calls:

- Execute each Java stored procedure following database startup. In the case of the AreasDML example, this may involve inserting and deleting a test record following each startup.

- Reduce the number of short-term database connections; for example, by connection pooling.

- Perform most of your direct database manipulation via standard SQL and PL/SQL.

Java is an appropriate technology to use for many computational processes and for display manipulation. In general, SQL and PL/SQL are slightly more efficient than Java for database connections and data manipulation. However, the performance of Java within Oracle makes it a strong alternative to PL/SQL; the primary source of the performance penalty for Java stored procedures is the time required to go through the PL/SQL wrapper. When designing applications that integrate Java, SQL, and PL/SQL, focus on using each language for the functions that it performs best.

If your code involves many loops and manipulations of data, Java should outperform PL/SQL. The costs of using Java—for Java object creation and the PL/SQL header interaction—will be offset by the improved performance Java yields during the actual work.

The calculation of a circle's area is simple arithmetic, handled easily by both PL/SQL and Java. Thus, you could put the area calculation in either part of the application—in a PL/SQL procedure that calculates the area prior to passing it to SQLJ to be inserted, or as part of the SQLJ class. In general, actions that involve selecting data from the database and manipulating it are best handled by PL/SQL and SQL. Computations on the selected data may be processed faster by Java. In your application design, be sure to use the proper tool for the proper function, and avoid unnecessary performance penalties.

# PART VI

# Hitchhiker's Guides

# CHAPTER
## 37

## The Hitchhiker's Guide to the Oracle9i Data Dictionary

racle's data dictionary stores all the information that is used to manage the objects in the database. Although the data dictionary is usually the domain of database administrators (DBAs), it also is a source of valuable information for developers and end users.

In this chapter, you will see the data dictionary—Oracle's internal directory—from the perspective of an end user; the data dictionary tables and views are not listed alphabetically, but rather are grouped by function (tables, security, and so on). This organization is designed to let you quickly find your way to the information you need. The most-used data dictionary views are all shown here, along with examples of their usage.

Depending on which Oracle configuration options you are using, some of the groups will not apply to your database. The most commonly used views are listed first. The groupings used in this chapter are, in order:

- The Road Maps: DICTIONARY (DICT) and DICT_COLUMNS

- Things You Select from: Tables (and Columns), Views, Synonyms, and Sequences

- Constraints and Comments

- Indexes and Clusters

- Abstract Datatypes, ORDBMS-Related Structures, and LOBs

- Database Links and Materialized Views

- Triggers, Procedures, Functions, and Packages

- Dimensions

- Space Allocation and Usage, Including Partitions and Subpartitions

- Users and Privileges

- Roles

- Auditing

- Miscellaneous

- Monitoring: The V$ Dynamic Performance Tables

**NOTE**
*As new features are added, it is expected that the data dictionary will be modified with each future release of Oracle.*

# A Note About Nomenclature

With some exceptions, the names of the objects in the Oracle data dictionary begin with one of three prefixes: "USER," "ALL," or "DBA." Records in the "USER" views usually show information about objects owned by the account performing the query. Records in the "ALL" views include the "USER" records plus information about objects on which privileges have been granted to

PUBLIC or to the user. "DBA" views encompass all of the database objects, regardless of owner. For most database objects, "USER," "ALL," and "DBA" views are available.

In keeping with the user focus of this guide, the emphasis will be on the "USER" views or those that are accessible to all users. The "ALL" and "DBA" views will be described when they are applicable.

# The Road Maps: DICTIONARY (DICT) and DICT_COLUMNS

Descriptions for the objects that make up the Oracle data dictionary are accessible via a view named DICTIONARY. This view, also accessible via the public synonym DICT, queries the database to determine which data dictionary views you can see. It also searches for public synonyms for those views.

The following example queries DICT for the names of all data dictionary views whose names include the string 'VIEWS'. Selecting from DICT via a non-DBA account, as shown in the following listing, returns the object name and comments for each data dictionary object that matches your search criteria. There are only two columns in this view: Table_Name and the table's associated Comments.

```
column Comments format a35 word_wrapped
column Table_Name format a25

select Table_Name, Comments
 from DICT
 where Table_Name like '%VIEWS%';
```

TABLE_NAME	COMMENTS
ALL_BASE_TABLE_MVIEWS	All materialized views with log(s) in the database that the user can see
ALL_MVIEWS	All materialized views in the database
ALL_REGISTERED_MVIEWS	Remote materialized views of local tables that the user can see
ALL_VIEWS	Description of views accessible to the user
USER_BASE_TABLE_MVIEWS	All materialized views with log(s) owned by the user in the database
USER_MVIEWS	All materialized views in the database
USER_REGISTERED_MVIEWS	Remote materialized views of local tables currently using logs owned by the user
USER_VIEWS	Description of the user's own views

You can query the columns of the dictionary views via the DICT_COLUMNS view. Like the DICTIONARY view, DICT_COLUMNS displays the comments that have been entered into the database for the data dictionary views. DICT_COLUMNS has three columns: Table_Name,

Column_Name, and Comments. Querying DICT_COLUMNS lets you determine which data dictionary views would be most useful for your needs.

For example, if you want to view space allocation and usage information for your database objects but are not sure which data dictionary views store that information, you can query DICT_COLUMNS, as shown in the following example, which looks for all the dictionary tables that have a column named Blocks:

```
select Table_Name
 from DICT_COLUMNS
 where Column_Name = 'BLOCKS'
 and Table_Name like 'USER%';

TABLE_NAME

USER_ALL_TABLES
USER_EXTENTS
USER_FREE_SPACE
USER_OBJECT_TABLES
USER_SEGMENTS
USER_TABLES
USER_TAB_PARTITIONS
USER_TAB_SUBPARTITIONS
USER_TS_QUOTAS
```

To list all of the available column names that you could have used in the last example, query DICT_COLUMNS:

```
select distinct Column_Name
 from DICT_COLUMNS
 order by Column_Name;
```

Whenever you're unsure about where to find the data you want, just check DICTIONARY and DICT_COLUMNS. If it appears that a large number of views could be useful, query DICTIONARY (as in the first example) to see the Comments on each view.

# Things You Select from: Tables (and Columns), Views, Synonyms, and Sequences

A user's catalog lists all of those objects that the user can **select** records from; that is, any object that can be listed in the **from** clause of a query. Although sequences are not referenced directly in **from** clauses, Oracle includes them in the catalog. In this section, you will see how to retrieve information about tables, columns, views, synonyms, sequences, and the user catalog.

## Catalog: USER_CATALOG (CAT)

Querying USER_CATALOG will display all tables, views, synonyms, and sequences the user owns. The Table_Name column shows the name of the object (even if it is not a table), and the Table_Type column shows the type of object:

```
select Table_Name, Table_Type
 from USER_CATALOG
 where Table_Name like 'T%';
```

USER_CATALOG may also be referred to by the public synonym CAT.

Two additional catalogs are available. ALL_CATALOG lists everything in your USER_CATALOG view plus any objects that you or PUBLIC have been granted access to. DBA_CATALOG is a DBA-level version of the catalog showing all tables, views, sequences, and synonyms in the database. In addition to the Table_Name and Table_Type columns shown in the USER_CATALOG query, ALL_CATALOG and DBA_CATALOG include an Owner column.

## Objects: USER_OBJECTS (OBJ)

USER_CATALOG only displays information for tables, views, sequences, and synonyms. To retrieve information on all types of objects, query USER_OBJECTS. You can use this view to find out about many types of objects, including clusters, database links, directories, functions, indexes, libraries, packages, package bodies, Java classes, abstract datatypes, resource plans, sequences, synonyms, tables, triggers, materialized views, LOBs, and views. USER_OBJECTS' columns are listed in Table 37-1.

USER_OBJECTS (also known by its public synonym OBJ) contains several vital pieces of information that are not found in other data dictionary views. It records the creation date of

Column Name	Description
Object_Name	The name of the object
SubObject_Name	The name of the subobject, such as a partition name
Object_ID	A unique, Oracle-assigned ID for the object
Data_Object_ID	The object number of the segment that contains the object's data
Object_Type	The object type ('TABLE', 'INDEX', 'TABLE PARTITION', and so on)
Created	The timestamp for the object's creation (a DATE column)
Last_DDL_Time	The timestamp for the last DDL command used on the object, including **alter**, **grant**, and **revoke**
Timestamp	The timestamp for the object's creation (same as Created, but stored as a character column)
Status	The status of the object ('VALID' or 'INVALID')
Temporary	A flag to indicate whether the object is a temporary table
Generated	A flag to indicate whether the object's name was system-generated
Secondary	A flag to indicate whether the object is a secondary index created by a domain index

**TABLE 37-1.**   *Columns in USER_OBJECTS*

objects (the Created column) and the last time an object was altered (the Last_DDL_Time column). These columns are very useful when trying to reconcile different sets of objects in the same application.

**NOTE**
*If you re-create objects in any way, such as via the Import utility (see Chapter 40), their Created values will change to the last time they were created.*

Two additional object listings are available. ALL_OBJECTS lists everything in your USER_OBJECTS view plus any objects for which access has been granted to you or PUBLIC. DBA_OBJECTS is a DBA-level version of the object listing, showing all of the objects in the database. In addition to the columns shown in the USER_OBJECTS view, ALL_OBJECTS and DBA_OBJECTS include an Owner column.

## Tables: USER_TABLES (TABS)

Although all of a user's objects are shown in USER_OBJECTS, few attributes of those objects are shown there. To get more information about an object, you need to look at the view that is specific to that type of object. For tables, that view is USER_TABLES. It can also be referenced via the public synonym TABS.

**NOTE**
*Earlier versions of Oracle included a view called TAB. That view, which is similar in function to TABS, is still supported because of Oracle products that reference it. However, TAB does not contain the columns that TABS contains. Use TABS in your data dictionary queries.*

The columns in USER_TABLES can be divided into four major categories (Identification, Space-Related, Statistics-Related, and Other), as shown in Table 37-2.

Identification	Space-Related	Statistics-Related	Other
Table_Name	Tablespace_Name	Num_Rows	Degree
Backed_Up	Cluster_Name	Blocks	Instances
Partitioned	Pct_Free	Empty_Blocks	Cache
IOT_Name	Pct_Used	Avg_Space	Table_Lock
Logging	Ini_Trans	Chain_Cnt	Buffer_Pool
IOT_Type	Max_Trans	Avg_Row_Len	Row_Movement
Temporary	Initial_Extent	Sample_Size	Duration

**TABLE 37-2.** *Columns in USER_TABLES*

Identification	Space-Related	Statistics-Related	Other
Nested	Next_Extent	Last_Analyzed	Skip_Corrupt
Secondary	Min_Extents	Avg_Space_ Freelist_Blocks	Monitoring
	Max_Extents	Num_Freelist_Blocks	Cluster_Owner
	Pct_Increase	Global_Stats	Dependencies
	Freelists	User_Stats	
	Freelist_Groups		

**TABLE 37-2.** *Columns in USER_TABLES* (continued)

The table's name is shown in the Table_Name column. The Backed_Up column shows whether or not the table has been backed up since its last modification. The Partitioned column will have a value of 'YES' if the table has been partitioned (data dictionary views related to partitions are described in the "Space Allocation and Usage" section of this chapter). If the table is an object table, then the Table_Type_Owner column will show the owner of the type.

The "Space-Related" columns are described in the "Storage" entry of the Alphabetical Reference. The "Statistics-Related" columns are populated when the table is analyzed.

Querying the Table_Name column from USER_TABLES will display the names of all of the tables in the current account. The following query lists all of the tables whose names begin with the letter 'L':

```
select Table_Name from USER_TABLES
 where Table_Name like 'L%';
```

The ALL_TABLES view shows all of the tables owned by the user as well as any to which the user has been granted access. Most third-party reporting tools that list available tables for queries obtain that list by querying ALL_TABLES. Since ALL_TABLES can contain entries for multiple users, it contains an Owner column in addition to the columns shown in Table 37-2. DBA_TABLES, which lists all tables in the database, has the same column definitions as ALL_TABLES.

The Degree and Instances columns in the "Other" category of Table 37-2 relate to how the table is queried during parallel queries. For information on Degree, Instances, and the other table parameters, see CREATE TABLE in the Alphabetical Reference.

**NOTE**
*For external tables, see USER_EXTERNAL_TABLES.*

# Columns: USER_TAB_COLUMNS (COLS)
Although users do not query from columns, the data dictionary view that shows columns is closely tied to the data dictionary view of tables. This view, called USER_TAB_COLUMNS, lists

information specific to columns. USER_TAB_COLUMNS can also be queried via the public synonym COLS.

The columns you can query from USER_TAB_COLUMNS can be separated into three major categories, as shown in Table 37-3.

The Table_Name and Column_Name columns contain the names of your tables and columns. The usage of the "Definition-Related" columns is described in the "Datatypes" entry in the Alphabetical Reference. The "Statistics-Related" columns are populated when the table is analyzed (see the **analyze** command in the Alphabetical Reference). Statistics for columns are also provided in the USER_TAB_COL_STATISTICS view (described shortly).

To see the column definitions for a table, query USER_TAB_COLUMNS, specify the Table_Name in the **where** clause:

```
select Column_Name, Data_Type
 from USER_TAB_COLUMNS
 where Table_Name = 'NEWSPAPER';

COLUMN_NAME DATA_TYPE
------------ ---------
FEATURE VARCHAR2
SECTION CHAR
PAGE NUMBER
```

Identification	Definition-Related	Statistics-Related
Table_Name	Data_Type	Num_Distinct
Column_Name	Data_Length	Low_Value
Column_ID	Data_Precision	High_Value
Character_Set_Name	Data_Scale	Density
Char_Col_Decl_Length	Nullable	Num_Nulls
	Default_Length	Num_Buckets
	Data_Default	Last_Analyzed
	Data_Type_Mod	Sample_Size
	Data_Type_Owner	Global_Stats
	Char_Length	User_Stats
	Char_Used	Avg_Col_Len
	V80_Fmt_Image	
	Data_Upgraded	

**TABLE 37-3.** *Columns in USER_TAB_COLUMNS*

The information in this example is also obtainable via the SQLPLUS **describe** command; however, **describe** does not give you the option of seeing the column defaults and statistics. The ALL_TAB_COLUMNS view shows the columns for all of the tables and views owned by the user as well as any to which the user has been granted access. Since ALL_TAB_COLUMNS can contain entries for multiple users, it contains an Owner column in addition to the columns shown in Table 37-3. DBA_TAB_COLUMNS, which lists the column definitions for all tables and views in the database, has the same column definitions as ALL_TAB_COLUMNS.

### Column Statistics

Most of the column statistics are available in both USER_TAB_COLUMNS (their former home) and USER_TAB_COL_STATISTICS. The columns available in USER_TAB_COL_STATISTICS are the "Statistics-Related" columns of USER_TAB_COLUMNS shown in Table 37-3 plus the Table_Name and Column_Name columns.

USER_TAB_COL_STATISTICS contains statistics columns that are also provided via USER_TAB_COLUMNS for backward-compatibility. You should access them via USER_TAB_COL_STATISTICS.

### Column Value Histograms

You can use histograms to improve the analysis used by the cost-based optimizer. The USER_TAB_HISTOGRAMS view contains information about each column's histogram, including the Table_Name, Column_Name, Endpoint_Number, Endpoint_Value, and Endpoint_Actual_Value. The values in USER_TAB_HISTOGRAMS are used by the optimizer to determine the distribution of the column values within the table. "ALL" and "DBA" versions of USER_TAB_HISTOGRAMS are available.

### Updatable Columns

You can update records in views that contain joins in their view queries, provided the join meets certain criteria. The USER_UPDATABLE_COLUMNS view lists all columns you can update. You can query the Owner, Table_Name, and Column_Name for the column; the Updatable column will have a value of YES if the column can be updated, and a value of NO if the column cannot be updated. You can also query to determine if you can insert or delete records from the view via the Insertable and Deletable columns.

## Views: USER_VIEWS

The base query of a view is accessible via the USER_VIEWS data dictionary view, which contains ten columns; the three main columns are as follows:

View_Name	The name of the view
Text_Length	The length of the view's base query, in characters
Text	The query that the view uses

The other columns, described later in this section, are related to object views.

**NOTE**
*This section only applies to traditional views. For materialized views, see "Database Links and Materialized Views" later in the chapter.*

The Text column is a LONG datatype. This may cause a problem when querying USER_VIEWS via SQLPLUS, because SQLPLUS truncates LONGs. The point at which truncation occurs, however, can be changed via the **set long** command. USER_VIEWS provides a mechanism for determining the proper setting for the LONG truncation point, as you'll see in the following example.

The Text_Length column shows the length of the view's query. Therefore, the SQLPLUS LONG truncation point must be set to a value equal to or greater than the view's Text_Length value. For example, the following listing shows a view whose View_Name is AGING and whose Text_Length is 355:

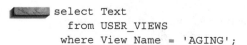

```
select View_Name, Text_Length
 from USER_VIEWS
 where View_Name = 'AGING';

View_Name Text_Length
---------------- -------------
AGING 355
```

Since the length of the view's text is 355 characters, use the **set long** command to increase the LONG truncation point to at least 355 (the default is 80) to see the full text of the view's query:

```
set long 355
```

You can then query USER_VIEWS for the view's Text, using the query shown in the following listing:

```
select Text
 from USER_VIEWS
 where View_Name = 'AGING';
```

If you had not used the **set long** command, then the output would have been truncated at 80 characters, with no message telling you why the truncation occurred. Before querying other views, you will need to recheck their Text_Length values.

**NOTE**
*You can query the column definitions for views from USER_TAB_COLUMNS, the same view you query for tables.*

If you use column aliases in your views, and your column aliases are part of the view's query, then your data dictionary queries for information about views will be simplified. Since the entire text of the view's query is displayed in USER_VIEWS, the column aliases will be displayed as well.

You can create views using this format:

```
create view NEWSPAPER_VIEW (SomeFeature, SomeSection)
 as select Feature, Section
 from NEWSPAPER;
```

Listing the column names in the header of the **create view** command removes the column aliases from the query and thus prevents you from seeing them via USER_VIEWS. The only way to see the view's column names would be to query USER_TAB_COLUMNS. If the column names are in the query, then you only need to query one data dictionary view (USER_VIEWS) for both the query and the column names.

For example, given the NEWSPAPER_VIEW view created in the last example, if you were to query USER_VIEWS, you would see

```
select Text
 from USER_VIEWS
 where View_Name ='NEWSPAPER_VIEW';

TEXT
--
select Feature, Section from NEWSPAPER
```

This query does *not* show you the new column names you assigned, since you did not make those column names part of the view's query. To make those column names show up in USER_VIEWS, add them as column aliases in the view's query:

```
create view NEWSPAPER_VIEW
 as select Feature AS SomeFeature, Section AS SomeSection
 from NEWSPAPER;
```

Now when you query USER_VIEWS, the column aliases will be displayed as part of the view's query text:

```
select Text
 from USER_VIEWS
 where View_Name ='NEWSPAPER_VIEW';

TEXT

select Feature SomeFeature, Section SomeSection
 from NEWSPAPER
```

To support object views, USER_VIEWS contains the following columns:

Type_Text	Type clause of the typed view
Type_Text_Length	Length of the type clause of the typed view
OID_Text	WITH OID clause of the typed view
OID_Text_Length	Length of the WITH OID clause of the typed view
View_Type_Owner	Owner of the view's type for typed views
View_Type	Type of the view

See Chapters 30 and 33 for information on object views and types.

The ALL_VIEWS view lists all of the views owned by the user as well as any views to which the user has been granted access. Since ALL_VIEWS can contain entries for multiple users, it contains an Owner column in addition to the columns listed earlier in this section. DBA_VIEWS, which lists all views in the database, has the same column definitions as ALL_VIEWS.

## Synonyms: USER_SYNONYMS (SYN)

USER_SYNONYMS lists all of the synonyms that a user owns. The columns are as follows:

Synonym_Name	The name of the synonym
Table_Owner	The owner of the table that the synonym refers to
Table_Name	The name of the table that the synonym refers to
DB_Link	The name of the database link used in the synonym

USER_SYNONYMS is useful when debugging programs or resolving problems with users' access to objects within applications. USER_SYNONYMS is also known by the public synonym SYN.

The DB_Link column will be **NULL** if the synonym does not use a database link. Therefore, if you want to see a list of the database links currently in use by the synonyms owned by your account, execute this query:

```
elect distinct DB_Link
 from USER_SYNONYMS
 where DB_Link is not null;
```

The ALL_SYNONYMS view lists all of the synonyms owned by the user, public synonyms, and all synonyms to which the user has been granted access. Since ALL_SYNONYMS can contain entries for multiple users, it contains an Owner column in addition to the columns listed earlier in this section. DBA_SYNONYMS, which lists all synonyms in the database, has the same column definitions as ALL_SYNONYMS.

## Sequences: USER_SEQUENCES (SEQ)

To display the attributes of sequences, you can query the USER_SEQUENCES data dictionary view. This view can also be queried using the public synonym SEQ. The columns of USER_SEQUENCES are listed in Table 37-4.

Column Name	Description
Sequence_Name	Name of the sequence
Min_Value	Minimum value of the sequence
Max_Value	Maximum value of the sequence

**TABLE 37-4.** *Columns in USER_SEQUENCES*

Column Name	Description
Increment_By	Increment between sequence values
Cycle_Flag	A flag to indicate whether the value should cycle back to the Min_Value once the Max_Value is reached
Order_Flag	A flag to indicate whether sequence numbers are generated in order
Cache_Size	The number of sequence entries cached in memory
Last_Number	The last sequence number written to disk or cached

**TABLE 37-4.**   *Columns in USER_SEQUENCES* (continued)

The Last_Number column is not updated during normal database operation; it is used during database restart/recovery operations.

ALL_SEQUENCES lists all of the sequences owned by the user or to which the user has been granted access. Since ALL_SEQUENCES can contain entries for multiple users, it contains a Sequence_Owner column in addition to the columns listed in Table 37-4. DBA_SEQUENCES, which lists all sequences in the database, has the same column definitions as ALL_SEQUENCES.

# Constraints and Comments

Constraints and comments help you to understand how tables and columns relate to each other. Comments are strictly informational; they do not enforce any conditions on the data stored in the objects they describe. Constraints, on the other hand, define the conditions under which that data is valid. Typical constraints include NOT NULL, UNIQUE, PRIMARY KEY, and FOREIGN KEY. In the following sections, you will see how to retrieve data about constraints and comments from the data dictionary.

## Constraints: USER_CONSTRAINTS

Constraint information is accessible via the USER_CONSTRAINTS view. This information is very useful when trying to alter data constraints or resolve problems with an application's data. The columns of this view are listed in Table 37-5.

Although this is a "USER" view, it contains an Owner column. In this view, Owner refers to the owner of the constraint, not the owner of the table (which is the user).

Valid values for the Constraint_Type column are shown in Table 37-5. Understanding the constraint types is crucial when you are trying to get useful information about your constraints.

FOREIGN KEY constraints will always have values for the R_Owner and R_Constraint_Name columns. These two columns will tell you which constraint the FOREIGN KEY references. A FOREIGN KEY references another *constraint,* not another column. NOT NULL constraints on columns are stored as CHECK constraints, so they have a Constraint_Type of 'C'.

Querying USER_CONSTRAINTS will give you the names of all the constraints on a table. This is important when trying to interpret error messages that only provide the name of the constraint that was violated.

Column Name	Description
Owner	The owner of the constraint.
Constraint_Name	The name of the constraint.
Constraint_Type	The type of constraint: 'C'   CHECK constraint; includes NOT NULLs 'P'   PRIMARY KEY constraint 'R'   FOREIGN KEY (reference) constraint 'U'   UNIQUE constraint 'V'   WITH CHECK OPTION constraint (for views) 'O'   WITH READ ONLY constraint (for views)
Table_Name	The name of the table associated with the constraint.
Search_Condition	The search condition used (for CHECK constraints).
R_Owner	The owner of the table referenced by a FOREIGN KEY constraint.
R_Constraint_Name	The name of the constraint referenced by a FOREIGN KEY constraint.
Delete_Rule	The action to take on the FOREIGN KEY tables when a PRIMARY KEY record is deleted (CASCADE or NO ACTION).
Status	The status of the constraint (ENABLED or DISABLED).
Deferrable	A flag to indicate whether the constraint can be deferred.
Deferred	A flag to indicate whether the constraint was initially deferred.
Validated	A flag (VALIDATED or NOT VALIDATED) to indicate whether all data obeys the constraint.
Generated	A flag to indicate whether the constraint name has been generated by the database.
Bad	A flag to indicate whether a date was used in the constraint creation without specifying a century value for CHECK constraints, resulting in ambiguous 2-digit years; applies only to constraints in databases upgraded from prior versions of Oracle. Such constraints may result in ORA-02436 errors if not dropped and re-created properly.
Rely	A flag to indicate if the constraint is enforced or unenforced.
Last_Change	The date the constraint was last enabled or disabled.
Index_Owner	Owner of the related index.
Index_Name	Name of the related index.
Invalid	Valid/Invalid flag.
View_Related	Yes/No flag to record if the constraint is view related.

**TABLE 37-5.**   *Columns in USER_CONSTRAINTS*

Once you know the name and type of a constraint, you can check the columns associated with it via the USER_CONS_COLUMNS view, described in the next section.

If you do not assign constraint names when creating them, Oracle will generate unique constraint names. See "Integrity Constraint" in the Alphabetical Reference for further details. If a constraint name has been system-generated, that fact will be indicated via the Generated column.

If you defer a constraint (as indicated by the Deferred column), the constraint will not be enforced for the duration of a transaction. For example, if you were performing bulk **update**s on related tables and could not guarantee the order of transactions, you may decide to defer constraint checking on the tables until all of the **update**s have completed.

ALL_CONSTRAINTS lists the constraints on all of the tables that the user can access. DBA_CONSTRAINTS lists all of the constraints in the database. Each of these views has the same set of columns as USER_CONSTRAINTS (since they all include the Owner column).

## Constraint Columns: USER_CONS_COLUMNS

You can view the columns associated with constraints via the USER_CONS_COLUMNS data dictionary view. If you have already queried USER_CONSTRAINTS to obtain the types and names of the constraints involved, you can use USER_CONS_COLUMNS to determine which columns are involved in the constraint. The columns in this view are the following:

Owner	The owner of the constraint
Constraint_Name	The name of the constraint
Table_Name	The name of the table associated with the constraint
Column_Name	The name of the column associated with the constraint
Position	The order of the column within the constraint definition

There are only two columns in USER_CONS_COLUMNS that are not in USER_CONSTRAINTS: Column_Name and Position. A sample query of this table is shown in the following listing:

```
select Column_Name, Position
 from USER_CONS_COLUMNS
 where Constraint_Name = 'SYS_C0008791';

COLUMN_NAME POSITION
----------- --------
FIRSTNAME 1
LASTNAME 2
```

As shown in the preceding listing, the combination of FirstName and LastName forms the constraint (in this case, a primary key).

The Position column is significant. When you create a UNIQUE or PRIMARY KEY constraint, Oracle automatically creates a unique index on the set of columns you specify. The index is created based on the column order you specify. The column order, in turn, affects the performance of the index. An index comprising multiple columns will be used most efficiently if the leading column of that index (Position=1) is used in the query's **where** clause. See Chapter 38 for further details on optimizers.

The ALL_CONS_COLUMNS and DBA_CONS_COLUMNS views have the same column definitions as USER_CONS_COLUMNS. ALL_CONS_COLUMNS can be used to display column information about constraints on all tables that the user can access regardless of owner. DBA_CONS_COLUMNS lists the column-level constraint information for the entire database.

## Constraint Exceptions: EXCEPTIONS

When enabling constraints on tables that already contain data, you may encounter constraint violations within the data. For example, you may attempt to create a PRIMARY KEY constraint on a column that contains the same value for multiple records, but such an attempt would fail due to uniqueness constraint violations.

You can capture information about the rows that cause constraint creations to fail. First, create a table called EXCEPTIONS in your schema; the SQL script that should be used to create this table is named utlexcpt.sql, and is usually located in the /rdbms/admin directory under the Oracle home directory.

The EXCEPTIONS table contains four columns: Row_ID (the RowID of each row that violated the constraint), Owner (the owner of the violated constraint), Table_Name (the table on which the violated constraint was created), and Constraint (the constraint violated by the row). After creating the EXCEPTIONS table, attempt to enable a PRIMARY KEY constraint:

```
alter table NEWSPAPER enable PRIMARY KEY
exceptions into EXCEPTIONS;

ORA-02437: cannot enable (NEWSPAPER.SYS_C00516) - primary key violated
```

The constraint creation fails, and a reference to all rows that violate the constraint is placed in the EXCEPTIONS table. For example, if the PRIMARY KEY constraint in the last example generated exceptions, then you could query the EXCEPTIONS table as shown in the following listing:

```
select Owner, Table_Name, Constraint from EXCEPTIONS;

OWNER TABLE_NAME CONSTRAINT
---------- ---------- ----------
PRACTICE NEWSPAPER SYS_C00516
PRACTICE NEWSPAPER SYS_C00516
```

Two rows violated the constraint named SYS_C00516 (which, in this example, is the constraint name given to the PRIMARY KEY constraint for the NEWSPAPER table). You can determine which rows of the NEWSPAPER table correspond to these exceptions by joining the Row_ID column of the EXCEPTIONS table to the RowID pseudo-column of the table on which the constraint was being placed (in this example, the NEWSPAPER table):

```
select *
 from NEWSPAPER
 where RowID in
 (select Row_ID from EXCEPTIONS);
```

The rows that caused the constraint violations will then be displayed.

**NOTE**
*Row_ID is an actual column in the EXCEPTIONS table, with a
datatype of ROWID. It is joined to the RowID pseudo-column
in the table from which the exceptions were generated.*

# Table Comments: USER_TAB_COMMENTS

You can add a comment to a table, view, or column after it has been created. Comments on
the data dictionary views are the basis for the records displayed via the DICTIONARY and
DICT_COLUMNS views. To display comments about your own tables, use the USER_TAB_
COMMENTS view.

USER_TAB_COMMENTS contains three columns:

Table_Name	The name of the table or view
Table_Type	The object type (table, object table, or view)
Comments	Comments that have been entered for the object

To add a comment to a table, use the **comment** command, as shown in the following listing:

```
comment on table BIRTHDAY is 'Birthday list for Blacksburg
 employees';
```

Query USER_TAB_COMMENTS by specifying the Table_Name you want to see the Comments
for, as shown in the following listing:

```
select Comments
 from USER_TAB_COMMENTS
 where Table_Name = 'BIRTHDAY';

COMMENTS

Birthday list for Blacksburg
 employees
```

To remove a comment, set the comment to two single quotes with no space between them:

```
comment on table BIRTHDAY is '';
```

You can view the comments on all of the tables you can access via the ALL_TAB_COMMENTS
view. ALL_TAB_COMMENTS has an additional column, Owner, which specifies the owner of
the table. DBA_TAB_COMMENTS lists all of the tables in the database, and it has an Owner
column as well.

## Column Comments: USER_COL_COMMENTS

USER_COL_COMMENTS displays the comments that have been entered for columns within your tables. These comments are added to the database via the **comment** command. USER_COL_COMMENTS contains three columns:

Table_Name	The name of the table or view
Column_Name	The name of the column
Comments	Comments that have been entered for the column

Query USER_COL_COMMENTS by specifying the Table_Name and Column_Name you want to see the Comments for:

```
select Comments
 from USER_COL_COMMENTS
 where Table_Name = 'BIRTHDAY'
 and Column_Name = 'AGE';
```

To add a comment to a column, use the **comment** command, as shown in the following listing:

```
comment on column BIRTHDAY.AGE is 'Age in years';
```

To remove a comment, set the comment to two single quotes with no space between them:

```
comment on column BIRTHDAY.AGE is '';
```

You can view the column comments on all of the tables you can access via the ALL_COL_COMMENTS view. ALL_COL_COMMENTS has an additional column, Owner, which specifies the owner of the table. DBA_COL_COMMENTS lists all of the columns in all of the tables in the database, and it has an Owner column as well.

# Indexes and Clusters

Indexes and clusters do not change the data that is stored in tables; however, they do change the way that data is stored and accessed. In the following sections, you will see data dictionary views that describe indexes and clusters. You will see descriptions of the data dictionary views related to partitioned indexes in "Space Allocation and Usage" in this chapter.

## Indexes: USER_INDEXES (IND)

In Oracle, indexes are very closely related to constraints. The PRIMARY KEY and UNIQUE constraints always have associated unique indexes. As with constraints, two data dictionary views are used to query information about indexes: USER_INDEXES and USER_IND_COLUMNS. USER_INDEXES is also known by its public synonym, IND.

The columns in USER_INDEXES can be grouped into four categories, as shown in Table 37-6. The name of the index is shown in the Index_Name column. The owner and name for the table being indexed are in the Table_Owner and Table_Name columns. The Uniqueness column

Identification	Space-Related	Statistics-Related	Other
Index_Name	Tablespace_Name	Blevel	Degree
Table_Owner	Ini_Trans	Leaf_Blocks	Instances
Table_Name	Max_Trans	Distinct_Keys	Include_Column
Table_Type	Initial_Extent	Avg_Leaf_Blocks_Per_Key	Buffer_Pool
Uniqueness	Next_Extent	Avg_Data_Blocks_Per_Key	Duration
Status	Min_Extents	Clustering_Factor	Pct_Direct_Access
Partitioned	Max_Extents	Num_Rows	Parameters
Index_Type	Pct_Increase	Sample_Size	Domidx_Status
Temporary	Pct_Free	Last_Analyzed	Domidx_Opstatus
Generated	Freelists	User_Stats	Funcidx_Status
Logging	Freelist_Groups	Global_Stats	Join_Index
Compression	Pct_Threshold		
Prefix_Length			
Secondary			
Ityp_Owner			
Ityp_Name			

**TABLE 37-6.** *Columns in USER_INDEXES*

will be set to UNIQUE for unique indexes and set to NONUNIQUE for nonunique indexes. Table_Type records whether the index is on a 'TABLE' or a 'CLUSTER'.

The "Space-Related" columns are described in the "Storage" entry in the Alphabetical Reference. The "Statistics-Related" columns are populated when the table is analyzed (see the **analyze** command in the Alphabetical Reference). The Degree and Instances columns refer to the degree of parallelism used when the index is created.

To see all of the indexes on a table, query USER_INDEXES using the Table_Owner and Table_Name columns in the **where** clause, as shown in the following listing:

```
select Index_Name, Uniqueness
 from USER_INDEXES
 where Table_Owner = 'PRACTICE'
 and Table_Name = 'BIRTHDAY';

INDEX_NAME UNIQUENES
---------------- ---------
PK_BIRTHDAY UNIQUE
```

The query output in the preceding example shows that an index named PK_BIRTHDAY exists on the BIRTHDAY table. By using the same naming standard for all of your indexes, you can make it very easy to identify the purpose and table for an index just by looking at the Index_Name. In this example, PK signifies PRIMARY KEY; the constraint name can be specified during constraint creation to supersede the system-generated constraint name.

The Clustering_Factor column is not directly related to clusters, but rather represents the degree to which the rows in the table are ordered. The more ordered those rows are, the more efficient range queries will be (*range queries* are those in which a range of values is given for a column, such as **where LastName like 'A%'**).

To discover which columns are part of the index, and their order within the index, you need to query the USER_IND_COLUMNS view, which is described in the next section.

ALL_INDEXES shows all of the indexes owned by the user as well as any created on tables to which the user has been granted access. Since ALL_INDEXES can contain entries for multiple users, it contains an Owner column in addition to the columns shown in Table 37-6. DBA_INDEXES, which lists all indexes in the database, has the same column definitions as ALL_INDEXES.

**NOTE**
*For function-based indexes, see USER_IND_EXPRESSIONS.*

## Indexed Columns: USER_IND_COLUMNS

You can determine which columns are in an index by querying USER_IND_COLUMNS. The columns available via this view are as follows:

Index_Name	The name of the index
Table_Name	The name of the indexed table
Column_Name	The name of a column within the index
Column_Position	The column's position within the index
Column_Length	The indexed length of the column
Char_Length	Maximum codepoint length of the column (Unicode)
Descend	A Y/N flag to indicate whether or not the column is sorted in descending order

Five columns in this view are not in USER_INDEXES: Column_Name, Column_Position, Column_Length, Char_Length, and Descend. Column_Length, like the statistics-related columns in USER_INDEXES, is populated when the index's base table is analyzed (see the **analyze** command in the Alphabetical Reference). A sample query of this table, using the Index_Name from the USER_INDEXES example, is shown in the following listing (in this example, the Column_Position column is given the alias Pos):

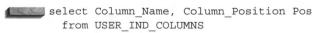
```
select Column_Name, Column_Position Pos
 from USER_IND_COLUMNS
 where Index_Name = 'PK_BIRTHDAY';
```

```
COLUMN_NAME POS
------------ ---
FIRSTNAME 1
LASTNAME 2
```

As you can see from this query, the PK_BIRTHDAY index consists of two columns: FirstName and LastName, in that order. See Chapter 38 for details on how the optimizer uses multicolumn indexes.

The ALL_IND_COLUMNS and DBA_IND_COLUMNS views have the same column definitions as USER_IND_COLUMNS. ALL_IND_COLUMNS can be used to display column information about indexes on all tables that the user can access regardless of owner. DBA_IND_COLUMNS lists the column-level index information for the entire database.

### Bitmap Join Index Columns: USER_JOIN_IND_COLUMNS

If you create a bitmap join index (introduced in Oracle9i), you can query USER_JOIN_IND_COLUMNS for the join details. USER_JOIN_IND_COLUMNS records the names of the tables involved in the join, the inner and outer join columns, and the dimension and fact tables involved.

## Clusters: USER_CLUSTERS (CLU)

The storage and statistics parameters associated with clusters are accessible via USER_CLUSTERS (also known by the public synonym CLU). The columns in this data dictionary view are shown in Table 37-7, separated by type.

Identification	Space-Related	Statistics-Related	Other
Cluster_Name	Tablespace_Name	Avg_Blocks_Per_Key	Degree
Cluster_Type	Pct_Free	Hashkeys	Instances
Function	Pct_Used		Cache
	Key_Size		Buffer_Pool
	Ini_Trans		Single_Table
	Max_Trans		Dependencies
	Initial_Extent		
	Next_Extent		
	Min_Extents		
	Max_Extents		
	Pct_Increase		
	Freelists		
	Freelist_Groups		

**TABLE 37-7.** *Columns in USER_CLUSTERS*

The Cluster_Name column contains the name of the cluster. Cluster_Type specifies whether the cluster uses a standard B-tree index or a hashing function for the cluster.

The usage of the "Space-Related" columns is described in the "Storage" entry in the Alphabetical Reference. The "Statistics-Related" columns are populated when the table is analyzed.

ALL_CLUSTERS and DBA_CLUSTERS have an additional column, Owner, since they list clusters in multiple schemas.

You can specify a hashing function for a cluster. User-specified hashing functions are most useful if the following conditions exist:

- The cluster key column is numeric.

- The cluster key column values are sequentially assigned.

- You know the maximum number of cluster key column values for the table.

If all three conditions are met, you can use the **hash is** clause of the **create cluster** command to specify your own hashing function (see **create cluster** in the Alphabetical Reference).

## Cluster Columns: USER_CLU_COLUMNS

To see the mapping of table columns to cluster columns, query USER_CLU_COLUMNS, whose columns are the following:

Cluster_Name	The name of the cluster
Clu_Column_Name	The name of the key column in the cluster
Table_Name	The name of a table within the cluster
Tab_Column_Name	The name of the key column in the table

Since a single cluster can store data from multiple tables, USER_CLU_COLUMNS is useful for determining which columns of which tables map to the cluster's columns.

There is no "ALL" version of this view. There are only USER_CLU_COLUMNS for the user's cluster columns, and DBA_CLU_COLUMNS, which shows the column mappings for all clusters in the database.

# Abstract Datatypes, ORDBMS-Related Structures, and LOBs

In the following sections, you will see the data dictionary views associated with object-relational structures such as abstract datatypes, methods, and large objects (LOBs). "ALL" and "DBA" versions of all of these data dictionary views are available. Because they contain records for multiple owners, the "ALL" and "DBA" versions of these views contain Owner columns as well as the columns listed in this section.

# Abstract Datatypes: USER_TYPES

Abstract datatypes created within your schema are listed in USER_TYPES, which includes columns for the Type_Name, number of attributes (Attributes), and number of methods (Methods) defined for the datatype.

For example, the ANIMAL_TY datatype has three attributes and one method (methods are defined via the **create type body** command), as shown in the following listing:

```
select Type_Name,
 Attributes,
 Methods
 from USER_TYPES;

TYPE_NAME ATTRIBUTES METHODS
-------------------------------- ---------- ----------
ANIMAL_TY 3 1
```

## Datatype Attributes: USER_TYPE_ATTRS

To see the attributes of a datatype, you need to query the USER_TYPE_ATTRS view. The columns in USER_TYPE_ATTRS are shown in Table 37-8.

Column Name	Description
Type_Name	Name of the type
Attr_Name	Name of the attribute
Attr_Type_Mod	The type modifier of the attribute
Attr_Type_Owner	Owner of the attribute's type, if the attribute is based on another datatype
Attr_Type_Name	Name of the type of the attribute
Length	Length of the attribute
Precision	Precision of the attribute
Scale	Scale of the attribute
Character_Set_Name	Character set of the attribute
Attr_No	Ordinal position of the attribute within the type definition
Inherited	YES/NO flag to indicate if the attribute is inherited from a supertype

**TABLE 37-8.** *Columns in USER_TYPE_ATTRS*

You can query USER_TYPE_ATTRS to see the relationships between nested abstract datatypes. For example, the PERSON_TY datatype uses the ADDRESS_TY datatype, as shown in the following listing:

```
select Attr_Name,
 Length,
 Attr_Type_Name
 from USER_TYPE_ATTRS
 where Type_Name = 'PERSON_TY';
```

```
ATTR_NAME LENGTH ATTR_TYPE_NAME
-------------------------------- ---------- ------------------
NAME 25 VARCHAR2
ADDRESS ADDRESS_TY
```

### Datatype Methods: **USER_TYPE_METHODS and USER_METHOD_PARAMS**

If a type has methods defined for it, then you query USER_TYPE_METHODS to determine the methods' names. USER_TYPE_METHODS contains columns showing the type name (Type_Name), method name (Method_Name), method number (Method_No, used for overloaded methods), and type of method (Method_Type). USER_TYPE_METHODS also includes columns that show the number of parameters (Parameters) and results (Results) returned by the method.

For example, the ANIMAL_TY datatype has one method, a member function named AGE. The AGE method has one input parameter (Birthdate) and one output result (the age, in days). Querying USER_TYPE_METHODS shows that *two* parameters are defined for AGE, not one as expected:

```
select Parameters,
 Results
 from USER_TYPE_METHODS
 where Type_Name = 'ANIMAL_TY'
 and Method_Name = 'AGE';
```

```
PARAMETERS RESULTS
---------- ----------
 2 1
```

Why does AGE have two parameters if it only has one input parameter defined? To find out, you can query USER_METHOD_PARAMS, which describes the parameters for your methods:

```
select Param_Name, Param_No, Param_Type_Name
 from USER_METHOD_PARAMS;
```

```
PARAM_NAME PARAM_NO PARAM_TYPE_NAME
-------------------------------- ---------- ------------------
SELF 1 ANIMAL_TY
BIRTHDATE 2 DATE
```

USER_METHOD_PARAMS shows that for each method, Oracle creates an implicit SELF parameter. The results of your methods are shown in USER_METHOD_RESULTS:

```
select Method_Name,
 Result_Type_Name
 from USER_METHOD_RESULTS
 where Type_Name = 'ANIMAL_TY';

METHOD_NAME RESULT_TYPE_NAME
------------------------------ --------------------------
AGE NUMBER
```

### Other Datatypes: USER_REFS, USER_COLL_TYPES, and USER_NESTED_TABLES

If you use REFs (see Chapter 33), you can query the USER_REFS data dictionary view to display the REFs you have defined. USER_REFS will show the name of the table containing the REF column (Table_Name) and the column name of the object column (Column_Name). The attributes of the REF—such as whether or not it is stored with the RowID—are also accessible via USER_REFS.

Collector types (nested tables and varying arrays) are described via the USER_COLL_TYPES data dictionary view. The columns of USER_COLL_TYPES include Type_Name, Upper_Bound (for varying arrays), and the Length and Precision of the elements. You can use USER_COLL_TYPES in conjunction with the abstract datatype data dictionary views shown earlier in this section to determine the type structure of a collector. You can also query USER_NESTED_TABLES and USER_VARRAYS to see details for your collections.

# LOBs: USER_LOBS

As described in Chapter 32, you can store large objects inside the database. The USER_LOBS view provides information on the LOBs defined in your tables, as shown in the following listing:

```
column column_name format A30

select Table_Name,
 Column_Name
 from USER_LOBS;

TABLE_NAME COLUMN_NAME
------------------------------ --------------------------
PROPOSAL PROPOSAL_TEXT
PROPOSAL BUDGET
```

USER_LOBS also shows the names of the segments used to hold the LOB data when it grows large; however, it does not show the datatypes of the LOB columns. To see the LOB datatypes, you can either **describe** the table that includes the LOBs or query USER_TAB_COLUMNS (as shown earlier in this chapter).

To use BFILE datatypes for LOBs, you have to create directories (see the entry for the **create directory** command in the Alphabetical Reference). The ALL_DIRECTORIES data dictionary shows the Owner, Directory_Name, and Directory_Path for each directory to which you have been granted access. A "DBA" version of this view is also available. No "USER" version of this view is available.

# Database Links and Materialized Views

Database links and materialized views are used to manage access to remote data. Depending on the type of materialized view you use, you may be able to use materialized view logs. In the following sections, you will see descriptions of the data dictionary views you can use to display information about database links and materialized views. For further information on database links, see Chapter 22. For further information on materialized views, see Chapter 23.

## Database Links: USER_DB_LINKS

To see the database links created under your account, query USER_DB_LINKS. The columns of this view, including the link name (DB_Link), username to connect to (Username), and the connection string (Host), show the information about the remote connection that the link will be used to establish. The Username and Password values will be used to log in to the remote database defined by the Host value.

The Host column stores the Oracle Net service names. This column stores the exact character string you specify during the **create database link** command, and does not alter its case. Therefore, you should be careful with the case you use when creating database links. Otherwise, your queries against USER_DB_LINKS will have to take into account inconsistencies in the case of the Host column. For example, looking for a database link that uses the 'HQ' service descriptor would require you to enter

```
select * from USER_DB_LINKS
 where UPPER(Host) = 'HQ';
```

since it is possible that there are entries with a Host value of 'hq' instead of 'HQ'.

**NOTE**
*If you are using default logins to the remote database, then Password will be **NULL**.*

The ALL_DB_LINKS view lists all of the database links that either are owned by the user or are PUBLIC database links. DBA_DB_LINKS lists all database links in the database. ALL_DB_LINKS and DBA_DB_LINKS share most of the same column definitions as USER_DB_LINKS; they have an Owner column in place of the Password column.

See Chapter 22 for further information on the uses of database links.

## Materialized Views

You can query USER_MVIEWS to display information about the materialized views owned by your account. This view, whose columns are listed in Table 37-9, shows the structural information about the materialized view as well as its refresh schedule.

**NOTE**
*See Chapter 23 for details on materialized views.*

Column Name	Description
Owner	The account that owns the materialized view
Mview_Name	The name of the materialized view
Container_Name	The base table (in the local database) for the materialized view's data; pre-Oracle8i, the Mview_Name preceded by "SNAP$_"
Query	The query that defines the materialized view
Query_Len	The length of the materialized view's base query
Updatable	A flag to indicate whether the snapshot can be updated
Update_Log	The name of the table that logs changes made to an updatable snapshot
Master_Rollback_Seg	The rollback segment to use during snapshot population and refresh operations
Master_Link	The database link used to access the master database
Rewrite_Enabled	A Y/N flag to indicate if query rewrite is enabled for the view
Rewrite_Capability	Rules and restrictions for query rewrites
Refresh_Mode	DEMAND, COMMIT, or NEVER, depending on the refresh mode for the view
Refresh_Method	Values used to drive a fast refresh of the view (Complete, Fast, Never, or Force)
Build_Mode	IMMEDIATE, DEFERRED, or PREBUILT instantiation of the materialized view data during its creation
Fast_Refreshable	What methods are available for fast refresh of the materialized view
Last_Refresh_Type	The most recent refresh type used
Last_Refresh_Date	A timestamp to record the last time the snapshot's data was refreshed
Staleness	The status of the materialized view's data relative to its master tables
After_Fast_Refresh	Staleness status following a fast refresh
Compile_State	Validity of the materialized view
Use_No_Index	Y/N flag to indicate if the materialized view was created with the USING NO INDEX clause

**TABLE 37-9.**   *Columns in USER_MVIEWS*

The name of the materialized view is found in the Mview_Name column of USER_MVIEWS. The local base table for the view is the Container_Name column.

To determine which database links are being used by your materialized views, query the Master_Link column, as shown in the following example:

```
select Master_Link
 from USER_MVIEWS;
```

The names of the database links returned by this query can be used as input for queries against USER_DB_LINKS. This query will display all of the database link information available for database links used in your materialized views:

```
select *
 from USER_DB_LINKS
 where DB_Link in
 (select Master_Link
 from USER_MVIEWS);
```

Additional queries that are useful in the management of materialized views are provided in Chapter 23.

The ALL_MVIEWS and DBA_MVIEWS views have the same column definitions as USER_MVIEWS. You can use ALL_MVIEWS to display information about all materialized views that the user can access regardless of owner. DBA_MVIEWS lists materialized view information for all users in the database.

Two related views—USER_REFRESH and USER_REFRESH_CHILDREN—display information about refresh groups. USER_MVIEW_REFRESH_TIMES shows the last time each materialized view was refreshed.

### Additional Materialized View Capabilities

You can query USER_MVIEW_ANALYSIS to see the materialized views that support query rewrite. If a materialized view had been created as a snapshot prior to Oracle8i, or if it contains references to a remote table, then it will not be listed in this view. You can query the owner of the materialized view, its name (Mview_Name), and the owner of the base table (Mview_Table_Owner). Many of the columns in this view are flags, such as Summary ('Y' if the view contains an aggregation), Known_Stale ('Y' if the view's data is inconsistent with the base table), and Contains_Views ('Y' if the materialized view references a view).

If the materialized view contains aggregations, you can query USER_MVIEW_AGGREGATES for details on the aggregations. Columns in this view are as follows:

Owner	Owner of the materialized view
Mview_Name	Name of the materialized view
Position_in_Select	Position within the query
Container_Column	Name of the column
Agg_Function	Aggregate function
DistinctFlag	'Y' if the aggregation uses the DISTINCT function
Measure	The SQL text of the measure, excluding the aggregate function

You can query details of the relations within materialized views from the USER_MVIEW_ DETAIL_RELATIONS and USER_MVIEW_KEYS data dictionary views. If the materialized view is based on joins, see USER_MVIEW_JOINS for the join details. In general, USER_MVIEW_ ANALYSIS will be the most commonly used data dictionary view related to materialized views.

## Materialized View Logs: USER_MVIEW_LOGS

Materialized view logs can be used by many materialized views to determine which records in the master table need to be refreshed in the materialized view of that table. You can query USER_MVIEW_LOGS for information about a user's logs, including the name of the master table (Master), the table holding the log records (Log_Table), and whether the materialized view is based on the primary key or the RowID (the Primary_Key and Rowids columns). USER_MVIEW_ LOGS is usually queried for maintenance purposes, such as to determine the name of the trigger used to create the materialized view log records.

There is no "ALL" version of this view. DBA_MVIEW_LOGS has the same column definitions as USER_MVIEW_LOGS, and shows all materialized view logs in the database. You can query USER_BASE_TABLE_MVIEWS for a listing of the materialized view master tables using materialized view logs.

# Triggers, Procedures, Functions, and Packages

You can use procedures, packages, and triggers—blocks of PL/SQL code stored in the database— to enforce business rules or to perform complicated processing. Triggers are described in Chapter 28. Procedures, functions, and packages are described in Chapter 29. In the following sections, you will see how to query the data dictionary for information about triggers, procedures, packages, and functions.

## Triggers: USER_TRIGGERS

USER_TRIGGERS contains information about the triggers owned by your account. This view, whose columns are listed in Table 37-10, shows the trigger type and body.

Column Name	Description
Trigger_Name	Name of the trigger
Trigger_Type	The type of trigger (BEFORE STATEMENT, BEFORE EACH ROW, and so on)
Triggering_Event	The command that executes the trigger (INSERT, UPDATE, or DELETE)
Table_Owner	The owner of the table that the trigger is defined for
Base_Object_Type	The type of object on which the trigger is based (TABLE, VIEW, SCHEMA, or DATABASE)
Table_Name	The name of the table or view that the trigger is defined for

**TABLE 37-10.** *Columns in USER_TRIGGERS*

Column Name	Description
Column_Name	For nested table triggers, the name of the nested table column
Referencing_Names	Names used for referencing OLD and NEW values in the trigger
When_Clause	The **when** clause used for the trigger
Status	Whether the trigger is ENABLED or DISABLED
Description	The description for the trigger
Action_Type	Action type for the trigger body (CALL or PL/SQL)
Trigger_Body	The trigger text

**TABLE 37-10.**  *Columns in USER_TRIGGERS* (continued)

The ALL_TRIGGERS view lists the triggers for all tables to which you have access. DBA_TRIGGERS lists all of the triggers in the database. Both of these views contain an additional column, Owner, which records the owner of the trigger.

A second trigger-related data dictionary view, USER_TRIGGER_COLS, shows how columns are used by a trigger. It lists the name of each column affected by a trigger, as well as how the trigger is used. Like USER_TRIGGERS, "ALL" and "DBA" versions of this data dictionary view are available.

## Procedures, Functions, and Packages: USER_SOURCE

The source code for existing procedures, functions, packages, and package bodies can be queried from the USER_SOURCE data dictionary view. The Type column in USER_SOURCE identifies the procedural object as a 'PROCEDURE', 'FUNCTION', 'PACKAGE', 'PACKAGE BODY', 'TRIGGER', 'TYPE', 'TYPE BODY', or 'JAVA SOURCE'. Each line of code is stored in a separate record in USER_SOURCE.

You can select information from USER_SOURCE via a query similar to the one shown in the following listing. In this example, the Text column is selected and ordered by Line number. The Name of the object and the object Type are used to specify which object's source code to display.

```
select Text
 from USER_SOURCE
 where Name = '&procedure_name'
 and Type = 'PROCEDURE'
 order by Line;
```

**NOTE**
*The sequence of the lines is maintained by the Line column;
therefore, the Line column should be used in the **order by** clause.*

The ALL_SOURCE and DBA_SOURCE views have all of the columns found in USER_SOURCE plus an additional Owner column (the owner of the object). ALL_SOURCE can be used to display the source code for all procedural objects that the user can access regardless of owner. DBA_ SOURCE lists the source code for all users in the database.

**NOTE**
*To see the persistent parameter settings for PL/SQL units, query*
*USER_STORED_SETTINGS.*

### Code Errors: USER_ERRORS

The **show errors** command in SQLPLUS checks the USER_ERRORS data dictionary view for the errors associated with the most recent compilation attempt for a procedural object. **show errors** will display the line and column number for each error, as well as the text of the error message.

To view errors associated with previously created procedural objects, you may query USER_ERRORS directly. You may need to do this when viewing errors associated with package bodies, since a package compilation that results in an error may not display the package body's error when you execute the **show error** command. You may also need to query USER_ERRORS when you encounter compilation errors with multiple procedural objects.

The following are the columns available in USER_ERRORS:

Name	The name of the procedural object
Type	The object type ('PROCEDURE', 'FUNCTION', 'PACKAGE', 'PACKAGE BODY', 'TRIGGER', 'TYPE', 'TYPE BODY', or 'JAVA SOURCE')
Sequence	The line sequence number, for use in the query's **order by** clause
Line	The line number within the source code at which the error occurs
Position	The position within the Line at which the error occurs
Text	The text of the error message

Queries against this view should always include the Sequence column in the **order by** clause. "ALL" and "DBA" versions of this view are also available; they feature an additional column, Owner, which records the owner of the object.

### Code Size: USER_OBJECT_SIZE

You can query the amount of space used in the SYSTEM tablespace for a procedural object from the USER_OBJECT_SIZE data dictionary view. As shown in the following listing, the four separate size areas can be added together to determine the total space used in the SYSTEM data dictionary tables to store the object. The four Size columns, along with the Name and Type columns, constitute all of the columns in this view.

```
select Source_Size+Code_Size+Parsed_Size+Error_Size Total
 from USER_OBJECT_SIZE
 where Name = '&procedure_name'
 and Type = 'PROCEDURE';
```

There is also a "DBA" version of this view available: DBA_OBJECT_SIZE lists the sizes for all objects in the database.

# Dimensions

You can create and maintain dimensions and hierarchies. For example, you may have a table named COUNTRY, with columns named Country and Continent. A second table, named CONTINENT, may have a column named Continent. If you have the CREATE DIMENSION system privilege, you can create a dimension to reflect the relationship between these elements:

```
create dimension GEOGRAPHY
 level COUNTRY_ID is COUNTRY.Country
 level CONTINENT_ID is CONTINENT.Continent
 hierarchy COUNTRY_ROLLUP (
 COUNTRY_ID child of
 CONTINENT_ID
 join key COUNTRY.Continent references CONTINENT_id);
```

You can query the Dimension_Name column of the USER_DIMENSIONS view to see the names of your dimensions. USER_DIMENSIONS also contains columns for the dimension owner (Owner), state (the Invalid column, set to 'Y' or 'N'), and revision level (the Revision column). The attributes of a dimension are accessed via additional data dictionary views.

To see the hierarchies within a dimension, query USER_DIM_HIERARCHIES. This view has only three columns: Owner, Dimension_Name, and Hierarchy_Name. Querying USER_DIM_HIERARCHIES for the GEOGRAPHY dimension returns the name of its hierarchies:

```
select Hierarchy_Name
 from USER_DIM_HIERARCHIES;

HIERARCHY_NAME

COUNTRY_ROLLUP
```

You can see the hierarchy details for COUNTRY_ROLLUP by querying USER_DIM_CHILD_OF, as shown in the following listing:

```
column join_key_id format a4

select Child_Level_Name,
 Parent_Level_Name,
 Position, Join_Key_Id
 from USER_DIM_CHILD_OF
where Hierarchy_Name = 'COUNTRY_ROLLUP';

CHILD_LEVEL_NAME PARENT_LEVEL_NAME POSITION JOIN
-------------------- ------------------------------ -------- ----
COUNTRY_ID CONTINENT_ID 1 1
```

To see the join key for a hierarchy, query USER_DIM_JOIN_KEY:

```
select Level_name, Child_Join_Column
 from USER_DIM_JOIN_KEY
 where Dimension_Name = 'GEOGRAPHY'
 and Hierarchy_Name = 'COUNTRY_ROLLUP';

LEVEL_NAME CHILD_JOIN_COLUMN
------------------------------ ------------------------------
CONTINENT_ID CONTINENT
```

You can see the levels of a dimension by querying the USER_DIM_LEVELS data dictionary view, and see the key columns for the levels via USER_DIM_LEVEL_KEY. Attribute information for dimensions is accessible via USER_DIM_ATTRIBUTES.

There are "ALL" and "DBA" views of all of the data dictionary views related to dimensions. Because the "USER" views for dimensions contain an Owner column, there are no additional columns found in the corresponding "ALL" and "DBA" views.

# Space Allocation and Usage, Including Partitions and Subpartitions

You can query the data dictionary to determine the space that is available and allocated for database objects. In the following sections, you will see how to determine the default storage parameters for objects, your space usage quota, available free space, and the way in which objects are physically stored. For information on Oracle's methods of storing data, see Chapters 20 and 40.

## Tablespaces: USER_TABLESPACES

You can query the USER_TABLESPACES data dictionary view to determine which tablespaces you have been granted access to and the default storage parameters in each. A tablespace's default storage parameters will be used for each object stored within that tablespace unless the **create** or **alter** command for that object specifies its own storage parameters. The storage-related columns in USER_TABLESPACES, listed in Table 37-11, are very similar to the storage-related columns in USER_TABLES. See the "Storage" entry of the Alphabetical Reference for further details.

Column Name	Description
Tablespace_Name	The name of the tablespace.
Block_Size	Database block size in use for this tablespace.
Initial_Extent	The default INITIAL parameter for objects in the tablespace.
Next_Extent	The default NEXT parameter for objects in the tablespace.
Min_Extents	The default MINEXTENTS parameter for objects in the tablespace.
Max_Extents	The default MAXEXTENTS parameter for objects in the tablespace.

**TABLE 37-11.** *Columns in USER_TABLESPACES*

Column Name	Description
Pct_Increase	The default PCTINCREASE parameter for objects in the tablespace.
Min_Extlen	The minimum extent size for objects in the tablespace.
Status	The tablespace's status ('ONLINE', 'OFFLINE', 'INVALID', 'READ ONLY'). An "invalid" tablespace is one that has been dropped; its record is still visible via this view.
Contents	A flag to indicate whether the tablespace is used to store permanent objects ('PERMANENT') or only temporary segments ('TEMPORARY').
Logging	A flag to indicate the default LOGGING/NOLOGGING parameter value for objects in the tablespace.
Extent_Management	Where extent management is performed for the tablespace ('DICTIONARY' or 'LOCAL').
Allocation_Type	Type of extent allocation in effect.
Segment_Space_ Management	Flag to indicate if free space is managed via free lists (MANUAL) or bitmaps (AUTO).

**TABLE 37-11.** *Columns in USER_TABLESPACES* (continued)

There is no "ALL" version of this view. DBA_TABLESPACES shows the storage parameters for all tablespaces.

## Space Quotas: USER_TS_QUOTAS

USER_TS_QUOTAS is a very useful view for determining the amount of space you have currently allocated and the maximum amount of space available to you by tablespace. A sample query of USER_TS_QUOTAS is shown in the following listing:

```
select * from USER_TS_QUOTAS;

TABLESPACE_NAME BYTES MAX_BYTES BLOCKS MAX_BLOCKS
--------------- ---------- ---------- ---------- ----------
USERS 67584 0 33 0
```

USER_TS_QUOTAS contains one record for each Tablespace_Name. The Bytes column reflects the number of bytes allocated to objects owned by the user. Max_Bytes is the maximum number of bytes the user can own in that tablespace; if there is no quota for that tablespace, then Max_Bytes will display a value of 0. The Bytes and Max_Bytes columns are translated into Oracle blocks in the Blocks and Max_Blocks columns, respectively.

There is no "ALL" version of this view. DBA_TS_QUOTAS shows the storage quotas for all users for all tablespaces and is a very effective way to list space usage across the entire database.

# Segments and Extents: USER_SEGMENTS and USER_EXTENTS

As described in Chapter 20, space is allocated to objects (such as tables, clusters, and indexes) in *segments*, the physical counterparts to the logical objects created in the database. You can query USER_SEGMENTS to see the current storage parameters and space usage in effect for your segments. USER_SEGMENTS is very useful when you are in danger of exceeding one of the storage limits; its columns are listed in Table 37-12.

Segments consist of contiguous sections called *extents*. The extents that constitute segments are described in USER_EXTENTS. In USER_EXTENTS, you will see the actual size of each extent within the segment; this is very useful for tracking the impact of changes to the **next** and **pctincrease** settings. In addition to the Segment_Name, Segment_Type, and Tablespace_Name

Column Name	Description
Segment_Name	The name of the segment
Partition_Name	**NULL** if the object is not partitioned; otherwise, the segment's partition name
Segment_Type	The type of segment ('TABLE', 'CLUSTER', 'INDEX', 'ROLLBACK', and so on)
Tablespace_Name	The name of the tablespace in which the segment is stored
Bytes	The number of bytes allocated to the segment
Blocks	The number of Oracle blocks allocated to the segment
Extents	The number of extents in the segment
Initial_Extent	The size of the initial extent in the segment
Next_Extent	The value of the NEXT parameter for the segment
Min_Extents	The minimum number of extents in the segment
Max_Extents	The value of the MAXEXTENTS parameter for the segment
Pct_Increase	The value of the PCTINCREASE parameter for the segment
Freelists	The number of process freelists (lists of data blocks in the segment that can be used during inserts) allocated to the segment; if a segment has multiple freelists, then contention for free blocks during concurrent **inserts** will be lessened
Freelist_Groups	The number of freelist groups (the number of groups of freelists, for use with the Parallel Server option) allocated to the segment
Buffer_Pool	Buffer pool into which the segment will be read ('DEFAULT', 'KEEP', or 'RECYCLE') if you have defined multiple buffer pools

**TABLE 37-12.** *Columns in USER_SEGMENTS*

columns, USER_EXTENTS has four new columns: Extent_ID (to identify the extent within the segment), Bytes (the size of the extent, in bytes), Blocks (the size of the extent, in Oracle blocks), and Partition_Name (if the segment is part of a partitioned object).

Both USER_SEGMENTS and USER_EXTENTS have "DBA" versions, which are useful for listing the space usage of objects across owners. Both DBA_SEGMENTS and DBA_EXTENTS have an additional Owner column. If you want to list all of the owners who own segments in a tablespace, you can query based on the Tablespace_Name column in DBA_SEGMENTS, and list all of the owners of segments in that tablespace.

## Partitions and Subpartitions

A single table's data can be stored across multiple partitions. See Chapter 20 for examples of partitions and descriptions of the indexing options available. To see how a table is partitioned, you should query the USER_PART_TABLES data dictionary view, whose columns are listed, by category, in Table 37-13.

Most of the columns of USER_PART_TABLES define the default storage parameters for the table partitions. When a partition is added to the table, it will by default use the storage parameters shown in USER_PART_TABLES. USER_PART_TABLES also shows the number of partitions in the table (Partition_Count), the number of columns in the partition key (Partitioning_Key_Count), and the type of partitioning (Partitioning_Type).

USER_PART_TABLES stores a single row for each table that has been partitioned. To see information about each of the individual partitions that belong to the table, you can query USER_TAB_PARTITIONS. In USER_TAB_PARTITIONS, you will see one row for each of the table's partitions. The columns of USER_TAB_PARTITIONS are shown, by category, in Table 37-14.

Identification	Storage-Related
Table_Name	Def_Tablespace_Name
Partitioning_Type	Def_Pct_Free
Subpartitioning_Type	Def_Pct_Used
Partition_Count	Def_Ini_Trans
Def_Subpartition_Count	Def_Max_Trans
Partitioning_Key_Count	Def_Initial_Extent
Subpartitioning_Key_Count	Def_Next_Extent
Def_Logging	Def_Min_Extents
Def_Buffer_Pool	Def_Max_Extents
	Def_Pct_Increase
	Def_Freelists
	Def_Freelist_Groups

**TABLE 37-13.** *Columns in USER_PART_TABLES*

Identification	Storage-Related	Statistics-Related
Table_Name	Tablespace_Name	Num_Rows
Composite	Pct_Free	Blocks
Partition_Name	Pct_Used	Empty_Blocks
Subpartition_Count	Ini_Trans	Avg_Space
High_Value	Max_Trans	Chain_Cnt
High_Value_Length	Initial_Extent	Avg_Row_Len
Partition_Position	Next_Extent	Sample_Size
Logging	Min_Extent	Last_Analyzed
Buffer_Pool	Max_Extent	Global_Stats
	Pct_Increase	User_Stats
	Freelists	
	Freelist_Groups	

**TABLE 37-14.** *Columns in USER_TAB_PARTITIONS*

USER_TAB_PARTITIONS contains columns that identify the table to which the partition belongs and shows the partition's storage parameters and the statistics for the partition. The "Statistics-Related" columns are populated when the table is analyzed (see the **analyze** command in the Alphabetical Reference). The "Identification" columns show the high value for the range used to define the partition (High_Value) and the position of the partition within the table (Partition_Position).

The columns used for the partition key are accessible via the USER_PART_KEY_COLUMNS data dictionary view. USER_PART_KEY_COLUMNS contains only four columns:

Name	The name of the partitioned table or index
Object_Type	Object type (TABLE or INDEX)
Column_Name	The name of the column that is part of the partition key
Column_Position	The position of the column within the partition key

Statistics for the partition columns are accessible via the USER_PART_COL_STATISTICS data dictionary view. The columns in USER_PART_COL_STATISTICS closely mirror those in USER_TAB_COL_STATISTICS.

Data distribution within the partitions is recorded during the processing of the **analyze** command. The data histogram information for partitions is accessible via the USER_PART_HISTOGRAMS data dictionary view. The columns of this view are Table_Name, Partition_Name, Column_Name, Bucket_Number, Endpoint_Value, and Endpoint_Actual_Value.

Since indexes may be partitioned, there is a USER_IND_PARTITIONS data dictionary view available. The columns in USER_IND_PARTITIONS can be grouped into three categories, as shown in Table 37-15.

The columns in USER_IND_PARTITIONS parallel those in USER_INDEXES, with a few modifications to the "Identification" columns. The "Identification" columns for partitioned indexes show the name of the partition, the high value for the partition, and the position of the partition within the table. The "Statistics-Related" columns are populated when the partition is analyzed (see the **analyze** command in the Alphabetical Reference). The "Space-Related" columns describe the space allocation for the index; see the "Storage" entry in the Alphabetical Reference for information on storage parameters.

If a partition has subpartitions, you can see the details for the subpartitions via data dictionary views. USER_IND_SUBPARTITIONS contains the "Space-Related" and "Statistics-Related" columns of USER_IND_PARTITIONS, along with columns to identify the subpartition (Subpartition_Name and Subpartition_Position). Similarly, USER_TAB_SUBPARTITIONS contains the "Space-Related" and "Statistics-Related" columns of USER_TAB_PARTITIONS along with Subpartition_Name and Subpartition_Position columns. Thus, you can determine the space definitions of each of your partitions and subpartitions.

As shown earlier in this section, you can query the USER_PART_COL_STATISTICS and USER_PART_HISTOGRAMS data dictionary views for statistical information regarding partitions. For subpartitions, you can query USER_SUBPART_COL_STATISTICS and USER_SUBPART_HISTOGRAMS, whose structures mirror that of the partition statistics views. To see the

Identification	Space-Related	Statistics-Related
Index_Name	Tablespace_Name	Blevel
Composite	Ini_Trans	Leaf_Blocks
Partition_Name	Max_Trans	Distinct_Keys
Subpartition_Count	Initial_Extent	Avg_Leaf_Blocks_Per_Key
High_Value	Next_Extent	Avg_Data_Blocks_Per_Key
High_Value_Length	Min_Extent	Clustering_Factor
Partition_Position	Max_Extent	Num_Rows
Status	Pct_Increase	Sample_Size
Logging	Pct_Free	Last_Analyzed
Buffer_Pool	Freelists	User_Stats
Compression	Freelist_Groups	Pct_Direct_Access
Domidx_Opstatus		Global_Stats
Parameters		

**TABLE 37-15.** *Columns in USER_IND_PARTITIONS*

subpartition key columns, you can query USER_SUBPART_KEY_COLUMNS, whose column structure is identical to that of USER_PART_KEY_COLUMNS.

## Free Space: USER_FREE_SPACE

In addition to viewing the space you have used, you can also query the data dictionary to see how much space is currently marked as "free" space. USER_FREE_SPACE lists the free extents in all tablespaces accessible to the user. It lists by Tablespace_Name the File_ID, Block_ID, and relative file number of the starting point of the free extent. The size of the free extent is listed in both bytes and blocks. DBA_FREE_SPACE is frequently used by DBAs to monitor the amount of free space available and the degree to which it has become fragmented.

# Users and Privileges

Users and their privileges are recorded within the data dictionary. In the following sections, you will see how to query the data dictionary for information about user accounts, resource limits, and user privileges.

## Users: USER_USERS

You can query USER_USERS to list information about your account. The USER_USERS view includes your Username, User_ID (a number assigned by the database), Default_Tablespace, Temporary_Tablespace, and Created date (when your account was created). The Account_Status column in USER_USERS displays the status of your account, whether it is locked, unlocked ('OPEN'), or expired. If the account is locked, the Lock_Date column will display the date the account was locked and the Expiry_Date column will display the date of expiration. You can also query information about the resource consumer group (Initial_Rsrc_Consumer_Group) assigned to you by the DBA, and your External_Name value.

ALL_USERS contains only the Username, User_ID, and Created columns from USER_USERS, but it lists that information for all accounts in the database. ALL_USERS is useful when you need to know the usernames that are available (for example, during **grant** commands). DBA_USERS contains all of the columns in USER_USERS, plus two additional columns: Password (the encrypted password for the account) and Profile (the user's resource profile). DBA_USERS lists this information for all users in the database.

## Resource Limits: USER_RESOURCE_LIMITS

In Oracle, *profiles* can be used to place limits on the amount of system and database resources available to a user. If no profiles are created in a database, the default profile, which specifies unlimited resources for all users, will be used. The resources that can be limited are described in the **create profile** entry of the Alphabetical Reference. Profiles enforce additional security measures, such as expiration dates on accounts and the minimum length of passwords.

To view the limits that are in place for your current session, you can query USER_RESOURCE_LIMITS. Its columns are the following:

Resource_Name	The name of the resource (for example, SESSIONS_PER_USER)
Limit	The limit placed on this resource

USER_PASSWORD_LIMITS describes the password profile parameters for the user. It has the same columns as USER_RESOURCE_LIMITS.

There is no "ALL" or "DBA" version of this view; it is limited to the user's current session. To see the cost associated with each available resource, you can query the RESOURCE_COST view. DBAs can access the DBA_PROFILES view to see the resource limits for all profiles. The Resource_Type column of DBA_PROFILES indicates whether the resource profile is a 'PASSWORD' or 'KERNEL' profile.

# Table Privileges: USER_TAB_PRIVS

To view grants for which you are the grantee, the grantor, or the object owner, query USER_TAB_PRIVS (user table privileges). In addition to its Grantee, Grantor, and Owner columns, this view contains columns for the Table_Name, Privilege, and a flag (set to 'YES' or 'NO') to indicate whether the privilege was granted **with admin option** (Grantable).

USER_TAB_PRIVS_MADE displays the USER_TAB_PRIVS records for which the user is the owner (it therefore lacks an Owner column). USER_TAB_PRIVS_RECD (user table privileges received) displays the USER_TAB_PRIVS records for which the user is the grantee (it therefore lacks a Grantee column). Since both USER_TAB_PRIVS_ MADE and USER_TAB_PRIVS_RECD are simply subsets of USER_TAB_PRIVS, you can duplicate their functionality simply by querying against USER_TAB_PRIVS with an appropriate **where** clause to view the subset you want.

There are "ALL" versions available for USER_TAB_PRIVS, USER_TAB_PRIVS_MADE, and USER_TAB_PRIVS_RECD. The "ALL" versions list those objects for which either the user or PUBLIC is the grantee or grantor. There is a "DBA" version of USER_TAB_PRIVS named DBA_TAB_PRIVS that lists all object privileges granted to all users in the database. DBA_TAB_PRIVS and ALL_ TAB_PRIVS have the same column definitions as USER_TAB_PRIVS.

### Column Privileges: USER_COL_PRIVS

In addition to granting privileges on tables, you can also grant privileges at the column level. For example, you can grant users the ability to **update** only certain columns in a table. See Chapter 19 and the **grant** command in the Alphabetical Reference for further details.

The data dictionary views used to display column privileges are almost identical in design to the table privileges views described in the previous section. There is an additional Column_Name column in each of the COL views, and the Hierarchy column is not found there. USER_COL_PRIVS is analogous to USER_TAB_PRIVS, USER_COL_PRIVS_MADE is analogous to USER_TAB_ PRIVS_MADE, and USER_COL_PRIVS_RECD is analogous to USER_TAB_PRIVS_RECD. Also, the following tables have a Hierarchy column that the related COL_PRIVS tables do not have: USER_TAB_PRIVS, USER_TAB_PRIVS_MADE, and USER_TAB_PRIVS_RECD.

"ALL" versions are available for all of the column privileges views. DBA_COL_PRIVS lists all column privileges that have been granted to users in the database (just as DBA_TAB_PRIVS lists all table privileges granted to users).

# System Privileges: USER_SYS_PRIVS

USER_SYS_PRIVS lists the system privileges that have been granted to the user. Its columns are Username, Privilege, and Admin_Option (a flag set to 'YES' or 'NO' to indicate whether the privilege was granted **with admin option**). All system privileges directly granted to a user are displayed via this view. System privileges granted to a user via a role are not displayed here. The following query shows sample output for the PRACTICE account:

 `select * from USER_SYS_PRIVS;`

```
USERNAME PRIVILEGE
--------------------------------- -----------------------
PRACTICE CREATE DIMENSION
PRACTICE UNLIMITED TABLESPACE
```

There is no "ALL" version of this view. To see the system privileges granted to all users in the database, query DBA_SYS_PRIVS, which has the same column definitions as USER_SYS_PRIVS.

# Roles

In addition to privileges granted directly to users, sets of privileges may be grouped into roles. Roles may be granted to users or to other roles, and may consist of both object and system privileges. For information on the use and management of roles, see Chapter 19.

To see which roles have been granted to you, query the USER_ROLE_PRIVS data dictionary view. Any roles that have been granted to PUBLIC will also be listed here. The available columns for USER_ROLE_PRIVS are as follows:

Username	The username (may be 'PUBLIC')
Granted_Role	The name of the role granted to the user
Admin_Option	A flag to indicate whether the role was granted **with admin option** ('YES' or 'NO')
Default_Role	A flag to indicate whether the role is the user's default role ('YES' or 'NO')
OS_Granted	A flag to indicate whether the operating system is being used to manage roles ('YES' or 'NO')

To list all of the roles available in the database, you need to have DBA authority; you can then query DBA_ROLES to list all roles. DBA_ROLE_PRIVS lists the assignment of those roles to all of the users in the database.

Roles may receive three different types of grants, and each has a corresponding data dictionary view:

Table/column grants	ROLE_TAB_PRIVS. Similar to USER_TAB_PRIVS and USER_COL_PRIVS, except that it has a Role column instead of a Grantee column
System privileges	ROLE_SYS_PRIVS. Similar to USER_SYS_PRIVS, except that it has a Role column instead of a Username column
Role grants	ROLE_ROLE_PRIVS. Lists all roles that have been granted to other roles

**NOTE**
*If you are not a DBA, these data dictionary views list only those roles that have been granted to you.*

In addition to these views, there are two views, each with a single column, that list the privileges and roles enabled for the current session:

SESSION_PRIVS     The Privilege column lists all system privileges available to the session, whether granted directly or via roles.

SESSION_ROLES     The Role column lists all roles that are currently enabled for the session.

SESSION_PRIVS and SESSION_ROLES are available to all users.

**NOTE**
*See Chapter 19 for information on enabling and disabling roles and the setting of default roles.*

# Auditing

As a non-DBA user within an Oracle database, you cannot enable the database's auditing features. If auditing has been enabled, there are data dictionary views that anyone can use to view the audit trail.

Many different audit trail data dictionary views are available. Most of these views are based on a single audit trail table in the database (SYS.AUD$). The most generic of the audit trail views available is named USER_AUDIT_TRAIL. Its columns are described in Table 37-16. Since this

Column Name	Description
OS_Username	The audited user's operating system account
Username	The Oracle username of the audited user
UserHost	A numeric ID for the instance used by the audited user
Terminal	The user's operating system terminal identifier
TimeStamp	The date and time the audit record was created
Owner	The owner of the object affected by an action (for action audits)
Obj_Name	The name of the object affected by an action (for action audits)
Action	The numeric code for the audited action
Action_Name	The name of the audited action
New_Owner	The owner of the object named in the New_Name column
New_Name	The new name of an object that has been **rename**d
Obj_Privilege	The object privilege that has been **grant**ed or **revoke**d

**TABLE 37-16.**    *Columns in USER_AUDIT_TRAIL*

Column Name	Description
Sys_Privilege	The system privilege that has been **grant**ed or **revoke**d
Admin_Option	A flag to indicate whether the role or system privilege was **grant**ed **with admin option** ('Y' or 'N')
Grantee	The username specified in a **grant** or **revoke** command
Audit_Option	The auditing options set via an **audit** command
Ses_Actions	A string of characters serving as a session summary, recording success and failure for different actions
Logoff_Time	The date and time the user logged off
Logoff_LRead	The number of logical reads performed during the session
Logoff_PRead	The number of physical reads performed during the session
Logoff_LWrite	The number of logical writes performed during the session
Logoff_DLock	The number of deadlocks detected during the session
Comment_Text	A text comment on the audit trail entry
SessionID	The numeric ID for the session
EntryID	A numeric ID for the audit trail entry
StatementID	The numeric ID for each command that was executed
ReturnCode	The return code for each command that was executed; if the command was successful, then the ReturnCode will be 0
Priv_Used	The system privilege used to execute the action
Client_ID	Client ID
Session_CPU	Session CPU used

**TABLE 37-16.** *Columns in USER_AUDIT_TRAIL* (continued)

view shows the audit records for many different types of actions, many of the columns may be inapplicable for any given row. The "DBA" version of this view, DBA_AUDIT_TRAIL, lists all entries from the audit trail table; USER_AUDIT_TRAIL lists only those that are relevant to the user.

As shown in Table 37-16, a vast array of auditing capabilities is available (see the **audit** command in the Alphabetical Reference for a complete listing). Each type of audit can be accessed via its own data dictionary view. The following are the available views:

USER_AUDIT_OBJECT	For statements concerning objects
USER_AUDIT_SESSION	For connections and disconnections
USER_AUDIT_STATEMENT	For **grant**, **revoke**, **audit**, **noaudit**, and **alter system** commands issued by the user

There are "DBA" versions available for each of the "USER" views in the previous list; the "DBA" versions show all of the audit trail records that fit into the view's category.

You can view the auditing options that are currently in effect for your objects by querying USER_OBJ_AUDIT_OPTS. For each object listed in USER_OBJ_AUDIT_OPTS, the audit options for each command that may be performed on that object (identified by the Object_Name and Object_Type columns) are listed in USER_OBJ_AUDIT_OPTS. The column names of USER_OBJ_AUDIT_OPTS correspond to the first three letters of the command (for example, Alt for **alter**, Upd for **update**, and so on). Each column will record whether that command is audited for that object when the command is successful ('S'), unsuccessful ('U'), or both. The default auditing options in effect for any new objects in the database can be displayed via the ALL_DEF_AUDIT_OPTS view, which has the same column naming conventions as USER_OBJ_AUDIT_OPTS.

The commands that can be audited are stored in a reference table named AUDIT_ACTIONS, which has two columns: Action (the numeric code for the action) and Name (the name of the action/command). Action and Name correspond to the Action and Action_Name columns of USER_AUDIT_TRAIL.

DBAs can use several additional auditing views that do not have "USER" counterparts, including DBA_AUDIT_EXISTS, DBA_PRIV_AUDIT_OPTS, DBA_STMT_AUDIT_OPTS, and STMT_AUDIT_OPTION_MAP. See the *Oracle Server Administrator's Guide* for details on these DBA-only views.

# Miscellaneous

In addition to the data dictionary views described earlier in this chapter, several miscellaneous views and tables may be available within your data dictionary. These views and tables include DBA-only views and the table used when the **explain plan** command is executed. In the following sections, you will see brief descriptions for each of the miscellaneous view types.

# Monitoring: The V$ Dynamic Performance Tables

The views that monitor the database environment performance are called the *system statistics views.* The system statistics tables, also called the dynamic performance tables, are commonly referred to as the *V$* (pronounced "Vee-Dollar") tables, because they all begin with the letter *V* followed by the dollar sign ($).

The definitions and usage of columns within the monitoring views are subject to change with each version of the database that is released. Correctly interpreting the results of ad hoc queries against views usually requires referring to the *Oracle9i Database Administrator's Guide.* The V$ tables are normally used only by the DBA. Consult the *Oracle9i Database Reference* and the *Oracle9i DBA Handbook* for details on the use of the V$ views.

# CHAINED_ROWS

When a row no longer fits within the data block its row header is stored in, that row may store the remainder of its data in a different block or set of blocks. Such a row is said to be *chained,* and chained rows may cause poor performance due to the increased number of blocks that must be read to read a single row.

The **analyze** command can be used to generate a listing of the chained rows within a table. This listing of chained rows can be stored in a table called CHAINED_ROWS. To create the CHAINED_ROWS table in your schema, run the utlchain.sql script (usually found in the /rdbms/ admin subdirectory under the Oracle home directory).

To populate the CHAINED_ROWS table, use the **list chained rows into** clause of the **analyze** command, as shown in the following listing:

```
analyze TABLE BIRTHDAY list chained rows into CHAINED_ROWS;
```

The CHAINED_ROWS table lists the Owner_Name, Table_Name, Cluster_Name (if the table is in a cluster), Partition_Name (if the table is partitioned), Subpartition_Name (if the table contains subpartitions), Head_RowID (the RowID for the row), and an Analyze_TimeStamp column that shows the last time the table or cluster was analyzed. You can query the table based on the Head_RowID values in CHAINED_ROWS, as shown in the following example:

```
select * from BIRTHDAY
 where RowID in
 (select Head_RowID
 from CHAINED_ROWS
 where Table_Name = 'BIRTHDAY');
```

If the chained row is short in length, then it may be possible to eliminate the chaining by deleting and reinserting the row.

# PLAN_TABLE

When tuning SQL statements, you may want to determine the steps that the optimizer will take to execute your query. To view the query path, you must first create a table in your schema named PLAN_TABLE. The script used to create this table is called utlxplan.sql, and is usually stored in the /rdbms/admin subdirectory of the Oracle software home directory.

After you have created the PLAN_TABLE table in your schema, you can use the **explain plan** command, which will generate records in your PLAN_TABLE, tagged with the Statement_ID value you specify for the query you want to have explained:

```
explain plan
set Statement_ID = 'MYTEST'
for
select * from BIRTHDAY
 where LastName like 'S%';
```

The ID and Parent_ID columns in PLAN_TABLE establish the hierarchy of steps (Operations) that the optimizer will follow when executing the query. See Chapter 38 for details on the Oracle optimizer and the interpretation of PLAN_TABLE records.

# Interdependencies: USER_DEPENDENCIES and IDEPTREE

Objects within Oracle databases can depend upon each other. For example, a stored procedure may depend upon a table, or a package may depend upon a package body. When an object

within the database changes, any procedural object that depends upon it will have to be recompiled. This recompilation can take place either automatically at runtime (with a consequential performance penalty) or manually (see Chapter 29 for details on compiling procedural objects).

Two sets of data dictionary views are available to help you track dependencies. The first is USER_DEPENDENCIES, which lists all *direct* dependencies of objects. However, this only goes one level down the dependency tree. To fully evaluate dependencies, you must create the recursive dependency-tracking objects in your schema. To create these objects, run the utldtree.sql script (usually located in the /rdbms/admin subdirectory of the Oracle home directory). This script creates two objects you can query: DEPTREE and IDEPTREE. They contain identical information, but IDEPTREE is indented based on the pseudo-column Level, and is thus easier to read and interpret.

## DBA-Only Views

Since this chapter is intended for use by developers and end users, the data dictionary views available only to DBAs are not covered here. The DBA-only views are used to provide information about distributed transactions, lock contention, rollback segments, and other internal database functions. For information on the use of the DBA-only views, see the *Oracle9i Database Administrator's Guide*.

## Oracle Label Security

Users of Oracle Label Security can view additional data dictionary views, including ALL_SA_ GROUPS, ALL_SA_POLICIES, ALL_SA_USERS, and ALL_SA_USER_PRIVS. For details on the usage of these views, see the *Oracle Label Security Administrator's Guide*.

## SQL*Loader Direct Load Views

To manage the direct load option within SQL*Loader, Oracle maintains a number of data dictionary views. These generally are only queried for debugging purposes, upon request from Oracle Customer Support. The SQL*Loader direct load option is described under the "SQLLDR" entry in the Alphabetical Reference; its supporting data dictionary views are listed here:

- LOADER_COL_INFO
- LOADER_CONSTRAINT_INFO
- LOADER_FILE_TS
- LOADER_PARAM_INFO
- LOADER_PART_INFO
- LOADER_REF_INFO
- LOADER_TAB_INFO
- LOADER_TRIGGER_INFO

For details on the use of these views, see the catldr.sql script, usually located in the /rdbms/admin subdirectory of the Oracle home directory.

# National Language Support (NLS) Views

Three data dictionary views are used to display information about the National Language Support parameters currently in effect in the database. Nonstandard values for the NLS parameters (such as NLS_DATE_FORMAT and NLS_SORT) can be set via the database's parameter file or via the **alter session** command. (See the **alter session** command in the Alphabetical Reference for further information on NLS settings.) To see the current NLS settings for your session, instance, and database, query NLS_SESSION_PARAMETERS, NLS_INSTANCE_PARAMETERS, and NLS_DATABASE_PARAMETERS, respectively.

# Libraries

Your PL/SQL routines (see Chapter 27) can call external C programs. To see which external C program libraries are owned by you, you can query USER_LIBRARIES, which displays the name of the library (Library_Name), the associated file (File_Spec), whether or not the library is dynamically loadable (Dynamic), and the library's status (Status). ALL_LIBRARIES and DBA_LIBRARIES are also available; they include an additional Owner column to indicate the owner of the library. For further information on libraries, see the entry for the **create library** command in the Alphabetical Reference.

# Heterogeneous Services

To support the management of heterogeneous services, Oracle provides 16 data dictionary views. All of the views in this category begin with the letters HS instead of DBA. In general, these views are used primarily by DBAs. For details on the HS views, see the *Oracle9i Database Reference.*

# Indextypes and Operators

Operators and indextypes are closely related. You can use the **create operator** command to create a new operator and define its bindings. You can reference operators in indextypes and in SQL statements. The operators, in turn, reference functions, packages, types, and other user-defined objects.

You can query the USER_OPERATORS view to see each operator's Owner, Operator_Name, and Number_of_Binds values. Ancillary information for operators is accessible via USER_OPANCILLARY, and you can query USER_OPARGUMENTS to see the operator arguments. You can query USER_OPBINDINGS to see the operator bindings.

USER_INDEXTYPE_OPERATORS lists the operators supported by indextypes. Indextypes, in turn, are displayed via USER_INDEXTYPES. There are "ALL" and "DBA" views of all the operator and indextype views.

# Outlines

When you use stored outlines, you can retrieve the name of, and details for, the outlines via the USER_OUTLINES data dictionary views. To see the hints that make up the outlines, query USER_OUTLINE_HINTS. There are "ALL" and "DBA" versions of USER_OUTLINES and USER_OUTLINE_HINTS.

# CHAPTER
# 38

## The Hitchhiker's Guide to the Oracle Optimizer

ithin the relational model, the physical location of data is unimportant. Within Oracle, the physical location of your data and the operation used to retrieve the data are unimportant—until the database needs to find the data. If you query the database, you should be aware of the operations Oracle performs to retrieve and manipulate the data. The better you understand the execution path Oracle uses to perform your query, the better you will be able to manipulate and tune the query.

In this chapter, you will see the operations Oracle uses to query and process data, presented from a user's perspective. First, the operations that access tables are described, followed by index access operations, data set operations, joins, and miscellaneous operations. For each type of operation, relevant tuning information is provided to help you use the operation in the most efficient and effective manner possible.

The focus of this chapter is the operations Oracle goes through when executing SQL statements. If you are attempting to tune an application, you should evaluate the application architecture and operating environment to determine if they are appropriate for your users' requirements before examining the SQL. An application that performs a large number of queries across a slow network just to display a data entry screen will be perceived as slow even if the database activity portion is fast; tuning the SQL in that example may yield little in the way of performance improvement.

Before beginning to tune your queries, you need to decide which optimizer you will be using.

# Which Optimizer?

The Oracle optimizer has two primary modes of operation: cost-based or rule-based. To set the optimizer goal, you can specify CHOOSE (for cost-based) or RULE (for rule-based) for the OPTIMIZER_MODE parameter in your database's initialization parameter file. You can override the optimizer's default operations at the query and session level, as shown later in this chapter.

**NOTE**
*As of Oracle9i, you can store parameters in a system parameter file, replacing the init.ora parameter file used in prior versions.*

Setting OPTIMIZER_MODE to RULE invokes the *rule-based optimizer (RBO),* which evaluates possible execution paths and rates the alternative execution paths based on a series of syntactical rules. In general, the RBO is seldom used by new applications, and is found primarily in applications developed and tuned for earlier versions of Oracle.

Setting OPTIMIZER_MODE to CHOOSE invokes the *cost-based optimizer (CBO).* You can use the **analyze** command and the DBMS_STATS package to generate statistics about the objects in your database. The generated statistics include the number of rows in a table and the number of distinct keys in an index. Based on the statistics, the CBO evaluates the cost of the available execution paths and selects the execution path that has the lowest relative cost. If you use the CBO, you need to make sure that you analyze the data frequently enough for the statistics to accurately reflect the data within your database. If a query references tables that have been analyzed and tables that have not been analyzed, the CBO selects values for the missing statistics—and it may

decide to perform an inappropriate execution path. To improve performance, you should use either the RBO or the CBO consistently throughout your database. Since the CBO supports changes in data volumes and data distribution, you should favor its use.

To use the CBO, you should first analyze your tables and indexes. You can analyze individual tables, indexes, partitions, or clusters via the **analyze** command (see the Alphabetical Reference for the full syntax). When analyzing, you can scan the full object (via the **compute statistics** clause) or part of the object (via the **estimate statistics** clause). In general, you can gather adequate statistics by analyzing 10 to 20 percent of an object—in much less time than you would need to compute the statistics. Here is a sample **analyze** command:

```
analyze table BOOKSHELF estimate statistics;
```

Once you have analyzed an object, you can query the statistics-related columns of the data dictionary views to see the values generated. See Chapter 37 for a description of those views and their statistics-related columns.

The DBMS_STATS package is a replacement for the **analyze** command, and is the recommended method as of Oracle9i. The GATHER_TABLE_STATS procedure within DBMS_STATS requires two parameters: the schema owner and the name of the table; all other parameters (such as partition name and the percent of the table to be scanned via the estimate statistics method) are optional. The following command gathers the statistics for the BOOKSHELF table in the PRACTICE schema:

```
execute DBMS_STATS.GATHER_TABLE_STATS('PRACTICE','BOOKSHELF');
```

Other procedures within DBMS_STATS include GATHER_INDEX_STATS (for indexes), GATHER_SCHEMA_STATS (for all objects in a schema), GATHER DATABASE_STATS (for all objects in the database), and GATHER_SYSTEM_STATS (for system statistics). You can use other procedures within the DBMS_STATS package to migrate statistics from one database to another, avoiding the need to recalculate statistics for different copies of the same tables. See Oracle's *Supplied PL/SQL Packages and Types Reference* for further information on the DBMS_STATS package.

The examples in this section assume that the cost-based optimizer is used and that the tables and indexes have been analyzed.

# Operations That Access Tables

Two operations directly access the rows of a table: a full table scan and a RowID-based access to the table. For information on operations that access table rows via clusters, see "Queries That Use Clusters," later in this chapter.

## TABLE ACCESS FULL

A full table scan sequentially reads each row of a table. The optimizer calls the operation used during a full table scan a TABLE ACCESS FULL. To optimize the performance of a full table scan, Oracle reads multiple blocks during each database read.

A full table scan is used whenever there is no **where** clause on a query. For example, the following query selects all of the rows from the BOOKSHELF table:

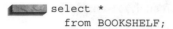

```
select *
 from BOOKSHELF;
```

To resolve the preceding query, Oracle will perform a full table scan of the BOOKSHELF table. If the BOOKSHELF table is small, a full table scan of BOOKSHELF may be fairly quick, incurring little performance cost. However, as BOOKSHELF grows in size, the cost of performing a full table scan grows. If you have multiple users performing full table scans of BOOKSHELF, then the cost associated with the full table scans grows even faster.

With proper planning, full table scans need not be performance problems. You should work with your database administrators to make sure the database has been configured to take advantage of features such as the Parallel Query Option and multiblock reads. Unless you have properly configured your environment for full table scans, you should carefully monitor their use.

**NOTE**
*Depending on the data being selected, the optimizer may choose to use a full scan of an index in place of a full table scan.*

You can display Oracle's chosen execution path via a feature called an "explain plan." You will see how to generate explain plans later in this chapter. For this example, the explain plan would look like this:

```
Execution Plan
--
 0 SELECT STATEMENT Optimizer=CHOOSE (Cost=1 Card=31 Bytes=1209
)
 1 0 TABLE ACCESS (FULL) OF 'BOOKSHELF' (Cost=1 Card=31 Bytes=1
 209)
```

The TABLE ACCESS (FULL) operation shown in the explain plan shows that the optimizer chose to perform a full table scan of the BOOKSHELF table. Each step has an ID (in this case, 0 and 1) with step 0 being the step that returns data to the user. Steps may have parent steps (in this case, step 1 provides its data to step 0, so it is listed as having a parent ID of 0). As queries grow more complicated, the explain plans grow more complicated. The emphasis in this chapter is on the operations Oracle uses; you can verify the steps by generating the explain plans. To simplify the discussion, a walkthrough of the generation and interpretation of complex explain plans will be deferred until later in the chapter; a graphical method of depicting the explain plan will be used to describe the major execution path steps and data flow.

## TABLE ACCESS BY ROWID

To improve the performance of table accesses, you can use Oracle operations that access rows by their RowID values. The RowID records the physical location where the row is stored. Oracle uses indexes to correlate data values with RowID values—and thus with physical locations of the data. Given the RowID of a row, Oracle can use the TABLE ACCESS BY ROWID operation to retrieve the row.

When you know the RowID, you know exactly where the row is physically located. However, you do not need to memorize the RowIDs for your rows; instead, you can use indexes to access the RowID information, as described in the next major section, "Operations That Use Indexes." Because indexes provide quick access to RowID values, they help to improve the performance of queries that make use of indexed columns.

## Related Hints

Within a query, you can specify hints that direct the CBO in its processing of the query. To specify a hint, use the syntax shown in the following example. Immediately after the **select** keyword, enter the following string:

```
/*+
```

Next, add the hint, such as

```
FULL(bookshelf)
```

Close the hint with the following string:

```
*/
```

Hints use Oracle's syntax for comments within queries, with the addition of the "+" sign at the start of the hint. Throughout this chapter, the hints relevant to each operation will be described. For table accesses, there are two relevant hints: FULL and ROWID. The FULL hint tells Oracle to perform a full table scan (the TABLE ACCESS FULL operation) on the listed table, as shown in the following listing:

```
select /*+ FULL(bookshelf) */ *
 from BOOKSHELF
 where Title like 'T%';
```

If you did not use the FULL hint, Oracle would normally plan to use the primary key index on the Title column to resolve this query. Since the table is presently small, the full table scan is not costly. As the table grows, you would probably favor the use of a RowID-based access for this query.

The ROWID hint tells the optimizer to use a TABLE ACCESS BY ROWID operation to access the rows in the table. In general, you should use a TABLE ACCESS BY ROWID operation whenever you need to return rows quickly to users and whenever the tables are large. To use the TABLE ACCESS BY ROWID operation, you need to either know the RowID values or use an index.

## Operations That Use Indexes

Within Oracle are two major types of indexes: *unique indexes,* in which each row of the indexed table contains a unique value for the indexed column(s), and *nonunique indexes,* in which the rows' indexed values can repeat. The operations used to read data from the indexes depend on the type of index in use and the way in which you write the query that accesses the index.

Consider the BOOKSHELF table:

```
create table BOOKSHELF
(Title VARCHAR2(100) primary key,
Publisher VARCHAR2(20),
CategoryName VARCHAR2(20),
Rating VARCHAR2(2),
constraint CATFK foreign key (CategoryName)
references CATEGORY(CategoryName));
```

The Title column is the primary key for the BOOKSHELF table—that is, it uniquely identifies each row, and each attribute is dependent on the Title value.

Whenever a PRIMARY KEY or UNIQUE constraint is created, Oracle creates a unique index to enforce uniqueness of the values in the column. As defined by the **create table** command, a PRIMARY KEY constraint will be created on the BOOKSHELF table. The index that supports the primary key will be given a system-generated name, since the constraint was not explicitly named.

You can create indexes on other columns of the BOOKSHELF table manually. For example, you could create a nonunique index on the CategoryName column via the **create index** command:

```
create index BOOKSHELF$CATEGORY
 on BOOKSHELF(CategoryName)
tablespace INDEXES
compute statistics;
```

The BOOKSHELF table now has two indexes on it: a unique index on the Title column, and a nonunique index on the CategoryName column. One or more of the indexes could be used during the resolution of a query, depending on how the query is written and executed. As part of the index creation, its statistics were gathered via the **compute statistics** clause. Since the table is already populated with rows, you do not need to execute a separate command to analyze the index.

# INDEX UNIQUE SCAN

To use an index during a query, your query must be written to allow the use of an index. In most cases, you allow the optimizer to use an index via the **where** clause of the query. For example, the following query could use the unique index on the Title column:

```
select *
 from BOOKSHELF
 where Title = 'INNUMERACY';
```

Internally, the execution of the preceding query will be divided into two steps. First, the Title column index will be accessed via an INDEX UNIQUE SCAN operation. The RowID value that matches the title 'INNUMERACY' will be returned from the index; that RowID value will then be used to query BOOKSHELF via a TABLE ACCESS BY ROWID operation.

If all of the columns selected by the query had been contained within the index, then Oracle would not have needed to use the TABLE ACCESS BY ROWID operation; since the data would

be in the index, the index would be all that is needed to satisfy the query. Because the query selected all columns from the BOOKSHELF table, and the index did not contain all of the columns of the BOOKSHELF table, the TABLE ACCESS BY ROWID operation was necessary.

# INDEX RANGE SCAN

If you query the database based on a range of values, or if you query using a nonunique index, then an INDEX RANGE SCAN operation is used to query the index.

Consider the BOOKSHELF table again, with a unique index on its Title column. A query of the form

```
select Title
 from BOOKSHELF
 where Title like 'M%';
```

would return all Title values beginning with 'M'. Since the **where** clause uses the Title column, the primary key index on the Title column can be used while resolving the query. However, a unique value is not specified in the **where** clause; a range of values is specified. Therefore, the unique primary key index will be accessed via an INDEX RANGE SCAN operation. Because INDEX RANGE SCAN operations require reading multiple values from the index, they are less efficient than INDEX UNIQUE SCAN operations.

In the preceding example, only the Title column was selected by the query. Since the values for the Title column are stored in the primary key Index—which is being scanned—there is no need for the database to access the BOOKSHELF table directly during the query execution. The INDEX RANGE SCAN of the primary key index is the only operation required to resolve the query.

The CategoryName column of the BOOKSHELF table has a nonunique index on its values. If you specify a limiting condition for CategoryName values in your query's **where** clause, an INDEX RANGE SCAN of the CategoryName index may be performed. Since the BOOKSHELF$CATEGORY index is a nonunique index, the database cannot perform an INDEX UNIQUE SCAN on BOOKSHELF$CATEGORY, even if CategoryName is equated to a single value in your query.

## When Indexes Are Used

Since indexes have a great impact on the performance of queries, you should be aware of the conditions under which an index will be used to resolve a query. The following sections describe the conditions that can cause an index to be used while resolving a query.

### If You Set an Indexed Column Equal to a Value

In the BOOKSHELF table, the CategoryName column has a nonunique index named BOOKSHELF$CATEGORY. A query that compares the CategoryName column to a value will be able to use the BOOKSHELF$CATEGORY index.

The following query compares the CategoryName column to the value 'ADULTNF':

```
select Title
 from BOOKSHELF
 where CategoryName = 'ADULTNF';
```

Since the BOOKSHELF$CATEGORY index is a nonunique index, this query may return multiple rows, and an INDEX RANGE SCAN operation may be used when reading data from it. Depending on the table's statistics, Oracle may choose to perform a full table scan instead.

If it uses the index, the execution of the preceding query may include two operations: an INDEX RANGE SCAN of BOOKSHELF$CATEGORY (to get the RowID values for all of the rows with 'ADULTNF' values in the CategoryName column), followed by a TABLE ACCESS BY ROWID of the BOOKSHELF table (to retrieve the Title column values).

If a column has a unique index created on it, and the column is compared to a value with an "=" sign, then an INDEX UNIQUE SCAN will be used instead of an INDEX RANGE SCAN.

### If You Specify a Range of Values for an Indexed Column

You do not need to specify explicit values in order for an index to be used. The INDEX RANGE SCAN operation can scan an index for ranges of values. In the following query, the Title column of the BOOKSHELF table is queried for a range of values (those that start with *M*):

```
select Title
 from BOOKSHELF
 where Title like 'M%';
```

A range scan can also be performed when using the "<"or ">" operators:

```
select Title
 from BOOKSHELF
 where Title > 'M';
```

When specifying a range of values for a column, an index will not be used to resolve the query if the first character specified is a wildcard. The following query will *not* perform an INDEX RANGE SCAN on the available indexes:

```
select Publisher
 from BOOKSHELF
 where Title like '%M%';
```

Since the first character of the string used for value comparisons is a wildcard, the index cannot be used to find the associated data quickly. Therefore, a full table scan (TABLE ACCESS FULL operation) will be performed instead. Depending on the statistics for the table and the index, Oracle may choose to perform a full scan of the index instead. In this example, if the selected column is the Title column, the optimizer may choose to perform a full scan of the primary key index rather than a full scan of the BOOKSHELF table.

### If No Functions Are Performed on the Column in the where Clause

Consider the following query, which will use the BOOKSHELF$CATEGORY index:

```
select COUNT(*)
 from BOOKSHELF
 where CategoryName = 'ADULTNF';
```

What if you did not know whether the values in the CategoryName column were stored as uppercase, mixed case, or lowercase values? In that event, you may write the query as follows:

```
select COUNT(*)
 from BOOKSHELF
 where UPPER(CategoryName) = 'ADULTNF';
```

The **UPPER** function changes the Manager values to uppercase before comparing them to the value 'ADULTNF'. However, using the function on the column may prevent the optimizer from using an index on that column. The preceding query (using the **UPPER** function) will perform a TABLE ACCESS FULL of the BOOKSHELF table unless you have created a function-based index on UPPER(CategoryName); see Chapter 20 for details on function-based indexes.

If you concatenate two columns together or a string to a column, then indexes on those columns will not be used. The index stores the real value for the column, and any change to that value will prevent the optimizer from using the index.

### If No IS NULL or IS NOT NULL Checks Are Used for the Indexed Column

**NULL** values are not stored in indexes. Therefore, the following query will not use an index; there is no way the index could help to resolve the query:

```
select Title
 from BOOKSHELF
 where CategoryName is null;
```

Since CategoryName is the only column with a limiting condition in the query, and the limiting condition is a **NULL** check, the BOOKSHELF$CATEGORY index will not be used and a TABLE ACCESS FULL operation will be used to resolve the query.

What if an **IS NOT NULL** check is performed on the column? All of the non-**NULL** values for the column are stored in the index; however, the index search would not be efficient. To resolve the query, the optimizer would need to read every value from the index and access the table for each row returned from the index. In most cases, it would be more efficient to perform a full table scan than to perform an index scan (with associated TABLE ACCESS BY ROWID operations) for all of the values returned from the index. Therefore, the following query may not use an index:

```
select Title
 from BOOKSHELF
 where CategoryName is not null;
```

If the selected columns are in an index, the optimizer may choose to perform a full index scan in place of the full table scan.

### If Equivalence Conditions Are Used

In the examples in the prior sections, the Title value was compared to a value with an "=" sign, as in this query:

```
select *
 from BOOKSHELF
 where Title = 'INNUMERACY';
```

What if you wanted to select all of the records that did not have a Title of 'INNUMERACY'? The **=** would be replaced with **!=**, and the query would now be

```
select *
 from BOOKSHELF
 where Title != 'INNUMERACY';
```

When resolving the revised query, the optimizer may not use an index. Indexes are used when values are compared exactly to another value—when the limiting conditions are equalities, not inequalities. The optimizer would only choose an index in this example if it decided the full index scan (plus the TABLE ACCESS BY ROWID operations to get all the columns) would be faster than a full table scan.

Another example of an inequality is the **not in** clause, when used with a subquery. The following query selects values from the BOOKSHELF table for books that aren't written by Stephen Jay Gould:

```
select *
 from BOOKSHELF
 where Title NOT IN
(select Title
 from BOOKSHELF_AUTHOR
 where AuthorName = 'STEPHEN JAY GOULD');
```

In some cases, the query in the preceding listing would not be able to use an index on the Title column of the BOOKSHELF table, since it is not set equal to any value. Instead, the BOOKSHELF.Title value is used with a **not in** clause to eliminate the rows that match those returned by the subquery. To use an index, you should set the indexed column equal to a value. In many cases, Oracle now internally rewrites the **not in** as a **not exists** clause, allowing the query to use an index. The following query, which uses an **in** clause, could use an index on the BOOKSHELF.Title column or could perform a nonindexed join between the tables; the optimizer will choose the path with the lowest cost based on the available statistics:

```
select *
 from BOOKSHELF
 where Title IN
(select Title
 from BOOKSHELF_AUTHOR
 where AuthorName = 'STEPHEN JAY GOULD');
```

### If the Leading Column of a Multicolumn Index Is Set Equal to a Value

An index can be created on a single column or on multiple columns. If the index is created on multiple columns, the index will be used if the leading column of the index is used in a limiting condition of the query.

If your query specifies values for only the nonleading columns of the index, the index will not be used to resolve the query prior to Oracle9i. As of Oracle9i, the index skip-scan feature enables the optimizer to potentially use a concatenated index even if its leading column is not listed in the **where** clause.

## If the MAX or MIN Function Is Used

If you select the **MAX** or **MIN** value of an indexed column, the optimizer may use the index to quickly find the maximum or minimum value for the column.

## If the Index Is Selective

All of the previous rules for determining if an index will be used consider the syntax of the query being performed and the structure of the index available. If you are using the CBO, the optimizer can use the selectivity of the index to judge whether using the index will lower the cost of executing the query.

In a highly selective index, a small number of records are associated with each distinct column value. For example, if there are 100 records in a table and 80 distinct values for a column in that table, the selectivity of an index on that column is 80/100 = 0.80. The higher the selectivity, the fewer the number of rows returned for each distinct value in the column.

The number of rows returned per distinct value is important during range scans. If an index has a low selectivity, then the many INDEX RANGE SCAN operations and TABLE ACCESS BY ROWID operations used to retrieve the data may involve more work than a TABLE ACCESS FULL of the table.

The selectivity of an index is not considered by the optimizer unless you are using the CBO and have analyzed the index. The optimizer can use histograms to make judgments about the distribution of data within a table. For example, if the data values are heavily skewed so that most of the values are in a very small data range, the optimizer may avoid using the index for values in that range while using the index for values outside the range.

# Combining Output from Multiple Index Scans

Multiple indexes—or multiple scans of the same index—can be used to resolve a single query. For the BOOKSHELF table, two indexes are available: the unique primary key index on the Title column, and the BOOKSHELF$CATEGORY index on the CategoryName column. In the following sections, you will see how the optimizer integrates the output of multiple scans via the AND-EQUAL and INLIST ITERATOR operations.

## AND-EQUAL of Multiple Indexes

If limiting conditions are specified for multiple indexed columns in a query, the optimizer may be able to use multiple indexes when resolving the query.

The following query specifies values for both the Title and CategoryName columns of the BOOKSHELF table:

```
select *
 from BOOKSHELF
 where Title > 'M'
 and CategoryName > 'B';
```

The query's **where** clause contains two separate limiting conditions. Each of the limiting conditions corresponds to a different index: the first to the primary key and the second to BOOKSHELF$CATEGORY. When resolving the query, the optimizer may use both indexes, or it may perform a full table scan.

If the indexes are used, each index will be scanned via an INDEX RANGE SCAN operation. The RowIDs returned from the scan of the primary key index will be compared with those returned from the scan of the BOOKSHELF$CATEGORY index. The RowIDs that are returned from both indexes will be used during the subsequent TABLE ACCESS BY ROWID operation. Figure 38-1 shows the order in which the operations are executed.

The AND-EQUAL operation, as shown in Figure 38-1, compares the results of the two index scans. In general, accesses of a single multicolumn index (in which the leading column is used in a limiting condition in the query's **where** clause) will perform better than an AND-EQUAL of multiple single-column indexes.

## INLIST ITERATION of Multiple Scans

If you specify a list of values for a column's limiting condition, the optimizer may perform multiple scans and concatenate the results of the scans. For example, the query in the following listing specifies two separate values for the BOOKSHELF.CategoryName value. An INDEX hint, as described in the next section, advises the optimizer to use the available index in place of a full table scan.

```
select *
 from BOOKSHELF
 where CategoryName in ('ADULTNF', 'CHILDRENPIC');
```

Since a range of values is not used, a single INDEX RANGE SCAN operation may be inefficient when resolving the query. Therefore, the optimizer may choose to perform two separate scans of the same index and concatenate the results.

When resolving the query, the optimizer may perform an INDEX RANGE SCAN on BOOKSHELF$CATEGORY for each of the limiting conditions. The RowIDs returned from the index scans would be used to access the rows in the BOOKSHELF table (via TABLE ACCESS BY

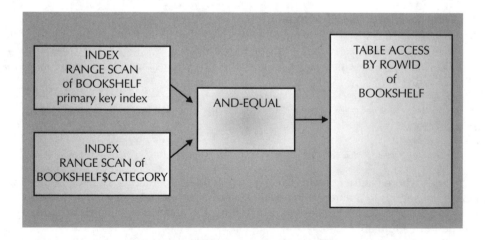

**FIGURE 38-1.** *Order of operations for an AND-EQUAL operation*

ROWID operations). The rows returned from each of the TABLE ACCESS BY ROWID operations may be combined into a single set of rows via the CONCATENATION operation.

Alternatively, the optimizer could use a single INDEX RANGE SCAN operation followed by a TABLE ACCESS BY ROWID, with an INLIST ITERATOR operation used to navigate through the selected rows from the table.

## Related Hints

Several hints are available to direct the optimizer in its use of indexes. The INDEX hint is the most commonly used index-related hint. The INDEX hint tells the optimizer to use an index-based scan on the specified table. You do not need to mention the index name when using the INDEX hint, although you can list specific indexes if you choose.

For example, the following query uses the INDEX hint to suggest the use of an index on the BOOKSHELF table during the resolution of the query:

```
select /*+ index(bookshelf bookshelf$category) */ Title
 from BOOKSHELF
 where CategoryName = 'ADULTNF';
```

According to the rules provided earlier in this section, the preceding query should use the index without the hint being needed. However, if the index is nonselective or the table is small and you are using the CBO, then the optimizer may choose to ignore the index. If you know that the index is selective for the data values given, you can use the INDEX hint to force an index-based data access path to be used.

In the hint syntax, name the table (or its alias, if you give the table an alias) and, optionally, the name of the suggested index. The optimizer may choose to disregard any hints you provide.

If you do not list a specific index in the INDEX hint, and multiple indexes are available for the table, the optimizer evaluates the available indexes and chooses the index whose scan is likely to have the lowest cost. The optimizer could also choose to scan several indexes and merge them via the AND-EQUAL operation described in the previous section.

A second hint, INDEX_ASC, functions the same as the INDEX hint: It suggests an ascending index scan for resolving queries against specific tables. A third index-based hint, INDEX_DESC, tells the optimizer to scan the index in descending order (from its highest value to its lowest). To suggest an index fast full scan, use the INDEX_FFS hint. The ROWID hint is similar to the INDEX hint, suggesting the use of the TABLE ACCESS BY ROWID method for the specified table. The AND_EQUAL hint suggests the optimizer merge the results of multiple index scans.

## Additional Tuning Issues for Indexes

When you're creating indexes on a table, two issues commonly arise: should you use multiple indexes or a single concatenated index, and if you use a concatenated index, which column should be the leading column of the index?

In general, it is faster for the optimizer to scan a single concatenated index than to scan and merge two separate indexes. The more rows returned from the scan, the more likely the concatenated index scan will outperform the merge of the two index scans. As you add more columns to the concatenated index, it becomes less efficient for range scans.

For the concatenated index, which column should be the leading column of the index? The leading column should be very frequently used as a limiting condition against the table, and it

should be highly selective. In a concatenated index, the optimizer will base its estimates of the index's selectivity (and thus its likelihood of being used) on the selectivity of the leading column of the index. Of these two criteria—being used in limiting conditions and being the most selective column—the first is more important. If the leading column of the index is not used in a limiting condition (as described earlier in this chapter), the index will not be used unless you take advantage of Oracle9i's index skip-scan capability. You may need to use an INDEX hint to force the optimizer to use the skip-scan method.

A highly selective index based on a column that is never used in limiting conditions will never be used. A poorly selective index on a column that is frequently used in limiting conditions will not benefit your performance greatly. If you cannot achieve the goal of creating an index that is both highly selective and frequently used, then you should consider creating separate indexes for the columns to be indexed.

Many applications emphasize online transaction processing over batch processing; there may be many concurrent online users but a small number of concurrent batch users. In general, index-based scans allow online users to access data more quickly than if a full table scan had been performed. When creating your application, you should be aware of the kinds of queries executed within the application and the limiting conditions in those queries. If you are familiar with the queries executed against the database, you may be able to index the tables so that the online users can quickly retrieve the data they need. When the database performance directly impacts the online business process, the application should perform as few database accesses as possible.

# Operations That Manipulate Data Sets

Once the data has been returned from the table or index, it can be manipulated. You can group the records, sort them, count them, lock them, or merge the results of the query with the results of other queries (via the **UNION**, **MINUS**, and **INTERSECT** operators). In the following sections, you will see how the data manipulation operations are used.

Most of the operations that manipulate sets of records do not return records to the users until the entire operation is completed. For example, sorting records while eliminating duplicates (known as a SORT UNIQUE operation) cannot return records to the user until all of the records have been evaluated for uniqueness. On the other hand, index scan operations and table access operations can return records to the user as soon as a record is found.

When an INDEX RANGE SCAN operation is performed, the first row returned from the query passes the criteria of the limiting conditions set by the query—there is no need to evaluate the next record returned prior to displaying the first record. If a set operation—such as a sorting operation—is performed, then the records will not be immediately displayed. During set operations, the user will have to wait for all rows to be processed by the operation. Therefore, you should limit the number of set operations performed by queries used by online users (to limit the perceived response time of the application). Sorting and grouping operations are most common in large reports and batch transactions.

## Ordering Rows

Three of Oracle's internal operations sort rows without grouping the rows. The first is the SORT ORDER BY operation, which is used when an **order by** clause is used in a query. For example, the BOOKSHELF table is queried and sorted by Publisher:

```
select Title from BOOKSHELF
 order by Publisher;
```

When the preceding query is executed, the optimizer will retrieve the data from the BOOKSHELF table via a TABLE ACCESS FULL operation (since there are no limiting conditions for the query, all rows will be returned). The retrieved records will not be immediately displayed to the user; a SORT ORDER BY operation will sort the records before the user sees any results.

Occasionally, a sorting operation may be required to eliminate duplicates as it sorts records. For example, what if you only want to see the distinct Publisher values in the BOOKSHELF table? The query would be as follows:

```
select DISTINCT Publisher from BOOKSHELF;
```

As with the prior query, this query has no limiting conditions, so a TABLE ACCESS FULL operation will be used to retrieve the records from the BOOKSHELF table. However, the **DISTINCT** function tells the optimizer to only return the distinct values for the Publisher column.

To resolve the query, the optimizer takes the records returned by the TABLE ACCESS FULL operation and sorts them via a SORT UNIQUE operation. No records will be displayed to the user until all of the records have been processed.

In addition to being used by the **DISTINCT** function, the SORT UNIQUE operation is invoked when the **MINUS**, **INTERSECT**, and **UNION** (but not **UNION ALL**) functions are used.

A third sorting operation, SORT JOIN, is always used as part of a MERGE JOIN operation and is never used on its own. The implications of SORT JOIN on the performance of joins is described in "Operations That Perform Joins," later in this chapter.

## Grouping Rows

Two of Oracle's internal operations sort rows while grouping like records together. The two operations—SORT AGGREGATE and SORT GROUP BY—are used in conjunction with grouping functions (such as **MIN**, **MAX**, and **COUNT**). The syntax of the query determines which operation is used.

In the following query, the maximum Publisher value, alphabetically, is selected from the BOOKSHELF table:

```
select MAX(Publisher)
 from BOOKSHELF;
```

To resolve the query, the optimizer will perform two separate operations. First, a TABLE ACCESS FULL operation will select the Publisher values from the table. Second, the rows will be analyzed via a SORT AGGREGATE operation, which will return the maximum Publisher value to the user.

If the Publisher column were indexed, the index could be used to resolve queries of the maximum or minimum value for the index (as described in "Operations That Use Indexes," earlier in this chapter). Since the Publisher column is not indexed, a sorting operation is required. The maximum Publisher value will not be returned by this query until all of the records have been read and the SORT AGGREGATE operation has completed.

The SORT AGGREGATE operation was used in the preceding example because there is no **group by** clause in the query. Queries that use the **group by** clause use an internal operation named SORT GROUP BY.

What if you want to know the number of titles from each publisher? The following query selects the count of each Publisher value from the BOOKSHELF table using a **group by** clause:

```
select Publisher, COUNT(*)
 from BOOKSHELF
 group by Publisher;
```

This query returns one record for each distinct Publisher value. For each Publisher value, the number of its occurrences in the BOOKSHELF table will be calculated and displayed in the COUNT(*) column.

To resolve this query, Oracle will first perform a full table scan (there are no limiting conditions for the query). Since a **group by** clause is used, the rows returned from the TABLE ACCESS FULL operation will be processed by a SORT GROUP BY operation. Once all the rows have been sorted into groups and the count for each group has been calculated, the records will be returned to the user. As with the other sorting operations, no records are returned to the user until all of the records have been processed.

The operations to this point have involved simple examples—full table scans, index scans, and sorting operations. Most queries that access a single table use the operations described in the previous sections. When tuning a query for an online user, avoid using the sorting and grouping operations that force users to wait for records to be processed. When possible, write queries that allow application users to receive records quickly as the query is resolved. The fewer sorting and grouping operations you perform, the faster the first record will be returned to the user. In a batch transaction, the performance of the query is measured by its overall time to complete, not the time to return the first row. As a result, batch transactions may use sorting and grouping operations without impacting the perceived performance of the application.

If your application does not require all of the rows to be sorted prior to presenting query output, consider using the FIRST_ROWS hint. FIRST_ROWS tells the optimizer to favor execution paths that do not perform set operations.

## Operations Using RowNum

Queries that use the RowNum pseudo-column use either the COUNT or COUNT STOPKEY operation to increment the RowNum counter. If a limiting condition is applied to the RowNum pseudo-column, such as

```
where RowNum < 10
```

then the COUNT STOPKEY operation is used. If no limiting condition is specified for the RowNum pseudo-column, then the COUNT operation is used. The COUNT and COUNT STOPKEY operations are not related to the **COUNT** function.

The following query will use the COUNT operation during its execution, since it refers to the RowNum pseudo-column:

```
select Title,
 RowNum
 from BOOKSHELF;
```

To resolve the preceding query, the optimizer will perform a full index scan (against the primary key index for BOOKSHELF), followed by a COUNT operation to generate the RowNum values for each returned row. The COUNT operation does not need to wait for the entire set of records to be available. As each record is returned from the BOOKSHELF table, the RowNum counter is incremented and the RowNum for the record is determined.

In the following example, a limiting condition is placed on the RowNum pseudo-column:

```
select Title,
 RowNum
 from BOOKSHELF
 where RowNum < 10;
```

To enforce the limiting condition, the optimizer replaces the COUNT operation with a COUNT STOPKEY operation, which compares the incremented value of the RowNum pseudo-column with the limiting condition supplied. When the RowNum value exceeds the value specified in the limiting condition, no more rows are returned by the query.

## UNION, MINUS, and INTERSECT

The **UNION**, **MINUS**, and **INTERSECT** functions allow the results of multiple queries to be processed and compared. Each of the functions has an associated operation—the names of the operations are UNION, MINUS, and INTERSECTION.

The following query selects all of the Title values from the BOOKSHELF table and from the BOOK_ORDER table:

```
select Title
 from BOOKSHELF
 UNION
select Title
 from BOOK_ORDER;
```

When the preceding query is executed, the optimizer will execute each of the queries separately, then combine the results. The first query is

```
select Title
 from BOOKSHELF
```

There are no limiting conditions in the query, and the Title column is indexed, so the primary key index on the BOOKSHELF table will be scanned.

The second query is

```
select Title
 from BOOK_ORDER
```

There are no limiting conditions in the query, so the BOOK_ORDER table will be accessed via a TABLE ACCESS FULL operation.

Since the query performs a **UNION** of the results of the two queries, the two result sets will then be merged via a UNION-ALL operation. Using the **UNION** operator forces Oracle to eliminate duplicate records, so the result set is processed by a SORT UNIQUE operation before

the records are returned to the user. The UNION-ALL optimizer operation, shown in Figure 38-2, is used when both **union** and **union all** queries are executed. The order of operations for the **UNION** operator is shown in Figure 38-2.

If the query had used a **UNION ALL** function in place of **UNION**, the SORT UNIQUE operation (seen in Figure 38-2) would not have been necessary. The query would be

```
select Title
 from BOOKSHELF
 UNION ALL
select Title
 from BOOK_ORDER;
```

When processing the revised query, the optimizer would perform the scans required by the two queries, followed by a UNION-ALL operation. No SORT UNIQUE operation would be required, since a **UNION ALL** function does not eliminate duplicate records.

When processing the **UNION** query, the optimizer addresses each of the **UNION**ed queries separately. Although the examples shown in the preceding listings all involved simple queries with full table scans, the **UNION**ed queries can be very complex, with correspondingly complex execution paths. The results are not returned to the user until all of the records have been processed.

**NOTE**
*UNION ALL is a row operation. UNION, which includes a SORT UNIQUE, is a set operation.*

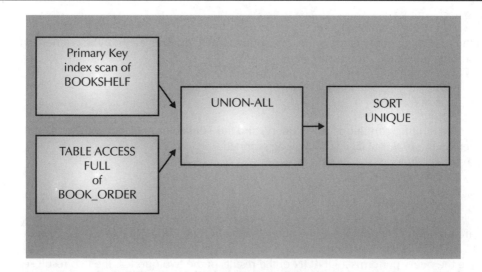

**FIGURE 38-2.** *Order of operations for the UNION function*

When a **MINUS** function is used, the query is processed in a manner very similar to the execution path used for the **UNION** example. In the following query, the Title values from the BOOKSHELF and BOOK_ORDER tables are compared. If a Title value exists in BOOK_ORDER but does not exist in BOOKSHELF, then that value will be returned by the query. In other words, we want to see all of the Titles on order that we don't already have.

```
select Title
 from BOOK_ORDER
 MINUS
select Title
 from BOOKSHELF;
```

When the query is executed, the two **MINUS**ed queries will be executed separately. The first of the queries,

```
select Title
 from BOOK_ORDER
```

requires a full table scan of the BOOK_ORDER table. The second query,

```
select Title
 from BOOKSHELF
```

requires a full index scan of the BOOKSHELF primary key index.

To execute the **MINUS** function, each of the sets of records returned by the full table scans is sorted via a SORT UNIQUE operation (in which rows are sorted and duplicates are eliminated). The sorted sets of rows are then processed by the MINUS operation. The order of operations for the **MINUS** function is shown in Figure 38-3.

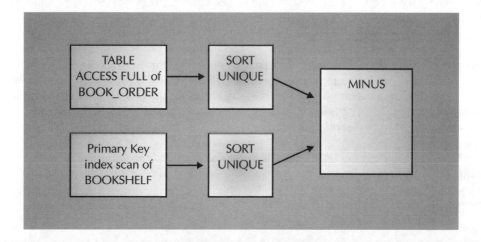

**FIGURE 38-3.** *Order of operations for the MINUS function*

As shown in Figure 38-3, the MINUS operation is not performed until each set of records returned by the queries is sorted. Neither of the sorting operations returns records until the sorting operation completes, so the MINUS operation cannot begin until both of the SORT UNIQUE operations have completed. Like the **UNION** query example, the example query shown for the MINUS operation will perform poorly for online users who measure performance by the speed with which the first row is returned by the query.

The **INTERSECT** function compares the results of two queries and determines the rows they have in common. The following query determines the Title values that are found in both the BOOKSHELF and BOOK_ORDER tables:

```
select Title
 from BOOK_ORDER
INTERSECT
select Title
 from BOOKSHELF;
```

To process the **INTERSECT** query, the optimizer starts by evaluating each of the queries separately. The first query,

```
select Title
 from BOOK_ORDER
```

requires a TABLE ACCESS FULL operation against the BOOK_ORDER table. The second query,

```
select Title
 from BOOKSHELF
```

requires a full scan of the BOOKSHELF primary key index. The results of the two table scans are each processed separately by SORT UNIQUE operations. That is, the rows from BOOK_ORDER are sorted, and the rows from BOOKSHELF are sorted. The results of the two sorts are compared by the INTERSECTION operation, and the Title values returned from both sorts are returned by the **INTERSECT** function.

Figure 38-4 shows the order of operations for the **INTERSECT** function for the preceding example.

As shown in Figure 38-4, the execution path of a query that uses an **INTERSECT** function requires SORT UNIQUE operations to be used. Since SORT UNIQUE operations do not return records to the user until the entire set of rows has been sorted, queries using the **INTERSECT** function will have to wait for both sorts to complete before the INTERSECTION operation can be performed. Because of the reliance on sort operations, queries using the **INTERSECT** function will not return any records to the user until the sorts complete.

The **UNION**, **MINUS**, and **INTERSECT** functions all involve processing sets of rows prior to returning any rows to the user. Online users of an application may perceive that queries using these functions perform poorly, even if the table accesses involved are tuned; the reliance on sorting operations will affect the speed with which the first row is returned to the user.

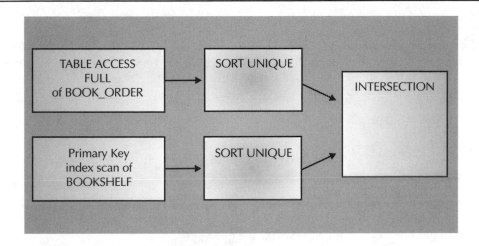

**FIGURE 38-4.** *Order of operations for the INTERSECT function*

## Selecting Rows for Update

You can lock rows by using the **select for update** syntax. For example, the following query selects the rows from the BOOK_ORDER table and locks them to prevent other users from acquiring update locks on the rows. Using **select for update** allows you to use the **where current of** clause in **insert**, **update**, and **delete** commands. A **commit** will invalidate the cursor, so you will need to reissue the **select for update** after every **commit**.

```
select *
 from BOOK_ORDER
 for update of Title;
```

When the preceding query is executed, the optimizer will first perform a TABLE ACCESS FULL operation to retrieve the rows from the BOOK_ORDER table. The TABLE ACCESS FULL operation returns rows as soon as they are retrieved; it does not wait for the full set to be retrieved. However, a second operation must be performed by this query. The FOR UPDATE optimizer operation is called to lock the records. It is a set-based operation (like the sorting operations), so it does not return any rows to the user until the complete set of rows has been locked.

## Selecting from Views

When you create a view, Oracle stores the query that the view is based on. For example, the following view is based on the BOOKSHELF table:

```
create or replace view ADULTFIC as
select Title, Publisher
```

```
 from BOOKSHELF
 where CategoryName = 'ADULTFIC';
```

When you select from the ADULTFIC view, the optimizer will take the criteria from your query and combine them with the query text of the view. If you specify limiting conditions in your query of the view, those limiting conditions will—if possible—be applied to the view's query text. For example, if you execute the query

```
select Title, Publisher
 from ADULTFIC
 where Title like 'T%';
```

the optimizer will combine your limiting condition

```
where Title like 'T%';
```

with the view's query text, and it will execute the query

```
select Title, Publisher
 from BOOKSHELF
 where CategoryName = 'ADULTFIC'
 and Title like 'T%';
```

In this example, the view will have no impact on the performance of the query. When the view's text is merged with your query's limiting conditions, the options available to the optimizer increase; it can choose among more indexes and more data access paths.

The way that a view is processed depends on the query on which the view is based. If the view's query text cannot be merged with the query that uses the view, the view will be resolved first before the rest of the conditions are applied. Consider the following view:

```
create or replace view PUBLISHER_COUNT as
select Publisher, COUNT(*) Count_Pub
 from BOOKSHELF
 group by Publisher;
```

The PUBLISHER_COUNT view will display one row for each distinct Publisher value in the BOOKSHELF table along with the number of records that have that value. The Count_Pub column of the PUBLISHER_COUNT view records the count per distinct Publisher value.

How will the optimizer process the following query of the PUBLISHER_COUNT view?

```
select *
 from PUBLISHER_COUNT
 where Count_Pub > 1;
```

The query refers to the view's Count_Pub column. However, the query's **where** clause cannot be combined with the view's query text, since Count_Pub is created via a grouping operation. The **where** clause cannot be applied until *after* the result set from the PUBLISHER_COUNT view has been completely resolved.

Views that contain grouping operations are resolved before the rest of the query's criteria are applied. Like the sorting operations, views with grouping operations do not return any records until the entire result set has been processed. If the view does not contain grouping operations, the query text may be merged with the limiting conditions of the query that selects from the view. As a result, views with grouping operations limit the number of choices available to the optimizer and do not return records until all of the rows are processed—and such views may perform poorly when queried by online users.

When the query is processed, the optimizer will first resolve the view. Since the view's query is

```
select Publisher, COUNT(*) Count_Pub
 from BOOKSHELF
 group by Publisher;
```

the optimizer will read the data from the BOOKSHELF table via a TABLE ACCESS FULL operation. Since a **group by** clause is used, the rows from the TABLE ACCESS FULL operation will be processed by a SORT GROUP BY operation. An additional operation—FILTER—will then process the data. The FILTER operation is used to eliminate rows based on the criteria in the query:

```
where Count_Pub > 1
```

If you use a view that has a **group by** clause, rows will not be returned from the view until all of the rows have been processed by the view. As a result, it may take a long time for the first row to be returned by the query, and the perceived performance of the view by online users may be unacceptable. If you can remove the sorting and grouping operations from your views, you increase the likelihood that the view text can be merged with the text of the query that calls the view—and as a result, the performance may improve (although the query may use other set operations that negatively impact the performance).

## Selecting from Subqueries

Whenever possible, the optimizer will combine the text from a subquery with the rest of the query. For example, consider the following query:

```
select Title
 from BOOKSHELF
 where Title in
(select Title from BOOK_ORDER);
```

The optimizer, in evaluating the preceding query, will determine that the query is functionally equivalent to the following join of the BOOKSHELF and BOOK_ORDER tables:

```
select BOOKSHELF.Title
 from BOOKSHELF, BOOK_ORDER
 where BOOKSHELF.Title = BOOK_ORDER.Title;
```

With the query now written as a join, the optimizer has a number of operations available to process the data (as described in "Operations That Perform Joins," later in this chapter).

If the subquery cannot be resolved as a join, it will be resolved before the rest of the query text is processed against the data—similar in function to the manner in which the FILTER operation is used for views. As a matter of fact, the FILTER operation is used for subqueries if the subqueries cannot be merged with the rest of the query!

Subqueries that rely on grouping operations have the same tuning issues as views that contain grouping operations. The rows from such subqueries must be fully processed before the rest of the query's limiting conditions can be applied.

When the query text is merged with the view text, the options available to the optimizer increase. For example, the combination of the query's limiting conditions with the view's limiting conditions may allow a previously unusable index to be used during the execution of the query.

The automatic merging of the query text and view text can be disabled via the NO_MERGE hint. The PUSH_PRED hint forces a join predicate into a view; PUSH_SUBQ causes nonmerged subqueries to be evaluated as early as possible in the execution path.

## Additional Tuning Issues

If you are tuning queries that will be used by online users, you should try to reduce the number of sorting operations. When using the operations that manipulate sets of records, you should try to reduce the number of nested sorting operations.

For example, a **UNION** of queries in which each query contains a **group by** clause will require nested sorts; a sorting operation would be required for each of the queries, followed by the SORT UNIQUE operation required for the **UNION**. The sort operation required for the **UNION** will not be able to *begin* until the sorts for the **group by** clauses have completed. The more deeply nested the sorts are, the greater the performance impact on your queries.

If you are using **UNION** functions, check the structures and data in the tables to see if it is possible for both queries to return the same records. For example, you may be querying data from two separate sources and reporting the results via a single query using the **UNION** function. If it is not possible for the two queries to return the same rows, then you could replace the **UNION** function with **UNION ALL**—and avoid the SORT UNIQUE operation performed by the **UNION** function.

If you are using the Parallel Query Option, work with your database administrator to make sure your database and tables are configured properly to take advantage of parallelism. The optimizer can parallelize many operations, including table scans, index scans, and sorts. Most join operations, described in the next section, can also be executed in parallel.

# Operations That Perform Joins

Often, a single query will need to select columns from multiple tables. To select the data from multiple tables, the tables are joined in the SQL statement—the tables are listed in the **from** clause, and the join conditions are listed in the **where** clause. In the following example, the BOOKSHELF and BOOK_ORDER tables are joined, based on their common Title column values:

```
select BOOKSHELF.Title
 from BOOKSHELF, BOOK_ORDER
 where BOOKSHELF.Title = BOOK_ORDER.Title;
```

which can be rewritten using the join syntax introduced with Oracle9i as:

```
select Title
 from BOOKSHELF inner join BOOK_ORDER
 using (Title);
```

or:

```
select Title
 from BOOKSHELF natural inner join BOOK_ORDER;
```

The join conditions can function as limiting conditions for the join. Since the BOOKSHELF.Title column is equated to a value in the **where** clause, the optimizer may be able to use an index on the BOOKSHELF.Title column during the execution of the query. If an index is available on the BOOK_ORDER.Title column, that index would be considered for use by the optimizer as well.

Oracle has three methods for processing joins: MERGE JOIN operations, NESTED LOOPS operations, and HASH JOIN operations. Based on the conditions in your query, the available indexes, and (for CBO) the available statistics, the optimizer will choose which join operation to use. Depending on the nature of your application and queries, you may want to force the optimizer to use a method different from its first choice of join methods. In the following sections, you will see the characteristics of the different join methods and the conditions under which each is most useful.

## How Oracle Handles Joins of More than Two Tables

If a query joins more than two tables, the optimizer treats the query as a set of multiple joins. For example, if your query joined three tables, then the optimizer would execute the joins by joining two of the tables together, and then joining the result set of that join to the third table. The size of the result set from the initial join impacts the performance of the rest of the joins. If the size of the result set from the initial join is large, then many rows will be processed by the second join.

If your query joins three tables of varying size—such as a small table named SMALL, a medium-sized table named MEDIUM, and a large table named LARGE—you need to be aware of the order in which the tables will be joined. If the join of MEDIUM to LARGE will return many rows, then the join of the result set of that join with the SMALL table may perform a great deal of work. Alternatively, if SMALL and MEDIUM were joined first, then the join between the result set of the SMALL-MEDIUM join and the LARGE table may minimize the amount of work performed by the query. Later in this chapter, the section "Displaying the Execution Path," which describes the **explain plan** and **set autotrace on** commands, will show how you can interpret the order of joins.

## MERGE JOIN

In a MERGE JOIN operation, the two inputs to the join are processed separately, sorted, and joined. MERGE JOIN operations are commonly used when there are no indexes available for the limiting conditions of the query.

In the following query, the BOOKSHELF and BOOKSHELF_AUTHOR tables are joined. If neither table has an index on its Title column, then there are no indexes that can be used during

the query (since there are no other limiting conditions in the query). The example uses a hint to force a merge join to be used:

```
select /*+ USE_MERGE (bookshelf, bookshelf_author)*/
 BOOKSHELF_AUTHOR.AuthorName
 from BOOKSHELF, BOOKSHELF_AUTHOR
 where BOOKSHELF.Title = BOOKSHELF_AUTHOR.Title
 and BOOKSHELF.Publisher > 'T%';
```

or

```
select /*+ USE_MERGE (bookshelf, bookshelf_author)*/
 BOOKSHELF_AUTHOR.AuthorName
 from BOOKSHELF inner join BOOKSHELF_AUTHOR
 on BOOKSHELF.Title = BOOKSHELF_AUTHOR.Title
 where BOOKSHELF.Publisher > 'T%';
```

To resolve the query, the optimizer may choose to perform a MERGE JOIN of the tables. To perform the MERGE JOIN, each of the tables is read individually (usually by a TABLE ACCESS FULL operation or a full index scan). The set of rows returned from the table scan of the BOOKSHELF_AUTHOR table is sorted by a SORT JOIN operation. The set of rows returned from the index scan and table access by RowID of the BOOKSHELF table is already sorted (in the index), so no additional SORT JOIN operation is needed for that part of the execution path. The data from the SORT JOIN operations is then merged via a MERGE JOIN operation. Figure 38-5 shows the order of operations for the MERGE JOIN example. The explain plan is as follows:

```
Execution Plan
--
 0 SELECT STATEMENT Optimizer=CHOOSE (Cost=7 Card=5 Bytes=320)
 1 0 MERGE JOIN (Cost=7 Card=5 Bytes=320)
 2 1 TABLE ACCESS (BY INDEX ROWID) OF 'BOOKSHELF' (Cost=2 Car
 d=4 Bytes=120)
 3 2 INDEX (FULL SCAN) OF 'SYS_C002547' (UNIQUE) (Cost=1 Ca
 rd=4)
 4 1 SORT (JOIN) (Cost=5 Card=37 Bytes=1258)
 5 4 TABLE ACCESS (FULL) OF 'BOOKSHELF_AUTHOR' (Cost=1 Card
 =37 Bytes=1258)
```

When a MERGE JOIN operation is used to join two sets of records, each set of records is processed separately before being joined. The MERGE JOIN operation cannot begin until it has received data from both of the SORT JOIN operations that provide input to it. The SORT JOIN operations, in turn, will not provide data to the MERGE JOIN operation until all of the rows have been sorted. If indexes are used as data sources, the SORT JOIN operations may be bypassed.

If the MERGE JOIN operation has to wait for two separate SORT JOIN operations to complete, a join that uses the MERGE JOIN operation will typically perform poorly for online users. The perceived poor performance is due to the delay in returning the first row of the join to the users. As the tables increase in size, the time required for the sorts to be completed increases dramatically. If the tables are of greatly unequal size, then the sorting operation performed on the larger table will negatively impact the performance of the overall query.

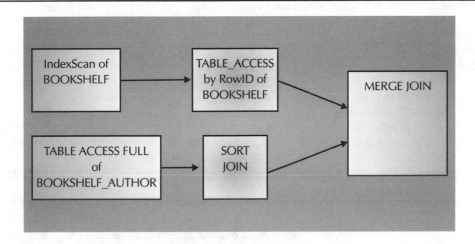

**FIGURE 38-5.** *Order of operations for the MERGE JOIN operation*

Since MERGE JOIN operations involve full scanning and sorting of the tables involved, you should only use MERGE JOIN operations if both tables are very small or if both tables are very large. If both tables are very small, then the process of scanning and sorting the tables will complete quickly. If both tables are very large, then the sorting and scanning operations required by MERGE JOIN operations can take advantage of Oracle's parallel options.

Oracle can parallelize operations, allowing multiple processors to participate in the execution of a single command. Among the operations that can be parallelized are the TABLE ACCESS FULL and sorting operations. Since a MERGE JOIN uses the TABLE ACCESS FULL and sorting operations, it can take full advantage of Oracle's parallel options. Parallelizing queries involving MERGE JOIN operations frequently improves the performance of the queries (provided there are adequate system resources available to support the parallel operations).

# NESTED LOOPS

NESTED LOOPS operations join two tables via a looping method: The records from one table are retrieved, and for each record retrieved, an access is performed of the second table. The access of the second table is performed via an index-based access.

A form of the query from the preceding MERGE JOIN section is shown in the following listing. A hint is used to recommend an index-based access of the BOOKSHELF table:

```
select /*+ INDEX(bookshelf) */
 BOOKSHELF_AUTHOR.AuthorName
 from BOOKSHELF, BOOKSHELF_AUTHOR
 where BOOKSHELF.Title = BOOKSHELF_AUTHOR.Title;
```

Since the Title column of the BOOKSHELF table is used as part of the join condition in the query, the primary key index can resolve the join. When the query is executed, a NESTED LOOPS operation can be used to execute the join.

To execute a NESTED LOOPS join, the optimizer must first select a *driving table* for the join, which is the table that will be read first (usually via a TABLE ACCESS FULL operation, although index scans are commonly seen). For each record in the driving table, the second table in the join will be queried. The example query joins BOOKSHELF and BOOKSHELF_AUTHOR, based on values of the Title column. During the NESTED LOOPS execution, an operation will select all of the records from the BOOKSHELF_AUTHOR table. The primary key index of the BOOKSHELF table will be probed to determine if it contains an entry for the value in the current record from the BOOKSHELF_AUTHOR table. If a match is found, then the Title value will be returned from the BOOKSHELF primary key index. If other columns were needed from BOOKSHELF, the row would be selected from the BOOKSHELF table via a TABLE ACCESS BY ROWID operation. The flow of operations for the NESTED LOOPS join is shown in Figure 38-6.

As shown in Figure 38-6, at least two data access operations are involved in the NESTED LOOPS join: an access of the driving table and an access, usually index-based, of the driven table. The data access methods most commonly used—TABLE ACCESS FULL, TABLE ACCESS BY ROWID, and index scans—return records to successive operations as soon as a record is found; they do not wait for the whole set of records to be selected. Because these operations can provide the first matching rows quickly to users, NESTED LOOPS joins are commonly used for joins that are frequently executed by online users.

When implementing NESTED LOOPS joins, you need to consider the size of the driving table. If the driving table is large and is read via a full table scan, then the TABLE ACCESS FULL operation performed on it may negatively affect the performance of the query. If indexes are available on both sides of the join, Oracle will select a driving table for the query. The method of selection for the driving table depends on the optimizer in use. If you are using the CBO, then the optimizer will check the statistics for the size of the tables and the selectivity of the indexes and will choose the path with the lowest overall cost. If you are using the RBO, and indexes are available for all join conditions, then the driving table will usually be the table that is listed *last* in the **from** clause.

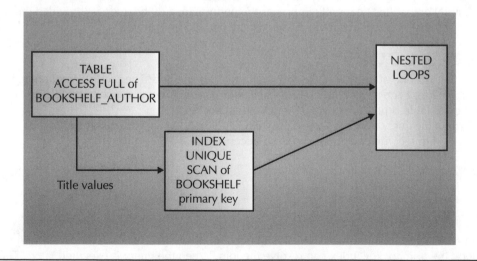

**FIGURE 38-6.** *Order of operations for NESTED LOOPS*

When joining three tables together, Oracle performs two separate joins: a join of two tables to generate a set of records, and then a join between that set of records and the third table. If NESTED LOOPS joins are used, then the order in which the tables are joined is critical. The output from the first join generates a set of records, and that set of records is used as the driving table for the second join.

The size of the set of records returned by the first join impacts the performance of the second join—and thus may have a significant impact on the performance of the overall query. You should attempt to join the most selective tables first so that the impact of those joins on future joins will be negligible. If large tables are joined in the first join of a multijoin query, then the size of the tables will impact each successive join and will negatively impact the overall performance of the query.

NESTED LOOPS joins are useful when the tables in the join are of unequal size—you can use the smaller table as the driving table and select from the larger table via an index-based access. The more selective the index is, the faster the query will complete.

# HASH JOIN

The optimizer may dynamically choose to perform joins using the HASH JOIN operation in place of either MERGE JOIN or NESTED LOOPS. The HASH JOIN operation compares two tables in memory. During a hash join, the first table is scanned and the database applies "hashing" functions to the data to prepare the table for the join. The values from the second table are then read (typically via a TABLE ACCESS FULL operation), and the hashing function compares the second table with the first table. The rows that result in matches are returned to the user.

**NOTE**
*Although they have similar names, hash joins have nothing to do with hash clusters or with the TABLE ACCESS HASH operation discussed later in this chapter.*

The optimizer may choose to perform hash joins even if indexes are available. In the sample query shown in the following listing, the BOOKSHELF and BOOKSHELF_AUTHOR tables are joined on the Title column:

```
select /*+ USE_HASH (bookshelf) */
 BOOKSHELF_AUTHOR.AuthorName
 from BOOKSHELF, BOOKSHELF_AUTHOR
 where BOOKSHELF.Title = BOOKSHELF_AUTHOR.Title;
```

The BOOKSHELF table has a unique index on its Title column. Since the index is available and can be used to evaluate the join conditions, the optimizer may choose to perform a NESTED LOOPS join of the two tables as shown in the previous section. If a hash join is performed, then each table will be read via a separate operation. The data from the table and index scans will serve as input to a HASH JOIN operation.

The order of operations for a hash join is shown in Figure 38-7. As shown, the hash join does not rely on operations that process sets of rows. The operations involved in hash joins return records quickly to users. Hash joins are appropriate for queries executed by online users if the tables are small and can be scanned quickly.

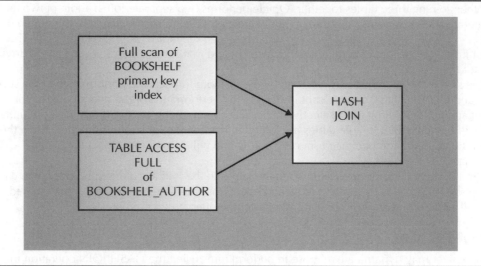

**FIGURE 38-7.** *Order of operations for the HASH JOIN operation*

## Processing Outer Joins

When processing an outer join, the optimizer will use one of the three methods described in the previous sections. For example, if the sample query were performing an outer join between BOOK_ORDER and CATEGORY (to see which categories had no books on order), a NESTED LOOPS OUTER operation may be used instead of a NESTED LOOPS operation. In a NESTED LOOPS OUTER operation, the table that is the "outer" table for the outer join is typically used as the driving table for the query; as the records of the inner table are scanned for matching records, **NULL** values are returned for rows with no matches.

## Related Hints

You can use hints to override the optimizer's selection of a join method. Hints allow you to specify the type of join method to use or the goal of the join method.

In addition to the hints described in this section, you can use the FULL and INDEX hints, described earlier, to influence the way in which joins are processed. For example, if you use a hint to force a NESTED LOOPS join to be used, then you may also use an INDEX hint to specify which index should be used during the NESTED LOOPS join and which table should be accessed via a full table scan.

### Hints About Goals

You can specify a hint that directs the optimizer to execute a query with a specific goal in mind. The available goals related to joins are the following:

■ **ALL_ROWS**   Execute the query so that all of the rows are returned as quickly as possible.

■  **FIRST_ROWS**  Execute the query so that the first row will be returned as quickly as possible.

By default, the optimizer will execute a query using an execution path that is selected to minimize the total time needed to resolve the query. Thus, the default is to use ALL_ROWS as the goal. If the optimizer is only concerned about the total time needed to return all rows for the query, then set-based operations such as sorts and MERGE JOIN can be used. However, the ALL_ROWS goal may not always be appropriate. For example, online users tend to judge the performance of a system based on the time it takes for a query to return the first row of data. The users thus have FIRST_ROWS as their primary goal, with the time it takes to return all of the rows as a secondary goal.

The available hints mimic the goals: the ALL_ROWS hint allows the optimizer to choose from all available operations to minimize the overall processing time for the query, while the FIRST_ROWS hint tells the optimizer to select an execution path that minimizes the time required to return the first row to the user.

**NOTE**
*You should only use the ALL_ROWS or FIRST_ROWS hint if you have first analyzed the tables.*

In the following example, the query from the join examples is modified to include the ALL_ROWS hint:

```
select /*+ ALL_ROWS */
 BOOKSHELF_AUTHOR.AuthorName
 from BOOKSHELF, BOOKSHELF_AUTHOR
 where BOOKSHELF.Title = BOOKSHELF_AUTHOR.Title;
```

You could modify this query to use the FIRST_ROWS hint instead:

```
select /*+ FIRST_ROWS */
 BOOKSHELF_AUTHOR.AuthorName
 from BOOKSHELF, BOOKSHELF_AUTHOR
 where BOOKSHELF.Title = BOOKSHELF_AUTHOR.Title;
```

If you use the FIRST_ROWS hint, the optimizer will be less likely to use MERGE JOIN and more likely to use NESTED LOOPS. The join method selected partly depends on the rest of the query. For example, the join query example does not contain an **order by** clause (which is a set operation performed by the SORT ORDER BY operation). If the query is revised to contain an **order by** clause, as shown in the following listing, how does that change the join processing?

```
select /*+ FIRST_ROWS */
 BOOKSHELF_AUTHOR.AuthorName
 from BOOKSHELF, BOOKSHELF_AUTHOR
 where BOOKSHELF.Title = BOOKSHELF_AUTHOR.Title
 order by BOOKSHELF_AUTHOR.AuthorName;
```

With an **order by** clause added to the query, the SORT ORDER BY operation will be the last operation performed before the output is shown to the user. The SORT ORDER BY operation will not complete—and will not display any records to the user—until all of the records have been sorted. Therefore, the FIRST_ROWS hint in this example tells the optimizer to perform the join as quickly as possible, providing the data to the SORT ORDER BY operation as quickly as possible. The addition of the sorting operation (the **order by** clause) in the query may negate or change the impact of the FIRST_ROWS hint on the query's execution path (since a SORT ORDER BY operation will be slow to return records to the user regardless of the join method chosen).

## Hints About Methods

In addition to specifying the goals the optimizer should use when evaluating join method alternatives, you can list the specific operations to use and the tables to use them on. If a query involves only two tables, you do not need to specify the tables to join when providing a hint for a join method to use.

The USE_NL hint tells the optimizer to use a NESTED LOOPS operation to join tables. In the following example, the USE_NL hint is specified for the join query example. Within the hint, the BOOKSHELF table is listed as the inner table for the join.

```
select /*+ USE_NL(bookshelf) */
 BOOKSHELF_AUTHOR.AuthorName
 from BOOKSHELF, BOOKSHELF_AUTHOR
 where BOOKSHELF.Title = BOOKSHELF_AUTHOR.Title;
```

If you want all of the joins in a many-table query to use NESTED LOOPS operations, you could just specify the USE_NL hint with no table references. In general, you should specify table names whenever you use a hint to specify a join method, because you do not know how the query may be used in the future. You may not even know how the database objects are currently set up—for example, one of the objects in your **from** clause may be a view that has been tuned to use MERGE JOIN operations.

If you specify a table in a hint, you should refer to the table alias or the unqualified table name. That is, if your **from** clause refers to a table as

```
from FRED.HIS_TABLE, ME.MY_TABLE
```

then you should *not* specify a hint such as

```
/*+ USE_NL(ME.MY_TABLE) */
```

Instead, you should refer to the table by its name, without the owner:

```
/*+ USE_NL(my_table) */
```

If multiple tables have the same name, then you should assign table aliases to the tables and refer to the aliases in the hint. For example, if you join a table to itself, then the **from** clause may include the text shown in the following listing:

```
from BOOKSHELF B1, BOOKSHELF B2
```

A hint forcing the BOOKSHELF-BOOKSHELF join to use NESTED LOOPS would be written to use the table aliases, as shown in the following listing:

```
/*+ USE_NL(b2) */
```

The optimizer will ignore any hint that isn't written with the proper syntax. Any hint with improper syntax will be treated as a comment (since it is enclosed within the **/\*** and **\*/** characters).

**NOTE**
*USE_NL is a hint, not a rule. The optimizer may recognize the hint and choose to ignore it, based on the statistics available when the query is executed.*

If you are using NESTED LOOPS joins, then you need to be concerned about the order in which the tables are joined. The ORDERED hint, when used with NESTED LOOPS joins, influences the order in which tables are joined.

When you use the ORDERED hint, the tables will be joined in the order in which they are listed in the **from** clause of the query. If the **from** clause contains three tables, such as

```
from BOOK_ORDER, BOOKSHELF, BOOKSHELF_AUTHOR
```

then the first two tables will be joined by the first join, and the result of that join will be joined to the third table.

Since the order of joins is critical to the performance of NESTED LOOPS joins, the ORDERED hint is often used in conjunction with the USE_NL hint. If you use hints to specify the join order, you need to be certain that the relative distribution of values within the joined tables will not change dramatically over time; otherwise, the specified join order may cause performance problems in the future.

You can use the USE_MERGE hint to tell the optimizer to perform a MERGE JOIN between specified tables. In the following listing, the hint instructs the optimizer to perform a MERGE JOIN operation between BOOKSHELF and BOOKSHELF_AUTHOR:

```
select /*+ USE_MERGE (bookshelf, bookshelf_author)*/
 BOOKSHELF_AUTHOR.AuthorName
 from BOOKSHELF, BOOKSHELF_AUTHOR
 where BOOKSHELF.Title = BOOKSHELF_AUTHOR.Title
 and BOOKSHELF.Publisher > 'T%';
```

You can use the USE_HASH hint to tell the optimizer to consider using a HASH JOIN method. If no tables are specified, then the optimizer will select the first table to be scanned into memory based on the available statistics.

```
select /*+ USE_HASH (bookshelf) */
 BOOKSHELF_AUTHOR.AuthorName
 from BOOKSHELF, BOOKSHELF_AUTHOR
 where BOOKSHELF.Title = BOOKSHELF_AUTHOR.Title;
```

If you are using the CBO but have previously tuned your queries to use rule-based optimization, you can tell the CBO to use the rule-based method when processing your query. The RULE hint tells the optimizer to use the RBO to optimize the query; all other hints in the query will be ignored. In the following example, the RULE hint is used during a join:

```
select /*+ RULE */
 BOOKSHELF_AUTHOR.AuthorName
 from BOOKSHELF, BOOKSHELF_AUTHOR
 where BOOKSHELF.Title = BOOKSHELF_AUTHOR.Title;
```

In general, you should only use the RULE hint if you have tuned your queries specifically for the RBO. Although the RULE hint is still supported, you should investigate using the CBO in its place for your queries.

You can set the optimizer goal at the session level via the **alter session** command. In the following example, the session's optimizer_goal parameter is changed to RULE:

```
alter session set optimizer_goal = RULE;
```

Other settings for the session's optimizer_goal parameter include COST, CHOOSE, ALL_ROWS, and FIRST_ROWS.

Additional hints for influencing joins include LEADING (to tell Oracle to use the specified table first in the join order) and ORDERED (join tables in the order they are listed in the **from** clause).

## Additional Tuning Issues

As noted in the discussions of NESTED LOOPS and MERGE JOIN operations, operations differ in the time they take to return the first row from a query. Since MERGE JOIN relies on set-based operations, it will not return records to the user until all of the rows have been processed. NESTED LOOPS, on the other hand, can return rows to the user as soon as rows are available.

Because NESTED LOOPS joins are capable of returning rows to users quickly, they are often used for queries that are frequently executed by online users. Their efficiency at returning the first row, however, is often impacted by set-based operations applied to the rows that have been selected. For example, adding an **order by** clause to a query adds a SORT ORDER BY operation to the end of the query processing—and no rows will be displayed to the user until all of the rows have been sorted.

As described in "Operations That Use Indexes," earlier in this chapter, using functions on a column prevents the database from using an index on that column during data searches unless you have created a function-based index. You can use this information to dynamically disable indexes and influence the join method chosen. For example, the following query does not specify a join hint, but it disables the use of indexes on the Title column by concatenating the Title values with a null string:

```
select BOOKSHELF_AUTHOR.AuthorName
 from BOOKSHELF, BOOKSHELF_AUTHOR
 where BOOKSHELF.Title||'' = BOOKSHELF_AUTHOR.Title||'';
```

The dynamic disabling of indexes allows you to force MERGE JOIN operations to be used even if you are using the RBO (in which no hints are accepted).

As noted during the discussion of the NESTED LOOPS operation, the order of joins is as important as the join method selected. If a large or nonselective join is the first join in a series, the large data set returned will negatively impact the performance of the subsequent joins in the query as well as the performance of the query as a whole.

Depending on the hints, optimizer goal, and statistics, the optimizer may choose to use a variety of join methods within the same query. For example, the optimizer may evaluate a three-table query as a NESTED LOOPS join of two tables, followed by a MERGE JOIN of the NESTED LOOPS output with the third table. Such combinations of join types are usually found when the ALL_ROWS optimizer goal is in effect.

To see the order of operations, you can use the **set autotrace on** command to see the execution path, as described in the next section.

# Displaying the Execution Path

You can display the execution path for a query in either of two ways:

- Use the **explain plan** command
- Use the **set autotrace on** command

In the following sections, both commands are explained; for the remainder of the chapter, the **set autotrace on** command will be used to illustrate execution paths as reported by the optimizer.

## Using set autotrace on

You can have the execution path automatically displayed for every transaction you execute within SQLPLUS. The **set autotrace on** command will cause each query, after being executed, to display both its execution path and high-level trace information about the processing involved in resolving the query.

To use the **set autotrace on** command, you must have first created a PLAN_TABLE table within your account. The PLAN_TABLE structure may change with each release of Oracle, so you should drop and re-create your copy of PLAN_TABLE with each Oracle upgrade. The commands shown in the following listing will drop any existing PLAN_TABLE and replace it with the current version.

**NOTE**
*In order for you to use **set autotrace on**, your DBA must have first created the PLUSTRACE role in the database and granted that role to your account. The PLUSTRACE role gives you access to the underlying performance-related views in the Oracle data dictionary. The script to create the PLUSTRACE role is called plustrce.sql, usually found in the /sqlplus/admin directory under the Oracle software home directory.*

The following example refers to $ORACLE_HOME. Replace that symbol with the home directory for Oracle software on your operating system. The file that creates the PLAN_TABLE table is located in the /rdbms/admin subdirectory under the Oracle software home directory.

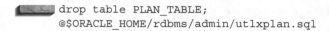

```
drop table PLAN_TABLE;
@$ORACLE_HOME/rdbms/admin/utlxplan.sql
```

When you use **set autotrace on**, records are inserted into your copy of the PLAN_TABLE to show the order of operations executed. After the query completes, the selected data is displayed. After the query's data is displayed, the order of operations is shown followed by statistical information about the query processing. The following explanation of **set autotrace on** focuses on the section of the output that displays the order of operations.

> **NOTE**
> *To show only the explain plan output, use the **set autotrace on explain** command.*

If you use the **set autotrace on** command, you will not see the explain plan for your queries until *after* they complete. The **explain plan** command (described next) shows the execution paths without running the queries first. Therefore, if the performance of a query is unknown, you may choose to use the **explain plan** command before running it. If you are fairly certain that the performance of a query is acceptable, use **set autotrace on** to verify its execution path.

In the following example, a full table scan of the BOOKSHELF table is executed. The rows of output are not displayed in this output, for the sake of brevity. The order of operations is displayed below the query.

```
select *
 from BOOKSHELF;
Execution Plan
--
 0 SELECT STATEMENT Optimizer=CHOOSE (Cost=1 Card=31 Bytes=1209
)
 1 0 TABLE ACCESS (FULL) OF 'BOOKSHELF' (Cost=1 Card=31 Bytes=1
 209)
```

The "Execution Plan" shows the steps the optimizer will use to execute the query. Each step is assigned an ID value (starting with 0). The second number shows the "parent" operation of the current operation. Thus, for the preceding example, the second operation—the TABLE ACCESS (FULL) OF 'BOOKSHELF'—has a parent operation (the **select** statement itself). Each step displays a cumulative cost for that step plus all of its child steps. Note that the line breaks are not word-wrapped; the Bytes value for step 1 is 1,209.

You can generate the order of operations for DML commands, too. In the following example, a **delete** statement's execution path is shown:

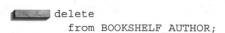

```
delete
 from BOOKSHELF_AUTHOR;
```

```
Execution Plan
--
 0 DELETE STATEMENT Optimizer=CHOOSE (Cost=1 Card=37)
 1 0 DELETE OF 'BOOKSHELF_AUTHOR'
 2 1 TABLE ACCESS (FULL) OF 'BOOKSHELF_AUTHOR' (Cost=1 Card=3
 7)
```

The **delete** command, as expected, involves a full table scan. If you have analyzed your tables, the Execution Plan column's output shows the number of rows from each table, the relative cost of each step, and the overall cost of the operation. You could use that information to pinpoint the operations that are the most costly during the processing of the query.

In the following example, a slightly more complex query is executed. An index-based query is made against the BOOKSHELF table, using its primary key index.

```
select /*+ INDEX(bookshelf) */ *
 from BOOKSHELF
 where Title like 'M%';
```

```
Execution Plan
--
 0 SELECT STATEMENT Optimizer=CHOOSE (Cost=2 Card=2 Bytes=78)
 1 0 TABLE ACCESS (BY INDEX ROWID) OF 'BOOKSHELF' (Cost=2 Card=
 2 Bytes=78)
 2 1 INDEX (RANGE SCAN) OF 'SYS_C002547' (UNIQUE) (Cost=1 Car
 d=2)
```

This listing includes three operations. Operation #2, the INDEX RANGE SCAN of the BOOKSHELF primary key index (its name was system-generated), provides data to operation #1, the TABLE ACCESS BY INDEX ROWID operation. The data returned from the TABLE ACCESS BY ROWID is used to satisfy the query (operation #0).

The preceding output also shows that the optimizer is automatically indenting each successive step within the execution plan. In general, you should read the list of operations from the inside out and from top to bottom. Thus, if two operations are listed, the one that is the most indented will usually be executed first. If the two operations are at the same level of indentation, then the one that is listed first (with the lowest operation number) will be executed first.

In the following example, BOOKSHELF and BOOKSHELF_AUTHOR are joined without the benefit of indexes:

```
select /*+ USE_MERGE (bookshelf, bookshelf_author)*/
 BOOKSHELF_AUTHOR.AuthorName
 from BOOKSHELF, BOOKSHELF_AUTHOR
 where BOOKSHELF.Title = BOOKSHELF_AUTHOR.Title
 and BOOKSHELF.Publisher > 'T%';
```

```
Execution Plan
--
 0 SELECT STATEMENT Optimizer=CHOOSE (Cost=7 Card=5 Bytes=320)
 1 0 MERGE JOIN (Cost=7 Card=5 Bytes=320)
 2 1 TABLE ACCESS (BY INDEX ROWID) OF 'BOOKSHELF' (Cost=2 Car
```

```
 d=4 Bytes=120)
 3 2 INDEX (FULL SCAN) OF 'SYS_C002547' (UNIQUE) (Cost=1 Ca
 rd=4)
 4 1 SORT (JOIN) (Cost=5 Card=37 Bytes=1258)
 5 4 TABLE ACCESS (FULL) OF 'BOOKSHELF_AUTHOR' (Cost=1 Card
 =37 Bytes=1258)
```

The indentation here may seem confusing at first, but the operational parentage information provided by the operation numbers clarifies the order of operations. The innermost operations are performed first—the TABLE ACCESS FULL and INDEX FULL SCAN operations. Next, the full table scan's data is processed via a SORT JOIN operation (in operation 4), while the output from the index scan (which is sorted already) is used as the basis for a TABLE ACCESS BY ROWID (step 2). Both step 2 and step 4 have operation #1, the MERGE JOIN, as their parent operations. The MERGE JOIN operation provides data back to the user via the **select** statement. The picture of this data flow was shown in Figure 38-5. You should be comfortable reading the execution path and picturing its matching data flow.

If the same query were run as a NESTED LOOPS join, a different execution path would be generated. As shown in the following listing, the NESTED LOOPS join would be able to take advantage of the primary key index on the Title column of the BOOKSHELF table:

```
select /*+ INDEX(bookshelf) */
 BOOKSHELF_AUTHOR.AuthorName
 from BOOKSHELF, BOOKSHELF_AUTHOR
 where BOOKSHELF.Title = BOOKSHELF_AUTHOR.Title;
Execution Plan
--
 0 SELECT STATEMENT Optimizer=CHOOSE (Cost=1 Card=37 Bytes=1924
)
 1 0 NESTED LOOPS (Cost=1 Card=37 Bytes=1924)
 2 1 TABLE ACCESS (FULL) OF 'BOOKSHELF_AUTHOR' (Cost=1 Card=3
 7 Bytes=1258)
 3 1 INDEX (UNIQUE SCAN) OF 'SYS_C002547' (UNIQUE)
```

NESTED LOOPS joins are among the few execution paths that do not follow the "read from the inside out" rule of indented execution paths. To read the NESTED LOOPS execution path correctly, examine the order of the operations that directly provide data to the NESTED LOOPS operation (in this case, operations #2 and #3). Of those two operations, the operation with the lowest number (#2, in this example) is executed first. Thus, the TABLE ACCESS FULL of the BOOKSHELF_AUTHOR table is executed first (BOOKSHELF_AUTHOR is the driving table for the query).

Once you have established the driving table for the query, the rest of the execution path can be read from the inside out and from top to bottom. The second operation performed is the INDEX UNIQUE SCAN of the BOOKSHELF primary key index. The NESTED LOOPS operation is then able to return rows to the user.

If a hash join had been selected instead of a NESTED LOOPS join, the execution path would have been

```
select /*+ USE_HASH (bookshelf) */
 BOOKSHELF_AUTHOR.AuthorName
```

```
 from BOOKSHELF, BOOKSHELF_AUTHOR
where BOOKSHELF.Title = BOOKSHELF_AUTHOR.Title;

Execution Plan

 0 SELECT STATEMENT Optimizer=CHOOSE (Cost=3 Card=37 Bytes=1924
)
 1 0 HASH JOIN (Cost=3 Card=37 Bytes=1924)
 2 1 INDEX (FULL SCAN) OF 'SYS_C002547' (UNIQUE) (Cost=1 Card
 =31 Bytes=558)
 3 1 TABLE ACCESS (FULL) OF 'BOOKSHELF_AUTHOR' (Cost=1 Card=3
 7 Bytes=1258)
```

The hash join execution path shows that two separate scans are performed. Since the two operations are listed at the same level of indentation, the BOOKSHELF table's primary key index is scanned first (since it has the lower operation number).

> **NOTE**
> When using the **set autotrace on** command, you do not have to manage the records within the PLAN_TABLE. Oracle will automatically delete the records it inserts into PLAN_TABLE once the execution path has been displayed.

If you use the parallel query options or query remote databases, an additional section of the **set autotrace on** output will show the text of the queries executed by the parallel query server processes or the query executed within the remote database.

To disable the autotrace feature, use the **set autotrace off** command.

## Using explain plan

You can use the **explain plan** command to generate the execution path for a query without first running the query. To use the **explain plan** command, you must first create a PLAN_TABLE table in your schema (see the previous instructions on creating the table). To determine the execution path of a query, prefix the query with the following SQL:

```
explain plan
set Statement_ID = 'TEST'
for
```

To make the tuning process simpler, always use the same Statement_ID value and delete the records for each execution path before using the **explain plan** command a second time.

An example of the execution of the **explain plan** command is shown in the following listing. The query shown in the listing will not be run during the command; only its execution path steps will be generated, and they will be inserted as records in PLAN_TABLE.

```
explain plan
set Statement_ID = 'TEST'
for
select /*+ USE_HASH (bookshelf) */
```

```
 BOOKSHELF_AUTHOR.AuthorName
 from BOOKSHELF, BOOKSHELF_AUTHOR
 where BOOKSHELF.Title = BOOKSHELF_AUTHOR.Title;

Explained.
```

When the **explain plan** command is executed, records will be inserted into PLAN_TABLE. You can query PLAN_TABLE using the following query. The results of the query will show the operations performed at each step and the parent-child relationships between the execution path steps, similar to the indented display of the **set autotrace on** command.

```
select ID ID_plus_exp,
Parent_ID parent_id_plus_exp,
LPAD(' ',2*(level-1))|| /* Indent for the level */
Operation|| /* The operation */
DECODE(other_tag,null,'','*')|| /* will display an '*' if parallel */
DECODE(options,null,'',' ('||options||')')|| /* display the options */
DECODE(object_name,null,'',' of '''||object_name||'''')||
DECODE(object_type,null,'',' '||object_type||')')||
DECODE(id,0,decode(optimizer,null,'',' optimizer='||optimizer))||
DECODE(cost,null,'',' (cost='||cost|| /* display cost info. */
DECODE(cardinality,null,'',' card='||cardinality)|| /* cardinality */
DECODE(bytes,null,'',' bytes='||bytes)||')') plan_plus_exp,
object_node object_node_plus_exp /* parallel and remote info */
from PLAN_TABLE
start with ID=0 and Statement_ID='TEST'
connect by prior ID=Parent_ID and Statement_ID='TEST'
order by ID,Position;
```

The query shown in the preceding listing uses the **connect by** operator to evaluate the hierarchy of steps in the query's execution path. The query in the listing assumes the Statement_ID field has been set to 'TEST'. The execution path steps will be displayed in the column given the Execution_Path alias.

The output from the preceding query is shown in the following listing:

```
 i p PLAN_PLUS_EXP OBJECT_N
---- ---- --- --------
 0 SELECT STATEMENT optimizer=CHOOSE (cost=3 card=37 bytes=1924
)
 1 0 HASH JOIN (cost=3 card=37 bytes=1924)
 2 1 INDEX (FULL SCAN) of 'SYS_C002547' UNIQUE) (cost=1 card=
 31 bytes=558)
 3 1 TABLE ACCESS (FULL) of 'BOOKSHELF_AUTHOR' (cost=1 card=3
 7 bytes=1258)
```

The first two columns show the ID and the parent ID for each step. The output includes the Cost column, which displays the relative "cost" of each step. You cannot compare the costs of dissimilar queries during your tuning process.

## Implementing Stored Outlines

As you migrate from one database to another, the execution paths for your queries may change. Your execution paths may change for several reasons:

- You may be using a different optimizer in different databases (cost-based in one, rule-based in another).

- You may have enabled different optimizer features in the different databases.

- The statistics for the queried tables may differ in the databases.

- The frequency with which statistics are gathered may differ among the databases.

- The databases may be running different versions of the Oracle kernel.

The effects of these differences on your execution paths can be dramatic, and can have a significant negative impact on your query performance as you migrate or upgrade your application. To minimize the impact of these differences on your query performance, Oracle introduced a feature called a *stored outline* in Oracle8i.

A stored outline stores a set of hints for a query. Those hints will be used every time the query is executed. Using the stored hints will increase the likelihood that the query will use the same execution path each time. Hints do not mandate an execution path (they're hints, not commands) but do decrease the impact of database moves on your query performance.

To start creating hints for all queries, set the CREATE_STORED_OUTLINES initialization parameter to TRUE; thereafter, all the outlines will be saved under the DEFAULT category. As an alternative, you can create custom categories of outlines and use the category name as a value in the initialization parameter file, as shown in the following listing:

```
CREATE_STORED_OUTLINES = development
```

In this example, stored outlines will be stored for queries within the DEVELOPMENT category.

You must have the CREATE ANY OUTLINE system privilege in order to create an outline. Use the **create outline** command to create an outline for a query, as shown in the following listing:

```
create outline REORDERS
 for category DEVELOPMENT
 on
select BOOKSHELF.Title
 from BOOKSHELF, BOOK_ORDER
 where BOOKSHELF.Title = BOOK_ORDER.Title;
```

**NOTE**
*If you do not specify a name for your outline, the outline will be given a system-generated name.*

If you have set CREATE_STORED_OUTLINES to TRUE in your initialization parameter file, the RDBMS will create stored outlines for your queries; using the **create outline** command gives you more control over the outlines that are created.

**NOTE**
*You can create outlines for DML commands
and for **create table as select** commands.*

Once an outline has been created, you can alter it. For example, you may need to alter the outline to reflect significant changes in data volumes and distribution. You can use the **rebuild** clause of the **alter outline** command to regenerate the hints used during query execution:

```
alter outline REORDERS rebuild;
```

You can also rename an outline via the **rename** clause of the **alter outline** command:

```
alter outline REORDERS rename to BOOK_REORDERS;
```

You can change the category of an outline via the **change category** clause, as shown in the following example:

```
alter outline REORDERS change category to DEFAULT;
```

For the stored outlines to be used by the optimizer, set the USE_STORED_ OUTLINES initialization parameter to TRUE or to a category name (such as DEVELOPMENT in the earlier examples). If stored outline use is enabled, any query with a stored outline will use the hints generated when the outline was created. You can also enable USE_STORED_OUTLINES at the session level via the **alter session** command.

To manage stored outlines, use the OUTLN_PKG package, which gives you three capabilities:

- Drop outlines that have never been used
- Drop outlines within a specific category
- Move outlines from one category to another

Each of these three capabilities has a corresponding procedure within OUTLN_PKG. To drop outlines that have never been used, execute the DROP_UNUSED procedure, as shown in the following listing:

```
execute OUTLN_PKG.DROP_UNUSED;
```

To drop all of the outlines within a category, execute the DROP_BY_CAT procedure, which has the name of the category as its only input parameter. The following example drops all of the outlines within the DEVELOPMENT category:

```
execute OUTLN_PKG.DROP_BY_CAT -
 (cat => 'DEVELOPMENT');
```

To reassign outlines from an old category to a new category, use the UPDATE_BY_CAT procedure, as shown in the following example.

```
execute OUTLN_PKG.UPDATE_BY_CAT -
 (old_cat => 'DEVELOPMENT', -
 new_cat => 'TEST');
```

To drop a specific outline, use the **drop outline** command.

# Miscellaneous Operations

In addition to the operations shown previously in this chapter—table access, index access, data set manipulation, and joins—a number of other operations are used by the optimizer when executing a query. The operations described in the following sections can impact your query's performance, but they tend to be less tunable or less frequently used than the operations previously described.

## Filtering Rows

When a **where** clause is used to eliminate rows for a query, Oracle may use a FILTER operation to select the rows that meet the **where** clause criteria. The FILTER operation is not always shown in the **set autotrace on** output, even though it may be used. See the View example earlier in this chapter for an illustration of the FILTER operation. When a FILTER operation is listed explicitly in a query's execution path, it usually indicates that no index is available to assist in the processing of a limiting condition. FILTER operations are commonly seen in queries that use the **connect by** clause and occasionally during the processing of VIEW operations.

## Queries That Use connect by Clauses

When a query uses a **connect by** clause, Oracle uses a CONNECT BY operation to execute the query. The execution path will show that the CONNECT BY operation usually takes three inputs as it progresses up and down a "tree" of records. For best performance from a **connect by** query, you should create a set of indexes that can be used by the columns in the **connect by** clause.

For example, the **connect by** examples shown throughout this book use the BREEDING table to illustrate the family history of cows and bulls. The following query travels from the root node of the family tree (the cow named 'EVE') to the descendants. A **connect by** query can be written to travel either from the root to its descendants or from a descendant to its ancestors.

```
select Cow,
 Bull,
 LPAD(' ',6*(Level-1))||Offspring Offspring,
 Sex,
 Birthdate
 from BREEDING
 start with Offspring = 'EVE'
connect by Cow = PRIOR Offspring;
```

With no indexes on the BREEDING table, the following execution path is generated for this query (as reported via **set autotrace on**, with the table analyzed):

```
Execution Plan

 0 SELECT STATEMENT Optimizer=CHOOSE (Cost=1 Card=16 Bytes=320)
 1 0 CONNECT BY (WITH FILTERING)
 2 1 NESTED LOOPS
 3 2 TABLE ACCESS (FULL) OF 'BREEDING' (Cost=1 Card=1 Bytes
 =5)
 4 2 TABLE ACCESS (BY USER ROWID) OF 'BREEDING'
 5 1 HASH JOIN
 6 5 CONNECT BY PUMP
 7 5 TABLE ACCESS (FULL) OF 'BREEDING' (Cost=1 Card=16 Byte
 s=320)
```

The CONNECT BY operation has multiple inputs: an initial table scan to determine the location of the root node, followed by a pair of table access operations to traverse the data tree. Of the data access operations that supply data to the CONNECT BY operation, two are TABLE ACCESS FULL operations.

To reduce the number of TABLE ACCESS FULL operations required by the CONNECT BY operation, you should create a pair of concatenated indexes on the columns used in the **connect by** clause. For the query of the BREEDING table, the **connect by** clause is

```
connect by Cow = PRIOR Offspring
```

To properly index the data for the query, you can create two concatenated indexes of the Cow and Offspring columns. In the first index, the Cow column should be the leading column. In the second index, reverse the order of the columns in the index. The pair of indexes created on the Cow and Offspring columns can be used regardless of the direction used when traversing the data tree. As of Oracle9i, you can create just one concatenated index and use the skip-scan feature to quickly scan the index.

In the following listing, the two concatenated indexes are created:

```
create index Cow$Offspring
on BREEDING(Cow,Offspring);

create index Offspring$Cow
on BREEDING(Offspring, Cow);
```

With those two indexes available, the execution path for the query of the BREEDING table will now use index-based accesses instead of full table scans, as shown in the following listing. Note that you may need to hint the optimizer to use the specific index, as shown here:

```
select /*+ INDEX(breeding offspring$cow) */
 Cow,
 Bull,
 LPAD(' ',6*(Level-1))||Offspring Offspring,
 Sex,
 Birthdate
 from BREEDING
 start with Offspring = 'EVE'
connect by Cow = PRIOR Offspring;
```

```
Execution Plan
--
 0 SELECT STATEMENT Optimizer=CHOOSE (Cost=148 Card=3 Bytes=60)
 1 0 CONNECT BY (WITH FILTERING)
 2 1 NESTED LOOPS
 3 2 TABLE ACCESS (FULL) OF 'BREEDING' (Cost=1 Card=1 Bytes
 =5)
 4 2 TABLE ACCESS (BY USER ROWID) OF 'BREEDING'
 5 1 NESTED LOOPS
 6 5 BUFFER (SORT)
 7 6 CONNECT BY PUMP
 8 5 TABLE ACCESS (BY INDEX ROWID) OF 'BREEDING' (Cost=148
 Card=3 Bytes=60)
 9 8 INDEX (SKIP SCAN) OF 'OFFSPRING$COW' (NON-UNIQUE) (C
 ost=18 Card=3)
```

In the preceding listing, one of the TABLE ACCESS FULL operations for the BREEDING table has been replaced by index-based accesses. A hint was used to force the optimizer to use the OFFSPRING$COW index, illustrating the Oracle9i skip scan feature (see operation #9 in the listing). In general, index-based accesses will perform better than full table scans for **connect by** queries, particularly if there are multiple levels in the data tree.

## Queries That Use Sequences

When a query selects values from a sequence, a SEQUENCE operation will appear in the execution path for the query. In general, sequence values are selected by querying DUAL (the public synonym for the SYS.DUAL table). If another table is already involved in the query, you do not need to add DUAL to the query in order to select from the sequence.

The use of DUAL as a base table for the query is arbitrary; the important criteria are that the table be accessible and that it have one row in it for each sequence number you want returned.

To improve the performance of queries that generate values from sequences, you can "cache" a preallocated set of sequence values in memory. By default, 20 sequence values will be cached. When caching sequence values, Oracle will not replenish the cache until all 20 values have been used. If the database is shut down, any cached sequence values will be lost; on database startup, the next 20 values will be cached.

For example, if you select 12 values from a sequence, 8 will still be left in the cache. If you then shut down the database, those 8 values will be lost. When the database is restarted, another 20 sequence values—starting after the last previously cached value—will be cached. Thus, there will be a gap of eight sequence values in the values selected from the sequence. See the Alphabetical Reference for the syntax of the **create sequence** and **alter sequence** commands.

## Queries That Use Database Links

If a query uses a database link to access remote data, the optimizer will show that a REMOTE operation is used. When a REMOTE operation is used, the Other column of the PLAN_TABLE table will record the query that is executed in the remote database. When tuning a query that uses remote objects, you should seek to minimize the amount of traffic between the instances. Minimizing the traffic between databases includes limiting both the size of the data sent from

the remote database to the local database and the number of times the remote database is accessed during the query.

## Queries That Use Clusters

If a table is stored in a cluster, a TABLE ACCESS CLUSTER operation can be used to access the table. In general, data manipulation against clustered tables performs poorly when compared to data manipulation against nonclustered tables. If your tables will be frequently modified by **insert**, **update**, and **delete**, then using clusters may negatively impact the performance of your application. Clusters are most appropriate when the data stored in them is static.

For the NESTED LOOPS join example, the BOOKSHELF_AUTHOR table was used as the driving table and an index-based access was used to find matching records in the BOOKSHELF table. During the access to the BOOKSHELF data, the primary key index was used. If the BOOKSHELF table was stored in a cluster, and the Title column was the cluster key column, then the operations used to access the data within the NESTED LOOPS join would have changed slightly.

If BOOKSHELF were in a cluster, then BOOKSHELF_AUTHOR could still be the driving table for the join. The access to the BOOKSHELF table's data would be at most a two-step process: an INDEX UNIQUE SCAN of the cluster key's index, followed by a TABLE ACCESS CLUSTER of the BOOKSHELF table. A TABLE ACCESS CLUSTER operation is used whenever data is read from a table after selecting index values from the cluster index for the table's cluster.

If BOOKSHELF were in a hash cluster, the method of reading the data from the table would change completely. In a hash cluster, the physical location of a row is determined by the values in the row. If BOOKSHELF were in a hash cluster, and the Title column values were used as the hashing function for the hash cluster, then the query

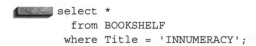

```
select *
 from BOOKSHELF
 where Title = 'INNUMERACY';
```

would use a TABLE ACCESS HASH operation to read the data. Since the physical location of the data would already be known by the optimizer, no index-based accesses would be necessary.

## Related Hints

You can use the HASH hint to tell the optimizer to use a TABLE ACCESS HASH operation when scanning a table. When you specify the HASH hint, you should provide the name (or alias) of the table to be read via the TABLE ACCESS HASH operation.

**NOTE**
*There is no relation between hash clusters and hash joins.*
*To specify the use of hash joins, use the USE_HASH hint.*

If you are using non-hash clusters, then you can specify that a table be read via a TABLE ACCESS CLUSTER operation via the CLUSTER hint. In general, the CLUSTER and HASH hints are mostly used when the queries being modified do not contain joins. If a query contains a join, you should use the join-related hints to have the greatest impact on the query's chosen execution path.

## Additional Tuning Issues

In addition to the operations and hints listed in the previous sections, you can use two other sets of hints to influence the query processing. The additional hints allow you to control the parallelism of queries and the caching of data within the System Global Area (SGA).

If your server has multiple processors, and the data being queried is distributed across multiple devices, then you may be able to improve the processing of your queries by parallelizing the data access and sorting operations. When a query is parallelized, multiple processes are run in parallel, each of which accesses or sorts data. A query coordinator process distributes the workload and assembles the query results for the user.

The *degree of parallelism*—the number of scanning or sorting processes started for a query—can be set at the table level (see the **create table** command in the Alphabetical Reference). The optimizer will detect the table-level settings for the degree of parallelism and will determine the number of query server processes to be used during the query. The optimizer will dynamically check the number of processors and devices involved in the query and will base its parallelism decisions on the available resources.

You can influence the parallelism of your queries via the PARALLEL hint. In the following example, a degree of parallelism of four is set for a query of the BOOKSHELF table:

```
select /*+ PARALLEL (bookshelf,4) */ *
 from BOOKSHELF;
```

If you are using the Real Application Clusters option, you can specify an "instances" parameter in the PARALLEL hint. In the following query, the full table scan process will be parallelized, with a proposed degree of parallelism of four across two instances:

```
select /*+ PARALLEL(bookshelf,4,2) */ *
 from BOOKSHELF
 order by Publisher;
```

In the preceding query, a second operation—the SORT ORDER BY operation for the **order by Publisher** clause—was added. Because the sorting operation can also be parallelized, the query may use nine query server processes instead of five (four for the table scan, four for the sort, and one for the query coordinator). The optimizer will dynamically determine the degree of parallelism to use based on the table's settings, the database layout, and the available system resources.

If you want to disable parallelism for a query, you can use the NOPARALLEL hint. The NOPARALLEL hint may be used if you want to execute serially a query against a table whose queries are typically executed in a parallelized fashion.

If a small table (less than five database blocks in size) is read via a full table scan, that table's data is marked to be kept in the SGA for as long as possible. Data read via index scans and TABLE ACCESS BY ROWID operations is also kept in the SGA for as long as possible and is removed only when necessary by additional memory requests from the application. If a table is larger than five blocks, and it is read via a full table scan, its blocks will normally be marked for removal from the SGA as early as possible. If the table read by a full table scan is larger than five blocks, and you want its data to be kept in memory for as long as possible, you can mark the table as a "cached" table, using the **cache** clause of the **create table** or **alter table** command.

If a large table has not been marked as a cached table, and you want its data to stay in the SGA after the query completes, you can use the CACHE hint to tell the optimizer to keep the data in the SGA for as long as possible. The CACHE hint is usually used in conjunction with the FULL hint.

In the following listing, the BOOKSHELF table is queried; although its data will be read via a TABLE ACCESS FULL operation, the data will not be immediately removed from the SGA:

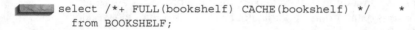

```
select /*+ FULL(bookshelf) CACHE(bookshelf) */ *
 from BOOKSHELF;
```

If a table is commonly used by many queries or users, and there is no appropriate indexing scheme available for the query, then you should use caching to improve the performance of accesses to that table. Caching is most useful for static tables. To dynamically disable the cache settings for a table, use the NOCACHE hint.

# Review

The preceding sections have shown the methods used by the optimizer to access and manipulate data. When tuning queries, you need to keep in mind several factors:

- **The goal of the user**   Do you want rows to be quickly returned, or do you care more about the total throughput time for the query?

- **The type of joins used**   Are the tables properly indexed to take advantage of NESTED LOOPS operations?

- **The size of the tables**   How large are the tables that are being queried? If there are multiple joins, how large is the set of data returned from each join?

- **The selectivity of the data**   How selective are the indexes in use?

- **The sorting operations**   How many sorting operations are performed? Are nested sorting operations being performed?

If you can carefully manage the issues related to performance, then the number of "problem" queries within your database should diminish. If a query appears to be taking more resources than it should, then you should use the **set autotrace on** or **explain plan** command to determine the order of operations used for the query. You can use the tips and discussions provided throughout this chapter to then tune the operations or the set of operations. The tuned query will then be able to meet your goals.

# CHAPTER
## 39

# The Hitchhiker's
# Guide to Oracle9iAS

ith the introduction of Oracle9i Application Server (9iAS), Oracle presents the development community with a full-featured suite of tools and applications to develop, deploy, manage, and tune applications for the Web. Oracle9iAS is a reliable, scalable, middle-tier application server that enables you and your organization to benefit from the true power of the Internet. Rather than being a single product, Oracle9iAS is a collection of services designed to work together to deliver content dynamically to the Web. You can pick and choose the services you need, and can add new services as you grow and change. Oracle9iAS is designed to enable the newest web development methods, tools, and standards, supporting Java J2EE, XML, PL/SQL, or JavaServer Pages, and many others. Oracle9iAS also provides services for configuring the other application services, configuring web and database caching, and a host of other application components.

**NOTE**
*Thanks to Brad Brown of TUSC for his contributions to this chapter. For further details on the development of 9iAS-based applications, see Brad's book* Oracle9i Web Development *(Osborne/McGraw-Hill–Oracle Press, 2001).*

Oracle classifies the 9iAS services into several groups according to the type of support they provide:

- **Communication Services**   Web servers to handle requests to and from the Web

- **Business Logic Services**   Development tools and languages for building custom applications

- **Presentation Services**   Dynamic web page development tools

- **Caching Services**   Tools to improve web site performance by caching common data or pages

- **Content Management Services**   Internet File System (IFS) for managing documents in the database

- **Business Intelligence Services**   Useful for creating reports and ad-hoc queries of user activity on your sites

- **Database Services**   Oracle9i database for storing your application data

As part of the 9iAS Suite, Oracle also provides several developer kits to aid in creating dynamic, flexible applications, tools to manage the database, and security once the web sites are deployed.

The openness of this suite affords you and your site designers and developers tremendous flexibility and scalability in the tools and services you want to use. As your needs grow, you can add services or change development direction without leaving the integrated Oracle environment. For example, if you're well-versed in Oracle Forms, but don't have much experience with the Web, you might choose to deploy your forms and reports on the Web today, and add Java or PL/SQL Server Pages as you gain more experience. If you have static pages you want to make dynamic, you can gain management control of the static content using IFS, deploy them today,

and add Java tags to create JavaServer Pages (JSPs) that query their dynamic content from the database later. As your site traffic grows, you might find caching most-used data or pages beneficial to increase performance. When your web sites become *really* popular, you can deploy your applications and data across multiple servers, add more caching, and manage everything using the Enterprise Manager and the Advanced Security system services. Of course, as your sites gain attention and prestige, others will want to incorporate your content, which you can easily provide through the use of XML and Enterprise Java Beans.

Oracle9iAS currently comes in three editions: Standard Edition, Enterprise Edition, and Wireless Edition. *Standard Edition* provides the tools needed to get started with your application development efforts and to grow to a medium-size web site. *Enterprise Edition* adds extra services to grow your site from a medium to a large web presence. For deploying content to cell phones and small web appliances using the Wireless Access Protocol (WAP) interface, Oracle provides the *Wireless Edition,* which adds Portal-to-Go.

In 9iAS release 2, Oracle has further enhanced the functionality of the 9iAS toolset and has recategorized some of the features. In 9iAS release 2, the solutions and components are

Solution	Oracle9iAS Components
J2EE and Internet Applications	Oracle HTTP Server Oracle9iAS Containers for J2EE Oracle9iAS Web Services Oracle PL/SQL Oracle9iAS Forms Services Oracle XML Developer Kit Oracle9i Client
Portals	Oracle9iAS Portal Oracle9iAS Portal Developer Kit
Wireless	Oracle9iAS Wireless
Caching	Oracle9iAS Web Cache
Business Intelligence	Oracle9iAS Reports Services Oracle9iAS Discoverer Oracle9iAS Personalization Oracle9iAS Clickstream Intelligence
E-Business Integration	Oracle9iAS InterConnect Oracle9iAS Unified Messaging Oracle Internet File System
Management and Security	Oracle Enterprise Manager Oracle9iAS Single Sign-On Oracle Internet Directory Oracle9iAS Infrastructure

**NOTE**
*The Oracle9iAS Database Cache is no longer part of 9iAS as of Release 2.*

In the following sections, you will see descriptions of the major components of 9iAS. This is not an exhaustive list, but rather a high-level description of the most commonly used features. Please see the full production documentation set for detailed descriptions of all components.

# Communication Services

*Communication Services* provide Internet connectivity to your users. The Web is the most visible facet and interface of the Internet today, consisting of client and server computers, which can handle multimedia documents. The Internet follows a standard set of protocols and conventions, and has become a universe of network-accessible information. The communication is based on the Hypertext Transfer Protocol (HTTP). Communication Services are the components, protocols, and procedures that provide multimedia communication services—real-time audio, video, and data communications—over packet networks, including Internet Protocol (IP)-based networks. The bottom line is that Communication Services are, in effect, the Web server.

Oracle9iAS provides you with several options for your Communication Services. These services continue to expand with each release of 9iAS.

## Communication Services—Powered by Apache

Oracle supports the following Oracle Apache Modules in the current release:

mod_ssl	Secure Sockets Layer (SSL) message encryption support.
mod_perl	Support for writing Apache modules in Perl.
mod_jserv	Communication with Java servlet engine (J2EE).
mod_plsql	PL/SQL toolkit support.
mod_ose	Delegates URLs to stateful Java and PL/SQL servlets in Oracle Servlet Engine (OSE). This module —keeps session IDs in cookies or redirected URLs —routes requests to the appropriate OSE sessions —communicates with OSE over Network Services (that is, SQL*Net), which gives firewall support between Oracle HTTP Server and OSE, and connection pooling.
http_core	Core Apache features.
mod_access	Host-based access control; provides access control based on client hostname or IP address.
mod_actions	Filetype/method-based script execution; provides for CGI scripts based on media type or request method.
mod_alias	Aliases and redirects; provides for mapping different parts of the host filesystem in the document tree and for URL redirection.
mod_auth	User authentication using text files, Basic and Digest Authentication.
mod_auth_anon	Anonymous user authentication, FTP-style.

mod_autoindex	Automatic directory listings.
mod_cgi	Execution of CGI scripts; processes any file with MIME type application/x-httpd-cgi.
mod_define	Enables the Define directive, which defines a variable that can be expanded on any configuration line. The Define directive has the status Extension, which means that it is not compiled into the server by default.
mod_digest	MD5 authentication; provides for user authentication using MD5 Digest Authentication.
mod_dir	Basic directory handling; provides for "trailing slash" redirects and serving directory index files.
mod_dms	Enables you to monitor performance of site components with Oracle's Dynamic Monitoring Service.
mod_env	Passing of environments to CGI scripts; provides for passing environment variables to CGI/SSI scripts.
mod_expires	Apply Expires: headers to resources; provides for the generation of Expires headers according to user-specified criteria.
mod_fastcgi	This third-party module supports the fastcgi protocol, which enables you to maintain a pool of running servers for CGI applications (thereby eliminating startup and initialization overhead).
mod_headers	Add arbitrary HTTP headers to resources; document headers can be merged, replaced, or removed.
mod_include	Server-parsed documents; provides for server-parsed HTML documents.
mod_info	Summarizes the entire server configuration, including all installed modules and directive settings.
mod_log_config	User-configurable logging replacement for mod_log_common.
mod_log_common	Provides for logging requests made to the server, using the Common Log Format or a user-specified format.
mod_mime	Determines and registers document types using file extensions.
mod_negotiation	Content negotiation.
mod_oc4j	Routes requests from the Oracle HTTP Server to Oracle9iAS Containers for J2EE (OC4J), providing the ajp13 protocol for communication with the servlet engine.
mod_oradav	The Oracle module (an OCI application written in C) that is an extended implementation of mod_dav, and is integrated with the Oracle HTTP Server. mod_oradav performs read/write activity to local files and to Oracle databases.

mod_ossl	Sets security parameters for mod_oc4j. This Oracle module enables strong cryptography for the HTTP Server.
mod_osso	Enables single sign-on for the Oracle HTTP Server. mod_osso examines incoming requests and determines whether the resource requested is protected, and if so, retrieves the HTTP Server cookie for the user.
libproxy (mod_proxy)	Caching proxy capabilities; provides for an HTTP 1.0 caching proxy server.
mod_rewrite	Powerful URL-to-file name mapping using regular expressions; provides a rule-based rewriting engine to rewrite requested URLs on-the-fly.
mod_setenvif	Sets environment variables based on client information; provides for the capability to set environment variables based on attributes of the request.
mod_so	Support for loading modules at runtime; provides for loading of executable code and modules into the server at startup or restart time.
mod_speling	Automatically corrects minor typographical errors in URLs; attempts to correct misspellings of URLs users enter, by ignoring capitalization and allowing up to one misspelling.
mod_status	Server status display; enables a Webmaster, DBA, or server administrator to find out how well the server is performing, presenting an HTML page that gives the current server statistics in an easily readable form.
mod_unique_id	Creates a unique ID for each request.
mod_userdir	User home directories; provides for user-specific directories.
mod_usertrack	User tracking using cookies.
mod_vhost_alias	Enables dynamically configured mass virtual hosting.

## Communication Services—IIS

Incoming requests are handled by the Oracle Communication Services, more commonly known as the *Web Server*. Oracle9iAS comes bundled with the Apache Web Server and also supports Microsoft Internet Information Server (IIS). With the Oracle Plug-in for Microsoft IIS, you can directly invoke PL/SQL and Java Web-stored objects from an Oracle database. Oracle Plug-in for Microsoft IIS provides functionality in a Microsoft IIS environment that's similar to the Oracle HTTP Server Modules: *mod_plsql* and *mod_ose*. Using it, you can access web application components in one of the following two ways:

- ■ Passing a preconfigured virtual directory prefix (PL/SQL access)
- ■ Passing a predefined file extension and virtual directory prefixes, which are stored in the Java configuration file (Java access)

### PL/SQL Web Component Access

Oracle Plug-in for Microsoft IIS supports accessing PL/SQL server pages and PL/SQL stored procedures written with the Oracle PL/SQL Web Toolkit. If you have an existing PL/SQL application, you should have no problem invoking it from IIS. PL/SQL requests are filtered using a predefined prefix and are executed using pooled database connections. Developers have the ability to configure PL/SQL component access from multiple databases.

### Java Web Component Access

Oracle Plug-in for Microsoft IIS supports accessing JSPs and servlets. Java requests are filtered using a Java configuration file.

For more information, see *Oracle Plug-in for Microsoft IIS Configuration and User's Guide* in the Oracle9i Application Server Documentation Library.

# Content Management Services

*Content Management Services* make all your content, regardless of the file type, accessible in one heterogeneous file hierarchy through web browsers, Microsoft Windows networking, File Transfer Protocol (FTP), or an e-mail client. In addition, you can use these services to configure sophisticated file searching capabilities, event alerts, and check-in, check-out functionality to support collaborative projects. On Windows NT- or Windows 2000-based servers, many of these services are available through Microsoft IIS. To enable these same services on all operating systems, Oracle introduced Internet File System.

## Oracle Internet File System

Oracle Internet File System (IFS) is a service that stores files in an Oracle database. From the user's viewpoint, Oracle IFS appears like any other file system accessible through web browsers, Microsoft Windows Explorer, FTP, NFS, or an e-mail client. The fact that files are stored in the database is transparent to users because users don't directly interact with the database.

**NOTE**
*The latest 9iAS Release 2 iFS must use an Oracle9i database;*
*Release 1 can use Oracle8i or Oracle9i.*

Unlike other file systems, Oracle IFS stores all your document files in the same file system. For example, you can display e-mail message files and address books, web files, and word processing or spreadsheet files within a single file hierarchy, or you can perform a single search to locate all references to a topic.

### File System Management

As with most traditional operating system-based file systems, you can manage the files you own or those for which you have the proper permissions. The main file management features include

- **Renaming files** You can rename files you own.

- **Deleting files** You can delete files for which you have the correct permissions.

- **Uploading files**   You can upload files using FTP, NFS, Windows Explorer (by using Server Message Block and Web Folders), and the Web.

- **Setting automatic expiration on files**   You can set an expiration date for each file you upload to Oracle IFS. The file is automatically deleted on that date.

- **Modifying file attributes**   You can view and modify file attributes such as description, filename, and the access control permissions.

Unlike most traditional operating system-based file systems, IFS is built to support collaborative team development and management of documents. These additional features include

- **Check-in, check-out (CICO)**   For group projects, you can check out files, so others can't overwrite your work. Files remain locked until you check them back in or an administrator releases the lock.

- **Versioning**   Developers can decide to make a file versioned. Each time the versioned file is checked in, a new version is created and stored. File versions can be kept or purged as needed.

- **Searching**   Oracle IFS includes a Find utility that uses Oracle Text extensions to search across multiple file types. This advanced search utility enables you to search quickly without having to know database syntax.

- **Multiple folders per file**   This feature allows multiple folders to be assigned to files, avoiding making multiple copies of files when the same document fits into a number of categories. This feature reduces maintenance when files are updated and also saves storage space.

- **Extensible file attributes**   Application developers can extend Oracle IFS to manage new types for custom information. For each new type, you can define custom attributes about the information, which are then used to track and search for the information. This is especially useful for tracking binary or proprietary application-owned file types that, traditionally, are difficult to search.

# Ultra Search

Oracle *Ultra Search* is new in the Oracle9i database release and enables you to search inside databases, as well as static HTML pages. Other search engines cannot see content inside a database and wouldn't be able to find, for example, documents, newspaper articles, and so forth stored inside a database. Ultra Search unifies search areas across heterogeneous corporate repositories, web sites, and groupware content. Oracle Ultra Search includes a web interface, web crawling, and search administration facilities to provide a unified interface for enterprise and vertical portal search applications.

# Business Logic Services

*Business Logic Services* are the development tools and languages that support your application logic. With Business Logic Services, you can build and run custom web applications. The following sections describe the major elements that provide Business Logic Services in Oracle9iAS.

## Oracle Business Components for Java

Oracle *Business Components* for Java is a 100 percent pure Java and XML framework that enables productive development, portable deployment, and flexible customization of multitiered database applications from reusable business components. Application developers can use this framework to

- Author and test business logic in components that automatically integrate with databases
- Reuse business logic through multiple SQL views of data that support different application tasks
- Access and update the views from servlets, JSPs, and Thin-Java Swing clients
- Customize application functionality in layers without modifying the delivered application

See Chapter 34 for an introduction to Java.

## Oracle PL/SQL

Oracle *PL/SQL* is a scalable engine for running business logic against data in Oracle Database Cache and Oracle databases. It enables you to invoke PL/SQL procedures stored in Oracle databases through your web browsers. The stored procedures retrieve data from tables in the database and generate HTML pages, which include the data that is then returned to the client browser. See Chapter 27 for an introduction to PL/SQL.

## Oracle Forms Services

If you have the Enterprise Edition of Oracle9iAS installed, you can run applications based on Oracle Forms technology either over the Internet or over your company intranet. On the application server tier, Oracle *Forms Services* consists of a listener and a runtime engine, where the application logic is stored. On the client tier, Oracle Forms Services consists of a Java applet, which provides the user interface for the runtime engine, and Oracle JInitiator (a Java plug-in), which provides the capability to specify the use of a specific Java virtual machine on the client.

In Oracle9iAS, when you submit a URL to launch an Oracle Forms-based application, the Web listener accepts the request and downloads the Oracle Forms applet to your browser. The Oracle Forms applet then establishes a persistent connection to an Oracle Forms runtime engine. All processing takes place between the Oracle Forms applet and the Oracle Forms Services runtime engine, which seamlessly handles any queries or commits to the database.

# Presentation Services

*Presentation Services* deliver dynamic content to client browsers, supporting servlets, JavaServer Pages, Perl/CGI scripts, PL/SQL Server Pages, forms, and business intelligence. You can use Presentation Services to build your presentation layer for your web applications. While Oracle puts these services into a separate group, you can think of them grouped with the Business Logic Services, in that your application logic can reside within these components. You can break your business logic into executable components, which can then be called or invoked by these services.

# Apache JServ

*Apache JServ* is a 100 percent pure Java servlet engine that is fully compliant with the following Sun Microsystems Java specifications:

- Java Servlet APIs version 2.0
- Java Runtime Environment (JRE) version 1.1

Beginning with version 1.0.2.2 of Oracle9iAS, Oracle offers the J2EE servlet engine. Apache JServ works on any Java Virtual Machine that's compliant with this JRE and executes any Java servlet that's compliant with this version of the Java Servlet APIs specification. When the HTTP server receives a servlet request, it's routed to mod_jserv, which forwards the request to the Apache JServ servlet engine.

# OracleJSP (JavaServer Pages)

*JSP* technology extends Java Servlet technology, and supports the use of Java calls and scriptlets within HTML and XML pages. By using JSP pages, you can create user interfaces by combining static template data with dynamic content. JSP pages support component-based development, separating business logic (usually in JavaBeans or PL/SQL-stored procedure calls) from the presentation, thus enabling you to focus on your areas of expertise. Consequently, JSP developers (who may not know Java) can focus on presentation logic, while Java developers can focus on business logic. For general information about JSPs, refer to the JavaServer Pages Specification (available from http://java.sun.com).

OracleJSP is an implementation of JavaServer Pages version 1.1 (along with some features of HSP 1.2) as specified by Sun Microsystems and extends this specification to provide the following benefits:

- **Portability between servlet environments**   OracleJSP pages are supported on all web servers that support Java servlets built to the version 2.0 or higher specification. Consequently, you can migrate your existing JSP pages that are compliant with the version 1.0 specifications to Oracle9i Application Server without needing to rewrite them.

- **Support for SQLJ**   *SQLJ* is a standard syntax for embedding SQL commands directly into Java code. OracleJSP supports SQLJ programming in JSP scriptlets. This includes support for an additional filename extension, sqljsp, which causes the OracleJSP translator to invoke the Oracle SQLJ translator. See Chapter 35 for examples of SQLJ programming.

- **Oracle JSP Markup Language (JML)**   Oracle provides the JML tag set as a sample tag library, which enables developers unfamiliar with Java syntax to jumpstart by using looping, conditionals, and other high-level programming logic.

- **Extended National Language Support (NLS)**   OracleJSP provides extended NLS support for servlet environments that cannot encode multibyte request parameters and bean property settings. For such environments, OracleJSP offers the *translate_params* configuration parameter, which can be enabled to direct OracleJSP to override the servlet container and do the encoding itself.

■ **Extended datatypes**   OracleJSP provides the *JmlBoolean, JmlNumber, JmlFPNumber,* and *JmlString* JavaBean classes in the *oracle.jsp.jml* package to wrap the most common Java datatypes. These extended datatypes provide a way to work around the limitations of Java primitive types and wrapper classes in the standard *java.lang* package.

■ **Custom JavaBeans**   OracleJSP includes a set of custom JavaBeans for quickly accessing the Oracle database.

As of Oracle9iAS Release 2, the new name for OracleJSP is "OC4J JSP Container," combining the old OracleJSP with Ironflare's Orion.

## Oracle PL/SQL Server Pages (PSP)

Oracle *PSPs* are one of the most exciting new features offered to traditional Oracle PL/SQL developers in Oracle9iAS. PSPs are analogous to JavaServer Pages, but they use PL/SQL, rather than Java, for the server-side scripting. Unlike the other server page offerings, PSPs are fully compiled components executed as Oracle stored procedures. The Oracle PSP service includes the PSP Compiler and the PL/SQL Web Toolkit.

By using this service when developing applications, you can separate page formatting from application logic. Starting with either an existing web page or a stored procedure, you can create dynamic web pages by embedding PL/SQL tags. These dynamic web pages can perform database operations and display the results as HTML, XML, or plain text. Typically, a PL/SQL server page is intended to display in a web browser. It can also be retrieved and interpreted by a program that can make HTTP requests, such as a Java or Perl application, enabling you to improve your application's modular development and reuse.

If you plan to use PSPs as your presentation layer solution, it's important to understand that unless you use a Database Cache Server, the PL/SQL will be executed on the database server, not on the application server. Java and most other languages execute their code on the application server, making those solutions scalable without using a Database Cache Server.

## Perl Interpreter

The *Perl Interpreter* is a persistent Perl runtime environment, which is embedded in the Apache HTTP Server, thus saving the overhead of starting an external interpreter, as in a traditional CGI call. When Oracle HTTP Server receives a Perl request, it's routed through *mod_perl* to the Perl Interpreter for processing.

# Business Intelligence Services

Oracle *Business Intelligence Services* enables you to manage and analyze your business and your web site daily by enabling you to deploy and share business intelligence over the Web or over your corporate intranet.

## Oracle Reports Services

Using Oracle *Reports Services* and its *Reports Servlet Services,* you can create and run new or existing Oracle Reports on an internal company intranet, an external company extranet, or publish them to the Internet. Oracle Reports Services is optimized to deploy Oracle Reports applications (reports and graphics) in a multitiered environment. The Reports Services consist

of the server component, runtime engines, and the servlet runner. In Oracle9iAS, when a client submits a request for a report, the Oracle HTTP Server Web listener routes that request to the Oracle Reports Services server component. The server routes the request to the Oracle Reports Services runtime engine, which runs the report. The report output is then sent back to the client through the Oracle HTTP Server Web listener. Reports can be formatted as HTML, Adobe Acrobat, or as plain text for the user. Developers can also easily customize the report for import into Microsoft Excel or any other commonly supported document type, such as Multipurpose Internet Mail Extensions (MIME).

## Oracle Discoverer 4i Viewer/Oracle9iAS Discoverer

Oracle9iAS Discoverer (previously known as *Discoverer 4i Viewer*) is a tool for running and viewing workbooks (reports) created with Oracle Discoverer 4i Plus over the Web. Targeted at power users, Discoverer enables you to access information from the database and embed it in your site using graphic user interface (GUI) tools and a What You See Is What You Get (WYSIWYG) data display, without being experienced SQL developers. You can publish live reports to web sites by creating a linkable URL that indicates to Discoverer which workbooks to open. Clicking the URL invokes the workbook query to the database and returns live results to the browser. Users interact with the query results to drill up or down, to enter values into optional parameters, or to follow links to other workbooks or applications.

# Portal Services

You can use *Portal Services* to build portal sites that integrate all your content on a single web page. Portal sites give your users a single, centralized, personalized view of relevant applications and data. By using Oracle9iAS Portal Services and Portal-to-Go, you can make your portal sites accessible to both fixed and mobile clients. While building simple applications within Oracle Portal is also possible, its real purpose is in offering applications to users through a subscription model.

## Oracle Portal

An *enterprise portal* is a Web-based application that provides a common, integrated entry point for accessing dissimilar data types on a single web page. For example, you can create portals that give users access to web applications, business documents, business intelligence reports, charts, and links that reside both inside and outside your corporate intranet. You can manage the user experience, creating and administering portal pages that contain portlets. To users, *portlets* on a page appear as regions of an HTML page that present text or graphics as links to more information or applications. Portlets provide access to web resources, such as applications, web pages, or syndicated content feed. Portlets are owned by *portlet providers,* which provide the communication link between the portal page and the portlets. When an application is ready for the user, it's *published,* and the portal administrator makes it available to the intended audience. Users then *subscribe* to the portlet, effectively putting it on their personalized pages.

## Portal-to-Go

*Portal-to-Go* is a translation layer available on the Enterprise Edition of the database that enables web content to be displayed on Wireless Application Protocol (WAP)-enabled devices, such as browser-enabled cell phones and hand-held devices. Portal-to-Go works by isolating content

acquisition from content delivery. It works like an XSLT style sheet, providing an intermediary format layer—Portal-to-Go XML—between the source format and the target format. Portal-to-Go XML is a set of Document Type Definitions (DTDs) and XML document conventions used to define content and internal objects in Oracle Portal-to-Go.

## 9i Dynamic Services

*Dynamic Services* use XML, XSLT, and a common Java or PL/SQL client API to turn any web content or legacy application accessible via the Web into a service, usable by other applications or the end user. Services are application calls or web data sources wrapped in an XML service package that defines the input and output APIs, the properties of the data source, and the execution flow. Thinking of each dynamic service as an application component, the services can be grouped and published together to form a coherent web application interface. Dynamic Services offer support for most web protocols (for example, HTTP, UDDI, LDAP, SMTP, XML Schema, or SOAP) and enable developers also to wrap legacy applications with custom APIs, giving them a new standards-based interface. As part of the Dynamic Services architecture, Oracle provides a central registry for managing and defining the properties, rights, syntax, and execution flow of the applications contained within Dynamic Services. Oracle also provides a Dynamic Services Adapter to incorporate management of the Dynamic Services into the 9iAS Portal registry, so any services defined in Dynamic Services are immediately available for publication as a portlet.

# Developer's Toolkits

To support application development and deployment, Oracle has provided in Oracle9iAS several toolkits containing libraries and tools. Using these *Developer's Toolkits,* you can build web applications that can access your database.

## Oracle Java Messaging Service (JMS) Toolkit

Oracle Java Messaging Service (JMS) extends the standard Sun Microsystems Java Message Service version 1.02 specification. In addition to the standard JMS features, Oracle JMS provides a Java API for Oracle Advanced Queuing (AQ). This API supports the AQ administrative operations and other AQ features including

- **An administrative API** to create queue tables, queues, and topics.

- **Point-to-multipoint communication** that extends the standard point-to-point by using recipient lists for topics.

- **Message propagation between destinations**, which allows applications to define remote subscribers.

- **Transacted sessions** so you can perform JMS, as well as SQL operations in one common transaction.

- **Message retention** after messages are dequeued.

- **Message delay** to make messages visible after a specified time.

- ■ **Exception handling** so messages can be moved to exception queues if they cannot be processed successfully.

- ■ **Oracle8i or Oracle9i AdtMessages** message types, which are stored in the database as Oracle objects. Consequently, the payload of the message can be queried after it's enqueued. Subscriptions can be defined on the contents of these messages in addition to the message properties.

## Oracle SQLJ

Oracle *SQLJ* is a preprocessor that developers can use to embed *static* SQL operations in Java code. A *SQLJ program* is a Java method containing embedded static SQL statements that comply with the ANSI-standard SQLJ Language Reference syntax. Static SQL operations are predefined. The operations themselves don't change in real time as a user runs the application, although the data values returned can change dynamically.

Oracle SQLJ consists of a translator and a runtime component. The *translator* converts embedded SQL into calls to the SQLJ *runtime component,* which performs the SQL operations. In standard SQLJ, this is typically done through calls to a JDBC driver. In the case of Oracle9iAS, it's done through an Oracle JDBC driver. When you run SQLJ applications, the runtime component is invoked to handle the SQL operations. See Chapter 35 for more on using SQLJ.

## Oracle XML Developer's Kit

Extensible Markup Language (XML) is quickly becoming the new standard for web development, especially among business-to-business (B2B) content and service providers. Oracle XML Developer's Kit (XDK) contains XML component libraries and utilities you can use to enable applications and web sites with XML. Using Java stored procedures, the API to call the components is available to either Java or PL/SQL-based applications. See Chapter 41 for more on XML.

Oracle9i features several enhanced database operations to store XML through SQL and render traditional database data as XML. These functionalities are required to support B2B and business-to-customer (B2C) e-business, packaged applications, and Internet content management. The main area of XML support in Oracle9i is built-in XML XDKs.

With Java preloaded and the C XDK linked into Oracle9i, developers can easily access World Wide Web Consortium (W3C) functionalities that generate, manipulate, render, and store XML-formatted data in Oracle9i. Also available in PL/SQL and C++, the XDKs offer XML/XSLT parsers, XML Schema processors, XML Class Generators, XML Transviewer Beans, and the XSQL Servlet, providing basic building block features that let developers quickly enable their applications for XML.

## Oracle LDAP Developer's Kit

The Lightweight Directory Access Protocol (LDAP) Developer's Kit supports client connectivity with Oracle Internet Directory, the Oracle LDAP directory server. Oracle Internet Directory combines a native implementation of the Internet Engineering Task Force's (IETF) LDAPv3 standard with an Oracle8i or Oracle9i back-end data store. Specifically, you can use Oracle LDAP Developer's Kit to develop and monitor LDAP-enabled applications. It supports encrypted connections and client calls to directory services, and you can use it to manage your directory data.

# Caching Services

To scale your e-business web site, Oracle9iAS provides *Caching Services* in the Enterprise Edition of the suite. These services include Oracle Web Cache and, in 9iAS Release 1, Oracle Database Cache. Oracle Web Cache is a content-aware service that improves the performance, scalability, and availability of web sites by caching both static and dynamic pages. Oracle Database Cache, which is not available with Oracle9iAS Release 2, is a middle-tier database cache that reduces the load between the application and database tiers by caching frequently requested data, avoiding unnecessary network round-trips for read-only data.

## Oracle Database Cache

Oracle *Database Cache* resides on the middle tier as a service of 9iAS. It improves the performance and scalability of applications that access Oracle databases by caching frequently used data on the middle-tier machine. With Oracle Database Cache, your applications can process several times as many requests as their original capacity because round-trips to the back-end database are greatly reduced. Oracle Database Cache service supports running stateful servlets, JavaServer Pages, Enterprise JavaBeans, and CORBA objects in Oracle8i and Oracle9i JVM.

### Who Should Use Oracle Database Cache?

If your applications meet the following criteria, you can use Oracle Database Cache to boost the scalability of your web sites and the performance of your applications:

- Your applications access an Oracle database.

- You use a multitiered environment, where the clients, Application Server, and Oracle database servers are located on separate machines.

- Your applications communicate with an Oracle database through Oracle Call Interface (OCI) or an access layer built on OCI, like JDBC-OCI, ODBC, or OLE.

- Your web or application users generate mostly read-only queries.

- Your applications can tolerate some synchronization delay with data in the source database. That is, the cache doesn't need to be as up-to-date as the real-time data in the master database. (You decide how often to refresh the data.)

### Oracle Database Cache Environment

In the Oracle *Database Cache environment,* the cache software consists of a thin middle-tier database instance for caching frequently accessed data and running intelligent software that routes queries. The source database is on the back end running in its own tier. It is the original and primary storage for the data. Currently, Oracle Database Cache can cache data from only one source database.

### Example of How Requests Are Served by Oracle Database Cache

When users request frequently accessed data, the request passes from the client to the Oracle Database Cache, through the web server, and the database cache returns the data. Because the data is stored on the same tier, the data is returned quickly and the request doesn't need to pass

to the source database server for retrieval of the data. If a new user requests the same information, the request is again served in the middle-tier database cache, which returns the data quickly. If the data doesn't reside in the cache, the request is then routed through to the source database for resolution, cached in the middle tier, and served to the user. Any subsequent request for the same data is served from the cache.

### How Oracle Database Cache Is Different Than the Source Database

Although Oracle Database Cache looks like a regular database instance placed in the middle tier, important differences exist.

- Oracle Database Cache does cache data, but it isn't a persistent store for data.

- You cannot perform backup and recovery on it. If you need to back up your data, then you must store it on the source database.

- Oracle Database Cache cannot be used to create tables or other database objects. The only way you can put data into this environment is by caching data from the source database to the middle-tier instance.

- Oracle Database Cache doesn't provide transparent application fail-over (TAF) guarantees if it fails because Oracle Database Cache isn't a true persistent store for data. It's only a mirror of the source instance.

- Oracle Database Cache cannot be treated as an enlisted database in global transactions to avoid an unnecessary and expensive two-phase commit.

### How Do Applications Make Use of Oracle Database Cache?

To take advantage of the benefits of Oracle Database Cache, you only need to configure the environment of your applications. You needn't make any modifications to your applications if they use SQL statements to access the database or are linked with OCI using dynamic libraries and are layered directly on OCI. If your applications satisfy either criterion, queries are routed to the middle-tier database cache automatically.

## Oracle Web Cache

Oracle *Web Cache* is a web server caching service that improves the performance, scalability, and availability of busy web sites that run on Oracle9iAS and the Oracle database. Most Webmasters run statistics on their sites and have a good idea what pages are hit most often. By storing frequently accessed pages in virtual memory, Oracle Web Cache reduces the need to repeatedly process requests for those URLs on the web server. Unlike legacy proxy servers and other web server products that only handle static images and text, Oracle Web Cache caches both static and dynamically generated HTTP content from one or more application web servers. Using Oracle Web Cache, web clients experience faster page retrieval, and the load on the HTTP servers is significantly reduced.

Oracle Web Cache is positioned in front of Oracle HTTP Servers to cache their pages and to provide content to web users who request it. When web browsers access your web sites, they send HTTP requests to Oracle Web Cache, which acts as a virtual server or virtual request router to the Oracle HTTP Servers. If the requested content has changed or aged off, Oracle Web Cache retrieves the new content from an Oracle HTTP Server.

### Oracle Web Cache Main Features

The main features of Oracle Web Cache make it ideal for dynamic e-commerce web sites that host online catalogs, news services, B2B services, and portals:

- **Static and dynamically generated content caching**  Caches documents according to rules and timetables you specify.

- **Cache invalidation**  Supports page invalidation as a means to keep Oracle Web Cache pages consistent with the content on Oracle9iAS.

- **Performance assurance**  Built-in performance measurement handles performance issues, while maintaining cache consistency. These statistics assign a priority order to contents and determine which documents can be served old and which must be retrieved fresh.

- **Surge protection**  Lets you set limits on the number of concurrent requests passed to Oracle Web Cache to avoid overburdening it.

- **Load balancing**  Dynamically distributes requests over many web servers that Oracle Web Cache cannot serve itself. Oracle Web Cache is designed to manage HTTP requests for up to 100 Oracle9iAS server machines.

- **Backend fail-over**  Automatically redistributes the load over the remaining web servers when one server fails or is taken offline. When the failed server returns to operation, Oracle Web Cache automatically includes it in the server pool.

- **Session tracking**  Supports web sites that use session ID tracking to track users.

- **Security**  Provides password authentication for administration tasks, control over which ports operations can be requested from, and timeout for inactive connections.

## Oracle9iAS Clickstream Analysis

Oracle9iAS Clickstream Intelligence is a web-based, comprehensive analytical tool that enables you to acquire, analyze, and report on web interactions with customers, suppliers, and employees. It is one of the key Business Intelligence components of Oracle9iAS Release 2. Clickstream Intelligence leverages the business intelligence tools in Oracle9iAS and the Oracle9i database to provide an integrated and extensible solution for measuring web traffic and improving web site effectiveness.

The Runtime Administrator simplifies the setup, management, and deployment of clickstream data sources. This web-based tool enables you to define how Clickstream Intelligence interprets web log file data, determine which types of data you want to track, and configure and populate the database for optimal storage of clickstream data. The Oracle9iAS Clickstream Intelligence Administrator's Guide describes in detail how to use the Runtime Administrator.

Oracle9iAS Clickstream Intelligence Analytics (Clickstream Analytics) provides more than 150 preconfigured reports that display data acquired from your web sites. Clickstream Analytics reports, called worksheets, are grouped with other reports of a similar nature to form workbooks that can be accessed and viewed with Oracle9iAS Discoverer. You can use Oracle9iAS Discoverer Viewer as well as Oracle9iAS Discoverer Plus to view and analyze data related to web site traffic.

Oracle9iAS Clickstream Intelligence can be installed into the Oracle9i database included in Oracle9i Application Server, or may be installed into a standalone Oracle9i Enterprise Edition database. The Oracle9iAS Clickstream Intelligence database model is built via Oracle9i Warehouse Builder, a tool for designing and deploying databases.

# System Services

Oracle9iAS includes Oracle Enterprise Manager and Oracle Advanced Security to provide system management and security services for your applications. These services manage your Oracle environment and network security through encryption and authentication.

## Oracle Enterprise Manager

*Oracle Enterprise Manager* has been enhanced from a database administration tool into a system management tool that provides an integrated environment for centrally managing your Oracle platform. This service is also available in the Enterprise Edition, and combines a GUI console, Oracle Management Servers, Oracle Intelligent Agents, common services, and administrative tools. In Oracle9iAS, you use the console to manage Oracle Database Cache, Oracle Forms Services, and the host operating system. From the console, you can perform the following tasks:

- Centrally administer and diagnose Oracle Database Cache and Oracle Forms Services

- Monitor the status of your Oracle products and third-party services

- Schedule maintenance activities on multiple machines at varying time intervals

- Monitor networked services for scheduled and unusual events

- Customize your display by organizing your server components into logical groups according to your unique system architecture; as your system grows and changes, you can rearrange the services to fit the new architecture

## Oracle Advanced Security

*Oracle Advanced Security* provides a "soup-to-nuts" suite of security services for Oracle Database Cache, Oracle8i and Oracle9i JVM, and Oracle8i and Oracle9i PL/SQL. Its functionality is two-fold: first, network security features protect enterprise networks and securely extend corporate networks to the Internet; second, it integrates security and directory services, combining to provide enterprise user management and single sign-on.

**Network security features** ensure data privacy, data integrity, and user authentication between the multiple servers in the network. They also provide users single sign-on where the user authenticates once, and then authentication occurs transparently in subsequent connections to other databases or services on the network. Using a single sign-on, users can access multiple schemas and applications with a single password.

**Security and Directory Services** provide you or your systems administrator tools to manage users centrally on a central directory service, rather than repeatedly managing the same users on individual databases and servers. Using Oracle Enterprise Security Manager, a tool accessible through Oracle Enterprise Manager, enterprise users and their authorizations are managed in Oracle Internet Directory or other LDAP directory services.

# Database Services

Oracle9i *Database Services* provide distinct advantages over the Oracle8i database. The Oracle9i database contains many important new features that optimize traditional business applications and facilitate critical advancement for web applications. Oracle9i database's new features deliver the performance, scalability, and availability essential to your applications. These features are covered throughout this book, including partitioning options, external tables, flashback queries, online object reorganization, dynamic parameter management, new functions, new packages (such as DBMS_METADATA for extracting DDL) and new datatypes (such as TIMESTAMP).

## iSQL*Plus

*iSQL*Plus* is a browser-based implementation of SQLPLUS, which can be used over the Internet to connect to an Oracle RDBMS to perform the same actions as through the SQLPLUS command line. The iSQL*Plus implementation uses a web browser, an Oracle HTTP Server with the iSQL*Plus Server, and an Oracle RDBMS Server.

# Starting, Stopping, and Restarting iAS (Apache)

The Oracle9iAS control program is named **apache** on NT and **apachectl** on UNIX. To start Oracle9iAS on NT at the command line, verify that the **apache** executable is in the system PATH environment variable. To check this, find the **apache** executable, typically located in the ORACLE_HOME\Apache\Apache directory, and then check the path by selecting the system icon in the Control Panel and selecting the Environment tab (NT) or Advanced tab (Win 2000 or Win XP Pro). Add the directory for the **apache** executable in the PATH environment variable if it is not set.

To start Oracle9iAS from the command line, enter the following:

```
apache -k start
```

To stop Oracle9iAS from the command line, enter the following:

```
apache -k shutdown
```

You can also start and stop Oracle9iAS using the Oracle HTTP Server shortcuts under Start | Programs | Oracle | Oracle HTTP Server. Additionally, the Services icon in the Control Panel (Administrative Tools/Services under Win XP Pro) has an entry for Oracle HTTP Server, allowing you to start and stop Oracle9iAS here, or you can set the service startup to automatic and have the Oracle HTTP Server started at system startup.

To start Oracle9iAS on UNIX, use the following command to check if your path has been set containing the directory that holds the **httpd** executable:

```
echo $PATH
```

To start Oracle9iAS on UNIX from the command line, enter

```
apachectl
```

or enter

> `httpd`

To have Oracle9iAS start automatically when the server is rebooted, edit the /etc/rc.d/rc.local file and add the following command:

> `$ORACLE_HOME/Apache/Apache/bin/httpd`

To shut down Oracle9iAS, enter

> `apachectl shutdown`

or

> `kill -9 'cat $ORACLE_HOME/Apache/Apache/logs/httpd.pid'`

Command-line syntax for **apache** and **apachectl** is

> ```
> Usage: APACHE [-D name] [-d directory] [-f file] [-n service]
>               [-C "directive"] [-c "directive"] [-k signal]
>               [-v] [-V] [-h] [-l] [-L] [-S] [-t] [-T]
> ```

Command-line options for UNIX and NT are shown in Table 39-1.

Option	Description
**-D** *name*	Define a name for use in <IfDefine *name*> directives
**-d** *directory*	Specify an alternate initial ServerRoot
**-f** *file*	Specify an alternate ServerConfigFile
**-C** *"directive"*	Process directive before reading config files
**-c** *"directive"*	Process directive after reading config files
**-v**	Show version number
**-V**	Show compile settings
**-h**	List available command-line options
**-l**	List compiled-in modules
**-L**	List available configuration directives

**TABLE 39-1.** *UNIX and NT Apache Command-Line Options*

Option	Description	
**-S**	Show parsed settings (currently only vhost settings)	
**-t**	Run syntax check for config files (with docroot check)	
**-T**	Run syntax check for config files (without docroot check)	
**-n** *name*	Name the Oracle9iAS service for **-k** options	
**-k stop	shutdown**	Tell running Oracle9iAS to shut down
**-k restart**	Tell running Oracle9iAS to do a graceful restart	
**-k start**	Tell Oracle9iAS to start	
**-k install	-i**	Install an Oracle9iAS service
**-k config**	Reconfigure an installed Oracle9iAS service	
**-k uninstall	-u**	Uninstall an Oracle9iAS service

**TABLE 39-1.** *UNIX and NT Apache Command-Line Options* (continued)

# CHAPTER
## 40

# The Hitchhiker's Guide to Database Administration

n this chapter, you will see the basic steps involved in administering an Oracle database. There are many components to the database administrator (DBA) job, and there are books written specifically for DBAs. This chapter will provide an overview of the tasks of a DBA, along with guidance on the usage of standard DBA tools.

In earlier chapters, you have already seen many of the functions of a DBA, such as creating tables, indexes, views, users, synonyms, database links, and packages. The DBA topics described in this chapter will therefore focus on the production-control functions of the DBA role:

- Creating a database

- Starting and stopping the database

- Sizing and managing the memory areas for the database

- Allocating and managing space for the objects

- Creating and managing undo

- Performing backups

For each of these topics, many options are available to developers and DBAs. The following sections of this chapter should provide you with enough information to get started, and to learn what questions to ask of your DBAs and system administrators. For further details on all of these topics, see *Oracle9i DBA Handbook*.

# Creating a Database

The simplest way to generate a **create database** script is via the Oracle Universal Installer (OUI). When you install Oracle, OUI gives you the option to create a database. If you use that option, OUI will create a small database that is useful for practice, and can be deleted once you are done practicing. The **create database** scripts provided by Oracle give you a solid template for your standard **create database** scripts. A sample **create database** script is found in the build_db.sql file in the /rdbms/admin subdirectory under the Oracle software home directory. See the **create database** entry in the Alphabetical Reference for the full command syntax.

The **create database** command is issued from within SQLPLUS, via an account with the SYSDBA system privilege:

```
SQL> connect system/manager as sysdba
SQL> startup nomount
SQL> create database...
```

To issue **connect as SYSDBA** successfully, you must have the proper authorization at the operating system and database levels. See your operating system-specific Oracle documentation for information on the operating system rights needed.

## Using the Oracle Enterprise Manager

Oracle Enterprise Manager (OEM), a graphical user interface (GUI) tool, is supplied as part of the standard Oracle toolset to enable DBAs to manage databases from a personal computer. The

OEM toolset provides a robust interface for remote database administration. All DBAs can use the same central OEM repository (a set of tables created in a database) to perform their work. In addition to those changes, OEM includes task scheduling and assignment features to enable around-the-clock database coverage.

You must make several key decisions before installing and configuring OEM. You need to decide where the OEM repository is to be created and how and when you are going to perform backups to protect this repository. Since you can use OEM as an interface to Oracle Recovery Manager (RMAN), recovery information can be stored in the OEM repository. You may want to create a small, separate database in which to store the OEM repository. You should ensure that this database is backed up frequently so that recovery of the repository itself is assured.

If you are the only DBA working with the OEM toolset, you will not have to consider who will handle administration of specific databases in your environment. If there are several DBAs at the site, you will need to determine task definitions, database responsibilities, and schedules. With OEM, you can grant levels of access and privilege to each DBA in the group on a task-by-task basis. You can configure OEM to enable you to send e-mail requests and assignments to other DBAs or take control of a problem to speed resolution.

If you have a previous version of OEM installed, migrate that repository to the newest version to take advantage of the new features. If you have more than one repository on your system, you will need to take precautions to ensure that you migrate each version of the repository without damaging currently stored information.

Oracle supports the Simple Network Messaging Protocol (SNMP). By supporting SNMP, Oracle products can be easily integrated into monitoring tools for systems and networks.

Although you do not have to use OEM, it provides a common GUI for managing your databases. As your enterprise grows in size (and in number of databases and DBAs), the consistency of the DBA interface will support consistent implementation of your change-control and production-control processes.

# Starting and Stopping the Database

To start a database, issue the **startup** command from within SQLPLUS, as shown in the following listing. In the examples in this chapter, the name of the database is MYDB.

```
SQL> connect system/manager as sysdba;
SQL> startup open MYDB;
```

Alternatively, you can first mount the database and then open it via an **alter database** command:

```
SQL> connect system/manager as sysdba;
SQL> startup mount MYDB;
SQL> alter database open;
```

When the database is mounted but not open, you can manage its files. For example, if you moved some of the database's files while the database was shut down, you need to let Oracle know where to find them before it will restart. To give the new locations of the files, you can mount the database (as shown in the preceding listing) and then use the **alter database** command to rename the old files to their new locations. Once you have finished telling Oracle the new locations for the files, you can open the database via the **alter database open** command.

Four primary options are available for shutting down the database. In a normal shutdown (the default), Oracle waits for all users to log out of the database before shutting down. In a transactional shutdown, Oracle waits for active transactions to complete before shutting down. In an immediate shutdown, Oracle rolls back all existing uncommitted transactions and logs out any users currently logged in. In an abort shutdown, the database immediately shuts down, and all uncommitted transactions are lost.

**NOTE**
*While the database is in the process of shutting down or starting up, no new logins are permitted.*

To perform a normal shutdown, use the **shutdown** command. An immediate shutdown, as shown in the following listing, uses the **shutdown immediate** version of the **shutdown** command. To abort the database, use **shutdown abort**.

```
SQL> connect system/manager as sysdba;
SQL> shutdown immediate
```

If you use **shutdown abort**, Oracle will automatically perform recovery operations during the next database startup. In normal and immediate **shutdown**s, your shutdown process may stop if deadlocks exist between multiple users. In those cases, you may need to stop the **shutdown** and issue a **shutdown abort** in its place. A **shutdown abort** may also be useful in situations where the database needs to be stopped in the shortest possible time, for example, for an impending power failure. During the subsequent startup, Oracle will perform any necessary recovery operations.

**NOTE**
*If you are shutting down the database to make a backup, you should use either **shutdown** or **shutdown immediate**. If you have problems during your shutdowns, you may use the following sequence: **shutdown abort**, **startup**, and then **shutdown**.*

You may also use OEM to start up and shut down the instance, via the General tab on the Instance Manager/Configuration screen.

# Sizing and Managing Memory Areas

When you start a database, Oracle allocates a memory area (the System Global Area, or SGA) shared by all of the database users. The two largest areas of the SGA are the *database buffer cache* and the *Shared Pool*; their size will directly impact the memory requirements for the database and the performance of database operations. Their sizes are controlled by parameters in the database's initialization file.

The database buffer cache is an area in the SGA used to hold the data blocks that are read from the data segments in the database, such as tables, indexes, and clusters. The size of the database buffer cache is determined by the DB_CACHE_SIZE parameter (expressed in terms of number of bytes) in the initialization parameter file for the database. The default size for the

database blocks is set via the DB_BLOCK_SIZE parameter specified in the parameter file during database creation. Managing the size of the database buffer cache is an important part of managing and tuning the database.

The database has a default block size, but you can establish cache areas for different database block sizes and then create tablespaces to use those caches. For example, you can create a 4K database block size database with some tablespaces set to 8K. The size of the 8K cache would be set via the DB_8K_CACHE_SIZE parameter. To create tablespaces to use that cache, specify **blocksize 8K** as part of the **create tablespace** command. If the default block size for the database is 4K, you would not set a value for DB_4K_CACHE_SIZE; the size specified for DB_CACHE_SIZE would be used for the 4K cache.

The different cache areas can be resized while the database is running. The caches must be increased or decreased in *granules*. For a database with an SGA less than 128M, the granule size is 4M—so DB_8K_CACHE_SIZE can be 4M, 8M, 12M, and so on. If you attempt to use any other setting, Oracle will round it up to the next granule size. The following listing shows the setting of the DB_8K_CACHE_SIZE parameter.

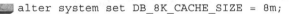

```
alter system set DB_8K_CACHE_SIZE = 8m;
```

If you create a tablespace that uses a non-default database block size, you must be sure that the related cache size parameter (such as DB_8K_CACHE_SIZE) is updated in your database parameter file. If you are using an init.ora file, you must update it with the new value. If you are using a system parameter file, it will be automatically updated when you execute the **alter system** command.

**NOTE**
*You cannot alter the SGA_MAX_SIZE or JAVA_POOL_SIZE parameter values while the database is open.*

Typically, the data block buffer cache is about 1 to 2 percent of the allocated size of the database. Oracle will manage the space available by using an algorithm that keeps the most actively used blocks in memory for as long as possible. When free space is needed in the cache, the new data blocks will either use the space occupied by infrequently accessed blocks or the space occupied by a modified block once it has been written out to disk.

If the SGA is not large enough to hold the most frequently used data, different objects will contend for space within the data block buffer cache. This is particularly likely when multiple applications use the same database and thus share the same SGA. In that case, the most recently used tables and indexes from each application constantly contend for space in the SGA with the most recently used objects from other applications. As a result, requests for data from the data block buffer cache will result in a lower ratio of "hits" to "misses." Data block buffer cache misses result in physical I/Os for data reads, resulting in performance degradation.

The Shared Pool stores the data dictionary cache (information about the database structures) and the *library cache* (information about statements that are run against the database). While the data block buffer and dictionary cache enable sharing of structural and data information among users in the database, the library cache allows the sharing of commonly used SQL statements.

The Shared Pool contains the execution plan and parse tree for SQL statements run against the database. The second time that an identical SQL statement is run (by any user), Oracle is able

to take advantage of the parse information available in the Shared Pool to expedite the statement's execution. Like the data block buffer cache, the Shared Pool is managed via an LRU algorithm. As the Shared Pool fills, less recently used execution paths and parse trees will be removed from the library cache to make room for new entries. If the Shared Pool is too small, statements will be continually reloaded into the library cache, affecting performance.

The size (in bytes) of the Shared Pool is set via the SHARED_POOL_SIZE initialization parameter. Like the other caches, the Shared Pool size can be altered while the database is open.

## The Initialization Parameter File

The characteristics of the database instance—such as the size of the SGA and the number of background processes—are specified during startup. These parameters are stored in a binary file called the system parameter file. To generate the system parameter file for an open database, use the **create spfile** command. You can generate a readable version of the system parameter file via the **create pfile from spfile** command. See the Alphabetical Reference for the command syntax for these commands. The "pfile" version of the parameter file, formerly known as the init.ora file, usually contains the database name as part of the filename. For example, a database named MYDB may have a pfile file named initmydb.ora.

# Allocating and Managing Space for the Objects

To understand how space should be allocated within the database, you first have to know how the space is used within the database. In this section, you will see an overview of the Oracle database space usage functions.

When a database is created, it is divided into multiple logical sections called *tablespaces*. The SYSTEM tablespace is the first tablespace created. You can then create additional tablespaces to hold different types of data (such as tables, indexes, and rollback segments).

When a tablespace is created, *datafiles* are created to hold its data. These files immediately allocate the space specified during their creation. Each datafile can support only one tablespace. Datafiles can be set to automatically extend when they run out of space; you can set the increment by which they extend and their maximum size. A database can have multiple users, each of whom has a *schema*. Each user's schema is a collection of logical database objects, such as tables and indexes, that refer to physical data structures that are stored in tablespaces. Objects from a user's schema may be stored in multiple tablespaces, and a single tablespace can contain objects from multiple schemas.

When a database object (such as a table or index) is created, it is assigned to a tablespace via user defaults or specific instructions. A *segment* is created in that tablespace to hold the data associated with that object. The space that is allocated to the segment is never released until the segment is dropped, manually shrunk, or truncated.

A segment is made up of sections called *extents*—contiguous sets of Oracle blocks. Once the existing extents can no longer hold new data, the segment will obtain another extent. The extension process will continue until no more free space is available in the tablespace's datafiles or until an internal maximum number of extents per segment is reached. If a segment is composed of multiple extents, there is no guarantee that those extents will be contiguous.

Tablespaces can be created as locally managed (the default) or dictionary-managed. In a dictionary-managed tablespace, the extent location information is stored in the data dictionary. In a locally managed tablespace, that data is stored in the datafile headers. Oracle encourages the use of locally managed tablespaces. To review, databases have one or more tablespaces, and

tablespaces consist of one or more datafiles. Within those tablespaces, Oracle stores segments for database objects. Each segment can have multiple extents.

Managing the space used by tablespaces, datafiles, segments, and database objects is one of the basic functions of the DBA. The intent of this overview is to aid you in the planning of their physical storage.

## Implications of the storage Clause

The amount of space used by a segment is determined by its storage parameters. These parameters are determined by the database at segment-creation time; if no specific storage parameters are given in the **create table**, **create index**, **create cluster**, or **create rollback segment** command, then the database will use the default storage parameters for the tablespace in which the segment is to be stored.

**NOTE**
*You can assign default tablespaces to users, and assign space quotas within those tablespaces, via the **create user**, **alter user**, and **grant** commands. See the Alphabetical Reference for the command syntax.*

When you create a table, index, or other segment, you can use the default values for a locally managed tablespace (the recommended option) or specify a **storage** clause as part of the **create** command. You can also specify a **tablespace** clause, enabling you to direct Oracle to store the data in a particular tablespace. For example, a **create table** command in a dictionary-managed tablespace may include the following clauses:

```
tablespace USERS
storage (initial 1M next 1M pctincrease 0
minextents 1 maxextents 200)
```

For a locally managed USERS tablespace, the **create table** command would only need to include

```
tablespace USERS
```

The storage parameters specify the **initial** extent size, the **next** extent size, the **pctincrease** (a factor by which each successive extent will geometrically grow), the **maxextents** (maximum number of extents), and the **minextents** (minimum number of extents). After the segment has been created, the **initial** and **minextents** values cannot be altered unless you perform a reorganization of the object. The default values for the storage parameters for each tablespace are available in the DBA_TABLESPACES and USER_TABLESPACES views.

When you create a tablespace, you specify its default storage parameters. The following command creates a dictionary-managed tablespace and specifies its default storage parameters. See the syntax for **create tablespace** in the Alphabetical Reference.

```
create tablespace CODES_TABLES
datafile '/u01/oracle/VLDB/codes_tables.dbf' size 10M
extent management dictionary
default storage
 (initial 1M next 1M maxextents 200 pctincrease 0);
```

When a segment is created, it will acquire at least one extent. The initial extent will be used to store data until it no longer has any free space available (the **pctfree** clause can be used to reserve a percentage of space within each block in the segment to remain available for updates of existing rows). When additional data is added to the segment, the segment will extend by obtaining a second extent of the size specified by the **next** parameter. There is no guarantee that the second extent will be physically contiguous to the first extent. In the **storage** clause shown in the preceding listing, the **initial** extent is 1MB in size, and the **next** extent is 1MB. Because **pctincrease** is set to 0, every later extent will be 1MB as well, up to a maximum of 200 extents (the **maxextents** setting).

The **pctincrease** parameter is designed to minimize the number of extents in growing tables. A non-zero value for this parameter can be very dangerous—it causes the size of each successive extent to increase geometrically by the **pctincrease** factor specified.

**NOTE**
*pctincrease cannot be used with locally managed tablespaces.*

To create a locally managed tablespace, specify the **local** option for the **extent management** clause in the **create tablespace** command. An example of the **create tablespace** command declaring a locally managed tablespace is shown here:

```
create tablespace CODES_TABLES
datafile '/u01/oracle/VLDB/codes_tables.dbf'
size 10M
extent management local uniform size 256K;
```

Assuming that the block size for the database in which this tablespace is created is 4KB in this example, the tablespace is created with the extent management declared as **local** and with a uniform size of 256KB. Each bit in the bitmap describes 64 blocks (256/4). If the **uniform size** clause is omitted, the default is **autoallocate**. The default **size** for **uniform** is 1MB.

**NOTE**
*If you specify **local** in a **create tablespace** command, you cannot specify a **default storage** clause, **minextents**, or **temporary**.*

Locally managed tablespaces can take over some of the space management tasks performed by DBAs in dictionary-managed tablespaces. Because of their architecture, they are less likely to be fragmented, and their objects are less likely to have space-related problems.

**NOTE**
*You cannot create the SYSTEM tablespace as locally managed in Oracle8i or in Oracle9i Release 1 when you create the database, and it cannot be converted at a later time. As of Oracle9i Release 2 (version 9.2), you can create a locally managed SYSTEM tablespace.*

You can create a set of locally managed tablespaces with a small number of storage parameters and resolve most of the space requests in your database. For example, you could create three DATA tablespaces as shown here:

```
create tablespace DATA_SMALL
datafile '/u01/oracle/VLDB/data_small.dbf'
size 10M
extent management local uniform size 1M;

create tablespace DATA_MEDIUM
datafile '/u01/oracle/VLDB/data_medium.dbf'
size 100M
extent management local uniform size 4M;

create tablespace DATA_LARGE
datafile '/u01/oracle/VLDB/data_large.dbf'
size 1000M
extent management local uniform size 16M;
```

In this example, the DATA_SMALL tablespace creates objects with extent sizes that are each 1MB; DATA_MEDIUM uses 4MB extent sizes, and DATA_LARGE uses 16MB extent sizes. If you have a small table, simply place it in the DATA_SMALL tablespace. If it grows significantly in size, you can move it to the DATA_MEDIUM or DATA_LARGE tablespace.

Within each of these example tablespaces, all objects will have the same storage parameters, simplifying any future maintenance you perform. Using consistent extent sizes also improves the reuse of space once an object has been dropped from the tablespace or moved.

The following sections describe space management of each major object type. Note that if you use locally managed tablespaces, many of the **storage** clause issues do not apply; you rely on the tablespace to manage the space based on the parameters defined at the tablespace level. Although this may result in some overallocation of space, it will greatly simplify the space management operations in your database.

## Table Segments

*Table segments*, also called *data segments*, store the rows of data associated with tables or clusters. Each data segment contains a header block that serves as a space directory for the segment.

Once a data segment acquires an extent, it keeps that extent until the segment is either dropped or **truncate**d. Deleting rows from a table via the **delete** command has no impact on the amount of space that has been allocated to that table. The number of extents will increase until either (1) the **maxextents** value is reached (if one is set), (2) the user's quota in the tablespace is reached, or (3) the tablespace runs out of space (if the datafiles cannot autoextend).

To minimize the amount of wasted space in a data segment, tune the **pctfree** parameter. The **pctfree** parameter specifies the amount of space that will be kept free within each data block. The free space can then be used when **NULL**-valued columns are updated to have values, or when updates to other values in the row force the total length of the row to increase. The proper setting of **pctfree** is application-specific since it is dependent on the nature of the updates that are being performed.

You can use the **alter table** command to alter most storage parameters for an existing table. You can use the **move** option of the **alter table** command to change the tablespace assignment for a table.

# Index Segments

Like table segments, *index segments* hold the space that has been allocated to them until they are dropped; however, they can also be indirectly dropped if the table or cluster they index is dropped. To minimize contention, indexes should be stored in a tablespace that is different from the tablespace that holds their associated tables.

Index segments in dictionary-managed tablespaces have **storage** clauses that specify their **initial**, **next**, **minextents**, **maxextents**, and **pctincrease** values, and they are as likely to be fragmented as their tables are.

You can use the **rebuild** option of the **alter index** command to alter the **storage** and **tablespace** settings for an index. For example, if you create an index with an overly large **initial** extent, you can reclaim the space from that extent by rebuilding the index and specifying a new value for **initial**, as shown in the following example. In the following listing, the JOB_PK index is rebuilt with an **initial** extent of 10MB.

```
alter index JOB_PK rebuild
tablespace INDEXES
storage (initial 10M next 10M pctincrease 0);
```

During the index **rebuild** process, both the old and the new indexes will temporarily coexist in the database. Therefore, you must have enough space available to store both indexes prior to executing the **alter index rebuild** command.

While the index is being built, the optimizer can gather statistics about the index's contents. Use the **compute statistics** clause of the **create index** and **alter index rebuild** commands to generate the statistics while the index is being built; the combined operation will be faster than separate creation and statistics-gathering commands.

# Rollback Segments and System-Managed Undo

Rollback segments can dynamically shrink to a specified size, or they can be manually shrunk to a size of your choosing. The **optimal** clause, which allows rollback segments to shrink to an **optimal** size after extending, helps to provide interim support to systems that have not been properly implemented for the way they are being used. For system-managed undo (SMU), Oracle automatically allocates and deallocates undo segments as processing requires.

As of Oracle9i, you can use automatic *undo management* to place all undo data in a single tablespace. When you create an undo tablespace, Oracle manages the storage, retention, and space utilization for your rollback data via system-managed undo (SMU).

To start using SMU, you must first create an undo tablespace using the following command:

```
create undo tablespace UNDO_TBS datafile 'filespec' size 20m;
```

Next, set the UNDO_MANAGEMENT initialization parameter in your system parameter file or init.ora file to AUTO. Specify your undo tablespace via the UNDO_TABLESPACE initialization parameter. You will not need to create or manage any rollback segments within the undo tablespace. Shut down the database and use the updated init.ora or spfile.ora to start up the database.

## Setting Undo Retention

You can explicitly manage how long Oracle retains undo data in the undo tablespace via the UNDO_RETENTION initialization parameter. Retaining undo serves two purposes: it supports the retention of inactive, in-use (IIU) data for long-running queries, and it supports queries that show the prior state of current data (Oracle Flashback queries).

For example, if you set

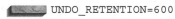

```
UNDO_RETENTION=600
```

then Oracle will make a best effort to retain all committed undo data in the database for 600 seconds. With that setting, any query taking less than 10 minutes should not result in an ORA-1555 ("Snapshot too old") error. While the database is running, you can change the UNDO_RETENTION parameter value via the **alter system** command.

## Creating an Undo Tablespace

You can create an undo tablespace during the database creation process, as shown in the following listing:

```
create database UNDODB
undo tablespace UNDO_TBS
...
```

In an existing database, you can use the **create tablespace** command to create an undo tablespace:

```
create undo tablespace UNDO_TBS
datafile '/u01/oracle/undodb/undo_tbs_1.dbf'
size 100m;
```

See the Alphabetical Reference for the full syntax of the **create tablespace** command.

Once you have created an undo tablespace, you can manage it via the **alter tablespace** command. For example, you can add datafiles to the undo tablespace or rename existing datafiles the same as you would for any other tablespace. To stop using a tablespace as your undo tablespace, use the **alter system** command to set a new value for the UNDO_TABLESPACE initialization parameter, or change that parameter during a database shutdown/startup.

**NOTE**
*You cannot have more than one active undo tablespace within a database at any given time.*

# Temporary Segments

*Temporary segments* store temporary data during sorting operations (such as large queries, index creations, and **union**s). Each user has a temporary tablespace specified when the account is created via **create user**, or altered via **alter user**. The user's temporary tablespace must be a tablespace that has been designated as a temporary tablespace; as of Oracle9i, permanent tablespaces cannot be used for this purpose.

When you create a database, you can specify a default temporary tablespace for all users. For an existing database, you can change the default tablespace via the **alter database** command, as shown in the following listing:

```
alter database default temporary tablespace TEMP;
```

When you alter the database's default temporary tablespace assignment, users who had been assigned the old default temporary tablespace will be redirected to the new default temporary tablespace. To see the current default temporary tablespace, execute the following query:

```
select Property_Value
 from DATABASE_PROPERTIES
 where Property_Name = 'DEFAULT_TEMP_TABLESPACE';
```

You can specify a tablespace as a "temporary" tablespace via the **create temporary tablespace** command. A temporary tablespace cannot be used to hold any permanent segments, only temporary segments created during operations. The first sort to use the temporary tablespace allocates a temporary segment within the temporary tablespace; when the query completes, the space used by the temporary segment is not dropped. Instead, the space used by the temporary segment is available for use by other queries, allowing the sorting operation to avoid the costs of allocating and releasing space for temporary segments. If your application frequently uses temporary segments for sorting operations, the sorting process should perform better if a dedicated temporary tablespace is used.

To dedicate an existing tablespace for temporary segments, specify the **temporary** clause of the **create tablespace** or **alter tablespace** command, as shown in the following listing:

```
alter tablespace TEMP temporary;
```

**NOTE**
*If there are any permanent segments (tables or indexes, for example)
stored in TEMP, the command shown in the preceding listing will fail.*

To enable the TEMP tablespace to store permanent (nontemporary) objects, use the **permanent** clause of the **create tablespace** or **alter tablespace** command, as shown in the following listing:

```
alter tablespace TEMP permanent;
```

The Contents column in the DBA_TABLESPACES data dictionary view displays the status of the tablespace as either "TEMPORARY" or "PERMANENT."

# Free Space

A *free extent* in a tablespace is a collection of contiguous free blocks in the tablespace. A tablespace may contain multiple data extents and free extents. When a segment is dropped, its extents are deallocated and marked as free. In dictionary-managed tablespaces, these free extents are not always recombined with neighboring free extents; the barriers between these free extents may be

maintained. The SMON background process periodically coalesces neighboring free extents, provided the default **pctincrease** for the tablespace is nonzero.

**NOTE**
*The SMON background process only coalesces tablespaces whose default* **pctincrease** *value is nonzero. A* **pctincrease** *of 1 will force SMON to coalesce the adjacent free space in a tablespace but will only coalesce eight areas of adjoining extents at a time. Each of the eight coalesces will join two or more extents together to create one larger extent. For best space management, use locally managed tablespaces so that you never have to worry about coalescing. If you must use dictionary-managed tablespaces, maintain a* **pctincrease** *of 0 and periodically coalesce any dropped extents manually.*

To force the tablespace to coalesce its free space, use the **coalesce** clause of the **alter tablespace** clause, as shown in the following listing:

```
alter tablespace DATA coalesce;
```

The preceding command will force the neighboring free extents in the DATA tablespace to be coalesced into larger free extents. The command will coalesce up to eight separate areas, just like SMON.

**NOTE**
*The* **alter tablespace** *command will not coalesce free extents that are separated by data extents.*

Locally managed tablespaces do not require the same degree of free space management. Since locally managed tablespaces can be configured to have consistent extent sizes for all segments, dropped extents are easily reused.

When allocating a new extent, Oracle will not merge contiguous free extents unless there is no alternative. In dictionary-managed tables, this can result in the large free extent at the rear of the tablespace being used while the smaller free extents toward the front of the tablespace are relatively unused. The small free extents become "speed bumps" in the tablespace because they are not, by themselves, of adequate size to be of use. As this usage pattern progresses, the amount of space wasted in the tablespace increases.

In an ideal database, all objects are created at their appropriate size, and all free space is always stored together, a resource pool waiting to be used. If you can avoid dynamic space allocation during application usage, you remove both a performance impact and a source of potential application failure.

# Sizing Database Objects

Choosing the proper space allocation parameters for database objects is critical. Developers should begin estimating space requirements before the first database objects are created. Afterward, the

space requirements can be refined based on actual usage statistics. The following sections discuss the space estimation methods for tables, indexes, and clusters.

## Why Size Objects?

You should size your database objects for three reasons:

- To preallocate space in the database, thereby minimizing the amount of future work required to manage object space requirements

- To reduce the amount of space wasted due to overallocation of space

- To improve the likelihood of a dropped free extent being reused by another segment

You can accomplish all of these goals by following the sizing methodology shown in the following sections. This methodology is based on Oracle's internal methods for allocating space to database objects. Rather than rely on detailed calculations, the methodology relies on approximations that will dramatically simplify the sizing process while simplifying the long-term maintainability of the database.

## The Golden Rule for Space Calculations

*Keep your space calculations simple, generic, and consistent across databases.* There are far more productive ways to spend your work time than performing extremely detailed space calculations that Oracle may ignore anyway. Even if you follow the most rigorous sizing calculations, you cannot be sure how Oracle will load the data into the table or index.

Consider an index on a table with 100,000 rows. During tests, loading the data into the table in sorted order required 920 blocks for the index. The table and index were then truncated and the data was reloaded in a nonsorted order; the index now required 1,370 blocks. The 49 percent increase in space required by the index was due to Oracle's internal index management processes. If you can't reliably be within 49 percent of the correct answer, why spend a lot of time on sizing exercises?

In the following section, you'll see how to simplify the space estimation process, freeing you to perform much more useful DBA functions. These processes should be followed whether you are generating the **default storage** values for a dictionary-managed tablespace or the extent sizes for locally managed tablespaces.

## The Ground Rules for Space Calculations

Oracle follows a set of internal rules when allocating space:

- Oracle only allocates whole blocks, not parts of blocks.

- Oracle allocates sets of blocks, usually in multiples of five blocks.

- Oracle may allocate larger or smaller sets of blocks depending on the available free space in the tablespace.

The first two rules can serve as the basis for fairly exact space estimates, but the third overrides the first two. Even if you try to allocate exactly 20 blocks for a table, Oracle may find a free extent that is 22 blocks and use it rather than leave a 2-block free extent.

Your goal should be to work with Oracle's space allocation methods instead of against them. If you use consistent extent sizes, you can largely delegate the space allocation to Oracle.

## The Impact of Extent Size on Performance

*There is no direct performance benefit gained by reducing the number of extents in a table.* In some situations (such as in parallel query environments), having multiple extents in a table can significantly reduce I/O contention and enhance your performance. Regardless of the number of extents in your tables, the extents need to be properly sized.

Oracle reads data from tables in two ways: by RowID (usually immediately following an index access) and via full table scans. If the data is read via RowID, then the number of extents in the table is not a factor in the read performance. Oracle will read each row from its physical location (as specified in the RowID) and retrieve the data.

If the data is read via a full table scan, then the size of your extents can impact performance to a very small degree. When reading data via a full table scan, Oracle will read multiple blocks at a time. The number of blocks read at a time is set via the DB_FILE_MULTIBLOCK_READ_COUNT database initialization parameter, and is limited by the operating system's I/O buffer size. For example, if your database block size is 4KB and your operating system's I/O buffer size is 64KB, then you can read up to 16 blocks per read during a full table scan. In that case, setting DB_FILE_MULTIBLOCK_READ_COUNT to a value higher than 16 will not change the performance of the full table scans.

Your extent sizes should take advantage of Oracle's ability to perform multiblock reads during full table scans. Thus, if your operating system's I/O buffer is 64KB, then your extent sizes should be a multiple of 64KB.

Consider a table that has ten extents, each of which is 64KB in size. For this example, the operating system's I/O buffer size is 64KB. To perform a full table scan, Oracle must perform ten reads (since 64KB is the operating system I/O buffer size). If the data is compressed into a single 640KB extent, Oracle still must perform ten reads to scan the table. Compressing the extents results in no gain in performance.

If the table's extent size is not a multiple of the I/O buffer size, then the number of reads required may increase. For the same 640KB table, you could create eight extents that are 80KB each. To read the first extent, Oracle will perform two reads: one for the first 64KB of the extent, and a second read for the last 16KB of the extent (reads cannot span extents). To read the whole table, Oracle must therefore perform two reads per extent, or 16 reads. Reducing the number of extents from ten to eight increased the number of reads by 60 percent.

To avoid paying a performance penalty for your extent sizes, you must therefore choose between one of the following strategies:

1. Create extents that are significantly larger than your I/O size. If the extents are very large, then very few additional reads will be necessary even if the extent size is not a multiple of the I/O buffer size.

2. Set DB_FILE_MULTIBLOCK_READ_COUNT to take full advantage of the I/O buffer size for your operating system. Note that setting it too high may make the optimizer think that full table scans are more efficient than they actually are, resulting in changes to existing execution plans.

3. If you must create small extents, choose extent sizes that are a multiple of the I/O buffer size for your operating system.

If the I/O buffer size for your operating system is 64KB, then your pool of extent sizes to choose is 64KB, 128KB, 256KB, 512KB, 1MB, and so on. In the next section, you will see how to further reduce the pool of extent sizes from which to choose.

To maximize the reuse of dropped free extents in dictionary-managed tablespaces, use a pool of extent sizes that meets the following criterion: *Every extent size will hold an integral multiple of every smaller extent size.* The simplest implementation of this rule is to create extent sizes that increase by doubling: 1MB, 2MB, 4MB, 16MB, 32MB. To reduce the number of extent sizes to manage, you can quadruple the values instead of doubling: 1MB, 4MB, 16MB, and so on. Using those values for extent sizes will eliminate I/O problems and will enhance the likelihood that dropped extents will be reused.

## Sizing the Objects

To effectively manage your space, all you need to do is select a set of space values that meet the criteria described in the preceding sections. Once the space allocations are finalized, separate them by tablespace. For example:

```
create tablespace DATA_1M
datafile '/u01/oracle/VLDB/data_1m.dbf'
size 100M
extent management local uniform size 1M;

create tablespace DATA_4M
datafile '/u02/oracle/VLDB/data_4m.dbf'
size 400M
extent management local uniform size 4M;

create tablespace DATA_16M
datafile '/u03/oracle/VLDB/data_16m.dbf'
size 16000M
extent management local uniform size 16M;
```

In this example, three separate DATA tablespaces are created, with extent sizes of 1MB, 4MB, and 16MB. If you need to create a table 3MB in size, you can either create it with three 1MB extents in DATA_1M or with one 4MB extent in DATA_4M. A table that will grow to 10MB can be placed in DATA_16M.

As your tables grow in size, your default storage clauses will grow in a consistent fashion, following the space rules and your standards for extent sizes. DATA_64M would be next, followed by DATA_256M and DATA_1G. Use the same extent sizes across your databases to ease space management of your entire database environment.

As the extent sizes grow, the distribution of extent sizes across tablespaces will usually result in a separation of table types—small static tables will be isolated in the tablespaces with small extent sizes. Large transaction processing tables (or their partitions) will be segregated to the large extent size tables, simplifying later management and tuning activities.

In the following sections you will see guidelines for estimations of the space usage for your objects. Since the target sizes (1MB, 4MB, 16MB, and so on) are not close together, the following estimations do not include highly detailed calculations.

**NOTE**
*As of Oracle9i, the database block size may change at the tablespace level. Be sure the extent sizes you choose account for the largest block size in use in the database. Limiting the usage of nonstandard block sizes in the database will simplify cross-database maintenance and your sizing procedures.*

# Creating and Managing Rollback Segments

As noted in the section on rollback segments and system-managed undo in the space management section of this chapter, rollback segments dynamically expand and contract to support your transactions. When a database is created, Oracle automatically creates a SYSTEM rollback segment that supports transactions within the data dictionary. A second rollback segment must be created and brought online prior to the use of any non-SYSTEM tablespaces. See the **create database** command scripts created by OUI for examples of the **create rollback segment** command.

In general, you should be aware of the following procedures involving rollback segments:

- How to take them online and offline
- How to determine their maximum size
- How to assign transactions to specific rollback segments

These three steps will allow developers to properly support the transaction sizes required for the batch and online portions of applications.

## Activating Rollback Segments

*Activating* a rollback segment makes it available to the database users. A rollback segment may be deactivated without being dropped. A deactivated rollback segment will maintain the space already allocated to it, and can be reactivated at a later date. The following examples provide the full set of rollback segment activation commands.

An active rollback segment can be deactivated via the **alter rollback segment** command.

```
alter rollback segment SEGMENT_NAME offline;
```

To drop a rollback segment, use the **drop rollback segment** command.

```
drop rollback segment SEGMENT_NAME;
```

To create a rollback segment, use the **create rollback segment** command, as shown in the following listing:

```
create rollback segment SEGMENT_NAME
tablespace RBS;
```

Note that the example **create rollback segment** command creates a private rollback segment (since the **public** keyword was not used) and that it creates it in a non-SYSTEM tablespace called

RBS. Since no storage parameters are specified, the rollback segment will use the default storage parameters for that tablespace. (You will see the space management details for rollback segments later in this chapter.)

Although the rollback segment has been created, it is not yet in use by the database. To activate the new rollback segment, bring it online using the following command:

```
alter rollback segment SEGMENT_NAME online;
```

Once a rollback segment has been created, you should list it in the database's initialization parameter file. A sample initialization entry for rollback segments is shown in the following listing:

```
rollback_segments = (r0,r1,r2)
```

**NOTE**
*The SYSTEM rollback segment should never be listed in the initialization parameter file. The SYSTEM rollback segment can never be dropped; it is always acquired along with any other rollback segments that the instance may acquire.*

In the preceding example, the rollback segments named r0, r1, and r2 are online. If you take a rollback segment offline, remove its entry from the parameter file. When you take a rollback segment offline, it will remain online until its active transactions complete.

## How to Determine the Maximum Size of a Rollback Segment

A rollback segment is a segment in the database, so you can query its storage values from the DBA_SEGMENTS data dictionary view. When working with rollback segments, it is important to know how large the rollback segment can grow. Since a transaction cannot span rollback segments, rollback segments must be large enough to support the largest transaction you will be executing. As described in the next section, you can force Oracle to use a specific rollback segment for your transactions.

The maximum size of a rollback segment can be determined by querying DBA_SEGMENTS:

```
select Segment_Name,
 Tablespace_Name,
 Bytes AS Current_Size,
 Initial_Extent + Next_Extent*(Max_Extents-1)
 AS Max_Size
 from DBA_SEGMENTS
 where Segment_Type = 'ROLLBACK';
```

The result of this query tells you the maximum size for the rollback segments, based on the segment definitions. You should then compare that value to the free space within the datafiles for the rollback segment's tablespace. If the datafiles have **autoextend** enabled, the size of the rollback segment datafiles may be limited by either the available disk space or the **maxsize** setting for the datafiles.

Whenever possible, limit the size of batch transactions. The smaller a transaction, the more manageable it is within the database. If you must have a large transaction, then you should isolate that transaction to a specific tablespace, as described in the next section. If you cannot assign the transaction to a rollback segment, then all of the non-SYSTEM rollback segments must be large enough to support the transaction.

If a rollback segment must frequently extend beyond its **optimal** setting, the performance of your transactions may be impacted by this dynamic space management. Set the **optimal** storage parameter for your rollback segments to reflect the average space usage within the segment.

## Monitoring an Undo Tablespace

For system-managed undo, the primary view for gathering statistics on the undo tablespace usage is V$UNDOSTAT. The V$UNDOSTAT view provides a histogram of the retained data usage. In ten-minute intervals, Oracle records the total number of undo blocks consumed in the UndoBlks column of V$UNDOSTAT, and the number of transactions supported in the TxnCount column. You can use the data from V$UNDOSTAT to determine if the undo tablespace is properly sized for the transaction volume of the application. Oracle maintains 144 rows in V$UNDOSTAT, reflecting the past day's statistics.

Other columns of interest in V$UNDOSTAT include MaxQuerylen, which records the duration in seconds of the longest query executed; the undo retention must be greater than this value. If the NoSpaceErrCnt column of V$UNDOSTAT has a nonzero value, you should add space to the undo tablespace to avoid future space-related errors.

## How to Assign Transactions to Specific Rollback Segments

You can use the **set transaction** command to specify which rollback segment a transaction should use. You should execute the **set transaction** command before large transactions to ensure that they use rollback segments that are created specifically for them.

The settings that are specified via the **set transaction** command will be used only for the current transaction. The following example shows a series of transactions. The first transaction is directed to use the ROLL_BATCH rollback segment. The second transaction (following the second **commit**) will be randomly assigned to a production rollback segment.

```
commit;

set transaction use rollback segment ROLL_BATCH;
insert into TABLE_NAME
select * from DATA_LOAD_TABLE;

commit;

REM* The commit command clears the rollback segment assignment.
REM* Implicit commits, like those caused by DDL commands, will
REM* also clear the rollback segment designation.

insert into TABLE_NAME select * from SOME_OTHER_TABLE;
```

# Performing Backups

Like the rest of the material in this chapter, this section provides an overview. Backup and recovery is a complex topic, and all backup and recovery methods should be thoroughly tested and practiced before being implemented in a production environment. The purpose of this section is to give developers an understanding of Oracle's capabilities, along with the impact of the backup decisions on recovery efforts and availability. Before using backup and recovery methods in a production environment, you should refer to books that are dedicated to that topic, including Oracle's documentation.

The backup methods provided by Oracle can be categorized as follows:

- Logical backups, using Export (and its companion utility, Import)

- Physical file system backups: offline backups and online backups

- Incremental physical file system backups via Recovery Manager (RMAN)

The following sections describe each of these methods and their capabilities.

## Export and Import

Oracle's Export utility queries the database, including the data dictionary, and writes the output to a binary file called an *export dump file*. You can export the full database, specific users, or specific tables. During exports, you may choose whether or not to export the data dictionary information associated with tables, such as the grants, indexes, and constraints associated with them. The file written by Export will contain the commands necessary to completely re-create all of the chosen objects and data.

As of Oracle9i, you can perform tablespace-level exports to export all of the objects contained in a tablespace. Any indexes defined on the exported tables would also be exported. Tablespace-level exports use the **tablespaces** clause of the Export utility, as described later in this chapter.

Once data has been exported, it may be imported via Oracle's Import utility. The Import utility reads the binary export dump file created by Export and executes the commands found there. For example, these commands may include a **create table** command, followed by an **insert** command to load data into the table.

The data that has been exported does not have to be imported into the same database, or the same schema, as was used to generate the export dump file. You may use the export dump file to create a duplicate set of the exported objects under a different schema or in a separate database.

You can import either all or part of the exported data. If you import the entire export dump file from a Full export, then all of the database objects—including tablespaces, datafiles, and users—will be created during the import. However, it is often useful to pre-create tablespaces and users in order to specify the physical distribution of objects in the database.

If you are only going to import part of the data from the export dump file, then the tablespaces, datafiles, and users that will own and store that data should be set up prior to the import.

Exported data may be imported into an Oracle database created under the next higher version of the Oracle software. The reverse capability—importing from an export file created by a more recent major release—is commonly supported, but extra actions may be required to support the older version of the views Export uses. The README.doc files that accompany Oracle releases detail the requirements for using Export and Import across specific versions.

# Export

The Export utility has four levels of functionality: Full mode, Tablespace mode, User mode, and Table mode. You can export partitions via a modified version of Table mode exports.

In Full mode, the full database is exported. The entire data dictionary is read, and the DDL needed to re-create the full database is written to the export dump file. This file includes creation commands for all tablespaces, all users, and all of the objects, data, and privileges in their schemas.

In Tablespace mode, all of the objects contained in the specified tablespace(s) will be exported, including the definition of indexes on the contained objects, even if they are in another tablespace.

In User mode, a user's objects are exported, as well as the data within them. All grants and indexes created by the user on the user's objects are also exported. Grants and indexes created by users other than the owner are not exported.

In Table mode, a specified table is exported. The table's structure, indexes, and grants are exported along with or without its data. Table mode can also export the full set of tables owned by a user (by specifying the schema owner but no table names). You can also specify partitions of a table to export.

Export can be run interactively, through Oracle Enterprise Manager, or via command files. The run-time options that can be specified for Export are listed in Table 40-1, along with their default values in Oracle9i.

Keyword	Description
**userid**	Username/password of the account running the export. **Userid** must be the first parameter on the command line.
**buffer**	Size of the buffer used to fetch data rows. The default is system dependent; this value is usually set to a high value (> 64,000).
**file**	Name of the export dump file; default is expdat.dmp.
**compress**	A Y/N flag to indicate whether export should compress fragmented segments into single extents. This affects the **storage** clauses that will be stored in the export file for those objects. Default is Y. Having objects in one large extent is not always the best choice. For large tables, you should use **compress = N**.
**grants**	A Y/N flag to indicate whether **grant**s on database objects will be exported. Default is Y.
**indexes**	A Y/N flag to indicate whether indexes on tables will be exported. Default is Y.
**direct**	A Y/N flag to indicate if a direct export should be performed. A direct export bypasses the buffer cache during the export, generating significant performance gains for the export process. Default is N.
**log**	The name of a file to which the log of the export will be written.

**TABLE 40-1.** *Export Run-Time Options*

Keyword	Description
**rows**	A Y/N flag to indicate whether rows should be exported. If this is set to N, then only the DDL for the database objects will be created in the export file. Default is Y.
**consistent**	A Y/N flag to indicate whether a read-consistent version of all exported objects should be maintained. This is needed when tables that are related to each other are being modified by users during the export process.
**full**	If set to Y, then a Full database export is performed. Default is N.
**owner**	A list of database accounts to be exported; User exports of those accounts may then be performed.
**tables**	A list of tables to be exported; Table exports of those tables may then be performed. As of Oracle9i, this parameter supports the use of the % and _ wildcards for pattern matching.
**recordlength**	The length, in bytes, of the export dump file record. Usually not specified unless you are going to transfer the export file between different operating systems.
**triggers**	A Y/N flag to indicate if triggers should be exported. Default is Y.
**statistics**	A parameter to indicate whether **analyze** commands for the exported objects should be written to the export dump file. Valid values are COMPUTE, ESTIMATE (the default), and N. In earlier versions of Oracle, this parameter was called **analyze**.
**parfile**	The name of a parameter file to be passed to Export. This file may contain entries for all of the parameters listed here.
**constraints**	A Y/N flag to indicate whether constraints on tables are exported. Default is Y.
**feedback**	The number of rows after which to display progress during Table exports. The default value is 0, so no feedback is displayed until a table is completely exported.
**filesize**	The maximum size for an export dump file. If multiple files are listed in the **file** entry, the export will be directed to those files based on the **filesize** setting.
**flashback_scn**	Specifies the SCN Export will use to enable flashback. The export is performed with data consistent as of this SCN.
**flashback_time**	Time used to get the SCN closest to the specified time. The export is performed with data consistent as of this SCN.
**query**	A **where** clause that will be applied to each table during the export.

**TABLE 40-1.** *Export Run-Time Options* (continued)

Keyword	Description
**resumable**	A Y/N flag to indicate if the session is resumable following errors. Default is N.
**resumable_name**	The specified value is inserted into the DBA_RESUMABLE view to help identify the resumable statement.
**resumable_timeout**	The wait time for resumable statements.
**tts_full_check**	Perform full or partial dependency check for transportable tablespaces.
**volsize**	Number of bytes to write to each tape volume.
**tablespaces**	In Oracle9i, the tablespaces whose tables should be exported, including all tables that have a partition located in the specified tablespaces.
**transport_tablespace**	Set to Y if you are using the pluggable tablespace option available as of Oracle8i. Use in conjunction with the **tablespaces** keyword. Default is N.
**template**	Template name used to invoke iAS mode export.

**TABLE 40-1.**   *Export Run-Time Options* (continued)

A number of the parameters conflict with each other or may result in inconsistent instructions for Export. For example, setting **full**=Y and **owner**=HR would fail, since the **full** parameter calls for a Full export, while the **owner** parameter specifies a User export.

**NOTE**
*The default values and available parameters may change with each release of Oracle.*

You can display the Export parameters online via the following command:

```
exp help=Y
```

The **compress**=Y option alters the **initial** parameter of the **storage** clause for segments that have multiple extents. During a subsequent import, the total allocated space for that segment will be compressed into a single extent. There are two important points to note concerning this functionality:

- First, it is the *allocated,* not the *used,* space that is compressed. An empty table with 300MB allocated to it in three 100MB extents will be compressed into a single empty 300MB extent. No space will be reclaimed.

- Second, if the tablespace has multiple datafiles, a segment may allocate space that is greater than the size of the largest datafile. In that case, using **compress**=Y would change the **storage** clause to have an **initial** extent size that is greater than any datafile size. Since a single extent cannot span more than one datafile, the object creation will fail during import.

In the following example, the **compress**=Y option is used, as the HR and THUMPER owners are exported:

```
exp system/manager file=expdat.dmp compress=Y owner=(HR,THUMPER)
```

**NOTE**
*You can avoid space fragmentation problems through the use of locally managed tablespaces.*

## Consistent Exports

During the process of writing the database's data to the export dump file, Export reads one table at a time. Thus, although Export started at a specific point in time, each table is read at a different time. The data as it exists in each table at the moment Export starts to read *that table* is what will be exported. Since most tables are related to other tables, this may result in inconsistent data being exported if users are modifying data during the export. The export dump file may contain inconsistent data, such as foreign key records from one table without matching primary key records from a related table.

To avoid inconsistency in your exports, there are two options:

■ First, you should schedule exports to occur when no one is making modifications to tables. If feasible, you can use the **startup restrict** option to make sure only DBAs are logged in while the export is occurring.

■ Second, you can use the **consistent** parameter. This parameter is only available for complete exports. During a consistent export, Oracle will try to create a read-consistent version of the exported data as of the time the export started. You will get "snapshot too old" errors if Oracle cannot re-create the read-consistent version of the tables. To guarantee you will not encounter "snapshot too old" errors, you must create large rollback segments or a large undo tablespace because Oracle will overwrite old rollback segment entries without regard to your **consistent**=Y setting.

■ Third, you could quiesce the database, which restricts logins to SYSDBA-privileged users. While the database is quiesced, all ongoing transactions and queries appear to hang, and no new user logins are permitted.

Whenever possible, guarantee the consistency of exported data by running exports while the database is not being used or is mounted in restricted mode. If you are unable to do this, restrict the database usage during the export and perform a **consistent**=Y export.

Another alternative is to create two parameter files (**parfile**). One file will contain the names of the majority of tables within your database or schema. You can use this file for your first export with the default of **consistent**=N. The second file, containing the names of the tables whose consistency must be maintained, is used to perform an export with **consistent**=Y. Using this approach, the size of your rollback segments will not need to be as large, and the performance of your system will not suffer as much.

## Exporting Tablespaces

The better you have distributed your application schema owners and their objects across tablespaces, the easier it will be to export them. For example, if you want to export all of the objects in the AP_DATA schema, you can execute a User export if only a single user owns objects in that tablespace. If multiple users own objects in the DATA tablespace, you can export all of the objects within the tablespace using one command (starting with Oracle9i) regardless of which schema owns the object:

```
exp demo/demo tablespaces=DATA
```

The following query maps users to tablespaces to determine the distribution of their tables and indexes:

```
break on Owner on Tablespace_Name
column Objects format A20
select
 Owner,
 Tablespace_Name,
 COUNT(*)||' tables' Objects
 from DBA_TABLES
where Owner <> 'SYS'
group by
 Owner,
 Tablespace_Name
union
select
 Owner,
 Tablespace_Name,
 COUNT(*)||' indexes' Objects
 from DBA_INDEXES
where Owner <> 'SYS'
group by
 Owner,
 Tablespace_Name;
```

Sample output from this query is shown in the following listing:

```
OWNER TABLESPACE_NAME OBJECTS
------------- ------------------ --------------------
FLOWER USERS 3 tables
 2 indexes
HR HR_TABLES 27 tables
 HR_INDEXES 35 indexes
THUMPER USERS 5 tables
```

The sample output shown in the preceding listing shows that the user account FLOWER owns tables and indexes in the USERS tablespace, and that THUMPER owns several tables in

that tablespace as well. The user HR owns objects in both the HR_TABLES and the HR_INDEXES tablespaces.

Before determining the proper combinations of users to export for a tablespace, the inverse mapping—of tablespaces to users—should be reviewed via the following query:

```
break on Tablespace_Name on Owner
column Objects format A20
select
 Tablespace_Name,
 Owner,
 COUNT(*)||' tables' Objects
 from DBA_TABLES
where Owner <> 'SYS'
group by
 Tablespace_Name,
 Owner
union
select
 Tablespace_Name,
 Owner,
 COUNT(*)||' indexes' Objects
 from DBA_INDEXES
where Owner <> 'SYS'
group by
 Tablespace_Name,
 Owner;
```

Sample output from this query is shown in the following listing:

```
TABLESPACE_NAME OWNER OBJECTS
----------------- ----------- --------------------
HR_INDEXES HR 35 indexes
HR_TABLES HR 27 tables
USERS FLOWER 3 tables
 2 indexes
 THUMPER 5 tables
```

The sample output shown in the preceding listing shows that the HR_TABLES tablespace contains objects from just one user (the HR account). The HR_INDEXES tablespace is similarly isolated. The USERS tablespace, on the other hand, contains both tables and indexes from several accounts.

The results of the preceding queries illustrate the importance of properly distributing users' objects among tablespaces. Since the HR_TABLES tablespace only contains tables owned by the HR account (from the second query), exporting the HR tables will export all of the objects in the HR_TABLES tablespace. As seen from the first query, HR does not own any tables anywhere else in the database. Because HR's tables are isolated to the HR_TABLES tablespace, and because that tablespace is only used by the HR account, a User export of HR will export all of the tables in HR_TABLES. Since the indexes on those tables are stored in HR_INDEXES, that tablespace can be re-created at the same time from the same export dump file.

As of Oracle9i, you can use the **tablespaces** parameter to export all tables located in a specific tablespace. If any table has a partition in the specified tablespace, the entire table will be exported. If you set **indexes**=Y, the tables' associated indexes will be exported regardless of their tablespace location.

### Exporting Partitions

You can reference partitions and subpartitions within tables when you perform Table exports. For example, if the SALES table in the THUMPER schema is partitioned into PART1, PART2, and PART3, then you can export the entire table or its partitions.

To export the entire table, use the **tables** parameter of Export:

```
exp system/manager FILE=expdat.dmp TABLES=(Thumper.SALES)
```

To export a specific partition or subpartition, list the partition or subpartition name following the table name. The table name and the partition name should be separated by a colon (:). In the following listing, the PART1 partition is exported:

```
exp system/manager FILE=expdat.dmp TABLES=(Thumper.SALES:Part1)
```

If you export a partition, all of its subpartitions will be exported.

# Import

The Import utility reads the export dump file and runs the commands stored there. Import may be used to selectively bring back objects or users from the export dump file.

You can run Import either interactively or via command files. The run-time options that can be specified for Import and their default values are listed in Table 40-2.

Keyword	Description
**userid**	Username/password of the account running the import; this must be the first parameter, and the "**userid=**" text is optional.
**buffer**	Size of the buffer used to fetch data rows. The default is system dependent; this value is usually set to a high value (>100,000).
**file**	Name of the export dump file to be imported.
**show**	A Y/N flag to specify whether the file contents should be displayed rather than executed. Default is N.
**ignore**	A Y/N flag to indicate whether the import should ignore errors encountered when issuing **create** commands. This flag is used if the objects being imported already exist. Default is N.
**grants**	A Y/N flag to indicate whether grants on database objects will be imported. Default is Y.

**TABLE 40-2.** *Import Parameters and Default Values*

Keyword	Description
**indexes**	A Y/N flag to indicate whether indexes on tables will be imported. Default is Y.
**rows**	A Y/N flag to indicate whether rows should be imported. If this is set to N, then only the DDL for the database objects will be executed. Default is Y.
**log**	The name of a file to which the log of the import will be written.
**full**	A Y/N flag; if set to Y, then the Full export dump file is imported. Default is N.
**fromuser**	A list of database accounts whose objects should be read from the export dump file (when FULL=N).
**touser**	A list of database accounts into which objects in the export dump file will be imported. **fromuser** and **touser** do not have to be set to the same value.
**tables**	A list of tables to be imported. As of Oracle9i, the % and _ wildcards are supported for table names.
**recordlength**	The length, in bytes, of the export dump file record. Usually left at the default value unless you are going to transfer the export file between different operating systems.
**commit**	A Y/N flag to indicate whether Import should **commit** after each array (whose size is set by **buffer**). If this is set to N (the default), then Import will **commit** after every table is imported. For large tables, **commit**=N requires equally large undo segments.
**parfile**	The name of a parameter file to be passed to Import. This file may contain entries for all of the parameters listed here.
**constraints**	A Y/N flag to indicate whether constraints on tables will be imported. Default is Y.
**destroy**	A Y/N flag to indicate whether the **create tablespace** commands found in dump files from Full exports will be executed (thereby destroying the datafiles in the database being imported into). Default is N.
**indexfile**	This option writes all of the **create table**, **create cluster**, and **create index** commands to a file, rather than running them. All but the **create index** commands will be commented out. If **constraints**=Y, then constraints will be written to the file as well. This file can then be run (with slight modifications) after importing with **indexes**=N. It is useful for separating tables and indexes into separate tablespaces.

**TABLE 40-2.** *Import Parameters and Default Values* (continued)

Keyword	Description
skip_unusable_indexes	A Y/N flag that indicates if Import should skip partition indexes marked as "unusable." You may want to skip the indexes during import and manually create them later to improve index creation performance. Default is N.
feedback	The number of rows after which to display progress during table imports. The default value is 0, so no feedback is displayed until a table is completely imported.
toid_novalidate	Enables Import to skip validation of specified object types.
filesize	The maximum dump size that was specified on export if the parameter **filesize** was used on export.
statistics	A flag to indicate if precomputed statistics should be imported. Default is ALWAYS; other values are NONE, SAFE (for nonquestionable statistics), and RECALCULATE (recalculate during the import).
resumable	A Y/N flag to indicate if the session is resumable following errors. Default is N.
resumable_name	The specified value is inserted into the DBA_RESUMABLE view to help identify the resumable statement.
resumable_timeout	The wait time for resumable statements.
compile	A Y/N flag to indicate if procedures, functions, and packages should be recompiled during import. Default is Y.
volsize	Maximum number of bytes in a file on each volume of tape.
transport_tablespace	A Y/N flag to indicate that transportable tablespace metadata is to be imported into the database. Default is N.
tablespaces	The name or list of names of tablespaces to be transported into the database.
datafiles	The list of datafiles to be transported into the database.
tts_owners	The name or list of names of owners of data in the transportable tablespace.

**TABLE 40-2.** *Import Parameters and Default Values* (continued)

A number of the Import parameters conflict with each other or may result in inconsistent instructions for Import. For example, setting **full**=Y and **owner**=HR would fail, since the **full** parameter calls for a Full import, while the **owner** parameter specifies a User import.

### Undo Segment Requirements

By default, the database will issue a **commit** after every table is completely imported. As a result, the rollback segment will contain a RowID for each row imported. To reduce the sizes of the undo segment entries, specify **commit=Y** along with a value for **buffer**. A **commit** will then be executed after every **buffer** worth of data, as shown in the following example. In the first **import** command shown, a **commit** is executed after every table is loaded. In the second command shown, a **commit** is executed after every 64,000 bytes of data are inserted.

```
imp system/manager file=expdat.dmp
imp system/manager file=expdat.dmp buffer=64000 commit=Y
```

How large should **buffer** be? **buffer** should be large enough to handle the largest single row to be imported. If you do not know the longest row length that was exported, start with a reasonable value (such as 50,000) and run the import. If an IMP-00020 error is returned, then the **buffer** size is not large enough. Increase it and try the import again.

When using **commit=Y**, remember that a **commit** is being performed for each **buffer** array. This implies that if the import of a table fails, it is possible that some of the rows in that table may have already been imported and **commit**ted. The partial load may then be either used or **delete**d prior to running the import again.

In tables with BFILE, LONG, LOB, REF, ROWID, and UROWID columns, rows are inserted individually. The **buffer** value does not have to accommodate the LONG and LOB portions of the row; Import will attempt to allocate additional buffer areas as needed for those portions.

### Importing into Different Accounts

To move objects from one user to another user via Export/Import, perform a User export of the owner of the objects. During the import, specify the owner as the **fromuser** and the account that is to own the objects as the **touser**.

For example, to copy THUMPER's objects into the FLOWER account, you could execute the following commands. The first command exports the THUMPER owner, and the second command imports the THUMPER objects into the FLOWER account.

```
exp system/manager file=thumper.dat owner=thumper grants=N
 indexes=Y compress=Y rows=Y

imp system/manager file=thumper.dat FROMUSER=thumper TOUSER=flower
 rows=Y indexes=Y
```

See the *Oracle9i Utilities Guide* for further details on Export and Import, along with data recovery examples.

## Offline Backups

An offline backup (sometimes called a cold backup) is a physical backup of the database files, made after the database has been shut down via either a **shutdown normal** or a **shutdown immediate** or a **shutdown transactional**. While the database is shut down, each of the files that

is actively used by the database is backed up. These files provide a complete image of the
database as it existed at the moment it was shut down.

**NOTE**
*You should not rely on an offline backup performed following a*
***shutdown abort****, since it may be inconsistent. If you must perform
a **shutdown abort**, you should restart the database and perform a
normal **shutdown** or a **shutdown immediate** or a **shutdown
transactional** prior to beginning your offline backup.*

The following files should be backed up during cold backups:

- All datafiles
- All control files
- All online redo logs

You may optionally choose to back up the database initialization parameter file, particularly
if the backup will serve as the basis for a disaster recovery process.

Having all of these files backed up *while the database is closed* provides a complete image
of the database as it existed at the time it was closed. The full set of these files could be retrieved
from the backups at a later date and the database would be able to function. It is *not* valid to
perform a file system backup of the database while it is open unless an online backup is being
performed (as discussed later in this chapter).

Ideally, all of the datafiles are located in directories at the same level on each device. For
example, all database files may be stored in an instance-specific subdirectory under an /oracle
directory for each device (such as /db01/oracle/MYDB). Directories such as these should contain
all of the datafiles, redo log files, and control files for a database. The only file you may optionally
add to the offline backup that will not be in this location is the production initialization parameter
file, which should be in either the /app/oracle/admin/*INSTANCE_NAME*/pfile subdirectory under the
Oracle software base directory or the /database directory under the Oracle software home directory.

If you use the directory structure in the prior example, your backup commands are greatly
simplified, since you will be able to use wildcards in the filenames. After shutting down the
database, back up the files to the backup destination area (either a tape or a separate disk area).

**NOTE**
*If necessary, you can also back up the init.ora and config.ora files at
the same time.*

Since offline backups involve changes to the database's availability, they are usually
scheduled to occur at night.

Offline backups are very reliable. To reduce their impact on the database's availability,
you may use online backups. As described in the following section, online backups use Oracle's
ARCHIVELOG mode to allow consistent file system backups during database usage.

# Online Backups

You can use online backups for any database that is running in ARCHIVELOG mode. In this mode, the online redo logs are archived, creating a full log of all transactions within the database.

Oracle writes to the online redo log files in a cyclical fashion; after filling the first log file, it begins writing to the second log until that one fills, and then begins writing to the third. Once the last online redo log file is filled, the LGWR (Log Writer) background process begins to overwrite the contents of the first redo log file.

When Oracle is run in ARCHIVELOG mode, the ARC0-ARC9 (Archiver) background processes make a copy of each redo log file before overwriting it. These archived redo log files are usually written to a disk device. The archived redo log files may also be written directly to a tape device, but this tends to be very operator-intensive.

You can perform file system backups of a database while that database is open, provided the database is running in ARCHIVELOG mode. An online backup involves setting each tablespace into a backup state, backing up its datafiles, and then restoring the tablespace to its normal state.

**NOTE**
*When using the Oracle-supplied RMAN utility, you do not have to place each tablespace into a backup state. The utility will put the tablespace into and take it out of the backup state automatically.*

The database can be fully recovered from an online backup, and can, via the archived redo logs, be rolled forward to any point in time. When the database is then opened, any committed transactions that were in the database at that time will have been restored and any uncommitted transactions will have been rolled back.

While the database is open, the following files are backed up:

- All datafiles
- All archived redo log files
- One control file, via the **alter database** command

Online backup procedures are very powerful for two reasons. First, they provide full point-in-time recovery. Databases that are not running in ARCHIVELOG mode can only be recovered to the point in time when the backup occurred. Second, they allow the database to remain open during the file system backup. Thus, even databases that cannot be shut down due to user requirements can still have file system backups.

## Getting Started

To make use of the ARCHIVELOG capability, the database must first be placed in ARCHIVELOG mode. The following listing shows the steps needed to place a database in ARCHIVELOG mode. Run SQLPLUS and mount the database (providing its name in place of "mydb" in these examples), then alter it as shown here:

```
SQL> connect system/manager as sysdba
SQL> startup mount mydb;
SQL> alter database archivelog;
SQL> alter database open;
```

The following command will display the current ARCHIVELOG status of the database from within SQLPLUS:

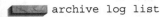

```
archive log list
```

**NOTE**
*To see the currently active online redo log and its sequence number,
query the V$LOG dynamic view.*

To change a database back to NOARCHIVELOG mode, use the following set of commands after shutting down the database:

```
SQL> connect system/manager as sysdba
SQL> startup mount mydb;
SQL> alter database noarchivelog;
SQL> alter database open;
```

A database that has been placed in ARCHIVELOG mode will remain in that mode until it is placed in NOARCHIVELOG mode. The location of the archived redo log files is determined by the settings in the database's parameter file. The parameters to note in Oracle9i are as follows (with sample values):

```
log_archive_dest_1 = /db01/oracle/arch/CC1/arch
log_archive_dest_state_1 = ENABLE
log_archive_start = TRUE
log_archive_format = arch%s.arc
```

In this example, the archived redo log files are being written to the directory /db01/oracle/arch/CC1. The archived redo log files will all begin with the letters "arch," followed by a sequence number. For example, the archived redo log file directory may contain the following files:

```
arch_170.arc
arch_171.arc
arch_172.arc
```

Each of these files contains the data from a single online redo log. They are numbered sequentially, in the order in which they were created. The size of the archived redo log files varies, but does not exceed the size of the online redo log files.

If the destination directory of the archived redo log files runs out of space, then ARCH will stop processing the online redo log data and the database will temporarily hang. This situation can be resolved by adding more space to the archived redo log file destination disk or by backing up the archived redo log files and then removing them from this directory.

**NOTE**
*Never delete archived redo log files until you have backed them up
and verified that you can restore them successfully.*

Although the initialization parameter LOG_ARCHIVE_START parameter may be set to TRUE, the database will *not* be in ARCHIVELOG mode unless you have executed the **alter database archivelog** command shown earlier in this section. Once the database is in ARCHIVELOG mode, it will remain in that mode through subsequent database shutdowns and startups until you explicitly place it in NOARCHIVELOG mode via the **alter database noarchivelog** command.

## Performing Online Database Backups

Once a database is running in ARCHIVELOG mode, you can back it up while it is open and available to users. This capability allows round-the-clock database availability to be achieved while still guaranteeing the recoverability of the database.

Although online backups can be performed during normal working hours, they should be scheduled for the times of the least user activity for several reasons. First, the online backups will use operating system commands to back up the physical files, and these commands will use the available I/O resources in the system (impacting the system performance for interactive users). Second, while the tablespaces are being backed up, the manner in which transactions are written to the archived redo log files changes. When you put a tablespace in "backup" mode, the DBWR process writes all of the blocks in the buffer cache that belong to any file that is part of the tablespace back to disk. When the blocks are read back into memory and then changed, they will be copied to the log buffer the first time that a change is made to them. As long as they stay in the buffer cache, they will not be recopied to the online redo log file. This will use a great deal more space in the archived redo log file destination directory.

The command file for a hot backup has three parts:

1. A tablespace-by-tablespace backup of the datafiles, which in turn consists of

   a. Setting the tablespace into backup state

   b. Backing up the tablespace's datafiles

   c. Restoring the tablespace to its normal state

2. Backup of the archived redo log files, which consists of

   a. Recording which files are in the archived redo log destination directory

   b. Backing up the archived redo log files, then (optionally) deleting or compressing them

3. Backup of the control file via the **alter database backup controlfile** command.

**NOTE**
*The online backup process is automated via the RMAN utility.*

You should create a script to perform the backups. The script should run at the operating system level, with SQLPLUS commands executed for Steps 1a, 1c, and 3.

When the datafiles are being backed up, you may back them up directly to tape or to disk. If you have enough disk space available, choose the latter option, since it will greatly reduce the time necessary for the backup procedures to complete.

# Recovery Manager

Beginning in Oracle8.0, a Recovery Manager toolset called RMAN has been supplied to enable you to back up and recover your databases in an automated manner using either a command-line mode or the Recovery Manager from within the Oracle Enterprise Manager. You can use either approach to back up, restore, and recover database files.

Recovery Manager keeps track of backups either through a Recovery Catalog or by placing the required information into the control file for the database being backed up. Recovery Manager adds new backup capabilities that are unavailable in the other Oracle backup utilities. There are four components within the Recovery Manager: the RMAN executable, one or more target databases, the Recovery catalog database, and the Media management software. The only components that you must have are the RMAN executable and a target database. Since RMAN automatically stores its metadata in the target database's control file, you do not have to have a recovery catalog.

The most significant new capability provided via Recovery Manager is the ability to perform incremental physical backups of datafiles. During a full (called a *level 0*) datafile backup, all of the blocks ever used in the datafile are backed up. During a cumulative (*level 1*) datafile backup, all of the blocks used since the last full datafile backup are backed up. An incremental (*level 2*) datafile backup backs up only those blocks that have changed since the most recent cumulative or full backup. You can define the levels used for incremental backups.

The ability to perform incremental and cumulative backups of datafiles may greatly improve the performance of backups. The greatest performance improvements will be realized by very large databases in which only a small subset of a large tablespace changes. Using the traditional backup methods, you would need to back up all of the datafiles in the tablespace. Using Recovery Manager, you only back up the blocks that have changed since the last backup.

During database recovery using Recovery Manager, you need to know which files are current, which are restored, and the backup method you plan to use. If you use the recover catalog, Recovery Manager stores its catalog of information in an Oracle database—and you need to back up that database or else you may lose your entire backup and recovery catalog of information.

Recovery Manager is only used by DBAs, who need to make the decisions regarding the Recovery Manager architecture for your environment (for example, deciding on the location of the recovery catalog). You should work with your DBA to understand the recovery options in use and their implications for database availability and recovery time.

## Performing a Backup with Oracle Enterprise Manager (OEM)

To perform any level backup using the OEM tool, connect to the OEM Server Manager console, select the appropriate database and right-click to bring up the database options. From the database options, select the Backup option from the Backup Manager menu. The Backup Wizard will activate.

To perform a backup operation, the target database must be running and available. After the initial Welcome screen, you are prompted to select a Strategy choice. You can select a predefined backup strategy or customize your own backup strategy. OEM displays the Backup Frequency options screen with three choices:

1. A Decision Support System (DSS) with a backup frequency of once a week

2. A moderately updated system (OLTP) that is not very large with a backup frequency of every day

3. A frequently updated, medium to large database with a backup frequency of full backups weekly and incremental backups nightly

The default option is a DSS system backed up once a week on Sunday. Once you have selected a strategy, you will be prompted for the time to execute the backup, and the databases to back up. To perform an immediate backup, you can choose the Customize option from the initial Strategy screen.

# Where to Go from Here

In this chapter, you've seen a high-level overview of the topics that production DBAs deal with every day. In addition to the topics discussed here, DBAs monitor databases, tune databases, install software, maintain database connectivity, and many other tasks. If you are interested in learning more about those tasks, see your Oracle documentation set or the *Oracle9i DBA Handbook* (Oracle Press, 2001). The more developers understand about database administration, the more likely they are to build applications that take advantage of the database's inherent capabilities.

# CHAPTER
## 41

# The Hitchhiker's Guide to XML in Oracle

ML (eXtensible Markup Language) is a standardized syntax for describing hierarchical data. Rather than being a programming language, XML is a universal format for structured documents and data. Its tag-based syntax will be familiar to those familiar with HTML (HyperText Markup Language) and gives it the flexibility to handle complex data. Whereas HTML tells a Web browser how to present data, XML tells applications what the data means.

XML is well suited to solving data interchange problems among heterogeneous systems; database-resident data is easily accessed, converted, and stored. In this chapter, you will see an overview of the XML access methods available in Oracle9i. XML and its toolsets are evolving; see http://www.w3.org for the most current information.

**NOTE**
*Thanks to Mike Holder of TUSC for his contributions to this chapter.*

# Document Type Definitions, Elements, and Attributes

In XML, application-specific tags or "elements" wrap around the data they describe. The syntax for these tags is defined in a special kind of XML document called a Document Type Definition (DTD). The DTD defines the structure for a valid XML document. The structure is strictly hierarchical.

Each XML document is an instantiation of an "infoset"—the abstract data model consisting of a document and its information items. Information items are mostly elements, attributes, and content. For example, an XML infoset may contain the following:

```
<book>
 <title>MY LEDGER</title>
 <chapter num="1">
 <title>Beginning</title>
 <text>&chapter1;</text>
 </chapter>
</book>
```

In this example, the tags <book> and </book> define the starting and ending points of the infoset. The XML document describes a book named "MY LEDGER". That book has chapters, and the first chapter's title is "Beginning". The text of the chapter is not stored inside the XML document; instead, a pointer is created to an external file.

In addition to being a tag in the file, "title" is an element. It has content, in this example, "MY LEDGER". As shown in this example, you can set the content of elements by providing values between tags (for the title) or within the tag (as in the chapter number setting). Elements can contain content, child elements, or both, or they may be empty. For data interchange, you should avoid creating elements that contain both content and child elements. To create an empty element, its tag would be in the format:

```
<name/>
```

**NOTE**
*Element names are case-sensitive.*

Each element has exactly one parent, and a parent can have any number of children. The strict hierarchical nature of XML means that if an element starts within another element (such as "chapter" within "book"), its ending tag must precede the ending tag for the parent element.

As shown in the book example, elements have attributes. For example, the chapter element has an attribute named *num*. The attribute value is enclosed in double quotes:

```
<chapter num="1">
```

**NOTE**
*Like element names, attribute names are case-sensitive.*

In general, applications use element attributes for specific items (such as the chapter number) and element content for the bulk of the data (in this case, the chapter text).

An XML document is said to be well-formed if the following conditions are met:

- Every start tag has a matching end tag.

- Elements do not overlap.

- There is one root element.

- Attribute values are always within quotes.

- An element cannot have two attributes within the same name.

- Comments and processing instructions do not appear inside tags.

- There are no unescaped < or & signs in an element's or attribute's character data.

These are the basic syntax rules. If an XML document conforms to these rules, it may still not be valid. To be valid, the XML document must conform to the rules of a Document Type Definition (DTD). The DTD is a formal way of describing what elements and entities may appear in an XML document, and what each element's contents and attributes are.

For example, consider the following XML document.

```
<?xml version="1.0" encoding="UTF-8"?>
<!DOCTYPE CustomerList SYSTEM "Example1.dtd">
<CustomerList>
 <Customer preferredCustomer="">
 <ID>12345</ID>
 <Address>
 <Name>TUSC</Name>
 <Street>377 E BUTTERFIELD RD</Street>
 <City>LOMBARD</City>
 <State>IL</State>
 <Country>USA</Country>
```

```
 <ZIP_CODE>60148</ZIP_CODE>
 <PHONE>630-960-2909</PHONE>
 </Address>
 <CreditRating>EXCELLENT</CreditRating>
 <SalesRepID></SalesRepID>
 <RegionID>5</RegionID>
 <Comments>THIS IS A TEST XML DOCUMENT</Comments>
 <ShippingMethod>M</ShippingMethod>
 </Customer>
</CustomerList>
```

The first line is an XML declaration, which starts with "<?" and ends with "?>":

```
<?xml version="1.0" encoding="UTF-8"?>
```

The *version* attribute should be set to 1.0 for now. The *encoding* attribute is optional; its default value is UTF-8. You can also set a third attribute, *standalone*. In this case, the XML document is not standalone; it has a related DTD, as specified in the second line:

```
<!DOCTYPE CustomerList SYSTEM "Example1.dtd">
```

The related DTD file Example1.dtd for this example is shown in the following listing:

```
<?xml version="1.0" encoding="UTF-8"?>
<!ELEMENT CustomerList (Customer*)>
<!ELEMENT Customer (ID, Address, CreditRating*, SalesRepID*,
 RegionID, Comments*, ShippingMethod)>
<!ATTLIST Customer preferredCustomer CDATA #IMPLIED>
<!ELEMENT ID (#PCDATA)>
<!ELEMENT Address (Name, Street*, City, County,
 State, Country, ZIP_CODE, PHONE)>
<!ELEMENT Name (#PCDATA)>
<!ELEMENT Street (#PCDATA)>
<!ELEMENT City (#PCDATA)>
<!ELEMENT County (#PCDATA)>
<!ELEMENT State (#PCDATA)>
<!ELEMENT Country (#PCDATA)>
<!ELEMENT ZIP_CODE (#PCDATA)>
<!ELEMENT PHONE (#PCDATA)>
<!ELEMENT CreditRating (#PCDATA)>
<!ELEMENT SalesRepID (#PCDATA)>
<!ELEMENT RegionID (#PCDATA)>
<!ELEMENT Comments (#PCDATA)>
<!ELEMENT ShippingMethod (#PCDATA)>
```

The DTD is analogous to the control file specifications for external tables. It tells applications what they will find in the XML document—the element names and the hierarchy of elements. An XML document can have only one DTD.

The syntax for the element declarations is

```
<!ELEMENT element_name (content_model)>
```

where *content_model* specifies what children an element can or must have and the order they are in. The simplest content model is #PCDATA, which says that the element can contain only parsed character data. For example:

```
<!ELEMENT Name (#PCDATA)>
```

In this example, the CustomerList element contains zero or more "Customer" elements, as indicated by the * suffix:

```
<!ELEMENT CustomerList (Customer*)>
```

The allowable suffixes are

*	Permits zero or more occurrences
+	Permits one or more occurrences
?	Permits zero or one occurrences

As shown in the Address element specification, you can specify a sequence of multiple elements by separating them with commas:

```
<!ELEMENT Address (Name, Street*, City, County,
 State, Country, ZIP_CODE, PHONE)>
```

You can provide multiple options within the specification, separated by the vertical bar (|) character. For example, a point on a two-dimensional graph may be specified via its horizontal and vertical measurements or its distance and angle from the center:

```
<!ELEMENT Point ((x,y) | (distance, angle))>
```

For real-world applications, DTDs can quickly become very complex. You can have attribute lists, external references, entity attributes, IDs, conditional inclusions, and other structures within your DTD. Refer to XML documentation for a thorough review of DTD structures and options.

**NOTE**
*Before creating a DTD for a standard business operation, see if one is already available for your purpose. Web sites such as http://www.xml.org/xml/registry.jsp provide many examples of DTDs. These registries provide a valuable resource for the documentation of industry standard DTDs and their components.*

# XML Schema

The XML Schema specification is an alternative to DTDs. It includes data typing, which is particularly helpful when working with relational databases. Whereas DTDs are not extensible (they're just control files), XML Schema is extensible in the following ways:

- Parts of schemas can be reused in other schemas.
- Complex structures can be reused in other schemas.

- Derived datatypes can be created based on existing datatypes.

- A single document instance can reference multiple schemas.

Within XML Schema, elements are declared using xsd:element, as shown in the following listing:

```
<xsd:element name="Date">
```

The element's datatype can be declared via the *type* attribute:

```
<xsd:element name="Date" type="date">
```

You can specify the minimum and maximum number of occurrences for the element via the *minOccurs* and *maxOccurs* attributes:

```
<xsd:element name="Date" type="date" minOccurs="0" maxOccurs="1">
```

Built-in XML Schema types include primitive types (such as string, Boolean, number, float, date, time, and datetime) and derived types (such as normalizedString, integer, token, and language). The full list of types can be found at http://www.w3.org/TR/xmlschema-2/.

You can create and name complex types, just as you can create abstract datatypes in Oracle. The following code creates the "Address" type:

```
<xsd:complexType name="Address">
 <xsd:sequence>
 <xsd:element name="Street1"/>
 <xsd:element name="Street2"/>
 <xsd:element name="City"/>
 <xsd:element name="State"/>
 <xsd:element name="Zip"/>
 </xsd:sequence>
</xsd:complexType>
```

You can then refer to the "Address" complex type when defining your elements:

```
<xsd:element name="mailingAddress" type="Address"/>
<xsd:element name="billingAddress" type="Address"/>
```

If you are declaring a content model for a single element, use an anonymous type, as shown in the following listing.

```
<xsd:element name="Name">
 <xsd:complexType>
 <xsd:sequence>
 <xsd:element name="First"/>
 <xsd:element name="MiddleInitial"/>
 <xsd:element name="Last"/>
 </xsd:sequence>
 </xsd:complexType>
</xsd:element>
```

Attributes are declared using xsd:attribute, as shown in the following example:

```
<xsd:attribute name="paid" type="boolean"/>
```

You can create attributes within a complex type:

```
<xsd:element name="Invoice">
 <xsd:complexType>
 <xsd:attribute name="paid" use="optional" default="True"/>
 </xsd:complexType>
</xsd:element>
```

In addition to creating attributes, you can create attribute groups and model groups. Model groups are groups or element definitions, named for reuse. The "group" element must be a top-level schema component (a child of the "schema" element). For example, the following listing shows the creation of a MealOptions group, referenced by the "FlightDinner" element.

```
<xsd:element name="FlightDinner">
 <xsd:sequence>
 <xsd:element ref="Name"/>
 <xsd:group ref="MealOptions"/>
 </xsd:sequence>
</xsd:element>

<xsd:group name="MealOptions">
 <xsd:choice>
 <xsd:element name="Fish" type="Meal"/>
 <xsd:element name="Meat" type="Meal"/>
 <xsd:element name="Vegetarian" type="Meal"/>
 </xsd:choice>
</xsd:group>
```

Attributes are commonly grouped together if elements often use the same set of attributes. This is similar to the approach described in Part IV of this book, in which common attributes were combined to form new datatypes. For example, the following definition for a "Product" element uses an attribute group named *productDetails*. Other elements can reuse this same attribute group, improving your ability to enforce a standardized representation of this data.

```
<xsd:element name="Product">
 <xsd:complexType>
 <xsd:attributeGroup ref="productDetails"/>
 </xsd:complexType>
</xsd:element>

<xsd:attributeGroup name="productDetails">
 <xsd:attribute name="productID" use="required" type="xsd:ID"/>
 <xsd:attribute name="name" use="required" type="xsd:string"/>
 <xsd:attribute name="description" use="required" type="xsd:string"/>
 <xsd:attribute name="unit" type="xsd:positiveInteger"/>
```

```
 <xsd:attribute name="price" use="required" type="xsd:decimal"/>
 <xsd:attribute name="stock" type="xsd:integer"/>
</xsd:attributeGroup>
```

You can enforce uniqueness within a document instance by using xsd:unique:

```
<xsd:unique name="uniqueProductID">
 <xsd:selector xpath="tc:Product/"/>
 <xsd:field xpath="tc:@productID"/>
</xsd:unique>
```

Uniqueness is declared at the same level as the complex type definition for the "Product" element. The *tc:* namespace is for the schema we are creating and is declared in the xsd:schema element. The xsd:selector value specifies the elements to constrain (the "Product" elements), and xsd:field specifies the attribute to constrain (productID).

You can use xsd:key and xsd:keyref to create references between elements. For example, you can create a "Customer" element and then reference it from multiple "Invoice" elements:

```
<xsd:key name="customerID">
 <xsd:selector xpath="tc:SalesData/"/>
 <xsd:field xpath="tc:Customer/@CustID"/>
</xsd:key>

<xsd:keyref name="item" refer="customerID">
 <xsd:selector xpath="tc:SalesData/"/>
 <xsd:field xpath="tc:Invoice/@CustID"/>
</xsd:keyref>
```

To allow an element to be NULL, use the *nillable* attribute:

```
<xsd:element name="FlightDinner" nillable="true"/>
```

# Using XSU to Select, Insert, Update, and Delete XML values

You can use Oracle's XML-SQL Utility (XSU) to convert the result of a SQL query to XML. XSU supports dynamic generation of DTDs and the insertion of XML into database tables. You can also use XSU to update or delete rows from database objects.

You can access XSU via Java and PL/SQL APIs (application programming interfaces). The XSU Java classes are part of the Oracle kernel software. The PL/SQL API is a wrapper that publishes the Java classes to PL/SQL (see Chapter 36). Because the XSU classes are stored in the database, you can write new stored procedures to directly access XSU's Java classes. Since there is a PL/SQL API available, XSU's functionality can be accessed directly through SQL.

For example, you can generate the XML version of the RATING table via the XSU PL/SQL procedures. The following listing creates a procedure named PRINTCLOBOUT that will be called as part of the data output process. The data will be read in as a CLOB.

```
create or replace procedure PRINTCLOBOUT(result IN OUT NOCOPY CLOB)
 is
xmlstr varchar2(32767);
line varchar2(2000);
begin
 xmlstr := dbms_lob.SUBSTR(result,32767);
 loop
 exit when xmlstr is null;
 line := substr(xmlstr,1,instr(xmlstr,chr(10))-1);
 dbms_output.put_line('| '||line);
 xmlstr := substr(xmlstr,instr(xmlstr,chr(10))+1);
 end loop;
end;
```

Now that the PRINTCLOBOUT procedure exists, run the following anonymous PL/SQL block. This block queries the RATING table, so that table must be accessible from your schema (see the accompanying CD-ROM):

```
declare
 queryCtx DBMS_XMLquery.ctxType;
 result CLOB;
begin
 -- set up the query context...
 queryCtx := DBMS_XMLQuery.newContext('select * from rating');
 -- get the result..
 result := DBMS_XMLQuery.getXML(queryCtx);
 -- Now you can use the result to put it in tables/send as messages..
 printClobOut(result);
 DBMS_XMLQuery.closeContext(queryCtx); -- you must close the query..
end;
```

The result is the RATING table, formatted with XML tags:

```
| <?xml version = '1.0'?>
| <ROWSET>
| <ROW num="1">
| <RATING>1</RATING>
| <RATINGDESCRIPTION>ENTERTAINMENT</RATINGDESCRIPTION>
| </ROW>
| <ROW num="2">
| <RATING>2</RATING>
| <RATINGDESCRIPTION>BACKGROUND INFORMATION</RATINGDESCRIPTION>
| </ROW>
| <ROW num="3">
| <RATING>3</RATING>
| <RATINGDESCRIPTION>RECOMMENDED</RATINGDESCRIPTION>
| </ROW>
| <ROW num="4">
```

```
| <RATING>4</RATING>
| <RATINGDESCRIPTION>STRONGLY RECOMMENDED</RATINGDESCRIPTION>
| </ROW>
| <ROW num="5">
| <RATING>5</RATING>
| <RATINGDESCRIPTION>REQUIRED READING</RATINGDESCRIPTION>
| </ROW>
| </ROWSET>

PL/SQL procedure successfully completed.
```

## Insert, Update, and Delete Processing with XSU

To insert a document into a table or view, use the DBMS_XMLSave package. XSU will parse the document and create an **insert** statement that inserts the values into all the columns of the table or view. An absent element is treated as a **NULL** value.

```
create or replace procedure INSPROC(xmlDoc IN CLOB,
tableName IN VARCHAR2) is
 insCtx DBMS_XMLSave.ctxType;
 rows number;
 begin
 insCtx := DBMS_XMLSave.newContext(tableName); -- get the context
 rows := DBMS_XMLSave.insertXML(insCtx,xmlDoc); -- insert the doc
 DBMS_XMLSave.closeContext(insCtx); -- close the handle
end;
```

You can now pass in XML documents as CLOB input values to the INSPROC procedure, along with the table name. INSPROC will take the XML document and insert its values into the table. Updates can be executed via calls to a separate procedure, UPDATEPROC, shown in the following listing.

```
create or replace procedure UPDATEPROC (xmlDoc IN clob) is
 updCtx DBMS_XMLSave.ctxType;
 rows number;
begin
 updCtx := DBMS_XMLSave.newContext('RATING'); -- get context
 DBMS_XMLSave.clearUpdateColumnList(updCtx); -- clear settings
 DBMS_XMLSave.setKeyColumn(updCtx,'RATING'); -- set RATING as key
 rows := DBMS_XMLSave.updateXML(updCtx,xmlDoc); -- update
 DBMS_XMLSave.closeContext(updCtx); -- close context
end;
```

In this example, the Rating column is the key column used for the update's **where** clause:

```
DBMS_XMLSave.setKeyColumn(updCtx,'RATING'); -- set RATING as key
```

The new values are passed in as an XML document in CLOB format, and the RATING table values are updated based on the contents of the XML document.

**Delete**s function in much the same way. The following procedure takes an XML document as its input, establishes the Rating column as the key for the RATING table, and performs the **delete** based on the key values in the input document. Note that newContext takes the table name RATING as its input value, while setKeyColumn takes the key column name (which in this case happens to also be Rating).

```
create or replace procedure DELETEPROC(xmlDoc IN clob) is
 delCtx DBMS_XMLSave.ctxType;
 rows number;
begin
 delCtx := DBMS_XMLSave.newContext('RATING');
 DBMS_XMLSave.setKeyColumn(delCtx,'RATING');
 rows := DBMS_XMLSave.deleteXML(delCtx,xmlDoc);
 DBMS_XMLSave.closeContext(delCtx);
end;
```

# XSU and Java

If you prefer, you can perform the XSU DML operations via calls to Java classes instead of the PL/SQL procedures. In place of the DBMS_XMLQuery package, you should execute the oracle.xml.sql.query.OracleXMLQuery class. In place of the DBMS_XMLSave package, use oracle.xml.sql.dml.OracleXMLSave.

For example, the Oracle-provided sample Java program for XML queries is customized slightly in the following listing. It relies on connection management in a fashion very similar to that shown in the SQLJ and JDBC examples (see Chapter 35). The program imports the oracle.xml.sql.query.OracleXMLQuery class, enabling it to get the XML string; Java's System.out.println method is then called to display the output.

```
import oracle.xml.sql.query.OracleXMLQuery;
import java.lang.*;
import java.sql.*;

// class to test the String generation!
class testXMLSQL {

 public static void main(String[] argv)
 {

 try{
 // create the connection
 Connection conn = getConnection("practice","practice");

 // Create the query class.
 OracleXMLQuery qry = new OracleXMLQuery(conn, "select * from rating");

 // Get the XML string
 String str = qry.getXMLString();

 // Print the XML output
```

```
 System.out.println(" The XML output is:\n"+str);
 // Always close the query to get rid of any resources..
 qry.close();
 }catch(SQLException e){
 System.out.println(e.toString());
 }
 }

 // Get the connection given the user name and password..!
 private static Connection getConnection(String username,
 String password)
 throws SQLException
 {
 // register the JDBC driver..
DriverManager.registerDriver(new oracle.jdbc.OracleDriver());

 // Create the connection using the OCI8 driver
 Connection conn =
DriverManager.getConnection("jdbc:oracle:oci8:@or90",username,password);

 return conn;
 }
}
```

For details on SQLJ, connection management, and Java, see Part V of this book.

## Customizing the Query Process

You can create your own procedures to simplify the interaction with the DBMS_XMLQuery and DBMS_XMLSave packages. For example, the following listing creates a function named GET_XML. GET_XML will select the rows from the table and display it in XML format.

```
create function GET_XML (in_SQL varchar2)
 return CLOB
is queryCtx DBMS_XMLQuery.ctxType;
 result CLOB;
begin queryCtx := DBMS_XMLQuery.newContext(in_SQL);
 result := DBMS_XMLQuery.getXML(queryCtx);
 DBMS_XMLQuery.closeContext(queryCtx);
 return result;
end;
```

The data will be returned in CLOB format, so you can use the **set long** command to set the maximum display length (the default is 80 characters). You can call GET_XML from within SQL queries, as shown in the following listing.

```
set pagesize 100 long 2000

select GET_XML('select * from category') from DUAL;
```

```
GET_XML('SELECT*FROMCATEGORY')
--
<?xml version = '1.0'?>
<ROWSET>
 <ROW num="1">
 <CATEGORYNAME>ADULTREF</CATEGORYNAME>
 <PARENTCATEGORY>ADULT</PARENTCATEGORY>
 <SUBCATEGORY>REFERENCE</SUBCATEGORY>
 </ROW>
 <ROW num="2">
 <CATEGORYNAME>ADULTFIC</CATEGORYNAME>
 <PARENTCATEGORY>ADULT</PARENTCATEGORY>
 <SUBCATEGORY>FICTION</SUBCATEGORY>
 </ROW>
 <ROW num="3">
 <CATEGORYNAME>ADULTNF</CATEGORYNAME>
 <PARENTCATEGORY>ADULT</PARENTCATEGORY>
 <SUBCATEGORY>NONFICTION</SUBCATEGORY>
 </ROW>
 <ROW num="4">
 <CATEGORYNAME>CHILDRENPIC</CATEGORYNAME>
 <PARENTCATEGORY>CHILDREN</PARENTCATEGORY>
 <SUBCATEGORY>PICTURE BOOK</SUBCATEGORY>
 </ROW>
 <ROW num="5">
 <CATEGORYNAME>CHILDRENFIC</CATEGORYNAME>
 <PARENTCATEGORY>CHILDREN</PARENTCATEGORY>
 <SUBCATEGORY>FICTION</SUBCATEGORY>
 </ROW>
 <ROW num="6">
 <CATEGORYNAME>CHILDRENNF</CATEGORYNAME>
 <PARENTCATEGORY>CHILDREN</PARENTCATEGORY>
 <SUBCATEGORY>NONFICTION</SUBCATEGORY>
 </ROW>
</ROWSET>
```

# Using XMLType

As of Oracle9i, you can use XMLType as a datatype in your tables. XMLType can be used to store
and query XML data in the database. As a type, XMLType has member functions (see Chapter 30)
to access, extract, and query XML data using a class of operations known as Xpath expressions.
The SYS_XMLGEN, SYS_XMLAGG, and DBMS_XMLGEN packages create XMLType values from
existing object-relational data. When you designate a column as using the XMLType datatype,
Oracle will store the data internally in a CLOB datatype.

The following listing shows the creation of a table using the XMLType datatype:

```
create table MY_XML_TABLE
(Key1 NUMBER,
Xml_Column SYS.XMLTYPE);
```

If you describe the table, you will see its columns:

```
desc MY_XML_TABLE
```

```
Name Null? Type
-- -------- ------------
KEY1 NUMBER
XML_COLUMN SYS.XMLTYPE
```

If you increase the describe depth, you will see the member functions for the XMLType column as well:

```
set describe depth 5
```

```
desc MY_XML_TABLE
Name Null? Type
-- -------- ------------
KEY1 NUMBER
XML_COLUMN SYS.XMLTYPE

METHOD

 STATIC FUNCTION CREATEXML RETURNS XMLTYPE
 Argument Name Type In/Out Default?
 ------------------------------ ------------------- ------ --------
 XMLDATA CLOB IN

METHOD

 STATIC FUNCTION CREATEXML RETURNS XMLTYPE
 Argument Name Type In/Out Default?
 ------------------------------ ------------------- ------ --------
 XMLDATA VARCHAR2 IN

METHOD

 MEMBER FUNCTION EXTRACT RETURNS XMLTYPE
 Argument Name Type In/Out Default?
 ------------------------------ ------------------- ------ --------
 XPATH VARCHAR2 IN

METHOD

 MEMBER FUNCTION EXISTSNODE RETURNS NUMBER
 Argument Name Type In/Out Default?
 ------------------------------ ---------------------- ------ --------
 XPATH VARCHAR2 IN
```

```
METHOD

 MEMBER FUNCTION ISFRAGMENT RETURNS NUMBER

METHOD

 MEMBER FUNCTION GETCLOBVAL RETURNS CLOB

METHOD

 MEMBER FUNCTION GETSTRINGVAL RETURNS VARCHAR2

METHOD

 MEMBER FUNCTION GETNUMBERVAL RETURNS NUMBER
```

You can now insert values into MY_XML_TABLE by calling XMLType's CREATEXML method:

```
insert into MY_XML_TABLE (Key1, Xml_Column)
values (1, SYS.XMLTYPE.CREATEXML
 ('<book>
 <title>MY LEDGER</title>
 <chapter num= "1 ">
 <title>Beginning</title>
 <text>This is the ledger of G.B. Talbot</text>
 </chapter>
</book>'));
```

You can query the data by calling the GETCLOBVAL method. This query

```
select M.Xml_Column.GETCLOBVAL() as XML_Data
 from MY_XML_TABLE M
 where Key1 = 1;
```

returns this data:

```
XML_DATA

<book>
 <title>MY LEDGER</title>
 <chapter num="1">
 <title>Beginning</title>
 <text>This is the ledger of G.B. Talbot</text>
 </chapter>
|</book>
```

**NOTE**
*You can create functional indexes on columns created with the
XMLType datatype to improve performance of queries.*

## Other Features

This chapter has shown a very high-level view of the interaction of XML data with the Oracle database. There are many other possibilities, including the use of style sheets for data formatting, and creating XSQL pages. You can even create text indexes on XMLType columns:

```
create index XML_INDEX on MY_XML_TABLE (Xml_Column)
 indextype is ctxsys.context;
```

**NOTE**
*See Chapter 24 for further details on text indexes.*

Oracle provides additional packages to interact with XML data, including:

DBMS_XMLGEN	Converts the results of SQL queries to canonical XML format, returning them as a CLOB. DBMS_XMLGEN is implemented in C, and compiled in the database kernel. DBMS_XMLGEN is similar in functionality to DBMS_XMLQuery package.
SYS_XMLGEN	Generates XML within SQL queries. DBMS_XMLGEN and other packages operate at a query level, giving aggregated results for the *entire* query. SYS_XMLGEN operates on a *single* argument inside a SQL query and converts the result to XML. SYS_XMLGEN takes in a scalar value, object type, or an XMLType instance to be converted to an XML document. It also takes an optional XMLGenFormatType object to specify formatting options for the result. SYS_XMLGEN returns an XMLType.
SYS_XMLAGG	Aggregates over a set of XMLTypes. SYS_XMLAGG aggregates all the input XML documents/fragments and produces a single XML document by concatenating XML fragments, and adding a top-level tag that defaults to ROWSET.

Oracle provides utilities to support additional uses, such as oraxml (a command-line interface to parse an XML document) and oraxsl (a command-line interface used to apply a style sheet on multiple XML documents). A full discussion of every utility and data access method is beyond the scope of this book; please see the *Oracle9i Application Developer's Guide – XML* for additional options and sample programs.

# PART
# VII

# Alphabetical Reference

his chapter contains references for most major Oracle commands, keywords, features, and functions, with cross-referencing of topics. The reference is intended for use by both developers and users of Oracle, but assumes some familiarity with the products. Reading the first four pages of this reference will help you make the most productive use of the entries.

# What This Alphabetical Reference Includes

This alphabetical reference contains entries for virtually every Oracle command in SQL, PL/SQL, and SQLPLUS, as well as definitions of all relevant terms used in Oracle and SQL. Each command is listed with its correct format or syntax, an explanation of its purpose and use, the product or products in which it is used, and important details, restrictions, and hints about it, along with examples to illustrate proper usage. Topics are in alphabetical order, and are cross-referenced, both within the alphabetical reference and to preceding chapters in the book.

# What This Alphabetical Reference Does Not Include

This is not a tutorial; it does not explain the screen-oriented development tools. Additionally, there are a few areas where usage is likely to be so specialized or infrequent that inclusion here did not seem of much benefit. In these instances, the text refers you to the Oracle manual where you can find the needed information.

# General Format of Entries

Entries in this reference are typically either definitions of terms or descriptions of functions, commands, and keywords. These are usually structured in seven sections: the keyword, its type, the products in which it is used, a "See also" cross-reference, the format in which the keyword appears, a description of its components, and an example of its use. A typical entry looks like the following:

## RPAD
**SEE ALSO**    CHARACTER FUNCTIONS, **LPAD**, **LTRIM**, **RTRIM**, **TRIM**, Chapter 7
**FORMAT**    RPAD(*string,length* [,'*set*'])
**DESCRIPTION**    Right **PAD.** RPAD makes a string a certain length by adding a certain set of characters to the right. If set is not specified, the default pad character is a space.
**EXAMPLE**

```
select RPAD('HELLO ',24,'WORLD') from DUAL;
```

produces this:

```
HELLO WORLDWORLDWORLDWOR
```

## The Sections of Each Entry

The **KEYWORD** usually appears on a line by itself. In some cases a brief definition follows. If a keyword has more than one definition, either in different Oracle tools or in different Oracle versions, the keyword will be followed by a brief qualifier in order to indicate that more than one listing exists for this keyword.

**SEE ALSO** suggests other topics that are closely related to the keyword, or gives the chapter or chapters in the book that give detailed descriptions of how the keyword is used in practice. Occasionally you will be referred to the Oracle manual or other reference book that contains detail beyond the scope of this reference.

**FORMAT** generally follows the notation of Oracle manuals, with all SQL and other keywords in uppercase. In actual use, these must be entered exactly as they are shown (except that case is irrelevant). Variables and variable parameters are shown in lowercase *italic*. This indicates that some appropriate value should be substituted. When parentheses are shown, they must be entered where they appear, just as are words shown in uppercase.

## Standard Usages for Variables

Some standard usages for variables follow:

This Variable	Indicates
*Column*	The name of a column
*Database*	The name of a database
*Link*	The name of a link in Oracle Net
*Password*	A password
*Segment*	The name of a segment
*Table*	The name of a table
*Tablespace*	The name of a tablespace
*User*	The name of a user or owner
*View*	The name of a view

## Other Formatting Guidelines

Some other guidelines for formatting follow:

- *character* means the value must be a single character.
- *string* typically represents a character column or an expression or column that can be treated like a CHAR or VARCHAR2 column after automatic data conversion.
- *value* usually represents a NUMBER column or an expression or column that can be treated like a NUMBER column after automatic data conversion.
- *date* usually represents a date column or an expression or column that can be treated like a date column after automatic data conversion.
- *integer* must be a whole number, such as -3, 0, or 12.
- *expression* means any form of a column. This could be a literal, a variable, a mathematical computation, a function, or virtually any combination of functions and columns whose final result is a single value, such as a string, a number, or a date.
- Occasionally other notation is used as well, such as *condition* or *query*. This is explained or is apparent in context.
- **Optional** items are enclosed in square brackets, as in **[user.]**, meaning that *user* is not necessarily required.

■ **Alternative** items in a list are separated by a single broken vertical bar, as in OFF | ON, which should be read "OFF or ON." On some systems this vertical bar is displayed as a solid vertical bar.

■ **Required** options, where one item of a list of items is required, are surrounded by curly braces, as in {OFF | ON}.

■ The **default** item in a list, if there is one, will be listed first.

■ Three periods (or ellipses) indicate that the previous expression can be repeated any number of times, as in **column** *[,column]. . .*, which means that *,column* may be any number of additional columns separated by commas.

■ In rare instances, normal notation is either insufficient or inappropriate for what is being shown. In these cases, the **Description** will spell out more fully what is intended in the **Format**.

## Other Elements of a Listing

A few commands have a **Return type**, which indicates the datatype of the value returned by a function.

**DESCRIPTION** is a verbal explanation of the command and its parts. **Boldface** words within the description usually direct references to either commands or variables shown in the **Format** section.

Examples will show either the results of a function, or how a keyword is used in a real command. The style of the examples is not the same as that of the **Format** section. Instead, it follows the style of the first part of this book (described in Chapter 3), since this is more typical of real coding practice.

# The Order of the Keywords

This reference is in alphabetical order, with all entries that begin with symbols coming before the first entry beginning with the letter A.

Words that are hyphenated or that have an underscore character in them are alphabetized as if the hyphen or underscore were a space.

## Symbols

The symbols are listed in order of appearance with a short definition or name. Those symbols with definitions in **boldface** have full entries dedicated to them, or are prefixes to words that are covered in the pages that follow.

_	**underline (also called underscore, underbar)**
!	**exclamation mark**
"	**double quotation mark**
#	**pound sign**
$	**dollar sign**
?	**question mark**
%	**percent sign**
&	**ampersand**
&&	**double ampersand**
'	**single quotation mark or apostrophe**
( )	**parentheses**

*	asterisk or multiplication
**	exponentiation in PL/SQL
+	plus
-	subtraction or hyphen
- -	double hyphen, SQL comment minus or hyphen
.	period or dot, a name or variable separator
..	to
/	division or slash
/*	slash asterisk, SQL comment divided by or slash
:	colon
:=	is set equal to in PL/SQL
;	semicolon
<< >>	label name delimiter in PL/SQL
<	less than
<=	less than or equal to
< >	not equal
!=	not equal
=	equal
>	greater than
>=	greater than or equal to
@	at sign
@@	double at sign
[]	square brackets
^	caret
^=	not equal
{}	curly braces
\|	broken vertical bar
\|\|	concatenation

# _ (Underscore)

The underscore represents a single position with the **LIKE** operator. *See* **LIKE**.

# _EDITOR

*See* **EDIT**.

# ! (Exclamation Mark)

**SEE ALSO**     =, **CONTAINS, SOUNDEX,** Chapter 24

**FORMAT**   Within SQL, **!** is used as part of the "not equal" expression **!=**. For example, you can select all the city values that are not in the continent of Asia:

```
select City
 from LOCATION
 where Continent != 'ASIA';
```

For CONTEXT text indexes, **!** signals the text engine to perform a SOUNDEX search. The terms to search for will be expanded to include terms that sound like the search term, using the text's SOUNDEX value to determine possible matches.

```
select Title
 from BOOK_REVIEW_CONTEXT
 where CONTAINS(Review_Text, '!grate')>0;
```

## " (Double Quotation Mark)

**SEE ALSO**   **ALIAS, TO_CHAR**, Chapters 7 and 9

**DESCRIPTION**   **"** surrounds a table or column alias that contains special characters or a space, or surrounds literal text in a date format clause of **TO_CHAR**.

**EXAMPLE**   Here it is used as an alias:

```
select NEXT_DAY(CycleDate,'FRIDAY') "Pay Day!"
 from PAYDAY;
```

and here it is used as a formatting portion of **TO_CHAR**:

```
select FirstName, Birthdate, TO_CHAR(BirthDate,
 '"Baby Girl on" fmMonth ddth, YYYY, "at" HH:MI "in the Morning"')
 "Formatted"
 from BIRTHDAY
 where FirstName = 'VICTORIA';
```

```
FIRSTNAME BIRTHDATE Formatted
--------------- --------- ------------------------------
VICTORIA 20-MAY-49 Baby Girl on May 20th, 1949,
 at 3:27 in the Morning
```

## # (Pound Sign)

**SEE ALSO**   **DOCUMENT, REMARK**, /* */, Chapter 6

**DESCRIPTION**   **#** completes a block of documentation in a SQLPLUS start file where the block is begun by the word DOCUMENT. SQL*PLUS ignores all lines from the line where it sees the word DOCUMENT until the line after the **#**.

## $ (Dollar Sign)

**SEE ALSO**   **@,@@, HOST, START, CONTAINS,** Chapter 24

**FORMAT**   For SQL*PLUS:

```
$ host_command
```

For CONTEXT text indexes:

```
select column
 from table
 where CONTAINS(text_column, '$search_term') >0;
```

**DESCRIPTION**    $ passes any host command back to the operating system for execution without exiting SQL*PLUS. **$** is shorthand for **HOST**. This doesn't work on all hardware or operating systems. For a CONTEXT text index, **$** instructs the search engine to perform a stem expansion on the search term. A stem expansion includes in the search words that have the same word stem. For example, a stem expansion of the word 'sing' would include 'singing,' 'sang,' and 'sung.'

## ? (Question Mark)
**SEE ALSO**    **CONTAINS**, Chapter 24
**FORMAT**

```
select column
 from table
 where CONTAINS(text_column, '?term')>0;
```

**DESCRIPTION**    For CONTEXT text indexes, **?** instructs the text engine to perform a fuzzy match search. The terms to search for will be expanded to include terms that are spelled similarly to the search term, using the text index as the source for possible matches.

## % (Percent)
% is a wild card used to represent any number of positions and characters with the **LIKE** operator. *See* **LIKE**.

## %FOUND
**SEE ALSO**    %ISOPEN, %NOTFOUND, %ROWCOUNT, **CURSOR, SQL CURSOR**, Chapter 27
**FORMAT**

```
cursor%FOUND
```

or

```
SQL%FOUND
```

**DESCRIPTION**    %FOUND is a success flag for **select**, **insert**, **update**, and **delete**. *cursor* is the name of an explicit cursor **declared** in a PL/SQL block, or the implicit cursor named **SQL**. %FOUND can be attached to a cursor name as a suffix. The two together are a success flag for the execution of **select**, **insert**, **update**, and **delete** statements in PL/SQL blocks.

PL/SQL temporarily sets aside a section of memory as a scratchpad for the execution of SQL statements, and for storing certain kinds of information (or *attributes*) about the state of that execution. If the SQL statement is a **select**, this area will contain one row of data.

%FOUND is one of those attributes. %FOUND is typically tested (via IF/THEN logic) after an explicit **fetch** has been performed from the cursor. It will be TRUE if the **fetch** retrieved a row, and FALSE otherwise. It always evaluates TRUE, FALSE, or NULL. **%NOTFOUND** is the logical opposite. It is FALSE when **%FOUND** is TRUE, TRUE when **%FOUND** is FALSE, and NULL when **%FOUND** is NULL.

Testing **%FOUND** for the condition of an explicit cursor before it is **OPEN**ed raises an EXCEPTION (error code ORA-01001, INVALID CURSOR).

## %ISOPEN

**SEE ALSO**    SQL CURSOR, Chapter 27
**FORMAT**

```
cursor%ISOPEN
```

**DESCRIPTION**    *cursor* must be either the name of an explicitly declared cursor or the implicit cursor named **SQL**. Evaluates to TRUE if the named cursor is open, FALSE if it is not. **SQL%ISOPEN** will *always* evaluate FALSE, because the SQL cursor is opened and closed automatically when a SQL statement not explicitly declared is executed (*see* **SQL CURSOR**). **%ISOPEN** is used in PL/SQL logic; it cannot be a part of a SQL statement.

## %NOTFOUND

*See* %**FOUND**.

## %ROWCOUNT

**SEE ALSO**    **CLOSE, DECLARE, DELETE, FETCH, INSERT, OPEN, SELECT, UPDATE**, Chapter 27
**FORMAT**

```
cursor%ROWCOUNT
```

**DESCRIPTION**    *cursor* must be either the name of an explicitly declared cursor, or the implicit cursor named SQL. **cursor%ROWCOUNT** contains the cumulative total number of rows that have been **fetch**ed from the active set in this cursor. This can be used to intentionally process only a fixed number of rows, but is more commonly used as an exception handler for **select**s that are intended to return just one row (for example **select. . . into**). In these cases, **%ROWCOUNT** is set to 0 if no rows are returned (**%NOTFOUND** can make this test as well), and to 2 if more than one row is returned, regardless of the actual number.

   **%ROWCOUNT** is used in PL/SQL logic; it cannot be a part of a SQL statement. If **SQL%ROWCOUNT** is used, it can only refer to the most recently opened implicit cursor. If no implicit cursor has been opened, **SQL%ROWCOUNT** returns NULL.

## %ROWTYPE

**SEE ALSO**    **FETCH**, Chapter 27
**FORMAT**

```
{[user.]table | cursor}%ROWTYPE
```

**DESCRIPTION**    **%ROWTYPE** declares a record variable to have the same structure as an entire row in a table (or view), or as a row retrieved by the named cursor. **%ROWTYPE** is used as part of a variable declaration and assures that the variable will contain the appropriate fields and datatypes to handle all of the columns being fetched. If [*user.*]*table* is used, the table (or view) must exist in the database.

   To create a variable that will contain corresponding fields, use **declare**, a variable name, and **%ROWTYPE** with the table name, and then select a row into the record. Because the variable has the same structure as the table, you can reference the fields as variable.field, using notation similar to table.column used in SQL statements. **select. . .into** and **fetch. . .into** are the only methods for loading an entire record variable. Individual fields within the record can be loaded using := as shown here.

```
BOOKSHELF_RECORD.Publisher := 'PANDORAS';
```

If a cursor is used as the prefix for **%ROWTYPE**, then it can contain a **select** statement with only as many columns as are needed. However, if a column that is **fetch**ed from a named cursor is an expression, rather than a simple column name, the expression must be given an alias in the **select** statement before it can be referenced using this technique.

# %TYPE

**SEE ALSO**      %ROWTYPE, Chapter 27

**FORMAT**

```
{[user.]table.column | variable}%TYPE
```

**DESCRIPTION**      %TYPE is used to declare a variable to be of the same type as a previously declared variable, or as a particular column in a table that exists in the database you're connected to.

**EXAMPLE**      In this example a new variable, Writer, is declared to be the same type as the AuthorName column in the AUTHOR table. Since Writer now exists, it can be used to declare yet another new variable, Coauthor:

```
Writer AUTHOR.AuthorName%TYPE;
Coauthor Writer%TYPE;
```

# & or && (Ampersand or Double Ampersand)

**SEE ALSO**      :, ACCEPT, DEFINE, START, CONTAINS, Chapters 14 and 24

**FORMAT**      For SQL*PLUS:

```
&integer
&variable
&&variable
```

For CONTEXT indexes:

```
select Title
 from BOOK_REVIEW_CONTEXT
 where CONTAINS(Review_Text, 'property & harvests')>0;
```

**DESCRIPTION**      & and && can be used in several ways (&& applies only to the second definition below):

- ■ Prefix for parameters in a SQL*PLUS start file. Values are substituted for &1, &2, etc. *See* **START**.
- ■ Prefix for a substitution variable in a SQL command in SQL*PLUS. SQL*PLUS will prompt for a value if an undefined **&** or **&&** variable is found. **&&** will define the variable and thereby preserve its value; **&** will not define or preserve the value, but only substitute what is entered one time. *See* **ACCEPT** and **DEFINE**.
- ■ When using CONTEXT indexes, **&** is used to signal an AND condition for text searches involving multiple search terms. If any of the search terms is not found, the text will not be returned by the search.

# ' (Single Quotation Mark)

**SEE ALSO**      " (Double Quotation Mark), Chapter 7

**FORMAT**

```
'string'
```

**DESCRIPTION**    ' surrounds a literal, such as a character string or date constant. To use one quotation mark or an apostrophe in a string constant, use two ' marks (not a double quotation mark). Avoid the use of apostrophes in data (and elsewhere) whenever possible.

**EXAMPLE**

```
select 'William' from DUAL;
```

produces this:

```
William
```

whereas this:

```
select 'William''s brother' from DUAL;
```

produces this:

```
William's brother
```

# ( ) (Parentheses)

**SEE ALSO**    **PRECEDENCE, SUBQUERY, UPDATE**, Chapters 4, 12, and 15

**DESCRIPTION**    encloses subqueries or lists of columns, or controls precedence within expressions.

# * (Multiplication)

**SEE ALSO**    +, -, /, Chapters 8 and 24

**FORMAT**

```
value1 * value2
```

**DESCRIPTION**    *value1 * value2* means *value1* multiplied by *value2*. For CONTEXT indexes, * is used to weight the individual search terms differently.

# ** (Exponentiation)

**SEE ALSO**    POWER

**FORMAT**

```
x ** y
```

**DESCRIPTION**    *x* is raised to the power *y*. *x* and *y* may be constants, variables, columns, or expressions. Both must be numeric.

**EXAMPLE**    4**4 = 256

# + (Addition)

**SEE ALSO**    -, *, /, Chapter 8

**FORMAT**

```
value1 + value2
```

**DESCRIPTION**     *value1* + *value2* means *value1* plus *value2*.

## - (Subtraction [Form 1])

**SEE ALSO**     +, *, /, Chapter 8, **CONTAINS, MINUS,** Chapter 24

**FORMAT**

```
value1 - value2
```

**DESCRIPTION**     *value1* - *value2* means *value1* minus *value2*. For CONTEXT indexes, a '-' tells the text search of two terms to subtract the score of the second term's search from the score of the first term's search before comparing the result to the threshold score. For CTXCAT indexes, a '-' tells the text search engine to exclude the row from the result set if the term following the '-' is found.

## - (Hyphen [Form 2])

**SEE ALSO**     Chapter 14

**FORMAT**

```
command text -
 text -
 text
```

**DESCRIPTION**     SQL*PLUS command continuation. - continues a command on the following line.

**EXAMPLE**

```
ttitle left 'Current Portfolio' -
right 'November 1st, 1999' skip 1 -
center 'Industry Listings ' skip 4;
```

## - (Comment)

**SEE ALSO**     /* */, **REMARK**, Chapter 6

**FORMAT**

```
-- any text
```

**DESCRIPTION**     -- tells Oracle a comment has begun. Everything from that point to the end of the line is treated as a comment. These delimiters are used only within SQL itself or in PL/SQL and must appear before the SQLTERMINATOR.

**EXAMPLE**

```
select Feature, Section, Page
-- this is just a comment
 from NEWSPAPER -- this is another comment
 where Section = 'F';
```

## . (Period or Dot [Form 1])

**FORMAT**

```
&variable.suffix
```

**DESCRIPTION**     The . is a variable separator, used in SQL*PLUS to separate the variable name from a suffix, so that the suffix is not considered a part of the variable name.

**EXAMPLE**     Here the suffix "st" is effectively concatenated to the contents of the variable &Avenue.

```
define Avenue = 21
select '100 &Avenue.st Street' from DUAL;
```

produces this:

```
100 21st Street
```

This same technique might also be used in a **where** clause.

# . (Period or Dot [Form 2])

**SEE ALSO**    SYNTAX OPERATORS, Chapters 4, 21

**FORMAT**

```
[user.][table.]column
```

**DESCRIPTION**    The . is a name separator, used to specify the complete name of a column, including (optionally) its table or user. The . is also used to address columns within abstract datatypes during **select**s, **update**s, and **delete**s.

**EXAMPLE**

```
select Practice.BOOKSHELF.Title
 from Practice.BOOKSHELF, Practice.BOOKSHELF_AUTHOR
 where Practice.BOOKSHELF.Title = Practice.BOOKSHELF_AUTHOR.Title;
```

If the table contains columns based on an abstract datatype, the datatype's attributes may be accessed via the . notation.

```
select C.Person.Address.City
 from Company C
 where C.Person.Address.State = 'FL';
```

*See* Chapter 4 for further examples.

# .. (To)

*See* **LOOP**.

# / (Division [Form 1])

**SEE ALSO**    +, -, *, Chapter 8

**FORMAT**

```
value1 / value2
```

**DESCRIPTION**    *value1* / *value2* means *value1* divided by *value2*.

# / (Slash [Form 2])

**SEE ALSO**    ;, **BUFFER**, **EDIT**, **GET**, **RUN**, **SET**, SQLTERMINATOR, Chapter 14

**DESCRIPTION**    / executes the SQL in the SQL buffer without displaying it, unlike **RUN**, which displays it first.

# /* */ (Comment)

**SEE ALSO**    **REMARK**, Chapter 6

**FORMAT**

```
/* any text */
```

**DESCRIPTION**    /* tells Oracle a comment has begun. Everything Oracle sees from that point forward, even for many words and lines, it regards as a comment until it sees the ending */, which ends the comment. Comments cannot be embedded within comments; that is, a /* is terminated by the first following */, even if there is an intervening /*.

**EXAMPLE**

```
select Feature, Section, Page
 /* this is a multi-line comment
 used to extensively document the code */
 from NEWSPAPER
 where Section = 'F';
```

# : (Colon, Host Variable Prefix)

**SEE ALSO**    INDICATOR VARIABLE

**FORMAT**

```
:name
```

**DESCRIPTION**    *name* is the name of a host variable. When PL/SQL is embedded in a host language through an Oracle precompiler, host variables can be referenced from within the PL/SQL blocks by prefixing their host language names with a colon. In effect, this is the host variable. If PL/SQL changes its value through an assignment (:=), the value of the host variable is changed. They may be used anywhere a PL/SQL variable can be used. The one exception is in assigning the value NULL to a host variable, which is not supported directly, but requires the use of an indicator variable.

**EXAMPLE**

```
int BookCount;
...
 select COUNT(*) into :BookCount from BOOKSHELF;
```

# := (Set Equal To)

**SEE ALSO**    DECLARE, FETCH, SELECT INTO, Chapter 27

**FORMAT**

```
variable := expression
```

**DESCRIPTION**    The PL/SQL *variable* is set equal to the *expression*, which may be a constant, **NULL**, or a calculation with other variables, literals, and PL/SQL functions.

**EXAMPLE**

```
Extension := Quantity * Price;
Title := 'BARBERS WHO SHAVE THEMSELVES';
Name := NULL;
```

# ; (Semicolon)

**SEE ALSO**    / (Slash), **BUFFER, EDIT, GET, RUN, SQLTERMINATOR, CONTAINS, NEAR**, Chapter 24

**DESCRIPTION**   ; executes the SQL or the command that precedes it. For CONTEXT indexes, **;** indicates that a proximity search should be executed for the specified text strings. If the search terms are 'summer' and 'lease', then a proximity search for the two terms could be

```
select Text
 from SONNET
 where CONTAINS(Text,'summer;lease') >0;
```

When evaluating the text search results, text with the words 'summer' and 'lease' near to each other in the text will have higher scores than text with the words 'summer' and 'lease' farther apart.

## < < > > (PL/SQL Label Name Delimiter)
*See* **BEGIN**, BLOCK STRUCTURE, **END**, **GOTO**, **LOOP**, Chapter 27.

## @ ("At" Sign [Form 1])
**SEE ALSO**   @@, START
**FORMAT**   @*file*
**DESCRIPTION**   @ starts the SQL*PLUS start file named *file*. @ is similar to **START**, but does not allow command line arguments.

## @ ("At" Sign [Form 2])
**SEE ALSO**   **CONNECT**, **COPY**, **DATABASE LINK**, Chapter 22
**FORMAT**

```
CON[NECT] user[/password] [@database];
COPY [FROM user/password@database]
 [TO user/password@database]
 {APPEND | CREATE | INSERT | REPLACE}
 table [(column, [column]...)]
 USING query;
SELECT... FROM [user.]table[link] [, [user.]table[@link]]...
```

**DESCRIPTION**   @ prefixes a database name in a **CONNECT** or **COPY** command, or a link name in a **from** clause.

## @@ (Double "At" Sign)
**SEE ALSO**   @ (Form 1), START
**FORMAT**

```
@@file
```

**DESCRIPTION**   @@ starts a nested SQL*PLUS start file named *file*. @@ is similar to @, but differs in that @@, when used in a command file, will search for a start file in the same directory as the command file that called it (rather than in the directory you are in when you execute the command file).

## {} (Curly Braces)
**SEE ALSO**   **CONTAINS**, Chapter 24, Chapter 34
**FORMAT**   For text searches, {} indicate that the enclosed text should be considered part of the search string even if it is a reserved word. For example, if the search term is 'in and out,' and you want to search for the entire phrase, then you must enclose the word 'and' within braces:

```
REM CONTAINS method for CONTEXT indexes:
select Title
 from BOOK_REVIEW_CONTEXT
 where CONTAINS(Review_Text, 'transactions {and} finances')>0;
```

Within Java, {} indicate the beginning and ending of a block. See Chapter 34 for examples of Java blocks.

# | (Vertical Bar)
**SEE ALSO**    **BTITLE**, **HEADSEP**, **TTITLE**, Chapter 6, Chapter 24
**FORMAT**

```
text|text
```

**DESCRIPTION**    When used in a SQL*PLUS **column, ttitle** or **btitle** command, I is the default **headsep** character, and is used to denote the splitting of a line onto a second line. (When used in listings in this Reference, I denotes a break between alternative choices: *variable* I *literal* would be read "variable or literal." On some machines this shows as a solid vertical bar.) Within text queries, I signals an OR condition for searches involving multiple search terms. If either of the search terms is found, and its search score exceeds the specified threshold value, the text will be returned by the search.

**EXAMPLE**    Here's how I is used as a **headsep** character.

```
TTITLE 'This is the First Line|and This is the Second'
```

produces this:

```
This is the First Line
and This is the Second
```

Here's how I is used as an OR clause in a text search query:

```
REM CONTAINS method for CONTEXT indexes:
select Title
 from BOOK_REVIEW_CONTEXT
 where CONTAINS(Review_Text, 'property | harvests')>0;
REM CATSEARCH method for CTXCAT indexes:
select Title
 from BOOK_REVIEW_CTXCAT
 where CATSEARCH(Review_Text, 'property | harvests', NULL)>0;
```

# || (Concatenation)
**SEE ALSO**    . (Period or Dot [Form 1]), **CONCAT, SUBSTR**, Chapter 7
**FORMAT**

```
expression1 || expression2
```

**DESCRIPTION**    II concatenates two strings together.

**EXAMPLE**    Use II to display a column of cities, followed by a comma, a space, and the country:

```
select City||', '||Country from LOCATION;
```

# ABS (Absolute Value)
**SEE ALSO**    NUMBER FUNCTIONS, Chapter 8

**FORMAT**

```
ABS(value)
```

   *value* must be a number, whether a literal number, the name of a number column, a literal character string containing a valid number, or a character column containing only a valid number.

**DESCRIPTION**    Absolute value is the measure of the magnitude of something, and is always a positive number.

**EXAMPLES**

```
ABS(146) = 146
ABS(-30) = 30
ABS('-27.88') = 27.88
```

# ABSTRACT DATATYPE

*Abstract datatypes* are datatypes that consist of one or more attributes. Rather than being constrained to the standard datatypes of NUMBER, DATE, and VARCHAR2, abstract datatypes can consist of multiple attributes and/or other, previously defined abstract datatypes. Abstract datatypes are also known as *user-defined types* (UDTs). See Chapters 4 and 30 for examples, and **CREATE TYPE** for creation syntax.

# ACCEPT

**SEE ALSO**    **&**, **&&**, **DEFINE**, Chapter 14

**FORMAT**

```
ACC[EPT] variable [NUM[BER]|CHAR|DATE] [FOR[MAT] format]
 [DEF[AULT] default] [PROMPT text | NOPR[OMPT]] [HIDE]
```

**DESCRIPTION**    **ACCEPT** takes input from a user's keyboard and puts it in the named variable. If the variable has not been previously **DEFINE**d, it is created. NUMBER, CHAR, or DATE determines the datatype of the variable as it is input. CHAR will accept any numbers or characters. DATE accepts character strings in valid date formats (or an error message will be returned). NUMBER will accept only numbers and an optional decimal point and minus sign, otherwise **ACCEPT** will produce an error message. FORMAT specifies the input format for the reply (such as A20). DEFAULT sets the default value if a reply is not given. PROMPT displays the text to the user before accepting the input. NOPROMPT skips a line and waits for input without displaying any prompt. Using neither PROMPT nor NOPROMPT causes ACCEPT to invent a prompt asking for the value of the variable. HIDE suppresses the user's entry, and is valuable for passwords and the like.

**EXAMPLE**    The following prompts the user with "How hot?" and puts the user's entry in a number variable named Temperature:

```
ACCEPT Temperature NUMBER PROMPT 'How hot? '
```

# ACCUMULATE

*See* CONTAINS.

# ACOS

**SEE ALSO**    **ASIN, ATAN, ATAN2, COS, COSH, EXP, LN, LOG, SIN, SINH, TAN, TANH**

**FORMAT**

ACOS(*value*)

**DESCRIPTION** ACOS returns the arc cosine of a value. Input values range from -1 to 1; outputs are expressed in radians.

# ADD_MONTHS

**SEE ALSO** DATE FUNCTIONS, Chapter 9

**FORMAT**

ADD_MONTHS(*date*,*integer*)

**DESCRIPTION** ADD_MONTHS adds a number of months to *date*, and returns the date that is that many months in the future. *date* must be a legitimate Oracle date. *integer* must be an integer; a non-integer value will be truncated to the next smallest integer. A negative value for *integer* will return a date in the past.

**EXAMPLE** ADD_MONTHS adds 1 month and 0.3 months to April 22, 2001:

```
select ADD_MONTHS(TO_DATE('22-APR-01'),1),
 ADD_MONTHS(TO_DATE('22-APR-01'),.3) from DUAL;

ADD_MONTH ADD_MONTH
--------- ---------
22-MAY-01 22-APR-01
```

# ALIAS

Alias is a temporary name assigned to a table or a column within a SQL statement and used to refer to it elsewhere in the same statement (if a table) or in a SQL*PLUS command (if a column). You can use the AS keyword to separate the column definition from its alias. *See* " (Double Quotation Mark), **AS**, and **SELECT**. When used for a table, the alias is referred to as a *correlation name*.

# ALL

**SEE ALSO** ANY, **BETWEEN**, **EXISTS**, **IN**, LOGICAL OPERATORS, Chapter 12

**FORMAT**

*operator* ALL *list*

**DESCRIPTION** != **ALL** is the equivalent of **NOT IN**. *operator* can be any one of =, >, >=, <, <=, != and *list* can be a series of literal strings (such as 'Talbot', 'Jones', 'Hild'), or a series of literal numbers (such as 2, 43, 76, 32.06, 444), or a column from a subquery, where each row of the subquery becomes a member of the list, such as this:

LOCATION.City != ALL (select City from WEATHER)

It also can be a series of columns in the **where** clause of the main query, as shown here:

Prospect != ALL (Vendor, Client)

**RESTRICTIONS** *list* cannot be a series of columns in a subquery, such as this:

Prospect != ALL (select Vendor, Client from . . .)

Many people find this operator and the ANY operator very difficult to remember, because the logic for some of their cases is not immediately intuitive. As a result, some form of EXISTS is usually substituted. The combination of an operator with ALL and a list can be illustrated with the following explanations:

Page = ALL (4,2,7)	Page is equal to every item in the list—no number qualifies. A subquery *could* return a list where all the items were identical, and a value of Page could be equal to every one of them, but this would be very rare.
Page > ALL (4,2,7)	Page is greater than the greatest item in the list (4,2,7)—anything larger than 7 qualifies.
Page >= ALL (4,2,7)	Page is greater than or equal to the greatest item in the list (4,2,7)—anything equal to or larger than 7 qualifies.
Page < ALL (4,2,7)	Page is less than the lowest item in the list (4,2,7)—anything below 2 qualifies.
Page <= ALL (4,2,7)	Page is less than or equal to the lowest item in the list (4,2,7)—anything equal to or lower than 2 qualifies.
Page != ALL (4,2,7)	Page is not equal to any item in the list—any number qualifies except 4, 2, and 7

# ALLOCATE (Embedded SQL)

**SEE ALSO**    DECLARE CURSOR, Precompiler documentation
**FORMAT**

```
EXEC SQL [AT { db_name | :host_variable }]
 ALLOCATE { :cursor_variable | :host_ptr }
 [[INDICATOR] :ind_ptr]
```

**DESCRIPTION**    The **ALLOCATE** clause allocates a cursor variable that will be referenced in a PL/SQL block. See the precompiler documentation for details on **ALLOCATE** and related clauses such as the host pointer.

# ALTER CLUSTER

**SEE ALSO**    **CREATE CLUSTER**, **CREATE TABLE**, **STORAGE**, Chapter 20
**FORMAT**
alter_cluster::=

**physical_attributes_clause::=**

**allocate_extent_clause::=**

**deallocate_unused_clause::=**

**parallel_clause::=**

**DESCRIPTION**     Descriptions of the parameters can be found under **CREATE TABLE**. They have the same purpose and effect, except that here they are used to alter a cluster. Size is described under **CREATE CLUSTER**. In order to alter a cluster, you must either own the cluster or have ALTER ANY CLUSTER system privilege.

All tables in a cluster use the values for **PCTFREE**, **PCTUSED**, **INITRANS**, **MAXTRANS**, **TABLESPACE**, and **STORAGE** set by **CREATE CLUSTER**. **ALTER CLUSTER** changes these values for future cluster blocks, but does not affect those that already exist. **ALTER CLUSTER** does not allow changing the **extent** parameters in **STORAGE**. The **DEALLOCATE UNUSED** clause allows the cluster to shrink in size, freeing unused space.

**EXAMPLE**

```
alter cluster BOOKandAUTHOR size 1024;
```

# ALTER DATABASE

**SEE ALSO**    ALTER ROLLBACK SEGMENT, CREATE DATABASE, RECOVER, START UP, SHUTDOWN, Chapter 40

**FORMAT**

alter_database::=

startup_clauses::=

recovery_clauses::=

**general_recovery::=**

**full_database_recovery::=**

**partial_database_recovery::=**

**parallel_clause::=**

**managed_standby_recovery::=**

**recover_clause::=**

**cancel_clause::=**

**finish_clause::=**

**database_file_clauses::=**

**autoextend_clauses::=**

**maxsize_clause::=**

**logfile_clauses::=**

**logfile_descriptor::=**

**controlfile_clauses::=**

**trace_file_clause::=**

**standby_database_clauses::=**

**commit_switchover_clause::=**

**default_settings_clauses::=**

**set_time_zone_clause::=**

**conversion_clauses::=**

**redo_thread_clauses::=**

**security_clause::=**

**DESCRIPTION**    To alter a database, you must have the ALTER DATABASE system privilege. *database* is the database name, and must be eight or fewer characters long.

When a database is first created, it is **MOUNT**ed in **EXCLUSIVE** mode, meaning no one but its creator has access to it. To allow multiple instances to access the database, use **MOUNT PARALLEL** if you have installed the Oracle Real Application Clusters option.

After mounting a database, you **OPEN** it. **RESETLOGS** resets the redo log, cleaning out any redo entries. You use this option to restore a database after a partial recovery from a media failure. The **NORESETLOGS** option leaves everything the same when you **OPEN** the database.

You can **RECOVER** the database with a recover clause. This command performs media recovery for a lost database. You can use multiple recovery processes to apply redo entries to datafiles for each instance. *See* **RECOVER**. You can **BACKUP** a **CONTROLFILE** to the specified file or to a trace file.

**STANDBY** databases provide a mechanism for automated failover in the event of a database failure. See the *Oracle9i Database Administrator's Guide* for details on the creation and management of standby databases.

**RENAME** changes the name of an existing database or log file. DBAs can also **CREATE DATAFILE**s and **CREATE TEMPFILE**s and manage the increments by which datafiles autoextend. The **AUTOEXTEND** clause can be used to dynamically extend datafiles as needed, in increments of **NEXT** size, to a maximum of **MAXSIZE** (or **UNLIMITED**). You can use the **RESIZE** clause to increase or decrease the size of an existing datafile. You can bring a file **ONLINE** or take it **OFFLINE** with the *datafile* clause. You can **CREATE** a new **DATAFILE** to replace an old one to re-create a data file lost without backup.

**ARCHIVELOG** and **NOARCHIVELOG** define the way redo log files are used. **NOARCHIVELOG** is the default, and using it means that redo files will be reused without saving their contents elsewhere. This provides instance recovery except from a media failure, such as a disk crash. **ARCHIVELOG** forces redo files to be archived (usually to another disk or a tape), so that you can recover from a media failure. This mode also supports instance recovery.

**ADD LOGFILE** adds a redo file or files to the database. *file_definition* specifies the **LOGFILE** names and sizes. **SIZE** is the number of bytes set aside for this file. Suffixing this with **K** multiplies the value by 1024; using **M** multiplies it by 1048576. **REUSE** (without **SIZE**) means destroy the contents of any file by this name and give the name to this database. **SIZE** with **REUSE** creates the file if it doesn't exist, and checks its size if it does. **SIZE** alone will create the file if it doesn't exist, but will return an error if it does. The log file is assigned to a thread, either explicitly with the thread clause or to the thread assigned to the current instance of Oracle. A **GROUP** is a collection of log files. You can add a **GROUP** of log files by listing them, and you can name the group with an integer.

**ADD LOGFILE MEMBER** adds new files to an existing log file group, either by specifying the **GROUP** integer or by listing all the log files in the group.

**DROP LOGFILE** drops an existing redo log file group. **DROP LOGFILE MEMBER** drops one or more members of a log file group.

You can **RENAME GLOBAL_NAME** to change the name of the database. If you specify a domain, tell Oracle where the database is on the network. You must change references to the database from remote databases as well.

You can use the **RESET COMPATIBILITY** option, in conjunction with the **COMPATIBLE** parameter in the initialization parameter file, to revert from compatibility with one version of Oracle to a previous version.

You can **ENABLE** or **DISABLE** a **THREAD**. **PUBLIC** makes the thread available to any instance not requesting a specific thread.

# ALTER DIMENSION

**SEE ALSO**    CREATE DIMENSION, DROP DIMENSION

**FORMAT**

alter_dimension::=

level_clause::=

hierarchy_clause::=

**join_clause::=**

**attribute_clause::=**

**DESCRIPTION**    **ALTER DIMENSION** modifies the attributes, hierarchy, and levels of an existing dimension. *See* **CREATE DIMENSION**.

**EXAMPLE**

```
alter dimension TIME drop hierarchy MONTH_TO_DATE;
```

# ALTER FUNCTION

**SEE ALSO**    **CREATE FUNCTION**, **DROP FUNCTION**, Chapter 29

**FORMAT**

**alter_function::=**

**DESCRIPTION**    **ALTER FUNCTION** recompiles a PL/SQL function. You can avoid runtime overhead and error messages by explicitly compiling a function in advance. To alter a function, you must either own the function or have the ALTER ANY PROCEDURE system privilege.

# ALTER INDEX

**SEE ALSO**    **CREATE INDEX**, **DROP INDEX**, **STORAGE**, Chapters 18 and 20

**FORMAT**

**alter_index::=**

**deallocate_unused_clause::=**

**allocate_extent_clause::=**

**parallel_clause::=**

**physical_attributes_clause::=**

**logging_clause::=**

**rebuild_clause::=**

**key_compression::=**

**alter_index_partitioning::=**

**modify_index_default_attrs::=**

**modify_index_partition::=**

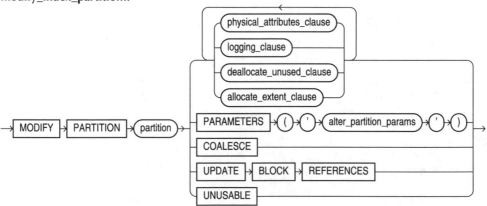

**rename_index_partition::=**

**drop_index_partition::=**

**split_index_partition::=**

**index_partition_description::=**

**segment_attributes_clause::=**

**modify_index_subpartition::=**

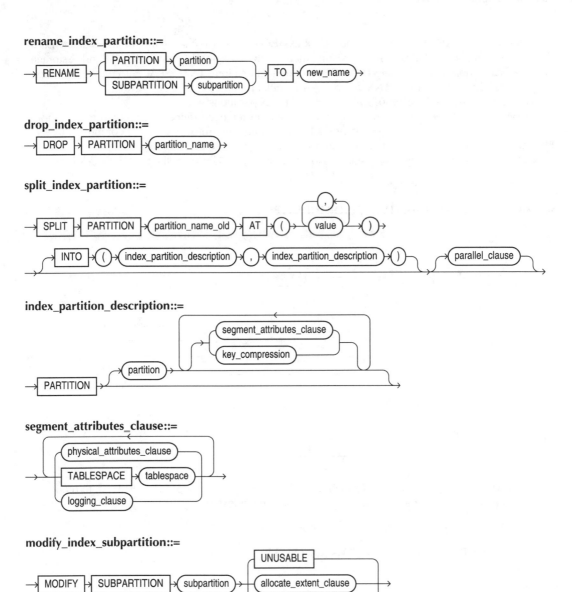

**DESCRIPTION**    *user* is the user who owns the index you wish to alter (if you are not that user, you must have DBA privileges). *index* is the name of an existing index. *See* **CREATE TABLE** for a description of **INITRANS** and **MAXTRANS**. The default for **INITRANS** for indexes is 2; **MAXTRANS** is 255. **STORAGE** contains subclauses that are described under **STORAGE**. You must have INDEX privilege on the table in order to create an index, and you must also either own the index or have the ALTER ANY INDEX system privilege.

You can use the **REBUILD** clause of the **ALTER INDEX** command to change the storage characteristics of an existing index. **REBUILD** uses the existing index as the basis for the new index. All index storage commands are supported, such as **STORAGE** (for extent allocation), **TABLESPACE** (to move the index to a new tablespace), and **INITRANS** (to change the initial number of entries).

You can modify, rename, drop, split, or rebuild index partitions.

**COMPRESS** enables key compression, eliminating repeated occurrence of key column values for nonunique indexes. *integer* specifies the prefix length (number of prefix columns to compress). By default, indexes are not compressed. You cannot compress a bitmapped index.

**COMPUTE STATISTICS** generates statistics for the cost based optimizer at the time the index is rebuilt.

# ALTER INDEXTYPE

**SEE ALSO**     CREATE INDEXTYPE, DROP INDEXYPE

**FORMAT**

alter_indextype::=

using_type_clause::=

**DESCRIPTION**     Use **ALTER INDEXTYPE** to add or drop an operator of the indextype, to modify the implementation type, or to change the properties of the indextype.

# ALTER JAVA

**SEE ALSO**     CREATE JAVA, DROP JAVA, Chapter 34

**FORMAT**

alter_java::=

**invoker_rights_clause::=**

**DESCRIPTION**    ALTER JAVA recompiles a Java source schema object. You can also use this command to change the authorization enforced (definer or current user). To alter Java source schema objects, you must either own the source or class or have the ALTER ANY PROCEDURE system privilege.

# ALTER MATERIALIZED VIEW

**SEE ALSO**    CREATE MATERIALIZED VIEW, DROP MATERIALIZED VIEW, MATERIALIZED VIEW, Chapter 23

**FORMAT**

**alter_materialized_view::=**

**physical_attributes_clause::=**

**data_segment_compression::=**

**LOB_storage_clause::=**

**LOB_parameters::=**

**modify_LOB_storage_clause::=**

**modify_LOB_parameters::=**

**parallel_clause::=**

**logging_clause::=**

**allocate_extent_clause::=**

**deallocate_unused_clause::=**

**alter_iot_clauses::=**

**index_org_table_clause::=**

**index_org_overflow_clause::=**

**alter_overflow_clause::=**

**add_overflow_clause::=**

**scoped_table_ref_constraint::=**

**alter_mv_refresh::=**

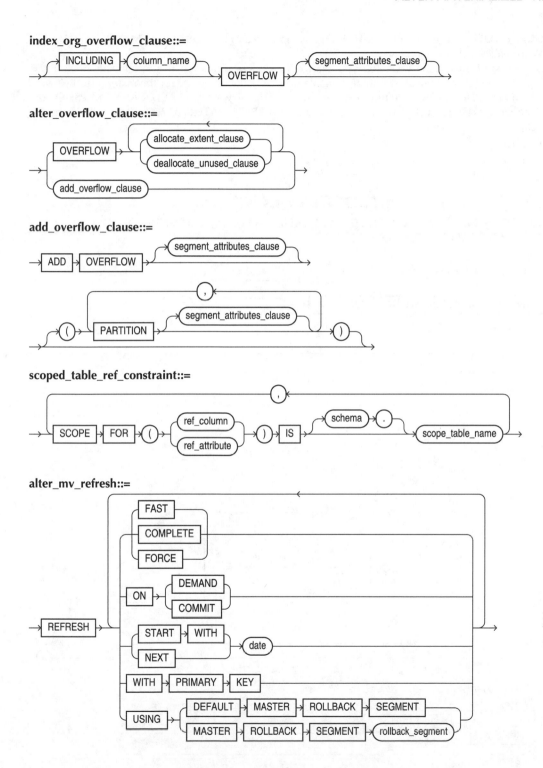

**DESCRIPTION** The keyword **SNAPSHOT** is supported as a replacement for **MATERIALIZED VIEW** for backward compatibility.

**ALTER MATERIALIZED VIEW** lets you change the storage characteristics or refresh mode and times of a materialized view. You can also enable or disable query rewrite for the materialized view. To alter a materialized view, you must own the materialized view or have ALTER ANY SNAPSHOT or ALTER ANY MATERIALIZED VIEW system privilege. *See* **CREATE MATERIALIZED VIEW** and Chapter 23 for details.

**EXAMPLE**

```
alter materialized view MONTHLY_SALES
 enable query rewrite;
```

# ALTER MATERIALIZED VIEW LOG

**SEE ALSO** **CREATE MATERIALIZED VIEW, CREATE MATERIALIZED VIEW LOG, DROP MATERIALIZED VIEW LOG**, Chapter 23

**FORMAT**

alter_materialized_view_log::=

new_values_clause::=

**physical_attributes_clause::=**

**allocate_extent_clause::=**

**parallel_clause::=**

**DESCRIPTION**    The keyword **SNAPSHOT** is supported as a replacement for **MATERIALIZED VIEW** for backward compatibility.

　　**ALTER MATERIALIZED VIEW LOG** lets you change the storage characteristics of a materialized view log. To alter the log, you must either have ALTER privilege on the log table, or you must have the ALTER ANY TABLE system privilege. *See* **CREATE MATERIALIZED VIEW LOG** and Chapter 23.

# ALTER OUTLINE

**SEE ALSO**    **CREATE OUTLINE, DROP OUTLINE**

**FORMAT**

alter_outline::=

**DESCRIPTION**    You can use **ALTER OUTLINE** to rename a stored outline or to assign it to a different category. Stored outlines maintain sets of hints for previously executed queries. See the *Oracle9i DBA Handbook*.

# ALTER PACKAGE

**SEE ALSO**    **CREATE PACKAGE**, **DROP PACKAGE**, Chapter 29

**FORMAT**

alter_package::=

**DESCRIPTION**    **ALTER PACKAGE** recompiles a package specification and/or body. If you recompile the specification using **PACKAGE**, you recompile both the specification and the body. Recompiling the specification will cause referencing procedures to be recompiled. You can recompile the **BODY** without affecting the specification. To alter a package, you must either be the owner of the package or have ALTER ANY PROCEDURE system privilege.

# ALTER PROCEDURE

**SEE ALSO**    **CREATE PROCEDURE**, **DROP PROCEDURE**, Chapter 29

**FORMAT**

alter_procedure::=

**DESCRIPTION**    **ALTER PROCEDURE** recompiles a PL/SQL procedure. You can avoid runtime overhead and error messages by explicitly compiling a procedure in advance. To alter a procedure, you must either own the procedure or have ALTER ANY PROCEDURE system privilege.

# ALTER PROFILE

**SEE ALSO**    **CREATE PROFILE**, **DROP PROFILE**, Chapter 19

**FORMAT**

alter_profile::=

**resource_parameters::=**

**password_parameters::=**

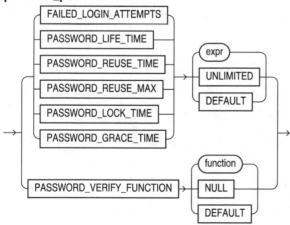

**DESCRIPTION**     **ALTER PROFILE** lets you modify a particular profile setting. *See* **CREATE PROFILE** for details.

# ALTER RESOURCE COST

**SEE ALSO**    CREATE PROFILE

**FORMAT**

alter_resource_cost::=

**DESCRIPTION**    The resource cost formula calculates the total cost of resources used in an Oracle session. **ALTER RESOURCE COST** lets you assign a weight to several resources. CPU_PER_SESSION is the amount of CPU used in a session in hundredths of a second. CONNECT_TIME is the elapsed time of the session in minutes. LOGICAL_READS_ PER_SESSION is the number of data blocks read from both memory and disk during a session. PRIVATE_SGA is the number of bytes in a private System Global Area (SGA), which is only relevant if you are using the shared server architecture. By assigning weights, you change the formula used to calculate total resource cost.

# ALTER ROLE

**SEE ALSO**    CREATE ROLE, DROP ROLE, Chapter 19

**FORMAT**

alter_role::=

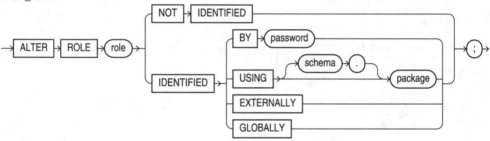

**DESCRIPTION**    **ALTER ROLE** lets you modify a role. *See* **CREATE ROLE** and Chapter 19 for details.

# ALTER ROLLBACK SEGMENT

**SEE ALSO**    CREATE DATABASE, CREATE ROLLBACK SEGMENT, CREATE TABLESPACE, DROP ROLLBACK SEGMENT, STORAGE, Chapter 40

**FORMAT**
alter_rollback_segment::=

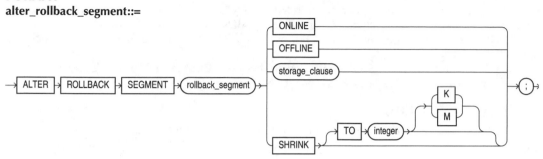

**DESCRIPTION**   *segment* is a name assigned to this rollback segment. **STORAGE** contains subclauses that are described under **STORAGE**. The **INITIAL** and **MINEXTENTS** options are not applicable. A rollback segment can be taken **ONLINE** or **OFFLINE** while the database is open. You can **SHRINK** it to a specified size (the default is its **OPTIMAL** size).

# ALTER SEQUENCE

**SEE ALSO**   **AUDIT, CREATE SEQUENCE, DROP SEQUENCE, GRANT, REVOKE, NEXTVAL** and **CURRVAL** under PSEUDO-COLUMNS, Chapter 20
**FORMAT**
alter_sequence::=

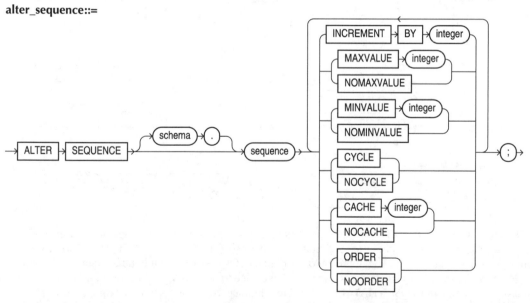

**DESCRIPTION**   All of these options affect the future use of an existing sequence with the name *sequence*. (Note that **start with** is not available. To change the value with which a sequence starts, you must **DROP** the sequence and **CREATE** it again.)

A new **MAXVALUE** cannot be specified that is lower than the existing **CURRVAL** on an ascending sequence (one which has a positive number as its **INCREMENT BY**). A similar rule applies for **MINVALUE** on a descending sequence (which has a negative **INCREMENT BY**).

To alter a sequence, you must have ALTER privilege on the sequence or have the ALTER ANY SEQUENCE system privilege.

All other features of **ALTER SEQUENCE** work as they do in **CREATE SEQUENCE**, except that they apply to an existing sequence. *See* **CREATE SEQUENCE** for details.

# ALTER SESSION

**SEE ALSO**     *Oracle9i Performance Guide and Reference, Oracle9i Database Administrator's Guide*
**FORMAT**
alter_session::=

alter_session_set_clause::=

**DESCRIPTION**     The **ALTER SESSION** command alters settings in effect for the current user session. To generate performance statistics for SQL statement processing by Oracle, set SQL_TRACE to TRUE. To turn them off, set it to FALSE. The initialization parameter SQL_TRACE sets the initial value for this trace.

**ADVISE** allows you to send transaction handling advice to remote databases involved in distributed transactions. You can **CLOSE** a **DATABASE LINK** to eliminate the session's link to a remote database.

You can specify whether procedures can **COMMIT** or not, the degree to which DML operations are parallelized, and whether resumable operations are enabled. If you enable parallel DML or DDL for your session, you still must specify the PARALLEL hint for the operations to be executed in parallel.

# ALTER SNAPSHOT

*See* **ALTER MATERIALIZED VIEW**

## ALTER SNAPSHOT LOG

*See* **ALTER MATERIALIZED VIEW LOG**

## ALTER SYSTEM

**SEE ALSO**     **ALTER SESSION, ARCHIVE_LOG, CREATE PROFILE**
**FORMAT**
alter_system::=

**archive_log_clause::=**

**end_session_clause::=**

**alter_system_set_clause::=**

**alter_system_reset_clause::=**

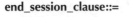

**DESCRIPTION** **ALTER SYSTEM** lets you configure your Oracle instance in many ways. Via the **SET** options, you can change many of the initialization parameter values while the database is running. If you are using a system parameter file, the changes will be saved and will be in effect the next time the database is started. If you are using an initialization parameter file (such as init.ora), you will need to modify that file so the change is in effect during subsequent database startups.

You can also use the **ALTER SYSTEM** command to **SWITCH LOGFILE**, forcing Oracle to change log file groups.

**CHECKPOINT** performs a checkpoint for (**GLOBAL**) all instances or (**LOCAL**) your instance of Oracle. **CHECK DATAFILES** verifies that every instance (**GLOBAL**) or your instance (**LOCAL**) of Oracle can access all online data files.

**ENABLE** or **DISABLE RESTRICTED SESSION** turns on or off a restricted session, accessible only to users with that system privilege.

**ENABLE** or **DISABLE DISTRIBUTED RECOVERY** turns this option on or off, respectively.

**FLUSH SHARED_POOL** clears all data from the SGA shared pool.

**SUSPEND** suspends database activity; **RESUME** re-enables the database.

**QUIESCE RESTRICTED** places the database into a consistent state during which only SYS and SYSTEM, connected as SYSDBA, can perform operations. **UNQUIESCE** returns the database to its normal mode.

**ARCHIVE LOG** manually archives the redo log files or enables automatic archiving.

**KILL SESSION** ends a session with both the SID column and the SERIAL# column of the V$SESSION table identifying the session. **DISCONNECT SESSION**, unlike **KILL SESSION**, gives you the option of forcing the session's outstanding transactions to be posted prior to the termination of the session.

# ALTER TABLE

**SEE ALSO** **CREATE TABLE, DISABLE, DROP, ENABLE**, Chapters 18, 20, 31, and 32

**FORMAT**

alter_table::=

**alter_table_properties::=**

**physical_attributes_clause::=**

**logging_clause::=**

**data_segment_compression::=**

**supplemental_lp_grp_clauses::=**

**allocate_extent_clause::=**

**deallocate_unused_clause::=**

**upgrade_table_clause::=**

**records_per_block_clause::=**

**parallel_clause::=**

**row_movement_clause::=**

**alter_iot_clauses::=**

**index_org_table_clause::=**

**mapping_table_clauses::=**

**key_compression::=**

**index_org_overflow_clauses::=**

**segment_attributes_clause::=**

**alter_overflow_clauses::=**

**add_overflow_clause::=**

**alter_mapping_table_clause::=**

**column_clauses::=**

**add_column_clause::=**

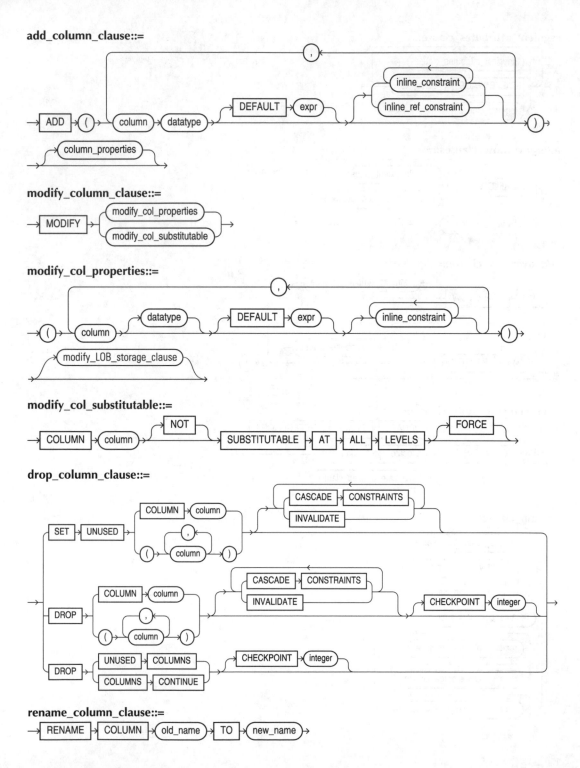

**modify_column_clause::=**

**modify_col_properties::=**

**modify_col_substitutable::=**

**drop_column_clause::=**

**rename_column_clause::=**

**modify_collection_retrieval::=**

**constraint_clauses::=**

**drop_constraint_clause::=**

**column_properties::=**

**object_type_col_properties::=**

**substitutable_column_clause::=**

**nested_table_col_properties::=**

**object_properties::=**

**supplemental_logging_props::=**

**physical_properties::=**

**varray_col_properties::=**

**LOB_storage_clause::=**

**LOB_parameters::=**

**modify_LOB_storage_clause::=**

**modify_LOB_parameters::=**

**alter_varray_col_properties::=**

**LOB_partition_storage::=**

**XMLType_column_properties::=**

**XMLType_storage::=**

**XMLSchema_spec::=**

**alter_external_table_clause::=**

**external_data_properties::=**

**alter_table_partitioning::=**

**modify_table_default_attrs::=**

**set_subpartition_template::=**

**modify_table_partition::=**

**modify_range_partition::=**

**modify_hash_partition::=**

**modify_list_partition::=**

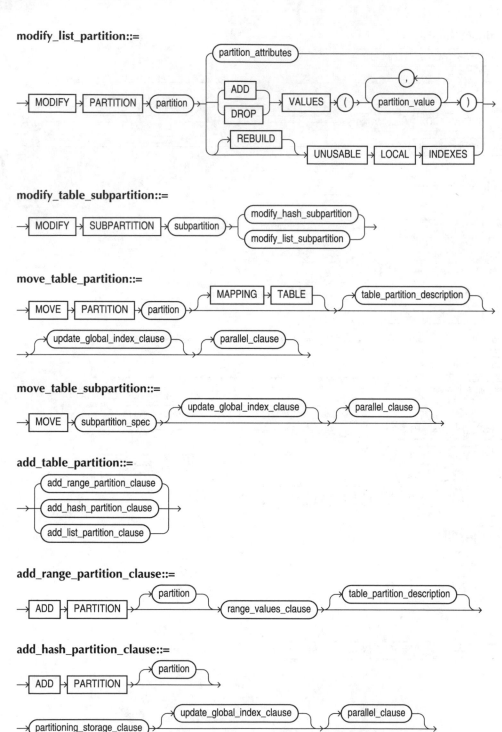

**modify_table_subpartition::=**

**move_table_partition::=**

**move_table_subpartition::=**

**add_table_partition::=**

**add_range_partition_clause::=**

**add_hash_partition_clause::=**

**add_list_partition_clause::=**

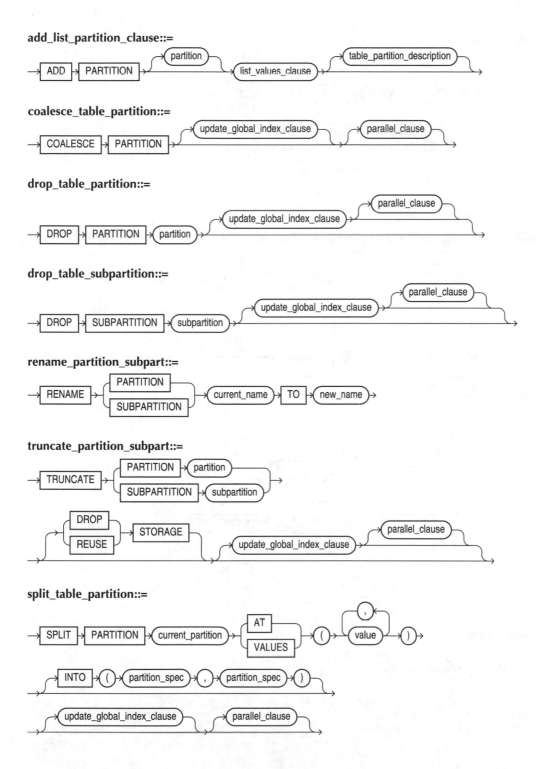

**coalesce_table_partition::=**

**drop_table_partition::=**

**drop_table_subpartition::=**

**rename_partition_subpart::=**

**truncate_partition_subpart::=**

**split_table_partition::=**

**split_table_subpartition::=**

**merge_table_partitions::=**

**merge_table_subpartitions::=**

**exchange_partition_subpart::=**

**exceptions_clause::=**

**list_values_clause::=**

**range_values_clause::=**

**partitioning_storage_clause::=**

**partition_attributes::=**

**add_hash_subpartition::=**

**add_list_subpartition::=**

**modify_hash_subpartition::=**

**modify_list_subpartition::=**

**table_partition_description::=**

**partition_level_subpartition::=**

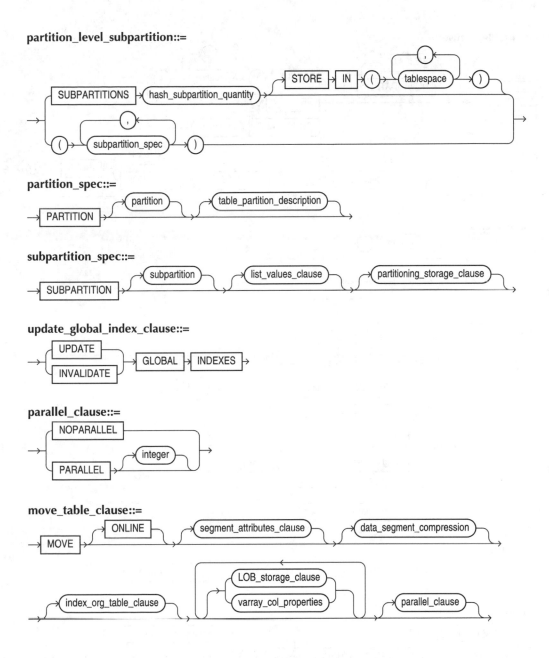

**partition_spec::=**

**subpartition_spec::=**

**update_global_index_clause::=**

**parallel_clause::=**

**move_table_clause::=**

**enable_disable_clause::=**

**using_index_clause::=**

**global_partitioned_index::=**

**index_partitioning_clause::=**

**DESCRIPTION**    **ALTER TABLE** changes the definition of an existing table. **ADD** allows you to add a new column to the end of an existing table, or add a constraint to the table's definition. These follow the same format used in **CREATE TABLE**.

**MODIFY** changes an existing column, with some restrictions:

- You may change the type of column or decrease its size only if the column is NULL in every row of the table.
- A NOT NULL column may be added only to a table with no rows.
- An existing column can be modified to NOT NULL only if it has a non-NULL value in every row or a default value is specified during the alteration.
- Increasing the length of a NOT NULL column without specifying NULL will leave it NOT NULL.

You can use the **SET UNUSED** clause to mark columns as unused. When you use the **DROP UNUSED COLUMNS** clause, the table will be reorganized and all unused columns will be dropped.

**ALLOCATE EXTENT** lets you allocate a new extent explicitly. **ENABLE** and **DISABLE** enable and disable constraints. All other features of **ALTER TABLE** work as they do in **CREATE TABLE**, except that they apply to an existing table. *See* **CREATE TABLE** for details.

In order to alter a table, you must either have the ALTER privilege for that table or the ALTER ANY TABLE system privilege.

**CACHE** specifies that the blocks for this table, when read, are to be marked as "most recently used" and kept in the data block buffer cache for as long as possible. This option is useful if the tables are small and fairly static. **NOCACHE** (the default) reverts the table back to the normal LRU list behavior.

**PARALLEL**, along with **DEGREE** and **INSTANCES**, specifies the parallel characteristics of the table (for databases using the Real Application Clusters option). **DEGREE** specifies the number of query servers to use; **INSTANCES** specifies how the table is to be split among instances of Real Application Clusters for parallel query processing. An integer *n* specifies that the table is to be split among the specified number of available instances.

You can use **ALTER TABLE** to ADD, DROP, EXCHANGE, MODIFY, MOVE, SPLIT, or TRUNCATE partitions. *See* Chapter 18 and **CREATE TABLE**.

The LOB storage clauses specify the storage area to be used for LOB data that will not be stored in the table itself (out-of-line).

The **MOVE ONLINE** option allows you to access a table for DML operations during an online table reorganization. The **MOVE** and **MOVE ONLINE** options are only available for non-partitioned index-organized tables. During a **MOVE ONLINE** operation, parallel DML operations against the table are not supported.

# ALTER TABLESPACE

**SEE ALSO**    **CREATE TABLESPACE, DROP TABLESPACE, STORAGE**, Chapters 20, 40

**FORMAT**
alter_tablespace::=

datafile_tempfile_clauses::=

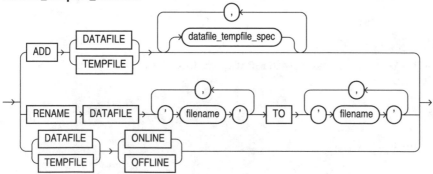

**DESCRIPTION**    *tablespace* is the name of an existing tablespace. **ADD DATAFILE** adds to the tablespace a file or series of files described according to a *file_definition*, which specifies the database file names and sizes.

The file name format is operating system specific. **SIZE** is the number of bytes set aside for this file. Suffixing this with K multiplies the value by 1024; using M multiplies it by 1048576. **REUSE** (without **SIZE**) means destroy the contents of any file by this name and assign it for use by this tablespace. **SIZE** and **REUSE** create the file if it doesn't exist, and check its size if it does. **SIZE** alone will create the file if it doesn't exist, but will return an error if it does.

You can use the **AUTOEXTEND** clause to dynamically resize your datafiles as needed, in increments of **NEXT** size, to a maximum of **MAXSIZE** (or UNLIMITED).

**NOLOGGING** specifies the default action for the writing of redo log entries for certain types of transactions in the tablespace. You can override this setting at the object level. *See* Chapter 18.

**RENAME** changes the name of an existing tablespace file. The tablespace should be offline while the renaming takes place. Note that **RENAME** does not actually rename the files; it only associates their new names with this tablespace. Actually renaming operating system files must be done with the operating system itself. To properly rename files, first **ALTER TABLESPACE OFFLINE**, rename the files in the operating system, **RENAME** them with **ALTER TABLESPACE**, and then **ALTER TABLESPACE ONLINE**.

**DEFAULT STORAGE** defines the default storage for all future objects created in this tablespace, unless those defaults are overridden, such as by **CREATE TABLE**. **ONLINE** brings the tablespace back online. **OFFLINE** takes it offline, either without waiting for its users to logoff (**IMMEDIATE**), or after they've all stopped using it (**NORMAL**).

**MINIMUM EXTENT** sets the minimum size for any extent created in the tablespace. **COALESCE** combines neighboring free extents in the tablespace into fewer, larger free extents.

**READ ONLY** tablespaces are never updated by Oracle, and can be placed on read-only media. Read-only tablespaces do not need repeated backups. All tablespaces are created read-write. To change a read-only tablespace back to read-write status, use the **READ WRITE** clause.

**BEGIN BACKUP** can be executed at any time. It puts the tablespace in a state such that an online backup can occur while users are accessing the tablespace. **END BACKUP** indicates the system backup is finished. If the tablespace is online, any system backup must also back up archive redo logs. If it is offline, this is unnecessary.

**TEMPORARY** tablespaces cannot contain any permanent objects (such as tables or indexes); they can only hold the temporary segments used by Oracle during the processing of sorting operations and index creations. A **PERMANENT** tablespace can hold every type of Oracle segment.

# ALTER TRIGGER
**SEE ALSO**    CREATE TRIGGER, DROP TRIGGER, ENABLE, TRIGGER, Chapter 28
**FORMAT**
alter_trigger::=

**DESCRIPTION**    **ALTER TRIGGER** enables, disables, renames or recompiles a PL/SQL trigger. *See* **CREATE TRIGGER** and Chapter 28 for a discussion of triggers. To use the **ALTER TRIGGER** command, you must either own the trigger or have ALTER ANY TRIGGER system privilege.

You can use the **COMPILE** clause to manually recompile an invalid trigger object. Since triggers have dependencies, they can become invalid if an object the trigger depends on changes. The **DEBUG** clause allows PL/SQL information to be generated during trigger recompilation.

# ALTER TYPE

**SEE ALSO**    **CREATE TYPE, CREATE TYPE BODY**, Chapters 4 and 30
**FORMAT**
alter_type::=

invoker_rights_clause::=

element_spec::=

inheritance_clauses::=

**subprogram_clauses::=**

**procedure_spec::=**

**function_spec::=**

**constructor_spec::=**

**map_order_function_spec::=**

**pragma_clause::=**

**alter_method_spec::=**

**alter_attribute_definition::=**

**dependent_handling_clause::=**

**exceptions_clause::=**

**DESCRIPTION**    **ALTER TYPE** allows you to modify existing abstract datatypes. When you create a method that acts on the abstract datatype, you use the **CREATE TYPE BODY** command (see entry in this chapter). Each method defined in the type body must first be listed in the type. Member functions typically use the PRAGMA RESTRICT_REFERENCES option with the WNDS (Write No Database State) constraint.

# ALTER USER
**SEE ALSO**    **CREATE TABLESPACE, GRANT, CREATE PROFILE, CREATE USER,** Chapter 19
**FORMAT**

**alter_user::=**

**proxy_clause::=**

**DESCRIPTION**     You use **ALTER USER** to change a user's password, or the **DEFAULT** tablespace (for objects the user owns) or **TEMPORARY** tablespace (for temporary segments used by the user). Without **ALTER USER**, the defaults for both of these are set by the defaults of the first tablespace (both for objects and temporary segments) to which the user is **GRANT**ed resource and the default temporary tablespace defined at the database level. **ALTER USER** can also change the quota, the resource profile, or the default role (*see* **CREATE USER**). You can use the **PASSWORD EXPIRE** clause to force a user's password to expire, in which case the user must change his or her password during the next login. The **ACCOUNT UNLOCK** clause allows you to unlock an account that has exceeded its maximum number of consecutive failed login attempts. *See* **CREATE PROFILE** for details on password control. To alter a user, you must have the ALTER USER system privilege.

   You can use the **PROXY** clause to connect as the specified user and to activate all, some, or none of the user's roles. **PROXY** is typically used in three-tier applications involving application servers.

# ALTER VIEW
**SEE ALSO**     **CREATE VIEW, DROP VIEW**, Chapter 18
**FORMAT**
**alter_view::=**

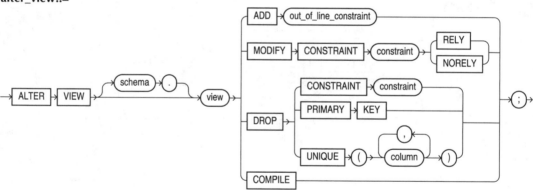

**DESCRIPTION**     ALTER VIEW recompiles a view or alters its constraints. To alter a view, you must either own the view or have ALTER ANY TABLE system privilege.

# ANALYZE
**SEE ALSO**     Chapter 38
**FORMAT**

**analyze::=**

**compute_statistics_clause::=**

**estimate_statistics_clause::=**

**validation_clauses::=**

**for_clause::=**

**into_clause::=**

**DESCRIPTION**    Oracle recommends you use the DBMS_STATS package in place of the **ANALYZE** command, but **ANALYZE** offers capabilities not yet found in DBMS_STATS. **ANALYZE**, unlike DBMS_STATS, supports the ability to sample a specific number of rows, to validate an index, to list chained rows, and to collect data on freelist blocks.

**ANALYZE** lets you collect statistics about a table, cluster, partition, or index for the optimizer, storing them in the data dictionary; it lets you delete these statistics; it validates the structure of an object; and it identifies migrated and chained rows of a table or cluster with a listing in a local table. Estimating is usually faster and pretty much as accurate as **COMPUTE** for optimizer statistics. You use the **VALIDATE STRUCTURE** clause to test an object for possible data corruption. To analyze a table, you must either own the table or have the ANALYZE ANY system privilege.

You can use the **FOR** clause with **COMPUTE STATISTICS** and **ESTIMATE STATISTICS**. The **FOR** clause allows you to alter the default behavior of **ANALYZE**. You can analyze a table without its indexes (**FOR TABLE**), a table and all of its indexed columns (**FOR TABLE FOR INDEXED COLUMNS**), just the indexed columns (**FOR ALL INDEXED COLUMNS**), or just specific columns. The **SIZE** parameter is used to populate data histograms used by the cost-based optimizer during advanced tuning efforts.

The **LIST CHAINED ROWS** clause records information about row chaining in a table you specify.

# AND
*See* LOGICAL OPERATORS, PRECEDENCE, **CONTAINS**.

# ANSI
The American National Standards Institute sets standards for the SQL language and its many elements.

# ANY
**SEE ALSO**    ALL, BETWEEN, EXISTS, IN, LOGICAL OPERATORS, Chapter 12
**FORMAT**

```
operator ANY list
```

**DESCRIPTION**    = **ANY** is the equivalent of **IN**. *operator* can be any one of =, >, >=, <, <=, != and *list* can be a series of literal strings (such as 'Talbot', 'Jones', or 'Hild'), or series of literal numbers (such as 2, 43, 76, 32.06, or 444), or a column from a subquery, where each row of the subquery becomes a member of the list, as shown here:

```
LOCATION.City = ANY (select City from WEATHER)
```

It also can be a series of columns in the **where** clause of the main query, as shown here:

```
Prospect = ANY (Vendor, Client)
```

**RESTRICTIONS**    *list* cannot be a series of columns in a subquery, like this:

```
Prospect = ANY (select Vendor, Client from . . .)
```

Many people find this operator and the **ALL** operator very difficult to remember, because the logic for some of their cases is not immediately intuitive. As a result, some form of **EXISTS** is usually substituted.

The combination of an operator with **ANY** and a list can be illustrated with these explanations:

Page = ANY (4,2,7)	Page is in the list (4,2,7)—2, 4, and 7 all qualify.
Page > ANY (4,2,7)	Page is greater than any single item in the list (4,2,7)—even 3 qualifies, because it is greater than 2.
Page >= ANY (4,2,7)	Page is greater than or equal to any single item in the list (4,2,7)—even 2 qualifies, because it is equal to 2.
Page < ANY (4,2,7)	Page is less than any single item in the list (4,2,7)—even 6 qualifies, because it is less than 7.
Page <= ANY (4,2,7)	Page is less than or equal to any single item in the list (4,2,7)—even 7 qualifies.
Page != ANY (4,2,7)	Page is not equal to any single item in the list (4,2,7)—any number qualifies so long as the list has more than one value. With only one value, != ANY is the equivalent of !=.

# APPEND

**SEE ALSO**    **CHANGE, DEL, EDIT, LIST,** Chapter 6
**FORMAT**

```
A[PPEND] text
```

**DESCRIPTION**    **APPEND** is a feature of the SQL*PLUS command line editor. **APPEND** places the text at the end of the current line in the current buffer, with no intervening spaces. If you want a space between the end of the current line and *text*, put two spaces between **APPEND** and *text*. If you want to append a semicolon at the end of a line, put two of them together (one of them will be regarded as a command terminator and discarded).

**EXAMPLE**

```
APPEND ;;
```

# APPLICATION

An application is a set of forms, menus, reports, and other components that satisfies a particular business function. For example, you might build an application to serve as an order entry system.

# ARCH PROCESS

One of the background processes used by Oracle, ARCH performs automatic archiving of redo log files when the database is used in **ARCHIVELOG** mode. *See* BACKGROUND PROCESS.

# ARCHIVE

In a general sense, archiving means to save data for possible later use. In a specific sense, it means to save the data found in the online redo logs, in the event that the logs are needed to restore the database due to a media failure.

# ARCHIVE LOG

**SEE ALSO**    **ALTER DATABASE, RECOVER**, Chapter 40

**FORMAT**

```
ARCHIVE LOG {LIST|STOP}|{START|NEXT|ALL|integer} [TO destination]
```

**DESCRIPTION**    **ARCHIVE LOG** starts or stops automatic archiving of online redo log files, manually archives specific redo log files, or displays information about redo log files. **START** enables automatic archiving; **STOP** disables it. **LIST** shows the archive status for the online redo logs. **NEXT** manually archives the next online redo log file group that has been filled but not yet archived. **ALL** manually archives all filled but not yet archived redo log file groups. You can specify the online redo log group number and the destination area for the archived files.

**EXAMPLE**

```
ARCHIVE LOG ALL
ARCHIVE LOG LIST
```

# ARGUMENT

An argument is an expression within the parentheses of a function or procedure, supplying a value for the function or procedure to use.

# ARRAY PROCESSING

Array processing is processing performed on batches of data rather than one row at a time. In some Oracle utilities such as Export/Import and the precompilers, users can set the size of the array; increasing the array size will generally improve performance.

# ARRAYSIZE (SQL*PLUS)

*See* **SET**.

# AS

**SEE ALSO**    **ALIAS, TO_CHAR**, Chapters 7 and 9

**DESCRIPTION**    AS is used to separate column formulas from column aliases.

**EXAMPLE**    Here AS separates the column alias PayDay from its column formula:

```
select NEXT_DAY(CycleDate,'FRIDAY') AS PayDay
from PAYDAY;
```

# ASCII

**SEE ALSO**   CHARACTER FUNCTIONS, **ASCIISTR**, **CHR**

**FORMAT**

```
ASCII(string)
```

**DESCRIPTION**   ASCII is an acronym for "American Standard Code for Information Interchange." It is a convention for using digital data to represent printable characters.

The **ASCII** function will return the ASCII value of the first (leftmost) character in the string. The ASCII value of a character is an integer between 0 and 255. Those between 0 and 127 are well defined. Those above 127 ("extended ASCII set") tend to differ by country, application, and computer manufacturer. The letter A, for instance, is equal to the ASCII number 65; B is 66; C is 67, and so on. The decimal point is 46. A minus sign is 45. The number 0 is 48; 1 is 49; 2 is 50, and so on.

**EXAMPLE**

```
select ASCII('.'), ASCII(.5),
 ASCII('E'), ASCII('EMILY')
 from DUAL;

ASCII('.') ASCII(.5) ASCII('E') ASCII('EMILY')
---------- --------- ---------- --------------
 46 46 69 69
```

# ASCIISTR

**SEE ALSO**   CHARACTER FUNCTIONS, **ASCII**, **CHR**

**FORMAT**

```
ASCIISTR(string)
```

**DESCRIPTION**   The **ASCII** function takes a string and returns its ASCII equivalent in the database character set.

**EXAMPLE**

```
select ASCIISTR('E'), ASCIISTR('EMILY')
 from DUAL;

A ASCII
- -----
E EMILY
```

# ASIN

**SEE ALSO**   ACOS, ATAN, ATAN2, COS, COSH, EXP, LN, LOG, SIN, SINH, TAN, TANH

**FORMAT**   ASIN(value)

**DESCRIPTION**   ASIN returns the arc sine of a value. Input values range from -1 to 1; outputs are expressed in radians.

# ASSOCIATE STATISTICS

**SEE ALSO**   ANALYZE

**FORMAT**
**associate_statistics::=**

**column_association::=**

**function_association::=**

**using_statistics_type::=**

**default_cost_clause::=**

**default_selectivity_clause::=**

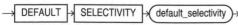

**DESCRIPTION**    **ASSOCIATE STATISTICS** associates a set of statistics functions with one or more columns, standalone functions, packages, types, or indexes. You must have the required privileges to **ALTER** the object being modified.

You can view associations in USER_USTATS after you analyze the object with which you are associating your statistics functions.

# ATAN

**SEE ALSO**    ACOS, ASIN, ATAN2, COS, COSH, EXP, LN, LOG, SIN, SINH, TAN, TANH
**FORMAT**

```
ATAN(value)
```

**DESCRIPTION**    ATAN returns the arc tangent of a value. Input values are unbounded; outputs are expressed in radians.

# ATAN2

**SEE ALSO**    ACOS, ASIN, ATAN, COS, COSH, EXP, LN, LOG, SIN, SINH, TAN, TANH
**FORMAT**

```
ATAN2(value1, value2)
```

**DESCRIPTION**    ATAN2 returns the arc tangent of two values. Input values are unbounded; outputs are expressed in radians.

# ATTRIBUTE

An attribute can be one of three things:

- A synonym of "characteristic" or "property"
- Another name for column
- A part of an abstract datatype

**SEE ALSO**    COLUMN, Chapter 30
**FORMAT**

```
ATTRIBUTE [type_name.attribute_name [option ...]]
```

*Option* can be one of the following:

```
ALI[AS] alias
CLE[AR]
FOR[MAT] format
LIKE {type_name.attribute_name|alias}
ON|OFF
```

**DESCRIPTION**    ATTRIBUTE sets the display attributes for attributes of a user-defined type column in SQL*PLUS.
**EXAMPLE**

```
ATTRIBUTE ADDRESS_TY.Street FORMAT A50
```

# AUDIT

**SEE ALSO**    CREATE DATABASE LINK, DATA DICTIONARY, **NOAUDIT,** PRIVILEGE

**FORMAT**
**audit::=**

**sql_statement_clause::=**

**auditing_by_clause::=**

**schema_object_clause::=**

**auditing_on_clause::=**

**DESCRIPTION**   You can AUDIT statements executed by users and statements that access specific objects.

The *statement options* are:

Option	Audits
CLUSTER	Create, alter, drop, or truncate cluster
CONTEXT	Create or drop context
DATABASE LINK	Create or drop database link
DIMENSION	Create, alter, or drop dimension
DIRECTORY	Create or drop directory
INDEX	Create, alter, or drop index
NOT EXISTS	SQL statements that fail because an object does not exist
PROCEDURE	Create or drop procedure, function, library or package; create package body
PROFILE	Create, alter, or drop profile
PUBLIC DATABASE LINK	Create or drop public database link
PUBLIC SYNONYM	Create or drop public synonym
ROLE	Create, alter, drop, or set role
ROLLBACK SEGMENT	Create, alter, or drop rollback segment
SEQUENCE	Create, alter, or drop sequence
SESSION	Logon attempts
SYNONYM	Create or drop synonym
SYSTEM AUDIT	Audit or noaudit of SQL statements
SYSTEM GRANT	Grant or Revoke of system privileges and roles
TABLE	Create, drop, or truncate table
TABLESPACE	Create, alter, or drop tablespace
TRIGGER	Create, alter, or drop trigger; alter table with ENABLE\|DISABLE ALL TRIGGERS
TYPE	Create, alter, or drop type or type body
USER	Create, alter, or drop user
VIEW	Create or drop view

**ALL** audits all of these facilities but not the following:

ALTER SEQUENCE	ALTER SEQUENCE
ALTER TABLE	ALTER TABLE
COMMENT TABLE	COMMENT ON TABLE *table, view, materialized view* COMMENT ON COLUMN *table.column, view.column,* *materialized view.column*
DELETE TABLE	DELETE FROM *table, view*

EXECUTE PROCEDURE	CALL Execution of any procedure or function or access to any variable, library, or cursor inside a package
GRANT DIRECTORY	GRANT privilege ON directory REVOKE privilege ON directory
GRANT PROCEDURE	GRANT privilege ON procedure, function, package REVOKE privilege ON procedure, function, package
GRANT SEQUENCE	GRANT privilege ON sequence REVOKE privilege ON sequence
GRANT TABLE	GRANT privilege ON table, view, materialized view REVOKE privilege ON table, view, materialized view
GRANT TYPE	GRANT privilege ON TYPE REVOKE privilege ON TYPE
INSERT TABLE	INSERT INTO table, view
LOCK TABLE	LOCK TABLE table, view
SELECT SEQUENCE	Any statement containing sequence.CURRVAL or sequence.NEXTVAL
SELECT TABLE	SELECT FROM table, view, materialized view
UPDATE TABLE	UPDATE table, view

**BY** *user* audits only SQL statements issued by particular users. The default is to audit all users.

**WHENEVER [NOT] SUCCESSFUL** writes a row to an audit table only when an attempted access to an audited table or system facility is (or is **NOT**) successful. Omitting this optional clause causes a row to be written whether an access is successful or not.

Auditing information is written to a table named SYS.AUD$ and accessed via views; *see* DATA DICTIONARY VIEWS.

**EXAMPLE**    This audits all updates by a user named CLERK_USER:

```
audit UPDATE TABLE by clerk_user;
```

# AUDIT TRAIL

An audit trail is a physical record of the rows written when auditing is enabled. If you have enabled auditing (via the AUDIT_TRAIL initialization parameter) and auditing commands have been issued by users or the DBA, the internal audit trail table AUD$, owned by SYS, contains all audit trail rows.

# AUDITING

Auditing is a set of Oracle features that allow the DBA and users to track usage of the database. The DBA can set default auditing activity. The auditing information is stored in the data dictionary, and SQL statements control which information is stored. For example, you can have all attempts to update a table's data be recorded, or only unsuccessful attempts. Alternatively, you can have all logins to Oracle be recorded, or only unsuccessful attempts to do DBA activities.

# AUTOCOMMIT

**AUTOCOMMIT** is a SQL*PLUS setting used to automatically commit changes to the database following any SQL command that **insert**s, **update**s, or **delete**s data in the database. *See* **SET**.

# AUTORECOVERY (SQL*PLUS)

*See* **SET**.

# AVG

**SEE ALSO**    **COMPUTE**, GROUP FUNCTIONS, Chapter 8
**FORMAT**

```
AVG ([DISTINCT | ALL] expr) [OVER (analytic_clause)]
```

**DESCRIPTION**    **AVG** is the average of value for a group of rows. **DISTINCT** forces only unique values to be averaged. **NULL** rows are ignored by this function, which may affect results.

# B-TREE

B-TREE is a high performance indexing structure used by Oracle to create and store indexes.

# BACKGROUND PROCESS

A background process is one of the processes used by an instance of Oracle to perform and coordinate tasks on behalf of concurrent users of a database.

# BEGIN

**SEE ALSO**    **BLOCK STRUCTURE, DECLARE, END, EXCEPTION, TERMINATOR**, Chapter 27
**FORMAT**

```
[<<block label>>]
[DECLARE]
BEGIN
 ... block logic ...
END [block label];
```

**DESCRIPTION**    **BEGIN** is the opening statement of a PL/SQL block's executable section. It can be followed with any legal PL/SQL logic, and an exception handler, and is closed with the **END** statement. At least one executable statement is required between **BEGIN** and **END**. *See* **BLOCK STRUCTURE**.

*block label* is a name given to a PL/SQL block that starts with the word **BEGIN** and finishes with the word **END**. The word **END** is followed by a terminator, usually a semicolon (*see* **TERMINATOR** for exceptions). *block label* follows normal naming conventions for objects, and must be bracketed by << and >>. These symbols tell PL/SQL that this is a label. **BEGIN** may optionally be preceded by a section called **DECLARE** (which follows the block label) and may optionally contain a section called **EXCEPTION**.

# BETWEEN

*See* **LOGICAL OPERATORS**.

# BFILE

BFILE is a datatype (*see* DATA TYPES) used for binary LOB data stored outside the database. Oracle does not maintain read consistency or data integrity for the externally stored data. Within the database, a LOB locator value is stored to point to the external file. Before creating a BFILE entry, you must first create a directory. *See* **CREATE DIRECTORY**.

## BFILENAME

**SEE ALSO**     **BFILE**, **CREATE DIRECTORY**, Chapter 32
**FORMAT**

```
BFILENAME ('directory' , 'filename')
```

**DESCRIPTION**     BFILENAME returns a BFILE locator associated with the specified filename and directory object.

## BIN_TO_NUM

**SEE ALSO**     NUMBER FUNCTIONS, Chapter 8
**FORMAT**

```
BIN_TO_NUM (expr [, expr]...)
```

**DESCRIPTION**     BIN_TO_NUM converts a bit vector to its equivalent number.
**EXAMPLE**

```
select BIN_TO_NUM(1,0,0,1) from DUAL;

BIN_TO_NUM(1,0,0,1)

9
```

## BIND VARIABLE

A bind variable is a variable in a SQL statement that must be replaced with a valid value or address of a value in order for the statement to successfully execute.

## BITAND

**SEE ALSO**     **DECODE**, Chapter 17
**FORMAT**

```
BITAND (argument1, argument2)
```

**DESCRIPTION**     BITAND computes an AND operation on the bits of `argument1` and `argument2`, both of which must resolve to nonnegative integers, and returns an integer. This function is commonly used with the **DECODE** function.

## BITMAP INDEX

A bitmap index is a type of index best suited for columns with few distinct values (and thus, poor selectivity). If there are few distinct values for a column, and it is frequently used as a limiting condition in queries, you should consider using a bitmap index for the column. *See* Chapter 20 for further details on bitmap indexes. For full syntax information, *see* **CREATE INDEX**.

## BLOB

A BLOB is a binary large object, stored inside the database. *See* Chapter 32.

# BLOCK

A block is the basic unit of storage (physical and logical) for all Oracle data. The Oracle block size varies by operating system and may differ from the block size of the host operating system. Common block sizes are 4K, 8K, and 16 K. For the size of a block on your specific operating system, refer to your *Installation and User's Guide*. Database block sizes can differ at the tablespace level.

# BLOCK STRUCTURE

A block structure is a structure of block sections in PL/SQL.

**PRODUCTS**     PL/SQL

**SEE ALSO**      **BEGIN, DECLARE, END, EXCEPTION, GOTO**, Chapter 27

**DESCRIPTION**      PL/SQL blocks can be embedded in SQL*PLUS and any of several programming languages, through the use of the Oracle precompilers. PL/SQL blocks are structured like this:

```
[<<block label>>]
[DECLARE
.. declarations (CURSOR, VARIABLE and EXCEPTION)...]

BEGIN

... block logic (executable code)...

[EXCEPTION

... exception handling logic (for fatal errors)...]

END [block label];
```

As the brackets show, both the **DECLARE** and **EXCEPTION** sections are optional. A block may optionally be labeled by a block name, which must be bracketed by << and >>.

The sections of a block must be in this order, although blocks may nest inside of other blocks in either the block logic or exception handling logic sections. *blocks* may be used for branching using a **GOTO**, or as a prefix in referencing a variable in another block (*see* **DECLARE** for details on this). If a variable will be referenced in a cursor declaration, it must be declared before the cursor is declared. *See* Chapter 27 for examples of block structures and loops.

**EXAMPLE**

```
<<calc_areas>>
DECLARE
 pi constant NUMBER(9,7) := 3.14159;
 area NUMBER(14,2);
 cursor rad_cursor is
 select * from RADIUS_VALS;
 rad_val rad_cursor%ROWTYPE;
BEGIN
 open rad_cursor;
 loop
 fetch rad_cursor into rad_val;
 exit when rad_cursor%NOTFOUND;
 area := pi*power(rad_val.radius,2);
 insert into AREAS values (rad_val.radius, area);
 end loop;
 close rad_cursor;
END calc_areas;
```

# BRANCH

Branches are a series of connected nodes of a logical tree. *See* **CONNECT BY**.

# BREAK

**SEE ALSO**     **CLEAR**, **COMPUTE**, Chapters 6 and 14
**FORMAT**

```
BRE[AK] [ON report_element [action [action]]] ...
```

Where *report_element* is

```
{column|expr|ROW|REPORT}
```

and *action* is

```
[SKI[P]n|[SKI[P]] PAGE] [NODUP[LICATES]|DUP[LICATES]]
```

**DESCRIPTION**     A break occurs when SQL*PLUS detects a specified change, such as the end of a page or a change in the value of an expression. A break will cause SQL*PLUS to perform some action you've specified in the **BREAK** command, such as **SKIP**, and to print some result from a **COMPUTE** command, such as averages or totals for a column. Only one **BREAK** command may be in effect at a time. A new **BREAK** command may specify changes, and their associated actions, that are to cause a break.

A break **ON REPORT** causes a break at the end of a report or query.

A change in the value of an expression may occur at any time prior to the **REPORT** break, and there may be several **ON** expression clauses in a single **BREAK** statement; however, their order in the **BREAK** command should be the same as in the **order by** of the **select** statement. That is, each expression that appears in the **BREAK** command also should be placed in the **order by** clause of select, in identical sequence, or the result will be meaningless. In addition, their order should be from the largest grouping to the smallest (for example, ON Corporation, ON Division, ON Project).

**ON ROW** causes a break for every row selected.

**ON PAGE** causes a break at the end of each page, and is independent of breaks caused by *expression*, ON ROW, or ON REPORT.

**SKIP** skips a number of *lines*, and PAGE or SKIP PAGE skips to a new page, before printing the result of the associated **COMPUTE** for the break.

**NODUPLICATES** suppresses the printing of the values in the expression or column in the **BREAK** for every row except the first one after the **BREAK** occurs.

**BREAK** by itself will display the current break settings.

**CLEAR BREAKS** will remove any existing **BREAK**s.

For examples of these in use, *see* Chapter 14.

# BTITLE (bottom title)

**SEE ALSO**     **ACCEPT, DEFINE, PARAMETERS, REPFOOTER, REPHEADER, SET HEADSEP, TTITLE,** Chapter 14
**FORMAT**

```
BTI[TLE] [printspec [text|variable]... | OFF | ON]
```

**DESCRIPTION**     **BTITLE** puts *text* (may be multiline) at the bottom of each page of a report. OFF and ON suppress and restore the display of the *text* without changing its contents. **BTITLE** by itself displays the current **btitle** options and text or variable. *text* is a bottom title you wish to give this report,

and *variable* is a user-defined variable or a system-maintained variable, including SQL.LNO, the current line number, SQL.PNO, the current page number, SQL.RELEASE, the current Oracle release number, SQL.SQLCODE, the current error code, and SQL.USER, the username.

*options* are described next:

- **COL** *n* skips directly to position *n* (from the left margin) of the current line.
- **S[KIP]** *n* prints *n* blank lines. If no *n* is specified, one blank line is printed. If *n* is 0, no blank lines are printed and the current position for printing becomes position 1 of the current line (leftmost on the page).
- **TAB** *n* skips forward *n* positions (backward if *n* is negative).
- **BOLD** prints the output data in bold print.
- **LE[FT], CE[NTER]**, and **R[IGHT]**. Left-justify, center, and right-justify data respectively on the current line. Any text or variables following these commands are justified as a group, up to the end of the command, or a LEFT, CENTER, RIGHT, or COL. CENTER and RIGHT use the value set by the **SET LINESIZE** command to determine where to place the text or variable.
- **FORMAT** string specifies the format model that will control the format of following text or variables, and follows the same syntax as **FORMAT** in a **COLUMN** command, such as **FORMAT** A12 or **FORMAT** $999,999.99. Each time a **FORMAT** appears, it supersedes the previous one that was in effect. If no **FORMAT** model has been specified, the one set by **SET NUMFORMAT** is used. If **NUMFORMAT** has not been set, the default for SQL*PLUS is used.

Data values are printed according to the default format unless a variable has been loaded with a date reformatted by **TO_CHAR**.

Any number of options, text, and variables may be used in a single **btitle**. Each is printed in the order specified, and each is positioned and formatted as specified by the clauses that precede it.

# BUFFER

Generally speaking, a buffer is a scratchpad, usually in the computer's memory, where commands are staged for editing and execution.

In SQL*PLUS, a buffer is an area in memory for editing SQL commands. *See* **EDIT** and **SET**.

# BUFFERS (DATABASE)

Buffers are temporary storage places for database blocks that are currently being accessed and changed by database users.

# BUFFERS (REDO LOG)

Buffers are temporary storage places for redo log entries that are created by transactions within the database.

# C LANGUAGE

C is a programming language popular for its portability to many different types of computers. Oracle is itself written primarily in C.

# CACHES

Caches are temporary holding places for either database data that is currently being accessed or changed by users or data that Oracle requires to support users.

# CALL

**SEE ALSO**     **EXECUTE**, Chapter 36
**FORMAT**
call::=

**DESCRIPTION**     You can use **CALL** to execute a stored procedure or function from within SQL. You must have EXECUTE privilege on the procedure or function, or on the package in which the procedure or function exists.

# CALL, RECURSIVE

*See* RECURSIVE CALL.

# CASE

**SEE ALSO**     OTHER FUNCTIONS, **DECODE**, **TRANSLATE**, Chapter 17
**FORMAT**
case_expression::=

simple_case_expression::=

searched_case_expression::=

else_clause::=

**DESCRIPTION**    **CASE** supports if-then-else logic within SQL statements. Use **WHEN/THEN** clauses to tell the database what to do for each condition. You can use an **ELSE** clause to handle exceptions to your WHEN clauses.

**EXAMPLE**

```
select distinct
 CASE CategoryName
 when 'ADULTFIC' then 'Adult Fiction'
 when 'ADULTNF' then 'Adult Nonfiction'
 when 'ADULTREF' then 'Adult Reference'
 when 'CHILDRENFIC' then 'Children Fiction'
 when 'CHILDRENNF' then 'Children Nonfiction'
 when 'CHILDRENPIC' then 'Children Picturebook'
 else CategoryName
 end
 from BOOKSHELF;
```

# CAST

**SEE ALSO**    NESTED TABLE, Chapter 31

**FORMAT**

```
CAST ({ expr | (subquery) | MULTISET (subquery) } AS type_name)
```

**DESCRIPTION**    You can use **CAST** to convert one datatype to another. **CAST** is most commonly used when working with collectors such as nested tables.

# CATSEARCH

**CATSEARCH** is used for text searches against CTXCAT text indexes created within Oracle Text. See Chapter 24 for index creation and text search examples. Supported text search operators include the following:

Operator	Description
\|	Returns a record if either search term has a score that exceeds the threshold.
AND	Returns a record if both search terms have a score that exceeds the threshold. This is the default action.
-	Returns rows that contain the term preceding the "-" that do not contain the term following it.
NOT	Same as -.
()	Specifies the order in which search criteria are evaluated.
" "	Encloses phrases

# CEIL

**SEE ALSO**    **FLOOR**, NUMBER FUNCTIONS

**FORMAT**

```
CEIL(value)
```

**DESCRIPTION**    **CEIL** is the smallest integer higher than or equal to *value*.

### EXAMPLE

```
CEIL(1.3) = 2
CEIL(-2.3) = -2
```

# CHAINED ROW

A chained row is a row that is stored in more than one database block, and therefore has several row pieces. Long rows (or inline LOBs) whose data is greater than the size of a block always have multiple row pieces. The **ANALYZE** command can identify chained rows and can also provide statistics on the number of chained rows. *See* **ANALYZE**.

# CHANGE

**SEE ALSO**    APPEND, **DEL**, **EDIT**, **LIST**, Chapter 6
**FORMAT**

```
C[HANGE] /old text/new text/
```

**DESCRIPTION**    **CHANGE** is a feature of the SQL*PLUS command line editor. It changes *old text* to *new text* in the current line of the current buffer (the line marked with an * in the LIST).
  **CHANGE** ignores case in searching for old text. Three dots are a wild card. If *old text* is prefixed with '. . .', everything up to and including the first occurrence of old text is replaced by new text. If old text is suffixed with '. . .', everything including and after the first occurrence of old text is replaced by new text. If old text has . . . embedded in it, everything from the part of old text before the dots, through the part of old text after the dots, is replaced by new text.
  The space between the **CHANGE** and the first / may be omitted; the final delimiter is unnecessary if no trailing spaces need to be inserted. A delimiter other than / may be used. Any character following the word **CHANGE** (other than a space) is assumed to be the delimiter.
**EXAMPLES**    If this is the current line of the current buffer:

```
where CategoryName = 'ADULTFN'
```

then this:

```
C /ADULTTN/ADULTNF
```

would change the line to this:

```
where CategoryName = 'ADULTNF'
```

# CHAR DATA TYPE

*See* DATA TYPES.

# CHARACTER FUNCTIONS

**SEE ALSO**    CONVERSION FUNCTIONS, NUMBER FUNCTIONS, OTHER FUNCTIONS, Chapter 7
**DESCRIPTION**    This is an alphabetical list of all current character functions in Oracle's SQL. Each of these is listed elsewhere in this reference under its own name, with its proper format and use.

## Function Name and Use

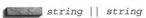
```
string || string
```

|| concatenates two strings. The | symbol is called a broken vertical bar, although on some computers it may be a solid bar.

ASCII(*string*)

> **ASCII** gives the ASCII value of the first character of a string.

CHR(*integer*)

> **CHR** gives the character with ASCII value equal to a given positive integer.

CONCAT(*string1*, *string2*)

> **CONCAT** concatenates two strings. It is equivalent to ||.

INITCAP(*string*)

> This stands for **INIT**ial **CAP**ital. It changes the first letter of a word or series of words into uppercase.

INSTR(*string*, *set* [, *start* [ , *occurrence* ] ])

> **INSTR** finds the location of the beginning of a set of characters **IN** a **STR**ing.

LENGTH(*string*)

> This tells the **LENGTH** of a string.

LOWER(*string*)

> **LOWER** converts every letter in a string to lowercase.

LPAD(*string*, *length* [, '*set*'])

> **LPAD** stands for **L**eft **PAD**. It makes a string a specific length by adding a specified set of characters to the left.

LTRIM(*string* [, '*set*'])

> **LTRIM** stands for **L**eft **TRIM**. It trims all the occurrences of any one of a set of characters off of the left side of a string.

NLS_INITCAP(*string*[, 'NLS_SORT=*sort*'])

> **NLS_INITCAP** stands for **N**ational **L**anguage **S**upport **Init**ial **Cap**ital. This version of **INITCAP** uses the collating sequence *sort* to do the case conversion.

NLS_LOWER(*string*[, 'NLS_SORT=*sort*'])

> **NLS_LOWER** stands for **N**ational **L**anguage **S**upport **Lower** case. This version of **LOWER** uses the collating sequence *sort* to do the case conversion.

NLS_UPPER(*string*[, 'NLS_SORT=*sort*'])

> **NLS_UPPER** stands for **N**ational **L**anguage **S**upport **Upper** case. This version of **UPPER** uses the collating sequence *sort* to do the case conversion.

NLSSORT(*string*[, 'NLS_SORT=*sort*'])

Oracle uses **N**ational **L**anguage **S**upport **SORT.** This gives the collating sequence value of the given string based on the collating sequence *sort,* or if omitted, the National Language Support option chosen for the site.

REPLACE(*string, if* [*,then*])

**REPLACE** returns *string* with every occurrence of *if* replaced with *then* (zero or more characters). If no *then* string is specified, then all occurrences of *if* are removed. *See* **TRANSLATE**.

RPAD(*string,length* [ *,'set'*])

**RPAD** stands for **R**ight **PAD**. It makes a string a specific length by adding a specified set of characters to the right.

RTRIM(*string* [*,'set'*])

**RTRIM** stands for **R**ight **TRIM**. It trims all the occurrences of any one of a set of characters off of the right side of a string.

SOUNDEX(*string*)

**SOUNDEX** converts a string to a code value. Names with similar sounds tend to have the same code value. You can use **SOUNDEX** to compare names that might have small spelling differences but are still the same.

SUBSTR(*string, start* [*,count*])

**SUBSTR**ing clips out a piece of a string beginning at *start* position and counting for *count* characters from *start.*

TRANSLATE(*string,if,then*)

This **TRANSLATE**s a string, character by character, based on a positional matching of characters in the *if* string with characters in the *then* string. *See* **REPLACE**.

TRIM
```
([{ { LEADING | TRAILING | BOTH } [trim_character])
 | trim_character
 } FROM] trim_source)
```

**TRIM** removes all the occurrences of any one of a set of characters off of the right side, left side, or both sides of a string.

UPPER(*string*)

**UPPER** converts every letter in a string into uppercase.

USERENV(*option*)

**USERENV** returns information about the **USER ENV**ironment, usually for an audit trail. Options include 'ENTRYID', 'SESSIONID', and 'TERMINAL'. **USERENV** is still supported but has been replaced by SYS_CONTEXT's UserEnv namespace.

VSIZE(*string*)

**VSIZE** gives the storage size of *string* in Oracle.

## CHARTOROWID

**SEE ALSO**     CONVERSION FUNCTIONS, **ROWIDTOCHAR**
**FORMAT**

```
CHARTOROWID(string)
```

**DESCRIPTION**     This stands for **CHAR**acter **TO ROW ID**entifier. It changes a character string to act like an internal Oracle row identifier, or **ROWID**.

## CHECKPOINT

A checkpoint is a point in time at which changed blocks of data are written from the SGA to the database.

## CHILD

In tree-structured data, a child is a node that is the immediate descendant of another node. The node that the child descends from is called the *parent.*

## CHR

**SEE ALSO**     **ASCII**, CHARACTER FUNCTIONS
**FORMAT**

```
CHR(integer)
```

**DESCRIPTION**     **CHR** will return the character with the ASCII value of *integer*. (*integer* means an integer between 0 and 255, since the ASCII value of a character is an integer between 0 and 255.) Those between 0 and 127 are well defined. Those above 127 (called the extended ASCII set) tend to differ by country, application, and computer manufacturer. The letter A, for instance, is equal to the ASCII number 65, B is 66, C is 67, and so on. The decimal point is 46. A minus sign is 45. The number 0 is 48, 1 is 49, 2 is 50, and so on.

**EXAMPLE**

```
select CHR(77), CHR(46), CHR(56) from DUAL;

C C C
- - -
M . 8
```

## CLAUSE

A clause is a major section of a SQL statement and begins with a keyword such as **select**, **insert**, **update**, **delete**, **from**, **where**, **order by**, **group by**, or **having**.

## CLEAR

**SEE ALSO**     BREAK, COLUMN, COMPUTE
**FORMAT**

```
CL[EAR] option
```

**DESCRIPTION**     **CLEAR** clears the option.
    **BRE[AKS]** clears breaks set by the **BREAK** command.
    **BUFF[ER]** clears the current buffer.

**COL[UMNS]** clears options set by the **COLUMN** command.
**COMP[UTES]** clears options set by the **COMPUTE** command.
**SCR[EEN]** clears the screen.
**SQL** clears the SQL buffer.
**TIMI[NG]** deletes all timing areas created by the **TIMING** command.
**EXAMPLES**    To clear computes, use this:

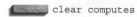
```
clear computes
```

To clear column definitions, use this:

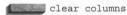
```
clear columns
```

# CLIENT

Client is a general term for a user, software application, or computer that requires the services, data, or processing of another application or computer.

# CLOB

CLOB is a datatype that supports character large objects. *See* Chapter 32.

# CLOSE

**SEE ALSO**    **DECLARE**, **FETCH**, **FOR**, **OPEN**, Chapter 27
**FORMAT**

```
CLOSE cursor;
```

**DESCRIPTION**    **CLOSE** closes the named cursor, and releases its resources to Oracle for use elsewhere. *cursor* must be the name of a currently open cursor.

Even though a cursor has been closed, its definition has not been lost. You can issue **OPEN** *cursor* again, so long as the cursor was explicitly declared. A FOR loop will also implicitly **OPEN** a declared cursor. *See* CURSOR FOR LOOP.

# CLOSED DATABASE

A closed database is a database that is associated with an instance (the database is mounted) but not open. Databases must be closed for some database maintenance functions. This can be accomplished via the SQL statement **ALTER DATABASE**.

# CLUSTER

A cluster is a means of storing together data from multiple tables, when the data in those tables contains common information and is likely to be accessed concurrently. You can also cluster an individual table. *See* **CREATE CLUSTER** and Chapter 20.

# CLUSTER INDEX

A cluster index is one manually created after a cluster has been created and before any DML (**select**, **insert**, **update**, or **delete**) statements can operate on the cluster. This index is created on the cluster key columns with the SQL statement **CREATE INDEX**. In Oracle, you can define a hash cluster to index on the primary key. *See* HASH CLUSTER.

# CLUSTER KEY

A cluster key is the column or columns that clustered tables have in common, and which is chosen as the storage/access key. For example, two tables, BOOKSHELF and BOOKSHELF_AUTHOR, might be clustered on the column Title. A cluster key is the same thing as a CLUSTER COLUMN.

# CMDSEP (SQL*PLUS)

*See* **SET**.

# COALESCE

**SEE ALSO**     **DECODE**, Chapter 17

**FORMAT**

```
COALESCE(value1, value2, ...)
```

**DESCRIPTION**     **COALESCE** will return the first non-NULL value encountered in the list of values provided.

# COALESCE (space)

To coalesce space is to unite adjoining free extents into a single extent. For example, if two 100-block extents are next to each other within a tablespace, then they can be coalesced into a single 200-block extent. The SMON background process will coalesce free space within tablespaces whose default **pctincrease** value is non-zero. You can manually coalesce the free space within a tablespace via the **coalesce** option of the **alter tablespace** command. *See* **ALTER TABLESPACE**.

# COLLATION

**SEE ALSO**     **GROUP BY, INDEX, ORDER BY**, Chapter 9

**DESCRIPTION**     The collation or collating sequence is the order in which characters, numbers, and symbols will be sorted because of an **order by** or **group by** clause. These sequences differ based on the collation sequence of the computer's operating system or the national language. EBCDIC (usually IBM and compatible mainframes) and ASCII (most other computers) sequences differ significantly. In spite of these differences, the following rules always apply:

- A number with a larger value is considered "greater" than a smaller one. All negative numbers are smaller than all positive numbers. Thus, -10 is smaller than 10; -100 is smaller than -10.

- A later date is considered greater than an earlier date.

Character strings are compared position by position, starting at the leftmost end of the string, up to the first character that is different. Whichever string has the "greater" character in that position is considered the greater string. One character is considered greater than another if it appears after the other in the computer's collation sequence. Usually this means that a B is greater than an A, but the value of A compared to a, or compared to the number 1, will differ by computer.

The collation comparison varies slightly depending on whether you are using CHAR or VARCHAR2 strings.

If two VARCHAR2 strings are identical up to the end of the shorter one, the longer string is considered greater. If two strings are identical and the same length, they are considered equal.

With CHAR strings, the shorter string is padded with blanks out to the length of the longer string. If the strings are not identical after this padding, the comparison treats the padded blanks as less than any other character, resulting in the same truth value as the VARCHAR2 comparison. If the strings are

identical after, but not before the padding, the CHAR comparison would treat them as equal whereas the VARCHAR2 comparison would not.

In SQL it is important that literal numbers be typed without enclosing single quotes, as '10' would be considered smaller than '6', since the quotes will cause these to be regarded as character strings rather than numbers, and the '6' will be seen as greater than the '1' in the first position of '10'.

## COLSEP (SQL*PLUS)
*See* **SET**.

## COLUMN (Form 1-Definition)
A column is a subdivision of a table with a column name and a specific datatype. For example, in a table of workers, all of the worker's ages would constitute one column. *See* **ROW**.

## COLUMN (Form 2-SQL*PLUS)
**SEE ALSO**    ALIAS, Chapters 6 and 14
**FORMAT**

```
COL[UMN] {column | expression}
 [ALI[AS] alias]
 [CLE[AR] | DEF[AULT]]
 [ENTMAP {ON|OFF}]
 [FOLD_A[FTER]]
 [FOLD_B[EFORE]]
 [FOR[MAT] format]
 [HEA[DING] text
 [JUS[TIFY] {L[EFT]|C[ENTER]|C[ENTRE]|R[IGHT]}]]
 [LIKE {expression | alias}]
 [NEWL[INE]]
 [NEW_V[ALUE] variable]
 [NOPRI[NT]|PRI[NT]]
 [NUL[L] text]
 [ON | OFF]
 [OLD_V[ALUE] variable]
 [WRA[PPED]|WOR[D_WRAPPED]|TRU[NCATED]]...
```

**DESCRIPTION**    **COLUMN** controls column and column heading formatting. The options are all cumulative, and may be entered either simultaneously on a single line, or on separate lines at any time; the only requirement is that the word **COLUMN** and the column or expression must appear on each separate line. If one of the options is repeated, the most recent specified will be in effect. **COLUMN** by itself displays all the current definitions for all columns. **COLUMN** with only a column or expression will show that column's current definition.

*column* or *expression* refers to a column or expression used in the **select**. If an expression is used, the expression must be entered exactly the same way that it is in the **select** statement. If the expression in the **select** is **Amount * Rate**, then entering **Rate * Amount** in a **COLUMN** command will not work. If a column or expression is given an alias in the **select** statement, that alias must be used here.

If you **select** columns with the same name from different tables (in sequential selects), a **COLUMN** command for that column name will apply to both. Avoid this by assigning the columns different aliases

in the **select** (not with the **COLUMN** command's **alias** clause), and entering a **COLUMN** command for each column's alias.

**ALIAS** gives this column a new name, which then may be used to reference the column in **BREAK** and **COLUMN** commands.

**CLEAR** drops the column definition.

**DEFAULT** leaves the column defined and ON, but drops any other options.

**ENTMAP** allows entity mapping to be turned on or off for selected columns in HTML output.

**FOLD_A[FTER]** and **FOLD_B[EFORE]** instruct Oracle to fold a single row of output across multiple rows when printed. You can choose to fold the row either before or after the column.

**FORMAT** specifies the display format of the column. The format must be a literal like A25 or 990.99. Without format specified, the column width is the length as defined inthe table.

A LONG column's width defaults to the value of the **SET LONG**. Both regular CHAR and LONG fields can have their width set by a format like **FORMAT A***n*, where *n* is an integer that is the column's new width.

A number column's width defaults to the value of **SET NUMWIDTH**, but is changed by the width in a **format** clause such as FORMAT 999,999.99. These options work with both **set numformat** and the **column format** commands:

Format	Result
9999990	The count of nines and zeros determines the maximum digits that can be displayed.
999,999,999.99	Commas and decimals will be placed in the pattern shown.
999990	Displays a zero if the value is zero.
099999	Displays numbers with leading zeros.
$99999	A dollar sign is placed in front of every number.
B99999	The display will be blank if the value is zero.
99999MI	If the number is negative, a minus sign follows the number. The default is for the negative sign to be on left.
S9999	Returns "+" for positive values, "-" for negative values.
99999PR	Negative numbers are displayed within < and >.
99D99	Displays the decimal in the position indicated.
9G999	Displays the group separator in the position shown.
C9999	Displays the ISO currency symbol in this position.
L999	Displays the local currency symbol.
,	Displays a comma.
.	Displays a period.
9.999EEEE	The display will be in scientific notation (4 E's are required).
999V99	Multiplies number by 10$n$, where $n$ is the number of digits to the right of V. 999V99 turns 1234 into 123400.
RN	Displays Roman numeral values, for numbers between 1 and 3999.
DATE	Displays value as a date in MM/DD/YY format, for NUMBER columns used storing Julian dates.

**HEADING** relabels a column heading. The default is the column name or the expression. If text has blanks or punctuation characters, it must be in single quotes. The **HEADSEP** character (usually '|') in text makes SQL*PLUS begin a new line. The **COLUMN** command will remember the current **HEADSEP** character when the column is defined, and continue to use it for this column unless the column is redefined, even if the **HEADSEP** character is changed.

**JUSTIFY** aligns the heading over the column. By default this is RIGHT for number columns and LEFT for anything else.

**LIKE** replicates the column definitions of a previously defined column for the current one, where either the expression or label was used in the other column definition. Only those features of the other column that have not been explicitly defined in the current column command are copied.

**NEWLINE** starts a new line before printing the column value.

**NEW_VALUE** names a variable to hold the column's value for use in the **ttitle** command. *See* Chapter 14 for usage information.

**NOPRINT** and **PRINT** turn the column's display off or on.

**NULL** sets text to be displayed if the column has a **NULL** value. The default for this is a string of blanks as wide as the column is defined.

**OFF** or **ON** turns all these options for a column off or on without affecting its contents.

**OLD_VALUE** names a variable to hold the column's value for use in the **btitle** command. *See* Chapter 13 for usage information.

**WRAPPED**, **WORD_WRAPPED**, and **TRUNCATED** control how SQL*PLUS displays a heading or string value too wide to fit the column. **WRAP** folds the value to the next line. **WORD_WRAP** folds similarly, but breaks on words. **TRUNCATED** truncates the value to the width of the column definition.

## COLUMN CONSTRAINT

A column constraint is an integrity constraint placed on a specific column of a table. *See* INTEGRITY CONSTRAINT.

## COMMAND

*See* STATEMENT.

## COMMAND LINE

A command line is a line on a computer display where you enter a command.

## COMMENT

**SEE ALSO**      DATA DICTIONARY VIEWS, Chapter 37
**FORMAT**

```
COMMENT ON
{ TABLE [schema .] { table | view | materialized view }
| COLUMN [schema .] { table . | view . | materialized view . } column
| OPERATOR [schema .] operator
| INDEXTYPE [schema .] indextype
}
IS 'text';
```

**DESCRIPTION** **COMMENT** inserts the comment text about an object or column into the data dictionary.

You drop a comment from the database only by setting it to an empty string (set *text* to '').

# COMMIT

To commit means to make changes to data (**insert**s, **update**s, and **delete**s) permanent. Before changes are stored, both the old and new data exist so that changes can be made, or so that the data can be restored to its prior state ("rolled back"). When a user enters the Oracle SQL command **COMMIT**, all changes from that transaction are made permanent.

## COMMIT (Form 1-Embedded SQL)

**SEE ALSO** **ROLLBACK, SAVEPOINT, SET TRANSACTION**, Precompiler programmer's guides

**FORMAT**

```
EXEC SQL [AT { database| :host variable}] COMMIT [WORK]
 [[COMMENT 'text'] [RELEASE]
 | FORCE 'text' [, integer]]
```

**DESCRIPTION** You use **COMMIT** to commit work at various stages within a program. Without the explicit use of **COMMIT**, an entire program's work will be considered one transaction, and will not be committed until the program terminates. Any locks obtained will be held until that time, blocking other users from access. **COMMIT** should be used as often as logically feasible.

**WORK** is optional and has no effect on usage; it is provided for ANSI compatibility. **AT** references a remote database accessed by the **DECLARE DATABASE** command. **RELEASE** disconnects you from the database, whether remote or local. **FORCE** manually commits an in-doubt distributed transaction.

## COMMIT (Form 2-PL/SQL Statement)

**SEE ALSO** **ROLLBACK, SAVEPOINT**

**FORMAT**

```
COMMIT [WORK] [COMMENT 'text' | FORCE 'text' [, integer]];
```

**DESCRIPTION** **COMMIT** commits any changes made to the database since the last **COMMIT** was executed implicitly or explicitly. **WORK** is optional and has no effect on usage.

**COMMENT** associates a text comment with the transaction. The comment can be viewed via the data dictionary view DBA_2PC_PENDING in the event a distributed transaction fails to complete. **FORCE** manually commits an in-doubt distributed transaction.

# COMMUNICATIONS PROTOCOL

Communications protocol is any one of a number of standard means of connecting two computers together so that they can share information. Protocols consist of several layers of both software and hardware, and may connect homogeneous or heterogeneous computers.

## COMPOSE

**SEE ALSO**    CONVERSION FUNCTIONS, Chapter 10

**FORMAT**

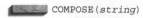

```
COMPOSE(string)
```

**DESCRIPTION**    **COMPOSE** takes as its argument a string in any datatype, and returns a unicode string in its fully normalized form in the same character set as the input.

**EXAMPLE**    To display an o with an umlaut:

```
select COMPOSE ('o' || UNISTR('\0308')) from DUAL;
```

```
C
-
ö
```

## COMPOSITE KEY

A composite key is a primary or foreign key composed of two or more columns.

## COMPOSITE PARTITION

A composite partition involves the use of multiple partition methods, such as a range-partitioned table in which the range partitions are then hash partitioned. *See* Chapter 18.

## COMPRESSED INDEX

A compressed index is an index for which only enough index information is stored to identify unique index entries; information that an index stores with the previous or following key is "compressed" (truncated) and not stored to reduce the storage overhead required by an index. *See also* NONCOMPRESSED INDEX.

## COMPUTE

**SEE ALSO**    **BREAK**, GROUP FUNCTIONS

**FORMAT**

```
COMP[UTE] [AVG|COU[NT]|MAX[IMUM]|MIN[IMUM]|NUM[BER]|STD|SUM|VAR[IANCE]]...
 [function LABEL label_name
 OF {expression | column | alias} ...
 ON {expression | column | alias | REPORT | ROW}...]
```

**DESCRIPTION**    *expression* is a column or expression. **COMPUTE** performs computations on columns or expressions selected from a table. It works only with the **BREAK** command.

By default, Oracle will use the function name (SUM, AVG, etc.) as the label for the result in the query output. **LABEL** allows you to specify a *label_name* that overrides the default value.

**OF** names the column or expression whose value is to be computed. These columns also must be in the **select** clause, or the **COMPUTE** will be ignored.

ON coordinates the **COMPUTE** with the **BREAK** command. **COMPUTE** prints the computed value and restarts the computation when the ON *expression*'s value changes, or when a specified ROW or REPORT break occurs. *See* **BREAK** for coordination details.

**COMPUTE** by itself displays the computes in effect.

**AVG, MAXIMUM, MINIMUM, STD, SUM**, and **VARIANCE** all work on expressions that are numbers. **MAXIMUM** and **MINIMUM** also work on character expressions, but not DATEs. **COUNT** and **NUMBER** work on any expression type.

All of these computes except **NUMBER** ignore rows with **NULL** values:

**AVG**	Gives average value
**COUNT**	Gives count of non-**NULL** values
**MAXIMUM**	Gives maximum value
**MINIMUM**	Gives minimum value
**NUMBER**	Gives count of all rows returned
**STD**	Gives standard deviation
**SUM**	Gives sum of non-**NULL** values
**VARIANCE**	Gives variance

Successive computes are simply put in order without commas, such as in this case:

```
compute sum avg max of Amount Rate on report
```

This will compute the sum, average, and maximum of both Amount and Rate for the entire report.

**EXAMPLE**    To calculate for each Item classification and for the entire report, enter this:

```
break on Report on Industry skip 1
compute sum of Volume on Industry Report
```

# CONCAT

*See* **SET**, ||.

# CONCATENATED INDEX (or KEY)

A concatenated index is one that is created on more than one column of a table. It can be used to guarantee that those columns are unique for every row in the table and to speed access to rows via those columns. *See* COMPOSITE KEY.

# CONCURRENCY

Concurrency is a general term meaning the access of the same data by multiple users. In database software, concurrency requires complex software programming to assure that all users see correct data and that all changes are made in the proper order.

# CONDITION

A condition is an expression whose value evaluates to either TRUE or FALSE, such as Age > 65.

# CONNECT

To connect is to identify yourself to Oracle by your user name and password, in order to access the database.

## CONNECT (Form 1)

**SEE ALSO**      **COMMIT**, **DISCONNECT**, Chapter 22

**FORMAT**

```
CON[NECT] [{user[/password] [@database] |/} [AS SYSOPER|SYSDBA}]];
```

**DESCRIPTION**      You must be in SQL*PLUS to use this command, although you don't need to be logged on to Oracle (*see* **DISCONNECT**). **CONNECT** commits any pending changes, logs you off of Oracle, and logs on as the specified *user*. If the *password* is absent, you are prompted for it. It is not displayed when you type it in response to a prompt.

   *@database* connects to the named database. It may be on your host, or on another computer connected via Oracle Net.

## CONNECT (Form 2-Embedded SQL)

**SEE ALSO**      **COMMIT**, **DECLARE DATABASE**, Chapter 22

**FORMAT**

```
EXEC SQL CONNECT
 { :user IDENTIFIED BY :password | :user_password }
 [AT { database | :host_variable}]
 [USING :connect_string]
 [ALTER AUTHORIZATION :new_password
 | IN {SYSDBA | SYSOPER } MODE]
```

**DESCRIPTION**      **CONNECT** connects a host program to a local or remote database. It may be used more than once to connect to multiple databases. *:user_password* is a host variable that contains the Oracle user name and password separated by a slash (/). Alternatively, *:user* and *:password* can be entered separately by using the second format.

   **AT** is used to name a database other than the default for this user. It is a required clause to reach any databases other than the user's default database. This name can be used later in other SQL statements with **AT**. This database must be first identified with **DECLARE DATABASE**. **USING** specifies an optional Oracle Net string (such as a service name) used during the connect operation. Without the **USING** string, you will be connected to the user's default database, regardless of the database named in the **AT** line.

# CONNECT BY

**SEE ALSO**     Chapter 13

**FORMAT**

```
SELECT expression [,expression]...
 FROM [user.]table
 WHERE condition
CONNECT BY [PRIOR] expression = [PRIOR] expression
 START WITH expression = expression
 ORDER BY expression
```

**DESCRIPTION**     **CONNECT BY** is an operator used in a **select** statement to create reports on inheritance in tree-structured data, such as company organization, family trees, and so on. **START WITH** tells where in the tree to begin. These are the rules:

- ■ The position of **PRIOR** with respect to the **CONNECT BY** expressions determines which expression identifies the root and which identifies the branches of the tree.
- ■ A **where** clause will eliminate individuals from the tree, but not their descendants (or ancestors, depending on the location of **PRIOR**).
- ■ A qualification in the **CONNECT BY** (particularly a not equal instead of the equal sign) will eliminate both an individual and all of its descendants.
- ■ **CONNECT BY** cannot be used with a table join in the **where** clause.

**EXAMPLE**

```
select Cow, Bull, LPAD(' ',6*(Level-1))||Offspring AS Offspring,
 Sex, Birthdate
 from BREEDING
connect by Offspring = PRIOR Cow
 start with Offspring = 'DELLA'
 order by Birthdate;
```

In this example, the following clause:

```
connect by Offspring = PRIOR Cow
```

means the offspring is the cow **PRIOR** to this one.

# CONSTRAINT

A rule or restriction concerning a piece of data (such as a **NOT NULL** restriction on a column) that is enforced at the data level, rather than the object or application level. *See* INTEGRITY CONSTRAINT.

## constraints

**SEE ALSO**     **CREATE TABLE**, INTEGRITY CONSTRAINT, Chapter 18, Chapter 20.

## FORMAT

**constraints::=**

**inline_constraint::=**

**out_of_line_constraint::=**

**inline_ref_constraint::=**

**out_of_line_ref_constraint**

**references_clause::=**

**constraint_state::=**

**using_index_clause::=**

**global_partitioned_index::=**

**index_partitioning_clause::=**

**segment_attributes_clause**

**physical_attributes_clause::=**

**exceptions_clause::=**

**DESCRIPTION**     *constraints* are defined with the *relational_properties* clause of the **CREATE TABLE** and **ALTER TABLE** commands. You use the constraints clauses to create a constraint or to alter an existing constraint. You can enable and disable constraints. If you disable a constraint and then try to re-enable it, Oracle will check the data. If the constraint cannot be re-enabled, Oracle can write the exceptions out to a separate table for review.

For PRIMARY KEY and UNIQUE constraints, Oracle will create indexes. As part of the constraint clause for those constraints, you can use the **USING INDEX** clause to specify the tablespace and storage for the index.

# CONTAINS

**CONTAINS** is used to evaluate text searches that use CONTEXT indexes within Oracle Text. *See* Chapter 24. Supported text search operators for CONTAINS are shown in the following table:

Operator	Description
OR	Returns a record if either search term has a score that exceeds the threshold.
I	Same as OR.
AND	Returns a record if both search terms have a score that exceeds the threshold.
&	Same as AND.
ACCUM	Returns a record if the sum of the search terms' scores exceeds the threshold.
,	Same as ACCUM.
MINUS	Returns a record if the score of the first search minus the score of the second search exceeds the threshold.
-	Same as MINUS.
*	Assigns different weights to the score of the searches.
NEAR	The score will be based on how near the search terms are to each other in the searched text.
;	Same as NEAR.
{}	Encloses reserved words such as AND if they are part of the search term.
%	Multiple-character wildcard.
_	Single-character wildcard.
$	Performs stem expansion of the search term prior to performing the search.
?	Performs a fuzzy match (allowing for misspellings) of the search term prior to performing the search.
!	Performs a SOUNDEX (phonetic) search.
()	Specifies the order in which search criteria are evaluated.

# CONTEXT INDEX

Oracle Text supports three types of text indexes; CONTEXT indexes, CTXCAT indexes and CTXRULE indexes. CONTEXT indexes use the **CONTAINS** operator and support a wider array of text search capabilities. CTXCAT indexes support a narrower set of search operators but support the creation of index sets. CTXRULE indexes are indexes on columns that contain a set of text queries. See Chapter 24 for details.

# CONTEXT AREA

A context area is work area in memory where Oracle stores the current SQL statement, and if the statement is a query, one row of the result. The context area holds the state of a cursor.

# CONTROL FILE (DATABASE)

A control file is a small administrative file required by every database, necessary to start and run a database system. A control file is paired with a database, not with an instance. Multiple identical control files are preferred to a single file.

# CONTROL FILE (SQL*LOADER)

A SQL*Loader control file tells the SQL*Loader executable where to find the data to be loaded, and how to process the data during the load. Every SQL*Loader session has an associated control file. For control file syntax, see SQLLDR. For details on the use of SQL*Loader, see Chapter 21.

# CONVERSION FUNCTIONS

**SEE ALSO**    CHARACTER FUNCTIONS, NUMBER FUNCTIONS, Chapter 10

**DESCRIPTION**    The following is an alphabetical list of all current conversion and transformation functions in Oracle's SQL.

Function Name	Definition
ASCIISTR	Translates a string in any character set and returns an ASCII string in the database character set.
BIN_TO_NUM	Converts a BINary value TO its NUMerical equivalent.
CAST	CASTs one built-in or collection type to another; commonly used with nested tables and varying arrays.
CHARTOROWID	CHARacter TO ROW IDentifier. Changes a character string to act like an internal Oracle row identifier, or RowID.
COMPOSE	Translates a string in any datatype to a unicode string in its fully normalized form in the same character set as the input.
CONVERT	CONVERTs a character string from one national language character set to another.
DECODE	DECODEs a CHAR, VARCHAR2, or NUMBER into any of several different character strings or NUMBERs, based on value. This is a very powerful *if, then, else* function. Chapter 17 is devoted to DECODE.
DECOMPOSE	Translates a string in any datatype to a unicode string after canonical decomposition in the same character set as the input.

Function Name	Definition
**HEXTORAW**	HEXadecimal TO RAW. Changes a character string of hex numbers into binary.
**NUMTODSINTERVAL**	Converts a NUMber to an INTERVAL DAY TO SECOND literal.
**NUMTOYMINTERVAL**	Converts a NUMber to an INTERVAL YEAR TO MONTH literal.
**RAWTOHEX**	RAW TO HEXadecimal. Changes a string of binary numbers to a character string of hex numbers.
**RAWTONHEX**	RAW TO NHEX. Converts raw to an NVARCHAR2 character value containing its hexadecimal equivalent.
**ROWIDTOCHAR**	ROW Identifier TO CHARacter. Changes an internal Oracle row identifier, or RowID, to a character string.
**ROWIDTONCHAR**	RAW TO NCHAR. Converts a RowID value to an NVARCHAR2 datatype.
**TO_CHAR**	TO CHARacter. Converts a NUMBER or DATE to a character string.
**TO_CLOB**	TO CLOB. Converts NCLOB values in a LOB column or other character strings to CLOB values.
**TO_DATE**	TO DATE. Converts a NUMBER, CHAR, or VARCHAR2 to a DATE (an Oracle datatype).
**TO_DSINTERVAL**	Converts a character string of CHAR, VARCHAR2, NCHAR, or NVARCHAR2 datatype to an INTERVAL DAY TO SECOND type.
**TO_LOB**	TO LOB. Converts a LONG to a LOB as part of an **insert as select**.
**TO_MULTI_BYTE**	TO MULTI_BYTE. Converts the single-byte characters in a character string to multibyte characters.
**TO_NCHAR**	TO NCHAR. Converts a character string, NUMBER, or DATE from the database character set to the national character set.
**TO_NCLOB**	TO NCLOB. Converts CLOB values in a LOB column or other character strings to NCLOB values.
**TO_NUMBER**	TO NUMBER. Converts a CHAR or VARCHAR2 to a number.
**TO_SINGLE_BYTE**	TO SINGLE BYTE. Converts the multibyte characters in a CHAR or VARCHAR2 to single bytes.
**TO_YMINTERVAL**	Converts a character string of CHAR, VARCHAR2, NCHAR, or NVARCHAR2 datatype to an INTERVAL YEAR TO MONTH type.
**TRANSLATE**	TRANSLATEs characters in a string into different characters.
**UNISTR**	Converts a string into unicode in the database unicode character set.

# CONVERT

**SEE ALSO** CONVERSION FUNCTIONS

**FORMAT**

```
CONVERT(string, [destination_set, [source_set]])
```

**DESCRIPTION** **CONVERT**s the characters in *string* from one standard bit representation to another, such as from US7ASCII (the default if either set isn't entered) to WE8DEC. This is typically

done when data entered into a column on one computer contains characters that can't be properly displayed or printed on another computer. **CONVERT** allows a reasonable translation of one to the other in most cases. The most common sets include:

F7DEC	DEC's 7-bit ASCII set for France
US7ASCII	Standard US 7-bit ASCII set
WE8DEC	DEC's 8-bit ASCII set for Western Europe
WE8HP	HP's 8-bit ASCII set for Western Europe
WE8ISO8859P1	ISO 8859-1 Western Europe 8-bit character set
WE8EBCDIC500	IBM West European EBCDIC Code Page 500
WE8PC850	IBM PC Code Page 850

# COPY

**SEE ALSO**     **CREATE DATABASE LINK**, Chapter 22

**FORMAT**

```
COPY [FROM user/password@database]
 [TO user/password@database]
 {APPEND | CREATE | INSERT | REPLACE}
 table [(column [,column]...)]
 USING query
```

**DESCRIPTION**     **COPY** copies **FROM** a table **TO** a table in another computer using Oracle Net. **FROM** is the user name, password, and database of the source table, and **TO** is the destination table. Either **FROM** or **TO** may be omitted, in which case the user's default database will be used for the missing clause. The source and destination databases must not be the same, so only one of the **from** and **to** clauses may be absent.

APPEND adds to the destination table; if the table does not exist, it is created. **CREATE** requires that the destination table be created; if it already exists, a 'table already exists' error occurs. **INSERT** adds to the destination table; if the table does not exist, a 'table does not exist' error occurs. **REPLACE** drops the data in the destination table and replaces it with the data from the source table; if the table does not exist, it is created.

*table* is the name of the destination table. *column*, is the name(s) of the column(s) in the destination table. If named, the number of columns must be the same as in the query. If no columns are named, the copied columns will have the same names in the destination table as they had in the source table. *query* identifies the source table and determines which rows and columns will be copied from it.

**SET LONG** (*see* **SET**) determines the length of a long field that can be copied. Long columns with data longer than the value of LONG will be truncated. **SET COPYCOMMIT** determines how many sets of rows get copied before a commit. **SET ARRAYSIZE** determines how many rows are in a set.

**EXAMPLE**     This example copies bookshelf checkout from the EDMESTON database to the database the local SQL*PLUS user is connected to. The table LOCAL_CHECKOUT is created by the copy. The columns may be renamed at the destination. Note the use of the dash (-) at the end of each line. This is required. The command does not end with a semicolon (since it is a SQL*Plus command, not a SQL command). *See* the **SET** command for options related to the **COPY** command.

```
copy from PRACTICE/PRACTICE@EDMESTON -
create LOCAL_CHECKOUT (Borrower, Title) -
```

```
using select Name, Title -
 from BOOKSHELF_CHECKOUT
```

# COPYCOMMIT (SQL*PLUS)

*See* **SET**.

# COPYTYPECHECK (SQL*PLUS)

*See* **SET**.

# CORR

**SEE ALSO**    GROUP FUNCTIONS

**FORMAT**

```
CORR (expr1 , expr2) [OVER (analytic_clause)]
```

**DESCRIPTION**    **CORR** returns the coefficient of correlation of a set of number pairs. Both *expr1* and *expr2* are number expressions. Oracle applies the function to the set of (*expr1* , *expr2*) after eliminating the pairs for which either *expr1* or *expr2* is **NULL**. Then Oracle makes the following computation:

```
COVAR_POP(expr1, expr2) / (STDDEV_POP(expr1) * STDDEV_POP(expr2))
```

The function returns a value of type NUMBER. If the function is applied to an empty set, it returns **NULL**.

# CORRELATED QUERY

A correlated query is a subquery that is executed repeatedly, once for each value of a candidate row selected by the main query. The outcome of each execution of the subquery depends on the values of one or more fields in the candidate row; that is, the subquery is correlated with the main query. *See* Chapter 12.

# COS

**SEE ALSO**    ACOS, ASIN, ATAN, ATAN2, COSH, EXP, LN, LOG, SIN, SINH, TAN, TANH

**FORMAT**

```
COS(value)
```

**DESCRIPTION**    **COS** returns the cosine of a value, an angle expressed in radians. You can convert a degree angle into radians by multiplying it by pi/180.

# COSH

**SEE ALSO**    ACOS, ASIN, ATAN, ATAN2, COS, EXP, LN, LOG, SIN, SINH, TAN, TANH

**FORMAT**

```
COSH(value)
```

**DESCRIPTION**    **COSH** returns the hyperbolic cosine of a *value*.

# COUNT

**SEE ALSO**    GROUP FUNCTIONS, Chapter 8, Chapter 11

**FORMAT**

COUNT ( { * | [ DISTINCT | ALL ] *expr* } ) [OVER ( *analytic_clause* )]

**DESCRIPTION**    **COUNT** counts the number of rows where *expression* is non-**NULL**, which are then returned by the query. With **DISTINCT**, **COUNT** counts only the distinct non-**NULL** rows. With **\***, it counts all rows, whether **NULL** or not.

# COVAR_POP

**SEE ALSO**    GROUP FUNCTIONS

**FORMAT**

COVAR_POP ( *expr1* , *expr2* ) [OVER ( *analytic_clause* )]

**DESCRIPTION**    **COVAR_POP** returns the population covariance of a set of number pairs. You can use it as an aggregate or analytic function.

Both *expr1* and *expr2* are number expressions. Oracle applies the function to the set of (*expr1* , *expr2*) pairs after eliminating all pairs for which either *expr1* or *expr2* is **NULL**. Then Oracle makes the following computation:

(SUM(*expr1* * *expr2*) - SUM(*expr2*) * SUM(*expr1*) / n) / n

where *n* is the number of (*expr1* , *expr2*) pairs where neither *expr1* nor *expr2* is **NULL**.

# COVAR_SAMP

**SEE ALSO**    GROUP FUNCTIONS

**FORMAT**

COVAR_POP ( *expr1* , *expr2* ) [OVER ( *analytic_clause* )]

**DESCRIPTION**    **COVAR_SAMP** returns the sample covariance of a set of number pairs. You can use it as an aggregate or analytic function.

Both *expr1* and *expr2* are number expressions. Oracle applies the function to the set of (*expr1* , *expr2*) pairs after eliminating all pairs for which either *expr1* or *expr2* is **NULL**. Then Oracle makes the following computation:

(SUM(*expr1* * *expr2*) - SUM(*expr1*) * SUM(*expr2*) / n) / (n-1)

where *n* is the number of (*expr1* , *expr2*) pairs where neither *expr1* nor *expr2* is **NULL**.

# CREATE CLUSTER

**SEE ALSO**    **CREATE INDEX**, **CREATE TABLE**, Chapter 20

**FORMAT**

**create_cluster::=**

**physical_attributes_clause::=**

**parallel_clause::=**

**DESCRIPTION**    **CREATE CLUSTER** creates a cluster for one or more tables. Tables are added to the cluster using **CREATE TABLE** with the **cluster** clause. **CREATE CLUSTER** requires at least one cluster column from each of the tables. These must have the same datatype and size, but are not required to have the same name. For the tables in a cluster, rows with the same cluster column values are kept together on disk in the same area, the same logical block(s). This can improve performance when the cluster columns are the columns by which the tables are usually joined.

   Each distinct value in each cluster column is stored only once, regardless of whether it occurs once or many times in the tables and rows. This typically can reduce the amount of disk space needed to store the tables, but each table continues to appear as if it contained all of its own data. Tables with LONG columns cannot be clustered.

*cluster* is the name created for the cluster. *column* and *datatype* follow the method of **CREATE TABLE**, except that **NULL** and **NOT NULL** cannot be specified. However, in the actual **CREATE TABLE** statement, at least one cluster column in a cluster must be **NOT NULL**. **SIZE** sets the size in bytes for a logical block (not a physical block). **SPACE** is the cluster's initial disk allocation, as used in **CREATE TABLE**.

**SIZE** should be the average amount of space needed to store all the rows from all the clustered tables that are associated with a single cluster key. A small **SIZE** value may increase the time needed to access tables in the cluster, but can reduce disk space usage. **SIZE** should be a proper divisor of the physical block size. If not, Oracle will use the next larger divisor. If **SIZE** exceeds the physical block size, Oracle will use the physical block size instead.

By default, the cluster is indexed, and you must create an index on the cluster key before putting any data in the cluster. If you specify the hash cluster form, however, you don't need to (and can't) create an index on the cluster key. Instead, Oracle uses a hash function to store the rows of the table.

You can create your own hash value as a column of the table and use that for hashing with the **HASH IS** clause to tell Oracle to use that column as the hash value. Otherwise, Oracle uses an internal hash function based on the columns of the cluster key. The **HASHKEYS** clause actually creates the hash cluster and specifies the number of hash values, rounded to the nearest prime number. The minimum value is 2.

See the *storage_clause* entry in the Alphabetical Reference for details on the common storage clause parameters.

# CREATE CONTEXT

**SEE ALSO**    **ALTER CONTEXT**

**FORMAT**

```
CREATE [OR REPLACE] CONTEXT NAMESPACE USING [SCHEMA .] PACKAGE
[INITIALIZED { EXTERNALLY | GLOBALLY }
| ACCESSED GLOBALLY] ;
```

**DESCRIPTION**    A context is a set of attributes used to secure an application. **CREATE CONTEXT** creates a namespace for a **context** and associates the namespace with the externally created package that sets the context. To create a context namespace, you must have CREATE ANY CONTEXT system privilege.

# CREATE CONTROLFILE

**SEE ALSO**    **ALTER DATABASE, CREATE DATABASE**

**FORMAT**

create_controlfile::=

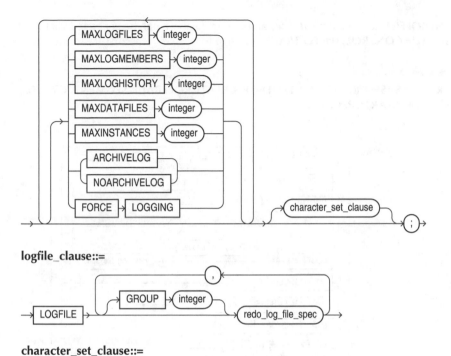

**logfile_clause::=**

**character_set_clause::=**

**DESCRIPTION**    The **CREATE CONTROLFILE** command re-creates a control file when you have either lost your current control file to media failure, you want to change the name of your database, or you want to change one of the options for the log file or a datafile. In general, this command should only be used by experienced database administrators.

**NOTE**
*Perform a full offline backup all of your database files before using this command.*

The **REUSE** option lets existing control files be reused rather than giving an error if any exist. The **SET** option changes the name of the database, specified by the database clause. The **LOGFILE** clause specifies the redo log file groups, all of which must exist. The **RESETLOGS** versus **NORESETLOGS** clause tells Oracle to reset the current logs or not. The **DATAFILE** line specifies the data files for the database, all of which must exist.

The **MAXLOGFILES** option specifies the maximum number of redo log file groups that can be created. The **MAXLOGMEMBERS** option specifies the number of copies for a redo log group. The **MAXLOGHISTORY** option specifies the number of archived redo log file groups for Real Application Clusters. The **MAXDATAFILES** option specifies the maximum number of data files that can ever be created for the database. The **MAXINSTANCES** option gives the maximum number of Oracle instances that can mount and open the database. The **ARCHIVELOG** and **NOARCHIVELOG** options turns archiving of the redo log files on and off, respectively.

The **CREATE CONTROLFILE** command needed for an existing database can be generated via the **ALTER DATABASE BACKUP CONTROLFILE TO TRACE** command.

# CREATE DATABASE

**SEE ALSO**    **ALTER DATABASE**, **CREATE CONTROLFILE**, **CREATE ROLLBACK SEGMENT**, **CREATE TABLESPACE**, **SHUTDOWN**, **STARTUP**, Chapter 40

**FORMAT**

**create_database::=**

**default_temp_tablespace::=**

**temp_tablespace_extent::=**

**undo_tablespace_clause::=**

**set_time_zone_clause::=**

**DESCRIPTION**     *database* is the database name, and must have eight characters or fewer. DB_NAME in init.ora contains the default database name. In general, this command should only be used by experienced database administrators.

**NOTE**
*Using this command in an existing database will erase the specified datafiles.*

*file_definition* specifies the LOGFILE and DATAFILE names and sizes:

```
'file' [SIZE integer [K | M] [REUSE]
```

**SIZE** is the number of bytes set aside for this file. Suffixing this with K multiplies the value by 1024; M multiplies it by 1048576. **REUSE** (without **SIZE**) means destroy the contents of any file by this name and associate the name with this database. **SIZE** with **REUSE** creates the file if it doesn't exist, and checks its size if it does. **CONTROLFILE REUSE** overwrites the existing control files defined by CONTROL_FILES parameter in the initialization parameter file.

**LOGFILE** names the files to be used as redo log files. If this parameter is not used, Oracle creates two by default. **MAXLOGFILES** overrides the LOG_FILES initialization parameter, and defines the maximum number of redo log files that can ever be created for this database. This number cannot be increased later except by re-creating the control file. Minimum is 2. A high number only makes a somewhat larger control file.

**DATAFILE** names the files to be used for the database itself. **MAXDATAFILES** sets the absolute upper limit for files that can be created for this database, and overrides the DB_FILES initialization parameter. A high number only makes a somewhat larger control file.

When the **AUTOEXTEND** option is turned ON for a datafile, the datafile will dynamically extend as needed in increments of **NEXT** size, to a maximum of **MAXSIZE** (or UNLIMITED).

**MAXINSTANCES** overrides the INSTANCES parameter in init.ora and sets the maximum number of simultaneous instances that can mount and open this database.

**ARCHIVELOG** and **NOARCHIVELOG** define the way redo log files are used when the database is first created. **NOARCHIVELOG** is the default, and means that redo files will get reused without saving their contents elsewhere. This provides instance recovery but will not recover from a media failure, such as a disk crash. **ARCHIVELOG** forces redo files to be archived (usually to another disk or a tape), so that you can recover from a media failure. This mode also supports instance recovery. This parameter can be reset by **ALTER DATABASE**.

The **MAXLOGMEMBERS** option specifies the maximum number of copies of a redo log file group. The **MAXLOGHISTORY** option specifies the maximum number of archived redo log files, useful only for the Real Application Cluster when you are archiving log files. The **CHARACTER SET** option specifies the character set used to store data, which depends on the operating system.

For more automated handling of undo (rollback) segments, you can specify the **UNDO TABLESPACE** clause to allocate a tablespace specifically to hold undo data. The database must be started in Automatic Undo Management (AUM) mode.

You can use the **DEFAULT TEMPORARY TABLESPACE** clause to designate a non-SYSTEM tablespace as the default temporary tablespace for all new users created in the database.

## CREATE DATABASE LINK

**SEE ALSO**     **CREATE SYNONYM**, **SELECT**, Chapter 22
**FORMAT**

```
CREATE [SHARED] [PUBLIC] DATABASE LINK dblink
[CONNECT TO { CURRENT_USER | user IDENTIFIED BY password
[AUTHENTICATED BY user IDENTIFIED BY password] }
| AUTHENTICATED BY user IDENTIFIED BY password]
[USING 'connect_string'];
```

**DESCRIPTION**     *dblink* is the name given to the link. *connect_string* is the definition of the remote database that can be accessed through Oracle Net and defines the link between a local database and a username on a remote database. **PUBLIC** links can only be created by a user with the CREATE PUBLIC DATABASE LINK system privilege, but are then available to all users except those who have created a private link with the same name. If **PUBLIC** isn't specified, the link is only available to the user who executed the **CREATE DATABASE LINK** statement. *connect_string* is the Oracle Net service name for the remote database.

Remote tables can be accessed just like local tables, except that the table name must be suffixed by @*link* in the **from** clause of the **select** statement. Most systems set the maximum number of simultaneous links to four. The DBA can increase this number with the OPEN_LINKS parameter in init.ora.

Tree-structured queries are limited. They may not use the **PRIOR** operator except in the **connect by** clause. **START WITH** cannot contain a subquery. **CONNECT BY** and **START WITH** cannot use the function **USERENV**('ENTRYID'), or the pseudo-column RowNum.

To create a database link, you must have CREATE DATABASE LINK privilege in the local database, and the CREATE SESSION privilege in a remote database. To create a public database link, you must have CREATE PUBLIC DATABASE LINK system privilege.

If you use the **CONNECT TO CURRENT_USER** clause, the link will attempt to open a connection in the remote database using your current username and password. You will therefore need to coordinate any password changes you make between the local database and the remote database or database links may stop working.

If you use the shared server architecture, you can create **SHARED** database links that eliminate the need for many separate dedicated connections via links. When you create a **SHARED** link, you must supply a valid username and password in the remote database to use as an authentication for the connection.

**EXAMPLES**    The following defines a link named EDMESTON_BOOKS that connects to the Practice username in the EDMESTON database:

```
create database link EDMESTON_BOOKS
connect to Practice identified by Practice
 using 'EDMESTON';
```

You now can query Practice's tables like this:

```
select Title, Publisher
 from BOOKSHELF@EDMESTON_BOOKS;
```

A synonym could also be created to hide the remoteness of the tables:

```
create synonym BOOKSHELF for BOOKSHELF@EDMESTON_BOOKS;
```

# CREATE DIMENSION

**SEE ALSO**    **ALTER DIMENSION, DROP DIMENSION**

**FORMAT**

create_dimension::=

level_clause::=

hierarchy_clause::=

**join_clause::=**

**attribute_clause::=**

**DESCRIPTION**   **CREATE DIMENSION** creates hierarchies among related columns in tables, for use by the optimizer. The optimizer will use dimension values when determining whether a materialized view will return the same data as its base table. To create a dimension, you must have CREATE DIMENSION privilege; to create a dimension in another user's schema, you must have the CREATE ANY DIMENSION privilege.

**LEVEL** defines the level within the dimension. **HIERARCHY** defines the relationships among the levels. **ATTRIBUTE** assigns specific attributes to levels within the dimension. **JOIN_KEY** defines the join clauses between the levels.

**EXAMPLES**   For a table named COUNTRY, with columns Country and Continent, and a second table named CONTINENT, with a column named Continent:

```
create table CONTINENT (
 Continent VARCHAR2(30));

create table COUNTRY (
Country VARCHAR2(30) not null,
Continent VARCHAR2(30));

create dimension GEOGRAPHY
 level COUNTRY_ID is COUNTRY.Country
 level CONTINENT_ID is CONTINENT.Continent
 hierarchy COUNTRY_ROLLUP (
 COUNTRY_ID child of
 CONTINENT_ID
 join key COUNTRY.Continent references CONTINENT_ID);
```

# CREATE DIRECTORY
**SEE ALSO**   BFILE, Chapters 25 and 30
**FORMAT**

```
CREATE [OR REPLACE] DIRECTORY directory AS 'path_name';
```

**DESCRIPTION**   Within Oracle, a "directory" is an alias for an operating system directory. You must create a directory prior to accessing BFILE datatype values or external tables. See Chapter 25 for details on the creation and management of external tables.

# CREATE FUNCTION

**SEE ALSO**     **ALTER FUNCTION**, BLOCK STRUCTURE, **CREATE LIBRARY**, **CREATE PACKAGE**, **CREATE PROCEDURE**, DATA TYPES, **DROP FUNCTION**, Chapters 27, 29 and 36

**FORMAT**

create_function::=

invoker_rights_clause::=

parallel_enable_clause::=

streaming_clause::=

**call_spec::=**

**Java_declaration::=**

**C_declaration::=**

**DESCRIPTION**     *function* is the name of the function being defined. A function may have parameters, named arguments of a certain datatype, and every function returns a value of a certain datatype as specified by the RETURN clause. The PL/SQL block defines the behavior of the function as a series of declarations, PL/SQL program statements, and exceptions.

The IN qualifier means that you have to specify a value for the parameter when you call the function, but since you always have to do this for a function, the syntax is optional. In a procedure, you can have other kinds of parameters. The difference between a function and a procedure is that a function returns a value to the calling environment.

In order to create a function, you must have the CREATE PROCEDURE system privilege. To create a function in another user's account, you must have CREATE ANY PROCEDURE system privilege.

Your function can use C libraries that are stored outside of the database (see **CREATE LIBRARY**). If you use Java within your function, you can provide a Java declaration within the **LANGUAGE** clause. The *invoker_rights* clause lets you specify whether the function executes with the privileges of the function owner (the definer) or the current user (the invoker).

# CREATE INDEX
**SEE ALSO**     ANALYZE, **ALTER INDEX**, **DROP INDEX**, INTEGRITY CONSTRAINT, **STORAGE**, Chapters 18 and 20
**FORMAT**
**create_index::=**

**cluster_index_clause::=**

**table_index_clause::=**

**bitmap_join_index_clause::=**

**index_expr::=**

**index_attributes::=**

**physical_attributes_clause::=**

**logging_clause::=**

**key_compression::=**

**domain_index_clause::=**

**global_partitioned_index::=**

**global_partitioning_clause::=**

**local_partitioned_index::=**

**on_range_partitioned_table::=**

**on_list_partitioned_table::=**

**segment_attributes_clause::=**

**on_hash_partitioned_table::=**

**on_comp_partitioned_table::=**

**index_subpartition_clause::=**

**parallel_clause::=**

**DESCRIPTION**    *index* is a name you assign to this index. It's usually a good idea to make it reflect the table and columns being indexed. *table* and *column*(s) are the table and column(s) for which the index is to be created. A **UNIQUE** index guarantees that each indexed row is unique on the values of the index columns. You can use the unique constraint on the columns to automatically create unique indexes. Specifying multiple columns will create a composite index. **ASC** and **DESC** mean ascending and descending; descending indexes are supported as of Oracle8i. **CLUSTER** is the name of the cluster key that is indexed for a cluster. Clusters must have their keys indexed for their associated tables to be accessed. (*See* **CREATE TABLE** for a description of **INITRANS** and **MAXTRANS**.) The default for **INITRANS** for indexes is 2; **MAXTRANS** is 255. **PCTFREE** is the percentage of space to leave free in the index for new entries and updates. The minimum is zero.

TABLESPACE is the name of the tablespace to which this index is assigned. The physical attributes section contains subclauses that are described under **STORAGE**. **NOSORT** is an option whose primary value is in reducing the time to create an index if, and only if, the values in the column being indexed are already in ascending order. It doesn't harm anything if they later fall out of ascending order, but

**NOSORT** will only work if they are in order when the index is created. If the rows are not in order, **CREATE INDEX** will return an error message, will not damage anything, and will allow you to rerun it without the **NOSORT** option.

**PARALLEL**, along with **DEGREE** and **INSTANCES**, specifies the parallel characteristics of the index. **DEGREE** specifies the number of query servers to use to create the index; **INSTANCES** specifies how the index is to be split among instances of Real Application Clusters for parallel query processing. An integer *n* specifies that the index is to be split among the specified number of available instances.

In order to create an index, you must either own the indexed table, have INDEX privilege on the table, or have CREATE ANY INDEX system privilege. To create a function-based index, you must have the QUERY REWRITE privilege.

**BITMAP** creates a bitmap index, which can be useful for columns with few distinct values. The **PARTITION** clauses create indexes on partitioned tables.

**REVERSE** stores the bytes of the indexed value in reverse order. You cannot reverse a bitmap index.

**COMPRESS** saves storage space by compressing non-unique non-partitioned indexes. During data retrieval, the data will be displayed as if it were uncompressed. You can turn off index compression; re-create the index using the clause **NOCOMPRESS**.

# CREATE INDEXTYPE

**FORMAT**
create_indextype::=

**DESCRIPTION**    **CREATE INDEXTYPE** specifies the routines used by a domain index. To create an indextype, you must have the CREATE INDEXTYPE system privilege. To create an indextype in another user's schema, you must have CREATE ANY INDEXTYPE system privilege.

# CREATE JAVA

**SEE ALSO**    **ALTER JAVA**, **DROP JAVA**, Chapters 34, 35 and 36
**FORMAT**
create_java::=

**invoker_rights_clause::=**

**DESCRIPTION** **CREATE JAVA** creates a Java source, class, or resource. You must have the CREATE PROCEDURE system privilege or (to create the object in another user's schema) CREATE ANY PROCEDURE. To replace such a schema object in another user's schema, you must have ALTER ANY PROCEDURE system privilege.

The **JAVA SOURCE**, **JAVA CLASS**, and **JAVA RESOURCE** clauses load sources, classes, and resources.

The **AUTHID** lets you specify whether the function executes with the privileges of the function owner or the current user.

**EXAMPLE** The following command creates a Java source:

```
create java source named "Hello" as
 public class Hello (
 public static String hello() (
 return "Hello World";));
```

# CREATE LIBRARY

**SEE ALSO**     **CREATE FUNCTION, CREATE PACKAGE BODY, CREATE PROCEDURE,** Chapter 29
**FORMAT**

```
CREATE [OR REPLACE] LIBRARY [schema .] libname
{ IS | AS } 'filespec' [AGENT 'agent_dblink'];
```

**DESCRIPTION**     **CREATE LIBRARY** creates a library object, allowing you to reference an operating-system shared library, from which SQL and PL/SQL can call external 3GL functions and procedures. To use the procedures and functions stored in the library, you must have been granted EXECUTE privilege on the library. Specify the **AGENT** clause if you want external procedures to be run from a database link other than the server. Oracle will use the database link specified by *agent_dblink* to run external procedures. If you omit this clause, the default agent on the server (extproc) will run external procedures.

# CREATE MATERIALIZED VIEW

**SEE ALSO**     **ALTER MATERIALIZED VIEW, CREATE MATERIALIZED VIEW LOG, DROP MATERIALIZED VIEW, STORAGE,** Chapter 23
**FORMAT**
**create_materialized_view::=**

**materialized_view_props::=**

**prebuilt_table_clause::=**

**scoped_table_ref_constraint::=**

**index_org_table_clause::=**

**key_compression::=**

**index_org_overflow-clause::=**

**create_mv_refresh:=**

**segment_attributes_clause::=**

**physical_attributes_clause::=**

**logging_clause::=**

**data_segment_compression::=**

**column_properties::=**

**object_type_col_properties::=**

**substitutable_column_clause::=**

**nested_table_col_properties::=**

**varray_col_properties::=**

**LOB_storage_clause::=**

**LOB_parameters::=**

**LOB_partition_storage::=**

**parallel_clause::=**

**build_clause::=**

**DESCRIPTION**    The keyword **SNAPSHOT** is supported in place of **MATERIALIZED VIEW** for backward compatibility.

**CREATE MATERIALIZED VIEW** creates a materialized view, a table that holds the results of a query, usually on one or more tables, called master tables. The master tables may be in a local database or in a remote database. You can have the data refreshed at intervals using the **REFRESH** clause.

To enable a materialized view for query rewrite, you must have the QUERY REWRITE system privilege. If the materialized view is based on objects in other schemas, you must have the GLOBAL QUERY REWRITE privilege.

Materialized views cannot contain LONG columns or reference any objects owned by SYS.

A **FAST** refresh uses the materialized view log associated with the master table(s) to refresh the materialized view. A **COMPLETE** refresh reexecutes the query. A **FORCE** refresh lets Oracle make the choice between a **FAST** or a **COMPLETE** refresh. Oracle first refreshes the materialized view on the **START WITH** *date*. If you give a **NEXT** *date*, Oracle refreshes the materialized view at intervals specified by the difference between the **START WITH** and **NEXT** dates.

A simple materialized view selects data from a single master table using a simple query. A complex materialized view selects data using a **GROUP BY**, **CONNECT BY**, subquery, join, or set operation in the query. Oracle can do a **FAST** refresh only on simple materialized views that have materialized view logs.

Because of the local objects which materialized views create, the name of a materialized view should not exceed 19 characters in length. In order to create a materialized view in your schema, you must have the CREATE SNAPSHOT or CREATE MATERIALIZED VIEW system privilege. To create a materialized view in another user's schema, you must have the CREATE ANY SNAPSHOT or CREATE ANY MATERIALIZED VIEW system privilege.

**EXAMPLE**

```
create materialized view LOCAL_BOOKSHELF
storage (initial 100K next 100K pctincrease 0)
tablespace USERS
refresh force
start with SysDate next SysDate+7
with primary key
```

```
as
select * from BOOKSHELF@REMOTE_CONNECT;
```

# CREATE MATERIALIZED VIEW LOG

**SEE ALSO** **ALTER MATERIALIZED VIEW LOG**, **CREATE MATERIALIZED VIEW**, **DROP MATERIALIZED VIEW LOG**, **STORAGE**, Chapter 23

**FORMAT**

**create_materialized_vw_log::=**

**physical_attributes_clause::=**

**logging_clause::=**

**parallel_clause::=**

**new_values_clause::=**

**DESCRIPTION**    The keyword **SNAPSHOT** is supported in place of **MATERIALIZED VIEW** for backward compatibility.

**CREATE MATERIALIZED VIEW LOG** creates a table associated with the master table of a materialized view that tracks changes to the master table's data. Oracle uses the materialized view log to **FAST** refresh the materialized views of a master table. The storage options specify the storage of the table. Oracle logs database changes only if there is a simple materialized view based on the master table.

You can have only one log for a given master table, and the log is stored in the same schema as the master table. In order to create a materialized view log on your own master table, you must have the CREATE TABLE system privilege. If the master table is in another user's schema, you must have the CREATE ANY TABLE and COMMENT ANY TABLE system privileges as well as SELECT privilege on the master table.

# CREATE OPERATOR

**FORMAT**

**create_operator::=**

**binding_clause::=**

**implementation_clause::=**

**context_clause::=**

**using_function_clause::=**

**DESCRIPTION**    **CREATE OPERATOR** creates a new operator and defines its bindings. You can reference operators in indextypes and in SQL statements. The operators, in turn, reference functions, packages, types, and other user-defined objects.

To create an operator, you must have EXECUTE privilege on the functions and operators referenced by the operator, and CREATE OPERATOR system privilege. If the operator is created in another user's schema, you must have CREATE ANY OPERATOR system privilege.

# CREATE OUTLINE

**SEE ALSO**    Chapter 38

**FORMAT**

```
CREATE [OR REPLACE] [PUBLIC | PRIVATE] OUTLINE [outline]
[FROM [PUBLIC | PRIVATE] source_outline]
[FOR CATEGORY category]
[ON statement];
```

**DESCRIPTION**    **CREATE OUTLINE** creates a stored outline, which is a set of hints used to create the execution plan of the associated query. Later executions of the query will use the same set of hints. You can group stored outlines into categories.

To create an operator, you must have CREATE ANY OUTLINE system privilege.

**EXAMPLE**

```
create outline TEST
 for category DEVELOPMENT
 on select AuthorName, COUNT(AuthorName) from BOOKSHELF_AUTHOR group by AuthorName;
```

## CREATE PACKAGE
**SEE ALSO**    **ALTER PACKAGE**, **CREATE FUNCTION**, **CREATE PACKAGE BODY**, **CREATE PROCEDURE**, CURSOR, **DROP PACKAGE**, EXCEPTION, RECORD, TABLE, VARIABLE DECLARATION, Chapter 29
**FORMAT**

```
CREATE [OR REPLACE] PACKAGE [schema .] package
[AUTHID { CURRENT_USER | DEFINER }]
{ IS | AS } pl/sql_package_spec;
```

**DESCRIPTION**    **CREATE PACKAGE** sets up the specification for a PL/SQL package, a group of public procedures, functions, exceptions, variables, constants, and cursors. Adding **OR REPLACE** replaces the package specification if it already exists, which invalidates the package and initiates a recompilation of the package body and any objects that depend on the package specification.

Packaging your procedures and functions lets them share data through variables, constants, and cursors. It gives you the ability to grant the whole collection at once as part of a role. Oracle accesses all the elements of a package more efficiently than it would if they were separate. If you change the package body, which Oracle stores separately from the package specification, you do not have to recompile anything that uses the package.

In order to create a package, you must have the CREATE PROCEDURE system privilege; to create a package in another user's account, you must have the CREATE ANY PROCEDURE system privilege.

The **AUTHID** clause lets you specify whether the package code executes with the privileges of the package owner or the user who runs the package's code.

## CREATE PACKAGE BODY
**SEE ALSO**    **ALTER PACKAGE**, **CREATE FUNCTION**, **CREATE LIBRARY**, **CREATE PACKAGE**, **CREATE PROCEDURE**, CURSOR, **DROP PACKAGE**, EXCEPTION, RECORD, TABLE, VARIABLE DECLARATION, Chapters 27 and 29
**FORMAT**

```
CREATE [OR REPLACE] PACKAGE BODY [schema .] package
{ IS | AS } pl/sql_package_body;
```

**DESCRIPTION**    **CREATE PACKAGE BODY** builds the body of a previously specified package created with **CREATE PACKAGE**. Adding **OR REPLACE** replaces the package body if it already exists. You must have the CREATE PROCEDURE system privilege to create a package body; to create a package body in another user's account, you must have CREATE ANY PROCEDURE system privilege.

## CREATE PFILE
**SEE ALSO**    **CREATE SPFILE**, init.ora
**FORMAT**

```
CREATE PFILE [= 'pfile_name'] FROM SPFILE [= 'spfile_name'];
```

**DESCRIPTION**    **CREATE PFILE** exports a binary server parameter file into a text-initialization parameter file (init.ora). Creating a text parameter file is a convenient way to get a listing of the current parameter settings being used by the database, and it lets you edit the file easily in a text editor and then convert it back into a server parameter file using the **CREATE SPFILE** statement. You can specify the name of both the source binary server parameter file and the target text parameter file.

**EXAMPLE**

```
create pfile from spfile;
```

# CREATE PROCEDURE

**SEE ALSO**    **ALTER PROCEDURE**, BLOCK STRUCTURE, **CREATE LIBRARY**, **CREATE FUNCTION**, **CREATE PACKAGE**, DATA TYPES, **DROP PROCEDURE**, Chapters 27, 29, and 36

**FORMAT**

create_procedure::=

invoker_rights_clause::=

call_spec::=

Java_declaration::=

C_declaration::=

**DESCRIPTION** **CREATE PROCEDURE** creates the specification and body of a procedure. A procedure may have parameters, named arguments of a certain datatype. The PL/SQL block defines the behavior of the procedure as a series of declarations, PL/SQL program statements, and exceptions.

The IN qualifier means that you have to specify a value for the argument when you call the procedure. The OUT qualifier means that the procedure passes a value back to the caller through this argument. The IN OUT qualifier combines the meaning of both IN and OUT-you specify a value, and the procedure replaces it with a value. If you don't have any qualifier, the argument defaults to IN. The difference between a function and a procedure is that a function returns a value to the calling environment in addition to any arguments that are OUT arguments.

The PL/SQL block can refer to programs in an external C library or to a Java call specification. The *invoker_rights* (**AUTHID**) clause lets you specify whether the procedure executes with the privileges of the function owner or the user calling the function.

# CREATE PROFILE

**SEE ALSO** **ALTER PROFILE, ALTER RESOURCE COST, ALTER SYSTEM, ALTER USER, CREATE USER, DROP PROFILE,** Chapter 19

**FORMAT**

**create_profile::=**

**resource_parameters::=**

**password_parameters::=**

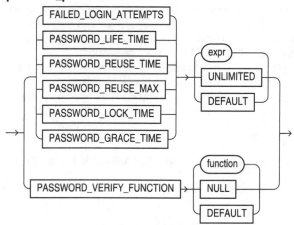

**DESCRIPTION**    **CREATE PROFILE** creates a set of limits on the use of database resources. When you associate the profile with a user with **CREATE** or **ALTER USER**, you can control what the user does via those limits. To use **CREATE PROFILE**, you must enable resource limits through the initialization parameter RESOURCE_LIMIT or through the **ALTER SYSTEM** command.

SESSIONS_PER_USER limits the user to *integer* concurrent SQL sessions. CPU_PER_SESSION limits the CPU time in hundredths of seconds. CPU_PER_CALL limits the CPU time for a parse, execute, or fetch call in hundredths of seconds. CONNECT_TIME limits elapsed time of a session in minutes. IDLE_TIME disconnects a user after this number of minutes; this does not apply while a query is running. LOGICAL_READS_PER_SESSION limits the number of blocks read per session; LOGICAL_READS_PER_CALL does the same thing for parse, execute, or fetch calls. PRIVATE_SGA limits the amount of space you can allocate in the SGA as private; the K and M options apply only to this limit. COMPOSITE_LIMIT limits the total resource cost for a session in service units based on a weighted sum of CPU, connect time, logical reads, and private SGA resources.

UNLIMITED means there is no limit on a particular resource. DEFAULT picks up the limit from the DEFAULT profile, which you can change through the **ALTER PROFILE** command.

If a user exceeds a limit, Oracle aborts and rolls back the transaction, then ends the session. You must have CREATE PROFILE system privilege in order to create a profile. You associate a profile to a user with the **ALTER USER** command.

# CREATE ROLE

**SEE ALSO**    **ALTER ROLE**, **ALTER USER**, **CREATE USER**, **DROP ROLE**, **GRANT**, **REVOKE**, **ROLE**, **SET ROLE**, Chapter 19

**FORMAT**

```
CREATE ROLE role
[NOT IDENTIFIED
| IDENTIFIED { BY password |
 USING [schema .] package | EXTERNALLY | GLOBALLY }];
```

**DESCRIPTION** With **CREATE ROLE**, you can create a named role or set of privileges. When you grant the role to a user, you grant him or her all the privileges of that role. You first create the role with **CREATE ROLE**, then grant privileges to the role using the **GRANT** command. When a user wants to access something that the role allows, he or she enables the role with **SET ROLE**. Alternatively, the role can be set as the user's DEFAULT role via the **ALTER USER** or **CREATE USER** command.

If you put password protection on the role, the user who wants to use the privileges must supply the password in the **SET ROLE** command to enable the role. The **USING** *package* clause lets you create an application role, which is a role that can be enabled only by applications using an authorized package. If you do not specify *schema*, Oracle assumes the package is in your own schema.

## CREATE ROLLBACK SEGMENT

**SEE ALSO** **ALTER ROLLBACK SEGMENT, CREATE DATABASE, CREATE TABLESPACE, DROP ROLLBACK SEGMENT, STORAGE**, Chapter 40
**FORMAT**

```
CREATE [PUBLIC] ROLLBACK SEGMENT rollback_segment
[{ TABLESPACE tablespace | storage_clause }
[TABLESPACE tablespace | storage_clause]...];
```

**DESCRIPTION** *rollback_segment* is a name assigned to this rollback segment. *tablespace* is the name of the tablespace to which this rollback segment is assigned. One tablespace may have multiple rollback segments.

*Storage_clause* contains subclauses that are described under **STORAGE**. If **PUBLIC** is used, this rollback segment can be used by any instance that requests it; otherwise it is available only to instances that named it in their initialization parameter files. *See* Chapter 40 for details concerning the use and management of rollback segments.

## CREATE SCHEMA

**SEE ALSO** **CREATE TABLE, CREATE VIEW, GRANT**
**FORMAT**

```
CREATE SCHEMA AUTHORIZATION schema
{ create_table_statement | create_view_statement | grant_statement }
[create_table_statement | create_view_statement | grant_statement]...;
```

**DESCRIPTION** The **CREATE SCHEMA** command creates a collection of tables, views, and privilege grants as a single transaction. The schema name is the same as your Oracle username. The **CREATE TABLE, CREATE VIEW**, and **GRANT** commands are the standard commands, and the order in which the commands appear is not important, even if there are internal dependencies.

## CREATE SEQUENCE

**SEE ALSO** **ALTER SEQUENCE, AUDIT, DROP SEQUENCE, GRANT, REVOKE, NEXTVAL** and **CURRVAL** under PSEUDO-COLUMNS, Chapter 20
**FORMAT**

```
CREATE SEQUENCE [schema .] sequence
[{ { INCREMENT BY | START WITH } integer
 | { MAXVALUE integer | NOMAXVALUE }
 | { MINVALUE integer | NOMINVALUE }
```

```
 | { CYCLE | NOCYCLE }
 | { CACHE integer | NOCACHE }
 | { ORDER | NOORDER }
 }
 [{ INCREMENT BY | START WITH } integer
 | { MAXVALUE integer | NOMAXVALUE }
 | { MINVALUE integer | NOMINVALUE }
 | { CYCLE | NOCYCLE }
 | { CACHE integer | NOCACHE }
 | { ORDER | NOORDER }]...];
```

**DESCRIPTION** *sequence* is the name given to the sequence. The default **INCREMENT BY** is 1. A positive number will increment the sequence number in an interval equal to the integer. A negative number will cause decrement (decrease the value of) the sequence in the same way. **START WITH** is the number with which the sequence will begin. The default **START WITH** is **MAXVALUE** for descending sequences and **MINVALUE** for ascending; use **START WITH** to override this default.

MINVALUE is the lowest number the sequence will generate. The default is 1 for ascending sequences. MAXVALUE is the highest number the sequence will generate. For descending sequence the default is -1. To allow sequences to progress without limitation, specify only **MINVALUE** for ascending and **MAXVALUE** for descending sequences. To stop creating sequence numbers and force an error when an attempt is made to get a new one, specify a **MAXVALUE** on an ascending sequence, or a **MINVALUE** on a descending sequence, plus **NOCYCLE**. To restart either type of sequence where its **MAXVALUE** or **MINVALUE** made it begin, specify **CYCLE**.

CACHE allows a preallocated set of sequence numbers to be kept in memory. The default is 20. The value set must be less than **MAXVALUE** minus **MINVALUE**.

ORDER guarantees that sequence numbers will be assigned to instances requesting them in the order the requests are received. This is only required in applications using Real Application Clusters.

To create a sequence in your own schema, you must have the CREATE SEQUENCE system privilege; to create a sequence in another user's schema, you must have the CREATE ANY SEQUENCE system privilege.

# CREATE SNAPSHOT

*See* CREATE MATERIALIZED VIEW

# CREATE SNAPSHOT LOG

*See* CREATE MATERIALIZED VIEW LOG

# CREATE SPFILE

**SEE ALSO** **CREATE PFILE,** init.ora

**FORMAT**

```
CREATE SPFILE [= 'spfile_name'] FROM PFILE [= 'pfile_name'];
```

**DESCRIPTION** **CREATE SPFILE** creates a server parameter file from a client-side text-based initialization parameter file. Server parameter files are binary files that exist only on the server and are called from client locations to start up the database. Server parameter files let you make persistent changes to individual parameters; parameter changes made via **ALTER SYSTEM** commands are retained across database shutdowns and startups even if no external parameter file is manually updated.

## CREATE SYNONYM

**SEE ALSO**    CREATE DATABASE LINK, **CREATE TABLE**, **CREATE VIEW**, Chapters 19 and 22

**FORMAT**

```
CREATE [PUBLIC] SYNONYM [schema .] synonym
 FOR [schema .] object [@ dblink];
```

**DESCRIPTION**    **CREATE SYNONYM** creates a synonym for a table, view, sequence, stored procedure, function, package, materialized view, java class object, or synonym, including those on a remote database. **PUBLIC** makes the synonym available to all users, but can only be created by a DBA. Without **PUBLIC**, users must prefix the synonym with your user name. *synonym* is the synonym name. *user.table* is the name of the table, view, or synonym to which the synonym refers. You can have a synonym of synonym. @*database_link* is a database link to a remote database. The synonym refers to a table in the remote database as specified by the database link.

**EXAMPLE**

```
create synonym LOCAL_BOOKSHELF for BOOKSHELF@REMOTE_CONNECT;
```

## CREATE TABLE

**SEE ALSO**    ALTER TABLE, **CREATE CLUSTER**, **CREATE INDEX**, **CREATE TABLESPACE**, **CREATE TYPE**, DATA TYPES, **DROP TABLE**, INTEGRITY CONSTRAINT, **OBJECT NAMES**, **STORAGE**, Chapters 3, 18, 20, 25, 30, 31, and 33

**FORMAT**

**create_table::=**

**relational_table::=**

**object_table::=**

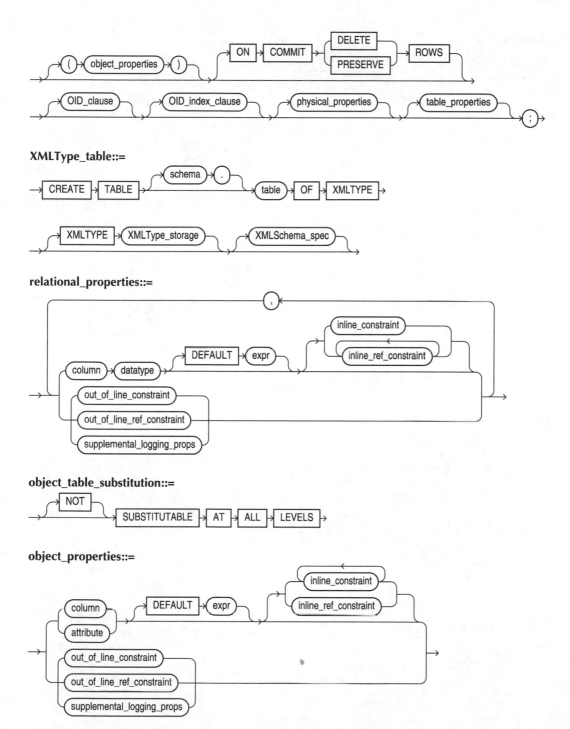

**XMLType_table::=**

**relational_properties::=**

**object_table_substitution::=**

**object_properties::=**

**OID_clause::=**

**OID_index_clause::=**

**physical_properties::=**

**segment_attributes_clause::=**

**physical_attributes_clause::=**

**data_segment_compression::=**

**table_properties::=**

**column_properties::=**

**object_type_col_properties::=**

**substitutable_column_clause::=**

**nested_table_col_properties::=**

**varray_col_properties::=**

**LOB_storage_clause::=**

**LOB_parameters::=**

**logging_clause::=**

**LOB_partition_storage::=**

**XMLType_column_properties::=**

**XMLType_storage::=**

**XMLSchema_spec::=**

**row_movement_clause::=**

**index_org_table_clause::=**

**mapping_table_clause::=**

**key_compression::=**

**index_org_overflow_clause::=**

**supplemental_logging_props::=**

**external_table_clause::=**

**external_data_properties::=**

**table_partitioning_clauses::=**

**range_partitioning::=**

**hash_partitioning::=**

**list_partitioning::=**

**composite_partitioning::=**

**subpartition_by_hash::=**

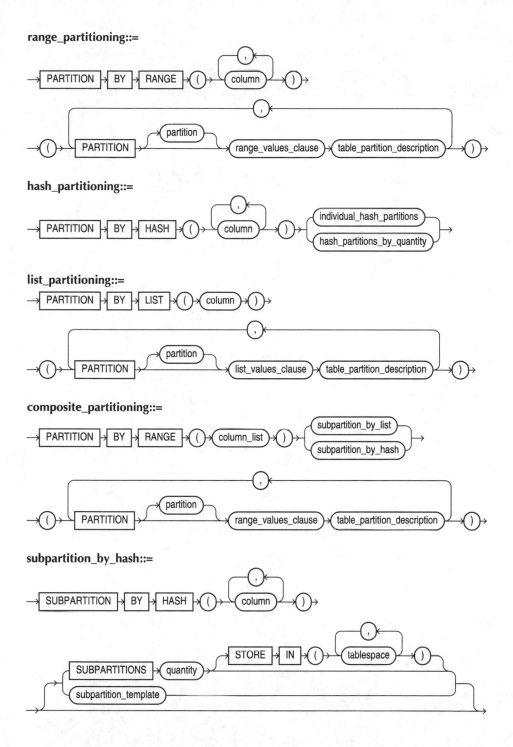

**individual_hash_partitions::=**

**hash_partitions_by_quantity::=**

**subpartition_by_list::=**

**subpartition_template::=**

**range_values_clause::=**

**list_values_clause::=**

**table_partition_description::=**

**partition_level_subpartition::=**

**subpartition_spec::=**

**partitioning_storage_clause::=**

**parallel_clause::=**

**enable_disable_clause::=**

**using_index_clause::=**

**global_partitioned_index::=**

**global_partitioning_index::=**

**DESCRIPTION**    *user* is the table owner. If the table owner is absent, *user* defaults to the user issuing this command. *table* is the table name, and follows Oracle naming conventions.

*column* is the name of a column, and *datatype* is one of the Oracle-supplied datatypes (*see* DATA TYPES) or a user-defined type (see CREATE TYPE). **DEFAULT** specifies a value to be assigned to the

column if a row is inserted without a value for this column. The value can be a simple literal or the result of an expression. The expression, however, cannot include a reference to a column, to Level, or to RowNum.

For an existing abstract datatype, you can create an object table. The following example creates an object table called ANIMAL, based on the ANIMAL_TY datatype:

```
create table ANIMAL of ANIMAL_TY;
```

*See* Chapter 33 for details on the usage of object tables.

*See* INTEGRITY CONSTRAINT for a full description of the column and table constraints.

**CLUSTER** includes this table in the named cluster. The table columns listed must correspond in order and datatype to the cluster's cluster columns. The names need not be the same as the corresponding cluster's columns, although matching names can help the user to understand what is being done.

**INITRANS** specifies the initial number of transactions that can update a data block concurrently (**select**s are not counted). **INITRANS** ranges from 1 to 255. 1 is the default. Every transaction takes space (23 bytes in most systems) in the data block itself until the transaction is completed. When more than the **INITRANS** number of transactions are created for the block, space is automatically allocated for them, up to **MAXTRANS**.

**MAXTRANS** specifies the maximum number of transactions that can update a data block concurrently (**select**s are not counted). **MAXTRANS** ranges from 1 to 255. 255 is the default. Every transaction takes space (23 bytes in most systems) in the data block itself until the transaction is completed. Transactions queuing up for execution will occupy more and more free space in the block, although usually there is more free space than is needed for all concurrent transactions.

Whenever Oracle inserts a row into a table, it first looks to see how much space is available in the current block (the size of a block is operating system dependent-see the *Oracle Installation and User's Guide* for your system). If the size of the row will leave less than **PCTFREE** percent in the block, it puts the row in a newly allocated block instead. Default is 10; 0 is the minimum.

**PCTUSED** defaults to 40. This is the percentage minimum of available space in a block that will make it a candidate for insertion of new rows. Oracle tracks how much space in a block has been made available by deletions. If it falls below **PCTUSED**, Oracle makes the block available for insertions.

**STORAGE** contains subclauses that are described under STORAGE. **TABLESPACE** is the name of the tablespace to which this table is assigned.

The **ENABLE** and **DISABLE** clauses enable or disable constraints.

**PARALLEL**, along with **DEGREE** and **INSTANCES**, specifies the parallel characteristics of the table. **DEGREE** specifies the number of query servers to use; **INSTANCES** specifies how the table is to be split among instances of Real Application Clusters for parallel query processing. An integer *n* specifies that the table is to be split among the specified number of available instances.

The **PARTITION** clauses control how the table's data is partitioned—by range, by hash, or by a composite of multiple partition methods. *See* Chapter 18 for details on partitioning.

A **TEMPORARY** table contains data that is only visible to the session that creates it. If a temporary table is defined as **GLOBAL**, its definition may be seen by all users. Temporary tables may not be partitioned and cannot support many standard table features (such as varying array datatypes, LOB datatypes, and index organization). For example, the following command creates a table whose rows will be deleted at the end of the current session

```
create global temporary table WORK_SCHEDULE (
 StartDate DATE,
 EndDate DATE,
 PayRate NUMBER)
 on commit preserve rows;
```

The **AS** clause creates the rows of the new table through the returned query rows. The columns and types of the query must match those defined in the **CREATE TABLE**. The query used in the AS clause may not contain any LONG datatype columns. You can turn off logging during the **create table ... as select** operation via the **NOLOGGING** keyword. This option disables the redo log entries that would normally be written during the population of the new table, thus improving performance while impacting your ability to recover that data if an instance failure occurs prior to the next backup.

The **LOB** clause specifies the out-of-line data storage used for internally-stored LOB (BLOB, CLOB, and NCLOB) data. See Chapter 32 for details on LOB management.

The object table definition section applies to object tables, in which each row has an object ID (OID). *See* Chapter 33.

# CREATE TABLESPACE
**SEE ALSO**   **ALTER TABLESPACE, DROP TABLESPACE**, Chapters 20 and 40
**FORMAT**
create_tablespace::=

**logging_clause::=**

**data_segment_compression::=**

**extent_management_clause::=**

**segment_management_clause::=**

**DESCRIPTION**    *tablespace* is the name of the tablespace, and follows Oracle naming conventions. The DATAFILE is a file or series of files described according to a *file_definition*, which specifies the file names and sizes:

```
'file' [SIZE integer [K | M] [REUSE]
```

The file format is operating-system specific. **SIZE** is the number of bytes set aside for this file. Suffixing this with K multiplies the value by 1024; M multiplies it by 1048576. **DEFAULT STORAGE** defines the default storage for all objects created in this tablespace, unless those defaults are overridden in the **CREATE TABLE** command itself. **ONLINE**, the default, indicates that this tablespace will become available to users as soon as it is created. **OFFLINE** prevents access to it until **ALTER TABLESPACE** changes it to **ONLINE**. DBA_TABLESPACES gives the status of all the tablespaces.

**SIZE** and **REUSE** together tell Oracle to reuse the file if it already exists (anything it contains will be wiped out), or create it if it doesn't already exist. **SIZE** without **REUSE** will create a file that does not exist, but return an error if it does. Without **SIZE**, the file must already exist.

The **MINIMUM EXTENT** size parameter specifies the minimum size for extents within the tablespace. The default is operating system and database block size-specific.

When turned ON, the **AUTOEXTEND** option will dynamically extend a datafile as needed in increments of **NEXT** size, to a maximum of **MAXSIZE** (or UNLIMITED). If a tablespace will only be used for temporary segments created during query processing, you can create it as a **TEMPORARY** tablespace. If the tablespace will contain permanent objects (such as tables), then you should use the default setting of **PERMANENT**.

**EXTENT MANAGEMENT** controls the manner in which the extent management data for a tablespace is recorded. By default, extent usage is **LOCAL**—the extent location information is stored in a bitmap within the tablespace's datafiles.

# CREATE TEMPORARY TABLESPACE

**SEE ALSO**    **CREATE TABLE, CREATE TABLESPACE**

**FORMAT**

create_temporarary_tablespace::=

temp_tablespace_extent::=

**DESCRIPTION**    **CREATE TEMPORARY TABLESPACE** creates a tablespace that will be used to store temporary tables. The temporary tables stored in this tablespace are not the temporary segments created during sort operations; rather, they are tables created via the **create temporary table** command. *See* **CREATE TABLESPACE** for the tablespace parameters, and **CREATE TABLE** for the syntax for temporary tables.

# CREATE TRIGGER

**SEE ALSO**    **ALTER TABLE, ALTER TRIGGER**, BLOCK STRUCTURE, **DROP TRIGGER**, Chapters 28 and 30

**FORMAT**

create_trigger::=

**dml_event_clause::=**

**referencing_clause::=**

**DESCRIPTION**    **CREATE TRIGGER** creates and enables a database trigger, a stored procedure block associated with a table, specified in the **on** clause, that Oracle automatically executes when the specified SQL statement executes against the table. You can use triggers to enforce complex constraints and to propagate changes throughout the database instead of doing this in your applications. That way you implement the triggered code once instead of having to do it in every application.

The main clause of the **CREATE TRIGGER** command specifies the SQL operation that triggers the block (such as **delete**, **insert**, or **update**) and when the trigger fires (**BEFORE**, **AFTER**, or **INSTEAD OF** executing the triggering operation). If you specify an **OF** clause on an **UPDATE** trigger, the trigger fires only when you update one or more of the specified columns. Note that you can also create triggers that fire when DDL events occur (including **create**, **alter**, and **drop**) and when specific database events occur (logons, logoffs, database startups, shutdowns, and server errors).

The **REFERENCING** clause specifies a correlation name for the table for the OLD and NEW versions of the table. This lets you use the name when referring to columns to avoid confusion, particularly when the table name is OLD or NEW. The default names are OLD and NEW.

The **FOR EACH ROW** clause specifies the trigger to be a row trigger, a trigger fired once for each row affected by the triggering operation. The **WHEN** clause restricts the execution of the trigger to happen only when the *condition* is met. This condition is a SQL condition, not a PL/SQL condition.

You can disable and enable triggers through the **ALTER TRIGGER** and **ALTER TABLE** commands. If a trigger is disabled, Oracle does not fire the trigger when a potentially triggering operation occurs. The **CREATE TRIGGER** command automatically enables the trigger.

To create a trigger on a table you own, you must have the CREATE TRIGGER system privilege. To create a trigger on another user's table, you must have the CREATE ANY TRIGGER system privilege. The user must have been directly granted all privileges necessary to execute the stored procedure.

# CREATE TYPE

**SEE ALSO**    **CREATE TABLE**, **CREATE TYPE BODY**, Chapters 4, 30, and 31

**FORMAT**

**create_type::=**

**create_incomplete_type::=**

**create_object_type::=**

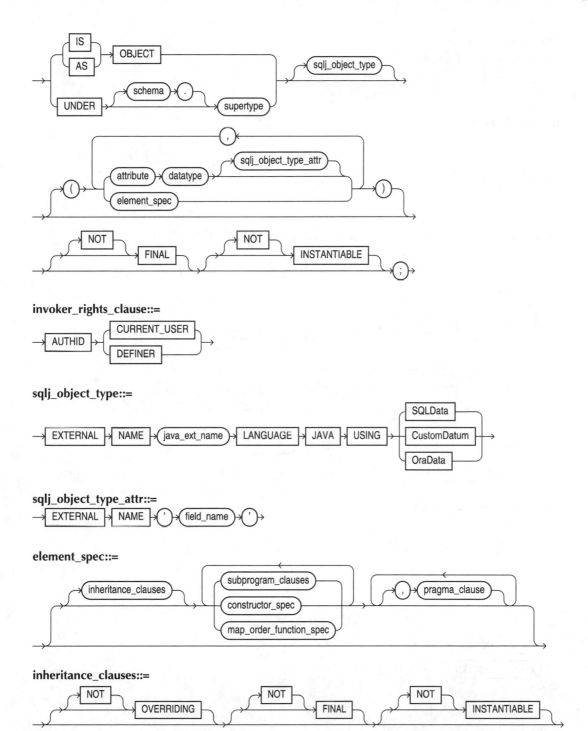

**invoker_rights_clause::=**

**sqlj_object_type::=**

**sqlj_object_type_attr::=**

**element_spec::=**

**inheritance_clauses::=**

**subprogram_clauses::=**

**procedure_spec::=**

**function_spec::=**

**constructor_spec::=**

**map_order_function_spec::=**

**return_clause::=**

**sqlj_object_type_sig::=**

**pragma_clause::=**

**call_spec::=**

**Java_declaration::=**

**C_declaration::=**

**create_varray_type::=**

**create_nested_table_type::=**

**DESCRIPTION**    **CREATE TYPE** creates an abstract datatype, named varying array (VARRAY), nested table type, or an incomplete object type. To create or replace a type, you must have CREATE TYPE privilege. To create a type in another user's schema, you must have CREATE ANY TYPE system privileges.

When creating an abstract datatype, you can base it on Oracle's provided datatypes (such as DATE and NUMBER) and on previously defined abstract datatypes.

An "incomplete" type has a name but no attributes or methods. However, it can be referenced by other object types, and so can be used to define object types that refer to each other. If you have two types that refer to each other, you must create one as an incomplete type, then create the second, then re-create the first with its proper definition.

If you plan to create methods for the type, you need to declare the method names in the type specification. When naming the methods, restrict their ability to modify the database via the **PRAGMA RESTRICT_REFERENCES** clause. The available options are shown in the syntax diagram. At a minimum, your methods should use the WNDS restriction. *See* Chapter 30. For details on VARRAYs and nested tables, see Chapter 31.

**EXAMPLES**    Creating a type that will have associated methods:

```
create or replace type ANIMAL_TY as object
(Breed VARCHAR2(25),
 Name VARCHAR2(25),
 BirthDate DATE,
member function AGE (BirthDate IN DATE) return NUMBER,
PRAGMA RESTRICT_REFERENCES(AGE, WNDS));
```

Creating a varying array:

```
create or replace type TOOLS_VA as varray(5) of VARCHAR2(25);
```

Creating a type with no methods:

```
create type ADDRESS_TY as object
(Street VARCHAR2(50),
 City VARCHAR2(25),
 State CHAR(2),
 Zip NUMBER);
```

Creating a type that uses another type:

```
create type PERSON_TY as object
(Name VARCHAR2(25),
 Address ADDRESS_TY);
```

# CREATE TYPE BODY

**SEE ALSO**    **CREATE FUNCTION, CREATE PROCEDURE, CREATE TYPE**, Chapters 4, 25, 29, 30, and 31

**FORMAT**

create_type_body::=

procedure_declaration::=

function_declaration::=

constructor_declaration::=

**call_spec::=**

**Java_declaration::=**

**C_declaration::=**

**DESCRIPTION**    **CREATE TYPE BODY** specifies the methods to be applied to types created via **CREATE TYPE**. You must have the CREATE TYPE privilege in order to create type bodies. To create a type body in another user's schema, you must have the CREATE ANY TYPE privilege.

*See* Chapter 30 for examples of methods.

**EXAMPLE**

```
create or replace type body ANIMAL_TY as
member function Age (BirthDate DATE) return NUMBER is
 begin
 RETURN ROUND(SysDate - BirthDate);
 end;
end;
```

# CREATE USER

**SEE ALSO**    ALTER USER, CREATE PROFILE, CREATE ROLE, CREATE TABLESPACE, GRANT, Chapter 19

**FORMAT**

```
CREATE USER user IDENTIFIED
{ BY password | EXTERNALLY | GLOBALLY AS 'external_name' }
[{ DEFAULT TABLESPACE tablespace
 | TEMPORARY TABLESPACE tablespace
 | QUOTA { integer [K | M] | UNLIMITED } ON tablespace
 [QUOTA { integer [K | M] | UNLIMITED } ON tablespace]...
 | PROFILE profile
 | PASSWORD EXPIRE
 | ACCOUNT { LOCK | UNLOCK } }
 [DEFAULT TABLESPACE tablespace
 | TEMPORARY TABLESPACE tablespace
 | QUOTA { integer [K | M] | UNLIMITED } ON tablespace
 [QUOTA { integer [K | M] | UNLIMITED } ON tablespace]...
 | PROFILE profile
```

```
| PASSWORD EXPIRE
| ACCOUNT { LOCK | UNLOCK }]...] ;
```

**DESCRIPTION**   **CREATE USER** creates a user account that lets you log into the database with a certain set of privileges and storage settings. If you specify a password, you must supply that password to log on; if you specify the **EXTERNALLY** option, access is verified through operating system security. External verification uses the OS_AUTHENT_PREFIX initialization parameter to prefix the operating system user id, so the user name you specify in **CREATE USER** should contain that prefix (usually, OPS$).

The **DEFAULT TABLESPACE** is the tablespace in which the user creates objects. The **TEMPORARY TABLESPACE** is the tablespace in which temporary objects are created for the user's operations.

You can put a **QUOTA** on either of these tablespaces that limits the amount of space, in bytes (kilobytes or megabytes for K or M options, respectively), that a user can allocate. The **profile** clause assigns a named profile to the user to limit usage of database resources. Oracle assigns the DEFAULT profile to the user if you don't specify a profile.

When you first create a user, the user has no privileges. You must use the **GRANT** command to grant roles and privileges to the user. You should usually grant **CREATE SESSION** as a minimal privilege.

For information on password expirations and account locking, see **CREATE PROFILE** and Chapter 19.

# CREATE VIEW

**SEE ALSO**   **CREATE SYNONYM, CREATE TABLE, DROP VIEW, RENAME**, INTEGRITY CONSTRAINT, Chapters 18 and 30

**FORMAT**

**create_view::=**

**object_view_clause::=**

**XMLType_view_clause::=**

**XMLSchema_spec::=**

**subquery_restriction_clause::=**

**DESCRIPTION**    **CREATE VIEW** defines a view named *view*. *user* is the name of the user for whom the view is created. The **OR REPLACE** option re-creates the view if it already exists. The **FORCE** option creates the view regardless of whether the tables to which the view refers exist or whether the user has privileges on them. The user still can't execute the view, but he or she can create it. The **NO FORCE** option creates the view only if the base tables exist and the user has privileges on them.

If an alias is specified, the view uses the alias as the name of the corresponding column in the query. If an alias is not specified, the view inherits the column name from the query; in this case each column in a query must have a unique name, one that follows normal Oracle naming conventions. It cannot be an expression. An alias in the query itself also can serve to rename the column.

**AS** *query* identifies the columns of tables and other views that are to appear in this view. Its **where** clause will determine which rows are to be retrieved.

**WITH CHECK OPTION** restricts **insert**s and **update**s performed through the view to prevent them from creating rows that the view cannot itself select, based on the **where** clause of the **CREATE VIEW** statement. **WITH CHECK OPTION** may be used in a view that is based on another view; however, if the underlying view also has a **WITH CHECK OPTION**, it is ignored.

*constraint* is a name given to the **CHECK OPTION**. *constraint* is an optional name assigned to this constraint. Without it, Oracle will assign a name in the form **SYS_C***n*, where *n* is an integer. An Oracle-assigned name will usually change during an import, while a user-assigned name will not change.

**update** and **delete** will work on rows in a view if the view is based on a single table and its query does not contain the **group by** clause, the **distinct** clause, group functions, or references to the pseudo-column RowNum. You may **update** views containing other pseudo-columns or expressions, as long as they are not referenced in the **update**.

You may **insert** rows through a view if the view is based on a single table and if its query does not contain the **group by** clause, the **distinct** clause, group functions, references to any pseudo-columns, or any expressions; rows may also be inserted through a view with more than one table by using INSTEAD OF triggers. If the view is created **WITH READ ONLY**, then only selects are allowed against the view; no data manipulation is allowed.

You can create object views to superimpose abstract datatypes on existing relational tables. *See* Chapter 30.

In order to create a view, you must have the CREATE VIEW system privilege. To create a view in another user's schema, you must have the CREATE ANY VIEW system privilege.

## CREATING A DATABASE

Creating a database is the process of making a database ready for initial use. It includes clearing the database files and loading initial database tables required by the RDBMS. This is accomplished via the SQL statement **CREATE DATABASE**.

## CTXCAT INDEX

A CTXCAT text index, available in Oracle Text, supports text queries executed with the CATSEARCH operator. *See* Chapter 24 for information on Oracle Text.

## CUBE

**SEE ALSO**     **GROUPING**, **ROLLUP**, Chapter 13

**FORMAT**

```
GROUP BY CUBE (column1, column2)
```

**DESCRIPTION**     **CUBE** groups rows based on the values of all possible combinations of expressions for each row, and returns a single row of summary information for each group. You can use the **CUBE** operation to produce cross-tab reports. *See* Chapter 13.

## CUME_DIST

**SEE ALSO**     GROUP FUNCTIONS

**FORMAT**     For aggregates:

```
CUME_DIST (expr [, expr]...) WITHIN GROUP
(ORDER BY
 expr [DESC | ASC] [NULLS { FIRST | LAST }]
 [, expr [DESC | ASC] [NULLS { FIRST | LAST }]]...)
```

For analytics:

```
CUME_DIST () OVER ([query_partition_clause] order_by_clause)
```

**DESCRIPTION**     **CUME_DIST** calculates the cumulative distribution of a value in a group of values. The range of values returned by **CUME_DIST** is >0 to <=1. Tie values always evaluate to the same cumulative distribution value.

## CURRENT_DATE

**SEE ALSO**     DATE FUNCTIONS

**FORMAT**

```
CURRENT_DATE
```

**DESCRIPTION** **CURRENT_DATE** returns the current date in the session time zone, in a value in the Gregorian calendar of datatype DATE.

**EXAMPLE**

```
SELECT CURRENT_DATE FROM DUAL;
```

# CURRENT_TIMESTAMP

**SEE ALSO** DATE FUNCTIONS

**FORMAT**

```
CURRENT_TIMESTAMP [(precision)]
```

**DESCRIPTION** **CURRENT_TIMESTAMP** returns the current date and time in the session time zone, in a value of datatype TIMESTAMP WITH TIME ZONE. The time zone displacement reflects the current local time of the SQL session. If you omit precision, the default is 6. The difference between this function and **LOCALTIMESTAMP** is that **CURRENT_TIMESTAMP** returns a TIMESTAMP WITH TIME ZONE value while LOCALTIMESTAMP returns a TIMESTAMP value.

*precision* specifies the fractional second precision of the time value returned.

**EXAMPLE**

```
select CURRENT_TIMESTAMP from DUAL;
```

# CURRVAL

*See* PSEUDO-COLUMNS.

# CURSOR

Cursor is also a synonym for context area—a work area in memory where Oracle stores the current SQL statement. For a query, the area in memory also includes column headings and one row retrieved by the query.

# CURSOR-PL/SQL

**SEE ALSO** **CREATE PACKAGE, CREATE PACKAGE BODY**, Chapter 27

**FORMAT**

```
CURSOR cursor [(parameter datatype[,parameter datatype]...]
 [IS query]
```

**DESCRIPTION** You can specify a cursor in a PL/SQL package and declare its body. The specification contains only the list of parameters with their corresponding datatypes, not the **IS** clause, while the body contains both. The parameters may appear anywhere in the query that a constant could appear. You can specify the cursor as a part of the public declarations of the package specification, and then the cursor body as part of the hidden package body.

## CURSOR FOR LOOP

In FOR loops, the loop executes a specified number of times. In a cursor FOR loop, the results of a query are used to dynamically determine the number of times the loop is executed. In a cursor FOR loop, the opening, fetching, and closing of cursors is performed implicitly; you do not need to explicitly code these actions.

The following listing shows a cursor FOR loop that queries the RADIUS_VALS table and inserts records into the AREAS table.

```
declare
 pi constant NUMBER(9,7) := 3.1415927;
 area NUMBER(14,2);
 cursor rad_cursor is
 select * from RADIUS_VALS;
begin
 for rad_val in rad_cursor
 loop
 area := pi*power(rad_val.radius,2);
 insert into AREAS values (rad_val.radius, area);
 end loop;
end;
```

In a cursor FOR loop, there is no **open** or **fetch** command. The

```
for rad_val in rad_cursor
```

command implicitly opens the *rad_cursor* cursor and fetches a value into the *rad_val* variable. Note that the *rad_val* variable is not explicitly declared when you use a cursor FOR loop. When there are no more records in the cursor, the loop is exited and the cursor is closed. In a cursor FOR loop, there is no need for a **close** command. *See* Chapter 27 for further information on cursor management within PL/SQL.

## DATA CONTROL LANGUAGE (DCL) STATEMENTS

DCL statements are one category of SQL statements. DCL statements, such as **grant**, **grant select**, **grant update**, and **revoke all**, control access to the data and to the database. The other categories are data definition language (DDL) and data manipulation language (DML) statements.

## DATA DEFINITION LANGUAGE (DDL) STATEMENTS

DDL statements are one category of SQL statements. DDL statements define (create) or delete (drop) database objects. Examples are **create view**, **create table**, **create index**, **drop table**, **create function**, and **rename table**. Executing any DDL command commits any pending changes to the database. The other categories of SQL statements are data control language (DCL) and data manipulation language (DML) statements.

## DATA DEFINITION LOCKS

Data definition locks are locks placed on the data dictionary during changes to the structures (definitions) of database objects (such as tables, indexes, views, and clusters) so that those changes occur with no negative impact on the database data. There are three kinds of locks: dictionary operation locks, dictionary definition locks, and table definition locks.

## DATA DICTIONARY

The data dictionary is a comprehensive set of tables and views owned by the DBA users SYS and SYSTEM, which activates when Oracle is initially installed, and is a central source of information for the Oracle RDBMS itself and for all users of Oracle. The tables are automatically maintained by Oracle, and hold a set of views and tables containing information about database objects, users, privileges, events, and use. *See* Chapter 37.

## DATA DICTIONARY VIEWS

**SEE ALSO**      Chapter 37

**DESCRIPTION**      The Oracle data dictionary views are described in Chapter 37. Most of the following listing, describing the available data dictionary views, was generated by selecting records from the DICTIONARY view in Oracle, via a non-DBA account. The views are listed here in alphabetical order; Chapter 37 groups and describes them by function. For details on the use of the DBA views in the data dictionary, see the *Oracle9i DBA Handbook*.

TABLE_NAME	Comments
ALL_ALL_TABLES	Description of all object and relational tables accessible to the user
ALL_ARGUMENTS	Arguments in object accessible to the user
ALL_ASSOCIATIONS	All associations available to the user
ALL_AUDIT_POLICIES	All fine grained auditing policies in the database
ALL_BASE_TABLE_MVIEWS	All materialized views with log(s) in the database that the user can see
ALL_CATALOG	All tables, views, synonyms, sequences accessible to the user
ALL_CLUSTERS	Description of clusters accessible to the user
ALL_CLUSTER_HASH_EXPRESSIONS	Hash functions for all accessible clusters
ALL_COLL_TYPES	Description of named collection types accessible to the user
ALL_COL_COMMENTS	Comments on columns of accessible tables and views
ALL_COL_PRIVS	Grants on columns for which the user is the grantor, grantee, owner, or an enabled role or PUBLIC is the grantee
ALL_COL_PRIVS_MADE	Grants on columns for which the user is owner or grantor
ALL_COL_PRIVS_RECD	Grants on columns for which the user, PUBLIC or enabled role is the grantee
ALL_CONSTRAINTS	Constraint definitions on accessible tables
ALL_CONS_COLUMNS	Information about accessible columns in constraint definitions
ALL_CONTEXT	Description of all active context namespaces under the current session
ALL_DB_LINKS	Database links accessible to the user
ALL_DEF_AUDIT_OPTS	Auditing options for newly created objects
ALL_DEPENDENCIES	Dependencies to and from objects accessible to the user
ALL_DIMENSIONS	Description of the dimension objects accessible to the DBA

TABLE_NAME	Comments
ALL_DIM_ATTRIBUTES	Representation of the relationship between a dimension level and a functionally dependent column
ALL_DIM_CHILD_OF	Representation of a 1:n hierarchical relationship between a pair of levels in a dimension
ALL_DIM_HIERARCHIES	Representation of a dimension hierarchy
ALL_DIM_JOIN_KEY	Representation of a join between two dimension tables
ALL_DIM_LEVELS	Description of dimension levels visible to DBA
ALL_DIM_LEVEL_KEY	Representation of columns of a dimension level
ALL_DIRECTORIES	Description of all directories accessible to the user
ALL_ERRORS	Current errors on stored objects that user is allowed to create
ALL_EXTERNAL_LOCATIONS	Description of the external tables locations accessible to the user
ALL_EXTERNAL_TABLES	Description of the external tables accessible to the user
ALL_HISTOGRAMS	Synonym for ALL_TAB_HISTOGRAMS
ALL_INDEXES	Descriptions of indexes on tables accessible to the user
ALL_INDEXTYPES	All indextypes available to the user
ALL_INDEXTYPE_COMMENTS	Comments for user-defined indextypes
ALL_INDEXTYPE_OPERATORS	All operators available to the user
ALL_IND_COLUMNS	COLUMNs comprising INDEXes on accessible TABLES
ALL_IND_EXPRESSIONS	FUNCTIONAL INDEX EXPRESSIONs on accessible TABLES
ALL_IND_PARTITIONS	All index partitions
ALL_IND_SUBPARTITIONS	All index subpartitions
ALL_INTERNAL_TRIGGERS	Description of the internal triggers on the tables accessible to the user
ALL_JOBS	Synonym for USER_JOBS
ALL_JOIN_IND_COLUMNS	Join Index columns comprising the join conditions
ALL_LIBRARIES	Description of libraries accessible to the user
ALL_LOBS	Description of LOBs contained in tables accessible to the user
ALL_LOB_PARTITIONS	All LOB partitions
ALL_LOB_SUBPARTITIONS	All LOB subpartitions
ALL_LOG_GROUPS	Log group definitions on accessible tables
ALL_LOG_GROUP_COLUMNS	Information about columns in log group definitions
ALL_METHOD_PARAMS	Description of method parameters of types accessible to the user
ALL_METHOD_RESULTS	Description of method results of types accessible to the user
ALL_MVIEWS	All materialized views in the database
ALL_MVIEW_AGGREGATES	Description of the materialized view aggregates accessible to the user
ALL_MVIEW_ANALYSIS	Description of the materialized views accessible to the user

TABLE_NAME	Comments
ALL_MVIEW_DETAIL_RELATIONS	Description of the materialized view detail tables accessible to the user
ALL_MVIEW_JOINS	Description of a join between two columns in the WHERE clause of a materialized view accessible to the user
ALL_MVIEW_KEYS	Description of the columns that appear in the GROUP BY list of a materialized view accessible to the user
ALL_MVIEW_LOGS	All materialized view logs in the database that the user can see
ALL_MVIEW_REFRESH_TIMES	Materialized views and their last refresh times for each master table that the user can look at
ALL_NESTED_TABLES	Description of nested tables in tables accessible to the user
ALL_OBJECTS	Objects accessible to the user
ALL_OBJECT_TABLES	Description of all object tables accessible to the user
ALL_OPANCILLARY	All ancillary operators available to the user
ALL_OPARGUMENTS	All arguments of the operators available to the user
ALL_OPBINDINGS	All binding functions for operators available to the user
ALL_OPERATORS	All operators available to the user
ALL_OPERATOR_COMMENTS	Comments for user-defined operators
ALL_OUTLINES	Synonym for USER_OUTLINES
ALL_OUTLINE_HINTS	Synonym for USER_OUTLINE_HINTS
ALL_PARTIAL_DROP_TABS	All tables with partially dropped columns accessible to the user
ALL_PART_COL_STATISTICS	Column statistics for partitions
ALL_PART_HISTOGRAMS	Histograms for partitions
ALL_PART_INDEXES	Partition index definitions
ALL_PART_KEY_COLUMNS	Partition key columns
ALL_PART_LOBS	Partition LOB details
ALL_PART_TABLES	Partitioned table definitions
ALL_PENDING_CONV_TABLES	All tables accessible to the user which are not upgraded to the latest type version
ALL_POLICIES	All policies for objects if the user has system privileges or owns the objects
ALL_POLICY_CONTEXTS	All policy groups defined for all tables or views accessible to the user
ALL_POLICY_GROUPS	All policy groups defined for any tables or views accessible to the user
ALL_PROBE_OBJECTS	All probe objects
ALL_PROCEDURES	Description of all procedures available to the user
ALL_QUEUES	All queues accessible to the user
ALL_QUEUE_TABLES	All queue tables accessible to the user
ALL_REFRESH	All the refresh groups that the user can touch

TABLE_NAME	Comments
ALL_REFRESH_CHILDREN	All the objects in refresh groups, where the user can touch the group
ALL_REFRESH_DEPENDENCIES	Description of the detail tables that materialized views depend on for refresh
ALL_REFS	Description of REF columns contained in tables accessible to the user
ALL_REGISTERED_MVIEWS	Remote materialized views of local tables that the user can see
ALL_REGISTERED_SNAPSHOTS	Remote snapshots of local tables that the user can see
ALL_REPAUDIT_ATTRIBUTE	Information about attributes automatically maintained for replication
ALL_REPAUDIT_COLUMN	Information about columns in all shadow tables for replicated tables which are accessible to the user
ALL_REPCAT	Replication catalog
ALL_REPCATLOG	Information about asynchronous administration requests
ALL_REPCOLUMN	Replicated top-level columns (table) sorted alphabetically in ascending order
ALL_REPCOLUMN_GROUP	All column groups of replicated tables which are accessible to the user
ALL_REPCONFLICT	All conflicts with available resolutions for user's replicated tables
ALL_REPDDL	Arguments that do not fit in a single repcat log record
ALL_REPFLAVORS	Flavors defined for replicated object groups
ALL_REPFLAVOR_COLUMNS	Replicated columns in flavors
ALL_REPFLAVOR_OBJECTS	Replicated objects in flavors
ALL_REPGENERATED	Objects generated to support replication
ALL_REPGENOBJECTS	Objects generated to support replication
ALL_REPGROUP	Information about replicated object groups
ALL_REPGROUPED_COLUMN	Columns in the all column groups of replicated tables which are accessible to the user
ALL_REPGROUP_PRIVILEGES	Information about users who are registered for object group privileges
ALL_REPKEY_COLUMNS	Primary columns for a table using column-level replication
ALL_REPOBJECT	Information about replicated objects
ALL_REPPARAMETER_COLUMN	All columns used for resolving conflicts in replicated tables which are accessible to the user
ALL_REPPRIORITY	Values and their corresponding priorities in all priority groups which are accessible to the user
ALL_REPPRIORITY_GROUP	Information about all priority groups which are accessible to the user
ALL_REPPROP	Propagation information about replicated objects
ALL_REPRESOLUTION	Description of all conflict resolutions for replicated tables which are accessible to the user
ALL_REPRESOLUTION_METHOD	All conflict resolution methods accessible to the user

TABLE_NAME	Comments
ALL_REPRESOLUTION_STATISTICS	Statistics for conflict resolutions for replicated tables which are accessible to the user
ALL_REPRESOL_STATS_CONTROL	Information about statistics collection for conflict resolutions for replicated tables which are accessible to the user
ALL_REPSCHEMA	N-way replication information
ALL_REPSITES	N-way replication information
ALL_SECONDARY_OBJECTS	All secondary objects for domain indexes
ALL_SEQUENCES	Description of SEQUENCEs accessible to the user
ALL_SNAPSHOTS	Snapshots the user can access
ALL_SNAPSHOT_LOGS	All snapshot logs in the database that the user can see
ALL_SNAPSHOT_REFRESH_TIMES	Synonym for ALL_MVIEW_REFRESH_TIMES
ALL_SOURCE	Current source on stored objects that user is allowed to create
ALL_SOURCE_TABLES	Source tables
ALL_SOURCE_TAB_COLUMNS	Source columns
ALL_SQLJ_TYPES	Description of types accessible to the user
ALL_SQLJ_TYPE_ATTRS	Description of attributes of types accessible to the user
ALL_SQLJ_TYPE_METHODS	Description of methods of types accessible to the user
ALL_STORED_SETTINGS	Parameter settings for objects accessible to the user
ALL_SUBPART_COL_STATISTICS	Subpartition statistics
ALL_SUBPART_HISTOGRAMS	Subpartition histograms
ALL_SUBPART_KEY_COLUMNS	Subpartition keys
ALL_SUBSCRIBED_COLUMNS	Columns subscribed to
ALL_SUBSCRIBED_TABLES	Tables subscribed to
ALL_SUBSCRIPTIONS	All subscriptions
ALL_SUMDELTA	Direct path load entries accessible to the user
ALL_SUMMARIES	Description of the summaries accessible to the user
ALL_SYNONYMS	All synonyms accessible to the user
ALL_TABLES	Description of relational tables accessible to the user
ALL_TAB_COLS	Columns of user's tables, views and clusters
ALL_TAB_COLUMNS	Columns of user's tables, views and clusters
ALL_TAB_COL_STATISTICS	Columns of user's tables, views and clusters
ALL_TAB_COMMENTS	Comments on tables and views accessible to the user
ALL_TAB_HISTOGRAMS	Histograms on columns of all tables visible to user
ALL_TAB_MODIFICATIONS	Information regarding modifications to tables
ALL_TAB_PARTITIONS	All table partitions
ALL_TAB_PRIVS	Grants on objects for which the user is the grantor, grantee, owner, or an enabled role or PUBLIC is the grantee
ALL_TAB_PRIVS_MADE	User's grants and grants on user's objects

TABLE_NAME	Comments
ALL_TAB_PRIVS_RECD	Grants on objects for which the user, PUBLIC or enabled role is the grantee
ALL_TAB_SUBPARTITIONS	All table subpartitions
ALL_TRIGGERS	Triggers accessible to the current user
ALL_TRIGGER_COLS	Column usage in user's triggers or in triggers on user's tables
ALL_TYPES	Description of types accessible to the user
ALL_TYPE_ATTRS	Description of attributes of types accessible to the user
ALL_TYPE_METHODS	Description of methods of types accessible to the user
ALL_TYPE_VERSIONS	Description of each type version accessible to the user
ALL_UNUSED_COL_TABS	All tables with unused columns accessible to the user
ALL_UPDATABLE_COLUMNS	Description of all updatable columns
ALL_USERS	Information about all users of the database
ALL_USTATS	All statistics
ALL_VARRAYS	Description of varrays in tables accessible to the user
ALL_VIEWS	Description of views accessible to the user
AUDIT_ACTIONS	Description table for audit trail action type codes. Maps action type numbers to action type names
CAT	Synonym for USER_CATALOG
CLU	Synonym for USER_CLUSTERS
COLS	Synonym for USER_TAB_COLUMNS
COLUMN_PRIVILEGES	Grants on columns for which the user is the grantor, grantee, owner, or an enabled role or PUBLIC is the grantee
DATABASE_COMPATIBLE_LEVEL	Database compatible parameter set via init.ora
DBMS_ALERT_INFO	
DBMS_LOCK_ALLOCATED	
DICT	Synonym for DICTIONARY
DICTIONARY	Description of data dictionary tables and views
DICT_COLUMNS	Description of columns in data dictionary tables and views
DUAL	A one-row, one-column table
GLOBAL_NAME	Global database name
IND	Synonym for USER_INDEXES
INDEX_HISTOGRAM	Statistics on keys with repeat count
INDEX_STATS	Statistics on the b-tree
NLS_DATABASE_PARAMETERS	Permanent NLS parameters of the database
NLS_INSTANCE_PARAMETERS	NLS parameters of the instance
NLS_SESSION_PARAMETERS	NLS parameters of the user session
OBJ	Synonym for USER_OBJECTS
RESOURCE_COST	Cost for each resource
ROLE_ROLE_PRIVS	Roles which are granted to roles

TABLE_NAME	Comments
ROLE_SYS_PRIVS	System privileges granted to roles
ROLE_TAB_PRIVS	Table privileges granted to roles
SEQ	Synonym for USER_SEQUENCES
SESSION_PRIVS	Privileges which the user currently has set
SESSION_ROLES	Roles which the user currently has enabled.
SM$VERSION	Synonym for SM_$VERSION
SYN	Synonym for USER_SYNONYMS
TABLE_PRIVILEGES	Grants on objects for which the user is the grantor, grantee, owner, or an enabled role or PUBLIC is the grantee
TABS	Synonym for USER_TABLES
USER_ALL_TABLES	Description of all object and relational tables owned by the user
USER_ARGUMENTS	Arguments in object accessible to the user
USER_ASSOCIATIONS	All associations defined by the user
USER_AUDIT_OBJECT	Audit trail records for statements concerning objects, specifically: table, cluster, view, index, sequence, [public] database link, [public] synonym, procedure, trigger, rollback segment, tablespace, role, user
USER_AUDIT_POLICIES	All fine grained auditing policies for objects in user schema
USER_AUDIT_SESSION	All audit trail records concerning CONNECT and DISCONNECT
USER_AUDIT_STATEMENT	Audit trail records concerning grant, revoke, audit, noaudit and alter system
USER_AUDIT_TRAIL	Audit trail entries relevant to the user
USER_BASE_TABLE_MVIEWS	All materialized views with log(s) owned by the user in the database
USER_CATALOG	Tables, Views, Synonyms and Sequences owned by the user
USER_CLUSTERS	Descriptions of user's own clusters
USER_CLUSTER_HASH_EXPRESSIONS	Hash functions for the user's hash clusters
USER_CLU_COLUMNS	Mapping of table columns to cluster columns
USER_COLL_TYPES	Description of the user's own named collection types
USER_COL_COMMENTS	Comments on columns of user's tables and views
USER_COL_PRIVS	Grants on columns for which the user is the owner, grantor or grantee
USER_COL_PRIVS_MADE	All grants on columns of objects owned by the user
USER_COL_PRIVS_RECD	Grants on columns for which the user is the grantee
USER_CONSTRAINTS	Constraint definitions on user's own tables
USER_CONS_COLUMNS	Information about accessible columns in constraint definitions
USER_DB_LINKS	Database links owned by the user
USER_DEPENDENCIES	Dependencies to and from a user's objects
USER_DIMENSIONS	Description of the dimension objects accessible to the DBA

TABLE_NAME	Comments
USER_DIM_ATTRIBUTES	Representation of the relationship between a dimension level and a functionally dependent column
USER_DIM_CHILD_OF	Representation of a 1:n hierarchical relationship between a pair of levels in a dimension
USER_DIM_HIERARCHIES	Representation of a dimension hierarchy
USER_DIM_JOIN_KEY	Representation of a join between two dimension tables.
USER_DIM_LEVELS	Description of dimension levels visible to DBA
USER_DIM_LEVEL_KEY	Representations of columns of a dimension level
USER_ERRORS	Current errors on stored objects owned by the user
USER_EXTENTS	Extents comprising segments owned by the user
USER_EXTERNAL_LOCATIONS	Description of the user's external tables locations
USER_EXTERNAL_TABLES	Description of the user's own external tables
USER_FREE_SPACE	Free extents in tablespaces accessible to the user
USER_HISTOGRAMS	Synonym for USER_TAB_HISTOGRAMS
USER_INDEXES	Description of the user's own indexes
USER_INDEXTYPES	All user indextypes
USER_INDEXTYPE_COMMENTS	Comments for user-defined indextypes
USER_INDEXTYPE_OPERATORS	All user indextype operators
USER_IND_COLUMNS	COLUMNs comprising user's INDEXes and INDEXes on user's TABLES
USER_IND_EXPRESSIONS	Functional index expressions in user's indexes and indexes on user's tables
USER_IND_PARTITIONS	User index partitions
USER_IND_SUBPARTITIONS	The user's index subpartitions
USER_INTERNAL_TRIGGERS	Description of the internal triggers on the user's own tables
USER_JAVA_POLICY	Java security permissions for current user
USER_JOBS	All jobs owned by this user
USER_JOIN_IND_COLUMNS	Join Index columns comprising the join conditions
USER_LIBRARIES	Description of the user's own libraries
USER_LOBS	Description of the user's own LOBs contained in the user's own tables
USER_LOB_PARTITIONS	User LOB partitions
USER_LOB_SUBPARTITIONS	User LOB subpartitions
USER_LOG_GROUPS	Log group definitions on user's own tables
USER_LOG_GROUP_COLUMNS	Information about columns in log group definitions
USER_METHOD_PARAMS	Description of method parameters of the user's own types
USER_METHOD_RESULTS	Description of method results of the user's own types
USER_MVIEWS	All materialized views in the database
USER_MVIEW_AGGREGATES	Description of the materialized view aggregates created by the user

TABLE_NAME	Comments
USER_MVIEW_ANALYSIS	Description of the materialized views created by the user
USER_MVIEW_DETAIL_RELATIONS	Description of the materialized view detail tables of the materialized views created by the user
USER_MVIEW_JOINS	Description of a join between two columns in the WHERE clause of a materialized view created by the user
USER_MVIEW_KEYS	Description of the columns that appear in the GROUP BY list of a materialized view created by the user
USER_MVIEW_LOGS	All materialized view logs owned by the user
USER_MVIEW_REFRESH_TIMES	Materialized views and their last refresh times for each master table that the user can look at
USER_NESTED_TABLES	Description of nested tables contained in the user's own tables
USER_OBJECTS	Objects owned by the user
USER_OBJECT_SIZE	Sizes, in bytes, of various pl/sql objects
USER_OBJECT_TABLES	Description of the user's own object tables
USER_OBJ_AUDIT_OPTS	Auditing options for user's own tables and views
USER_OPANCILLARY	All ancillary operators defined by user
USER_OPARGUMENTS	All operator arguments of operators defined by user
USER_OPBINDINGS	All binding functions or methods on operators defined by the user
USER_OPERATORS	All user operators
USER_OPERATOR_COMMENTS	Comments for user-defined operators
USER_OUTLINES	Stored outlines owned by the user
USER_OUTLINE_HINTS	Hints stored in outlines owned by the user
USER_PARTIAL_DROP_TABS	User tables with unused columns
USER_PART_COL_STATISTICS	Partition column statistics
USER_PART_HISTOGRAMS	Partition column histograms
USER_PART_INDEXES	Index partition definitions
USER_PART_KEY_COLUMNS	Partition keys
USER_PART_LOBS	Partition LOBs
USER_PART_TABLES	Partition table definitions
USER_PASSWORD_LIMITS	Display password limits of the user
USER_PENDING_CONV_TABLES	All user's tables which are not upgraded to the latest type version
USER_POLICIES	All row level security policies for tables or views owned by the user
USER_POLICY_CONTEXTS	All policy groups defined for tables or views in current schema
USER_POLICY_GROUPS	All policy groups defined for any tables or views
USER_PROCEDURES	Description of the user's own procedures
USER_PROXIES	Description of connections the user is allowed to proxy

TABLE_NAME	Comments
USER_QUEUES	All queues owned by the user
USER_QUEUE_SCHEDULES	User queue schedules
USER_QUEUE_TABLES	All queue tables created by the user
USER_REFRESH	All the refresh groups
USER_REFRESH_CHILDREN	All the objects in refresh groups, where the user owns the refresh group
USER_REFS	Description of the user's own REF columns contained in the user's own tables
USER_REGISTERED_MVIEWS	Remote materialized views of local tables currently using logs owned by the user
USER_REGISTERED_SNAPSHOTS	Remote snapshots of local tables currently using logs owned by the user
USER_REPAUDIT_ATTRIBUTE	Information about attributes automatically maintained for replication
USER_REPAUDIT_COLUMN	Information about columns in all shadow tables for user's replicated tables
USER_REPCAT	Replication catalog
USER_REPCATLOG	Information about the current user's asynchronous administration requests
USER_REPCOLUMN	Replicated columns for the current user's table in ascending order
USER_REPCOLUMN_GROUP	All column groups of user's replicated tables
USER_REPCONFLICT	Replication conflicts
USER_REPDDL	Arguments that do not fit in a single repcat log record
USER_REPFLAVORS	Flavors current user created for replicated object groups
USER_REPFLAVOR_COLUMNS	Replicated columns from current user's tables in flavors
USER_REPFLAVOR_OBJECTS	Replicated user objects in flavors
USER_REPGENERATED	Objects generated for the current user to support replication
USER_REPGENOBJECTS	Objects generated for the current user to support replication
USER_REPGROUP	Replication information about the current user
USER_REPGROUPED_COLUMN	Columns in the all column groups of user's replicated tables
USER_REPGROUP_PRIVILEGES	Information about users who are registered for object group privileges
USER_REPKEY_COLUMNS	Primary columns for a table using column-level replication
USER_REPOBJECT	Replication information about the current user's objects
USER_REPPARAMETER_COLUMN	All columns used for resolving conflicts in user's replicated tables
USER_REPPRIORITY	Values and their corresponding priorities in user's priority groups
USER_REPPRIORITY_GROUP	Information about user's priority groups
USER_REPPROP	Propagation information about the current user's objects

TABLE_NAME	Comments
USER_REPRESOLUTION	Description of all conflict resolutions for user's replicated tables
USER_REPRESOLUTION_METHOD	All conflict resolution methods accessible to the user
USER_REPRESOLUTION_STATISTICS	Statistics for conflict resolutions for user's replicated tables
USER_REPRESOL_STATS_CONTROL	Information about statistics collection for conflict resolutions for user's replicated tables
USER_REPSCHEMA	N-way replication information about the current user
USER_REPSITES	N-way replication information about the current user
USER_RESOURCE_LIMITS	Display resource limit of the user
USER_RESUMABLE	Resumable session information for current user
USER_ROLE_PRIVS	Roles granted to current user
USER_RSRC_CONSUMER_GROUP_PRIVS	Switch privileges for consumer groups for the user
USER_RSRC_MANAGER_SYSTEM_PRIVS	System privileges for the resource manager for the user
USER_RULESETS	Rulesets owned by the user
USER_SECONDARY_OBJECTS	All secondary objects for domain indexes
USER_SEGMENTS	Storage allocated for all database segments
USER_SEQUENCES	Description of the user's own SEQUENCEs
USER_SNAPSHOTS	Snapshots the user can look at
USER_SNAPSHOT_LOGS	All snapshot logs owned by the user
USER_SNAPSHOT_REFRESH_TIMES	Synonym for USER_MVIEW_REFRESH_TIMES
USER_SOURCE	Source of stored objects accessible to the user
USER_SOURCE_TABLES	Source tables
USER_SOURCE_TAB_COLUMNS	Source columns
USER_SQLJ_TYPES	Description of the user's own types
USER_SQLJ_TYPE_ATTRS	Description of attributes of the user's own types
USER_SQLJ_TYPE_METHODS	Description of methods of the user's own types
USER_STORED_SETTINGS	Parameter settings for objects owned by the user
USER_SUBPART_COL_STATISTICS	Subpartition column stats
USER_SUBPART_HISTOGRAMS	Subpartition histograms
USER_SUBPART_KEY_COLUMNS	Subpartition keys
USER_SUBSCRIBED_COLUMNS	Subscribed columns
USER_SUBSCRIBED_TABLES	Subscribed tables
USER_SUBSCRIPTIONS	User subscriptions
USER_SUMMARIES	Description of the summaries created by the user
USER_SYNONYMS	The user's private synonyms
USER_SYS_PRIVS	System privileges granted to current user
USER_TABLES	Description of the user's own relational tables
USER_TABLESPACES	Description of accessible tablespaces
USER_TAB_COLS	Columns of user's tables, views and clusters

TABLE_NAME	Comments
USER_TAB_COLUMNS	Columns of user's tables, views and clusters
USER_TAB_COL_STATISTICS	Columns of user's tables, views and clusters
USER_TAB_COMMENTS	Comments on the tables and views owned by the user
USER_TAB_HISTOGRAMS	Histograms on columns of user's tables
USER_TAB_MODIFICATIONS	Information regarding modifications to tables
USER_TAB_PARTITIONS	User table partitions
USER_TAB_PRIVS	Grants on objects for which the user is the owner, grantor or grantee
USER_TAB_PRIVS_MADE	All grants on objects owned by the user
USER_TAB_PRIVS_RECD	Grants on objects for which the user is the grantee
USER_TAB_SUBPARTITIONS	User table subpartitions
USER_TRANSFORMATIONS	User transformations
USER_TRIGGERS	Triggers owned by the user
USER_TRIGGER_COLS	Column usage in user's triggers
USER_TS_QUOTAS	Tablespace quotas for the user
USER_TYPES	Description of the user's own types
USER_TYPE_ATTRS	Description of attributes of the user's own types
USER_TYPE_METHODS	Description of methods of the user's own types
USER_TYPE_VERSIONS	Description of each version of the user's types
USER_UNUSED_COL_TABS	User tables with unused columns
USER_UPDATABLE_COLUMNS	Description of updatable columns
USER_USERS	Information about the current user
USER_USTATS	All statistics on tables or indexes owned by the user
USER_VARRAYS	Description of varrays contained in the user's own tables
USER_VIEWS	Description of the user's own views
V$ACTIVE_INSTANCES	Synonym for V_$ACTIVE_INSTANCES
V$ACTIVE_SESS_POOL_MTH	Synonym for V_$ACTIVE_SESS_POOL_MTH
V$BH	Synonym for V_$BH
V$LOADCSTAT	Synonym for V_$LOADCSTAT
V$LOADISTAT	Synonym for V_$LOADISTAT
V$LOADPSTAT	Synonym for V_$LOADPSTAT
V$LOADTSTAT	Synonym for V_$LOADTSTAT
V$LOCK_ACTIVITY	Synonym for V_$LOCK_ACTIVITY
V$MAX_ACTIVE_SESS_TARGET_MTH	Synonym for V_$MAX_ACTIVE_SESS_TARGET_MTH
V$MLS_PARAMETERS	Synonym for V_$MLS_PARAMETERS
V$NLS_PARAMETERS	Synonym for V_$NLS_PARAMETERS
V$NLS_VALID_VALUES	Synonym for V_$NLS_VALID_VALUES
V$OPTION	Synonym for V_$OPTION

TABLE_NAME	Comments
V$PARALLEL_DEGREE_LIMIT_MTH	Synonym for V_$PARALLEL_DEGREE_LIMIT_MTH
V$PQ_SESSTAT	Synonym for V_$PQ_SESSTAT
V$PQ_TQSTAT	Synonym for V_$PQ_TQSTAT
V$QUEUEING_MTH	Synonym for V_$QUEUEING_MTH
V$RSRC_CONSUMER_GROUP	Synonym for V_$RSRC_CONSUMER_GROUP
V$RSRC_CONSUMER_GROUP_CPU_MTH	Synonym for V_$RSRC_CONSUMER_GROUP_CPU_MTH
V$RSRC_PLAN	Synonym for V_$RSRC_PLAN
V$RSRC_PLAN_CPU_MTH	Synonym for V_$RSRC_PLAN_CPU_MTH
V$SESSION_CONNECT_INFO	Synonym for V_$SESSION_CONNECT_INFO
V$SESSION_LONGOPS	Synonym for V_$SESSION_LONGOPS
V$TEMPORARY_LOBS	Synonym for V_$TEMPORARY_LOBS
V$TIMEZONE_NAMES	Synonym for V_$TIMEZONE_NAMES
V$VERSION	Synonym for V_$VERSION

# DATA INDEPENDENCE

Data independence is the property of well-defined tables that allows the physical and logical structure of a table to change without affecting applications that access the table.

# DATA MANIPULATION LANGUAGE (DML) STATEMENTS

DML statements are one category of SQL statements. DML statements, such as **select**, **insert**, **delete**, and **update**, query and update the actual data. The other categories are data control language (DCL) and data definition language (DDL) statements.

# DATA TYPES

**SEE ALSO**   CHARACTER FUNCTIONS, CONVERSION FUNCTIONS, DATE FUNCTIONS, LIST FUNCTIONS, NUMBER FUNCTIONS, OTHER FUNCTIONS

**DESCRIPTION**   When a table is created and the columns in it are defined, they must each have a datatype specified. Oracle's primary datatypes are VARCHAR2, CHAR, DATE, LONG, LONG RAW, NUMBER, RAW, and ROWID, but for compatibility with other SQL databases, its **create table** statements will accept several versions of these. The following table summarizes the built-in Oracle datatypes:

Datatype	Definition
VARCHAR2(*size*)	Variable length character string having a maximum of *size* bytes (up to 4000).
NVARCHAR2(*size*)	Variable length character string having a maximum of *size* bytes (up to 4000) or characters, depending on the choice of national character set.
NUMBER(*size,d*)	For NUMBER column of specified *size* with *d* digits after the decimal point. For example, NUMBER(5,2) could contain nothing larger than 999.99 without an error.

Datatype	Definition
LONG	Character data of variable size up to 2Gb in length. Only one LONG column may be defined per table. LONG columns may not be used in subqueries, functions, expressions, **where** clauses, or indexes. A table containing a LONG column may not be clustered.
DATE	Valid dates range from January 1, 4712 B.C. to December 31, 9999 A.D.
TIMESTAMP (*precision*)	Date plus time, where *precision* is the number of digits in the fractional part of the Seconds field (default is 6).
TIMESTAMP (*precision*) WITH TIME ZONE	TIMESTAMP plus time zone displacement value.
TIMESTAMP (*precision*) WITH LOCAL TIME ZONE	TIMESTAMP, normalized to local time zone.
INTERVAL YEAR (*precision*) TO MONTH	Period of time in years and months, where *precision* is the number of digits in the YEAR datetime field (default is 2).
INTERVAL DAY (*day_precision*) TO SECOND (*second_precision*)	Period of time in days, hours, minutes, and seconds, where *day_precision* is the number of digits in the DAY datetime field (default is 2) and *second_precision* is the number of digits in the fractional part of the Seconds field (default is 6).
RAW(*size*)	Raw binary data, *size* bytes long. Maximum size is 255 bytes.
LONG RAW	Raw binary data; otherwise the same as LONG.
ROWID	A value that uniquely identifies a row in an Oracle database. It is returned by the pseudo-column ROWID.
UROWID (*size*)	Hex string for the logical address of a row in an index-organized table; maximum *size* is 4000 bytes.
CHAR(*size*)	Fixed-length character data, *size* characters long. Maximum size is 2000. Default is 1 byte. Padded on the right with blanks to full length of size.
NCHAR(*size*)	Multi-byte character set version of CHAR.
CLOB	Character large object, up to 4Gb in length.
NCLOB	Same as CLOB, but for multi-byte character sets.
BLOB	Binary large object, up to 4Gb in length.
BFILE	Pointer to a binary operating system file.

# DATABASE

Database can have one of two definitions:

- A set of dictionary tables and user tables that are treated as a unit.
- One or more operating system files in which Oracle stores tables, views, and other objects; also, the set of database objects used by a given application.

# DATABASE ADMINISTRATOR (DBA)

A DBA is an Oracle user authorized to **grant** and **revoke** other users' access to the system, modify Oracle options that affect all users, and perform other administrative functions. *See* Chapter 40.

## DATABASE LINK

A database link is an object stored in the local database that identifies a remote database, a communication path to the remote database, and, optionally, a username and password for it. Once defined, the database link is used to perform queries on tables in the remote database. *See* Chapter 22.

## DATABASE NAME

A database name is a unique identifier used to name a database. It is assigned in the **create database** command or in the initialization parameter file.

## DATABASE OBJECT

A database object is something created and stored in a database. Tables, views, synonyms, indexes, sequences, clusters, and columns are all types of database objects.

## DATAFILE

A datafile is any file used to store data in a database. A database is made up of one or more tablespaces, which in turn are made up of one or more datafiles.

## DATATYPE

*See* DATA TYPES.

## DATE

DATE is a standard Oracle datatype to store date and time data. Standard date format is 22-APR-02. A DATE column may contain a date and time between January 1, 4712 B.C. and December 31, 9999 A.D.

## DATE FORMATS

**SEE ALSO**     DATE FUNCTIONS, Chapter 9

**DESCRIPTION**     These date formats are used with both **TO_CHAR** and **TO_DATE**:

MM	Number of month: 12
RM	Roman numeral month: XII
MON	Three-letter abbreviation of Month: AUG
MONTH	Month fully spelled out: AUGUST
DDD	Number of days in year, since Jan 1: 354
DD	Number of days in month: 23
D	Number of days in week: 6
DY	Three-letter abbreviation of day: FRI
DAY	Day fully spelled out, padded to 9 characters
YYYY	Full four-digit year: 1946
Y,YYY	Year, with comma
SYYYY	Signed year: 1000 B.C.=-1000
YYY	Last three digits of year: 946

YY	Last two digits of year: 46
Y	Last one digit of year: 6
IYYY	Four-digit year from ISO standard*
IYY	Three-digit year from ISO standard
IY	Two-digit year from ISO standard
I	One-digit year from ISO standard
RR	Last two digits of year relative to current date
RRRR	Rounded year, accepting either two- or four-digit input
CC	Century: (20 for 1999)
SCC	Century, with BC dates prefixed with -
YEAR	Year spelled out: NINETEEN-FORTY-SIX
SYEAR	Year, with - before BC dates
Q	Number of quarter: 3
WW	Number of weeks in year, where week 1 starts on the first day of the year
IW	Weeks in year from ISO standard
W	Number of weeks in month where week 1 starts on the first day of the month
J	"Julian"—days since December 31, 4712 B.C.: 2422220
HI I	Hours of day, always 1-12: 11
HH12	Same as HH
HH24	Hours of day, 24-hour clock: 17
MI	Minutes of hour: 58
SS	Seconds of minute: 43
SSSSS	Seconds since midnight, always 0-86399: 43000
FF	Fractional seconds as in HH.MI.SS.FF
X	Local radix character
/,-:.;	Punctuation to be incorporated in display for **TO_CHAR** or ignored in format for **TO_DATE**
A.M.	Displays A.M. or P.M., depending upon time of day
P.M.	Same effect as A.M.
AM or PM	Same as A.M. but without periods
B.C.	Displays B.C. or A.D., depending upon date
A.D.	Same as B.C.
BC or AD	Same as B.C. but without periods
E	Abbreviated era name, for Asian calendars
EE	Full era name, for Asian calendars
TZD	Daylight savings time information
TZH	Time zone hour
TZM	Time zone minute
TZR	Time zone region

* ISO is the International Standards Organization, which has a different set of standards for dates than the U.S. formats.

These date formats work only with **TO_CHAR**. They do not work with **TO_DATE**:

"string"	*string* is incorporated in display for **TO_CHAR**.
Fm	Prefix to Month or Day: fmMONTH or fmday. Suppresses padding of Month or Day (defined earlier) in format. Without fm, all months are displayed at same width. Similarly true for days. With fm, padding is eliminated. Months and days are only as long as their count of characters.
Fx	Format Exact: Specifies exact format matching for the character argument and the date format model.
TH	Suffix to a number: ddTH or DDTH produces 24th or 24TH. Capitalization comes from the case of the number—DD—not from the case of the TH. Works with any number in a date: YYYY, DD, MM, HH, MI, SS, and so on.
SP	Suffix to a number that forces number to be spelled out: DDSP, DdSP, or ddSP produces THREE, Three, or three. Capitalization comes from case of number—DD—not from the case of SP. Works with any number in a date: YYYY, DD, MM, HH, MI, SS, and so on.
SPTH	Suffix combination of TH and SP that forces number to be both spelled out and given an ordinal suffix: Ddspth produces Third. Capitalization comes from case of number—DD—not from the case of SP. Works with any number in a date: YYYY, DD, MM, HH, MI, SS, and so on.
THSP	Same as SPTH.

# DATE FUNCTIONS

**SEE ALSO**   DATE FORMATS, Chapter 9

**DESCRIPTION**   This is an alphabetical list of all current date functions in Oracle's SQL. Each of these is listed elsewhere in this reference under its own name, with its proper format and use.

- **ADD_MONTHS**(*date,count*)   **Add**s *count* **months** to *date*.
- **CURRENT_DATE**   Returns the **current date** in the session's time zone.
- **CURRENT_TIMESTAMP**   Returns the **current timestamp** with the active time zone information
- **DBTIMEZONE**   Returns the current **database timezone**, in UTC format.
- **EXTRACT**   (*datetime*) **Extract**s a portion of a date from a date value – such as extracting the month value from a date column's values.
- **FROM_TZ**   Converts a timestamp value to a timestamp with timezone value.
- **GREATEST**(*date1,date2,date3,...*)   Picks latest date from list of dates.
- **LEAST**(*date1,date2,date3,...*)   Picks earliest date from list of dates.
- **LAST_DAY**(*date*)   Gives date of **last day** of month that *date* is in.
- **LOCALTIMESTAMP**   Returns the **local timestamp** in the active time zone, with no time zone information shown.
- **MONTHS_BETWEEN**(*date2,date1*)   Gives *date2–date1* in **months** (can be fractional months).
- **NEW_TIME**(*date*, '*this*', '*other*')   Gives the *date* (and time) in *this* time zone. *this* will be replaced by a three-letter abbreviation for the current time zone. *other* will be replaced by a three-letter abbreviation for the other time zone for which you'd like to know the time and date.

Time zones are as follows:

AST/ADT	Atlantic standard/daylight time
BST/BDT	Bering standard/daylight time
CST/CDT	Central standard/daylight time
EST/EDT	Eastern standard/daylight time
GMT	Greenwich mean time
HST/HDT	Alaska-Hawaii standard/daylight time
MST/MDT	Mountain standard/daylight time
NST	Newfoundland standard time
PST/PDT	Pacific standard/daylight time
YST/YDT	Yukon standard/daylight time

- **NEXT_DAY**(*date*,'*day*') Gives date of **next day** after *date*, where '*day*' is 'Monday', '*Tuesday*', and so on.

- **NUMTODSINTERVAL**(*n*,'*value*') Converts a number or expression *n* to an INTERVAL DAY TO SECOND literal where *value* is the unit of *n*: 'DAY', 'HOUR', 'MINUTE', 'SECOND'.

- **NUMTOYMINTERVAL** (*n*,'*value*') Converts a number or expression *n* to an INTERVAL YEAR TO MONTH literal where *value* is the unit of *n*: 'YEAR', 'MONTH'.

- **ROUND**(*date*,'*format*') Without *format* specified, **rounds** a *date* to 12 A.M. (midnight, the beginning of that day) if time of *date* is before noon; otherwise, **rounds** up to next day. For use of *format* for rounding, see ROUND in the Alphabetical Reference.

- **SESSIONTIMEZONE** Returns the value of the current **session**'s **timezone**.

- **SYS_EXTRACT_UTC**(*datetime_with_timezone*) Extracts the Coordinated Universal Time (UTC) from a datetime with time zone displacement.

- **SYSTIMESTAMP** Returns the system date, including fractional seconds and time zone of the database.

- **SYSDATE** Returns the current date and time.

- **TO_CHAR**(*date*,'*format*') Reformats *date* according to *format*.

- **TO_DATE**(*string*,'*format*') Converts a *string* in a given '*format*' into an Oracle date. Will also accept a *number* instead of a *string*, with certain limits. '*format*' is restricted.

- **TO_DSINTERVAL**('*value*') Converts *value* of CHAR, VARCHAR2, NCHAR, or NVARCHAR2 datatype to an INTERVAL DAY TO SECOND type.

- **TO_TIMESTAMP**('*value*') converts *value* of CHAR, VARCHAR2, NCHAR, or NVARCHAR2 datatype to a value of TIMESTAMP datatype.

- **TO_TIMESTAMP_TZ**('*value*') Converts *value* of CHAR, VARCHAR2, NCHAR, or NVARCHAR2 datatype to a value of TIMESTAMP WITH TIMEZONE datatype.

- **TO_YMINTERVAL**('*value*') Converts *value* of CHAR, VARCHAR2, NCHAR, or NVARCHAR2 datatype to a value of INTERVAL YEAR TO MONTH datatype.

- **TRUNC**(*date*,'*format*') Without *format* specified, sets a *date* to 12 A.M. (midnight, the beginning of that day). For use of *format* for truncating, see TRUNC in the Alphabetical Reference.

- **TZ_OFFSET**('*value*') Returns the time zone offset corresponding to the value entered based on the date the statement is executed.

## DBA
*See* DATABASE ADMINISTRATOR (DBA).

## DBTIMEZONE
**SEE ALSO**    DATE FUNCTIONS
**FORMAT**

```
DBTIMEZONE
```

**DESCRIPTION**    DBTIMEZONE returns the value of the database time zone.
**EXAMPLE**

```
select DBTIMEZONE from DUAL;
```

## DBWR PROCESS
One of the background processes used by Oracle. The **Database Wr**iter process writes new data to the database. Also referred to as DBWn.

## DCL
*See* DATA CONTROL LANGUAGE (DCL) STATEMENTS.

## DDL
*See* DATA DEFINITION LANGUAGE (DDL) STATEMENTS.

## DDL LOCK
When a user executes a DDL command, Oracle locks the objects referred to in the command with DDL locks. A DDL lock locks objects in the data dictionary. (Contrast this to parse locks, the other type of dictionary lock.)

## DEADLOCK
A deadlock is a rare situation in which two or more user processes of a database cannot complete their transactions. This occurs because each process is holding a resource that the other process requires (such as a row in a table) in order to complete. Although these situations occur rarely, Oracle detects and resolves deadlocks by rolling back the work of one of the processes.

## DECLARE
The DECLARE command allows you to declare cursors, variables, and exceptions for use within PL/SQL blocks. *See* Chapter 27.

## DECLARE CURSOR (Form 1-Embedded SQL)
**SEE ALSO**    **CLOSE, DECLARE DATABASE, DECLARE STATEMENT, FETCH, OPEN, PREPARE, SELECT, SELECT** (Embedded SQL), *Precompiler Programmer's Guide*
**FORMAT**

```
EXEC SQL [AT {database | :host_variable}]
DECLARE cursor CURSOR
 FOR {SELECT command | statement}
```

**DESCRIPTION**    The **DECLARE CURSOR** statement must appear before any SQL that references this cursor, and must be compiled in the same source as procedures that reference it. Its name must be unique to the source.

*database* is the name of a database already declared in a **DECLARE DATABASE** and used in a SQL CONNECT; *host_variable* is a variable with such a name as its value. *cursor* is the name you assign to this cursor. **SELECT** *command* is a query with no **INTO** clause. Alternatively, a SQL statement or a PL/SQL block already declared in a SQL **DECLARE STATEMENT** statement can be used.

When the **FOR UPDATE OF** clause is included in the **SELECT** statement, an **update** can reference the cursor with **where current of cursor**, although the cursor must still be open, and a row must be present from a **FETCH**.

## DECLARE CURSOR (Form 2-PL/SQL)
**SEE ALSO**    CLOSE, FETCH, OPEN, SELECT. . .INTO, Chapter 27
**FORMAT**

```
DECLARE
CURSOR cursor (parameter datatype [,parameter datatype]...)
 IS select_statement
 [FOR UPDATE OF column [,column]...];
```

**DESCRIPTION**    A cursor is a work area that Oracle uses to control the row currently being processed. **DECLARE CURSOR** names a cursor and declares that it IS (the result of) a certain *select_statement*. The *select_statement* is required, and may not contain an **INTO** clause. The cursor must be declared. It can then be **OPEN**ed, and rows can then be **FETCH**ed into it. Finally, it can be **CLOSE**d.

Variables cannot be used directly in the **where** clause of the *select_statement* unless they've first been identified as parameters, in a list that precedes the select. Note that DECLARE CURSOR does not execute the **select** statement, and the parameters have no values until they are assigned in an **OPEN** statement. Parameters have standard object names, and datatypes, including VARCHAR2, CHAR, NUMBER, DATE, and BOOLEAN, all without size or scale, however.

**FOR UPDATE OF** is required if you wish to affect the current row in the cursor using either **update** or **delete** commands with the **CURRENT OF** clause.

## DECLARE DATABASE (Embedded SQL)
**SEE ALSO**    **COMMIT RELEASE** (Embedded SQL), **CONNECT** (Embedded SQL), *Precompiler Programmer's Guide*
**FORMAT**

```
EXEC SQL DECLARE database DATABASE
```

**DESCRIPTION**    **DECLARE DATABASE** declares the name of a remote database for use in later AT clauses of SQL statements, including **COMMIT, DECLARE CURSOR, DELETE, INSERT, ROLLBACK, SELECT**, and **UPDATE**.

## DECLARE STATEMENT (Embedded SQL)
**SEE ALSO**    CLOSE, FETCH, OPEN, PREPARE, *Precompiler Programmer's Guide*
**FORMAT**

```
EXEC SQL [AT {database | :host_variable}]
DECLARE STATEMENT {statement | block_name} STATEMENT
```

**DESCRIPTION**    *statement* is the name of the statement in a **DECLARE CURSOR**, and must be identical to the statement name here. *database* is the name of a database previously declared with **DECLARE DATABASE**; *host_variable* may contain such a name as its value. This command is only needed if **DECLARE CURSOR** will come before a **PREPARE**. When it is used, it should come prior to **DECLARE**, **DESCRIBE**, **OPEN**, or **PREPARE**, and must be compiled in the same source as procedures that reference it.

# DECLARE TABLE

**SEE ALSO**    **CREATE TABLE,** *Precompiler Programmer's Guide*

**FORMAT**

```
EXEC SQL DECLARE table TABLE
(column datatype [NULL|NOT NULL],
 ...);
```

**DESCRIPTION**    *table* is the name of the table being declared. *column* is a column name and *datatype* is its datatype. This structure is nearly identical to that of **create table**, including the use of **NULL** and **NOT NULL**.

You use **DECLARE TABLE** to tell precompilers to ignore actual Oracle database table definitions when running with SQLCHECK=FULL. The precompilers will regard the table description here as relevant to the program and ignore the table definitions in the database. Use this when table definitions will change, or when a table has not yet been created. If SQLCHECK is not equal to FULL (which means tables and columns will not be checked against the database anyway), this command is ignored by the precompiler and becomes simply documentation.

**EXAMPLE**

```
EXEC SQL DECLARE COMFORT TABLE (
 City VARCHAR2(13) NOT NULL,
 SampleDate DATE NOT NULL,
 Noon NUMBER(3,1),
 Midnight NUMBER(3,1),
 Precipitation NUMBER
);
```

# DECODE

**SEE ALSO**    OTHER FUNCTIONS, **CASE**, **TRANSLATE**, Chapter 17

**FORMAT**

```
DECODE(value,if1,then1[,if2,then2,]... ,else)
```

**DESCRIPTION**    *value* represents any column in a table, regardless of datatype, or any result of a computation, such as one date minus another, a **SUBSTR** of a character column, one number times another, and so on. For each row, *value* is tested. If it equals *if1*, then the result of the **DECODE** is *then1*; if value equals *if2*, then the result of the **DECODE** is *then2*, and so on, for virtually as many if/then pairs as you can construct. If *value* equals none of the *if*s, then the result of the **DECODE** is *else*. Each of the *if*s, *then*s, and the *else* also can be a column or the result of a function or computation. Chapter 16 is devoted entirely to **DECODE**.

**EXAMPLE**

```
select DISTINCT City,
 DECODE(City, 'SAN FRANCISCO', 'CITY BY THE BAY', City)
```

```
 from COMFORT;

CITY DECODE(CITY,'SA
-------------- ----------------
KEENE KEENE
SAN FRANCISCO CITY BY THE BAY
```

# DECOMPOSE

**SEE ALSO**   CONVERSION FUNCTIONS

**FORMAT**

DECOMPOSE ('*string*')

**DESCRIPTION**   DECOMPOSE translates a string in any datatype to a unicode string after canonical decomposition in the same character set as the input.

# DEFAULT

Default is a clause or option value that is used if no alternative is specified. You can specify the default value for a column in a table via a DEFAULT column constraint.

# DEFAULT VALUE

The default value is a value that is used unless a different one is specified or entered.

# DEFERRED ROLLBACK SEGMENT

A deferred rollback segment is one containing entries that could not be applied to the tablespace, because the given tablespace was offline. As soon as the tablespace comes back online, all the entries are applied.

# DEFINE (SQL*PLUS)

*See* **SET**.

# DEFINE PHASE

The define phase is one phase of executing a SQL query, in which the program defines buffers to hold the results of a query to be executed.

# DEL

**SEE ALSO**   **APPEND, CHANGE, EDIT, INPUT, LIST**, Chapter 6

**FORMAT**

DEL

**DESCRIPTION**   DEL deletes the current line of the current buffer. You can delete multiple lines with a single DEL command.

**EXAMPLE**

del

deletes the current line in the SQLPLUS buffer.

To delete a range of lines with one command, specify the line numbers of the beginning and ending of the range in the **DEL** command. The following command would delete lines 2 through 8 in the current buffer.

```
del 2 8
```

# DELETE (Form 1-PL/SQL)

**SEE ALSO**   **DECLARE CURSOR, UPDATE**, Chapter 27

**DESCRIPTION**   In PL/SQL, **DELETE** follows the normal SQL command rules, with these added features:

- A PL/SQL function and/or variable can be used in the **where** clause just as a literal could be.
- **DELETE. . .WHERE CURRENT OF cursor** can be used in conjunction with a SELECT FOR UPDATE to delete the last row **FETCH**ed. The **FETCH** can either be explicit or implicit from a FOR LOOP.
- Like **update** and **insert**, the **delete** command executes only within the SQL cursor. The SQL cursor's attributes can be checked for the success of the **delete**. SQL%ROWCOUNT will contain the number of rows deleted. If this is 0, none were **delete**d. (Also, SQL%FOUND will be FALSE if none were **delete**d.)

# DELETE (Form 2-SQL Command)

**SEE ALSO**   **DROP TABLE, FROM, INSERT, SELECT, UPDATE, WHERE**, Chapter 15

**FORMAT**

delete::=

DML_table_expression_clause::=

**subquery_restriction_clause::=**

**table_collection_expression::=**

**where_clause::=**

**returning_clause::=**

**DESCRIPTION**    **DELETE** deletes from *table* all rows that satisfy *condition*. The *condition* may include a correlated query and use the alias for correlation. If the table is remote, a database link has to be defined. @*link* specifies the link. If *link* is entered, but *user* is not, the query seeks a table owned by the same user on the remote database.

   When using the **DELETE** command, you may specify a partition or subpartition. In order to delete rows from a table, you must have DELETE privileges on the table. If the SQL92_SECURITY initialization parameter is set to TRUE, then you must also have SELECT privileges if the **DELETE** refers to columns in the table itself.

**EXAMPLE**    This example deletes all rows for the city of Keene from the COMFORT table:

```
delete from COMFORT
 where City = 'KEENE';
```

# DELETE (Form 3-Embedded SQL)
## FORMAT

```
EXEC SQL [AT {db_name | :host_variable}] [FOR :host_integer | integer]
 DELETE [FROM]
 [(subquery)
 | [user.] {table / view } [@dblink |PARTITION (partition_name)]]
[alias] [WHERE {condition | CURRENT OF cursor}]
[{ RETURN | RETURNING } expr [, expr]... INTO
 :host_variable [[INDICATOR] :ind_variable]
 [, :host_variable [[INDICATOR] :ind_variable]]...]
```

**DESCRIPTION**    This form of the **DELETE** command allows you to delete rows (from a table, view, or index-only table) from within a precompiler program.

## DENSE_RANK

**SEE ALSO**   GROUP FUNCTIONS, Chapter 13

**FORMAT**

```
DENSE_RANK (expr [, expr]...) WITHIN GROUP
(ORDER BY
 expr [DESC | ASC] [NULLS { FIRST | LAST }]
 [, expr [DESC | ASC] [NULLS { FIRST | LAST }]]...)
```

For analytics:

```
DENSE_RANK () OVER ([query_partition_clause] order_by_clause)
```

**DESCRIPTION**   **DENSE_RANK** computes the rank of a row in an ordered group of rows. See Chapter 13 for related examples.

## DEREF

The **DEREF** operator returns the value of a referenced object. *See* Chapter 31.

## DESCRIBE (Form 1-SQL*PLUS Command)

**SEE ALSO**   **CREATE TABLE**

**FORMAT**

```
DESC[RIBE] [user.]table
```

**DESCRIPTION**   **DESCRIBE** displays a specified table's definition. If *user* is omitted, SQL*PLUS displays the table owned by you. The definition includes the table and its columns, with each column's name, **NULL** or **NOT NULL** status, datatype, and width or precision. **DESCRIBE** can also be used on views, synonyms, or function and procedure specifications.

**EXAMPLE**

```
describe COMFORT
```

```
Name Null? Type
------------------------------ --------- ------------
CITY NOT NULL VARCHAR2(13)
SAMPLEDATE NOT NULL DATE
NOON NUMBER(3,1)
MIDNIGHT NUMBER(3,1)
PRECIPITATION NUMBER
```

## DESCRIBE (Form 2-Embedded SQL)

**SEE ALSO**   PREPARE

**FORMAT**

```
EXEC SQL DESCRIBE [BIND VARIABLES FOR
 | SELECT LIST FOR]
 statement_name INTO descriptor
```

**DESCRIPTION**     The **DESCRIBE** command initializes a descriptor to hold descriptions of host variables for a dynamic SQL statement or PL/SQL block. The **DESCRIBE** command follows the **PREPARE** command.

# DICTIONARY CACHE

The dictionary cache stores data dictionary information in the SGA. Caching dictionary information improves performance because the dictionary information is used frequently. The dictionary cache is part of the Shared SQL Pool.

# DICTIONARY LOCKS

A dictionary lock is a shared lock owned by users parsing DML statements, or an exclusive lock owned by users doing DDL commands, to prevent a table from being altered while the dictionaries are queried. There may be many such locks concurrently.

# DIMENSION

A dimension is a named set of hierarchies among columns of tables. For example, in the geography dimension, countries are parts of continents, and states are parts of countries. When you define the dimension relationships, Oracle can use that information when evaluating optimizer choices. If there are materialized views that contain aggregated data, the optimizer can use the dimension definitions to determine if the materialized view can be accessed instead of the base table. *See* **CREATE DIMENSION**.

# DIRECTORY

A logical name that points to a physical directory, used by BFILE LOBs and external tables. *See* **CREATE DIRECTORY** and Chapter 25.

# DISASSOCIATE STATISTICS

**SEE ALSO**     **ASSOCIATE STATISTICS**

**FORMAT**

```
DISASSOCIATE STATISTICS FROM
{ COLUMNS [schema .] table . column [, [schema .] table . column]...
| FUNCTIONS [schema .] function [, [schema .] function]...
| PACKAGES [schema .] package [, [schema .] package]...
| TYPES [schema .] type [, [schema .] type]...
| INDEXES [schema .] index [, [schema .] index]...
| INDEXTYPES [schema .] indextype [, [schema .] indextype]...}
[FORCE];
```

**DESCRIPTION**     **ASSOCIATE STATISTICS** associates a set of statistics functions with one or more columns, standalone functions, packages, types, or indexes. **DISASSOCIATE STATISTICS** revokes the associations. You must have ALTER privilege on the base object.

# DISCONNECT

**SEE ALSO**     **CONNECT, EXIT, QUIT**

**FORMAT**

```
DISC[ONNECT]
```

**DESCRIPTION**    **DISCONNECT** commits pending changes to the database and logs you off of Oracle. Your SQL*PLUS session remains active and the features of SQL*PLUS continue to function, but without any connection to the database. You can edit buffers, use your own editor, spool and stop spooling, or connect to Oracle again, but until a connection is established, no SQL can be executed.

   **EXIT** or **QUIT** will return you to your host's operating system. If you are still connected when you **EXIT** or **QUIT**, you will be automatically disconnected and logged off of Oracle.

# DISTINCT

Distinct means unique. It is used as a part of **select** statements and group functions. *See* GROUP FUNCTIONS, **SELECT**.

# DISTRIBUTED DATABASE

A distributed database is a collection of databases that can be operated and managed separately and also share information.

# DISTRIBUTED PROCESSING

Distributed processing is performing computation on multiple CPUs to achieve a single result.

# DISTRIBUTED QUERY

A distributed query is one that selects data from multiple databases, usually across multiple nodes of a network.

# DML

*See* DATA MANIPULATION LANGUAGE (DML) STATEMENTS.

# DML LOCK

When a user executes a SQL statement, the data to which the statement refers is locked in one of several lock modes. The user can also lock data explicitly with a **LOCK** statement.

# DROP CLUSTER

**SEE ALSO**    **CREATE CLUSTER**, **DROP TABLE**, Chapter 20
**FORMAT**

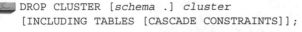

```
DROP CLUSTER [schema .] cluster
[INCLUDING TABLES [CASCADE CONSTRAINTS]];
```

**DESCRIPTION**    **DROP CLUSTER** deletes a cluster from the database. You must have DROP ANY CLUSTER privilege if the cluster is not in your own schema. You cannot drop a cluster that contains tables. The tables must be dropped first. The INCLUDING TABLES clause will drop all the clustered tables automatically. The **CASCADE CONSTRAINTS** option drops all referential integrity constraints from tables outside the cluster that refer to keys in the clustered tables.

   Individual tables cannot be removed from a cluster. To accomplish the same effect, copy the table under a new name (use **CREATE TABLE** with AS SELECT), drop the old one (this will remove it from the cluster), **RENAME** the copy to the name of the table you dropped, and then issue the appropriate **GRANT**S, and create the needed indexes.

# DROP CONTEXT

**SEE ALSO**     **CREATE CONTEXT**
**FORMAT**

```
DROP CONTEXT namespace;
```

**DESCRIPTION**     **DROP CONTEXT** deletes a context namespace from the database. You must have the DROP ANY CONTEXT system privilege.

# DROP DATABASE LINK

**SEE ALSO**     **CREATE DATABASE LINK**, Chapter 22
**FORMAT**

```
DROP [PUBLIC] DATABASE LINK link;
```

**DESCRIPTION**     **DROP DATABASE LINK** drops a database link you own. For a public link, the optional **PUBLIC** keyword must be used, and you must be a DBA to use it. **PUBLIC** cannot be used when dropping a private link. *link* is the name of the link being dropped. You must have DROP PUBLIC DATABASE LINK system privilege to drop a public database link. You may drop private database links in your account.

**EXAMPLE**     The following will drop a database link named ADAH_AT_HOME:

```
drop database link ADAH_AT_HOME;
```

# DROP DIMENSION

**SEE ALSO**     **CREATE DIMENSION**
**FORMAT**

```
DROP DIMENSION [schema .] dimension;
```

**DESCRIPTION**     **DROP DIMENSION** drops a dimension you own. You must have DROP ANY DIMENSION system privilege.

**EXAMPLE**     The following will drop the GEOGRAPHY dimension:

```
drop dimension GEOGRAPHY;
```

# DROP DIRECTORY

**SEE ALSO**     **CREATE DIRECTORY**, Chapters 25, 32
**FORMAT**

```
DROP DIRECTORY directory_name;
```

**DESCRIPTION**     **DROP DIRECTORY** drops an existing directory. You must have DROP ANY DIRECTORY privilege to drop a directory.

**NOTE**
*Do not drop a directory while its files are in use.*

**EXAMPLE**     The following will drop a directory called REVIEWS:

```
drop directory REVIEWS;
```

## DROP FUNCTION

**SEE ALSO**    **ALTER FUNCTION**, **CREATE FUNCTION**, Chapter 29

**FORMAT**

```
DROP FUNCTION [schema .] function_name;
```

**DESCRIPTION**    **DROP FUNCTION** drops the specified function. Oracle invalidates any objects that depend on or call the function. You must have DROP ANY PROCEDURE system privilege to drop a function that you do not own.

## DROP INDEX

**SEE ALSO**    **ALTER INDEX**, **CREATE INDEX**, **CREATE TABLE**, Chapter 20

**FORMAT**

```
DROP INDEX [schema .] index [FORCE];
```

**DESCRIPTION**    **DROP INDEX** drops the specified index. You must either own the index or have DROP ANY INDEX system privilege. **FORCE** applies only to domain indexes. This clause drops the domain index even if the indextype routine invocation returns an error or the index is marked **IN PROGRESS**.

## DROP INDEXTYPE

**SEE ALSO**    **CREATE INDEXTYPE**

**FORMAT**

```
DROP INDEXTYPE [schema .] indextype [FORCE];
```

**DESCRIPTION**    **DROP INDEXTYPE** drops the specified indextype and any association with statistics types. You must have the DROP ANY INDEXTYPE system privilege.

## DROP JAVA

**SEE ALSO**    **CREATE JAVA**, Chapter 36

**FORMAT**

```
DROP JAVA { SOURCE | CLASS | RESOURCE } [schema .] object_name;
```

**DESCRIPTION**    **DROP JAVA** drops the specified Java class, source, or resource. You must have the DROP PROCEDURE system privilege. If the object is in another user's schema, you must have the DROP ANY PROCEDURE system privilege.

## DROP LIBRARY

**SEE ALSO**    **CREATE LIBRARY**, Chapter 29

**FORMAT**

```
DROP LIBRARY library_name;
```

**DESCRIPTION**    **DROP LIBRARY** drops the specified library. You must have the DROP ANY LIBRARY system privilege.

# DROP MATERIALIZED VIEW

**SEE ALSO**   ALTER MATERIALIZED VIEW, CREATE MATERIALIZED VIEW, Chapter 23
**FORMAT**

```
DROP MATERIALIZED VIEW [schema .] materialized_view;
```

**DESCRIPTION**   DROP MATERIALIZED VIEW drops the indicated materialized view. You must either own the materialized view or you must have DROP ANY SNAPSHOT or DROP ANY MATERIALIZED VIEW system privilege.

The keyword **SNAPSHOT** is supported in place of **MATERIALIZED VIEW** for backward compatibility.

# DROP MATERIALIZED VIEW LOG

**SEE ALSO**   ALTER MATERIALIZED VIEW LOG, CREATE MATERIALIZED VIEW LOG, Chapter 23
**FORMAT**

```
DROP MATERIALIZED VIEW LOG ON [schema .] table;
```

**DESCRIPTION**   DROP MATERIALIZED VIEW LOG drops the indicated log table. To drop a materialized view log, you must have the privileges to drop a table. After dropping the log, any materialized views on the master table will get complete refreshes, not fast refreshes.

The keyword **SNAPSHOT** is supported in place of **MATERIALIZED VIEW** for backward compatibility.

# DROP OPERATOR

**SEE ALSO**   ALTER OPERATOR
**FORMAT**

```
DROP OPERATOR [schema .] operator [FORCE];
```

**DESCRIPTION**   DROP OPERATOR drops a user-defined operator. You must either own the operator or have DROP ANY OPERATOR system privilege. Specify **FORCE** to drop the operator even if it is currently being referenced by one or more schema objects (indextypes, packages, functions, procedures, and so on), and marks those dependent objects **INVALID**.

# DROP OUTLINE

**SEE ALSO**   CREATE OUTLINE
**FORMAT**

```
DROP OUTLINE outline;
```

**DESCRIPTION**   DROP OUTLINE drops a stored outline from the database. You must have the DROP ANY OUTLINE system privilege. Subsequent executions of SQL statements that used the outline will have their execution paths evaluated at runtime.

# DROP PACKAGE

**SEE ALSO**   ALTER PACKAGE, CREATE PACKAGE, Chapter 29
**FORMAT**

```
DROP PACKAGE [BODY] [schema .] package;
```

**DESCRIPTION** DROP PACKAGE drops the specified package. Using the optional **BODY** clause drops only the body without dropping the package specification. Oracle invalidates any objects that depend on the package if you drop the package specification but not if you just drop the body. You must either own the package or have DROP ANY PROCEDURE system privilege.

## DROP PROCEDURE
**SEE ALSO** **ALTER PROCEDURE, CREATE PROCEDURE**, Chapter 29
**FORMAT**

```
DROP PROCEDURE [schema .] procedure;
```

**DESCRIPTION** DROP PROCEDURE drops the specified procedure. Oracle invalidates any objects that depend on or call the procedure. You must either own the procedure or have DROP ANY PROCEDURE system privilege.

## DROP PROFILE
**SEE ALSO** **ALTER PROFILE, CREATE PROFILE**, Chapter 19
**FORMAT**

```
DROP PROFILE profile [CASCADE];
```

**DESCRIPTION** DROP PROFILE drops the specified profile. You must have DROP PROFILE system privilege.

## DROP ROLE
**SEE ALSO** **ALTER ROLE, CREATE ROLE**, Chapter 19
**FORMAT**

```
DROP ROLE role;
```

**DESCRIPTION** DROP ROLE drops the specified role. You must have either been granted the role WITH ADMIN OPTION or you must have DROP ANY ROLE system privilege.

## DROP ROLLBACK SEGMENT
**SEE ALSO** **ALTER ROLLBACK SEGMENT, CREATE ROLLBACK SEGMENT, CREATE TABLESPACE, SHUTDOWN, STARTUP**, Chapter 40
**FORMAT**

```
DROP ROLLBACK SEGMENT rollback_segment;
```

**DESCRIPTION** *rollback_segment* is the name of an existing rollback segment to be dropped. The segment must not be in use when this statement is executed. **PUBLIC** is required for dropping public rollback segments.

The Status column of the data dictionary view DBA_ROLLBACK_SEGS can reveal which rollback segments are in use. If the segment is in use, you can either wait until it no longer is in use, or SHUTDOWN the database using IMMEDIATE, and then bring it up in EXCLUSIVE mode using **STARTUP**. You must have the DROP ROLLBACK SEGMENT system privilege in order to drop a rollback segment.

# DROP SEQUENCE

**SEE ALSO**    **ALTER SEQUENCE, CREATE SEQUENCE**, Chapter 20
**FORMAT**

```
DROP SEQUENCE [schema .] sequence_name;
```

**DESCRIPTION**    *sequence_name* is the name of the sequence being dropped. To drop a sequence, you must either own the sequence or have DROP ANY SEQUENCE system privilege.

# DROP SNAPSHOT

*See* **DROP MATERIALIZED VIEW**

# DROP SNAPSHOT LOG

*See* **DROP MATERIALIZED VIEW LOG**

# DROP SYNONYM

**SEE ALSO**    **CREATE SYNONYM**, Chapter 22
**FORMAT**

```
DROP [PUBLIC] SYNONYM [schema .] synonym;
```

**DESCRIPTION**    **DROP SYNONYM** drops the specified synonym. To drop a public synonym, you must have DROP ANY PUBLIC SYNONYM system privilege. To drop a private synonym, you must own the synonym or have DROP ANY SYNONYM system privilege.

# DROP TABLE

**SEE ALSO**    **ALTER TABLE, CREATE INDEX, CREATE TABLE, DROP CLUSTER**, Chapter 18
**FORMAT**

```
DROP TABLE [schema .] table [CASCADE CONSTRAINTS];
```

**DESCRIPTION**    **DROP TABLE** drops the specified table. To drop a table, you must either own the table or have DROP ANY TABLE system privilege. Dropping a table also drops indexes and grants associated with it. Objects built on dropped tables are marked invalid and cease to work.

The **CASCADE CONSTRAINTS** option drops all referential integrity constraints referring to keys in the dropped table.

You can drop a cluster and all of its tables by using the INCLUDING TABLES clause on **DROP CLUSTER**.

# DROP TABLESPACE

**SEE ALSO**    **ALTER TABLESPACE, CREATE DATABASE, CREATE TABLESPACE**, Chapters 20 and 40.
**FORMAT**

```
DROP TABLESPACE tablespace
[INCLUDING CONTENTS [AND DATAFILES] [CASCADE CONSTRAINTS]];
```

**DESCRIPTION**    *tablespace* is the name of the tablespace being dropped. The **INCLUDING CONTENTS** option allows you to drop a tablespace that contains data. Without **INCLUDING**

**CONTENTS**, only an empty tablespace can be dropped. Tablespaces should be offline (*see* **ALTER TABLESPACE**) before dropping, or the drop operation will be prevented by any users accessing data, index, rollback, or temporary segments in the tablespace. You must have DROP TABLESPACE system privilege to use this command.

# DROP TRIGGER

**SEE ALSO**    **ALTER TRIGGER**, **CREATE TRIGGER**, Chapters 28 and 30
**FORMAT**

```
DROP TRIGGER [schema .] trigger;
```

**DESCRIPTION**    **DROP TRIGGER** drops the specified trigger. You must either own the trigger or you must have the DROP ANY TRIGGER system privilege.

# DROP TYPE

**SEE ALSO**    **CREATE TYPE**, Chapters 4 and 30
**FORMAT**

```
DROP TYPE [schema .] type_name [FORCE | VALIDATE];
```

**DESCRIPTION**    **DROP TYPE** drops the specification and body of an abstract datatype. You must either own the type or have DROP ANY TYPE system privilege. You cannot drop a type if a table or other object references it.

# DROP TYPE BODY

**SEE ALSO**    **CREATE TYPE**, **CREATE TYPE BODY**, **DROP TYPE**, Chapter 30
**FORMAT**

```
DROP TYPE BODY [schema .] type_name;
```

**DESCRIPTION**    **DROP TYPE BODY** drops the body of the specified type. You must either own the type or have DROP ANY TYPE system privilege.

# DROP USER

**SEE ALSO**    **ALTER USER**, **CREATE USER**, Chapter 19
**FORMAT**

```
DROP USER user [CASCADE];
```

**DESCRIPTION**    **DROP USER** drops the specified user. You must have DROP USER system privilege. The **CASCADE** option drops all the objects in the user's schema before dropping the user, and you *must* specify **CASCADE** if the user has any objects in the schema.

# DROP VIEW

**SEE ALSO**    **CREATE SYNONYM**, **CREATE TABLE**, **CREATE VIEW**, Chapter 18
**FORMAT**

```
DROP VIEW [schema .] view [CASCADE CONSTRAINTS];
```

**DESCRIPTION**    **DROP VIEW** drops the specified view. The view must either be in your schema or you must have DROP ANY VIEW system privilege.

# DROPJAVA

DROPJAVA is a utility for removing Java classes from the database. *See* LOADJAVA.

# DUAL

**SEE ALSO**    **FROM**, **SELECT**, Chapter 9

**DESCRIPTION**    DUAL is a table with only one row and one column in it. Since Oracle's many functions work on both columns and literals, it is possible to demonstrate some of its functionality by using just literals or pseudo-columns. When doing this, the **select** statement doesn't care which columns are in the table, and a single row is more than sufficient to demonstrate a point.

**EXAMPLE**    The following shows the current User and SysDate:

```
select User, SysDate from DUAL;
```

# DUMP

**SEE ALSO**    **RAWTOHEX**

**FORMAT**

```
DUMP(string [,format [,start [,length]]])
```

**DESCRIPTION**    DUMP displays the value of *string* in internal data format, in ASCII, octal, decimal, hex, or character format. *format* defaults to ASCII or EBCDIC, depending upon your machine; 8 produces octal, 10 decimal, 16 hex, and 17 character (the same as ASCII or EBCDIC). *start* is the beginning position in the string, and *length* is the number of characters to display. *string* can be a literal or an expression.

**EXAMPLE**    The following shows how characters 1 through 8 are represented in hex for just the City in the first row of the COMFORT table:

```
select City, dump(City,16,1,8) from COMFORT where rownum < 2;

CITY DUMP(CITY,16,1,8)
------------- ------------------------------------
SAN FRANCISCO Typ=1 Len= 13: 53,41,4e,20,46,52,41,4e
```

# EBCDIC

EBCDIC is an acronym for **E**xtended **B**inary **C**oded **D**ecimal **I**nterchange **C**ode—the collation sequence used by IBM's mainframe computers and other computers compatible with them.

# ECHO (SQL*PLUS)

*See* **SET**.

# EDIT

**SEE ALSO**    **DEFINE**, **SET**, Chapter 6

**FORMAT**

```
EDIT [file[.ext]]
```

**DESCRIPTION** **EDIT** calls an external standard text editor and passes to it the name of the file. If *.ext* is omitted, the extension SQL is appended. If *file* and *ext* are both omitted, the editor is called and passed the name of a file (invented by SQLPLUS) that contains the contents of the current buffer. The local user variable _EDITOR determines which text editor is used by **EDIT**. _EDITOR can be changed with **DEFINE**, and this is usually best done in the LOGIN.SQL file, which is read whenever SQL*PLUS is invoked.

     **EDIT** will fail if the current buffer is empty and **EDIT** is called without a file name. You can use the **SET EDITFILE** command to set the default name of the file created by the **EDIT** command.

# EMBEDDED (SQL*PLUS)

*See* **SET**.

# EMPTY_BLOB

**SEE ALSO** Chapter 32

**FORMAT**

```
EMPTY_BLOB()
```

**DESCRIPTION** **EMPTY_BLOB** returns an empty LOB locator that can be used to initialize a LOB variable or, in an INSERT or UPDATE statement, to initialize a LOB column or attribute to EMPTY. EMPTY means that the LOB is initialized, but not populated with data.

**EXAMPLE**

```
UPDATE BOOK_TEXT set BlobCol = EMPTY_BLOB();
```

# EMPTY_CLOB

**SEE ALSO** Chapter 32

**FORMAT**

```
EMPTY_CLOB()
```

**DESCRIPTION** **EMPTY_CLOB** returns an empty LOB locator that can be used to initialize a LOB variable or, in an INSERT or UPDATE statement, to initialize a LOB column or attribute to EMPTY. EMPTY means that the LOB is initialized, but not populated with data.

**EXAMPLE**

```
UPDATE BOOK_TEXT set ClobCol = EMPTY_CLOB();
```

# END

**SEE ALSO** **BEGIN**, BLOCK STRUCTURE, Chapter 27

**FORMAT**

```
END [block label] ;
```

**DESCRIPTION** **END** is unrelated to the END IF and END LOOP statements. *See* IF and LOOP for details on either of them.

     **END** is the closing statement of a PL/SQL block's executable section (and the entire block). If the block is named at the **BEGIN**, the name must also follow the word **END**. At least one executable

statement is required between **BEGIN** and **END**. *See* BLOCK STRUCTURE and Chapters 27 and 29 for more details.

# ENQUEUE

Enqueue is the lock on a given resource. Those waiting for a given resource have not yet gotten the enqueue. Enqueues exist for many database resources.

# ENTITY

An entity is a person, place, or thing represented by a table. In a table, each row represents an occurrence of that entity.

# ENTITY-RELATIONSHIP MODEL

An entity-relationship model is a framework used to model systems for a database. It divides all elements of a system into two categories: entities or relationships.

# EQUI-JOIN

An equi-join is a join in which the join comparison operator is an equality, such as

```
where BOOKSHELF.Title = BOOKSHELF_CHECKOUT.Title
```

# ESCAPE (SQL*PLUS)

*See* **SET**.

# EXCEPTION

**SEE ALSO**     BLOCK STRUCTURE, **DECLARE EXCEPTION**, **RAISE**, Chapter 27
**FORMAT**

```
EXCEPTION
 {WHEN {OTHERS | exception [OR exception]...}
 THEN statement; [statement;]...}
 [WHEN {OTHER | exception [OR exception]...}
 THEN statement; [statement;]...]...
```

**DESCRIPTION**     The EXCEPTION section of a PL/SQL block is where program control is transferred whenever an exception flag is raised. Exception flags are either user-defined or system exceptions raised automatically by PL/SQL. *See* **RAISE** for details on user-defined exception flags. The system exception flags are all, in effect, BOOLEAN variables that are either TRUE or FALSE. The **WHEN** clause is used to test these. For example, the NOT_LOGGED_ON flag is raised if you attempt to issue a command to Oracle without being logged on. You do not need to have **DECLARE**d an exception, or **RAISE**d this flag yourself. PL/SQL will do it for you.

When any exception flag is raised, the program immediately halts whatever it was doing and jumps to the EXCEPTION section of the current block. This section, however, doesn't know automatically which exception flag was raised, nor what to do. Therefore, you must code the EXCEPTION section first to check all of the exception flags that are likely to have occurred, and then give action instructions for each. This is what the **WHEN...THEN** logic does. You can use WHEN OTHERS as a catch-all to handle unanticipated errors for which you have not declared exceptions.

**EXAMPLE**   Here one exception flag is tested in the EXCEPTION section. The ZERO_DIVIDE flag is raised when any calculation attempts to divide by zero.

```
declare
 pi constant NUMBER(9,7) := 3.1415927;
 radius INTEGER(5);
 area NUMBER(14,2);
 some_variable NUMBER(14,2);
begin
 radius := 3;
 loop
 some_variable := 1/(radius-4);
 area := pi*power(radius,2);
 insert into AREAS values (radius, area);
 radius := radius+1;
 exit when area >100;
 end loop;
exception
 when ZERO_DIVIDE
 then insert into AREAS values (0,0);
end;
```

The system-raised exception flags are:

ACCESS_INTO_NULL	Your program attempts to assign values to the attributes of an uninitialized (atomically null) object.
CASE_NOT_FOUND	None of the choices in the WHEN clauses of a CASE statement is selected, and there is no ELSE clause.
COLLECTION_IS_NULL	Your program attempts to apply collection methods other than EXISTS to an uninitialized (atomically null) nested table or varray, or the program attempts to assign values to the elements of an uninitialized nested table or varray.
CURSOR_ALREADY_OPEN	Your program attempts to open an already open cursor. A cursor must be closed before it can be reopened. A cursor FOR loop automatically opens the cursor to which it refers. So, your program cannot open that cursor inside the loop.
DUP_VAL_ON_INDEX	Your program attempts to store duplicate values in a database column that is constrained by a unique index.
INVALID_CURSOR	Your program attempts an illegal cursor operation such as closing an unopened cursor.
INVALID_NUMBER	In a SQL statement, the conversion of a character string into a number fails because the string does not represent a valid number. (In procedural statements, VALUE_ERROR is raised.) This exception is also raised when the LIMIT-clause expression in a bulk FETCH statement does not evaluate to a positive number.
LOGIN_DENIED	Your program attempts to log on to Oracle with an invalid username and/or password.

NO_DATA_FOUND	A SELECT INTO statement returns no rows, or your program references a deleted element in a nested table or an uninitialized element in an index-by table. SQL aggregate functions such as AVG and SUM always return a value or a null. So, a SELECT INTO statement that calls an aggregate function never raises NO_DATA_FOUND. The FETCH statement is expected to return no rows eventually, so when that happens, no exception is raised.
NOT_LOGGED_ON	Your program issues a database call without being connected to Oracle.
PROGRAM_ERROR	PL/SQL has an internal problem.
ROWTYPE_MISMATCH	The host cursor variable and PL/SQL cursor variable involved in an assignment have incompatible return types. For example, when an open host cursor variable is passed to a stored subprogram, the return types of the actual and formal parameters must be compatible.
SELF_IS_NULL	Your program attempts to call a MEMBER method on a null instance. That is, the built-in parameter SELF (which is always the first parameter passed to a MEMBER method) is null.
STORAGE_FRROR	PL/SQL runs out of memory or memory has been corrupted.
SUBSCRIPT_BEYOND_COUNT	Your program references a nested table or varray element using an index number larger than the number of elements in the collection.
SUBSCRIPT_OUTSIDE_LIMIT	Your program references a nested table or varray element using an index number (-1 for example) that is outside the legal range.
SYS_INVALID_ROWID	The conversion of a character string into a universal rowid fails because the character string does not represent a valid rowid.
TIMEOUT_ON_RESOURCE	A time-out occurs while Oracle is waiting for a resource.
TOO_MANY_ROWS	A SELECT INTO statement returns more than one row.
VALUE_ERROR	An arithmetic, conversion, truncation, or size-constraint error occurs. For example, when your program selects a column value into a character variable, if the value is longer than the declared length of the variable, PL/SQL aborts the assignment and raises VALUE_ERROR. In procedural statements, VALUE_ERROR is raised if the conversion of a character string into a number fails. (In SQL statements, INVALID_NUMBER is raised.)
ZERO_DIVIDE	Your program attempts to divide a number by zero.

The associated Oracle error numbers and SQLCode values are:

Exception	Oracle Error #	SQLCode
ACCESS_INTO_NULL	ORA-06530	-6530
CASE_NOT_FOUND	ORA-06592	-6592
COLLECTION_IS_NULL	ORA-06531	-6531
CURSOR_ALREADY_OPEN	ORA-06511	-6511
DUP_VAL_ON_INDEX	ORA-00001	-1

Exception	Oracle Error #	SQLCode
INVALID_CURSOR	ORA-01001	-1001
INVALID_NUMBER	ORA-01722	-1722
LOGIN_DENIED	ORA-01017	-1017
NO_DATA_FOUND	ORA-01403	+100
NOT_LOGGED_ON	ORA-01012	-1012
PROGRAM_ERROR	ORA-06501	-6501
ROWTYPE_MISMATCH	ORA-06504	-6504
SELF_IS_NULL	ORA-30625	-30625
STORAGE_ERROR	ORA-06500	-6500
SUBSCRIPT_BEYOND_COUNT	ORA-06533	-6533
SUBSCRIPT_OUTSIDE_LIMIT	ORA-06532	-6532
SYS_INVALID_ROWID	ORA-01410	-1410
TIMEOUT_ON_RESOURCE	ORA-00051	-51
TOO_MANY_ROWS	ORA-01422	-1422
VALUE_ERROR	ORA-06502	-6502
ZERO_DIVIDE	ORA-01476	-1476

OTHERS is the catch-all for any exception flags you did not check for in your EXCEPTION section. It must always be the last WHEN statement, and must stand alone. It cannot be included with any other exceptions.

Exception handling, particularly as it relates to exceptions you declare, should really be reserved for errors that are fatal—that means normal processing should stop.

If an exception flag is raised that is not tested for in the current block, the program will branch to the EXCEPTION block in the enclosing block, and so on, until either the exception raised is found, or control falls through to the host program.

EXCEPTION sections can reference variables in the same manner that the execution block can. That is, they can reference local variables directly, or variables from other blocks by prefixing them with the other block's name.

Use caution in testing for certain kinds of exceptions. For instance, if the EXCEPTION section takes the error message and inserts it into a database table, a NOT_LOGGED_ON exception would put the EXCEPTION section into an infinite loop. Design the statements that follow THEN not to duplicate the error that got the program there in the first place. You also may use **RAISE** without an exception name. This will automatically pass control to the next outer exception block, or the main program. *See* **RAISE** for further details.

# EXCEPTION_INIT

**SEE ALSO**    **DECLARE EXCEPTION, EXCEPTION, SQLCODE**, *Precompiler Programmer's Guide*
**FORMAT**

```
PRAGMA EXCEPTION_INIT(exception,integer);
```

**DESCRIPTION**   The standard system exceptions, such as ZERO_DIVIDE, which are referenced by name, are actually no more than the association of a name with the internal Oracle error number. There are hundreds of these error numbers, and only the most common have been given names. Any that are not named will still raise an exception flag and transfer control to the EXCEPTION block, but they will all be caught by OTHERS, rather than by name.

You can change this by assigning your own names to other Oracle error numbers. EXCEPTION_INIT allows you to do this. *exception* is the one-word name you assign to the integer error number (*see* Oracle's *Error Messages and Codes Manual* for a complete list). *integer* should be negative if the error code is negative (true for fatal errors), and *exception* must follow normal object naming rules.

Note that the format of this command requires the word PRAGMA before EXCEPTION_INIT. A pragma is an instruction to the PL/SQL compiler, rather than executable code. The pragma must be in the DECLARE section of a PL/SQL block, and must be preceded by an exception declaration.

**EXAMPLE**

```
DECLARE
 some_bad_error exception;
 pragma exception_init(some_bad_error, -660);
BEGIN
 ...
 EXCEPTION
 when some_bad_error
 then ...
END;
```

# EXCLUSIVE LOCK

An exclusive lock is one that permits other users to query data, but not change it. It differs from a SHARE lock because it does not permit another user to place any type of lock on the same data; several users may place SHARE locks on the same data at the same time.

# EXECUTE

**SEE ALSO**   **CALL, CREATE PROCEDURE, CREATE FUNCTION, CREATE PACKAGE, CREATE PACKAGE BODY, GRANT,** Chapters 28 and 29

**FORMAT**

```
EXECUTE procedural_object_name [arguments];
```

**DESCRIPTION**   EXECUTE executes a procedure, package, or function. To execute a procedure within a package, specify both the package name and the procedure name in the execute command, as shown in the following example. This example executes a procedure named NEW_BOOK, in a package named BOOKSHELF_PACKAGE; the value 'TALE OF TWO CITIES' is passed as input to the procedure.

```
execute BOOKSHELF_PACKAGE.NEW_BOOK('TALE OF TWO CITIES');
```

To execute a procedural object, you must have been granted the EXECUTE privilege on that object. *See* **GRANT.**

# EXECUTE (Dynamic Embedded SQL)

**SEE ALSO**   **EXECUTE IMMEDIATE, PREPARE,** *Precompiler Programmer's Guide*

**FORMAT**

```
EXEC SQL [FOR { integer | :array_size }]
 EXECUTE statement_id
 [USING
 { DESCRIPTOR SQLDA_descriptor
 | :host_variable [[INDICATOR] :indicator_variable]
 [, :host_variable [[INDICATOR] :indicator_variable]]... }]
```

**DESCRIPTION**        :*integer* is a host variable used to limit the number of iterations when the **where** clause uses arrays. *statement_id* is the identifier for a prepared **insert**, **delete**, or **update** statement to be executed (**select** is not allowed). **USING** introduces a list of substitutions into the host variables of the previously prepared statement.

## EXECUTE IMMEDIATE (Dynamic Embedded SQL)

**SEE ALSO**        **EXECUTE, PREPARE,** *Precompiler Programmer's Guide*

**FORMAT**

```
EXEC SQL [AT {database | :host_variable}]
 EXECUTE IMMEDIATE {:string | literal}
```

**DESCRIPTION**        *database* is the name of a database connection other than the default; *host_variable* may contain such a name as its value. :*string* is a host variable string containing a SQL statement. *literal* is a character string containing a SQL statement. The **EXECUTE IMMEDIATE** statement cannot contain host variable references other than an executable SQL statement in :*string*. The SQL statement is parsed, put into executable form, executed, and the executable form is destroyed. It is intended only for statements to be executed just once. Statements that require multiple executions should use **PREPARE** and **EXECUTE**, as this eliminates the overhead of parsing for each execution.

## EXISTS

**SEE ALSO**        **ANY, ALL, IN, NOT EXISTS,** Chapter 12

**FORMAT**

```
select ...
 where EXISTS (select...)
```

**DESCRIPTION**        **EXISTS** returns *true* in a **where** clause if the subquery that follows it returns at least one row. The **select** clause in the subquery can be a column, a literal, or an asterisk—it doesn't matter. (Convention suggests an asterisk or an 'x'.)

   Many people prefer **EXISTS** over **ANY** and **ALL** because it is easier to remember and understand, and most formulations of **ANY** and **ALL** can be reconstructed using **EXISTS**.

**EXAMPLE**        The query shown in the following example uses EXISTS to list from the BOOKSHELF table all Publishers that have had books checked out:

```
select Publisher
 from BOOKSHELF B
 where EXISTS
 (select 'x' from BOOKSHELF_CHECKOUT
 where BOOKSHELF_CHECKOUT.Title = B.Title);
```

# EXISTSNODE
**SEE ALSO**    Chapter 41
**FORMAT**

EXISTSNODE ( *XMLType_instance* , *Xpath_string* )

**DESCRIPTION**    **EXISTSNODE** determines whether traversal of the document using the path results in any nodes. It takes as arguments the XMLType instance containing an XML document and a VARCHAR2 string designating a path.

The return value is NUMBER: 0 if no nodes remain after applying the XPath traversal on the document, >0 if any nodes remain.

# EXIT (Form 1-PL/SQL)
**SEE ALSO**    END, LOOP, Chapter 27
**FORMAT**

EXIT [*loop*] [WHEN *condition*];

**DESCRIPTION**    Without any of its options, **EXIT** simply takes you out of the current loop, and branches control to the next statement following the loop. If you are in a nested loop, you can exit from any enclosing loop simply by specifying the loop name. If you specify a condition, you will exit when the condition evaluates to TRUE. Any cursor within a loop is automatically closed when you **EXIT**.

# EXIT (Form 2-SQL*PLUS)
**SEE ALSO**    COMMIT, DISCONNECT, QUIT, START
**FORMAT**

{EXIT | QUIT} [SUCCESS|FAILURE|WARNING|*integer*|*variable*] [COMMIT|ROLLBACK]

**DESCRIPTION**    **EXIT** ends a SQL*PLUS session and returns user to the operating system, calling program, or menu. Unless ROLLBACK is specified, **EXIT** commits pending changes to the database. A return code is also returned. SUCCESS, FAILURE, and WARNING have values that are operating-system specific; FAILURE and WARNING may be the same on some operating systems.

*integer* is a value you can pass back explicitly as the return code; *variable* allows you to set this value dynamically. This can be a user-defined variable, or a system variable, such as sql.sqlcode, which always contains the sqlcode of the last SQL statement executed, either in SQL*PLUS or an embedded PL/SQL block.

# EXP
**SEE ALSO**    LN, NUMBER FUNCTIONS, Chapter 8
**FORMAT**

EXP(*n*)

**DESCRIPTION**    **EXP** returns *e* raised to the *n*th power; e = 2.718281828....

# EXPLAIN PLAN
**SEE ALSO**    Chapter 38

**FORMAT**

```
EXPLAIN PLAN [SET STATEMENT_ID = 'name']
[INTO [schema .] table [@ dblink]]
FOR statement;
```

**DESCRIPTION**    *name* identifies this plan explanation for this *statement* when it appears in the output table, and follows normal object naming conventions. If *name* is not specified, the STATEMENT_ID column in the table will be NULL. *table* is the name of the output table into which the plan explanation will go. It must be previously created before this procedure can be executed. The start file UTLXPLAN.SQL contains the format and can be used to create the default table, named PLAN_TABLE. If *table* is not specified, EXPLAIN PLAN will use PLAN_TABLE. *sql_statement* is the simple text of any **select**, **insert**, **update**, or **delete** statement you wish to have analyzed for Oracle's execution plan for it.

# EXPORT

Export can have either of two definitions:

- Export is the Oracle utility used to store Oracle database data in export format files for later retrieval into an Oracle database via Import.
- To export is to use the Export utility to write selected table data to an export file.

For information on the Export utility, *see* the *Oracle9i Utilities User's Guide* and Chapter 40.

# EXPRESSION

An expression is any form of a column. This could be a literal, a variable, a mathematical computation, a function, or virtually any combination of functions and columns whose final result is a single value, such as a string, a number, or a date.

## External Table

An external table is a file outside the database that is accessible via SQL commands. See Chapter 25 for details on the creation and use of external tables.

## EXTRACT (datetime)

**SEE ALSO**    DATE FUNCTIONS, Chapter 9

**FORMAT**

```
EXTRACT
({ { YEAR
 | MONTH
 | DAY
 | HOUR
 | MINUTE
 | SECOND }
 | { TIMEZONE_HOUR
 | TIMEZONE_MINUTE }
 | { TIMEZONE_REGION
 | TIMEZONE_ABBR
 } }
 FROM { datetime_value_expression | interval_value_expression })
```

**DESCRIPTION**      EXTRACT extracts and returns the value of a specified datetime field from a datetime or interval value expression.

**EXAMPLE**

```
select BirthDate,
 EXTRACT(Month from BirthDate) AS Month
 from BIRTHDAY
 where FirstName = 'VICTORIA';

BIRTHDATE MONTH
--------- ----------
20-MAY-49 5
```

# EXTRACT (XML)

**SEE ALSO**      Chapter 41

**FORMAT**

```
EXTRACT (XMLType_instance , Xpath_string)
```

**DESCRIPTION**      EXTRACT is similar to the **EXISTSNODE** function. It applies a VARCHAR2 XPath string and returns an XMLType instance containing an XML fragment.

# FEEDBACK (SQL*PLUS)

*See* **SET**.

# FETCH

One phase of query execution is the fetch phase, where actual rows of data meeting all search criteria are retrieved from the database.

# FETCH (Form 1-Embedded SQL)

**SEE ALSO**      CLOSE, DECLARE CURSOR, **DESCRIBE**, INDICATOR VARIABLE, **OPEN**, **PREPARE**, *Precompiler Programmer's Guide*

**FORMAT**

```
EXEC SQL [FOR { integer | :array_size }]
 FETCH { cursor | :cursor_variable }
 { USING DESCRIPTOR SQLDA_descriptor
 | INTO :host_variable [[INDICATOR] :indicator_variable]
 [, :host_variable [[INDICATOR] :indicator_variable]]... }
```

**DESCRIPTION**      *integer* is a host variable that sets the maximum number of rows to fetch into the output variables. *cursor* is the name of a cursor previously set up by **DECLARE CURSOR**. :*host_variable* is one or more host variables into which fetched data will be placed. If any of the host variables is an array, then all of them (in the **INTO** list) must be arrays. The **INDICATOR** keyword is optional.

# FETCH (Form 2-PL/SQL)

**SEE ALSO**      %FOUND, %ROWTYPE, CLOSE, DECLARE CURSOR, LOOP, OPEN, SELECT. . .INTO, Chapter 27

**FORMAT**

```
FETCH cursor INTO {record | variable [,variable]...};
```

**DESCRIPTION**     **FETCH** gets a row of data. The named cursor's select statement determines which columns are retrieved, and its **where** statement determines which (and how many) rows can be retrieved. This is called the "active set," but it is not available to you for processing until you fetch it, row by row, using the **FETCH** statement. The **FETCH** gets a row from the active set and drops the row's values into the record (or string of variables), which has been defined in the **DECLARE.**

If you use the variable list method, each column in the select list of the cursor must have a corresponding variable, and each of them must have been declared in the DECLARE section. The datatypes must be the same or compatible.

If you use the record method, the record is DECLAREd using the %ROWTYPE attribute, which declares the structure of the record to be the same (with the same datatypes) as the column list in the select. Each variable within this record can then be accessed individually using the record name as a prefix, and a variable name that is the same as the column name.

**EXAMPLE**

```
declare
 pi constant NUMBER(9,7) := 3.1415927;
 area NUMBER(14,2);
 cursor rad_cursor is
 select * from RADIUS_VALS;
 rad_val rad_cursor%ROWTYPE;
begin
 open rad_cursor;
 loop
 fetch rad_cursor into rad_val;
 exit when rad_cursor%NOTFOUND;
 area := pi*power(rad_val.radius,2);
 insert into AREAS values (rad_val.radius, area);
 end loop;
 close rad_cursor;
end;
```

# FIELD

In a table, a field is the information stored at the intersection of a row and a column. Field is generally synonymous with a column, but also can mean an actual column value.

# FILE TYPES

Files usually have a name and an extension, for example **comfort.tab** where **comfort** is the file name, and **tab** is the extension, or file "type." In SQL*PLUS, **start** files that are created using **EDIT** are given the default extension SQL if no extension is specified. In other words, this:

```
edit misty
```

will create or edit a file named **misty.sql**, while this:

```
start misty
```

will attempt to start a file named **misty.sql** because no extension was specified. Similarly, this:

```
spool bellwood
```

will create an output file named **bellwood.lst**, because **lst** is the default extension for spooled files. Of course, if either **edit** or **spool** is followed by both a file name and extension, the given extension will be used, not the default.

# file_specification

**SEE ALSO**    ALTER TABLESPACE, CREATE CONTROLFILE, CREATE DATABASE, CREATE LIBRARY, CREATE TABLESPACE

**FORMAT**

**file_specification::=**

**datafile_tempfile_spec::=**

**redo_log_file_spec::=**

**autoextend_clause::=**

**maxsize_clause::=**

**DESCRIPTION**    *file_specification* defines the name, location, and size of a file used by the database. For example, when you create a tablespace you must specify at least one datafile for the tablespace to use. *file_specification* provides the format for the datafile portion of the **CREATE TABLESPACE** command.

# FIRST

**SEE ALSO**    DENSE_RANK, LAST

**FORMAT**

```
aggregate_function KEEP
(DENSE_RANK FIRST ORDER BY
 expr [DESC | ASC] [NULLS { FIRST | LAST }]
 [, expr [DESC | ASC] [NULLS { FIRST | LAST }]]...
) [OVER query_partitioning_clause]
```

**DESCRIPTION**    FIRST is both an aggregate and analytic function that operates on a set of values from a set of rows that rank as the first with respect to a given sorting specification. *aggregate_function* is one of the standard numeric grouping functions (such as MIN, MAX, AVG, and STDDEV).

# FIRST_VALUE

**SEE ALSO**    LAST_VALUE

**FORMAT**

```
FIRST_VALUE (expr) OVER (analytic_clause)
```

**DESCRIPTION**    **FIRST_VALUE** is an analytic function. It returns the first value in an ordered set of values.

# FLASHBACK QUERY

A flashback query shows data as it existed prior to a commit. You cannot perform DML while in flashback query mode. See Chapter 26 for examples and restrictions related to flashback queries.

# FLOOR

**SEE ALSO**    CEIL, NUMBER FUNCTIONS, Chapter 8

**FORMAT**

```
FLOOR(value)
```

**DESCRIPTION**    **FLOOR** is the largest integer smaller than or equal to *value*.

**EXAMPLE**

```
FLOOR(2) = 2
FLOOR(-2.3) = -3
```

# FLUSH (SQL*PLUS)

*See* **SET**.

# FOR

*See* **LOOP** and CURSOR FOR LOOP.

# FOREIGN KEY

A foreign key is one or more columns whose values are based on the primary or candidate key values from another table.

# FORMAT

*See* **BTITLE**, CHAR FORMAT, **COLUMN**, DATE FORMAT, **TO_CHAR**, **TO_DATE**, **TTITLE**.

# FORMAT MODEL

A format model is a clause that controls the appearance of numbers, dates, and character strings. Format models for DATE columns are used in date conversion functions such as **TO_CHAR** and **TO_DATE**.

# FREE EXTENTS

Free extents are extents of database blocks that have not been allocated to any table or index segment. *Free extents* is another term for free space.

# FROM

**SEE ALSO**    **DELETE**, **SELECT**, Chapter 3

**FORMAT**

```
DELETE FROM [user.]table[@link] [alias]
 WHERE condition

SELECT... FROM [user.]table[@link] [, [user.]table[@link]]...
```

**DESCRIPTION**    *table* is the name of the table used by **delete** or **select**. *link* is the link to a remote database. Both **delete** and **select** commands require a **from** clause to define the tables from which rows will be deleted or selected. If the table is owned by another user, its name must be prefixed by the owner's user name.

    If the table is remote, a database link has to be defined. *@link* specifies the link. If *link* is entered, but *user* is not, the query seeks a table owned by the user on the remote database. The *condition* may include a correlated query and use the *alias* for correlation.

# FROM_TZ

**SEE ALSO**    TIMESTAMP WITH TIME ZONE, Chapter 9

**FORMAT**

```
FROM_TZ (timestamp_value , time_zone_value)
```

**DESCRIPTION**    **FROM_TZ** converts a timestamp value at a time zone to a TIMESTAMP WITH TIME ZONE value. *time_zone_value* is a character string in the format 'TZH:TZM' or a character expression that returns a string in TZR with optional TZD format.

# FULL OUTER JOIN

A full outer join performs an outer join in which both tables are used as the "outer" table in the join. Thus A FULL OUTER JOIN B returns all rows in common between A and B, all rows from A not matched in B matched to **NULL** values, and all rows in B not matched in A matched to **NULL** values.

# FULL TABLE SCAN

A full table scan is a method of data retrieval in which Oracle directly searches in a sequential manner all the database blocks for a table (rather than using an index), when looking for the specified data. *See* Chapter 38.

# FUNCTION

A function is a predefined operation, such as "convert to uppercase," which may be performed by placing the function's name and arguments in a SQL statement. *See* CHARACTER FUNCTIONS, CONVERSION FUNCTIONS, DATE FUNCTIONS, GROUP FUNCTIONS, LIST FUNCTIONS, NUMBER FUNCTIONS, and individual functions.

# FUZZY MATCH

A fuzzy match is a type of text search that allows for misspellings or variant spellings. *See* CONTAINS and Chapter 24.

# GET

**SEE ALSO**    EDIT, SAVE

**FORMAT**

```
GET file [LIST | NOLIST]
```

**DESCRIPTION**    **GET** loads a host system file named *file* into the current buffer (whether the SQL buffer or a named buffer). If the file type is not included, **GET** assumes a file type of SQL. **LIST** makes SQL*PLUS list the lines being loaded into the buffer. This is the default. **NOLIST** gets the file without listing its contents.

**EXAMPLE**    This example gets a file called **work.sql**:

```
get work
```

# GLOBAL INDEX

When a table is partitioned, its data is stored in separate segments. When an index is created on the partitioned table, the index can be partitioned so that each of the table partitions has a matching index

partition. If the index partitions do not match the table partitions, then the index is a global index. *See* Chapter 18.

# GOTO

**SEE ALSO**    BLOCK STRUCTURE, Chapter 27
**FORMAT**

```
GOTO label;
```

**DESCRIPTION**    **GOTO** transfers control to a section of code preceded by the named *label*. Such a label can be used to precede any legitimate statement within an execution block, or within an EXCEPTION section. There are certain restrictions:

■  A **GOTO** cannot transfer control to a block enclosed in the current block, or inside of a FOR LOOP or an IF statement.

■  A **GOTO** cannot transfer to a label outside of its own block unless it is to a block that encloses its block.

**EXAMPLE**    Here's an informal loop built from a **GOTO** that, without actually knowing ahead of time what the top number will be, **insert**s a geometric progression from 1 to about 10,000 into a table:

```
DECLARE
 ...
BEGIN
 x := 0;
 y := 1;
 <<alpha>>
 x := x + 1;
 y := x*y;
 insert ...
 if y > 10000
 then goto beta;
 goto alpha;
<<beta>>
 exit;
```

# GRANT

**SEE ALSO**    **ALTER USER**, **CREATE USER**, PRIVILEGE, **REVOKE**, ROLE, Chapter 19
**FORMAT**
**grant::=**

**grant_system_privileges::=**

**grant_object_privileges::=**

**on_object_clause::=**

**grantee_clause::=**

**DESCRIPTION**    The first form of **GRANT** extends one or more system privileges to users and roles. A system privilege is an authorization to perform one of the various data definition or control commands, such as **ALTER SYSTEM, CREATE ROLE**, or **GRANT** itself. *See* PRIVILEGE for details of these privileges. A user is created by **CREATE USER** and is then granted system privileges to enable logging into the database and other operations. A user without grants is unable to do anything at all in Oracle. A *role* is a collection of privileges created by **CREATE ROLE**. As with a user, a role has no privileges when created, but gets them through one or more **GRANT**s. One can grant one role to another role to create a nested network of roles, which gives the database administrator a great deal of flexibility in managing the security of the system.

The **WITH ADMIN OPTION** option lets the granted user or role (the grantee) grant the system privilege or role to other grantees. The grantee can also alter or drop a role granted **WITH ADMIN OPTION**.

The second form of the **GRANT** command grants object privileges, privileges that affect specific kinds of objects in Oracle databases, to any user or role. *object* can be a table, view, sequence, procedure, function, package, materialized view, or a synonym for one of these objects. **GRANT**s on a synonym actually become grants on the underlying object that the synonym references. *See* PRIVILEGE for a complete list of object privileges and a discussion of which can be granted for the various objects.

If you are granting INSERT, REFERENCES, or UPDATE privileges on a table or view, **GRANT** can also specify a list of columns of the table or view to which the **GRANT** applies. The **GRANT** applies only to those columns. If **GRANT** has no list of columns, the **GRANT** applies to all columns in the table or view.

**PUBLIC** grants the privileges to all users present and future.

The **WITH GRANT OPTION** passes along the right to grant the granted privileges to another user or role.

# GREATEST

**SEE ALSO**    COLLATION, **LEAST, MAX**, LIST FUNCTIONS, Chapters 8 and 9
**FORMAT**

```
GREATEST(value1, value2, ...)
```

**DESCRIPTION**    **GREATEST** chooses the greatest of a list of values. These can be columns, literals, or expressions, and CHAR, VARCHAR2, NUMBER, or DATE datatypes. A number with a larger value is considered greater than a smaller one. All negative numbers are smaller than all positive numbers. Thus, -10 is smaller than 10; -100 is smaller than -10.

A later date is considered greater than an earlier date.

Character strings are compared position by position, starting at the leftmost end of the string, up to the first character that is different. Whichever string has the greater character in that position is considered the greater string. One character is considered greater than another if it appears after the other in the computer's collation sequence. Usually this means that a B is greater than an A, but the value of A compared to a, or compared to the number 1, will differ by computer.

If two strings are identical through to the end of the shorter one, the longer string is considered greater. If two strings are identical and the same length, they are considered equal. In SQL, it is important that literal numbers be typed without enclosing single quotes, as '10' would be considered smaller than '6', since the quotes will cause these to be regarded as character strings rather than numbers, and the '6' will be seen as greater than the 1 in the first position of '10'.

Unlike many other Oracle functions and logical operators, the **GREATEST** and **LEAST** functions will not evaluate literal strings that are in date format as dates. In order for **LEAST** and **GREATEST** to work properly, the **TO_DATE** function must be applied to the literal strings.

# GROUP BY

**SEE ALSO**    CUBE, **HAVING**, **ORDER BY**, **ROLLUP**, WHERE, Chapter 11

**FORMAT**

```
SELECT expression [,expression]...
 GROUP BY expression [,expression]...
HAVING condition
 ...
```

**DESCRIPTION**    **GROUP BY** causes a **select** to produce one summary row for all selected rows that have identical values in one or more specified columns or expressions. Each expression in the **select** clause must be one of these things:

- A constant
- A function without parameters (SysDate, User)
- A group function like **SUM**, **AVG**, **MIN**, **MAX**, **COUNT**
- Matched identically to an expression in the **GROUP BY** clause

Columns referenced in the **GROUP BY** clause need not be in the **select** clause, though they must be in the table.

You use **HAVING** to determine which groups the **GROUP BY** is to include. A **where** clause, on the other hand, determines which rows are to be included in groups.

**GROUP BY** and **HAVING** follow **WHERE**, **CONNECT BY**, and **START WITH**. The **ORDER BY** clause is executed after the **WHERE**, **GROUP BY**, and **HAVING** clauses (which execute in that order). It can employ group functions, or columns from the **GROUP BY**, or a combination. If it uses a group function, that function operates on the groups, then the **ORDER BY** sorts the *results* of the function in order. If the **ORDER BY** uses a column from the **GROUP BY**, it sorts the rows that are returned based on that column. Group functions and single columns can be combined in the **ORDER BY** (so long as the column is in the **GROUP BY**).

In the **ORDER BY** clause you can specify a group function and the column it affects even though they have nothing at all to do with the group functions or columns in the **SELECT**, **GROUP BY**, or **HAVING** clause. On the other hand, if you specify a column in the **ORDER BY** that is not part of a group function, it must be in the **GROUP BY** clause.

**EXAMPLE**

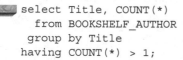
```
select Title, COUNT(*)
 from BOOKSHELF_AUTHOR
 group by Title
having COUNT(*) > 1;
```

# GROUP FUNCTIONS

**SEE ALSO**    AVG, **COUNT**, **MAX**, **MIN**, NUMBER FUNCTIONS, **STDDEV**, **SUM**, VARIANCE, Chapter 8

**DESCRIPTION**    A GROUP FUNCTION computes a single summary value (such as sum or average) from the individual number values in a group of values. This is an alphabetical list of all current group

functions in Oracle's SQL. Each of these is listed elsewhere in this reference under its own name, with its proper format and use. Group functions are useful only in queries and subqueries. **DISTINCT** makes a group function summarize only distinct (unique) values.

**FUNCTION NAME AND USE**

**AVG** gives the average of the values for group of rows.

**CORR** returns the coefficient of correlation of a set of number pairs

**COUNT** gives the count of rows for a column, or for a table (with *).

**COVAR_POP** returns the population covariance of a set of number pairs.

**COVAR_SAMP** returns the sample covariance of a set of number pairs.

**CUME_DIST** calculates the cumulative distribution of a value in a group of values.

**DENSE_RANK** computes the rank of a row in an ordered group of rows.

**FIRST** operates on a set of values from a set of rows that rank as the first with respect to a given sorting specification.

**FIRST_VALUE** returns the first value in an ordered set of values.

**GROUP_ID** distinguishes duplicate groups resulting from a GROUP BY specification.

**GROUPING** distinguishes superaggregate rows from regular grouped rows.

**GROUPING_ID** returns a number corresponding to the GROUPING bit vector associated with a row.

**LAST** operates on a set of values from a set of rows that rank as the last with respect to a given sorting specification.

**MAX** gives the maximum of all values for a group of rows.

**MIN** gives the minimum of all values for a group of rows.

**PERCENT_RANK** performs a percent ranking calculation.

**PERCENTILE_CONT** is a percentile calculation function that assumes a continuous distribution model.

**PERCENTILE_DISC** is a percentile calculation function that assumes a discrete distribution model.

**RANK** calculates the rank of a value in a group of values.

**REGR** functions perform linear regression analysis on a group of values.

**STDDEV** gives the standard deviation of all values for a group of rows.

**STDDEV_POP** computes the population standard deviation and returns the square root of the population variance.

**STDDEV_SAMP** computes the cumulative sample standard deviation and returns the square root of the sample variance.

**SUM** gives the sum of all values for a group of rows.

**VAR_POP** returns the population variance of a set of numbers after discarding the nulls in this set.

**VAR_SAMP** returns the sample variance of a set of numbers after discarding the nulls in this set.

**VARIANCE** gives the variance of all values for a group of rows.

# GROUP_ID

**SEE ALSO**     **GROUP BY, GROUPING_ID**, GROUP FUNCTIONS, Chapter 13

**FORMAT**

```
GROUP_ID ()
```

**DESCRIPTION**     **GROUP_ID** distinguishes duplicate groups resulting from a GROUP BY specification.

# GROUPING

**GROUPING** is a function used in conjunction with **ROLLUP** and **CUBE** functions to detect **NULL**s. *See* **ROLLUP**.

## GROUPING_ID

GROUPING_ID returns a number corresponding to the GROUPING bit vector associated with a row. See **ROLLUP**, **CUBE**, and Chapter 13.

## HASH CLUSTER

A hash cluster is a cluster stored by a hash key instead of by an index key. A hash key is a value computed from the key values that represents the location on disk. An index key requires Oracle to look up the location in the index, while a hash key lets Oracle calculate the location.

## HASH JOIN

A hash join is a method of performing a join of two tables. A hash join uses hash algorithms (similar to those used for hash clusters) to evaluate rows that meet the join criteria. Although they use similar algorithms, there is no direct relation between hash joins and hash clusters.

## HASH PARTITION

In a hash partition, data to be partitioned is processed by a hash algorithm rather than simply being partitioned by range. Hash partitioning will therefore spread small sets of sequential data over more partitions than range partitioning. *See* **CREATE TABLE**.

## HAVING

*See* GROUP BY.

## HEADING (SQL*PLUS)

*See* **SET**.

## HEADSEP (SQL*PLUS)

*See* **SET**.

## HELP (SQL*PLUS)

**FORMAT**

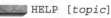
```
HELP [topic]
```

**DESCRIPTION**     The **HELP** command accesses the SQL*PLUS help system. **HELP INDEX** displays a list of topics.

## HEXADECIMAL NOTATION

Hexadecimal notation is a numbering system with a base of 16 instead of the decimal base of 10. The numbers 10 through 15 are represented by the letters A through F. This system is often used to display the internal data stored in a computer.

## HEXTORAW

**SEE ALSO**     **RAWTOHEX**
**FORMAT**

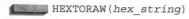
```
HEXTORAW(hex_string)
```

**DESCRIPTION**   HEXadecimal **TO RAW**, **HEXTORAW** changes a character string of hex numbers into binary.

# HINT

Within a query, you can specify hints that direct the cost-based optimizer in its processing of the query. To specify a hint, use the following syntax. Immediately after the **select** keyword, enter the string:

```
/*+
```

Next, add the hint, such as

```
FULL(bookshelf)
```

Close the hint with the following string:

```
*/
```

*See* Chapter 38 for a description of the available hints and their impact on query processing.

# HISTOGRAM

A histogram shows the distribution of data values for a column. The Oracle optimizer can use histograms to determine the efficiency of indexes for specific data value ranges. *See* **ANALYZE**.

# HOST (SQL*PLUS)

**SEE ALSO**   $, @, @@, **START**
**FORMAT**

```
HO[ST] host command
```

**DESCRIPTION**   A host is a computer on which the Oracle RDBMS is running. The **HOST** command in SQL*PLUS passes any host command back to the operating system for execution without exiting SQL*PLUS. SQL*PLUS permits embedding local or PL/SQL variables in the host command string. This doesn't work on all hardware or operating systems.

# IF

**SEE ALSO**   **LOOP**, Chapter 27
**FORMAT**

```
IF condition
 THEN statement; [statement;]...
 [ELSIF condition THEN statement; [statement;]...
 [ELSIF condition THEN statement; [statement;]...]...]
[ELSE statement; [statement;]...]
END IF;
```

**DESCRIPTION**   The IF statement will execute one or more *statements* if *condition* evaluates to TRUE, after which the program branches to END IF. If the *condition* is FALSE, then any number of a series of optional ELSIF conditions are tested. If any one is TRUE, the associated *statements* (following THEN) are executed, and then the program branches to END IF. If none of the ELSIF conditions are TRUE (and the original IF condition was not TRUE), then the statements following the optional ELSE are executed. Note that the final ELSE does not have a condition.

**EXAMPLE**

```
declare
 pi constant NUMBER(9,7) := 3.1415927;
 area NUMBER(14,2);
 cursor rad_cursor is
 select * from RADIUS_VALS;
 rad_val rad_cursor%ROWTYPE;
begin
 open rad_cursor;
 fetch rad_cursor into rad_val;
 area := pi*power(rad_val.radius,2);
 if area >30
 then
 insert into AREAS values (rad_val.radius, area);
 end if;
 close rad_cursor;
end;
```

# IMPORT

Import is the Oracle utility used to retrieve Oracle database data found in export format files into an Oracle database. To import is to use the Import utility to move data from an export file into database table(s). *See* EXPORT. For details on using Import, *see* the *Oracle9i Utilities Guide* and Chapter 40.

# IN

**SEE ALSO**   ALL, ANY, LOGICAL OPERATORS, **WHERE**, Chapter 3

**FORMAT**

```
WHERE expression IN ({'string' [,'string']... | select...})
```

**DESCRIPTION**   **IN** is equivalent to **=ANY**. In the first option, **IN** means the expression is equal to any member of the following list of literal *strings*. In the second option, it means the expression is equal to any value in any row selected from the subquery. The two are logically equivalent, with the first giving a list made of literal strings, and the second building a list from a query. **IN** works with VARCHAR2, CHAR, DATE, and NUMBER datatypes, as well as RowID.

# INDEX

Index is a general term for an Oracle/SQL feature used primarily to speed execution and impose uniqueness upon certain data. In general, indexes provide a faster access method to table data than doing a full table scan. There are several types of indexes; *see* CONCATENATED INDEX, COMPRESSED INDEX, and UNIQUE INDEX. An index has an entry for each value found in the table's indexed field(s) (except those with a **NULL** value) and pointer(s) to the row(s) having that value.

# INDEX SEGMENT

The index segment is the storage that is allocated for an index, as compared to storage allocated to the data in a table.

# INDEX-ORGANIZED TABLE

An *index-organized table* keeps its data sorted according to the primary key column values for the table. An index-organized table allows you to store the entire table's data in an index. A normal index only stores the indexed columns in the index; an index-organized table stores all of the table's columns in the index.

To create an index-organized table, use the **organization index** clause of the **create table** command, as shown in the following example:

```
create table TROUBLE (
City VARCHAR2(13),
SampleDate DATE,
Noon NUMBER(4,1),
Midnight NUMBER(4,1),
Precipitation NUMBER,
constraint TROUBLE_PK PRIMARY KEY (City, SampleDate))
organization index;
```

In order to create TROUBLE as an index-organized table, you must create a PRIMARY KEY constraint on it.

In general, index-organized tables are appropriate for associative tables in many-to-many relationships. Ideally, an index-organized table will have few (or no) columns that are not part of its primary key.

*See* Chapter 18 and **CREATE TABLE**.

# INDICATOR VARIABLE

**SEE ALSO**    : (colon, the host variable prefix), *Precompiler Programmer's Guide*

**FORMAT**

```
:name [INDICATOR] :indicator
```

**DESCRIPTION**    An indicator variable—used when both name and indicator are host language variable names—is a data field whose value indicates whether a host variable should be regarded as **NULL**. (The INDICATOR keyword is for readability and has no effect.)

*name* may be any legitimate host variable data name used in the host program and included in the precompiler's DECLARE SECTION. *indicator* is defined in the precompiler's DECLARE SECTION as a two-byte integer.

Few procedural languages directly support the idea of a variable with a **NULL** or unknown value, although Oracle and SQL do so easily. In order to extend languages for which Oracle has developed precompilers to support the **NULL** concept, an indicator variable is associated with the host variable, almost like a flag, to indicate whether it is **NULL**. The host variable and its indicator variable may be referenced and set separately in the host language code, but are always concatenated in SQL or PL/SQL.

**EXAMPLE**

```
BEGIN
 select Title, AuthorName into :Title, :AuthorName:AuthorNameInd
 from BOOKSHELF_AUTHOR;

 IF :AuthorName:AuthorNameInd IS NULL
```

```
 THEN :AuthorName:AuthorNameInd := 'No Auth'
 END IF;
END;
```

Note that the test to see if the variable is **NULL**, and the assignment of 'No Auth' to it if it is, are both done with the concatenated variable name. PL/SQL knows enough to check the indicator in the first case, and set the variable value in the second case. The two variables together are treated just like a single Oracle column. These important points must be noted:

- Within any single PL/SQL block, a host variable must either always stand alone, or always be concatenated with its indicator variable.

- An indicator variable cannot be referenced alone within PL/SQL, although it can be in the host program.

When setting host variables within the host program, but outside of PL/SQL, note these points:

- Setting the indicator variable equal to -1 will force the concatenated variable to be regarded within PL/SQL as **NULL**, both in logic tests and for **insert**s or **update**s.

- Setting the indicator variable greater than or equal to 0 will force the concatenated variable to be regarded as equal to the value in the host variable, and **NOT NULL**.

- PL/SQL tests the value of all indicator variables on entering a block, and sets them on exiting the block.

When loading concatenated host variables within PL/SQL, via a SQL statement with an INTO clause, the following rules apply when checking the indicator variable within the host program, but outside of PL/SQL:

- The indicator variable will be equal to -1 if the value loaded from the database was **NULL**. The value of the host variable is uncertain, and should be treated as such.

- The indicator variable will be equal to 0 if the value from the database is loaded completely and correctly into the host variable.

- The indicator variable will be greater than 0 and equal to the actual length of the data in the database column if only a portion of it could fit in the host variable. The host variable will contain a truncated version of what was in the database column.

## init.ora

**init.ora** is a database system parameter file that contains settings and file names used when a system is started using the **CREATE DATABASE**, **STARTUP**, or **SHUTDOWN** command. In Oracle9i, you can use an init.ora file or you can create a system parameter file via the **CREATE SPFILE** command. *See* **CREATE PFILE** and **CREATE SPFILE**.

## INITCAP

**SEE ALSO**   CHARACTER FUNCTIONS, **LOWER**, **UPPER**, Chapter 7
**FORMAT**

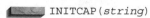

```
INITCAP(string)
```

**DESCRIPTION**   INITial CAPital changes the first letter of a word or series of words into uppercase. It also notes the presence of symbols, and will **INITCAP** any letter that follows a space or a symbol, such as a comma, period, colon, semicolon, !, @, #, $, and so on.

**EXAMPLE**

```
INITCAP('this.is,an-example of!how@initcap#works')
```

produces this:

```
This.Is,An-Example Of!How@Initcap#Works
```

# INNER JOIN

Inner joins return rows based on the key values two tables have in common. They support both the **ON** and **USING** clauses. For example, the following query joins BOOK_ORDER to BOOKSHELF based on their Title column values:

```
select BO.Title
 from BOOK_ORDER BO inner join BOOKSHELF B
 on BO.Title = B.Title;
```

That query can be rewritten as:

```
select Title
 from BOOK_ORDER BO inner join BOOKSHELF B
 using (Title);
```

# INPUT

**SEE ALSO**     APPEND, CHANGE, DEL, EDIT, Chapter 6
**FORMAT**

```
I[NPUT] [text]
```

**DESCRIPTION**     INPUT adds a new line of text after the current line in the current buffer. Using **INPUT** by itself allows multiple lines to be keyed in after the current line, which stops when the system encounters ENTER with nothing else on the line. The space between **INPUT** and *text* will not be added to the line but any additional spaces will be. *See* **DEL** for a discussion of current line.

# INSERT (Form I-Embedded SQL)

**SEE ALSO**     EXECUTE, FOR, *Precompiler Programmer's Guide*
**FORMAT**

```
EXEC SQL [AT { db_name | :host_variable }]
 [FOR { :host_integer | integer }]
 INSERT INTO
 [(subquery)
 | [schema.] { table | view }
 [@db_link | PARTITION (part_name)]]
 [(column) [, (column)]...]
 { VALUES (expr [, expr]...) | subquery }
[{ RETURN | RETURNING } expr [, expr]... INTO
 :host_variable [[INDICATOR] :ind_variable]
 [, :host_variable [[INDICATOR] :ind_variable]]...]
```

**DESCRIPTION** *db_name* is a database other than the user's default, and *host_variable* contains the name of the database. *:host_integer* is a host value that limits the number of times the **INSERT** will be processed (*see* **FOR**). *table* is any existing table, view, or synonym, and *db_link* is the name of a remote database where the table is stored. (*See* the **INSERT** Form 3 definition for a discussion of the **VALUES** clause, columns, and query.) *expression* here can be an expression or a host variable in the form *:variable[:indicator]*.

# INSERT (Form 2-PL/SQL)

**SEE ALSO** SQL CURSOR, Chapter 27

**FORMAT**

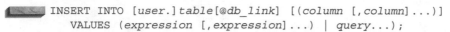

```
INSERT INTO [user.] table[@db_link] [(column [,column]...)]
 VALUES (expression [,expression]...) | query...);
```

**DESCRIPTION** PL/SQL's use of **INSERT** is identical to its general form (Form 3 in the following section), with these exceptions:

- You may use a PL/SQL variable in an expression for the value in the VALUES list.
- Each variable will be treated in the same way that a constant, with the value of the variable, would be treated.
- If you use the *query*. . . version of the **INSERT**, you cannot use the **INTO** clause of the **select**.

# INSERT (Form 3-SQL Command)

**SEE ALSO** **CREATE TABLE**, Chapters 4, 15, 30 and 31

**FORMAT**

insert::=

single_table_insert::=

insert_into_clause::=::=

**values_clause::=**

**returning_clause::=**

**multi_table_insert::=**

**conditional_insert_clause::=**

**DML_table_expression_clause::=**

**subquery_restriction_clause::=**

**table_collection_expression::=**

**DESCRIPTION**    **INSERT** adds one or more new rows to the table or view. The optional *schema* must be a user to whose table you have been granted insert authority. *table* is the table into which rows are to be inserted. If a list of columns is given, an expression (SQL expression) must be matched for each of those columns. Any columns not in the list receive the value **NULL**, and none of them can be defined **NOT NULL** or the **INSERT** will fail. If a list of columns is not given, values must be given for all columns in the table.

    **INSERT** with a subquery adds as many rows as the query returns, with each query column being matched, position for position, with columns in the column list. If no column list is given, the tables must have the same number and type of columns. The USER_TAB_COLUMNS data dictionary view shows these, as does DESCRIBE in SQL*PLUS.

**EXAMPLE**    The following inserts a row into the COMFORT table:

```
insert into COMFORT values ('KEENE','23-SEP-01',99.8,82.6,NULL);
```

    The following inserts City, SampleDate (both NOT NULL columns), and Precipitation into COMFORT:

```
insert into COMFORT (City, SampleDate, Precipitation) values
 ('KEENE','22-DEC-01',3.9);
```

    To copy just the data for the city of KEENE into a new table named NEW_HAMPSHIRE, use this:

```
insert into NEW_HAMPSHIRE
select * from COMFORT
 where City = 'KEENE';
```

    *See* Chapters 4 and 30 for information on inserting rows into tables that use abstract datatypes. *See* Chapter 31 for details on inserting rows into nested tables and varying arrays.

# INSTANCE

An instance is everything required for Oracle to run: background processes (programs), memory, and so on. An instance is the means of accessing a database.

# INSTANCE IDENTIFIER

An instance identifier is a means of distinguishing one instance from another when multiple instances exist on one host.

## INSTANCE RECOVERY

Instance recovery is recovery in the event of software or hardware failure. This occurs if the software aborted abnormally due to a severe bug, deadlock, or destructive interaction between programs. *See also* MEDIA RECOVERY.

## INSTEAD OF TRIGGER

An INSTEAD OF trigger executes a block of PL/SQL code in place of the transaction that causes the trigger to be executed. INSTEAD OF triggers are commonly used to redirect transactions against views. *See* **CREATE TRIGGER** and Chapters 28 and 30.

## INSTR

**SEE ALSO**    CHARACTER FUNCTIONS, **SUBSTR**, Chapter 7
**FORMAT**

```
INSTR(string,set[,start[,occurrence]])
```

**DESCRIPTION**    INSTR finds the location of a *set* of characters in a *string*, starting at position *start* in the string, and looking for the first, second, third, and so on, *occurrence* of the *set*. This function will also work with NUMBER and DATE datatypes. *start* also can be negative, meaning the search begins with the characters at the end of the string and searches backward.

**EXAMPLE**    To find the third occurrence of PI in this string, use this:

```
INSTR('PETER PIPER PICKED A PECK OF PICKLED PEPPERS','PI',1,3)
```

The result of this function is 30, the location of the third occurrence of 'PI'.

## INTEGRITY CONSTRAINT

An integrity constraint is a rule that restricts the range of valid values for a column. It is placed on a column when the table is created. For the syntax, see the ***constraints*** entry in the Alphabetical Reference.

   If you do not name a constraint, Oracle assigns a name in the form SYS_C*n*, where *n* is an integer. An Oracle-assigned name will usually change during an import, while a user-assigned name will not change.

   **NULL** permits **NULL** values. **NOT NULL** specifies that every row must have a non-**NULL** value for this column.

   **UNIQUE** forces column values to be unique. There can be only one PRIMARY KEY constraint on a table. If a column is UNIQUE it cannot also be declared the PRIMARY KEY (PRIMARY KEY also enforces uniqueness). An index enforces the unique or primary key, and the USING INDEX clause and its options specify the storage characteristics of that index. *See* **CREATE INDEX** for more information on the options.

   **REFERENCES** identifies this column as a foreign key from [*user.*]*table* [*(column)*]. Omitting *column* implies that the name in the *user.table* is the same as the name in this table. Note that when REFERENCES is used in a *table_constraint* (described shortly) it must be preceded by FOREIGN KEY. This is not used here, as only this column is referenced; *table_constraint* can reference several columns for FOREIGN KEY. ON DELETE CASCADE instructs Oracle to maintain referential integrity automatically by removing foreign key rows in the dependent tables if you remove the primary key row in this table.

**CHECK** assures that the value for this column passes a condition such as this:

```
Amount number(12,2) CHECK (Amount >= 0)
```

*condition* may be any valid expression that tests TRUE or FALSE. It can contain functions, any columns from this table, and literals.

The **EXCEPTIONS INTO** clause specifies a table into which Oracle puts information about rows that violate an enabled integrity constraint. This table must be local.

The **DISABLE** option lets you disable the integrity constraint when you create it. When the constraint is disabled, Oracle does not automatically enforce it. You can later enable the constraint with the **ENABLE** clause in **ALTER TABLE**.

You can also create constraints at the table level. Table constraints are identical to column constraints except that a single constraint can reference multiple columns—for example in declaring a set of three columns as a primary or foreign key.

# INTERSECT

**SEE ALSO**    **MINUS**, QUERY OPERATORS, **UNION**, Chapter 12

**FORMAT**

```
select...
INTERSECT
select...
```

**DESCRIPTION**    **INTERSECT** combines two queries and returns only those rows from the first **select** statement that are identical to at least one row from the second **select** statement. The number of columns and datatypes must be identical between **select** statements, although the names of the columns do not need to be. The data, however, must be identical in the rows produced for the **INTERSECT**ion to pass them.

# INTERVAL DAY TO SECOND

The INTERVAL DAY (*day_precision*) TO SECOND (*second_precision*) datatype stores the period of time in days, hours, minutes, and seconds. You can specify a *day_precision* as the number of digits in the DAY datetime field (default is 2) and a *second_precision* as the number of digits in the fractional part of the Seconds field (default is 6).

# INTERVAL YEAR TO MONTH

The INTERVAL YEAR (precision) TO MONTH datatype stores the period of time in years and months, where *precision* is the number of digits in the YEAR datetime field (default is 2).

# IS NULL

**SEE ALSO**    LOGICAL OPERATORS, Chapters 3 and 8

**FORMAT**

```
WHERE column IS [NOT] NULL
```

**DESCRIPTION**    **IS NULL** tests column (or an expression) for the absence of any data. A **NULL** test is distinctly different from a test for equality, because **NULL** means that the value is unknown or irrelevant, and it therefore cannot be said to be equal to anything, including another **NULL**.

# JAVA

Java is a programming language originally developed by Sun Microsystems. You can write stored procedural objects in either PL/SQL or Java. See Chapter 34.

# JDBC

JDBC is an acronym for Java Database Connectivity, an industry standard application programming interface to databases. Oracle supports JDBC connections. See Chapter 35.

# JOIN

**SEE ALSO**    **SELECT**, Chapter 3
**FORMAT**

```
WHERE TableA.column = TableB.column
```

or

```
FROM TableA INNER JOIN TableB
 on TableA.Column = TableB.Column
```

or

```
 FROM TableA INNER JOIN TableB
using(Column)
```

or

```
FROM TableA NATURAL JOIN TableB
```

**DESCRIPTION**    A join combines columns and data from two or more tables (and in rare cases, of one table with itself). The tables are all listed in the **from** clause of the **select** statement, and the relationship between the two tables may specified in the **where** clause, usually by a simple equality, such as this:

```
where BOOK_ORDER.Title = BOOKSHELF.Title
```

This is often called an *equi-join* because it uses the equal sign in the **where** clause. You could join tables using other forms of equality, such as >=, <, and so on, but the results are seldom meaningful. There also are cases in which one or both sides of the equal sign contain an expression, perhaps a **SUBSTR** or a combination of columns, which is used for equality with the other side. This is a fairly common usage.

Joining two tables together without a join clause—either in the **from** clause or in the **where** clause—produces a Cartesian product, which combines every row in one table with every row in the other table. An 80-row table combined with a 100-row table would produce an 8000-row result (which is usually quite meaningless).

An *outer join* is a method for intentionally retrieving selected rows from one table that don't match rows in the other table. As of Oracle9i, you can use the ANSI standard outer join syntax options (LEFT OUTER JOIN, RIGHT OUTER JOIN, and FULL OUTER JOIN). See Chapter 12 for examples of the syntax for outer joins.

# JOIN COLUMN

A join column is a column used to join one table to another. You identify a join column by using it in a **where** clause, **using** clause, or **on** clause that specifies the relationship between the two tables.

# JULIAN DATE

Julian dates are a means of converting date data so that every date can be expressed as a unique integer. Julian dates can be obtained by using the format mask 'J' with functions on date data. *See* DATE FORMATS.

# KERNEL

Kernel is the base Oracle RDBMS program code (a collection of many modules) that can be called by the background processes.

# KEY

A key is a column or columns used to identify rows; it is not the same as an index, although indexes are often used with such columns. *See* FOREIGN KEY, PRIMARY KEY, and UNIQUE KEY.

# LABEL (PL/SQL)

A label is a word associated with an executable statement, usually for the purpose of being the target of a GOTO statement.

# LAG

**SEE ALSO** LEAD

**FORMAT**

```
LAG (value_expr [, offset] [, default])
 OVER ([query_partition_clause] order_by_clause)
```

**DESCRIPTION** **LAG** provides access to more than one row of a table at the same time without a self-join. Given a series of rows returned from a query and a position of the cursor, **LAG** provides access to a row at a given physical offset prior to that position.

# LAST

**SEE ALSO** **DENSE_RANK, FIRST**

**FORMAT**

```
aggregate_function KEEP
(DENSE_RANK LAST ORDER BY
 expr [DESC | ASC] [NULLS { FIRST | LAST }]
 [, expr [DESC | ASC] [NULLS { FIRST | LAST }]]...
) [OVER query_partitioning_clause]
```

**DESCRIPTION** **LAST** is both an aggregate and analytic function that operates on a set of values from a set of rows that rank as the last with respect to a given sorting specification. *aggregate_function* is one of the standard numeric grouping functions (such as MIN, MAX, AVG, and STDDEV).

# LAST_DAY

**SEE ALSO** **ADD_MONTHS**, DATE FUNCTIONS, **NEXT_DAY**, Chapter 9

**FORMAT**

```
LAST_DAY (date)
```

**DESCRIPTION**  **LAST_DAY** gives the date of the last day of the month that *date* is in.

**EXAMPLE**  This:

```
LAST_DAY ('05-NOV-01')
```

produces a result of 30-NOV-01.

# LAST_VALUE

**SEE ALSO**  **FIRST_VALUE**

**FORMAT**

```
LAST_VALUE (expr) OVER (analytic_clause)
```

**DESCRIPTION**  **LAST_VALUE** is an analytic function. It returns the last value in an ordered set of values.

# LEAD

**SEE ALSO**  LAG

**FORMAT**

```
LEAD (value_expr [, offset] [, default])
 OVER ([query_partition_clause] order_by_clause)
```

**DESCRIPTION**  **LEAD** provides access to more than one row of a table at the same time without a self-join. Given a series of rows returned from a query and a position of the cursor, **LEAD** provides access to a row at a given physical offset beyond that position.

# LEAF

In a tree-structured table, a leaf is a row that has no child row.

# LEAST

**SEE ALSO**  **GREATEST**, LIST FUNCTIONS, Chapter 9

**FORMAT**

```
LEAST(value1, value2, ...)
```

**DESCRIPTION**  **LEAST** is the value of a list of columns, expressions, or values. Values may be VARCHAR2, CHAR, DATE, or NUMBER datatypes, although **LEAST** will not properly evaluate literal dates (such as '20-MAY-49') without the **TO_DATE** function. *See* **GREATEST** for a discussion of evaluating relative values.

# LENGTH

**SEE ALSO**  CHARACTER FUNCTIONS, **VSIZE**, Chapter 7

**FORMAT**

```
LENGTH(string)
```

**DESCRIPTION**  **LENGTH** tells the length of a string, a number, date, or expression.

## LEVEL

**SEE ALSO**    **CONNECT BY**, PSEUDO-COLUMNS, Chapter 13

**FORMAT**

```
LEVEL
```

**DESCRIPTION**    Level is a pseudo-column, used with **CONNECT BY**, that is equal to 1 for a root node, 2 for a child of a root, 3 for a child of a child of a root, and so on. Level tells basically how far down a tree you've traveled.

## LGWR

**LGWR** (LoG WRiter process) writes redo log entries from the System Global Area to the online redo logs. *See* BACKGROUND PROCESS.

## LIBRARY

PL/SQL blocks can reference external subprograms, stored in libraries. *See* **CREATE LIBRARY**.

## LIKE

**SEE ALSO**    LOGICAL OPERATORS, Chapter 3

**FORMAT**

```
WHERE string LIKE string
```

**DESCRIPTION**    **LIKE** performs pattern matching. An underline represents exactly one space. A percent sign represents any number of spaces or characters, including zero. If **LIKE** uses either the _ or % in the first position of a comparison (as in the second and third examples following), any index on the column is ignored.

**EXAMPLES**

```
Feature LIKE 'MO%' "Feature begins with the letters MO."
Feature LIKE '_ _I%' "Feature has an I in the third position."
Feature LIKE '%0%0%' "Feature has at least two 0's in it."
```

## LINESIZE (SQL*PLUS)

*See* **SET**.

## LIST

**SEE ALSO**    APPEND, **CHANGE**, **EDIT**, **INPUT**, **RUN**, Chapter 6

**FORMAT**

```
L[IST] [{start|*} [end|*]]
```

**DESCRIPTION**    **LIST** lists lines of the current buffer starting at *start* and ending at *end*, both of which are integers. The end line becomes the current line of the buffer, and is flagged with an asterisk. **LIST** without *start* or *end* lists all lines. An asterisk in either place will set it to the current line. **LIST** with a single number will display just that line, and **LIST** with just an asterisk will display just the current line. The space between **LIST** and *start* is not necessary but it does help readability.

**EXAMPLE**     Use this to list the current SQL buffer:

    LIST

An asterisk will designate the current line. To list just the second line, use this:

    LIST 2

This also makes 2 the current line in the current buffer.

## LIST FUNCTIONS

**SEE ALSO**     All other function lists, Chapter 9

**DESCRIPTION**     The following is an alphabetical list of all current list functions in Oracle's SQL. Each of these is listed elsewhere in this reference under its own name, with its proper format and use.
    This gives the first non-NULL value in the set:

    COALESCE(*value1*, *value2*, ...)

    This gives the greatest value of a list:

    GREATEST(*value1*, *value2*, ...)

    This gives the least value of a list:

    LEAST(*value1*, *value2*, ...)

## LN

**SEE ALSO**     NUMBER FUNCTIONS, Chapter 8

**FORMAT**

    LN(*number*)

**DESCRIPTION**     **LN** is the "natural," or base *e*, logarithm of a **number**.

## LOADJAVA

LOADJAVA is a utility for loading Java classes, resources, and sources into the database. You must load your Java classes into the database if you plan to use them in stored procedures. To remove the Java classes from the database, use the DROPJAVA utility.

## LOB

A LOB is a large object. Oracle supports several large object datatypes, including BLOB (binary large object), CLOB (character large object), and BFILE (binary file, stored outside the database). *See* Chapter 32 and the **LOB** clause of **CREATE TABLE**.

## LOBOFFSET (SQL*PLUS)

*See* **SET**.

## LOCAL DATABASE

The local database is usually a database on your host computer. *See* REMOTE DATABASE.

## LOCAL INDEX

When a table is partitioned, its data is stored in separate tables. When an index is created on the partitioned table, the index can be partitioned so that each of the table partitions has a matching index partition. The matching index partitions are called local indexes. *See* Chapter 18.

## LOCALTIMESTAMP

**SEE ALSO**    DATE FUNCTIONS, Chapter 9

**FORMAT**

```
LOCALTIMESTAMP [(timestamp_precision)]
```

**DESCRIPTION**    **LOCALTIMESTAMP** returns the current date and time in the session time zone as a value of datatype TIMESTAMP.

**EXAMPLE**

```
SELECT LOCALTIMESTAMP FROM DUAL;
```

## LOCALLY MANAGED TABLESPACE

A locally managed tablespace maintains its extent usage information in bitmaps within the tablespace's datafiles. By default, tablespaces store their extent usage information in the data dictionary (and are referred to as "dictionary-managed"). See **CREATE TABLESPACE**.

## LOCK

To lock is to temporarily restrict other users' access to data. The restriction that is placed on such data is called "a lock." Lock modes are SHARE, SHARE UPDATE, EXCLUSIVE, SHARE EXCLUSIVE, ROW SHARE, and ROW EXCLUSIVE. Not all locks can be acquired in all modes.

## LOCK TABLE

**SEE ALSO**    COMMIT, DELETE, INSERT, ROLLBACK, SAVEPOINT, UPDATE

**FORMAT**

```
LOCK TABLE
[schema .] { table | view }
[{ PARTITION (partition) | SUBPARTITION (subpartition) }
| @ dblink]
[, [schema .] { table | view }
 [{ PARTITION (partition) | SUBPARTITION (subpartition) }
 | @ dblink]]...
IN lockmode MODE [NOWAIT];
```

**DESCRIPTION**    **LOCK TABLE** locks a table in one of several specified modes, allowing it to be shared, but without loss of data integrity. Using **LOCK TABLE** allows you to give other users continued but restricted access to the table. Regardless of which option you choose, the table will remain in that lock mode until you **commit** or **rollback** your transactions.

Lock modes include ROW SHARE, ROW EXCLUSIVE, SHARE UPDATE, SHARE, SHARE ROW EXCLUSIVE, and EXCLUSIVE.

EXCLUSIVE locks permit users to query the locked table but not to do anything else. No other user may lock the table. SHARED locks permit concurrent queries but no updates to the locked table.

With a ROW SHARE or SHARE UPDATE lock, no user can lock the whole table for exclusive access, allowing concurrent access for all users to the table. The two types of lock are synonymous, and SHARE UPDATE exists for compatibility with previous versions of Oracle.

ROW EXCLUSIVE locks are similar to ROW SHARE but they prohibit shared locking, so only one user may access the table at a time.

If a **LOCK TABLE** command cannot be completed (usually because someone else has executed a prior and competing **LOCK TABLE** of some sort) then your **LOCK TABLE** will wait until it can complete. If you wish to avoid this, and simply have control returned to you, use the **NOWAIT** option. Note that you can lock specific partitions and subpartitions.

# LOG

**SEE ALSO**     NUMBER FUNCTIONS, Chapter 8

**FORMAT**

```
LOG(base, number)
```

**DESCRIPTION**     **LOG** gives the logarithm of a *number* for a specified *base*.

**EXAMPLE**

```
LOG(EXP(1),3) = 1.098612 -- log(e) of 3
LOG(10,100) = 2 -- log(10) of 100
```

# LOG WRITER PROCESS (LGWR)

*See* **LGWR**.

# LOGICAL EXPRESSION

A logical expression is one whose value evaluates to either TRUE or FALSE. It is a synonym for CONDITION.

# LOGICAL OPERATORS

**SEE ALSO**     PRECEDENCE

**FORMAT**     The following lists all current logical operators in Oracle's SQL. Most of these are listed elsewhere in this reference under their own names with their proper format and use. All of these operators work with columns or literals.

## Logical Operators that Test a Single Value

```
= expression is equal to expression
> expression is greater than expression
>= expression is greater than or equal to expression
< expression is less than expression
<= expression is less than or equal to expression
!= expression is not equal to expression
^= expression is not equal to expression
<> expression is not equal to expression

EXISTS (query)
NOT EXISTS (query)
```

```
LIKE expression
NOT LIKE expression

expression IS NULL
expression IS NOT NULL
```

## Logical Operators that Test More than a Single Value

```
ANY (expression [,expression]... | query)
ALL (expression [,expression]... | query)
```

ANY and ALL require an equality operator as a prefix, such as **>ANY**, **=ALL**, and so on.

```
IN (expression [,expression]... | query)
NOT IN (expression [,expression]... | query)

BETWEEN expression AND expression
NOT BETWEEN expression AND expression
```

## Other Logical Operators

```
+ Addition
- Subtraction
* Multiplication
/ Division
** Exponentiation
|| Concatenation
() Overrides normal precedence rules, or encloses a
 subquery
NOT Reverses logical expression
AND Combines logical expressions
OR Combines logical expressions
UNION Combines results of queries
UNION ALL Combines results of queries without eliminating duplicates
INTERSECT Combines results of queries
MINUS Combines results of queries
```

# LOGICAL UNIT OF WORK

*See* TRANSACTION.

# LOGIN ACCOUNT

A login account is a username and password that allows people to use the Oracle RDBMS. This account is usually separate from your operating system account.

# LOBSOURCE (SQL*PLUS)

*See* SET.

# LONG (SQL*PLUS)

*See* SET.

## LONG DATATYPE

*See* DATA TYPES.

## LONG RAW DATATYPE

A LONG RAW column contains raw binary data, but is otherwise the same as a LONG column. Values entered into LONG RAW columns must be in hex notation.

## LOOP

You can use loops to process multiple records within a single PL/SQL block. PL/SQL supports three types of loops:

Simple Loops    A loop that keeps repeating until an **exit** or **exit when** statement is reached within the loop

FOR Loops       A loop that repeats a specified number of times

WHILE Loops     A loop that repeats until a condition is met

You can use loops to process multiple records from a cursor. The most common cursor loop is a cursor FOR loop. *See* CURSOR FOR LOOP and Chapter 27 for details on using loops for both simple and cursor-based processing logic.

## LOWER

**SEE ALSO**    CHARACTER FUNCTIONS, **INITCAP**, **UPPER**, Chapter 7

**FORMAT**

LOWER(*string*)

**DESCRIPTION**    **LOWER** converts every letter in a string to lowercase.

**EXAMPLE**

LOWER('PeninSula') = peninsula

## LPAD

**SEE ALSO**    CHARACTER FUNCTIONS, **LTRIM**, **RPAD**, **RTRIM**, Chapter 7

**FORMAT**

LPAD(*string*,*length* [,'*set*'])

**DESCRIPTION**    Left **pad** makes a *string* a certain *length* by adding a certain *set* of characters to the left of the string. If *set* is not specified, the default pad character is a space.

**EXAMPLE**

LPAD('>',11,'- ')

produces

- - - - - >

## LTRIM

**SEE ALSO**    CHARACTER FUNCTIONS, **LPAD**, **RPAD**, **RTRIM**, Chapter 7

**FORMAT**

```
LTRIM(string [,'set'])
```

**DESCRIPTION**    Left **TRIM** trims all the occurrences of any one of a *set* of characters off of the left side of a *string*.

**EXAMPLE**

```
LTRIM('NANCY','AN')
```

produces this:

```
CY
```

# MAKE_REF

The **MAKE_REF** function constructs a REF (reference) from the foreign key of a table that references the base table of an object view. **MAKE_REF** allows you to construct references superimposed on existing foreign key relationships. *See* Chapter 33.

# MAIN QUERY

A main query is the outermost or top query in a query containing a subquery. It's the query whose columns produce a result.

# MAINTENANCE RELEASE

The maintenance release is the second number in Oracle software version numbering. In Oracle version 9.0.1, the maintenance release is 0.

# MATERIALIZED VIEW

You can use materialized views to pre-aggregate data and improve query performance. When you create a materialized view, Oracle creates a physical table to hold data that would usually be read via a view. When you create a materialized view, you specify the view's base query as well as a schedule for the refreshes of its data. You can then index the materialized view to enhance the performance of queries against it. As a result, you can provide data to your users in the format they need, indexed appropriately. *See* **CREATE MATERIALIZED VIEW** and Chapter 23.

# MATERIALIZED VIEW LOG

When you refresh a materialized view, you can perform a full or incremental refresh. An incremental refresh, called a "fast" refresh, sends only the DML changes from the master table to the materialized view. To track changes to the master table for the materialized view, you must create a materialized view log. The materialized view log must be in the same schema as the master table for the materialized view. Fast refreshes are not available for complex materialized views. *See* **CREATE MATERIALIZED VIEW LOG** and Chapter 23.

# MAX

**SEE ALSO**    COMPUTE, GROUP FUNCTIONS, **MIN**, Chapter 8

**FORMAT**

```
MAX([DISTINCT | ALL] value)
```

**DESCRIPTION**     MAX is the maximum of all *values* for a group of rows. **MAX** ignores **NULL** values. The **DISTINCT** option is not meaningful, since the maximum of all values is identical to the maximum of the distinct values.

## MEDIA RECOVERY

Media recovery is recovery in the event of hardware failure, which would prevent reading or writing of data and thus operation of the database. *See also* INSTANCE RECOVERY.

## METHOD

A method is a block of code. In reference to abstract datatypes, a method is a block of PL/SQL code used to encapsulate the data access method for an object. Methods are specified as part of the abstract datatype specification (*see* CREATE TYPE) and their body is specified as part of the CREATE TYPE BODY command. Users can execute methods on the datatypes for which the methods are defined. The constructor method created for each abstract datatype is an example of a method. *See* Chapter 30 for examples of methods.

In Java, a method is a member of a class. You can call a class method and pass parameters to it for it to use when executing its commands. See Chapter 30 for examples.

## MIN

**SEE ALSO**     **COMPUTE**, GROUP FUNCTIONS, **MAX**, Chapter 8
**FORMAT**

```
MIN([DISTINCT | ALL] value)
```

**DESCRIPTION**     **MIN** is the minimum of all *values* for a group of rows. **MIN** ignores **NULL** values. The **DISTINCT** option is not meaningful, since the minimum of all values is identical to the minimum of the distinct values.

## MINUS

**SEE ALSO**     **INTERSECT**, QUERY OPERATORS, **UNION**, TEXT SEARCH OPERATORS, Chapters 12 and 24
**FORMAT**

```
select
MINUS
select
```

within Oracle Text queries against CONTEXT indexes:

```
select column
 from TABLE
 where CONTAINS(Text,'text MINUS text') >0;
```

**DESCRIPTION**     MINUS combines two queries. It returns only those rows from the first **select** statement that are not produced by the second **select** statement (the first **select** MINUS the second **select**). The number of columns and datatypes must be identical between **select** statements, although the names of the columns do not need to be. The data, however, must be identical in the rows produced for the **MINUS** to reject them. *See* Chapter 12 for a discussion of the important differences and effects of **INTERSECT**, **MINUS**, and **UNION**.

Within text searches against CONTEXT indexes, **MINUS** tells the text search of two terms to subtract the score of the second term's search from the score of the first term's search before comparing the result to the threshold score.

# MOD
**SEE ALSO**    NUMBER FUNCTIONS, Chapter 8
**FORMAT**

```
MOD(value, divisor)
```

**DESCRIPTION**    **MOD** divides a *value* by a *divisor*, and gives the remainder. **MOD**(23,6) = 5 means divide 23 by 6. The answer is 3 with 5 left over, so 5 is the result of the modulus. *value* and *divisor* can both be any real number, except that *divisor* cannot be 0.

**EXAMPLES**

```
MOD(100,10) = 0
MOD(22,23) = 22
MOD(10,3) = 1
MOD(-30.23,7) = -2.23
MOD(4.1,.3) = .2
```

The second example shows what **MOD** does whenever the divisor is larger than the dividend (the number being divided). It produces the dividend as a result. Also note this important case:

```
MOD(value,1) = 0
```

if *value* is an integer. This is a good test to see if a number is an integer.

# MONTHS_BETWEEN
**SEE ALSO**    ADD_MONTHS, DATE FUNCTIONS, Chapter 9
**FORMAT**

```
MONTHS_BETWEEN(date2,date1)
```

**DESCRIPTION**    **MONTHS_BETWEEN** gives *date2 - date1* in months. The result is usually not an integer.

# MOUNT A DATABASE
To mount a database is to make it available to the database administrator.

# MOUNT AND OPEN A DATABASE
To mount and open a database is to make it available to users.

# MULTI-THREADED SERVER
*See* Shared Server.

# NATURAL JOIN
A NATURAL JOIN joins two tables based on the key columns they have in common. The syntax is

```
FROM TableA NATURAL JOIN TableB
```

which is equivalent to

```
FROM TableA, TableB
WHERE TableA.KeyColumn = TableB.KeyColumn
```

See Chapter 12 for examples of different types of join syntax.

# NCHAR

NCHAR is a multibyte version of the CHAR datatype. It stores fixed-length character data up to 2000 bytes in length. *See* DATA TYPES.

# NCHR

**SEE ALSO**   CHR

**FORMAT**

```
NCHR (number)
```

**DESCRIPTION**   **NCHR** returns the character having the binary equivalent to *number* in the national character set.

# NCLOB

The NCLOB datatype is the multibyte version of the CLOB datatype. NCLOB stores character large objects containing UNICODE characters, up to a maximum length of 4GB. *See* DATA TYPES.

# NEAR

**SEE ALSO**   **CONTAINS**, Chapter 24

**DESCRIPTION**   Within CONTEXT indexes, **NEAR** indicates that a proximity search should be executed for the specified text strings. If the search terms are 'summer' and 'lease', then a proximity search for the two terms could be

```
select Text
 from SONNET
 where CONTAINS(Text,'summer NEAR lease') >0;
```

When evaluating the text search results, text with the words 'summer' and 'lease' near each other in the text will have higher scores than text with the words 'summer' and 'lease' farther apart.

# NESTED TABLE

A nested table is, as its name implies, a table within a table. In this case, it is a table that is represented as a column within another table. You can have multiple rows in the nested table for each row in the main table. There is no limit to the number of entries per row. *See* Chapter 31 for details on creating, using, and querying nested tables.

# NESTING

Nesting is the practice of placing a statement, clause, query, and so on, within another statement, clause, query, and so on.

## NEWPAGE (SQL*PLUS)
*See* **SET**.

## NEW_TIME
*See* DATE FUNCTIONS.

## NEXT_DAY
*See* DATE FUNCTIONS.

## NEXTVAL
*See* PSEUDO-COLUMNS.

## NLS_CHARSET_DECL_LEN
**SEE ALSO**　　NCHAR
**FORMAT**

```
NLS_CHARSET_DECL_LEN (byte_count , char_set_id)
```

**DESCRIPTION**　　**NLS_CHARSET_DECL_LEN** returns the declaration width (in number of characters) of an NCHAR column.

## NLS_CHARSET_ID
**SEE ALSO**　　NLS_CHARSET_NAME
**FORMAT**

```
NLS_CHARSET_ID (text)
```

**DESCRIPTION**　　**NLS_CHARSET_ID** returns the character set ID number corresponding to character set name *text*.

## NLS_CHARSET_NAME
**SEE ALSO**　　NLS_CHARSET_ID
**FORMAT**

```
NLS_CHARSET_NAME (number)
```

**DESCRIPTION**　　NLS_CHARSET_NAME returns the name of the character set corresponding to ID number *number*.

## NLS_INITCAP
**SEE ALSO**　　CHARACTER FUNCTIONS, **INITCAP**, Chapter 8
**FORMAT**

```
NLS_INITCAP(number[, nls_parameters])
```

**DESCRIPTION**　　**NLS_INITCAP** is like the **INITCAP** function except with the addition of a parameter string. The *NLS parameters* string, enclosed in single quotation marks, gives a sort sequence for capitalizing

special linguistic sequences. You would usually use **INITCAP** with the default sort sequence for the session, but this function lets you specify the exact sort sequence to use.

## NLS_LOWER

**SEE ALSO**    CHARACTER FUNCTIONS, **LOWER**, Chapter 8

**FORMAT**

```
NLS_LOWER(number[, nls_parameters])
```

**DESCRIPTION**    **NLS_LOWER** is like the **LOWER** function except with the addition of a parameter string. The *NLS parameters* string, enclosed in single quotation marks, gives a sort sequence for lowercasing special linguistic sequences. You would usually use **LOWER** with the default sort sequence for the session, but this function lets you specify the exact sort sequence to use.

## NLSSORT

**SEE ALSO**    *Oracle9i Database Administrator's Guide,* Chapter 37

**FORMAT**

```
NLSSORT(character[, nls_parameters])
```

**DESCRIPTION**    National **L**anguage **S**upport **SORT** gives the collating sequence value (an integer) of the given *character* based on the National Language Support option chosen for the site. The *NLS parameters* string, enclosed in single quotation marks, gives a sort sequence for special linguistic sequences if you do not want to use the session or database default.

## NLS_UPPER

**SEE ALSO**    CHARACTER FUNCTIONS, **UPPER**, Chapter 8

**FORMAT**

```
NLS_UPPER(number[, nls_parameters])
```

**DESCRIPTION**    **NLS_UPPER** is like the **UPPER** function except with the addition of a parameter string. The *NLS parameters* string, enclosed in single quotation marks, gives a sort sequence for capitalizing special linguistic sequences. You would usually use **UPPER** with the default sort sequence for the session, but this function lets you specify the exact sort sequence to use.

## NOAUDIT

**SEE ALSO**    **AUDIT**, PRIVILEGE

**FORMAT**

noaudit::=

**sql_statement_clause::=**

**auditing_by_clause::=**

**schema_object_clause::=**

**auditing_on_clause::=**

**DESCRIPTION**   **NOAUDIT** stops auditing of SQL statements being audited as a result of the **AUDIT** command. It stops auditing either a statement (*see* **AUDIT**) or a statement authorized by a system privilege (*see* PRIVILEGE). If there is a BY clause with a list of users, the command stops the auditing of statements issued by these users. If there is no BY clause, Oracle stops auditing the statements for all users. The **WHENEVER SUCCESSFUL** option stops auditing only for those statements that successfully complete; **WHENEVER NOT SUCCESSFUL** stops only for those statements that result in an error.

**NOAUDIT** also stops the audit for an option of the use of a table, view, or synonym. To stop the audit of any table, view, or synonym, you must either own them or have DBA authority. *option* refers to the options described shortly. *user* is the username of the object owner. *object* is a table, view, or synonym. *option* specifies what commands the audit should be stopped for. For a table or materialized view, options are **ALTER**, **AUDIT**, **COMMENT**, **DELETE**, **GRANT**, **INDEX**, **INSERT**, **LOCK**, **RENAME**, **SELECT**, and **UPDATE**. For procedures, functions, types, libraries, and packages, **EXECUTE** and **GRANT** commands can be audited. For directories, **AUDIT**, **GRANT**, and **READ** can be audited. **GRANT** audits both **GRANT** and **REVOKE** commands. **NOAUDIT GRANT** stops both of them. **ALL** stops the audits of all of these.

ON *object* names the object being audited, and includes a table, view, or a synonym of a table, view or sequence.

For views, **ALTER** and **INDEX** cannot be used. The default options of a view are created by the union of the options of each of the underlying tables plus the DEFAULT options.

For synonyms, the options are the same as tables.

For sequences, the options are **ALTER**, **AUDIT**, **GRANT**, and **SELECT**.

**WHENEVER SUCCESSFUL** turns off auditing for successful writes to the table. **WHENEVER NOT SUCCESSFUL** turns auditing off for unsuccessful writes to the table. Omitting this optional clause turns off both kinds of auditing.

Both formats commit any pending changes to the database. If remote tables are accessed through a database link, any auditing on the remote system is based on options set there. Auditing information is written to a table named SYS.AUD$. *See* Chapter 37 for details on the auditing views.

**EXAMPLES**    The following stops auditing of all attempts at **update** or **delete** on the BOOKSHELF table:

```
noaudit update, delete on BOOKSHELF;
```

This stops auditing of all unsuccessful access to BOOKSHELF:

```
noaudit all on BOOKSHELF whenever not successful;
```

# NODE

Node can be either of two definitions:

- In a tree-structured table, a node is one row.
- In a network, a node is the location in the network where a computer is attached.

# NOLOGGING

The **NOLOGGING** clause for object creation (tables, LOBs, indexes, partitions, etc.) specifies that the creation of the object will not be logged in the online redo log files, and thus will not be recoverable following a media failure. The object creation is not logged, and neither are certain types of transactions against the object. **NOLOGGING** takes the place of the **UNRECOVERABLE** keyword introduced in Oracle7.2. See Chapters 21 and 40.

# NON-EQUI-JOIN

A non-equi-join is a join condition other than "equals" (=). *See* EQUI-JOIN.

# NOT

**SEE ALSO**    LOGICAL OPERATORS, Chapter 3

**DESCRIPTION**    **NOT** comes before and reverses the effect of any of these logical operators: **BETWEEN**, **IN**, **LIKE**, and **EXISTS**. **NOT** can also come before **NULL**, as in **IS NOT NULL**.

## NOT EXISTS

**SEE ALSO**    ANY, ALL, EXISTS, IN, Chapter 12

**FORMAT**

```
select ...
where NOT EXISTS (select...);
```

**DESCRIPTION**    NOT EXISTS returns false in a **where** clause if the subquery that follows it returns one or more rows. The **select** clause in the subquery can be a column, a literal, or an asterisk—it doesn't matter. The only part that matters is whether the **where** clause in the subquery will return a row.

**EXAMPLE**    NOT EXISTS is frequently used to determine which records in one table do not have matching records in another table. See Chapter 12 for examples of the use of NOT EXISTS.

## NTILE

**SEE ALSO**    WIDTH_BUCKET

**FORMAT**

```
NTILE (expr) OVER ([query_partition_clause] order_by_clause)
```

**DESCRIPTION**    NTILE is an analytic function. It divides an ordered dataset into a number of buckets indicated by an expression and assigns the appropriate bucket number to each row. The buckets are numbered and the expression must resolve to a positive constant for each partition.

## NULL (Form 1-PL/SQL)

**SEE ALSO**    BLOCK STRUCTURE

**FORMAT**

```
NULL;
```

**DESCRIPTION**    The **NULL** statement has nothing to do with **NULL** values. Its main purpose is to make a section of code more readable by saying, in effect, "do nothing." It also provides a means of having a null block (since PL/SQL requires at least one executable statement between **BEGIN** and **END**). It is usually used as the statement following one (usually the last) of a series of condition tests.

**EXAMPLE**

```
IF Age > 65 THEN
 ...
ELSEIF AGE BETWEEN 21 and 65 THEN
 ...
ELSE
 NULL;
ENDIF;
```

## NULL (Form 2-SQL Column Value)

**SEE ALSO**    **CREATE TABLE**, GROUP FUNCTIONS, INDICATOR VARIABLE, **NVL**, Chapter 3

**DESCRIPTION**    A **NULL** value is one that is unknown, irrelevant, or not meaningful. Any Oracle datatype can be **NULL**. That is, any Oracle column in a given row can be without a value (unless the table was created with **NOT NULL** for that column). **NULL** in a NUMBER datatype is not the same as zero.

Few procedural languages directly support the idea of a variable with a **NULL** or unknown value, although Oracle and SQL do so easily. In order to extend languages for which Oracle has developed precompilers to support the **NULL** concept, an INDICATOR VARIABLE is associated with the host variable, almost like a flag, to indicate whether it is **NULL**. The host variable and its indicator variable may be referenced and set separately in the host language code, but are always concatenated in SQL or PL/SQL.

You use the **NVL** function to detect the absence of a value for a column, and convert the **NULL** value into a real value of the datatype of the column. For instance, **NVL(Name,'NOT KNOWN')** converts a **NULL** value in the column Name into the words NOT KNOWN. For a non-**NULL** value (that is, where a name is present), the **NVL** function simply returns the name. **NVL** works similarly with NUMBERs and DATEs.

Except for **COUNT(*)** and **COMPUTE NUMBER**, group functions ignore null values. Other functions return a null value when a **NULL** is present in the value or values they are evaluating. Thus, the following example:

```
NULL + 1066 is NULL.
LEAST(NULL,'A','Z') is NULL.
```

Since **NULL** represents an unknown value, two columns that are each **NULL** are not equal to each other. Therefore, the equal sign and other logical operators (except for **IS NULL** and **IS NOT NULL**) do not work with **NULL**. For example, this:

```
where Name = NULL
```

is not a valid **where** clause. **NULL** requires the word **IS**:

```
where Name IS NULL
```

During **order by** sorts, **NULL** values always come first when the order is ascending, and last when it is descending.

When **NULL** values are stored in the database, they are represented with a single byte if they fall between two columns that have real values, and no bytes if they fall at the end of the row (last in the column definition in the **create table**). If some of the columns in a table are likely to often contain **NULL** values, those columns can be usefully grouped near the end of the **create table** column list; this will save disk space.

**NULL** values do not appear in indexes, except in the single case where all the values in a cluster key are **NULL**.

# NULLIF

**SEE ALSO**  **COALESCE, DECODE, NULL**, Chapter 17

**FORMAT**

```
NULLIF (expr1 , expr2)
```

**DESCRIPTION**  **NULLIF** compares *expr1* and *expr2*. If they are equal, the function returns **NULL**. If they are not equal, the function returns *expr1*. You cannot specify the literal **NULL** for *expr1*.

The **NULLIF** function is logically equivalent to the following **CASE** expression:

```
CASE WHEN expr1 = expr2 THEN NULL
ELSE expr1 END
```

## NUMBER DATATYPE

A NUMBER datatype is a standard Oracle datatype that may contain a number, with or without a decimal point and a sign. Valid values are 0, and positive and negative numbers with magnitude 1.0E-130 to 9.99.. E125.

## NUMBER FORMATS

**SEE ALSO**     COLUMN, Chapter 14

**DESCRIPTION**     These options work with both **set numformat** and the **column format** command:

9999990	The count of nines and zeros determines the maximum digits that can be displayed.
999,999,999.99	Commas and decimals will be placed in the pattern shown.
999990	Displays a zero if the value is zero.
099999	Displays numbers with leading zeros.
$99999	A dollar sign is placed in front of every number.
B99999	The display will be blank if the value is zero. This is the default.
99999MI	If the number is negative, a minus sign follows the number. The default is for the negative sign to be on left.
S9999	Returns "+" for positive values, "-" for negative values
99999PR	Negative numbers are displayed within < and >.
99D99	Displays the decimal in the position indicated
9G999	Displays the group separator in the position shown
C9999	Displays the ISO currency symbol in this position
L999	Displays the local currency symbol
,	Displays a comma
.	Displays a period
9.999EEEE	The display will be in scientific notation (4 E's are required).
999V99	Multiplies number by $10n$, where $n$ is the number of digits to the right of V. 999V99 turns 1234 into 123400.
RN	Displays Roman numeral values, for numbers between 1 and 3999
DATE	Displays value as a date in MM/DD/YY format, for NUMBER columns used storing Julian dates.

## NUMBER FUNCTIONS

This is an ordered list of all current single-value number functions in Oracle's SQL. Each of these is listed elsewhere in this reference under its own name, with its proper format and use. Each can be used as a regular SQL function as well as a PL/SQL function. See GROUP FUNCTIONS and LIST FUNCTIONS.

Function	Definition
*value1* + *value2*	Addition
*value1* - *value2*	Subtraction

Function	Definition
value1 * value2	Multiplication
value1 / value2	Division
ABS(value)	ABSolute value
ACOS(value)	Arc COSine of value, in radians
ASIN(value)	Arc SINe of value, in radians
ATAN(value)	Arc TANgent of value, in radians
BITAND (value1, value2)	BITwise AND of value1 and value2, both of which must resolve to nonnegative integers, and returns an integer
CEIL(value)	Numeric CEILing: the smallest integer larger than or equal to value
COS(value)	COSine of value
COSH(value)	Hyperbolic COSine of value
EXP(value)	e raised to value EXPonent
FLOOR(value)	Largest integer smaller than or equal to value
LN(value)	Natural Logarithm of value
LOG(value)	Base 10 LOGarithm of value
MOD(value, divisor)	MODulus
NVL(value, substitute)	substitute for value if value is NULL
POWER(value, exponent)	value raised to an exponent POWER
ROUND(value, precision)	ROUNDing of value to precision
SIGN(value)	1 if value is positive, −1 if negative, 0 if zero
SIN(value)	SINe of value
SINH(value)	Hyperbolic SINe of value
SQRT(value)	SQuare RooT of value
TAN(value)	TANgent of value
TANH(value)	Hyperbolic TANgent of value
TRUNC(value, precision)	value TRUNCated to precision
VSIZE(value)	Storage SIZE of value in Oracle

# NUMTODSINTERVAL

**SEE ALSO**     DATA TYPE, Chapter 10
**FORMAT**

```
NUMTODSINTERVAL (n , 'char_expr')
```

**DESCRIPTION**     **NUMTODSINTERVAL** converts n to an INTERVAL DAY TO SECOND literal. n can be a number or an expression resolving to a number. char_expr can be of CHAR, VARCHAR2, NCHAR, or NVARCHAR2 datatype. The value for char_expr specifies the unit of n and must resolve to one of the following string values: 'DAY', 'HOUR', 'MINUTE', or 'SECOND'.

## NUMTOYMINTERVAL

**SEE ALSO**     DATA TYPE, Chapter 10

**FORMAT**

```
NUMTOYMINTERVAL (n , 'char_expr')
```

**DESCRIPTION**     **NUMTOYMINTERVAL** converts number *n* to an INTERVAL YEAR TO MONTH literal. *n* can be a number or an expression resolving to a number. *char_expr* can be of CHAR, VARCHAR2, NCHAR, or NVARCHAR2 datatype. The value for *char_expr* specifies the unit of *n*, and must resolve to either 'YEAR' or 'MONTH'.

## NUMWIDTH (SQL*PLUS)

*See* **SET**.

## NVARCHAR2

NVARCHAR2 is the multibyte equivalent of the VARCHAR2 datatype. Its maximum length is 4000 bytes. *See* DATA TYPES.

## NVL

**SEE ALSO**     GROUP FUNCTIONS, NULL, OTHER FUNCTIONS, Chapter 8

**FORMAT**

```
NVL(value, substitute)
```

**DESCRIPTION**     If *value* is **NULL**, this function returns *substitute*. If *value* is not **NULL**, this function returns *value*. *value* can be any Oracle datatype. *Substitute* can be a literal, another column, or an expression, but must be the same datatype as *value*.

## NVL2

**SEE ALSO**     GROUP FUNCTIONS, NULL, OTHER FUNCTIONS, Chapter 8

**FORMAT**

```
NVL2 (expr1 , expr2 , expr3)
```

**DESCRIPTION**     **NVL2** is an extended form of **NVL**. In **NVL2**, *expr1* can never be returned; either *expr2* or *expr3* will be returned. If *expr1* is not **NULL**, **NVL2** returns *expr2*. If *expr1* is **NULL**, **NVL2** returns *expr3*. The argument *expr1* can have any datatype. The arguments *expr2* and *expr3* can have any datatypes except LONG.

## OBJECT

An object is a named element in the Oracle database, such as a table, index, synonym, procedure, or trigger.

## OBJECT NAMES

These database objects may be given names: tables, views, synonyms, aliases, columns, indexes, users, sequences, tablespaces, and so on. The following rules govern naming objects:

- The name of an object can be from 1 to 30 characters long, except for database names, which are up to eight characters, and host file names, whose length is operating system dependent.

- A name may not contain a quotation mark.
- A name must:
  Begin with a letter
  Contain only the characters A-Z, 0-9, $, #, and _
  Not be an Oracle reserved word (*see* RESERVED WORDS)
  Not duplicate the name of another database object owned by the same user

Object names are not case sensitive. Object names should follow a sensible naming convention, such as is discussed in Chapter 2.

## OBJECT TABLE

An object table is a table in which each of its rows is a row object. *See* Chapter 33 and the CREATE TABLE command entry.

## OBJECT VIEW

An object view superimposes abstract datatypes on existing relational tables. Object views allow you to access the relational table's data either via normal SQL commands or via its abstract datatype structures. Object views provide a technological bridge between relational and object-relational databases. *See* Chapters 30 and 33 for examples of object views.

## OBJECT-RELATIONAL DATABASE MANAGEMENT SYSTEM

An object-relational database management system (ORDBMS) supports both relational database features (such as primary keys and foreign keys) and object-oriented features (such as inheritance and encapsulation). *See* Chapter 4 for a description of Oracle's implementation of an ORDBMS.

## OEM

*See* ORACLE ENTERPRISE MANAGER

## OFFLINE BACKUP

An offline backup is a physical backup of the database files while the database is shutdown.

## OID

An OID is an object identifier, assigned by Oracle to each object in a database. For example, each row object within an object table has an OID value assigned to it; the OID is used to resolve references to the row objects. Oracle does not reuse OID values after an object is dropped. *See* Chapter 33.

## ONLINE BACKUP

Online backup is the ability of Oracle to archive data while the database is still running. The DBA does not need to shut down the database to archive data. Even data currently being accessed can be archived.

## ONLINE REDO LOG

Online redo logs are redo log files that are not yet archived. They may be available to the instance for recording activity, or have previously been written but are awaiting archiving.

## OPEN

**SEE ALSO**     **CLOSE, DECLARE CURSOR, FETCH, LOOP**, Chapter 27

**FORMAT**

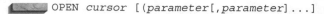

```
OPEN cursor [(parameter[,parameter]...]
```

**DESCRIPTION**   **OPEN** works in conjunction with **DECLARE** cursor and **FETCH**. The **DECLARE** cursor sets up a **SELECT** statement to be executed, and establishes a list of parameters (PL/SQL variables) that are to be used in its **where** clause, but it does not execute the query.

   **OPEN** *cursor*, in effect, executes the query in the named cursor and keeps its results in a staging area, where they can be called in, a row at a time, with **FETCH**, and their column values put into local variables with the INTO clause of the **FETCH**. If the cursor **SELECT** statement used parameters, then their actual values are passed to the **SELECT** statement in the parameter list of the **OPEN**. They must match in number and position and have compatible datatypes.

   There is also an alternative method of associating the values in the **OPEN** with those in the **SELECT** list:

```
DECLARE
 cursor mycur(Title, Publisher) is select ...
BEGIN
 open my_cur(new_book => Title, 'PANDORAS' => Publisher);
```

   Here, *new_book*, a PL/SQL variable, loaded perhaps from a data entry screen, is pointed to Title, and therefore loads it with whatever is currently in the variable *new_book*. Publisher is loaded with the value 'PANDORAS', and these then become the parameters of the cursor *my_cur*. (*See* **DECLARE CURSOR** for more details on parameters in cursors.)

   You also may combine pointed associations with positional ones, but the positional ones must appear first in the **OPEN**'s list.

   You cannot reopen an open cursor, though you can **CLOSE** it and re**OPEN** it, and you cannot use a cursor for which you have a current **OPEN** statement in a cursor FOR LOOP.

## OPEN CURSOR (Embedded SQL)

**SEE ALSO**   **CLOSE, DECLARE CURSOR, FETCH, PREPARE**, *Precompiler Programmer's Guide*

**FORMAT**

```
EXEC SQL [FOR { integer | :array_size }]
OPEN cursor
 [USING
 {DESCRIPTOR SQLDBA_descriptor
 | :variable[[INDICATOR]:indicator_variable
 [,:variable[INDICATOR]:indicator_variable]]... }]
```

**DESCRIPTION**   *cursor* is the name of a cursor previously named in a **DECLARE CURSOR** statement. The optional USING references either the host variable list of variables that are to be substituted in the statement in the **DECLARE CURSOR**, based on position (the number and type of variables must be the same), or a descriptor name that references the result of a previous DESCRIBE.

   **OPEN** *cursor* allocates a cursor, defines the active set of rows (the host variables are substituted when the cursor is opened), and positions the cursor just before the first row of the set. No rows are retrieved until a **FETCH** is executed. Host variables do not change once they've been substituted. To change them, you must reopen the cursor (you don't have to **CLOSE** it first).

## OPERATOR

An operator is a character or reserved word used in an expression to perform an operation, such as addition or comparison, on the elements of the expression. Some examples of operators

are * (multiplication), > (greater than comparison), and **ANY** (compares a value to each value returned by a subquery).

## OPS$ LOGINS

OPS$ LOGINS are a type of Oracle username in which OPS$ is prefixed to the user's operating system account ID, to simplify logging into Oracle from that ID.

## OPTIMIZER

An optimizer is the part of an Oracle kernel that chooses the best way to use the tables and indexes to complete the request made by a SQL statement. *See* Chapter 38.

## OR

**SEE ALSO**　　AND, CONTAINS, Chapters 3 and 24

**DESCRIPTION**　　OR combines logical expressions so that the result is true if either logical expression is true.

**EXAMPLE**　　The following will produce data for both KEENE and SAN FRANCISCO:

```
select * from COMFORT
 where City = 'KEENE' OR City = 'SAN FRANCISCO'
```

Within CONTEXT queries, an **OR** operator can be used for searches involving multiple search terms. If either of the search terms is found, and its search score exceeds the specified threshold value, the text will be returned by the search. *See* Chapter 24.

## ORACLE ENTERPRISE MANAGER

Oracle Enterprise Manager (OEM) is a product from Oracle Corporation. OEM provides a graphical interface for common DBA tasks, and has add-on features for extended performance tuning and data management capabilities.

## ORACLE REAL APPLICATION CLUSTER

In an Oracle Real Application Cluster (RAC) environment, multiple instances (usually on a cluster of servers) access a single set of datafiles. RAC provides server failover capability in a high-availability environment, since users can be directed to multiple servers to access the same data.

## ORACLE9i APPLICATION SERVER

Oracle9i Application Server (9iAS) allows developers to access Oracle databases from Web-based applications. The developers call procedures from within the database. The procedures, in turn, retrieve or manipulate data, and return results to the developers. See Chapter 39.

## ORDBMS

*See* OBJECT-RELATIONAL DATABASE MANAGEMENT SYSTEM.

## ORDER BY

**SEE ALSO**　　COLLATION, FROM, GROUP BY, HAVING, SELECT, WHERE

## FORMAT

```
ORDER BY { expression [,expression]... |
 position [,position]... }
 alias [,alias]... }
[ASC | DESC]
```

**DESCRIPTION**   The **ORDER BY** clause causes Oracle to sort the results of a query before they are displayed. This can be done either by *expression*, which can be a simple column name or a complex set of functions, an *alias* (*see* Note below), or a column *position* in the **select** clause (*see* Note below). Rows are ordered first by the first expression or position, then by the second, and so on, based on the collating sequence of the host. If **ORDER BY** is not specified, the order in which rows are selected from a table is indeterminate, and may change from one query to the next.

**NOTE**
*Oracle still supports the use of column positions in ORDER BY clauses, but this feature is no longer part of the SQL standard and is not guaranteed to be supported in future releases. Use column aliases instead.*

**ASC** or **DESC** specifies ascending or descending order, and may follow each expression, position, or alias in the **ORDER BY**. **NULL** values precede ascending and follow descending rows in Oracle.
**ORDER BY** follows any other clauses except FOR UPDATE OF.
If **ORDER BY** and **DISTINCT** are both specified, the **ORDER BY** clause may only refer to columns or expressions that are in the **SELECT** clause.
When the **UNION**, **INTERSECT**, or **MINUS** operator is used, the names of the columns in the first **select** may differ from the names in subsequent **selects**. **ORDER BY** must use the column name from the first **select**.
Only CHAR, VARCHAR2, NUMBER, and DATE datatypes—and the special datatype RowID—can appear in an **ORDER BY**.

## EXAMPLE

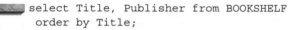

```
select Title, Publisher from BOOKSHELF
 order by Title;
```

# OTHER FUNCTIONS

This is an alphabetical list of all current functions in Oracle's SQL that do not readily fall into any other function category. Each of these is listed elsewhere in this reference under its own name, with its proper format and use.

```
DUMP(string [,format [,start [,length]]])
```

**DUMP** displays the value of *string* in internal data format, in ASCII, octal, decimal, hex, or character format.

```
NVL(value, substitute)
```

If *value* is **NULL**, the **NVL** function returns *substitute*. Otherwise it returns *value*.

```
NVL2 (expr1 , expr2 , expr3)
```

If *expr1* is not **NULL**, **NVL2** returns *expr2*. If *expr1* is **NULL**, **NVL2** returns *expr3*.

```
VSIZE(expression)
```

**VSIZE** tells how many bytes Oracle needs in order to store the *expression* in its database.

# OUTER JOIN

*See* JOIN for a detailed explanation. As of Oracle9i, you can use the ANSI standard outer join syntax options (LEFT OUTER JOIN, RIGHT OUTER JOIN, and FULL OUTER JOIN). See Chapter 12 for details and examples.

# PACKAGE

A package is a PL/SQL object that groups PL/SQL types, variables, SQL cursors, exceptions, procedures, and functions. Each package has a specification and a body. The specification shows the objects you can access when you use the package. The body fully defines all the objects and can contain additional objects used only for the internal workings. You can change the body (for example, by adding procedures to the package) without invalidating any object that uses the package.

*See* **CREATE PACKAGE, CREATE PACKAGE BODY**, CURSOR, EXCEPTION, FUNCTION, TABLE (PL/SQL), RECORD (PL/SQL), PROCEDURE, and Chapter 29.

# PAGESIZE (SQL*PLUS)

*See* **SET**.

# PARAMETER

A parameter is a value, a column name, or an expression, usually following a function or module name, specifying additional functions or controls that should be observed by the function or module. *See* PARAMETERS for an example.

# PARAMETERS

**SEE ALSO** &, &&, **ACCEPT, DEFINE**, Chapter 16

**DESCRIPTION** Parameters allow the execution of a start file with values passed on the command line. These are simply spaced apart following the name of the start file. Within the file they are referenced by the order in which they appeared on the command line. &1 is the first, &2 the second, and so on. Aside from this, the rules for use are the same as for variables loaded using **DEFINE** or **ACCEPT**, and they may be used in SQL statements in the same way.

There is one limitation, however. There is no way to pass a multiple word argument to a single variable. Each variable can take only one word, date, or number. Attempting to solve this by putting the parameters in quotes on the command line results in the words being concatenated.

**EXAMPLE** Suppose you have a start file named **fred.sql** that contains this SQL:

```
select Title, Publisher
 from BOOKSHELF
 where Title > &1;
```

Starting it with this command line:

```
start fred.sql M
```

produces a report of all titles that start with a character > 'M'.

# PARENT

In tree-structured data, a parent is a node that has another node as a descendent, or child.

# PARENT QUERY

The parent query is the outermost query (the one that displays a result) in a main query containing a subquery. *See* MAIN QUERY.

# PARENTHESES

*See* LOGICAL OPERATORS and PL/SQL KEY WORDS AND SYMBOLS.

# PARSE

Parsing is the mapping of a SQL statement to a cursor. At parse time, several validation checks are made, such as, do all referenced objects exist, are grants proper, and is statement syntax correct? Also, decisions regarding execution and optimization are made, such as which indexes will be used.

# PASSWORD

A password is a set of characters that you must enter when you connect to the host computer's operating system or to an Oracle database. Passwords should be kept confidential.

## PASSWORD (SQL*PLUS Command)

**SEE ALSO**    **ALTER USER**, Chapter 19

**FORMAT**

```
PASSW[ORD] [username]
```

**DESCRIPTION**    You can use the **password** command in SQL*Plus to change the password on your account or another account (if you have ALTER ANY USER privilege). If you use the **password** command, your new password will not be displayed on the screen as you type. Users with dba authority can change any user's password via the **password** command; other users can change only their own password.

When you enter the **password** command, you will be prompted for the old and new passwords.

**EXAMPLE**

```
password
Changing password for dora
Old password:
New password:
Retype new password:
```

When the password has been successfully changed, you will receive the feedback:

```
Password changed
```

# PARALLEL QUERY OPTION

The Parallel Query Option (PQO) splits a single database task into multiple coordinated tasks, enabling the task to use multiple processors. For example, a full table scan or a large sort may be parallelized, enabling multiple processors to take part in the completion of the operation. If there are adequate

resources available on the server, then the parallelized operation may complete faster than if it ran as a single task.

The number of parallel query server processes used to execute an operation is called the *degree of parallelism*, and is set via the **DEGREE** parameter of hints. See Chapter 38.

# PARTITION

To partition a table is to systematically divide its rows among multiple tables, each with the same structure. You can direct the database to automatically partition a table and its indexes. *See* Chapter 18.

# PARTITIONED TABLE

A partitioned table is a table whose rows have been partitioned across multiple smaller tables.

# PAUSE (Form 1-SQL*PLUS)

*See* **SET**.

# PAUSE (Form 2-SQL*PLUS)

**SEE ALSO**    **ACCEPT**, **PROMPT**, Chapter 6

**FORMAT**

```
PAU[SE] [text];
```

**DESCRIPTION**    **PAUSE** is similar to **PROMPT**, except **PAUSE** first displays an empty line, then a line containing *text*, then waits for the user to press RETURN. If *text* is not entered, **PAUSE** displays two empty lines, then waits for user to press RETURN.

> **NOTE**
> *PAUSE waits for a* RETURN *from the terminal even if the source of command input has been redirected to be from a file, which means a start file with SET TERMOUT OFF could hang, waiting for a* RETURN, *with no message as to why it was waiting (or that it was waiting). Use* **PAUSE** *with caution.*

**EXAMPLE**

```
prompt Report Complete.
pause Press RETURN to continue.
```

# PCTFREE

PCTFREE is a portion of the data block that is not filled by rows as they are inserted into a table, but is reserved for later updates made to the rows in that block.

# PCTUSED

PCTUSED is the percentage of space in a data block which Oracle attempts keep filled. If the percent used falls below PCTUSED, then block is added to the list of free blocks in the segment. PCTUSED may be set on a table-by-table basis.

## PERCENT_RANK

**SEE ALSO** GROUP FUNCTIONS, Chapter 13

**FORMAT** For aggregates:

```
PERCENT_RANK (expr [, expr]...) WITHIN GROUP
(ORDER BY
 expr [DESC | ASC] [NULLS { FIRST | LAST }]
 [, expr [DESC | ASC] [NULLS { FIRST | LAST }]]...)
```

For analytics:

```
PERCENT_RANK () OVER ([query_partition_clause] order_by_clause)
```

**DESCRIPTION** As an aggregate function, **PERCENT_RANK** calculates, for a hypothetical row R identified by the arguments of the function and a corresponding sort specification, the rank of row R minus 1 divided by the number of rows in the aggregate group. This calculation is made as if the hypothetical row R were inserted into the group of rows over which Oracle is to aggregate. The arguments of the function identify a single hypothetical row within each aggregate group. Therefore, they must all evaluate to constant expressions within each aggregate group. The constant argument expressions and the expressions in the **ORDER BY** clause of the aggregate match by position. Therefore the number of arguments must be the same and their types must be compatible.

The range of values returned by **PERCENT_RANK** is 0 to 1, inclusive. The first row in any set has a **PERCENT_RANK** of 0.

As an analytic function, for a row R, **PERCENT_RANK** calculates the rank of R minus 1, divided by 1 less than the number of rows being evaluated (the entire query result set or a partition).

See Chapter 13 for an example of the use of **PERCENT_RANK**.

## PERCENTILE_CONT

**SEE ALSO** GROUP FUNCTIONS, **PERCENTILE_DISC**, Chapter 13

**FORMAT**

```
PERCENTILE_CONT (expr) WITHIN GROUP (ORDER BY expr [DESC | ASC])
[OVER (query_partition_clause)]
```

**DESCRIPTION** **PERCENTILE_CONT** is an inverse distribution function that assumes a continuous distribution model. It takes a percentile value and a sort specification, and returns an interpolated value that would fall into that percentile value with respect to the sort specification. Nulls are ignored in the calculation.

The first *expr* must evaluate to a numeric value between 0 and 1, because it is a percentile value. This *expr* must be constant within each aggregation group. The **ORDER BY** clause takes a single expression that must be a numeric or datetime value, as these are the types over which Oracle can perform interpolation.

## PERCENTILE_DISC

**SEE ALSO** GROUP FUNCTIONS, **PERCENTILE_CONT**, Chapter 13

**FORMAT**

```
PERCENTILE_DISC (expr) WITHIN GROUP (ORDER BY expr [DESC | ASC])
[OVER (query_partition_clause)]
```

**DESCRIPTION**    **PERCENTILE_DISC** is an inverse distribution function that assumes a discrete distribution model. It takes a percentile value and a sort specification and returns an element from the set. Nulls are ignored in the calculation.

The first *expr* must evaluate to a numeric value between 0 and 1, because it is a percentile value. This expression must be constant within each aggregate group. The **ORDER BY** clause takes a single expression that can be of any type that can be sorted.

For a given percentile value P, **PERCENTILE_DISC** function sorts the values of the expression in the **ORDER BY** clause, and returns the one with the smallest **CUME_DIST** value (with respect to the same sort specification) that is greater than or equal to P.

## PMON PROCESS

The **Process MON**itor is a background process used for recovery when a process accessing a database fails. *See* BACKGROUND PROCESS.

## POWER

**SEE ALSO**    **SQRT**, Chapter 8
**FORMAT**

```
POWER(value,exponent)
```

**DESCRIPTION**    **POWER** is *value* raised to an *exponent*.
**EXAMPLE**

```
POWER(2,4) = 16
```

## PRAGMA

A pragma statement is a directive to the compiler, rather than a piece of executable code. Even though a pragma statement looks like executable code, and appears in a program (such as a PL/SQL block), it is not actually executable and doesn't appear as a part of the execution code of that block. Rather, it gives instructions to the compiler. *See* **EXCEPTION_INIT** and Chapter 30.

## PRECEDENCE

**SEE ALSO**    LOGICAL OPERATORS, QUERY OPERATORS, Chapter 12
**DESCRIPTION**    The following operators are listed in descending order of precedence. Operators with equal precedence are on the same line. Operators of equal precedence are evaluated in succession from left to right. All **AND**s are evaluated before any **OR**. Each of these is listed and described separately under its own symbol or name in this alphabetical reference.

Operator	Function
-	SQL*PLUS command continuation. Continues a command on the following line.
&	Prefix for parameters in a SQL*PLUS start file. Words are substituted for &1, &2, and so on. *See* START.
& &&	Prefix for a substitution in a SQL command in SQL*PLUS. SQL*PLUS will prompt for a value if an undefined & or && variable is found. && also defines the variable and saves the value; '&' does not. *See* & and &&, DEFINE, and ACCEPT.
:	Prefix for a host variable in PL/SQL.

Operator	Function
.	Variable separator, used in SQL*PLUS to separate the variable name from a suffix, so that the suffix is not considered a part of the variable name.
( )	Surrounds subqueries or lists of columns.
'	Surrounds a literal, such as a character string or date constant. To use a ' in a string constant, use two ' marks (not a double quotation mark).
"	Surrounds a table or column alias that contains special characters or a space.
"	Surrounds literal text in a date format clause of **TO_CHAR**.
@	Precedes a database name in a COPY, or a link name in a **from** clause.
( )	Overrides normal operator precedence.
+ -	Prefix sign (positive or negative) for a number or number expression.
* /	Multiplication and division.
+ -	Addition and subtraction.
\|\|	Char value concatenation.
NOT	Reverses result of an expression.
AND	True if both conditions are true.
OR	True if either condition is true.
UNION	Returns all distinct rows from both of two queries.
INTERSECT	Returns all matching distinct rows from two queries.
MINUS	Returns all distinct rows in first query that are not in the second.

# PRECOMPILER

A precompiler program reads specially structured source code, and writes a modified (precompiled) source program file that a normal compiler can read.

# PREDICATE

The predicate is the **where** clause and, more explicitly, a selection criteria clause based on one of the operators (=, !=, **IS**, **IS NOT**, >, >=) and containing no **AND**, **OR**, or **NOT**.

# PREPARE (Embedded SQL)

**SEE ALSO**  CLOSE, DECLARE, CURSOR, FETCH, OPEN, *Precompiler Programmer's Guide*
**FORMAT**

```
EXEC SQL [AT { db_name | :host_variable }] PREPARE statement_id
 FROM { :host_string | 'text' | select_command }
```

**DESCRIPTION**  **PREPARE** parses SQL in the host variable *:host_string* or the literal *text*. It assigns a *statement_id* as a reference to the SQL. If the *statement_id* has been used previously, this reference replaces it. The SQL is a select statement, and may include a **for update of** clause. *:host_string* is not the actual name of the host variable used, but a placeholder. **OPEN CURSOR** assigns input host variables in its **using** clause, and **FETCH** assigns output host variables in its **into** clause, based on position. A statement only needs to be **PREPARE**d once. It can then be executed multiple times.

**EXAMPLE**

```
query_string : string(1..100)
get(query_string);
EXEC SQL prepare FRED from :query_string;
EXEC SQL execute FRED;
```

# PRIMARY KEY

The primary key is the column(s) used to uniquely identify each row of a table.

# PRINT

**SEE ALSO**     BIND VARIABLE, **VARIABLE**, Chapter 26
**FORMAT**

```
PRINT variable1 variable2
```

**DESCRIPTION**     Displays the current value of the specified variable (which is created via the **VARIABLE** command). You can **print** the current values of multiple variables in a single command.

# PRIOR

*See* CONNECT BY.

# PRIVILEGE

A privilege is a permission granted to an Oracle user to execute some action. In Oracle, no user can execute any action without having the privilege to do so.

There are two kinds of privileges: system privileges and object privileges. System privileges extend permission to execute various data definition and data control commands such as **CREATE TABLE** or **ALTER USER**, or even to log onto the database. Object privileges extend permission to operate on a particular named database object.

System privileges in Oracle include CREATE, ALTER, and DROP privileges for the various **CREATE**, **ALTER**, and **DROP** commands. Privileges with the keyword **ANY** in them mean that the user can exercise the privilege on any schema for which the privilege has been granted, not just his or her own schema. The standard privileges in the list following just give permission to execute the indicated command, and don't require further explanation. Some of the privileges aren't intuitively clear; these are explained here.

System privileges include:

Privilege	Permission to
**CLUSTERS**	
CREATE CLUSTER	Create clusters in grantee's schema.
CREATE ANY CLUSTER	Create a cluster in any schema. Behaves similarly to CREATE ANY TABLE.
ALTER ANY CLUSTER	Alter clusters in any schema.
DROP ANY CLUSTER	Drop clusters in any schema.
**CONTEXTS**	
CREATE ANY CONTEXT	Create any context namespace.

Privilege	Permission to
DROP ANY CONTEXT	Drop any context namespace.
**DATABASE**	
ALTER DATABASE	Alter the database.
ALTER SYSTEM	Issue ALTER SYSTEM statements.
AUDIT SYSTEM	Issue AUDIT *sql_statements* statements.
**DATABASE LINKS**	
CREATE DATABASE LINK	Create private database links in grantee's schema.
CREATE PUBLIC DATABASE LINK	Create public database links.
DROP PUBLIC DATABASE LINK	Drop public database links.
**DIMENSIONS**	
CREATE DIMENSION	Create dimensions in the grantee's schema.
CREATE ANY DIMENSION	Create dimensions in any schema.
ALTER ANY DIMENSION	Alter dimensions in any schema.
DROP ANY DIMENSION	Drop dimensions in any schema.
**DIRECTORIES**	
CREATE ANY DIRECTORY	Create directory database objects.
DROP ANY DIRECTORY	Drop directory database objects.
**INDEXTYPES**	
CREATE INDEXTYPE	Create an indextype in the grantee's schema.
CREATE ANY INDEXTYPE	Create an indextype in any schema.
ALTER ANY INDEXTYPE	Modify indextypes in any schema.
DROP ANY INDEXTYPE	Drop an indextype in any schema.
EXECUTE ANY INDEXTYPE	Reference an indextype in any schema.
**INDEXES**	
CREATE ANY INDEX	Create in any schema a domain index or an index on any table in any schema.
ALTER ANY INDEX	Alter indexes in any schema.
DROP ANY INDEX	Drop indexes in any schema.
**LIBRARIES**	
CREATE LIBRARY	Create external procedure/function libraries in grantee's schema.
CREATE ANY LIBRARY	Create external procedure/function libraries in any schema.
DROP ANY LIBRARY	Drop external procedure/function libraries in any schema.

Privilege	Permission to
**MATERIALIZED VIEWS**	
CREATE MATERIALIZED VIEW	Create a materialized view in the grantee's schema.
CREATE ANY MATERIALIZED VIEW	Create materialized views in any schema.
ALTER ANY MATERIALIZED VIEW	Alter materialized views in any schema.
DROP ANY MATERIALIZED VIEW	Drop materialized views in any schema.
QUERY REWRITE	Enable rewrite using a materialized view, or create a function-based index, when that materialized view or index references tables and views that are in the grantee's own schema.
GLOBAL QUERY REWRITE	Enable rewrite using a materialized view, or create a function-based index, when that materialized view or index references tables or views in any schema.
ON COMMIT REFRESH	Create a refresh-on-commit materialized view on any table in the database. Alter a refresh-on-demand materialized view on any table in the database to refresh-on-commit.
**OPERATORS**	
CREATE OPERATOR	Create an operator and its bindings in the grantee's schema.
CREATE ANY OPERATOR	Create an operator and its bindings in any schema.
DROP ANY OPERATOR	Drop an operator in any schema.
EXECUTE ANY OPERATOR	Reference an operator in any schema.
**OUTLINES**	
CREATE ANY OUTLINE	Create public outlines that can be used in any schema that uses outlines.
ALTER ANY OUTLINE	Modify outlines.
DROP ANY OUTLINE	Drop outlines.
SELECT ANY OUTLINE	Create a clone private outline from a public outline.
**PROCEDURES**	
CREATE PROCEDURE	Create stored procedures, functions, and packages in grantee's schema.
CREATE ANY PROCEDURE	Create stored procedures, functions, and packages in any schema.
ALTER ANY PROCEDURE	Alter stored procedures, functions, or packages in any schema.
DROP ANY PROCEDURE	Drop stored procedures, functions, or packages in any schema.
EXECUTE ANY PROCEDURE	Execute procedures or functions (standalone or packaged). Reference public package variables in any schema.
**PROFILES**	
CREATE PROFILE	Create profiles.
ALTER PROFILE	Alter profiles.
DROP PROFILE	Drop profiles.

Privilege	Permission to
**ROLES**	
CREATE ROLE	Create roles.
ALTER ANY ROLE	Alter any role in the database.
DROP ANY ROLE	Drop roles.
GRANT ANY ROLE	Grant any role in the database.
**ROLLBACK SEGMENTS**	
CREATE ROLLBACK SEGMENT	Create rollback segments.
ALTER ROLLBACK SEGMENT	Alter rollback segments.
DROP ROLLBACK SEGMENT	Drop rollback segments.
**SEQUENCES**	
CREATE SEQUENCE	Create sequences in grantee's schema.
CREATE ANY SEQUENCE	Create sequences in any schema.
ALTER ANY SEQUENCE	Alter any sequence in the database.
DROP ANY SEQUENCE	Drop sequences in any schema.
SELECT ANY SEQUENCE	Reference sequences in any schema.
**SESSIONS**	
CREATE SESSION	Connect to the database.
ALTER RESOURCE COST	Set costs for session resources.
ALTER SESSION	Issue ALTER SESSION statements.
RESTRICTED SESSION	Logon after the instance is started using the SQL*Plus STARTUP RESTRICT statement.
**SYNONYMS**	
CREATE SYNONYM	Create synonyms in grantee's schema.
CREATE ANY SYNONYM	Create private synonyms in any schema.
CREATE PUBLIC SYNONYM	Create public synonyms.
DROP ANY SYNONYM	Drop private synonyms in any schema.
DROP PUBLIC SYNONYM	Drop public synonyms.
**TABLES**	
CREATE TABLE	Create tables in grantee's schema.
CREATE ANY TABLE	Create tables in any schema. The owner of the schema containing the table must have space quota on the tablespace to contain the table.
ALTER ANY TABLE	Alter any table or view in any schema.
BACKUP ANY TABLE	Use the Export utility to incrementally export objects from the schema of other users.
DELETE ANY TABLE	Delete rows from tables, table partitions, or views in any schema.
DROP ANY TABLE	Drop or truncate tables or table partitions in any schema.

Privilege	Permission to
INSERT ANY TABLE	Insert rows into tables and views in any schema.
LOCK ANY TABLE	Lock tables and views in any schema.
SELECT ANY TABLE	Query tables, views, or materialized views in any schema.
UPDATE ANY TABLE	Update rows in tables and views in any schema.

**TABLESPACES**

CREATE TABLESPACE	Create tablespaces.
ALTER TABLESPACE	Alter tablespaces.
DROP TABLESPACE	Drop tablespaces.
MANAGE TABLESPACE	Take tablespaces offline and online and begin and end tablespace backups.
UNLIMITED TABLESPACE	Use an unlimited amount of any tablespace. This privilege overrides any specific quotas assigned. If you revoke this privilege from a user, the user's schema objects remain but further tablespace allocation is denied unless authorized by specific tablespace quotas. You cannot grant this system privilege to roles.

**TRIGGERS**

CREATE TRIGGER	Create a database trigger in grantee's schema.
CREATE ANY TRIGGER	Create database triggers in any schema.
ALTER ANY TRIGGER	Enable, disable, or compile database triggers in any schema.
DROP ANY TRIGGER	Drop database triggers in any schema.
ADMINISTER DATABASE TRIGGER	Create a trigger on DATABASE. (You must also have the CREATE TRIGGER or CREATE ANY TRIGGER privilege.)

**TYPES**

CREATE TYPE	Create object types and object type bodies in grantee's schema.
CREATE ANY TYPE	Create object types and object type bodies in any schema.
ALTER ANY TYPE	Alter object types in any schema.
DROP ANY TYPE	Drop object types and object type bodies in any schema.
EXECUTE ANY TYPE	Use and reference object types and collection types in any schema, and invoke methods of an object type in any schema if you make the grant to a specific user. If you grant EXECUTE ANY TYPE to a role, users holding the enabled role will not be able to invoke methods of an object type in any schema.
UNDER ANY TYPE	Create subtypes under any nonfinal object types.

**USERS**

CREATE USER	Create users. This privilege also allows the creator to: Assign quotas on any tablespace Set default and temporary tablespaces Assign a profile as part of a CREATE USER statement
ALTER USER	Alter any user. This privilege authorizes the grantee to: Change another user's password or authentication method Assign quotas on any tablespace Set default and temporary tablespaces Assign a profile and default roles
BECOME USER	Become another user. (Required by any user performing a full database import.)

Privilege	Permission to
DROP USER	Drop users.
**VIEWS**	
CREATE VIEW	Create views in grantee's schema.
CREATE ANY VIEW	Create views in any schema.
DROP ANY VIEW	Drop views in any schema.
UNDER ANY VIEW	Create subviews under any object views.
**MISCELLANEOUS**	
ANALYZE ANY	Analyze any table, cluster, or index in any schema.
AUDIT ANY	Audit any object in any schema using AUDIT *schema_objects* statements.
COMMENT ANY TABLE	Comment on any table, view, or column in any schema.
EXEMPT ACCESS POLICY	Bypass fine-grained access control. This is a very powerful system privilege, as it lets the grantee bypass application-driven security policies. Database administrators should use caution when granting this privilege.
FORCE ANY TRANSACTION	Force the commit or rollback of any in-doubt distributed transaction in the local database. Induce the failure of a distributed transaction.
FORCE TRANSACTION	Force the commit or rollback of grantee's in-doubt distributed transactions in the local database.
GRANT ANY PRIVILEGE	Grant any system privilege.
RESUMABLE	Enable resumable space allocation.
SELECT ANY DICTIONARY	Query any data dictionary object in the SYS schema. This privilege lets you selectively override the default FALSE setting of the O7_DICTIONARY_ACCESSIBILITY initialization parameter. This privilege must be granted individually. It is not included in GRANT ALL PRIVILEGES, nor can it be granted through a role.
SYSDBA	Perform STARTUP and SHUTDOWN operations. ALTER DATABASE: open, mount, back up, or change character set. CREATE DATABASE. ARCHIVELOG and RECOVERY. CREATE SPFILE. Includes the RESTRICTED SESSION privilege.
SYSOPER	Perform STARTUP and SHUTDOWN operations. ALTER DATABASE OPEN \| MOUNT \| BACKUP. ARCHIVELOG and RECOVERY. CREATE SPFILE. Includes the RESTRICTED SESSION privilege.

**NOTE**
*For external tables, the only valid privileges are CREATE ANY TABLE, ALTER ANY TABLE, DROP ANY TABLE, and SELECT ANY TABLE.*

Object privileges apply only to certain kinds of objects. The following table shows the relationships and the grantable object privileges.

Object Privilege	Table	View	Sequence	Procedures, Functions, Packages[a]	Materialized View	Directory	Library	User-defined Type	Operator	Index-type
ALTER	X		X							
DELETE	X	X			X[b]					
EXECUTE				X			X	X	X	X
INDEX	X									
INSERT	X	X			X[b]					
ON COMMIT REFRESH	X									
QUERY REWRITE	X									
READ						X				
REFERENCES	X	X								
SELECT	X	X	X		X					
UNDER		X						X		
UPDATE	X	X			X[b]					
WRITE						X				

[a] Oracle treats a Java class, source, or resource as if it were a procedure for purposes of granting object privileges.
[b] The DELETE, INSERT, and UPDATE privileges can be granted only to updatable materialized views.

# PRO*C

PRO*C is an extension to C that lets you develop user exits and other programs that access the Oracle database. A precompiler converts PRO*C code into normal C code, which can then be compiled. See the *Pro*C/C++ Precompiler Programmer's Guide*.

# PROCEDURE

A procedure is a set of instructions (usually combining SQL and PL/SQL commands) saved for calling and repeated execution. *See* **CREATE PROCEDURE**.

# PRODUCT_USER_PROFILE

A PRODUCT_USER_PROFILE is a SYSTEM table in Oracle used to restrict use of individual Oracle products, by disabling one or more commands available in the product. *See SQL*Plus User's Guide and Reference*.

# PROFILE

A profile is a collection of settings in Oracle that limit database resources. *See* **CREATE PROFILE** and Chapter 19.

# PROMPT

**SEE ALSO** ACCEPT

## FORMAT

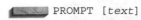

```
PROMPT [text]
```

**DESCRIPTION**    Displays the *text* to the user's screen. If no *text* is specified, then a blank line will be displayed. To display a variable, *see* **PRINT**.

# PSEUDO-COLUMNS

**DESCRIPTION**    A pseudo-column is a "column" that yields a value when selected, but which is not an actual column of the table. An example is RowID or SysDate. Here are the current Oracle pseudo-columns:

Pseudo-column	Value Returned
sequence.CurrVal	Current value for this sequence name.
Level	Equal to 1 for a root node, 2 for a child of a root, and so on. Tells basically how far down a tree you've traveled.
sequence.NextVal	Next value for this sequence name. Also increments the sequence.
NULL	A null value.
RowID	Returns the row identifier for a row. Use the RowID in the UPDATE ... WHERE and SELECT ... FOR UPDATE. This guarantees that only a certain row is updated, and no others.
RowNum	Returns the sequence number in which a row was returned when selected from a table. The first row RowNum is 1, the second is 2, and so on.

# PUBLIC

Public can have either of two definitions:

- Something public can be visible or available to all users. Synonyms and database links can be public. In Oracle, a user must have CREATE PUBLIC SYNONYM or CREATE PUBLIC DATABASE LINK privilege. Users may GRANT PUBLIC access to their own objects.
- A group to which every database user belongs—the name of that group.

# PUBLIC SYNONYM

A public synonym is a synonym for a database object that a user with CREATE PUBLIC SYNONYM privilege has created for use by all Oracle users.

# QUERY

A query is a SQL instruction to retrieve data from one or more tables or views. Queries begin with the SQL keyword **select**.

# QUERY OPERATORS

The following is an alphabetical list of all current query operators in Oracle's SQL. Each of these is listed elsewhere in this reference under its own name, with its proper format and use. *See also* Chapter 12.

Operator	Purpose
UNION	Returns all distinct rows from both of two queries
UNION ALL	Returns all rows from both of two queries
INTERSECT	Returns all matching distinct rows from two queries
MINUS	Returns all distinct rows in first query that are not in the second

# QUIT

**SEE ALSO**   COMMIT, DISCONNECT, EXIT, SET AUTOCOMMIT, START

**FORMAT**

```
QUIT
```

**DESCRIPTION**   QUIT ends a SQL*PLUS session and returns the user to an operating system, calling program, or menu.

# QUOTA

A quota is a resource limit. Quotas can limit the amount of storage used by each user of the database. *See* **CREATE USER** and **ALTER USER**.

# RAISE

**SEE ALSO**   DECLARE EXCEPTION, EXCEPTION, EXCEPTION_INIT

**FORMAT**

```
RAISE [exception]
```

**DESCRIPTION**   RAISE names the exception flag you want to raise, based on a condition that is being tested. The exception must either be one you've explicitly **DECLARE**d, or an internal system exception such as DIVIDE_BY_ZERO (*see* EXCEPTION for a complete list).

A **RAISE** statement causes control to be transferred to the EXCEPTION section of the current block, where you must test to see which exception was raised. If no EXCEPTION section is present, control is passed to the nearest EXCEPTION section of an enclosing block (basically backward through the nesting of the blocks). If no logic is found to handle the exception, control is passed from the PL/SQL to the calling program or environment with an unhandled exception error. (The use of OTHERS can avoid this. *See* EXCEPTION.)

**RAISE** without an explicitly named exception can only be used in one circumstance: within an EXCEPTION section, in order to force the current exception to be handled by an enclosing block's EXCEPTION section, rather than the current one. If, for instance, a NOT_LOGGED_ON error had occurred, and your local EXCEPTION section says this:

```
when not_logged_on
 then raise;
```

it would pass control back to the EXCEPTION section of the next enclosing block that had one, or to the program if none were found. That EXCEPTION block could also test for NOT_LOGGED_ON. The benefit here is that for a certain class of errors, particularly where the recovery, tracing, or error-logging steps you want to take may be extensive, you can set every nested block's EXCEPTION section to simply hand the EXCEPTION backward to a single spot for disposition.

## RATIO_TO_REPORT

**SEE ALSO**   GROUP FUNCTIONS

**FORMAT**

```
RATIO_TO_REPORT (expr) OVER ([query_partition_clause])
```

**DESCRIPTION**   RATIO_TO_REPORT is an analytic function. It computes the ratio of a value to the sum of a set of values. If *expr* evaluates to **NULL**, the ratio-to-report value also evaluates to **NULL**.

## RAW DATATYPE

A RAW column contains binary data in whatever form the host computer stores it. Raw columns are useful for storing binary (non-character) data.

## RAWTOHEX

**SEE ALSO**   HEXTORAW

**FORMAT**

```
RAWTOHEX(binary_string)
```

**DESCRIPTION**   RAW TO HEXadecimal changes a string of binary numbers to a character string of hex numbers.

## RAWTONHEX

**SEE ALSO**   RAWTOHEX

**FORMAT**

```
RAWTONHEX (raw)
```

**DESCRIPTION**   RAW TO NHEXadecimal converts *raw* to an NVARCHAR2 character value containing its hexadecimal equivalent

## RDBMS

*See* RELATIONAL DATABASE MANAGEMENT SYSTEM.

## READ CONSISTENCY

Read consistency is a state that guarantees that all data encountered by a statement/transaction is a consistent set throughout the duration of the statement/transaction. *See* **SET TRANSACTION.**

## RECORD

Record is a synonym for row.

## RECORD (PL/SQL)

**SEE ALSO**   TABLE (PL/SQL), DATA TYPES

**FORMAT**

```
TYPE new_type IS RECORD
 (field {type | table.column%TYPE}[NOT NULL]
 [,field {type | table.column%TYPE}[NOT NULL]...]);
```

**DESCRIPTION** A RECORD declaration declares a new type that can then be used to declare variables of that type. The individual components of the record are fields, and each has its own datatype. That datatype can either be one of the standard PL/SQL datatypes (including another RECORD but not a TABLE), or it can be a reference to the type of a particular column in a specific table. Each field also may have a NOT NULL qualifier that specifies that the field must always have a non-null value.

You can refer to the individual fields in a record using dot notation.

## RECORD LOCKING

Record locking protects two users from updating the same row of data at the same time.

## RECOVER

**SEE ALSO** **ALTER DATABASE**, Chapter 40

**FORMAT**

```
RECOVER {general | managed | END BACKUP}
```

where the *general* clause has the following syntax:

```
[AUTOMATIC] [FROM location]
{ {full_database_recovery | partial_database_recovery |LOGFILE filename}
[{TEST | ALLOW integer CORRUPTION } [TEST | ALLOW integer CORRUPTION]...]
|CONTINUE [DEFAULT] |CANCEL}
```

where the *full_database_recovery* clause has the following syntax:

```
[STANDBY] DATABASE
[{UNTIL {CANCEL | TIME date | CHANGE integer} | USING BACKUP CONTROLFILE}
[UNTIL {CANCEL | TIME date | CHANGE integer} | USING BACKUP CONTROLFILE]...]
```

where the *partial_database_recovery* clause has the following syntax:

```
{TABLESPACE tablespace [, tablespace]... | DATAFILE datafilename [, datafilename]...
| STANDBY
{TABLESPACE tablespace [, tablespace]... | DATAFILE datafilename [, datafilename]...}
UNTIL [CONSISTENT] [WITH] CONTROLFILE }
```

and the *managed* clause has the following syntax:

```
MANAGED STANDBY DATABASE
[{NODELAY | [TIMEOUT] integer | CANCEL [IMMEDIATE] [NOWAIT] }
| [DISCONNECT [FROM SESSION]] [FINISH [NOWAIT]]]
```

**DESCRIPTION** The **RECOVER** command, like the **RECOVER** clause of the **ALTER DATABASE** command recovers a database using various options. **AUTOMATIC** recovery generates the redo log file names automatically during recovery. The **FROM** clause specifies the location of the archived redo log file group and must be a fully qualified filename. The default is set by the initialization parameter LOG_ARCHIVE_DEST.

The **DATABASE** option recovers the entire database and is the default. The **UNTIL CANCEL** alternative recovers the database until you cancel the recovery with the **CANCEL** option. The **UNTIL TIME** alternative recovers to a specified date and time. The **UNTIL CHANGE** alternative recovers up to a *system change number* (SCN, a unique number assigned to each transaction) specified by an integer. The **USING BACKUP CONTROLFILE** alternative recovers by applying the redo log in a backup control file.

## RECOVERY MANAGER

Recovery Manager (RMAN) is a product from Oracle Corporation. RMAN is used by DBAs to perform database backups. The information about the backups is stored either in an RMAN repository database or in the control files of the databases being backed up.

## RECSEP (SQL*PLUS)

*See* **SET**.

## RECSEPCHAR (SQL*PLUS)

*See* **SET**.

## RECURSIVE CALL

A recursive call is a nested invocation of the RDBMS; for example, auditing information is recorded in system tables using a recursive call. That is, during a normal database operation, such as an **update**, another database operation is executed to write log, auditing, or other vital information *about* the normal database operation underway. *See* CALL, RECURSIVE.

## REDO LOG

A redo log is a sequential log of actions in the database. The log always consists of at least two files; one is optionally being archived while the other is being written. When the one currently being written fills, the next one is reused.

## REDO LOG SEQUENCE NUMBER

The redo log sequence number is a number used to identify a redo log, used when applying the log file for recovery.

## REF

A reference datatype used with object tables. *See* Chapter 33.

## REFERENTIAL INTEGRITY

Referential integrity is the property that guarantees that values from one column depend on values from another column. This property is enforced through integrity constraints. *See* INTEGRITY CONSTRAINT.

## REFERENTIAL INTEGRITY RULE

A referential integrity rule is an integrity constraint that enforces referential integrity.

## REFTOHEX

**SEE ALSO**    Chapter 33

**FORMAT**

```
REFTOHEX (expr)
```

**DESCRIPTION**    **REFTOHEX** converts argument *expr* to a character value containing its hexadecimal equivalent. *expr* must return a REF.

# REGRESSION FUNCTIONS

As of Oracle9i, Oracle supports the following regression functions: REGR_SLOPE, REGR_INTERCEPT, REGR_COUNT, REGR_R2, REGR_AVGX, REGR_AVGY, REGR_SXX, REGR_SYY, and REGR_SXY. See the *Oracle SQL Reference Guide* for syntax and examples for these analytic functions.

# RELATION

*See* TABLE and Chapter 1.

# RELATIONAL DATABASE MANAGEMENT SYSTEM

An RDBMS is a computer program for general-purpose data storage and retrieval that organizes data into tables consisting of one or more units of information (rows), each containing the same set of data items (columns). Oracle is a relational database management system.

# RELATIONAL OPERATOR

A relational operator is a symbol used in search criteria to indicate a comparison between two values, such as the equal sign in "where Amount = .10". Only those rows are returned (fetched) for which the comparison results in TRUE.

# REMARK

**SEE ALSO**      /* */, - -, DOCUMENT, Chapter 6

**FORMAT**

```
REM[ARK] text
```

**DESCRIPTION**      **REMARK** begins a single line of remarks, usually documentation, in a start file. It is not interpreted as a command. **REMARK** cannot appear within a SQL statement.

**EXAMPLE**

```
REM Reduce the default column width for this data field:
column ActionDate format a6 trunc
```

# REMOTE COMPUTER

A remote computer refers to any computer in a network other than one's own host computer.

# REMOTE DATABASE

A remote database is one that resides on a remote computer, in particular, one that you use through a database link.

# RENAME

**SEE ALSO**      **COPY, CREATE SEQUENCE, CREATE SYNONYM, CREATE TABLE, CREATE VIEW**

**FORMAT**

```
RENAME old TO new;
```

**DESCRIPTION**      **RENAME** changes the name of a table, view, sequence, or synonym from its old name to a new one. No quotes are used around the names, and the new name must be neither a reserved word nor the name of an existing object for the user.

**EXAMPLE** The following changes the BOOKSHELF table to the BOOK table:

```
rename BOOKSHELF to BOOK;
```

# REPFOOTER

**SEE ALSO** ACCEPT, **BTITLE**, **DEFINE**, PARAMETERS, **REPHEADER**, Chapter 14
**FORMAT**

```
REPF[OOTER] [PAGE] [option [text|variable]... | OFF|ON]
```

**DESCRIPTION** REPFOOTER (REPort FOOTER) puts a footer (may be multi-line) on the last page of a report. OFF and ON suppress and restore the display of the text without changing its contents. **REPFOOTER** by itself displays the current **REPFOOTER** options and *text* or *variable*. **PAGE** begins a new page before printing the specified report footer.

*text* is a footer you wish to give this report, and *variable* is a user-defined variable or a system-maintained variable, including SQL.LNO, the current line number; SQL.PNO, the current page number; SQL.RELEASE, the current Oracle release number; SQL.SQLCODE, the current error code; and SQL.USER, the username.

Valid values for option are

- **COL** *n* skips directly to position *n* from the left margin of the current line.

- **S[KIP]** *n* prints *n* blank lines. If no *n* is specified, one blank line is printed. If *n* is 0, no blank lines are printed and the current position for printing becomes position 1 of the current line (leftmost on the page).

- **TAB** *n* skips forward *n* positions (backward if *n* is negative).

- **LE[FT], CE[NTER]**, and **R[IGHT]** left-justify, center, and right-justify data on the current line. Any text or variables following these commands are justified as a group, up to the end of the command, or a LEFT, CENTER, RIGHT, or COL. CENTER and RIGHT use the value set by the **SET LINESIZE** command to determine where to place the text or variable.

- **BOLD** prints data in bold print. SQL*PLUS represents bold print on your terminal by repeating the data on three consecutive lines.

- **FORMAT** string specifies the format model that will control the format of subsequent text or variables, and follows the same syntax as FORMAT in a **COLUMN** command, such as FORMAT A12 or FORMAT $999,990.99. Each time a FORMAT appears, it supersedes the previous one that was in effect. If no FORMAT model has been specified, the one set by **SET NUMFORMAT** is used. If NUMFORMAT has not been set, the default for SQL*PLUS is used.

Date values are printed according to the default format unless a variable has been loaded with a date reformatted by **TO_CHAR**.

# REPHEADER

**SEE ALSO** ACCEPT, **BTITLE**, **DEFINE**, PARAMETERS, **REPFOOTER**, Chapter 14
**FORMAT**

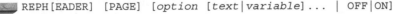
```
REPH[EADER] [PAGE] [option [text|variable]... | OFF|ON]
```

**DESCRIPTION** REPHEADER (REPort HEADER) puts a header (may be multi-line) on the first page of a report. OFF and ON suppress and restore the display of the text without changing its contents.

**REPHEADER** by itself displays the current **REPHEADER** options and *text* or *variable*. **PAGE** begins a new page after printing the report header.

*text* is a header you wish to give this report, and *variable* is a user-defined variable or a system-maintained variable, including SQL.LNO, the current line number; SQL.PNO, the current page number; SQL.RELEASE, the current Oracle release number; SQL.SQLCODE, the current error code; and SQL.USER, the username.

Valid values for option are

- **COL** *n* skips directly to position *n* from the left margin of the current line.
- **S[KIP]** *n* prints *n* blank lines. If no *n* is specified, one blank line is printed. If *n* is 0, no blank lines are printed and the current position for printing becomes position 1 of the current line (leftmost on the page).
- **TAB** *n* skips forward *n* positions (backward if *n* is negative).
- **LE[FT]**, **CE[NTER]**, and **R[IGHT]** left-justify, center, and right-justify data on the current line. Any text or variables following these commands are justified as a group, up to the end of the command, or a LEFT, CENTER, RIGHT, or COL. CENTER and RIGHT use the value set by the **SET LINESIZE** command to determine where to place the text or variable.
- **BOLD** prints data in bold print. SQL*PLUS represents bold print on your terminal by repeating the data on three consecutive lines.
- **FORMAT** string specifies the format model that will control the format of subsequent text or variables, and follows the same syntax as FORMAT in a **COLUMN** command, such as FORMAT A12 or FORMAT $999,990.99. Each time a FORMAT appears, it supersedes the previous one that was in effect. If no FORMAT model has been specified, the one set by **SET NUMFORMAT** is used. If NUMFORMAT has not been set, the default for SQL*PLUS is used.

Date values are printed according to the default format unless a variable has been loaded with a date reformatted by **TO_CHAR**.

# REPLACE

**SEE ALSO**   CHARACTER FUNCTIONS, **TRANSLATE**, Chapter 16

**FORMAT**

```
REPLACE(string,if,then)
```

**DESCRIPTION**   **REPLACE** replaces a character or characters in a string with 0 or more characters. *if* is a character or characters. Every time it appears in *string*, it is replaced by the contents of *then*.

**EXAMPLE**

```
REPLACE('GEORGE','GE',null) = OR
REPLACE('BOB','BO','TA') = TAB
```

# REPLICATION

Replication is the process of copying data from one database to another. The target to which the replicated data is copied is called the replica. To manage replication, you will need to determine:

- The location, structure, and ownership of the source data
- The update frequency of the source data
- The timeliness requirements for the replica data

- The volatility of the source data
- The intended uses of the replica

If the replica will also be able to make changes, and those changes must be propagated back to the original source database, then you have a *multi-master* configuration, and you will have to manage conflict resolution and error handling for the environment. In general, single-site ownership of data with multiple read-only replicas will be simpler to manage than a multi-master configuration.

See **CREATE MATERIALIZED VIEW, CREATE DATABASE LINK**

## RESERVED WORDS

**SEE ALSO**   OBJECT NAMES

**DESCRIPTION**   A reserved word is one that has a special meaning to SQL, and therefore may not be used as the name of an object. Contrast this to keyword, which may be used as an object name, but may become a reserved word in the future. Not every word is reserved in all products, so this list is structured to show which products reserve which words. In the following table, the entries with *s are reserved in SQL and in PL/SQL. The entries without *s are reserved only in PL/SQL.

ACCESS	ALL*	ALTER*	AND*	ANY*
ARRAY	AS*	ASC*	AT	AUDIT
AUTHID	AVG	BEGIN	BETWEEN*	BINARY_INTEGER
BODY	BOOLEAN	BULK	BY*	CASE
CHAR*	CHAR_BASE	CHECK*	CLOSE	CLUSTER*
COALESCE	COLLECT	COLUMN	COMMENT*	COMMIT
COMPRESS*	CONNECT*	CONSTANT	CREATE*	CURRENT*
CURRVAL	CURSOR	DATE*	DAY	DECLARE
DECIMAL*	DEFAULT*	DELETE*	DESC*	DISTINCT*
DO	DROP*	ELSE*	ELSIF	END
EXCEPTION	EXCLUSIVE*	EXECUTE	EXISTS*	EXIT
EXTENDS	EXTRACT	FALSE	FETCH	FILE
FLOAT*	FOR*	FORALL	FROM*	FUNCTION
GOTO	GROUP*	HAVING*	HEAP	HOUR
IDENTIFIED	IF	IMMEDIATE*	IN*	INCREMENT
INDEX*	INDICATOR	INITIAL	INSERT*	INTEGER*
INTERFACE	INTERSECT*	INTERVAL	INTO*	IS*
ISOLATION	JAVA	LEVEL*	LIKE*	LIMITED
LOCK*	LONG*	LOOP	MAX	MAXEXTENTS
MIN	MINUS*	MINUTE	MLSLABEL*	MOD
MODE*	MODIFY	MONTH	NATURAL	NATURALN
NEW	NEXTVAL	NOCOMPRESS	NOCOPY	NOT*
NOWAIT*	NULL*	NULLIF	NUMBER*	NUMBER_BASE

OCIROWID	OF*	OFFLINE	ON*	ONLINE
OPAQUE	OPEN	OPERATOR	OPTION*	OR*
ORDER*	ORGANIZATION	OTHERS	OUT	PACKAGE
PARTITION	PCTFREE*	PLS_INTEGER	POSITIVE	POSITIVEN
PRAGMA	PRIOR*	PRIVATE	PROCEDURE	PUBLIC*
RAISE	RANGE	RAW*	REAL	RECORD
REF	RELEASE	RENAME	RESOURCE	RETURN
REVERSE	ROLLBACK	ROW*	ROWID*	ROWNUM*
ROWTYPE	SAVEPOINT	SECOND	SELECT*	SEPARATE
SET*	SHARE*	SMALLINT*	SPACE	SQL
SQLCODE	SQLERRM	START*	STDDEV	SUBTYPE
SUCCESSFUL*	SUM	SYNONYM*	SYSDATE*	TABLE*
THEN*	TIME	TIMESTAMP	TIMEZONE_REGION	TIMEZONE_ABBR
TIMEZONE_MINUTE	TIMEZONE_HOUR	TO*	TRIGGER*	TRUE
TYPE	UI	UID	UNION	UNIQUE
UPDATE	USER	VALIDATE	VALUES	VARCHAR
VARCHAR2	VIEW	WHENEVER	WHERE	WITH

# RESOURCE

Resource is a general term for a logical database object or physical structure that may be locked. Resources that users can directly lock are rows and tables; resources that the RDBMS can lock are numerous and include data dictionary tables, caches, and files.

RESOURCE is also the name of a standard role in Oracle. *See* ROLE.

# REVERSE-KEY INDEX

In a reverse-key index, the bytes of the indexed value are reversed prior to being stored in the index. Thus, values 1234 and 1235 are indexed as if they were 4321 and 5321. As a result of this reversal, those two values will be stored farther apart. If you are frequently querying the column for an exact match (*column=1234*) then a reverse-key index may reduce block contention within your index. If you are frequently performing range queries (*column>1234* or *column like '123%'*) then traditional indexes should be more appropriate for your needs. *See* **CREATE INDEX**.

# REVOKE
**SEE ALSO**    **DISABLE**, **ENABLE**, **GRANT**, PRIVILEGE, Chapter 19
**FORMAT**
revoke::=

**revoke_system_privileges::=**

**revoke_object_privileges::=**

**grantee_clause::=**

**on_object_clause::=**

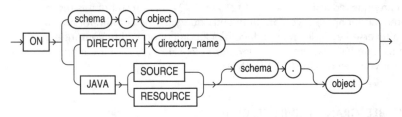

**DESCRIPTION** The **REVOKE** command takes privileges and roles away from users or privileges away from roles. Any system privilege may be revoked; *see* PRIVILEGE.

If you revoke a privilege from a user, the user can no longer execute the operations allowed by the privilege. If you revoke a privilege from a role, no user granted the role can execute the allowed operations, unless they are permitted by another role or directly as a user. If you revoke a privilege from **PUBLIC**, no user granted the privilege through **PUBLIC** can execute the operations allowed by the privilege.

If you revoke a role from a user, the user can no longer enable the role (*see* **ENABLE**) but may continue exercising the privilege in a current session. If you revoke a role from a role, users granted the role can no longer enable the role but may continue using the privilege during the current session. If you revoke a role from **PUBLIC**, users granted the role through **PUBLIC** can no longer enable the role.

For object access, the **REVOKE** command takes object privileges on a specific object away from a user or role. If a user's privileges are revoked, the user may not execute the operations allowed by the privilege on the object. If a role's privileges are revoked, no user granted the role may execute those operations unless they are granted through another role or directly to the user. If the PUBLIC's privileges are revoked, no user granted the privilege through **PUBLIC** may execute those operations.

The **CASCADE CONSTRAINTS** clause drops any referential integrity constraints defined by the user or by users granted the role. This applies to a REFERENCES privilege.

# ROLE

A role is a set of privileges that a user can grant to another user. Oracle has many system-supplied roles, including CONNECT, RESOURCE, and DBA. You can verify the privileges assigned to the roles via the ROLE_SYS_PRIVS and DBA_SYS_PRIVS data dictionary views. You should not rely on the system-provided roles in your application development, since the names and privileges for these roles may change with future releases of Oracle. See **CREATE ROLE** for role creation syntax.

*See* Chapter 19 for examples of creating and using roles.

# ROLL FORWARD

Roll forward is the reapplying of changes to the database. You sometimes need it for media recovery and sometimes for instance recovery. The **REDO LOG** contains the redo entries used for roll forward.

# ROLLBACK

A rollback discards part or all of the work you have done in the current transaction, since the last **COMMIT** or **SAVEPOINT**.

# ROLLBACK (Form 1-SQL)

**SEE ALSO**     **COMMIT, SET AUTOCOMMIT**, Chapter 15
**FORMAT**

```
ROLLBACK [WORK] [TO [SAVEPOINT] savepoint | FORCE 'text'];
```

**DESCRIPTION**     **ROLLBACK** reverses all changes made to tables in the database since changes were last committed or rolled back and releases any locks on the tables. An automatic rollback occurs whenever a transaction is interrupted, such as by an execution error, a power failure, and so on. **ROLLBACK** affects not just the last **insert**, **update**, or **delete** statement but any that have occurred since the last **COMMIT**. This allows you to treat blocks of work as a whole and only **COMMIT** when all of the changes you want are completed.

With **SAVEPOINT**, **ROLLBACK** goes to a specific, named place in the sequence of transactions being processed, the **SAVEPOINT**. It erases any interim **SAVEPOINT**s and releases any table or row locks that occurred after the **SAVEPOINT** was made.

With **FORCE**, **ROLLBACK** manually rolls back an in-doubt transaction identified by the literal text, which is a local or global transaction ID from the data dictionary view DBA_2PC_PENDING.

**NOTE**
*If **SET AUTOCOMMIT** is ON, every **insert**, **update**, or **delete** will
immediately and automatically commit the changes to the database.
Typing the word **ROLLBACK** will produce a 'ROLLBACK COMPLETE'
message but it won't mean anything since **ROLLBACK** only rolls back
to the last **COMMIT**.*

**NOTE**
*All DDL commands cause a **COMMIT**.*

## ROLLBACK (Form 2-Embedded SQL)

**SEE ALSO**    COMMIT, SAVEPOINT, SET TRANSACTION, *Precompiler Programmer's Guide*
**FORMAT**

```
EXEC SQL [AT {database | :variable }]
ROLLBACK [WORK]
[TO [SAVEPOINT] savepoint] | [FORCE text] | [RELEASE]]
```

**DESCRIPTION**    ROLLBACK ends the current transaction, reverses any changes resulting from the
current transaction, and releases any locks being held, but does not affect host variables or program
flow. *database* indicates the name of the database where the **ROLLBACK** should take effect. Its absence
indicates the default database for the user. **SAVEPOINT** allows a rollback to a named **SAVEPOINT** that
has been previously declared. (*See **SAVEPOINT**.*)

   **FORCE** manually rolls back an in-doubt transaction specified by a literal text containing the
transaction ID from the DBA_2PC_PENDING data dictionary view. WORK is entirely optional and is
for readability only.

   Both **ROLLBACK** and **COMMIT** have **RELEASE** options. **RELEASE** should be specified by one of them
after the last transaction, otherwise locks put on during the program will block other users. **ROLLBACK**
occurs automatically (with a **RELEASE**) if the program abnormally terminates.

## ROLLBACK SEGMENT

A rollback segment is a storage space within a tablespace that holds transaction information that is used
to guarantee data integrity during a rollback and to provide read consistency across multiple transactions.
See Chapter 40.

## ROLLUP

**SEE ALSO**    GROUPING, CUBE, Chapter 13
**FORMAT**

```
GROUP BY ROLLUP(column1, column2)
```

**DESCRIPTION**    ROLLUP generates subtotals for groups of rows within a query. See Chapter 13.

## ROOT

In a table with tree-structured data, the root is the origin of the tree, a row that has no parent, and whose
children, grandchildren, and so on, constitute the entire tree. In a tree-structured query, the root is the
row specified by the **START WITH** clause.

# ROUND (Form 1-for Dates)

**SEE ALSO**    DATE FUNCTIONS, **ROUND** (NUMBER), **TRUNC**, Chapter 9
**FORMAT**

ROUND (`date, 'format'`)

**DESCRIPTION**    **ROUND** is the rounding of date according to format. Without a format, date is rounded to the next day if the time is 12:00:00 P.M. (exactly noon) or later, or to today's date if before noon; in other words, it is rounded to the nearest day The resulting date has its time set to 12 A.M., the very first instant of the day.

**FORMATS AVAILABLE FOR ROUNDING**

Format	Meaning
CC,SCC	century (rounds up to January 1st of next century, as of midnight exactly on the morning of January 1st of 1950, 2050, and so on).
SYEAR,SYYY,Y,YY,YYY,YYYY and YEAR	year (rounds up to January 1st of the next year as of midnight exactly on the morning of July 1st).
IYYY, IYY, IY, I	ISO year
Q	quarter (rounds up in the 2nd month of the quarter as of midnight exactly on the morning of the 16th, regardless of the number of days in the month).
MONTH,MON,MM,RM	month (rounds up as of midnight exactly on the morning of the 16th regardless of the number of days in the month).
WW	same day of the week as the first day of the year
IW	same day of the week as the first day of the ISO year
W	rounds to closest day which is the same day as the first day of the month
DDD,DD,J	rounds up to the next day as of noon exactly. This is the same as ROUND with no format.
DAY,DY,D	rounds up to next Sunday (first day of the week) as of noon exactly on Wednesday.
HH,HH12,HH24	rounds up to the next whole hour as of 30 minutes and 30 seconds after the hour.
MI	rounds up to the next whole minute as of 30 seconds of this minute.

When **ww** and **w** round, the time of the date being rounded is compared to a date which is set to 12 A.M., the very beginning of the day. The result of **ROUND** is a new date, which is also set to 12 A.M.

# ROUND (Form 2-for Numbers)

**SEE ALSO**    CEIL, **FLOOR**, NUMBER FUNCTIONS, **ROUND** (DATE), **TRUNC**, Chapter 8
**FORMAT**

ROUND(`value,precision`)

**DESCRIPTION**    ROUND rounds *value* to *precision*. *precision* is an integer and may be positive, negative, or zero. A negative integer rounds to the given number of places to the left of the decimal point, a positive integer rounds to the given number of places to the right of the decimal point.

### EXAMPLE

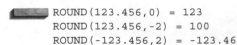
```
ROUND(123.456,0) = 123
ROUND(123.456,-2) = 100
ROUND(-123.456,2) = -123.46
```

# ROW

Row can have either of two definitions:

■ One set of fields in a table; for example, the fields representing one worker in the table WORKER.

■ One set of fields in the output of a query. RECORD is a synonym.

# ROW HEADER

A row header is the portion of each row that contains information about the row other than row data, such as the number of row pieces, columns, and so on.

# ROW-LEVEL LOCKING

Row-level locking is a type of locking in which **update**s to data occur through locking rows in a table and not the entire page.

# ROW SEQUENCE NUMBER

A row sequence number is a number assigned to a row as it is inserted into a data block for a table. This number is also stored as row overhead and forms a part of the ROWID.

# ROW_NUMBER

**SEE ALSO**    ROWNUM

**FORMAT**

```
ROW_NUMBER () OVER ([query_partition_clause] order_by_clause)
```

**DESCRIPTION**    ROW_NUMBER is an analytic function. It assigns a unique number to each row to which it is applied (either each row in the partition or each row returned by the query), in the ordered sequence of rows specified in the *order_by_clause*, beginning with 1.

# ROWID

ROWID is the logical address of a row, and it is unique within the database.

ROWID can be **select**ed, or used in a **where** clause, but cannot be changed by an **insert**, **update**, or **delete**. It is not actually a data column, but merely a logical address, made of the database address information. ROWID is useful when used in a **where** clause for rapid **update**s or **delete**s of rows. However, it can change if the table it is in is exported and imported.

The ROWID datatype is a hexadecimal string representing the unique address of a row in a table. This datatype is primarily used for values returned by the ROWID pseudocolumn.

# ROWIDTOCHAR

**SEE ALSO**    **CHARTOROWID**, CONVERSION FUNCTIONS

**FORMAT**

ROWIDTOCHAR(*RowId*)

**DESCRIPTION**    **ROW ID**entifier **TO CHAR**acter changes an internal Oracle row identifier, or RowID, to act like a character string. However, Oracle will do this kind of conversion automatically, so this function isn't really needed. It seems to be a debugging tool that has made its way into general availability.

# ROWIDTONCHAR

**SEE ALSO**    **CHARTOROWID**, **ROWIDTOCHAR**, CONVERSION FUNCTIONS

**FORMAT**

ROWIDTONCHAR(*RowId*)

**DESCRIPTION**    **ROW ID**entifier **TO NCHAR**acter changes an internal Oracle row identifier, or RowID, to a NVARCHAR2 datatype.

# ROWNUM

**SEE ALSO**    PSEUDO-COLUMNS, Chapter 16

**FORMAT**

ROWNUM

**DESCRIPTION**    ROWNUM returns the sequence number in which a row was returned when first selected from a table. The first row has a ROWNUM of 1, the second is 2, and so on. Note, however, that even a simple **order by** in the **select** statement may *disorder* the ROWNUMs, which are assigned to the rows before any ordering takes place.

# RPAD

**SEE ALSO**    CHARACTER FUNCTIONS, **LPAD**, **LTRIM**, **RTRIM**, **TRIM**, Chapter 7

**FORMAT**

RPAD(*string*,*length* [,'*set*'])

**DESCRIPTION**    **R**ight **PAD** makes a string a certain length by adding a certain *set* of characters to the right. If *set* is not specified, the default pad character is a space.

**EXAMPLE**

select RPAD('HELLO ',24,'WORLD') from DUAL;

produces this:

HELLO WORLDWORLDWORLDWOR

# RTRIM

**SEE ALSO**    CHARACTER FUNCTIONS, **LPAD**, **LTRIM**, **RPAD**, **TRIM**, Chapter 7

**FORMAT**

RTRIM(*string* [,'*set*'])

**DESCRIPTION** Right **TRIM** trims all the occurrences of any one of a *set* of characters off of the right side of a string.

**EXAMPLE**

```
RTRIM('GEORGE','OGRE')
```

produces *nothing*, an empty string with zero length! On the other hand, this:

```
RTRIM('EDYTHE','HET')
```

produces this:

```
EDY
```

# RUN

**SEE ALSO** /, @, @@, **EDIT, START**

**FORMAT**

```
R[UN]
```

**DESCRIPTION** **RUN** displays the SQL command in the SQL buffer, and then executes it. **RUN** is similar to the **/** command, except that the **/** doesn't display the SQL first.

# SAVE

**SEE ALSO** **EDIT, GET**, Chapter 6

**FORMAT**

```
SAV[E] file[.ext] [CRE[ATE] | REP[LACE] | APP[END]]
```

**DESCRIPTION** **SAVE** saves the contents of the current buffer into a host file with the name *file*. If no file type (extension) is specified, the file type SQL is added to the file name. This default extension can be changed with **SET SUFFIX**. **SAVE** commits pending work to the database.

If the file already exists, the **CREATE** option will force **SAVE** to abort and will produce an error message. The **REPLACE** option will replace any existing file, or create a new one if none exists.

The **APPEND** option adds this file to the end of any existing file, or creates a new one if none exists.

**EXAMPLE** The following saves the contents of the current buffer into a file named lowcost.sql:

```
save lowcost
```

# SAVEPOINT

**SEE ALSO** **COMMIT, ROLLBACK, SET TRANSACTION**

**FORMAT**

```
SAVEPOINT savepoint;
```

**DESCRIPTION** **SAVEPOINT** is a point within a transaction to which you may rollback. Savepoints allow you to **ROLLBACK** portions of your current transaction. *See* **ROLLBACK**.

The first version here is typical of SQL*PLUS. The purpose of **SAVEPOINT** is to be able to assign a name to the beginning of a group of SQL statements and later, if necessary, **ROLLBACK** to that name, thus undoing the results of *just that group*. These can be nested or sequenced, allowing great control over recovery from errors. The idea here is to collect together a series of SQL statements that make up one logical transaction, and hold the **COMMIT** until all the steps within it have been completed successfully. It may be that an attempted step will fail, but you'll want to be able to try it again without having to undo everything else prior to it. Here is an example:

```
insert into COMFORT
values ('WALPOLE', '22-APR-01',50.1, 24.8, 0);

savepoint A;

insert into COMFORT
values ('WALPOLE', '27-MAY-01',63.7, 33.8, 0);

savepoint B;

insert into COMFORT
values ('WALPOLE', '07-AUG-01',83.0, 43.8, 0);
```

You can rollback just the last insert by returning to savepoint B:

```
rollback to savepoint B;
```

This shows that SQL statements, or groups of them, can be collected together and undone in sets or singly. In a host program, or using PL/SQL or SQL*PLUS, you may want to set up SAVEPOINTs that you can **ROLLBACK** to, based on the results of your most recent SQL statement or condition test. **ROLLBACK** allows you to return to a specific step where you named a SAVEPOINT.

If a function, a section of logic, or an attempted SQL statement fails, you can return the data in the database back to the state it was in before the local step began. You can then try it again.

**SAVEPOINT** names must be unique to a transaction (defined by where it ends, with either a **COMMIT** or unconditional **ROLLBACK**) but do not have to be unique to all of your database objects. You can give a **SAVEPOINT** the same name as a table, for instance (this might even result in more understandable code if the **SAVEPOINT** had the name of the table being updated). Names for **SAVEPOINT**s follow object-naming conventions.

If you give a new **SAVEPOINT** the same name as a previous one, the new one replaces the earlier one. The earlier one is lost, and you can no longer roll back to it.

Once a **COMMIT** or an unconditional **ROLLBACK** (not to a SAVEPOINT) is issued, all previous **SAVEPOINT**s are erased. Recall that all DDL statements (such as **DISCONNECT**, **CREATE TABLE**, **CREATE INDEX**, and so on) automatically issue an implicit **COMMIT**, and any severe failure (if the program terminates abnormally or the computer goes down), will result in an automatic **ROLLBACK**.

# SCAN (SQL*PLUS)

*See* **SET**.

## SCORE

The **SCORE** function is used by CONTEXT indexes in Oracle Text to evaluate how well a text string met the specified search criteria. You can display the score of an individual search; more often, the score is compared to a threshold value. *See* Chapter 24.

## SEGMENT

A segment is the physical storage for the space allocated to a table, index, or cluster. A table has one segment that consists of all of its extents. Every index has one segment similarly defined. A cluster has at least two segments, one for its data and one for its cluster key index.

## SEGMENT HEADER BLOCK

The segment header block is the first block in the first extent of a segment.

## SELECT (Form 1-SQL)

**SEE ALSO** COLLATION, **CONNECT BY, DELETE**, DUAL, **FROM, GROUP BY, HAVING, INSERT, JOIN**, LOGICAL OPERATORS, **ORDER BY**, QUERY OPERATORS, SUBQUERY, SYNTAX OPERATORS, **UPDATE, WHERE**

**FORMAT**

select::=

subquery::=

**subquery_factoring_clause::=**

**select_list::=**

**table_reference::=**

**flashback_clause::=**

**query_table_expression::=**

**sample_clause::=**

**subquery_restriction_clause::=**

**table_collection_expression::=**

**joined_table::=**

**join_type::=**

**hierarchical_query_clause::=**

**group_by_clause::=**

**rollup_cube_clause::=**

**grouping_sets_clause::=**

**grouping_expression_list::=**

**expression_list::=**

**order_by_clause::=**

**for_update_clause::=**

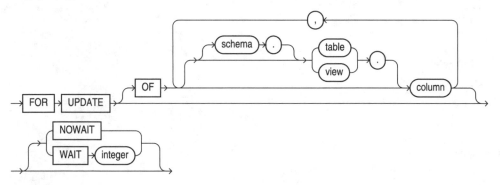

**DESCRIPTION** **SELECT** retrieves rows from one or more tables or views, either as a command, or as a subquery in another SQL command (within limitations), including **select**, **insert**, **update**, and **delete**. **ALL** means that all rows satisfying the conditions will be returned (this is the default). **DISTINCT** means that only rows that are unique will be returned; any duplicates will be weeded out first.

An * (asterisk) by itself results in all columns from all tables in the **from** clause being displayed. *table.** means that all columns from this table will be displayed. An asterisk by itself cannot be combined with any other columns, but a *table.** can be followed by column names and expressions, including ROWID.

*select_list* can include any form of a column. This could be a column name, a literal, a mathematical computation, a function, or several functions combined. The most common version is a simple column name, or a column name prefixed by a table name or table alias. *c_alias* is a renaming of the column or expression. The column alias can be preceded by the word AS. The column alias will become the column heading in the display, and may be referenced by the **column**, **ttitle**, and **btitle** commands in SQL*PLUS. The column alias may be used in the **order by** clause. If it is more than one word, or will contain characters that are neither numbers nor letters, it must be enclosed in double quotation marks.

*schema, table*, and *dblink* denote the table or view from which the rows will be drawn. *schema* and *dblink* are optional, and their absence makes Oracle default to the current user. However, specifying the user in a query may reduce Oracle's overhead and make the query run more quickly. A subquery can be specified in the FROM clause. Oracle will execute the subquery and the resulting rows will be treated as if they came from a view.

A table *t_alias* here will rename the table for this query. This alias, unlike the expression alias, can be referenced elsewhere within the **select** statement itself, for instance as a prefix to any column name coming from that table. In fact, if a table has an alias, the alias *must* be used whenever a column from that table has a table name prefix. Tables are typically aliased when two tables with long names are joined in a query, and many of their columns have the same name, requiring them to be unambiguously named in the **select** clause. Aliases are also commonly used in correlated subqueries, and when a table is being joined to itself.

*condition* may be any valid expression that tests true or false. It can contain functions, columns (from these tables), and literals. *position* allows the **order by** to identify the expressions based on their relative position in the **select** clause, rather than on their names. This is valuable for complicated expressions. You should discontinue the use of ordinal positions in **order by** clauses; column aliases may be used in their place. The current SQL standard does not include support for ordinal positions in **order by** clauses, and Oracle may not support them in the future. **ASC** and **DESC** specify whether it is an ascending or descending sequence for each expression in the **order by**. *See* COLLATION for a discussion of what these sequences are.

*column* is a column in a table listed in the **from** clause. This cannot be an expression, but must be a real column name. **NOWAIT** means that a **select for update** attempt that encounters a locked row will terminate and return immediately to the user, rather than wait and attempt to update the row again in a few moments.

The **for update of** clause puts locks on the rows that have been selected. **select . . . for update of** should be followed immediately by an **update. . .where** command, or, if you decide not to update anything, by a **COMMIT** or **ROLLBACK**. The **for update of** also includes the actions of **insert** and **delete**. Once you have locked a row, other users cannot update it until you free it with a **COMMIT** command (or **AUTOCOMMIT**) or **ROLLBACK**. **select . . . for update of** cannot include **DISTINCT**, **GROUP BY**, **UNION**, **INTERSECT**, **MINUS**, or any group function, such **MIN**, **MAX**, **AVG**, or **COUNT**. The columns named have no effect and are present for compatibility with other dialects of SQL. Oracle will lock only the tables that appear in the **for update** clause. If you don't have an **of** clause listing any tables, Oracle will lock all the tables in the **from** clause for update. All the tables must be on the same database, and if there are references to a LONG column or a sequence in the **select**, the tables must be on the same database as the LONG or the sequence.

If you are querying from a partitioned table, you can list the name of the partition you are querying as part of the **from** clause of the query. *See* Chapter 18.

The other individual clauses in the **select** statement are all described under their own names elsewhere in this reference. *flashback_clause* is available as of Oracle9i Release 2.

**OTHER NOTES**    Clauses must be placed in the order shown, except for these:

- **connect by**, **start with**, **group by**, and **having**, which may be in any order in relation to each other.

- **order by** and **for update of**, which may be in any order in relation to each other.

# SELECT (Form 2-Embedded SQL)

**SEE ALSO**    **CONNECT, DECLARE CURSOR, DECLARE DATABASE, EXECUTE, FETCH, FOR, PREPARE, UPDATE** (Form 1), **WHENEVER**, *Precompiler Programmer's Guide*

**FORMAT**

```
EXEC SQL [AT { db_name | :host_variable }]
 SELECT select_list INTO
 :host_variable [[INDICATOR] :indicator_variable]
 [, :host_variable [[INDICATOR] :indicator_variable]]...
 FROM table_list [WHERE condition]
 { [START WITH condition] CONNECT BY condition
 | CONNECT BY condition [START WITH condition]
 | GROUP BY expr [, expr]... [HAVING condition] }
 [[START WITH condition] CONNECT BY condition
 | CONNECT BY condition [START WITH condition]
 | GROUP BY expr [, expr]... [HAVING condition]]...
 [WITH READ ONLY | WITH CHECK OPTION]
 [{ UNION | UNION ALL | INTERSECT | MINUS } SELECT command]
[ORDER BY
 { expr | position } [ASC | DESC]
 [, { expr | position } [ASC | DESC]]...
 | FOR UPDATE
 [OF [[schema.] { table. | view. | materialized view. }] column
 [, OF [[schema.] { table. | view. | materialized view. }] column]...] [NOWAIT]]
 [ORDER BY
 { expr | position } [ASC | DESC]
 [, { expr | position } [ASC | DESC]]...
 | FOR UPDATE
 [OF [[schema.] { table. | view. | materialized view. }] column
 [, OF [[schema.] { table. | view. | materialized view. }] column]...]
 [NOWAIT]]...
```

**DESCRIPTION**     *See* the description of the various clauses in **SELECT** (Form 1). The following are the elements unique to embedded SQL:

- **AT** database, which optionally names a database from a previous **CONNECT** statement, for a database name from a previous **DECLARE DATABASE** statement.

- **INTO** :*host_variable* [,:*host_variable*] is the list of host variables into which the results of the **select** statement will be loaded. If any variable in this list is an array, all of the variables in the list must be arrays, though they need not all be the same size arrays.

- The **where** clause may reference non-array host variables.

- The **select** clause may reference host variables anywhere a constant would have been used.

You can use the embedded **SQL SELECT** with variable arrays to return multiple rows with a single **FETCH**. You also can use it to either **DECLARE CURSOR** or **PREPARE** statements for use with a later **FETCH**, and may include the **for update of** clause. The later **update** statement can then reference the columns named in the **for update of** using its own **current of** clause. *See* **DECLARE CURSOR** and **UPDATE** (Form 2).

If the embedded **select** returns no rows, SQLCODE is set to +100, and the host variables are left unchanged. In that case, **WHENEVER** lets you change the program flow.

All rows that meet the **select** criteria are locked at the **OPEN**. **COMMIT** releases the locks, and no further **FETCH**ing is permitted. This means you must **FETCH** and process all of the rows you wish to update before you issue a **COMMIT**.

## SELECT. . .INTO

**SEE ALSO**      %ROWTYPE, %TYPE, DECLARE VARIABLE, FETCH
**FORMAT**

```
SELECT expression [,expression]...
 INTO {variable [,variable]... | record}
 FROM [user.]table [,[user.]table]...
[where...][group by... [having...]] [order by...];
```

**DESCRIPTION**      This is not the form of the **select** statement used in **DECLARE CURSOR**. This form utilizes the implicit cursor named SQL, executes within an execution section of a block (between **BEGIN** and **END**), and copies the values from a single row being returned into either a string of named variables, or a record whose structure is declared by **%ROWTYPE** to be just like the columns being selected. If the form that uses variables is used, they must each be **DECLARE**d and have compatible datatypes with those being retrieved. The order in which they appear in the **into** clause must correspond to the order of the associated columns in the **select** clause.

This **select** may be used in a loop with PL/SQL variables appearing in the **where** clause (or even acting like constants in the **select** clause), but each time the **select** executes it must return only one row. If it produces more than one row, the TOO_MANY_ROWS exception will be **RAISE**d, and SQL%ROWCOUNT will be set to 2 (*see* EXCEPTION for details). SQL%FOUND will be TRUE.

If it produces no rows, the NO_DATA_FOUND exception is **RAISE**d, and SQL%ROWCOUNT will be set to 0. SQL%FOUND will be FALSE.

## SEQUENCE

A sequence is a database object used to generate unique integers for use as primary keys. *See* **CREATE SEQUENCE**.

## SERVICE NAME

A service name, found in the tnsnames.ora file, is an alias for a database accessed by Oracle Net. Within the tnsnames.ora file, the service name is mapped to a host, port, and instance. You can therefore change the service name for a database without changing the database name, and you can move a database to a different host without changing its service name.

## SESSION

The session is the series of events that happens between the time a user connects to SQL and the time he or she disconnects.

## SESSIONTIMEZONE

**SEE ALSO**      Chapter 8
**FORMAT**

```
SESSIONTIMEZONE
```

**DESCRIPTION**      **SESSIONTIMEZONE** returns the value of the current session's time zone.
**EXAMPLE**

```
select SESSIONTIMEZONE from DUAL;
```

# SET

**SEE ALSO**   **SET TRANSACTION, SHOW**, Chapter 6
**FORMAT**

```
SET feature value
```

where feature and value are from the following list. The default values are underlined.

APPI[NFO]{ON|OFF|text} enables the registering of command files via the DBMS_APPLICATION_INFO package. The registered name appears in the Module column of the V$SESSION dynamic performance table.

ARRAY[SIZE] {15|n} will set the size of the batch of rows that SQL*PLUS will fetch at one time. The range is 1 to 5000. Larger values improve the efficiency of queries and subqueries where many rows will be fetched, but use more memory. Values above 100 generally do not produce much improvement. ARRAYSIZE has no other effect on the workings of SQL*PLUS.

AUTO[COMMIT]{ON|OFF|IMM[EDIATE]|n} makes SQL immediately commit any pending changes to the database upon the completion of every SQL command. *n* allows you to specify the number of commands after which a commit will occur. OFF stops automatic committing, and you must instead commit changes intentionally with the **COMMIT** command. Many commands, such as **QUIT**, **EXIT**, **CONNECT**, and all DDL commands will cause a **COMMIT** of any pending changes.

AUTOP[RINT] {ON|OFF} sets whether SQL*Plus automatically displays bind variables used in a PL/SQL block or EXECUTEd procedure.

AUTORECOVERY [ON|OFF] tells the **RECOVER** command to automatically apply the default filenames of archived redo log files needed during recovery.

AUTOT[RACE] {ON|OFF|TRACE[ONLY]} [EXP[LAIN]] [STAT[ISTICS]] allows you to see the execution path for a query after the query has completed. To see the execution path, you first must have the PLAN_TABLE table created in your schema (it can be created by running the UTLXPLAN.SQL file in the /rdbms/admin directory under your Oracle software directory).

BLO[CKTERMINATOR] {.|c} sets the symbol used to denote the end of a PL/SQL block. This cannot be a letter or a number. To execute the block, use **RUN** or **/** (slash).

CMDS[EP] {;|c|ON|OFF} sets the character used to separate multiple SQL*PLUS commands entered on a line. ON or OFF controls whether multiple commands may be entered on a line.

COLSEP {_|text} sets a value to be printed between columns.

COM[PATIBILITY]{V7|V8|NATIVE} specifies the version of Oracle to which you are currently connected.

CON[CAT] {.|c|ON|OFF} sets a symbol that may be used to terminate or delimit a user variable that is followed by a symbol, character, or word that would otherwise be interpreted as a part of the user variable name. Setting CONCAT ON resets its value to '.'.

COPYC[OMMIT] {0|n} commits rows to the destination database on a cycle of *n* batches of rows (the number of rows in a batch is **SET** by ARRAYSIZE). Valid values are 0 to 5000. If value is 0, a **COMMIT** will occur only at the end of a copy operation.

COPYTYPECHECK {ON|OFF} enables the suppression of datatype checks when using the COPY command.

DEF[INE] {&|c|ON|OFF} determines whether SQL*PLUS will look for and substitute commands for substitution variables and load them with their DEFINEd values.

DESCRIBE [DEPTH {1|n|ALL}][LINENUM {ON|OFF}][INDENT {ON|OFF}] sets the depth of the level to which you can recursively describe an object. The valid range of the DEPTH clause is from 1 to 50.

ECHO {ON|OFF} **ECHO ON** makes SQL*PLUS echo (display) commands to the screen as they execute from a start file. OFF makes SQL*PLUS execute them without displaying them. The results of the commands, on the other hand, are controlled by **TERMOUT**.

EDITF[ILE] *file_name[.ext]* sets the default filename created by the EDIT command.

EMB[EDDED] {ON|OFF} allows a new report in a series of reports to begin anywhere on a page, just after the previous one ended. OFF forces the new report to start at the top of a new page.

ESC[APE] {\|c|ON|OFF} defines the character you enter as the escape character. OFF undefines the escape character. ON enables the escape character. ON changes the value of c back to the default "\". You can use the escape character before the substitution character (set through SET DEFINE) to indicate that SQL*Plus should treat the substitution character as an ordinary character rather than as a request for variable substitution.

FEED[BACK] {6|n|ON|OFF} makes SQL*PLUS show "records selected" after a query if at least *n* records are selected. ON or OFF turns this display on or off. **SET FEEDBACK** to 0 is the same as OFF.

FLAGGER {OFF|ENTRY |INTERMED[IATE]|FULL} sets the FIPS level for SQL92 compliance.

FLU[SH] {ON|OFF} is used when a start file can be run without needing any display or interaction until it has completed. The OFF lets the operating system avoid sending output to the display. ON restores output to the user's display. OFF may improve performance.

HEA[DING] {ON|OFF} suppresses the headings, both text and underlines, that normally appear above columns. ON allows them to be displayed.

HEADS[EP] {|c|ON|OFF} defines the character you enter as the heading separator character. ON or OFF turns heading separation on or off.

INSTANCE [*instance_path*|LOCAL] changes the default instance for your session to the specified instance path. Using the SET INSTANCE command does not connect to a database. The default instance is used for commands when no instance is specified.

LIN[ESIZE] {80|n} sets the line width, the total number of characters on a line that can be displayed before wrapping down to the next line. This number is also used when SQL*PLUS calculates the proper position for centered or right-aligned titles. The maximum value of *n* is 999.

LOBOF[FSET] {n|1} sets the starting position from which CLOB and NCLOB data is retrieved and displayed.

LOGSOURCE [*pathname*] specifies the location from which archive logs are retrieved during recovery. The default value is set by the LOG_ARCHIVE_DEST initialization parameter in the Oracle initialization file. Using the SET LOGSOURCE command without a pathname restores the default location.

LONG {80|n} is the maximum width for displaying or copying (spooling) LONG, CLOB, and NCLOB values. *n* may range from 1 to 2 GB.

LONGC[HUNKSIZE] {80|n} sets the size, in characters, of the increments in which SQL*Plus retrieves a LONG, CLOB, or NCLOB value.

MARK[UP] HTML [ON|OFF] [HEAD *text*] [BODY *text*] [TABLE *text*] [ENTMAP {ON|OFF}] [SPOOL {ON|OFF}] [PRE[FORMAT] {ON|OFF}] outputs HTML marked up text. SET MARKUP only specifies that SQL*Plus output will be HTML encoded. You must use SET MARKUP HTML ON SPOOL ON and the SQL*Plus SPOOL command to create and name a spool file, and to begin writing HMTL output to it. SET MARKUP has the same options and behavior as SQLPLUS -MARKUP.

NEWP[AGE] {1|n|NONE} sets the number of blank lines to be printed between the bottom of one page and the top title of the next. A 0 (zero) sends a form feed at the top of each page. If the output is being displayed, this will usually clear the screen.

NULL *text* sets the text that will be substituted when SQL*PLUS discovers null value. NULL without text displays blanks.

NUMF[ORMAT] *format* sets the default number format for displaying number data items. *See* NUMBER FORMATS for details.

NUM[WIDTH] {10|*n*} sets the default width for number displays.

PAGES[IZE] {24|*n*} sets the number of lines per page.

PAU[SE] {ON|OFF|*text*} ON makes SQL*PLUS wait for you to press RETURN after it displays each page of output. OFF means no pause between pages of display. *text* is the message SQL*PLUS will display at the bottom of the screen as it waits for you to hit the RETURN key. Pause will wait before the very first page is displayed; you'll have to hit RETURN to see it.

RECSEP {WR[APPED]|EA[CH]|OFF}: Each row SQL*PLUS brings back can be separated from other rows by a character, defined by RECSEPCHAR (*see also* SET). By default, the character is a space, and this only happens for records (and therefore columns) that wrap.

RECSEPCHAR works with RECSEP. The default is a space, but you can set it to another symbol if you wish.

SERVEROUT[PUT] {ON|OFF} [SIZE *n*] [FOR[MAT] {WRA[PPED] | WOR[D_WRAPPED]|TRU[NCATED]}] allows you to display the output of PL/SQL procedures (from the DBMS_OUTPUT package—*see* the *Application Developer's Guide*). WRAPPED, WORD_WRAPPED, TRUNCATED, and FORMAT determine the formatting of the output text.

SHIFT[INOUT] {VIS[IBLE]|INV[ISIBLE]} allows correct alignment for terminals that display shift characters. Use VISIBLE for terminals that display shift characters as a visible character (for example, a space or a colon). INVISIBLE is the opposite and does not display any shift characters.

SHOW[MODE] {ON|OFF} ON makes SQL*PLUS display the old and new settings of a SET feature and its value when it is changed. OFF stops the display of both of these.

SQLBL[ANKLINES] {ON|OFF} controls whether SQL*Plus allows blank lines within a SQL command or script. ON interprets blank lines and new lines as part of a SQL command or script. OFF, the default value, does not allow blank lines or new lines in a SQL command or script.

SQLC[ASE] {MIX[ED]|LO[WER]|UP[PER]} converts all the text, including literals and identifiers, in either SQL or PL/SQL blocks, before it is executed by Oracle. MIXED leaves case just as it is typed. LOWER converts everything to lowercase; UPPER converts it all to uppercase.

SQLCO[NTINUE] {> |*text*} sets the character sequence to be displayed as a prompt for a long line that must continue on the next line. When you enter a - (hyphen) at the end of a SQL*PLUS command line, the SQLCONTINUE symbols or text will prompt you from the left of the next screen line.

SQLN[UMBER] {ON|OFF}: If this is ON, then lines of SQL beyond the first one you enter will have line numbers as prompts. If this is OFF, the SQLPROMPT will appear only on additional lines.

SQLPLUSCOMPAT[IBILITY] {*x.y*[*.z*]} sets the behavior or output format of VARIABLE to that of the release or version specified by x.y[.z]. Where *x* is the *version* number, *y* is the *release* number, and *z* is the *update* number. In later releases, SQLPLUSCOMPATIBILITY may affect features other than VARIABLE. Setting the value of SQLPLUSCOMPATIBILITY to a version less than 9.0.0 will result in VARIABLE definition of NCHAR or NVARCHAR2 datatypes to revert to Oracle8i behavior whereby the size of the variable is in bytes or characters depending on the chosen national character set.

SQLPRE[FIX] {#|*c*} sets the SQL*Plus prefix character. While you are entering a SQL command or PL/SQL block, you can enter a SQL*Plus command on a separate line, prefixed by the SQL*Plus prefix character. SQL*Plus will execute the command immediately without affecting the SQL command or PL/SQL block that you are entering. The prefix character must be a non-alphanumeric character.

SQLP[ROMPT] {SQL>|*text*} sets the SQL*Plus command prompt.

SQLT[ERMINATOR] {;|*c*|ON|OFF} sets the character used to end and execute SQL commands to c.

SUF[FIX] {SQL|*text*} sets the default file extension that SQL*Plus uses in commands that refer to command files. SUFFIX does not control extensions for spool files.

TAB {ON|OFF} determines how SQL*Plus formats white space in terminal output. OFF uses spaces to format white space in the output. ON uses the TAB character. TAB settings are every eight characters.

TERM[OUT] {ON|OFF}: OFF suppresses the display so that you can spool output from a command file without seeing the output on the screen. ON displays the output.

TI[ME] {ON|OFF} **ON** displays the current time before each command prompt. **OFF** suppresses the time display.

TIMI[NG] {ON|OFF} **ON** displays timing statistics on each SQL command or PL/SQL block run. **OFF** suppresses timing of each command.

TRIM[OUT] {ON|OFF} **ON** removes blanks at the end of each line, improving performance especially when you access SQL*Plus from a slow communications device. **OFF** allows SQL*Plus to display trailing blanks.

TRIMS[POOL] {ON|OFF} **ON** removes blanks at the end of each line. **OFF** allows SQL*Plus to include trailing blanks.

UND[ERLINE] {-|c|ON|OFF} sets the character used to underline column headings in SQL*Plus reports.

VER[IFY] {ON|OFF} controls whether SQL*Plus lists the text of a SQL statement or PL/SQL command before and after SQL*Plus replaces substitution variables with values. **ON** lists the text; **OFF** suppresses the listing.

WRA[P] {ON|OFF} controls whether SQL*Plus truncates the display of a SELECTed row if it is too long for the current line width. **OFF** truncates the SELECTed row; **ON** allows the SELECTed row to wrap to the next line.

**DESCRIPTION**     **SET** turns a SQL*PLUS feature ON or OFF or to a certain value. All of these features are changed with the **SET** command and displayed with the **SHOW** command. **SHOW** will display a particular command if its name follows the word **SHOW**, or all commands if **SHOW** is entered by itself.

# SET CONDITION

Set condition is a logical expression containing a query, for example "Name IN (select. . . )". The name derives from the idea that the query condition will produce a set of records.

# SET CONSTRAINTS

**SEE ALSO**     INTEGRITY CONSTRAINT
**FORMAT**

```
SET { CONSTRAINT | CONSTRAINTS }
{ constraint [, constraint]... | ALL }
{ IMMEDIATE | DEFERRED };
```

**DESCRIPTION**     **SET CONSTRAINTS DEFERRED** tells Oracle not to check the validity of a constraint until the transaction is committed. This allows you to temporarily defer integrity checking of data. Deferred constraints are usually used when performing DML against multiple related tables when you cannot guarantee the order of the transactions. You must either own the table modified by the constraint or you must have SELECT privilege on the table.

The default setting is **SET CONSTRAINTS IMMEDIATE**, in which case the constraints are checked as soon as a record is inserted into the table.

# SET OPERATOR

The set operator is either **UNION**, **INTERSECT**, or **MINUS**. *See also* QUERY OPERATORS.

# SET ROLE

**SEE ALSO**     **ALTER USER, CREATE ROLE**, Chapter 19

**FORMAT**

```
SET ROLE
{ role [IDENTIFIED BY password] [, role [IDENTIFIED BY password]]...
| ALL [EXCEPT role [, role]...]
| NONE };
```

**DESCRIPTION**     **SET ROLE** enables or disables roles granted to a user for the current SQL session. The first option lets the user enable specific roles, optionally giving a password if the role has one (*see* **CREATE ROLE**). The second option lets the user enable **ALL** roles **EXCEPT** for specific ones; these roles must be directly granted to the user, not roles granted through other roles. The **ALL** option does not enable roles with passwords. The third option, **NONE**, disables all roles for the current session.

## SET TRANSACTION

**SEE ALSO**     **COMMIT, ROLLBACK, SAVEPOINT, TRANSACTION**, Chapter 40

**FORMAT**

```
SET TRANSACTION
{ { READ { ONLY | WRITE }
 | ISOLATION LEVEL { SERIALIZABLE | READ COMMITTED }
 | USE ROLLBACK SEGMENT rollback_segment }
 [NAME 'test']
| NAME 'test' } ;
```

**DESCRIPTION**     **SET TRANSACTION** starts a transaction. The standard SQL transaction guarantees statement level read consistency, making sure that the data from a query is consistent while the statement is executing. But some transactions need a stronger guarantee that a series of **select** statements, accessing one or more tables, will see a consistent snapshot of all of the data in one instant in time. **SET TRANSACTION READ ONLY** specifies this stronger read consistency. No changes to the queried data by other users will affect the transaction's view of the data. In a read-only transaction, you can use only the **select**, **lock table**, **set role**, **alter session**, and **alter system** commands.

For transactions that include **insert**, **update**, or **delete** commands, Oracle assigns a rollback segment to the transaction. **SET TRANSACTION USE ROLLBACK SEGMENT** specifies that the current transaction will use a specific rollback segment.

**SET TRANSACTION** must be the first SQL statement in a transaction. Placing a **COMMIT** just before **SET TRANSACTION** assures that this is true. The **COMMIT** at the end releases the snapshot of the data. This is important because Oracle needs to release the resources it has set aside to maintain consistency.

## SGA

*See* System Global Area.

## SHARED POOL

An area in the Oracle SGA that contains both the dictionary cache and a shared area for the parsed versions of all SQL commands within the database. Its size is determined by the SHARED_POOL_SIZE parameter in the database's initialization parameter file.

## SHARED SERVER

The Oracle Shared Server, formerly known as the multithreaded server (MTS), supports connections to Oracle via dispatcher processes and shared server processes. Dispatcher processes accept connection

requests from users, and shared server processes communicate with the database. Shared Server allows many users to share a small number of shared server processes, potentially reducing the amount of memory required to support the database's users. Shared Server is most effective when there are many users initiating connections, and when the application users frequently interrupt their data input activity.

# SHOW

**SEE ALSO**     SET

**FORMAT**

```
SHO[W] { option }
```

*option* may be any parameter set via the **SET** command or the following:

```
system_variable
ALL
BTI[TLE]
ERR[ORS] [{ FUNCTION | PROCEDURE | PACKAGE | PACKAGE BODY |
 TRIGGER| VIEW | TYPE | TYPE BODY | DIMENSION | JAVA CLASS } [schema.]name]
LNO
PARAMETERS [parameter_name]
PNO
REL[EASE]
REPF[OOTER]
REPH[EADER]
SGA
SPOO[L]
SQLCODE
TTI[TLE]
USER
```

**DESCRIPTION**     **SHOW** displays the value of a feature of **SET**, or **ALL** features of **SET**, or of the other SQL*PLUS items. More than one of these (including more than one **SET** feature) can follow the word **SHOW**, and each will be displayed on a separate line. The rows returned will be ordered alphabetically.

   *system_variable* is any variable set with the **SET** command.

   BTI[TLE] displays the current **btitle** definition.

   ERR[ORS] shows the latest errors encountered with the compilation of a stored object.

   LNO shows the current line number (the line in the current page being displayed).

   PARAMETERS shows the setting of a specific parameter, or all if none is specified.

   PNO displays the page number.

   REL[EASE] gives the release number of this version of Oracle.

   REPF[OOTER] shows the report footer.

   REPH[EADER] shows the report header.

   SGA shows the current memory allocations for the SGA.

   SPOO[L] tells whether output is being spooled (ON or OFF). *See* **SPOOL**.

   SQLCODE shows the error message number of the most recent Oracle error.

   TTI[TLE] displays the current **ttitle** definition.

   USER shows the user's ID.

# SHOWMODE (SQL*PLUS)

*See* **SET**.

# SHUTDOWN

To shut down is to disconnect an instance from the database and terminate the instance. *See* (and contrast with) STARTUP. As a Server Manager command, **SHUTDOWN**'s options are **NORMAL**, **IMMEDIATE**, and **ABORT**. See Chapter 40.

# SIGN

**SEE ALSO**    +, **PRECEDENCE**, Chapter 8

**FORMAT**

```
SIGN(value)
```

**DESCRIPTION**    It equals 1 if *value* is positive, -1 if negative, 0 if zero.

**EXAMPLE**

```
SIGN(33) = 1
SIGN(-.6) = -1
SIGN(0) = 0
```

# SIN

**SEE ALSO**    ACOS, ASIN, ATAN, ATAN2, COS, COSH, NUMBER FUNCTIONS, **SINH**, **TAN**, Chapter 8

**FORMAT**

```
SIN(value)
```

**DESCRIPTION**    SIN returns the sine of an angle *value* expressed in radians.

**EXAMPLE**

```
select SIN(30*3.141593/180) Sine -- sine of 30 degrees in radians
from DUAL;
```

# SINH

**SEE ALSO**    ACOS, ASIN, ATAN, ATAN2, COS, NUMBER FUNCTIONS, **SIN**, **TAN**, Chapter 8

**FORMAT**

```
SINH(value)
```

**DESCRIPTION**    SINH returns the hyperbolic sine of an angle *value*.

# SMON

The System Monitor Process is one of the Oracle background processes used to perform recovery and clean up unused temporary segments. *See* BACKGROUND PROCESS.

# SNAPSHOT

"Snapshot" is an old name for a materialized view. *See* Chapter 23, **CREATE MATERIALIZED VIEW**, and **CREATE MATERIALIZED VIEW LOG**.

## SNAPSHOT REFRESH GROUP

A snapshot refresh group is a set of local materialized views that are all refreshed as a group. Refresh groups allow data consistency to be enforced between materialized views. *See* Chapter 23.

## SOUNDEX

**SEE ALSO**     **LIKE**, Chapters 7 and 24

**FORMAT**

```
SOUNDEX(string)
```

**DESCRIPTION**     **SOUNDEX** finds words that **SOUND** like an **EX**ample *string*. **SOUNDEX** makes certain assumptions about how letters and combinations of letters are usually pronounced. The two words being compared must begin with the same letter. You can perform **SOUNDEX** searches of individual words within text strings in CONTEXT indexes.

**EXAMPLE**

```
select LastName, FirstName, Phone from ADDRESS
 where SOUNDEX(LastName) = SOUNDEX('SEPP');
```

```
LASTNAME FIRSTNAME PHONE
------------------------ ------------------------ ------------
SZEP FELICIA 214-522-8383
SEP FELICIA 214-522-8383
```

## SPACE (SQL*PLUS)

*See* **SET**.

## SPOOL

**SEE ALSO**     **SET**, Chapter 6

**FORMAT**

```
SPO[OL] [file|OFF|OUT];
```

**DESCRIPTION**     **SPOOL** starts or stops spooling (copying) of SQL*PLUS output to a host system file or the system printer. **SPOOL** *file* makes SQL*PLUS spool all output to the named file. If the file type is not specified, **SPOOL** adds a default, similar to what **SAVE** does, usually .LST, but with some variation by host. OFF stops spooling. OUT stops spooling and sends the file to the printer. To spool output to a file without displaying it, **SET TERMOUT OFF** in the start file prior to the SQL statement, but before the **SPOOL** command. **SPOOL** by itself shows the name of the current (or most recent) spool file.

## SQL

SQL (Structured Query Language) is the ANSI industry-standard language, used to manipulate information in a relational database and used in Oracle and IBM DB2 relational database management systems. SQL is formally pronounced "sequel," although common usage also pronounces it "S.Q.L."

## SQL CURSOR

**SEE ALSO**       %FOUND, %ISOPEN, %NOTFOUND, %ROWCOUNT, Chapter 27

**DESCRIPTION**       *SQL* is the name of the cursor opened implicitly any time the SQL statement being processed is not part of an explicitly named and opened cursor (*see* **DECLARE**). There is only one of these at any time. The cursor attributes **%FOUND** and **%NOTFOUND** can be tested by checking SQL%FOUND and SQL%NOTFOUND before or after an **insert**, **update**, or **delete** (which are never associated with an explicit cursor) or a single-row **select** that happened to be executed without an explicit cursor.

See **%FOUND** for details on these tests. *See* **%ROWCOUNT** for details on the values this attribute has under different conditions. SQL%ISOPEN always evaluates to FALSE because Oracle closes the SQL cursor automatically after executing the SQL statement.

## SQL*LOADER

SQL*LOADER is a utility for loading data into an Oracle database. *See* **SQLLDR** and Chapter 21.

## SQL*PLUS

*See* SQLPLUS.

## SQLCASE (SQL*PLUS)

*See* **SET**.

## SQLCODE

**SEE ALSO**       EXCEPTION, SQLERRM

**FORMAT**

```
variable := SQLCODE
```

**DESCRIPTION**       SQLCODE is an error function that returns the latest error number, but outside of an exception handler (*see* EXCEPTION WHEN) always returns 0. This is because the occurrence of an exception (that is, when SQLCODE would be nonzero) is expected to immediately transfer control to the EXCEPTION part of the PL/SQL block. Once there, SQLCODE can be tested for its value, or used to assign a value to a variable.

SQLCODE cannot be used as a part of a SQL statement (such as to insert the value of the error code into a error table). However, you can set a variable equal to SQLCODE, and then use the variable in a SQL statement:

```
sql_error := sqlcode;
insert into PROBLEMLOG values (sql_error);
```

## SQLCONTINUE (SQL*PLUS)

*See* **SET**.

## SQLERRM

**SEE ALSO**       EXCEPTION, EXCEPTION_INIT, PRAGMA, SQLCODE

**FORMAT**

```
SQLERRM[(integer)]
```

**DESCRIPTION**     Without *integer* supplied, SQLERRM returns the error message related to the current SQLCODE. With an integer supplied, it returns the error message related to that integer value. Like SQLCODE, this function cannot be used directly in a SQL statement, but can be used in an assignment:

```
error_message := sqlerrm;
```

or, to retrieve the error message associated with the error code 1403:

```
error_message := sqlerrm(1403);
```

Outside of an exception handler (*see* SQLCODE), this function without an integer argument will always return "normal, successful completion." In an exception handler, you will get one of these messages:

- The message associated with an Oracle error.
- The words "User-defined exception" for an explicitly raised user-exception where you did not assign a message text.
- A user-defined message text, loaded using the PRAGMA EXCEPTION_INIT.

# SQLJ

SQLJ is a pre-processor that generates JDBC-compatible code. In general, SQLJ code is simpler to write and debug than JDBC code.

# SQLLDR

**SEE ALSO**     Chapter 21

**FORMAT**     Parameters for the SQLLDR command:

Userid	Username and password for the load, separated by a slash.
Control	Name of the control file.
Log	Name of the log file.
Bad	Name of the bad file.
Discard	Name of the discard file.
Discardmax	Maximum number of rows to discard prior to stopping the load. Default is to allow all discards.
Skip	Number of logical rows in the input file to skip prior to starting to load data. Usually used during re-loads from the same input file following a partial load. Default is 0.
Load	Number of logical rows to load. Default is all.
Errors	Number of errors to allow. Default is 50.
Rows	Number of rows to commit at a time. Use this parameter to break up the transaction size during the load. Default for conventional path loads is 64, for Direct Path loads is all rows.
Bindsize	Size of conventional path bind array in bytes. Default is operating system-dependent.
Silent	Suppress messages during the load.
Direct	Use Direct Path loading. Default is FALSE.

Parfile	Name of the parameter file that contains additional load parameter specifications.
Parallel	Perform parallel loading. Default is FALSE.
File	File to allocate extents from (for parallel loading).
Skip_Unusable_Indexes	Allows loads into tables that have indexes in unusable states. Default is FALSE.
Skip_Index_Maintenance	Stops index maintenance for Direct Path loads, leaving them in unusable states. Default is FALSE.
Readsize	Size of the Read buffer in bytes; default is 1048576.
External_Table	Use external table for load. Default is NOT_USED, other values are GENERATE_ONLY and EXECUTE.
ColumnArrayRows	Number of rows for direct path column array. Default is 5000.
StreamSize	Size of direct path stream buffer in bytes. Default is 256000.
Multithreading	Use multithreading in direct path
Resumable	Enable or disable resumable for current session; default is FALSE.
Resumable_Name	Text string used to identify resumable statements.
Resumable_Timeout	Wait time, in seconds, for Resumable. Default is 7200.

**DESCRIPTION**    SQL*LOADER loads data from external files into tables in the Oracle database. See Chapter 21 for examples. The syntax for the control file is:

**Options clause::=**

**Load statement::=**

**infile_clause::=**

**on_file_proc_clause::=**

**concatenate_clause::=**

**into_table_clause::=**

**cond_spec::=**

**delim_spec::=**

**full_fieldname::=**

**termination_spec::=**

**enclosure_spec::=**

**OID_spec::=**

**SID_spec::=**

**field_list::=**

**d_gen_fld_spec::=**

**REF_spec::=**

**init_spec::=**

**BFILE_spec::=**

**filler_fld_spec::=**

**scalar_fld_spec::=**

**LOBFILE_spec::=**

**pos_spec::=**

**datatype_spec::=**

**col_obj_fld_spec::=**

**collection_fld_spec::=**

**nested_table_spec::=**

**VARRAY_spec::=**

**SDF_spec::=**

**count_spec::=**

# SQLNUMBER (SQL*PLUS)

*See* **SET**.

# SQLPLUS

**SEE ALSO**     Chapters 6, 14

**FORMAT**

```
SQLPLUS [user[/password] [@database] [@file]] [-SILENT] |
 [/NOLOG] [-SILENT] | [-?]
```

**DESCRIPTION**     SQLPLUS starts up SQL*PLUS. Entering both username and password will log you onto your default database. Entering just your username will cause SQL*PLUS to prompt you for your password, which will not be displayed as you enter it. Entering *@database* will connect you to the named

database instead of your default. The *@database* can be anywhere, so long as the computer you are logging onto is connected to it through Oracle Net. There must be no space between *password* and *@database*. For more information about Oracle Net, see Chapter 22. *@file* will run the start file immediately after SQL*PLUS is loaded. There must be a space before *@file*. If the username and password are not entered on the command line with SQLPLUS, they must be the first line in the file. If they are in the file, and you enter them on the command line, you'll get an error message but the start file will run correctly anyway. To put user and password at the top of the file, separate them with a slash (/):

```
GEORGE/MISTY
```

**/NOLOG** makes SQL*PLUS start, but does not log you onto the Oracle database. You must then use **CONNECT** to attach to Oracle. (*See* **CONNECT**).

**-SILENT** suppresses all of SQL*PLUS's screen displays, including the command prompts and even the SQL*PLUS logon and copyright information. It makes the use of SQL*PLUS by another program invisible to the program's user.

**-?** displays the current version and level number for SQL*PLUS without actually starting it up.

**EXAMPLE**   Normal startup of SQL*PLUS follows:

```
sqlplus george/misty
```

To start up on the database EDMESTON, use this:

```
sqlplus george/misty@EDMESTON
```

To start the report file REPORT6, which includes the name and password as its first line, use this:

```
sqlplus @report6
```

To start the report file REPORT6, which includes the name and password as its first line, on the database EDMESTON, use this:

```
sqlplus george/misty@EDMESTON @report6
```

# SQLPREFIX (SQL*PLUS)
*See* **SET**.

# SQLPROMPT (SQL*PLUS)
*See* **SET**.

# SQLTERMINATOR (SQL*PLUS)
*See* **SET**.

# SQRT
**SEE ALSO**   POWER
**FORMAT**

```
SQRT(value)
```

**DESCRIPTION**   **SQRT** finds the square root of value.

**EXAMPLES**

```
SQRT(64) = 8
```

The square root of negative numbers is not available in Oracle.

# START

**SEE ALSO**    **@,@@, ACCEPT, DEFINE, SPOOL**, Chapter 6

**FORMAT**

```
STA[RT] file [parameter] [parameter]...
```

**DESCRIPTION**    **START** executes the contents of the specified start file (so called because it is started by this command). The file may contain any SQL*PLUS commands. If no file type is specified, START assumes it is **.sql**. Any parameters following the file name are substituted into variables in the start file; the variables must be named &1, &2, &3, and so on, and will receive the parameters in order, from left to right. Every occurrence in the start file of &1 will get the first parameter. Parameters consisting of more than one word may be enclosed in single quotes (''); otherwise, parameters are limited to a single word or number each.

**EXAMPLE**

```
start checkout INNUMERACY
```

where the file **checkout.sql** contains a variable named &1, into which the string 'INNUMERACY' will be substituted.

# STARTUP

Starting up is the process of starting an instance, presumably with the intent of mounting and opening a database in order to make a database system available for use. See Chapter 40.

# STDDEV

**SEE ALSO**    GROUP FUNCTIONS, VARIANCE, Chapter 8

**FORMAT**

```
STDDEV([DISTINCT | ALL] value) [OVER (analytic_clause)]
```

**DESCRIPTION**    **STDDEV** gives the standard deviation from the norm of values in a group of rows. It ignores **NULL** values in its calculation.

# STDDEV_POP

**SEE ALSO**    GROUP FUNCTIONS, STTDEV, STDDEV_SAMP

**FORMAT**

```
STDDEV_POP (expr) [OVER (analytic_clause)]
```

**DESCRIPTION**    **STDDEV_POP** computes the population standard deviation and returns the square root of the population variance.

# STDDEV_SAMP

**SEE ALSO**    GROUP FUNCTIONS, STTDEV, STDDEV_POP

**FORMAT**

STDDEV_POP ( *expr* ) [OVER ( *analytic_clause* )]

**DESCRIPTION** **STDDEV_SAMP** computes the cumulative sample standard deviation and returns the square root of the sample variance.

# STORAGE

**SEE ALSO** **BLOCK, CREATE CLUSTER, CREATE INDEX, CREATE ROLLBACK SEGMENT, CREATE MATERIALIZED VIEW, CREATE MATERIALIZED VIEW LOG, CREATE TABLE, CREATE TABLESPACE**, as well as the **ALTER** statement for each of these.

**FORMAT**
**storage_clause::=**

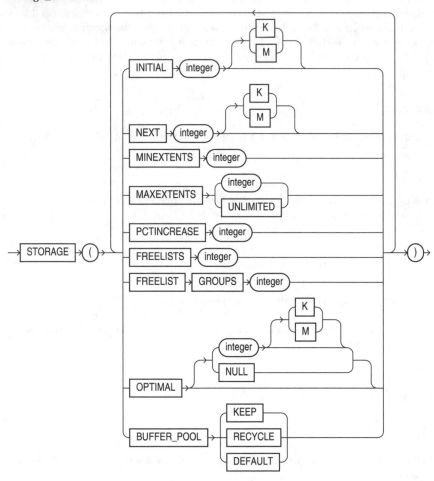

**DESCRIPTION** The **STORAGE** clause is optional in any of the **CREATE** and **ALTER** statements listed under the "See also" section. It is not a SQL statement, and cannot stand alone. In the following

paragraphs, a block is a database block (*see* **BLOCK**) with a size depending on the operating system and the database initialization parameters.

**INITIAL** allocates the first extent of space to the object. If **INITIAL** is not specified, it defaults to five data blocks. The smallest initial extent you can allocate is two data blocks, and the largest depends on your operating system. You can express these numbers either as a simple integer or as an integer followed by K or M to indicate kilobytes or megabytes, respectively.

**NEXT** is the size of the extent allocated after the initial extent has been filled. If not specified, it defaults to five data blocks. The smallest next extent you can allocate is one data block, and the largest depends on the operating system. You can use K and M for kilobytes and megabytes.

**PCTINCREASE** controls the rate of growth of extents beyond the second. If set to 0, every additional extent will be the same size as the second extent, specified by **NEXT**. If **PCTINCREASE** is a positive integer, each succeeding extent will be that percentage larger than the previous one. For example, if **PCTINCREASE** was 50 (the default, if it is not specified), each additional extent would be 50 percent larger than the previous one. **PCTINCREASE** cannot be negative. The minimum **PCTINCREASE** is 0, and the maximum depends on the operating system. Oracle rounds the extent size up to the next multiple of the operating system block size.

**MINEXTENTS** defaults to 1 (or 2 for a rollback segment) if it is not specified, meaning that when the object is created, only the initial extent is allocated. A number larger than 1 will create that many total extents (which don't need to be contiguous on disk, as each extent itself does), and the size of each of them will be determined by the values set with **INITIAL**, **NEXT**, and **PCTINCREASE**. All of these will be allocated when the object is created.

**MAXEXTENTS** sets the limit on the total number of extents that can be allocated. The minimum limit is 1, with the default and maximum depending on the operating system. You can specify a **MAXEXTENTS** value of **UNLIMITED**.

**OPTIMAL** sets an optimal size in bytes for a rollback segment. You can use K and M for kilobytes and megabytes. Oracle will dynamically deallocate extents in the rollback segment to maintain the optimal size. **NULL** means that Oracle never deallocates the rollback segment extents, and this is the default behavior. You must supply a size greater than or equal to the initial space allocated for the rollback segment by the **MINEXTENTS**, **INITIAL**, **NEXT**, and **PCTINCREASE** parameters.

**FREELIST GROUPS** gives the number of groups of free lists, with a default value of 1. This setting applies to the Real Application Clusters option of Oracle for tables, clusters, or indexes.

**FREELISTS** sets the number of free lists for each free list group.

**BUFFER_POOL** sets the buffer pool into which the table's blocks will be read. By default, all blocks are read into the **DEFAULT** pool. You can create separate pools for blocks you want to keep in memory longer (the **KEEP** pool) or for those you wish to age out of memory quickly (the **RECYCLE** pool). *See* the *Oracle9i DBA Handbook* for details.

# STORE

**SEE ALSO** **SAVE**, **START**, Chapter 14
**FORMAT**

```
STORE SET file[.ext] [CRE[ATE] | REP[LACE] | APP[END]]
```

**DESCRIPTION** **STORE** saves all of your SQLPLUS environment settings to a file.

**EXAMPLE** The following command saves the current SQLPLUS environment settings to a file named SETTINGS.SQL.

```
store settings.sql
```

## STRUCTURED QUERY LANGUAGE

*See* **SQL**.

## SUBPARTITION

A subpartition is a partition of a partition. Typically, a range partition is hash partitioned, creating multiple hash subpartitions for each of the range partitions. *See* Chapter 18.

## SUBQUERY

A query (that is, a **select** statement) may be used as a part of another SQL statement (called the parent, or outer statement), including **CREATE TABLE**, **delete**, **insert**, **select**, and **update**, or in the SQL*PLUS **COPY** command, in order to define the rows or columns that the parent will use in its execution. The results of the child query (also called a subquery) are not themselves displayed, but are passed to the parent SQL statement for its use. The following rules apply:

- In an **update** or **CREATE TABLE** command, the subquery must return one value for each column to be inserted or updated. The value or values are then used by the parent SQL statement to **insert** or **update** the rows.

- A subquery cannot contain **order by** and **for update of** clauses.

- A "correlated" subquery is used in the **where** clause of a **select** statement, and references an alias for the table used by the parent select command. It is tested once for each row evaluated for selection by the parent select statement (a standard subquery evaluated just once for the parent query). *See* Chapter 12 for further details.

Other than these restrictions, normal rules for a **select** statement apply.

## SUBSTITUTION

*See* **&, &&, ACCEPT, DEFINE**

## SUBSTR

**SEE ALSO**    ||, CHARACTER FUNCTIONS, **INSTR**, Chapter 7
**FORMAT**

```
SUBSTR(string, start [,count])
```

**DESCRIPTION**    **SUBSTR**ing clips out a piece of a string beginning at *start* and going for *count* characters. If *count* is not specified, the string is clipped from *start* and goes to the end of the string.
**EXAMPLE**

```
SUBSTR('NEWSPAPER',5)
```

produces this:

```
PAPER
```

## SUFFIX (SQL*PLUS)

*See* **SET**.

## SUM

**SEE ALSO**    **COMPUTE**, GROUP FUNCTIONS, Chapter 8
**FORMAT**

SUM([DISTINCT | ALL] `value`) [OVER (analytic_clause)]

**DESCRIPTION**    **SUM** is the sum of all *values* for a group of rows. **DISTINCT** makes SUM add each unique value to the total only once; this is usually not very meaningful.

## SYNONYM

A synonym is a name assigned to a table, view, or sequence that may thereafter be used to refer to it. If you have access to another user's table, you may create a synonym for it and refer to it by the synonym alone, without entering the user's name as a qualifier. *See* Chapter 22 and Chapter 37.

## SYNTAX

Syntax is a set of rules that determine how to construct a valid statement in a computer language such as SQL.

## SYNTAX OPERATORS

**SEE ALSO**    LOGICAL OPERATORS, PRECEDENCE
**DESCRIPTION**    Syntax operators have the highest precedence of all operators, and may appear anywhere in a SQL statement. Here they are listed in descending order of precedence. Operators of equal precedence are evaluated from left to right. Most of these are listed and described separately under their own symbols.

Operator	Function
-	SQL*PLUS command continuation. Continues a command on the following line.
&	Prefix for parameters in a SQL*PLUS start file. Words are substituted for &1, &2, and so on. *See* START.
& &&	Prefix for a substitution variable in a SQL command in SQL*PLUS. SQL*PLUS will prompt for a value if an undefined & or && variable is found. && also defines the variable and saves the value; '&' does not. *See* **&** and **&&**, **DEFINE**, and **ACCEPT**.
:	Prefix for a variable in SQL*FORMS and for a host variable in PL/SQL.
.	Variable separator, used in SQL*PLUS to separate the variable name from a suffix, so that the suffix is not considered a part of the variable name, and in SQL between user, table, and column names.
( )	Surrounds subqueries, lists of columns, or controls precedence.
'	Surrounds a literal, such as a character string or date constant. To use a ' in a string constant, use two ' marks (not a double quotation mark).
"	Surrounds a table or column alias that contains special characters or a space.
"	Surrounds literal text in a date format clause of **TO_CHAR**.
@	Precedes a database name in a COPY, or a link name in a **from** clause.

# SYS (ORACLE USER)

SYS is one of the DBA users that is created when a database system is installed and initialized (the other is SYSTEM). SYS owns most of the data dictionary tables, while SYSTEM owns the views created on those base tables.

## SYS_CONNECT_BY_PATH

**SEE ALSO**     **CONNECT BY**, Chapter 13
**FORMAT**

```
SYS_CONNECT_BY_PATH (column, char)
```

**DESCRIPTION**     **SYS_CONNECT_BY_PATH** is valid only in hierarchical queries. It returns the path of a column value from root to node, with column values separated by *char* for each row returned by **CONNECT BY** condition.

## SYS_CONTEXT

**SEE ALSO**     **CREATE CONTEXT**
**FORMAT**

```
SYS_CONTEXT (namespace , parameter [, length])
```

**DESCRIPTION**     **SYS_CONTEXT** returns the value of *parameter* associated with the context *namespace*.

## SYS_DBURIGEN

**SEE ALSO**     Chapter 41
**FORMAT**

```
SYS_DBURIGEN
({ column | attribute } [rowid]
 [, { column | attribute } [rowid]]...
 [, 'text ()'])
```

**DESCRIPTION**     **SYS_DBURIGEN** takes as its argument one or more columns or attributes, and optionally a rowid, and generates a URL of datatype **DBUriType** to a particular column or row object. You can then use the URL to retrieve an XML document from the database.

All columns or attributes referenced must reside in the same table. They must perform the function of a primary key. That is, they need not actually match the primary keys of the table, but they must reference a unique value. If you specify multiple columns, all but the final column identify the row in the database, and the last column specified identifies the column within the row.

By default the URL points to a formatted XML document. If you want the URL to point only the text of the document, specify the optional 'text()'. (In this XML context, the lowercase 'text' is a keyword, not a syntactic placeholder.)

## SYS_EXTRACT_UTC

**SEE ALSO**     Chapter 8
**FORMAT**

```
SYS_EXTRACT_UTC (datetime_with_timezone)
```

**DESCRIPTION**    **SYS_EXTRACT_UTC** extracts the UTC (Coordinated Universal Time) from a datetime with time zone displacement.

# SYS_GUID

**FORMAT**

```
SYS_GUID ()
```

**DESCRIPTION**    **SYS_GUID** generates and returns a globally unique identifier (RAW value) made up of 16 bytes. On most platforms, the generated identifier consists of a host identifier and a process or thread identifier of the process or thread invoking the function, and a nonrepeating value (sequence of bytes) for that process or thread.

# SYS_TYPEID

**SEE ALSO**    Chapter 33

**FORMAT**

```
SYS_TYPEID (object_type_value)
```

**DESCRIPTION**    **SYS_TYPEID** returns the typeid of the most specific type of the operand. This value is used primarily to identify the type-discriminant column underlying a substitutable column. For example, you can use the value returned by SYS_TYPEID to build an index on the type-discriminant column.

# SYS_XMLAGG

**SEE ALSO**    SYS_XMLGEN, Chapter 41

**FORMAT**

```
SYS_XMLAGG (expr [fmt])
```

**DESCRIPTION**    **SYS_XMLAGG** aggregates all of the XML documents or fragments represented by *expr* and produces a single XML document. It adds a new enclosing element with a default name ROWSET. If you want to format the XML document differently, specify *fmt*, which is an instance of the SYS.XMLGenFormatType object.

# SYS_XMLGEN

**SEE ALSO**    SYS_XMLAGG, Chapter 41

**FORMAT**

```
SYS_XMLGEN (expr [fmt])
```

**DESCRIPTION**    **SYS_XMLGEN** takes an expression that evaluates to a particular row and column of the database, and returns an instance of type SYS.XMLType containing an XML document. The *expr* can be a scalar value, a user-defined type, or an XMLType instance.

If *expr* is a scalar value, the function returns an XML element containing the scalar value. If *expr* is a type, the function maps the user-defined type attributes to XML elements. If *expr* is an XMLType instance, then the function encloses the document in an XML element whose default tag name is ROW.

By default the elements of the XML document match the elements of *expr*. For example, if *expr* resolves to a column name, the enclosing XML element will be the same column name. If you want to format the XML document differently, specify *fmt*, which is an instance of the SYS.XMLGenFormatType object.

## SYSDATE
**SEE ALSO**    Chapter 9
**FORMAT**

```
SYSDATE
```

**DESCRIPTION**    **SYSDATE** returns the current date and time.
**EXAMPLE**

```
select SYSDATE from DUAL;
```

## SYSTEM (ORACLE TABLESPACE)
SYSTEM is the name given to the first tablespace in a database. It contains the data dictionary.

## SYSTEM (ORACLE USER)
SYSTEM is one of the DBA users that is created when database system is installed and initialized (the other is SYS). While SYS owns most of the data dictionary tables, SYSTEM owns the views created on those base tables.

## SYSTEM GLOBAL AREA (SGA)
*SGA* is a shared storage area in memory that is the center of Oracle activity while the database is running. The size of the SGA (and performance of the system) depends on the values of the variable initialization parameters. The SGA provides communication between the user and the background processes.

## SYSTIMESTAMP
**SEE ALSO**    Chapter 9
**FORMAT**

```
SYSTIMESTAMP
```

**DESCRIPTION**    **SYSTIMESTAMP** returns the current date and time.
**EXAMPLE**

```
select SYSTIMESTAMP from DUAL;
```

## TABLE
A table is the basic data storage structure in a relational database management system. A table consists of one or more units of information (rows), each of which contains the same kinds of values (columns). *See* **CREATE TABLE**.

## TABLE-PL/SQL
**SEE ALSO**    DATA TYPES, **RECORD** (PL/SQL)
**FORMAT**

```
TYPE new_type IS TABLE OF
{type | table.column%TYPE}[NOT NULL]
INDEX BY BINARY_INTEGER;
```

**DESCRIPTION**    A TABLE declaration declares a new type that can then be used to declare variables of that type. A PL/SQL table has one column and an integer key and can have any number of rows. The datatype of the column can either be one of the standard PL/SQL datatypes (including another RECORD but not a TABLE), or it can be a reference to the type of a particular column in a specific database table. Each field may also have a NOT NULL qualifier that specifies that the field must always have a non-null value.

The **index by binary integer** clause is required and reminds you that the index is an integer. You can refer to any row of the table with the index in parentheses.

If you refer to an index to which you have not assigned any data, PL/SQL raises the NO_DATA_FOUND exception.

## TABLE ALIAS

A table alias is a temporary substitute for a table name, defined in the **from** clause of a **select** statement. *See* **AS** and Chapter 11.

## TABLE CONSTRAINT

A table constraint is an integrity constraint that applies to multiple columns of the same table. *See* INTEGRITY CONSTRAINT.

## TABLESPACE

A tablespace is a file or set of files that is used to store Oracle data. An Oracle database is composed of the SYSTEM tablespace and most likely other tablespaces. *See* Chapters 20 and 40.

## TAN

**SEE ALSO**    ACOS, ASIN, ATAN, ATAN2, COS, COSH, NUMBER FUNCTIONS, **SIN**, **TANH**, Chapter 8
**FORMAT**

```
TAN(value)
```

**DESCRIPTION**    **TAN** returns the tangent of an angle *value* expressed in radians.
**EXAMPLE**

```
select TAN(135*3.141593/180) Tan -- tangent of 135 degrees in radians
from DUAL;
```

## TANH

**SEE ALSO**    ACOS, ASIN, ATAN, ATAN2, COS, COSH, NUMBER FUNCTIONS, **SIN**, **TAN**, Chapter 8
**FORMAT**

```
TANH(value)
```

**DESCRIPTION**    **TANH** returns the hyperbolic tangent of an angle *value*.

## TEMPORARY SEGMENT

A temporary segment is a storage space within a tablespace used to hold intermediate results of a SQL statement. For example, temporary segments are used when sorting large tables. Temporary segments are usually stored in tablespaces dedicated to them; *see* **CREATE TABLESPACE**.

## TERMINAL NODE

In a tree-structured table, a terminal node is a row that has no child row. It's the same as LEAF.

## TERMOUT (SQL*PLUS)

*See* **SET**.

## TEXT INDEX

A text index is a set of tables and indexes used by text search programs. Like the index in a book, a text index contains tables of text entries and their locations. See Chapter 24.

## THEME

A theme is a category of a text document. Text entries may contain themes that do not appear as words within the document. For example, a document about mortgages could have 'banking' as one of its themes even if the word 'banking' did not appear in the document. See Chapter 24.

## THROW

In Java, programs throw exceptions via the **try** clause, and process exceptions via the **catch** and **finally** clauses. See Chapter 34.

## TIME (SQL*PLUS)

*See* **SET**.

## TIMESTAMP

The TIMESTAMP (*fractional_seconds_precision*) datatype records year, month, and day values of date, as well as hour, minute, and second values of time, where *fractional_seconds_precision* is the number of digits in the fractional part of the SECOND datetime field. Accepted values of *fractional_seconds_precision* are 0 to 9. The default is 6. See DATA TYPES and Chapter 9.

## TIMESTAMP WITH TIME ZONE

The TIMESTAMP (*fractional_seconds_precision*) WITH TIME ZONE datatype records year, month, and day values of date, as well as hour, minute, and second values of time, where *fractional_seconds_precision* is the number of digits in the fractional part of the SECOND datetime field. Accepted values of *fractional_seconds_precision* are 0 to 9. The default is 6.

## TIMESTAMP WITH LOCAL TIME ZONE

The TIMESTAMP (*fractional_seconds_precision*) WITH LOCAL TIME ZONE datatype records the TIMESTAMP WITH TIME ZONE values, normalized to the database time zone when the data is stored. When the data is retrieved, users see the data in the session time zone.

## TIMING (Form 1-SQL*PLUS)

*See* **SET**.

## TIMING (Form 2-SQL*PLUS)

**SEE ALSO**    CLEAR, SET

**FORMAT**

```
TIMI[NG] [START area | STOP | SHOW];
```

**DESCRIPTION**    **TIMING** keeps track of elapsed time from START to STOP by area name. **START** opens a timing area and makes *area* its title. *area* must be a single word. Several areas may exist at once. The most recently created one is the current timing area until it is deleted, when the previously created one becomes current. Timing areas are, in effect, nested. The most recently created will always show the least amount of time, because the elapsed time of those before it will be, by definition, longer. Total time for any timing area is its own net time plus those of all the timing areas that followed it.

SHOW gives the current timing area's name and elapsed time.

STOP gives the current timing area's name and elapsed time, deletes the area, and makes the one previous to it (if there was one) the current timing area. *See* the *SQL\*Plus User's Guide and Reference* for your host operating system for details on the precise meaning of time on your machine.

**EXAMPLE**    To create a timing area named 1, you enter this:

```
timing start 1
```

To see the current area name and time, but allow it to continue running, enter the following:

```
timing show
```

To see the current timing area's name and accumulated time, stop it, and make the previous one current, use this:

```
timing stop
```

# TO_CHAR (character formats)

**SEE ALSO**    TO_CHAR (date and number formats)

**FORMAT**

```
TO_CHAR (nchar | clob | nclob)
```

**DESCRIPTION**    The **TO_CHAR** (*character*) function converts NCHAR, NVARCHAR2, CLOB, or NCLOB data to the database character set.

**EXAMPLE**

```
SELECT TO_CHAR(Title) FROM BOOKSHELF;
```

# TO_CHAR (date and number formats)

**SEE ALSO**    DATE FORMATS, DATE FUNCTIONS, NUMBER FORMATS, **TO_DATE**, Chapter 9

**FORMAT**

```
TO_CHAR(date,'format')
TO_CHAR(number,'format')
```

**DESCRIPTION**    **TO_CHAR** reformats number or date according to *format*. *date* must be a column defined as an Oracle DATE datatype. It cannot be a string even if it is in the default date format of DD-MON-YY. The only way to use a string in which *date* appears in the **TO_CHAR** function is to enclose it within a **TO_DATE** function. The formats possible for this function are numerous. They are listed under NUMBER FORMATS and DATE FORMATS.

**EXAMPLE** Note the format in the following example. This is necessary in SQL*PLUS to avoid the current default date width produced by **TO_CHAR**, which is about 100 characters wide:

```
column Formatted format a30 word_wrapped heading 'Formatted'

select BirthDate, TO_CHAR(BirthDate,'MM/DD/YY') Formatted
 from BIRTHDAY
 where FirstName = 'VICTORIA';

BIRTHDATE Formatted
--------- ------------------------------
20-MAY-49 05/20/49
```

# TO_CLOB
**SEE ALSO**   Chapters 18 and 32
**FORMAT**

```
TO_CLOB (lob_column | char)
```

**DESCRIPTION**   **TO_CLOB** converts NCLOB values in a LOB column or other character strings to CLOB values. *char* can be any of the datatypes CHAR, VARCHAR2, NCHAR, NVARCHAR2, CLOB, or NCLOB. Oracle executes this function by converting the underlying LOB data from the national character set to the database character set. Note that LONG values can be converted directly to CLOB columns via **ALTER TABLE**.

# TO_DATE
**SEE ALSO**   DATE FORMATS, DATE FUNCTIONS, **TO_CHAR**, Chapter 8
**FORMAT**

```
TO_DATE(string,'format')
```

**DESCRIPTION**   **TO_DATE** converts a *string* in a given format into an Oracle date. It also will accept a number instead of a string, with certain limits. *string* is a literal string, a literal number, or a database column containing a string or a number. In every case but one, the format must correspond to that which is described by the *format*. Only if a string is in the format 'DD-MON-YY' can the format be omitted. Note that *format* is restricted. *See* DATE FORMATS for a list of acceptable formats for **TO_DATE**.
**EXAMPLE**

```
select TO_DATE('02/22/02','MM/DD/YY') from DUAL;

TO_DATE('

22-FEB-02
```

# TO_DSINTERVAL
**SEE ALSO**   DATA TYPES
**FORMAT**

```
TO_DSINTERVAL (char ['nlsparam'])
```

**DESCRIPTION**    **TO_DSINTERVAL** converts a character string of CHAR, VARCHAR2, NCHAR, or NVARCHAR2 datatype to an INTERVAL DAY TO SECOND type. *char* is the character string to be converted. The only valid NLS parameter you can specify in this function is NLS_NUMERIC_CHARACTERS. This argument can have the form: NLS_NUMERIC_CHARACTERS = "dg" where *d* and *g* represent the decimal character and group separator respectively.

# TO_LOB
**SEE ALSO**    INSERT, Chapter 32
**FORMAT**

```
TO_LOB(long_column)
```

**DESCRIPTION**    **TO_LOB** converts LONG values in *long_column* to LOB values. You can apply this function only to a LONG column, and only in the **select** list of a subquery in an **insert** command.

# TO_MULTI_BYTE
**SEE ALSO**    CONVERSION FUNCTIONS, Chapter 10
**FORMAT**

```
TO_MULTI_BYTE(string)
```

**DESCRIPTION**    **TO_MULTI_BYTE** converts the single-byte characters in a character *string* to their multi-byte equivalents. If a character has no multi-byte equivalent, the function returns the character unconverted.

# TO_NCHAR (character)
**SEE ALSO**    CONVERSION FUNCTIONS, **TRANSLATE ...USING**
**FORMAT**

```
TO_NCHAR ({char | clob | nclob} [, fmt [, 'nlsparam']])
```

**DESCRIPTION**    **TO_NCHAR** (*character*) converts a character string, CLOB, or NCLOB from the database character set to the national character set. This function is equivalent to the **TRANSLATE ... USING** function with a **USING** clause in the national character set.

# TO_NCHAR(datetime)
**SEE ALSO**    CONVERSION FUNCTIONS
**FORMAT**

```
TO_NCHAR ({ datetime | interval } [, fmt [, 'nlsparam']])
```

**DESCRIPTION**    **TO_NCHAR** (*datetime*) converts a character string of DATE, TIMESTAMP, TIMESTAMP WITH TIME ZONE, TIMESTAMP WITH LOCAL TIME ZONE, INTERVAL MONTH TO YEAR, or INTERVAL DAY TO SECOND datatype from the database character set to the national character set.

# TO_NCHAR(number)
**SEE ALSO**    CONVERSION FUNCTIONS

**FORMAT**

```
TO_NCHAR (n [, fmt [, 'nlsparam']])
```

**DESCRIPTION**     TO_NCHAR (*number*) converts a number to a string in the NVARCHAR2 character set. The optional *fmt* and *nlsparam* corresponding to *n* can be of DATE, TIMESTAMP, TIMESTAMP WITH TIME ZONE, TIMESTAMP WITH LOCAL TIME ZONE, INTERVAL MONTH TO YEAR, or INTERVAL DAY TO SECOND datatype.

## TO_NCLOB

**SEE ALSO**     CONVERSION FUNCTIONS, Chapter 32

**FORMAT**

```
TO_NCLOB (lob_column | char)
```

**DESCRIPTION**     TO_NCLOB converts CLOB values in a LOB column or other character strings to NCLOB values. *char* can be any of the datatypes CHAR, VARCHAR2, NCHAR, NVARCHAR2, CLOB, or NCLOB. Oracle implements this function by converting the character set of the LOB column from the database character set to the national character set.

## TO_NUMBER

**SEE ALSO**     CONVERSION FUNCTIONS, Chapter 10

**FORMAT**

```
TO_NUMBER(string [, fmt [, 'nlsparam']])
```

**DESCRIPTION**     TO_NUMBER converts a character *string* to a number datatype. It requires that the characters in the string be a properly formatted number with only the characters 0-9, -, +, and . included. This function is largely unnecessary due to automatic data conversion done by Oracle, except when used for a character column containing numbers in an **order by** or a comparison.

**EXAMPLE**

```
TO_NUMBER('333.46')
```

## TO_SINGLE_BYTE

**SEE ALSO**     CONVERSION FUNCTIONS, Chapter 10

**FORMAT**

```
TO_SINGLE_BYTE(string)
```

**DESCRIPTION**     TO_SINGLE_BYTE converts the multi-byte characters in a character *string* to their single-byte equivalents. If a multi-byte character has no single-byte equivalent, the function returns the character unconverted.

## TO_TIMESTAMP

**SEE ALSO**     CONVERSION FUNCTIONS, **TO_CHAR**, TIMESTAMP, **TO_TIMESTAMP_TZ**

**FORMAT**

```
TO_TIMESTAMP (char [, fmt ['nlsparam']])
```

**DESCRIPTION**    TO_TIMESTAMP converts *char* of CHAR, VARCHAR2, NCHAR, or NVARCHAR2 datatype to a value of TIMESTAMP datatype, using a *fmt* format if *char* is not in the default format of the TIMESTAMP datatype. The optional *nlsparam* has the same purpose in this function as in the **TO_CHAR** function for date conversion.

## TO_TIMESTAMP_TZ

**SEE ALSO**    CONVERSION FUNCTIONS, **TO_TIMESTAMP**, TIMESTAMP WITH TIME ZONE
**FORMAT**

```
TO_TIMESTAMP_TZ (char [, fmt ['nlsparam']])
```

**DESCRIPTION**    **TO_TIMESTAMP_TZ** converts *char* of CHAR, VARCHAR2, NCHAR, or NVARCHAR2 datatype to a value of TIMESTAMP WITH TIME ZONE datatype.

## TO_YMINTERVAL

**SEE ALSO**    CONVERSION FUNCTIONS, INTERVAL YEAR TO MONTH
**FORMAT**

```
TO_YMINTERVAL (char)
```

**DESCRIPTION**    **TO_YMINTERVAL** converts a character string of CHAR, VARCHAR2, NCHAR, or NVARCHAR2 datatype to an INTERVAL YEAR TO MONTH type, where *char* is the character string to be converted.

## TRANSACTION

A transaction is a sequence of SQL statements that Oracle treats as a single unit. The set of changes is made permanent with the **COMMIT** statement. Part or all of a transaction can be undone with the **ROLLBACK** statement.

Oracle manages transactions both with locking (*see* LOCK) and a *multiversion consistency model,* which essentially behaves as though each transaction had its own copy of the database—that is, that there are multiple, overlapping versions of the database in existence at any given time. A transaction starts with the execution of the first SQL statement in the transaction and ends with either the **COMMIT** or **ROLLBACK** statement. By default, Oracle guarantees that a transaction has *statement-level read consistency,* which means that when you execute a query, the data stays the same while Oracle is gathering and returning it. But if a transaction has multiple queries, each query is consistent but not with each other. If you want to be able to maintain a consistent view of the data throughout such a transaction, the transaction needs to have *transaction-level read consistency,* which guarantees that the transaction will not see the effects of the committing of other transactions. This read-only transaction, started with **SET TRANSACTION READ ONLY**, can only execute queries and certain control commands (*see* **SET TRANSACTION**).

## TRANSACTION PROCESSING

Transaction processing is a form of processing oriented toward logical units of work, rather than separate and individual changes, in order to keep the database consistent.

## TRANSLATE

**SEE ALSO**    **REPLACE**, Chapter 10

**FORMAT**

```
TRANSLATE(string,from,to)
```

**DESCRIPTION**    **TRANSLATE** looks at each character in *string*, and then checks *from* to see if that character is there. If it is, **TRANSLATE** notes the position in *from* where it found the character, and then looks at the same position in *to*. Whatever character it finds there, it substitutes for the character in *string*.

**EXAMPLE**

```
select TRANSLATE('I LOVE MY OLD THESAURUS','AEIOUY','123456')
from DUAL;

TRANSLATE('ILOVEMYOLDTH

3 L4V2 M6 4LD TH2S15R5S
```

# TRANSLATE ... USING

**SEE ALSO**    CONVERSION FUNCTIONS, **CONVERT**, **TO_NCHAR**, **UNISTR**

**FORMAT**

```
TRANSLATE (text USING { CHAR_CS | NCHAR_CS })
```

**DESCRIPTION**    **TRANSLATE ... USING** converts *text* into the character set specified for conversions between the database character set and the national character set. The *text* argument is the expression to be converted.

Specifying the **USING CHAR_CS** argument converts *text* into the database character set. The output datatype is VARCHAR2.

Specifying the **USING NCHAR_CS** argument converts *text* into the national character set. The output datatype is NVARCHAR2.

This function is similar to the Oracle **CONVERT** function, but must be used instead of **CONVERT** if either the input or the output datatype is being used as NCHAR or NVARCHAR2. If the input contains UCS2 codepoints or backslash characters (\), use the **UNISTR** function.

# TRANSPORTABLE TABLESPACE

A transportable tablespace is a tablespace that can be "unplugged" from one database and "plugged into" another. To be transportable, a tablespace—or a set of tablespaces—must be self-contained. The tablespace set cannot contain any objects that refer to objects in other tablespaces. Thus, if you transport a tablespace containing indexes, you must move the tablespace containing the indexes' base tables as part of the same transportable tablespace set. The better you have organized and distributed your objects among tablespaces, the easier it is to generate a self-contained set of tablespaces to transport.

To transport tablespaces, you need to generate a tablespace set, copy or move that tablespace set to the new database, and plug the set into the new database. The databases must be on the same operating system, with the same version of Oracle and character set.

**GENERATING A TRANSPORTABLE TABLESPACE SET**    A transportable tablespace set contains all of the datafiles for the tablespaces being moved, along with an export of the metadata for those tablespaces. You can optionally choose whether to include referential integrity constraints as part of the transportable tablespace set. If you choose to use referential integrity constraints, the transportable tablespace set will increase to include the tables required to maintain the key relationships. Referential integrity is optional because you may have the same codes tables in multiple databases. For example, you may be planning to move a tablespace from your test database to your production database. If you

have a COUNTRY table in the test database, then you may already have an identical COUNTRY table in the production database. Since the codes tables are identical in the two databases, you do not need to transport that portion of the referential integrity constraints. You could transport the tablespace and then re-enable the referential integrity in the target database once the tablespace has been moved, simplifying the creation of the transportable tablespace set.

To determine if a tablespace set is self-contained, execute the TRANSPORT_SET_CHECK procedure of the DBMS_TTS package. This procedure takes two input parameters: the set of tablespaces and a Boolean flag set to TRUE if you want referential integrity constraints to be considered. In the following example, referential integrity constraints are not considered for the combination of the AGG_DATA and AGG_INDEXES tablespaces:

```
execute DBMS_TTS.TRANSPORT_SET_CHECK('AGG_DATA,AGG_INDEXES','FALSE');
```

If there are any self-containment violations in the specified set, Oracle will populate the TRANSPORT_SET_VIOLATIONS data dictionary view. If there are no violations, the view will be empty.

Once you have selected a self-contained set of tablespaces, make the tablespaces read only, as shown here:

```
alter tablespace AGG_DATA read only;
alter tablespace AGG_INDEXES read only;
```

Next, export the metadata for the tablespaces, using the TRANSPORT_TABLESPACES and TABLESPACES Export parameters:

```
exp TRANSPORT_TABLESPACE=Y TABLESPACES=(AGG_DATA,AGG_INDEXES) CONSTRAINTS=N
GRANTS=Y TRIGGERS=N
```

As shown in the example, you can specify whether triggers, constraints, and grants are exported along with the tablespace metadata. You should also note the names of the accounts that own objects in the transportable tablespace set. You can now copy the tablespaces' datafiles to a separate area. If needed, you can put the tablespaces back into read-write mode in their current database. After you have generated the transportable tablespace set, you can move its files (including the export) to an area that the target database can access.

**PLUGGING IN THE TRANSPORTABLE TABLESPACE SET**  Once the transportable tablespace set has been moved to an area accessible to the target database, you can plug the set into the target database. First, use Import to import the exported metadata:

```
imp TRANSPORT_TABLESPACE=Y DATAFILES=(agg_data.dbf, agg_indexes.dbf)
```

In the import, you specify the datafiles that are part of the transportable tablespace set. You can optionally specify the tablespaces (via the TABLESPACES parameter) and the object owners (via the OWNERS parameter).

After the import completes, all tablespaces in the transportable tablespace set are left in read-only mode. You can issue the **ALTER TABLESPACE READ WRITE** command in the target database to place the new tablespaces in read-write mode.

```
alter tablespace AGG_DATA read write;
alter tablespace AGG_INDEXES read write;
```

Note that you cannot change the ownership of the objects being transported.

Transportable tablespaces support very fast movement of large datasets. In a data warehouse, you could use transportable tablespaces to publish aggregations from core warehouse to data mart,

or from the data marts to a global data warehouse. Any read-only data can be quickly distributed to multiple databases—instead of sending SQL scripts, you can send datafiles and exported metadata. This modified data movement process may greatly simplify your procedures for managing remote databases, remote data marts, and large data movement operations.

# TREAT

**SEE ALSO**    **DEREF**, **REF**, Chapter 33

**FORMAT**

```
TREAT (expr AS [REF] [schema.] type)
```

**DESCRIPTION**    **TREAT** changes the declared type of an expression.

If the declared type of *expr* is *source_type*, then type must be some supertype or subtype of *source_type*. If the most specific type of *expr* is *type* (or some subtype of *type*), then **TREAT** returns *expr*. If the most specific type of *expr* is not *type* (or some subtype of *type*), then TREAT returns **NULL**.

If the declared type of *expr* is **REF** *source_type*, then *type* must be some subtype or supertype of *source_type*. If the most specific type of **DEREF**(*expr*) is *type* (or a subtype of *type*), **TREAT** returns *expr*. If the most specific type of **DEREF**(*expr*) is not *type* (or a subtype of *type*), then **TREAT** returns **NULL**.

# TREE-STRUCTURED QUERY

A tree-structured query is one whose result shows hierarchical relationships among rows in a table. *See* **CONNECT BY**.

# TRIGGER

A database trigger is a stored procedure associated with a table that Oracle automatically executes on one or more specified events (**BEFORE, AFTER,** or **INSTEAD OF** an **insert**, **update**, or **delete**) affecting the table. Triggers can execute for the table as a whole or for each affected row in the table. *See* Chapter 28 for a full discussion of triggers and examples, and **CREATE TRIGGER** in this Alphabetical Reference for syntax.

# TRIM

**SEE ALSO**    **LTRIM, RTRIM**, Chapter 7

**FORMAT**

```
TRIM
([{ { LEADING | TRAILING | BOTH } [trim_character])
 | trim_character
 } FROM] trim_source)
```

**DESCRIPTION**    **TRIM** enables you to trim leading or trailing characters (or both) from a character string. If *trim_character* or *trim_source* is a character literal, you must enclose it in single quotes.

If you specify **LEADING**, Oracle removes any leading characters equal to *trim_character*. If you specify **TRAILING**, Oracle removes any trailing characters equal to *trim_character*. If you specify **BOTH** or none of the three, Oracle removes leading and trailing characters equal to *trim_character*.

If you specify only *trim_source*, Oracle removes leading and trailing blank spaces. If either *trim_source* or *trim_character* is a **NULL** value, then the TRIM function returns a **NULL**.

**EXAMPLE**

```
select TRIM('"' from Title) from MAGAZINE;
select TRIM(leading '"' from Title) from MAGAZINE;
select TRIM(trailing '"' from Title) from MAGAZINE;
```

# TRIMOUT (SQL*PLUS)
*See* **SET**.

# TRUNC (Form 1-for Dates)
**SEE ALSO**    **COLUMN**, DATE FUNCTIONS, **TRUNC** (Form 2 - for Numbers), Chapter 9
**FORMAT**

```
TRUNC(date,'format')
```

**DESCRIPTION**    **TRUNC** is the truncating of *date* according to *format*. Without a *format*, *date* is truncated to 12 A.M. (midnight) in the morning, with the first moment of the new day, today's date, for any time up to and including 11:59:59 P.M. (just before midnight). See DATE FORMATS for that valid date *format* values.

    The result of **TRUNC** is always a date with its time set to 12 A.M., the first moment of the day.

# TRUNC (Form 2-for Numbers)
**SEE ALSO**    **COLUMN**, NUMBER FUNCTIONS, **TRUNC** (Form 1-for Dates), Chapter 8
**FORMAT**

```
TRUNC(value,precision)
```

**DESCRIPTION**    TRUNC is value truncated to precision.
**EXAMPLES**

```
TRUNC(123.45,0) = 123
TRUNC(123.45,-1) = 120
TRUNC(123.45,-2) = 100
```

# TRUNCATE
**SEE ALSO**    **CREATE CLUSTER, DELETE, DROP TABLE**, TRIGGER, Chapter 18
**FORMAT**

```
TRUNCATE
{ TABLE [schema .] table [{ PRESERVE | PURGE } MATERIALIZED VIEW LOG]
| CLUSTER [schema .] cluster }
[{ DROP | REUSE } STORAGE];
```

**DESCRIPTION**    **TRUNCATE** removes all the rows from a table or cluster. You can only truncate an indexed cluster, not a hash cluster (*see* **CREATE CLUSTER**). If you add the **DROP STORAGE** option, **TRUNCATE** will deallocate the space from the deleted rows; if you add the **REUSE STORAGE** option, **TRUNCATE** will leave the space allocated for new rows in the table. **DROP STORAGE** is the default.

The **TRUNCATE** command is faster than a **DELETE** command because it generates no rollback information, does not fire any **DELETE** triggers (and therefore must be used with caution), and does not record any information in a materialized view log. In addition, using **TRUNCATE** does not invalidate the objects depending on the deleted rows or the privileges on the table.

**NOTE**
*You cannot roll back a* **TRUNCATE** *statement.*

# TTITLE
**SEE ALSO**   **ACCEPT**, **BTITLE**, **DEFINE**, PARAMETERS, **REPFOOTER**, **REPHEADER**, Chapter 14
**FORMAT**

```
TTI[TLE] [option [text|variable]... | OFF | ON]
```

**DESCRIPTION**   **TTITLE** (**T**op **TITLE**) puts a title (may be multiline) at the top of each page of a report. OFF and ON suppress and restore the display of the text without changing its contents. **TTITLE** by itself displays the current **TTITLE** options and *text* or *variable.*

*text* is a title you wish to give this report, and *variable* is a user-defined variable or a system-maintained variable, including SQL.LNO, the current line number; SQL.PNO, the current page number; SQL.RELEASE, the current Oracle release number; SQL.SQLCODE, the current error code; and SQL.USER, the username.

SQL*PLUS uses **ttitle** in the new form if the first word after **ttitle** is a valid option. The valid options are

- **COL** *n* skips directly to position *n* from the left margin of the current line.

- **S[KIP]** *n* prints *n* blank lines. If no *n* is specified, one blank line is printed. If *n* is 0, no blank lines are printed and the current position for printing becomes position 1 of the current line (leftmost on the page).

- **TAB** *n* skips forward *n* positions (backward if *n* is negative).

- **BOLD** prints the output data in bold print.

- **LE[FT]**, **CE[NTER]**, and **R[IGHT]**. left-justify, center, and right-justify data on the current line. Any text or variables following these commands are justified as a group, up to the end of the command, or a LEFT, CENTER, RIGHT, or COL. CENTER and RIGHT use the value set by the **SET LINESIZE** command to determine where to place the text or variable.

- **FORMAT** string specifies the format model that will control the format of subsequent text or variables, and follows the same syntax as FORMAT in a **COLUMN** command, such as FORMAT A12 or FORMAT $999,990.99. Each time a FORMAT appears, it supersedes the previous one that was in effect. If no FORMAT model has been specified, the one set by **SET NUMFORMAT** is used. If NUMFORMAT has not been set, the default for SQL*PLUS is used.

Date values are printed according to the default format unless a variable has been loaded with a date reformatted by **TO_CHAR**.

Any number of options, pieces of text, and variables may be used in a single **ttitle**. Each is printed in the order specified, and each is positioned and formatted as specified by the clauses that precede it.

# TUPLE
TUPLE is a synonym for row. It rhymes with "couple."

## TWO-PHASE COMMIT

Oracle manages distributed transactions with a special feature called *two-phase commit*. Two-phase commit guarantees that a transaction is valid at all sites by the time it commits or rolls back. All sites either commit or roll back together, no matter what errors occur in the network or on the machines tied together by the network. You don't need to do anything special to have your applications use a two-phase commit.

## TYPE

*See* ABSTRACT DATATYPE and **CREATE TYPE**.

## TYPE (Embedded SQL)

**SEE ALSO**     *Precompiler Programmer's Guide*

**FORMAT**

```
EXEC SQL TYPE type IS datatype
```

**DESCRIPTION**     PL/SQL lets you assign an Oracle external datatype to a user-defined datatype. The datatype may include a length, precision, or scale. This external datatype is equivalenced to the user-defined type and assigned to all host variables assigned to the type. For a list of external datatypes, see *Precompiler Programmer's Guide*.

## TYPE BODY

*See* ABSTRACT DATATYPE, **CREATE TYPE**, and METHOD.

## TZ_OFFSET

**SEE ALSO**     SESSIONTIMEZONE, DBTIMEZONE

**FORMAT**

```
TZ_OFFSET
({ 'time_zone_name'
 | '{ + | - } hh : mi'
 | SESSIONTIMEZONE
 | DBTMEZONE
 })
```

**DESCRIPTION**     **TZ_OFFSET** returns the time zone offset corresponding to the value entered based on the date the statement is executed. You can enter a valid time zone name, a time zone offset from UTC (which simply returns itself), or the keyword **SESSIONTIMEZONE** or **DBTIMEZONE**. For a listing of valid values, query the TZNAME column of the V$TIMEZONE_NAMES dynamic performance view.

## UID

**SEE ALSO**     SESSION

**FORMAT**

```
UID
```

**DESCRIPTION**     **UID** returns an integer that uniquely identifies the session user (the user who logged on).

# UNDEFINE

**SEE ALSO**     **ACCEPT**, **DEFINE**, PARAMETERS, Chapters 14 and 16
**FORMAT**

```
UNDEF[INE] variable
```

**DESCRIPTION**     UNDEFINE deletes the definition of a user variable that has been defined by **ACCEPT**, **DEFINE**, or as a parameter to the **START** command. You can **undefine** the current values of multiple variables in a single command. The format is shown in the following listing:

```
undefine variable1 variable2 ...
```

**EXAMPLE**     To undefine a variable named Total, use this:

```
undefine Total
```

# UNDERLINE (SQL*PLUS)

*See* **SET**.

# UNDO SEGEMENT

As of Oracle9i, you can use automatic undo management to provide read consistency in place of rollback segments. If you use this option, Oracle will maintain undo segments to track changes and provide rollback capabilities. See ROLLBACK SEGMENT and Chapter 40.

# UNION

**SEE ALSO**     **INTERSECT**, **MINUS**, QUERY OPERATORS, Chapter 12
**FORMAT**

```
select...
 UNION [ALL]
select...
```

**DESCRIPTION**     UNION combines two queries. It returns all distinct rows for both **select** statements, or, when **ALL** is specified, all rows regardless of duplication. The number of columns and datatypes must be identical between **select** statements, although the names of the columns do not need to be. *See* Chapter 12 for a discussion of the important differences and effects of **INTERSECT**, **UNION**, and **MINUS**, and the role that precedence plays in the results.

# UNISTR

**SEE ALSO**     CONVERSION FUNCTIONS, **CONVERT**, **TRANSLATE...USING**
**FORMAT**

```
UNISTR ('string')
```

**DESCRIPTION**     UNISTR takes as its argument a string in any character set and returns it in unicode in the database unicode character set. To include UCS2 codepoint characters in the string, use the escape backslash (\) followed by the next number. To include the backslash itself, precede it with another backslash (\\).

     This function is similar to the **TRANSLATE ... USING** function, except that **UNISTR** offers the escape character for UCS2 codepoints and backslash characters.

# UNIQUE INDEX

A unique index is an index that imposes uniqueness on each value it indexes. The index may be one single column or concatenated (multiple columns). *See* INTEGRITY CONSTRAINT.

# UNIQUE KEY

A unique key is one or more columns that must be unique for each row of the table. *See* KEY, PRIMARY KEY, and INTEGRITY CONSTRAINT.

# UNIT OF WORK

In Oracle, a transaction is equivalent to a logical unit of work, which includes all SQL statements since you either logged on, last committed, or last rolled back your work. Thus, a transaction can encompass numerous SQL statements, or only one.

# UPDATE (Form I-Embedded SQL)

**SEE ALSO**     **EXECUTE IMMEDIATE, FOR, PREPARE, SELECT** (Form 2), *Precompiler Programmer's Guide*

**FORMAT**

```
EXEC SQL [AT { dbname | :host_variable }]
 [FOR { :host_integer | integer }]
 UPDATE
 [(subquery)
 | [schema .] { table | view } [@db_link | PARTITION (part_name)]]
 SET
 { column = { expr | (subquery_2) }
 | (column [, column]...) = (subquery_1) }
 [, { column = { expr | (subquery_2) }
 | (column [, column]...) = (subquery_1) }]...
 [WHERE { condition | CURRENT OF cursor }]
 [{ RETURN | RETURNING } expr [, expr]... INTO
 :host_variable [[INDICATOR] :ind_variable]
 [, :host_variable [[INDICATOR] :ind_variable]]...]
```

**DESCRIPTION**     See the description of the various clauses in **UPDATE** (Form 3). The elements unique to Embedded SQL follow:

- **AT *dbname***, which optionally names a database from a previous **CONNECT** statement for a database name from a previous **DECLARE DATABASE** statement.

- **FOR *:host_integer***, which sets the maximum number of rows that can be fetched. *integer* is a named host variable.

- *expr* may include a host :*variable*[:*indicator*].

- The **WHERE** clause may include host variables or arrays.

- **CURRENT OF** updates the last row fetched for the named *cursor*. However, the cursor must be open and positioned on the row. If it isn't, the **CURRENT OF**, which is a part of the **WHERE** clause, causes the **WHERE** to find no rows, and none will be updated. The cursor must have previously been named in a **DECLARE CURSOR** statement with a **SELECT. . .FOR UPDATE OF**.

If any host variable in either the **SET** or **WHERE** is an array, then all host variables in both must be arrays, though they do not all need to be the same size arrays. If they are arrays, **UPDATE** is executed once for each set of components in the array, and may update zero or more rows. The maximum number depends on either the size of the smallest array, or the integer value in the **FOR** clause, if one is specified. *See* **FOR** for additional details.

# UPDATE (Form 2-PL/SQL)

**SEE ALSO**   **DECLARE CURSOR**, SUBQUERY
**FORMAT**

```
UPDATE [user.]table[@dblink]
SET { column = expression | column = (select expression...)
 [[,column = expression]... |
 [,column = (select
expression...)]...] |
 (column [,column]...) = (subquery)}
 [WHERE {condition | CURRENT OF cursor}];
```

**DESCRIPTION**   **UPDATE** in PL/SQL works identically to the normal SQL UPDATE statement, with the exception of the alternative **where** clause **WHERE CURRENT OF** cursor. In this instance, the **update** statement affects just the single row currently in the cursor as a result of the last **FETCH**. The cursor **select** statement must have included the words FOR UPDATE.

Like **insert**, **delete**, and **select. . .into**, the **update** statement always uses the implicit cursor named SQL. This is never declared (although the **select. . .for update** statement must be **DECLARE**d in a cursor for **WHERE CURRENT OF cursor** to be used). Its attributes are set as follows:

- SQL%ISOPEN is irrelevant.
- SQL%FOUND is TRUE if one or more rows is updated, FALSE if no rows are updated. SQL%NOTFOUND is the opposite of SQL%FOUND.
- SQL%ROWCOUNT is the number of rows updated.

# UPDATE (Form 3-SQL Command)

**SEE ALSO**   **DELETE**, **INSERT**, **SELECT**, SUBQUERY, **WHERE**, Chapter 15
**FORMAT**
update::=

**DML_table_expression_clause::=**

**subquery_restriction_clause::=**

**table_collection_expression::=**

**update_set_clause::=**

**where_clause::=**

**returning_clause::=**

**DESCRIPTION**   **UPDATE** updates (changes) the values in the listed columns in the specified table. The **where** clause may contain a correlated subquery. A subquery may select from the table that is being updated, although it must return just one row. Without a **where** clause, all rows will be updated. With a **where** clause, only those rows it selects will be updated. The expressions are evaluated as the command is executed, and their results replace the current values for the columns in the row(s).

A subquery must select the same number of columns (with compatible datatypes) as are in parentheses on the left side of the **set** clause. Columns that are set to equal an expression may precede columns in parentheses set equal to a subquery, all within a single **update** statement.

**EXAMPLE**   To set **NULL** all Publisher values:

```
update BOOKSHELF set Publisher = NULL ;
```

The following will update the city of Walpole in the COMFORT table, setting the precipitation for all Walpole rows to **NULL**, the noon temperature equal to that in Manchester, and the midnight temperature equal to the noon temperature minus 10 degrees.

```
update COMFORT set Precipitation = NULL,
 (Noon, Midnight) =
 (select Temperature, Temperature - 10
 from WEATHER
 where City = 'MANCHESTER')
 where City = 'WALPOLE';
```

# UPPER

**SEE ALSO**   **LOWER**, Chapter 7
**FORMAT**

```
UPPER(string)
```

**DESCRIPTION**   **UPPER** converts every letter in a *string* into uppercase.
**EXAMPLE**

```
upper('Look what you''ve done!')
```

produces this:

```
LOOK WHAT YOU'VE DONE!
```

# UROWID

UROWID is the datatype for index-organized tables' primary keys, also known as a Universal RowID. The maximum and default size is 4000 bytes. See DATA TYPES and **CREATE TABLE**.

# USED EXTENTS

Used extents are those that either have been allocated to a data (table) segment—and thus have data in them—or have been reserved for data.

# USER

**SEE ALSO**    UID

**FORMAT**

```
USER
```

**DESCRIPTION**    *User* is the name by which the current user is known to Oracle. *User* is a function, and as such can be queried in any **SELECT** statement.

**EXAMPLE**

```
select USER from DUAL;
```

# USER VARIABLES

*See* **ACCEPT**, **DEFINE**, PARAMETERS

# USERENV

**SEE ALSO**    CHARACTER FUNCTIONS

**FORMAT**

```
USERENV(option)
```

**DESCRIPTION**    USERENV is a legacy function, replaced by SYS_CONTEXT's UserEnv namespace. The options and their return values are:

'CLIENT_INFO'	CLIENT_INFO returns up to 64 bytes of user session information that can be stored by an application using the DBMS_APPLICATION_INFO package.
'ENTRYID'	ENTRYID returns available auditing entry identifier. You cannot use this attribute in distributed SQL statements. To use this keyword in USERENV, the initialization parameter AUDIT_TRAIL must be set to true.
'INSTANCE'	INSTANCE returns the instance identification number of the current instance.
'ISDBA'	ISDBA returns 'TRUE' if the user has been authenticated as having DBA privileges either through the operating system or through a password file.
'LANG'	LANG returns the ISO abbreviation for the language name, a shorter form than the existing 'LANGUAGE' parameter.
'LANGUAGE'	LANGUAGE returns the language and territory currently used by your session along with the database character set in this form: language_territory.characterset

'SESSIONID'	SESSIONID returns your auditing session identifier. You cannot use this attribute in distributed SQL statements.
'TERMINAL'	TERMINAL returns the operating system identifier for your current session's terminal. In distributed SQL statements, this attribute returns the identifier for your local session. In a distributed environment, this is supported only for remote SELECT statements, not for remote INSERT, UPDATE, or DELETE operations.

# USERNAME

*Username* is a word that identifies you as an authorized user of your host computer's operating system or of Oracle. Associated with each username is a password.

# VALUE

**SEE ALSO**   **DEREF**, **REF**, Chapter 33

**FORMAT**

```
VALUE (correlation_variable)
```

**DESCRIPTION**      In a SQL statement, **VALUE** takes as its argument a correlation variable (table alias) associated with a row of an object table and returns object instances stored in the object table. The type of the object instances is the same type as the object table. See Chapter 33.

# VAR (Embedded SQL)

**SEE ALSO**   *See* **SELECT (Form 2)**, VARIABLE DECLARATION.

**FORMAT**

```
EXEC SQL VAR host_variable
 { IS dtyp [({ length | precision, scale })]
 [CONVBUFSZ [IS] (size)]
 | CONVBUFSZ [IS] (size) }
```

**DESCRIPTION**      PL/SQL lets you override the default datatype assignment of a variable via the **VAR** command. Once a variable has been declared, it uses the datatype assigned to it in the **declare** command. **VAR** allows you to change the datatype of a declared variable within a PL/SQL block.

# VAR_POP

**SEE ALSO**   GROUPING FUNCTIONS, VAR_SAMP, VARIANCE

**FORMAT**

```
VAR_POP (expr) [OVER (analytic_clause)]
```

**DESCRIPTION**      **VAR_POP** returns the population variance of a set of numbers after discarding the **NULL**s in this set.

# VAR_SAMP

**SEE ALSO**   GROUPING FUNCTIONS, VAR_POP, VARIANCE

**FORMAT**

```
VAR_SAMP (expr) [OVER (analytic_clause)]
```

**DESCRIPTION**    VAR_SAMP returns the sample variance of a set of numbers after discarding the NULLs in this set.

# VARCHAR2

*See* DATA TYPES.

# VARIABLE

**SEE ALSO**    PRINT

**FORMAT**

```
VAR[IABLE] [variable_name {NUMBER|CHAR|CHAR (n)}]
```

**DESCRIPTION**    **VARIABLE** declares a bind variable which can be referenced in PL/SQL. Each variable is assigned a *variable_name* and a type (NUMBER or CHAR). For CHAR variables, a maximum length (*n*) can be specified.

**EXAMPLES**    In the following example, a variable named *bal* is created and is set equal to the result of a function.

```
variable bal NUMBER
begin
 :bal := LATE_FEE('DORAH TALBOT');
end;
```

# VARIABLE DECLARATION (PL/SQL)

**FORMAT**

```
variable [CONSTANT]
{type | identifier%TYPE | [user.]table%ROWTYPE}
 [NOT NULL]
 [{DEFAULT | :=} expression];
```

**DESCRIPTION**    PL/SQL lets you declare variables in a PL/SQL block. If you declare the variable to be CONSTANT, you must initialize the variable with a value in the declaration and you cannot assign a new value to the variable.

The type of the variable can be a PL/SQL type (*see* DATA TYPES), the type of another PL/SQL variable or database column given by an identifier, or a ROWTYPE (*see* **%ROWTYPE**) that lets you refer to a record corresponding to a database table.

If you add **NOT NULL** to the declaration, you cannot assign a NULL to the variable and you must initialize the variable. The initialization (following a DEFAULT or assignment :=) expression is any valid PL/SQL expression that results in a value of the type declared.

# VARIANCE

**SEE ALSO**    ACCEPT, **COMPUTE**, **DEFINE**, GROUP FUNCTIONS, **PARAMETERS**, **STDDEV**, **VAR_POP**, **VAR_SAMP**, Chapter 8

**FORMAT**

```
VARIANCE ([DISTINCT | ALL] expr) [OVER (analytic_clause)]
```

**DESCRIPTION** **VARIANCE** gives the variance of all *values* for a group of rows. Like other group functions, **VARIANCE** ignores **NULL** values.

# VARRAY

VARRAY is a clause within the **CREATE TYPE** command that tells the database the limit to the number of entries within the varying array. *See* Chapter 31 for detailed examples of varying arrays. *See* CREATE TYPE for syntax information.

# VARYING ARRAY

A varying array is a collector—for a single row in a table, it can contain multiple entries. The maximum number of varying array entries per row is set when the varying array is created (via **CREATE TYPE**). *See* Chapter 31.

# VERIFY (SQL*PLUS)

*See* **SET**.

# VERSION NUMBER

The version number is the primary identifying number of Oracle software. In Oracle9i Release 9.0.1.0, 9 is the version number.

# VIEW

A view is a database object that is a logical representation of a table. It is derived from a table but has no storage of its own and often may be used in the same manner as a table. *See* **CREATE VIEW** and Chapter 18.

# VIRTUAL COLUMN

A virtual column is a column in a query result whose value is calculated from the value(s) of other column(s).

# VSIZE

**SEE ALSO** CHARACTER FUNCTIONS, **LENGTH**, NUMBER FUNCTIONS, Chapter 8
**FORMAT**

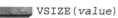

```
VSIZE(value)
```

**DESCRIPTION** **VSIZE** is the storage size of value in Oracle. For character columns, **VSIZE** is the same as LENGTH. For numbers it is usually smaller than the apparent length, because less space is required to store numbers in the database.
**EXAMPLES**

```
VSIZE(12.345) = 4
```

# WALKING A TREE

Walking a tree is the process of visiting each node of a tree in turn. *See* **CONNECT BY**.

# WHENEVER

**SEE ALSO**     EXECUTE, FETCH

**FORMAT**

```
EXEC SQL WHENEVER {NOT FOUND | SQLERROR | SQL WARNING}
 {CONTINUE |
 GOTO label |
 STOP |
 DO routine |
 DO BREAK |
 DO CONTINUE}
```

**DESCRIPTION**     **WHENEVER** is not an executable SQL statement, but rather an instruction to the Oracle language processor to embed an "IF *condition* THEN GOTO *label* " statement after every SQL statement to follow. As each SQL statement executes, its results are tested to see if they meet the *condition*. If they do, the program branches to the *label*.

     **WHENEVER** may be used with **CONTINUE** or a different label for each of the three possible conditions. Each of these will be in effect for all subsequent SQL statements. A new **WHENEVER** with one of these conditions will completely replace its predecessor for all subsequent SQL statements.

     The **NOT FOUND** condition is raised any time SQLCODE is 100, meaning, for instance, that a **FETCH** failed to return any rows (this includes subqueries in **insert** statements).

     **SQLERROR** occurs whenever SQLCODE is less than 0. These are typically fatal errors and require serious error handling.

     **SQLWARNING** occurs when a nonfatal "error" occurs. These include truncation of character strings being loaded into host variables, a select list of columns that doesn't match the INTO list of host variables, and **delete** or **update** statements without **where** clauses.

     Usually initial branching, continuation, stopping, or routine execution is set up at the very beginning of a program, before any executable SQL statements. However, within particular blocks of logic in the body of the program, any or all of these could be replaced depending upon local needs. Note that **WHENEVER** knows nothing about the host languages scoping rules, calls, or branching. From the moment a **WHENEVER** is asserted, its rules remain in effect until another **WHENEVER** (with the same condition) replaces it. On the other hand, your program must obey language scoping rules with regard to the **GOTO** and label.

     The **STOP** option stops program execution; the **DO** option calls a host language routine of some kind, the syntax of which depends on your host language. **DO BREAK** performs a break from a loop; **DO CONTINUE** performs a continue statement from a loop when the condition is met.

     Lastly, in an error-handling routine, particularly one that may contain SQL statements, **WHENEVER SQLERROR** should probably contain **CONTINUE** or **STOP** or should call an exit routine in order to avoid an infinite loop back into the same error-handling routine.

# WHENEVER OSERROR

**SEE ALSO**     WHENEVER SQLERROR

**FORMAT**

```
WHENEVER OSERROR
{EXIT [SUCCESS|FAILURE|n|variable|:BindVariable] [COMMIT|ROLLBACK]
|CONTINUE [COMMIT|ROLLBACK|NONE] }
```

**DESCRIPTION**    **WHENEVER OSERROR** handles processing logic within SQL*PLUS if an operating system error occurs. **EXIT** directs SQL*PLUS to exit, and **CONTINUE** turns off **EXIT**. **COMMIT** tells SQL*PLUS to issue a **COMMIT** prior to exiting, and **ROLLBACK** tells it to issue a **ROLLBACK** before exiting. The default behavior is **NONE**.

# WHENEVER SQLERROR

**SEE ALSO**    WHENEVER OSERROR

**FORMAT**

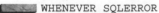
```
WHENEVER SQLERROR
{EXIT [SUCCESS|FAILURE|WARNING|n|variable|:BindVariable]
[COMMIT|ROLLBACK]|CONTINUE [COMMIT|ROLLBACK|NONE]}
```

**DESCRIPTION**    **WHENEVER SQLERROR** handles processing logic within SQL*PLUS if a SQL command or a PL/SQL block encounters an error. **EXIT** directs SQL*PLUS to exit, and **CONTINUE** turns off **EXIT**. **COMMIT** tells SQL*PLUS to issue a **COMMIT** prior to exiting, and **ROLLBACK** tells it to issue a **ROLLBACK** before exiting. The default behavior is **NONE**.

**NOTE**
*SQL and PL/SQL errors initiate WHENEVER SQLERROR processing.*
*SQL*Plus errors do not.*

You may place WHENEVER SQLERROR in a start file in front of as many SQL statements as you wish. Each WHENEVER SQLERROR will supersede the one before, and will remain in effect until it is itself superseded.

**EXAMPLE**    When the **CREATE TABLE** in the following example fails because the literal KEENE is not enclosed in single quotation marks, the subsequent **UPDATE** and **SELECT** will never even execute. The WHENEVER SQLERROR will exit SQL*PLUS immediately, and pass the **SQL.SQLCODE** back to the host:

```
WHENEVER SQLERROR EXIT SQL.SQLCODE;

create table KEENE as
select * from COMFORT
 where City = KEENE;

update KEENE set Noon = 75;

select * from KEENE;
```

# WHERE

**SEE ALSO**    **DELETE**, LOGICAL OPERATORS, PRECEDENCE, **SELECT**, SYNTAX OPERATORS, UPDATE

**FORMAT**

```
DELETE FROM [user.]table ...
 [WHERE condition]
```

```
SELECT ...
 [WHERE condition]
UPDATE [user.]table [alias] ...
 [WHERE condition]
```

**DESCRIPTION** **WHERE** defines those logical conditions that will control which rows a **select** statement will return, a **delete** statement will delete, or an **update** statement will update.

A condition may be defined in one of several ways:

- A comparison between expressions (=, >, !=, and so on).
- A comparison between an expression and a query.
- A comparison between a list of expressions and a list of expressions from a query.
- A comparison between an expression and **ANY** or **ALL** members of a list or between an expression and the values brought back from a query.
- A test to see if an expression is **IN** or **NOT IN** a list, or the results of a query.
- A test for being **BETWEEN** or **NOT BETWEEN** one value and another.
- A test to see if an expression **IS NULL** or **IS NOT NULL**.
- A test to see if there **EXISTS** (or **NOT EXISTS**) any results for a query.
- A combination of any of the above, using the conjunctions **AND** and **OR**.

**EXAMPLES**

```
where Section >ANY ('A','C','D');
where City !=ALL (select City from LOCATION);
where Section IN ('A','C','D');
where City NOT IN (select City from LOCATION);
where Page BETWEEN 4 and 7;
where Skill IS NULL;
where EXISTS (select * from WORKER where Age > 90);
where Section = 'A' or Section = 'B' and Page = 1;
```

# WHILE (PL/SQL)

*See* **LOOP**, Chapter 27

# WIDTH_BUCKET

**SEE ALSO** NTILE

**FORMAT**

```
WIDTH_BUCKET (expr , min_value , max_value , num_buckets)
```

**DESCRIPTION** **WIDTH_BUCKET** constructs equiwidth histograms, in which the histogram range is divided into intervals that have identical size. (Compare this function with **NTILE**, which creates equiheight histograms.) Ideally each bucket is a "closed-open" interval of the real number line. For a given expression, **WIDTH_BUCKET** returns the bucket number into which the value of this expression would fall after being evaluated. *expr* is the expression (a number or datetime value) for which the histogram is being created. If *expr* evaluates to **NULL**, the expression returns **NULL**. *min_value* and

*max_value* are expressions that resolve to the end points of the acceptable range for *expr*. Both of these expressions must also evaluate to number or datetime values, and neither can evaluate to **NULL**. *num_buckets* is an expression that resolves to a constant indicating the number of buckets. This expression must evaluate to a positive integer.

# WRAP (SQL*PLUS)

*See* **SET**.

# WRAPPING

Wrapping is moving the end of a heading or title, or the contents of a column, down to a new line when it is too long to fit on one line. (Contrast with **TRUNCATE**.) *See* **COLUMN**.

# XML

XML (eXtensible Markup Language) is a standardized syntax for describing hierarchical data. XML provides a universal format for structured documents and data. Its tag-based syntax gives it the flexibility to handle complex data. Whereas HTML tells a Web browser how to present data, XML tells applications what the data means. See Chapter 41 for examples.

# XMLType

XMLType is a datatype available as of Oracle9i to store and query XML data in the database. As a type, XMLType has member functions to access, extract, and query XML data using a class of operations known as Xpath expressions. The SYS_XMLGEN, SYS_XMLAGG, and DBMS_XMLGEN packages create XMLType values from existing object-relational data. When you designate a column as using the XMLType datatype, Oracle will internally store the data in a CLOB datatype.

The following listing shows the creation of a table using the XMLType:

datatype:

```
create table MY_XML_TABLE
(Key1 NUMBER,
Xml_Column SYS.XMLTYPE);

insert into MY_XML_TABLE (Key1, Xml_Column)
values (1, SYS.XMLTYPE.CREATEXML
 ('<book>
 <title>Complete Reference</title>
 <chapter num= "43">
<title>Ending</title>
 <text>This is the end of the book.</text>
 </chapter>
</book>'));
```

You can retrieve the data from the XMLType column via the GETCLOBVAL method:

```
select M.Xml_Column.GETCLOBVAL() as XML_Data
 from MY_XML_TABLE M
 where Key1 = 1;
```

See Chapter 41 for additional details on XMLType and its related methods.

# Index

## Symbols

\# (pound sign), 848
\$ (dollar sign), 458, 848–849
% (percent sign), 54–55, 849
& (ampersand), 309, 453, 851
&& (double ampersand), 851
: (colon), 855
; (semicolon), 855–856
. (period or dot)
    as name separator, 854
    as variable separator, 853–854
_ (underscore), 847
! (exclamation mark), 847–848
? (question mark), 849
' (single quotation mark), 851–852
" (double quotation mark), 848
{}(curly braces)
    Java classes, 640, 857
    Oracle Text reserved word, 456,
      856–857
[] (square brackets), 115
() (parentheses), 162–163, 852
@ ("at" sign), 856
@@ (double "at" sign), 856
* (multiplication), 852
** (exponentiation), 852
+ (addition), 852–853

++ (Java operator), 630–631
- (subtraction), 853
- (hyphen), 853
-- (comment), 93, 853
/* */ (comment), 93, 103, 854–855
/ (division), 854
/ (slash), 854
:= (set equal to), 855
| (vertical bar), 453, 857
|| (concatenation), 116, 117–118, 857

## A

abbreviations, 18, 25
ABORT_REDEF_TABLE procedure, 352
ABOUT operator, 461
ABS function, 148, 857–858
absolute value, 148, 857–858
abstract datatypes, 72, 552–557, 858
    alter type command, 914–916
    attributes, 695–696
    collectors and, 566, 568
    constructor methods, 78
    create type command, 74–75, 552,
      553, 1006–1010
    data dictionary views, 695–697

# E

## F

## U

# INTERNATIONAL CONTACT INFORMATION

**AUSTRALIA**
McGraw-Hill Book Company Australia Pty. Ltd.
TEL +61-2-9415-9899
FAX +61-2-9415-5687
http://www.mcgraw-hill.com.au
books-it_sydney@mcgraw-hill.com

**CANADA**
McGraw-Hill Ryerson Ltd.
TEL +905-430-5000
FAX +905-430-5020
http://www.mcgrawhill.ca

**GREECE, MIDDLE EAST,**
**NORTHERN AFRICA**
McGraw-Hill Hellas
TEL +30-1-656-0990-3-4
FAX +30-1-654-5525

**MEXICO (Also serving Latin America)**
McGraw-Hill Interamericana Editores S.A. de C.V.
TEL +525-117-1583
FAX +525-117-1589
http://www.mcgraw-hill.com.mx
fernando_castellanos@mcgraw-hill.com

**SINGAPORE (Serving Asia)**
McGraw-Hill Book Company
TEL +65-863-1580
FAX +65-862-3354
http://www.mcgraw-hill.com.sg
mghasia@mcgraw-hill.com

**SOUTH AFRICA**
McGraw-Hill South Africa
TEL +27-11-622-7512
FAX +27-11-622-9045
robyn_swanepoel@mcgraw-hill.com

**UNITED KINGDOM & EUROPE**
**(Excluding Southern Europe)**
McGraw-Hill Education Europe
TEL +44-1-628-502500
FAX +44-1-628-770224
http://www.mcgraw-hill.co.uk
computing_neurope@mcgraw-hill.com

**ALL OTHER INQUIRIES Contact:**
Osborne/McGraw-Hill
TEL +1-510-549-6600
FAX +1-510-883-7600
http://www.osborne.com
omg_international@mcgraw-hill.com

# free
## development software

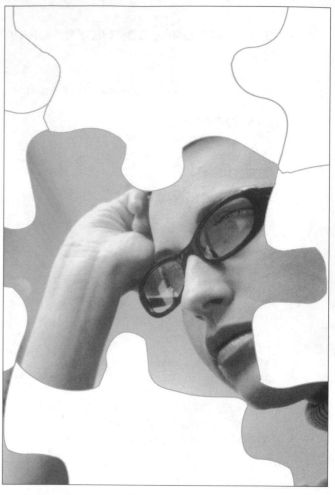

# free
## membership
Solve every technical puzzle.

ORACLE
Technology
NETWORK

ORACLE

# GET YOUR FREE SUBSCRIPTION TO ORACLE MAGAZINE

*Oracle Magazine* is essential gear for today's information technology professionals. Stay informed and increase your productivity with every issue of *Oracle Magazine*. Inside each free bimonthly issue you'll get:

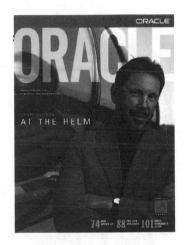

- Up-to-date information on Oracle Database, E-Business Suite applications, Web development, and database technology and business trends
- Third-party news and announcements
- Technical articles on Oracle Products and operating environments
- Development and administration tips
- Real-world customer stories

## Three easy ways to subscribe:

### ① Web

Visit our Web site at www.oracle.com/oraclemagazine. You'll find a subscription form there, plus much more!

### ② Fax

Complete the questionnaire on the back of this card and fax the questionnaire side only to +1.847.647.9735.

### ③ Mail

Complete the questionnaire on the back of this card and mail it to P.O. Box 1263, Skokie, IL 60076-8263

IF THERE ARE OTHER ORACLE USERS AT YOUR LOCATION WHO WOULD LIKE TO RECEIVE THEIR OWN SUBSCRIPTION TO ORACLE MAGAZINE, PLEASE PHOTOCOPY THIS FORM AND PASS IT ALONG.

**Oracle Publishing**

ORACLE

# FREE SUBSCRIPTION

○ Yes, please send me a FREE subscription to *Oracle Magazine*          ○ NO

To receive a free subscription to *Oracle Magazine*, you must fill out the entire card, sign it, and date it (incomplete cards cannot be processed or acknowledged). You can also fax your application to +1.847.647.9735.
Or subscribe at our Web site at www.oracle.com/oraclemagazine/

○ From time to time, Oracle Publishing allows our partners exclusive access to our e-mail addresses for special promotions and announcements. To be included in this program, please check this box.

○ Oracle Publishing allows sharing of our mailing list with selected third parties. If you prefer your mailing address not to be included in this program, please check here. If at any time you would like to be removed from this mailing list, please contact Customer Service at +1.847.647.9630 or send an e-mail to oracle@halldata.com.

signature (required)

X

date

name                                         title

company                                      e-mail address

street/p.o. box

city/state/zip or postal code                telephone

country                                      fax

## YOU MUST ANSWER ALL NINE QUESTIONS BELOW

**① WHAT IS THE PRIMARY BUSINESS ACTIVITY OF YOUR FIRM AT THIS LOCATION?**
(check one only)

- ☐ 01 Application Service Provider
- ☐ 02 Communications
- ☐ 03 Consulting, Training
- ☐ 04 Data Processing
- ☐ 05 Education
- ☐ 06 Engineering
- ☐ 07 Financial Services
- ☐ 08 Government (federal, local, state, other)
- ☐ 09 Government (military)
- ☐ 10 Health Care
- ☐ 11 Manufacturing (aerospace, defense)
- ☐ 12 Manufacturing (computer hardware)
- ☐ 13 Manufacturing (noncomputer)
- ☐ 14 Research & Development
- ☐ 15 Retailing, Wholesaling, Distribution
- ☐ 16 Software Development
- ☐ 17 Systems Integration, VAR, VAD, OEM
- ☐ 18 Transportation
- ☐ 19 Utilities (electric, gas, sanitation)
- ☐ 98 Other Business and Services

**② WHICH OF THE FOLLOWING BEST DESCRIBES YOUR PRIMARY JOB FUNCTION?**
(check one only)

*Corporate Management/Staff*
- ☐ 01 Executive Management (President, Chair, CEO, CFO, Owner, Partner, Principal)
- ☐ 02 Finance/Administrative Management (VP/Director/ Manager/Controller, Purchasing, Administration)
- ☐ 03 Sales/Marketing Management (VP/Director/Manager)
- ☐ 04 Computer Systems/Operations Management (CIO/VP/Director/ Manager MIS, Operations)

*IS/IT Staff*
- ☐ 05 Systems Development/ Programming Management
- ☐ 06 Systems Development/ Programming Staff
- ☐ 07 Consulting
- ☐ 08 DBA/Systems Administrator
- ☐ 09 Education/Training
- ☐ 10 Technical Support Director/Manager
- ☐ 11 Other Technical Management/Staff
- ☐ 98 Other

**③ WHAT IS YOUR CURRENT PRIMARY OPERATING PLATFORM?** (select all that apply)

- ☐ 01 Digital Equipment UNIX
- ☐ 02 Digital Equipment VAX VMS
- ☐ 03 HP UNIX
- ☐ 04 IBM AIX

- ☐ 05 IBM UNIX
- ☐ 06 Java
- ☐ 07 Linux
- ☐ 08 Macintosh
- ☐ 09 MS-DOS
- ☐ 10 MVS
- ☐ 11 NetWare
- ☐ 12 Network Computing
- ☐ 13 OpenVMS
- ☐ 14 SCO UNIX
- ☐ 15 Sequent DYNIX/ptx
- ☐ 16 Sun Solaris/SunOS
- ☐ 17 SVR4
- ☐ 18 UnixWare
- ☐ 19 Windows
- ☐ 20 Windows NT
- ☐ 21 Other UNIX
- ☐ 98 Other
- 99 ☐ None of the above

**④ DO YOU EVALUATE, SPECIFY, RECOMMEND, OR AUTHORIZE THE PURCHASE OF ANY OF THE FOLLOWING?** (check all that apply)

- ☐ 01 Hardware
- ☐ 02 Software
- ☐ 03 Application Development Tools
- ☐ 04 Database Products
- ☐ 05 Internet or Intranet Products
- 99 ☐ None of the above

**⑤ IN YOUR JOB, DO YOU USE OR PLAN TO PURCHASE ANY OF THE FOLLOWING PRODUCTS?** (check all that apply)

*Software*
- ☐ 01 Business Graphics
- ☐ 02 CAD/CAE/CAM
- ☐ 03 CASE
- ☐ 04 Communications
- ☐ 05 Database Management
- ☐ 06 File Management
- ☐ 07 Finance
- ☐ 08 Java
- ☐ 09 Materials Resource Planning
- ☐ 10 Multimedia Authoring
- ☐ 11 Networking
- ☐ 12 Office Automation
- ☐ 13 Order Entry/Inventory Control
- ☐ 14 Programming
- ☐ 15 Project Management
- ☐ 16 Scientific and Engineering
- ☐ 17 Spreadsheets
- ☐ 18 Systems Management
- ☐ 19 Workflow

*Hardware*
- ☐ 20 Macintosh
- ☐ 21 Mainframe
- ☐ 22 Massively Parallel Processing

- ☐ 23 Minicomputer
- ☐ 24 PC
- ☐ 25 Network Computer
- ☐ 26 Symmetric Multiprocessing
- ☐ 27 Workstation

*Peripherals*
- ☐ 28 Bridges/Routers/Hubs/Gateways
- ☐ 29 CD-ROM Drives
- ☐ 30 Disk Drives/Subsystems
- ☐ 31 Modems
- ☐ 32 Tape Drives/Subsystems
- ☐ 33 Video Boards/Multimedia

*Services*
- ☐ 34 Application Service Provider
- ☐ 35 Consulting
- ☐ 36 Education/Training
- ☐ 37 Maintenance
- ☐ 38 Online Database Services
- ☐ 39 Support
- ☐ 40 Technology-Based Training
- ☐ 98 Other
- 99 ☐ None of the above

**⑥ WHAT ORACLE PRODUCTS ARE IN USE AT YOUR SITE?** (check all that apply)

*Software*
- ☐ 01 Oracle9i
- ☐ 02 Oracle9i Lite
- ☐ 03 Oracle8
- ☐ 04 Oracle8i
- ☐ 05 Oracle8i Lite
- ☐ 06 Oracle7
- ☐ 07 Oracle9i Application Server
- ☐ 08 Oracle9i Application Server Wireless
- ☐ 09 Oracle Data Mart Suites
- ☐ 10 Oracle Internet Commerce Server
- ☐ 11 Oracle interMedia
- ☐ 12 Oracle Lite
- ☐ 13 Oracle Payment Server
- ☐ 14 Oracle Video Server
- ☐ 15 Oracle Rdb

*Tools*
- ☐ 16 Oracle Darwin
- ☐ 17 Oracle Designer
- ☐ 18 Oracle Developer
- ☐ 19 Oracle Discoverer
- ☐ 20 Oracle Express
- ☐ 21 Oracle JDeveloper
- ☐ 22 Oracle Reports
- ☐ 23 Oracle Portal
- ☐ 24 Oracle Warehouse Builder
- ☐ 25 Oracle Workflow

*Oracle E-Business Suite*
- ☐ 26 Oracle Advanced Planning/Scheduling
- ☐ 27 Oracle Business Intelligence
- ☐ 28 Oracle E-Commerce
- ☐ 29 Oracle Exchange
- ☐ 30 Oracle Financials

- ☐ 31 Oracle Human Resources
- ☐ 32 Oracle Interaction Center
- ☐ 33 Oracle Internet Procurement
- ☐ 34 Oracle Manufacturing
- ☐ 35 Oracle Marketing
- ☐ 36 Oracle Order Management
- ☐ 37 Oracle Professional Services Automation
- ☐ 38 Oracle Projects
- ☐ 39 Oracle Sales
- ☐ 40 Oracle Service
- ☐ 41 Oracle Small Business Suite
- ☐ 42 Oracle Supply Chain Management
- ☐ 43 Oracle Travel Management
- ☐ 44 Oracle Treasury

*Oracle Services*
- ☐ 45 Oracle.com Online Services
- ☐ 46 Oracle Consulting
- ☐ 47 Oracle Education
- ☐ 48 Oracle Support
- ☐ 98 ther
- 99 ☐ None of the above

**⑦ WHAT OTHER DATABASE PRODUCTS ARE IN USE AT YOUR SITE?** (check all that apply)

- ☐ 01 Access     ☐ 08 Microsoft Access
- ☐ 02 Baan       ☐ 09 Microsoft SQL Server
- ☐ 03 dbase      ☐ 10 PeopleSoft
- ☐ 04 Gupta      ☐ 11 Progress
- ☐ 05 BM DB2     ☐ 12 SAP
- ☐ 06 Informix   ☐ 13 Sybase
- ☐ 07 Ingres     ☐ 14 VSAM
- ☐ 98 Other
- 99 ☐ None of the above

**⑧ DURING THE NEXT 12 MONTHS, HOW MUCH DO YOU ANTICIPATE YOUR ORGANIZATION WILL SPEND ON COMPUTER HARDWARE, SOFTWARE, PERIPHERALS, AND SERVICES FOR YOUR LOCATION?** (check only one)

- ☐ 01 Less than $10,000
- ☐ 02 $10,000 to $49,999
- ☐ 03 $50,000 to $99,999
- ☐ 04 $100,000 to $499,999
- ☐ 05 $500,000 to $999,999
- ☐ 06 $1,000,000 and over

**⑨ WHAT IS YOUR COMPANY'S YEARLY SALES REVENUE?** (please choose one)

- ☐ 01 $500, 000, 000 and above
- ☐ 02 $100, 000, 000 to $500, 000, 000
- ☐ 03 $50, 000, 000 to $100, 000, 000
- ☐ 04 $5, 000, 000 to $50, 000, 000
- ☐ 05 $1, 000, 000 to $5, 000, 000

123101

# About the CD

## How to Use the *Oracle9i: The Complete Reference* CD-ROM

The CD that accompanies this book contains a special electronic Adobe Acrobat pdf-format edition of *Oracle9i: The Complete Reference*. With this electronic version, you can easily transport all of the valuable information contained in the book on your PC while the printed version of the book remains in your office or home.

**Note:** *To view the electronic edition of the book and other documentation on this CD, you will need the Adobe Acrobat Reader program. If you do not already have it pre-installed on your system, you may locate and launch* **rp505enu.exe** *from your CD to install.*

## Viewing and Navigating the Book

You can easily view and navigate specific areas of interest within the book using the hyperlinked Table of Contents provided.

### Viewing

1. Insert the CD-ROM into the CD drive of your computer (if you have not already done so).
2. Locate and launch the file **Book.pdf** from your CD drive. This displays the book's Table of Contents on the left side of the screen and actual book pages on the right.

### Navigating

1. To view a chapter, click the triangle to the left of the Part in which the chapter resides. This displays all chapters in the selected Part.
2. Click the name of the chapter you want to view (displays first page of chapter at right).
3. To view a section within a chapter, click the triangle to the left of the chapter name to display the sections of the chapter, and click the name of the section you want to view.

### Searching

1. Choose the Search | Query option from the Edit menu.
2. In the Adobe Acrobat Search dialog box, click Indexes.
3. In the Index Selection dialog box, make sure the box next to "Oracle9i: The Complete Reference" is checked. Click Add.
4. In the Add Index dialog box, highlight "Index for Oracle9i: The Complete Reference.pdx." Click Open.
5. In the Index Selection dialog box, click OK.
6. In the Adobe Acrobat Search dialog box, type in the text for which you want to search. Click the Search button.
7. In the Search Results dialog box, click the View button. This takes you to the first instance of found text matching the search criteria. Alternatively, you can double-click each occurrence of found text in the Results field to be taken to a specific match.

## Using the Code

The tables used in this book are available for you to access and use without retyping! You can use these to easily work your way through the examples and experiment with the many techniques illustrated in this book. Simply locate and open **Tables.txt**. You can freely select, copy, and paste the desired text from this file.

## Bonus Content Found on the CD-ROM

In addition to the great convenience and flexibility offered by the fully searchable electronic version of the book and the tables from the book, we are happy to offer you added value in the form of an Oracle9i Release 2 *Information & Documentation Kit* and a Special Offer from Oracle University.

### Information & Documentation Kit

In the Information & Documentation folder, you will find the following White Paper and documentation for Oracle9i Release 2 in pdf-format reproduced with the permission of Oracle Corporation:

- Oracle9i Database Release 2 New Features, An Oracle White Paper
- Oracle9i SQL Reference Release 2
- SQL*Plus User's Guide and Reference Release 9.2
- Oracle9i Database Utilities Release 2 (9.2)
- Oracle9i XML API Reference—XDK and Oracle XML DB Release 2
- Oracle9i XML Database Developer's Guide—Oracle XML DB Release 2
- Oracle9i XML Developer's Kits Guide—XDK Release 2

### SPECIAL OFFER from Oracle University

Learn Oracle from Oracle and keep your career on track with this special offer for a 90-day Oracle University Professional Subscription, a 100-percent online learning offering that enables you to take self-paced, instructor-led courses on a variety of advanced Oracle technology topics, all at your convenience, 24x7. For details, go to the Special Offer folder and click on **opress.htm**.

NO TECHNICAL SUPPORT IS PROVIDED WITH THIS CD-ROM.